Unsuccessful Arab siege of Byzantium: high-water mark of Moslem expansion toward eastern Europe — **717**

Battle of "Tours": high-water mark of Moslem expansion toward western Europe — **732**

(Christmas Day) Charlemagne crowned emperor at Rome — **800**

Mamun caliph at Baghdad: Abbasid power at height — **813**

Otto the Great of Germany crowned emperor at Rome: "Holy Roman Empire" — **962**

Basil II emperor at Byzantium: peak of Byzantine power; Bulgarians defeated and Russians converted during his reign — **976**

Hugh Capet King of France — **987**

Formal schism between Greek and Roman Churches — **1054**

Conquest of England by William and the Normans — **1066**

Double defeat of Byzantine Empire: at Bari by Normans, at Manzikert by Seljuk Turks — **1071**

Pope Gregory VII against Emperor Henry IV: opening of Investiture Controversy — **1075**

First Crusade preached by Pope Urban II — **1095**

Henry II King of England: Angevin Empire — **1154**

Sack of Byzantium by "Fourth" Crusade: Latin Empire established in the East — **1204**

A
HISTORY
OF
CIVILIZATION

CRANE

McLean Professor of Ancient and Modern History, Harvard University

JOHN B.

University of Rochester

ROBERT LEE

Harvard University

Englewood Cliffs, New Jersey • 1960

PRENTICE-HALL, INC.

A

BRINTON

HISTORY

CHRISTOPHER

OF

WOLFF

CIVILIZATION

VOLUME ONE: *Prehistory to 1715*

Second Edition

Grateful acknowledgment is made to the following publishers for granting permission to use the material quoted on the pages indicated: Basil Blackwell, 215; Cambridge University Press, 126, 314; Chatto & Windus, Ltd., 189; James Clarke & Company, Ltd., 503; Columbia University Press, 107, 120; E. P. Dutton & Company, Inc., 267, 328, 423, 536; Faber and Faber, 73; Harcourt, Brace and Company, Inc., 455; Harvard University Press, 78, 99, 103, 109, 126, 127, 128, 129, 131, 148, 149, 242, 243, 244, 316, 325; Alfred A. Knopf, Inc., 151; Macmillan & Company, Ltd., 153, 630; The Macmillan Company, 433; New Directions, 330; W. W. Norton & Company, Inc., 470; Oxford University Press (London), 79, 81, 83, 84, 156, 184, 185, 307, 482, 483, 484, 505, 507; Oxford University Press (New York), 128, 129, 273, 383; Penguin Books, Ltd.. 78, 90, 340, 443; Princeton University Press, 359, 449; Random House, Inc., 424, 425, 426, 445; Routledge & Kegan Paul, Ltd., 221, 232, 233; St. Martin's Press, Inc., 153, 630; Sheed & Ward, Inc., 403; University Books, Inc., 544; University of Chicago Press, 40, 56, 75, 255, 444, 448; The Viking Press, Inc., 544, 545; Yale University Press, 447, 473.

A History of Civilization: VOLUME ONE: *to* 1715, *Second Edition*

Brinton, Christopher, and Wolff

Color plates by arrangement with Harry N. Abrams, Inc.

Design by Walter Behnke

Current printing (last digit):

19   18   17   16   15   14   13   12   11   10

38974-C

Preface

IN PREPARING this revised edition of *A History of Civilization* we have had a triple aim in view. We have sought to record and interpret the fast-moving events that have occurred since the publication of the first edition in 1955; to incorporate the new discoveries that continue to revolutionize man's knowledge of his past, notably the remote past; and to profit by the suggestions for improvement offered by readers of the first edition. The result represents not a mere tinkering with the original work but a thorough revision and, we hope, a better and more useful book.

In particular, in Volume I we have recast large sections treating the first civilizations and the ancient Greeks, and have extended the political narrative of the Medieval West over three chapters rather than two (see Chapters V, VII, and X). We have also rearranged the two chapters (VI and IX) on the Medieval East so that they come directly after their western counterparts. In Volume II, we have reorganized the chapters on developments since the First World War and have greatly expanded our accounts of the non-western world and of the intellectual and cultural history of the twentieth-century West. Throughout the two volumes we have endeavored to trim off some of the "fat" of the original book without, we trust, cutting into the meat or impairing the flavor. The reading suggestions have been brought up to date, and the maps and illustrations have been considerably changed, specifically by the addition of the new color plates.

A revision of these dimensions would never have been possible without the help of the large number of people who have contributed suggestions. We wish to thank all the teachers—and students—who have taken the trouble to write us. We wish to express our special appreciation to the following gentlemen for their critiques of the first edition: Professors Paul J. Alexander, University of Michigan; the Reverend John Francis Bannon, St. Louis University; William A. Baumgartner, Paterson State College; William Bouwsma, University of California, Berkeley; Roderic H. Davison, George Washington University; Harold S. Fink, University of Tennessee; Franklin L. Ford, Harvard University; Carl Hammond, Flint Junior College; Arthur R. Hogue, Indiana University; H. Stuart Hughes, Harvard University; and Dun Li, Benjamin Matelson, and Alfred Young, all Paterson State College. And, as the second edition goes to press, we thank again the expert readers who five years ago contributed so substantially to the improvement of the original manuscript: Professors Richard V. Burks, Wayne State University; Leland H. Carlson, Northwestern University; Myron P. Gilmore, Harvard University; E. H. Harbison, Princeton University; Harry Kimber, Michigan State University; Harry R. Rudin, Yale University; Kenneth Setton, University of Pennsylvania; Robert A. Spiller, University of Pennsylvania; and Henry R. Winkler, Rutgers University.

Finally, we wish to record our especially heavy debt to those with whom we have worked most closely: to the late Donald C. McKay of Amherst College, the editor of the parent volumes, whose untimely death occurred just as the revision was beginning to take shape; to the members of the staff both at Prentice-Hall, Inc., and at Harry N. Abrams, Inc., who have applied their skills and energies most generously and effectively; and to our families and colleagues whose sympathy, understanding, and aid have demonstrated anew that authors' tributes are no mere courteous gestures but are based on solid historical facts.

CRANE BRINTON · JOHN B. CHRISTOPHER · ROBERT L. WOLFF

A Note on the Endpapers

Some day psychologists may be able to tell us just what and how to remember. But at present we know little more than this: though a few exceptional people can absorb and tap at will large stores of systematically arranged facts—say the list of popes from St. Peter on—most human beings cannot remember great systems of facts for very long unless they make fairly regular use of them. Indeed, if we never did any figuring at all, most of us would forget the multiplication table. Few of us make any regular use of history. Fortunately, the modern world is admirably supplied with works of ready reference that can free our minds for more useful work than just memorizing. The engineer, for example, does not need to keep in mind all the formulas and equations he might need; he has his engineer's handbook. So anyone using history has a host of reference books available in libraries, and on his desk he may have for immediate use such a storehouse of information as the one-volume *Encyclopaedia of World History* (Houghton Mifflin, 1948), edited by W. L. Langer.

Yet we do need something like a historian's equivalent of the multiplication table, if only to give us a frame of reference. The trouble with most historical tables, however, is that they are much too long and contain far too many facts for the average person. It is as if our multiplication table, instead of stopping with twelve times twelve, or even ten times ten, went on to fifty times fifty. The list of dates beginning in the front endpaper of this volume and continuing in the other endpapers is an attempt to construct the historian's equivalent of the multiplication table. It is a simple list of approximately a hundred dates, a kind of rough map of historic time. It is worth memorizing bit by bit and keeping in memory.

The list is not necessarily meant to include all the "hundred great dates." It is meant rather to assist the reader to keep his mind on the course of history by focusing on two threads that serve to put an order, a pattern, into a complex set of facts.

First, there is the concept of recorded history as a series of streams which have different sources on this earth, but which finally flow together in the One World of the present. Of course, some of the streams—the Chinese, the East Indian, the African, for example—have by no means wholly mingled, and are still present as separate currents. We take as the main stream in the endpapers, as we do in this book, our western civilization with its sources in the river valleys of the ancient Near East.

Second, there is the concept of a specific region or nation as a leader, a center, a focal point of historic change in our own western civilization at a given period. Periclean Athens, the Rome of the Caesars, and Victorian Britain are classic examples. Very broadly speaking, these centers of leadership have since 3000 B.C. swung westward and northward in a huge arc, from Egypt and Mesopotamia to Greece, Rome, western and central Europe, the United States. But the metaphor is imperfect. As we have taken pains to point out in this book, in the thousand years after the "fall" of the western Roman Empire, the Byzantines, the Slavs, and even perhaps the Moslems were in some ways quite as focal to western history as the medieval westerners. Moreover, leadership, especially in politics, may pass from one region to another, and former leaders like ancient Athens may fall almost to the status of ghost towns. Yet on the whole the area of western civilization constantly widens. Those parts left behind in the march of history do not lapse into an entirely separate existence; they remain a part, though only a subsidiary part, of the West.

A Note on the Reading Suggestions

A LIST OF READING SUGGESTIONS is appended to each chapter of this book. Almost all historical bibliographies nowadays begin apologetically with the statement that they are highly selective and do not, of course, aspire to be exhaustive. This apology is hardly necessary, for the fact is that in most fields of history we have outrun the possibility of bringing together in one list all the books and articles in all languages on a given topic. There are for the wide fields of this book, and in English alone, thousands of volumes and hundreds of thousands of articles in periodicals. The brief lists following each chapter are simply suggestions to the reader who wishes to explore a given topic further.

Each list attempts to give important and readable books for each chapter. Special attention has been paid to inexpensive editions, often paper-backed, in such series as Mentor Books (published by the New American Library), Penguin and Pelican Books, Anchor Books (published by Doubleday), the Teach-Yourself-History Library (published by Macmillan), Torchbooks (published by Harper's), Vintage Books (published by Knopf), and many, many others. A useful guide to paper-backs is *Paperbound Books in Print,* which appears twice a year (Bowker).

Good readings in original sources, the contemporary documents and writings of an age, are sometimes listed, though the reader can supplement these listings from the text itself and from the footnotes. In addition, there are many good collections of sources for European history, notably the *Introduction to Contemporary Civilization in the West* (1954), prepared by faculty members at Columbia University; this begins with the Middle Ages and gives much longer selections from the sources than such compilations usually do. Other good collections are to be found in the Portable Readers (published by Viking). There are also many source books and pamphlets on central or controversial problems in European history. A good example is K. M. Setton and H. R. Winkler, eds., *Great Problems in European Civilization* (Prentice-Hall, 1954).

Our lists also include historical novels and, occasionally, dramas. Professional historians are likely to be somewhat severe in their standards for a historical novel. They naturally want its history to be sound; and at bottom they are likely to be somewhat prejudiced against the form as a painting of their lily or a sweetening of their pill. The historical novels listed here are all readable and all reasonably good as history. But note that historical novels, like historical films, though accurate on such material matters as

authentic settings and appropriate costumes, often fail to capture the immaterial aspects
—the psychology, the spirit—of the age they are written about. Many such novels moti-
vate their characters, especially in love, as if they were modern Europeans and
Americans. Exceptions to this rule are noted in the lists.

It is not hard to assemble more material on a given topic than is furnished by our
reading lists. American libraries, large and small, have catalogues with subject and title
listings, as well as a section of reference books with encyclopaedias and bibliographies.
Many libraries have open shelves where, once a single title is discovered, many others
may be found in the immediate area. Perhaps the first printed list of books to be consulted is *A Guide to Historical Literature* (Macmillan, 1931), a revised edition of which
is promised for the near future. For more recent books one can turn, for American
history, to the *Harvard Guide to American History* (Belknap, 1954), edited by
O. Handlin and others. And for the history of Europe and other areas there are many
good bibliographies; see, for example, those in the volumes of "The Rise of Modern
Europe" series edited by W. L. Langer and published by Harper; in the multi-volumed
Oxford History of England; and in R. R. Palmer and J. Colton, *A History of the Modern
World* (Knopf, 1956). For historical fiction, one may consult two older specialized
guides: E. A. Baker, *A Guide to Historical Fiction* (Macmillan, 1914) and J. Nield, *A
Guide to the Best Historical Novels and Tales* (Elkins, Mathews, and Marrot, 1929).
The more recent *Fiction Catalogue* (Wilson, 1951) covers much besides historical
fiction but does furnish keys to books that cover particular countries and particular
historical eras.

What is much more difficult than assembling titles is securing an evaluation of
individual books. For older books the *Guide to Historical Literature,* already mentioned,
gives the most useful references to critical reviews of the titles it discusses. *The Book
Review Digest* gives capsule reviews and references to longer ones. For current books
the weekly book section of *The New York Times* and *The Times Literary Supplement*
(published in London) usually provide informative reviews of historical works soon
after they are published. Later—sometimes as much as three years later—full scholarly
appraisals are published in the *American Historical Review,* its British equivalent the
English Historical Review, and in many more specialized reviews, such as the *Journal
of Modern History* and, for medieval studies, *Speculum.* By reading a few reviews of a
book one can usually get an indication of its scope and quality. In the reading suggestions
for these volumes we have tried, within a brief compass, to give our readers comparable
indications.

Contents

INTRODUCTION The Uses of History, *3*

I

The First Men and the First Civilizations, *9*

I. BEFORE WRITTEN HISTORY. *Prehistoric Man. The Chronology of Prehistoric Man. The Culture of Prehistoric Man. Some Conclusions about Man. II.* OUR NEAR EASTERN ORIGINS. *When Did Civilization and History Begin? The Challenge of the River Valleys. The Near Eastern States. Common Denominators of Near Eastern Civilization. Our Debt to the Near East. III.* EGYPT. *The Setting. An Outline of Egyptian History. Egyptian Society. Religion. Culture. The Egyptian Style.´ IV.* MESOPOTAMIA. *The Setting. An Outline of Mesopotamian History. Culture. The Assyrian, Babylonian, and Persian Styles. V.* THE PERIPHERY—THE JEWS. *The Peoples Outside the Valleys. The History of the Jews. The Uniqueness of the Jews. The Beginnings of a Universal Faith.*

II

The Greeks, *49*

I. THE BACKGROUND. *The Natural Setting. Minoan Civilization. II.* EARLY GREEK HISTORY. *Mycenaean Civilization. The Dorian Invasion and Its Results. Homer. The City-State. The Age of Colonization. Changing Forms of Government. III.* SPARTA AND ATHENS. *The Spartan Régime. Spartan Institutions Evaluated. The Athenian Régime. The Early History of Athens. Pisistratus and Cleisthenes. The Institutions of Athenian Democracy. Athenian Democracy Evaluated. The Persian Wars. The Athenian Empire. IV.* GREEK CIVILIZATION. *Religion. Tragic Drama. Comedy. Poetry. The Arts. Science. Philosophy: Socrates. Philosophy: Plato. Philosophy: Aristotle. Everyday Life. The Greek Style. V.* THE DECLINE AND TRANSFORMATION OF GREEK CIVILIZATION. *The Peloponnesian War. The Aftermath of War. The Rise of Macedon. Alexander the Great. The Hellenistic States. Hellenistic Culture. The Hellenistic Style.*

III

The Romans, 95

I. INTRODUCTION. *The Setting. The Etruscans.* II. RISE OF THE REPUBLIC. *The Army. Government. Liberalization of the Republic. Expansion in Italy. Rome and Carthage. Rome and the Hellenistic World.* III. THE CRISIS AND COLLAPSE OF THE REPUBLIC. *Signs of Trouble. The Reforms of the Gracchi. The Road to Autocracy. Marius and Sulla. Pompey and Caesar. The End of the Republic.* IV. THE FIRST TWO CENTURIES OF THE ROMAN EMPIRE (27 B.C.-180 A.D.). *Augustus (Octavian) 27 B.C.-14 A.D. The Successors of Augustus to 180 A.D. The Provinces of the Empire. The Administration of the Empire.* V. ROMAN CIVILIZATION. *Law. Science and Engineering. The Fine Arts. Religion and Philosophy. Literature. Standard of Living.* VI. THE DECLINE OF ROME. *Unsuccessful Emperors (180-284). The Reforms of Diocletian and His Successors. Why Rome Declined.* VII. CONCLUSION.

IV

Christianity, 141

I. JESUS AND PAUL. *The Historical Jesus. The Teachings of Jesus. The First Christians. Saint Paul. The Early Spread of Christianity.* II. CHRISTIANITY IN THE PAGAN WORLD. *The Reasons for Persecution. The Persecutions. The Problems of Christianity's Triumph.* III. THE ORGANIZATION OF CHRISTIANITY. *The Need for Organization. The Hierarchy. The Supremacy of Rome. The Regular Clergy. Monasticism Evaluated. Church Government in Review.* IV. THE IDEAS OF CHRISTIANITY. *The Eucharist. The Doctrine of Salvation. The Seven Sacraments. The Problem of Heresy. Gnosticism. Arianism and the Trinity. The Dispute over the Nature of Christ. Other Heresies. Saint Augustine.* V. THE CHRISTIAN WAY OF LIFE. *The Flesh and the Spirit. The Individual and Society. Reason and Faith. Attitude toward This World.*

V

The West: *Early Middle Ages,* 173

I. THE GERMANIC INVASIONS. *The Nature of the Germanic Invasions. Losses and Survivals in the Dark Ages. Early German Expansion. The Visigoths. The Ostrogoths. The Vandals. The Huns. Burgundians and Lombards. The Anglo-Saxons.* II. THE FRANKS— THE BUILDING OF AN EMPIRE. *Clovis. The Merovingians after Clovis. Pepin and Italy. Significance of the Frankish-Papal Alliance. Expansion under Charlemagne. The Revival of the Empire. Charlemagne the Man. The Decay of the Carolingian Empire. Anglo-Saxon Britain.* III. EUROPE AND THE NORTHMEN. *The Norse Invasions: Causes and Character. The Norse Invasions: Consequences. Ireland. Germany and Italy. A Bird's-*

Eye View of the West about 1000.   IV. WESTERN INSTITUTIONS, 500-1000. *The Problem of Origins. The Breakdown into Local Units. Early Feudalism. Vassals and Lords. The Feudal Pyramid. Manorialism. Manorial Society.*   V. WESTERN CULTURE, 500-1000. *The Breakdown in Culture. The Fine Arts. Literature and Thought. The Status of the Church. The Early Feudal Way of Life.*

VI

Eastern Christendom and Islam:
To the Late Eleventh Century,   211

I. THE HISTORICAL ROLE OF BYZANTIUM. *The Character of Byzantine History. Byzantium as Preserver of the Classics. Original Writing. The Arts. War. Diplomacy. Economic Prosperity.*   II. BYZANTINE GOVERNMENT AND SOCIETY. *The Emperor. The Law. The Capital and the Factions.*   III. CHURCH AND STATE. *Religion at Byzantium. Contrast with the West. The Great Theological Controversies. Ritual and Monasticism. The Schism. Antagonism between East and West.*   IV. THE FORTUNES OF EMPIRE, 330-1081. *The Main Periods of Byzantine History, 330-1081. 330-717. The Reorganization of the Seventh and Eighth Centuries. 717-867. 867-1081.*   V. BYZANTIUM AND THE SLAVS. *Conversion of the Bulgarians. The Early Russian State. Conversion of the Russians. Effects of Conversion. Kievan Russia.*   VI. ISLAM BEFORE THE CRUSADES. *Mohammed. Expansion of Islam. Disunity in Islam. Islamic Civilization. Science. Philosophy, Literature, and the Arts.*

VII

Monarchy in the Medieval West:
To the Early Fourteenth Century,   259

I. INTRODUCTION.   II. THE DEVELOPMENT OF FRANCE, HUGH CAPET TO PHILIP THE FAIR. *The Capetians. The Contest with Normans and Angevins. The Albigensian Crusade and the Winning of the South. Royal Administration. Saint Louis. The System Hardens: Philip the Fair. Philip the Fair's Struggle for Money. Protest in France.*   III. THE DEVELOPMENT OF ENGLAND, 1066-1307. *The Norman Conquest. Henry I and Henry II: Administration and Law. Henry II and Becket. Richard I and John. John and the Barons: Magna Carta. Henry III and the Barons. The Origins of Parliament. Knights of the Shire and Burgesses. Edward I.*   IV. THE DEVELOPMENT OF GERMANY AND THE EMPIRE, 911-1273. *Dukes and King. Saxon Administration. The Empire. Salian Administration. The Investiture Controversy to 1077. The Investiture Controversy, 1077-1122. The Investiture Controversy: Aftermath. Frederick Barbarossa. The Struggle with the Italian Towns. Barbarossa's German Policies. Consequences of Henry VI's Sicilian Marriage. Frederick II. Frederick II and the Papacy.*   V. CONCLUSION.

CONTENTS

VIII

Medieval Civilization in the West, 301

I. INTRODUCTION. *The Material Basis. The Towns. The Growth of Central Authority.* II. THE MEDIEVAL CHURCH. *Medieval and Modern Christianity Contrasted. The Cluniac Reform Movement. Significance of the Cluniac Movement. St. Bernard and the Cistercians. The Friars. Lollards and Hussites. The Challenge of the New Dynastic States. The Conciliar Movement.* III. MEDIEVAL THOUGHT. *Education. The Church and Public Opinion. Medieval Formal Thought. Nominalism and Realism. Saint Thomas Aquinas. Political Thought. Economic Thought. The Law of Nature. The Medieval and the Modern Outlooks Contrasted. Mysticism. Science.* IV. LAY CULTURE. *Early Chivalry. Later Chivalry. Popular Culture.* V. MEDIEVAL ART. *The Stamp of the Community. Gothic Architecture. Gothic Architecture Evaluated. The Other Fine Arts. Music.* VI. CONCLUSION: THE MEDIEVAL WAY OF LIFE.

IX

The East: *Late Middle Ages,* 345

I. THE MAIN THREADS. *The Crusades. The Downfall of Byzantium. The Ottoman Turks. Post-Kievan Russia.* II. THE CRUSADES. *The Idea of a Holy War. Pilgrimages. The Late-Eleventh-Century Crisis. The First Crusade. The Crusader States. The Military Orders. The Moslem Reconquest. The Later Crusades. The Meeting of East and West. Impact of the Crusades on the West.* III. THE FORTUNES OF EMPIRE, 1081-1453. *Western Influences at Byzantium. Byzantine Feudalism. The Fourth Crusade. The Latin Empire. Byzantium after 1261. The Advance of the Ottoman Turks.* IV. THE OTTOMAN SUCCESSOR-STATE, 1453-1699. *A Slave System. The "Four Pillars" of Administration. Weaknesses of the Ottoman System. Ottoman Expansion to 1566. Ottoman Decline, 1566-1699. The End of an Era.* V. RUSSIA FROM THE THIRTEENTH TO THE END OF THE SEVENTEENTH CENTURY. *The Western Lands. The North. The Northeast: Moscow and the Tartars. Tartar Impact on Russian Civilization. The Development of the Muscovite State. The Autocracy. Nobles and Serfs. The Reign of Ivan the Terrible. The Time of Troubles. The Role of the Zemski Sobor. The Role of the Church. The Expansion of Russia. Russia and the West.* VI. CONCLUSION.

X

Politics and Economics: *Late Medieval West,* 393

I. INTRODUCTION. *The Pattern of Late Medieval Politics.* II. THE EMERGING NATIONAL MONARCHIES. *The Hundred Years' War: The First Round. The Aftermath of Defeat in France. The Hundred Years' War: The Second Round. France: Louis XI. England: Edward II and Edward III. The Evolution of Parliament. Richard II. Lancaster and York. Henry VII: The First Tudor. Spain. Ferdinand and Isabella.* III. PARTICULARISM IN GERMANY AND ITALY. *The German Interregnum and Its Results. Elective Monarchy: The Golden Bull of 1356. The Consolidation of Princely Power. The Italian States. Milan. Florence. Venice. The "School of Europe." Machiavelli.* IV. ECONOMIC CHANGES. *Trade. The Hanse. Venice. Industry. Banking. Jacques Coeur and the Fuggers. Social Impact of Economic Change. Political and Cultural Impact of Economic Change.*

XI

The Renaissance, 439

I. INTRODUCTION: THE PROBLEM OF THE RENAISSANCE. II. LITERATURE AND THOUGHT. The Rise of the Vernaculars. Humanism. Dante. Petrarch. Boccaccio. Preservation of the Classics. Chaucer and Rabelais. The Platonic Academy. Erasmus. III. THE ARTS: PAINTING. Main Characteristics of Renaissance Art. Giotto. Patronage, Subject Matter, and Technique. Leonardo. Michelangelo and Titian. Northern European Painting. IV. THE OTHER ARTS. Sculpture. Architecture. Music. V. SCIENCE. The Place of the Renaissance in the History of Science. Technology and Invention. Medicine and Anatomy. Astronomy. VI. RELIGION. The Relationship between the Renaissance and Religion. The Condition of the Church. Proposals for Reform. VII. CONCLUSION: THE RENAISSANCE STYLE.

XII

The Protestant Reformation, 479

I. PROTESTANT ORIGINS—LUTHER. The End of Medieval Religious Unity. Luther and the Ninety-Five Theses. Luther's Revolt. The Reasons for Luther's Success. The Opposition to Luther. The Lutheran Church. Knights' War and Peasants' Rebellion. II. PROTESTANT ORIGINS—ZWINGLI, CALVIN, AND OTHER FOUNDERS. Zwingli. Calvin. The English Reformation. The Anabaptists. Unitarianism. III. PROTESTANT BELIEFS AND PRACTICES. Common Denominators. Anglicanism. Lutheranism. Calvinism: Predestination. Calvinist Practice: Puritanism. The Left Wing. IV. THE CATHOLIC REFORMATION. The Jesuits. The Inquisition. The Council of Trent. V. THE PLACE OF PROTESTANTISM IN HISTORY. Protestantism and Progress. Protestantism and Capitalism. Protestantism and Nationalism

XIII

Dynastic and Religious Wars, 515

I. INTERNATIONAL POLITICS—THE MODERN EUROPEAN STATE-SYSTEM. The Competitive State-System. Dynastic State and Nation State. Diplomacy. The Armed Forces. II. HABSBURG AND VALOIS. The Italian Wars of Charles VIII and Louis XII. Charles V and Francis I: The First Round. Charles V and Francis I: The Second Round. The Peace of Augsburg. The Wars of Philip II. The Dutch Revolt. The End of Philip II. The Dutch Republic. III. THE THIRTY YEARS' WAR. Nature and Causes. The Bohemian Period, 1618-1625. The Danish Period, 1625-1629. The Swedish Period, 1630-1635. The Swedish and French Period, 1635-1648. Effects on Germany. The Peace of Westphalia. IV. THE NEW MONARCHIES—SPAIN AND FRANCE. The "Age of Absolutism." Power and Limits of Spanish Absolutism. The Spanish Economy. The Spanish Style. The French Monarchy. The French Wars of Religion, 1562-1598. The Victory of Henry of Navarre. The Politiques. V. THE NEW MONARCHIES—ENGLAND. Henry VIII, 1509-1547. Tudor Parliaments. Religious Difficulties. Elizabeth the Queen. The English Renaissance.

CONTENTS

XIV

The Expansion of Europe:

Fifteenth through Seventeenth Centuries, 561

> I. INTRODUCTION. *Ancient and Modern Expansion Contrasted. The Motives and Nature of Modern Expansion.* II. EAST BY SEA TO THE INDIES. *Prince Henry and the Portuguese. Africa. India. China. The Portuguese Empire.* III. WEST BY SEA TO THE INDIES. *Columbus. Later Explorers. The Foundation of the Spanish Empire. The First True Colonial Empire. The Balance Sheet of Latin-American Empire.* IV. THE LATECOMERS —FRANCE, HOLLAND, ENGLAND. *Early French and English Activity. The Thirteen Colonies: Settlement. The Thirteen Colonies: Institutions. New France. The Indies, West and East. Africa. The Far East.* V. THE BEGINNINGS OF ONE WORLD. *The Black Side of the Record. The Economic Record. Effects of Expansion on the West. The One World of 1700.*

XV

Divine-Right Monarchy — and Revolution, 597

> I. INTERNATIONAL POLITICS—FRANCE AS AGGRESSOR. *Before Louis XIV: Henry IV and Sully. Before Louis XIV: Richelieu and Mazarin. The Successes of Louis XIV. The Failures of Louis XIV. The Utrecht Settlement. French Aggression in Review.* II. THE FRANCE OF LOUIS XIV. *Divine-Right Monarchy. The Nobility. The Clergy. The Royal Administration. Mercantilism in Theory. Mercantilism in Practice: Colbert.* III. ENGLAND IN REVOLUTION. *The Constitutional Tradition. The Role of the Crown. Issues between Crown and Parliament. The Reign of James I (1603-1625). The Troubles of Charles I. The Road to Civil War, 1638-1642. The Civil War, 1642-1649. Cromwell and the Interregnum, 1649-1660. The Revolution in Review. The Restoration, 1660-1688. The Glorious Revolution of 1688-1689.* IV. THE CENTURY OF GENIUS. *Natural Science. The Implications of Scientific Progress. The Classical Spirit. The Arts. Seventeenth-Century Culture in Review.*

Index, 641

Maps *by Vaughn Gray*

Cradles of Civilization, *19*

Ancient Greece, *50*

Greek Colonial World, *58*

Alexander's Empire and the Hellenistic World, *88*

Growth of Roman Dominions under the Republic, *105*

Growth of Roman Dominions under the Empire, *118*

Roman Empire under Diocletian, *134*

Germanic Invasion Routes, *178*

Germanic Kingdoms in 526, *181*

Carolingian Empire, *186*

Invasions of Europe—7th through 11th Centuries, *192*

Byzantine Empire, *220*

Moslem Expansion, *250*

Medieval France and England, *263*

German "Drang nach Osten," *285*

Medieval Germany and Italy, *296*

Religious Situation about 1100, *306*

Crusader States, *354*

Medieval and Early Modern Russia— 1190-1689, *377*

England and France during the Hundred Years' War, *396*

Burgundian Dominions, *401*

Christian Reconquest of Spain, *411*

Germany and the Baltic in the 15th Century, *416*

Renaissance Italy, *418*

Religious Situation about 1600, *507*

Political Situation about 1560, *525*

Europe in 1648, *538-539*

Growth of Empires to 1715, *562*

India about 1715, *587*

Europe in 1715, *604-605*

Illustrations

ABBREVIATIONS: *AMNH*, Courtesy of the American Museum of Natural History; *BA*, The Bettman Archive; *BIS*, British Information Services; *BM*, Courtesy of the Trustees of the British Museum; *BMFA*, Courtesy of the Boston Museum of Fine Arts; *EG*, Ewing Galloway; *ENIT*, Italian State Tourist Office; *FTO*, French Government Tourist Office; *MMA*, Courtesy of the Metropolitan Museum of Art; *NYPL*, New York Public Library; *NYPLPC*, New York Public Library Picture Collection; *PAA*, Pan American World Airways; *TWA*, Trans World Airlines; *VAM*, Courtesy of the Victoria and Albert Museum, Crown Copyright.

CHAPTER I: Early Human Tools (*AMNH*), 12; Early Men (*AMNH*), 13; Reindeer (*AMNH*), 15; Pyramids (*TWA*), 24; Rosetta Stone (*BM*), 26; Ikhnaton and Nefertiti (*both formerly State Museums, Berlin*), 30; Temple at Karnak (*TWA*), 31; Egyptian Scribe (*Louvre*), 32; Ruins of Ur (*NYPLPC*), 35; Assyrians Attacking (*BM*), 38; Audience Hall at Persepolis (*Courtesy Oriental Institute of the University of Chicago*), 39.

CHAPTER II: Toreador Fresco (*Cnossos Museum, Candia, Crete*), 51; Snake *Goddess* (*BMFA*), 52; Temple at Paestum (*Sawders from Cushing*), 57; Greek Vase (*BMFA*), 63; Athenian Coin (*BMFA*), 68; Acropolis (*Greek Embassy Press and Information Service*), 71; Epidaurus Theater (*EG*), 73; Parthenon Frieze, 76; Discobolus (*Museo delle Terme, Rome*), 77; Alexander the Great, 87; Old Market Woman (*MMA*), 90.

CHAPTER III: Etruscan Wall Painting (*Tarquinia, Italy*), 97; Roman Soldier (*Courtesy of the Museum, York, England*), 98; Augustus (*MMA*), 113; Maison Carrée (*Nimes, France*), 116; Roman Surgical Instruments (*MMA*), 121; Pont du Gard (*French Embassy Press and Information Division*), 122; Temple at Baalbek (*PAA*), 123; Vespasian (*BA*), 124; Ostia Mosaic (*ENIT*), 125; Street in Pompeii (*ENIT*), 130; Colosseum, 131.

CHAPTER IV: Good Shepherd (*Lateran Museums, Rome*), 143; Madonna and Child (*Catacomb of Priscilla, Rome*), 149; Santa Maria Maggiore, 155; Bishop's Chair (*Archiepiscopal Museum, Ravenna*), 159; Marys at Sepulchre (*Castello Sforzesco, Milan*), 162; Sarcophagus (*Sant'Apollinare in Classe, Ravenna*), 170.

CHAPTER V: Mounted Soldier (*BA*), 179; Charlemagne (*NYPL*), 187; Viking Ship (*Norwegian Information Service*), 190; Bayeux Tapestry (*VAM*), 193; Queen Mary's Psalter (*BM*), 197; Plan of Medieval Manor (*adapted from* Introduction to English Industrial History *by Henry Allsop*, G. Bell & Sons, Ltd.), 202; Purse Cover (*BM*), 205; Merovingian Tombstone, 206.

CHAPTER VI: Santa Sophia (*PAA*), 216; St. Mark's Exterior (*PAA*), 218; St. Mark's Interior, 219; Constantine and Justinian with Madonna (*The Byzantine Institute, Inc.*), 228; Silver Plate with Theodosius (*NYPL*), 235; Church of the Savior (*Sovfoto*), 244; Mohammed (*BA*), 248; Umayyad Mosque (*Arab Information Center*), 252; Cordova Mosque (*News Bureau, Spanish National Tourist Department*), 256.

CHAPTER VII: Palais de Justice, 266; Carcassonne (*FTO*), 268; Bayeux Tapestry (*VAM*), 274-275; *Parliament under Edward I* (*BA*), 282; Frederick Barbarossa (*NYPLPC*), 291; Tomb of Henry the Lion (*Cathedral, Brunswick, Germany*), 293.

CHAPTER VIII: Fountains Abbey (*BIS*), 309; King's College (*BIS*), 313; Scenes of Student Life (*from* Statutenbuch des Collegium Sapientiae, *The Pierpont Morgan Library*), 314; Medieval Society (*NYPL*), 321; Chartres Cathedral (*EG*), 332; St. Sernin, Toulouse, 333; Notre Dame Cathedral (*TWA*), 334; Beauvais Cathedral (*Ward-Princehorn*), 335; Church of Saint-Maclou, Rouen, 336; Mont-St.-Michel (*FTO*), 337; Portal, Chartres Cathedral, 338; Romanesque Capital at Vézelay, 339; "October" (*from* Les très riches heures du duc de Berry), 341.

CHAPTER IX: Battle between Crusaders and Moslems (*BA*), 353; Krak des Chevaliers (*Arab Information Center*), 357; St. Mark's Horses (*ENIT*), 365; Anastasis (*The Byzantine Institute, Inc.*), 366; Golden Gate in Vladimir, 378; Muscovite Soldiers (*BA*), 381; Ivan the Terrible (*National Museum, Copenhagen*), 385; St. Basil Cathedral, 388; Seventeenth-century Moscow House (*NYPLPC*), 389.

CHAPTER X: Peasants' Revolt, 406; Henry VII (*Courtesy of the National Portrait Gallery, London*), 409; Scenes from Der Sachsenspiegel (*by permission of Insel-Verlag*), 414-415; Burning of Savonarola, 421; Lorenzo de' Medici (*NYPLPC*), 422; Venice in the Sixteenth Century (*from* Civitates Orbis Terrarum, 1573, *by G. Braun, NYPL, Reserve Division*), 429; House of Jacques Coeur, Bourges, 432; Jacob Fugger (*BA*), 433; Fuggerei (*German Tourist Information Office*), 434.

CHAPTER XI: Erasmus by Dürer, 449; Giotto, "The Lamentation" (*Arena Chapel, Padua*), 452; Botticelli, "Primavera" (*Uffizi Gallery, Florence*), 453; Masaccio, "Expulsion" (*S. Maria del Carmine, Florence*), 454; Leonardo, "Madonna of the Rocks" (*Louvre*), 456; Michelangelo, "Creation" (*Sistine Chapel, Rome*), 457; Breughel, "Peasant Wedding" (*Kunsthistorisches Museum, Vienna*), 459; Donatello, "Gattamelata", 460; Donatello, "Mary Magdalen" (*Baptistery, Florence*), 461; Michelangelo, "Pietà," 462; St. Peter's Cathedral (*BA*), 464; Grimani Palace, Venice, 465; Leonardo, Drawing of Crossbow, 467; Michelangelo, "Moses" (*S. Pietro in Vincoli, Rome*), 472.

CHAPTER XII: Luther, by Cranach (*MMA*), 481; Pope in Hell (*Courtesy of the Museum of Modern Art*), 484; Rebelling German Peasants (*NYPLPC*), 487; Zwingli (*NYPLPC*), 490; Henry VIII, by Holbein (*National Gallery, Rome*), 492; Anabaptists (*NYPLPC*), 494; Page from a Catechism (*NYPL*), 498; Sketches of Calvin (*from* Iconographie calvinienne *by Emile Doumergue, NYPL*), 500; John of Leyden (*NYPL*), 502; Loyola (*BA*), 505.

CHAPTER XIII: Dürer, Engraving of Cannon (*MMA*), 520; Francis I (*Courtesy of the John G. Johnson Collection, Philadelphia*), 523; Philip II (*MMA*), 527; English Fleet and Spanish Armada (*BM*), 529; Dutch Family (*NYPL*), 530; Siege of Magdeburg (*BA*), 535; Escorial (*News Bureau, Spanish National Tourist Department*), 541; Chenonceaux (*FTO*), 546; Henry IV (*NYPL*), 548; Elizabeth I (*Courtesy of the National Portrait Gallery, London*), 553; Compton Wynyates (*BIS*), 555.

CHAPTER XIV: Polo Brothers (*BA*), 567; Ma Yüan, "Sage under a Pine Tree" (*MMA*), 570; Departure from Lisbon (*BA*), 572; Jesuit Missionary (*BA*), 574; Columbus, by Sebastiano del Piombo, 575; Machu Picchu (*EG*), 578; Coatlicue (*National Museum, Mexico City*), 579; Ortelius' Map of America (*The Weyhe Gallery*), 583; Hōryūji Monastery, 589; People in Unknown Lands (*NYPL, Prints Division*), 592.

CHAPTER XV: Cardinal Richelieu (*Reproduced by Courtesy of the Trustees, National Gallery, London*), 599; Versailles (*FTO*), 609; Charles I, by Van Dyck, 614; Cromwell Dissolving Parliament (*BIS*), 620; St. Paul's Cathedral (*BIS*), 625; Descartes, by Frans Hals, 629; The Baldacchino, St. Peter's, Rome, 633; Velasquez, "The Maids of Honor," 634; Rubens, Self-Portrait (*Pinakothek, Munich*), 635; Rembrandt, "The Night Watch" (*Rijksmuseum, Amsterdam*), 636.

ILLUSTRATIONS

A
HISTORY
OF
CIVILIZATION

Introduction:

The Uses of History

THE WORD HISTORY has two broad general meanings. It can mean everything that has happened, past history, even just the Past, as contrasted with the Present and the Future; and it can mean the study of the past and the resulting oral or written record of what has happened in that past. For several thousand years now, both the making and the study of the historical record have interested many individuals. But they have clearly never interested everybody. Now that universal education requires nearly everyone to study some history, hundreds of thousands of people are obliged to fill their heads, for a while at least, not merely with the tales and heroes of their nation, but with facts about the Code of Hammurabi, the faith of Ikhnaton, the trade routes of medieval Europe, the influence on American political institutions of the writings of John Locke, and a very great deal more. Since some people dislike the study of history, just as others dislike the study of mathematics, an introduction to the study of history must begin with some justification of that study. In the United States, especially, the historian is confronted with the forceful "Hammurabi —so what?"

Yet the historian ought not to be apologetic, and above all he ought not to yield to the temptation, so natural in modern arguments, to rest his entire case on the practical value of history. Some people love the study of history. Some actually enjoy storing their memories with lists of kings and battles; some are moved by the endless skeins of association the past affords, by the sickle-curve of the beach at Marathon, by the gargoyles of Notre Dame de Paris, by the rude bridge that arches the flood at Concord, by the wheat field at Gettysburg; others are fascinated by the inexhaustible resources the historical record offers for research, for the exercise of the detective instinct. These lovers of Clio, the muse of history, have seemed a bit odd to those who do not share their enthusiasm. They have been called "antiquarians," a term of gentle reproach on the lips of those busied with the details of daily life. Yet, in a world where so much human activity is directed toward making others conform, the activity of historians is a refreshing reminder that human beings are not identical, that their interests vary. The pursuit of history is essentially a quiet occupation. Historians are rarely disturbers of the peace. Historians—most of them, one hopes—enjoy reading and writing history. Surely this alone would be a full justification for the study of history.

There is, however, no sense in maintaining that the study of history ought to be a pleasure for all. Moreover, even those who do find it a pleasure are not above consoling themselves by finding it also useful and edifying. Yet, in comparison with the natural sciences, history is not readily shown to be useful in our contemporary American common-sense meaning of "useful." For example, the study of history and the practice of politics have not as yet scored over the disease of race discrimination the kind of victory that the study of biology and the practice of medicine have scored over typhoid fever. And it must be admitted that, in comparison with literature and the arts, history as it is written nowadays—including history as written in this book—does not serve clear aesthetic or moral ends. History in its usual academic form is seldom either a good story or a good sermon. If you want to hold your breath as the blade of the guillotine falls on Marie Antoinette, you will have to go to older histories, to fiction, or to the movies. Nor will you find in the work of good historians that virtue is always rewarded.

Furthermore, and most important for the many "practical" people who will read this book, the study of history will not produce exact or "correct" answers to problems, answers of the sort that the scientists or engineers or perhaps even the practicing physician expect. Nor, so long as history does not turn into theology, philosophy, or just plain preaching, will it give the kind of answers to questions about man's fate that you would expect from your spiritual guides in Church or State. History, to be specific, will not tell you whether to use steel or aluminum for a given gadget. It will not choose for you between Browning's

> God's in his heaven—
> All's right with the world

and James Russell Lowell's

> Truth forever on the scaffold,
> Wrong forever on the throne.

In our time there has been a powerful current of thought, commonly called "historicism," which seeks to find in the historical record *and in it alone* the clue to man's fate—in short, to find in history alone, as the record of how man makes himself and his society, a cosmology, a philosophy, indeed a theology, a substitute for revealed religion. This book will record this attempt to make Clio not merely a muse, but a priestess, prophet, even a sole godhead. It will not, we hope, contribute to this attempt.

What history can do, however, is supply a series of case histories or clinical reports not quite as full as the best medical case histories, but still extensions of human experience, from which certain notions of how to go about handling cases in the present may be obtained. Thus at the very outset of western historical writing the Athenian Thucydides gives a case history of the struggle between Athens and Sparta, a case history of which the late General George Marshall said, "I doubt seriously whether a man can think with full wisdom and deep convictions regarding certain of the basic international issues today who has not at least reviewed in his mind the period of the Peloponnesian War and the fall of Athens." * General Marshall was not repeating the old chestnut that history repeats itself. History is full of repetition and of novelty, of similarities and differences, for history is no more than the imperfect record of the lives of millions of human beings *each like, and each unlike,* the others.

What the individual does with the materials his experience offers him is another matter. Another old chestnut asserts that all we learn from history is that we never learn from history. Certainly there exists in the United States today a tendency to feel that somehow or other we should have learned from the so-called World War I how to avoid World War II, with the panicky addition that apparently we have not learned from the first two how to avoid World War III. Yet to expect such clear-cut lessons, to expect immediate widespread effective action to follow any lesson in human relations, is precisely what a knowledge of history can show to be unwise, unreasonable, unprofitable.

For history can do more than present a mere random collection of human experiences. It can, though only roughly, only approximately, show the range—or the spectrum—of human behavior, with some indication of its extremes and averages. It can, though again by no means perfectly, show how and within what limits human behavior changes. This last is especially important

---

* Quoted in *Life,* Jan. 1, 1951, p. 96.

for the social scientist, for the economist, the sociologist, the applied anthropologist. For if these experts studied only the people and institutions existing today, they would have but imperfect notions of the real capacities of human beings. They would be like biologists with no knowledge of the contributions of historical geology and paleontology to their understanding of organic evolution. History, then, provides materials that the social scientist has to master. It provides materials that even the inspiring leader of men into new ways and new worlds—the prophet, the reformer, or the columnist—will do well to master before he tries to lead us into new ways.

For it can tell us something—not all—we need to know about the capacities and the limitations of human beings. To use a crude and to some religious temperaments an offensive analogy: history can help us understand what human material can stand and what it cannot stand, as the many contributory sciences and technologies involved can tell the engineer what stresses his metals can stand. The historian, incidentally, knows that human beings can stand a lot—much more than any metal.

At the very least, history can give an awareness of the depth of time and space that should check the optimism and the overconfidence of the reformer. Reason can show the inefficiency of many of our ways of doing things—our calendar, for example, or our Anglo-Saxon system of measurements. Millions of man-hours are wasted in the process of teaching children to read English, with its absurd spelling and its over-refined punctuation. Only in English, for instance, could one joke about *ghoti* as a spelling for "fish" (gh = f as in "rough," o = i as in "women," ti = sh as in "notion"). Yet the slightest background of history will show that human societies usually resist changes like the reform of spelling and accept them only in times of revolution, as when the metric system was introduced during the French Revolution, or under dictatorship, as when the Turkish alphabet was changed from Arabic to Roman by the twentieth-century dictator Kemal. You may still wish to reform our spelling, even though you know its history; but if you have learned anything at all from history, you will never look at the problem of getting English-speaking peoples to change their spelling as if it were a problem like that of designing a superhighway.

The historical record is most imperfect, and even the labors of generations of scholars have not filled it out. Notably, historians until quite recently have usually been more interested in the pomp and drama of the lives of the great than in the conditions of life for the masses. They have studied with care political and religious institutions, it is true, and within the last few generations they have studied economic institutions. They have paid less attention to social institutions and to folkways. Since the historians of one generation make the historical record that is handed down to later historians, our record is very faulty and cannot always be improved. No one can ever conduct a sort of retrospective Gallup Poll, for instance, to find out just what millions of fifteenth-century Frenchmen thought about Joan of Arc. Yet our ignorance must not be exaggerated either. As you can learn from any manual of historiography—that is, the history of the writing of history—historians have in the last few hundred years built up a technique and a body of verifiable facts that have lifted history far beyond Voltaire's familiar reproach that history cannot be truth, but only a story agreed upon.

Furthermore, historians have in the last two generations turned increasingly to the study of what the gifted American historian James Harvey Robinson called the "new history"—that is, to social, economic, intellectual, cultural history, to the study of the behavior of the many as well as the behavior of the conspicuous few, the rulers, warriors, priests, courtiers, and their women-folk who made the stuff of most recorded history. History is no longer merely "past politics"—and past wars; it is "past everything." Geographically, it is no longer just the history of Europe and North America; it is the history of the whole world.

Now no sensible person will deny that these newer interpretations have greatly enriched and deepened the study of history. On the other hand, this new history is much more complex, difficult, and unwieldy than was the old. To use a nice old-fashioned figure of speech out of the old "classical" education, adding China, India, the Aztecs, and a lot more in space, adding the centuries back to ancestral sub-humans in time, adding all the innumerable activities of all men to the dramatic activities of a few in politics and war—adding all this is piling Pelion on Ossa indeed. What happens, of course, is that in the ordinary "introduction" to history more ground is now covered, but it is covered less thoroughly. We have what is sometimes wryly called a "gallop through the centuries."

Often, indeed, historians pile up even more material in a given space than did their predecessors. The result is sometimes a longer and more arid catalogue of details than the lists of kings, queens, presidents, consuls, generals, popes, and cardinals that used to fill the older histories. After all, a list of poets, or even of inventors, is not in itself very illuminating; and even a hasty epithet or two—"ethereal" Shelley, "sweet-voiced" Keats, "ingenious and laborious" Edison—adds very little.

The present book is in part—though only in part—a reaction against the attempt to cover all the past everywhere on earth. We hope to retain the best of the old and add the best of the new. As for space, we shall concentrate on the history of one part of the world, the Europe sometimes scornfully called a "small peninsula of Asia." We shall trace the expansion of Europe as Europeans explored, settled, colonized, and traded in all parts of the globe. But we shall be concerned with non-European peoples only as they and their histories impinged on the development of European cultures. We are not motivated by any "self-worship," by any contempt for Asians or Africans, but simply by a desire to get our own record straight. As for time, after a very brief look at the ages-long prehistoric past of western man and the beginnings of his history in the Near East, we shall be mostly concerned with the last two thousand years or so.

Obviously, this is not all a good American citizen of the second half of the twentieth century needs to know about the past of *homo sapiens*. But it is an essential part of what he needs to know, probably the part he *most* needs to know if he is to face the problems of human relations on this planet. Now for the first time, as a result of modern transportation and communication, we are physically at least part of One World.

Finally, though we hope to do justice to the complexity and variety of man's activities during these centuries, we shall still find the center of our history in his political and military record. A general history must, it seems to us, focus on these activities, for without them "what really happened" cannot be understood. No doubt a general history must also give important clues to what are labeled economic history, intellectual history, social history, history of science, history of religions, and so on. We shall do our best to give such clues. But all written history must omit vast amounts of information, facts, "coverage"; indeed, in these days the cluttered modern mind needs the kind of cleaning a general survey can afford.

Reading Suggestions
on the Uses of History

(Asterisk indicates paperbound edition.)

G. J. Renier, *History, Its Purpose and Method* (Beacon, 1950). The most readable of the many current manuals on historical writing.

J. Barzun and H. F. Graff, *The Modern Researcher* (Harcourt, Brace, 1957). An admirable introduction to the study of history, as well as a practical manual for research in history and allied fields.

There are several other useful manuals. Among them are: the old and classic account by C. V. Langlois and C. Seignobos, *Introduction to the Study of History* (Holt, 1904); G. J. Garraghan, S. J., *A Guide to Historical Method* (Fordham Univ. Press, 1946); Allan Nevins, *The Gateway to History* (Heath, 1938); and Sherman Kent, *Writing History* (Appleton-Century-Crofts, 1941).

On the study of history in general, and on the philosophy of history and the relations of history and the social sciences in particular, there is an excellent bibliography in *Bulletin No. 54* (1946) of the Social Science Research Council, "Theory and Practice in Historical Study."

I. Berlin, *Historical Inevitability* (Oxford Univ. Press, 1955). A fine introduction to the contemporary problem of "historicism," but not easy reading.

A. J. Toynbee, *Civilization on Trial* (Oxford Univ. Press, 1948; °Meridian). Several essays in this collection introduce the reader to the central views of the most famous philosopher of history in our own day. His views are presented at full length in *A Study of History*, 10 vols. (Oxford Univ. Press, 1934-1954), and in shorter form in the abridgment of the first six volumes by D. C. Somervell (Oxford Univ. Press, 1947).

P. Geyl, *Debates with Historians* (*Meridian, 1957). Contains interesting essays by a historian firmly opposed to Toynbee.

H. E. Barnes, *A History of Historical Writing* (Univ. of Oklahoma Press, 1938); J. T. Shotwell, *The History of History* (Columbia Univ. Press, 1939); J. W. Thompson, *A History of Historical Writing* (Macmillan, 1942). Three fairly recent treatments of the topic.

J. S. Black, *The Art of History: A Study of Four Great Historians of the Eighteenth Century* (Macmillan, 1926); G. P. Gooch, *History and Historians in the Nineteenth Century*, rev. ed. (Longmans, Green, 1952; *Beacon). Two good examples of special studies of historians of a particular period.

M. Bloch, *The Historian's Craft* (Knopf, 1953). A thoughtful essay, written at an advanced level, by a distinguished French historian.

S. E. Morison, *History as a Literary Art: An Appeal to Young Historians* ("Old South Leaflet," Series 2, No. 1, n. d.). Brief, witty, and very instructive; by one of the few twentieth-century historians who are at once scholars and literary artists.

J. Tey (pseudonym of E. Mackintosh), *The Daughter of Time* (Macmillan, 1953). Unusual exercise in historical detective work by a distinguished writer of detective fiction.

The First Men and the First Civilizations

CHAPTER I

Opposite. WALL PAINTING FROM THE TOMB OF NAKHT, *official under Pharaoh Thutmosis IV. Egyptian, Dynasty XVIII (fifteenth century B.C.), Thebes (across the Nile from Luxor). The scene illustrates the funeral banquet commemorating Nakht, who was a scribe, astronomer, and priest of the god Amon. The dancers and musicians suggest the lighter side of the Egyptian "style" and the relatively wide range of its art.*

I: Before Written History

THE GREAT-GRANDPARENTS, certainly the great-great grandparents, of almost everyone who reads this book believed without questioning that the entire course of history, not only of human beings, but of the organic and inorganic universe, had lasted about 6,000 years. Indeed the Anglican Archbishop Ussher in the seventeenth century had worked out the exact date of the creation: 4004 B.C. Almost all who read this book, even those who do not unreservedly accept the theories of organic evolution, have grown familiar with the idea that the age of the earth is to be measured in billions of years, the duration of organic life on earth in millions of years, and that of human beings in tens of thousands of years. Relatively few people in western society still hold to the earlier time-scale, which rested essentially on the Old Testament of the Christian faith. The new time-scale and the accompanying classification of present human beings as members of the species *homo sapiens* have been accepted by many believers in western higher religion, but by no means by all such believers, as congruous with a belief in a God above nature—and above natural science.

This remarkable change in our time-sense, occurring in the course of a very few generations, has not yet had its full repercussions on our attitude toward the world. We have not yet fully assimilated this knowledge. The evidence that has caused us to revise our time-scale is essentially what we call "scientific evidence." More specifically, this evidence is the existence of fossils, remains of plants and animals embedded in rocks and loose earth. The pioneer geologists of the eighteenth century assumed that these rocks and deposits of gravel and sand had been produced by the very long and very slow processes of wear and tear essentially like those now going on around us. Thus it was possible to show clearly that if a given fossil in a given layer of rock were a part of the regular processes of nature as we know them from observation, then life on earth, and the earth itself, had existed for millions of years before 4004 B.C.

For several generations now, the experts have also been working in astronomy, geophysics, and allied fields; and within the last few decades they have been greatly aided by discoveries, such as radiocarbon (Carbon 14), which enable them to estimate more exactly the age of many deposits under 30,000 years old. Their timetable is not exact, nor are they all agreed on it. The tendency has been to estimate the age of the planet as greater and greater; most experts would now put that age as over, perhaps very much over, two billion years. Life in simple one-celled forms may be over a billion years old; mammals, a hundred million years; and man-like creatures, *though not present man,* at least five or six hundred thousand years. All these are approximations on which not even trained specialists are in complete agreement; in fact, if the subject is distant in geological time, specialists with a conventional sense of humor will use phrases like "give or take a million years."

Historical records—that is, written accounts that we can read—go back no more than 5,000 to 6,000 years. The ratio of the time manlike creatures have been on earth before history to the time since history began is something like the ratio of three hours to one minute. If we accept the ordinary scientific assumptions concerning the regularity of natural processes such as causation, then it should follow that man behaves as he does in the mid-twentieth century as much because of what went on in the three hours of prehistory as because of what went on in the single minute of written history. It seems quite possible that much of the physical and even the cultural base of our behavior—our appetites, our emotions, our unconscious and our subconscious lives, even our boasted thinking—was largely formed in the long centuries of prehistory, and not in the brief years that have seen the triumphs of civilization. That is the lesson most of us have not yet learned from the new time-scale the sciences of life on earth have brought us.

Prehistoric Man

Scientists have learned a great deal about those hundreds of thousands of years during which man, or a creature much like man, has been on this earth. They have had to work with very imperfect material evidences. Once man began to practice formal burial, he made quite a good fossil. But for long ages he no more practiced burial than did other mammals, and bodies were at the mercy of the elements, surviving often in merest fragments, a tooth, a bit of a jawbone or skull. Nevertheless, with infinite patience and with great help from comparative anatomy, the anthropologist can use these fragments to reconstruct within tolerable limits of error the whole body.

In a somewhat similar way, the student of the culture of prehistoric men is obliged to piece together a representation of their way of life from material fragments that have been recovered, usually only after very delicate and costly excavations of archaeological sites. What has survived are mostly tools, weapons (after all, only a special sort of tool), pottery, and, toward the end of the prehistoric period in Europe, some remarkable wall paintings. From these scattered material remains the student of prehistory has to infer what kind of men their users were. The student of prehistory has one further main resource: he can study at first hand the ways of primitive people still existing—Australian bushmen, African pygmies, and many others. Formal anthropology, which began in the nineteenth century, makes the assumption—and it is an assumption rather than a fully proved truth—that prehistoric men and modern primitives are in rather similar stages of development and share common ideas and feelings, just as they share certain material things.

The scientists who have studied prehistoric men have widened our human horizon immensely. They have brought home to us how long and how hard men have struggled to get that slight margin over daily needs without which invention, innovation, and civilization could not have begun. But they cannot tell us much about the sum total of conditions that make invention (or innovation, or "progress") successful in a society. Nor can they tell us nearly all we should like to know about the religion, the morals, and the sense of values of prehistoric men. Suppose, for example, almost all vestiges of the present American culture had vanished —all Americans, all historical records, all knowledge of the language. Suppose there were left only the more durable objects from several dozen Main Streets scattered from the Atlantic to the Pacific. Intelligent students of prehistory in the eightieth century could learn a lot about Americans, and would be struck by the identity of many articles in all the sites. They would almost certainly infer that the United States was a single culture or civilization. They might well infer from the number and complexity of the objects that it was a "materialistic" culture. But what guesses, lacking verbal accounts, they would have to make about

American religion, art and literature, political beliefs and habits, family life! Even were they helped by excavating several dozens of cemeteries, they could hardly do more than make ingenious stabs at describing Americans as they really were. Similarly, we today can do little more than make ingenious stabs at describing prehistoric man as he really was.

The Chronology of Prehistoric Man

The very first manlike creatures, or "hominids," may well go back some million years to the beginning of the Pleistocene period. Indeed, a discovery of fossil bones in soft-coal mines in Tuscany, Italy, announced in November, 1959, puts a hominid, *oreopithecus*, almost incredibly far back, some twelve million years ago. This assigned date will probably be disputed among the experts; but such discoveries keep being made, and keep disturbing established time-schemes. The hominids had, we assume, no tools; but they had the hand with the opposable thumb which they share with other primates. No anthropologist today, however, would be bothered by the problem that worried the nineteenth-century public: Is man descended from the apes? Man and apes are believed to have a very distant common ancestor. But there is no "missing link" between man and ape, because there are no links of descent between them.

Archaeologists have worked out the chronological pattern of prehistoric man by a very careful study of artifacts—that is, the objects made by primitive man. They have constructed a sequence of periods, based on the type of material used for artifacts, starting with the Paleolithic or Old Stone Age, and continuing through the Neolithic or New Stone Age and the Bronze Age to the Iron Age. Since these archaeological studies were made in western and central Europe, later excavations in other parts of the world have made possible alterations or additions to the chronological pattern. It now appears, for instance, that in parts of Asia men had reached the latest of the chronological periods, the Iron Age, when men in Europe were still in the New Stone Age, and when men in Australia were almost certainly in the Old Stone Age. Moreover, the recent use of radiocarbon to date materials tends to shorten somewhat our estimate of the length of these prehistoric ages. But they remain thousands of years in length.

The Old Stone Age began in Europe and the Near East some million years ago, though the first tools came later. These first tools were *eoliths,* rough stones held in the fist and so crudely shaped that archaeologists cannot be sure that they really are man-made tools. But slowly, in more recent deposits, the tools become unmistakably shaped for specific tasks. We can recognize them as hatchets, awls, scrapers, needles, spear and arrow heads, increasingly well made from flint, a hard stone capable of being given a sharp cutting edge. At some point during this period, evidences of camp-fires show that man had mastered the use of fire, and that by the end of the age he could start a fire by friction with a stick. These centuries of the Old Stone Age were long, and technological change within their cultures was very slow.

In contrast with the aeons of the Paleolithic Age, the Neolithic or New Stone Age is only yesterday. It began in Europe no more than ten or twelve thousand years ago, and persists today in isolated parts of the globe. The new stone tools were ground and polished, technically far superior to the old. Moreover, Neolithic man produced pottery, cooked cereals, and made new tools of bone and horn, and new textiles. He domesticated animals—dogs, sheep, and finally horses and cattle. He made the very great invention, whose specific inventor or inventors are unknown, the wheel. In the centuries of this "Neolithic revolution," and

under conditions we shall probably never quite understand, men made cultural and technological changes which, given what they started from, are more astonishing than ours in modern times.

From the scanty remains of bodies left from these ages of prehistory, the anthropologist has constructed a sequence of species that become progressively more human. But this progression is by no means as clear and as detailed as the cultural progression built up from artifacts. *Pithecanthropus erectus* (erect ape-man), established at first on fragmentary fossils found in Java in 1891, long seemed the first man-

Early human tools. Eoliths at the bottom; paleoliths (from the Old Stone Age), a bit more shaped, in the middle; neoliths (from the New Stone Age) at the top.

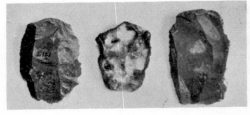

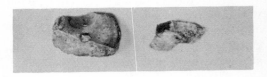

CHAPTER I

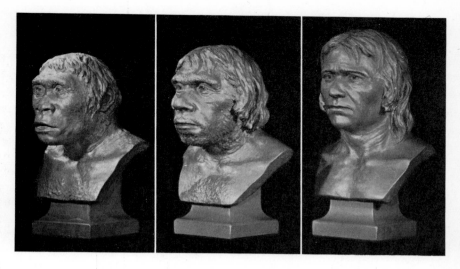

Restorations of (left to right) Pithecanthropus erectus, *Neanderthal man, and Cro-Magnon man.*

like creature. Discoveries beginning in 1925 in South Africa of fossils known as *Australopithecines* (southern apes or apelike creatures) may or may not establish an even earlier manlike creature. These hominids, labeled with long Latin-Greek names, are certainly not quite man, *homo sapiens,* of today. They go on two feet, but stoop or slouch a bit; they have a face rather than a snout, but the chin, nose, and forehead are conspicuously more apelike and less human than ours.

Manlike species apparently existed in Europe, Asia, and Africa through most of the glacial age. This age, some million years in duration, was marked by successive advances and retreats of great ice sheets, and by alternating mild and severe climates. Just before the last advance of the glacier in western Europe, probably less than fifty thousand years ago, there appeared types known as *homo,* though not quite *homo sapiens.* Of these, the best known is *homo neandertalensis,* Neanderthal man, named from the little gorge near Düsseldorf in Germany where the first find was made in the mid-nineteenth century. The type is now well established, and is a favorite one for restoration in museums. Neanderthal men—and women—were solidly built, with big heads, somewhat receding chins and prognathous jaws, and sloping foreheads.

These people had tools and knew the use of fire; they were, in short, men of the Old Stone Age.

Finally, still in the Old Stone Age, there are true men, *homo sapiens,* men who could breed with us today, men who would not surprise us greatly were we to meet them in the street properly clothed and barbered. The best-known of these is Cro-Magnon man, named from the cave in France where his remains were discovered. He was a white man, a European, and the creator of some remarkable works of art. Cro-Magnon man probably does not exist on earth today. He represents a variety, a subspecies, or in our ordinary language, a *race* of men. He was long-headed and fairly tall, and seems most closely related to the present long-headed peoples of Europe.

The first appearance on earth of our species, *homo sapiens,* cannot be dated very exactly. The contributing sciences—anthropology, historical geology, especially its branch called glaciology, chemistry, especially the use of radioactive elements like Carbon 14—progress rapidly these days. From 20,000 to 50,000 years ago, perhaps more, will have to do as a guess. Recent discoveries, notably at Fontechevade in France in 1947, have given some support to the theory that the shaggy-browed Neanderthal man himself was rather an early cousin of ours, so to speak, and not an ancestor. The formal recognition by British authorities in 1953 that the so-called "Piltdown man" depended on a hoax perpetrated in 1911 at least cleared away some difficulties for the anthropologist. The Piltdown remains combined a very human skull with a very apelike jaw, and had taxed the experts' ingenuity to reconstruct an ape-man contemporary with, or even later than, much more manlike creatures. We now know that the Piltdown jaw was that of a modern ape, chemically doctored to appear very old, and that it did not give off the amount of radiation of uranium salts which an authentic object of great antiquity would. The natural science that made the hoax possible was in turn used by contemporary scientists to expose the hoax.

Prehistoric man did come to the New World, but most experts agree that he came late, since none of the earlier types of man, such as Neanderthal man, has as yet been found in America. Nor have hominid remains been found in the New World. When man first appears here he is already *homo sapiens*. A find of fossilized human bones near Midland, Texas, in 1953 has tentatively been interpreted as establishing human settlement there well before 10,000 years ago, but not quite 20,000 years ago. In the opinion of most anthropologists, man first came into these continents from Asia across the Bering Strait, or a then-existing land bridge, or even over the ice farther north, not earlier than 20,000 years ago.

The Culture
of Prehistoric Man

We know, then, directly or by inference, a fair amount about prehistoric man. Perhaps the most important thing we can learn from the scientific study of prehistory is that there are no simple affirmative or negative answers to the questions about the nature of man that political and moral thinkers of the last few hundred years liked to ask—and answer so as to bolster their own desires and values. To judge from primitive men, for instance, which is more "natural" to our human race, peace or war? common ownership of property or individual ownership of property? monogamous marriage or promiscuity? subordination of women to men or sex equality? equal distribution of goods or economic inequalities between rich and poor?

None of these questions makes sense in terms of prehistory. Almost all the extremes, and much in between, can be found during these millennia. Primitive men (especially when primitive people existing today are brought in for comparison) display a very wide range of behavior. *Homo sapiens* can behave, and has behaved, very differently at various times and in various places. If you are looking for peoples who do not make war in groups against other groups, you can find them. The earliest men were probably not well enough organized—in a sense, not rich enough—to make war. Some of the prehistoric pastoral and agricultural peoples seem to have led generally peaceful lives, but some of the earliest wall paintings apparently show raiding bands. The Zuñi Indian tribe of the American southwest is notably peaceful, but the Zuñi live in the same part of the world as the warlike Apache. If you are looking for rough economic equality, you can find it. Especially in primitive groups on the margin of subsistence, everyone shares a common poverty. But very early some individuals manage to assemble better and richer objects than others. You can find a very great variety of marriage customs, religious beliefs, and property and inheritance arrangements.

A simple and clear indication of the range of possible ways of life for *homo sapiens* can be found in his eating habits. Human teeth are suited both to grinding and to cutting and tearing, both to vegetable and to animal food. Man, therefore, is an *omnivore,* an eater of everything. Perhaps one can say that his "natural" diet is a balanced one, a mixture of starches, fats, and proteins. Yet many peoples have lived —and the coolies of the East still do—on an almost strictly vegetarian diet low in proteins and high in starches. In the very exceptional environment of the Far North, Eskimos live where no good vegetables grow and eat animal food exclusively—that is, fat and proteins.

Obviously, men have been able to adapt their eating habits to very great extremes. The physical environment, one may argue, has forced the Eskimos to make this adaptation. Economic need has perhaps dictated the diet of the coolies. And yet even in this down-to-earth matter, the will of men is not always powerless before the physical and economic environment. We eat certain kinds of food today in part because we like to preserve a slender figure. Perhaps some primitive men anticipated our eating habits. We know that most modern primitives are very fond of ornaments. There are no grounds for believing that even prehistoric man was always the slave of a narrow necessity.

The study of prehistoric art reinforces these conclusions on the nature of prehistoric man. The last period of Paleolithic culture in Europe, called the Magdalenian, represented a kind of prehistoric flowering of the arts. About 10,000 B.C. Magdalenian man engraved, and later painted, on the walls of caves some remarkable reindeer, bisons, mammoths, and other animals. The best of these magnificent animals are not "primitive," in the sense of being awkwardly or childishly drawn, or obviously nonrealistic or in any way crude. They are as clearly in the western tradition of realistic art as anything we have from the Greeks, though these unknown artists flourished almost ten thousand years before the Age of Pericles. The human form, however, is a less favorite subject than animals in these caves and is much less realistically drawn. Where it does appear, usually in simple black, it is crude or stylized, often with emphasis on the sexual parts. Magdalenian men also carved admirable tools of bone, engraved as skillfully as the best of the wall paintings. But they also sculptured female figures with grossly exaggerated breasts, thighs, and buttocks. Finally, in some of the caves there appear what are probably tracings of the human

Two reindeer from cavern at Font-de-Gaume, France. Cave paintings probably more than 10,000 years old.

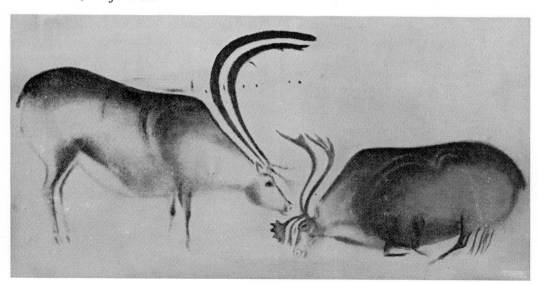

hand, often with one or more fingers missing.

These concrete details suggest two important generalizations. First is the fact, confirmed by work on remains of human bodies from the period, that about twelve thousand years ago Europe was filled with different types of human beings, with different tastes and different ways of life, and with now one group dominant, now another. We cannot trace the ups and downs of these groups in prehistory; indeed the experts are not wholly agreed on the sequence of peoples and cultures. But it is clear that something like the later rise and fall of societies and cultures in the historic era did fill these prehistoric ages, or the prehistorian could not find names for his periods, Aurignacian, Solutrean, Magdalenian, and many more.

Second, these prehistoric people had the kind of ideas that we call religious. It seems plausible that some part of the energy that went into drawing was in the service of magic. The hunter who had made an image of an animal was on his way to kill one. The exaggerated emphasis on human sexual differences inevitably suggests a cult of fertility. The mutilated hands suggest some sort of ritual sacrifice, perhaps a sacrifice modified from the surrender of life to the mere loss of a finger. These men and women, it would seem, lived in no simple world of common sense. Since we have to infer the religion of prehistoric men from their burial practices, their wall paintings, and other physical remains, we can never be sure that we have understood their beliefs.

One further generalization is much more risky. It may be that the artists who drew those remarkable cave animals were not solely occupied with the practical task of adding to the tribe's kill by magic means. They were also—perhaps they were mainly —displaying their ability to put those beasts on the wall. They were, in short, enjoying themselves as artists; they were inspired

with the splendid vanity of the artist, more enduring than bronze.

Two hundred years ago, in the Age of Enlightenment, it was fashionable to find in prehistoric cultures the Golden Age, an era of honesty, simplicity, and natural enjoyment from which men later declined. Few of us are likely to hold such views nowadays. Nor can many of us find in prehistoric cultures simple and ordered anticipations of our own culture—ourselves when young, so to speak. The greatest pitfall today is that we should see prehistoric man as fear-ridden, quaking before wild beasts and wilder gods, stupid, custom-ridden, dirty, maladjusted, and neurotic, a nasty, savage, overgrown child. Such a view is at least as erroneous as the notion of a past Golden Age. Alexander Pope could have written of Magdalenian man as he wrote of his own eighteenth-century contemporaries:

Chaos of Thought and Passion, all confus'd;
Still by himself abus'd, or dis-abus'd;
Created half to rise, and half to fall;
Great lord of all things, yet a prey to all;
Sole judge of Truth, in endless Error hurl'd:
The glory, jest, and riddle of the world!

Or so one must believe who looks at Magdalenian art.

Some Conclusions about Man

From this brief survey of prehistory, then, our most useful conclusion is that even thousands of years ago men in society displayed that great variety of behavior which is always the despair of the dogmatic simplifiers of human nature. We may now list a few more positive conclusions, with the caution that in this field, even more than in that of written history, the experts disagree.

First, from the point of view of those who accept current theories of organic evolution, the study of these millennia definitely puts man in the general evolutionary history of the primates, a subdivision of the mammals. *Homo sapiens* is clearly the product of a long development. Although the exact relation between his family tree and that of such apes as the chimpanzee is not clear, the scientists concerned with the problem hold that existing apes are, as it were, our cousins many times removed rather than our ancestors. Just as the scientific doctrine of the immense age of the earth does not invalidate arguments for the existence of God, so the zoological cataloguing of *homo sapiens* does not necessarily conflict with theological doctrines which insist that man has a soul and is thus not *merely* an animal.

Second, man is unique among animals in two broad ways. Man alone among animals has the ability to use words and symbols, and therefore to communicate his thoughts —and, indeed, to *have* thoughts that separate out individual experiences and enable him to list, to compare, and to remember these experiences. And in some sense related to this power of thinking, man alone can *teach* his young certain complicated forms of behavior, or ways of living, which we may loosely call "culture."

Third, over the long ages of prehistory material culture unquestionably shows what we call *progress*. Man progressively secured more food, better housing, and fuller satisfaction of his physical wants. Indeed, the very names that we give to the various ages —stone, bronze, and iron—suggest that man's tools progressed from the very simple to the more elaborate. They suggest the increasing adaptation of means to ends that we are familiar with today as technological improvement. Again, all this can be treated quite separately from man's moral and spiritual improvement or progress. We may or may not be more virtuous than the Magdalenians; we may or may not be "happier" than they; a modern painting may or may not be better than a Magdalenian cave painting. There is, however, no doubt that our modern tools are better tools than those of Magdalenian man, just as Magdalenian tools were better, did their work more *effi-*

ciently, than those of Neanderthal man thousands of years before him.

Fourth, man has long existed on this earth as a single species. Apparently throughout human wanderings separate groups of men have stayed long enough in a given area to produce the kind of subspecies called a race. Thus white, yellow, and Negro races developed, but, since they did not remain "pure," they did not become separate species. Or, put another way, man is and long has been a mongrel. So far at least, hardly does he get started breeding a variant that might become a new species when others come into the group, or else the group forces itself onto others, and the process is ended. Established human variations such as races are vastly smaller than the variations men have deliberately bred in the dog, *canis familiaris*. Most of the variations that stand out in human achievement seem to be individual variations rather than group variations. Thus great artistic or athletic ability is a matter of individual gift and skill, not one of the marks of the subspecies or race. Prehistory, like history, does not back up modern notions of racism, the doctrine that one race is as a whole "superior" to another. As we shall see later (p. 25), terms like Semitic and Aryan that racists use so frequently refer properly not to well-defined races, "superior" or "inferior," nor to any clear-cut biological factor, but only to families of human languages.

Finally, to return to a point made already, the abiding impression one gets from a study of prehistory is of the great range of potentialities in human beings and in human cultures. Above all, one is aware of a basic paradox of human behavior: men are creatures of custom, reluctant to change, yet quite unable to take this world as they find it. They will daydream another world, if nothing better comes up. Ever since the first rude, manlike creature banged off a few awkward protuberances from his eolithic fist-hatchet, some men have always been dissatisfied with things as they are. Man is no doubt much more, but at a minimum he is the inventive animal. That is, he changes his environment—his tools, his society, his art, his religion. He does not, as far as we know, greatly change his body. Anthropologists do not believe that *homo sapiens* has evolved physically in the few thousand years of history; yet changes such as an increase in average height of American youth in the last few generations are real enough. Better diet and other improvements in environment probably explain such changes.

Perhaps the future will establish them genetically. Meanwhile, man's ability to change his environment without altering his body is the most extraordinary of his inventions, something no other animal has ever attained. Other land mammals have indeed learned to fly and to live in the water, but only by becoming bats or whales. Twentieth-century man—*homo sapiens,* still anatomically almost identical with our Magdalenian of thousands of years ago—flies in airplanes and sails in ships.

II: Our Near Eastern Origins

When Did Civilization and History Begin?

It is barely possible that the first manlike creatures who came down out of the trees to live on the ground were beasts without language, without social structure, without culture. But the question of the origins of man the social animal is probably unanswerable. Very early, prehistoric man leaves us evidence that he did live in organized groups, and that he systematically practiced and transmitted very elaborate economic, artistic, and religious habits and attitudes that no animal lacking in language could possibly practice and transmit. In one of the looser senses of the word, prehistoric man was "civilized." By the end of the Neolithic period in the Near East, say 4000 B.C., men lived in villages, wove cloth, made pots, plowed with animal power, grew grain, navigated small boats, and built monumentally—that is, they built not just for shelter or comfort or even ordinary display, but to honor gods or a god, to give great men appropriate tombs, and to provide for ceremonial.

Although the point at which a "culture" becomes a "civilization" is always to some degree a matter of individual opinion, the transition from "prehistory" to "history" is clear. It occurs whenever men *write* their language and so are able to preserve written records. So far as we know, this acquisition of the art of writing coincided roughly with the establishment of *cities*. Gatherings of men in such numbers necessitated considerable division of labor, some kind of police force, and the beginnings of civil administration, social and economic classes, organized religion and kingship. From the start, war and military organization seem inseparably woven into this fabric of city life.

The start is fairly definite in place and time. From about 4500 to 4000 B.C., true cities rise in the valleys of the Nile, the Tigris-Euphrates, and perhaps the Indus. Authentic Chinese history does not begin quite so early. Nevertheless, it is pretty certain that in the valleys of the Wei and the Hoang Ho in China city life and all that goes with it were beginning to take shape in the fourth millennium before Christ. Finally, much later, city life starts inde-

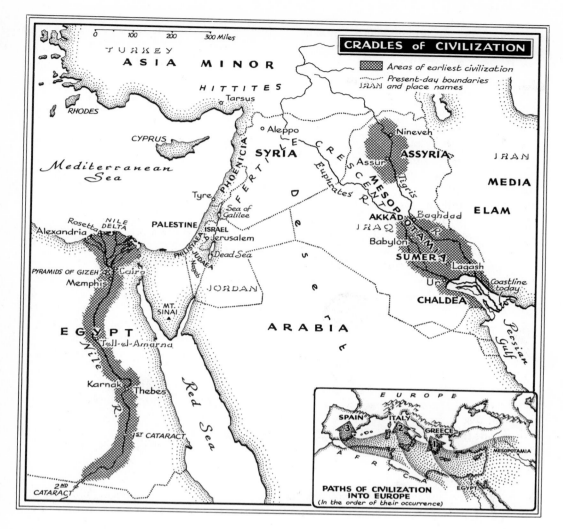

CRADLES of CIVILIZATION

▨ Areas of earliest civilization
Present-day boundaries and place names

PATHS OF CIVILIZATION INTO EUROPE
(In the order of their occurrence)

pendently, it is assumed, in Mexico and Peru. We shall be obliged in this book, if only from consideration of space, to neglect the histories of these urban cultures in China, India, and America. Except perhaps for the Asian Indian, they do not play a part in our own distant civilized origins. The two centers in the Nile and in the Tigris-Euphrates valleys were geographically close, for both lay in the region traditionally known as the Near East but now called the Middle East. These Near Eastern valleys were, in the time-honored phrase, the "cradles of our western civilization."

The Challenge of the River Valleys

It is impossible to say for certain why the people of the Nile and Tigris-Euphrates valleys were able to take the important steps leading from a peasant-pastoral culture to a true city culture. These river valleys do indeed have rich soils, but so do hundreds of other river valleys on earth. One thing is clear: The experts are greatly modifying the old view that the fertility and the good living conditions of the Near Eastern valleys somehow sucked men into them and allowed them to multiply sufficiently to attain the density of city populations. It is more likely that in prehistoric times these valleys were marshes overgrown with a junglelike vegetation, and subject to uncontrolled floods. Gradually, perhaps beginning about 11,000 years ago, there was a change in climate, a drying up as the glaciers northward melted, a change in the winds that had brought moisture, so that the arid and semi-arid conditions that now prevail in a vast area from the Sahara to Central Asia began to make life impossibly difficult in much of the region. The farmers and herders, feeling the pressure of diminishing crops and grasses, may have gone as colonists to the valleys, where at least there was water. They may have gone because of the simple pressure of overpopulation, or possibly even for adventure.

In the process of taming marshes and jungles by digging canals, building levees, and settling water rights, they gathered themselves into groups big enough, and above all disciplined enough, to do the job. This meant that they had some sort of political and economic *organization*. Many anthropologists believe that the transition from a pastoral, hunting, and nomadic culture to settled farming villages took place in the foothills of Mesopotamia (northern Iraq) rather than in the great valleys. These villagers, they believe, then advanced into the great valleys along tributary streams as the climate grew steadily drier. Whatever the process of settlement, there is no doubt that the great river valleys of the Near East brought men together into large cities and true political organizations, perhaps as early as 4500 B.C.

The Near Eastern States

The ancient Near East produced the first known system of states, the first collection of independent political units to conduct formal international relations. The great powers were Egypt, along the Nile, and a succession of states—Chaldea, Babylon, Assyria, Persia—in Mesopotamia, "the land between the rivers," as the Greeks called the valleys of the Tigris and Euphrates. Between Egypt and Mesopotamia stretches the "Fertile Crescent," running through modern Palestine and Syria and skirting the desert of Arabia. In ancient times, as today, the middle part of the Fertile Crescent formed a zone of fragmentation, which was divided politically into small and medium-sized states like Judea and Phoenicia. The small powers in this zone of fragmentation carried on constant rivalry among themselves, but they also maintained close contact with the wealth and culture of the great powers. Mesopotamia itself, though it later saw the rise of imperial "powers" like Assyria, Babylonia, and Persia, was in much of these millennia a zone of fragmentation, with individual city-states loosely held together by trade and political hegemonies. Finally, almost surrounding the great valleys and the zone of fragmentation, lay the vast areas which today form the Balkan states, Russia, Turkey, Arabia, Central Asia, Ethiopia, and the Sudan, and which were inhabited at the dawn of history by nomads or semi-nomads. Bands of these primitive peoples that lived near the borders of the civilized Near Eastern states were tempted to attack by their neighbors' wealth and apparent ease of life.

Every one of the great and small powers of the civilized Near East had its own life-history, and many of them developed distinctive individual styles and cultures. Later sections of this chapter will discuss the specific characteristics of Egyptians, Babylonians, Assyrians, Persians, and Jews. Here we shall first indicate what these peoples shared, the common denominators of Near Eastern civilization. For, different as they were, these peoples of the Ancient Near East did at least trade, war, and otherwise interact one with another.

Common Denominators
of Near Eastern Civilization

The political history of the ancient Near East may be explained partly in terms of two interacting forces. The first force is the push of nomadic or semi-nomadic tribes along the frontiers into the civilized areas, constantly as the migration of individuals or groups, and also from time to time as mass eruptions in violent conquest. The second force is the effort of certain great Near Eastern states to conquer their neighbors, thus threatening the rough equilibrium between great and small states that later ages have termed the balance of power. The first sort of push often resulted in the triumph of the invaders, as in the repeated attacks of Arabian nomads upon Mesopotamia (see below, p. 34). Invasion caused violence and a loss of prosperity. Then came the absorption of the invaders into the more advanced culture of the old state, and often a renewed period of flourishing for the invaded area.

The efforts to upset and maintain the balance of power caused many centuries of international rivalry. Occasionally some one great power, like Assyria in the eighth and seventh centuries B.C., exercised a wide domination. But on the whole a precarious balance of power was maintained, and the various individual states, big and little, preserved for centuries their identities and in some sense their "independence." Nevertheless, the balance was always precarious, and as time went on this unstable international system showed an increasing tendency to break down. Egyptians, Assyrians, and Babylonians successively aspired to universal rule in the Near East. Finally, at the very end of the period with which this chapter is concerned, about 500 B.C., the Persians brought almost the whole of the Near East under their sway. As simple tribesmen, little more than nomads, they broke into Mesopotamia, seized power there, and soon conquered the whole area from farthest Egypt to the edges of Russia and India.

The political and social structures of the great states in the valleys tended to follow a common pattern. This was the bureaucratically administered state headed by a king who was also a priest if not actually a god, who ruled through a privileged class of nobles and priests, who commanded a professional army, and—this is most important—who was a despot in the sense that none of his subjects could habitually go beyond the royal authority to some higher authority, to a god or a "constitution." Indeed, they probably could not think or feel at all that there was such an authority.

These first large-scale political organizations demanded from the people hard work, discipline, and the surrender as "taxes" of a considerable part of their crops. On this surrendered surplus king, nobles, priests, and—a new thing—expert administrators, engineers, even scientist-priests, were able to live. More, some of the surplus could be used to procure goods, especially metals, not available in the great valleys. Merchants, skilled craftsmen, domestic and foreign commerce all developed until in the city-states of Mesopotamia and in the Egyptian unified state there came to be societies in many ways like "modern" societies.

It must not be assumed that these societies were held together by what we Americans would think of as the threat of force from above and the reality of fear among the masses. The great and difficult shift from Neolithic village life, in which we must assume there were village and tribal councils of elders, and some discussion, some rough equality, to city life, irrigation engineering, taxation, written records, including law cases, was accompanied by, accomplished through, the new despotic state. But the masses seem to have submitted at first to this despotism because they believed they were in so doing submitting to a god; and they continued for centuries to so submit because they had been conditioned to an acceptance of tradition. This is a state of mind hard for an American to understand. But we may approximate understanding if we realize that to these early peoples a slogan like "taxation without representation is tyranny" would have been totally incomprehensible. To them, taxation was almost certainly a part of nature, part of the way the gods ran the universe, no more subject to change by "politics" than is the weather to us.

There must have been some social mobility in these societies, if only because commerce carries with it travel, new experiences, immigration. A merchant class is almost always a less fixed and custom-bound class than a priesthood or a nobility. Save for Egypt, there was a merchant class in all these early civilizations; and even the Egyptians conducted considerable trade through a somewhat bureaucratized economy. On the whole, however, these are societies that changed very slowly indeed, that after their very great innovation of urban civilization made no great innovations. But they must not be thought of as societies in which the majority of the people were simply blocks, cogs, not really participating emotionally at all in the common thing of the state. A concept like "citizens" will surely not do for Babylonian or Egyptian masses. We do not really know enough about them to say whether they had strong loyalties, as the Chinese and Hindus in great despotic states had, to lesser groups within the state—subcaste, family, village community, and the like; but if only as religious believers, the masses were "members" of a common thing. It seems hard to believe that even the Egyptian pyramids were built wholly under the lash or threat of the lash, that they were mere monuments to the pharaohs' vanity and superstition, that they were in no sense community undertakings. Indeed, a recent Egyptian-inspired theory holds that they were actually relief projects, and that construction was carried on only during the flood season, when the peasants were driven off the land.

Recent research, especially on the earliest Mesopotamian civilization of Sumer, makes it clear that the older notion of a simple, rigid "despotic" government and society in the Ancient Near East was wrong. The varieties of political life included an earlier period of "primitive democracy" (or primitive monarchy) not unlike that of Homeric Greece, or perhaps that of the Iroquois Indians, later an oligarchy or aristocracy of the well-born, and an "enlightened" despotism favoring public works and attempting to make life more secure for the masses. Yet it must be repeated that the developed "style" of these societies is more nearly what we Americans can think of as "authoritarian" than it is "libertarian"; above all, these societies were *relatively* conservative, slow to change, early hardened into conformities.

Our Debt to the Near East

In these eastern monarchies, so alien and so distant to us in so many ways, there none the less grew up habits, techniques, beliefs, and institutions that are still a part of our lives today. Most conspicuously, there grew up an elaborate structure of domestic and international trade. Merchants, though not clearly at the top of the social order with priests and nobles, were, especially at times in Mesopotamia, almost at the top. In Phoenicia and in other parts of the zone of fragmentation, we find genuinely commercial societies, states in which the merchant is the leader. From such a society came the great contribution of the ancient Near East to our daily living, the alphabet.

Writing itself was in large part an achievement of priests, who needed to keep records of the wealth in their temples. It must have been a difficult invention, and neither the Nile nor the Tigris-Euphrates valleys took the final steps. The first step was ideographic writing, still in use in China. Our familiar + sign for a crossroad is a simple example. The next step was to use the sign for the *sound* of a whole syllable, regardless of its picture meaning, as if we used a simplified picture of a sheep (ewe) for the sound of "you," another for "night," and put the two together to make "unite." In Mesopotamia these picture-signs were simplified out of all recognition as pictures by the use of little wedge-shaped imprinters on wet clay to make "cuneiform" writing.

The last important step, that of using a single letter for each sound, was apparently taken first by the Phoenicians, a Semitic trading people in the zone of fragmentation, and came to us through the Greeks. Anthropologists believe that the alphabet, which has now spread around the world, is an example of the diffusion of an invention that was made only once. All true alphabets, not only our own but also such very different ones as the Hebrew, Arabic, and Sanskrit, seem to go back to this one source.

The alphabet is not the only great invention we owe to the ancient Near East. Even before the cities were established, it may well be that inventions like the wheel came

from this area. The historically established list of "firsts" in this area that are still important to us is a very long one. Here were the first sure beginnings of science—astronomy, mathematics, and in particular the calendar; and here in drainage, irrigation, and construction, technology and science first appear in some kind of relation, though we must not believe that "pure" science in our modern sense made technological advance possible. Here was the first codified set of laws, the famous Code of Hammurabi of the nineteenth century B.C. Here were probably the first books, the first paper, and the first architecture that has come down to us as something like an understandable aesthetic whole. Here, finally, were the first religions that we can know from something more than simple material remains, religions that we can begin to know as theologies and as organized churches. From here came the Christianity which, after two thousand years, is still the religion professed by the overwhelming majority of men and women in the western world. All these, it must be noted, came to us westerners not directly, but filtered through and in part transformed by Greeks, Romans, and Hebrews.

III: Egypt

The Setting

Historic Egypt is made up of Upper Egypt, the narrow valley of the Nile, for some eight hundred miles between the second cataract and the Delta, and Lower Egypt, the Delta itself, a wedge-shaped area one hundred miles long. In prehistoric times, the wadies, lateral valleys that are now wholly dry, were probably wet enough to permit effective agriculture. Once the

settlement of the flood-plain of the Nile and the Delta had been achieved, probably between 5000 and 4000 B.C., the stage was set for the long and amazingly stable course of Egyptian history. The Nile flooded regularly and quietly once a year over fields that had been prepared for the flooding, so that what is still in many parts of the world a handicap to farming became a help. Indeed, it flooded so regularly that Egyptian leaders, probably priests, early were able to calculate the solar year as 365 days; the

The pyramids of Gizeh, photographed from the air.

more obvious lunar month had hitherto been the basis for reckoning time. Each year, the Nile silt provided enough new soil for fertilizing. Moreover, inhospitable deserts shielded the Nile on both the eastern and western sides. Southward, the Nile flowed from the sparsely settled lands of primitive peoples, and even the Delta was protected by the sea and the desert. Here was a setting well suited to a stable and isolated society.

Yet the isolation of Egypt may easily be exaggerated. Once she became an effective political unit, Egypt expanded—or tried to expand—chiefly in the direction that was the most tempting because it was the richest and the most civilized—that is, toward the Fertile Crescent and Mesopotamia. Moreover, Egyptians early traced a good route across the desert to the Red Sea, and began to trade with the countries of the Indian Ocean. Egypt was never for long a "Hermit Kingdom," but fully a part of the international state system of the Near East.

Egypt was peopled by a mixed population. The dominant part used to be called Hamitic, as Jews and Arabs were called Semitic, and the Indo-Europeans or Aryans were called Japhetic, after the three sons of Noah—Ham, Shem, and Japhet. This quaint

CHAPTER I

terminology is now discredited, particularly with respect to race. Apparently, there have never been·clearly marked Hamitic, Semitic, and Japhetic, or Aryan, races. In language, however, the threefold distinction has more validity, and we may properly speak of human linguistic groups where we may not speak with certainty of races. It is true that the ancient Egyptian language is not like the Semitic tongues of Jews, Arabs, Phoenicians, Babylonians, and many other Near Eastern peoples. It is also true that both Hamitic and Semitic languages differ from the Indo-European languages, which cover a wide range from the Sanskrit and Persian of the Middle East through Greek and Latin to most of the modern European tongues with which we are familiar.

An Outline
of Egyptian History

The conquest of the marshes and jungles of the Nile Valley for agriculture must have been the slow work of relatively small communities. The Egyptians themselves attributed the union of Upper and Lower Egypt in one great kingdom to a certain Menes, the shadowy founder of the first dynasty. (The Egyptians early developed a calendar and in time began the custom of dating their histories by "dynasties" of pharaohs or kings.) There is among our Egyptologists controversy over the date of Menes, but he cannot have been much earlier than 3000 B.C. There are many archaeological discoveries indicating a high culture well before that date, though it is likely that the city and all it implies came later in Egypt than in Mesopotamia. As in the history of China, the first dynasties are more or less mythical, and the dates are uncertain. But Dynasty III, about 2700 B.C., is by no means mythical. From its capital at Memphis it ruled the so-called "Old Kingdom," which united Upper and Lower Egypt. Under the next dynasty, the fourth,

about 2600 to 2500 B.C., the famous pyramids of Gizeh appeared, built by Cheops and other pharaohs for their burial places. The dynasties go on and on until the thirtieth, in the fourth century B.C. After that, Egypt fell to Alexander the Great and continued under the Greek dynasty of the Ptolemies until, with the defeat of Antony and Cleopatra, it passed into Roman hands in 30 B.C.

We know a great deal about ancient Egypt, thanks to fragments of Egyptian histories that were translated into Greek, to careful archaeology, and above all to vast numbers of inscriptions and papyri in the Egyptian language (papyrus is a kind of paper made from reeds and preserved in the dry air). The language was first deciphered by the Frenchman Champollion from the famous Rosetta Stone, which was found in the Delta in 1799. The same inscription was repeated on this stone in Greek and in two forms of Egyptian writing. We do not, however, know enough about Egypt to make the narrative of its political and military history very real. Nor can we reconstruct many of the living personalities, except in such rare cases as that of the idealistic Pharaoh Ikhnaton. Thutmosis III, great conqueror though he was, is scarcely more than a name, even to special students of ancient Egypt. In fact, until we come to the Greek historians Herodotus and Thucydides, we can learn more from a glance at an Egyptian statue or the Great Pyramid or a few lines from the collection of lore on the after-world called the Book of the Dead than we can from conventional narrative history.

Yet the bare political and military narrative is worth a paragraph or two, for the pattern of Egyptian history is a familiar one. Egypt had periods of firm government, prosperity, and expansion; relatively brief semi-"feudal" periods of political disintegration when the central power of the pharaohs was greatly weakened; periods of conquest by foreign masters; and, finally, periods of re-

Rosetta Stone. Egyptian hieroglyphics at the top; demotic characters in the middle; Greek characters at the bottom.

26

vival and attempted reconquest. Through all these shifts, however, Egyptian culture remained surprisingly stable. The "Old Kingdom," ruled by Dynasties III to VI, lasted from 2700 to 2200 B.C., and was followed by a hundred years of decentralization. Dynasty XI (2100-2000 B.C.) reestablished the pharaoh's authority in the "Middle Kingdom," which had its capital at Thebes and which declined after 1800 B.C. Under Dynasties XV-XVI (1680-1580), the rule of Egypt fell to foreign conquerors, the Hyksos ("Rulers of Countries"), who came apparently from Palestine and Asia Minor. The native Egyptian Dynasty XVII drove out the Hyksos and established the "New Kingdom," which endured from 1580 to 1090 B.C. Thutmosis III (1501-1447), of Dynasty XVIII, conquered Phoenicia, Palestine, and Syria and made Egypt a great imperial power. This dynasty also saw the attempts at radical religious and political reform of the Pharaoh Ikhnaton. But Egypt failed to maintain her rule in Asia, and after warrior pharaohs named Rameses flourished in the thirteenth and twelfth centuries B.C. her greatest days of expansion were over.

It was again Egypt's turn to be conquered. For more than two centuries (945-712 B.C.) Egypt was ruled by Dynasties XXII-XXIV, whose leaders came from Libya, farther west along the Mediterranean. It fell next to Dynasty XXV (712-663 B.C.), which sprang from its southern neighbor, Ethiopia. Yet both the Hyksos and the later foreign rulers from Libya and Ethiopia, like those who have established "foreign" dynasties in China, were absorbed by the weight of the Egyptian people and the Egyptian culture. They never really remade the country. Native Egyptian forces again won power after the Ethiopian dynasty, and Dynasty XXVI (the Saite dynasty, 663-625 B.C.) marked a revival strong enough for the Egyptians to attempt, though vainly, the reconquest of their former possessions in Asia.

The high points of Egyptian culture tended to coincide with periods of political greatness or at least of native rule. Although this correlation is far from perfect, much of the best of Egyptian art comes from the dynasties of the Old, Middle, and New Kingdoms—the great pyramids from the Old Kingdom, and the richly furnished tomb of Tutankhamen (discovered in 1922) from the early part of the New Kingdom. Nevertheless, arts and letters, indeed all patterns of Egyptian culture, tended to grow stale and repetitious as the centuries went on—a tendency paralleled by Egypt's increasing inability to stand up in war against Babylonians, Persians, and Greeks. In fact, almost all lovers of Egypt would agree that the first two thousand years are much richer in achievements of all sorts, from wall painting to poetry, than the last fifteen hundred. The Saite revival of the seventh and sixth centuries attempted to check the decline by deliberately restoring the good old ways in literature, art, religion, and morals. This pathetic effort was a failure.

Egyptian Society

One thing stands out in these four thousand years of Egyptian history. Underneath the ebb and flow of dynasty and empire, centralization and decentralization, foreign invasion and native reconquest, cultural flourishing and decline—underneath all this there is a great continuity in the life of Egyptians. Indeed, some experts maintain that the *fellaheen* of twentieth-century Egypt, the toilers of the land, are still essentially like their remote ancestors of dynastic Egypt, despite later Hellenistic, Roman, Byzantine, Moslem, and modern western influences. (No one, of course, would say that of the modern urban masses of cities like Cairo and Alexandria.)

The Egyptian society that endured throughout antiquity was shaped into a rigidly controlled economy. Egypt had a small priestly and noble class at the top of the social pyramid, and a toiling mass of peasants at the bottom. Much of the economic life in Egypt, from the control of the Nile floods to the distribution of the crops, was planned and regulated from above, by the agents of the pharaoh. The land was in rather more than mere theory the property of the pharaoh, who was so sacred that his very name, "per-o," meant Great House, the temple in which the god lived. The familiar story in Chapter 41 of the Book of Genesis shows how complete was the pharaoh's control of land through his bureaucrats. Joseph interpreted the pharaoh's dreams to mean that after seven good crop years, seven bad years would bring famine, and he therefore advised the monarch to set aside regularly in storage granaries the crops of one-fifth of the land in the good years. This was done, and Egypt came through the bad years without famine. The point for us is not whether the biblical story is exactly true, but rather that it shows how centralized the land system was. In the whole history of the continent of Europe up to quite modern times no government could have done what the pharaoh's government is said to have done, for agricultural production and distribution could not have been so controlled from a national center, nor grain transported effectively to such granaries.

Egypt, then, was an authoritarian state and a planned society, with a kind of state capitalism, and a well-organized bureaucracy. We use these contemporary terms so understandable in our twentieth century deliberately; they do describe the Egyptian society. But they are also, in themselves, if unsupplemented, misleading and anachronistic. The Egyptian was an early society in which "individualism," government by discussion, civil rights in our sense, had never been experienced; and it was a society based on religious beliefs most effective in the preservation of a hierarchically organized society.

Religion

The most striking feature of ancient Egyptian religion, after its doctrine of the pharaoh's unlimited power, is its obsessive preoccupation with life after death. We think immediately of elaborate tombs and carefully mummified bodies. The earlier graves—including the pyramids themselves —and the accompanying inscriptions suggest a complicated concept of body and soul. The body had a double, called *ka*, which survived the death of the body of daily life; the grave, the mummy, and the symbolic statues were all provided for the sake of this undying *ka*. This is almost a belief in literal not-dying rather than a belief that the soul is immortal and that man has a choice between heaven and hell. This belief later did take on moral notions that one would be rewarded and punished in an afterlife for what one did in this life. Witness this prayer to the Sun-god Amon (Amunrē in this transliteration):

Amunrē, who wast the first to be king! The god of the Beginning! The vizier of the poor! He taketh not unrighteous reward, and he speaketh not to him that bringeth testimony, and looketh not on him that maketh promises(?).
Amunrē judgeth the earth with his finger, and speaketh to the heart. He assigneth the sinner to hell, but the righteous to the West.°

Ultimately, the Egyptian cult of immortality was centered in the worship of a specific god, Osiris, who was identified with the Nile. His sister, Isis, whom he married, was identified with earth and fertility.

That the Egyptians believed in a moral judgment of the soul after death we know from the *Book of the Dead*, the most important surviving piece of their literature. The suppliant to Osiris, judge of the dead, urges at length, almost as if before an earthly law-court, evidence that he did no wrong on earth. Here is a sample:

° A. Erman, *Literature of the Ancient Egyptians* (London, 1927), 308.

Hail to thee, great god, lord of Truth [Osiris]. I have come to thee, my lord, and I am led (hither) in order to see thy beauty. I . . . have committed no sin against people. . . . I have not done evil in the place of truth. I knew no wrong. I did no evil thing. . . . I did not do that which the god abominates. I did not report evil of a servant to his master. I allowed no one to hunger. I caused no one to weep. I did not murder. . . . I did not decrease the offerings of the gods. I did not take away the food-offerings of the dead. I did not commit adultery. I did not commit self-pollution in the pure precinct of my city-god. I did not diminish the grain measure. . . . I did not take milk from the mouth of the child. I did not drive away the cattle from their pasturage. I did not snare the fowl of the gods. I did not catch the fish in their pools. I did not hold back the water in its time. I did not dam the running water [i.e. did not tamper with the irrigation system].[*]

Note that the Jew at Yom Kippur, the Christian at confession, do something very different: they recite their sins. Note also, by inference, that even in well-run Egypt, men must have *done* wicked things!

Popular Egyptian religion appears to have been a fairly routine kind of polytheism. There was, in addition to Osiris, Isis, and their son Horus, a sun-god Amon, with whom Horus was often identified. Amon died and was resurrected, and was the lord and father of other gods, in the manner of the Roman Jupiter. There were gods with animal heads and animal bodies, suggesting—though this is not certain—totemic origins. There were gods and goddesses who were closely concerned with love. The whole repertory that anthropologists look for was present—the cycle of birth, death, and rebirth; animal totemism; fertility cult. To the "Egyptian-in-the-street," these gods and goddesses were doubtless extremely powerful and in constant need of being appeased. But they were probably not considered to be particularly righteous or particularly concerned with the spiritual health of their worshipers.

The upper classes undertook a process of

[*] J. H. Breasted, *The Dawn of Conscience* (New York, 1933), 255-256.

refining polytheistic beliefs that culminated in the monotheism of Ikhnaton (1375-1358 B.C.). This pharaoh preached the religion of Aton, the sun-disk, represented in art as a disk emanating rays, each of which ended in a human hand. The other sun-god, Amon, together with most of the chief Egyptian deities, was represented in human form. Ikhnaton had changed his own name from Amenophis in honor of Aton. He made Aton not just the father of the gods, as Amon was, but the *sole god,* and a god concerned that men do good and avoid evil, a god who could be worshiped with intense devotion. A glance at the great hymn to the sun which has come down to us from Ikhnaton's day shows how close this pharaoh's faith was to our own biblical faith:

How manifold are thy works!
They are hidden before men
O sole God, beside whom there is no other.
Thou didst create the earth according to thy heart.[*]

Ikhnaton moved his capital to a wholly new site some two hundred miles north of the old city of Thebes, which remained a center of conservative priestly opposition to the new god, Aton. Here at a modern village named Tell el-Amarna were discovered in 1887 the royal diplomatic archives: correspondence with other Near Eastern rulers, inscribed in Mesopotamian cuneiform writing on tablets (see p. 23 above). Later excavations have added to our knowledge of this reign, which was marked by a flourishing realistic art, such as the famous portrait head of Ikhnaton's queen Nefertiti.

Ikhnaton is the first person in our history to stand out clearly as an idealistic reformer. Since he was born to the pharaoh's position of absolute power, he could initiate reforms without having to organize pressure groups or to prepare public opinion in some other way. But even in so apparently despotic a state as Egypt, Ikhnaton failed miserably. His attempt to establish the new and purer

[*] J. H. Breasted, *The Dawn of Conscience,* 284.

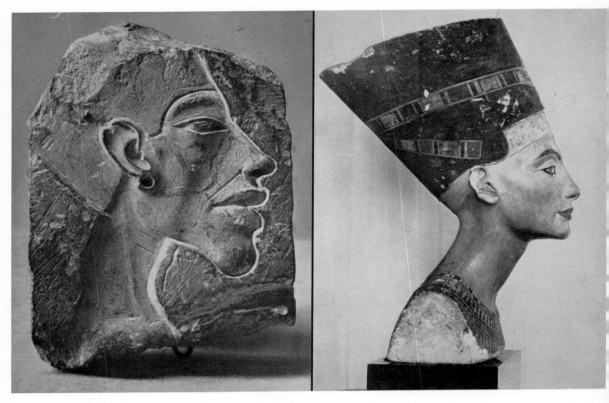

Bas-relief of Ikhnaton (1375-1358 B.C.) and painted limestone bust of his wife and sister, Nefertiti. Both pieces date from about 1360 B.C.

belief in Aton offended the priests of the older religion and, one may guess, also offended most of the faithful. Ikhnaton died in circumstances not clear to us, and under his successor Tutankhamen the old religion was brought back and the capital returned to Thebes. The priests of Amon had had their revenge:

> The sun of him (Ikhnaton) who knows
> thee not goes down, O Amon!
> The temple of him who assailed thee is in
> darkness.*

Almost nothing in the long record of Egyptian religion indicates a current of thought of the kind that we call rationalist —that is, an attempt to explain the universe in terms of reason or natural science. Some Egyptians did, however, as early as the end of the third millennium before Christ, reach the stage of disillusionment and disbelief in the old religion that appears in later cultures as one of the phases of rationalism. The poet of the Song of the Harp-player, after referring to the nobles "entombed in their pyramids," casts doubt on immortality —"None cometh from thence that he may tell us how they fare"—and concludes with a sentiment that hardly seems four thousand years old:

> Celebrate the glad day,
> Be not weary therein.
> Lo, no man taketh his goods with him.
> Yea, none returneth again that is gone
> thither.*

---

* J. H. Breasted, *The Dawn of Conscience,* 308.

* *Ibid.,* 163-164.

Culture

With the cave men of Magdalenian times we have the first human achievements in the plastics arts that we moderns can still enjoy without a sense of patronizing, without a sense of great strangeness. Then, with the Egyptians, we come to a whole series of achievements that are unquestionably a part of our heritage. The pyramids, the ruins of the monumental hall at Karnak (Thebes), the Sphinx, the rock tombs, the wall decorations, the smaller sculptures, even the jewelry and objects of daily use are familiar to most of us through reproductions and museums. In the beginning, this art was stiff and primitive, but it moved on to several periods of blossoming after it had solved its main technical problems. It then became, very simply, great art. Eventually, a decline set in, a lapse into mere copying and repeating, with certain refinements. In short, Egypt went through that cycle of the arts that is discernible in many times and places—in the classical Mediter-ranean world, in China, and in medieval Europe. The Egyptians had different con-ventions—different basic artistic assump-tions—from ours, notably in the matter of perspective and draftsmanship, but there is no sense at all in saying that their art is therefore necessarily inferior to ours, or that it is more "primitive."

Some of their sculpture, in particular, is in so direct a line with Greek and Renais-sance sculpture that few of us have any trouble with it. The head of Queen Nefer-titi is as familiar to us as any piece of sculp-ture. The representation of the scribe on page 32 is for us clearly in the tradition of the realistic (not, however, exact or photo-graphic) portrayal of the external world of men and things. The colossal statues are—despite our own Goddess of Liberty and our giant heads on Dakotan and Georgian mountains—rather more alien to us, and the wall paintings seem definitely strange. But most of their art, as we can clearly see for ourselves, is the work of admirable crafts-men who were thoroughly trained masters of their art.

Pillars in temple at Karnak, Egypt.

Only a few examples of Egyptian secular literature have come down to us, yet there is enough to show that such literature existed and that it produced such varying forms as poetry, short tales, history, and even some elementary mathematical and astronomical works. The Egyptians, it would seem from their literature, were not always gloomy and miserable, or obsessed with death and the commands of the pharaoh in this world. They were often carefree and happy, willing to enjoy themselves. Here are some fragments from an Egyptian love poem:

If I kiss her and her lips are open, I am happy (even) without beer. . . .

Ah, would I were her negress that is her handmaid, then would I behold the colour of all her limbs.°

Here, from the Middle Kingdom four thousand years ago, is a lyric still more unmistakably in the great tradition of the West:

° A. Erman, *Literature of the Ancient Egyptians* (London, 1927), 244.

Egyptian scribe with roll of papyrus. Limestone sculpture from about 2400 B.C.

Death is before me to-day
As the odour of myrrh,
As when one sitteth under the sail on a
  windy day.

.   .   .

Death is before me to-day
As when a man longeth to see his house
  again,
After he hath spent many years in captivity.°

Egyptian literature, particularly its somewhat disillusioned aphorisms, or moral sayings, almost certainly influenced the authors of the Book of Proverbs in the Old Testament. In fact, the list of Egyptian influences upon the Jews and the Greeks and so, ultimately, upon ourselves is very long indeed. It includes not only religion and art but also such practical skills as masonry and surveying, bookkeeping and accounting, metalworking and textiles, pottery, cookery, and embalming. The Egyptians learned a lot about human anatomy from embalming and mummifying, and it is not farfetched to credit them with the origins of modern medicine. Although a good deal of magic and superstition doubtless entered into the practice of the Egyptians, they made significant contributions to medical skill and knowledge.

The Egyptian Style

In part because of the dry climate, in which mummies, papyrus, and inscriptions are well preserved, we know a lot about the ancient Egyptians. We know enough to be able to recognize an Egyptian "style" or "character." How to put that style, or any other national, local, even family, style or character in words is always a problem; indeed, there are those today who think that so much nonsense is written about "group style" or "group character" that we had better give up the effort to describe it—besides there's no such thing, these skeptics say, only concrete, individual

---

° *Ibid.*, 91-92.

persons and things. But most of us know that French art, French literature, French men and women, for instance, are not just isolated concrete "things," but share something in common; this something we Americans do not share—we have our own something. In this book, we propose to try to put in words from time to time the way these varying historical styles strike us. We must all judge such matters in part for ourselves, for the description can never have the kind of exactness of, say, a cook's recipe or a draftsman's blueprint. The interested reader, making use of our suggestions for further reading, may well decide our description in a given instance needs amending, or even radical revision.*

Now there is throughout Egyptian art and culture an unmistakable strain of simple attachment to the good things of this earth, to food and drink and lovemaking, an interest in things as they appear to common sense to be. There is a strain of realism in the Egyptian—witness the statue of the scribe. The Egyptian is a practical fellow, so practical that he does not on the whole make a very good conqueror or soldier. He

has an almost Parisian or Athenian feeling for the art of living. He is at home in this world. And yet—the other world is very near, very threatening, and very much a part of this world. The other world is not just death, though death must always seem its most threatening phase. It is what we call transcendence, something more—bigger even in the sense of "monumental," more enduring, indeed everlasting, and not to be caught by the camera eye of realism and common sense. It is that other world toward which strive the pyramids, the colossal statues, the impatient purity of Ikhnaton, and the so much more than human beauty of the sculptured face of Nefertiti.

This drive to transcend the world of common sense is not unique with the Egyptians. But what gives them their style is perhaps above all the immediacy, the directness, the innocence with which they try to *make this world the next one*. Their other world is a heightening and intensification of this familiar one. It is not a repudiation of this world, as in much of Hindu and some even of Christian thought, nor is it quite the ennobling and humanizing of this world which the Greeks and much of Christian aspiration attempted. The Egyptians' striving after the infinite resembled their *ka:* the thing beyond is a curious double of the thing here. It has something of the simplicity of the pyramids—one ordinary stone is placed on another—but the result is most extraordinary.

---

* The matter discussed in elementary terms in the above paragraph is a major problem in what philosophers call "epistemology," or the "theory of knowledge." In our story, it comes out most sharply, perhaps, in the medieval debate between "nominalists" and "realists" (see below, p. 317). To a layman, it would seem that the philosophers have not yet solved the problem; perhaps it is insoluble, at least in traditional terms.

IV: Mesopotamia

The Setting

The taming of Mesopotamia, the "land between the rivers," and its maintenance at a high state of agricultural yield

presented harder natural problems than did the adaptation of the Nile Valley to human use. In all the ups and downs of its history the Nile has continued to be cultivated and populated, whereas the valleys of the Tigris and Euphrates relapsed into marsh and malaria after the great days of medieval Baghdad and continue as twentieth-century Iraq to be a relatively backward area. The two rivers flooded erratically and sometimes dangerously, unlike the predictable Nile. Indeed, the Old Testament account of the Flood is sometimes held to be a Jewish version of old Mesopotamian tales based on one or more particularly notable floods in the valleys. Again, the climate of the valleys is much less equable than that of the Nile; in modern Iraq there is a spread from 120° in summer to below freezing in the winter. Finally, the Mesopotamian region is much less isolated than Egypt. Invasion is easy from the mountainous regions to the north and east, and even the deserts to the west and southwest have proved no barrier to nomads tempted by the wealth of the valleys.

Ancient Mesopotamia, then, unlike Egypt, shows a succession of separate states, not just of dynasties. Invaders in the Tigris-Euphrates valleys were ultimately absorbed into a culture that was in a sense continuous for more than three thousand years before Christ. But they disrupted the political continuity so completely that we must talk of different states in the valleys, and not merely as in Egypt of Old, Middle, and New Kingdoms.

An Outline of Mesopotamian History

The earliest of these states were apparently city-states in the lower valleys, each of which may have been independently responsible for the irrigation work and maintenance without which the valleys were unusable. They were, however, often in conflict and subject to the hegemony or leadership of one or another, such as the "Ur of the Chaldees" of the Old Testament. The first of these grew up in land reclaimed from swamps at the mouth of the Tigris-Euphrates in the "land of Sumer," which now, after five thousand years of river delta deposits, is some hundred and fifty miles from the head of the Persian Gulf. We do not know of what race the Sumerians were; their language, however, is *not* a form of Semitic, the language of most other peoples of the area.

Sumerian cities like Ur and Lagash go back beyond 3000 B.C., and are thus older than the organized state of Egypt. These cities were centered around the temple of the god who was literally the "owner" of the city (see above, p. 28). In the flat place his temple arose as an artificial mountain or "ziggurat" now crumbled, but still identifiable, and a fine clue for archaeologists looking for sites to excavate. Our biblical tale of the Tower of Babel is almost certainly a Hebrew reflection of these Mesopotamian monumental temples.

North of the Sumerians a Semitic-speaking people, the Akkadians, early appear and war with the Sumerians, whom they seem ultimately to have absorbed. The great city of the Akkadians, Babylon, "Gate of God," was the most famous of ancient Mesopotamian cities. Its "Hanging Gardens" in its later days (seventh century B.C.) were one of the "seven wonders" of the ancient world. The culture of this Sumerian-Babylonian area has left us innumerable bequests— more perhaps, if the sum could be worked out, than Egypt. Here arose the duodecimal system of time measurement we still use, the science of mathematics and the science of astronomy (and its disreputable twin-brother, astrology, still alive, though a bit enfeebled, in the mid-twentieth century A.D.), myths of creation, of a dying and resurrected god, epics, law codes, and much else.

The first Babylonian greatness may have been due in part to an injection of new blood, that of the nomadic Amorites from Syria. After about 1800 B.C., Babylonian power declined. Then came a thorough conquest from the desert, that of the Kassites, a mixed people about whom little is known.

Air view of the ruins of Ur, showing the remains of the great Ziggurat that dominated the city.

During the Kassite rule, the valleys fell into a period of decentralization. In the twelfth century, native Babylonian rule revived briefly under the first Nebuchadrezzar. Another invasion of desert peoples followed, and then Babylon fell to her northern upstart neighbor, Assyria.

The Assyrian Empire was a true military expansion. Under successive rulers from the ninth to the seventh centuries, Assyria brought the whole of the ancient Near East under one rule, though only briefly and incompletely. Although the Assyrians defeated Egyptian armies several times, they never really absorbed Egypt. Assyria wiped out the northern of the two Jewish kingdoms, Israel, but failed to take Jerusalem. The Assyrians seem to have initiated the policy of wholesale transfers of populations in an effort to prevent uprisings. Babylon enjoyed another revival in the late seventh century, and, after having joined with a new power in the mountains on the east, the Medes, destroyed Nineveh, the Assyrian

capital. Under the second Nebuchadrezzar, Babylon took Jerusalem itself and, in an attempt to destroy Jewish nationalism, deported several thousands of the Jewish élite to Babylon. This is the "Babylonian Captivity" of biblical history.

The new Babylonian Empire lasted only a short time. In the mountains of Persia there was a rising new power. The Medes and the Persians, semi-nomadic tribes speaking a tongue related to those of modern Europe, invaded the great valley from the mountains east of it, and from that base conquered all the lands we have dealt with in this chapter. Under Darius I (521-485 B.C.) this empire was one of the really great empires of western history; as a continuous land empire it has been rivaled only by those of Alexander the Great, Rome, the Tartars, and the present U.S.S.R. The rule of Darius ran from Libya to the Indus, from the Caspian Sea to the Indian Ocean. He made military expeditions into the Danube region and Greece and established a

European "satrapy" (province) in Thrace; but the Persians never really held continental European lands. With Darius we seem almost into modern history. His empire was not a unified state, but it was well administered by imperial governors (satraps) and a regular civil service, tied together by roads and a well-organized postal system. Indeed Woodrow Wilson had an eloquent encomium of the Persian postal system by Herodotus inscribed on the entrance to the main post office in New York City:

Neither snow nor rain nor heat nor gloom of night stays these couriers from the swift completion of their appointed rounds.

Culture

In these long millennia of the rise and fall of states, certain cultural patterns persist. The basic agricultural skills needed in Mesopotamia were never actually destroyed for long, nor were the administrative and political skills which were needed to preserve sufficient order to allow irrigation farming at all. On this agricultural basis there flourished one of the great urban cultures of history, urban in the rather special sense of a materialistic drive to wealth and display, to a kind of metropolitan-mindedness. Since we have absorbed much of what we know of Mesopotamia from Jewish sources, Babylon has come down to us as a wicked, sensual city, quite properly destroyed by an angry God. Actually, it was probably the first great urban center with a big ruling class, merchants and professional men of all sorts, and a common working people absorbed into the life of the metropolis. Until Alexandria (see Chapter II), which after all was a Greek city, Egyptian cities seem not to have shared this metropolitan atmosphere; they were administrative centers overshadowed by a nobility and a bureaucracy.

The sciences were on the whole carried further in Mesopotamia than in Egypt. Astronomy and mathematics in particular developed a definite body of knowledge which the Greeks later took over. Theories on why this development took place in just this area can hardly be verified. The land system and methods of irrigation certainly called for and got the skills of surveyor and engineer, but no more than in Egypt. Chaldean religious beliefs may have fostered the study of the stars as determinants of human destiny. There may even be something in the poetic notion that astronomy really began on the desert fringes of the river valleys where the idle shepherds lay watching the clear night skies. We do not know.

Law, too, was developed in Mesopotamia to a point where it was actually published. It remained no longer, as primitive law tends to do, the secret and semi-magical possession of a special class of men. The Code of Hammurabi was "published" about 1800 B.C. by being engraved in cuneiform characters on an eight-foot column of very hard stone which has survived intact for almost four thousand years. It almost certainly was preceded by earlier Sumerian codes. It is a primitive code in many ways, notably in its punishments, which fit the crime with a vengeance. Here is a sample that those familiar with our Bible will recognize:

If a man destroy the eye of another man, they shall destroy his eye.[*]

Even on the subject of assault and battery, however, Hammurabi's Code is not always as barbarous as this sample suggests. For example, a little further on there is this provision:

If a man strike another man in a quarrel and wound him, he shall swear: 'I struck him without intent,' and he shall be responsible for the physician.[†]

_____
[*] R. F. Harper, _Code of Hammurabi_ (Chicago, 1904), §196.
[†] _Ibid._, §206.

The Code of Hammurabi is based on a caste society: injuries to men of the upper class are fined more heavily than injuries to a "freeman," and injuries to a freeman come higher than injuries to a slave. But it is not by any means a society in which some individuals are wholly without rights, without personality in the eyes of the law. The slaves were also protected by the law; they had a status; they could be emancipated under certain conditions; even a gentleman had to pay a fine if he injured or killed a slave. Domestic relations are covered in many provisions. Here is one set that will not seem altogether unreasonable to many of us.

> If a woman hate her husband, and say: 'Thou shalt not have me,' they shall inquire into her antecedents for her defects; and if she have been a careful mistress and be without reproach and her husband have been going about and greatly belittling her, that woman has no blame. She shall receive her dowry and shall go to her father's house.
> If she have not been a careful mistress, have gadded about, have neglected her house and have belittled her husband, they shall throw that woman into the water.*

Incest brings out the full horror that most peoples have always felt for it—though only a few hundred miles away brother-sister marriage was to grow up in the families of the pharaohs.

> If a man lie in the bosom of his mother after (the death of) his father, they shall burn both of them.†

Mesopotamian religion has the usual gods to represent war, daily business, and sex, and one god who serves as ruler or father of a very turbulent family of gods. In Babylon this god was Marduk, whose name was given to the great planet which Roman astrologers called Jupiter because they thought Marduk was the Babylonian equivalent of Jupiter. There is little sign of a sense of sin in this polytheism—or these polytheisms, for the constant invasions of the valley meant a steady process of absorbing new gods.

The Mesopotamian afterlife was at first a vague limbo, like the old Hebrew *sheol* or the Greek Hades. Yet it seems clear that as the varied gods of the separate city-states got organized into a pantheon, and as the city-states got organized into successive empires, there came into being a religion that anticipates much in later Greco-Roman, and indeed Judaeo-Christian, religion. Notably the family relations and attributes of gods and goddesses came to represent a sort of parallel to human ones, an explanation of the universe in terms understandable by men, yet beyond, above them, gods to be worshiped, reconciled, and—in our eyes, perhaps—bribed and cajoled. And around the god, Tammuz, who died and was born again, there grew up a cult through which the worshipers—probably a minority of the people—came to believe that they might share the deathless existence of the god himself.

As we have already noted (p. 34), the story of the Biblical Flood is probably of Mesopotamian origin, as is that of the Tower of Babel (p. 34). The ruins of the library of the Assyrian kings have yielded the great epic of Gilgamesh, a legendary Mesopotamian hero. On the eleventh tablet of the epic, there is an account of a great flood, of the ship Utnapishtim built to withstand it, how the floods came, and how the ship stuck fast on Mount Nisir. Then:

> When the seventh day drew nigh
> I sent out a dove, and let her go.
> The dove flew hither and thither,
> but as there was no resting-place for her, she returned.
> Then I sent out a swallow, and let her go.
> The swallow flew hither and thither,
> but as there was no resting-place for her she also returned.
> Then I sent out a raven, and let her go.
> The raven flew away and saw the abatement of the waters.

---

* *Ibid.*, §§142-143.
† *Ibid.*, §157.

Assyrians attacking a city. Relief from about 750 B.C.

She settled down to feed, went away, and returned no more.*

The Assyrian, Babylonian, and Persian Styles

In spite of the many historic "firsts" we find earlier among Sumerians, perhaps the most striking development in ancient Mesopotamia was the Assyrian culture, the first culture to which we can certainly apply the derogatory adjective "militaristic." The Assyrians can hardly have been the first militarists, the first men to live by organized warfare; but they are the first group so to live in a great area of civilized culture, the first who have a "style." This style stands out in all Assyrian sculpture, which is mostly in

*R. F. Harper, *Assyrian and Babylonian Literature: Selected Translations* (New York, 1904), 356.

bas-relief. The bearded fighters, the impaled lions, and the lines of captives look out at us with exaggerated masculinity. These are tough people, with no nonsense about them except the impractical belief that military force is all that is needed for a people to succeed on this earth.

We do not really know enough about the Assyrians to be sure they were in fact the caricatures of some of our notions of militarism that they appear to be. Here is a passage from the *Annals of Ashurbanipal,* an Assyrian king of the seventh century B.C. The king speaks:

By the command of Ashur, Sin, Shamash, Ramman, Bel, Nabu, Ishtar of Nineveh, Ninib, Nergal, and Nusku, I entered the land of Mannai and marched through it victoriously. Its cities, great and small, which were without number, as far as Izirtu, I captured, I destroyed,

CHAPTER I

I devastated, I burned with fire. I brought forth people, horses, asses, cattle, and sheep from within those cities, and counted them as spoil. Ahsheri heard of the progress of my campaign and abandoned Izirtu, his royal city. He fled to Ishtatti, a city in which he trusted, and took refuge there. I conquered that region, laid it waste for a distance of fifteen days' march, and poured disaster upon it. As for Ahsheri, . . . the people of his land made a revolt against him. On the street of his city they cast his corpse and left his body lie. With my weapons I struck down his brother, his family, and the members of his father's house. Afterward I placed Ualli, his son, upon his throne.*

Ashurbanipal's gods are dead and meaningless, but note in that last sentence the technique that we might call setting up a "satellite" state.

The Assyrians were clearly an energetic people, with a kind of hybrid vigor. They were a new people, from the hitherto back-

---

* *Ibid.*, 103.

ward mountainous regions of upper Mesopotamia. They probably represent a cross between an older non-Semitic people, the Hurrians, and a Semitic folk. The hooked nose, which is sometimes but wrongly thought to be peculiarly Jewish, appears clearly on some of these bearded fighters. They had great gifts not only for fighting but also for military organization and plunder. In Nineveh, their capital, the great Assyrian kings gathered the spoils of the world, including—for even this early, conquerors paid tribute to science and learning—a great library of thousands of clay tablets. But, unless the Assyrians were just victims of hard luck, they must have lacked something, some touch of understanding of other peoples, or of political moderation, or of respect for law. Otherwise their rule could hardly have been so ephemeral, for at its peak or second phase, it lasted not much more than a century (745-625 B.C.). As it is,

The Audience Hall of Darius at Persepolis (about 500 B.C.).

they stand in our memory mainly through a line of Byron's:

The Assyrian came down like the wolf on the fold.

To balance this Assyrian militarism there is Babylon, the city of pleasure. The psalmist of the Old Testament tells us: "By the rivers of Babylon . . . they that led us captive required of us songs; and they that watched us required of us mirth." But, since with all its hanging gardens, all its luxury, Babylon was a city built of adobe-like brick, its ruins are not so impressive as those of a provincial Roman town, and not nearly so impressive as the ruins of Mayan cities in Mexico. For Babylon we have not, as we have for Egypt, scraps of papyri in which the trivia, the love notes, the unpaid bills, and the private woes and delights of ordinary folk survive. We cannot be sure just what Babylonian life was really like. But it does seem to have been the first true metropolis in western history, a business as well as an administrative center. One may guess that its people felt a touch of something like what we call urban sophistication.

Western historians have tended to neglect the Persians of the great period, that of the Achaemenid Empire (550-330 B.C.). Archaeological discoveries of the last seventy-five years have centered on earlier peoples, and have made their histories more exciting than that of the Persians; moreover, our interests have always been on the Greek side as against the Persians, as they have been on the Roman side as against the Carthaginian. Persians and Carthaginians have not appealed to us as part of our heritage. Yet the Persians built an empire with an admirable administrative system, the first successful empire to rule over many ethnically different peoples; they "pacified" the Near East under conditions that made possible a fascinating cosmopolitan culture; the ruins of their ceremonial capital, Persepolis (Greek for "city of the Persians") have been excavated to the great benefit of archaeology; they produced a higher revealed religion and a great prophet, Zoroaster (in Persian, Zarathushtra, sixth century B.C.), which had a part in the making of Christianity.

Persian art looks oriental, somewhat stiff and heavy, and does indeed owe much to the Assyrians. But Persian ethics and religion have gone far beyond the original polytheism of the Aryans with their sky-god father of a quarrelsome brood, and well beyond the fleshly fertility cults of Mesopotamia. Here is Zoroaster addressing the God of Light, Ahura-Mazdah, probably once two gods, now one:

> As the Holy One then I acknowledged
> thee, Mazdah-Ahura,
> When Good Thought once came to me,
> Best Silent Thought bade me proclaim:
> Let not man seek to please the many Liars,
> For they make all the Righteous foes to thee.
>
> Thus, Ahura, Zarathushtra chooses for
> himself,
> Mazdah, whatever Spirit of thine is Holiest.
> May Righteousness be incarnate, might in
> life's strength,
> May Piety be in the Kingdom that beholds
> the sun,
> With Good Thought may he assign Destiny
> to men for their deeds.°

° Quoted in A. T. Olmstead, *History of the Persian Empire* (Univ. of Chicago Press, 1948), p. 95.

CHAPTER I

V: The Periphery—The Jews

The Peoples
Outside the Valleys

The lands on the periphery of the great river valleys in which urban civilizations first grew up would be important to history if only because invaders from these lands repeatedly overran the settled valleys. From the first, Egypt, Mesopotamia, and Palestine-Syria were melting pots in something like the sense in which Americans use that phrase. In recent years, scholarly research has added greatly to our knowledge of these people in Asia Minor, in the deserts, and on the coast of Syria. Whole peoples, some known hitherto only by name from mention in our Bible, now take on reality for the specialist. Notably, we have learned that early in the second millennium before Christ the Hyksos kings of Egypt were leaders of a mixed people based in Asia Minor. This people used the horse, which they appear to have brought to Egypt for the first time.

We have also learned that a people called the Mitanni ruled in upper Mesopotamia a few centuries earlier. The Mitanni too were a warrior people, and some of their descendants were the fighting Assyrians of the seventh century. We do not know much about the Mitanni, but their ruling classes, at least, seem to have spoken an Aryan, or Indo-European, tongue related to those of most of our modern West. The archaeological experts have almost given up the attempt to find an "original" Aryan tribe or race; but the linguist can tell an Aryan language, though again, he cannot tell us anything final about where and when the "original" language grew up.

We have learned a lot about the Hittites, a people who held together, perhaps as a ruling minority, a major state in Asia Minor about 1500 B.C. The Hittites, or at the very least their ruling aristocracy, were quite conceivably of European origin, and certainly spoke an Aryan tongue that the experts have now succeeded in deciphering pretty completely. They introduced iron to the area, previously limited to copper and brass, and tried to hold a monopoly on some of the processes of iron-making. They had the horse, war chariots, and a rather heavy monumental style in art.

Then there were the Phoenicians, a people of Semitic tongue, who built a series of very busy trading cities at the eastern end of the Mediterranean. They invented the alphabet probably before 1300 B.C., were great traders, and founded colonies elsewhere in the Mediterranean, notably at Carthage, near the modern North African city of Tunis. Carthage is said to have been settled in 814 B.C.

On the western fringe of the area there grew up in the second millennium B.C. on the island of Crete the first true *urban* civilization we can locate in Europe proper. This civilization depended in large part on sea-borne trade, and there are many remains which show that these Minoans, as they are known, had commercial and cultural relations with Egyptians and other peoples of the area we have been studying. But the Minoans raise the curtain, so to speak, on Greek history, and we must postpone them to the next chapter (p. 51).

The History of the Jews

The Jews have left us a remarkable account of their part in the ancient history of the Near East. This account is known to Christians as the Old Testament. For fundamentalists of both Christian and Jewish faiths today it is the word of God, an exact account of the creation of the earth and of the subsequent history of God's chosen people, the sons of Abraham. For the ancient Jews, of course, these writings were revelations of God's will; for those scholars today who take the naturalistic-historical approach the Old Testament is simply the Jewish national record, more complete and consecutive in a single work than any other record we possess from that region, but nevertheless a historical document and one to be criticized by the canons of historical science. This critical task was carried out by nineteenth-century scholars, led by the Germans from E. Reuss (1804-1891) to Julius Wellhausen (1844-1918), who developed what is called the "higher criticism" of the Bible. These scholars sought not merely to establish accurate texts (which is the "lower criticism") but to put these texts in what they considered the proper historical setting. Broadly speaking, the scholars who produced this nineteenth-century higher criticism tended to find the Jewish holy writings historically inaccurate; the Old Testament appeared to them to be a set of legends, myths, genealogies, priestly prescriptions, all edited later by far from disinterested ancient Hebrew scholars. Some of the work of these pioneers of higher criticism has been generally accepted, especially in Protestant, Reformed Jewish, and freethinking circles. But the latest such scholarship, greatly helped by modern archaeological research, has tended to be critical of these earlier critics, and to regard the Jewish holy writings as on the whole much more historically accurate than they appeared to be to scholars only a generation ago. A leading American Hebraist has written of the first chapters of Genesis, for instance: "Aside from a few die-hards among older scholars, there is scarcely a biblical historian who has not been impressed by the rapid accumulation of data supporting the substantial historicity of pa-

triarchial tradition." * Thus it seems to scholars now that Abraham did live, that Terah his father did migrate from Ur of the Chaldees to northwestern Mesopotamia, that Abraham did migrate southward, that the Jews did live long in the hill country now Transjordan, and that they were also long established in the Delta region of Egypt, that they there sank into a state of servitude, that there was a historical Moses (the name is Egyptian), and that he did lead the Israelites out of bondage at least to the edge of Canaan, the Promised Land.

Nevertheless, what Christians call the Old Testament remains, from the point of view of the naturalistic historian, a great but varied body of writings. The account of the patriarchs, and of the age of Moses, remains an epic. To this epic material have been added some actual historical chronicles, a great deal of material on ritual and other priestly concerns, and material more purely literary—lyrical poems like the Song of Solomon, tales like that of Ruth, philosophical poems like the Book of Job, aphorisms and reflections on man's fate like the "wisdom" books. Finally, to all these was added the work of the prophets. These spiritual leaders sought to understand why the Jews were being overcome by the great powers round about them, and sought to spur their people to resistance, or to spiritual conquests. The Old Testament as we know it was thus put together—*edited*, in fact—by Jewish scholars who had known the dark days of the exile in Babylon, who had seen the beginnings of the uprooting of the Jews from their homeland, or, as it is tamely called, the Diaspora or "scattering abroad."

Seen in the light of history, the Jews were a Semitic tribe that may have originated in the Arabian desert, and that was closely related to such nomads as the Arabs of later history. About the third quarter of

---

* W. F. Albright, "The Biblical Period," in Louis Finkelstein, ed., *The Jews* (New York, 1949), 3.

CHAPTER I

the twentieth century B.C. they left the region of Ur for the western hill country and the Negeb. Some of them later settled in Egypt. Under Moses the Israelites emerged from Egypt some time shortly after 1300 B.C. They were still simple folk, semi-nomads, herdsmen, without the skills of townsmen, with no clear and important noble class, and already with a monotheistic god, Yahweh, our Jehovah. In the next few centuries they invaded the more urban and more sophisticated land of Canaan; were tempted by the Canaanite wealth and Canaanite polytheistic religion; in short, were ready to assume the full burden of their history as religious pioneers. An established Jewish kingdom reached its height of prestige in the tenth century under David and Solomon. Even at its height, however, this ancient kingdom was no more than a relatively minor state, which, under Solomon, enjoyed particularly good commercial and diplomatic relations with neighboring Egypt and Phoenicia.

This prosperity and unity did not last. In the tenth century the northern tribes seceded and formed the Kingdom of Israel (933-722 B.C.). The southern tribes, retaining the sacred city of Jerusalem, formed the Kingdom of Judah (933-586 B.C.). The two rival kingdoms struggled together and took part in the balance-of-power politics in the Near East, which as we have seen was dominated by the rivalry of great powers in Mesopotamia and in Egypt. Had the power-centers in these two great valleys remained substantially equal, the Jews, like the modern Swiss, might have continued independent. As it was, Assyria, Babylonia, and Persia all rose to international supremacy, and, as we should say, "annexed" Palestine, the land of the Jews. Israel fell in 722 to Assyria, and Judah fell to Nebuchadrezzar II of Babylonia in 586. Because the Jews had been particularly stiff-necked in their resistance in Jerusalem, Nebuchadrezzar determined to stamp out the Jewish nuisance once and for all. He destroyed city and temple, and

deported ten thousand or more Jews—the intellectuals, the élite—to Babylon.

Under Persian rule, the Jews sifted back and restored Jerusalem after a fashion. Under Nehemiah in the fifth century the walls were rebuilt, and Jerusalem was started on a new period of material prosperity as part of the increasingly mature world of trade, war, and advanced culture that culminated in the One World of the Roman Empire. But the restored Jewish kingdom, though politically independent from 142 to 63 B.C., was for most of this period no more than a client or satellite state, a subordinate part of some great imperial system, Persian, Hellenistic, or Roman. The political greatness of Solomon was never restored.

The Uniqueness of the Jews

Yet the Jews, unlike the hundreds of tribes of the Near East, persisted. Their survival is hardly to be explained in terms of any single factor. Certainly no simple geographical or other environmental factor will do at all, for these they shared with the forgotten tribes. Modern biological and historical knowledge makes it unlikely that the sons of Abraham enjoyed a hereditary racial toughness, or that they kept their race pure. The fact is that the Jews have been held together by their *beliefs*, by a faith, by a hard core within the individual Jew that has been toughened, not worn away, by persecution.

The Jews were the first people of our western civilization to attain a belief in one God: this belief was brought home to every Jew, and lodged firmly in his whole personality, by the full ritual and legal force of community education. The Jewish tribal God, Yahweh, the Jehovah of our biblical transliteration, was at first no more than another tribal god, the protector of his own, but still no more than one god in a Near East full of roving peoples, settled peoples, and gods of all sorts. Very early, however, the worship of Jehovah became an exclusive worship enjoined on the Jews. No Jew could even hedge a bit by an occasional sacrifice to some other god. The first commandment reads: Thou shalt have no other gods before me.

The second commandment forbids the children of Israel to make graven images or idols, "for I the Lord thy God am a jealous God." That is, not only was the developed Jewish faith monotheistic, it was also resolutely turned against naturalistic or anthropomorphic (manlike) notions of divinity. Jehovah was not only the sole God of the Jews; he was a being so awful, so majestic, so unlike us humans that he must not be conceived in any earthly form or symbol, let alone portrayed. This was a greater emancipation from things of this earth than Ikhnaton had attained; for his one god, Aton, though a pure and powerful being, was none the less a sungod who was plainly symbolized by a sun and rays, and was therefore nearer the material universe than the developed Jewish concept of Jehovah.

The Old Testament records at length the Law of the Jews, the religious practices that made and kept the Jew aware of his membership in the faith, of the burden and discipline put upon him by the choice of Jehovah. We know that the Jew may not eat pork, that the Jewish boy must be circumcised, and that the Jew must fast on certain holy days. How far this religious organization, as contrasted with religious ideas, or theology, is responsible for the way the Jews have held together is a question of the kind that human beings love to ask. But there is no effective religion without *both* theology and church organization, *both* spirit and letter, faith and works. The Jewish faith was built over the centuries into a kind of prescribed but freely accepted behavior that most Jews would rather die than abandon. This faith survived, and the Jews survived.

It was a faith that foreshadows much of the later religion of the West. Its God, though infinitely above men, was also close to them, bound to them by a covenant (agreement) which men could rely on; if men lived up to the covenant—that is, if they lived up to moral standards and to ideas of justice recognizably like our own —they would be justified, they would be good men; later, perhaps under some eastern influences, that justification came to be seen as a personal immortality in another and happier world; finally, some generations before the birth of Christ, this concept of the future state (an "eschatology") came to include a Messiah, a divinely appointed leader who should bring the Jewish people, as leaders of humanity, into the New Jerusalem, the perfect state on earth.

The Beginnings
of a Universal Faith

One more element was added to Jewish faith at the very end of the period with which this chapter is concerned. The earlier books of the Old Testament, even after their editing by later Jewish scholars, do not make Jehovah a universal God, nor even a God who was clearly more powerful *throughout the universe* than the pagan gods were. Jehovah is the sole God for a Jew, but not by any means for an Egyptian; the Egyptian had better stick to Isis and Osiris and their family. It was hardly a nice family, and the Jews, who had always some touch of what we call "puritanism," could not approve of its ways; but in these early days the Jews would not think of Isis and the rest as frauds. Yet by the time of the prophets, roughly in the years just before and just after the fall of Jerusalem in 586, writers like the author of the second part of the Book of Isaiah saw Jehovah as the sole God, the beginning and the end of the universe, a God for the whole human race.

Ye are my witnesses, saith the Lord, and my servant whom I have chosen: that ye may know and believe me, and understand that I am he; before me there was no God formed, neither shall there be after me. I, even I, am the Lord; and beside me there is no saviour. I have declared, and I have saved, and I have shewed, and there was no strange God among you: therefore ye are my witnesses, saith the Lord, and I am God.*

For some Jews this gospel of the one true God probably meant that this God would one day bring back the worldly glory of Solomon, that he would make the Jews the greatest of the earth's peoples. But for most Jews, this purified faith reinforced the Law and the settled Jewish way of life. What is important is that in this final form Jewish monotheism identified God with an ethical concept of the good life and, as the years wore on toward the birth of Christ, with the concept of an afterlife in which conformity with God's will would bring eternal happiness in heaven, and disobedience would bring eternal punishment in hell. Early Jewish beliefs were, apparently, like most of the religious beliefs of the Mesopotamian and Palestinian region, vague and uncertain on individual immortality. There is nothing like the Egyptian preoccupation with the *ka* and an afterlife (see above, p. 28). But by the time of the Persian Empire, the belief in an afterlife is common throughout the Near East. Nowhere is this belief so closely tied to a high ethical code as among the Jews.

It is difficult to exaggerate the moral earnestness and depth of the developed Jewish view of life. In the midst of the worldly superstitions, the fertility cults—including the familiar practice of "temple prostitution"—the cruel, cheating gods to be appeased, not worshiped, all the rank earthiness of the late ancient Near East, the Jew, in spite of the "primitive" touches of the Old Testament, must give a modern the "shock of recognition." And not only

for what we call his puritanism, but also for his joyous hope of a better world:

O Zion, that bringest good tidings, get thee up into the high mountain; O Jerusalem, that bringest good tidings, lift up thy voice with strength; lift it up, be not afraid; say unto the cities of Judah, Behold your God! Behold, the Lord GOD will come with strong hand, and his arm shall rule for him: behold, his reward is with him, and his work before him. He shall feed his flock like a shepherd: he shall gather the lambs with his arm, and carry them in his bosom, and shall gently lead those that are with young.*

The life of the good religious Jew was not just a series of adjustments to the desires and habits of gods who were no more than irresponsible men with unlimited powers, like the gods of neighboring peoples. Especially for the sensitive and intelligent, life became a series of adjustments to the will of a being so much above mere men that he could not be known at all in human terms, in terms of buying and selling, persuading other people to do what we want, contriving better ways of spinning or cooking or raising food. God's plan was not the plan of common sense, nor even of what under the Greeks became the plan of natural science. No man could really *know* God's plan.

This indeed is the conclusion of the philosophic poem we call the Book of Job. In this poem, Job is a rich and happy man whom God afflicts with disasters of all sorts. Job does not really rebel or lose faith, but he does begin to wonder why God has thus afflicted him, an innocent man, a righteous man. But he learns to regret the pride that made him question, and the book closes (save for a prose epilogue in which Job recovers wealth and happiness) with the words:

Therefore have I uttered that which I understood not,
Things too wonderful for me, which I knew not.

---

* Isaiah 43:11.

---

* Isaiah 40: 9-11.

Hear, I beseech thee, and I will speak.
I will demand of thee, and declare thou unto
    me.
I had heard of thee by the hearing of the ear;
But now mine eye seeth thee:
Wherefore I abhor myself, and repent
In dust and ashes.*

Christianity, which has so many and so close links to developed Judaism, which indeed came directly out of Judaism, is our greatest debt to the ancient Near East. There are thousands of other debts, from the alphabet to the domestic cat. But one thing that is most important to us did not exist in the ancient Near East. At the end of the long course of history we have just traced, Darius, the Persian king, master of the whole of the region, had crossed over

into the Balkans, and perhaps southern Russia. On his flank, a people who called themselves Hellenes, and whom we call Greeks, had given him trouble. Their city-states had started to spread into Asia. Darius went to war with them, and at Marathon in 490 his army was beaten by a numerically inferior group of soldiers of a new kind, *citizen*-soldiers. These men of Marathon had grown up in a society which, though it owed much to the Near East and to the hunters and farmers of prehistoric Europe, was something new on earth. That something new we still call by the Greek word, democracy. It was no mere "primitive" tribal or village democracy. That sort had existed even in the "despotic" older civilizations of the Near East. It was a sophisticated, urban, competitive society with a full-fledged government by discussion.

---

* Job 42:3-6.

Reading Suggestions
on the First Men and the First Civilizations

(Asterisk indicates paperbound edition.)

PREHISTORY

W. F. Albright, *From the Stone Age to Christianity*, 2nd ed. (°Anchor, 1957). A superb up-to-date survey of a field in which modern scholarship has made remarkable advances.

G. Gamow, *Biography of the Earth* (°Mentor). A very good introduction to the earth sciences, and an indispensable background for human history.

J. Pfeiffer, *From Galaxies to Man: A Story of the Beginnings of Things* (Macmillan, 1959). A good popular account of the most recent evolutionary concepts.

A. L. Kroeber, *Anthropology* (Harcourt, Brace, 1948). A masterly review of the subject in its general ramifications, with much material that is really philosophy of history.

C. Ceram, *Gods, Graves, and Scholars* (Knopf, 1951). A best-seller, deservingly so, for it makes clear to the reader what archaeology is all about.

R. J. Braidwood, *Prehistoric Men*, 3rd ed. (Chicago Museum of Natural History, Popular Series, 1957). An admirable introduction.

H. L. Shapiro, ed., *Man, Culture, and Society* (Oxford Univ. Press, 1956). A good collaboration; scholarly work, advanced but not difficult.

V. Gordon Childe, *What Happened in History* (°Penguin, 1946). Prehistory and ancient history down to the Greeks. A rapid but suggestive survey by an ethnologist and archaeologist, "rationalist" in point of view.

CHAPTER I

Ralph Linton, *The Tree of Culture* (Knopf, 1955; °Vintage). An admirable recent survey of cultural anthropology.

R. Coulborn, *The Origin of Civilized Societies* (Princeton Univ. Press, 1959). A scholarly, readable, and stimulating study.

P. L. Ralph, *The Story of Our Civilization: Ten Thousand Years of Western Man* (°Everyman, 1959). A thoughtful survey in 300 pages.

NEAR EASTERN HISTORY—GENERAL ACCOUNTS

H. B. Parkes, *Gods and Men: The Origins of Western Men* (Knopf, 1959). A perceptive survey, "rationalist" at bottom, but respectful, even warm, toward the early religions of the West. Fine brief reading lists.

M. Rostovtzev, *History of the Ancient World*, Vol. I (Clarendon, 1936). A splendidly illustrated short account, inevitably without the latest discoveries.

H. Frankfort, *The Birth of Civilization in the Near East* (Indiana Univ. Press, 1951; °Anchor). A brief and stimulating essay by an expert in the field.

H. Frankfort and others, *Before Philosophy* (°Penguin, 1952). Admirable essays in the intellectual history of the ancient Near East.

Christopher Dawson, *The Age of the Gods* (Sheed and Ward, 1934). An admirable introduction to these earliest western civilizations.

V. M. Scramuzza and P. L. MacKendrick, *The Ancient World* (Holt, 1958). A good up-to-date, standard textbook.

NEAR EASTERN HISTORY—ACCOUNTS BY AREAS AND PEOPLES

Egypt: The distinguished Egyptologist, J. H. Breasted, wrote several books on aspects of ancient Egyptian history. One of his last works was *The Dawn of Conscience* (Scribner's, 1933), a study of Egyptian religious and ethical beliefs.

J. A. Wilson, *The Burden of Egypt* (Univ. of Chicago Press, 1951). The best single-volume study of Egyptian culture.

A. Mekhitarian, *Egyptian Painting* (Skira, 1954). Expensively and superbly illustrated.

Mesopotamia: S. N. Kramer, *History Begins at Sumer* (°Anchor, 1959). Incorporates the latest research in this rapidly growing field.

A. T. Olmstead, *History of the Persian Empire* (Univ. of Chicago Press, 1948; °paperback edition by same press, 1959). The authoritative account.

C. W. Ceram, *The Secret of the Hittites*, trans. by R. C. Winston (Knopf, 1956). A most readable popular account of this people as resurrected by modern archaeology.

O. R. Gurney, *The Hittites* (°Penguin, 1952). An excellent scholarly summary, authoritative and condensed.

The Jews: The best introduction of all, of course, is the Old Testament itself, the national epic of the early Jews. Other helpful accounts are:

A. L. Sachar, *A History of the Jews* (Knopf, 1930). A balanced and scholarly account by the President of Brandeis University.

H. M. Orlinsky, *Ancient Israel* (Cornell Univ. Press, 1954). A good introductory manual.

W. F. Albright, "The Biblical Period," in L. Finkelstein, ed., *The Jews*, Vol. I, pp. 3-65 (Harper, 1949). A masterly treatment, extremely condensed but very specific—the best general view of contemporary scholarship in this important field.

James B. Pritchard, *Ancient Near Eastern Texts Relating to the Old Testament*, 2nd ed. (Princeton Univ. Press, 1955) and *The Ancient Near East in Pictures Relating to the Old Testament* (Princeton Univ. Press, 1954). Two splendid source-books, well edited.

HISTORICAL FICTION

J. V. Jensen, "Fire and Ice" and "The Cimbrians," in *The Long Journey* (Knopf, 1933). By a Dane; one of the few good fictional treatments of prehistory.

H. G. Wells, "A Story of the Stone Age," from his "Tales of Space and Time," in *The Short Stories of H. G. Wells* (Doubleday, 1929).

D. C. Wilson, *Prince of Egypt* (Westminster, 1949; °Pocket Books). Concerning Moses in Egypt; good on the Egyptian background.

M. T. Waltari, *The Egyptian* (Putnam's, 1949; °Pocket Books). The settings are authentic, though the story is much like a movie script.

I. Fineman, *Ruth* (Harper, 1949). One of the few good historical novels on the Jews before the time of Christ.

T. Mann, *Joseph and His Brothers, Young Joseph, Joseph in Egypt,* and *Joseph the Provider* (Knopf, 1934-1944). A series of novels by the distinguished German-American writer. Not easy reading; an ambitious attempt to plumb the philosophical and psychological depths of a biblical theme.

CHAPTER I

The
Greeks

CHAPTER II

I: The Background

ABOUT FOUR THOUSAND YEARS ago the Greeks descended into the peninsula at the southeastern extremity of Europe that still bears their name. With them the history of Europe and of western civilization begins. But the Greek civilization that reached maturity in the fifth century B.C. was by no means exclusively western or European in character; it borrowed much from the older cultures of the Near East. Long before the full flowering of their civilization, the Greeks had moved out into the islands of the Aegean Sea and across the Aegean to the western shores of Asia Minor. Although they planted many colonies farther afield, westward along the Mediterranean and northeastward along the Black Sea, their homeland was the Aegean world, the natural bridge, so to speak, between Asia and Europe, and between the ancient Near Eastern civilizations and the western civilizations still to come.

The Natural Setting

In climate and geography the Aegean world was—and still is—a part of the larger Mediterranean world. The summers are long, sunny, and almost rainless, but, thanks to sea breezes, not intolerably hot. The win-

Opposite. PART OF A BRONZE STATUE OF A GOD, *Greek, fifth century* B.C., *National Museum, Athens. This superb sculpture, recovered from the sea in the 1920's, dates from the Age of Pericles. Its identity is still a subject of controversy among experts, some of whom claim it is Zeus while others believe it is Poseidon, god of the sea.*

49

ters are mild, though snow falls at the higher elevations, and rainy spells are broken by frequent periods of sunny weather. Thus, men can live outdoors for much of the year and can grow olives and other semi-tropical fruit. The physical setting of the Aegean world is superb, with innumerable gulfs and bays, mountains and islands. The sea itself is an intense blue, more brilliant than that of more northerly waters.

Nature, however, has endowed Greece with little except scenery and a mild climate. Much of the land is too steep or too barren for farming; the valleys and plains are closely hemmed in by mountains and

the sea. The rivers and streams are too swift or too shallow for navigation; they flood in the rainy season, then dwindle to a trickle or dry up altogether. Local springs are too meager to allow extensive irrigation during the dry season. In ancient times, therefore, little could be grown in summer except drought-resistant fruits like olives and grapes. For the rest, the farms produced barley and other grains that could be harvested in the early summer, wine, honey, and very little else. Meat was a rarity. Since grain monopolized the best of the level land, the only pastures available were mountain slopes which could support small herds of goats and sheep but which were too steep for cattle.

Geography, in sum, has always denied the Greeks an easy living. But it did give them one considerable advantage in ancient times: it made navigation and commerce their natural occupations. The irregular coasts of the mainland and the islands provided sheltered anchorages; no part of the Aegean Sea was more than fifty miles from land, and vessels could journey hundreds of miles without losing sight of shore. Travel in ships propelled by sails or oars, or a combination of the two, was swifter, cheaper, and more comfortable than an up-hill and down-dale journey overland. Consequently, the Greeks quite early carried on an active maritime trade; they exchanged the olive oil and wine of the Aegean world for the metals, grains, and slaves needed in the homeland.

Minoan Civilization

The first sailors and traders in the Aegean world were not Greeks; they were inhabitants of the island of Crete, which lies across the southern entrance to the Aegean Sea. Located at the crossroads of the eastern Mediterranean, Crete was within fairly easy sailing distance of three continents—Asia, Africa, and Europe. Her seamen traded with Egypt and Phoenicia and also conducted piratical raids. Yet the relative isolation of Crete also gave some protection against invasion and conquest from abroad.

About 2800 B.C. copper and the manufacture of bronze were brought to Crete, probably from Phoenicia or Asia Minor. The civilization that developed thereafter is termed Minoan, from Minos, a legendary king. Scholars have divided this civilization into three main chronological periods:

Early Minoan—down to 2300 B.C.
Middle Minoan—2300 to 1600 B.C.
Late Minoan—1600 to 1300 B.C.

Each of these main periods is subdivided into three segments, from I through III. Culture seems to have reached its zenith during the Middle Minoan III and the Late Minoan I and II, between 1700 and 1400 B.C.

We must say "seems to have," for our

The Toreador Fresco from the Palace at Cnossos, from about 1550 B.C. *(A watercolor copy.)*

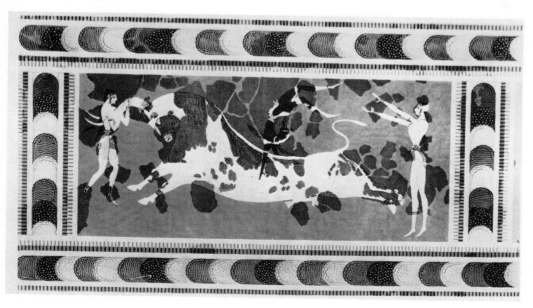

knowledge of ancient Crete is still fragmentary. Up to the beginning of the twentieth century, it consisted of little more than tantalizing references in Greek legends. Then the British archaeologist, Sir Arthur Evans, acting on a well-founded hunch, began excavations at Cnossos in central Crete. He struck "pay-dirt" almost at once and uncovered what was evidently a large and ancient palace, which he named the "palace of Minos." Subsequent digging by Evans and others disclosed the sites of more than a hundred towns that had existed before 1500 B.C., stretches of paved road, and enough pottery and other artifacts to stock a good-sized museum.

These archaeological remains provide convincing evidence that the Minoans were skillful builders, engineers, and artists. The palace at Cnossos was an unfortified structure several stories high, filling the area of an oversized city block. A city in miniature, it had running water, a drainage system, and a theater. The palace was begun in Middle Minoan I and was often repaired and altered, notably after a destructive earthquake in Middle Minoan III. Today the excavated palace is a maze of courtyards, corridors, storerooms, workshops, living quarters, council chambers, and government offices. Sir Arthur Evans realized that he had very likely discovered the actual building that inspired the old legend of the labyrinth to which the early Greeks were forced to send sacrificial victims.

Minoan potters, probably borrowing Egyptian techniques, produced work ranging from huge jars as tall as a man, for storing olive oil, to delicate cups, no thicker than an eggshell, decorated with birds, flowers, and fishes. Craftsmen employed ivory, gold, and jewels to make gaming boards for their kings, and exquisite statuettes, less than a foot high, of the bare-breasted snakegoddess who was apparently one of the chief objects of worship. Painters did elegant and flowing frescoes of plants, flowers, and dolphins, of cup-bearers and courtiers, and of

acrobats vaulting over a bull (see illustration on p. 51). The portrait of one court lady is now known as "La Parisienne" because of her obvious chic.

Some experts, therefore, have concluded that ancient Crete had a distinctive "style," carefree, opulent, gay; too little is known, however, about its political and social institutions to permit more than conjectures. What scholars have deduced about the politics of Crete suggests that the Minoan style also included a grimmer and rougher element. It is surmised that Crete, like Egypt, was ruled by despotic priest-kings with the aid of a central bureaucracy; that there were at first many little rival kingdoms; and that by Late Minoan I, the ruler of Cnossos had

Ivory and gold snake goddess from Crete, sixteenth century B.C.

come to dominate the whole island. About 1400 B.C., before the end of the Late Minoan period, Cnossos itself seems to have been captured by invaders from the European mainland. These invaders were Greeks from Mycenae, which lay on the Peloponnesus, the southern extremity of the Greek peninsula.

II: Early Greek History

A century ago the learned world would have rejected the hypothesis that the Greeks had invaded Crete as early as 1400 B.C. It was generally supposed that they had not appeared on the historical stage until much later. The earliest reference to them was in Homer's *Iliad*, probably written down in the eighth century B.C., the epic of the Greek siege of Troy; but there was no evidence that this Trojan War had actually occurred. Today we know that Homer's Greeks and Trojans were by no means entirely imaginary, and our knowledge of early Greek history has experienced a revolutionary expansion. Among the hundreds of archaeologists and scholars who made this expansion possible two were outstanding—Schliemann and Ventris.

Heinrich Schliemann (1822-1890) admired Homer so deeply that he devoted his life to proving that the Homeric Trojan War was more than poetic invention. Schliemann's biography makes a fine archaeological romance—early poverty in Germany, business success in California in the days of the gold rush, mastery of Greek and a dozen other languages, marriage to a Greek lady (she could recite Homer from memory), and finally two great discoveries. In 1873 Schliemann found the site of Troy, near the Hellespont in northwestern Asia Minor, although the remains that he uncovered turned out to be those of a later city built on the ruins of Homeric Troy.

Next, Schliemann went to the site of Mycenae overlooking the plain of Argos, one of the loveliest and most fertile areas of Greece. Here had stood the palace of Agamemnon, the leader of the Greek expedition against Troy in Homer's *Iliad*. In 1876 Schliemann dug up a fabulous treasure, a series of shaft-graves containing masks of gold and other objects fashioned with great artistry in gold and silver. Schliemann understandably thought he had found the burial place of Agamemnon himself; later experts have shown that the shaft-graves dated from an earlier era, probably the sixteenth century B.C. Obviously, a civilization had flourished on the Greek mainland hundreds of years before Homer.

Later excavations produced many other remains of this Mycenaean culture, including thousands of tablets found at various sites on the Peloponnesus and at Cnossos itself. The extraordinarily difficult feat of deciphering the writing on the tablets was accomplished in 1952 by a young English architect, Michael Ventris. As a lad in school, Ventris had been fascinated by Sir Arthur Evans' lectures on Linear B, the name given to the mysterious language of the tablets. Within twenty years Ventris had solved the mystery by using the techniques of cryptography and by enlisting the help of John Chadwick, a philologist at Cambridge University. His work proved that Linear B was an early form of the Greek language, a primitive script part way between the picture-writing of hieroglyphics and alphabetical writing. When Ventris died in 1956, in his mid-thirties, his work was already enabling scholars to undertake the first full appraisal of Mycenaean civilization.

Mycenaean Civilization

The task of appraisal is still under way. Enough work has already been accomplished, however, to make it clear that the Mycenaeans were Greeks who spoke an Indo-European language and who had first moved into Greece from the north about 2000 B.C. By the middle of the second millennium they had developed a prosperous and complex civilization. The shaft-graves found by Schliemann date from about 1600 B.C. A century or two later the Mycenaeans were constructing large beehive tombs and fortifying their cities with "Cyclopean" walls, composed of such huge stones that later tradition attributed their building to the mythical one-eyed giants called Cyclops. The tablets in Linear B were engraved about 1300-1200 B.C. and record the payments of tribute, the lists of supplies, and the other bookkeeping details of a bustling society.

The Mycenaeans already worshiped Zeus and the other Olympian deities made famous by the classical Greeks hundreds of years later. In other respects, however, Mycenaean culture bore a closer resemblance to that of Crete and the older Near Eastern societies than it did to the unborn world of classical Greece. Its arts and crafts were greatly influenced by the Minoans. Its political structure was monarchical with, at first, several separate kingdoms. Then, by the thirteenth century B.C., Agamemnon of Mycenae seems to have won recognition as overlord of the other monarchs. The social structure evidently included several well-defined classes arranged in the kind of hierarchy we have already encountered in the Near East. There were land-holding nobles; there were warriors, courtiers, merchants, and the clerks who compiled the accounts recorded on the tablets; and there were large

numbers of slaves, captured in war or rendered in tribute.

Mycenaean society, then, was both agrarian and commercial; it was also expansionist. The Mycenaeans traded with lands as distant as Sicily, established outposts on the shores of Syria, captured Crete, and raided the Aegean islands off the coast of Asia Minor. Their most celebrated exploit was the siege of Troy. We still have relatively little information about the Trojan War aside from Homer and from Schliemann's discovery of the site of Troy; we do not, for example, know who the Trojans really were. Expert opinion now rejects the date of about 1170 B.C. traditionally assigned to the war and suggests a date in the preceding century, perhaps 1250 or 1230.

The Dorian Invasion and Its Results

Soon after taking Troy, the Mycenaeans were themselves conquered by the Dorians. The new conquerors were, in effect, distant relatives of the Mycenaeans: they too spoke a Greek tongue and had first invaded Greece about 2000 B.C. After remaining for centuries in Epirus, a remote, rugged area of northwestern Greece, the Dorians began to expand about 1300 B.C. They took Crete first and then, between 1200 and 1100, captured most of the Mycenaean centers in the Peloponnesus, including Mycenae itself. There seems little doubt that the Dorians were rougher, cruder, and more destructive than their victims. Their invasion—"infiltration" is a more exact description of the gradual and piecemeal Dorian conquest—fatally undermined the foundations of Minoan and Mycenaean culture.

Not all of Greece experienced the blight of Dorian infiltration. The peninsula of Attica in the southeast for long escaped, and its chief city, Athens, attracted refugees from Dorian rule. Many of these refugees presently emigrated eastward across the Aegean to settle on the coast of Asia Minor and its offshore islands. This was the land called Ionia, and its new inhabitants became the Ionian Greeks. By 1100 B.C., however, most of the Greek world was entering a "Dark Age," which lasted for three centuries. Little is known about this period. Most of the refinements of the old Mycenaean culture seem to have vanished; some experts believe that the Linear B script went out of use and that the Greeks lapsed into illiteracy until the introduction of the alphabet from Phoenicia in the eighth century.

Homer

The first landmarks in Greek history after the Dark Age are the *Iliad* and the *Odyssey*. The date, the authorship, and the sources of these Homeric epics have been investigated and debated for more than a century. Although the debate is by no means closed, the informed consensus today is that the *Iliad* and the *Odyssey* were probably written in the eighth century B.C. They may have been the work of the blind poet Homer, an Ionian Greek, or of several unknown poets. They contain many echoes of far older writings, notably the Mesopotamian epic of Gilgamesh (see above, p. 37) and the items recorded on the tablets in Linear B.

The *Iliad* takes its title from Ilium (or Ilion), a poetic name for Troy, and recounts an episode in the Mycenaean siege of Troy. In the poem, the finest Greek warrior, Achilles, quarrels with his leader, Agamemnon, and sulks in his tent. The Greek forces then fare badly until Hector, the son of the Trojan king, slays Patroclus, the best friend of Achilles. The grief-stricken Achilles then avenges Patroclus by killing Hector. The *Odyssey* tells of the fantastic adventures of another Greek warrior, Odysseus (or Ulysses), King of Ithaca, who wanders for ten years after the defeat of Troy before he returns to his native island and his beloved wife, Penelope.

The two epics introduce us to the immense family of Greek gods who dwelled on snow-capped Mount Olympus at the northern edge of Greece. Homer's Olympians are neither remote nor perfect deities; they are, rather, supermen, all-powerful but not all-virtuous. As they intervene in human affairs, they are unruly, brawling, and jealous, yet they are also engaging and attractive. Poseidon, the sea-god, drives Odysseus on his wanderings. Zeus himself supports Achilles, the son of the goddess Thetis, after his quarrel with Agamemnon. When Achilles at length goes forth to slay Hector, he is provided with armor made by Hephaestus, god of the forge. And when he is dragging the corpse of Hector in triumph around the walls of Troy, the gods step in again and persuade him to hand Hector over to the Trojans for proper burial.

Homer's Greeks and Trojans behaved like their gods, quarreling and sulking but also respecting some of the basic decencies. Achilles did give over Hector's body for honorable burial, and Penelope did wait faithfully for Odysseus during his long absence. In sum, the pages of Homer present the heroic age of early Greece, and his warriors, half manlike, half godlike, resemble the legendary figures in other epics of other heroic ages. They call to mind Siegfried in the early German *Song of the Nibelung* or the Frankish knights in the *Chanson de Roland* (see Chapter VIII).

The following lines from the *Iliad*, rendered in a translation that preserves the rhythm of the Greek original, will illustrate Homer's imaginative similes and powerful descriptive passages. Zeus, dismayed by the possibility that Achilles' "sit-down strike" may bring defeat on the Greeks (or Achaians), appeals to his daughter, Athena, goddess of wisdom and champion of the Greek cause:

'My child, have you utterly abandoned the man of your choice?

Is there no longer deep concern in your heart
    for Achilleus?
Now he has sat down before the steep horned
    ships and is mourning
for his own beloved companion, while all the
    others
have gone to take their dinner, but he is fast-
    ing and unfed.
Go then to him and distil nectar inside his
    chest, and delicate
ambrosia, so the weakness of hunger will not
    come upon him.'

Speaking so, he stirred Athene, who was
    eager before this,
and she in the likeness of a wide-winged,
    thin-crying hawk
plummeted from the sky through the bright
    air. Now the Achaians
were arming at once along the encampment.
    She dropped the delicate
ambrosia and the nectar inside the breast of
    Achilleus
softly, so no sad weakness of hunger would
    come on his knees,
and she herself went back to the close house
    of her powerful
father, while they were scattering out away
    from the fast ships.
As when in their thickness the snowflakes of
    Zeus come fluttering
cold beneath the blast of the north wind
    born in the bright sky,
so now in their thickness the pride of the
    helms bright shining
were carried out from the ships, and shields
    massive in the middle
and the corselets strongly hollowed and the
    ash spears were worn forth.
The shining swept to the sky and all earth
    was laughing about them
under the glitter of bronze and beneath their
    feet stirred the thunder
of men, within whose midst brilliant Achil-
    leus helmed him.
A clash went from the grinding of his teeth,
    and his eyes glowed
as if they were the stare of a fire, and the
    heart inside him
was entered with sorrow beyond endurance.
    Raging at the Trojans
he put on the gifts of the god, that Hephais-
    tos wrought him with much toil.

First he placed along his legs the fair greaves
    linked with
silver fastenings to hold the greaves at the
    ankles.

Afterward he girt on about his chest the
    corselet,
and across his shoulders slung the sword with
    the nails of silver,
a bronze sword, and caught up the great
    shield, huge and heavy
next, and from it the light glimmered far, as
    from the moon.
And as when from across water a light shines
    to mariners
from a blazing fire, when the fire is burning
    high in the mountains
in a desolate steading, as the mariners are
    carried unwilling
by storm winds over the fish-swarming sea,
    far away from their loved ones;
so the light from the fair elaborate shield of
    Achilleus
shot into the high air. . . .°

Homer is a superb guide to the "style" of early Greek civilization, but he is not a fully reliable source for the evolution of particular Greek institutions. Since he wrote the *Iliad* five centuries after the historic Trojan war, it is almost impossible to distinguish what was Mycenaean from what developed centuries later. The politics and society depicted by Homer are basically aristocratic, dominated by noble families claiming descent from the god and goddesses. The strongest and bravest aristocrats became kings, as did Agamemnon at Mycenae. In religion, the kings served as the chief priests; but in politics they remained the first among equals, ruling with the help of aristocrats. This picture neglects important developments that had begun during the Dark Age, notably the formation of city-states.

The City-State

Around 1300 B.C., before the Dorian invasion, Greece seems to have been moving toward political unity under the overlordship of Mycenae. But as the Dark Age ended, in the eighth century, Greece was a

---

° *The Iliad*, Richmond Lattimore, trans. (Univ. of Chicago Press, 1951), 401-402.

collection of many disunited little states. The forces of geography surely fostered this political fragmentation. Cut off from each other by mountains, bays, and gulfs, the individual valleys and plains, both on the mainland and on the islands, were natural economic units. They became separate political units, too.

The political unit was the city-state or *polis*, including a city and the surrounding countryside, so that many of its citizens were in fact farmers. The average Greek city was a mere town, by modern standards, and most of the city-states were small in area. Greece contained well over a hundred of them. The nucleus of the *polis* was often some natural strong point, like the Athenian Acropolis (literally "high city") with its steep and rocky approaches. A more spectacular example is Acrocorinth, the small mountain dominating the city of Corinth on the isthmus of the same name connecting the Peloponnesus with the rest of Greece.

The history of the Greek city-states falls into three chronological periods, with the divisions coming approximately at various "century" years. First, the period from 800 to 600 B.C. was the age of colonization, marked not only by the founding of settlements abroad by individual city-states but also by the rapid development of new political institutions at home. Second, from 600 to 400 B.C., Greek civilization reached its golden age, with the maturity of its economic, social, and political institutions, and with the appearance of many of its finest artists and thinkers. Finally, after 400 B.C., decline set in, rapidly in politics, less rapidly in culture (Plato and Aristotle flourished during the first century of decline). In the second half of the fourth century B.C., the Greek city-states lost effective independence and became adjuncts of the Macedonian Empire under Philip, Alexander, and their Hellenistic successors. Two centuries later, Greece was absorbed in the still greater empire of Rome.

Interior of Temple of Poseidon, at Paestum in southern Italy. From about 460 B.C.

The Age of Colonization

The colonizing movement of the eighth and seventh centuries B.C. enlarged the Greek world, especially to the northeast and to the west. Byzantium (later Constantinople, and now Istanbul) and other Greek settlements lined the Hellespont, or Dardanelles, and the Bosporus, the famous Straits leading from the Aegean to the Black Sea. Around the Black Sea there were dozens of Greek trading settlements and fishing stations. In the Mediterranean, there were Greek colonies as far west as the coasts of Gaul and southern Spain. The modern French city of Marseilles was originally the

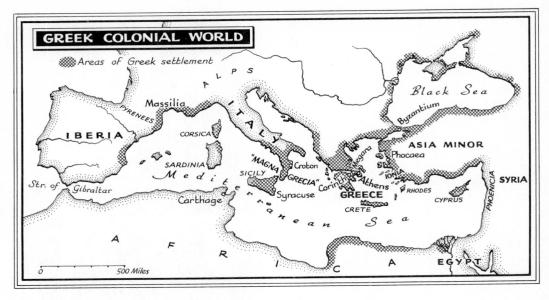

GREEK COLONIAL WORLD

Areas of Greek settlement

Greek Massilia, and the Riviera resort center of Nice derives its name from "Nike" the Greek word for victory. In eastern Sicily and along the southern shores of Italy, Greek colonies were so numerous that the Romans were later to call the region Magna Graecia (Great Greece): Naples, for example, is simply the Greek "Neapolis" (new town). Greek expansion from Magna Graecia across the narrow waist of the Mediterranean was checked by the Phoenician colony of Carthage, which pre-empted western Sicily and the choicest bits of North Africa. Egypt, however, permitted the planting of a Greek settlement in the Nile delta in the seventh century B.C.

This Greek movement differed from modern colonialism in two respects. First, it was the work not of the Greek people as a whole but of individual city-states. For example, Megara, lying half way between Athens and Corinth, founded Byzantium; Corinth founded Syracuse on Sicily; the Ionian Phocaea, near the present-day Turkish city of Izmir, founded Massilia. Sometimes an old colony itself founded one or more new colonies, as in Magna Graecia and along the shores of the Black Sea. In the second place,

the Greek colonies soon gained nearly complete independence from the mother *polis*. The ties that bound the colonist to the mother country were those of traditional sentiment, not those of colonial subjugation. The colonists were celebrated for the tenacity with which they maintained the sense of being Greeks and therefore of being superior to the peoples around their new homes in faraway lands.

Doubtless the impulse toward colonization sprang in part from the taste for spoils and adventure evident in the *Iliad* and in so much of early Greek history. It also reflected harsh political and economic realities. We have already seen how refugees from the Dorian invasions settled Ionia centuries earlier. Now there was a steady stream of refugees, victims of the frequent wars between city-states and of civil warfare within a state, victims, above all, of the chronic Greek afflictions of land-hunger and overpopulation. Despite internal strife, despite the widespread practice of homosexuality and the abandonment of unwanted babies, the number of Greeks steadily increased. It is probable that by the eighth century B.C. the population in some city-states had outgrown the meager local supplies of food and land.

The emigration of colonists, together with the importation of food, eased the pressure of overpopulation. But the expansion of foreign commerce created new tensions. In order to increase the exports of olive oil and wine needed to pay for the imports of fish and grain, Greek farmers concentrated on olive groves and vineyards. In this enterprise the wealthier landowners had a great advantage, for only they could afford the long and costly process of nurturing slow-growing olive trees until they reached the fruit-bearing stage. Many poor farmers borrowed extensively from their wealthier neighbors at heavy interest rates. If the borrower defaulted, he lost his property and sometimes his personal freedom as well, for he and his family were often forced to work off the debt by laboring in the lender's vineyard. The introduction of metallic coins in the seventh century aggravated the situation, increasing the riches of the few and the poverty of the many. The Greeks had their own "farm problem."

The widening gulf between wealthy landowners and poor peasants was not the only social and economic result of colonization. The growth of foreign trade gave rise to two new social groups: a business class of merchants, shipowners, weavers, potters, and blacksmiths; and a working class of stevedores and seamen. Both groups were restless and pushing; both resented the concentration of power in the aristocracy of well-to-do landowners; both were anxious to redress the political balance.

Changing Forms of Government

The political balance originally established by the Dorians appears to have been a combination of monarchy and aristocracy. During the age of colonization this balance was being upset in favor of the aristocrats, who either eliminated the king entirely or reduced his role to that of figurehead. At the same time the character of the aristocracy itself was changing. In this expanding and increasingly commercial society, wealth often replaced birth as the claim to noble position, and the aristocrats themselves lost the quality of *noblesse oblige* that had softened their rule in the old days. By the seventh century the aristocrats faced attack from both the debt-ridden farmers and the new commercial classes. In addition, they were often incompetent military leaders, unable to defend their cities in local wars.

In one *polis* after another, consequently, the aristocracy was overthrown, and one man seized power. This new form of government, which was in effect illegal monarchy, was called tyranny. The tyrant, like his modern counterpart, the dictator, usually acquired office by force rather than by the legal means of inheritance or election. But the tyrants were not necessarily tyrannical in the modern sense. In many city-states they instituted vigorous programs to reform the abuses and weaknesses of the aristocratic régime, and thus won the enthusiastic support of the discontented.

Tyrants were most common in Ionia, in the states near the Isthmus of Corinth, and in the Greek colonies of Sicily. Some states never experienced tyranny; others retained it as their characteristic form of government. In still others the tyrant reigned just long enough to establish a more enduring political system that did not depend on a single man. In these cases tyranny served as a bridge between the old aristocratic régime and the new more popular régime.

We shall now examine the two best-known examples of these new régimes—militaristic Sparta and democratic Athens. Remember, however, that Sparta and Athens were but two city-states among many, and that they by no means represented the full sweep and variety of Greek politics.

III: Sparta and Athens

The Spartan Régime

The constitution of Sparta—indeed, its whole life—was based on a rigid division of society into three castes. The upper caste of citizens, the Spartans proper, comprised some 5 to 10 per cent of the population; they were the rulers and soldiers and did no other work. The lower caste of *helots*, outnumbering the Spartans by perhaps 10 to 1, formed the majority of the population. They were bound to the land, serving as farm laborers, as the personal servants of the Spartans, and, on military campaigns, as their orderlies. The members of the third caste were known as *perioikoi,* literally "dwellers around," that is, neighbors, the inhabitants of a hundred or so towns and villages in the areas adjacent to Sparta. Some of the *perioikoi* were farmers; others were engaged in mining and trading and the other meager business activities of the *polis.* Unlike the helots, they enjoyed personal freedom. Neither the helots nor the *perioikoi* had any political rights; neither could expect admission to the ranks of the Spartans or permission to intermarry with them.

This social stratification was the product of Sparta's history. The Spartan citizens were the descendants of the Dorian conquerors who had invaded the southern Peloponnesus and occupied the plain of Laconia, one of the most fertile valleys in Greece. They had reduced the resident pre-Dorian population to the status of helots. During the age of colonization the Spartans met the problem of overpopulation in Laconia not by encouraging emigration abroad, as did so many other Greek city-states, but by annexing neighboring territories. The luckier descendants of Sparta's once independent neighbors became *perioikoi;* the rest became helots. By 600 B.C. the caste system was firmly entrenched in defense of the status quo against the possibility of rebellion from within or conquest from without. The threat of rebellion by the numerically preponderant helot masses obsessed the Spartan citizens; during the second half of the seventh century they had barely mastered a helot uprising in recently acquired territory.

By about 600 B.C. the Spartans had also completed their constitution, which they attributed to a single divinely inspired tyrant and law-giver, Lycurgus. Although Lycurgus may have been a wholly mythical personage, the constitution reflected the realities of Sparta's history and social system. Two kings, descendants of rival families of Dorian invaders, nominally headed the state. Actually, however, the executive authority rested with five *ephors* or overseers, elected annually by a popular assembly made up of all citizens over thirty years of age. In practice, the ephors dominated both this assembly and a smaller council representing the more illustrious families.

For the privileged minority, the Spartan citizens, this constitution contained monarchical, aristocratic, and democratic elements in the kings, council, and assembly, respectively. But for the helots and *perioikoi* it was an instrument of exploitation and repression, a device whereby the citizens made themselves "a garrison permanently stationed among a hostile population." For the historian, it is a classic example of oligarchy (from the Greek word meaning "rule of the few").

The military demands of the Spartan system shaped the training and traditions of the citizen class. The citizens led lives of self-denial and strict discipline. Unhealthy-looking or deformed babies were abandoned in a cave or a mountain wilderness, to die of exposure and neglect or perhaps to be adopted by a compassionate helot. At the age of seven, the Spartan boy was taken from his parents and subjected to a rigorous course of physical training and patriotic indoctrination. He learned reading and music, and above all he practiced wrestling, running, and the use of weapons. At times, all the boys had to eat was the food they could steal from the tables of the older Spartans. The important thing was to avoid being caught in the act or admitting the theft. Witness the story of the Spartan lad who stole a live fox and hid it under his clothing. When his elders questioned him, he let the fox gnaw at his belly until it killed him rather than confess to the theft. Girls, too, performed strenuous physical exercises under state supervision, presumably so that they would become healthier mothers. At any rate, they developed nerves of iron and sent their sons into war with the advice: "Return home with your shield or on it."

The adult citizen continued to undergo rigorous training and lived in barracks until he was thirty. Up to the age of sixty, though he lived at home, he took his main meal every day at a common mess, where, incidentally, the food is reported to have been singularly unappetizing. The citizen had to provide a quota for the mess and was "blackballed" if he failed to meet his obligation; consequently, he kept a tight rein on the helots who produced the food. All in all, war must have come as a relief to the Spartan, for then he could enjoy the comparative luxury of a campaign rather than the monotonous harshness of endless preparation.

Spartan Institutions Evaluated

This system had the merits that the adjective "Spartan" suggests. It fulfilled ad-

mirably the military purpose for which it was designed: the army was unequaled in courage and endurance. Military power enabled Sparta to dominate most of the states in the Peloponnesus, and in the course of the sixth century B.C. she allied with them in the Peloponnesian League, whose foreign policy was essentially her foreign policy. Her citizens were intensely patriotic and bore the news of military reverses and heavy casualties with fortitude. They were not addicted to idle talk: their economical use of words gives us the adjective "laconic" (from Laconia, the name of the Spartan plain).

Yet the very caste system designed to bolster Sparta's military power also undermined it. Sparta in her prime, in the fifth century B.C., is estimated to have had only about 4,000 adult male citizens. This was not enough for her to play a successful role in power politics indefinitely, and her tradition prevented the recruitment of new citizens from the other castes. The shortage of reliable manpower made Spartan policy conservative and defensive, and in the long run proved a fatal weakness.

The Spartan preoccupation with the army arrested the development of everything non-military. The city, which had had a flourishing culture in its early days, contributed almost nothing to the finest period of Greek sculpture, architecture, drama, and philosophy. When other states were thriving business centers, Sparta still had a backward economy, despite its fertile soil and its good deposits of iron ore. The Spartans checked the growth of commerce and industry at the point where they met the basic needs of the army. Long after more convenient gold and silver coins were circulating elsewhere, the Spartans deliberately kept on using cumbersome iron bars as money in order to discourage the accumulation of wealth and to foster the single-minded pursuit of military preparedness.

In her regimentation of economy and society, Sparta resembled the early Near Eastern monarchies. Still more did this barracks community resemble modern totalitarianism. The citizens discouraged visitors from other city-states, and they stationed secret police agents among the helots to head off uprisings by promptly killing the plotters. Fear was the foundation of the Spartan state —fear of money, fear of rebellion, fear of defeat by foreign troops, fear of foreign ideas.

The Athenian Régime

Fear was not the Athenian way. The apology for Athenian democracy is contained in the celebrated funeral speech of Pericles, the last in a series of notable Athenian statesmen. Dominating the *polis* from 461 to 429 B.C., Pericles gave his name to the greatest era of Athens—the Age of Pericles. His oration commemorated the Athenian soldiers who had fallen in battle against Sparta in 431; we have the oration, as Pericles may have delivered it, in the form reported by another famous Athenian, the historian Thucydides.

After opening with the customary tribute to the "founding fathers" of the city, Pericles goes on to define Athenian government:

. . . We are called a democracy, for the administration is in the hands of the many and not of the few. But while the law secures equal justice to all alike in their private disputes, the claim of excellence is also recognized; and when a citizen is in any way distinguished, he is preferred to the public service, not as a matter of privilege, but as the reward of merit. Neither is poverty a bar, but a man may benefit his country whatever be the obscurity of his condition.°

The funeral speech sharply contrasts the spirit of Athens and that of Sparta:

. . . Our city is thrown open to the world, and we never expel a foreigner or prevent him from seeing or learning anything of which the

secret if revealed to an enemy might profit him. We rely not upon management or trickery, but upon our own hearts and hands. And in the matter of education, whereas they [the Spartans] from early youth are always undergoing laborious exercises which are to make them brave, we live at ease, and yet are equally ready to face the perils which they face.

. . . For we are lovers of the beautiful, yet simple in our tastes, and we cultivate the mind without loss of manliness. Wealth we employ, not for talk and ostentation, but when there is a real use for it. To avow poverty with us is no disgrace; the true disgrace is in doing nothing to avoid it. An Athenian citizen does not neglect the state because he takes care of his own household; and even those of us who are engaged in business have a very fair idea of politics. We alone regard a man who takes no interest in public affairs, not as a harmless, but as a useless character . . .

. . . To sum up: I say that Athens is the school of Hellas [Greece], and the individual Athenian in his own person seems to have the power of adapting himself to the most varied forms of action with the utmost versatility and grace. This is no passing and idle word, but truth and fact; and the assertion is verified by the position to which these qualities have raised the state. For in the hour of trial Athens alone among her contemporaries is superior to the report of her. No enemy who comes against her is indignant at the reverses which he sustains at the hands of such a city; no subject complains that his masters are unworthy of him. . . . Such is the city for whose sake these men nobly fought and died; they could not bear the thought that she might be taken from them, and every one of us who survive should gladly toil on her behalf °

Pericles exaggerated somewhat, engaging in what Americans would call "Fourth of July oratory"; yet many of his boasts were well founded. Athens was indeed the "school of Hellas," the most attractive, the most influential, and the freest of the city-states. Its ascendancy, developing slowly at first, reached its height during the Age of Pericles. Four main causes contributed to this pre-eminence: first, the city's democratic institutions; second, its decisive leadership

---

° Thucydides, *History of the Peloponnesian War*, B. Jowett, trans. (Oxford, 1881), Bk. II, xxxvii.

° *Ibid.*, Bk. II, xxxix-xli.

in the wars between the Greeks and the Persians in the 490's and 480's; third, its subsequent hegemony over an empire of allied and subsidiary city-states; and fourth, its cultural leadership, the overwhelming part it played in setting the "style" of the Greeks.

The Early History of Athens

Athens lies a few miles from the sea, on the peninsula of Attica, one of the least fertile sections of Greece. The Athenian city-state arose from the fusion of many little states into a single *polis* that controlled most of Attica. Until the opening decades of the sixth century B.C. the government of Athens had grown along conventional aristocratic lines. Monarchy had disappeared, and the most important offices of state were monopolized by members of a few ancient landed families. From their ranks came the nine *archons* who served as the chief administrators. Former archons often joined the principal judicial and policy-making body. This was the Council of the Areopagus, named for the hill of Ares, the war god, which adjoined the Acropolis. There was also a more broadly representative body, the Assembly, but apparently it exercised no important authority.

As the age of colonization drew to a close, Athens experienced the political and economic discontent typical of the era. In particular, a heavy burden of debt oppressed the farmers. The dominant aristocrats seem to have made a gesture toward appeasing popular dissatisfaction about 621 B.C., when they permitted the first written statement of Athenian law. The code, according to tradition, was compiled by Draco; it marked a significant advance in so far as written laws were bound to be clearer and less capricious than those handed down orally by the aristocrats. The Draconian code, however, imposed the death penalty for acts of petty theft and

Greek vase, fifth century B.C., *showing hunter and dog.*

generally reflected the harsh outlook of a property-conscious aristocracy. We still use the term "Draconian" for laws of unusual severity.

Draco perhaps deserves better of history than the reputation he earned; the next major Athenian statesman, Solon has also won a misleading reputation. Traditionally, Solon has been regarded as the founder of Athenian democracy, and his name has become a synonym for the wise law-giver. Recent research, however, suggests that Solon was a rather cautious aristocratic reformer. Appointed as an archon about 594 B.C., Solon tried to alleviate the farm problem by canceling the debts owed by poor peasants and ending the practice of enslaving the debt-ridden. He widened the narrow agrarian base of the Athenian economy by encouraging such crafts as pottery-making, and for the first time he opened the most important political offices to well-to-do landowners who did not come from the old noble families. It is possible, though not yet established with certainty, that he also enlarged the role of the hitherto powerless Assembly and took the first steps toward the creation of more popular courts of justice that would reduce the jurisdiction of the aristocratic Council of the Areopagus. None the less, Solon did not succeed in easing the political and social tensions in Attica. Aristocrats criticized his reforms as too sweeping; the unprivileged found them too timid. By the time of Solon's retirement, Athens was ripe for tyranny.

Pisistratus and Cleisthenes

The tyrant was Pisistratus; like many other champions of the masses, he was no "man of the people," but a dissident aristocrat. He seized power about 560 B.C., was forced out of office more than once, but always came back. The historian Herodotus has left an entertaining account of the ruse adopted by Pisistratus to recoup his fortunes after his first loss of power. According to the story, the tyrant and his followers selected a woman "altogether comely to look upon," who was almost six feet tall:

This woman they clothed in complete armour, and, instructing her as to the carriage which she was to maintain in order to beseem

her part, they placed her in a chariot and drove to the city. Heralds had been sent forward to precede her, and to make proclamation to this effect: 'Citizens of Athens, receive again Pisistratus with friendly minds. Minerva [i.e., Athena], who of all men honours him the most, herself conducts him back to her own citadel.' This they proclaimed in all directions, and immediately the rumour spread throughout the country districts that Minerva was bringing back her favourite. They of the city also, fully persuaded that the woman was the veritable goddess, prostrated themselves before her, and received Pisistratus back.*

Whether true or not, this story is worthy of Pisistratus—the bold, resourceful, enlightened, and ruthless tyrant. He disarmed his aristocratic opponents by exiling them and distributing their estates to land-hungry peasants. He ruled that the Athenians should no longer try to grow grain on the meager soil of Attica; instead, they were to import grain and to specialize in the production of wine and olive oil for export. He exploited the silver mines of Attica and began to issue the famous coins stamped with the characteristic Athenian emblem of the owl. In short, Pisistratus solved the economic problems of Athens. More than that, his enthusiastic patronage of the arts prepared the way for the city's future cultural splendor.

Yet, Pisistratus and his two sons, who followed him in office, did little to democratize the machinery of government. In 510 B.C. exiled aristocrats, helped by Sparta, overthrew the second son of Pisistratus; the victors, in turn, were overthrown in 508 by Cleisthenes, the true founder of Athenian political democracy. Cleisthenes instituted sweeping administrative changes. He enlarged the authority of the Assembly; but this body, composed as it was of all the male citizens, was too unwieldy to carry on the day-to-day business of state. The routine of business was therefore entrusted to the Council of Five Hundred, represent-

---

* *The History of Herodotus,* G. Rawlinson, trans. (New York, 1861), I, 60.

ing the *demes*, the local units of Athenian government.

The demes were the keystone of Cleisthenes' reforms. Formerly, every Athenian citizen had belonged to one of four traditional tribes or clans, each with its own territorial basis, along the coast, on the plain, or in the hills. Consequently, local and factional interests had been favored at the expense of the welfare of the *polis* as a whole. Cleisthenes brushed aside the old geographical tribal divisions and set up ten new tribes, each composed of demes scattered about the Athenian territory. Under the new arrangement the tribes counted for little; what did count were the demes themselves, of which there were almost two hundred, and which corresponded roughly to such modern administrative subdivisions as parishes, villages, or wards. Cleisthenes thus destroyed the old tribal basis of aristocratic power. He allowed the demes the right of local self-government and augmented their popular character still more by permitting many non-citizens to acquire citizenship in a deme and thereby to participate in the workings of central government.

The Institutions
of Athenian Democracy

The liberal reforms of Cleisthenes virtually completed the democratization of Athenian politics. In the early decades of the next century (the fifth), the old aristocratic institutions, the archons and the Areopagus, were stripped of much of their former authority. We shall now examine in more detail the organs of Athenian government as they existed in their prime in the fifth century B.C.

Legislative power rested with the whole body of citizens convening in the Assembly. This enormous group met in the open air at least ten times a year, and sometimes as frequently as every ten days. It not only voted laws but also had the unique power to exile discredited leaders, usually for a period of ten years. This was the practice of ostracism, named after the pieces of tile, the *ostraka*, used in balloting. Though at times abused, ostracism proved an effective way of thwarting would-be-tyrants and stabilizing political life.

Executive power belonged to the Council of Five Hundred, whose members were chosen by lot from the citizens of the demes. So large a body proved cumbersome, however, and the Five Hundred were subdivided into ten 50-member groups, or committees, each of which guided the affairs of state for one-tenth of the year. The committee on duty transacted routine governmental business and referred the more important questions to the full Council, which, in turn, submitted the most important matters to the Assembly. Since no man could sit on the Council for more than two years, the average citizen had a good chance of serving on it during his lifetime. If chosen, he had an even better chance of becoming for one day what might almost be termed "President of Athens." The nominal head of the Athenian state was the "chairman" of the particular committee on duty, an office which changed hands daily.

Thus the administration was carried on by amateurs, ordinary citizens, rather than by a permanent staff of professional bureaucrats. There was one important exception to this rule: the ten generals commanding the army and the navy were elected annually by the Assembly, in part on the basis of their professional qualifications. Since generals could stand for annual re-election indefinitely, an accomplished incumbent might be chosen time and again and might well exert a decisive influence over governmental policy as well as over military affairs. Pericles, for instance, served as general for thirty years, enjoying an authority comparable with that of the President of the United States, the Secretary of State, and the Chief of

Staff all rolled into one. It should be borne in mind, however, that Pericles was no tyrant, that he did have to be elected anew every year.

Judicial power, unlike military power, rested directly with the mass of citizens; indeed, Athenian justice carried the principle of safety in numbers to an almost fantastic extreme. The various demes elected 6,000 men annually to act as judges and jurors combined. On every morning when there were cases to be heard, most of the 6,000 met in the city, and those needed for work that day were then chosen by lot. Hundreds upon hundreds were chosen, on the theory that the larger the number of justices considering a case the less the likelihood of personal prejudice affecting the outcome. In minor cases, the minimum complement for a legal court was 201; in weightier cases, it was 501 or even 1501!

Athenian Democracy Evaluated

In sum, many democratic practices matured in Periclean Athens, but they were the practices of direct democracy rather than of modern representative government. Though the election of officials was highly valued, it was usually election by lot, according to the principle that all citizens deserved an equal opportunity to hold office. The idea of electing the best-qualified man applied only to generals and was regarded by the Athenians themselves as a trifle undemocratic, a necessary but rather regrettable concession to older aristocratic ways. The most striking feature of the whole system was the direct participation of so many citizens in the essential tasks of government—legislative, executive, and judicial. In the United States, the town meetings of rural New England are the nearest equivalent of the direct democracy of ancient Athens. To be sure, such direct political activity by every citizen is quite impractical in the democracies of the twentieth cen-

tury, with their huge populations and complex problems. Nevertheless, it is enlightening—and chastening, too—for the modern democrat to recall Pericles' assertion that a man who shirked the responsibilities of citizenship was regarded as "a useless character."

Not all the citizens of Athens, however, responded to civic duty quite so readily as Pericles claimed. To induce men to attend sessions of the Council and of the courts, the state furnished daily allowances and free meals (thus anticipating the perquisites of American jurors). No such inducements applied to the Assembly, and only a fraction of the citizenry appear to have attended its meetings. Farmers who lived in the countryside doubtless found it a hardship to abandon their work and trudge to the city for a day. Men who lived in the city proper tended to dominate the Athenian government.

Women, of course, had no political rights. Their place was in the home, preparing meals, and bearing and raising children; nor did men generally accept them as social and intellectual equals. Occasionally an exceptional woman, like Pericles' brilliant mistress, Aspasia, surmounted the barrier. But she was a talented foreigner, not a native Athenian.

Nor were all the male residents in Athens citizens. Although precise statistical information is lacking, it seems likely that the number of citizens was nearly equaled, perhaps exceeded, by the number of *metics* and slaves. The metics were resident aliens, the Athenian counterparts of the Spartan *perioikoi*. Because of their connections abroad, they controlled the city's lucrative shipping and importing business. In the days of Solon and Cleisthenes metics had the opportunity of becoming in effect naturalized citizens. Then, in the middle of the fifth century B.C., Pericles closed the door to naturalization and to the ownership of property by aliens. Thereafter the metics continued to enjoy some rights, but their situation was probably less favorable than that of resident aliens in a modern democracy.

The Athenians got their slaves chiefly in Asia Minor and the lands around the Black Sea, as the chattels of trade or the booty of piracy. The lot of the slaves varied widely. The hapless creatures who mined the silver of Mount Laurium were manacled and overworked—examples of Aristotle's heartless definition of a slave as "a tool with life in it." Yet elsewhere in the Athenian state, especially in the city itself, slaves were well treated. Often they were accepted as full members of the master's household, as old and trusted family retainers, and later gained freedom with the status of metics.

In comparison with a modern democratic society, then, Athens still retained aristocratic elements, especially in its sharp division between citizens and non-citizens. This was at best democracy for the large minority. But in comparison with other ancient societies, Athens had made remarkable progress; Pericles had good reason to boast of his city's political greatness.

The Persian Wars

Pericles also claimed that, unlike the Spartans, "we live at ease, and yet are equally ready to face the perils which they face." Again he was justified, for Athens had proved her military ability—the second major element in her ascendancy—by her victories over the Persians in the early fifth century. During the sixth century the Persian Empire (see Chapter I) had subjugated the Greek city-states in Asia Minor. When these Ionian states attempted an unsuccessful revolt (499-494 B.C.), they received help from Athens and other states in European Greece. In revenge, the Persian Emperor Darius resolved to conquer the whole Greek world. In 490 B.C., guided by an exiled Athenian tyrant, a son of Pisistra-

tus, the forces of Darius landed on the beach at Marathon, twenty-six miles northeast of Athens. There, almost without aid from the other city-states, the soldiers of Athens expelled the invaders and endowed their city with the immense prestige of having defended Greek independence single-handed.

The Persians invaded again ten years later, this time under a new emperor, Xerxes, and with much larger forces. In this second campaign Athens was joined by Sparta and many other states. The Persians pushed into central Greece from the north through the pass of Thermopylae (480 B.C.), where the Spartans won lasting glory by fighting to the last man against hopeless odds. Now the enemy threatened to subjugate the rest of Greece. In the hour of crisis, the Athenians consulted the oracle of Apollo at Delphi (see below, p. 70) and were advised to seek safety from the Persians within "wooden walls." The Athenians had to decide whether the oracle meant them to retire to their fleet or to take refuge behind the timber palisade around the Acropolis. Luckily, they chose the former course, for the Persians soon overran Attica and burned the Acropolis. Fortunately, too, Athens had a fleet in readiness, thanks to the foresight of her able general, Themistocles, who had financed its construction with silver from a recently discovered deposit on Laurium. The Athenians defeated the Persians in a battle off Salamis, an island in the harbor of Athens (480). At Plataea (479), northwest of Attica, a Greek army under Spartan command overcame the army of Xerxes and forced the Persians to abandon their plans of conquest. The small city-states of Greece had triumphed over the greatest empire of the day.

The retreat of Xerxes, however, did not immediately liberate the Ionian cities from Persian control, nor did it end the threat of a new Persian assault on European Greece at some later time. Consequently the Greek states moved to put their emergency alliance of 480-479 on a permanent basis. The Spartans made the first bid to head such a permanent organization. But Sparta, despite its strong army, was hampered by its backward economy, by the limited provincial outlook of its leaders, and by the chronic danger of a helot revolt. Where Sparta failed, Athens succeeded. The Athenians now demonstrated the third major element in their ascendancy—their talent for empire-building.

The Athenian Empire

In 478, the year after Plataea, Athens organized a defensive alliance of city-states along the coasts and on the islands of the Aegean. Since its headquarters were on the small island of Delos, sacred to the god Apollo, the alliance was called the Delian Confederation. In theory, it was a confederation of equal partners; in practice, it became an Athenian empire, for Athens soon outdistanced the others in naval and commercial strength. She supplied most of the ships for the Confederation; the money to operate them came from lesser states that lacked the resources to develop individual fleets. Representatives of the allies assembled at Delos, supposedly to determine the disposition of these funds. Actually, the Athenians made the decisions, and the defense contributions were simply payment of tribute.

Under Pericles, Athens dropped the fiction of being merely the first among equals. In 454 B.C., the treasury of the Confederation was removed from Delos to the Acropolis, and Pericles grouped the allied states into provinces to facilitate the collection of the tribute money. Athenian coins, with their distinctive owl, were made the common medium of exchange within the Confederation. Athenian courts were given exclusive jurisdiction over any legal cases arising within the Confederation in which Athenians had a stake. Trade agreements

favorable to Athens were negotiated with the allies. Most significantly, members of the Confederation were denied the right of secession. The Athens of Pericles could, and did, intervene with force to prevent a city's withdrawing from the empire.

Imperialism sometimes brings advantages to the subject states. The satellites of Athens shared in Athenian prosperity and enjoyed protection against foreign aggressors. Although they also retained considerable self-government in local affairs, Athens often intervened in their internal political quarrels, and always on the side of the many

Athenian silver coin (fifth century B.C.), with the characteristic owl.

against the few. Unlike the Greek colonial world as a whole, these outposts of empire had to recast their constitutions in the image of the mother country's. Men of democratic leanings in the subject states often applauded Athenian intervention because it meant the triumph of their own party. Yet it is easy to sympathize with their aristocratic opponents who found loss of independence a high price to pay for economic and military security.

In the 440's, after years of intermittent warfare with Persia, the Delian Confederation finally attained its avowed goals of completing the liberation of Ionia and concluding a satisfactory peace with the enemy. By this time, however, it was evident that Athenian imperialism had overreached itself. A bold Athenian attempt to found a

CHAPTER II

new outpost in Egypt miscarried. Athens added many states in central Greece to her empire in the 450's, only to lose them in the next decade. These failures in themselves were not especially significant; far more significant were the aggressive policies behind the failures and the men behind the policies.

The chief Athenian policy-maker in these middle decades of the fifth century was Pericles himself, who seems to have been motivated by a genuine hope of uniting the Greek world under the leadership of its first city. But Pericles was also a politician responding to the demands of the multitude of citizens. The heart of the multitude, as we have already seen, lay in the city, Athens itself, among the merchants, craftsmen, and laborers who profited by Athenian expansion. What these men wanted was bigger and better imperialism, and Pericles gave it to them. The results were sometimes dazzling: the tribute of empire financed the glorious buildings on the Acropolis. But sometimes the results were disastrous: the ambitions of Athens and the fears they aroused among the other states brought on the ruinous Peloponnesian War in 431 B.C. (see below, pp. 84-85). It is a sobering fact that Athenian democracy, in effect, was to be destroyed by its own expansionist policies.

IV: Greek Civilization

The final major element in the ascendancy of Athens—her leadership of Greek culture—proved to be the most enduring. This leadership had begun in the sixth century under Pisistratus, reached its full flowering in the Age of Pericles, and continued on through the Peloponnesian War into the fourth century. The most famous single Greek building, the Parthenon, was erected on the Acropolis in Athens and dedicated to its patron goddess, Athena Parthenos (the virgin Athena). The Attic dialect won out over all rival dialects to become the standard literary language of the Greek world. A large proportion of the leading Greek writers, artists, and thinkers either were native Athenians or at least did their best work in the city. The list includes the historian, Thucydides; the finest of Greek sculptors, Phidias; the three masters of tragic drama, Aeschylus, Sophocles, and Euripides; the comic playwright, Aristophanes; and the philosophers, Socrates, Plato, and Aristotle. It has been estimated that the Athenian state of Pericles spent a very large part of its income (much of it, to be sure, was tribute money) on the rebuilding of the Acropolis after its destruction by the Persians. It is hard to escape the conclusion that never before—or since—have the arts played such a central role in a human community.

Almost equally remarkable is the fact that so many Greek city-states, from Sicily to Asia Minor, competed so closely with Athens for cultural leadership. Few of them were cultural deserts like Sparta. The tourist today will find some of the best specimens of Greek buildings not in Greece proper but in southern Italy and Sicily, the ancient Magna Graecia. And we could match the list of great Athenians with an almost equally impressive list of non-Athenian "greats"—in literature, Homer, from Asia Minor, and Sappho, from the Aegean island of Lesbos; in science, Pythagoras, from the island of Samos, and Hippocrates, from the island of Cos. Athens no more monopolized Greek culture than, say, New York City monopolizes American culture today.

Almost every activity that the Greeks pursued was linked in some fashion to religion. Their art, their architecture, and their literature all had religious significance, and such apparently secular institutions as the theater and the Olympic games actually developed from religious ceremonies. Politics and religion were intimately fused. The kings and aristocrats of the early Greek centuries based their claim to special power and privilege on their descent from one or another of the gods. Sometimes the claim was made by the whole citizenry of a *polis;* the Athenians, for example, boasted of their Ionian heritage, which they traced back to Ion, a son of Apollo.

Homer has already introduced us to Apollo, Zeus, and the other Olympians. The anthropomorphic qualities of these gods and goddesses may have been in part the inventions of Homer, but scholars have traced belief in somewhat similar deities all the way back to the ancient Near East and to the primitive peoples inhabiting Greece before the arrival of the Mycenaeans. The Homeric gods, then, were the result of a process that sociologists call syncretism—the borrowing, adapting, and fusing of a multitude of old beliefs. There are many traces of ancient fertility cults in the Homeric Olympians, and many examples of the attempts by primitive people to explain puzzling and often frightening phenomena. Thus, the passage of Apollo's fiery chariot across the sky explained the movement of the sun; the anger of Poseidon, the sea-god, accounted for Aegean storms; and the wrath of Zeus took the form of thunder and lightning. The Greeks also derived from their gods explanations of human emotions and human needs. For victory in fighting they prayed to Ares, the war-god, for success in love they appealed to Aphrodite, and for wisdom to Athena.

Apollo was a particular favorite of the Greeks. He had his own special shrine at Delphi, superbly located on the rocky slopes of Mount Parnassus in central Greece, overlooking an immense olive grove and an arm of the Gulf of Corinth. There the god spoke to his suppliants through the famous Delphic oracle, a prophetess who sat on a three-legged stool over a fissure in the rocks which was apparently an outlet for natural gas. The mumblings of the prophetess were translated into verse by a priest and presented as the admonitions of Apollo. The pronouncements of the Delphic oracle were celebrated for ambiguity, as in the advice to the Athenians in 480 to take refuge behind "wooden walls." On another occasion, a king learned at Delphi that, if he crossed a certain river, an empire would be destroyed; he followed this counsel, and brought on the fall of his own empire.

These well-known tales, however, do less than justice to the Delphic oracle, which frequently gave perfectly sound advice. Greeks high and low journeyed to Delphi for guidance on matters ranging from relatively trivial problems—household relations or real-estate purchases—to decisions of state like the founding of a colony or the formulation of a new constitution. Lycurgus himself was reported to have received the outlines of the Spartan constitution from the oracle. Delphi, in consequence, was one of the few Panhellenic centers, one of the rare places in the disunited Hellenic world respected by all Greeks, who temporarily put aside their chronic rivalries to visit the shrine of Apollo.

A second Panhellenic center was Olympia, in the western Peloponnesus. Here every four years, beginning, according to legend, in 776 B.C., were held the games honoring Zeus. The modern Olympics, for all their elaborate staging, miss much of the solemnity of their ancient counterpart. The games at Olympia were accompanied by religious rites, and the victorious contestants received crowns of leaves from the sacred laurel. For each festival the warring Greeks

The Acropolis, Athens. The Parthenon is in the center, with the Erechtheum behind it to the left; the Propylaea is at far left, and below it is the Roman theater of Herodes Atticus.

observed a truce long enough to permit all participants to journey safely to and from Olympia. In the games themselves naked athletes engaged in racing, jumping, and discus-throwing, and in contests of endurance like prolonged bouts of wrestling or running through sand. There were also competitions in musical composition, poetry, trumpet-playing, and even beauty and drinking.

A third Panhellenic center was Eleusis, a little town a dozen miles from Athens and joined to it by the Sacred Way. Here a very different sort of religious rite was celebrated—the Eleusinian Mysteries, so named because their essence was revealed only to a select group of initiates. When the playwright Aeschylus was accused of disclosing the secret in a few lines of a tragic drama, he had to undergo a formal trial in order to clear himself. We have no detailed account of the Eleusinian Mysteries, but it is conjectured that a solemn drama or pageant was staged, depicting the marriage of Zeus and Demeter and the fate of their daughter Persephone. Demeter, the god-

dess of the earth and its harvests, was so grieved when Persephone was snatched away by Hades, lord of the underworld, that the earth became frozen and barren. Zeus then intervened and arranged for Persephone to pass each winter with Hades and to spend the rest of the year, the seasons of growth and harvest, with Demeter.

Participants in the Eleusinian Mysteries thus shared in the annual miracle of spring and also may have experienced a renewal of their own spirit, a sense of purification and the promise of immortality. For, just as Demeter renewed annually the fertility of the fields, so too she might enable the dead to be reborn. We shall encounter this element of personal salvation in the mystery cults of the Near East and finally in Christianity itself (see Chapter IV).

In addition to these Panhellenic celebrations, every city and almost every deme had special festivals dedicated to its own particular god, like the Panathenea at Athens honoring the city's patroness. A host of lesser deities and spirits also commanded worship and propitiation, right down to the most primitive denizens of forests and springs. At this juncture the reader may well inquire why the Greeks continued religious practices that seem to us so childish and superstitious, so unworthy of the most intellectual people of antiquity. To this query we suggest two main answers.

First, what we identify as the religious aspects of Greek civilization represented to the Greeks themselves *both religion and something else*. The Olympic games, for example, not only expressed devotion to Zeus but also exemplified the decidedly worldly emphasis that the Greeks placed on intensive and disciplined physical training. The Panathenean festival honored both a goddess and a city. In common with other ancient peoples, the Greeks drew no clear-cut line between government and religion; instead of separating Church and State, they made them virtually identical. Religious feeling and patriotic feeling were often indistinguishable. The Athenian Acropolis was both a sacred place and a kind of municipal museum, where the laws passed by the Assembly were engraved on stones amid the temples. The priests officiating at the temples were public officials, as in many eastern civilizations, but with this important difference: they were the servants of the state, not its masters, as they would have been in an eastern theocracy. This feeling of religious and civic devotion helps explain why the old polytheism survived so long; the Athenians could not repudiate Athena without repudiating their own history and the whole *polis* that she protected.

Second, not all Greeks accepted the old polytheism with absolute literalness. The initiate at the Eleusinian Mysteries might pray for a fine harvest—or he might take the ceremony as a symbol of eternal life. Nor did the intellectuals accept the gods at face value. As we shall see, philosophers sought a higher morality than that prevailing on Olympus, and a more convincing explanation of the universe than that provided by the old polytheism. Playwrights transformed old legends about gods and men into poetic dramas that probed deeply into the human spirit.

Tragic Drama

Greek drama—the first plays of western history—originated in local religious festivals. The songs and the dances performed by the Athenians in honor of Dionysus, the wine god, were transformed into plays during the sixth century by the addition of characters and plots. The Greek word "tragedy" means "goat song," and the goat was a symbol of Dionysus and a popular form of sacrifice to him. In 534 B.C., Pisistratus established a competition and prizes for the plays written for the festival of Dionysus. Later prize-winners included the celebrated fifth-century playwrights— Aeschylus (525-456), Sophocles (496-406), and Euripides (*c.* 480-406).

Their tragedies retained a markedly religious character in theme, manner of presentation, and general purpose. They were performed in the open-air Theater of Dionysus on the slopes of the Acropolis, in a fashion very different from the realism of the modern stage. Instead of speaking naturally, the actors declaimed majestic verse through masks, and moved about on high-built shoes that made them appear abnormally tall. The singing and dancing of the old Dionysiac festival survived in the chorus, which periodically interrupted the action of the drama and commented on its significance.

In a famous definition, Aristotle assigned to tragedy the purpose of effecting a "catharsis" or purge of the spectators' emotions "through pity and terror." The formalized and ritualistic production of the tragedies helped to achieve this purpose. The dramatists chose subjects sure to arouse pity and terror—legends of kings and queens who, by their failings and unbridled behavior, brought down on themselves fearful and inevitable punishments. The vilest and most fatal of these human failings the Greeks called *hubris*, undue arrogance or pride. The *hubris* that cursed a whole family and caused a cycle of bloody crimes is the theme of the *Oresteia*, a trilogy by Aeschylus.

In the first of the three plays, the Chorus states the theme:

> Ancient self-glory is accustomed
> To bear to light in the evil sort of men
> A new self-glory and madness,
> Which sometime or sometime finds
> The appointed hour for its birth,
> And born therewith is the Spirit, intractable,
>   unholy, irresistible,
> The reckless lust that brings black Doom
>   upon the house,
> A child that is like its parents.°

Agamemnon, the leader of the expedition to besiege Troy, seeks to win the favor of the goddess Artemis, who has delayed the Greek forces by making the wind blow from the wrong quarter. He makes a sacrifice of his innocent daughter, Iphigenia. Clytemnestra, his unfaithful wife,

—————

° Aeschylus, *Agamemnon*, lines 763-771, Louis MacNeice, trans., in L. R. Lind, ed., *Ten Greek Plays* (Harcourt, Brace, 1957).

determines to avenge the death of Iphigenia and slays Agamemnon in his bath after his return from Troy. Vengeance for this second crime is plotted by Orestes and Electra, the surviving son and daughter. Orestes slays his mother and then goes mad and is pursued by the Furies, supernatural avengers, until finally Apollo and Athena intervene. They decide that Orestes has suffered long enough to be cleansed of his own and his parents' guilt. Aeschylus' *Oresteia*, though not conceived in Christian terms, is nevertheless a drama of *sin* and of *redemption* through suffering.

Sophocles used another legend, that of Creon and of Antigone, as the basis for a tragedy of the *hubris* that sets human law above the higher law. As the play opens, Creon, King of Thebes, has put down an uprising in which his rebellious nephew, Polyneices, was slain. In defiance of the hallowed custom of burying the dead, Creon orders that the corpse of Polyneices lie exposed, to be devoured by birds and beasts of prey. Antigone, the sister of Polyneices, insists on burying her brother, although she knows that she, too, will die for disobeying Creon. Antigone is put to death, and Creon, though belatedly recognizing his fault, is doubly punished. First his son,

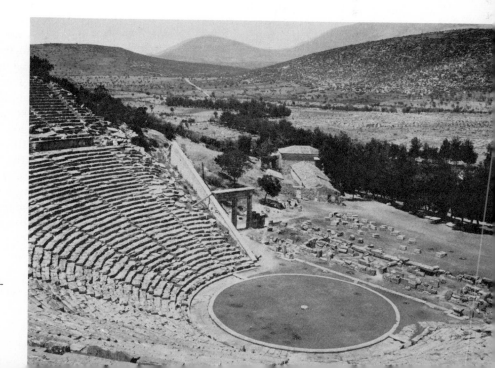

The fourth-century theater at Epidaurus.

in love with Antigone, and then his wife commit suicide. The chorus, in the closing verses of the drama, points up the lesson:

> Wise conduct hath command of happiness
> Before all else, and piety to Heaven
> Must be preserved. High boastings of the proud
> Bring sorrow to the height to punish pride:—
> A lesson men shall learn when they are old.°

The ethical values of *Antigone* are far removed from those of a crude polytheism. "High boastings of the proud bring sorrow to the height to punish pride"—this is one of the grand themes in the history of western moral teaching.

Comedy

Comedy as well as tragedy had its origins in Greek religious festivals. Comedy, too, stimulated the spectator to thought and gave him emotional release. The great comic playwright Aristophanes (*c.* 445-385 B.C.) specialized in topical satires, commenting on what he felt to be the weaknesses of his fellow Athenians. Athens was always ready to make war. So, in the *Lysistrata*, Aristophanes has a group of women, commanded by the shrewd Lysistrata, refuse their husbands until the men agree to give up war. Athenians were coming to favor the newer skeptical tragedies of Euripides over those of Aeschylus, who showed more reverence to the gods. So, in *The Frogs* (thus named because at one point a chorus of frogs is introduced, croaking "Brekekekex koax koax"), Aristophanes has the god Dionysus conduct a contest between the two playwrights, who weigh their verses on a gigantic pair of scales; the weightier and solider verses of Aeschylus win.

Athenians were taking an interest in Socrates and other philosophers who

seemed disrespectful of the old polytheistic teaching. So, in *The Clouds*, Aristophanes has Strepsiades, a newly impoverished man, enroll in the "thinking-shop" of Socrates to find a way of recovering his fortune. After having been shown around by a disciple, Strepsiades looks upward:

STREPSIADES And who is this man suspended up in a basket ?
DISCIPLE 'Tis *he himself.*
STREPSIADES Who himself?
DISCIPLE Socrates.
STREPSIADES Socrates! Oh! I pray you, call him right loudly for me.
DISCIPLE Call him yourself; I have no time to waste.
STREPSIADES Socrates! my little Socrates!
SOCRATES Mortal, what do you want with me?
STREPSIADES First, what are you doing up there? Tell me, I beseech you.
SOCRATES I traverse the air and contemplate the sun.
STREPSIADES Thus 'tis not on the solid ground, but from the height of this basket, that you slight the gods, if indeed . . .
SOCRATES I have to suspend my brain and mingle the subtle essence of my mind with this air, which is of the like nature, in order to clearly penetrate the things of heaven. I should have discovered nothing, had I remained on the ground to consider from below the things that are above; for the earth by its force attracts the sap of the mind to itself. 'Tis just the same with the water-cress.°

And thus Aristophanes goes on, ridiculing new-fangled ideas and, with Socrates suspended absurdly in his basket, starting on its way the perennial conservative gibe that liberals have both feet planted, not on the ground, but in mid-air.

Aristophanes, like most satirists, was a man with a message. He wanted the Athenians to return to the good old days before Pericles, when Athens was smaller and poorer, when the lower-class traders and workmen of the city had not yet pushed the Assembly into a policy of imperialism. Prosperity, empire, and war had corrupted the

---

° Sophocles, *Antigone,* Lewis Campbell, trans. (London, 1928), 16-17.

° Aristophanes, *The Eleven Comedies,* Athenian Society ed. (London, 1912), I, 319-320.

simple Athenian virtues, Aristophanes argued, just as Euripides and Socrates threatened to destroy the old belief in the gods of Olympus.

Poetry

The drama and the epic were but two of the forms of literature in which the Greeks excelled. We have already sampled the writing of the historian Thucydides in Pericles' funeral speech; we shall soon encounter the philosophical prose of Plato. In poetry the Greeks bequeathed not only the heroic verse of Homer and the tragic playwrights but also the lyric and the ode. Fragments of exquisite love lyrics are all that have been found of the writings of the poetess Sappho, who lived on the island of Lesbos in the early sixth century B.C. and ran a girls' school dedicated to the goddess of love, Aphrodite. From Pindar (518-c.438), on the other hand, we have a series of odes honoring the victorious runners, wrestlers, charioteers, and other champions of the Panhellenic festivals. Here are the first stanzas of Pindar's ode celebrating the success at Olympia by Diagoras, a boxer who came from the island of Rhodes, "bride of the sun":

As one who takes a cup from a lavish hand,
bubbling within the foam of the grape,
presenting it
to a young bridegroom, pledging hearth to
    hearth, the pride, sheer gold, of pos-
    session,
the joy of the feast, to honor his new son,
    render him
among friends present admired for the bride's
    consent:

so I, bringing poured nectar of victory,
gift of the Muses, the mind's sweet yield,
offer it up
to the conquerors at Olympia and Pytho.
    Blessed is he whom good fame sur-
    rounds.
Grace eyes one man, then another, bestowing
    favor

frequently to the melodious lyre and the
    manifold music of flutes;

and to both strains I keep company with
    Diagoras, singing
the sea's child, daughter of Aphrodite and
    bride of Helios, Rhodes,
and give praise, spoil of his boxing, to the
    onslaught of a man gigantic,
wreathed in victory beside Alpheus' water
and Kastalia; and to Damagetos his father,
    darling of Justice,
who dwell in the triple-citied island over
    against
the jut of broad Asia, by right of an Argive
    spear.*

The Arts

In the fine arts, too, the Greeks left a rich legacy, particularly in architecture and sculpture. The characteristic Greek building was a simple rectangle of marble supported by many columns. The kind of column used determined the architectural "order" of the whole structure. The oldest and plainest was the Doric, which employed sturdy, fluted columns terminating in simple block capitals; the fluting divided the surface into a series of shallow, curved depressions accenting the vertical line and conveying an impression of greater height than that given by the smooth, round Egyptian column. In the more elaborate Ionic order, the columns were more slender, the flutings were separated by narrow ribbons of stone, and the capitals were ornamented with simple curlicues. In the Corinthian order, an elaboration of the Ionic, acanthus leaves encrusted the capital.

A Greek temple, whether Doric, Ionic, or Corinthian, gives an impression of immense dignity and simplicity. We think at once of the Parthenon and the other monuments on the Acropolis. The Parthenon, a temple of the Doric order, was erected be-

---

* *The Odes of Pindar,* transl. Richmond Lattimore (Chicago, 1947), 19.

A part of the west frieze of the Parthenon, Athens.

northeastern Peloponnesus. Here is the finest remaining Greek theater built in the fourth century B.C., with long rows of stone benches, seating several thousand spectators, ranged in a semicircle on a beautiful hillside under the open sky (see illustration, page 73).

Although much of Greek sculpture has vanished since the Age of Pericles, enough remains in the way of original work or Roman copies to demonstrate the Greek artistry and versatility. We have only written descriptions of the three colossal statues by Phidias (c. 490-432), the most renowned Greek sculptor,—the Zeus at Olympia and two Athenas on the Acropolis. But parts of the frieze that Phidias designed to girdle the upper part of the Parthenon may still be seen in Athens or at the British Museum in London. These depictions of mythological scenes and of festival processions impress the viewer even in their present damaged condition; they must have been wonderfully striking in their original state, when they were apparently colored with a golden tint against blue-painted gables. Many Greek statues were painted, to minimize the white glare of marble in the bright Mediterranean sun. Experts conjecture that artists used a kind of sun-tan color for the body, a deep red for the hair, lips, eyebrows, and the irises of the eyes, and black for the pupils. Recent discoveries, fished up from the sea or dug from under modern Greek cities, make it clear that Greek sculptors did not always work in stone. Some of their very best statues were of bronze.

Clearly, then, it is wrong to suppose that Greek art possessed a unique "pure-white" quality, that it somehow embodied the "classical" attributes of serenity and restraint. In fact, the art of the Greeks was no more and no less restrained than the entirety of their civilization. For example, there is little serenity in the much-admired Discobolus, in which Myron, a contemporary of Phidias, portrays a nude athlete at

tween 447 and 432 as the crowning accomplishment of the rebuilding program undertaken by Pericles. It is not nearly so simple a building as it appears, for it was designed to look exactly right to the spectator standing in front of it. By means of many subtle distortions, it creates the illusion of perfection. The columns incline slightly inward, so that they look more stable; their diameter is not constant, but increases very slightly in the middle of the shaft, for otherwise they might seem concave; and the corner columns are a little thicker than the others, to stress their larger part in supporting the building.

The Parthenon was badly damaged in the fighting between Turks and Venetians three centuries ago, and many other masterpieces of classical Greek architecture have been totally destroyed. Enough remains, however, to suggest the scope of the Greek achievement. Two of the choicest survivals are quite small: the beautifully proportioned Treasury erected by the Athenian *polis* at Delphi, and the exquisite little temple to Victory in Athens perched on the very edge of the Acropolis. A splendid example of a very different sort of structure survives at Epidaurus in the

CHAPTER II

the moment before throwing the discus, poised between relaxation and extreme tension. On the other hand, great serenity may be found in the "archaic" statues of young men executed more than a hundred years earlier. These youths of the early sixth century are rather rigidly posed, their arms hanging down at their sides, the left foot forward, the head gazing straight ahead, and the lips formed into the curious smile called "archaic." The effect is most charming and not unlike that of an Egyptian statue, which probably furnished the model.

Jewelry, vase-decoration, and the other arts that had flourished in Mycenaean days also flourished in the later Greek centuries. By the close of the Dark Age, potters were producing large vases adorned with intricate geometrical patterns. Later craftsmen pictured ordinary human activities as well as religious and mythological scenes. The athlete, the cobbler, the miner, the fisherman, the carouser, the vomiting youth with

The Discobolus, by Myron. (A Roman copy.)

his head held by a sympathetic girl—these and a host of others may be found on bowls, plates, cups, and red and black vases.

Science

Greek artists were often scientists as well. Myron and Phidias reveal a knowledge of human anatomy in their muscular statues; the architects of the Parthenon employed geometry and physics to create subtle optical illusions for the spectator. In a wholly utilitarian endeavor, engineers employed by a tyrant on the island of Samos accomplished the remarkable feat of digging a water tunnel half a mile long and contriving to have the two bores meet almost exactly. Egypt and Mesopotamia, however, had already produced skillful builders, engineers, and embalmers; Rome, as the next chapter will show, was to be served by many of the ablest technicians in antiquity. The Greeks' claim to scientific originality resided more in their development of "pure" science, of theory rather than practice.

The pure scientist examines the world of nature and seeks natural, rather than supernatural, explanations for its behavior. He is interested in this knowledge or speculation for its own sake and is not necessarily concerned with its practical results. The pursuit of pure science began in the early sixth century B.C. among the Ionian Greeks, who were stimulated by their acquaintance with Egyptian scientific lore. The Ionians and, later, the European Greeks presently discovered many scientific facts, although they often lacked the instruments and the data to prove the validity of their discoveries. Geographers correctly traced the annual summer flood of the Nile in Egypt to the spring freshets at the river's headwaters in Ethiopia. They surmised that the Straits of Gibraltar and the separation of Sicily from the Italian mainland had resulted from an earthquake or some other cataclysm. Astronomers correctly accounted for eclipses and explained that the moon reflected but did not originate light. Thunder and lightning were attributed to natural causes rather than to the anger of Zeus.

At least a few Greeks apparently engaged in the kind of painstaking accumulation of data that we associate today with the scientific laboratory or clinic. The outstanding example is the school of medicine founded by Hippocrates (*c.* 460-377) from the island of Cos. Although almost nothing is known of the founder himself, we have some of the writings of his school, including the famous Hippocratic Oath, the solemn statement of the doctor's responsibilities that is still the core of the ethical code of the medical profession. The Hippocratic school made a thorough study of the symptoms and progress of diseases, as in this history of a case of epidemic fever:

> Philiscus lived by the wall. He took to his bed with acute fever on the first day and sweating; night uncomfortable.
> *Second Day.* General exacerbation, later a small clyster (enema) moved the bowels well. A restful night.
> *Third Day.* Early and until mid-day he appeared to have lost the fever, but towards evening acute fever with sweating; thirst; dry tongue; black urine. An uncomfortable night, without sleep; completely out of his mind.
> *Fourth Day.* All symptoms exacerbated.
> *Fifth Day.* . . . A distressing night, snatches of sleep, irrational talk; extremities everywhere cold, and would not get warm again; black urine; snatches of sleep toward dawn; speechless; cold sweat; extremities livid. About midday on the sixth day the patient died. The breathing throughout, as he were recollecting to do it, was rare and large. Spleen raised in a round swelling; cold sweats all the time. The exacerbations on even days.°

From these descriptions medical historians have identified cases of diphtheria, epilepsy, and typhoid fever. The school of Hippocrates, finally, experimented with new methods of treatment, chiefly purgatives and blood-letting; the new remedies, while often

crude and painful, did represent some advance over the older notion that prayer alone could cure sickness.

Medicine was taught also by Pythagoras (*c.* 580-500), who is, of course, better known for his contribution to mathematics. Like Hippocrates, Pythagoras is a rather obscure figure, and it is difficult to ascertain which of the Pythagorean teachings were the master's and which stemmed from his disciples. He founded a school of mathematics at Croton in Magna Graecia after the Persians had conquered his native island of Samos. It is believed that his concern with mathematics arose from the study of musical notation and of the mathematical differences in the strings needed to produce various tones on the lyre. His followers discovered essential laws of geometry, among them the well-known Pythagorean theorem that, in a right triangle, the square of the hypotenuse is equal to the sum of the squares of the other two sides. The Pythagoreans made the concept of numbers into a religious cult. One of them wrote that this concept

> . . . is great, all-powerful, all-sufficing, the first principle and the guide in life of Gods, of Heaven, of Men. Without it all is without limit, obscure, indiscernible. The nature of number is to be a standard of reference, of guidance, and of instruction in every doubt and difficulty.°

The Pythagorean religion of numbers was an early effort to explain the universe through that very abstract language we call mathematics. Pythagoras himself is said to have been the first to term the universe the *cosmos*—that is, a harmonious and beautiful order, as opposed to chaos.

Ionian thinkers of the sixth century also sought the key to the universe; they expected to find it, however, not in an abstraction but in some material substance. These early materialists tried to prove that nature could be reduced to a single essen-

---

° *Hippocrates,* W. H. S. Jones, trans. (London, 1923), I, 187.

° Philolaus, as quoted in Benjamin Farrington, *Greek Science* (Harmondsworth, Middlesex, 1944), I, 42.

tial substance, from which everything was formed. One selected water, another chose fire, another air. Finally, Democritus (*c.* 460-370) hit upon the theory that all matter consisted of minute, invisible atoms.

Philosophy: Socrates

Both the materialists and the Pythagoreans were as much philosophers as scientists. They were rational students of nature, and they were also lovers of wisdom (which is what the word "philosophers" means in Greek). They studied nature not just for its own sake, as the scientist does, but also in the hope of learning truth, as the philosopher does. Indeed, the Greeks may be said to have invented philosophy, and the credit for this Greek "first" belongs above all to the earliest of their great philosophers, Socrates.

Socrates (*c.* 469-399 B.C.), a stonemason by trade, wrote no books and held no formal teaching post. We know him only through the reports of his contemporaries and his students, pre-eminently through the dialogues of his pupil, Plato. He spent his life talking and arguing in the homes of Athenian citizens and in the Assembly and other public places of the city. Challenging everything that others said, he urged people to take nothing for granted and to put aside their prejudices and preconceptions. He described himself as a "gadfly," arousing and persuading and reproaching the citizens of Athens. The process of constant questioning, of never-ending debate, Socrates claimed, was the only avenue that might ultimately lead to knowledge. This was the famous "Socratic method," still used today as a most effective technique of teaching.

But what Socrates taught was more than a method; it was a new departure in human thought that has been called the "Socratic Revolution." Like the earlier Greek intellectuals, he sought wisdom and truth; significantly, however, he shifted the focus

from nature and the universe to man and humanity. In one of the Platonic dialogues, Socrates explains how he came to make the shift:

> When I was young, . . . I had a prodigious desire to know that department of philosophy which is called the investigation of nature; to know the causes of things, and why a thing is and is created or destroyed, appeared to me a lofty profession. . . .[*]

The materialistic investigation of nature, however, did not explain the causes of things to Socrates' satisfaction. He tried another approach:

> Then I heard someone reading . . . , from a book of Anaxagoras, that mind was the disposer and cause of all, and I was delighted at this notion. . . .

> How high were my hopes, and how quickly were they lost to me! As I proceeded, I found my philosopher altogether forsaking mind and making no appeal to any other principle of order, but having recourse to air, and ether, and water, and many other eccentricities. . . .[†]

Finally:

> I thought that I had better retreat to the domain of reasoning and seek there the truth of existence.[‡]

Reasoning led Socrates to the conclusion that man was more than an animal, that he had a mind and, above all, that he had a true self, a kind of soul or spirit. The cultivation and fulfillment of this true self were the proper business of man on earth. Once more the words of Plato may speak for his master:

> A man of sense ought not to assert that the description which I have given of the soul and her mansions is exactly true. But I do say that, inasmuch as the soul is shown to be immortal, he may venture to think, not improperly or unworthily, that something of the kind is true. The venture is a glorious one, and he ought to comfort himself with words of power like these,

---

[*] "Phaedo," B. Jowett, trans., *The Dialogues of Plato* (Oxford, 1953), I, 453.
[†] *Ibid.*, 454-455.
[‡] *Ibid.*, 457.

which is the reason why I lengthen out the tale. Wherefore, I say, let a man be of good cheer about his soul, who having cast away the pleasures and ornaments of the body as alien to him and working harm rather than good, has sought after the pleasures of knowledge; and has arrayed the soul, not in some foreign attire, but in her own proper jewels, temperance, and justice, and courage, and nobility, and truth—in these adorned she is ready to go on her journey to the world below. . . . °

Although this translation employs a vocabulary perhaps too strongly colored with Christian ideas of soul and immortality, Socrates unquestionably exalted many of the ethical values that are identified with Christianity—temperance, justice, courage, nobility, truth. It is easy to understand why another philosopher almost two thousand years later, Erasmus of the Renaissance, wanted to exclaim: "Pray for us, Saint Socrates!"

This "Socratic Revolution" offered man a new vision of his own potentialities and gave fresh meaning to the old Greek motto engraved at the shrine of Apollo in Delphi: "Know thyself." It went far beyond the old values of Homer's anthropomorphic Olympians—entirely too far, in the judgment of Socrates' conservative contemporaries. Aristophanes, as we have already seen (p. 74), bitterly attacked Socrates in *The Clouds*. When the philosopher was about seventy, the conservatives brought him to trial on the charge of being disrespectful to the gods and of corrupting the youth of Athens. Socrates argued that he faithfully observed religious customs and sought only to make men more useful and more honorable citizens. Moreover, he continued, a gadfly is needed, for "the state is a great and noble steed who is tardy in his motions owing to his very great size, and requires to be stirred into life. . . ." But one of those large Athenian courts voted the death penalty by a narrow margin. After drinking the poison cup of hemlock, Socrates awaited

the end with serene optimism, for he was to the last "of good cheer about his soul."

Philosophy: Plato

After Socrates' death, the "Socratic Revolution" was carried on by his disciple Plato (*c.* 427-347 B.C.), who spent a long and productive life traveling, teaching, and writing. Plato founded a school at Athens, the Academy, and wrote a celebrated series of dialogues—the *Republic,* the *Apology,* and *Phaedo,* from which we have already quoted, and many others. In these long intellectual conversations Plato enlarged upon the Socratic doctrine of the human spirit. Just as there is a "true self" within, and above, man's body, so there is a "true world" within, and above, the world experienced by our bodily senses. In this belief in a true world, a kind of invisible cosmos, Plato was influenced by Pythagorean teachings, which he encountered during a visit to Magna Graecia. He retained much of the Pythagorean reverence for mathematics and placed at the entrance of the Academy the inscription, "Let no man enter who knows no geometry."

But where the Pythagoreans found the cosmic reality to reside in numbers, Plato found it in what he called Ideas. He explained the relationship between the world of Ideas and that of the senses by means of the allegory, or parable, of the cave in the seventh book of the *Republic.* Socrates is the narrator:

. . . Behold! human beings housed in an underground cave . . . ; here they have been from their childhood, and have their legs and necks chained, so that they cannot move and can only see before them, being prevented by the chains from turning around their heads. Above and behind them a fire is blazing at a distance, and between the fire and the prisoners there is a raised way; and you will see, if you look, a low wall built along the way, like the screen which marionette players have in front of them, over which they show the puppets. . . . And do

---

° *Ibid.,* 474.

you see . . . men passing along the wall carrying all sorts of vessels, and statues . . . ?

You have shown me a strange image, and they are strange prisoners.

Like ourselves . . . ; for in the first place do you think they have seen anything of themselves, and of one another, except the shadows which the fire throws on the opposite wall of the cave? . . . And of the objects which are being carried in like manner they would see only the shadows? . . . And if they were able to converse with one another, would they not suppose that the things they saw were the real things? . . . To them . . . the truth would be literally nothing but the shadows of the images.

. . . And now look again, and see in what manner they would be released from their bonds, and cured of their error. . . . At first, when any of them is liberated and compelled suddenly to stand up and turn his neck round and walk and look towards the light, he will suffer sharp pains; the glare will distress him, and he will be unable to see the realities of which in his former state he had seen shadows. . . . Will he not fancy that the shadows which he formerly saw are truer than the objects which are now shown to him? . . . He will require to grow accustomed to the sight of the upper world. And first he will see the shadows best, next the reflections of men and other objects in the water, and then the objects themselves. . . . Last of all he will be able to see the sun, not turning aside to the illusory reflections of him in the water, but gazing directly at him in his own proper place, and contemplating him as he is.[*]

The meaning of the allegory is then explained:

. . . The prison-house is the world of sight, the light of the fire is the power of the sun, and you will not misapprehend me if you interpret the journey upwards to be the ascent of the soul into the intellectual world. . . . My opinion is that in the world of knowledge the Idea of good appears last of all, and is seen only with an effort; although, when seen, it is inferred to be the universal author of all things beautiful and right, parent of light and of the lord of light in the visible world, and the immediate and supreme source of reason and truth in the intellectual; and that this is the power upon which he who would act ration-

ally either in public or private life must have his eye fixed.[*]

Hence the chairs, tables, trees, and other familiar objects of this world are mere reflections of true realities, shadows of the Idea of the perfect chair, table, tree, and so on. Similarly, according to the Platonic theory, the virtues of men at their best are incomplete copies of ideal virtues of which the highest is the Idea of Good. But man can and should strive to know ultimate Ideas, especially the Idea of Good.

In exalting the Idea of Good as the final goal of existence, Plato was in effect teaching monotheism. On this basis his later followers, the neo-Platonists, constructed a mystical doctrine that contributed substantially to Christian thought. The Platonic theory of Ideas proved to be one of the great wellsprings of western thought. It helped to inspire the debates of the medieval Scholastics (see Chapter VIII) and to formulate many later philosophies.

The idealist naturally makes a critical appraisal of the political institutions of his own day. In his youth, Plato saw the Athenian democracy condemn Socrates and deteriorate generally under the crisis of the Peloponnesian War (see below, p. 85). Later, in Magna Graecia, he formed a favorable impression of the rule of tyrants. Therefore, when Plato delineated his ideal state in the *Republic*, he turned his back on Athenian democracy and proposed a system that bears many resemblances to an idealized Sparta. In his utopia, government would be entrusted to a small minority, an intellectual élite especially bred and trained to comprehend Ideas. These were to be the Guardians, and over them would rule the wisest man of all, the Philosopher King. The masses, on the other hand, would occupy their allotted stations as docile workers or soldiers, follow the lead of their intellectual and moral superiors, and have no political voice.

[*] *Republic*, B. Jowett, trans., *The Dialogues of Plato* (Oxford, 1953), II, 376-378.

[*] *Ibid.*, II, 379.

In evaluating the *Republic,* we should remember the forces that influenced its author and the fact that it was a blueprint for utopia and not for practical political reform. On the other hand, we may be grateful that, although echoes of the *Republic* may be heard in many later utopian theories, particularly those justifying an élite, the political theory of Plato never exerted an influence commensurate with that of his doctrine of Ideas.

Philosophy: Aristotle

Aristotle *(c.* 384-322 B.C.), Plato's most famous pupil, was the son of a physician at the court of Philip of Macedon (see below, p. 86). He left the Platonic Academy after twenty years of study and eventually conducted his own school in Athens, the Lyceum. A man of nearly universal interests, Aristotle mastered an amazing variety of subjects, including biology, logic, literary criticism, political theory, and ethics. Much of his original writing has been lost; the works that survive were in part compiled from notes taken by students at his lectures, so that they lack the literary polish of the Platonic dialogues. No matter: the writings of Aristotle as we have them constitute an encyclopedia of Greek learning at its prime. And his influence on later thinkers has been even more prodigious than that of Plato; for several centuries in the Middle Ages the reputation of Aristotle was so exalted that he was referred to simply as The Philosopher.

Plato's primary concern was with things as they ought to be; Aristotle's, with things as they were. In biology, for example, Aristotle arranged living things in groups according to a method somewhat resembling the modern classification into genus and species. In his *Politics,* he classified governments into three types, based on the number of rulers, with a good and bad form in each case. Good government by one man he called "monarchy" and bad, "tyranny"; good government by the few was "aristocracy" and bad, "oligarchy"; good government by the many he called "polity," meaning orderly popular rule, and bad he called "democracy," by which he meant the disorderly régime of the mob.

In his biological studies, in his *Politics, Logic, Poetics,* and still other works, Aristotle laid the indispensable foundations for later progress in a broad range of disciplines. He also revived the kind of thorough scientific observation associated with the school of Hippocrates. For his biological work he dissected animals; to prepare for writing the *Politics* he studied the régimes of more than a hundred city-states. But Aristotle never completely abandoned the philosophical tradition of Socrates and Plato. He, too, believed that men should strive and aspire; yet he defined the ideal more in terms of this workaday world.

Accordingly, the ethical code of Aristotle did not recommend the almost impossible ascent to the Idea of Good, nor the Socratic goal of self-knowledge. It advised the cultivation of the golden mean:

Virtue . . . is a mean between two vices, that which depends on excess and that which depends on defect; and again it is a mean because the vices respectively fall short of or exceed what is right in both passions and actions, while virtue both finds and chooses that which is intermediate.

. . . .

With regard to feelings of fear and confidence courage is the mean; of the people who exceed, he who exceeds in fearlessness has no name . . . , and he who exceeds in fear and falls short in confidence is a coward. With regard to pleasures and pains . . . the mean is temperance, the excess self-indulgence. Persons deficient with regard to the pleasures are not often found; hence such persons also have received no name. But let us call them 'insensible.' With regard to giving and taking of money the mean is liberality, the excess and the defect prodigality and meanness. . . . With regard to honor and dishonor, the mean is proper pride, the excess is known as a sort of 'empty vanity,' and the deficiency is undue humility. . . .

Everyday Life

The culture described in the last few pages was not the culture of the majority of Greeks. The new ideas of Plato or Pythagoras attracted comparatively few adherents. Everyday life was still superstitious: many citizens continued to worship the old gods and goddesses in the old ways. Moreover, relatively few Greeks, even among the favored Athenians, could afford to spend all their time preparing for festival games, listening to Socrates or Aristotle, and performing their military and political service. Except for a minority of wealthy landowners, most Greeks expended their best energies making a living.

By the criteria of the twentieth century, the ancient Greek standard of living was extremely low. The average Greek sometimes worked three hundred days during the year; yet he secured few of the comforts taken for granted as essential to existence today. In the city, and still more on the farm, Greek families made for themselves the necessities of life. The women of the household ground flour, baked bread, spun thread, wove cloth, and cut and sewed garments for the family. In the whole of Athens only one establishment employed more than a hundred workmen. Small business was the rule. Perfumers and jewelers catered to the wealthy; and potters, tanners, and shoemakers furnished the man of ordinary means with the few articles his family did not make at home.

Home, even for the wealthy Athenian, was a small, plain house made of stucco or of sun-dried brick. What we call "Greek architecture" today was reserved almost exclusively for temples and public buildings. The houses of Athens were crowded together on mean little streets, sanitary arrangements were sketchy, and inadequate lighting was furnished by ill-smelling olive-oil lamps. Open-air stalls or miserable shacks served as stores, and workshops were tiny and often suffocatingly hot. The potters and blacksmiths depicted on Greek vases as working naked were simply trying to be comfortable in the heat.

Most Greeks seem to have been reasonably content with this very modest life. They reconciled themselves to the meager diet forced on them by the natural poverty of their homeland. Musicians relieved the monotony, if not the heat, of workshops. A climate that made outdoor living possible during many months of the year did much to compensate for the absence of elaborate clothing and house furnishings. And relaxation from work was almost always close at hand in sports and festivals, at the theater, and even in the law suits so relished by the Athenians.

The Greek "Style"

Both the checkered actualities of everyday life and the marvelous achievements of writers, artists, and thinkers must enter into any attempt to define the Greek "style." And when the attempt is made, paradox and contradiction appear at once. The Greeks were remarkably inventive; as we have seen, their list of "firsts" includes drama, philosophy, and democracy. Yet they were also remarkably conservative: they clung to their old deities and rituals and remained faithful to the old system of warring city-states even when their failure to form "one Greece" threatened to deprive them of their cherished liberties. The Athenians were the firmest believers in freedom, the supreme individualists, of the ancient world; yet they ostracized able leaders and sentenced Socrates to death.

Greek ideals were summarized in Socrates' injunction, "Know thyself," and in

---

° *Ethica Nicomachea*, in W. D. Ross, ed., *The Works of Aristotle* (Oxford, 1932), Bk. II, Chs. 6-7.

Aristotle's golden mean—"Nothing in excess," as it was often phrased. And in some respects the Greeks did approach the ideal. Their temples were beautifully proportioned; except in Sparta, their education was balanced, as boys were trained to be at the same time athletes and soldiers, artists and intellectuals. But we have also seen the opposite of balance at work, *hubris*, the arrogance that demeaned Homer's gods and warriors, that ruined the heroes of the tragedies, and that beset the flesh-and-blood Greeks themselves. The hallmarks of the Greek style at its worst were bickering, parochialism and snobbery (even in democratic Athens), and selfish pride. But next to these must be juxtaposed the works of art, the ideas, and the ideals that represented the best of Greece. The flaws of the Greeks brought down on them a series of disasters, starting with the Peloponnesian War; their virtues, by contrast, have lived on to inspire and instruct men of culture and good will.

V: The Decline and Transformation of Greek Civilization

The Peloponnesian War

The ruinous Peloponnesian War (431-404 B.C.) produced only one figure of truly major stature: Thucydides (*c.* 470-396), who wrote the story of the war. Thucydides was not the first important Greek historian; a generation earlier, in Periclean Athens, Herodotus had composed an engaging, though not wholly reliable, world history, an account, that is, of the known world of his day—Persia, Egypt, and Mesopotamia, as well as Greece. Thucydides, however, wrote the first major work of objective history, based in part on his own direct observations. Although he himself was Athenian, his *History of the Peloponnesian War* is in general scrupulously accurate; more than that, Thucydides attempted to do for society what Hippocrates did for the ill—to diagnose human behavior.

Here is Thucydides' summary of the major specific cause of the war:

... The Athenians acquired a firmer hold over their empire and the city itself became a great power. The Lacedaemonians [i.e., the Spartans] saw what was going on, but during most of the time they remained inactive and hardly attempted to interfere. They had never been of temper prompt to make war unless they were compelled; and they were in some degree embarrassed by enemies near home. But the Athenians were growing too great to be ignored and were laying hands on their allies. They [the Spartans] could now bear it no longer; they made up their minds that they must put out all their strength and overthrow the Athenian power by force of arms. And therefore they commenced the Peloponnesian War.*

The Athenian empire, ambitious, dictatorial, and aggressive, had upset the balance of power. The other Greek city-states watched with mounting apprehension the increasing concentration of Greek trade in Athenian hands and the increasingly severe pressure exerted by Athens on her commercial and political rivals. And so, in 431, they joined with Sparta and the Peloponnesian League (see above, p. 61) to curb the aggressor.

It took the enemies of Athens a long time

---

* Thucydides, *History of the Peloponnesian War*, B. Jowett, trans. (Oxford, 1881), Bk. I, cxviii.

to force a decision. Athens, a sea power, and Sparta, a land power, found it hard to get at each other; it was harder still for one of them to deliver a decisive blow. The Spartans first tried to starve Athens out by sending their troops into Attica every year to cut down the olive trees and destroy the crops. The Athenians countered by assembling the whole population of Attica within the walls of the city and by importing food over the sea routes secured by the Athenian navy.

Meanwhile, Athens suffered the first in a series of damaging reverses. In 430 a deadly plague broke out, spread by the extremely unsanitary condition of the overcrowded city. The plague carried off perhaps a quarter of the population, including Pericles, who died in 429. After the death of Pericles, the old dissensions between Athenian factions broke out with redoubled intensity. During the remainder of the war, power shuttled back and forth between the aristocrats, who favored peace at almost any price, and the democrats, who wanted to continue the war at any cost. In the decade of the 410's the democratic faction found a new leader, Alcibiades, the nephew of Pericles and the favorite student of Socrates. He was a handsome and brilliant youth, idolized by the populace whom he was destined to betray.

Alcibiades proposed the risky strategy of attacking Syracuse, a powerful Greek city on the island of Sicily, and a potential ally of Sparta. The attack on Syracuse failed, and the Athenian expedition was wiped out (413); meantime, Alcibiades, forced out of Athens by his aristocratic opponents, fled to Sparta where he gave excellent advice on the best way to assist beleaguered Syracuse. Fresh outbreaks of factional violence within Athens enabled Alcibiades to regain control (411-406). But by this time a third power was about to intervene—Persia, still hoping to recover the Ionian lands lost after Salamis and Plataea. Subsidized by Persia, Sparta fitted out a

fleet capable of ending Athenian control of the sea. Cut off from seaborne food, besieged by a Spartan army, starving, Athens surrendered in 404.

The Aftermath of War

The Peloponnesian War brought neither victory nor peace. Sparta, the nominal victor, attempted and failed to reconquer the Ionian cities that she had handed back to Persia in return for Persian subsidies. She tried to take over former Athenian satellites but alienated them by her harsh, imperialistic rule. This new threat to the balance of power led Athens and some of Sparta's erstwhile allies in the Peloponnesian War to form a defensive league. Moreover, the ranks of the Spartans were so diminished by casualties that they lacked sufficient manpower to administer or defend an empire. In 371 B.C. the supposedly invincible Spartans met defeat at the hands of Thebes, a city located on the edge of the fertile plain of Boeotia, to the northwest of Attica. The new Theban hegemony, however, lasted less than a decade.

The half-century following the Peloponnesian War, though filled with shifting alliances and sporadic wars, was not an era of unmitigated decline. Plato was writing and teaching; Athens, though shorn of her empire, soon reconstituted her democratic government and re-established her old supremacy in commerce. Yet the same kinds of economic pressures that had made Greeks emigrate during the age of colonization were now at work in this period of postwar readjustment. In 401, ten thousand Greeks, many of them veterans, enlisted as mercenaries to support the rebellious brother of the Persian king. Although the rebellion failed, the ten thousand made a historic march from the heart of Mesopotamia north through wild mountainous country to the safety of the Black Sea. The journey was recorded for posterity by one of its participants, Xenophon (*c.* 430-345 B.C.), in the *Anabasis.*

The mercenary soldier, the professional fighting for pay rather than for a cause, was now becoming a fixture in the Greek homeland—another symptom of declining manpower and morale. The Greek states could scarcely afford to keep on fighting, but they never devised a way to live together in peace. They did make several promising starts at constructing genuine interstate leagues or confederations free of imperialistic domination, but all these experiments failed in the end. The Greeks were being penalized for their failure to transform their myriad city-states into "one Greece." The stage was set for the Macedonian conquest.

The Rise of Macedon

North of Greece, at the head of the Aegean Sea, lay Macedon, then as now a meeting place of divergent racial and cultural strains. The ancient Macedonians combined a mixture of Greek and more primitive characteristics. Until the fourth century B.C., Macedon was politically insignificant, weakened by strife among the ruling aristocratic families.

Then the great and ambitious Philip, king from 359 to 336 B.C., brought Macedon to the fore. By subduing the aristocrats, Philip made himself master of the country. He exploited its rich forests and gold deposits. He enlarged, strengthened, and incessantly drilled the army, copying the newest fighting techniques of the Greeks, such as the careful co-ordination of infantry and cavalry. He obtained outlets to the sea by capturing the Greek cities along the Macedonian coast of the Aegean.

Greece now faced the worst foreign threat since the Persian expeditions a century and a half earlier. The weak and disunited city-states were no match for Philip. He exploited their rivalries, bribed the disaffected, and

intervened in their disputes. Belatedly, Athens and Thebes recognized the threat to Greek independence and sent a joint force into the field. But this was not the century of Marathon and Salamis. In 338 B.C. at Chaeronea, between Thebes and Delphi, the Macedonians defeated the Greeks. Although Philip did not formally annex all the city-states, he organized them into a league under his domination and allowed them little more than nominal control over their own affairs.

Alexander the Great

In 336 B.C., Philip was assassinated, perhaps at the instigation of his estranged wife, in the course of a festival celebrating his daughter's marriage. His son Alexander, one of the most dramatic figures in history, succeeded him. Alexander, who reigned from 336 to 323 B.C., had no commonplace education: Aristotle had been his tutor. His interests and talents included war and politics, athletics, strong drink, literature (he particularly admired Homer and Pindar), medicine, and science. His armies were accompanied by medical auxiliaries, by biologists and other scientists, and by propagandists or, in the language of today, "public relations experts."

Alexander was only twenty when he inherited his father's domains. Within a dozen years he assembled the largest land empire recorded by history up to that time, larger even than the Achaemenian Empire of Persia (see Chapter I). The Persians, indeed, were repeatedly defeated by Alexander's armies. Their empire was already long past its prime, weakened by dynastic quarrels like the one in which Xenophon's ten thousand had participated. Philip had planned to attack Persia; on his death the Persians attempted to distract Alexander by bribing some of the Greek cities to rise against their new overlord. The distraction was short-lived, for Alexander taught the Greeks a forceful lesson by obliterating Thebes, the leader of the rebellion.

Alexander then wrested the Ionian Greek cities and the remainder of Asia Minor from Persian control. Moving south, he drove the Persians out of Syria, Palestine, and Egypt. At the western end of the Nile Delta, he founded a new city, designed as the major port of the eastern Mediterranean, destined soon to become that and much more, and named after himself—Alexandria. Next, Alexander took Babylon, moved east to occupy the Persian heartland, and still farther east into lands still little known today, like Afghanistan and Russian Central Asia. His armies then journeyed south across icy mountain passes and down into the valley of the Indus. Here, in the northwestern corner of the Indian subcontinent, Alexander had at last gone far enough; the possibility of further expansion was checked by the mutiny of his own forces, worn out by their arduous campaigning and by the rigors of a harsh climate, with its alternation of dry, blighting heat and monsoon floods. The strenuous life apparently weakened even the superb physique of Alexander himself. Soon after he returned from India to Babylon he was stricken; he died in 323 B.C. at the age of thirty-three.

Alexander's early death was perhaps a stroke of good fortune, for he did not live to experience the difficulty of governing his hastily built empire. To conquer was one thing; it was something else again to provide durable and workable institutions for vast territories largely lacking unifying forces. The policies Alexander did devise before his death suggest that he hoped to solve the problem by two methods. First, he ruled each area according to its own traditions. In Greece he governed through the *polis;* in Egypt he was worshiped as a god, as the pharaohs had been; in Persia he maintained the system of satraps or local governors; farther east, dealing with more primitive societies, he acted as a tribal overlord. Second, he hoped to make Greek cul-

Alexander the Great, with horns, on a four-drachma silver coin issued about 300 B.C.

ture the common denominator of the empire. To this end he founded more than a dozen cities called Alexandria in addition to the one already flourishing in Egypt. Each was settled by Greek colonists, and each was designed to be a center of Hellenization from which Greek economic and cultural achievements might radiate over the surrounding area.

Historians today are still debating the merits of Alexander's scheme for cementing together the known world of his day. Some claim that it was impractical and point to the fact that the empire actually did disintegrate after he died. Others counter that the policy of Hellenizing Egypt and western Asia—at least the upper classes of society—did actually work. They note also that the Romans later succeeded in organizing their own vast empire by following policies very much like Alexander's, although, of course, it took them centuries to do so (see Chapter III). Admirers of Alexander, therefore, see in him the first practical champion of the idea of the "brotherhood of man," seeking ways to diminish the

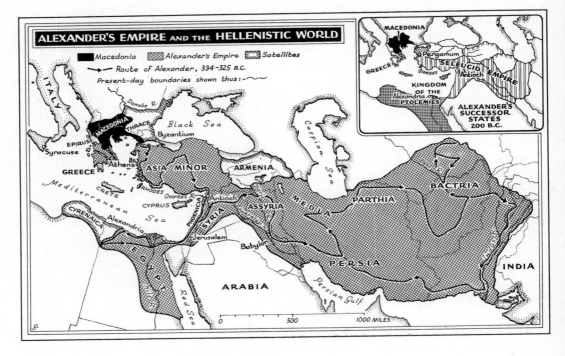

Macedonia   Alexander's Empire   Satellites
→ Route of Alexander, 334–325 B.C.
Present-day boundaries shown thus:

ALEXANDER'S SUCCESSOR STATES 200 B.C.

differences among men and to buttress the forces binding them together.

This last claim is indeed a bold one to make for a man who was a remarkable general and an imaginative and ruthless politician but who seems to have lacked the kind of inner fire and deep conviction that one expects in the proponent of a great idea. Although the facts will probably never become fully certain, legends depicting Alexander as a superman have long formed part of the western heritage. According to one story, on the eve of his first campaign, a wooden statue of the poet Orpheus broke into a sweat; this was taken to mean that poets would indeed have to sweat to record his marvelous accomplishments. A little later, in Asia Minor, Alexander confronted the Gordian knot, which had baffled the ingenuity of man up to then. It was said that he who managed to untie the tangled knot would rule Asia; Alexander cut the knot in two with a stroke of his sword. And the most beguiling legend of all portrays Alexander the Great as the first man to conceive the ideal of One World.

The Hellenistic States

The death of Alexander marks the beginning of the epoch called Hellenistic. This term, derived from Hellas (Greece), means Greek-like; it describes the institutions and civilization of the states formed out of Alexander's empire between 323 and the Roman conquest of the eastern Mediterranean in the second and first centuries B.C. Politically, the Hellenistic world was not One World. After Alexander died, rival generals struggled for control of the empire until, by the beginning of the third century, three major states emerged, each under a dynasty founded by one of Alexander's generals. One was Macedon, still the overlord of the European Greek states, which were as restless and quarrelsome as ever but no longer strong enough to assert their full independence. The second was Egypt, ruled by the Ptolemies from their capital at Alexandria, the biggest, richest, and most brilliant city in the Hellenistic world. The third was the Seleucid Empire, named for its founder, Seleucus, with its capital at Antioch on the Orontes River in northwestern Syria, where the Fertile Crescent arcs inland from the Mediterranean coast. The boundaries of Seleucid territories underwent frequent changes, but at one time or another they encompassed most of Alexander's Asian domains, notably Syria, Asia Minor, and Mesopotamia. Later on, toward the close of the third century B.C., two smaller states acquired significant power: the kingdom of Pergamum in western Asia Minor, and the island of Rhodes, a thriving commercial center off the southwestern corner of Asia Minor.

The three major Hellenistic states, born of warfare, lived and perished fighting one another. The chief stake in their struggle was control of the old Greek city-states and of the rich coastal areas along the eastern Mediterranean. The ultimate results, as the next chapter will show, were increasing intervention by Rome and the establishment of Roman hegemony. In this intensely competitive political climate, the old free institutions of Greek society met formidable competition from the still older Near Eastern institutions of absolutism. In Egypt, the Near Eastern tradition prevailed. The Ptolemies, with the assistance of a complex bureaucracy, ruled Egypt despotically. They owned outright, or else controlled, its land and its commerce, and imposed heavy taxes on its peasants. The colonies of Greeks in Alexandria and a few other towns retained but fragments of the rights enjoyed in their homeland. In the Seleucid Empire, Greek political traditions fared somewhat better. On the basis of rather skimpy evidence, it appears that the Seleucids would have liked to be as autocratic as the Ptolemies or as the former Persian masters of Asia, but they were thwarted by the vastness of their realm, the instability of their frontiers, and the mixture of cultures in their domains. They attempted a combination of East and West, of satrap and *polis*. Sometimes they used provincial governors of the Persian stamp; and sometimes they established Greek colonies which preserved part of the autonomous civic life of the *polis*. This interesting experiment in the fusion of two different traditions does not seem to have worked very well politically; the Greek settlements, however, acted as important conveyors of Greek culture.

In economics, as in politics, the focus of Hellenistic life shifted eastward and southward to Antioch and Alexandria. Although the Greek cities still retained some commercial vigor, they were quite overshadowed by their formidable new competitors, who also attracted some of the most enterprising Greeks as colonists. Athens, for example, was famous in Hellenistic days for its schools, not for its ships or its markets. Alexandria, by contrast, rapidly developed into the greatest metropolis of the ancient world, estimated to have reached a population of a million by the first century B.C. Through its harbor passed the commodities of a lucrative export trade, some transshipped from Arabia and tropical Africa, and some, like papyrus and grain, produced locally (North Africa, in ancient times unlike today, had a surplus of grain for export). Antioch ranked as a respectable, though not a close, second to Alexandria. It imported the wares of India and the Persian Gulf overland through the Tigris-Euphrates valley and sent them westward into the Mediterranean world.

The expanding Hellenistic economy made possible a high standard of living. Businessmen, high officials, and great landowners led a comfortable existence; their houses, for example, constructed around a central court, were airy and spacious and showed a notable advance over Greek domestic architecture. For society as a whole, however, there was no advance. The big Hellenistic cities were blighted by the big-city problems of slums and unemployment, somewhat mitigated by government doles of cheap grain to the poor. Labor was cheap, and the laborer was frequently overworked and overtaxed. As in older Greek days, the most brutal exploitation occurred among the slaves who worked in the mines.

Hellenistic Culture

Hellenistic society, then, with its broad gulf between rich and poor, marked a decline from Greek democracy. In the arts and sciences, however, much of the Greek tradition continued to live and flourish in the Hellenistic world. People of culture spoke Greek, even if they were not of Greek extraction. Libraries, administered by trained scholars, preserved the works of Greek writers; the Ptolemies established at Alexandria the greatest library of the ancient world, a splendid collection exceeding half a million rolls of papyrus, the equivalent of tens of thousands of books today.

Although Hellenistic architects and sculptors employed Greek forms, they treated their subjects in a more theatrical and emotional manner. The lighthouse at Alexandria was a spectacular example of Hellenistic taste; four hundred feet high, it was one of the "seven wonders of the ancient world." Another example is the celebrated sculpture of the Laocoön group created at Rhodes in the first century B.C., which shows a Trojan priest and his sons crushed by writhing serpents. Hellenistic sculptors also had a taste for the kind of art called *genre* —the realistic portrayal of ordinary people in everyday situations—as in the statues of a drunken crone and an old market woman. Their work, at its worst, is imitative and exaggerated; at its best, it includes such world-famous statues as the Venus de Milo and the Winged Victory.

The Hellenistic centuries produced few major works of literature. This was the "Silver Age" of Greek writing, a period of ebbing vigor and originality, yet not always inferior to the "Golden Age" of the fifth century. We may take as an example the "New Comedy," which was very different from the "Old Comedy" of Aristophanes. The leading dramatist of the New Comedy,

Menander (342-291), wrote plays of the type that would today be termed comedy of manners, civilized and gently satirical in contrast to the hard-hitting attacks of Aristophanes.

Hellenistic science prospered, thanks both to the patronage of the Ptolemies and to the influence of the Mesopotamian astronomical and mathematical tradition. Aristarchus, a third-century astronomer, advanced the following hypothesis:

The fixed stars and the sun remain unmoved, but the earth revolves about the sun in the circumference of a circle, the sun lying in the middle of the orbit.*

* Benjamin Farrington, *Greek Science* (Harmondsworth, Middlesex, 1949), II, 79.

Hellenistic sculpture. The old market woman.

This was the heliocentric theory of the universe, which was not generally accepted until almost two thousand years later (see Chapter XV). Eratosthenes, a younger contemporary of Aristarchus, believed the earth to be spherical, not flat, and made an estimate of the size of its circumference that is reasonably close to modern calculations. In mathematics, Euclid organized a school at Alexandria in the third century and systematically collected and arranged the geometrical propositions advanced earlier by the Greeks. Archimedes (c. 287-212 B.C.), a student at Euclid's school, continued the mathematical work of his master, formulated new laws of physics, and won an outstanding reputation as an engineer. He devised machines to be operated by slaves for removing water from mines and from irrigation ditches (Egyptian peasants still use "Archimedes' screw," a simple handcranked device, to raise water from ditch to field). In a striking display of the power of pulleys and levers, he pulled, single-handed, a loaded ship from the water onto land. Hence the reputed boast of Archimedes: "Give me a lever long enough and a place to stand on, and I will move the world."

Hellenistic religion and philosophy were deeply concerned with man's perennial search for fulfillment. The Olympian gods still attracted worshipers; in the second century B.C. Zeus was honored by the construction of a huge altar at Pergamum, one of the showiest productions of Hellenistic art. But Greek polytheism had really outlived its time. The dynamic religions were the mystery cults which, like the old Eleusinian rites, offered the promise of salvation and immortality. We shall examine two of the most significant cults—Asian Mithraism and the Egyptian cult of Isis—in Chapter IV when we consider the rivals of early Christianity.

In Hellenistic philosophy two schools in particular were to exert a lasting influence—the Epicurean and the Stoic. The Epicu-

reans found pleasure the key to happiness, but they emphatically did not advise the life of wine, women, and song that is today associated with the term "Epicurean." On the contrary, Epicurus (341-270 B.C.), the founder of the school, defined pleasure in a negative way as "absence of pain." He ranked the pleasures of the spirit above those of the body, although he recommended that bodily appetites should not be repressed but should receive satisfaction in moderation. The Epicurean code, with its counsels of temperance and common sense. reasserted the characteristically Greek concept of the golden mean and attracted an important following, especially among the Romans.

The Stoics (the name comes from the "stoa" or porch in Athens where they first taught) advised the repression of the physical side of life. For them the road to happiness lay in the triumph of spirit over flesh, reason over emotion. Some Stoics, finding it impossible to overcome bodily suffering, were driven to suicide by the logic of their own philosophy. But logic also led them to extend the Greek ideal of democracy to the whole of humanity. Only the inward man truly counted; outward differences, physical, social, or economic, mattered not at all. So the Stoics believed strongly that all men were brothers, and they championed slaves and other outcasts of society. In stressing the brotherhood of man and praising the virtues that we think of as stoical, Stoicism anticipated the moral teachings of Christianity.

The Hellenistic Style

The style of the Hellenistic world, then, had a markedly dualistic character, a kind of split personality. It strove to move beyond the merely physical, as in the mystery cults and in Stoicism, and it also strove to extract the maximum potentiality from the physical world. The symbol of Hellenistic worldliness was the great city of Alexandria, with its towering lighthouse and broad streets, its luxurious palaces and fine library, its scientists, bureaucrats, and merchants. The dualism of Hellenistic life arose from the attempt to fuse two older cultures —the Greek and the Near Eastern. The influence of Greece, though strong, was never all-pervasive; in the Hellenistic world, use of the Greek language never extended beyond the literate minority of the population. Behind an imposing Greek façade the Hellenistic lands preserved such deeply rooted eastern institutions as absolute political subservience to the dictates of godlike kings, and absolute spiritual subservience to the commands of mysterious deities.

Yet in these sprawling territories Greek civilization made many new conquests, even as it was becoming diluted and adulterated. Moreover, Philip, Alexander, and their successors tried to solve the problem that destroyed Greece—how to subdue the forces of political decentralization, fanatic local patriotism, and civil war. They sought a golden mean by using political units larger than city-states, but not impossibly large, and by tempering centralized absolutism with local self-rule. Although the experiment achieved only a very qualified success, it contained the germ of the system that was to bestow greatness and longevity upon the heir of the Hellenistic world—Rome.

Reading Suggestions on the Greeks

(Asterisk indicates paperbound edition.)

GENERAL ACCOUNTS

C. E. Robinson, *A History of Greece*, 9th ed. (Barnes and Noble, n.d.). An excellent survey, incorporating the most recent discoveries concerning Mycenaean Greece.

V. M. Scramuzza and P. L. MacKendrick, *The Ancient World* (Holt, 1958). A comprehensive and up-to-date textbook, covering the period from the beginnings of civilization to the fall of Rome.

J. B. Bury, *A History of Greece to the Death of Alexander the Great*, 3rd ed., revised by R. Meiggs (Macmillan, 1951). A famous longer political account.

Edith Hamilton, *The Greek Way to Western Civilization* (*Mentor). An engaging and enthusiastic popular treatment by a great admirer of the Greeks.

H. D. F. Kitto, *The Greeks* (*Penguin, 1951). An opinionated but useful introduction.

G. Lowes Dickinson, *The Greek View of Life* (*Univ. of Michigan, 1958). A widely used general introduction, rather old-fashioned in its point of view.

Will Durant, *The Life of Greece* (Simon and Schuster, 1939). A clear and careful introduction designed for the general public.

André Bonnard, *Greek Civilization*, 2 vols. (Allen and Unwin, 1957-59). A stimulating cultural survey.

C. M. Bowra, *The Greek Experience* (World, 1958). An enlightening interpretation for those already acquainted with the basic facts; handsomely illustrated.

H. J. Muller, *Loom of History* (Harper, 1958). A readable study of Asia Minor from ancient times to the present, with a special stress on the Ionian Greeks.

SPECIAL STUDIES—GREECE

Arthur Evans, *The Palace of Minos,* 4 vols. (Macmillan, 1921-1935). A detailed report of the excavations at Cnossos by the distinguished archaeologist.

A. E. Zimmern, *The Greek Commonwealth* (Modern Library, n.d.). A celebrated and sympathetic analysis of the *polis* by a British scholar.

G. Glotz, *The Greek City and Its Institutions* (Knopf, 1929). An excellent though outdated study by a French scholar.

W. S. Ferguson, *Greek Imperialism* (Houghton Mifflin, 1913). A series of brilliant lectures on the subject.

T. B. L. Webster, *From Mycenae to Homer* (Methuen, 1958). An up-to-date monograph on early Greek culture.

R. W. Livingstone, ed., *The Legacy of Greece* (Clarendon, 1921). Essays of unequal value on various aspects of the legacy.

W. Jaeger, *Paideia,* 3 vols. (Oxford Univ. Press, 1939-1944). An advanced study of Greek civilization and ideals.

E. Hamilton, *Mythology* (°Mentor, 1953). A popular introduction to famous myths; centered on Greece.

W. K. C. Guthrie, *The Greeks and Their Gods* (°Beacon, 1955). A detailed, rather difficult, but stimulating study of the origins and nature of Greek religion.

F. M. Cornford, *Before and After Socrates* (Cambridge Univ. Press, 1932). A capital short introduction to Greek science and philosophy.

B. Farrington, *Greek Science,* 2 vols. (°Penguin, 1944). A useful detailed account.

E. R. Dodds, *The Greeks and the Irrational* (°Beacon, 1957). An instructive study of an aspect of Greek culture often overlooked.

H. I. Marrou, *A History of Education in Antiquity* (Sheed & Ward, 1956). A useful account covering the Greeks, the Romans and the early Christians.

SPECIAL STUDIES—THE HELLENISTIC WORLD

W. W. Tarn, *Alexander the Great* (°Beacon, 1956). A sympathetic study by the foremost expert on the subject.

W. W. Tarn and G. T. Griffith, *Hellenistic Civilization,* rev. ed. (Arnold, 1952). An informative survey, covering all aspects of civilization under the successors of Alexander.

A. R. Burn, *Alexander the Great and the Hellenistic Empire* (Macmillan, 1948). A popular biography.

M. Rostovtzev, *The Social and Economic History of the Hellenistic World* (Clarendon, 1941). A detailed study by a great historian.

M. Hadas, *Hellenistic Culture* (Columbia Univ. Press, 1959). An up-to-date evaluation.

SOURCES IN TRANSLATION

Note: The following list includes only the most famous works; they are available in many editions besides those noted.

Homer, *The Iliad,* R. Lattimore, trans. (Univ. of Chicago Press, 1951). A good poetic translation.

Homer, *The Iliad,* W. H. D. Rouse, trans. (°Mentor, 1950). A rendition in modern prose.

W. J. Oates and E. O'Neill, Jr., eds., *The Complete Greek Drama* (Random House, 1938).

The Dialogues of Plato, B. Jowett, trans., new ed. (Clarendon, 1953).

The Works of Aristotle, W. D. Ross, ed. (Clarendon, 1908-1931).

Thucydides, *History of the Peloponnesian War,* B. Jowett, trans. (Clarendon, 1881).

A. J. Toynbee, ed., *Greek Civilization and Character* and *Greek Historical Thought* (°Mentor). Two volumes of selections from the works of historians and other Greek writers, affording a kaleidoscopic view of the Greek outlook.

W. H. Auden, ed., *Portable Greek Reader* (°Viking, 1948). An excellent short anthology of Greek writing.

HISTORICAL FICTION

Mary Renault, *The King Must Die* (Pantheon, 1958). A novel of Mycenaean and Minoan life.

Mary Renault, *The Last of the Wine* (Pantheon, 1956). A novel set in Athens at the time of the Peloponnesian War.

The
Romans

CHAPTER III

I: Introduction

In the war between the Greeks and the Trojans recounted by Homer, a great warrior named Aeneas, the son of a Trojan prince and the goddess Aphrodite, performed feats of valor second only to those of Hector. After the fall of Troy, Aeneas led a band of refugees on a long journey through the Mediterranean to Carthage and eventually to central Italy. There, on the banks of the River Tiber, the descendants of Aeneas' Trojan band founded a city that was to become the "eternal city" of the western world.

So runs, in bare outline, the legendary story of the founding of Rome as told in the *Aeneid* by the poet Vergil (see below, p. 128) at a time when Rome was nearing the height of her power. The story has no firm basis in historical fact, yet it forms a fitting preface to the actual history of Rome. Just as Vergil modeled the *Aeneid* in part on the great epics of Homer, so Rome borrowed extensively from the older civilizations of Greece and the Near East. Aeneas probably never set foot on Roman soil, but many Greeks and easterners eventually did. So many of their ideas, beliefs, and institutions were transplanted that historians speak of the broad Greco-Oriental or Hellenistic strain in Roman civilization. Some historians, in fact, conclude that, since

95

Rome owed such a large debt to her predecessors, there was but a single Greco-Roman civilization.

Rome, however, did not achieve greatness simply by operating on borrowed or confiscated cultural capital. From the first, her people showed a strong practical bent. The Romans had a remarkable capacity for military and political organization and for the equally practical tasks of engineering and the other applied sciences. It was this practicality above all that enabled a small city-state to expand and expand until it became the "One World" of antiquity.

The career of Rome as an independent state began about 500 B.C., when her citizens threw off the domination of foreign kings and set up a republic. The Roman Republic, which lasted until the middle of the first century B.C., conquered first its immediate neighbors, then the rest of Italy, and finally other Mediterranean lands. The Roman Empire, which succeeded the Republic, reached its peak during the first two centuries of the Christian Era when it brought most of the then-known world under the *Pax Romana*, the Roman peace.

The Setting

Geography gave Rome valuable assets. Built on the famous seven hills overlooking the Tiber River, the city was easily fortified and easily defended. It was centrally located, midway down the Italian peninsula and about fifteen miles from the western coast. It was close enough to the sea to participate in the commercial life of the Mediterranean.

The Italian peninsula as a whole is Mediterranean in climate and in terrain; most of it has never possessed really rich economic resources. But, compared with Greece, ancient Italy was relatively well favored by nature. The Italian mountains never formed quite the barrier to overland communication and political unification that the Greek mountains had. The Italian plains

were both more extensive and more fertile than those of Greece. One of the largest, the plain of Latium or the Latin plain, lay just to the south of Rome and stretched from the sea on the west to the Apennines, the mountainous backbone of the peninsula, on the east. Intensive farming of the Latin plain was possible when ditches were dug for drainage and irrigation; the hills nearby provided good pasturage and great stands of timber. Thus, food and fuel enough to support Rome in its early days were readily available.

Human beings had been settled in Italy for thousands of years before the emergence of the independent Roman Republic. The Latin tribes living in Rome and on the adjacent plain about 500 B.C. were apparently the descendants of these prehistoric Italians. Rome was to build the first strong native Italian state, but before its emergence two other civilizations, both originating abroad, had become firmly rooted in the peninsula. These were the Greek and the Etruscan. By 600 B.C., as we saw in the last chapter, Greek colonies dotted the shores of southern Italy and Sicily, and Magna Graecia had become an important center of Greek culture.

The Etruscans

The Etruscans are a fascinating example of an unsolved historical problem. They left hundreds of tombs, some containing inscriptions written in Greek letters but in a language that probably does not belong to the Indo-European family. Although scattered words have been translated, no general key to the Etruscan language has as yet been found, nothing comparable to the Rosetta Stone or to Ventris' deciphering of Linear B. The tombs, weapons, pottery, and other remains, however, strongly suggest that the Etruscans were foreign invaders, probably from Asia Minor, possibly the source of the Aeneas legend. The Etruscans apparently led piratical raids on

Etruscan wall painting. From the "Tomb of the Leopards," Tarquinia, late fifth century B.C.

Italy and then, between 800 and 700 B.C., conquered the region immediately north of the Tiber and the plain of Latium. There they settled down as a foreign minority ruling the native population.

Etruscan civilization seems to have had a distinctive style of its own, although some of its art and crafts reveal a marked Greek influence. The Etruscans were expert farmers and miners, and they fortified their cities with walls of great stones rather like those at Mycenae. To judge from their elaborate tombs, they held beliefs concerning the afterlife similar to those of the Egyptians. They also practiced divination, foretelling the future for example from the character of a flight of birds or from the arrangement of the entrails in an animal that had been slain as a sacrifice. To judge from the tomb decorations, Etruscan men

accorded women a higher status than was usual in ancient cultures, and the whole society had an attractive natural gaiety. Remember, however, that our evidence of the Etruscan style is fragmentary.

In the course of the seventh century B.C. the Etruscans extended their dominion southward along the western coast of Italy; first they bypassed Rome and then, soon after 600 B.C., conquered it. Ruled by Etruscan kings, Rome prospered and began to expand at the expense of her Latin neighbors. But her own Latin population, resenting the rule of foreigners, joined with other Latin tribes in a widespread rebellion and, toward the close of the sixth century—the traditional date is 509 B.C.—expelled the last Etruscan king, Tarquin the Proud. Thus began the historical career of the independent Latin city-state of Rome.

II: Rise of the Republic

The Roman Republic after the expulsion of Tarquin was a very small enterprise, far smaller than Athens or Sparta, which

were then approaching the peak of their power. Rome in the fifth century B.C. was only one of several Latin towns, newly liberated from Etruscan rule, that divided the control of the plain of Latium. The hostile Etruscans to the north, and marauding mountain tribesmen to the east and the south, constantly threatened its existence. To counter the threat, however, Rome had two assets of great value in addition to its good defensive site—its government and its army.

The Army

The basic unit of the first Roman armies was the phalanx, composed of about 8,000 footsoldiers, who marched into battle in a long line several rows deep. The phalanx was subdivided into centuries, each of which nominally contained a hundred men. Only some of the centuries could afford to furnish the expensive armor and weapons needed in the front line; these formed the first rows of the phalanx. The other centuries, more lightly armed, brought up the rear.

The early experiences of the Romans in warfare led to changes in the structure and the tactics of their army. The legion, consisting of 3600 men, replaced the larger phalanx. The legions were composed of groups of 60 or 120 men termed maniples (the word literally means "handful"). To the traditional equipment of the phalanx—the helmet and the shield, the lance and the sword—the legion added a potent assault weapon, the iron-tipped javelin, which was hurled at the enemy from a distance. The new organization permitted much greater elasticity on the battlefield. Whereas the phalanx was a cumbersome affair, hard to maneuver, the maniples of the legion could move more quickly and exploit the initiative more readily.

From the beginning of the Republic, almost all citizens of Rome were obliged to serve in the army. Many Greek city-states had discovered that citizen-soldiers resented being ordered about and were there-

fore almost impossible to discipline. The army of the Roman Republic, however, surmounted this difficulty and successfully enforced an iron discipline. Polybius, a Greek historian of the second century B.C., described the Roman method of dealing with the soldier who fell asleep on guard duty:

A court-martial composed of all the tribunes at once meets to try him, and if he is found guilty he is punished . . . as follows: The tribune takes a cudgel and just touches the condemned man with it, after which all in the camp beat or stone him, in most cases dispatching him in the camp itself. But even those who manage to escape are not saved thereby: impos-

Roman soldier. Statue discovered at York, England.

CHAPTER III

sible! for they are not allowed to return to their homes, and none of the family would dare to receive such a man in his house. So that those who have once fallen into this misfortune are utterly ruined. . . . Thus, owing to the extreme severity and inevitableness of the penalty, the night watches of the Roman army are most scrupulously kept.*

The successes of the Roman army, Polybius observed, depended on the distribution of generous rewards as well as on brutal punishments:

They also have an admirable method of encouraging the young soldiers to face danger. After a battle in which some of them have distinguished themselves, the general calls an assembly of the troops, and bringing forward those whom he considers to have displayed conspicuous valor, first of all speaks in laudatory terms of the courageous deeds of each . . . and afterwards distributes the following rewards. To the man who has wounded an enemy, a spear; to him who has slain and stripped an enemy, a cup. . . . To the first man to mount the wall at the assault on a city, he gives a crown of gold. . . . By such incentives they excite to emulation and rivalry in the field not only the men who are present and listen to their words, but those who remain at home also.†

Government

The young Republic not only commanded a resourceful and obedient army but also established effective political institutions. After the fall of Tarquin the Proud, Rome became an oligarchic republic, based on the division of the population into two classes, the patrician and the plebeian. The aristocracy of well-to-do families formed the class of *patricians* (from the Latin, *patres*, fathers); they alone were full citizens. Membership in the patrician class was limited to propertied families already well established in Etruscan days. The patricians were not necessarily "gentlemen

* Polybius, *The Histories*, W. R. Paton, trans. (New York, 1923), Bk. VI, Ch. 37.
† *Ibid.*, Bk. VIII, Ch. 39.

farmers" leading a leisurely life. According to a time-honored story, their military hero, Cincinnatus, left his plow in the field to lead the army to victory twice during the fifth century B.C.

The great majority—probably 90 per cent —of the population belonged to the inferior class of *plebeians* (from the Latin, *plebs*, the multitude). Merchants, laborers, small farmers (most of them very small, tilling tiny plots of land), the large group of debtors created by the economic upheaval following the expulsion of the Etruscans— all these were plebeians. The plebeians were denied full political rights, particularly access to high government office. They could amass wealth, however, and some of them did; well-to-do plebeians were to lead a prolonged campaign for the political emancipation of their class. The social and political situation in fifth-century Rome, with its marked class discrimination, bore a decided resemblance to that prevailing in Athens a century earlier, on the eve of the democratic reforms.

In the early days of the Roman Republic the patricians dominated the two most significant governmental institutions—the consulate and the Senate. Two consuls, chosen from the patrician class, served as the chief executives for the term of a year; more than that, they were granted full *imperium*, the Latin term for supreme political authority. In theory, the consuls were simply the republican equivalents of the Etruscan kings; in practice, however, their power was subject to limitations. Each consul, for instance, had the right of veto over his colleague, so that important policies had to win the support of both consuls. The consuls normally commanded the army; but in time of war, and with the advice of the Senate, they often turned over their powers to one man, for a maximum of six months. This man was the dictator, who differed from his modern namesake in that he gained office through normal constitutional means and retained it only for a short prescribed term. Cincinnatus served twice as dictator, once to defeat attacks by Rome's neighbors, and once to put down a rebellion.

In normal times, moreover, the consuls followed the lead of the Senate in transacting the daily business of state. The Senate had approximately 300 members, chosen largely from the patricians; all consuls became senators at the end of their term in office, and the reigning consuls appointed other senators. In theory, the functions of the Senate were merely advisory and supervisory; actually, it enjoyed great prestige and exerted great influence over the Republic. It was the most celebrated single Roman institution of government and came first in the political device of Rome, S.P.Q.R.—*Senatus Populusque Romanus* (The Senate and the Roman People).

The Roman People—for practical purposes, the *plebs*—could voice its views in another body, the Centuriate Assembly. This assembly, as its name suggests, was based on the centuries, the smallest units of the army; the various centuries simply met together to decide civil as well as military matters. Although the Centuriate Assembly apparently resembled a town meeting of citizen-soldiers, we do not know how democratic its procedures actually were. Both patricians and plebeians supplied centuries for the army, and some evidence suggests that the patrician centuries dominated the Centuriate Assembly. In any event, the Assembly seems to have enjoyed more legal prerogative but less actual power than did the Senate. In principle, it elected the consuls and other officials and approved or rejected legislation submitted to it by the consuls and the Senate.

The reigning patrician class took its political responsibilities seriously, and no man could rise to the high office of consul without first passing through an apprenticeship in other posts. Beginning as a minor official, the patrician might eventually become a praetor (*prae-itor*, he who goes before or in front), a position ranking next to consul

in the republican hierarchy. As the Republic grew, the number of praetors increased from one to eight, and their functions also multiplied. They served most frequently as judges, and they also became military commanders and, after the acquisition of territories abroad, provincial governors. In the absence of a consul the praetor might act in his place. The praetors, like the consuls, were elected by the Assembly and served for the fixed term of a year. Men seeking election as praetor or consul wore a robe whitened with chalk, the *toga candida* (whence the term "candidate").

The mounting burdens of government, particularly the need to keep the army at full strength, resulted in the creation of another high administrative post, that of censor. The censors, two in number and serving an eighteen-month term, were former consuls. They took a census of the population to determine who were qualified to serve in the army. The censors also secured the right to supervise public lands and public works, and to pass on the moral qualifications of men nominated for senator, barring those judged to be corrupt or unduly luxurious. This authority to assess private fitness for public office and to bar the unfit accounts for the modern connotation of the words "censor" and "censorship."

The early Roman Republic, in summary, had an aristocratic regime well designed to prosecute the chief business of state: defense and war. The institutions of the dictator, the censors, and the Centuriate Assembly all reflected the military preoccupations of Rome. The exercise of supreme authority by the patrician consuls and the patrician Senate reflected the predominance of the upper class. Since the qualifications for high office included ability, experience, and moral probity in addition to patrician birth, the government enlisted the best aristocratic talent available. All this, of course, did not satisfy the grievances of the plebeians, who resented the patrician monopoly and demanded increased political rights of their own. The patricians responded with a series of concessions that revealed the distinctive adaptability of Rome and liberalized the constitution of the Republic.

Liberalization of the Republic

The plebeians, however, had to struggle for these concessions. Very early, in the 490's, they found a weapon in the threat of secession, of withdrawing entirely from Rome and founding a new city-state nearby. This weapon proved to be a powerful one, and the plebeians were to employ it with great effect on several occasions during the fifth and fourth centuries B.C. The earliest use of the threat resulted in the forging of a second potent weapon, the creation of special plebeian officials, the Tribunes of the People. Originally, there were two tribunes, who had the primary duty of protecting the plebs from unduly harsh and discriminatory application of the laws by patrician magistrates. Eventually, the number of tribunes was increased to ten, and their functions expanded as they became the spearhead of agitation for further concessions.

After the creation of the tribunes, the plebeians complained that they still lacked adequate legal protection because the customs and traditions comprising the law were unwritten and could be manipulated by patrician judges for class purposes. To satisfy this grievance, the consuls had a statement of the laws engraved on twelve wooden tablets that were then exhibited in a public place. These were the Twelve Tables, formulated about 449 B.C. Their importance resided not so much in their specific provisions, which often prescribed crude punishments, as in the fact of their existence and "publication." With the Twelve Tables the Roman law began its epochal history.

Meantime, the plebeians developed their own assembly, which was known as the Tribal Assembly since the plebeian population was subdivided into geographical groupings called tribes. The Tribal Assembly chose the Tribunes of the People and gained the right to pass on new laws; the powers of the Tribal Assembly thus equaled those of the older Centuriate Assembly. In prestige and influence, however, the Senate remained supreme.

The plebeians obtained other important concessions during the fifth and fourth centuries B.C. They won the right to hold the offices of praetor, censor, and even consul and senator. They could marry patricians, a privilege originally denied them by aristocrats determined to keep the gulf between the two classes unbridgeable. They sponsored measures to deal with debts and with the land question. These problems were severe and chronic in the early Roman Republic, just as they had been in Greece. Many plebeian farmers lost their property and were forced into slavery because of their inability to pay debts. In order to keep more land from falling into the hands of the well-to-do, the Republic imposed a limit on the size of the estate that one man might accumulate. To reduce the number of debt-ridden plebeians, it abolished the heaviest penalties against debtors, notably enslavement, and opened newly acquired territories to resettlement by landless farmers.

These measures eased, but did not solve, the problems of farmers and debtors—problems that were to haunt the Republic for the rest of its days. Nor did the political emancipation of the plebeians end the political domination of the well-born and rich. Wealthy plebeians now gained entrance into the preserves of the old aristocracy, and the resulting fusion of the two groups created a new upper class, the *nobiles* or nobles. The nobles were to dominate the later Republic as the patricians had dominated the early Republic. Reforms had given

Rome not a democracy but a liberalized oligarchy.

It is enlightening to compare the institutions of republican Rome with those of Sparta. Like Sparta, Rome confided political and military leadership to the patrician class; the Roman army, like the Spartan, was strictly disciplined and highly organized; the chief purpose of Roman education was the training of brave, obedient soldiers. Yet the Roman boy did not have to leave his family, as did the Spartan, and the whole Roman regime was less rigid. Unlike the helots or *perioikoi*, plebeians could rise to the ranks of the upper class. Sufficient concessions were made to the plebeians so that they were not constantly on the verge of revolt, as were Sparta's helots. Rome had both the military and political strength for a successful career of territorial expansion.

Expansion in Italy

The first stage of expansion ended in 265 B.C., with Rome the dominant power in the Italian peninsula. A long series of wars had established Roman supremacy over the other Latin towns, the Etruscan cities, and the half-civilized tribes of the central Apennines. The decaying cities of Magna Graecia in the south, in an attempt to resist the Roman advance, had called in a redoubtable warrior, Pyrrhus, King of Epirus, in northwestern Greece. In a campaign between 281 and 275 B.C., Pyrrhus twice defeated the Roman armies, but his own losses were so heavy that he eventually lost the war (hence the term "Pyrrhic victory"). Southern Italy thus became Roman. Meanwhile, at the other end of the peninsula, Rome had checked the expansion of the Gauls, Celtic invaders from beyond the Alps, who had settled in the Po valley, in what we now call the Lombard plain. The Gauls, however, had not yet been mastered, so that after 265 B.C. the northern

frontier of Roman dominion lay along the little River Rubicon at the southern edge of the Lombard plain.

The expansion of Rome was partly a matter of self-defense. The Gauls and the mountain tribes had made repeated attacks on Rome, clearly aimed at the destruction of the city. Rome had to choose between conquering her enemies or being conquered herself. Sometimes, however, the objective of Roman campaigns was acquisition rather than defense. Additional farm lands and forests were needed, for the thin soil of the Latin plain was losing its fertility and the hills near Rome had been stripped of timber. Rome also sought territories in which to settle some of her land-hungry plebeians. For these reasons, and also for the purpose of securing the political loyalty of the non-Roman population, Roman colonies were sometimes planted in newly acquired lands.

On the whole, Rome followed a generous policy toward the other peoples of Italy, organizing them into a loosely controlled confederation rather than into a highly centralized empire. The ties that bound the weaker to the strong were generally the ties of alliance, not those of absolute subjection. Many of the conquered peoples were allowed at least a few rights of self-government; some, like the city-states of Magna Graecia, which had imported the tradition of the *polis* from their mother country, enjoyed considerable home-rule. In some cases, particularly among the closest neighbors of Rome, the conquered eventually secured full Roman citizenship; more frequently they became partial citizens, enjoying the protection of the Roman law but not sitting or voting in the assemblies at Rome.

The Romans were already demonstrating their capacity to create a complex political organism, nicely poised between the two extremes of excessive localism and excessive centralization. The wisdom of this statesmanlike policy was shown during the prolonged struggle with Carthage, when most of the Italians adhered faithfully to Rome even though Rome was facing almost certain defeat.

Rome and Carthage

Once the Greek cities of southern Italy had come within the Roman orbit, Rome and Carthage were bound to clash. The great Phoenician settlement in North Africa had long since outgrown the position of colony and had become the strongest power outside the Hellenistic East. It was an independent state ruled by a commercial oligarchy. It almost monopolized the trade of the western Mediterranean, and it controlled a long strip of the North African coast plus parts of Spain and of the islands of the western Mediterranean. The Carthaginians also ruled western Sicily and hoped to extend their control over the whole island. When they began to take over the Greek cities in eastern Sicily, the Sicilian Greeks appealed to Rome for protection. Rome responded and launched the First Punic War, 264-241 B.C. (Punic, from the Latin word for Phoenician).

Rome won the war. The citizen-fighters of a state that was largely agrarian, with little lucrative trade and almost no naval experience or tradition, defeated a state that for centuries had been a major commercial and naval power. The Romans succeeded in part because of Carthaginian blunders and, above all, because they speedily constructed a large fleet and vanquished the enemy on the sea. In the peace that ended the war, Carthage gave up all claims to eastern Sicily and ceded its territories in western Sicily. Thus Rome secured her first province outside the mainland of Italy and became a Mediterranean power rather than just a local Italian one.

The Carthaginians, humiliated by their defeat, now strengthened their hold over Spain as the base for an overland invasion of Italy. The invasion started the Second Punic War (218-201 B.C.). The Carthaginian commander was Hannibal, one of the most celebrated generals in history. Hannibal led his forces round the eastern edge of the Pyrenees, across southern Gaul, and thence over the Alps into the Po Valley. The Greek historian Polybius has left a detailed account of the march through the Alps in difficult autumn weather. On the way up, hostile tribes attacked the expedition; on the way down to Italy, Hannibal met further trouble:

During this he encountered no enemy, except a few skulking marauders, but owing to the difficulties of the ground and the snow his losses were nearly as heavy as on the ascent. The descending path was very narrow and steep, and, as both men and beasts could not tell on what they were treading owing to the snow, all that stepped wide of the path or stumbled were dashed down the precipice. . . . They at length reached a place where it was impossible for either the elephants or the pack-animals to pass owing to the extreme narrowness of the path. . . . The new snow, which had fallen on top of the old snow remaining since the previous winter, was itself yielding, . . . but when they had trodden through it and set foot on the congealed snow beneath it, they no longer sank in it, but slid along it with both feet, as happens to those who walk on ground with a coat of mud on it. . . . The animals, when they fell, broke through the lower layer of snow in their efforts to rise, and remained there with their packs as if frozen into it, owing to their weight and the congealed condition of this old snow.[*]

Few of the lumbering elephants used to transport supplies survived the Alpine crossing.

On reaching northern Italy, Hannibal filled up the depleted ranks of his foot-soldiers with recruits from the Gauls, who had recently been defeated by Rome and now sought revenge. Advancing southward, Hannibal won a series of battles. At Cannae (216 B.C.) he set a trap for the Romans by allowing them to attack the purposely

---

[*] Polybius, *The Histories*, W. R. Paton, trans. (New York, 1922), Bk. III, Chs. 54-55.

weakened center of his line; he then surrounded them by bringing together the two strong wings of his army, like two giant pincers. Seven-eighths of the Roman forces engaged were reported lost.

Although Rome had lost a campaign, she had not lost the war. Hannibal could not take the city itself because of its strong defenses, and his efforts to win over towns allied with Rome met with little success. The few towns that were disloyal to the Roman alliance later suffered terrible punishments, for Rome was to sell their inhabitants into slavery. Meantime, the Romans themselves met the crisis with admirable discipline. Their clever and patient general, Fabius Cunctator (Fabius the Delayer), refused to expose the newly recruited legions to the risk of a second Cannae. Avoiding any major engagement with Hannibal's forces, he harassed them by attacking their supplies and patrols. This Fabian strategy of eating away the enemy's strength bit by bit gradually exhausted the Carthaginians. Hannibal could not draw supplies and reinforcements from home because of Rome's command of the sea. He was still vainly attempting to subjugate Italy in 204 B.C. when a Roman force, commanded by Scipio, invaded North Africa. Hannibal was called back to defend Carthage. But Scipio prevailed and later, in honor of his victory, received the title "Africanus."

The power of Carthage as a major independent state ended in 201 B.C. with the conclusion of a one-sided peace. Carthage surrendered her Spanish possessions to Rome, paid a very large indemnity, and agreed to accept Roman tutelage in foreign policy. Some Romans, however, were alarmed by the continued existence of Carthage, particularly by the swift recovery of Carthaginian trade. Agitation for another Punic war mounted under the leadership of a belligerent censor and senator, Cato (234-149 B.C.), who once, it is said, brandished a magnificent cluster of North African figs before the senators to convince them of Carthaginian prosperity, and who habitually ended his speeches with the brutal exhortation, *Delenda est Carthago* (Carthage must be destroyed). Carthage was destroyed. In the Third Punic War (149-146 B.C.), its buildings were burned to the ground and its remaining territories were taken over by Rome.

Rome
and the Hellenistic World

The year 146 B.C. was a memorable one in the annals of Roman expansion; it marked not only the destruction of Carthage but also an important stage in the assertion of Roman hegemony over the Hellenistic world. The Second Punic War had embroiled Rome in the strife-ridden politics of the Hellenistic states (see Chapter II), for the ambitious King of Macedon had supported Carthage in the war. As soon as peace was made with Carthage in 201 B.C., Rome launched a preventive war against Macedon, to end the Macedonian ascendancy over Greece and thereby reduce the potential Macedonian threat to Roman security. This aim was achieved in 197 B.C., but a new threat to Greece was soon posed by the Seleucid Empire in Syria. The Seleucid ruler, egged on by Hannibal, now exiled from Carthage, menaced the Greek states on both the Asian and European shores of the Aegean. Again Rome undertook a defensive war, successfully concluded in 188 B.C.

By now the practice of Roman intervention had become a habit, fortified by appeals for help from the Greek states, which were still engrossed in their age-old petty rivalries. For a time the Roman Senate tried to act simply as the arbiter of the Hellenistic world, permitting the various states to run their own affairs except in matters of foreign policy where Roman interests were at stake. But this policy, which had

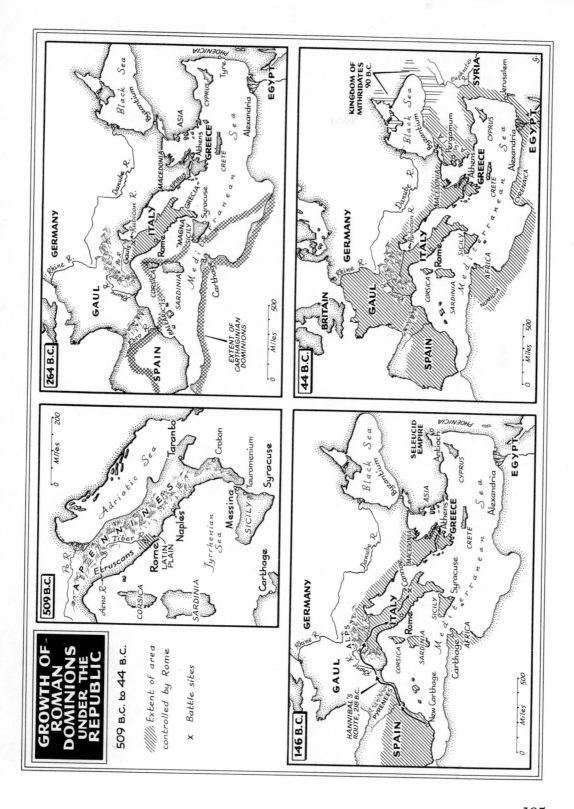

GROWTH OF ROMAN DOMINIONS UNDER THE REPUBLIC

509 B.C. to 44 B.C.

///// Extent of area controlled by Rome

x Battle sites

509 B.C.

Arno R.
CORSICA
SARDINIA
Etruscans
APPENNINES
Tiber R.
Rome
LATIN PLAIN
Naples
Adriatic Sea
Taranto
Tyrrhenian Sea
Croton
Messina
SICILY
Tauromenium
Syracuse
Carthage
Miles 0 200

264 B.C.

GERMANY
GAUL
SPAIN
Rhine R.
Rhone R.
Po R.
Danube R.
Ebro R.
BALEARICS
Gauls
Rubicon R.
Rome
ITALY
"MAGNA GRAECIA"
CORSICA
SARDINIA
SICILY
Syracuse
Carthage
Mediterranean Sea
CRETE
GREECE
Athens
EPIRUS
MACEDONIA
ASIA
Byzantium
Black Sea
CYPRUS
PHOENICIA
Tyre
Alexandria
EGYPT
EXTENT OF CARTHAGINIAN DOMINIONS
Miles 0 500

146 B.C.

GERMANY
GAUL
SPAIN
Rhine R.
Rhone R.
ALPS
PYRENEES
New Carthage
HANNIBAL'S ROUTE, 218 B.C.
CORSICA
SARDINIA
Rome
ITALY
Cannae
Carthage
AFRICA
SICILY
Syracuse
Mediterranean Sea
CRETE
GREECE
Athens
MACEDONIA
ASIA
Byzantium
Black Sea
Danube R.
CYPRUS
SELEUCID EMPIRE
Antioch
SYRIA
Alexandria
EGYPT
PHOENICIA
Miles 0 500

44 B.C.

BRITAIN
GERMANY
GAUL
SPAIN
Rhine R.
Rhone R.
Po R.
Danube R.
CORSICA
SARDINIA
Rome
ITALY
Rubicon R.
NUMIDIA
AFRICA
SICILY
Mediterranean Sea
CRETE
GREECE
Athens
MACEDONIA
Pergamum
ASIA
Byzantium
Black Sea
Euphrates R.
KINGDOM OF MITHRIDATES 90 B.C.
SYRIA
Jerusalem
CYPRUS
CYRENAICA
Alexandria
EGYPT
Miles 0 500

worked so well in Italy, did not work in Macedon and Greece, where rebellion against Roman directives became almost chronic. The result has been aptly described as a process of "muddling through to annexation." In 146 B.C. Rome, unable to control her unruly allies in the old way, made Macedon a province under a Roman governor and placed the Greek city-states under his supervision. The independence of the Hellenistic peoples was vanishing, partly because of their own incessant bickering and partly because of the mounting imperialism of Rome.

III: The Crisis and Collapse of the Republic

Signs of Trouble

After 146 B.C. the Roman Republic was the most powerful state of the day. She had already accumulated an extensive empire overseas—Sicily, Spain, Macedon and Greece, and the province of Africa, consisting of the home territories of Carthage (roughly equivalent to modern Tunisia). Fresh accumulations were to come in the next quarter-century—southern Gaul and the province of Asia, founded on the kingdom of Pergamum which the last ruler of that state bequeathed to Rome.

But as Rome's territory steadily increased, signs of impending trouble multiplied. Neither the old republican constitution nor the simple agrarian economy of Rome could deal effectively with the problems raised by the city's new imperial commitments. The Republic did not treat its overseas possessions generously, with the exception of a few favored cities that were allowed to retain some self-government. Most of the new acquisitions were organized as provinces, each with an all-powerful governor appointed by the Senate at Rome. Since the senators had little experience or interest in the complexities of provincial administration, they gave provincial governors a free rein so long as the latter raised recruits for the army and collected taxes and tributes of grain. Many governors executed their duties with a responsibility worthy of the finest republican tradition. Some, however, drained their provinces twice—once for the benefit of the Roman treasury, and once for their own private gain.

Italy itself, meantime, was undergoing a complex crisis, political as well as economic and social. Rome's allies, which had generally remained loyal during the great war with Hannibal, were now growing more and more restless. They requested full Roman citizenship in the hope of sharing in the new wealth and prestige that expansion had brought to the capital city. They resented the magnetic quality of Rome, which attracted so many of their own most enterprising inhabitants, and they complained of the high-handed treatment they received from some Roman officials, who seemed to be following the example of the worst provincial governors. Moreover, the perennial farm problem was now entering an acute phase. Soil exhaustion and the heavy damage caused by the Second Punic War had made much of the land in Italy unfit for grain. Grain was now imported from Africa, and old grainfields in Italy were turned into vineyards, orchards, and pastures. Only the operators of *latifundia*, large estates, profited, for they alone could afford to acquire the extensive acres and to provide the large amounts of slave labor needed to grow fruit and raise livestock. Veterans of fighting in the provinces and retired provincial governors had a special advantage, since they brought back money and slaves as the spoils of conquest.

A new social and economic cleavage resulted. For the first time in Roman history a class of very rich men appeared—successful generals and governors, the agricultural capitalists of the *latifundia*, merchants and businessmen, particularly the contractors who built roads for the state and furnished supplies for the army. Most of these wealthy men belonged not to the small and well-established aristocracy of the *nobiles* (see above, p. 101) but to the new class of *equites* or knights, so termed because they had sufficient money to equip themselves for service in the cavalry, the most costly branch of the army. In a pattern typical of the newly rich throughout history, the *equites* did not exert a political influence at all in proportion to their economic power. During the Punic Wars effective political authority in Rome had passed almost completely to the Senate, which, by its successful conduct of war, eclipsed the more representative bodies, the Centuriate Assembly and the Tribal Assembly. The Senate in turn was dominated by a small group of noble families which furnished not only the ranking senators but also a large proportion of the consuls and other executives. Tension was growing between the entrenched senatorial aristocracy and the new plutocracy. The old-fashioned senator Cato, for example, who fulminated against Carthage, also fulminated against what he considered to be the decadent taste of the wealthy for the soft, luxurious, and corrupting culture of the Hellenistic East.

Still more important tensions were developing further down the social and economic scale. Rome had her newly poor as well as her newly rich, for the growth of the *latifundia* left little place for the small farmer. The number of landless men grew rapidly, and many of them crowded into the city of Rome, seeking immediate relief and long-range reforms. The political machinery of a small city-state simply could not cope with these multifarious problems of a pan-Mediterranean power. The economic revolution of the second century B.C. was paving the way for a political revolution.

The Reforms of the Gracchi

The political revolution began with the reforms proposed by the Gracchus brothers; it ended with the downfall of the Republic. The Gracchi provide another illustration of high-born champions of the people. They came from a distinguished noble family (their mother, Cornelia, was the daughter of Scipio Africanus, the hero of the Second Punic War), yet they were determined to help the poor at the expense of the *nobiles*. Tiberius Gracchus served as a tribune of the people in 133 B.C.; Gaius, his younger brother, held the same post from 123 to 121 B.C. Both brothers strove to increase the political importance of the tribunes and the popular Tribal Assembly at the expense of the Senate. Both were eloquent pleaders on behalf of the unprivileged, as may be seen in this excerpt from a speech by Tiberius Gracchus:

The wild beasts that roam over Italy . . . have their dens, each has a place of repose and refuge. But the men who fight and die for Italy enjoy nothing but the air and light; without house or home they wander about with their wives and children. Their commanders lie when they exhort the soldiers in battle to defend sepulchers and shrines from the enemy, for not one of these many Romans has either hereditary altar or ancestral tomb; they fight and die to protect the wealth and luxury of others; they are styled masters of the world, and have not a clod of earth they can call their own. . . .*

By way of economic and social reform, the Gracchi proposed, first, to limit the size

---

* N. Lewis and M. Reinhold, *Roman Civilization* (New York, 1951), I, 236-237.

of estates held by one family in order to check the concentration of *latifundia* in the hands of relatively few agricultural capitalists. Second, farmers who had been dispossessed were to be resettled either in farm colonies abroad or on state-owned lands in Italy which had previously been leased to capitalist farmers. Third, the poor in the city of Rome were to obtain relief by being allowed to buy grain from the state at cost, well below the prevailing retail price. By way of political change, in addition to reducing the Senate's power, the Gracchi proposed giving increased responsibilities to the *equites*. They also favored the extension of full Roman citizenship to all Latins and to some other Italians. In sum, the Gracchi wanted to hurry the Republic along the road to democracy.

By and large, the Gracchi failed. Of their economic projects only the distribution of cheap grain was permanently adopted. In the following centuries the price of grain was steadily lowered until the poor in Rome finally received free bread from the state. The continuing need for the dole of bread revealed the failure of the resettlement program. If all evicted farmers had received new land allotments, the number of people in the city requiring cheap bread would have dropped sharply. As it was, the number on relief remained large. The agrarian capitalists, after being forced by the Gracchi to give up some of the land they rented from the state, were soon expanding their holdings once more. The *latifundia* had come to stay; it was impossible to restore the small farm as the economic foundation of Roman life.

Moreover, by attacking and attempting to browbeat the Senate, the Gracchi aroused its bitter hostility. The Senate resented the extension of political rights to the *equites*, and friction built up between the old privileged class and the new. Senators blocked the extension of Roman citizenship in Italy and played on popular superstitions to discredit the plan for new farms in the vicinity of Carthage. Claiming that the site had been cursed since the destruction of the city in the Third Punic War, they discouraged would-be colonists with stories of evil omens, such as the tale of hyenas digging up the stones that marked the boundaries of Carthaginian homesteads.

In the crisis, the political institutions of the Republic began to crumble. The Gracchi used methods of doubtful legality to promote their plans. Tiberius took the unprecedented step of ousting a tribune of the people who was a pawn of the Senate and was blocking his program. Again, in defiance of precedent, both brothers ran for re-election as tribune. The Senate, of course, capitalized on this chance to accuse the Gracchi of destroying the constitution. The senators themselves, however, resorted to the most violent of unconstitutional methods—murder. A mob of senators and their henchmen assassinated Tiberius Gracchus and three hundred of his followers in 133 B.C. Twelve years later, Gaius Gracchus, threatened by the same fate, had himself killed by a slave.

Today, more than two thousand years later, historians are still divided in their evaluation of the Gracchi. Liberals find them kindred spirits whose high-minded proposals for a "new deal in old Rome" ran afoul of the vested interests; if only the Senate had been more amenable to sweeping changes, then the Republic would have been preserved. Conservatives deplore the impatience of the Gracchi, their tactlessness, and the high-handed methods by which they added to the social and political discord; if only they had proceeded more cautiously, then the Republic would have been saved. The impartial historian must find a good deal of truth in both these opposing views but must also note that both "ifs" refer to conditions contrary to fact. The hard fact was that the deadlock between Gracchan reformism and senatorial conservatism set Rome on the road to autocracy.

The Road to Autocracy

The Republic never regained stability after the death of the Gracchi. Three competing groups dominated its political life: the *equites,* whose appetite for larger profits made them demand the constant expansion of Roman territories overseas; the *optimates,* "the best people," the new name for the conservative senatorial opponents of the Gracchan reforms; and the champions of democratic reforms, the *populares.* The continued antagonism among these groups—particularly between the *populares* and the *equites,* on the one hand, and the *optimates* on the other—was unsettling enough. More disruptive still, leadership of both *optimates* and *populares* passed to generals who showed less and less concern for the principles they were supposed to defend. The power of these generals, as we shall see, rested on their control of the army and on their ruthless use of military force.

Instability and misgovernment bedeviled not only Italy but also the outlying provinces, where much of the difficulty lay with the greedy *equites* and *optimates* charged with their administration. A classic indictment of provincial misrule was made by the rising young lawyer, Cicero, when he prosecuted Verres, the governor of Sicily (70 B.C.):

Countless sums of money, under a new and unprincipled regulation were wrung from the purses of the farmers; our most loyal allies were treated as if they were national enemies; Roman citizens were tortured and executed like slaves; the guiltiest criminals bought their legal acquittal, while the most honourable and honest men would be . . . condemned and banished unheard; strongly fortified harbours, mighty and well-defended cities, were left open to the assaults of pirates and buccaneers; Sicilian soldiers and sailors, our allies and our friends, were starved to death; fine fleets, splendidly equipped, were to the great disgrace of our nation destroyed and lost to us. Famous and ancient works of art, some of them the gifts of wealthy kings . . . —this same governor stripped and despoiled every one of them. Nor was it only the civic statues and works of art he treated thus; he also pillaged the holiest and most venerated sanctuaries; in fact, he has not left the people of Sicily a single god whose workmanship he thought at all above the average of antiquity or artistic merit.*

Such conditions provoked serious provincial revolts.

A second force disrupting the provinces was the long series of frontier wars. At the end of the second century B.C., Germanic tribes threatened to drive the Romans out of Spain and southern Gaul and to invade Italy. In 88 B.C. the powerful eastern king, Mithridates, who had assembled a large domain in Asia Minor and around the Black Sea, attacked the Roman province of Asia. The natives, incensed at Roman exploitation, rallied to Mithridates, and thousands of Italian immigrants were massacred. Ultimately Rome met successfully the grave threats to her empire posed by the Germans and by Mithridates.

Defense was not the only reason for the chronic fighting on the frontiers. The *equites* applauded the acquisition of new provinces and the fresh chance to obtain lucrative military contracts, to market slaves, and to collect taxes and tribute. Frontier warfare gave ambitious generals an opportunity to amass large fortunes and to further their political careers by staging triumphs in the city of Rome. These lavish parades of victorious legions, with the prisoners and riches they had taken, dazzled the inhabitants of the capital. And, finally, the generals, through their leadership and through the material rewards that they distributed to their armies, built up a devoted following of soldiers ready to serve in politics as well as in war. The key to political success was a victorious record as a general in distant provinces.

* Cicero, *First Part of the Speech against Gaius Verres at the First Hearing* (New York, 1928), Ch. V.

Marius and Sulla

The first general to take the Republic along the road to autocracy was Marius, a leader of the *populares*. He won military renown by suppressing a rebellion in North Africa (105 B.C.) and defeating the invading Germanic tribes (102 B.C.). Politically, Marius made two important innovations. Ignoring the law that required the lapse of ten years before a former consul might be re-elected to the consulate, Marius secured his own re-election as consul on five occasions between 108 and 100 B.C.·Thus he set a precedent whereby a strong man might hold high office almost indefinitely instead of relinquishing it after a short term. Second, Marius revolutionized the method of recruitment for the army along lines projected, but never established, by the Gracchi. Since Roman soldiers had been obliged to supply their own equipment, only citizens owning a certain minimum of property had traditionally been eligible for military service. Now Marius opened the ranks of the army for the first time to the propertyless, and had the state furnish their equipment. Thus the old army of citizen-soldiers, who returned to their normal peacetime occupations after a campaign, was vanishing. In its place appeared a new force of professionals, who made the army a permanent career, and who were intensely loyal to their general and benefactor.

Marius retired from office in 100 B.C.; the full implications of the revolutionary political changes he had made did not become evident for another decade. After his retirement, the *optimates* regained power for the Senate. Continued senatorial opposition to the old Gracchan policy of extending citizenship to the non-Roman population of Italy provoked a serious uprising (91-88 B.C.). The grant of Roman citizenship settled the revolt, renewed the loyalty of Italians to Rome, and showed that the

Senate could still be reasonable when it had to be.

Meanwhile, the depredations of Mithridates in Asia Minor (88 B.C.) demanded a new military effort by Rome and produced new political complications. Marius, emerging from retirement, claimed the right to lead the Roman forces in Asia Minor. The Senate, however, assigned the post to Sulla, a younger general and a firm supporter of senatorial conservatism. The two rival generals and their soldiers and henchmen were soon fighting for control of the government in Rome. As the advantage shifted from the side of Marius to that of Sulla and back again to Marius, riots, treachery, and bloodshed increased. Marius died in 86 B.C., and two years later Sulla defeated Mithridates. The *populares* could no longer resist the triumphant Sulla and his seasoned veterans; the bloody civil war came to an end in 82 B.C.

Sulla now assumed the office of dictator (see above, p. 99) and proceeded to revise the constitution of the Republic. He curtailed the powers of the Tribal Assembly and the tribunes of the people, and endeavored to restore the Senate to its old position as the arbiter of Roman politics. In fact, however, he took another long step along the road to autocracy. He exterminated the supporters of Marius and, contrary to precedent, continued as dictator for a period far exceeding the traditional six months. The real ruler of Rome was not the Senate but Sulla with his army.

Pompey and Caesar

After Sulla's retirement (80 B.C.), the Senate soon showed its inability to govern the decadent Republic, and the pattern of arbitrary rule was resumed. The nominal issue dividing Rome into rival political camps was the old struggle between the Senate and the *populares*. But the avowed programs of Roman politicians and generals now meant almost nothing. The real issue was the attempt of opportunists and their cliques to seize absolute control of Rome.

The first of these opportunists was Pompey, a young veteran of Sulla's army, who was given an important military command by the Senate. In 70 B.C. Pompey forced the Senate to repeal Sulla's constitution and restore the tribunes and the Tribal Assembly to their old power. Next, Pompey won new glory for himself and new provinces for Rome by conquering much of Mithridates' kingdom and the decayed Seleucid Empire (66-62 B.C.). Thus Rome gained control of western Asia. The Senate, however, thoroughly alarmed by the successes of its former protégé, tried to curtail his power. Pompey countered in 60 B.C. by forming an alliance with two other generals. Rome was now dominated by a triumvirate.

The triumvirate, in turn, was to prove a stepping stone to the ultimate triumph of one of its members. This was not Pompey but Julius Caesar (102-44 B.C.), the ablest and most ambitious of Roman generals. Though professing to champion the cause of the *populares* against the Senate, Caesar had one foot in each camp; his aunt had been the wife of Marius, but his daughter married Pompey and his own family was most patrician indeed. Soon after joining the triumvirate, Caesar went off to win new military laurels in Gaul. Between 58 and 50 B.C. he conquered the whole area between the older Roman settlements in Mediterranean Gaul, the English Channel, and the Rhine River. In the course of this campaign, he invaded the island of Britain to punish the Britons for aiding the Gauls (55-54 B.C.); however, no permanent Roman conquest of Britain was attempted until the middle of the next century. Caesar shrewdly publicized his achievements by writing the *Commentaries on the Gallic Wars*, a most effective piece of straightforward factual reporting.

Backed by the enormous prestige he had won in Gaul and by loyal veteran legions, Caesar made his bid for power in 49 B.C. When the Senate ordered him to remain in his province of Gaul, Caesar defied that body by leading his forces across the River Rubicon, the southern boundary of his province. Within a few weeks he had mastered Italy. Then he crossed the Adriatic to northern Greece, where he defeated Pompey, once his colleague and son-in-law and more recently his arch-rival. To consolidate his victory in this new civil war, Caesar now traveled the length of the Mediterranean. In Egypt he became enamored of the young Ptolemaic queen, Cleopatra, who bore him a son. In Asia Minor he celebrated a victory with the terse epigram: *veni, vidi, vici* (I came, I saw, I conquered). Finally, after further victories in North Africa and Spain, Caesar returned in triumph to Rome in 45 B.C. Less than a year later he was dead, stricken down on the Ides of March, 44 B.C., by the daggers of his senatorial opponents on the floor of the Senate itself at the foot of Pompey's statue.

During his brief years of triumph, Caesar carried one-man government to a point far beyond that reached by his predecessors. Caesarism, as his system is called, required the subversion of the Republic's institutions —in particular, the system of checks and balances among the various assemblies and executive officials. He himself held the post of dictator and assumed many of the powers usually allocated to the consuls, the tribunes, and the *pontifex maximus* (high priest —the chief religious official). He enlarged the Senate to accommodate his supporters and, until the fatal Ides of March, dominated this body and the assemblies. His opponents claimed that Caesar planned to be crowned king and worshiped as a god, like some oriental despot. These charges, which have never been fully substantiated or disproved, have left a cloud of ambiguity over Caesar's ultimate intentions.

At any rate, Caesar was an enlightened despot. Adopting the findings of a Greek astronomer in Alexandria, he discarded the old awkward calendar and instituted the 365-day year with an extra day in leap years, allowing the old fifth month to be renamed "July" after himself. This Julian calendar, as corrected by Pope Gregory XIII in the sixteenth century, remains in use today. Caesar tried with considerable success to solve the basic social and economic difficulties of the Republic, particularly the overcrowding and impoverishment of Italy. Like other political generals, he rewarded his followers with grants of land, especially in the outlying provinces where new colonies of veterans were encouraged to develop self-government. Since slaves, brought back as prisoners of war, were throwing free men out of work, he strove to limit the number of slaves. He made generous gifts to the Roman citizenry from his own private fortune and then sharply reduced the number of citizens eligible for the dole of grain first instituted by the Gracchi. This curtailment of relief required the creation of new jobs for the unemployed. At the time of his death, Caesar was projecting an impressive series of public works such as flood control along the Tiber, a trans-Apennine highway, and a canal through the Isthmus of Corinth in Greece. The rank and file of the Roman population seem to have regarded Caesar as a great benefactor, the restorer of order and prosperity.

The End of the Republic

Caesarism, therefore, did not die on the Ides of March. After Caesar's death, his blueprint served a new triumvirate, of which the two leading members were Octavian and Mark Antony. Octavian, young and precocious, was the grand-nephew, the adopted son, and the heir of Caesar; Antony was Caesar's most trusted lieutenant and the husband of Octavian's sister, Octavia. In a new civil war this second triumvirate soon routed the forces of its senatorial opponents led by Brutus, one of Caesar's assassins. Then the rivalry between Octavian and Antony broke up the triumvirate. Antony, deserting Octavia, withdrew to Egypt and the still alluring and ambitious Cleopatra; his followers, however, deserted to Octavian. In 30 B.C., utterly defeated by Octavian, Antony and Cleopatra committed suicide. A great turning point had been reached: Egypt at last became a Roman possession; Octavian gained sole mastery of Rome; and the Republic, so long on its death-bed, finally expired.

IV: The First Two Centuries of the Roman Empire (27 B.C.-180 A.D.)

Augustus (Octavian)
27 B.C.-14 A.D.

In 27 B.C., Octavian began the political transformation of Rome from a republican city-state to a system better suited to the needs of a farflung empire. The goal of his program was to preserve republican forms but to strengthen the authority of the government on the pattern of Caesarism. So .Octavian, who called himself "the restorer of the Roman Republic," was in fact the founder of the Roman Empire.

Playing the part of a good republican, Octavian avoided all ostentation. His house

A contemporary marble bust of Augustus (27 B.C. to 14 A.D.) as a youth.

in Rome was by no means the largest or the most sumptuous. He had his children learn the simple domestic arts of weaving and spinning, though it was unlikely that they would ever have to turn these accomplishments to practical account. He ate very moderately at official banquets to avoid any suggestion of vulgar capacity. And he claimed to prefer the innocuous republican title of "First Citizen" (*Princeps*) to his more grandiose title—"Revered Emperor and Son of the Godlike Caesar." But the latter title provided the names by which both the office and its first incumbent are known in history—Emperor, from *imperator*, meaning commander-in-chief; and Augustus, meaning revered.

The system of government set up by Augustus is often called the "dyarchy": that is, rule by two supreme authorities—himself and the Senate. In fact, however, the dyarchy came close to being the monarchy of Augustus. He reorganized the Senate, allowing it to retain all its old prestige but filling it with his friends and supporters. He gave the Senate rights of patronage in filling high government offices but deprived it of control over the two strongest levers in politics, the army and the tax-collecting power. Augustan government may be termed a partnership of Emperor and Senate, but the Emperor was the dominant partner and the Senate usually his docile servant.

Augustus showed less tenderness toward the other old republican institutions. Like Caesar before him, he himself assumed many of the prerogatives of consul and Tribune of the People, offices that now lost their former significance. He allowed the Centuriate and Tribal Assemblies to continue but only as powerless bodies.

The strength of Augustus derived not only from his firm grasp on the reins of government but also from his wealth and his command of the army. For all his simplicity of manner, Augustus was the richest man in Rome. He received a large inheritance from Caesar and added to it the spoils of his military campaigns and the fortunes that rich Romans bequeathed to him in a rather astonishing display of civic spirit. Augustus employed his fortune both for the public welfare and for his own political advantage. When he came to power, the tax machinery had broken down, and Rome was nearly bankrupt. He personally paid for soldiers' pensions and the dole of bread in Rome. He also financed the repair of Rome's water supply and the construction of handsome new public buildings in the capital, claiming that he had found Rome a city of brick and had left it a city of marble.

Augustus made a series of important innovations in the army. He ended the wasteful and politically dangerous practice of allowing rival independent generals to raise improvised armies. As the single commander-in-chief of all the Roman forces, he could discipline swiftly any would-be Caesar among the generals. Instead of the old practice of rushing troops out to provinces each time a threat arose, he stationed legions permanently in the frontier provinces to provide a ready defense against attack. And he instituted a small permanent navy—a kind of coast guard—to curb the pirates who had preyed on Mediterranean commerce at will during the last decades of the Republic.

In administration, too, Augustus ended the old hit-or-miss methods. Honest and able men replaced the corrupt officials of the decadent Republic. In filling public offices Augustus wisely made appointments not only from the protégés of the Senate but also from the *equites*, at last giving this important business class its political due and eliminating a source of social friction. Augustus also reformed and standardized taxes. Though there were many separate levies on real estate, salt, sales, imports, and a dozen other items, the total burden on the average individual was not unduly heavy. It has been estimated that the ordinary farmer, for instance, paid taxes amounting to about 10 per cent of the value of the crops he produced. The collection of taxes was now a state function, no longer the private business of grafting and extortionate tax-farmers.

Almost every policy of Augustus enlisted widespread support from his subjects. A century later, the reasons for his success were admirably summarized by the historian Tacitus, one of the relatively few Romans to regret the passing of the Republic and to take a critical view of Augustus:

He first conciliated the army by gratuities, the populace by cheapened corn [grain], the world by the amenities of peace, then step by step began to make his ascent and to unite in his own person the functions of the senate, the magistracy, and the legislature. Opposition there was none: the boldest spirits had succumbed on stricken fields or by proscription-lists; while the rest of the nobility found a cheerful acceptance of slavery the smoothest road to wealth and office, and, as they had thriven on revolution, stood now for the new order and safety in preference to the old order and adventure. Nor was the state of affairs unpopular in the provinces, where administration by the Senate and People had been discredited by the feuds of the magnates and the greed of the officials. . . .°

What Tacitus imputed to the nobility also applied to the great majority of the population: the Romans accepted "the new order and safety in preference to the old order and adventure." To obtain safety, they willingly sacrificed many of their old republican institutions. The price was high, but so was the Augustan achievement. At home there was no more civil war. The security of the provinces was broken only by a few frontier incidents, notably the defeat suffered in the Teutoburger Forest of northwestern Germany (9 A.D.) when the Germans under Herman (or Arminius) drove the Roman legions back westward to the Rhine. Occasional setbacks like this did not seriously mar the record of Augustus. His reign marked the beginning of the *Pax Romana,* the Roman Peace which lasted for two centuries (27 B.C.-180 A.D.), perhaps the longest span without a major war in the history of our western civilization.

The Successors of Augustus to 180 A.D.

The lasting qualities of the Augustan administrative revolution were impressively demonstrated by the events of the half-century after his death. The four emperors who followed him were quite unworthy successors and provoked crisis upon crisis. Yet the Empire weathered the storm, with relatively little of the disruption that had characterized comparable crises during the final century of the Republic.

The first successor, Tiberius (14-37), who was both the stepson and son-in-law of Augustus, had a remarkable talent for making himself unpopular. He finally retreated to the Isle of Capri for refuge from

° Tacitus, *Annals,* J. Jackson, trans. (New York, 1931), Bk. I, ii.

Rome and from the enemies who had unnerved him. Caligula (37-41), the grand-nephew of Tiberius, went insane and was assassinated. Claudius (41-54), the uncle of Caligula, and a fairly competent emperor, was fed poisonous mushrooms by his ambitious wife, who was scheming to secure the imperial throne for Nero, her son by a previous marriage. Nero (54-68), who murdered his mother, his wife, and his brother, was the worst of the lot. There is a grain of truth in the old saying that Nero fiddled while Rome burned. Nero's insistence on participating in musical contests and in theatrical performances scandalized the Romans, who thought this behavior beneath the dignity of an emperor. Contrary to the popular belief in Rome, however, Nero did not start the fire that devastated a large part of the city (64). In order to divert attention from himself, he put the blame on the Christians, whom he had slaughtered by the hundreds.

Through these hectic decades disorder at first infected only the summit of the government; further down, the administrative machinery had been so well oiled by Augustus that it kept on running smoothly. The misrule of Nero, however, finally provoked an army revolt and a civil war that led to the Emperor's suicide (68), and the transfer of the imperial office away from the dynasty of Augustus. The new emperor, Vespasian (69-79), an energetic soldier, soon re-established good government. He was followed by his two sons, the younger of whom, Domitian, ruled so brutally that he was assassinated (96). Thus another attempt to place the inheritance of the imperial office on a dynastic basis had failed.

The new emperor, Nerva (96-98), an astute old lawyer, at last solved the problem of succession and evolved a formula for a constant supply of capable emperors. He adopted as his son a man of proved talent and loyalty; the adopted son, on becoming emperor, repeated the process. This ingenious adoptive system made ability rather than heredity the decisive factor in selecting men for the imperial office. It accounted for four of the ablest emperors—Trajan (98-117), Hadrian (117-138), Antoninus Pius (138-161), and Marcus Aurelius (161-180).

From Tiberius through Marcus Aurelius, the emperors tampered little with the fundamentals of Augustan government. Following the example of Augustus, they kept in their own hands control over the army, the finances, and the bureaucracy. They did, however, introduce the significant new practice of emperor-worship. In theory, this was the worship not of the reigning emperor but of such of his predecessors as the Senate selected for deification. In practice, however, the Senate deified all the emperors except the most worthless, like Caligula, Nero, and Domitian. In the provinces of the East, long accustomed to equating emperors with gods, Augustus and others were venerated while they still lived. And in Rome itself, by the second century A.D., the reigning emperor was becoming surrounded by the kind of ceremonial easterners devoted to a god-king. Emperor-worship was, of course, basically more political than religious. It was a solemn patriotic act, expected of all Romans just as all Americans today salute the flag and sing the "Star-Spangled Banner."

The Provinces of the Empire

The Romans who participated in this cult of emperor-worship lived throughout a vast empire. Its expansion had continued under Augustus and during the first century A.D., reaching its peak in the next century. A good way to bring to life the sweep and variety of these territories is to call the roll of the provinces outside Italy at the height of Roman dominion in the second century A.D.

The Celtic-populated areas of western Europe were organized into thirteen provinces. There were two in Britain (Britannia), conquered under Claudius; Roman power extended over most of present-day England, as far north as the walls built by Hadrian and Antoninus to protect the border from raids by the hostile Scots. Gaul (Gallia) included six provinces, reaching north and east to the Rhine and taking in not only present-day France, Belgium, and Luxembourg but also the southern Netherlands and bits of Germany and Switzerland. The three provinces of Spain (Hispania) occupied the whole Iberian Peninsula. And

An early provincial monument of the Empire. The "Maison Carrée," a Roman temple at Nîmes, France, completed in 16 B.C.

the Alpine provinces of Raetia and Noricum roughly corresponded to today's Switzerland and Austria plus the southern fringe of Germany. All southeastern Europe to the south of the Danube River was under the domination of Rome. Eight provinces stretched from Pannonia, in modern Hungary, down to Thrace, Macedonia, and Greece.

Thus, the Rhine and Danube rivers, and a wall joining the two, formed the Roman frontier in Europe. The Roman attempt to push east of the Rhine was checked by Arminius and his Germans in 9 A.D. A century later, under Trajan, Roman forces did penetrate beyond the lower Danube to found the province of Dacia in the area of modern Rumania.

In Africa, Rome ruled the whole Mediterranean coast and its hinterland—from west to east, Mauretania (the land of the Moors, Morocco), then Numidia (in present-day Algeria), then the province of Africa around ancient Carthage and modern Tunis, then Cyrenaica (today in eastern Libya) and Egypt. In the Near East, Rome set up temporary provinces in Armenia and Mesopotamia and permanently organized an area reaching to the upper Euphrates River and the western edge of the Arabian desert. It was divided into about a dozen provinces, beginning with Asia proper on the eastern shore of the Aegean and then proceeding east and south through Bithynia, Galatia, Cappadocia, Cilicia, and other provinces, to Syria, Palestine, and the triangular province of Arabia jutting between the northern arms of the Red Sea.

The Administration of the Empire

This immense empire covered an equally immense range of human beings and human cultures, from the highly civilized Greeks and Egyptians to the near-barbarians of the frontiers who, like the Celts of northern Britain, sometimes still painted their bodies blue. Since no single pattern of government would have fitted all these diverse peoples, the imperial administration adjusted its policies to local needs and local customs. Along the borders, especially along the Rhine and the Danube where the Germans and other tribes threatened, Rome maintained a military administration. Some of the military camps became permanent towns as the soldiers married and settled down; a few of them long outlived the Roman Empire to become such great cities as Cologne and Vienna.

In the eastern parts of the Empire, with one exception, the emperors did not greatly alter the administration that they inherited from the Hellenistic states. Autocratic Roman governors ruled Egypt and other provinces accustomed to autocracy, and Greek city-states kept some of their traditional rights of self-government. North Africa was divided between partly autonomous city-states, some of them continuations of old Phoenician centers, and the enormous rural estates owned by the emperors or by wealthy Roman capitalists. The exception was Palestine, where Roman efforts to maintain a satellite kingdom met stubborn opposition from the Jews. The more the Romans intervened in Jewish life, the more the Jews rebelled, and the more blood was shed on both sides. Finally, in 70 A.D., after a Roman siege of Jerusalem lasting four years, the remnant of the old Jewish state was destroyed. The results were the persecution of Judaism as a religion and the gradual dispersion of the Jews abroad.

The provinces in Gaul, Spain, and elsewhere in the West, on the other hand, had few ancient cities and political traditions, so that the institution of the city and the machinery of local government were imported from Rome. Each province was subdivided into small units enjoying considerable autonomy in local affairs. These

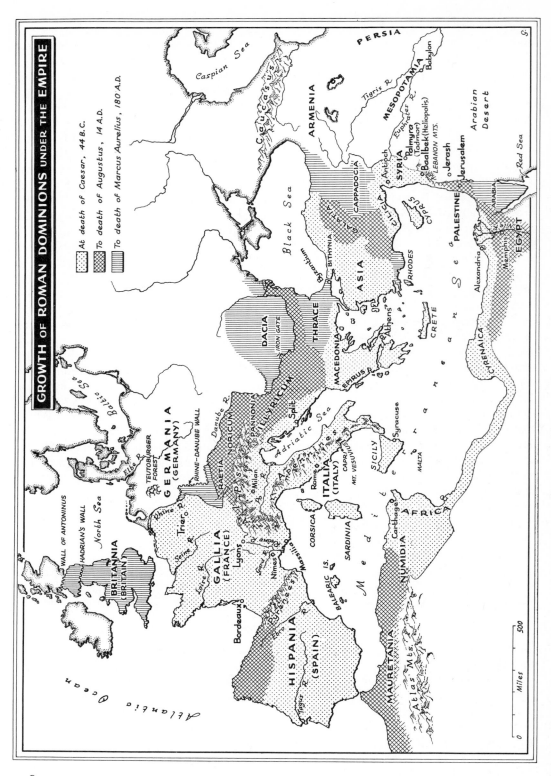

GROWTH OF ROMAN DOMINIONS UNDER THE EMPIRE

At death of Caesar, 44 B.C.
To death of Augustus, 14 A.D.
To death of Marcus Aurelius, 180 A.D.

small units were *civitates* (the plural of the Latin, *civitas*, city-state). Like the early Roman Republic, the *civitates* were small in area and were ruled by local equivalents of the old republican Senate and assemblies. A *curia* (council) dominated by the large landholders of the neighborhood ran the affairs of the typical *civitas*. Such important modern cities as Bordeaux and Lyons in France and Trier in western Germany trace their history back to Roman *civitates*.

Large areas of the Empire, particularly in the West, therefore constituted a federation of partially autonomous city-states under the watchful eye of the imperial regime at Rome. The *civitates* enjoyed their privileges so long as they paid their taxes, supplied army recruits, and observed the ceremonies of emperor-worship demanded by the central government in Rome. If a *civitas* failed in its duties, then the provincial governors or the emperor himself would intervene to set matters right. Ultimate sovereignty always rested with Rome, yet it was exercised with discrimination. The central government did not attempt to settle in the capital all the myriad local problems that arose hundreds or thousands of miles away. But this intelligent policy would never have succeeded without the development of an efficient civil service to administer it. One of the greatest achievements of the Empire was its efficient bureaucracy, no longer recruited chiefly from Rome herself as in the days of the Republic, but drawn from the best talents available throughout the Empire, especially in its western provinces.

Thus the Roman Empire of the first two centuries escaped in part the curse of bigness and unwieldiness. It struck a happy balance between centralization and decentralization, between unity and diversity. The Empire was distinctively Roman and at the same time cosmopolitan and heterogeneous. Within it diverse types of government flourished, diverse religions, and diverse cultures. It did not always satisfy all its subjects: the Egyptians, the Jews, and, as the next chapter will show, the Christians attempted rebellions. Nevertheless, such rebellions were the exception, not the rule. The forces that held the Empire together were the imperial civil service, the common practice of emperor-worship, a common coinage, common languages—Latin in the western provinces, Greek in the eastern—and a common regard for the benefits of the Roman law and the *Pax Romana*. To this list was added in 212 a common Roman citizenship bestowed on all provincials except the lowest class by the Emperor Caracalla. No prouder statement could be made from Britain to Egypt, from Mauretania to Pannonia, than the simple affirmation, "*Civis Romanus sum*"—"I am a Roman citizen."

V: Roman Civilization

Civis Romanus sum—the statement bears the stamp of the utilitarian political genius that marks the Roman "style." The Romans did not contribute a great deal that was new in the realm of art, drama, or philosophy; here they largely studied, imitated, and preserved the achievements of the Greeks. But in military organization, in government, in law, and in engineering the Romans stood head and shoulders above the other peoples of ancient times. The modern world owes a great debt to Rome's experts in the practical arts. Our survey of that debt begins with Roman law.

Law

Roman law had the merit of flexibility, of constant adjustment to new conditions. Its early statement in the Twelve Tables of the fifth century B.C. did not meet the requirements of an expanding empire. The Twelve Tables were superseded not by another formal code, which would soon have become obsolete also, but by a more complex accumulation of legal precepts from a variety of sources. This steady process of growth in the centuries of the later Republic and the *Pax Romana* produced an ever-changing law, to which contributions were made by the votes of the Senate and assemblies, the decrees of emperors, the decisions of praetors and other judges, the philosophy of the Stoics, and the opinions of expert lawyers. The great formal codifications embodying all these contributions came only after the decline of the Empire; the most famous was that of the eastern Emperor Justinian in the sixth century (see Chapter VI).

Expert lawyers were constantly consulted by the judges, who often had an inferior knowledge and understanding of the law. Under the Republic, these lawyers were private citizens; under the Empire, the state made them officials called *jurisconsults* (from the Latin, *iuris consulti—* those skilled in the law). Ulpian, a great jurisconsult of the early third century A.D., gave a splendid definition of the ideals of his profession when he wrote that

law is the art of the good and the fair. Of this art we may deservedly be called the priests; we cherish justice and profess the knowledge of the good and the fair, separating the fair from the unfair, discriminating between the permitted and the forbidden, desiring to make men good, not only by the fear of penalties, but also by the incentives of rewards, affecting, if I mistake not, a true and not a simulated philosophy.°

° N. Lewis and M. Reinhold, *Roman Civilization* (New York, 1955), II, 534.

The jurisconsults urged that the law always be adapted to the particular needs of particular cases, and in their concern for "the good and the fair" they fostered the growth of equity, the deciding of cases according to the spirit rather than the letter of the law. The liberal and humane precepts of the jurisconsults were fortified by the philosophy of the Stoics (see Chapter II), who taught that above the laws created by specific states there was a higher law—"natural law," they called it—divinely inspired, applying to all men in all states by virtue of their humanity.

Roman legal practice had its shortcomings. The judges, as we have already noted, had indifferent training; arbitrary emperors sometimes flouted the ideals of natural law and imposed barbarous and capricious punishments; and, as we shall find in medieval Europe, the Roman law could be used to exalt the authority of the state over the individual. On balance, however, the virtues of the Roman law far outweighed its defects. Though it stressed the majesty of the state, it also stressed the rights of its citizens. Though it recognized the institution of slavery (as did almost every other ancient civilization), it also afforded slaves legal redress against undue exploitation by a cruel master. The subject peoples of the Empire were not forced to adopt the law of Rome; they could abide by their own legal traditions. In cases between a citizen of Rome and the inhabitants of some outlying province, the judge did not make the use of Roman law obligatory. When the Roman law finally displaced other legal systems and was universally applied throughout the Empire, it won out principally on the basis of its own merits.

The law of Rome made a deep and permanent impression upon later civilizations. It has shaped to a greater or less degree the canon law of the Roman Catholic Church and the legal systems of most European countries. Its influence has been

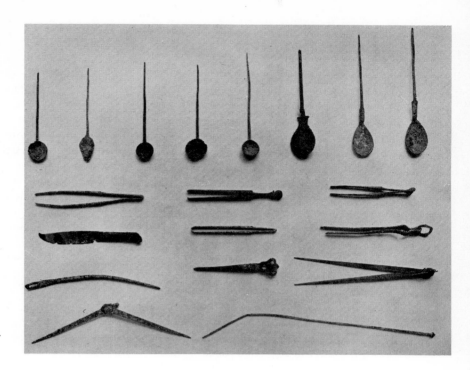

Roman surgical instruments.

particularly pervasive in the Latin nations of Italy, France, Spain, and Portugal, and in the states of Latin America. In North America the Roman civil law survives in the State of Louisiana and in the Province of Quebec, which were once ruled by France. The laws of the English-speaking countries, of course, derive mainly from the common law of medieval England rather than from the Roman law. But they, too, have shared in the enduring ideals of equity and natural law bequeathed by Rome.

Science and Engineering

The practical bent of the Romans was particularly evident in science. Although they made few new scientific discoveries, they showed both a natural curiosity and a zeal for the useful application of scientific findings. Contrary to the popular acceptance of the flatness of the earth, some learned Romans contended that the earth was spherical. It was characteristic of Roman science that this theory did not orig-

inate in Rome; it had been advanced at Alexandria in the third century B.C. by Eratosthenes. But it was also characteristic that Roman scientists observed natural facts supporting this hypothesis. Pliny the Elder, during the first century of the Empire, noted that when a ship was approaching the shore, first the tips of the masts, then the sails, and finally the hull came into view. This, Pliny argued, was a convincing demonstration that the earth had a curved surface. Pliny died of his curiosity, for he got too close to the hot lava while observing the great eruption of Vesuvius in 79 A.D.

Rome made substantial advances in surgery and public hygiene. Surgeons devised ingenious forceps and tweezers and other instruments for special operations. They extracted goiters, tonsils, and stones, apparently with considerable success. In the Caesarean operation (said to have been performed first at the birth of Julius Caesar) they developed a method for delivering babies who could not be born in the normal way. Surgeons were regularly attached to the Roman legions, and hospitals first appeared as establishments for the treatment of sick and wounded Roman soldiers. Cities then set up hospitals for civilians, the first public institutions of the sort in the history of Europe.

The Romans maintained high sanitary standards, the highest, indeed, known in Europe until the nineteenth century. They installed latrines (sometimes made of marble) and extensive systems of sewers and drainage ditches. The government went to great trouble and expense to provide cities with a pure and abundant water supply. A dozen aqueducts served Rome, conveying spring-water from the hills to the capital. These amenities were not restricted to Rome itself; elaborate pipes have been found in remote provincial villas. The most impressive aqueduct extant today is the Pont du Gard in southern France, a triple-tiered, arched bridge, 900 feet long and 160 feet high, which carried the water supply for the city of Nîmes over the Gard River. Many provincial cities had magnificent bathhouses, for the Romans, who were enthusiastic bathers, preferred the heated waters of indoor pools.

Roman progress in hygiene and medicine, however, was not uniform. For many ailments the Romans, like other peoples of the ancient world, relied on the useless prescriptions of quacks. For example, Cato (see above, p. 104) offered two remedies for dislocated joints: one relied on repeating a meaningless formula; the other recommended the use of cabbage, which was also Cato's panacea for dysentery, indigestion, drunkenness, ulcers, and warts. But, as a balance to this nonsense, there was the great work of Galen (131-201 A.D.), a Greek physician from Asia Minor who served several emperors and compiled a vast medical encyclopedia. Scholarly compilations of this kind were almost commonplace in the Greek-speaking provinces of the Empire. To cite only one instance, Galen's contemporary, Ptolemy of Alexandria, wrote excellent summations of ancient geographical and astronomical knowledge. Naturally, both Galen and Ptolemy made errors, but their prestige was so great that they were to be regarded as virtually infallible authorities right down to the beginning of modern times.

The Romans merited a still higher reputation for their achievements in engineering. They not only excelled in sanitary en-

The Pont du Gard. Roman aqueduct built early in the first century A.D. at Nîmes, France.

Ruins of the Temple of Jupiter at Baalbek, Lebanon.

gineering but also devised a formula for making a kind of concrete from sand, lime, silica, stone, and water. They combined concrete and large stones in the construction of roads and bridges which were so well designed and so well built that a few of them are still in service today. Roman roads, in fact, were seldom equaled until the development of macadam and other hard surfacing materials at the close of the eighteenth century. The best of Roman roads were stone-paved, all-weather highways, ten to twenty-five feet wide, with foundations several feet deep. They reached throughout the Empire and were designed, above all, to accelerate the movement of troops and military supplies. Travel overland became by ancient standards remarkably swift, safe, and easy, thanks in part also to the Roman practice of providing simple diagrammatic road maps.

The Fine Arts

The architecture of these great engineers naturally differed from that of the Greeks. Where the Greeks had devoted their highest skills to building temples, the Romans often turned theirs to more secular structures. Where the Greeks had made the column the basis of construction, the Romans frequently used the arch, though they also employed columns with ornate Corinthian capitals. The round arch, borrowed from the Etruscans, may be found everywhere in Roman remains—in bridges, baths, aqueducts, amphitheaters, and the freestanding triumphal arches honoring the conquests of victorious emperors. From the arch, the Romans developed the barrel vault, really a continuous series of arches like the roof of a tunnel, and capable of roofing over fairly large areas. The Romans were also experts in the use of the dome. The dome surmounting the Pantheon, erected in Rome to honor the supposedly divine ancestors of Augustus and still standing today in the heart of the city, is 142 feet in diameter, and stands 142 feet above the ground.

The Romans built on a large scale, both at home and abroad. In Rome the great amphitheater, the Colosseum, was indeed a colossal structure, a quarter of a mile in circumference, which could hold at least 45,000 spectators at gladiatorial contests. The baths built by the Emperor Caracalla accommodated thousands of bathers (in our own century they supplied the basic plan for the Pennsylvania Station in New York City, and the ruins of the baths themselves are still used for performances of opera on the grand scale). On the eastern shore of the Adriatic, the Emperor Diocletian erected a palace so vast that its ruins enclose the center of the modern Yugoslav city of Split. At Baalbek, high in a valley of Lebanon, six giant columns of the temple built for Jupiter still stand, each 65 feet high; the stone was quarried in Egypt, brought down the Nile and over the eastern Mediterranean, then hauled, apparently on greased runways, across a mile-high pass in Mount Lebanon! Few things Roman are more impressive and evocative than the remains that may still be seen today in remote corners of the Middle East. At Jerash in northern Jordan, which was only an ordinary provincial town, there are two theaters, a lovely elliptical forum, and a colonnaded main street, its paving still deeply scarred by the traffic of Roman carts and wagons. In the midst of the Syrian desert, by a pumping station on the oil pipeline from Iraq, are the long colonnades and ruined temples of Roman Palmyra. And in southwestern Iran there still stand the arches of a bridge across the Karun River built in the third century by Roman soldiers taken prisoner by a Persian

emperor. In a very literal sense, the Romans were indeed builders of empire.

In sculpture, the Romans at their best carried on the tradition of realism which they had inherited from the Hellenistic world. An appreciation of the values of publicity led the emperors to erect triumphal arches and busts and statues of themselves in Roman cities. The sculptors sometimes created works of notable realism, as in the bust of the Emperor Vespasian, which perfectly conveyed his earthy, soldierly intelligence. Yet they more often idealized and glorified their imperial subjects in an insipid fashion, as in the statues that make Augustus look less like an emperor than like the Roman counterpart of a model for men's clothing. On the whole, Roman artists seemed more at home in mosaics, elaborate designs of colored stones used generally to decorate the floors of public and private buildings. Many of the mosaics are pornographic in subject and

Bust of Vespasian, Emperor of Rome, 69-79 A.D.

CHAPTER III

Mosaic at Ostia, the seaport of Rome. A commercial sign for a ship-builder.

crude in execution. But the best of them have great vitality and charm and form an appropriate curtain-riser to the dramatic Byzantine achievement in the same medium (see Chapter VI).

Religion and Philosophy

The Roman contribution in religion and philosophy, by contrast, represents an end, not a beginning. Here the imitative quality of the Romans is most conspicuous. They adopted and transmitted the intellectual and spiritual heritage of Greece and the East, but added very little of their own. The early Romans had a religion natural to a small city-state inhabited by farmers. They took great stock in amulets and other charms; they worshiped the spirits that governed the household (the *lares* and *penates*) and those that ruled the springs, the fields, and other landmarks of the countryside.

The increasing wealth and complexity of the Roman world and its expanding contacts with the Greeks worked a change. The local agrarian spirits evolved into gods and goddesses identified with the Greek Olympians. The Greek Zeus became the Roman Jupiter; the Greek Hera, the Roman Juno; Poseidon, Neptune; Ares, Mars; Hephaestus, Vulcan; Aphrodite, Venus; Athena, Minerva; and so on. Transplantation, however, drained this polytheism of its vitality. Rome had no religious observances comparable in spontaneity, dignity, and mass participation with the Olympic games and the Athenian dramatic festivals. The individual Roman took little part in the ceremonies of worship; he left them to the official caste of priests, headed by the *pontifex maximus,* who performed the rites required for the cult of the Greco-Roman gods.

Under the later Republic and the Empire, Hellenistic philosophy and eastern mystery religions partly filled the vacuum left by the decay of the old polytheism. The intellectuals of Rome studied the teachings of the Epicurean and Stoic schools of Alexandria (see Chapter II). The principal Roman disciple of Epicurus was Lucretius (*c.* 95-55 B.C.), whose long philosophical poem, *De Rerum Natura* (On the Nature of Things), admirably states the

Epicurean ideal of the simple, well-balanced life:

> Can you not understand that Nature craves
> Nothing more for herself but this, that pain
> Be absent from the body, and that the mind,
> Released from care and terror, should enjoy
> The pleasures of the senses? Now we see
> That for the body's nature but few things
> Are indispensable, such things alone
> As dispel pain. Though sometimes luxuries
> May to our satisfaction minister
> Many delights, yet Nature for her part
> Will feel no lack, because about the halls
> There stand no golden images of youths
> In their right hands lifting fiery torches,
> That light may be supplied to nightly
>   banquets. . . .
>
> . . . Nor will hot fevers quit your body
> Any the sooner if you toss your limbs
> Beneath figured embroideries and sheets
> Of blushing purple, than if you must lie
> Under a poor man's coverlet. And so,
> Since useless to our body are hoarded wealth,
> Noble birth and the glory of regal power,
> We must believe moreover that such things
> Are of no profit likewise to the mind. . . .*

Lucretius offers more than a refutation of the mistaken notion that Epicureanism is mere hedonistic self-indulgence. He presents a thoroughgoing materialistic explanation of human life, divorced from any religious interpretation. The human body and the human soul, like everything else in the universe, represent temporary combinations of atoms. When death comes, the atoms separate and scatter; body and soul alike simply dissolve and can no longer feel anything. Death should not be feared, he concludes; it is an endless, dreamless sleep.

> So when we shall be no more,
> When body and soul, out of which we are
>   formed
> Into one being, shall have been torn apart,
> 'Tis plain nothing whatever shall have power
> To befall us, who shall then be no more,
> Or stir our feeling, no, not if earth with sea
> In ruin shall be mingled, and sea with sky.†

The Epicurean Lucretius, with his counsels of moderation and resignation, had much in common with the Roman Stoics. Yet the intellectual foundations of the two philosophies diverged entirely. For the Epicurean, man was transitory matter like the other animals of the universe; for the Stoic, he was a being apart, who should strive to be worthy of the divine elements in his soul. Stoicism proved to be more congenial to the temper of the Roman intellectuals during the last days of the Republic and the centuries of the *Pax Romana*. Among its distinguished exponents were the lawyer Cicero; Epictetus, the philosopher who was also a slave; Seneca, the wealthy dramatist and statesman; and the Emperor Marcus Aurelius, who scribbled down his *Meditations* in Greek on his military campaigns. Marcus Aurelius, in particular, faithfully practiced the Stoic ideal in his life of private virtue and of unflagging public service. He insisted that men must always do their duty:

> At daybreak, when loth to rise, have this thought read in thy mind: 'I am rising for a man's work.' Am I then still peevish that I am going to do that for which I was born and for the sake of which I came into the world? Or was I made for this, that I should nuzzle under the bed-clothes and keep myself warm? 'But this is pleasanter.' Hast thou then been made for pleasure . . . ? Consider each little plant, each tiny bird, the ant, the spider, the bee, how they go about their own work and do each his part for the building up of an orderly Universe. Does *thou* then refuse to do the work of a man? . . . 'But some rest, too, is necessary.' I do not deny it. Howbeit nature has set limits to this, and no less so to eating and drinking.*

Time and again Marcus Aurelius expounded the Stoic attitude toward oneself and one's fellows:

> . . . Above all, when thou findest fault with a man for faithlessness and ingratitude, turn

---

* Lucretius, *De Rerum Natura*, R. C. Trevelyan, trans. (Cambridge, England, 1937), 43–44.
  † *Ibid.*, 118.

* *The Communings with Himself of Marcus Aurelius Antoninus,* C. R. Haines, trans. (New York, 1924), 99.

thy thought to thyself. . . . For when thou hast done a kindness, what more wouldst thou have? Is not this enough that thou hast done something in accordance with thy nature? Seekest thou a recompense for it? As though the eye should claim a guerdon for seeing, or the feet for walking! For just as these latter were made for their special work, and by carrying this out according to their individual constitution they come fully into their own, so also man, formed as he is by nature for benefitting others, when he has acted as benefactor for the general weal, has done what he was constituted for, and has what is his.°

Neither Stoicism nor Epicureanism won a large popular following; both were too intellectual, too philosophical in outlook. The ordinary man wanted a religion of hope, not of resignation; he wanted to be able to identify himself with a deity who might improve a man's condition in the next world if not in this one. Christianity, in the long run, answered this need most successfully. But until Christianity came to predominate in the Roman world, during the last centuries of the Empire, it faced the competition of other mystery religions. Its triumph over the cults of Isis and Mithra will be examined in the next chapter.

Literature

Many Roman authors, like Roman artists and philosophers, copied Greek models; few writers felt the religious or speculative compulsion that drove the Greeks in search of final answers to the great questions. Latin literature, in consequence, lacks the creative excitement and some of the grandeur of the Greek; it shares in the earthbound qualities that made Rome such a practical success. Yet it also occupies a secure position at the very core of our classical heritage. Partly because Latin became the official language of the Roman Catholic Church, partly because the language itself is easier than Greek for west-

erners, and partly because the Roman writers themselves are so sensible and sometimes so obvious, the total influence of Latin literature over the centuries has probably surpassed that of Greek.

The flowering of Latin literature began during the last decades of the Republic, with the prose writings of Cicero and Caesar and the poetry of Lucretius. Then came its "Golden Age," the era of Vergil, Horace, and Ovid, also termed the "Augustan Age" because it largely coincided with the reign of the first emperor. The "Silver Age" followed, lasting through the early part of the second century A.D., with some decline in quality but with such notable writers as Juvenal, Tacitus, Pliny the Elder, and his nephew, Pliny the Younger.

Today the works of Caesar and Cicero are generally included in the curriculum wherever Latin is still studied. Caesar used the simple, straightforward writing of the reporter. Everyone is familiar with the opening words of his *Commentaries on the Gallic Wars*—"All Gaul is divided into three parts." They are typical of Caesar's way of taking the reader right into the subject without introductory fanfare. Cicero (106-43 B.C.) employed a richer style, of which the passage quoted earlier in this chapter (see page 109) furnishes a good sample. A lifelong student of philosophy and government and a practicing politician, Cicero was above all a successful lawyer and, as his attack on Verres showed, a courageous one, too. His voluminous letters, speeches, and essays tend to have the quality of special pleading that one associates with arguing a case; but they are always well organized, eloquent, and clear. Later writers in search of an effective prose style paid Cicero the high compliment of imitation.

Vergil (70-19 B.C.), the greatest of the Augustan writers, served as the poet laureate of the emperor. His immediate patron, Maecenas, was a rich and cultivated associate of Augustus, the imperial minister for cultural affairs, so to speak; his name is

---

° *Ibid.*, 259.

still sometimes applied to a wealthy patron of arts and letters. Vergil wrote on subjects close to the interests of Maecenas and Augustus. He drew on his own first-hand knowledge of farming for the *Georgics,* a poetic description of stock-raising, bee-keeping, and other homely agrarian tasks. By praising agriculture, Vergil enlisted in Augustus' campaign to make the farmer once again the foundation of Roman society. Vergil embellished his masterpiece, the *Aeneid,* with predictions of the glorious future in store for the new city under the descendants of Aeneas, of whom the greatest would be, of course, Augustus.

Yet Vergil was a great deal more than a propagandist and perhaps deserves to be called the Roman Homer. He really believed in the splendors of agriculture and Rome's political mission. The high patriotic tone sustained throughout the *Aeneid* is evident in the famous opening verses of the epic:

> I tell about war and the hero who first from Troy's frontier,
> Displaced by destiny, came to the Lavinian shores,
> To Italy—a man much travailed on sea and land
> By the powers above, because of the brooding anger of Juno,
> Suffering much in war until he could found a city
> And march his gods into Latium, whence rose the Latin race,
> The royal line of Alba and the high walls of Rome.°

Horace (65-8 B.C.), the second of the great Augustan poets, was also befriended by Maecenas, who endowed him with a comfortable country estate. Horace, too, wrote on the favorite themes of Augustus, moderation and the simple rural life, and expressed them in finely wrought Latin verses. The great worldling among the Augustans was Ovid (43 B.C.-17 A.D.), who

———
° *The Aeneid of Vergil,* C. Day Lewis, trans. (Garden City, 1953), 13.

was very much concerned with pleasures and very little with ethics. No favorite of Augustus, Ovid was eventually exiled from Rome because of a remote involvement in a scandal affecting the emperor's grand-daughter. A stern nineteenth-century critic has called Ovid's collection of poems, *The Art of Love,* "perhaps the most immoral and demoralizing work ever written, at least in ancient times, by a man of genius." The critic exaggerates, yet Ovid's light-hearted advice on the technique of seduction and his indifference to morals do make him seem far more "pagan" than Vergil or Horace.

Discontent and disillusionment, a sense that Rome had passed its prime, were the prominent themes of literature in the "Silver Age" following Augustus. The poet Juvenal, who flourished about 100 A.D., attacked in his *Satires* the shortcomings of his day. His epigrams sound a note of cynicism:

> Common sense among men of fortune is rare.
> There are few disputes in life, which do not originate with a woman.
> Why should you marry when it is easier to hang yourself?

Like Aristophanes, indeed like most great satirists, Juvenal was a moralist, deploring the passing of the old-fashioned ways. Significantly, the most famous line from his writings is *Mens sana in corpore sano*—the classical ideal of the sound mind in the sound body.

Moral and patriotic indignation is even more evident in the writings of Tacitus (*c.*55-*c.*117 A.D.), the greatest Roman historian. His celebrated *Germania* is less a history of the early Germans than an attack on contemporary Rome, for he praised the martial simplicity of the Germans extravagantly in order to point up the contrast with the effete depravity of his own times. Almost every subject Tacitus took prompted him to deliver a sermon on the virtues of Republican Rome and the vices of the Empire. His comment on the decline of Roman education is typical:

In the good old days, every man's son born in wedlock was brought up not in the chamber of some hireling nurse, but in his mother's lap, and at her knee. . . . Religiously and with the utmost delicacy she regulated not only the serious tasks of her youthful charges, but their recreations also and their games. It was in this spirit, we are told, that Cornelia, the mother of the Gracchi, directed their upbringing. . . .

Nowadays, on the other hand, our children are handed over at their birth to some silly little Greek serving-maid, with a male slave, who may be any one, to help her,—quite frequently the most worthless member of the whole establishment, incompetent for any serious service. It is from the foolish tittle-tattle of such persons that the children receive their earliest impressions, while their minds are still pliant and unformed; and there is not a soul in the whole house who cares a jot what he says or does in the presence of its lisping little lord. . . . These are the peculiar and characteristic vices of this metropolis of ours, taken on, as it seems to me, almost in the mother's womb,—the passion for play actors, and the mania for gladiatorial shows and horse-racing; and when the mind is engrossed in such occupations, what room is left over for higher pursuits? How few are to be found whose home-talk runs to any other subjects than these? What else do we overhear our younger men talking about whenever we enter their lecture-halls? And the teachers are just as bad. With them, too, such topics supply material for gossip with their classes more frequently than any others; for it is not by the strict administration of discipline, or by giving proof of their ability to teach that they get pupils together, but by pushing themselves into notice . . . by the tricks of toadyism.*

Angry, unbalanced, and didactic, Tacitus introduces us to a kind of history-writing which is very different from that of the dispassionate Thucydides but is, in its way, no less instructive.

Standard of Living

Even Tacitus would have agreed that Rome was at least a handsome city.

Here is a description of the capital as it was under Augustus:

The early Romans made but little account of the beauty of Rome, because they were occupied with other, greater and more necessary matters; whereas the later Romans, and particularly those of to-day . . . have filled the city with many beautiful structures. . . . The Campus Martius [Field of Mars] contains most of these. . . . The size of the Campus is remarkable, since it affords space at the same time and without interference, not only for the chariot-races and every other equestrian exercise, but also for all that multitude of people who exercise themselves by ball-playing, hoop-trundling, and wrestling; and all the works of art situated around the Campus Martius, and the ground, which is covered with grass throughout the year, and the crowns of those hills which are above the river and extend as far as its bed, which present to the eye the appearance of a stage-painting—all this, I say, affords a spectacle that one can hardly draw away from. And near this campus is still another campus, with colonnades round about it in very great numbers, and sacred precincts, and three theatres, and an amphitheatre, and very costly temples, in close succession to one another, giving you the impression that they are trying, as it were, to declare the rest of the city a mere accessory. . . . And again, if, on passing to the old Forum, you saw one forum after another ranged along the old one, and basilicas, and temples . . . , you would easily become oblivious to everything else outside. Such is Rome.*

Two hundred years later, when the building program of the emperors had added dozens of new temples, palaces, baths, and stadiums, Rome was more imposing still. Not only the capital but also Alexandria, Antioch, and the other large cities of the Empire presented a façade of magnificence.

Was "the grandeur that was Rome" only a façade, or did it extend far beneath the surface? To answer this question we must survey briefly some of the components that made up the Roman standard of living—the distribution of wealth, housing, food, education, the rights and privileges

---

* Tacitus, *A Dialogue on Oratory*, W. Paterson, trans. (New York, 1914), Chs. 28-29.

* Strabo, *Geography*, H. L. Jones, trans. (New York, 1917 ff.), II, 407, 409.

A street in Pompeii, lined with shops and private houses.

of ordinary men and women. During the first two centuries of the Empire, Roman society was prosperous; although the paucity of reliable statistics makes generalization risky, it was almost certainly the most prosperous era that had yet occurred in human history. The security of the *Pax Romana*, the excellent communications, the virtual absence of restrictions on trade, the sustained demand in Rome and Italy for imported food, luxury goods, and other commodities—all stimulated brisk business activity. But the profits of that activity were most unequally distributed. Like the Hellenistic world, Rome displayed striking contrasts between the wealth of the rich and the poverty of the poor.

Yet Rome must have the credit for remedying, or attempting to remedy, what seem to modern democrats some of the worst social deficiencies of antiquity. The Romans treated slaves with considerable generosity, allowing many to obtain eventual freedom and others to become tutors or to fill similar "white-collar" posts. Women, though possessing no political rights and few economic ones, otherwise enjoyed almost full equality. They were not considered to be household drudges in Rome, as they had so often been in Athens. The respected matriarch, like Cornelia the mother of the Gracchi, was a familiar personage in Roman history. By the end of the Republic, the father no longer had the right to snatch a new-born baby from the mother and order its exposure. Divorce was permitted and was resorted to more frequently, probably, than in any other period of history before the twentieth century. Many families, however, seem to have led a congenial existence, and Roman writers often praised the mutual devotion of husband and wife or of parents and children.

On the whole, the Romans were not a well-educated people; the strictures of Tacitus (see p. 129) were not completely exaggerated. Significantly, those who had the intellectual and economic wherewithal still secured their training in Athens. The schools of Rome did not match Plato's Academy or the best institutions of Hellenistic Alexandria.

When it came to creature comforts, the Romans quite surpassed their predecessors. The ruins of Pompeii show that the upper middle-class lived very comfortably, even luxuriously. Country villas, especially in the cold northern provinces, often had glass windows, water pipes, and a central heating system which conveyed hot air through tile pipes. Some, but by no means all, of these wealthy citizens were so coarse that they carried their appetite for food and wine to the point of mania, deliberately emptying the stomach after one course at a banquet in order to make room for the maximum intake of food during the next course. The peasants of the Empire enjoyed few

comforts, and the masses in the cities lived in jerry-built wooden tenements, six or seven stories high. A first-hand report on Roman real estate tells us:

The building of houses . . . goes on unceasingly in consequence of the fires and repeated sales (these last, too, going on unceasingly), and indeed the sales are intentional collapses, as it were, since the purchasers keep tearing down the houses and building new ones, one after another to suit their wishes. . . . Now Augustus Caesar concerned himself about such impairments of the city, organising for protection against fires a militia . . . whose duty it was to render assistance, . . . reducing the heights of the new buildings and forbidding that any structure on the public streets should rise higher than seventy feet.*

Despite the fire department and the building code instituted by Augustus, rickety slums continued to appear in Rome, and to burn down with depressing frequency.

The ill-housed poor of Rome often had no regular jobs. At the height of the *Pax Romana*, it is conjectured that half of the

---

* Strabo, *Geography*, II, 403, 405.

The Colosseum.

population of the capital was receiving a dole of free bread. This staggering estimate is somewhat misleading, for conditions were less severe in most other cities of the Empire, and some of the recipients of public charity in the capital undoubtedly could have afforded to buy their own flour. Even so, it is certain that a sizable fraction of the imperial population was always on relief. Although the Empire did not provide jobs for all its subjects, it did offer them all, rich and poor alike, free baths and free "circuses" in the form of chariot races and gladiatorial combats. Betting on the races, however, often took what little money the poor had, and many of the gladiators who performed in the Colosseum were killed. The Roman style was not always practical and progressive; it could also be brutal and callous.

VI: The Decline of Rome

Unsuccessful Emperors (180-284)

The *Pax Romana* and the most productive centuries of Roman civilization came to an end with the death of Marcus Aurelius in 180. The great Stoic, abandoning the practice of his predecessors, chose as his successor not an adopted son but his real son, Commodus (180-193), who had no talent for anything except chariot-racing and gladiatorial combats. His obsession with these sports swiftly lowered the prestige of the imperial office, and his neglect of his own personal safety cost him his life through assassination.

The policy of the emperors following Commodus made matters worse. Not only was there no return to the adoptive system; the emperors relied increasingly for support on the soldiers, to whom they extended more and more privileges. Now the soldiers became a specially favored caste, so powerful that they could neglect their proper military duties to intervene in politics. Political disaster resulted. During the aptly named era of military anarchy, 235-284, the army made and unmade emperors almost at will, and civil warfare became chronic. In this hectic half-century there were almost two dozen emperors, only one of whom died a natural death. The rest died fighting the peoples pressing on the frontiers of the Empire or were killed by the soldiers either for their wealth or because they were attempting to reassert control over the undisciplined army. All along the Rhine-Danube frontier the defenses sagged under increasing German pressure; the Germans raided Gaul, Britain, Spain, and other long-settled provinces; even the city of Rome had to be provided with a new defensive wall. In the East the old power of Persia revived under the vigorous Sasanid dynasty; in 259 the Persians inflicted a bitter humiliation on Rome by taking prisoner the Emperor Valerian and some of his legions.

The Reforms of Diocletian and His Successors

The military anarchy of the third century might have led to the total collapse of the Empire if a strong emperor had not appeared. The strong emperor was Diocletian (284-305), an army veteran, who began a series of drastic reforms that eventually transformed the Empire into a centralized autocracy of the eastern type. The reforms were continued by Galerius, Diocletian's lieutenant from 293 to 305 and the emperor from 305 to 311, and by the rival and co-emperor of Galerius, the famous Constantine (306-337). This whole period is somewhat confusing, and it is not always clear which policies should be attributed to Diocletian and which should be attributed to Galerius or Constantine.

Diocletian and his successors abandoned the deference to republican forms shown by Augustus and other early emperors. They destroyed the balance between centralization and decentralization, between Empire and *civitas,* wiping out the rights of self-government of the *civitates* and giving the provincial governors absolute power over local politics. During the era of military anarchy, however, the provincial governors had frequently used their right of commanding troops to raise the standard of revolt. Diocletian therefore sought to insure the loyalty of governors by pruning their military authority and by reducing the size of the average province. He more than doubled the number of provinces, raising the total to about a hundred. To provide an intermediate supervisory office between emperor and governor he instituted a dozen dioceses, each grouping several provinces, and each under a *vicarius* (vicar—that is, the emperor's deputy).

This elaborate administrative hierarchy was completed by organizational changes at the top. Diocletian appointed a co-emperor to share the burden of overseeing the administration and defense of the Empire; in addition, each emperor, or *augustus,* appointed a trusted lieutenant, or *caesar,* to assist him and perhaps also to be groomed as his successor on the pattern of the adoptive system. The Empire was now divided into eastern and western halves by a line passing through the Adriatic Sea. Each half had its own *augustus,* its own *caesar,* and its own capital. In 330 the eastern capital was fixed at the site of the Greek Byzan-tium, now named Constantinople, the city of Constantine, after its new founder. The western capital, meantime, had been moved from Rome to Milan in northern Italy. Milan was relatively free of the intriguing political cliques that infested Rome, and it was closer to the frontier where the emperor was striving to contain the barbarians.

Not all these new arrangements endured, but they foreshadowed the shape of things to come. Rome, supplanted by Milan and Constantinople, suffered a steady loss of population; its handsome buildings fell into disrepair. The end of this chapter in the city's history, however, marked the opening of a new chapter, with Rome the capital of Christendom. Although Constantine reunited the two halves of the Empire and ruled as sole emperor during the latter part of his reign, the bisection of the Empire into East and West became permanent in 395. The line of division followed that made by Diocletian and paralleled the linguistic division between the Greek-speaking and Latin-speaking halves of the Mediterranean world. Thus Diocletian helped fix the medieval pattern of a Europe split between eastern and western rulers, traditions, and cultures.

Diocletian's reforms inaugurated two further trends. First, to secure real fighting men for the army, he passed over the drones and cutthroats of the regular legions and relied heavily on Germans and other foreign mercenaries. Thus he discarded the age-old Roman custom of fighting with citizen-soldiers and encouraged the peaceful assimilation of Germans into the Roman Empire. Second, to lend a sacred majesty to the person of the emperor, Diocletian borrowed heavily from the pomp and circumstance of the Persian court. Tough old soldier though he was, Diocletian arrayed himself as a god, his nails gilded and his hair sprinkled with gold-dust to dazzle his subjects; the gold and blue of his court robes were supposed to show his identity with the sun and the

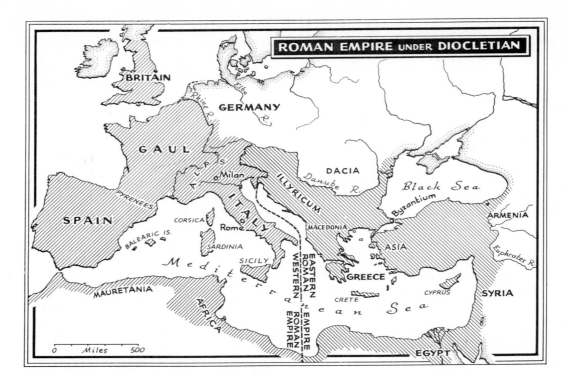

sky. The officers of government received high-sounding titles: the treasurer was now "count of the sacred largesses," and the imperial council became the "sacred consistory."

Diocletian tried in vain to salvage the economy of a bankrupt state. For many years the Empire had been experiencing an acute inflation; prices had been rising steadily and the value of money declining, partly because the emperors had reduced the quantity of precious metal in the coins. Diocletian attempted with some success to end this practice of debasement. Then, in a famous edict of 301, he sought to fix both prices and wages. The edict was extraordinarily detailed: it imposed different prices for sea fish and river fish and for the first and second qualities of each; it listed six types of boots and shoes—workers', soldiers', patrician, senatorial, equestrian, and women's—each with its own price; it spelled out transport charges for both passengers and freight; it allowed a scribe with the best writing to charge more than one with second-quality writing; it permitted the teacher of rhetoric to earn more than the teacher of geometry, and the geometer more than the teacher of arithmetic; it even put a ceiling on the fee of the check-room attendant at the baths! The edict offers many more fascinating glimpses into social history. But, although it decreed the death penalty for evaders, it failed in its main purpose of stemming inflation. Storekeepers and their customers rioted in protest against it; a widespread black market developed.

Diocletian took extraordinary steps to obtain the money and the manpower needed by the government. He assigned to each *civitas* a quota of taxes to be paid in money and commodities. If the *civitas* failed to fill its quota, then the *curiales* (the members of the local council, the *curia*) had to make up the difference out of their own pockets. The effect was catastrophic. Since the government set exorbitant quotas, in one city-state after another the *curiales* tried to resign so that they would not lose everything. The emperor forced them to remain in office and made membership in the *curia* hereditary. Once an honored group, the *curiales* became, as one authority puts it, "slaves of the administration."

The same sort of fate befell other social groups. Diocletian revised the tax on land, making it payable in produce rather than money. To pay the tax, the landowner required laborers to raise the necessary produce; but the number of *coloni* (tenant farmers) had dropped sharply as a consequence of the disorders of the third century. The government therefore fixed the *coloni* to the land they cultivated and made this status hereditary. In short, the *coloni* ceased being free peasants and became serfs. The *latifundia* operated by the state in Africa to supply grain for the dole of bread in Rome also experienced a shortage of labor. Here, too, the remaining *coloni* were "frozen" to their jobs in perpetuity. The policy of "freezing" jobs on a hereditary basis extended to other essential occupations: to bakers, for instance, to contractors, to the merchants who acted as business agents of the government, and to the workers building and repairing roads and aqueducts.

Diocletian and his successors thereby established what amounted to a caste system. But the Roman economy, staffed by so many involuntary and discontented workers, never achieved the full recovery that Diocletian had hoped for. The records of the fourth century are full of reports of *curiales* and *coloni* seeking escape from their intolerable burdens by joining the Christian clergy, enlisting in the army, or simply taking to the hills. The measures taken to cure the shortage of manpower made the disease worse.

Much the same judgment may be passed on the other policies of Diocletian. The vigorous autocracy he instituted did end the military anarchy, at least temporarily; it did for a time contain the pressure of Persians and Germans on the imperial frontiers. Yet, at most, his program delayed the downfall of the Empire; it did not avert it completely. Although the patient rallied briefly under the strong medicine, new complications were setting in, and the illness in the long run proved fatal.

From the time of Diocletian and Constantine until the final disappearance of Roman power in the West in 476, two rising institutions gradually took over control of the western Mediterranean world. These new forces were, first, the Christian Church and, second, the German tribes who organized the kingdoms that replaced the western empire. The story of the devitalized Rome of the fourth and fifth centuries will be told in connection with the Germanic invasions (see Chapter V). Here we may survey the fundamental reasons for the decline.

Why Rome Declined

The causes of Rome's decay reached far back into her history. In the army, the decline started during the third century with the degeneration of the legions into political and economic pressure groups. In politics, it had begun with the abandonment of the adoptive system in 180 and continued with the military anarchy and the imposition of Diocletian's autocracy. Long before Diocletian, the economy and society of Rome were showing alarming symptoms of serious deterioration. The partial caste system introduced in the fourth century was an attempt—a despairing, eleventh-hour attempt—to overcome the action of deeper forces that were corroding Roman society.

The social and economic crisis of the Empire resulted in part from the military anarchy and from the decreasing population. A generation or two ago it was often claimed that the Romans had committed "race suicide": the rich were too self-indulgent and vicious, the poor too downtrodden, to maintain the birth rate. Nowadays these moralistic views have given way to the more plausible theory that the severe losses in population may be traced to the civil warfare of the military anarchy and to widespread epidemics of plague, first under Marcus Aurelius and again in the third century.

Roman agriculture, crippled by the shortage of farm labor, also suffered from technological backwardness. Effective new techniques of tilling the soil were discovered from time to time, but farmers were slow to apply them. The methods of the fourth century B.C. often still served the fourth century A.D. Farm production may possibly have declined also because of a prolonged drought which dried up fertile grain lands. The evidence, however, suggests that changes of climate probably occurred at an almost imperceptible pace, far more slowly than the rate of Roman decline. Finally, the perennial trends toward the concentration of land in *latifundia* and the consequent reduction of independent small farmers to the status of *coloni* or unemployed inhabitants of a city undercut Roman prosperity. The inadequate purchasing power of the masses of people, compounded by inflation, impoverished the Roman economy.

And this was not all. What may be termed moral, spiritual, and psychological factors also entered into the Roman decline. The part taken by these intangible elements has caused much disagreement among historians. The dispute over the role of Christianity may serve as one example. In the eighteenth century, Edward Gibbon, a rationalist who admired Rome far more than he admired Christianity, wrote the celebrated *History of the Decline and Fall of the Roman Empire,* in which he suggested that Christianity was the real villain of the

Roman tragedy. Ever since then, followers of Gibbon have contended that, as Christianity spread throughout the Empire, it destroyed the civic spirit of the Romans. It turned their attention toward the afterlife and away from the taxes, the military service, and the other duties they owed to the earthly state. Defenders of Christianity, on the contrary, argue that the Empire fell not because it was too Christian but because it was not Christian enough. Paganism, they assert, culminated in the butchery of gladiators in the Colosseum and in the corruption of Roman morale.

Another example of disagreement over intangibles is the theory advanced by Professor Rostovtsev, a distinguished historian of the early twentieth century. Rostovtsev contended that Rome really collapsed when her underprivileged masses sought a share of the high living standards and cosmopolitan culture of the ruling classes. This revolt of the masses caused the bitter class tensions evident during the military anarchy and the reign of Diocletian. The tensions were never resolved because the comfortable life and culture of the well-to-do were not spread to the rest of society, and perhaps could not have been without being spread so thin, as it were, that they would have evaporated. Critics of Rostovtsev, however, point out that his views on Rome were strongly colored by events in his native Russia, where the tsarist regime was going down before the communists in the revolution of 1917.

Unquestionably, the Roman masses did become progressively disaffected from their rulers. Unquestionably, the culture of the rulers themselves did become old and devitalized. In literature and art, for example, the later centuries of the Empire were markedly less productive than the Golden Age or the Silver Age had been—a phenomenon of decline we have already observed in other civilizations, such as the Egyptian (see Chapter I). Writers of the fourth and fifth centuries were very conscious that they no longer lived in the good old days of the *Pax Romana*.

Except for the few statements made in the preceding paragraph, however, it is difficult to write with any certainty of the spiritual and psychological reasons for Roman decline. From these uncertainties we may draw two lessons: First, so long as there are historians, there will always be disagreement about such big, complex questions. Each generation will go on writing history in its own terms, as Gibbon wrote in terms of the anti-Christian bias of his own century, and as Rostovtsev wrote in the light of the collapse of tsarist Russia. Second, in explaining such a complex event, there are no simple answers. In the search for an explanation, all levels of society must be examined, from the economic foundations to its high politics and high culture. And all must be assumed to have played their part in shaping the course of history, even though we do not always fully comprehend the precise role that each of them may have played.

VII: Conclusion

The most remarkable thing about Rome was not that it declined and fell, but that it lasted as long as it did, for almost a thousand years. As a political institution, the Roman Empire ceased to exist in the West some fifteen hundred years ago. In the East, however, the Empire lived on to become the medieval Byzantine Empire, a new institution but one that always bore the marks of its Roman origins (see Chapter VI). And in the West, Roman civilization never died. The language of Rome, like the Roman law, has been of paramount importance in shaping the civilization of the Latin countries. Latin is the direct ancestor of the Romance (that is, Romanized) languages—French, Italian, Spanish, Portuguese, and Rumanian.

Modern English has derived much from Latin as well as from the Germanic Anglo-Saxon. A sentence in the preceding paragraph may be used as a case study: *The language of Rome, like the Roman law, has been of paramount importance in shaping the civilization of the Latin countries.* Most of the short, very common words of this sentence stem from the Anglo-Saxon spoken in England a thousand years ago. But the longer words, in addition to the obvious "Rome" and "Latin," all come from Latin: language from *lingua* (tongue); paramount from *mons* (mountain); importance, which suggests the notion of carrying weight, from *importare* (to carry into); civilization from *civis* (citizen); and countries, meaning literally those which lie opposite, from *contra* (against).

Moreover, Rome transmitted the Greek and eastern culture that might have perished if Rome had not established political order in the Mediterranean world, and if she had not been so cosmopolitan, so hospitable to older cultures. A great many Romans, fortunately, did not share the prejudices of Cato and Tacitus against things foreign. Even the Roman practice of outright imitation had its value. Roman copies of Myron's Discobolus, for example, are the only concrete evidence we have of the Greek sculptor's genius, for the original statue has disappeared.

As we shall see in later chapters, the Christian society of the Middle Ages owed a great deal to Rome, but it mistrusted Roman materialism and utilitarianism. With the waning of the Middle Ages, men's interests shifted away from the hereafter and back to the physical world. The men of the Renaissance turned again to the Roman concern for the practical and to the Roman taste for comfort and luxury. The legacy of this Roman "style" is one of the persistent strains in modern European and American culture.

Finally, the One World created by Rome has aroused nostalgia and admiration for almost twenty centuries. Later generations, living in an unstable and divided world, idealized the Roman Empire. To them it stood for the *Pax Romana,* for two hundred years of peace, progress, and prosperity. Whenever men have faced the problems of a universal organization they have studied the Roman example. Perhaps the highest tribute ever paid to the practical genius of the Romans is the fact that Roman foundations of law, language, and organization still support the oldest major institution in the western world—the Roman Catholic Church.

Reading Suggestions on the Romans

(Asterisk indicates paperbound edition.)

GENERAL ACCOUNTS

M. Rostovtzev, *History of the Ancient World,* Vol. II (Clarendon, 1928). An admirable survey, handsomely illustrated.

T. Frank, *A History of Rome* (Holt, 1923). A good, though opinionated, account by an American historian.

A. E. R. Boak, *A History of Rome to 565 A.D.,* 4th ed. (Macmillan, 1955). A sound American textbook.

C. E. Robinson, *A History of the Roman Republic* (Methuen, 1932). A good clear introduction.

W. Warde Fowler, *Rome,* 2nd ed. (Oxford Univ. Press, 1947). Brief and instructive account up to 180 A.D.

M. P. Charlesworth, *The Roman Empire* (Oxford Univ. Press, 1951). Informative general sketch.

R. H. Barrow, *The Romans* (*Penguin, 1951). A sound popular introduction.

E. Hamilton, *The Roman Way to Western Civilization* (*Mentor). A sympathetic estimate of the Roman spirit, based largely on literature.

W. C. Greene, *The Achievement of Rome* (Harvard Univ. Press, 1933). Useful cultural survey.

C. Bailey, ed., *The Legacy of Rome* (Oxford Univ. Press, 1923). Informative essays on Roman law and other topics.

T. Mommsen, *The History of Rome* (many editions). A celebrated older detailed account.

...g). A charming and enthusiastic introduction

SPECIAL STUDIES

D. H. Lawrence, Etruscan Places (°V... ... (Knopf, 1930). A scholarly survey.
by the well-known novelist.

L. Homo, Roman Political Ins...man Republic (Cambridge Univ. Press, 1955). A

R. E. Smith, The Failure ... acquainted with the facts; strongly critical of the

stimulating essay for th...on Old Rome (Knopf, 1939). A popular reinterpretation

Gracchi. ... the American experience of the 1930's; by a newspaper

H. J. Haskell, T'...'n Ancient Rome (Yale Univ. Press, 1940). A lively introduc-
of Roman refo...

editor and ? Social and Economic History of the Roman Empire, 2nd ed.,
J. C...957). A detailed scholarly study, magnificently illustrated; contains
...ions on the reasons for Rome's decline.

tio...Roman Imperial Civilization (Arnold, 1957; °Anchor). An instructive
...the illustrative material is derived from coins.

...nan Society from Nero to Marcus Aurelius (°Meridian). A classic of social

...bon, History of the Decline and Fall of the Roman Empire (many editions).
...lier chapters of this most famous account relate to the period under consideration

...Milner, The Problem of Decadence (Williams and Norgate, 1931). An inconclusive
but comprehensive introduction to the controversial topic of Roman decline.

M. Clarke, The Roman Mind (Cohen and West, 1956). Studies in the history of Roman thought from Cicero to Marcus Aurelius.

M. Hadas, A History of Roman Literature (Columbia Univ. Press, 1952). An encyclo-
paedic survey.

SOURCES

N. Lewis and M. Reinhold, Roman Civilization, 2 vols. (Columbia Univ. Press, 1951,
1955). A most useful compilation, with enlightening commentaries.

C. Bailey, ed., The Mind of Rome (Clarendon, 1926). A handy collection of representative writings.

The Communings with Himself of Marcus Aurelius Antoninus, C. R. Haines, ed. (Macmillan, 1924). A good edition of the Meditations of the philosopher-emperor.

Tacitus, On Britain and Germany, H. Mattingly, trans. (°Penguin, 1951).

Tacitus, The Annals of Imperial Rome, M. Grant, trans. (°Penguin, 1959).

Plutarch, Parallel Lives (many editions). The biographies of famous Greeks and Romans, written by a cultivated Greco-Roman gentleman who lived about 100 A.D.

Vergil, Aeneid, Rolfe Humphries, trans. (°Scribner's). A good modern translation of
the celebrated epic.

E. L. White, *Andivius Hedulio* (Dutt... nobleman in the days of the Empire. ...33). A novel of the adventures of a Roman

W. Bryher, *The Roman Wall* (Pantheon, ...ort novel of life on the frontier of the Roman Empire in the days of the declin...

A good imaginative reconstruction of Roma... three famous Roman tragedies by Shakespeare: J... ...may be found in the (with a devastating portrait of the ambitious young ... ...ny and Cleopatra ter commentary on politics in general and on popular gov... ...iolanus (a bit-

G. B. Shaw, *Caesar and Cleopatra* (°Penguin). Caesar ch... ...evo- lent, and talkative dictator.

CHAPTER III

Christianity

I: Jesus and Paul

CHAPTER IV

WE HAVE already had to note, in connection with early Jewish history, that there are difficulties in the way of a naturalistic-historical approach to the study of a revealed religion. Try as he may, the historian who does not fully accept given holy writings as the direct words of the divinity cannot understand and interpret those writings in just the way the true believer does. We shall in this book attempt consistently a naturalistic-historical approach, which we trust will not be identical with that hostile approach to religion usually known as "rationalistic." The reader must, however, not expect from us, or indeed from anyone, an account of Christianity equally acceptable to everyone in this modern western world, in which open and acknowledged differences over the whole range of Christian belief are simple facts of life. Indeed, in our western world there are those who openly reject all forms of Christian belief. All that can be expected at the present juncture is that due consideration will be maintained for the feelings of others, and that no partisan distortions will creep into the account. To such standards we hope our account will conform. But we must repeat that human emotions basic to religious feeling cannot be wholly repressed in dealing with religion.

Opposite. TWO WALL PAINTINGS, *dating from the fourth century* A.D., *in the Roman catacombs, the burial places of early Christians. The upper painting shows Shadrach, Meshack, and Abednigo, the Jewish youths who were thrown into the fiery furnace by Nebuchadrezzar during the Babylonian Captivity (see above, p. 35); the lower painting depicts Christ and the Apostles. The panels are typical of painting in the early Christian era; the debt to pagan Roman art is obvious.*

The Historical Jesus

About the accuracy of the biblical story of Jesus, his mission, his crucifixion and resurrection, there has been since the beginnings of modern scholarly studies in the eighteenth century much debate. Some of the more extreme of those who pursued in the nineteenth century the "higher criticism," such as the German, Bruno Bauer, denied that Jesus had ever existed; for Bauer, Jesus was a "myth." For the most part, however, these critics confined themselves to questioning the objectivity and accuracy of our historical "sources" for the life of Jesus. Closest to such sources are the "Synoptic Gospels," the New Testament books of Mark, Luke, and Matthew, which are called "synoptic" because they take the same general view. Scholars are now generally agreed that the Gospel according to St. Mark is the oldest, dating from about 60 A.D., and that Matthew and Luke, both of which show traces that their authors knew and used Mark and other sources now lost, date from twenty to thirty years later. One of these missing sources, known to scholars as "Q," seems to have been a collection of the words of Jesus himself, his parables and sermons.

The account of the life and ministry of Jesus as given in the Synoptic Gospels is, however, by no means false or legendary. The first generation or so of higher critics of the Bible in the nineteenth century— mostly Germans who were proud of their new techniques of historical research—went too far in their assumption that, because the life of Jesus is not *documented* in the sense, say, that the life of any modern great man is documented, we must assume that the gospel account is mostly fiction. The extremists who deny the historicity of Jesus have had few followers, even among the scholars who are outside Christian belief. Indeed the balance has now swung the other way, and most scholars believe that

our sources give us a faithful reflection of the life of Jesus as it seemed to the first generation of Christians.

Jesus came to a Palestine that was a satellite kingdom of the new world-state of the Romans. Like so much of the rest of the civilized world, the people of Palestine had been groping for firm religious beliefs. The mingling of men in this world of conquests and trade had been accompanied by an unsettling mingling of gods and creeds. Even the Jews, with their Jehovah and their Law (see Chapter I), were not wholly outside this melting pot of religious beliefs and emotions. Many members of their upper classes had been influenced by Greek philosophy, and the royal family of Herod the Great, King of Judea from 37 to 4 B.C., had been thoroughly Romanized and Hellenized.

Fragmentary but well-preserved documents, dating perhaps from 200 to 70 B.C. or so, discovered in 1947 and later in caves near the Dead Sea in Palestine, were carefully deciphered and by 1955 had been published and widely read. From these "Dead Sea Scrolls" we get a vivid sense of the living faith of Judaism at the time, and in particular we learn much of a Jewish sect or brotherhood, the Essenes. These people lived in retirement from the world in ascetic sharing of their common goods, much as did the early Christians. Centuries before, the prophets of the Old Testament had given sharp formulation to the concept of a Messiah, a God-sent leader who would fulfill the high destiny Jehovah intended for his chosen people. The Jewish faithful of the first century B.C. were torn between two sects, the Sadducees and the Pharisees. From a religious point of view the priestly Sadducees were conservative, and recognized only the Law of the Old Testament (see p. 44). The Pharisees, who were more progressive, recognized the authority of oral tradition and religious speculation as supplementing the Law. From these sources they developed ideas about resurrection from the dead, reward after death for the good and punishment for the wicked, and belief in a Messiah. All these beliefs are given later development in Christianity.

Jesus was born, it is now believed, between 8 and 4 B.C.° He preached in the towns and villages, and gathered small groups of followers. His doctrines brought him the enmity of influential Jewish groups, possibly also that of the Roman resident administrators. It might have seemed to the people in power that he was preaching social revolution; in the eyes of conventional Jews, he was pretty clearly a dangerous rebel. Jesus was crucified in Jerusalem, probably about 29 A.D. We can perhaps best put ourselves in the place of the Jewish countrymen of Jesus who condemned him to death if we think of Jesus as in their eyes an inciter to sedition, perhaps even a traitor.

The Teachings of Jesus

Just what Jesus did preach, just what the Gospel really was in those few years of his ministry, historians cannot determine fully. One modern interpretation—that Jesus was in fact a social reformer, a revolutionist, a democratic socialist two thousand years ago—is far too one-sided. There is little doubt that Jesus did appeal to the poor and unlearned, to the suffering, to the weak; the miraculous healing, the beatitudes (Matthew 8:5; 5:3), are proof enough of that appeal. But it is unfair to regard him simply as some sort of "nature-healer," as an emotional revivalist with no ideas. He seems to have preached not asceticism, but rather the enjoyment of the good things of this world, an enjoyment freed from rivalry, ostentation, vulgarity. He had a great gift for making himself understood by plain people, and for the cure of souls. But he

° The Gospel account has him born in the reign of Herod the Great, who died in 4 B.C., and who, moreover, had ordered at the time the killing of all children under two years of age (Matthew 2:16).

was no sentimentalist; there is a vein of iron.

And why call ye me, Lord, Lord, and do not the things which I say? Whosoever cometh to me, and heareth my sayings, and doeth them, I will show you to whom he is like: He is like a man which built a house, and digged deep, and laid the foundation on a rock: and when the flood arose, the stream beat vehemently upon that house, and could not shake it; for it was founded upon a rock. But he that heareth, and doeth not, is like a man that without a foundation built a house upon the earth; against which the stream did beat vehemently, and im-

Early Christian art. Statue of the Good Shepherd (about 350).

mediately it fell; and the ruin of that house was great.*

The ethics of the Sermon on the Mount (Matthew 5:1–7:28) and of the rest of Christ's preaching is an ethics of gentleness and loving-kindness. Christ urges on men the kind of moral conduct we know still to be *right* conduct, honesty, humility, fair-dealing, sobriety, all the long list; he teaches mutual toleration ("Judge not; that ye be not judged"), inner righteousness, charity, humility, all the virtues the higher religions have set as a human goal. Yet, as so often in Christianity, there comes the touch of iron, of tragedy. Jesus was no humanitarian optimist who believed that men *naturally* behaved as he would like them to behave:

> Enter ye in at the strait gate: for wide is the gate, and broad is the way, that leadeth to destruction, and many there be which go in thereat: Because strait is the gate, and narrow is the way, which leadeth unto life, and few there be that find it.†

Nor was he a pacifist—certainly not a preacher of absolute non-resistance, in spite of certain clashing texts: "Resist not evil: but whosoever shall smite thee on thy right cheek, turn to him the other also"; "Think not that I am come to send peace on earth: I came not to send peace, but a sword." ‡

Finally, from the teaching of Jesus there emerge theological doctrines of very great importance, notably what is called an eschatology (from the Greek, science of final things or purposes). Christ spoke often of his "Father which is in heaven," and called himself the "Son of man"; he had been sent by God the Father to lead sinful men to redemption; this redemption through conversion and right conduct on this earth was to bring the reward of an immortality of bliss in the Kingdom of Heaven; for those

---

* Luke 6:46-49.

† Matthew 7:13-14.

‡ Matthew 5:39; 10:34. The original text is in Greek, and therefore there are difficulties of translation. Note that Matthew 5:39 above is sometimes translated "resist not *him that is* evil."

who continued to do evil, there would be punishment of immortality in hell. The Gospels are even more specific as to an immediate eschatology: Christ died on the cross to fulfill his work of redemption, was resurrected and would return very shortly, during the lifetime of some of his hearers, to end this world as we know it in a final Judgment Day.

The First Christians

After the crucifixion of Jesus, a little group of his followers held together in Jerusalem. How soon among them there arose the belief in the Resurrection, in the divinity of Christ, in Christ as the promised Messiah, the Saviour, we cannot be sure. These first Christians were heretics of the Jewish faith and Law, and might well have remained no more than a humble Jewish sect or splinter group. But Christian belief had drawing powers that were bound to exceed the limits of the Jewish communities. The eschatology we have just noted was very specific: Christ had told his followers, "There be some standing here, which shall not taste of death, till they see the Son of man coming in his kingdom" (Matthew 16:28). This is the doctrine of the Second Coming of Christ, known technically as a "chiliastic" belief, for this promised reign of Christ on earth was to last a thousand (Greek chilo- or kilo-) years. It was no distant promise, heaven no mere hope, hell no mere threat, for all these to the Christian converts were certainties. Add to this the immediacy of the emotional tie which Christianity brought between the individual believer and Christ, and among individuals in the Christian brotherhood—all this so hard to put in the cold words of a history book —and you have indeed an Evangel, the "good news" that made Christians out of Jews, Greeks, Romans, all the varied folk of the Roman Empire.

The full social and psychological consequences of this widespread belief we cannot really know. Some of the first Christians were so obsessed with the idea of an almost immediate Day of Judgment that they gave up everything that touched the world of the senses and common sense and turned wholly to prayer, self-denial, and ecstasy. But clearly this chiliastic belief was useful in making converts to Christianity and, given the organizing gifts of the apostles and their successors, it was also useful in maintaining the loyalty and enthusiasm of converts. Quite as clearly, this belief in an immediate Second Coming began to prove an embarrassment after the first generation or so, and had to be spiritualized into a theological doctrine of salvation.

It has never been easy for the individual Christian to know whether or not he is a true Christian. But membership in the kind of organized society we call a church has always been for most Christians an indispensable accompanying condition of salvation. In the early and struggling years of Christianity, this condition was reasonably easy to fulfill. For in spite of doctrinal and disciplinary problems, problems complicated by the appeal of the Gospel to troubled and excitable souls, the early Christians were united to an extraordinary degree in the primitive Church.

Saint Paul

They owed that union in part to the tireless activities of the early organizers, of whom the most remarkable was Saul of Tarsus, a converted Jew who had never seen Christ. Saint Paul, as he is known in Christianity, after having helped to persecute the first little band of Christians in Jerusalem, himself experienced on a journey to Damascus a deep emotional conversion. Paul and his helpers have left behind them records in the Acts and the Pauline and other Epistles of the New Testament. From these we can learn how the new faith

was incorporated into an organized church, and we can come to know Paul as a person much more thoroughly and reliably than we know most personalities of the ancient world.

Paul is called the "Apostle to the Gentiles," and he seems to have led the way in taking the one step that had to be taken before Christianity could become a universal religion. The first Christians were religious Jews who thought of themselves as followers of Jehovah and his Law. This Law included among other things an elaborate set of ritual ways that a Jew mastered only slowly as he grew up among his people. It was a stumbling block in the way of Greeks and other Gentiles who might find the preachings of Jesus attractive. Even though Jesus himself had been what we call "liberal" in his interpretation of the Law, he had, according to the Gospels, made some strong statements, notably:

Think not that I am come to destroy the law, or the prophets: I am not come to destroy, but to fulfil. For verily I say unto you, Till heaven and earth pass, one jot or one tittle shall in no wise pass from the law, till all be fulfilled.*

The Jewish requirement of circumcision is a simple example of the hindrances that stood in the way of conversion to Christianity as long as it remained a Jewish sect. For an adult in those days, without antiseptics and without anesthesia, circumcision was a dangerous and dreaded operation. But Paul had a remedy: he announced that the Greek or Syrian convert to Christianity need not undergo circumcision. Similarly, he proclaimed that the convert need not abstain from pork or follow the detailed prescriptions of the Law. Paul said all this many times and in many ways:

For by one Spirit we are all baptized into one body, whether we be Jews or Gentiles, whether we be bond or free.†

---

* Matthew 5:17-18.
† Corinthians 12:13.

And most simply:

> For the letter killeth, but the Spirit giveth life.*

The Christian was to be saved, not by the letter of the Jewish Law, but by the spirit of the Jewish faith in a righteous God.

In a way that was surely never common in early history—one finds no such union in an Ikhnaton or a Plato—Paul united the mystic who would transcend the world and the flesh and the gifted spiritual adviser of ordinary men and women troubled in their everyday lives. In all Paul's writings there are passages which show him to have been ascetic in his morality and firmly convinced that Christian truth is not a matter of habit or reasoning, but of transcending faith:

> Howbeit we speak wisdom among them that are perfect: yet not the wisdom of this world, nor of the princes of this world, that come to nought: But we speak the wisdom of God in a mystery, even the hidden wisdom, which God ordained before the world unto our glory; Which none of the princes of this world knew: for had they known it, they would not have crucified the Lord of glory.†

Yet Paul was no oriental mystic who wholly denied the reality or goodness of this world; he never preached denial of this world in mystic ecstasy. Indeed he expresses clearly that characteristic Christian tension between this world and the next, between the real and the ideal, which has ever since firmly marked western society. This tension —better, this *awareness*—he expressed as the mystic union of Christ and Christian: "Always bearing about in the body the dying of the Lord Jesus, that the life also of Jesus might be made manifest in our body" (Corinthians 4:10), part of a magnificent passage much used in funeral services. Christians are not merely animals, or merely men: they are children of God who are destined, if they are true Christians, to eternal bliss. But on this earth they must live in the constant imperfection of the flesh, not wholly transcending it, always aware that they are at once mortal and immortal.

A large part of the Pauline Epistles deals with matters of church discipline. Here we see Paul charged with the cure of souls, keeping a firm but not despotic hand over the scattered and struggling Christian congregations in Corinth, in Rome, and in many parts of the Empire. We see him trying to tame the excesses to which the emotionally liberating new doctrines so readily gave rise. We find him urging the newly emancipated not to interpret Christian love as sexual promiscuity, not to take their new wisdom as an opportunity for wild ranting ("speaking with tongues"), not, in short, to indulge in excesses, but to accept the discipline of the Church, to lead quiet, faithful, but firmly Christian lives.

The Early Spread of Christianity

Paul, though not one of the twelve apostles, actual companions of Jesus, has been accepted as an equal. Christian tradition has the twelve (Matthias replacing the traitor, Judas) assembling in Jerusalem after the death of Jesus, and separating to preach the new faith in all four quarters of the earth. Peter, after working in the East, was believed to have gone to Rome, of which he was first Bishop, and there to have been martyred. Paul, too, went to Rome and was martyred. The Church of Rome had thus two of the greatest of the Apostles as co-founders, a very great source of prestige. The same sort of critical analysis that has been employed on the problem of the Synoptic Gospels has been directed to the problems of the Apostolic Age all over the Mediterranean world, and more especially in Rome. There have been even wider divergences of opinion on the historicity of the accounts of these missions, both in the New Testament and in other sources.

---

* Corinthians 3:6.
† Corinthians 2:6-9.

The new faith was gradually spread throughout the Roman Empire within the first two generations after the death of Christ. Some of the men who spread it had been members of the earliest Christian congregations in the Holy Land. The specific associations of Peter and Paul with Rome are now articles of faith for Roman Catholics and for many other Christians. Moreover, it is clear that very early, within a decade or two after the death of Jesus, there was a Christian congregation in Rome, capital of the Empire, indeed capital of the western world of that time. This mission to the Gentiles even in these earliest days, when Christianity was an obscure sect, hardly a threat to the imperial order, aroused opposition in many quarters. Peter and Paul in Christian tradition were martyred on the same day in Rome under Nero. Our earliest Latin sources show that the Christians were a despised sect, suspected of all sorts of horrid crimes, such as incest and infanticide as well as ritual murder.

Nevertheless, or indeed consequently, since the blood of the martyrs is the seed of the church, Christianity by about 100 A.D. had been sowed in the Empire well outside the old Jewish communities, and the seeds had begun to grow. Paul had been the most skillful of the gardeners nursing the young plants. They were already so hardy that not even the bitter winds of persecution could kill them.

II: Christianity in the Pagan World

The Reasons for Persecution

What to Christians is known as persecution was to the authorities of Rome simply their duty as defenders of public order against men and women who seemed to them traitors or irresponsible madmen. The Christians, like the Jews, ran afoul of the Roman civil law not so much for their positive beliefs and practices, but rather for their refusal to accept the divinity of the emperor, and to sacrifice to him as a god. It is true that to cultivated Greeks and Romans of these first centuries Christians seemed wild and indecent enthusiasts, and that to the masses they were dangerous cranks. But the Empire was not very concerned with the details of the morals and faiths of its hundreds of component city-states, tribes, and nations. Scores of gods and goddesses, innumerable spirits and demons, filled the minds of the millions under Roman rule, and the rulers, themselves usually Stoics with a philosophic, though scornful, toleration of mass superstitions, were willing to tolerate them all as part of the nature of things.

There was, however, a practical limit to this religious freedom, which after all was based on no ideal of religious liberty, and certainly not on any concept of separation of Church and State. To hold this motley collection of peoples in a common allegiance, to give them something like a national flag as a symbol of this unity, the emperor was deified (see Chapter III). Simple rites of sacrifice to him were added to local religions and local rites. After all, one more god gave no trouble to those who believed in the Greco-Roman pantheon or in Isis or Cybele or in any other conventional polytheism; one more pinch of incense on one more altar was simple enough. Those who did not believe in the customary local gods —and such disbelief was widespread in the Roman Empire—had no trouble in doing what was expected of them, for they did not take with undue seriousness any religion, new or old.

The Christians, however, were as rigorous monotheists as the Jews; they could not sacrifice to the emperor any more than the Jews of old could sacrifice to Baal. Indeed, they felt that in so far as the emperor pretended to be a god, he was in fact a devil. The more cautious administrators of the growing Christian Church were anxious to live down their reputation for disorderliness, and by no means sought to antagonize the civil authorities. These leaders may have been responsible for the fame of the text: "Render therefore unto Caesar the things that are Caesar's; and unto God the things that are God's" (Matthew 22:21). But sacrifice was a thing of God's. The true Christian, then, could not bring himself to make what to an outsider or a skeptic was merely a decent gesture, like raising one's hat today when the flag goes by in a parade. Moreover, if he was a very ardent Christian, he might feel that the very act of sacrifice to Caesar was a wicked thing, even when performed by non-Christians, and he might show these feelings in public.

The Persecutions

Even so, the imperial authorities by no means consistently sought to stamp out the Christian religion. The persecutions were sporadic. They came in some half-dozen major waves over three centuries, and they were subject to great local variations. The first persecution, and the one that is best known today, came very early indeed, in 64, under the Emperor Nero. This persecution is described by the upper-class historian Tacitus as a deliberate attempt by Nero to find a scapegoat for the disastrous fire in Rome. Rumor held that the dissolute Emperor himself had ordered the fire set. Tacitus continues in terms that

show clearly how some cultivated pagans regarded the new sect:

Therefore, to scotch the rumour, Nero substituted as culprits, and punished with the utmost refinements of cruelty, a class of men, loathed for their vices, whom the crowd styled Christians. Christus, the founder of the name, had undergone the death penalty in the reign of Tiberius, . . . and the pernicious superstition was checked for a moment, only to break out once more, not merely in Judaea, the home of the disease, but in the capital itself, where all things horrible or shameful in the world collect and find a vogue. First, then, the confessed members of the sect were arrested; next, on their disclosures, vast numbers were convicted, not so much on the count of arson as for hatred of the human race. And derision accompanied their end: they were covered with wild beasts' skins and torn to death by dogs; or they were fastened on crosses, and, when daylight failed, were burned to serve as lamps by night.[*]

There was no doubt in Tacitus' mind that the Christians were criminals, but a faint doubt did creep into the mind of an able and conscientious member of the imperial ruling class, Pliny the Younger. Pliny writes his Emperor Trajan (98-117) from Bithynia in Asia Minor that he is puzzled about the Christians. Shall he punish a Christian just because he admits to being a Christian, or must he have evidence of the horrid crimes that Christians were alleged to commit? Shall he trust an unknown informer who has furnished him with a list of alleged Christians? Many, he writes have actually recanted and worshiped Trajan's image. But, he goes on:

They affirmed, however, the whole of their guilt, or their error, was, that they were in the habit of meeting on a certain fixed day before it was light, when they sang in alternate verses a hymn to Christ, as to a god, and bound themselves by a solemn oath, not to any wicked deeds, but never to commit any fraud, theft or adultery, never to falsify their word, nor deny a trust when they should be called upon to deliver it up; after which it was their custom to separate, and then reassemble to partake of

[*] Tacitus, *The Annals*, John Jackson, trans. (Cambridge, Mass., 1937), XV, xliv.

food—but food of an ordinary and innocent kind. . . . I judged it so much the more necessary to extract the real truth, with the assistance of torture, from two female slaves, who were styled *deaconesses:* but I could discover nothing more than depraved and excessive superstition.*

Trajan's reply must be recorded, for it is the reply of an admirable representative of Roman law and order, and it should counteract the impression that Nero has made:

No search should be made for these people; when they are denounced and found guilty, they must be punished; with the restriction, however, that when the party denies himself to be a Christian, and shall give proof that he is not (that is, by adoring our Gods) he shall be pardoned on the ground of repentance, even though he may have formerly incurred suspicion. Informations without the accuser's name subscribed must not be admitted in evidence against anyone, as it is introducing a very dangerous precedent, and by no means agreeable to the spirit of the age.†

The men who directed that measures be taken against the Christians were not themselves men of passionate religious convictions; they were urbane, tolerant, and skeptical. At moments of crisis they sought to get rid of people like Christians, but they did not have the fanaticism of the true persecutor. They could not fight fire with fire of their own.

We must not, however, dismiss the persecutions as unimportant. They were at their climaxes most severe, and they claimed many Christian martyrs. But by going underground, by glorifying the memory of the martyrs, by persistent proselytizing, by taking advantage of the kind of good will evident in Trajan's letter, the Church grew stronger and its members more numerous throughout these centuries. After a final major persecution in the early fourth century, official toleration was achieved in 311

Madonna and Child, from the underground Catacomb of Priscilla, Rome, third century.

in an edict signed on his deathbed by the persecuting Emperor Galerius. The Emperor Constantine (306-337) confirmed the policy of toleration in an agreement with his rival Licinius about 313. More, the great Church Council of Nicaea in 325 (see below, p. 164) was held under imperial auspices. At the time of Constantine's death, the Church was on its way to becoming the official state religion of the Roman Empire.

One last major official attempt was made

---

* Pliny, *Letters*, W. Melmoth, trans. (London, 1915), Bk. X, xcvi.
† *Ibid.*, Bk. X, xcvii.

at a formal restoration—or, rather, reconstruction—of the old polytheism of the Empire. The Emperor Julian the Apostate (361-363) was sincerely attached to the traditions of the Roman ruling classes. He was genuinely persuaded that the "Galileans," as he called the Christians in contrast with his "Hellenes," were trying to put an inferior oriental superstition in the place of the hard-won decencies of Greco-Roman culture. But Julian's substitute for Christianity seems to have been a hopeless hodgepodge of Greek, Egyptian, and Persian religious ideas and practices.

At his death only two years after he had assumed the imperial crown, Christianity quickly regained and extended a position that had never been greatly threatened by Julian's activities. The Emperor Theodosius (379-395) made Christianity in effect the official Church and persecuted the pagan sects. Paganism continued among the upper classes and the intellectuals for another century or so, but it was no longer an organized force. Indeed, these cultivated gentlemen seem to have pretended that Christianity did not exist. There are few references to Christianity in the pagan imaginative literature of the dying empire. But snubbing is a poor way of fighting; paganism really had no fight left in it.

The Problem of Christianity's Triumph

This triumph of a once obscure, despised sect of simple religious enthusiasts in a mature, well-organized, rich, and intellectually sophisticated society is one of the dramatic facts and unsolved problems of history. No one has written of the period without attempting to explain the reasons why Christianity won out over its many rival creeds. But, as with the parallel problem of the reasons for the breakup of the Roman Empire, there is as yet no general agreement.

The historian has no simple answer. He may clear the ground somewhat by noting that the political unification of the Mediterranean had been achieved just before the Christian Era, and that this bringing together of men had, just as it had much earlier in the Near East, brought all sorts of rival creeds into conjunction in men's minds and practices. Isis, Mithra, Aphrodite, Osiris, Jupiter, and many other gods and goddesses all jostled for attention. Some of them were, served by wandering priests willing to make converts. Christianity had competitors in other new or newly adapted faiths, and not merely in the old set ways of men.

From such a statement it is tempting but dangerous to go on to the assertion that the total situation of society at this time—the economic, social, cultural configuration of the Roman world—required a unifying spiritual belief, a religion of love, consolation, and imaginative depth. Just because this was an old, relatively advanced materially, intellectually rather tired culture, it was ready for a vital and appealing emotional faith. The relatively small privileged upper class was so sophisticated that it was frankly rationalist or skeptic, and the huge proletarian lower class, in part composed of slaves, was uneducated but aware of the possibility of better things than its miserable life afforded. A world like that can be made to seem a world of misery, but also a world of yearning, a natural setting for a religion like Christianity. These great generalizations are tempting to many able minds. But they cannot be proved; we do not know all the conditions under which a "higher" religion—Christianity, Buddhism, Islam—is likely to emerge.

Even the narrower question—Why did Christianity triumph over its competitors in the first four centuries of our era?—can have no simple answer. One element in that answer is, however, fairly clear. On examination, Christianity's competitors turn out to be for the most part poor fighting creeds, often spread by priests who were no more than charlatans or mountebanks. Apuleius, a second-century Latin novelist, in the eighth book of his *Golden Ass*, describes a troupe of emasculated priests carrying about their "omnipotent and omniparent Syrian goddess" and behaving like a rowdy circus troupe. Apuleius himself appears fond of magic and new cults, and ends his story with a long account of his own initiation into the cult of Isis, an initiation in which one feels too much flubdubbery, too little real emotion.

Yet this cult of Isis, and the cult of Mithra, seem in retrospect to have been the only serious rivals of Christianity as proselytizing religions. The cult of Isis provided the consolations of a future life, a consoling mother-figure in Isis herself, mystic links with the great Egyptian past, and abundant miracles. But it lacked a fighting priesthood; it lacked drive and organization. The cult of Mithra, Persian in origin, was tied up with the characteristic Persian dualism between light and darkness, a good God and a satanic opponent. It had a core of hardness that the cult of Isis lacked. Its major ritual act, the taurobolium, involved the sacrifice of a bull. The believer was then baptized in the bull's blood. Mithraism also promised rewards in a future life, and Mithra himself was regarded as an intermediary between God and man. The cult was the favorite religion of the far-flung legions of the Empire, and it may well have been this identification with the military that handicapped its spread among other classes. Mithraism, like the cult of Isis, lacked an organized body of priests with an aggressive missionary spirit.

None of these competing faiths had either the moral spirit or the superb group organization that the Christians had. Whether Christianity won out because of its ideas and ideals or because of its organization, whether theology or church history gives the real clue to Christian success, is es-

sentially a false way of stating a historical problem. To understand the rise of Christianity one must think of both ideas and organization, *both the spiritual and the material*, as working together, as mutually determining factors.

The Christian holy writings, New and Old Testament, are admirably suited to the task of conversion. Here is a skeptical twentieth-century American, the late H. L. Mencken, commenting:

Try to imagine two evangelists on a street corner in Corinth or Ephesus, one expounding the Nicomachean ethics [of Aristotle] or a homily by Valentinus the Gnostic and the other reciting the Sermon on the Mount or the Twenty-third Psalm; certainly it is not hard to guess which would fetch the greater audience of troubled and seeking men.[*]

The good news (evangel) of the Gospels promised personal immortality, the rewards of heaven, sharing in loving-kindness with one's fellows on this earth; it provided a consoling ritual, a lofty moral code, above all, perhaps, a feeling the modern psychologist puts rather bleakly as personal "identification," becoming a part of a very great and noble thing, a fighting cause, masculinely fighting for peace, gentleness, good will to men. We are going to commit a bad anachronism: and yet, there *is* a touch of the early Christian in the lift of emotion still evident in that very modern hymn, "Onward, Christian Soldiers."

Indeed it is perhaps this fighting spirit, so congruous with much of what we know of western history, that helps explain why Christianity spread west and north from its cradle in Jerusalem, rather than east and south. Christianity, oriental in origin—at least geographically—never won far into lands of Zoroastrian, Hindu, and other eastern faiths, nor far into Africa. Those who prefer material to spiritual interpretations will here point out that Christianity spread in these crucial centuries essentially

---

[*] H. L. Mencken, *Treatise on Right and Wrong* (New York, 1934), 181.

within the Roman Empire, that it needed the political and cultural structure of the Empire to work within. And, of course, only a few centuries later a fiery and militant monotheism, Islam, arose and overwhelmed the eastern outposts of Christianity (see Chapter VI).

Finally, Christianity succeeded not only because it set itself against the earthly compromises and indecencies of pagan cults, but also because it contained so much of paganism, because, in short, it was by no means wholly new. This point is often referred to as the *syncretistic* nature of Christianity—that is, the new religion's capacity for borrowing and absorbing the doctrines and practices of older beliefs. Christian notions of immortality and resurrection are related to Egyptian, Greek, and Hebrew notions; Greek and Roman philosophies, especially mystical Neo-Platonism, contributed a great deal to developed Christianity. Even more important is the extent to which Christianity allowed the old uses, the old rites and habits, the unintellectual side of religion, to survive, and the extent to which it mastered and tamed pagan habits. So, when the crowds of Ephesus hailed the victory of the theologians who were defending the Virgin's motherhood, one might almost hear an echo, "Great is Diana of the Ephesians." And Easter is an echo of thousands of prehistoric years of celebrations of the coming of Spring.

Yet all these many causes pale into abstraction before the fact that Christianity prevailed because it won its way into the hearts of living men and women. Christianity brought to the confused millions of a world that was almost as self-conscious and worried as our own a feeling of belonging, of understanding, of loving and of being loved. Here is one of the many Christian inscriptions that have survived from early tombs:

I, Petronia, wife of a deacon, of modest countenance, here lay down my bones and place them in their resting place. Cease from weeping, my husband and sweet children, and believe that it is not right to mourn one that lives in God.*

Christianity, although it achieved the status of legal religion in the Roman Empire early in the fourth century, enjoyed no full and undisputed triumph. After the persecutions and the competition with pagan beliefs, long, serious struggles sprang up within Christianity itself over the forms and nature of its own beliefs and rituals. We may now follow the story of Christianity until the end of the historical period that our fathers called "Antiquity." For clarity of analysis, we shall treat separately the evolution of the two great elements in Christianity, ideas and spirit on one side, political and social organization on the other. But we must always remember that in real life the two elements were inseparable, each always conditioning and altering the other, a process of *reinforcement*.

* H. P. V. Nunn, *Christian Inscriptions* (London, 1920), No. 41.

III: The Organization of Christianity

Just what was the organization of the early Christian churches, and especially of the primitive churches of the first generation or two after the death of Christ? There has been the same kind of debate over this question as there has been over the problems of the historicity of Jesus and the sources of the New Testament. This debate has continued throughout Christian history ever since the late Middle Ages. Men have sought to find in the primitive Church a pattern, an authority, a confirmation of their own conceptions of what Christianity implies. In our own day, a scholarly and temperate English churchman has come to this tolerant conclusion:

For four hundred years theologians of rival churches have armed themselves to battle on the question of the Primitive Church. However great their reverence for scientific truth and historic fact, they have at least *hoped* that the result of their investigations would be to vindicate Apostolic authority for the type of Church Order to which they were themselves attached. The Episcopalian has sought to find episcopacy, the Presbyterian presbyterianism, and the Independent a system of independency, to be the form of Church government in New Testament times. But while each party to the dispute has been able to make out a case for his own view, he has never succeeded in demolishing the case of his opponent. The explanation of this deadlock, I have come to believe, is quite simple. It is the uncriticised assumption, made by all parties to the controversy, that in the first century there existed a single type of Church Order.

Approach the evidence without making that assumption and two conclusions come into sight:

(1) In the New Testament itself there can be traced an evolution in Church Order, comparable to the development in theological reflection detected by the scholarship of the last century.

(2) The most natural interpretation of the other evidence is that, at the end of the first century A.D., there existed, in different provinces of the Roman Empire, different systems of Church government. Among these, the Episcopalian, the Presbyterian, and the Independent can each discover the prototype of the system to which he himself adheres.[*]

The Need for Organization

Commentators on early Christian organization often differ on important details, such as the question of the role of St. Peter and St. Paul in the early Church at Rome.

----

[*] B. H. Streeter, *The Primitive Church* (London, 1929), viii–ix.

But almost all agree on two very broad generalizations. First, the primitive churches frequently had excited and excitable members who had somehow to be tamed, disciplined, and perhaps rejected if any kind of mundane order was to be maintained in the Church. Second, in all the primitive churches there gradually grew up a distinction between lay and clerical members.

It must never be forgotten that the disciplinarians, the organizers, of early Christianity had, in addition to the troubles that always face the worldly organizers of an other-worldly faith, the very grave difficulty of achieving this organization in the midst of a great bureaucratic empire that was committed in principle to the suppression of Christianity. The wild enthusiast—in the phrase of St. Paul, the "speaker with tongues"—was usually an unreliable member of an organized underground.

Yet Christianity did triumph, and its organization was already taking shape by the end of the second century. In the first churches, the little groups organized by the first missionaries, there were men called variously "prophets," "teachers," and the like. The names suggest that these men worked basically on the feelings of their co-religionists, that perhaps many of them were mystical believers rather than worldly organizers. But almost as early we also find that these groups have "elders," "overseers," and "presidents." And *these* names suggest in fact what we call "government"—church government, to be sure, and not political government, but essentially a source of law and authority.

The Hierarchy

From these early governing officials, who often merged their administrative abilities with more spiritual gifts and functions, there developed the government of the Church. This is a hierarchical organization, headed by the pope, who is Bishop of

Rome, and who claims authority over all the other bishops. This claim, however, was denied almost from the first by the bishops of such great centers of eastern Christianity as Antioch, Alexandria, and later Constantinople; it never quite established itself in the East. But in the West it was very firmly established by the time of the breakup of the Roman Empire and the Germanic invasions, and was to be a major factor in the growth of western civilization.

The key post in the government of the Church was that of the bishop (from the Greek *episcopos*, "overseer," whence the adjective "episcopal"), who was the head of a large administrative area called a see. The bishops gained particular prestige and authority through the doctrine of apostolic succession, which asserted that each episcopal church had been founded either directly by one of the apostles or by the agent of an apostle. A bishop thus became, in effect, a direct spiritual heir of Christ. The bishops, meeting in council, guided the policy of the early Church; their function was to distinguish true from false prophets, to accept or reject religious practices, to declare Christian writings divinely inspired or not.

Slowly under such governance, what is known as the Christian Canon was established. These are the twenty-seven books of the New Testament considered of divine inspiration. They are written in the *koine*, the current Greek of the time. So too the Christian Canon of the Old Testament was finally drawn up for the first Christians from an earlier Greek translation from the Hebrew known as the Septuagint (Latin, seventy) from the seventy translators who were said to have worked on it. This Greek version is still that used in the Greek Orthodox Church. In the Roman Church, an earlier Latin translation of both Testaments was revised and retranslated under the direction of St. Jerome, who did some of the translation himself, in the fourth century. This is the Vulgate, not a book about the Bible, but the Bible itself in Latin. Various writings, known as *apocrypha* and *pseudepigraphia*, have been rejected from the Canon, though Hebrew, Catholic, and Protestant rejections have not been identical. For the historian, the rejected writings are of interest as reflecting various phases of religious history.

Bishoprics were gathered into larger areas headed by an archbishop, sometimes called a "metropolitan." Within the bishopric, each church was headed by a priest (from the Greek *presbyteros*, "elder"), who had had formal training and had been "ordained" into the priesthood. Later, each church and its priest came to serve the local area known as the parish. By the fourth century, the older church office of deacon, which had been prominent in the primitive church, had become a preliminary step to full priesthood. In some of the early churches, officers were elected by the congregation, and the actual government was conducted by boards or committees of elders ("presbyteries"). In the developed western ecclesiastical system, however, clerical positions were basically determined by what we today understand as "appointment" from above—that is, by hierarchical superiors or elders already in office. Traces, and sometimes rather more than traces, of the early form of election by congregations persisted for centuries.

There is then a clear distinction between the *clergy*, who are trained for their task and are ordained when they are fully prepared, and the *laity*, the Christian faithful who worship in the churches guided by the clergy. Against this distinction reformers have revolted from time to time for two thousand years, always in the name of what they regard as a purer Christianity in which all men are priests. The Society of Friends (Quakers) notably refuses to have a formal clergy. Still, not only the Roman Catholic Church, but all Christian churches, sooner or later, have developed a practical distinction between clergy and laity. Even

An early Christian church. Interior of Santa Maria Maggiore in Rome (432-440 A.D.); the ceiling dates from about 1500.

among the Quakers, the most rigorous of the sects that have sought to eliminate a clerical order, there are in fact men who devote their lives to the guidance, here below at any rate, of the Society of Friends.

The Supremacy of Rome

The strength of its organization was one of the reasons for the triumph of the Church of Rome. Many forces were working toward the elevation of the ecclesiastical center of Rome to an exceptional position. The prestige of Rome, the City of cities, would perhaps alone have insured this result. The final success of Rome also owes a great deal to the prestige of Peter and Paul. The Gospels report Jesus as saying to Peter, "Thou art Peter; and upon this rock I will build my church." This celebrated sentence is, incidentally, a pun (in Greek *Petros* is Peter and *petra* is a ledge of rock). It is one of the foundations for the Petrine theory of the power of the popes, who are the successors of Peter as Bishop of Rome. In the fourth century, with the setting up of Constantinople in the East as a new administrative center, the pope gradually began to free himself from imperial controls. Finally, as the barbarian invasions became general after the sack of Rome in 410, the pope appeared more and more as the embodiment of those Roman regularities and certainties that were being threatened. In a much more literal sense than we usually give the text, he had indeed become a rock.

Moreover, since Rome was the center from which judicial decisions had come, it became a normal court of appeal in the many quarrels over ideas that fill the history of Christianity. These heresies we shall study in the next section of this chapter. Not all heretics respected Roman decisions, but Rome itself was hardly threatened by heresy. It was therefore natural for St. Jerome, a Latin father who knew the Greek world well, to write to Pope Damasus in 376:

> Since the East, rent asunder by feuds of long standing, is tearing to shreds the seamless robe of the Lord . . . I think it my duty to consult the chair of Peter. . . .
> It is to the successor of the fisherman that I address myself, to the disciple of the cross.
> As I follow no leader save Christ, so I communicate with none save your Beatitude, that is, with the chair of Peter. For this, I know, is the Rock on which the Church is built. This is Noah's ark, and he who is not found in it shall perish when the flood overwhelms all. . . .*

Finally, there were outstanding leaders among the early popes, and they were devoted to the furthering of the leadership that Rome had assumed. The greatest of them were men who combined what their contemporaries felt to be holiness (not softness) with great gifts of handling human beings and of taking full responsibility for the burdens of their world. Such was Damasus I (366-384), to whom Jerome addressed the letter quoted above. Such was Leo the Great (440-461), a well-born Roman of great firmness and executive ability, a theologian of great influence, and above all a legendary intercessor with the terrible Hun leader Attila, whom he was credited with persuading to turn aside from invading Italy (see Chapter V). Gregory the Great (590-604), pope in what were already the Dark Ages, was a nobleman of Rome who had once been prefect of the city. He carried over into the papacy his

---

* Quoted in *Documents of the Christian Church,* Henry Bettenson, ed. (New York, 1947), 113.

great talents as an administrator. Under Gregory, the papacy firmly took the place that it was, at its best, to occupy during the next thousand years, the period of the Middle Ages. Rapid loss of control was suffered after Gregory's pontificate, and there was a further lapse of papal prestige in the tenth century; but in the eleventh, twelfth, and thirteenth centuries many worthy and successful followers of Leo and Gregory occupied the chair of Peter. From the decay of the Roman Empire, the Church of Rome had emerged as the firmest of great organized institutions.

The Regular Clergy

One other kind of clergy remains to be mentioned. Gregory the Great came to his office, not through priesthood and episcopate, but through a monastery. Gregory had been a monk, a member of what in contrast to the *secular* priesthood that serves the laity of this world is called the *regular* clergy, men (and women) who follow a rule (in Latin, *regula*). The origins of monasticism are in the East, especially Egypt, where isolated individuals disgusted with this wicked world, and seeking salvation as far outside it as they could, left the cities to live in solitude on the edge of the desert. By the third century, some of these hermits were competing with one another for "records" in holiness and in the denial of the flesh that students of religion call asceticism. They tried to eat the least food, to sit for the longest time without moving, or to inflict the most horrible tortures on themselves, some of them, it would seem, in order to be known as the holiest of hermits. Some, like St. Simeon Stylites, lived in the tiny space on top of pillars or columns. Wise leaders of the Church, aware of this unChristian self-assertion under the cloak of holiness, sought to bring these hermits together under a common discipline. Moreover, around many hermits, like the greatest of them, St. Anthony, little groups of followers had begun to gather. From these origins there grew up communities of monks living under formally organized rules, devoted to celibacy and poverty, spending much of their time in religious ritual, but usually working enough to make their communities self-supporting.

From Egypt, this organized asceticism spread throughout the Empire. It came to Greek-speaking lands largely through St. Basil (329-379), whose rule has remained to this day fundamental to Greek and Slavic monasticism. Under St. Basil, the reaction against the life of the hermit went further than in Egypt, where the monks assembled usually only for religious services. In Greek monasticism, the monks not only worshiped but also ate and worked together. Although they were dedicated to a life outside this wicked world, they were also to do works of charity, such as setting up orphanages and hospitals near the monastery grounds. In the West, monasticism took firm shape under the hands of one of the greatest of Christian organizers, St. Benedict, whose great abbey at Monte Cassino in southern Italy, was founded about 520.

Monasticism Evaluated

One of the differences between eastern monasticism and western monasticism throws a good deal of light on the wider differences between eastern and western Europe. In the East, the monasteries tended to remain apart from the lay world, even though some of their officials were very active in ecclesiastical politics. In the West, the monks did not wholly retreat from the world, although during the best days of monasticism they always observed the fundamental rules of asceticism. In fact, during the early centuries of our era they did much hard work in clearing ground around new monasteries, invaluable missionary work among the heathen tribes of northern Europe, and a great deal of medical and charitable work among the poor, who were numerous indeed in those days. For centuries, as scholarship became one of the recognized forms of the monk's labor, the monasteries were the guardians of the western intellectual heritage. Especially in what we usually call the Dark Ages, roughly the five hundred years after 500 A.D., the Benedictine Order was at the front of the civilizing forces of the West.

Benedict's own Rule, which is one of the important documents of Christianity, should be read entire. Its spirit is evident in a short extract that points up the Benedictine solution to that form of pride which had arisen in the very first days of monasticism, the desire to outshine one's fellows in *something*:

As there is an evil and bitter emulation which separates from God and leads to hell, so there is a good spirit of emulation which frees from vices and leads to God and life everlasting. Let monks therefore practise this emulation with most fervent love; that is to say, let them in honour prevent one another, let them bear most patiently with each other's infirmities, whether of body or of manner. Let them contend with one another in their obedience. Let no one follow what he thinks most profitable to himself, but rather what is best for another. Let them show brotherly charity with a chaste love.[*]

We shall learn more about what sent men and women into the monastic movement when, in the final section of this chapter, we examine the Christian way of life. The New Testament sounds an ascetic note that is firm and clear, especially in some of the writings of St. Paul. First in emphasis among the renunciations of the monk and the nun is sexual intercourse; Christianity has always found sex one of those phases of human nature that need regulation. But the monastic movement also

---

[*] *The Rule of St. Benedict*, Cardinal Gasquet, ed. (London, 1936), Ch. LXXII.

meant renunciation of other pleasures of the flesh, and indeed of all pleasures in the ordinary sense. For many people, the monastic life has satisfied a strong need for security, communion, renunciation, and spiritual orderliness. This need has perhaps been more common in troubled times like those of the late Roman Empire, but during the last two thousand years it has never been absent from our society.

Although monasticism contributed great services to the Christian commonwealth, it also posed grave problems to those who had charge of the affairs of the Church. No body of men, even though they are very consecrated men, fails to develop some sense of what Benedict called "emulation." Both secular clergy and regular clergy have sometimes been tempted into emulation that has not always had holiness as its goal. The secular clergy have felt that they were the true soldiers of the Lord in this harsh world, and that the regular clergy were dodging their responsibilities. The regular, on the other hand, have felt that they were leading purer, more ascetic lives, which were nearer what Jesus had preached. The tension and rivalry between secular and regular clergy complicated the organization of the Church. The monasteries, and the abbots who headed them, needed to be integrated into that organization; in a sacramental religion such as Christianity, the bishop *had* to be brought into monastic life. Abbots, however, were often at odds with bishops and archbishops. They resented the attempts of the secular clergy to see that the high standards of monastic discipline were maintained.

In the long run, these difficulties were largely overcome. Later in the Middle Ages the monastic orders achieved a more centralized organization that made their own self-policing more effective. Meanwhile, though most of the monks lived in and for their monasteries, their officials, particularly the abbots, were integrated into the general government of the Church. These

officials took part in the councils or synods that were of such great importance in the formation of Church doctrine and discipline; sometimes, as did Gregory the Great, they rose to papal office. As centers of learning, the monasteries played a great part in building not only the structure of Christian theology but also the church or canon law that entered so essentially into medieval law and institutions, and thus into our own. In sum, the regular and secular clergy in the West were both recognized parts of a great whole.

Church Government in Review

By the seventh century the broad lines of church government in both the East and the West had been laid out. The organization was hierarchical—that is, there was a regular series of relations of subordinate to superior from priest to pope, somewhat, though by no means exactly, as military lines of command run from private to general. But this hierarchy was not without a principle of mutual consultation. At almost every level, in bishoprics, archbishoprics, and for the Church as a whole, there were councils made up of officials who met and debated problems and made decisions. Church government, then, was no simple relation of silent underling to commanding superior. Indeed, in these early centuries the critical decisions were made by assemblies rather than by individuals. Once the papacy had become firmly established, however, the popes maintained the position—when they could—that the pope was superior even to a general council, and was not bound by its decisions.

The conversion of the Emperor Constantine in the early fourth century had brought Church and State into close relations. As a result, political leaders began to take an interest in episcopal elections. Partly in defense against political encroachments, high church officials began the process that culminated in the election of the bishop by the chapter—that is, certain specific clergy attached to the cathedral that was the bishop's seat. But this process took a long time to perfect, and it was most uneven in practice. Some trace of election by the people remained in many parts of the

Bishop's chair, ivory on wood (about 520-550 A.D.), in Ravenna.

West. Especially the election of the most powerful of bishops, the bishops of Rome—the popes—was for a long time under the influence of Roman mobs, and, worse yet, of the rising Roman noble families. Not until 1059 did the Synod of the Lateran take action that led to the setting up of the College of Cardinals. This college, a specially constituted body of high clerical of-ficials, put the election of popes on the basis it has since retained.

The bishop, too, had to be consecrated, and this could only be done by another bishop, usually from a neighboring diocese. Gradually in the West the popes acquired definite influence over the selection of bishops and archbishops. Since these officials were of the greatest importance in the actual governing of their territories—in some cities they became the civil government—lay rulers refused to allow complete freedom to ecclesiastical authorities in making such appointments, and insisted on influencing the choice. All through the Middle Ages, the choice of bishops was a focal point in the struggle between lay and ecclesiastical authorities that forms one of the main threads of medieval history.

In a sense, however, this very struggle was one of the major sources of our present democratic institutions. The point becomes clear when we look at the very different history of Church and State in the East. The final formal separation, or schism, between Rome and Constantinople, between the Roman Catholic and the Orthodox Churches is usually reckoned as late as 1054, but the actual separation was foreshadowed by the time of Gregory the Great, in the sixth century or even earlier. In the Byzantine East, there grew up a form of government over Church and State alike which has the unwieldy name of caesaropapism (for details, see Chapter VI). The emperor was in fact head of both Church and State. No organized clerical body could tell him where to stop. Although religious disputes broke out in the Byzantine Empire, notably a long and bitter one over the use of images in worship, there emerged from them no clearcut moral or legal code to set limits to the emperor's *rights*. The Russian Church, which is the heir to that of Byzantium, shows some of this same caesaropapism. In the West, however, pope and emperor waged a fruitful, if sometimes bitter and cruel, struggle (see Chapter VII). From this struggle there gradually emerged in practice acceptance of a situation in which no absolute authority, at once political *and* religious, was combined in a single person or institution. This acceptance is one of the roots of what we now call "civil rights" of the individual and of smaller groups within the political state.

The Catholic Church of Gregory the Great had come a long way from the humble group of dissident Jews who gathered to mourn the death, and to rejoice at the resurrection, of Jesus Christ. Hostile critics of all sorts, both within and outside Christianity, have maintained that by engaging itself in the affairs of this world, by acquiring property, by taking over legal and administrative tasks, and by accepting rich and powerful men as members of the Christian communion, the Church has betrayed its founder. They quote such words of Jesus as "how hardly shall they that have riches enter into the kingdom of God" or "except ye . . . become as little children ye shall not enter into the kingdom of heaven." Yet Christianity has always held as a central mission its duty not to shun or deny or denigrate this world and this life, but to work in the world; not indeed to accept the world as it is, but to accept it as a challenge. But a challenge is a relation, and a relation means, for the living, some sort of compromise. Once the expectation of the immediate Second Coming had passed, the Church in a sense compromised with this world of living men and women. But this compromise must seem to most of us in the western tradition a strength, rather than a weakness.

IV: The Ideas of Christianity

The Christian clergy could hardly have attained their great power had they not been essential intermediaries between this visible world of actuality and the invisible other world that to the true Christian is as real as this one. In Christianity, certain important ideas about the other world are embodied in ritual acts called *sacraments*. These sacraments are central to Christianity, the chief of the many bridges that Christianity has sought to throw between this world and the other world, the imperfect and the perfect, the "real" and the "ideal."

The Eucharist

The sacrament of the Eucharist is the central mystery of Christianity. It is a mystery made available to simple men and women, as a part of ordinary living, by the services of the Church. Jesus, in his last supper with his disciples,

. . . took bread, and blessed it, and brake it, and gave it to the disciples, and said, Take, eat; this is my body. And he took the cup, and gave thanks, and gave it to them, saying, Drink ye all of it; for this is my blood of the new testament, which is shed for many for the remission of sins.*

In the Church of the third century, the Eucharist had become the miraculous ceremony that made the Christian believer feel emotionally his link with God, that made him feel the wonder of salvation. With undue simplification it may be stated: by the sacrament of *baptism* the individual was figuratively washed of the stain of original sin, and made a Christian; by the sacrament of the *Eucharist* he remained,

---

* Matthew 26:26-28.

subject always to good behavior, in the Christian communion, was sustained in his faith and fellowship. There have been many grave theological disputes over the doctrine of the Eucharist, notably at the time of the Protestant revolt (see Chapter XII). It remains central to the drama of the Christian faith even when, as with some Protestants, it is but a commemoration of the Lord's Supper.

The Doctrine of Salvation

Around this symbolic act of the Mass, or Eucharist, theological explanations were woven. For the common man, these explanations could be very simple; for theologians, they could be of great complexity. The reader must not expect from our account the kind of universally agreed-upon statements he would get in an elementary geometry, for example. We may start with the basic doctrine of original sin, according to which Adam was given the chance for a perfect life on earth but disobeyed God, was driven from Eden, and was exposed to death and suffering here on earth. All Adam's descendants shared this fate. But the Jews, in spite of individual and group backslidings, kept alive their faith in God; and after generations of suffering God took mercy and sent to earth his only begotten son, Jesus. By his sufferings on the cross, Jesus *atoned* for human sins, made redemption to God the Father, and made it possible in the future for those who believed in him to avoid the ultimate consequences of Adam's sin. He made it possible for good Christians to be saved, to enjoy in the other world after death the immortal happiness which they could anticipate, so to speak, in this one, but which they could not completely enjoy here because this earth is no longer the Garden of Eden. It should be noted, however, that for the very first Christians the belief in the immediate Second Coming of Christ amounted to a belief that this world of Adam's sons was about to end and that some would be transported to an eternal Eden, others to an eternal hell.

Even so elementary an outline of the doctrine of salvation bristles with the kind of difficulties Christians have been arguing about for centuries. What was the relation between God the Father and his only begotten son? In this context, what does the term "begotten" actually mean? What was Adam's original sin? How did a man go about the task of attaining salvation; was it enough to belong to the Church, or must he have some inward sign? This latter question raises what has been for two thousand years the central point of debate in Christianity, the problem of faith or good works.

If you hold strongly that salvation is purely inward and emotional, that it is the outflowing of the individual soul to its source in God, then outward acts, such as the sacraments, become superfluous—or worse, a possible refuge for hypocrites. If you hold strongly that God expects his true children to act on this earth in accordance with patterns he has laid down and given to his Church to administer, you may hold that doing prescribed things (i.e., "good works") is what really counts here on earth, since this is the only way a man can be known by his fellows. The first extreme could logically make the organized Church quite unnecessary, and could lead to the priesthood of the individual believer. The second extreme could make outward conformity the sole test of salvation, and could lead to the complete control of daily life by an all-powerful clergy. Neither *extreme* position has ever in fact been taken, except in words and on paper. In daily Christian living there is actually no conflict between faith and works. *To the orthodox Christian, one is impossible without the other.*

The Seven Sacraments

The seven sacraments are the core of the system of good works. They are:

(1) baptism, by which the infant was washed of the stain of original sin and brought into mystical union with Christ; (2) confirmation, by which on attaining an age at which he could understand Christian doctrine the child was formally brought into the discipline of the Church; (3) the Eucharist, the central act of the Christian drama; (4) penance, whereby the confessed and repentant sinner, granted absolution by the priest, had the guilt of his sin and *eternal* punishment remitted, subject to a *temporal* punishment assigned as penance; this temporal punishment might or might not be sufficient to satisfy God's justice, and hence a given penance itself could not *guarantee* the penitent's salvation; (5) extreme unction, "the last rites of the Church," a ceremony performed by the priest at the dying moments of the Christian to prepare him for the life to come; (6) ordination, the ceremony by which a candidate was made a priest; and (7) matrimony. Baptism and the Eucharist (the latter is often called the Lord's Supper or Communion) have remained as sacraments in almost all the Protestant groups. Of the other sacraments, the one that has been most heavily attacked and most vigorously rejected by Protestants generally is that of penance.

The Problem of Heresy

The early centuries of Christian history are a series of struggles to maintain a single church against disputes ranging over the whole field of Christian belief. In these disputes the accepted doctrine or interpretation is called *orthodoxy,* and the challenging interpretation is called *heresy.* By the sixth or seventh century, the western Church had won through to a unity that was not seriously menaced (though it never went quite unchallenged) until the Protestant Revolt of the sixteenth century (see Chapter XII).

The first heresies appear almost as soon

Early Christian art. The Marys at the Sepulchre, ivory leaf from a diptych, from about 400 A.D.

as the first clergy. In fact, the issue between those who wished to admit Gentiles who were outside the Law and those who wished to confine the gospel to the Jews foreshadowed the kind of issue that was to confront Christianity in the first few centuries, when heresy followed on heresy. The points at issue sometimes seem unreal and unimportant, even ludicrous to us today. But it is a grave error of understanding and of historical perspective for us to regard these religious debates as trivial or childish, on the assumption that we ourselves have outgrown such things.

These theological disputes of the first few Christian centuries concerned men's understanding of God's universe and of God's means of providing salvation for sinful man. Behind these disputes lay real differences of personality and of national and class interests. The very existence of these heresies is a sign of the vitality of youthful Christianity, of the wholeheartedness and energy with which men and women threw themselves into the new movement. To regard divisions and struggles over ideas and ideals as a weakness in a social movement is a superficial judgment. Western history indicates that such divisions, if not carried too far, are rather signs of strength and growth. The overcoming of these divisions was a part of the process by which the Church acquired the unity and the resiliency, the store of political skills, with which it was able to organize Europe after the barbarian invasions, and to salvage much of the culture of the Greco-Roman world.

Gnosticism

The first main crisis was brought on by a whole group of heresies, which are usually referred to as Gnostic, from the Greek word for knowledge. The Gnostics were mostly educated people of the Greco-Roman world who were in search of knowledge, indeed of magic—sophisticated magic. They knew about most of the competing cults of the Greco-Roman world, and about the philosophies of that world, especially Neo-Platonic philosophy. They tended, in spite of their bewildering variety, to have one thing in common, a belief that the physical world ("matter") is evil, or non-existent, or, more simply, that the everyday

world is an evil illusion. The figure of Jesus they found appealing, but it was Jesus the miracle-worker, Jesus the God, to whom they responded. His human nature, his participation in the familiar experiences of this world—this they could not for a moment admit.

One of the dangers from Gnosticism was that the Church would become too clearly and obviously divided into a body of ignorant faithful and a body of sophisticated initiates who felt themselves purer, wiser, and "deeper" than the rest of the flock. That danger has always existed in Christianity, even in the very distinction between clergy and laymen. But it has always been resisted as somehow a betrayal of the mission of Jesus. Another danger from the Gnostics was the belief that matter is evil: if this were so, then the Christian God who was also the God of the Old Testament, could not have created this wholly evil world of matter, and a rival God (Satan) had to be posited. Monotheism and the whole Judaic inheritance were thus threatened. The Gnostics were not conquered by any one dramatic council or decree; especially in the East, Gnosticism has been in a sense endemic. In the West, the Gnostics were never a real threat.

Arianism and the Trinity

The Arian heresy caused the greatest and best known of the crises suffered by the early Church. The critical issue here lay in the doctrine of the Trinity, that is, the concept of "God in three Persons"— God the Father, God the Son (Jesus), and God the Holy Ghost (or Holy Spirit). Arius, a learned priest of Alexandria who died in 336, was troubled by the intricate relationship among the three members of the Trinity, especially by the gospel word "begotten," which was used to describe the relation between the Father and the Son. If Jesus were begotten, he must be somehow inferior to, or dependent upon, or at least *later in time* than his begetter. Arius was not a Unitarian in our modern sense, which accepts only God the Father, which makes Jesus wholly mortal, no more than a supremely good and wise man, and which does away with the concept of the Holy Ghost as unnecessary metaphysics. But Arianism had *affinities* with the kind of reasoning that lies behind later Unitarianism. You might think of Arius as balking at the difficulty of understanding the Trinitarian doctrine of One God being at the same time Three.

Another modification of the Trinity, sometimes called tri-theism, made the members of the Trinity equal and separate, though co-operating and in a sense flowing together. Tri-theism, however, came close to preaching the existence of three gods. It meant the open abandonment of the claim that Christianity was truly monotheistic and above the crude pagan polytheisms. Tri-theism never took root except in Egypt and in some other border areas of the Roman Empire.

The orthodox solution to the problem of the Trinity is associated with the name of a great contemporary rival of Arius who also flourished in Alexandria, Bishop Athanasius. This solution asserts that the members of the Trinity are Three and yet at the same time One. The Father and Son are co-equals in eternity; neither is later in time than the other, and yet they are Father and Son.

In 325, under the auspices of the Emperor Constantine, some three hundred bishops gathered in the Council of Nicaea to settle the Arian-Athanasian controversy. The Council decided by a large majority against Arius. But it did not put an end to Arianism. From 325 to 381, thirteen church councils debated the rejected doctrine. The missionary Ulfilas (311-383) preached Arianism to the barbarian Goths on the outskirts of the Roman Empire, and the heresy continued to spread among these and other German tribes in spite of the official condemnation at Nicaea. Thus, when these tribes swarmed over the West a century later, they brought with them an Arian, not a Catholic, Christianity. This religious difference proved to be an important source of additional conflict between the invaders and the invaded (see Chapter V).

The kind of settlement that the Church reached in the Arian controversy, however, illustrates the way in which Christianity has tried to preserve its balance. It has always sought a careful balance between other-worldly idealism and practical acceptance of this imperfect world. Christianity can hardly afford the luxury of choosing logically between this world and the other, between what is and what ought to be. Gnosticism would have led it into magic and swooning, into *theosophy*, over-intellectual maundering, or into a denial of this world. Arianism might have led it into a mere common-sense acceptance of this world. Catholicism has kept a foot solidly planted in each world.

The Dispute over the Nature of Christ

In the East, controversy arose also over a problem that was closely related to Arianism, the problem of the nature of Christ. On this issue the two extreme positions were in complete opposition: either Christ was all-human and not God at all, or else he was all-divine and not human at all. Both extremes threatened a denial of the Trinity. Moreover, even the central orthodox position, that Jesus was *both* God and man, created difficulty. Infinite dispute arose over just how the divine and human natures were conjoined in Christ. Nestorius, Bishop of Constantinople in the early fifth century, advanced the doctrine that the two natures, human and divine, existed together in Christ in perfect harmony, but somehow distinct; it was a moral rather than a physical union. The Virgin was not, therefore, strictly speaking, the mother of God. Nestorianism was condemned at the Council of Ephesus in 431, but like tritheism it took refuge in the border areas of the Empire. In Syria, in Mesopotamia, in Persia, and even in China, the Nestorian Church flourished for centuries. A remnant still exists today in the Near East.

At the other extreme stood the Monophysites (the name comes from the Greek words for "single" and "nature"). The Monophysites believed that Christ had a single human-divine nature, that in him the human and divine were *of* two natures and not, as the Nestorians believed, *in* two natures. The bitter disputes over the implication of these two little prepositions, "of" and "in," may well seem to the modern layman an example of theological futility. Yet the "of," like Arianism, could lead to a form of Unitarianism, an excessive rationalism, an abandonment of the mystic, the miraculous, the other-worldly element in Christianity—and, above all, to an abandonment of the consoling intervention of the Virgin and the saints. Pope Leo the Great intervened decisively, in the Council of Chalcedon in 451, which condemned the Monophysite heresy, and saved the *dual* nature of the *one* Christ. But just as the Council of Nicaea did not dispose of Arianism by legislating against it, so the Council of Chalcedon did not dispose of Monophysitism. Its adherents, in Egypt and Syria particularly, continued vehemently to defend their case, and created for the Empire in the East a problem that remained unsettled at the time of the rise of Islam in the seventh century (see Chapter VI).

Other Heresies

In the Roman West, as contrasted with the Greek East, the serious heresies tend to involve less word-spinning and come closer to obvious moral and practical problems. Take, for example, the western heresy of Donatism, named for Donatus, a fourth-century Bishop of Carthage. This heresy was especially strong in North Africa during the fifth century. Donatism hinged on the problem of whether or not the validity of a sacrament depends on the personal purity of the minister. The Donatists, who were strict moralists, eventually maintained that a priest in a state of sin could not administer a sacrament efficaciously. This conception of the role of the priest introduced an element of uncertainty that was fatal to the communicant's sense of security. And in that troubled age a sense of security was one of the great sources of Christian strength. Moreover, by focusing on the personality of the minister rather than on the miracle of the sacrament, the Donatist heresy seemed to detract from the majesty of God. In orthodox doctrine, God can work even through an imperfect human vessel.

Another western heresy was Pelagianism, which, like Donatism, was strong in the fifth century. Pelagius was a British monk who argued that human beings held in their hands the control of their moral fate. They were not tainted by original sin; they did not need divine grace to obtain personal salvation. In short, Pelagius believed in complete freedom of will. But complete freedom of will is again a tipping of the complex balance that is orthodox Christianity. The idea tends to exalt human pride and human independence, and to lessen the majesty and supra-rational power of God. Pelagianism is simply too hopeful, without the note of tragedy, to be genuinely Christian. Yet in one form or another it has tended to crop up constantly in the history of western culture. The last major appearance was perhaps in the optimistic Enlightenment of the eighteenth-century.

One final heresy flourished in the West in the fifth and sixth centuries. It was hardly a heresy at all, but rather a separate religion, one of the many oriental cults that competed with Christianity, and was perhaps the longest-lived of them all. This was Manicheism, named after Mani, a Mesopotamian prophet of the third century. The Manicheans were dualists. They held that the universe is not in the power of a single God, all-powerful, all-good, all-knowing, but that it is torn between a God of light and a Devil of darkness, who fight it out on what to us mortals must seem equal terms. The Manicheans believed of course that they should enlist on the side of God. Their ethical values were not apparently greatly different from those of the Christians, although the Manicheans appear in Christian tradition as perversely wicked. The appeal of this dualism, like the appeal of Unitarianism, is too rational, easy, obvious, and "common-sensical" for the great Christian tradition. Yet Manicheism persisted, at least underground, and, as we shall see, cropped up as a major threat to the religious unity of the medieval world.

Saint Augustine

In St. Augustine (354-430), the Catholic Church found a great champion of orthodox Christianity against heresy. First a Stoic, then a Manichean and a Neo-Platonist, Augustine was converted to Catholicism as a mature man. He became a great preacher and organizer, a bishop, and in his most active years a full participant in the struggle to maintain orthodoxy in North Africa, which was the seat of some of the fiercest opposition to the orthodox Church. He combated Manicheism, Pelagianism, and Donatism with a zeal that makes him an outstanding example of the saying that converts are often the strongest pillars of the Church. Augustine was also a great writer and thinker, whose work is at the basis of western orthodoxy. It is impossible to do justice in our brief account to Augustine's theological, philosophical, and ethical

achievement. His *Confessions,* a mystical autobiography, are an important historical document as well as a revelation of a remarkable personality. Augustine codified with great skill the work of the early centuries of Christianity and set on a broad basis the major ideas of Christian orthodoxy in the medieval West.

He wrote his most influential work, the *City of God,* directly to rebut the pagan argument that Christianity, by undermining the old Roman virtues and by offending the old Roman gods, was responsible for the decline of the Empire. Augustine had little trouble in showing that in the past pagan empires had also risen and fallen. But he goes far beyond these polemics, and ends by outlining a complete Christian philosophy of history. For Augustine, Rome and its Empire were but one more phase of the *civitas terrena,* the city of earth, which could only beat back and forth in the confined round of earthly success and failure. But Christianity brought to men the possibility of citizenship in the *civitas Dei,* the City of God, which was something far better, far beyond the petty things of this world. Indeed, in the end, this citizenship led to peace, happiness, perfection, and salvation.

Augustine's City of God is not indeed of this earth, and it would be wrong to suggest that his philosophy "anticipates" the conventional modern doctrine of material progress, which he would have hardly been able to understand. But it is true that Augustine first clearly saw and presented human history as having a purposive development in time, as having a spiritual significance as struggle. Orthodox Christianity has never lost this feeling for the possibility of moral progress in mankind. The earthly city *can* be better; above all, for Augustine was a Roman, it can be ruled, under Christian dispensation by men who value order, decency, discipline, mutual trust, and forbearance among all men.

Augustine, then, set firmly the Christian

attitude toward history. The Church is in history, but it is also above and outside history. It changes, since it grows, makes converts on this earth; but it is no mere natural process; it is a goal, a purpose, as well as a way. Augustine also established the characteristic western Christian attitude toward the grave and unavoidable problem of the freedom of the will. Here again we encounter what to the unbeliever, or merely to the simplifier, is a contradiction, an effort to have one's cake and eat it. Augustine held that God is all-knowing, all-good, all-powerful; nothing could be that he had not known and intended; our actions are *determined*. Pelagius, who preached that men have full freedom of will, and can will independently of God's will, was to Augustine a dangerous heretic. And yet, Augustine had to preserve human moral responsibility; the Christian must be able to choose between doing right and doing wrong. The Christian may not say that when he does wrong it is because God made him do

wrong. God has put us on this earth for his glory and our eventual salvation; without the testing of our moral strength—without our being able to feel that *in a sense* we have "freedom of the will"—we should be poor creatures indeed, mere animals. But we are not gods ourselves, not free as God is free; we may not—as a twentieth-century anthropologist was to put it—believe that "Man makes himself." *

Our necessarily brief account of St. Augustine's position has made it seem more paradoxical, more contradictory in simple logic, than it is to the true believer. Christianity, as we shall see in the next section of this chapter, is a religion that holds in tension what seems to the outsider contradictions, opposites. But Augustine, like the later St. Thomas Aquinas (see p. 319) had a very great gift for ironing out these contradictions; he does not deliberately create and enjoy paradox.

---

* The title of a book: V. Gordon Childe, *Man Makes Himself* (London, 1936).

V: The Christian Way of Life

By the fourth and fifth centuries, it had become clear that East and West were interpreting much of the message of the Gospels in different ways. It is true that some fiction of unity continued to be maintained, and also that throughout the first Christian millennium Rome and Constantinople seem disputants within a common heritage. But the facts of the separation are clear enough to us now. We are here concerned above all with the spirit of *western* Christianity.

The Flesh and the Spirit

Western Christianity has sought to promote on this earth a life in which are

mingled (though not confused) the practical and the ideal, the commonplace and the heroic, sensual pleasure and ascetic self-denial. Like any other great effort of the human spirit, Christianity has never been in actuality quite what it is in ideal. It has, however, consistently maintained the relation between the ideal and the actual *as in fact a relation*, a coming together, not a flying apart. On the one hand, Christianity was often tempted, in an excess of idealism, to deny the reality or at any rate the importance of the actual, the sense world of our human experiences. On the other hand, in the dust of living it was often tempted to betray or simply to neglect its ideals. But it has on the whole maintained a fruitful tension between this world and the next. It has never quite, like some oriental cults, sought to escape from the sense world, or to suppress it by some continued magic. Nor has it ever quite, like crude hedonism or certain kinds of philosophical materialism, been willing to accept the sense world at whatever face value common sense or uncorrected human reason might give that world.

One of the clearest notes of Christianity is simply a distrust of the flesh, a rejection of the idea that the natural human appetites and instincts are adequate to serve as a sole guide to human conduct. This distrust inspires one of the major doctrines of Christianity, that of original sin, which is *not* a belief that man is naturally wicked, but rather a belief that without divine aid he must lapse into the wickedness which is a heritage from Adam. This profound distrust of the natural man of flesh and blood runs all through Christianity and takes many forms. Our Freudian time is tempted to believe that the early Christians were obsessed with sex, that the original sin of Adam and Eve was sexual intercourse, that the appetite in natural man most distrusted by Christianity is sexual appetite. Orthodoxy does not accept such a confined definition of original sin; for Christianity, pride is the great sin. Yet it is not unfair to say that most Christian thought distrusts the whole unaided natural man—his appetites for food, drink, gaming, fighting, and vainglory, as well as for sexual indulgence. Catholic Christianity has always provided a place for the rare individual who wishes to subdue the flesh by fleeing this world. Protestant Christianity has been less successful with such people, who under Protestantism have more generally had to turn their ascetic drive toward reforming the conduct of others on earth.

In practice, the traditional Christian way of life has not been wholly different from older ways, such as that of the Greeks of the great culture. We noted that for the Greek of the great age overeating and undereating, gluttony and abstinence, were *both* evils, and that the sensible man sought the golden mean by eating moderately but well. So too, in fact, with the good conventional Christian. Gluttony was for him worse than abstemiousness, because being more common, it was therefore more dangerous. There remains in the background of Christian feeling on this subject something that is reflected in the popular saying, "It is better to eat to live than to live to eat." But the view that Christianity is a gloomy faith, that the Christian may never under any conditions enjoy food, drink, and lovemaking on this earth is false. The note of asceticism is in Christianity, and if you listen for it with either a friendly or a hostile ear, you can always hear it. But there are many other notes, sounding simultaneously in chords of unbelievable complexity.

The Individual and Society

One of these other notes is that of unselfishness, un-selfconsciousness. From one point of view, Christianity is a very individualistic faith that is concerned with the salvation of the soul of each individual. The Christian at his highest moments is alone with God, responsible to God alone. State, vocation, family are all distractions of this world. Jesus himself spoke against family ties:

While he yet talked to the people, behold his mother and his brethren stood without, desiring to speak with him. Then one said unto him, Behold, thy mother and thy brethren stand without, desiring to speak with thee. But he answered and said unto him that told him, Who is my mother? And who are my brethren? And he stretched forth his hand toward his disciples, and said, Behold, my mother and my brethren! For whosoever shall do the will of my Father which is in heaven, the same is my brother, and sister, and mother.*

---

* Matthew 12:46-50.

Yet precisely this passage shows the way to the Christian emphasis on social responsibility. In the true Christian life all men are one, and subsidiary groups are a distraction—or, worse, a padding for the selfish ego. The important thing is for the individual to avoid all kinds of personal triumphs over others, all competitive successes, all the things that set off and sharpen his ego. Christianity as a great world religion, especially in its Catholic form, has never carried this annihilation of the individual ego to an extreme. Men who have competed very successfully with their fellows in this world have been professing Christians; even Napoleon was a professed Christian. Nevertheless, the ideal of unselfishness is there. Christianity tries to tame the more extravagant flights of the competitive human spirit, tries to subdue self-assertiveness, truculence, boasting, pride, and other manifestations of the "natural" man. It distrusts these manifestations quite as much as—indeed, properly, more than—it distrusts man's simpler appetites for food, drink, and sex, all the pleasures of the flesh.

A third note of Christianity is simply the other side of un-selfconsciousness. The Christian should not only subdue his own ego; he should open his heart in loving-kindness to all his fellow men. Modern rationalists have often been so shocked by the fact that some Christians burned, imprisoned, or otherwise silenced fellow men who disagreed with them on theological matters that they have refused to hear this note of love and charity in Christianity. But it is there, and without it Christianity is incomplete. The note is not quite the one we today recognize as sentimental humanitarianism, not quite the note of pity the crusading reformer feels for criminals, defectives, failures, and all other underdogs. The Christian is expected to love the "upperdog" as well as the underdog, a duty many humanitarian reformers seem not to acknowledge.

Christian loving-kindness, for all its affinities with gentler emotions, is also based on resignation in face of a universe that is not to be shaped wholly by man's will. For the Christian regards sin as a fact. He must forgive the truly repentant sinner, he must pity the sinner, he must indeed love the sinner. But he may not love the sinner for his sin. Above all, he may not regard sin as an illusion, nor as the result of bad physical and social environment alone, nor as the result of temporary and wholly human or physical influences. For the orthodox Christian loving-kindness can therefore never be optimistic about the perfectibility of man, nor can it ever be pure humanitarianism.

Reason and Faith

A fourth note of Christianity is its distrust of certain kinds of thinking. Christianity is by no means opposed to all thought. We have already seen that its theology is an intellectual structure of great subtlety and complexity; we shall see that at its medieval climax Christianity held reason in the highest esteem. But Christianity has always distrusted the kind of thinking we nowadays usually call "rationalism"; it has always been afraid that the human mind will *think away the supernatural*. Thus, though it is unfair to Christianity to say that it has always opposed full intellectual freedom, or to say that modern science has developed only in spite of Christian antagonism, there remains a grain of truth in these extreme statements. At the very least, the Christian must at some point begin to believe what his sense experience, his instruments, and his science give him no direct evidence for. Indeed, pure rationalism must remain for the Christian the indecent self-assertion of the rationalist, a sin perhaps worse than the self-assertion displayed by the sensualist or the show-off, a sin nearer the heart of pride. The natural man can think as well as lust. Only the spiritual man can have faith, "the substance

Early Christian art. Sixth-century marble sarcophagus of Archbishop Theodorus. From Sant'Apollinare in Classe, Ravenna, Italy.

of things hoped for, the evidence of things not seen."

Throughout the ages, Christianity has firmly maintained its belief that this world as presented by the conventional five senses is not the whole universe. The universe is for the Christian ultimately a problem, an intellectual as well as a moral and emotional problem. There is a God for whom nothing is a problem, a God who "understands" the universe. Men cannot possibly put themselves in God's place, and they cannot understand the universe by ordinary intellectual activity such as logic or common sense. But through the intercession of God they can by a different sort of activity acquire a kind of certainty quite different from worldly knowledge, which is the product of intellectual activity.

The kind of activity by which men arrive at this certainty we call *faith*. It is not thinking, not feeling, not anything the psychologist or physiologist in his laboratory can get at, any more than the chemist in his laboratory can get at the miracle of the Eucharist. Through faith, men cannot know the universe as they know, for instance, that oaks grow from acorns. Through faith they *can* be certain that God does exist, that the universe is not the puzzling, even hostile place it seems to a man thinking and worrying, and that the universe is indeed made for man and the drama of his salvation.

Attitude toward This World

But—and this is the last note we shall dwell on—Christianity also attaches a very great importance, a very great degree of reality, to this world of the senses. This world is the testing ground for entrance into the next world. The faith of the Christian, which we have above sought to separate sharply from other human activities, does teach him that these other activities are indispensable to his salvation, that they must be well conducted here on earth. But more than this, the good Christian wants other men to be good; he wants to make this imperfect world as nearly as possible like that perfect world his faith tells him about.

This emphasis on bettering mankind is called melioristic. Christianity is in many ways a pessimistic faith, with no concrete notions *of its own* about progress on this earth, indeed with quite definite notions about this earth as a vale of tears. And yet Christianity has been intensely melioristic in practice. It has been a reforming religion, anxious to make this world a better place for human beings, more peaceful, more prosperous, more friendly, more decent. It has believed in improvement, if not in formal progress.

Finally, Christianity has in its central tradition never really been strait-jacketed by formulas or dogmas that confined its appeal to one sort of person. It has been universal in its appeal. It has made room for mystics, for ascetics, for intellectuals, for soldiers, for rulers and administrators, for orators and salesmen, for artists and seers, and above all for ordinary men and women. In all these it has sought to tame the "natural" man (as Christianity must call him) of self-assertive pride, has sought to make him a Christian living a Christian life. Unlike the Greek polytheistic cults, which sought only to keep the gentlemanly few at the gentlemanly level, Christianity has sought to ennoble us all. Its standards of conduct are high—quite as high as, and indeed not so very different from, the best of Greek ideals. It seeks to extend these standards not just to an aristocracy, but to all mankind.

Reading Suggestions on Christianity

(Asterisk indicates paperbound edition.)

GENERAL ACCOUNTS

L. M. O. Duchesne, *Early History of the Christian Church*, 3 vols. (Longmans, Green, 1912-1924). A lengthy standard account; very readable.

K. Latourette, *History of Christianity* (Harper, 1953). A short survey; well-balanced, up-to-date, and sympathetic.

C. Guignebert, *Christianity Past and Present* (Macmillan, 1927). One of the best surveys, written by a French scholar who, though not sympathetic to Christianity, is fair-minded.

C. Dawson, *The Making of Europe* (Macmillan, 1933; °Meridian). A scholarly Catholic approach.

A. C. McGiffert, *A History of Christian Thought*, Vol. I (Scribner's, 1932). A good, brief account from a Protestant position.

H. B. Parkes, *Gods and Men: The Origins of Western Culture* (Knopf, 1959). A clear and sympathetic account with a fine up-to-date reading list.

SPECIAL STUDIES

F. Cumont, *The Oriental Religions in Roman Paganism* (Open Court, 1911; °Dover) An introduction to the general religious climate in which Christianity took root.

E. Renan, *Life of Jesus* (Modern Library). This famous book, written a century ago, was one of the first attempts to deal with Jesus as a historical figure. Its scholarship is now outdated, but it is interesting for its skeptical point of view.

M. Burrows, *The Dead Sea Scrolls* (Viking, 1955). Of the many books on the subject this is perhaps the most useful for the student of general history.

A. Schweitzer, *The Quest of the Historical Jesus*, new ed. (Macmillan, 1948). Somewhat detailed and specialized, but an excellent introduction to the fascinating question of the historicity of Jesus.

B. H. Streeter, *The Four Gospels* (Macmillan, 1930). A good middle-of-the-road study by a Protestant cleric.

S. J. Case, *The Social Origins of Christianity* (Univ. of Chicago Press, 1923). Fully lives up to its title; emphasizes interrelations of environment and ideas.

E. R. Goodenough, *The Church in the Roman Empire* (Holt, 1931). A "Berkshire study"; a brief, balanced account directed to the beginning student.

R. Bultman, *Primitive Christianity in Its Contemporary Setting*, trans. R. H. Fuller (°Meridian, 1956). An up-to-date scholarly treatment.

A. D. Nock, *St. Paul* (Oxford Univ. Press, 1955, Home University Library). A classic treatment, originally published in 1938.

SOURCES

The New Testament is, of course, the best source reading. The inquisitive reader may wish to compare several versions: The "Authorized" version (many editions) is substantially the King James version; the "Revised Standard" version (Nelson, 1952) has created some unfavorable comment both from literary reviewers and from fundamentalist Protestants; a recent American edition of the Douay (Roman Catholic) version was published in 1950 (Catholic Book Publishing Company); finally, there is an "American" Protestant version by Smith and Goodspeed (Univ. of Chicago Press, 1939).

Next to the New Testament may be ranked the writings of St. Augustine—his spiritual autobiography, *The Confessions*, J. F. Sheed, trans. (Sheed and Ward, 1947) and the more difficult *City of God*, G. E. McCracken, trans., now in course of publication in the Loeb Classical Library (Harvard Univ. Press, 1957—).

H. S. Bettenson, ed., *Documents of the Christian Church* (Oxford World Classics, 1947). An excellent collection, accompanied by enlightening summaries and editorial comments; useful not only for the early period but also for the whole history of Christianity.

CHAPTER IV

The
West:

Early Middle Ages

CHAPTER V

I: The Germanic Invasions

THE PERIOD from the collapse of the Roman Empire in the West down to about 1000 A.D. provides an outstanding example of the breakdown of a whole civilization. Historians used to call these early medieval centuries from 500 to 1000 the Dark Ages. This term suggests a unique barbarian interruption between an earlier classical flowering and a later slow recovery or renaissance. Today, however, historians often use the more neutral term, Early Middle Ages, in preference to the Dark Ages. For if much of Roman civilization was lost in these years, much, including above all Christianity, was retained; and much—new institutions, such as feudalism, new techniques, such as deeper plowing and better drainage, the horse-collar, a great improvement on the old yoke, the sea-worthy Norse ships, which could face the hazards of Atlantic navigation in a way the old Mediterranean vessels never could, and much more—was created.

The Nature of the Germanic Invasions

Viewed in the long perspective of world history, the fall of Rome to the barbarians is no more than another case of a

173

rich and settled country falling to simpler peoples of primitive background. It is one more example of the sort of thing the ancient Near East had often known, and of that eternal process of human cross-breeding or mongrelization that Americans call the "melting pot." Although some Germans broke through the Roman frontier in organized war bands, others were recruited as mercenaries for Roman armies, and others drifted in peacefully as individuals or in family groups. German agricultural workers quietly settled on big estates, especially in Gaul. In those days of primitive technology even the actual military invasions caused less destruction than we nowadays associate with warfare. They resulted in burnings and slaughterings, of course, but they were far from the bloodiest or most destructive invasions in history.

Thanks to many surviving chronicles and histories, almost all written by monks, we know a great deal about the routes of the invading bands, about their chiefs, and about the politics of the separate states they set up. Yet these historical accounts are inferior to the best Greek and Roman historical writings in depth and composition, in psychological insight and accuracy. Moreover, the modern student of social problems would like to know many things about the German wanderings which the sources do not tell him.

First, reliable statistics do not exist. We do not know how numerous the invaders were in proportion to the invaded population; we do not know to what degree the barbarians replaced peoples who were there before them; we do not know whether the total population of western Europe was greater or less under the barbarians than under the Late Empire. Modern research has generally tended to diminish the numerical importance of the German invaders. Almost certainly this general geographic rule holds true: there were more Germans in proportion to non-Germans in Britain and Belgium, with the proportion of Germans steadily diminishing from north to south, until in North Africa the raiding Vandals had no real effect on the structure of the population. In short, the German invasions did not wholly change the blood (or the genes) of western and southern Europe. Biologically, racially, the western world was just a bit more mixed after the invasions than before.

But may not this small German admixture have been *qualitatively* important? Much has been written about the tonic effect of this "new blood" on the tired old Empire. Proud patriots, especially in Germany and Britain during the nineteenth and early twentieth centuries, argued that the early Germans brought a youthful energy that ultimately made possible medieval and modern civilization. These are literary and moral metaphors, which cannot be given scientific proof. It is easy to picture the crude but energetic, somehow forward-looking, German barbarian chief and to contrast him with the refined, skeptical, impotent Roman aristocrat, just as it is easy for most Americans to picture the capable, ambitious immigrant in nineteenth-century New England and to contrast him with the snobbish, hidebound, proper Bostonian. Concrete experience, however, does not always confirm these stereotypes. The immigrant may be a gangster; the Bostonian may be an able, inventive Yankee. Bishop Gregory of Tours, himself apparently of pure Gallo-Roman noble stock, seems on the whole a far sounder and healthier person than many of the Frankish chiefs whose lives he records as historian of the Franks.

Losses and Survivals in the Dark Ages

The biggest and the most important problem created by the breakdown of Roman civilization in the West is also the most insoluble. How complete was the breakdown? Just what was really lost? The loss can be seen most clearly at the level of large-scale administration and organization. These centuries of the Dark Ages mark, with the brief but important interlude of Charlemagne's empire (see p. 186), a failure in human ability to organize and administer as an effective state and society any large territorial political or economic group. Only the Roman Catholic Church was able to transcend the relatively narrow limits of the incipient nation or province and to maintain an effective organization over millions of human beings. Even the Church was subject to grave lapses of discipline. Its local clergy were caught up in the web of local lay rule, and weakness and disorder appeared in its very heart at Rome. It struggled everywhere to preserve its unity and strength. Roads, postal systems, even sea transport declined from the Roman efficiency that had allowed both men and things an almost modern freedom and ease of circulation. Thousands of little districts came to depend on themselves for almost everything they used, and thus became *autarkic* (self-sufficient). And these same little districts took to fighting among themselves. Some invading Germanic tribes did exercise a rough control over sizable areas, but these areas were already much smaller than the old Empire had been, and the control was very rough indeed, not by any means an organized administration. Francia in 1000 was not as well run as Gallia had been under the *Pax Romana*.

With this loss of ability to run anything big there went a loss of discipline, a loss of morale, a loss of the older, orderly ways. The Dark Ages were not times of absolute chaos and anarchy. Had all order broken down, western civilization could not have survived at all, and we should now perhaps be speaking Hunnish or some such tongue. But, save for rare exceptions, mostly in the Church, the almost instinctive network of habits of command and obedience that keep a great, complex community together was rudely cut. It had to be reconstructed from

the local units that formed the foundation of the new society to come.

Finally, heavy losses occurred in the techniques of artistic and intellectual production. The artistic skills—sculpture, painting, architecture—tended to vanish, even though they by no means disappeared. Sculptors no longer carved the human body realistically, possibly because they did not want to, not because they did not know how. Their art may have rejected "realism." Still, it is hard to look at the scanty art that has survived from the earliest part of the Dark Ages without seeing signs that basic skills have been lost, presumably by interruptions in the process of handing them down from master to apprentice—that is, by a failure in *education*.

The Dark Ages lost command over the tools of scholarship and science. Spoken Latin broke down into the vernaculars— French, Italian, and Spanish in the making. Even where it survived as a learned tongue, written as well as spoken, Latin was debased and simplified. The general level of literature and philosophy was low; the few writers were no more than followers and imitators of the already enshrined "classics" like Cicero and Vergil.

But much of ancient civilization did survive the Dark Ages. Many basic useful skills were not lost. Men could weave, farm, use horses, and make pottery, swords, and spears quite as well in the year 1000 as in the year 100; in some ways and in some places, they could do these things better in 1000 than in 100. In the Church, too, there survived, not only in treasured libraries, but also in the whole intellectual and moral formation of its leaders, a large portion of the intellectual achievement of the ancient Near East, Greece, and Rome. Until very recently, this classical heritage formed the major part of all formal education in the West. Even among laymen, the memory of the One World of Rome never died. The barbarian chiefs so admired the Rome they were destroying that they retained something of its law and institutions. As we shall see, the most striking political event of the Dark Ages is the actual revival in the West, under Frankish kings, of the title and the claims of the Roman Empire.

Early German Expansion

Our sources for knowledge of the Germans, at least before the fourth century, are insufficient to bear the weight of specific generalizations about their primitive way of life. Both Caesar and Tacitus (see pp. 127-129) were more interested in impressing and influencing their Roman readers than in giving a full and accurate report on the Germans. The legends and poetry, the religious beliefs of these early Germans, were preserved at first orally, and were written down only much later in the Middle Ages. Finally, remnants or "fossils" or primitive German institutions remain in the working institutions as we know them in the years from 500 on. We have the beliefs and the institutions of the primitive Germans not in their original form but only as they were affected by intercourse with the civilized world of Rome and Christianity.

We do not know just where the original Germans came from, nor how many they were, nor just how they were related to other groups of Indo-European speech, the Celts, the Slavs, the Greeks, and the rest. Clues, such as the names of plants and animals or the frequency of blondness, which goes with mists and weak northern sun, make the shores of the Baltic the most likely point of origin for the Germans. By the time their tribal names come into Greek and Roman writing, the Germans had already started expanding, and they were already divided into tribes with no real political unity. They pushed eastward, perhaps in part as a ruling warrior class with subject Slavic populations. The Gothic tribes, for example, occupied the area that

is today Rumania and South Russia (the Ukraine). Others pushed westward, probably amalgamating with Celtic groups. The Belgae, for instance, whose name survives in Belgium, were apparently (though this is not certain) of mixed German and Celtic origins. As early as the end of the second century B.C., two tribes called by the Romans the Cimbri and the Teutones appeared somewhat prematurely on the stage of history and held a sort of preview of the later invasions. They ravaged Gaul, and even crossed the Alps, where in 102 B.C. they were defeated by the Roman Marius (see pp. 109-110).

For centuries, the Germans pressed upon the European land borders of the Roman state, but generally they were held on the line of the Rhine and the Danube. Then, in the fourth century A.D., they broke through. They were certainly pressed from behind—from the east—by waves of nomadic peoples pushing out from the great Eurasian steppes and semi-deserts, peoples of non-European stock and language, sometimes called rather vaguely Asiatics or Mongolians. The Huns were the most famous of these nomads and their name still suggests barbarian ruthlessness.

Although the fierce Huns and kindred tribes undoubtedly pushed the Germans on, it is quite likely that the Germans themselves were on the move because of a surplus of population. Still in economic terms barbarians, they were multiplying more rapidly than their resources. The Germans were attracted into the Roman Empire by its tempting wealth and by its obvious disorganization, of which they were well aware through generations of contact on the border and through the reports of their many fellows who had been in Roman service. We must now follow briefly the most important of their invasions of the Empire, remembering that in addition to these mass movements there went on constantly the peaceful immigration of individuals and small groups.

The Visigoths

The West Goths, or Visigoths, made the first and in many ways the most striking breakthrough. This tribe had wandered down from the Baltic to settle on the shores of the Black Sea, where they arrived about 200 A.D. Defeated by the onrushing Huns, the tribe—men, women, and children, perhaps all told 60,000 people—moved on across the Danube into Roman lands. On the South Russian plains the Visigoths had mastered the art of fighting on horseback. In 378, their cavalry decisively defeated the organized Roman army under the eastern co-emperor, Valens, near Adrianople. Valens himself was killed in this battle, which had grave psychological effects on the ruling classes of the Empire. The Visigoths, however, were not good enough at siege work before regular fortifications to take Adrianople, let alone Constantinople. So they turned south to invade and ravage the Balkan Peninsula from one end to the other.

Under their chieftain Alaric (370-410), they fought a series of actions with the Romans, who were themselves commanded by the German Stilicho. Finally reaching Italy, Alaric and his men succeeded in capturing the city of Rome itself in 410, after rather treacherous negotiations with some of the Romans; perhaps not even the great Alaric could have taken Rome from a determined garrison. Rome was sacked for three days, an event that spread a sense of doom and decay even more completely than had the defeat at Adrianople. It is against the background of Alaric and the Goths that you must read St. Augustine's *City of God* (see above, p. 166).

Alaric died in southern Italy, and was buried in the bed of the river Busento, the course of which was temporarily diverted to permit the interment. His successor, Ataulf, led the Visigoths across the Alps into Gaul, and thence into Spain.

Ataulf married the sister of the western co-emperor, Honorius, perhaps with her consent but certainly against the will of Honorius (though Honorius himself had married the daughter of the German Stilicho). Honorius bought off the Visigoths with the grant of Aquitaine in Gaul, roughly the lands between the Loire and the Garonne rivers, to which later Visigothic chieftains —we may now begin to call them *kings*— added Spain.

The Visigoths have left little permanent mark in history. Their kingdom of Toulouse in Aquitaine went down before the best organizers among the invading tribes, the Franks, in 507. Their Spanish kingdom kept on, not very successfully, until it was overwhelmed by the Moslems in the early eighth century. Like many other German tribes, the Visigoths were converted to the Arian form of Christianity and were thus additionally handicapped in the necessary task of accommodating themselves to the Roman Catholic majority among their Romanized "subjects."

The Visigoths were pioneers, signs of what was to come. They gained the first spectacular field victory over the Romans, and their kingdom of Toulouse in Aquitaine was the precedent for a whole subsequent series of barbarian "concessions" within the Empire. Most of these concessions became the territorial units of medieval and early modern history, and some of them became the nation-states of today.

The Ostrogoths

The East Goths, or Ostrogoths, kinsmen of the Visigoths, were subjected to the Huns and broke loose only after the decay of the Hunnish Empire in the mid-fifth century. They reached Italy soon after a minor barbarian chieftain, Odovacar, had profited by the general disorder to oust the western co-emperor, Romulus Augustulus (the little Augustus). This ousting of the

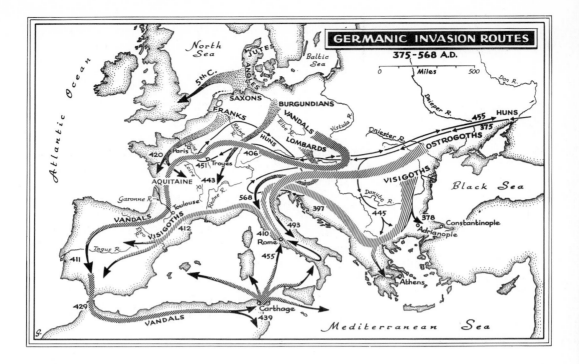

ironically named successor of the legendary founder of Rome is the traditional date for the "end" of the Roman Empire in the West—476 A.D. The Empire continued in Constantinople, however, and even in the West the traditions, the prestige, and the feeling of being part of some political whole lasted for generations.

The Ostrogoths, in fact, entered Italy as agents of the eastern Roman Empire. Their leader, Theodoric, who had been educated as a hostage in Constantinople, certainly thought of himself as belonging in some sense to Roman civilization. Theodoric was a good administrator and a cultivated man. He disposed easily of Odovacar, and in his long reign (489-526) he preserved comparative peace and order in Italy. As a person, he really deserved to be called Theodoric the Great. Yet he and his Ostrogoths remained essentially foreigners and heretics; their political, social, and Arian ecclesiastical institutions were superimposed on those of Catholic Italians. They were not given the time to do the work of recon-

struction thoroughly. After Theodoric's death, generals of the eastern Empire under Justinian (see below, Chapter VI) drove remnants of the main Ostrogothic bands over the Alps into oblivion, for history records no further trace of them. A few parts of Italy, however, remained under the control of groups of Ostrogothic descent.

The Vandals

Visigoths and Ostrogoths were major tribes who founded but did not perpetuate major states. There were other invaders who apparently did nothing but blaze a more or less spectacular path across the Empire. Of these, the best known are the Vandals, who crossed the Rhine into Gaul early in the fifth century and marauded down through Gaul into Spain, where they settled briefly in the south. Close to their new possession, across the narrow straits in Africa the Roman governor, Boniface was at odds with the central government.

CHAPTER V

Roman Africa—roughly what we now call North Africa—seems to have preserved from Punic days some sort of subdued endemic nationalism, perhaps a little like Welsh or Scottish nationalism in modern Britain. Moreover, the Donatist heresy (see above, p. 165) had become a schism in North Africa, and served to strengthen the separatist tendencies.

The discontented Boniface made the mistake that separatists have often made; he

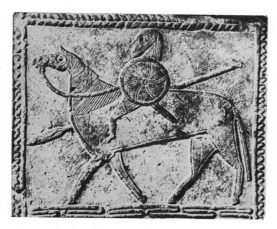

A mounted soldier of the period of barbarian invasions. Note the "primitive" character of this work.

invited in outside help. Thus the Vandals crossed into Africa in 429 and took it over for themselves. Under their chieftain Gaiseric, a gifted and unprincipled warrior, pirate, and politician, the Vandals organized what no other German tribe had yet had, a strong navy, and they took a leading part in the play of balance of power among the fragments of the fast-disintegrating Roman Empire. The Vandals, too, raided and sacked Rome, in 455. They acquired in the ancient world that special reputation for destructiveness which has made their tribal name a common noun in modern tongues; the vandal is the wanton destroyer and defacer. Perhaps they were in fact no worse than their kindred tribes. Their North African kingdom was

destroyed by the forces of the Emperor Justinian in the sixth century and the Vandals were absorbed into the population (see below, Chapter VI). In terms of institutions, they seem to have brought singularly little to the Africa they ruled.

The Huns

Even more spectacular and ephemeral than the course of the Vandals was the wild European career of the Huns. The Huns were not Germanic but Asiatic, and their pressure on the eastern German tribes had perhaps initiated the great German invasions. Pushing past the Slavs and Germans, in the fifth century they set up a short-lived empire in the great central Danubian plain. Under Attila, the horde pressed farther west, gathering mixed adherents, into the Rhineland and Gaul. The old Roman traditions, military and civil, were still strong enough in Gaul to enable the Roman general, Aëtius, to put together a composite force as mixed in blood and background as Attila's. In 451, Aëtius held the Huns near Troyes, at the battle often erroneously called that of Chalons. Thence the Huns passed into Italy, where tradition assigns to Pope Leo the Great credit for persuading Attila to give up his plans to take Rome.

Attila died soon after withdrawing from Italy, and the Huns, struck down by the plague, were dispersed. Attila had ruled not a state but an immense horde of professional cavalrymen and camp followers who were capable of living off the land like locusts. Undoubtedly many Germans, Slavs, and other non-Hunnic soldiers were added to the horde by accretion as it ate its way through Europe. The Huns were a horror to a generation that knew many horrors, and the name has survived as a term of abuse. (The Huns must not be confused with another group of Asiatic invaders, the Hungarians or Magyars, who were in effect distant relatives of the Huns and who came into central Danubia much later, at the end of the ninth century, to found there a permanent state.)

Burgundians and Lombards

The records show the names of many other tribes, such as the Sciri, Alans, and Suevi, who wandered and marauded, but who did not found true states. Individuals among them certainly settled down in a variety of places, and were absorbed into the indigenous population. Two other Germanic tribes, however, moved a relatively short way into the Empire and gave names to areas which, though not today identical with those settled originally by these tribes, are at least still on the map. About 443 the Burgundians moved into the Rhône-Saône region; their name is given to a later Merovingian kingdom, to an even later duchy and a "free county," and still survives as a French region noted for food, wine, and good living generally. The Lombards moved over the Alps into Italy, and gave their name to Lombardy in the Po Valley, a region most important in all later Italian history.

The Anglo-Saxons

Another Germanic tribe—or, better, a group of related tribes—also moved a relatively short distance, and set up several petty kingdoms and a society that have helped make modern Britain, and provided the modern name England, land of the Angles. The Angles, Saxons, and Jutes started from the eastern shore of the North Sea, and moved by sea—on which they had had a good training as pirates—to the great island known as Britain. As the Roman Empire in the West fell into graver difficulties, its rulers gradually abandoned the outpost province of Britannia between 410 and 442. The Roman civil and military government had maintained a kind of colonial rule over the only partly Romanized native Britons. The Anglo-Saxons—the Jutes are left out of the joint name—seeped into the disordered island, which was torn by its own tribal struggles and was threatened by invasion from the still heathen Picts and Scots in the north. Some of the Anglo-Saxon war bands were almost certainly invited for the purpose of redressing the balance among local groups, much as the Vandals had been invited into Africa.

Unlike the Vandals, however, the Anglo-Saxons gave their stamp to the land they invaded. They did not completely exterminate the Britons, some of whom almost certainly remained as a subject class that was gradually absorbed by the conquerors. None the less, Britain is unique among the invaded regions of the western Roman Empire in that it owes more to the Germanic barbarians than to the Romans. During four centuries of Roman rule, Britannia had been far less thoroughly integrated into Roman culture than had provinces like Gaul and Spain. Moreover, the Anglo-Saxons who came to Britannia were still heathen and had been less influenced by Rome than had other Germans.

II: The Franks—The Building of an Empire

The last of our list of German tribes is the Franks. Seen over fifteen centuries, they are the most important, the most successful in putting their imprint on history. Like the Anglo-Saxons, they moved but a short distance, steadily and cautiously. They

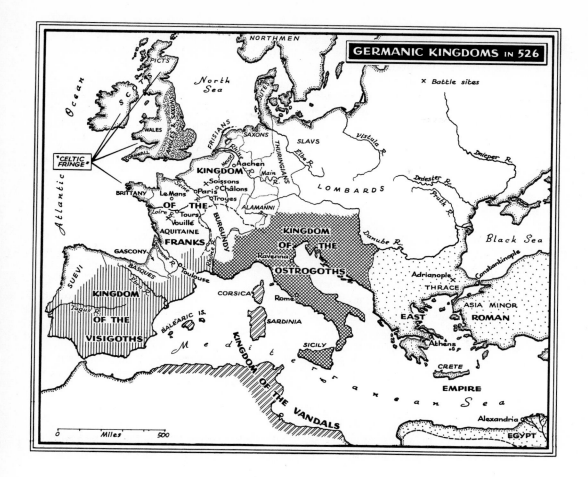

were probably a new tribe, a consolidation of older groups mentioned by Tacitus in the first century. They come on the stage of history in the lower Rhineland, divided into two groups, the Salian (dwellers by the sea) and the Ripuarian (dwellers by the rivers Meuse and Rhine). From the "Low Countries" (Holland, Belgium, the Rhineland), they pushed southward in wars and raids, but they never deserted their home base. The Franks, in short, expanded almost like a modern nation-state, by adding to a nucleus. Even after they had attained a West European hegemony, they kept a political center (one can hardly use here the modern word "capital") at Charlemagne's favorite residence, Aachen (in French, Aix-la-Chapelle). Their history

is the best thread through the story of the Dark Ages in the West.

In the last half of the fifth and the first half of the sixth centuries the Salian Franks, under the leadership of the House of Merovech—the Merovingians—consolidated Gaul and the Low Countries into the basis of the unit we call France. Under the succeeding House, that of Charles—the Carolingians—the Frankish kingdom was expanded into an empire which in theory represented a revival of the old western Roman Empire. At its height under Charlemagne, about 800, the new Carolingian Empire did in fact include many western Roman lands. But the new empire was short-lived, for under Charlemagne's successors in the ninth and tenth centuries it split into many independent or quasi-independent local units. These foreshadowed roughly in territory the modern states of France, Germany, and Italy—and that zone of fragmentation from Holland to Switzerland that still stands between the French and German nation-states.

Clovis

The first great figure in the building of the Frankish state is the Merovingian King Clovis, who reigned from 481 to 511. His success came partly from his long series of victorious military campaigns. At Soissons, in 486, he defeated the Gallo-Roman general Syagrius, one of the many who have been called the "last of the Romans." He then staved off another major German tribe, the Alamanni. Though never breaking permanently into Gaul, the Alamanni did settle in the partly Romanized area of Germany south of the River Main and have left their name in the French language to stand for all Germany, *l'Allemagne*. Clovis, in the crucial battle of Vouillé in 507, defeated the Visigoths and added to his realm most of their lands north of the Pyrenees. Burgundy had withstood him, but was conquered by his sons.

Perhaps the greatest single reason for the success of Clovis lay in his conversion from the heathen faith to Christianity. According to tradition, as so often happened with Germanic chiefs, Clovis was converted through his wife, who was already a Catholic. He embraced—and this is of great importance—not the Arian faith of so many tribes, but the orthodox faith of Rome, the religion of the great majority of the peoples he came to rule. The great power of the orthodox clergy in Gaul, and, most importantly, that of the Gallo-Roman bishops in the Visigoth-occupied South (Aquitaine) were cast on the Frankish side. The acquiescence in Frankish rule of the Catholic population was assured.

The Merovingians after Clovis

The Frankish state was by no means a monarchy of the modern type. The Merovingians followed the old tribal rules of succession, so that on the death of Clovis the kingdom did not go to his oldest son, but was partitioned among his four sons. This practice of partitioning, and the consequent chronic struggles to reunify the Frankish state, plagued not only the Merovingians but also their Carolingian successors. Later Merovingian history is a tale of hopeless warfare and steady decline, marked by melodramatic intrigues and ruthless rivalries. The conduct of the Merovingian ruling classes is surely one of the low points in the record of western society, as degraded as that of Nero in imperial Rome.

Here is a sample of what went on, as reported by the sixth-century historian, Gregory of Tours. A grandson of Clovis, King Chilperic, married Fredegund, who was not of noble birth. Fredegund determined to make herself queen in fact as well as in name. She stopped at nothing to achieve her ambitions and to eliminate her rivals. When her sons perished in an epidemic, she sent Chlodovech, Chilperic's son by an earlier marriage, to the same place "that he too might die the same death." Chlodovech survived, but only until his stepmother had him stabbed to death. Next, Fredegund tried to dispose of her sister-in-law, Brunhild, by sending "a cleric of her household to ensnare and slay that queen." Brunhild, however, discovered the would-be assassin and sent him back to Fredegund, who "punished him by having his hands and feet cut off." Finally, Fredegund turned against her own daughter, Rigunth:

Sometimes they even came to blows and buffets. One day her mother said to her: 'Why dost thou set thyself against me, O my daughter? Here are possessions of thy father which

I have under my control; take them and do with them as seemeth good to thee.' She then went into her treasure-room, and opened a chest full of necklets and precious ornaments, for a long time taking out one thing after another, and handing them to her daughter, who stood by. At last she said: 'I am weary; put thou in thy hand, and take out what thou mayst find.' Rigunth put her arm into the chest to take out more things, when her mother seized the lid and forced it down upon her neck. She bore upon it with all her strength, until the edge of the chest beneath pressed the girl's throat so hard that her eyes seemed about to start from her head. . . . The attendants outside . . . broke into the small chamber, and brought out the girl, whom they thus delivered from imminent death.*

The last Merovingian kings are known in history as *les rois fainéants,* the "do-nothing kings." They lived secluded in their harem palaces while their officials did the real work of governing. A family descended from Arnulf, Bishop of Metz (clerical celibacy was not enforceable among these barbarian converts), came into particular prominence as officials who were called "mayors of the palace." This position was very roughly analogous to that of prime minister. One mayor of the palace, Charles Martel (714-741), made himself king in all but name and established the ascendancy of the Carolingian (from Carolus, Latin for Charles) house. He organized the Frankish nobles into a dependable cavalry, and with them defeated a raiding band from Moslem Spain near Tours in 732. Tours, not much over a hundred miles from Paris, is the deepest penetration, north and west, into Europe attained by that extraordinary expansion of Moslem power which had begun in distant Arabia a century before (see Chapter VI). Modern historians are no doubt right to remind us that the Moslems at Tours were only a raiding band, and that probably France was not really in danger of being conquered and absorbed in 732. Still the battle of Tours

---

* Gregory of Tours, *History of the Franks,* O. M. Dalton, ed. (Oxford, 1927), Bk. IX, 34.

is a great landmark, not only in French, but in western history. France, the heart of the West, was never again so directly menaced by Moslem power.

Pepin and Italy

Pepin the Short (741-768), the son of Charles Martel, was the first Carolingian to assume the title of King of the Franks. He further consolidated the realm and took important steps to bring the Frankish power into what could already be called "international relations." Since the dispersal of the Ostrogoths in the mid-sixth century, Italy had been the scene of conflict among three major rivals—the Byzantines, the Lombards, and the papacy. The Byzantines, thanks to the conquests of Justinian (see Chapter VI), had held on to Sicily and the extreme south of the peninsula, and to the region around Ravenna, the seat of the Byzantine governors, or exarchs, in the north. They also maintained a kind of protectorate over the pope and Rome itself. The Lombards held quite securely their lands in the north and along the spine of Italy, and had shown signs of consolidating their rule somewhat as the Franks had done in France. In this laudable task the Lombards were soon balked by the Franks themselves, who intervened with almost modern balance-of-power methods to support the territorial independence of the papacy against the Lombards.

In the first part of the eighth century, the Lombards had slowly consolidated their North Italian holdings and added Ravenna and other parts of the peninsula outside Lombardy proper. Alarmed by this progress, Pope Stephen II in 753 made a fateful visit to Pepin, King of the Franks. He approved Pepin's appropriation of the royal title and entered into something not unremotely like what we today should call a "defensive pact" with the Frankish king. In two campaigns, Pepin defeated the Lombards and forced them to give up parts of their conquests in Italy, notably lands around Ravenna that had belonged to the eastern Empire. These lands Pepin handed over to the pope as the "Donation of Pepin." Together with territories closer to Rome they became the lands ruled by the pope as sovereign; even in the nineteenth century these lands were still known as the "States of the Church." Pepin's son Charlemagne finished off the Lombard kingdom in one campaign, and in 774 assumed the famous iron crown of Lombardy.

Significance
of the Frankish-Papal Alliance

Frankish intervention in Italy may actually be one of the most important turning points in western history, for it preserved and strengthened the Roman papacy as an independent temporal power. This papal independence seems to modern eyes essential to the maintenance of the western Church as an institution never wholly dominated by the state, in contrast to the caesaropapism of the East (see Chapter VI). Possibly the Roman see could have remained free from complete domination by a Lombard kingdom controlling all Italy. Possibly the Church in the eighth century was already strong enough to ward off caesaropapism. But as it happened it was the strong arm of the Carolingians, and their worldly desires for expansion and prestige, that enabled the papacy to maintain the temporal basis of its spiritual power.

The new Frankish patrons and protectors of the papacy might have become as great a menace to papal independence as the displaced Lombards had been. Vandal Africa offers an example of how the invited outsiders end as the masters of those who invited them. This did not happen with the Franks and the popes. The realistic explanation is that the Franks, occupied

with the whole western world, did not have the time or energy to concentrate on Italy; that, furthermore, the Frankish rulers in their ambitious aim of creating a super-state took on so many enemies that they had to make concessions to the popes to keep them on their side. Yet even the determined realist should perhaps grant that the Frankish leaders were not wholly unmoved by their status and responsibilities as protectors of the one true Church.

To strengthen papal claims, someone, or some group, in the papal chancellery, in the late 740's or 750's, forged documents to prove that the Donation of Pepin was only a confirmation of a donation that had been made long ago by the fourth-century Emperor Constantine. According to the forged "Donation of Constantine," the Emperor, on leaving Rome for his new capital of Constantinople, had made Pope Sylvester his successor. Indeed, he had made him more than his successor, for the Pope had divine as well as mundane powers:

And inasmuch as our imperial power is earthly, we have decreed that it shall venerate and honor his most holy Roman Church and that the sacred see of blessed Peter shall be gloriously exalted above our empire and earthly throne. We attribute to him the power and glorious dignity and strength and honor of the Empire, and we ordain and decree that he shall have rule as well over the four principal sees, Antioch, Alexandria, Constantinople, and Jerusalem, as also over all the churches of God in all the world. And the pontiff who for the time being presides over that most holy Roman Church shall be the highest and chief of all priests in the whole world, and according to his decision shall all matters be settled which shall be taken in hand for the service of God or the confirmation of the faith of Christians.*

The "Donation of Constantine," accepted in the Middle Ages as authentic, was proved to be a forgery in the fifteenth century by the Renaissance scholar, Lorenzo Valla (see Chapter XI). Valla demonstrated

* *Documents of the Christian Church*, Henry Bettenson, ed. (New York, 1947), 140.

that it contained many anachronisms—eighth-century usages and references in a supposedly fourth-century document. The forging itself was in many ways typical of the state of mind of early medieval intellectuals. One almost thinks that those who made the forgery believed it to have been in some sense "true": this is what Constantine *must* have done.

Expansion under Charlemagne

The man who brought to a climax the alliance between Franks and popes was the son of Pepin the Short, Charles, known to later generations as Charlemagne (from the early French vernacular form of Carolus Magnus, Charles the Great). Charlemagne (768-814) proceeded to extend his control over Italy, as we have seen. In the 780's he campaigned eastward, beginning a conquest of the Saxons that took him over thirty years to complete. Here for the first time the tide turned: Germany, the homeland of these swarming barbarian hordes, was invaded from the old Roman lands. Now for the first time Germany comes into our history as something more than an outside area reported on by an occasional historian or geographer. Some German tribes, especially the Saxons, were determined heathens, and Charlemagne had a hard time converting them to Christianity. Many of them were, in fact, converted only at sword's point. But the monks and priests followed with the learning and the regular services of the Church, and gradually Germany took its place among the lands of the Catholic Church.

As Charlemagne moved eastward, he came finally to the zone between Slavic and German populations, which is still today, as often before, a disputed zone between the two peoples. Roughly, Charlemagne's power, the power of the organized West, attained a line along the Elbe and then along the Danube where it turns sharply south below Vienna. Here Charlemagne set up special frontier provinces which he called marches or marks, and began that long historic German push which the Germans call the *Drang nach Osten*, the drive toward the East.

Even this early, the armed expansionist had to worry about protecting several fronts simultaneously. With Germany still not wholly conquered, Charlemagne had to take care of the Avars, an Asian (Mongol) tribe that had first appeared as invaders in the late sixth century and were now settled on the lower Danube and also fight the Moslems in Spain. He defeated the Avars, but, though he set up a Spanish march south of the Pyrenees in what is today Catalonia, he never really made a serious dent in Moslem power. Yet Charlemagne's name has gained most renown, perhaps, from an early (778) campaign in Spain, where his rear guard was defeated at Roncesvalles. This campaign was the theme of the unknown poet (or poets) who composed the epic *Chanson de Roland*. This *Song of Roland*, as we have it, dates from several centuries later, and is a chief source of our knowledge of the state of mind of the early medieval aristocracy in the West. In it and in other legends about the great Emperor, Charlemagne became the hero of romance.

The Revival of the Empire

By the end of the eighth century, the territories under the rule of Charlemagne included most of the old western Roman lands. The chief exceptions were Britain (in the hands of the Anglo-Saxons), North Africa and most of Spain (in the hands of the Moslems), and southern Italy and Sicily (partly "independent," partly under Byzantine control, and subject to Moslem raids). Significantly, the Carolingian state encompassed German lands between the Rhine and the Elbe that had never been part of the Roman Empire. On Christmas Day,

800, Charlemagne was crowned Emperor in Rome by the hand of the Pope himself, Leo III. Once more there was a Roman Empire in the West.

We cannot even be quite sure that Charlemagne wanted to be emperor. His admiring contemporary biographer Einhard tells us that Charlemagne regretted the step. The cautious historian should confess to ignorance here. It is possible that Pope Leo actually planned the coronation, and surprised Charlemagne with it. The papacy surely stood to gain by removing itself thus from the last vestige of control from Constantinople. The revival of the western imperial title did offend the eastern emperors, and later attempts of Charlemagne to mend the breach—at one time there were negotiations looking toward a marriage with the eastern Empress Irene—came to nothing.

Charlemagne's empire, as we shall see, hardly outlasted Charlemagne himself. Some historians say that it was all show and empty titles, that it had no real influence on the course of European history. They tend to deny the thesis, made famous by the English historian James Bryce, that

PARTITION of the EMPIRE
TREATY OF VERDUN, 843

CAROLINGIAN EMPIRE

Kingdom of Charlemagne, 768
Acquired by Charlemagne to 814
Areas tributary to Charlemagne's Empire
Byzantine Empire
×   Battle sites

Miles   400

there is any important continuity between Charlemagne's empire and the later medieval Holy Roman Empire of the German People. Others agree that Charlemagne's empire was but the impotent ghost of the old Roman Empire. But they add that as events turned out this vain and empty title lured later generations of German rulers over the Alps into Italy in search of a delusive honor, helped to keep them from forging Germany into a national unity, indeed helped to keep Italy and Germany tied together in an utterly unnatural relationship that prevented either from attaining national unity until the nineteenth century. More idealistic historians insist that Charlemagne's revival of the imperial title helped keep alive, even though in a tenuous and almost unreal form, the ideal of a Christian western society with something in common, not merely a collection of parochial states devoted to the cut-throat competition of war and so-called peace. Finally, some historians maintain that thanks to Charlemagne's act a lay power with universal or at least pan-western temporal aspirations was able through the medieval centuries to oppose the temporal claims of a spiritual power, the papacy; and, of course, a spiritual power well anchored in Italy could oppose the temporal power. The existence of these two claimants to supreme power, the pope and the emperor, saved the West from the extremes of caesaropapism on the one hand and theocracy on the other. This rivalry and tension helped promote such typically western institutions and attitudes as individual rights, the rule of law, and the dignity of man.

These are formidable results from a single act, and of course they cannot be "proved." Nevertheless, it is clear that the revival of the old Roman imperial idea is one of the great threads that run through all subsequent European history. The empire soon became a *German* one, but there always remained about the very name "empire" some suggestion of a common political

order within which war was somehow "unnatural," not right. In this sense, the medieval empire is a link, admittedly verbal, idealistic, even "ideological," rather than legal or institutional, between the One World of Rome and the One World of twentieth-century ideals.

Charlemagne the Man

Of the man who began all this we know tantalizingly little. Indeed, to work out the biography of medieval persons is a difficult matter; the thousands of intimate details we have for a Napoleon or a Lincoln, for instance—to say nothing of the subject's own letters, diaries, and the like—

Ninth-century bronze statuette presumed to represent Charlemagne.

simply do not exist. Many Greeks and Romans, such as Marcus Aurelius, are more real to us than any medieval figure save for a St. Augustine, an Abelard, a Dante, a St. Louis, and a very few others. This distance, so to speak, between us and medieval persons is no doubt in part a spiritual distance, since they lived in an age of faith in the immanence of the supernatural; but it is perhaps even more a simple lack of materials. Unlike Marcus Aurelius, Charlemagne has left us no authentic autobiographical work of his own.

We do have a good brief contemporary life by the monk Einhard, a member of the little inner circle of scholars Charlemagne kept with him at Aachen. Charlemagne clearly felt himself to be a Frankish chief— indeed he wore the Frankish national costume all his life. He was tall, and active in hunting and in such other activities as suited the new warrior aristocracy. According to the standards of his lusty age, he was temperate in food and drink, but even according to these standards he was perhaps rather intemperate in sex relations. Einhard lists nine wives or concubines, and in the middle of the passage he gives us a revealing parenthetical remark about a daughter "of a concubine who has escaped my memory." But Charlemagne was also an intelligent, able, inventive man, who by no means stumbled into an empire. He spoke Latin as well as his native Frankish (German). To make his vast empire a going concern, he put intelligence—his own and that of his helpers—to work on the available materials.

The available materials, however, were not adequate to the task. Here is what Einhard has to say:

When he had taken the imperial title he noticed many defects in the legal systems of his people; for the Franks have two legal systems, differing in many points very widely from one another, and he, therefore, determined to add what was lacking, to reconcile the differences, and to amend anything that was wrong or wrongly expressed. He completed

nothing of all his designs beyond adding a few capitularies, and those unfinished. But he gave orders that the laws and rules of all nations comprised within his domains which were not already written out should be collected and committed to writing.

He also wrote out the barbarous and ancient songs, in which the acts of the kings and their wars were sung, and committed them to memory. He also began a grammar of his native language.[*]

Yet Einhard has just told us that Charlemagne tried late in life to learn to write, and never succeeded at the "strange task," even though he kept writing materials under his pillow. He and his experts simply could not become expert enough. Nothing shows more plainly the basic fact that the "darkness" of the Dark Ages came largely from the loss of the accumulated knowledge and skills of the Greco-Roman world.

The Decay of the Carolingian Empire

Charlemagne had his son Louis the Pious crowned during his own lifetime, and at his death in 814 Louis took over the realm. But the old Frankish custom of partitioning the king's lands among all his sons now plagued the empire. As early as 817 the sons of Louis made a preliminary partitioning which led to the usual wars and further partitioning. In each generation, one Carolingian was marked out as emperor, but by now it had become almost an empty title. In the confusing sequence of wars and treaties there is a significant incident which shows that something more, however, than the Frankish law of succession was at work. This is the Strasbourg Oaths of 842, of which we have the text. Two of Charlemagne's grandsons, Louis the German and Charles the Bald, allied against a third, Lothair, who had the title of emperor. The brothers took an oath of

---

[*] Einhard, *Early Lives of Charlemagne*, A. J. Grant, ed. (London, 1922), 44-45.

alliance; each swore in a form of the prevailing language of the *other's* kingdom, Louis in Romance (Latin on the way to becoming French) and Charles in early German.

Modern France and modern Germany did not spring into being in 842, though the Strasbourg Oaths are a sign of the linguistic basis of these states to come. Nothing so large as these states could be maintained then. The political, economic, and psychological bases for such states simply did not exist; indeed, political and economic subdivision was soon to go much further all through the West. For example, in 879 and 888 two kingdoms of Burgundy arose in the old middle kingdom of Lothair; one was centered in the Rhone Valley, and the other in the region from Besançon to Geneva. In both France and Germany there grew up political ("feudal") entities, mostly duchies or counties (from "duke" and "count"), the names of which are still familiar to us as "provinces"—Champagne, Brittany, Aquitaine, Saxony, Bavaria, Franconia. In Italy the same process of political disintegration, which had already begun before the Carolingians, went on.

Anglo-Saxon Britain

Across the Channel, in the British Isles, the invading Angles, Saxons, and Jutes had all founded little states. These states warred among themselves and with the "Celtic fringe," the still independent Celts of Wales, Cornwall, and Scotland. In the Anglo-Saxon areas various small and middling "independent" states emerged. Christianity was introduced into the south by Roman missionaries in 597; it had been introduced into the north even earlier from Celtic Ireland.

Three of the Anglo-Saxon states made successive bids to "unify" England, or at least to gain a preponderant position in England. Northumbria and Mercia had brief supremacies. Then, as we shall soon see, a new wave of invaders broke over England—the Danes or Northmen. It was Wessex that led the resistance to the Danes and established an Anglo-Saxon state in the tenth century.

The Anglo-Saxon king governed through the officers of his household and the official clerical staffs. He had a great council, called the *witenagemot*, which was made up of important landholders, officials, and churchmen. Its functions were vague and unspecialized, but at times it gave advice, acted as a tribunal, and elected and deposed kings. The king's revenue came from his own estates, from a tax called the Danegeld for defense against the Danes, from fines imposed by local courts of which he could keep two-thirds, and from various tolls and customary dues. His army was still the old Germanic host (*fyrd*) in which every landholder was obliged to serve, but he also had additional household troops. The institutions of Anglo-Saxon England in the tenth century were not far different from those of the Franks two centuries before in the early Carolingian days or those of any settled Germanic tribe.

III: Europe and the Northmen

The whole problem of the breakdown of the One World of the Romans, with which we began this chapter, would be seriously misunderstood if we thought of the barbarian invasions of the West as limited to the Germanic waves of the fourth,

A Viking ship, as found at Oseberg, Norway, and as reconstructed.

fifth, and sixth centuries. Actually, there were two, in a sense, three, other waves of invasion: the one initiated by the extraordinary rise of Mohammed in Arabia in the seventh century, which threatened the West mainly through Spain in the eighth century (see Chapter VI); the invasions of the ninth and tenth centuries which originated in Scandinavia, a region that had hitherto been outside western history; and

a second series of Moslem attacks in Italy and Sicily, to which were added those of the Magyars in the central Danube region. The invasions of the Northmen, or Vikings, proved to be a severe blow for western Europe. For France, the Low Countries, and the British Isles, the ninth and tenth centuries were in some respects the low point, the period of greatest disintegration and darkness.

CHAPTER V

The Norse Invasions:
Causes and ·Character

The Northmen came at first by sea in little bands. They navigated in small ships with sail and oars that could easily penetrate estuaries and rivers like the Thames, the Seine, the Loire. These heathens were fierce fighters; they were masters of a hit-and-run technique of raiding that made it very difficult for the small land forces of a Europe already far gone in political subdivision to cope with them. At first, the Northmen came as mere piratical raiding bands who plundered the poorly protected coasts of Ireland and England. The booty they carried home to Norway and Denmark whetted their appetites, however, and soon they organized fleets of several hundred ships. With these fleets, they seized coastal lands and proceeded to winter there. Raiders prowled along the coasts of Spain, and even into the Mediterranean. Some of them turned westward, and reached Iceland and Greenland. A few may even have reached Canada or New England, although probably we shall never have positive evidence that this is so.

What brought about this sudden swarming of the Northmen out of Scandinavia we cannot know for certain. They were not pressed from behind in their homeland, as the Goths had been pressed by the Huns. It is most likely that they were attracted by the news that pickings were better to the south. The Northmen may even be a rather special case of emigration from an overpopulated district. One is struck throughout the history of Normandy, which became the base of operations for the most famous Scandinavian exiles, by the large families in the upper or noble classes, and by the younger sons' habit of going abroad to improve their fortunes. Since polygamy was common in the upper classes of heathen Scandinavia (the lower classes could not afford it), it seems likely that the sons of

Viking chiefs either had to leave home or else cease to live in the style to which they were accustomed.

The Northmen butchered the unfortunate people on whom they descended and destroyed their settlements. The chronicles of western Europe during this period are full of accounts of their horrible deeds. But they were too few in number to exterminate the other western Europeans, and their waves of invasion gradually subsided. By this time, however, many Northmen had settled permanently in France and in the British Isles.

The Norse Invasions:
Consequences

In France, the Northmen gradually gathered together in the region known as Normandy along the lower Seine River. There, beginning in 911, the French kings were obliged to grant them the same kind of political concession which the Romans had given the Goths centuries before. In Normandy, the Viking settlers became a ruling class operating under the system we know as feudalism. As Normans, they eventually organized a state that was more efficiently administered than was usual in the feudal age. From this base they launched out on a series of great accomplishments: they conquered England in 1066, they sent bands to form Norman states in Sicily and southern Italy, and they later set up crusader principalities in the Near East. Their remarkable career suggests that the Normans possessed an exceptional endowment for war and politics.

In the ninth and tenth centuries, the Danes, who were kinsmen of the Normans, came close to accomplishing in England what the Vikings had accomplished in Normandy. These men of Denmark first raided, then settled, and at last came to hold large portions of the east and north of England. Challenging the newly won

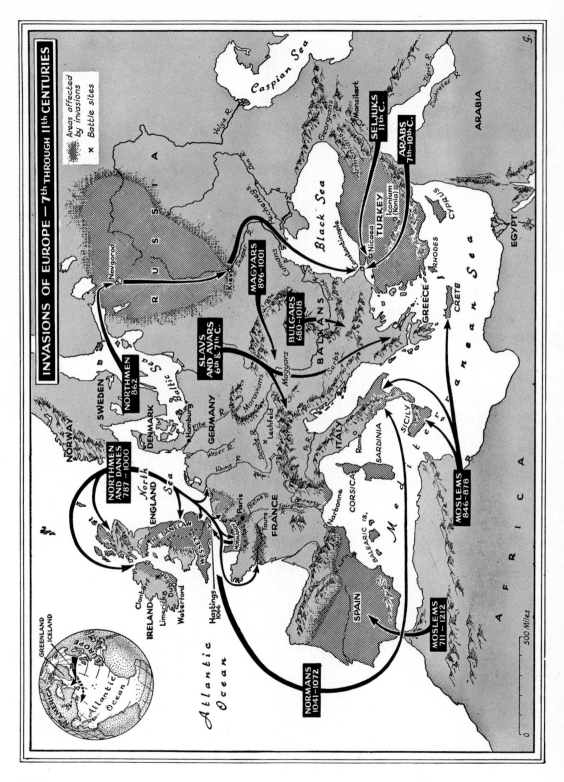

INVASIONS OF EUROPE — 7th THROUGH 11th CENTURIES

Areas affected by invasions
× Battle sites

Caspian Sea

ARABIA

SELJUKS 11th C.

ARABS 7th–10th C.

TURKEY
Iconium (Konia)
Manzikert
Nicaea
Constantinople

Black Sea

EGYPT

CYPRUS

RHODES

CRETE

GREECE

Mediterranean Sea

NORWAY

SWEDEN

NORTHMEN 862

DENMARK

Baltic Sea

Novgorod

R U S S I A

Volga R.

Dnieper R.

Kiev

MAGYARS 896–1001

BULGARS 680–1018

SLAVS AND AVARS 6th & 7th C.

BALKANS

GERMANY

Hamburg
Elbe
Weser R.
Rhine R.

Lechfeld ×

Danube R.

ITALY

Rome

SARDINIA

CORSICA

SICILY

MOSLEMS 846–878

North Sea

ENGLAND

THE DANELAW

WESSEX
Hastings 1066

Paris
Seine R.
Tours
FRANCE
Narbonne

BALEARIC IS.

NORTHMEN AND DANES 787–1000

IRELAND
Clontarf
Limerick
Dublin
Waterford

Atlantic Ocean

SPAIN

MOSLEMS 711–1212

NORMANS 1041–1072

A F R I C A

500 Miles

GREENLAND
ICELAND

AMERICA
EUROPE
Atlantic Ocean

Trees are felled to build a fleet.   *Building the fleet.*

The Bayeux Tapestry, illustrating preparations for the Norman expedition against England, 1066.

supremacy of Saxon Wessex, they were held off by the efforts of King Alfred (871-899), who has been suitably rewarded by history with the title of Alfred the Great. To satisfy the invaders, however, Alfred had to grant them the territorial concession of the "Danelaw," a large area in East Anglia, Mercia, and Northumbria, where place names still mark their settling. Under Alfred's successors the Danelaw was gradually absorbed, and many Danish warriors entered into the new fighting aristocracy of the Saxons. Then came other waves, this time from a Denmark that was better organized politically. In 1017, a Danish king, Canute, became King of England.

Canute, who was a very able man, ruled over a super-state that included England, Denmark, and Norway—a sort of northern "empire." It is tempting to speculate whether such a state, organized around the North Sea as the Roman Empire had been around the Mediterranean, could have been made to last. Geography was not in itself a barrier, for a small sea unites rather than divides a seafaring people. But Canute died young in 1035, and in 1042 his line was succeeded in England by the Saxon, Edward the Confessor. The Scandinavian lands went their own way. A few years later, in 1066, the Norman William seized the English throne by conquest, and England was tied once more to western rather than to northern Europe.

Ireland

A third victim of the Viking raids was Ireland, which first comes into western history in the Dark Ages. Ireland was known to the Romans, who called it Hibernia, but it never became a part of the Roman Empire. The Irish formed a loose society of warring clans and tribes, with a strong priestly class known as the druids. They were a Celtic people, related both to the Gauls of the Continent and to the Britons. Ireland had been converted peacefully to Christianity in the first half of the fifth century, under the leadership of a Romanized Christian Briton, St. Patrick. The increasing effects of the breakdown that soon followed, however, especially the disorders in Britain and Gaul, isolated the newly Christian Ireland from the Roman center of church government.

The next few centuries, from the fifth to the ninth, marked a great flourishing for Ireland, which somehow was spared from the barbarian inroads. Irish church organization was greatly affected by the whole structure of Irish society; the priest became the counterpart of the traditional druid.

The churches promoted learning, poetry, and the illumination of manuscripts. The illuminated *Book of Kells*, which dates from this era, is one of the artistic wonders of the Middle Ages. Some of its letters are elaborately decorated with interwoven traceries so delicate that they were reputed to have been drawn by angels. The illuminations in the *Book of Kells* also include fantastic and humorous pictures—human faces, imaginary creatures, and, in one instance, rats eating the communion wafer while cats look on.

In time, Irish monasticism became so strong that many Irish monks and scholars moved out of Ireland as missionaries to convert the heathen in Britain and elsewhere. St. Columban, for example, born in Leinster, headed missions from the Low Countries up to the Rhine to Switzerland and even into Italy in the seventh century. This "Celtic Christianity" developed several practices that differed from those of the Roman Church, notably in the method of determining the date of Easter. Yet it is probably wrong to think of a genuine corporate struggle between the Roman and the Celtic churches. The Synod of Whitby, which was held in England in 664, was a landmark in the reconciliation between the two churches. It could hardly have been successful had the two groups been opposed root and branch.

Later on, this early greatness of Irish culture helped to bolster the patriots who promoted Irish nationalism. They remembered that a civilized Ireland had once brought culture to an England of barbarous, heathen, Germanic tribesmen. But the civilized Ireland of the early Middle Ages developed little political and economic strength. When the Northmen descended on the coast at Dublin in 840, the Irish were perhaps even more helpless against them than were the English and the French. Soon the Northmen were firmly established, especially in the ports of Dub-

lin, Waterford, and in the Shannon river port of Limerick. But in the interior, the Celtic chieftains held on. Early in the tenth century, under the leadership of Brian of Munster, these chieftains won the battle of Clontarf against the Northmen and their native allies. Finally, the Northmen were absorbed into the texture of Irish society.

The two centuries of struggle had, however, put an end to the peaceful Ireland of monasteries and poetry, and had left a country divided into rival tribal areas. In the century following William's conquest of the English throne, one of the Irish chieftains rashly decided to invite outside aid to help him in his fight against his rivals. The King of England arrived in Ireland in 1167, and managed to establish half-independent feudal states in the eastern part of the island. Ireland was tied loosely to England and to the whole medieval world, and her isolation was ended. This was the beginning of the long history of antagonism between English masters and Irish subjects.

Germany and Italy

The waves of invasion from Scandinavia did not altogether spare Germany, which, as we have seen, became a political part of the West largely through the Carolingian expansion in the eighth century. Tempted by the estuaries of the Weser and Elbe, marauding bands of Northmen now added Hamburg to their list of victims. But the Northmen did not play a major part in the formation of Germany. When Charlemagne's empire broke up in the ninth century, its eastern part remained under Carolingian rulers who were unable to hold the country together. In the tenth century, consequently, large local units were able to gain strength—the duchies of Saxony, Bavaria, Swabia, Franconia, and Thuringia. On the eastern fringe of Germany—it might be better to say "the Germanies"—frontier states like Brandenburg and Austria with a large population of Slavic descent grew up in constant struggle with neighboring heathen Slavs.

The German Carolingian line in the east ended with the death of Louis the Child in 911, and the German nobles elected as their king Conrad, Duke of Franconia, to keep out the already "French" Carolingians from the west. But the rivalry of the duchies made a solid kingship impossible until the appearance of the extremely able Saxon king, Otto I, the Great (936-973). Otto defeated the rival dukes, and in 955 at the battle of the Lechfeld he won a great victory over the newest menace from the East, the Magyars or Hungarians who had settled in the land we call Hungary. At this point, Otto revived the imperial title and claim, which had become almost meaningless in the West.

In the first half of the tenth century, local Italian magnates had held the imperial title, even though they had been without power outside Italy. There was no strong hand like that of Charlemagne to preserve even the semblance of unity in Italy. The papacy itself had become a stake in Roman internal politics, and the Moslems were threatening from the south. Tenth-century Italy really does deserve the overworked adjective "anarchical." Yet the popes, even at this low point in church history, maintained some relations with all the West. And, at this lowest point in western trade, some merchandise still moved along the great trade routes, notably those across the Alps. Finally, Rome exerted a real pull of attraction on the North, and especially on the rulers of Germany. In 962, Otto the Great was crowned emperor by the pope. Now Germany and Italy were linked across the Alps, and one of the most serious medieval problems, that of the relation between pope and emperor, was firmly set.

A Bird's-eye View of the West about 1000

The eleventh century was roughly the dividing line between the Dark Ages and the Middle Ages proper. The Roman Church was now nearly supreme in the West; the Celtic and Scandinavian fringes had come into the fold; and the line against the heathen Slavs was being slowly pushed eastward. Most of Spain, and Sicily and southern Italy, were still under Moslem rule, but Christianity remained the faith of the native populations. In the long centuries of internal division and attacks from Germans, Moslems, Northmen and Asian tribes the discipline of the Church had weakened, but in the next age a great revival within the Church was to prepare the way for medieval Roman Christendom.

Something like the beginnings of the great states of our time had come into being, except perhaps in Italy, but they were all subdivided into local areas with a great degree of independence. England was the closest to being a modern centralized state. Ireland, Wales, and Scotland were all "independent," sharply divided into warring groups and areas. The accession of Hugh Capet, a local leader of the Parisian area (the Île de France), as King of France in 987 marks what we might regard as the founding of France. When Louis XVI went to the guillotine in 1793, he went as "Citizen Louis Capet." Yet his remote ancestor Hugh was hardly more than one feudal leader among others. The situation was much the same in Germany, although Otto the Great showed that a strong ruler could bring the dukes to heel and could make the position of emperor more than an empty title. Disunited Italy had no political head, save the German emperors, who claimed to be Kings of Italy. In Spain, the Christian kingdoms in the north—Galicia, the Asturias, Navarre, Leon—formed the nuclei of the future Spanish state, but the tide had not yet clearly turned against the Moslems. In the far north, the Viking period of expansion had run its course, and the kingdoms of Denmark, Norway, and Sweden had come into being.

On the east, Charlemagne's frontier against the Slavs had been the Elbe. In the next few centuries some of the Slavs were "integrated" with Europe by being conquered and absorbed by Germans. The process was chiefly one of gradual expansion of trade, the gradual establishment of Slav states, and, above all, their gradual conversion to Christianity. Here there is a fateful line, the line between conversion from Rome to Roman Catholicism and conversion from Byzantium to eastern Orthodoxy. The Poles, the Czechs, the Croats got with Roman Christianity the Roman alphabet, and inevitable ties of all sorts with the West. The Russians, the Ukrainians, the Bulgarians, and the Serbs got with Orthodox Christianity a different alphabet, the Cyrillic, invented by missionaries from Byzantium, and inevitable ties of all sorts with the East. That line of demarcation is still of major importance today.

IV: Western Institutions, 500-1000

The Problem of Origins

Out of the centuries between the fall of Rome and the last attacks of the Northmen there arose the institutions, the culture, and the way of life that we call medieval. Our documentation of these developments, however, is sparse and uncertain. We have almost no statistics on the Dark Ages. It is small wonder that such problems as the "origins of feudalism" have been the subject of learned treatise after learned treatise, and have engendered a great deal of scholarly debate still by no means ended.

One of these great debates about medieval origins is, we may hope, exhausted. This is the debate over whether the origins of basic medieval institutions like feudalism were "Roman" or "Germanic." During the nineteenth century, German historians and their British followers felt that the heroic men of the German forests, whom they supposed to be their ancestors, had provided everything worth while that persisted after 500. French historians and others of Roman sympathy took the opposite view: that what had really come through the turmoil and the darkness of the barbarian invasions was Roman and civilized and the German contribution slight or bad.

The facts of medieval origins are extremely complex. Many diverse elements combined to form the medieval reality, and they were combined in a way that cannot be analyzed exactly or mathematically. We can detect elements that persisted from Rome; elements brought in by the Germans, Moslems, and Northmen; the defense reactions of settled inhabitants against invaders; the long, slow mutual adjustments between invaders and invaded; the ideas and the emotional and intellectual attraction of Roman Christianity. The best thread through this complexity is the concept of the breakdown of man's ability to hold together large groups of human beings for political or economic purposes. The One World of Roman law, administration, and business was shattered into hundreds, indeed thousands, of little local units.

The Breakdown
into Local Units

The *manor* was a largely self-sufficient farm community that became the basis of medieval society and economy. This rural institution overshadowed in importance both urban and commercial units, although cities and towns never wholly disappeared and trade never wholly died out during the Dark Ages. The thousands of medieval manors were by no means uniform in area, in the produce they raised, in the number of people who lived and

Medieval farm occupations, from Queen Mary's Psalter (fourteenth century). Harvesting hay, treading grapes, killing pigs.

worked on them, or in any other respect. They varied greatly not only in size, productivity, and wealth, but also in internal organization and in their relations with the outside world.

The term *manorialism* describes the economic arrangements within the manor and the relationships—economic, social, and political—between the proprietor or lord of the manor and his tenants. The tenants were the farmers and herdsmen who worked on the land. They usually had homesteads of their own, perhaps grouped in villages, and plots of their own, which they cultivated for food. But they usually had to work for part of each week without pay, on the lord's land, and they usually had to pay him a percentage of their own crops. As a result, the lord enjoyed both free labor and free produce. Often the lord settled disputes between his tenants in his own court, and exercised what amounted to police powers over them.

The lord of a manor often did not own his manor (or manors, for the great lords usually held more than one) in our modern sense of ownership. It was not his real estate, except on special terms, and he was himself a tenant. Some other lord allowed him to hold and use the manor on certain military and political conditions. Viewed from this aspect, from above rather than from below, the manor was a *feudum* or fief, a grant made to a lord by a higher lord. The terms "feudal" and "feudalism" describe the relationships—military, political, and social—that existed between the lord of the manor and the person from whom he held it. Manor and fief are not the same thing, and do not necessarily coincide; keep in mind that the manor is basically a socio-economic unit, the fief, basically a socio-political unit. Upper-class persons, "nobles," "knights," have fiefs; "commoners" usually do not have fiefs, though they may well live on a manor.

Together, manorialism and feudalism describe an entire way of life during the

Middle Ages. This way of life is sometimes called the "feudal system," a name, however, that is just as misleading as "manorial system" would be. The word "system" suggests a neat arrangement the same everywhere, like the Dewey decimal or Library of Congress system of cataloguing books. It suggests a standardization that is quite un-medieval. It is also misleading to think of the Middle Ages as completely *lacking* in system. The institutions we are tracing were parts of the human attempt to organize life on this earth. They were not very successfully or efficiently systematic attempts, but they were more than random, makeshift efforts to keep humanity going until the happy day when the Renaissance, the Reformation, and Science would come along.

Early Feudalism

Feudalism was essentially a political device to preserve over many square miles of territory the chain of authority that the Romans had maintained in their army and their bureaucracy. That chain could no longer be preserved in its old form, because the individual members could not be paid or supervised from a common source. In the decay of the Roman Empire, large local landlords had already taken increasing responsibility for the people who lived on and near their estates. They came to be *magnates*, local bosses or chieftains, private persons performing a public function. As the barbarians seeped in, some of them displaced Roman magnates as great landholders. But they remained partly dependent on their own chiefs. The barbarian "concession" kingdoms that arose in all parts of the disintegrating Empire retained at least the basic principle that local government should be carried on by agents of the Crown, either barbarian or Roman.

Two of the most important formal titles of developed feudalism, count and duke, originated in the administration of the late Roman Empire. The count (in Latin *comes*; in German, *Graf*) was a local, or "county" official who was appointed by the Crown and who could be recalled by the Crown. The count acted as the agent of the Crown in fiscal, judicial, and, above all, military administration. The duke (in Latin, *dux*) came to perform most of the functions of the count for a larger and more important area, the duchy rather than the county. In the Middle Ages many dukes, and even a few counts, such as the Count of Champagne, came to be kings or kinglets in all but name. By a long, slow process, the public offices of duke, count, and other administrators fell into the hands of magnates and became hereditary. Thus the *control* (not our *ownership*) of real estate came to be inextricably mixed with the exercise of governmental functions.

An important transition to feudalism was the *beneficium* or benefice, the form of grant by which land and office were bestowed in Carolingian times. The benefice gave the holder, in return for performing governmental functions, certain rights or *immunities*. Notably, the possessor of the benefice ran his own law courts, collected his own taxes, and contributed his own armed quota to the armed forces of the granter. Although the benefice was not at first hereditary, holders of benefices often threatened to become independent of the Crown.

Charlemagne, therefore, tried to control his counts and other local officials by a familiar bureaucratic device—periodic inspections by traveling agents of the central power. His *missi dominici* (from the Latin, "those sent out by the lord") went about his empire in pairs, usually one layman and one cleric, to check on local administration. They then reported their findings to the Emperor. But, since travel and communication were slow, Charlemagne had trouble, especially on the frontiers of his vast empire, in controlling the counts and the special officials for the marches, the margraves (in German, *Markgraf*, the "march-count" or marquis). Charlemagne tried hard to build new institutions out of Roman and Germanic elements. But he simply did not have the authority or the technical means of enforcing his will throughout his empire. On his own private estates he kept careful watch, as we can see from the documents called capitularies. These are in effect his domestic executive instructions; they get down even to the most intimate details of farming.

The death of Charlemagne and the disintegration of his empire accelerated the process of feudalization. The new kings in France, Burgundy, and Germany, the leaders of the great duchies, and the local Italian lords—all needed men and money to carry on their wars. Under the conditions of breakdown the only way they could get men and money was to make concessions to the magnates who could provide them. These concessions meant that the magnates were granted full feudal status; they became hereditary holders of property and hereditary exercisers of governmental functions. By about 1000, the more or less temporary *beneficium* had become the hereditary *fief*, and feudalism was established in the medieval West.

Vassals and Lords

The holder of a fief was the *vassal* of the lord who had granted it, and the lord was the *suzerain* of the vassal. The term "vassal" now implies a somewhat degrading relationship of inferiority and dependence. In feudal usage, however, it has no such sense; indeed, it has rather a suggestion of superiority. For the non-noble populace, serfs, freemen, and the lower clergy, were not vassals. Knights and upper clergy usually, though not always, *were* vassals. Both suzerains and vassals came from the same class of fighting aristocrats; together they formed the new ruling class. This class was composed of descendants of the old

Roman imperial magnates and the barbarian chiefs, including representatives of the Northmen. It was held together by rules, traditions, and ethics that were already becoming the code of *chivalry*, to which we shall return in Chapter VIII.

After the vassal had done *homage* and had sworn *fealty* (fidelity), the suzerain proceeded to the act of *investiture*. He invested the vassal with a symbol, perhaps a staff or a bit of earth, signifying the transfer of the fief to the new holder. The fief could be any piece of land, small or large, a single manor, a group of manors, or a whole province. For example, the Norman dukes held Normandy as vassals of the French king. The fief could also be a building, such as a castle. Or it might not be real estate at all, but simply the right to collect taxes or tolls, to coin money, or to hold a court of justice and enjoy the fees levied by the court. Finally, especially in the earlier medieval centuries, lords had as dependants many "household knights" who held no fiefs, but were supported by their lord, for whom they fought.

The feudal contract imposed obligations on both parties. The lord contracted to protect the vassal and the fief, if necessary by arms; to respect the vassal's womenfolk; and to see that the vassal received justice at the hands of his "peers" (the other vassals, his social equals) in the lord's court. The vassal, in turn, promised to give the suzerain "aid and counsel." "Counsel" meant sitting in judgment on his peers in the lord's court as well as giving personal advice or counseling in our sense. "Aid" meant above all military aid, personal participation with full knightly equipment in the lord's wars. Since this obligation might prove time-consuming and costly to the vassal, it was usually limited to a certain period, often forty days a year.

Aid might also mean entertaining the lord and his retinue, for in those days of poor roads and meager trade it was sometimes simpler for the lord to move his household to the source of food on his vassals' manors than to move the food to his household. Here, too, a time limit was usually set on the vassal's obligation, lest it prove burdensome. Aid, finally, meant special payments by the vassal in produce or money whenever the suzerain faced an unusually expensive emergency—when he went on a crusade, or when he entertained at important family ceremonies. The marriage of the lord's eldest daughter or the coming-of-age and knighting of his eldest son occasioned weeks of costly feasting and entertainment.

The feudal contract was usually oral, but sometimes, in the later Middle Ages, it was written down in the form of a charter. The most famous document of English history, Magna Carta, is in part a written redefinition of the feudal contract between the lord, King John, and his vassals, the barons of the realm (see Chapter VII). Written or unwritten, the contract had to be renewed whenever one of the parties to it died. When a new vassal inherited the fief, he made his lord a special payment called *relief,* which was a part or even the whole of a year's revenue from the fief. The relief was the feudal counterpart of an inheritance tax.

The feudal contract gave the lord considerable control over the transmission of a fief. The vassal or his heir could take a bride only if she had been approved by the lord, and the lord could forbid a vassal to marry into a family that was on bad terms with his own. If a vassal died without an heir, the lord had the right of *escheat* —that is, the fief reverted to him to be disposed of as he wished. If the heir was a minor, the lord exercised *wardship* or guardianship until the minor came of age, a right that unscrupulous lords sometimes used to milk the fief dry. Finally, the lord had the right of *forfeiture*—that is, the right to seize the fief from a vassal who failed to live up to his contractual obligations.

In theory, a vassal had an equal right of redress against a faithless lord who demanded aid and counsel beyond his contractual due. Occasionally, the vassals called a grasping lord to account, as the English barons did with their king in Magna Carta. In practice, however, it was easier for the lord than for the vassal to declare the feudal contract broken, and it was easier for the suzerain to find a new vassal than for the vassal to find a new suzerain.

The Feudal Pyramid

According to feudal theory, all the lords and vassals in the kingdom were arranged in a neat and symmetrical hierarchy resembling a pyramid. At the summit of the feudal pyramid was the king; at the next level were the king's chief vassals, who were themselves feudal lords with vassals of their own. The king's *rear vassals,* as his vassals' vassals were called, thus occupied the third level of the pyramid. But they too might have vassals of their own. This process of *subinfeudation,* of vassals taking vassals, continued on down to the base of the pyramid, to the humblest vassals who had no vassals of their own but who were yet members of the ruling military aristocracy. Moreover, to complicate complications, some vassals holding directly from the king as "tenants-in-chief" were by no means great lords with their own vassals, but petty lords indeed. The pattern of landholding theoretically formed a similar pyramid. Only the king *owned* land; all vassals, so to speak, "leased" their fiefs hereditarily, either directly or indirectly from the king, and according to the terms of the feudal contract. No parcel of land was supposed to remain outside the feudal hierarchy of land tenure; *nulle terre sans seigneur,* no land without its lord, was the judgment, or more accurately the hope, of feudal lawyers.

All this was in accordance with feudal theory. But feudal practice was a far different and more complicated matter. Even in highly feudalized France, some pieces of land of different sizes always remained outside feudalism. These were termed *allods,* and they were in effect fully owned by the individuals who occupied them. Moreover, the practice of subinfeudation made the feudal pyramid of lords and vassals far from neat and symmetrical. In fact, it often became extremely untidy and unbalanced. Nothing, for example, prevented a vassal's becoming stronger than his suzerain; in fact, the Dukes of Normandy were for some centuries stronger than the Kings of France. Nothing, either, kept a single individual from holding several different fiefs, from being the vassal of different lords, and from occupying simultaneously positions on several levels of the feudal pyramid. In the twelfth century the Counts of Champagne held more than a score of fiefs from nine different lords, and one Bavarian count had twenty separate lords!

Attempts were made to iron out such complications by introducing the concept of a *liege lord,* the one lord among many to whom the vassal owed primary allegiance. Moreover, vassals sometimes devised a kind of "priority" system, listing which suzerains they would fight for and under what circumstances. These efforts, however, frequently failed. It was often both tempting and easy for an ambitious vassal to cut through feudal intricacies by seizing for his own whatever fiefs he could. Hence the endemic "private" wars, the chronic sieges of castles, which fill much of the history of the feudal West. Frequently the subtleties of contracts, subinfeudation, and liege lordship counted for little, and it was armed might that made feudal right.

Manorialism

Only the upper or ruling classes of the medieval West were directly a part of feudalism. Everyone, however, in a sense participated in manorialism, although, as we shall see in Chapter VIII, the clergy and the townsmen, especially the merchants, never fitted neatly into it. The lord might hold his manor as a fief from some higher lord, whose vassal he was. Or he might himself be king or duke, at or near the top of the feudal hierarchy. In the latter case, to maintain his kingly or ducal position, he depended heavily not only on the feudal "aid" of his vassals but also on the revenues in money and produce that he derived from his own manors.

The manor developed out of the late Roman *latifundia* or great estates. These estates were owned by a magnate and staffed by a household of fighters, who later became feudal vassals, and by a large number of *coloni,* who later became manorial serfs. The *coloni* were agricultural workers who were directly dependent on the magnates. They were often descendants of small landowners who had once been free and had farmed on their own. During the troubled times of the invasions and the Roman decline, they had turned their land over to the magnate and had sought his protection at the cost of their own free status. The manor also had Germanic origins, and it seems likely that its social structure bore some relation to that of the early German village community.

So far as there was a typical manor in the medieval West, it was the manor of the open champaign country—that is, cleared farmland. The grain-producing manors of the champaign country developed a three-field system. One field was used for spring planting, one for autumn planting, and one was allowed to lie fallow and recover its fertility. But the three-field system was not universal, even in the champaign country; the older two-field system, alternating crops and fallow, continued in use. Outside the great grain-growing areas—in the mountains, in wine-growing areas, in the "Celtic fringes" of Brittany, Wales, and elsewhere —there were many variant agricultural techniques. Here, as so often, there is no simple

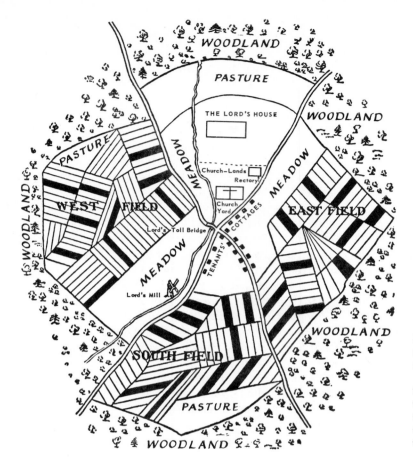

Plan of a medieval manor. The black strips are the lord's demesne. (This plan is no more than a generalized model; actual medieval manors varied enormously in size and make-up.)

"typical" medieval way. The open-field system generally prevailed in the champaign country. The people living on the manor had individual holdings in the big fields. These holdings were usually in the form of scattered long strips, each separated from neighboring strips by a narrow, unplowed "balk," but *not* by fence, wall, or hedge. The lord himself had a series of strips called his *demesne*, which was reserved to produce the food consumed by his household, and which was cultivated by the laborers who lived on the manor.

These manors of the open champaign country had certain characteristics that may be called equalitarian or even collectivist. The strips of each individual were, at least theoretically and perhaps originally, scat-

tered so that each would have some of the better land and some of the poorer. This was an application of the principle of share-and-share-alike. Moreover, since the great fields had to be plowed, sowed, and harvested at the same time, collective agreement and common labor were required. All the important decisions, plus the arrangements for common pasturage and for cultivating the lord's demesne, were made by agreement among the villagers and farmers and between them and the lord. Moreover, a great deal depended on custom; the medieval man really held that what had been done "time out of mind" was the right thing to do. And, since it often took talk and discussion to determine what actually had been done time out of mind, it is possible that these little medieval communities were schools for rural democracy, or at least for government by discussion. However, we must not overemphasize these features. The lord of the manor might himself be the autocratic arbiter of custom, and custom itself might block any effective improvement in agricultural techniques. For example, an enterprising peasant who got an idea for a new and better kind of grain to be sowed later than usual could not possibly experiment on his own strips, for he could not cross over the strips that had already been planted by his neighbors.

Not all manors were so ruled by custom as were those of the open champaign country. Vineyards, for instance, were more individualistic. On the Celtic fringes of the west, in Brittany and elsewhere, there remained small individual general farmers, who often supplemented their income by fishing. In the eastern frontier of Germany, new peasant colonists were attracted by generous land-grant terms, anticipating the westward expansion in America. The leaders of this early movement toward the east tended to become the owners of great estates that were operated along the lines of straightforward capitalist exploitation.

Manorial Society

If the lord resided on the manor, he lived in the manor house or castle, as his predecessor of late Roman days had lived in the great villa (whence our place-name ending, "ville"). Around him the lord gathered his household, not only his immediate family but also his private army of retainers, gentlemen like himself. The size of the household depended on the size and wealth of the manor, and fixed the number of men whom the lord of the manor, as vassal of a higher lord, could provide as military aid to his suzerain under the feudal contract. The whole establishment was kept running by large numbers of household servants, grooms, ostlers, and huntsmen. The

manor also had a priest; if the lord was a great lord, he might have several priests, including a chaplain for the household and a village priest for the local church. The majority of the manor's inhabitants were essentially agricultural workers. A few of them, however, were in a sense skilled laborers, especially the smiths, who worked in metals. But even the smiths did some farming and tended their own garden plots. Undoubtedly the bulk of the man-hours of labor on the manor went directly into farming, and the bulk of the farming was grain-farming.

The manor thus displayed considerable social diversity. In the early medieval West, except on the eastern frontier, you rarely find a social pattern anything like the capitalistic *latifundia* of Rome, or like the great cotton plantations of the American South before the Civil War, with master and family at one end of the social scale, a great mass of slave field hands at the other end, and only a few paid overseers in between. If we drew up the "social pyramid" of a big medieval manor, we should probably find that the bottom was occupied by the *serfs*. The serf was tied to the manor and to his job; he could not leave without the lord's consent. He had to spend perhaps half his working time on the lord's demesne. His status, moreover, was hereditary. He could not usually marry outside the manor unless he had the lord's consent, and when he inherited the use of certain strips in the field, he made the lord a special payment called *heriot*, the manorial counterpart of feudal relief. If his daughter were to marry outside the manor, he had to have the lord's consent and in addition pay a fine, called *merchet*. Merchet and heriot were the usual tests of serfdom, and go together in manorial custom.

Serfdom, however, was not slavery. In fact, slavery gradually died out in western Europe during the Middle Ages. The true slave is a chattel, like a horse or cow, to be disposed of as the master wishes. Although the medieval serf was tied to the land, the land, in effect, was also tied to the serf. The serf could not be dispossessed unless he failed to live up to his obligations. Thus he could claim certain rights, even if they were only customary rights—his share of the complex manorial farming operations, his use of the strips which he *felt* to be his own. Moreover, as a Christian, the serf had a soul and could not be treated as a mere animal. Christianity never fitted well with a slave society, and throughout the Middle Ages the Church helped to make the serf's customary rights into real rights. The serf was in a sense a party to a "manorial contract" between himself and his lord. The feudal contract, however, was concluded between social equals; not so the "manorial contract." The medieval aristocracy drew a sharp contrast between the honorable military aid of the vassal and the mere manual labor of the serf.

By no means all the peasants on every manor were serfs, however. Some of them were freemen, called "franklins" in England, who virtually owned the land they worked. And between the freemen and the serfs there were probably always a certain number of landless laborers who were not tied to the land as serfs, and some peasants with dues so light that they were almost freemen.

The manor was nearly, but not wholly, self-sustaining or autarkic. The picture of a self-sufficient manor suggests a little community in which nothing is used that comes from the outside, in which long hours of labor are required simply to feed and clothe the community. Yet we know that people fought lustily all through these years, and that they fought in armor, used swords, and built stone castles. Surely not every one of the thousands of manors could have produced steel and iron, or the salt, spices, building stones, lumber, furs, wines, and other commodities that never vanished altogether from western life. Some of these wares were luxuries, and others were durable goods that were needed only occasionally. But they were in demand, and they were produced and sold. The manor then was only *comparatively* self-sufficient and unspecialized. It had surpluses and deficiencies which gave it the motives and the means for trade with outsiders. It provided something above a bare minimum of livelihood for at least a minority of its residents. Even in the Dark Ages, western society was not reduced to a hand-to-mouth existence.

V: Western Culture, 500-1000

The Breakdown in Culture

Socially and politically, the effects of the breakdown of the *Pax Romana* were disruptive enough; culturally, they were almost disastrous. The Dark Ages were at their darkest in the realm of art, literature, and philosophy. The early medieval centuries stand up better if we compare their textiles, metal work, and grain-growing with those of Rome than if we compare their poetry, sculpture, and thought. Even the Dark Ages, however, did not hit a dead level of cultural stagnation. In the higher arts the eighth, ninth, and tenth centuries are definitely superior to the years immediately after the "fall" of Rome. Architecture, sculpture, wall painting, even Latin grammar, are generally—not always and everywhere—on a higher level in 950, say, than in 650. Indeed, by the year 1000 the bases of most of the great medieval arts are clearly laid.

One explanation of the rapid artistic decline in the centuries immediately after the Roman collapse is obvious. Artistic output, although it is often achieved by men born in the lower classes of a society, depends for its audience and its patronage on a certain minimum of taste and training among the well-to-do. Perhaps the businessmen who support the community symphony orchestra in a big American city do not really enjoy and appreciate Mozart and Beethoven, let alone contemporary composers of "serious" music; but they, and es-

scholars, philosophers, and teachers from books. Charlemagne even made an effort to restore formal culture. His palace school at Aachen was a center of studies and the arts; it was there that the biographer Einhard, the English monk Alcuin, and other scholars flourished. Charlemagne's efforts have been called the "Carolingian Renaissance," but it was really no rebirth. It was only one stage in the slow, continuous process of building medieval culture from the low point of the seventh century to the high point of the thirteenth.

Jewelry of the Dark Ages. Gold and enamel purse cover, from the Sutton Hoo Ship-Burial, Suffolk, England (before 655 A.D.).

pecially their wives, know what they ought to like, and in the whole community there are many trained musicians who know the tradition of great music. In the world of the sixth and seventh centuries the new barbarian masters were quite incapable of judging art and culture. The old aristocrats were fading out; the new intellectual class was the Christian clergy, who to a large extent were also crude, and who had the Christian contempt for, or distrust of, the sense-world in which the artist always has to work. The audience just wasn't there; naturally the play did not go on.

Or rather, an inferior play did go on. Men were building churches in the West all through the Dark Ages, often from the debris of ancient buildings. They decorated the churches with mosaics, wall paintings, and statues; they adorned themselves and their altars with jewelry; and they listened to poets and minstrels. A few of them were

The Fine Arts

In the fine arts, the Merovingians produced no great painting or sculpture. The Merovingian gravestone illustrated (p. 206) is probably typical of the technical level during the worst of the Dark Ages. Gravestones are not a wholly trustworthy test of high art; very crude work may be found in seventeenth-century New England graveyards. But in the great periods, Athens at her peak for instance, one is struck with the high technical level of the ordinary funeral tablets. The Merovingian stone-cutters could not do a satisfactory naturalistic job. Somewhat later, in Carolingian times, they begin to show a good deal of skill at carving capitals with conventionalized designs based on plants, but their sense of form was still defective. On the other hand, the illuminated manuscripts that have survived from the great age of Irish culture reveal a great capacity for drawing very intricate designs, and the jewelry of the age, though fairly barbarous, is the work of men with certain skills and traditions. As the Merovingian period merges into the Carolingian and then into the Middle Ages proper, the West gradually recovers the artistic techniques that had been partly lost and succeeds in achieving a style of its own, which is called the Romanesque (see Chapter VIII).

Literature and Thought

In the culture of the word—literature, philosophy, law, theology, and science—the late Romans had already lost much before the great barbarian invasions. Notably, natural science and technology had degenerated. Scientific investigation was almost nonexistent in the Dark Ages, although mathematics, including geometry, as applied above all to geography, never quite died out. We can see the degeneration in the recorded language itself. Here is how the distinguished American medievalist Henry Osborn Taylor has summed it up:

Merovingian tombstone, seventh century.

The diction falls away from what had been idiomatic and correct; it abandons the classic order of words and loses at the same time all feeling for the case endings of nouns and the conjugation of verbs, for which it substitutes prepositions and auxiliaries; many novel words are taken from the common speech. The substance also becomes somewhat debased and barbarized. It frequently consists in a recasting of what the fourth or fifth century had produced with the addition of whatever appealed to an insatiable credulity. As for literary form, as signifying the unity and artistic ordering rather than the diction of a composition, this does more than decline; judged by any antique standard, it ceases to exist.*

This falling off in substance is clear in almost everything that has survived, in Gregory of Tours, even in Einhard, who

* H. O. Taylor, *The Classical Heritage of the Middle Ages* (New York, 1911), 231.

tried so hard to write a classical biography of his master Charlemagne. It appears to us perhaps most conspicuously in the universal credulity that Taylor has noted. The miracles in the lives of the saints are almost too much for the most sympathetic of modern commentators. Again, these earlier writers suffer from an almost complete reverence for the authority of the works they had inherited from the classical writers and from the Fathers of the early Church. They copy, annotate, and expound, but they never, or rarely, question. And in their compiling they become absorbed in details and lose the sense of a given branch of learning as part of an organized cultural whole. It is not until the thirteenth century that men like Thomas Aquinas take all knowledge as their province (see Chapter VIII). Formlessness, repetitiousness, credulity, uncritical acceptance of earlier work—these are the marks of the literary culture of the early Middle Ages. These marks leave their traces in later medieval culture.

The Status of the Church

In these early medieval centuries, the Church had almost a monopoly of literary culture; if a man could prove that he was able to read and write, people assumed that he was a member of the clergy. This monopoly, as we have noted, contributed to the process of bringing the Church fully into the business of governing, since only clergymen had the necessary clerical skills. Our word "clerical" as a synonym for white-collar office work is in itself an indication of this old priestly monopoly.

With the barbarian invasions, the Church entered into one of its great periods of testing. The task of absorbing thousands of Germanic heathens into an organized faith that had still not won over all the old Greco-Roman ruling classes, the task of preserving high standards of human conduct—how high we have noted in Chapter IV—in a world of breakdown, the task of preserving learning in a world full of credulity, superstition, and violence—these tasks proved almost too much for the Church. And yet the historian true to his calling will hesitate to treat even the "substance" of these Dark Ages as blackness; certainly he will not make it a black one against a white of our own today. Credulity, superstition, violence, yes; but what—if they survive—will a historian of the thirtieth century make of our so-called "comics"? Our credulity, our violence (except in war), our debased taste is perhaps less widespread than theirs, perhaps less directly turned into action than theirs. It is perhaps a survival, a piece of "cultural lag"; but let us not forget it.

The Church, faced with these conditions, made temporary compromises, accepted in practice something less than universal clerical celibacy, permitted abbots and bishops to take direct part in war and politics. The abbot swinging his battle-axe against an enemy's skull is a fact, not a modern anti-clerical invention.

These compromises were not, however, major ones—and this is a point of great importance. German gods like Thor were not taken over and given a place in a Christian pantheon. Had such a completely syncretic process occurred in Christianity, we should indeed have had a very different western history. Rather, the compromises were minor. Pagan festivals were retained, but they were given a proper Christian interpretation; a new local saint could usually be discovered to make up for the loss of a local god; and concubinage was accepted among the great. In short, the Church managed to retain its basic monotheism, its basic hierarchical structure, and its basic doctrine.

For the Church, the worst centuries were not those of the Germanic invasions, but those that followed the Moslem invasions. For the papacy itself, the tenth century was the worst of all. The office had become a prize in local Roman politics, and the successors of St. Peter who held it were not always the most deserving of men. Monastic discipline had reached one of its lowest points in history, lower than it was to be on the eve of the Protestant Reformation. So entangled was the Church with the complex world of feudalism and manorialism that its offices were openly bought and sold on the market. In ecclesiastical terms this practice is known as *simony* (from the sin of Simon mentioned in the eighth chapter of the Book of Acts). Simony has probably never been more widespread in the West than it was in the tenth and early eleventh centuries.

The Early Feudal Way of Life

Outside the Church, there were few intellectuals. Yet the new ruling classes had a set of standards, a way of life. We can catch a glimpse of their ideals from the surviving epic poetry that the minstrels sang to them in their castles. These songs come to us, not from the Dark Ages, but from the Middle Ages proper, when they were written down, perhaps in modified form. Still it is clear that by Charlemagne's time there was an incipient chivalry, the code of a class of fighting men who were loyal to their chieftains and to God, and to whom God was a kind of distant but very powerful chieftain. These men were illiterate. and usually unintellectual. They took their Christianity straight, with no theological or ethical worries. They hoped to go to heaven and they were afraid to go to hell; the road to both places seemed to them fairly simple and clear. But they were violent men, men of quick temper and of barbaric, basically un-Christian, pride. They were easily insulted, and their remedy for an insult was either murder or mayhem. They had strong physical appetites, and the habit of indulging in them.

Some weary moderns—the disturbed Henry Adams in his *Mont-St.-Michel and Chartres*, for instance—have found in these paladins of the Dark Ages simple, fresh, dignified, serene, whole men, untouched by the sickness of an industrial age. But our sources of information on their actual behavior (their epic poetry is a source for their ideals rather than for what they really did) hardly bear out Henry Adams. If you read the *Song of Roland* you must also read Gregory of Tours, the Merovingian bishop whom we have already met. Roland reminds us of the very best of simple societies, that of Homer or the patriarchal Jews. But the Chilperics and Fredegunds of Gregory seem like unrepressed children who are grown up in body but not in mind. Perhaps the ordinary man of power in this society was neither as noble as in the *Song of Roland* nor as wicked as in the *History of the Franks*. But at any rate this was not one of the most admirable of our western ruling classes.

We know very little about the culture of the masses during the Dark Ages. Their material culture, as we have already noted, was by no means hopelessly poor. In most of the West, and throughout the West by the end of this period, the lower classes were formally Christian. By modern standards they were ignorant, superstitious, and remarkably unsanitary creatures. Their lives, statistically speaking, were far shorter than ours; the average span of life may well have been no longer than approximately thirty years, a figure in part accounted for by a very high infantile mortality. Yet at the worst of the Dark Ages they were not chattel slaves, but in some sense participating members of a society; and they were never an undifferentiated mass, but a varied group, out of which individuals could rise to conspicuous places in society.

On the whole, western society in the Dark Ages permitted something like the "career open to talents." Two kinds of talent in particular could lead upward even from serfdom: great intellectual and administrative gifts, which led to the top through membership in the clergy; and great gifts for fighting, which, especially if they were supplemented by the gift of getting along in male athletic circles, could take their possessor into the ruling classes, and make him a "noble." The first route tended to stay open throughout the Middle Ages; the second was easy enough in Merovingian and Carolingian times, but it grew harder and harder as the Middle Ages went on. At last, the class of *knights* had become something like a chivalric caste—a caste to which entrance was usually possible only through birth.

A final word. This culture of the West in the Dark Ages is a very difficult one to feel and to recognize in terms of *style*. As we shall see, the later Middle Ages produced one of the great styles of our long record, a style that we can feel as sharply as that of Egypt or Athens at their best. The reason is probably simple: the Dark Ages are ages of transition, in which men are culturally immature and uncertain of themselves. The elements of what was to ripen in the Middle Ages are there—in the earliest Romanesque churches, in the writings of Einhard, in the capitularies of Charlemagne. But they have not matured. In trying to hold the Dark Ages in mind, think of one of the last of the Romans, a poet, a patrician, a lover of the old culture, a formal Christian, but still a Hellenistic pagan at heart. Think of the barbarians at their crudest—Fredegund bent on killing her children and step-children. But think too of the best of the new men, of Charlemagne himself in his Frankish trousers trying to hold together thousands of square miles of land inhabited by men and women of scores of different dialects and scores of different local traditions, inventing schemes to keep his impossible realm together, checking accounts for his manors, talking over ideas with his palace circle in Aachen, enjoying his concubines, inventing new names for the months—and trying in vain to learn how to write!

Reading Suggestions
on the West in the Early Middle Ages

(Asterisk indicates paperbound edition.)

GENERAL ACCOUNTS

T. Hodgkin, *Italy and Her Invaders,* 8 vols. (Clarendon, 1885-1899). A detailed treatment of these centuries in Italy, a monumental work of nineteenth-century scholarship, by no means superseded.

J. B. Bury, *The Invasion of Europe by the Barbarians* (Macmillan, 1928). A helpful shorter account.

S. Painter, *A History of the Middle Ages, 284-1500* (Knopf, 1953). A textbook survey organized according to topics rather than chronology.

F. Lot, *The End of the Ancient World and the Beginnings of the Middle Ages* (Knopf, 1931). A balanced survey by a French historian.

The Cambridge Medieval History, Vol. II (Macmillan, 1913). One of the few scholarly surveys of the whole period in a single volume.

C. Dawson, *The Making of Europe* (Macmillan, 1933; *Meridian). A scholarly Catholic account.

J. R. Strayer and D. C. Munro, *The Middle Ages, 395-1500* (Appleton-Century-Crofts, 1942). A good American textbook.

SPECIAL STUDIES

J. H. Clapham and E. Power, eds., *The Cambridge Economic History,* Vol. I (Cambridge Univ. Press, 1941). A scholarly study of agrarian life in the Middle Ages.

A. Dopsch, *The Economic and Social Foundations of European Civilization* (Harcourt, 1937). An important work revising earlier notions of the breakdown that occurred after the "fall" of Rome.

S. Dill, *Roman Society in Gaul in the Merovingian Age* (Macmillan, 1926) and his *Roman Society in the Last Century of the Western Empire,* 2nd ed. (Macmillan, 1899; *Meridian). Both essential social history.

Carl Stephenson, *Medieval Feudalism* (°Great Seal Books, 1956). The best simple introductory manual.

A. C. Flick, *The Rise of the Medieval Church and Its Influence on the Civilization of Western Europe from the First to the Thirteenth Century* (Putnam's, 1909). A good survey.

C. H. Robinson, *The Conversion of Europe* (Longmans, Green, 1917). A convenient study of a topic hard to sort out in general histories.

H. Pirenne, *Mohammed and Charlemagne* (Norton, 1939; °Meridian). Advances the thesis that the worst breakdown in western Europe resulted from the Arab conquest of the Mediterranean rather than from the German invasions. One of the few new interpretations of the Dark Ages, and one that has been hotly debated.

R. Winston, *Charlemagne: From the Hammer to the Cross* (Bobbs-Merrill, 1952). The best biography available in English.

E. S. Duckett, *Alcuin, Friend of Charlemagne, His World and His Work* (Macmillan, 1951). A scholarly study.

C. H. Haskins, *The Normans in European History* (Houghton Mifflin, 1915). A very readable and sympathetic introduction.

F. M. Stenton, *Anglo-Saxon England,* 2nd ed. (Clarendon, 1950). The most recent standard account.

D. Whitelock, *The Beginnings of English Society* (°Penguin, 1952). A briefer introduction to Anglo-Saxon England.

M. L. W. Laistner, *Thought and Letters in Western Europe, A.D. 500 to 900* (Methuen, 1931). A good scholarly study.

E. K. Rand, *Founders of the Middle Ages* (Harvard Univ. Press, 1928). Engaging lectures on some of the cultural figures of the late classical period and the Dark Ages.

P. A. Allen and H. M. Jones, *The Romanesque Lyric* (Univ. of North Carolina Press, 1928). More generally informative than its title might suggest.

SOURCES

Gregory of Tours, *History of the Franks,* O. M. Dalton, ed. (Clarendon, 1927). The account of a sixth-century historian.

A. J. Grant, ed., *Early Lives of Charlemagne* (Chatto & Windus, 1922).

Sidonius, *Poems and Letters,* W. B. Anderson, trans. (Harvard Univ. Press, 1936). The observations of a fifth-century Roman aristocrat.

Venerable Bede (Beda Venerabilis), *Ecclesiastical History of the English Nation* (Dutton, 1954, Everyman ed.). An adequate translation.

HISTORICAL FICTION

H. Muntz, *The Golden Warrior* (Scribner's, 1949). A well-written, historically sound novel of the Norman conquest of England.

W. Bryher, *The Roman Wall* (Pantheon, 1954). A short novel of life on the frontier of the Roman Empire during the decline.

W. Bryher, *The Fourteenth of October* (Pantheon, 1952). Another good novel about the Norman conquest of England.

Eastern Christendom and Islam:

To the Late Eleventh Century

CHAPTER VI

I: The Historical Role of Byzantium

AT THE FAR southeastern corner of Europe, on a little tongue of land surrounded on three sides by water and still walled off on the land side by a long line of massive walls and towers, there stands a splendid city. Istanbul it is called now, which is simply a Turkish corruption of three Greek words meaning "to the city." For more than a thousand years, indeed it was *the* city to uncounted thousands of people: Greeks, Orientals, Slavs. The waters that lap against the remains of its sea walls are those of the Sea of Marmora, the Bosphorus, and its own sheltered harbor of the Golden Horn. A few miles up the narrow, swift-flowing Bosphorus lies the entrance into the otherwise land-locked Black Sea. Into the Black Sea flow the Danube from the west, and from the north the most westerly of the great Russian rivers—among them the Dnieper and the Don.

To the southwest of the city—a few more miles in the other direction—the Sea of Marmora narrows into the long passage of the Dardanelles, through which one emerges into the Aegean Sea, an island-studded inlet of the Mediterranean. The Dardanelles, the Sea of Marmora, and the Bosphorus together form the continuous water passage which not only connects the Black Sea with the Mediterranean but separates Europe from Asia. These are the famous "Straits," which the Russians have coveted so long, and which the Soviet Union still hopes to control. And dominating the straits is "the city." In the fifth century before Christ, a shrewd Persian general was told that the earliest Greek settlers had built a town across the Straits in Asia, some seventeen years before anyone had colonized the European site of Istanbul. "Then," said he, "they must have been laboring under blindness. Otherwise, when so excellent a site was open to them, they would never have chosen one so greatly inferior." [*]

Constantine the Great (324-337) made the critical decision to abandon Rome as the capital of the Empire, and after several years spent in rebuilding and redecorating, he dedicated this city as the new capital on May 11, 330. Thereafter it was often called Constantinople, Constantine's city. But it retained also its ancient name of Byzantium, after a half-mythical founder, Byzas. To the Slavs, both of Russia and the Balkans, who owe to it their religion and their culture, it has always been *Tsargrad*, city of the Emperor. After more than eleven hundred years as the capital of the Roman Empire, it fell to the Turks in 1453. In Constantine's day, Byzantium ruled over all the eastern provinces of the Roman Empire (see above, pp. 116-117). But after the seventh century, Egypt, North Africa, and Syria were permanently lost. Asia Minor and the Balkan peninsula always formed the core of these eastern imperial lands.

The Character of Byzantine History

Byzantium called itself "New Rome." Its emperors ruled in direct succession from Augustus, and the population, though predominantly Greek by race, called itself not Hellene (the traditional name of the ancient Greeks for themselves) but Rhomaean, that is to say Roman. But despite the importance of the continuous tradition derived from Rome, non-Roman elements —Christian, Greek, Armenian—became strikingly important in Byzantine society. A Roman of the time of Augustus, to say nothing of the Republic, would have found himself ill at ease and out of place in, say, eleventh-century Byzantium.

Until less than a century ago, the study of Byzantine history was under a cloud. German classical scholars felt that it was somehow not decent to investigate the history of a people who could not write good classical Greek. The French for their part usually referred to Byzantium as the "*bas-empire*," literally the low or degenerate empire, whose achievements they scornfully contrasted with the glorious literary and artistic performance of Greece and Rome. From Gibbon on, the English were equally indifferent or scornful. The Victorian scholar Lecky wrote:

Of that Byzantine Empire the universal verdict of history is that it constitutes, without a single exception, the most thoroughly base and despicable form that civilisation has yet assumed.... There has been no other enduring civilisation so absolutely destitute of all the forms and elements of greatness.... The history of the empire is a monotonous story of the intrigues of priests, eunuchs, and women, of poisonings, of conspiracies, of uniform ingratitude, of perpetual fratricides.[*]

Lecky was writing a history of European morals; and one must cheerfully admit that a Victorian moralist would find much to shudder at in the private life of the individual Byzantine emperors. Yet this is almost irrelevant to the historian's estimate of the Byzantine achievement.

[*] Herodotus, *History*, G. Rawlinson, trans. (New York, 1862), IV, 144.

[*] W. E. H. Lecky, *History of European Morals from Augustus to Charlemagne* (New York, 1869), II, 13-14.

CHAPTER VI

That achievement was varied, distinguished, and of major importance to the West. Byzantine literature does indeed suffer by comparison with the classics; but the appropriate society with which to compare medieval Byzantium is not classical antiquity but the Roman Catholic Europe of the Middle Ages. Medieval western European civilization and medieval Byzantine civilization are both Christian and both the direct heirs of Rome and Greece. Once these contemporary sister societies are compared, one sees immediately that the Byzantines created art as admirable in its way as anything produced in the West, that they maintained learning on a level much more advanced than did the West, and that the West itself owes a substantial cultural debt to Byzantium.

Byzantium as Preserver of the Classics

In the West, long centuries passed during which the knowledge of Greek had disappeared. Nobody in the West had access to the great works of philosophy, science, and literature written in Greek by the ancients. During all this time the Byzantines preserved these masterpieces, copied and re-copied them, by hand of course, and gave them constant study.

Again, in contrast to the West, study was not confined to monasteries, although the monks played a major role. It was also pursued in secular libraries and schools. The teacher occupied an important position in Byzantine society; books circulated widely among prominent men in public life; many of the emperors were scholars and lovers of literature. In the early days of the Empire, the greatest university was still at Athens, but because of its strong pagan tradition the deeply pious Christian Emperor Justinian closed the university there in the sixth century. The imperial university at Constantinople, which probably

dates from Constantine himself, supplied a steady stream of learned and cultivated men to the bureaucracy, the church, and the courts. The emphasis in its curriculum was on secular subjects: philosophy, astronomy, geometry, rhetoric, music, grammar, law, medicine, and arithmetic. The School of the Patriarch, the Archbishop of Constantinople, also in the capital, provided instruction in theology and other sacred subjects.

Had it not been for Byzantium, it seems certain that Plato and Aristotle, Homer and Sophocles, would have been lost. We cannot even imagine what such a loss would have meant to western civilization, how seriously it would have retarded us in science and speculation, in morals and ethics, how crippled we should have been in our efforts to deal with the fundamental problems of human relationships, how poor and meager our cultural inheritance would have been. That these living works of the dead past have been preserved to us we owe to Byzantium.

Original Writing

Too often, however, people have thought of the Byzantine cultural achievement as limited to preservation and transmission. The Byzantines were themselves creative. Although literature was not their strongest field, their literature has been insufficiently appreciated. We have, for instance, an epic poem, from the tenth or eleventh century, describing the heroic activity of a frontier warrior who had lived some two to three centuries earlier, Basil Digenes Akritas (Basil, of the two races, the frontiersman). Half Greek, half Arab, he fights wild beasts and brigands, preserves order on the border between Byzantine and Moslem territory, seizes a fair bride and forces her family to consent to the marriage, defeats a magnificent Amazon (female) warrior, and even tells the emperor how to behave. Though the creator of this hero was no Homer, he is fully comparable with the western authors who sang of Roland, of the Cid, and of the Scottish borderers. Like Basil, all these heroes were men of the frontiers, Daniel Boones of the Middle Ages, pursuing adventure and righting wrongs out where men are men, among the medieval equivalents of the Red Indians.

In prose, perhaps the most striking accomplishment is that scored by the almost unbroken line of those who over the long centuries wrote the history of the Empire. Writing in a popular style, the chroniclers took their story back to the Creation or continued the work of a predecessor who had done so. The true historians wrote for intellectuals, and limited themselves to the story of their own times, perhaps with an introduction describing a period immediately before their own about which they had some first-hand information. We must be careful to weigh what they tell us, because they were often violently partisan in the quarrels of their day, and may sometimes be found blackening the innocent or whitewashing the guilty for their own purposes. But if we proceed cautiously, the great series of Byzantine historians opens up for us a world as yet little known. There is no comparable body of literature to tell us about men and events in the medieval West, which all too often can be discovered only from the bare bones of legal documents or from a tantalizingly dry and brief mention in some book of annals.

In Byzantine society the Church played a central role. So, as we might expect, theological writing forms a substantial part of the prose literature. In the early period the Byzantine theologians hotly debated the great controversies that rent the Empire about the true relationship between God the Father and God the Son, or between the divine and human natures of Christ. In a society like the Byzantine, such works had the importance that may be ascribed, for example, to those of Freud or Marx in our own day. Too difficult for most people to read or understand, they none the less had enormous influence over the lives of everybody: the leaders of the society were directly or indirectly affected by their answers to the problems of human social and economic life in general, or of the life of the human individual in particular and of his prospects of eternal salvation or damnation. The early theologians also drew up appropriate rules for monks, balancing with reasonable opportunities for work the requirement that the desires of the flesh must be denied, an arrangement which worked in the East to prevent many of the difficulties which arose in western monasticism. Finally, under the influence of the Neo-Platonic philosophers, the theologians developed a mystic strain, in which they urged contemplation and purification as stages toward illumination and the final mystic union with God.

For the ordinary man, the mysteries of his faith were enhanced by the beauties of the church service, where magnificent hymns were sung, often especially by men whom we would consider to be major poets. Saints' lives, usually written for a popular audience, took the place of the novel in our society. They told a personal story, often including adventure, anxiety, deprivation, violence, and agony of various sorts, and they set forth the final triumph of virtue and piety. The eyes of the reader were elevated to consider his heavenly reward, since the hero of the story was often martyred here on earth. Exciting and edifying, these tales were not only immensely popular in their day, but help the scholar of our own, because they often supply valuable bits of information about daily life, especially among the humbler classes, and about the attitudes of the people, for which we sometimes have no other source.

The vivid and somewhat naive quality of these works is illustrated, for instance, in the following episode from the Life of

Theodore of Sykeon, a seventh-century saint who wrought miracles in Asia Minor:

> ... The holy Theodore sent his archdeacon to the capital, Constantinople, to buy a chalice and a paten of silver. ... The archdeacon went and bought from a silversmith a pure and well-finished vessel, so far as concerned the quality of the silver and the workmanship, and he brought it back to the monastery. ... When the saint looked at them, he ... condemned them as being useless and defiled. But the archdeacon who looked at the appearance and not at what was hidden, pointed out the perfect and well-wrought workmanship and the quality proved by the five-fold stamp upon it, and thought by these facts to convince the Saint. But the Saint said 'I know, yes, I know, son, that so far as eyes can see, it appears a beautiful specimen of craftsmanship and the worth of the silver is evident from the stamps on it, but it is another, an invisible cause which defiles it. I fancy the defilement comes from some impure use. But if you doubt it, pronounce the verse for our prayers and be convinced.' Then whilst the archdeacon chanted the verse of Invocation, the Saint bent his head in prayer, and after he had filled the chalice, the chalice and the paten turned black. ... Then the archdeacon returned to Constantinople and gave them back to the dealer in silver and told him the reason. The dealer made inquiries of ... his manager and his silversmith who fashioned the vessels, and found out that they came from the chamberpot of a prostitute. ... He gave him other and very beautiful vessels, and these the archdeacon carried to the Saint, and reported to him and to the monks the cause of defilement in the earlier vessels, and they all gave thanks unto God.[*]

From this passage we learn quite incidentally a good bit about the organization of the silver business in Byzantium: a merchant is shown employing a manager and an artisan, and we find that a five-fold hallmark was the Byzantine equivalent of our "sterling" stamped on an object. Also, quite incidentally, we discover that then as now ladies of easy virtue sometimes became quite prosperous.

Unique among these saints' lives is one extraordinary document of the tenth century: a highly polished tale of an Indian king, who shuts away his only son Ioasaph in a remote palace to protect him from the knowledge of the world and especially to prevent his being converted to Christianity. But the prince cannot be protected; he sees a sick man, a blind man, and a dead man; and when he is in despair at life's cruelties a wise monk in disguise, named Barlaam, succeeds in reaching him by pretending to have a precious jewel that he wishes to show. The jewel is the jewel of the Christian faith, and the rest of the long story is an account of the wise monk Barlaam's conversion of Prince Ioasaph. In the course of the conversion, Barlaam tells Ioasaph ten moral tales illustrating the Christian life. One of these is known to us as the "casket-story" of Shakespeare's *Merchant of Venice;* another is the tale of "Everyman," which later became common in all western literatures; others of Barlaam's stories were used by literally hundreds of other western authors and preachers of all nationalities.

Yet what is most fascinating about this piece of Byzantine literature is that it originally comes from India: the life of Ioasaph is a Christianized version of the life of Buddha, the great Indian religious leader of the sixth century B.C. His life story passed through Persia via the Arabs to the Caucasus Kingdom of Georgia before it was turned into Greek legend and transmitted to the West. And the stories that Barlaam tells to convert Ioasaph are also Indian in origin and are either Buddhist "birth-stories" (recitals of the Buddha's experiences in earlier incarnations used as comment upon what was going on around him), or Hindu moral-comic tales. Indeed the very name Ioasaph is the same as the Indian word Boddhisattva, which means a person destined to attain Buddhahood. Prince Ioasaph has been canonized as a saint of both the Orthodox and the Roman Catholic churches, and it is thus an odd but true fact that through this legend Buddha himself became and has remained a Christian saint.

---

[*] N. H. Baynes and E. A. S. Dawes, *Three Byzantine Saints* (Oxford, 1948), 117-118.

The Arts

It is when we turn to the field of the plastic arts, however, that we can see the Byzantine achievement with our own eyes. Description generally fails to do justice to great works of art, and reproductions can only suggest the color, which is so fundamental a part of Byzantine artistic creation. In Constantinople, the Church of Santa Sophia, built in the sixth century, was designed to be "a church the like of which has never been seen since Adam nor ever will be." The dome, "a work at once marvellous and terrifying," says a contemporary, "seems rather to hang by a golden chain from heaven than to be supported by solid masonry," and Justinian (527-565), the emperor who built it, was able to exclaim "I have outdone thee, O Solomon!" "On entering the church to pray," says Justinian's historian, Procopius, "one feels at once that it is the work not of man's effort or industry, but in truth the work of the divine power; and the spirit, mounting to heaven, realizes that here God is very near, and that He delights in this dwelling that He has chosen for Himself." The Turks themselves, who seized the city in 1453, ever since have paid Santa Sophia the sincerest compliment of imitation; the great mosques that throng present-day Istanbul are all more or less directly copied after the great church of the Byzantines.

Before Santa Sophia could be built, the other cities of the Empire, particularly Alexandria, Antioch, and Ephesus, had produced the necessary architectural synthesis: a fusion of the Hellenistic or Roman basilica with a dome taken from Persia. This is just one striking example of the way in which Greek and Oriental elements were to be blended in the new society. In decoration, the use of brilliantly colored marbles, enamel, silken and other fabrics, gold, silver, and jewels, and the paintings and glowing mosaics on the walls and ceilings, reflect the sumptuousness of the Orient.

The tourist of today wishing to see a Byzantine church of Justinian's time need not go all the way to Istanbul. On the Adriatic coast of Italy, south of Venice, at Ravenna, there are three wonderful smaller churches of the sixth century with superb mosaics still well preserved, including portraits of Justinian himself and of his Empress Theodora. And at Venice itself, first the client, then the equal, and finally the conqueror of Byzantium, St. Mark's is a true Byzantine church of the later period, whose richness and magnificence epitomize perhaps better than any surviving church in Istanbul itself the splendor of later Byzantine architecture.

The great church of Santa Sophia, Constantinople.

Along with the major arts of architecture, painting, and mosaics went the so-called minor arts, whose level the Byzantines raised so high that the term minor seems almost absurd. The silks, the ivories, the work of the goldsmiths and silversmiths, the enamel and jeweled book-covers, the elaborate containers made especially to hold the sacred relics of a saint, the great Hungarian sacred Crown of Saint Stephen, the superb miniatures of the illuminated manuscripts in half a hundred European libraries—all testify to the endless variety and fertility of Byzantine inspiration.

Even in those parts of western Europe where Byzantine political authority had disappeared, the influence of this Byzantine artistic flowering is often apparent. Sometimes we are dealing with actual creations by Byzantine artists produced in the West or ordered from Constantinople by a connoisseur. These are found in Sicily and southern Italy, in Venice, and in Rome itself. Sometimes the native artists work in the Byzantine manner, as in Spain, in Sicily, and in the great Romanesque domed churches of southern France. Often the new native product is not purely Byzantine, but rather a fusion of Byzantine with local elements, a new art diverse in its genius, but one of whose strands is clearly native to Constantinople.

War

Quite apart from its cultural achievements, however, Byzantium's military and economic achievements are so striking that any student of civilization needs to appreciate them. After the barbarian invasions of the fourth and fifth centuries, which shattered imperial unity in the West (see Chapter V), Europe was repeatedly threatened by other waves of invaders moving north and west from Asia. So the Persians in the seventh century, the Arabs from the seventh century on, and the Turks beginning in the eleventh century, beat against the Byzantine frontiers in an effort to break into Europe.

The Byzantine Empire was often shaken by these blows: the eastern Roman provinces of Syria and Egypt were lost forever in the seventh century as a result of the impact of Persians and Arabs. And western Europe was not entirely spared the effects of these invasions. The Arab expansion brought waves of Moslems into Sicily and southern Italy, and across the Straits of Gibraltar into Spain, whence a small force even challenged the Franks at Tours in 732. But Charles Martel's victory at Tours was a far less significant achievement in checking the Moslem tide at high-water mark than the victory of the Byzantine Emperor Leo III the Isaurian, who had repelled a major Arab attack on Byzantium itself in 717, fifteen years before.

We ought to ask: What might have been the fate of western Europe had not the Byzantines succeeded, with great losses and at great expense, in containing these Persian and Arab and Turkish attacks, down to the end of the eleventh century? During this entire period the western Europeans might well have proved unable to take care of themselves. The answer is clear: Had it not been for Byzantium, we might all be Moslems.

Byzantium thus served as a buffer that absorbed the heaviest shock of eastern invasions, and cushioned the West against them. The Byzantine state was also engaged on all its frontiers in almost constant warfare against a variety of other enemies. Sometimes they were Asiatics, who had drifted into Europe from what is now Russia. In this category belong the Huns of the fifth century, the Avars of the sixth and seventh, the Bulgars of the seventh and succeeding centuries, the Magyars of the ninth and later centuries, and the Pechenegs and Cumans of the eleventh, twelfth, and thirteenth centuries. All these peoples were initially Finnish or Mongoloid nomads, liv-

St. Mark's Cathedral, Venice, a western monument of Byzantine style.

ing in felt tents, drinking fermented mare's milk and eating cheese, and quite at home for days at a time on the backs of their swift horses.

Sometimes the enemies were native Europeans, like the Slavs, who first appear in the sixth century, and filter gradually into the Empire thereafter, in a steady human flow that covered the entire Balkan Peninsula, even Greece, with Slavic settlement. In the northeastern part of the Balkan Peninsula just south of the Danube, the Slavs were conquered by the Hunnic tribe of the Bulgars, but they slowly absorbed their conquerors. By the tenth century the Bulgarians had no recognizable Asiatic traces left, but were thoroughly Slavic.

These Bulgars and much later the Serbs to the west of them fought long and exhausting wars against the Empire. So did the Russians, another Slavic people, whose Scandinavian upper crust was gradually absorbed by a Slavic lower class. They first assaulted Byzantium from the water in 860, having floated in canoes down the river Dnieper and sailed across the Black Sea, and they several times repeated the attack. Sometimes, especially toward the end of the Byzantine period, the enemies were western Europeans: Normans from the southern Italian state in Italy and Sicily, Crusaders from France and Germany and Italy, freebooting commercial adventurers from the new Italian cities seeking to extract economic concessions by force or to increase the value of the concessions they already held (see Chapter IX).

Until the late eleventh century, when Turks and Normans alike inflicted serious defeats, the Byzantines were able to hold their own. Though hostile forces sometimes swarmed to the very foot of the land walls or threatened to launch a maritime invasion from across the Straits, the capital itself remained inviolable and secure until 1204. In that year it was taken for the first time by a mixed force of Venetian traders eager for profit and by French, Italian, and German Crusaders, who should have been fighting the infidel in Palestine.

This long record of military success could hardly have been scored by a state as degenerate as scholars once believed Byzantium to be. It can be accounted for only by the general excellence of the Byzantine military and naval establishment over a long period of years. We still have treatises on the art of war from all periods of Byzantine history, discussing innovations in weapons, in strategy, in tactics. Adaptability was the keynote of the Byzantines' attitude. They were always ready to apply to their own armed forces the lessons learned from each successive enemy. Often commanded by the emperor in person, carefully recruited and thoroughly trained, well armed and equipped, served by regular bands playing martial music, with medical and ambulance corps, signal corps with flashing mirrors, and intelligence services far ahead of those maintained by their rivals, the Byzantine armies, though occasionally defeated, were by and large superior to those which their enemies were able to put in the field.

The same is almost as true of the Byzantine navies. The appearance of a Moslem fleet in the eastern Mediterranean in the seventh century forced a naval reorganization by the Byzantines, who by the tenth century had recaptured their former control of these waters. In the eleventh century, like all other Byzantine institutions, the navy suffered a decline from which it never recovered. The Italian merchant cities replaced Byzantium as the great Mediterranean naval power, and this was one of the main causes of the Empire's downfall. At its height, however, the Byzantine fleet was a vital part of the military establish-

Interior of St. Mark's Cathedral in Venice.

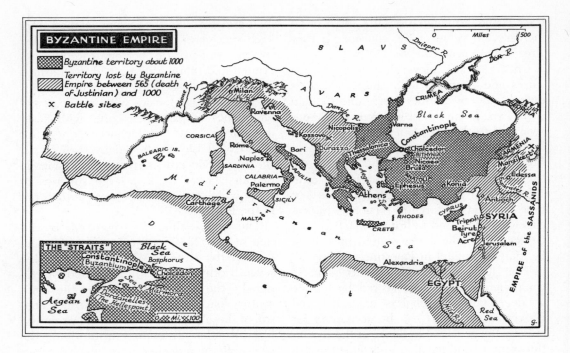

ment. It was equipped with one of the real secret weapons of the Middle Ages: Greek fire, a still mysterious chemical compound squirted from tubes or siphons in the shape of lions' heads of gilded bronze mounted on the prows of the Byzantine ships, which would set enemy vessels aflame and strike terror into the hearts of their sailors.

Diplomacy

The long-continued Byzantine success in war was due not only to good armies and navies but also to sound diplomacy. The Byzantine state always preferred negotiation to war, and achieved a remarkable record of success. We still have preserved the records and reports of a considerable number of Byzantine embassies, and can appreciate the delicacy of the instructions given the envoys, and the subtlety of the protocol involved. In the period before the Arab conquest, Persia was the only state which the Byzantines regarded as approaching their own in civilization, and whose rulers they treated as equals. To some extent, this was also true of the Moslem caliphs of the seventh century and later. All other monarchs were regarded with less respect, and when they claimed an imperial title, as in the case of the Franks or the later German emperors, the claim was usually passed over in scornful silence or openly disputed.

Yet, although the theory of empire proclaimed that the Empire was universal, in their constant effort to protect their frontiers the Byzantine emperors dealt realistically with those "barbarian" peoples, whom they could not conquer. They negotiated treaties securing to themselves military assistance, and graciously allowing the vassal peoples to bask in the reflected light of imperial prestige, and to enjoy the luxuries that Byzantine money could buy. A kind of "office of barbarian affairs" kept imperial officials supplied with intelligence reports on the internal conditions of each barbarian people so that a "pro-Byzantine" party might be created and any internal stresses and quarrels among the clients might be

CHAPTER VI

turned to the advantage of the Byzantines.

As in Roman times, when the emperor sent arms for the chieftain of a foreign tribe, the act was the equivalent of adoption, and the paternal relationship became even stronger, when, as often happened, the emperor stood sponsor to the ruler at his eventual baptism. The son of such a chief might be invited to Byzantium, educated there, and thus introduced to all the glories of Byzantine civilization. Titles in the hierarchy of the palace, with their rich and valuable insignia, were bestowed on barbarian rulers; and on occasion a royal crown might even be granted. Marriage was also a most useful instrument. Barbarian leaders were delighted to marry Byzantine girls of noble family; and when it was a question of a particularly desirable alliance, the emperor himself might marry a barbarian princess or arrange to give a princess of the imperial house to a foreigner.

A solemn and dazzling formal reception at the imperial court was always an extremely effective means of impressing a foreign ruler or envoy, even a sophisticated western bishop, like Liudprand, ambassador of Berengar, King of Italy, who has left us this account from the year 948:

Before the emperor's seat stood a tree made of bronze gilded over, whose branches were filled with birds, also made of gilded bronze, which uttered different cries, each according to its varying species. The throne itself was so marvellously fashioned that at one moment it seemed a low structure and at another it rose high into the air. It was of immense size and was guarded by lions, made either of bronze or of wood covered over with gold, who beat the ground with their tails and gave a dreadful roar with open mouth and quivering tongue. Leaning upon the shoulders of two eunuchs I was brought into the emperor's presence. At my approach the lions began to roar and the birds to cry out, each according to its kind. . . . After I had three times made obeisance to the emperor with my face upon the ground, I lifted my head and behold! the man whom just before I had seen sitting on a moderately elevated seat had now changed his raiment and was sitting on the level of the ceiling. How it was

done I cannot imagine, unless perhaps he was lifted up by some sort of device as we use for raising the timbers of a wine-press. On that occasion he did not address me personally, since even if he had wished to do so the wide distance between us would have rendered conversation unseemly, but by the intermediary of a secretary he enquired after Berengar's doings, and asked after his health. I made a fitting reply and then, at a nod from the interpreter, left his presence and retired to my lodging.*

Economic Prosperity

Good armies and navies and shrewd diplomacy are expensive, and depend directly upon the economic strength of the state that creates and uses them. Byzantium was enormously rich. In fact, the city was a great center of trade, to which came vessels from every quarter of the compass. From the countries around the shore of the Black Sea came furs and hides, grain, salt, and wine, and slaves from the Caucasus. From India, Ceylon, Syria, and Arabia came spices, precious stones, and silk; from Africa, slaves and ivory; from the West, especially Italy, merchants eager to buy the products sold in Constantinople, often the products of the imperial industries.

The Byzantine emperors themselves were able for a time to maintain a monopoly of the manufacture and sale of silk textiles, purple dye, and gold embroidery, which were not then merely luxuries, but absolute necessities for the dignitaries of church and state in the West as in the East. For long a closely guarded secret of the Persians, silk manufacture came to Byzantium in the middle of the sixth century, when two monks explained to the emperor that the mysterious cloth was the product of silkworms. Later—so the story goes—bribed by the promise of a great reward, they actually brought back silkworms' eggs hidden in a hollow cane. They taught the emperor that

* *Antapodosis*, VI, v, in *Works of Liudprand of Cremona*, F. A. Wright, trans. (London, 1930), 207-208.

the worms must be fed mulberry leaves; great plantations of mulberries were established, especially in Syria; and a mighty enterprise was under way.

The power that was derived from the control over the manufacture and sale of silk has rightly been compared with modern controls over strategic materials like coal, oil, and iron. But it was not only the imperial treasury that profited: the rich were able to embellish their persons and their homes; many middle-class merchants and craftsmen found a livelihood in the industry; and the flow of revenue into the imperial treasuries made it possible for the emperors to tax the lower classes less than would otherwise have been necessary for national defense and other official expenses. An elaborate system of control over manufacture (which was in the hands of carefully regulated imperial guilds) and over sales (which were permitted only in official salesrooms) safely secured the monopoly down to the eleventh century.

Besides controlling silk, the emperor forbade the export of gold, a measure obviously designed to prevent the depletion of reserves. In fact, one of the unmistakable signs of enduring Byzantine prosperity during the whole period from the fourth to the eleventh century is the Byzantine gold coinage. The *nomisma*, as the Byzantine gold coin was called, was standard all over the Mediterranean and even in the East. Until the late eleventh century it was almost never debased, and even then only under the impact of crisis brought about by civil strife and foreign invasion, and only gradually. But for eight hundred years this money was stable.

The wealth of Byzantium was noticed and envied by all visitors to the Empire, especially by visitors from the West, whose own largely rural society and meager way of life contrasted so strikingly with the urban glitter and sophistication of the imperial capital. This was not merely a matter of splendid silken garments embroidered

with gold, of palaces and churches aglow with mosaics and richly carved columns of semi-precious stones imported at great expense from distant lands, of treasures of jewelry and gold and ivory worn by the wealthy citizens and displayed in their houses. The impression created by these superficial externals was dazzling indeed. But beneath the splendor and the show lay the hard economic realities that preserved the state for centuries. These were a thriving commerce and industry and a substantial revenue.

Throughout Byzantine history, the sources of state income remained pretty much the same. There was the revenue from state property in land—farms, cattle ranches, gold and silver mines, marble quarries—as distinct from the money that came in from the emperor's personal estates. There was the revenue from liquid assets seized in war or confiscated from rich men in disgrace. There was also revenue from taxation: on land and persons, sales and profits, imports and exports, and inheritances.

Until the seventh century, the reigning concept of taxation on land and persons was that of Diocletian (284-305), who had linked the land tax with the tax on persons or head tax. The territory of the Empire was considered to be divided into units called *yokes,* each of which was defined as the amount of land that could feed a single laboring farmer. In order to be taxable as a unit of land, each yoke had to have its farmer to work it; in order to be taxable as a person, each farmer had to have a yoke to work. In a period of labor shortage, the government thus had to find a person to cultivate every yoke; otherwise there would have been no revenue.

It was this concept that led to the binding of the peasants to the soil, and to their slow degeneration into serfs. Large private landowners naturally flourished under such a system, since it was easier for the state to lease them large tracts of land and leave

CHAPTER VI

it to them to find the supply of labor. More-over, inferior land or abandoned or run-down farms were compulsorily assigned to nearby landowners, who were responsible for the taxes on this property as on their more productive acres. Only if a landowner had a substantial acreage of rich and pro-ductive farm land could he be expected to pay such taxes on the more marginal farms.

So this aspect of the system also contrib-uted to the growth of large private estates. Yet, though the large estate may have pre-dominated in the early period, the small private freeholder seems never to have dis-appeared. In later centuries, as we shall see, the balance between the two types of holding would several times swing one way or the other.

II: Byzantine Government and Society

The Emperor

Deeply conscious of the ties that bound them to Rome, the Byzantine em-perors believed in the divine mission of their empire. After Constantine had be-come a Christian, the Christian empire only slightly modified the old pagan tradition of the god-emperor. The emperor was no longer God, but he was ordained of God to rule, and his power was divine. There was but one God in heaven, so there could be but one emperor on earth. Though there were still nations left to conquer, it was the destiny of the Roman Empire to conquer them.

The will of God could, in theory, mani-fest itself only in the unanimous consent of the people, the senate, and the army to the choice of a new emperor. So there was no fixed custom that the Empire was heredi-tary. In practice, a reigning emperor often associated a colleague with him during his own reign, as had been done at Rome, and thus in effect he could choose his heir. The role of people, senate, and army then be-came a mere formality. Of course, when the colleague chosen was, as often happened, the emperor's son, the hereditary principle was operating, and at Byzantium it came to be felt as a necessity that, if a co-emperor

was not already the emperor's son, he should be adopted. Thus one encounters long-lasting dynasties on the Byzantine throne. Yet politicians and various social groups often intervened. They murdered emperors, blinded them (which made them ineligible to return to the throne), im-prisoned them or exiled them, and put their own candidates on the throne.

Once chosen, the Byzantine emperor re-ceived a collar and was raised aloft on a shield as a sign of army approval. This ceremony made him *imperator*, or com-mander in chief. By the mid-fifth century he was also formally crowned by the high-est dignitary of the Church, the patriarch. This was a Christian ceremony, which, by the seventh century, took place in Santa Sophia. At his coronation the emperor swore to defend the Christian faith. Be-sides the crown, the insignia of empire included a pair of high purple boots and a purple robe. In the seventh century also, the celebrated title *Basileus* was adopted, a Greek equivalent for the Persian King of Kings, whom the Byzantines had defeated. Still later, the additional title *autokrator* was added. At Byzantium, the empress bore feminine titles corresponding to those of her husband and was crowned as he was, but in one of the rooms of the palace. Her image appeared on the imperial coinage.

Occasionally she acted as regent. Three times during the course of Byzantine history women ruled without a male emperor, exercising full imperial power.

The emperor was an absolute ruler. Though now only the servant of the Christian God, he was still hedged by the old divinity. God bestowed his position upon him; God lent victory to his arms. Since the state was founded on the favor of heaven, there could be no need for change. Although the individual autocrat might be overthrown by the conspiracy of a rival, autocracy as such was never challenged. And of course these divinely awarded powers entailed immense earthly responsibilities: the "Imperial power," says an eighth-century text, "is a legal authority established for the good of all subjects. When it strikes a blow, it is not through hatred; if it grants a reward it is not through favoritism; but like the referee in a fight, it awards to each man the recompense he deserves." "And if," added a ninth-century patriarch more daring than most, "the Emperor, inspired by the devil, gives a command contrary to the divine law, no-one should obey him. Every subject can rebel against any administrative act which runs counter to the law, and even against the Emperor if he allows himself to be governed by his passions." Here is a statement of legalized revolution as the one recourse against absolutism, and over the years this theory was often put to the test in practice.

The emperor was bound by an elaborate and rigid code of etiquette that governed every movement he made every day of the year. So complex were the rules of his life that entire treatises were written to describe them. Silence in his presence was the rule. He spoke and gave his commands through simple, brief, and established formulas. When he gave gifts, his subjects hid their hands beneath their cloaks, a Persian ritual gesture implying that the touch of a mere human hand would soil his. As Liudprand reported (see p. 221, above), a person admitted to audience with the emperor was required to approach him with an official holding him by the arm on either side. When he came near to the divine presence, the suppliant fell on his face and made obeisance. On public occasions the emperor was acclaimed in song, to the sound of silver trumpets.

The Law

As the direct agent of God, the emperor was responsible for the preservation of the tradition of the Roman law. Since it was the emperor who ordered the periodic re-drafting and re-compiling of the statute books, and could modify the laws already in effect, he had ready to his hand an immensely powerful instrument for preserving and enhancing his power. Justinian (527-565) between 528 and 533 ordered his lawyers to dispose of obsolete, repetitious, and conflicting enactments, and thus to codify existing law. His *Code* included all legislation since Hadrian (117-138). Earlier authoritative opinions of legal experts were codified in the *Digest,* an even bulkier work. The *Institutes,* a handbook for students, served as an introduction to both compilations. All these were set down in Latin, but Justinian's own laws, the *Novels,* or newly passed enactments, appeared in Greek.

Not until the eighth century did a new collection appear—the *Ekloga*—which modified Justinian's work in accordance with Christian principles and with the decreasingly Roman character of the Empire. The *Ekloga* softened the death penalty provided for many offenses by earlier law, and substituted punishments less severe, though still often entailing cruel mutilations. The provisions with regard to marriage law and other matters connected with the family reflected the Christian attitude in these matters, and sanctioned some customs popular among Greeks and Orientals. Under Leo VI (886-912), a new collection, called the *Basilics,* made its appearance. This is remarkable especially for the new volume of Leo VI's own laws, in which the emperor himself rejected much that dated from an earlier period when the absolutism of the emperor had not been so fully developed.

In the Byzantine Empire, justice could be rendered only in the emperor's name. He was the supreme judge, and the rendering of justice was perhaps his most important function. Subordinate officials handed down decisions only by virtue of the power he had delegated to them, and could in theory always be overruled on appeal to him. The emperors themselves are found rendering judgment in person in quite ordinary cases brought to them by their subjects. Heraclius (610-641) punished an officer who had stolen the land of a poor widow and had beaten her son to death. Theophilus (829-842) appeared every week on horseback at a given church, rendering judgments so fair and equitable and unbiased that they have passed into legend:

One day when the Emperor appeared, a poor woman threw herself at his feet in tears, complaining that all light and air had been shut off from her house by a huge and sumptuous new palace which a high official of the police was building next door. Moreover, this official was the brother of the Empress. But the Emperor paid no heed to this. He ordered an instant inquiry, and when he found that the woman had told the truth, he had the guilty man stripped and beaten in the open street, commanded the palace to be torn down, and gave the land on which it stood to the woman. Another time, a woman boldly seized the bridle of the horse which the Emperor was riding, and told him that the horse was hers. As soon as Theophilus got back to the palace, he had her brought in, and she testified that the general of the province where she lived had taken the horse away from her husband by force, and had given it to the Emperor as a present to curry favor with him. Then he had sent the rightful owner of the horse into combat with

the infantry, where he had been killed. When the general was haled before the Emperor and was confronted by the woman, he finally admitted his guilt. He was dismissed from his post, and part of his property confiscated and given to the plaintiff.*

The emperors of the later ninth century took greater care in the systematic appointment of judges and created a kind of legal aid bureau to enable the poor of the provinces to make appeals to the capital. Judges were obliged to render written decisions, and to sign them all. New courts were set up and new officials were created. Later, even in the provinces, side by side with the martial law administered by the local commanding general, we find instances when even soldiers were tried in civil courts for civil offenses.

The "sacred palace," the emperor's residence, was the center of the state, and the officials of the palace were the most important functionaries of the state: administrative, civil, and military. All officials had a title that gave them a post in the palace, as well as a rank among the nobility. At Byzantium, many of the greatest and most influential officials were eunuchs, an oriental feature of the state that astonished westerners and made them uneasy. There was never a prime minister, but in practice an imperial favorite often controlled policy.

The Capital and the Factions

As the capital, Constantinople had its own special administration. Its leader was a high-ranking official called the "prefect of the city," or *eparch.* He was responsible for the maintenance of public order. His police arrested criminals and inspected the markets, and he himself wielded a variety of judicial and economic powers over lawyers, money-changers, no-

* C. Diehl, "La légende de Théophile," *Seminarium Kondakovianum,* IV (1931), 35. Our translation.

taries, and bankers as well as over merchants. The city artisans and tradesmen were organized into guilds or corporations, each with its own governor, under the authority of the prefect. Standards of quality in food supplies and in manufactured goods were upheld, and misrepresentations of quality by overenthusiastic or dishonest salesmen were punished. By the eleventh century, the eparch was often left in charge in the emperor's absence.

Byzantium inherited from Rome rival parties of chariot-racers, each with its own stables and equipment. We can best understand these circus factions if we imagine that in, let us say, present-day Chicago, the White Sox and the Cubs were not only the city's passionately loved baseball teams about whose rivalry the entire community was wildly concerned, but also represented opposing factions on all the political, religious, economic, and social issues of the day. At Byzantium, the two factions were called the Blues and the Greens. During the early centuries of the Empire, they were very influential. The emperor himself always became either a Green or a Blue. He fixed the days on which races were to be held at the Hippodrome, a vast stadium near Santa Sophia that was attached to the sacred palace. On the appointed day, the turbulent populace would throng the stands and root frantically for the charioteers of their party.

Blues and Greens seem to have come from different quarters of the city, but, more important, from different social classes. The Blues were the party of the aristocracy, the Greens of the lower classes; the Blues were the party of strict orthodoxy, the Greens were frequently the party of questionable orthodoxy, since new heresies naturally took root among the poor. Those emperors who were strictly orthodox themselves enrolled as Blues; those who leaned toward heterodoxy and felt the need for mob support enrolled as Greens. This division existed in the great provincial cities,

too, but at Constantinople it took on special virulence. The factional strife manifested itself sometimes in the Hippodrome, when the faction opposed to the emperor would riot against him; sometimes in the streets of the city, when roving bands belonging to one faction would invade the quarter of the other and burn down the houses.

The most celebrated riot in all Byzantine history was the "Nika" revolt of 532 (so called because of the cry of the rioters, meaning "victory"). On this occasion the two parties temporarily united in the Hippodrome to try to force Justinian to be merciful to two condemned criminals, one Green and one Blue, who had escaped execution by accident. When the emperor, who had been a Blue but who now tried to assume an impartially severe attitude toward both parties, failed to assent to their joint request, they revolted simultaneously, and burned most of the public buildings of the city. The seriousness of the riot was greatly increased by the presence in the city of a large number of poor peasants from the country, who had fled their farms as a result of heavy taxation, and who joined the factions in what became a revolution.

Justinian might well have lost his throne had it not been for the coolness and bravery of his celebrated Empress Theodora:

My opinion is that now, above all other times, is a bad time to flee, even if this should bring safety. Once a man has seen light, he must surely die; but for a man who has been an Emperor to become a refugee is not to be borne. May I never be separated from the purple [the symbol of imperial rank] and may I no longer live on that day when those who meet me shall not call me mistress. Now if you wish to save yourself, O Emperor, this is not hard. For we have much money; there is the sea, here are the boats. But think whether after you have been saved you may not come to feel that you would have preferred to die. As for me, I like a certain old proverb that says: royalty is a good shroud.[*]

_____
[*] Procopius, *History of the Wars,* I, xxiv, 35-38. Our translation.

The emperor took heart, and the revolt was put down. It was the destruction of the old cathedral in this riot that made necessary the construction of the new Santa Sophia.

The Nika affair was exceptional in its severity and in the combination of the rival factions. But every reign from the end of the fourth century to the middle of the seventh was marked by outbursts of disorder between the two parties. All this time, both the Blues and Greens also had military and municipal duties, helping with the construction of the walls, and bearing a heavy share of the responsibility for defense. This made for instability, since it was never certain that mutual hatred would yield in the face of common danger. We cannot be sure exactly when and how it happened, but we know that the emperors in the seventh and eighth centuries succeeded in clipping the wings of the factions. They took over the management of the public entertainments in the Hippodrome, and left only an unimportant role to the leaders of the Blues and Greens, who were restricted to acclaiming the emperor on public occasions.

III: Church and State

Religion at Byzantium

All aspects of Byzantine life were deeply permeated by Christianity. Religion pervaded social life: from birth until death, at every important moment in the life of every person, the Church played an important role, governing marriage and family relations, filling leisure time, helping determine any critical decision. Religion pervaded intellectual life: the most serious intellectual problems of the age were those of theology, and they were attacked with zest by brains second to none in power and subtlety. Religion pervaded aesthetic life: the arts were largely, though by no means entirely, devoted to the representation of ecclesiastical subjects, and serving the Church offered one of the best opportunities to exercise a creative talent. Religion pervaded economic life: business was carried on under the auspices of the Church, and a substantial part of the citizens' income went to support the Church.

Religion also pervaded political life. What we would call the domestic issues, about which the people got excited, were political issues centering on the theological problems we have mentioned. What was the relationship of the members of the Trinity to each other? What was the relationship of the human to the divine nature of Christ? Was it proper to worship the holy images? It was not only in monasteries and universities that such problems were argued, but also in barber shops and among the longshoremen on the docks. The factions rioted in the Hippodrome because the Emperor was taking the side opposed to them on such questions. The popular interest in these questions was as burning as that of Milwaukee fans in a local World Series, and the implications were somewhat more important, since the right answer meant salvation and future immortality, whereas the wrong answer meant damnation and eternal punishment.

What we would call the issues of foreign policy too were pervaded by religion: when the emperor went forth to war he went as the champion of the faith. Most often, the enemies were not Christians, or were heretics or schismatics. The emperor

Constantine and Justinian with the Madonna. Mosaic in Hagia Sophia (about 1000).

went into battle against them with a sacred picture borne before him, an icon (image) of the Virgin, perhaps one of those which legend said had been painted by Saint Luke, or not even made by human hands at all, but miraculously sent from heaven itself. In a sense, all Byzantine wars were crusades.

Contrast with the West

Yet the vast importance of religion in Byzantine society seems at first glance not very different from the parallel development in the West. The real contrast comes when one compares the relationship of Church and State in the West with the relationship in the East. During the early centuries of the Middle Ages, the very abandonment of Rome by the emperors and its transformation into a provincial town permitted the local bishops to assert their authority, until by the fifth century they had become popes, with considerable temporal authority; and by the seventh they had become powerful local rulers ready to challenge lay princes. The position of the popes was as we know strengthened by the grants from the Franks, and by their alliance with the empire of Charlemagne.

But contrast what happened in Constantinople. Here there was no chance for a papacy to grow up. Here the emperor was in residence. It was Constantine himself who summoned the Council of Nicaea. He paid the salaries of the bishops who attended, and he presided over their deliberations. Even more significant, he gave imperial sanction to their decrees. It was this precedent that was of tremendous importance for the developing relations between Church and State in Byzantium. When Constantine legislated effectively as head of the Christian church in matters of Christian dogma for the Christian populace, he was doing what no layman in the West would do. Church and Empire were felt as two different institutions, and yet neither could be conceived of without the other. When necessary, the emperor, who was still felt to possess some of the old quality of the Roman *pontifex*, was expected to play his part in church affairs, and, indeed, when necessary, the patriarch was expected to intervene in the affairs of state.

In contrast to the West, the emperors regularly deposed patriarchs, and punished clerics. The initiative for the reform of the Church was imperial initiative. Although distinct, canon and civil law were closely related: the faith was a principle of the civil law, and the emperor often participated in the preparation of canon law. At Byzantium, then, it has often been said, the Church was a department of state, and the emperor was the effective head of it as he was of the other departments. One of his titles is "equal to the Apostles." A single authority plays both the parts: the part of emperor and the part of pope. This is known as caesaropapism.

We have stated this proposition extremely in order to underline the contrast between Byzantium and the West. It is true that the Patriarch of Constantinople, the leading cleric in the eastern empire, was from time to time able to challenge the emperor; and it is also true that the emperor, absolute though he was, could not afford to impose new dogmas without church support or offend the religious susceptibilities of the people. For this reason, some scholars deny that caesaropapism existed and prefer the word "theocracy," a religious state in which the emperor's role was certainly preponderant but not all-powerful.

The Great Theological Controversies

However this may be, the emperors had been brought into the affairs of the Church by the need to settle the theological quarrel over Arianism, which was also tearing the Empire apart politically and socially. At first, Constantine himself did not want to intervene, and warned against speculation on theological problems as idle. But he soon realized that he would have to make a personal decision on the matter, and lend imperial authority to the eventual decision. From then on, the emperors were theologians themselves, and some of them preferred speculation and argument on these questions to any other pursuit.

The political storm was not claimed by the Council of Nicaea in 325, but raged during the reigns of Constantine's successors. The Empire was crossed and re-crossed by herds of mounted bishops galloping off to church councils. It was not until the end of the fourth century that the Arian controversy was really settled. Then, after a gap of only fifty years, began the new and even more desperately fought arguments over the relationship between the human and divine natures in Christ (see Chapter IV). This controversy was more concentrated in the eastern Mediterranean world, and did not affect the West. But in the East, the Egyptian, Syrian, Ethiopian, and Armenian Christians were "Monophysites," as they are to this day—that is, they believed that the human and divine natures in Christ are one. And they resisted vigorously attempts to force them to compromise.

The antagonism grew partly out of the jealousy felt by the older Mediterranean capitals of Antioch and Alexandria for the imperial city of Constantinople, an upstart from their point of view, which they blamed for the decline in their commerce. This jealousy was felt by churchmen as well as laymen. Antioch and Alexandria had been patriarchates, like Rome, from early days, whereas Byzantium had been only an obscure bishopric until it became the capital, under Constantine, and had become a patriarchate only after 381. It was only the presence of the emperor that won so great a rank for his city.

Just as the Council of Nicaea of 325 offered a solution to the Arian controversy that remained unacceptable, so the Council of Chalcedon of 451 offered a solution to the Monophysite controversy that was not acceptable. This internal dissension over theology and prestige in the Empire helped to soften the imperial defenses against the Moslems, whose success in Syria and Egypt is partly due to the failure of these provinces to develop a sense of solidarity with Byzantium. During the entire controversy, the emperors, especially Zeno (474-491), Justinian (527-565), and Heraclius (610-641), strove repeatedly to arrange compromises that would permit a settlement; but all efforts failed. Sometimes the emperors issued their own pronouncements on questions of dogma without summoning a council of bishops. In such instances, they were indeed caesaropapist.

In the course of the two great theological controversies, which lasted with intervals from the fourth to the late seventh century and which culminated in the loss of the eastern provinces of the Empire, almost every possible intellectual subtlety had been introduced into the discussion in the efforts at compromise. From the point of view of intellectual advance, of philosophical development, theology had reached a dead end. From here on, Byzantine Christianity takes on that unchanging quality that is so often associated with it. The important thing becomes the external rite, the magic of the ceremony, rather than the internal meaning of the act and the reasoning behind its performance. From now on, Byzantine Christianity is increasingly preoccupied with ritual.

In the eighth and ninth centuries there raged a new controversy over the use of sculptured and painted sacred images, and the nature of the reverence that might be paid to them. The struggle is called iconoclastic, from the word meaning "breaker of images." As usual, the emperors played a leading role. Twice, for long periods, they adopted the new puritanical rule that images must be banned, and each time in the end returned to their worship. This was not primarily a question of theology, however, but one of ritual, originating in the simple puritanism of the imperial soldiers, country boys from Anatolia and Armenia who harked back in their thinking to the Old Testament prohibition against worshiping graven images, and who were able to put their officers on the imperial throne itself.

It is interesting that this stagnation had set in before the Byzantines converted the Bulgarians and the Russians; as a result, none of the intellectual keenness or the sense for fine distinctions and closely reasoned argument that are associated with the earlier period of Byzantine church history was actually exported to Bulgaria or later to Russia. It was the newer Byzantine church, occupied with questions of ritual, from which they received their faith.

Ritual and Monasticism

In the Byzantine world the basic assumption was always that the individual has very little chance to be saved. One direct route to salvation was to become a monk. Thus in the East, more than in the West, monasticism came to be looked upon as *the* Christian life. Many entirely worldly men, including numerous emperors, became monks on their deathbeds in order to increase their chances of going to heaven. As a result, monks often enjoyed far more popular prestige and were able to exercise far more influence upon the course of politics than was possible in the West.

Monks frequently and increasingly supplied the highest ranks of the church hierarchy. Rich and powerful laymen, from the emperor down, founded new monasteries as an act of piety. Monasteries became possessed of enormous landed properties and many precious objects. They were frequently immune from taxation. Some emperors tried to check monastic growth, but all efforts of this sort failed, and in the later centuries of the Empire the monks became ever more powerful, virtually dictating policy, often most unwisely, by making use of their great influence over the loyalties of the population.

The other way to salvation for a Christian who did not choose to become a monk was through the sacraments of the Church. The West limited these sacraments to seven (see Chapter IV), but in the East every religious act had a sacramental quality. Every image, every relic of a saint, was felt to preserve the essence of the holy person in itself. And as the saint was present in the image or in the relic, so God was actually felt to be present in the sanctuary, and he could be reached through the proper performance of the ritual. So in the East the focus was on mystery, on magic, on a personal approach to the heavenly Saviour. Very little attention was devoted in the sermon to the teaching of Christ on ethical or moral questions. Once a magical act has been accepted as the proper way to God, no change in it can be permitted without admitting that the old way was wrong and that all one's ancestors are in hell.

The Schism

It is sometimes said that the schism, or split, between eastern and western churches, which took place in 1054, and which continues to exist in our own day, was due to a slight difference in wording between the two creeds. The Greek creed states that the Holy Ghost "proceeds" from the Father; the Latin adds the word *"filioque,"* meaning "and from the Son." There are of course other differences between the two churches in their manner of conducting Christian worship. But these differences on points of doctrine and ritual might never even have been noticed, and would surely not have been so emphasized, had not it been for underlying political questions at issue between the churches and for the increasing divergence of the two civilizations.

As early as the eighth century, the popes found themselves at odds with the iconoclastic Byzantine emperors on the question of image-worship, and supported the enemies of the Empire in Italy. By way of revenge, the Emperor Leo III (717-741), the first iconoclast, removed southern Italy and the Balkan provinces (Illyricum) from the jurisdiction of the papacy and attached them instead to the jurisdiction of the Patriarch of Constantinople. But even this blow to the papacy's prestige and treasury was not the decisive issue in splitting the papacy from Byzantium in this period. What was decisive was the Pope's political estimate that Byzantium could not defend Italy and the papacy against the Arabs invading from North Africa, or against the Lombards invading across the Alps. It was to secure the defense against the Lombards which the Byzantines could not supply that the Pope turned during the eighth century to Pepin and Charlemagne, and in 800 created the new empire in the West.

The subsequent disagreements between the papacy and the Byzantine Empire were equally political. In the 860's, they competed for the allegiance of the new Bulgarian church. At the same period and as part of the same complex of political rivalry, the Pope excommunicated the Byzantine Patriarch for refusing to return the Balkan province to Roman jurisdiction. It was only then, in the heat of the political quarrel, that the Greeks "discovered" the Roman "error" in adding *filioque* to the creed. Though the disagreement of the late ninth century was eventually settled, the underlying mistrust persisted. It was increased by the deep corruption into which the papacy fell during the tenth century. The Byzantines became accustomed to going their own way without reference to the Bishops of Rome. When the papacy was eventually reformed in the eleventh century, the Byzantines did not understand that they were no longer dealing with the slack and immoral popes they had grown used to.

Under these circumstances, they were unprepared for a revival of the old papal determination to recover jurisdiction over southern Italy, still a part of the Byzantine Empire and still therefore under the Patriarch of Constantinople. As the Norman adventurers, newly arrived in South Italy in the eleventh century, began to make conquests in this Byzantine territory, they turned over to the jurisdiction of the popes the churches and church revenues in the lands and cities they conquered. Naturally, the ambitious and vigorous popes welcomed the return of souls and revenues that they had never given up. Naturally, the Byzantine Patriarch was unhappy over his losses. A violent and powerful man, he dug up the *filioque* controversy again as a pretext for pushing his more solid grievances, and in answer to his complaints the Pope sent to Byzantium one of his most energetic and unbending cardinals. The interview ended in mutual excommunication. Cardinal Humbert shook the dust of Constantinople from his feet, and sailed for home. Despite numerous efforts at reconciliation since this famous episode of 1054, the churches have never been re-united for more than a very brief period.

Antagonism between East and West

Besides the political issues that contributed to the split between the churches, we must record the growing mutual dislike between easterner and westerner. To the visiting westerner, no doubt in part jealous of the Byzantine standard of living, the Greeks seemed soft, effeminate, and treacherous. To the Byzantine, the westerner seemed savage, fickle, and dangerous, a barbarian like all other barbarians. Nowhere is the western attitude shown any better than by our old acquaintance Liudprand, who returned to Constantinople, this time for the western Emperor Otto I in 969, some twenty-one years after his first mission. The Emperor Constantine VII Porphyrogenitus (913-959), who had then so mysteriously soared toward the ceiling and changed his clothes while still on the throne, had now been replaced by Nicephorus Phocas (963-969);

On the fourth of June we arrived at Constantinople, and after a miserable reception . . . we were given the most miserable and disgusting quarters. The palace where we were confined was certainly large and open, but it reither kept out the cold nor afforded shelter from heat. Armed soldiers were set to guard us and prevent my people from going out and any others from coming in. . . . To add to our troubles the Greek wine we found undrinkable because of the mixture in it of pitch, resin, and plaster. The house itself had no water, and we could not even buy any to quench our thirst. . . . On the sixth of June . . . I was brought before the Emperor's brother Leo . . . and there we tired ourselves with a fierce argument over your (Otto's) imperial title. He called you not emperor, which is Basileus in his tongue, but insultingly Rex, which is King in his. . . . On the seventh of June . . . I was brought before Nicephorus himself. . . . He is a monstrosity of a man, a dwarf, fat-headed and with tiny mole's eyes; disfigured by a short, broad thick beard half going gray; disgraced by a neck scarcely an inch long; piglike by reason of the big close bristles on his head; in color an Ethiopian, and, as the poet, says, 'you would not like to meet him in the dark.' *

As might have been expected, Liudprand, the defender of the West, and Nicephorus,

---

* *Works of Liudprand of Cremona*, F. A. Wright, trans. (London, 1930), 235-236.

the Byzantine, whose unattractiveness his guest certainly exaggerated in order to curry favor with his German imperial master, had a vigorous set-to on questions of prestige. Finally, when Liudprand was about to go home, he left behind him scrawled upon the wall of his uncomfortable quarters a long anti-Greek poem, which begins as follows:

Trust not the Greeks; they live but to betray;
Nor heed their promises, whate'er they say.
If lies will serve them, any oath they swear,
And when it's time to break it feel no fear.*

On the other side, the Byzantine reaction to westerners is illustrated by a document written by the princess Anna Comnena more than a century later, the famous *Alexiad,* a history of her father, Emperor Alexius I Comnenus (1081-1118). Here is what she says about the Norman crusader Bohemond:

Now, Bohemond took after his father in all things, in audacity, bodily strength, bravery, and untamable temper.... These two, father and son, might rightly be termed 'the caterpillar and the locust'; for whatever escaped Robert, that his son Bohemond took to him and devoured....

For by nature the man was a rogue and ready for any eventualities; in roguery and cunning he was far superior to all the Latins

* *Works of Liudprand,* 270.

[westerners].... But in spite of his surpassing them all in superabundant activity in mischief, yet fickleness like some natural appendage attended him too....

He was such a man, to speak briefly, as no one in the Empire had seen before, ... for he was a wonderful spectacle.... He was so tall that he surpassed the tallest man by a cubit (about eighteen inches); he was slender of waist and flank, broad of shoulder, and full-chested; his whole body was muscular.... His body as a whole was very white; his face was mingled white and ruddy-color. His hair was a shade of yellow, and did not fall upon his shoulders like that of other barbarians; the man avoided this foolish practice, and his hair was cut even to his ears. I cannot say whether his beard was red or some other color; his face had been closely shaved and seemed as smooth as chalk.... A certain charm hung about the man but was partly marred by a sense of the terrible. There seemed to be something untamed and inexorable about his whole appearance, ... and his laugh was like the roaring of other men.... His mind was many-sided, versatile, and provident. His speech was carefully worded and his answers guarded.*

The mutual dislike between Byzantines and westerners was to grow steadily more intense in the period after the late eleventh century, until it reached a climax in the tragedy of 1204 (see Chapter IX).

* Translation partly ours, partly from E. A. S. Dawes' translation of the *Alexiad* (London, 1928), 37-38, 266, 347.

IV: The Fortunes of Empire, 330-1081

When we are dealing with a stretch of more than eleven hundred years of history, as in the case of Byzantium from its dedication by Constantine in 330 to its capture by the Turks in 1453, it is useful to subdivide it into shorter periods. The late eleventh century provides the major break in Byzantine history: by then the decline in imperial strength can be plainly seen. So

in this chapter we shall bring the story down only as far as 1081. In each of the shorter periods that can be distinguished between 330 and 1081, we shall not only single out for emphasis the major trends of foreign and domestic policies but we shall also trace the more gradual course of changes to be found in government, society, and economic life.

The Main Periods
of Byzantine History, 330-1081

The first period runs from Constantine's dedication of his capital in 330 to the accession of the Emperor Leo III in 717. Despite their efforts, the Roman emperors at Constantinople could not reconquer the West and thus reconstitute the Roman Empire of Augustus. Indeed, theological controversy, reflecting internal political strain, and combined with Persian and Arab aggression, cost the Empire Syria and Egypt. The internal structure was modified in accordance with the new situation.

From 717 to 867, the threat of Arab conquest was safely contained, the Bulgarians were converted, a major religious and political struggle over church images was fought and decided, and the big landowners began to emerge as a threat to the financial and military system.

From 867 to 1025, the Byzantine Empire was at its height; the emperors went over to the counterattack against the Arabs and regained much territory and prestige; the grim Bulgarian struggle was fought to a bloody conclusion; the Russians were converted; and the emperors made every effort to check the growth of the great landowning aristocracy.

The years 1025-1081 represented a period of decline, slow at first, but accelerated as the period drew to a close: external military disaster accompanied, and was related to, the triumph of the landowners.

330-717

In the period from 330 to 717, the emperors immediately following Constantine were Arians. Theodosius the Great (379-395), the first truly orthodox emperor after Constantine, proclaimed Orthodox Nicene Christianity (381) to be the sole permitted state religion. All those who did not accept the Nicene Creed were to be driven from the cities of the Empire. Theodosius' enactment is a landmark along the road to the creation of the Orthodox eastern empire, and demonstrates once more the close relation of theology to politics and to imperial initiative in matters of faith. Although the Empire east and west was united under Theodosius, his sons Arcadius (395-408) and Honorius divided it, with Arcadius ruling at Constantinople. It was never again fully united in fact, although in theory it had never been divided.

Over the whole period until the accession of Justinian in 527, the eastern portion of the Empire was able to use the Germans as troops in its own armies, and at the same time usually managed to deflect the new blows of further invaders so that they fell chiefly upon the West. Though the Huns and the Persians presented a challenge, the cities of the East continued prosperous, and government operated undisturbed. Only the Monophysite controversy warned of the internal weakness that was threatening stability. The subtleties of theological argument only partly concealed the real issue: Would Alexandria successfully challenge Constantinople for leadership in the ecclesiastical world of the eastern Mediterranean?

With Justinian (527-565) we encounter an emperor so controversial that even his own historian Procopius, in addition to several works praising him to the skies, wrote a *Secret History*, never published in his own day, and discovered only much later. The *Secret History* denounces Justinian in the most unrestrained way, and tells some shocking stories about his past and that of his famous Empress Theodora, who in her youth had been an entertainer in the Hippodrome. On the basis of the full record we can safely conclude that Justinian was not greater than Cyrus the Great or Themistocles, as Procopius says when praising him. But we do not have to believe either that he was a demon who walked around

CHAPTER VI

Great silver plate, showing the Emperor Theodosius, with his sons Honorius and Arcadius on either side, bestowing the insignia of office on a local official. Found in the mid-nineteenth century in western Spain by two peasants, who, before they could be stopped, split it in order to divide the profits. Now in Real Academia de la Historia, Madrid.

the palace at night without his head, as Procopius tells us in the *Secret History.*

By strenuous military efforts, Justinian's armies reconquered North Africa from the Vandals, Italy from the Ostrogoths, and southern Spain from the Visigoths, a last desperate effort to reunite all of Rome's Mediterranean lands, and recreate a territorial unity that was by now in fact unmanageable. Both the long drawn-out campaigns and a vast new system of fortifications proved extremely costly. The focus of imperial attention on the West permitted the Persian danger on the eastern frontier to grow to the point where Justinian's immediate successors could not check it, while in Europe Slavs and Avars were able to dent the Danube line and filter into the Balkans.

Justinian began a process of administrative reorganization that his successors would finish. In the provinces of the Roman Empire, Constantine had seen to it that civil and military authority were never united in the hands of the same official. This was an obvious precaution against repeated revolts by ambitious generals like those that had characterized the third century. But now, Justinian's conquests in the West imposed so severe a strain on the system, and unrest in Egypt and elsewhere was so alarming, that the emperor occasionally entrusted both civil and military power to a single officer. After Justinian's death the military emergency caused in Italy by the invasion of the Lombards and in North Africa by the savage native Berbers forced the authorities to create in both places large military districts. Here the military commanders, called exarchs, also served as civil governors, and their areas of command were called exarchates. The exarchs of Italy and Africa, with their headquarters respectively at Ravenna and Carthage, became virtual vice-emperors.

The Empire did not have to pay the full bill for Justinian's policies until the early years of the seventh century. Under the reign of Phocas (602-610), internal bankruptcy and external attacks from the Persians seemed to threaten total destruction. It was Heraclius (610-641), the son of the Exarch of Africa, who sailed in the nick of time from Carthage to Constantinople and seized the throne. He spent the first years of his reign in military preparations, absorbing heavy losses as the Persians took Antioch, Damascus, and Jerusalem, bearing off the True Cross in triumph. Soon afterwards they entered Alexandria, and Egypt too was gone. After 622 Heraclius began his great counteroffensive. At one moment in 626 the Persians threatened Constantinople from the Asian side of the Straits while the Slavs and Avars were besieging it in Europe; but the Byzantines beat off the double threat. Heraclius defeated the Persians on their own territory, recaptured all the lost provinces, and returned the True Cross to Jerusalem in 629.

But only a few years later, the new movement of Islam, which we shall examine shortly, exploded out of Arabia, and took away once more the very provinces that Heraclius had recaptured from the Persians. In both the Persian and the Moslem victories over Byzantium the disaffection of the Monophysite Syrians and Egyptians played a major part. From Egypt the Moslems pushed on westward, and took Carthage in 698, putting an end to the North African exarchate. Moslem ships began to operate from Cyprus and Rhodes. In northern Italy the Lombard kingdom had increased its power, while Lombard duchies threatened in the center and south. Her-

aclius' work and that of Justinian were seemingly undone.

The Reorganization of the Seventh and Eighth Centuries

But despite the desperate crisis, the emperors, beginning with Heraclius, completely overhauled the administrative machinery of the state. They now extended to their remaining territories in Asia Minor and the Balkans the system of government previously introduced into the two exarchates. The loss of Syria and Egypt required the transformation of Asia Minor into a reservoir of military manpower and an orderly stronghold of defense. The perpetual raids of Slavs, Avars, and Bulgars into the Balkan provinces made the emergency the more acute and increased still more the dependence on Asia Minor. So now the emperors divided Asia Minor and the Balkans as well into what we would call army corps areas, with the local military commanders also exercising civil authority.

These new military districts were called *themes,* from a word meaning a permanent garrison. In each theme the troops were recruited from the native population; in return for their services, the sturdy, independent yeoman farmers were granted land, but they were not allowed to dispose of it or to evade their duties as soldiers. Their sons inherited the property along with the obligation to fight. The commanding generals of a theme, though in theory responsible to the emperor, often revolted, and in the seventh and eighth centuries many of them seized the throne. With time the imperial government strove to combat this danger, inevitable when broad military and civil powers were united in the same hands, by dividing up the large original themes into smaller ones. From seven big themes at the end of the seventh century, the number mounted to about thirty by the year

900. From the start, one of the themes was naval. In addition to the troops supplied by the commanders of the themes, the emperors had at their disposal other forces, both land and sea, quartered in the capital itself.

They also asserted more and more their direct supervisory authority over the civil service departments. As the reorganization proceeded, the old title of a formerly influential job was sometimes bestowed as a purely honorary reminder of past duties, much as the title of "Duke," for example, in England today, no longer means that the bearer is a true "Dux" or army commander. In this way a hierarchy of honorary titles came to exist side by side with the hierarchy of real jobs. Military and civil officials, eunuchs, clerics, and even foreign ambassadors to the Byzantine court all had their places both in the galaxy of honorary titles and in the hierarchy of real positions. Special treatises were needed to remind court officers of the proper precedence at banquets and other festivities.

The new system also embodied a change in concepts of taxation. New immigration and settlement had apparently put an end to the labor shortage of earlier centuries. It was now possible to separate the land tax from the tax on persons. The latter was transformed into a "hearth-tax," which fell on every peasant household without exception. For purposes of the land tax, each peasant village was considered a single unit. Imperial tax-assessors regularly visited each village, calculated its total tax, and assessed the individual inhabitants the portion of the tax that each would owe. The community as a whole was held responsible for the total tax, and often the neighbor of a poor peasant or of one who had abandoned his farm would have to pay the extra amount to make up the total. This obligation was onerous, and when the tax could not be collected the state itself sometimes had to take over the property and re-sell or re-lease it.

717-867

In 717, Leo III won a splendid victory over the Arabs, who were besieging the capital itself. Thereafter the struggle against the Moslems gradually became stabilized along a fixed frontier in Asia Minor. But the Moslem capture of Crete and Sicily opened the way for repeated pirate raids against the shores of imperial lands in Greece and southern Italy. In northern Italy, the Lombards extinguished the Exarchate of Ravenna in 751, and Byzantine rule was interrupted by the alliance between the Franks and the papacy. The Byzantine *dux* of Venetia moved his headquarters to the famous island of the Rialto, and thus became the forerunner of the *doges* of Venice. In the Balkans, the Bulgarian menace reached a new peak of severity (see below, pp. 240-242).

Most critical from the point of view of internal development are the two periods during which iconoclastic (image-breaking) emperors held the throne (726-787 and 813-842). Beginning in Anatolia as a puritan reaction against excessive or superstitious adoration of religious pictures and images, the movement took on in its later phases a violent anti-monastic aspect, since the monks at Byzantium were the great defenders of the images. During this phase of the struggle we find some of the monks actually challenging the right of the emperors to legislate in matters of religion. But the images were twice restored by imperial decree (each time by an empress) as they had twice been banned by imperial decree. The position of the emperor in church affairs remained supreme despite these murmurs against his authority, and the restoration of the images was a concession to the weight of public opinion. As a result of the struggle the Byzantines drew more careful distinctions between superstitious adoration paid to images and proper reverence. When the controversy closed, it was tacitly understood that no more religious statues would be sculptured in the round.

Although the new system of military small-holdings and the growth of a free peasantry retarded the development of large estates during the eighth and ninth centuries, we have clear evidence that once again large landlords were beginning to accumulate big properties. One cause may have been the ruin of the small farmers in Asia Minor as a result of the dreadful disorders incident to the rebellion of Thomas the Slav. After threatening to subvert the throne, this rebellion was put down in 823.

867-1081

Although intrigue and the violent overthrow of sovereigns remained a feature of Byzantine politics, the people developed a deep loyalty to the new ruling house that was established in 867 by the Armenian Basil I (867-886) and called the "Macedonian" dynasty. Even usurpers now took pains to legitimatize themselves by marrying into the imperial house. As political disintegration began to weaken the Moslem world, the Byzantines went over to the counteroffensive in the tenth century. Their fleets and armies recaptured Crete (961), and soon afterward Antioch and much of northern Syria after three centuries of Arab domination.

A new Moslem dynasty in Egypt, which took over in Palestine also, stopped the Byzantine advance short of Jerusalem. But, much like the later Crusaders from the West, the Byzantine emperors hoped to liberate Christ's city from the infidel. While pushing back the Moslems, the Byzantines allied themselves with the Armenians, penetrated the state of Armenia, and at the end of the period annexed it. This was almost surely an error in judgment: what had been a valuable buffer against the Turks of Central Asia, who were beginning to raid into eastern Asia Minor, now lay open to attack. Firmly re-established in southern Italy in the face of the Moslem threat from Sicily, the Byzantines dominated the neighboring Lombard duchies until after the advent of the Normans in the early eleventh century. These adventurers displayed their usual savagery in local warfare and their usual ability in carving out estates for themselves and gaining a foothold in the peninsula. With the critically important fight against the Bulgarians we shall deal below (pp. 240-241).

Under the early emperors of the Macedonian dynasty the large landowners continued to flourish. Whole dynasties of nobles came to exist on their great estates. They were "the powerful," who were constantly acquiring more land at the expense of "the poor." The more they got, the more they wanted. They bought up the holdings of "the poor" and made the peasantry once more dependent upon them. The growing power of "the powerful" threatened the state in two important ways: not only was it losing its best taxpayers, the free peasants, but also its best soldiers, the military settlers.

During the tenth and eleventh centuries, there developed a great struggle between the emperors and "the powerful," parallel in some ways to the struggle between the monarchy and the feudal nobility in France (see below, Chapter VII), but destined to end differently. For while in France over the centuries the nobility was curbed and a strong centralized monarchy was established in the East, where absolutism as such was never questioned, "the powerful" thwarted all the imperial attempts to check the growth of their economic and military power and eventually seized the throne itself. Repeated laws striving to put an end to the acquisition of land by "the powerful" could not be enforced; in times of bad harvest especially, the small free proprietor was forced to sell out to his rich neighbor.

The great Emperor Basil II (976-1025) made the most sustained efforts to reverse this process. A law of Basil has been preserved, with marginal notes and comments of his own, which vividly illustrates the problem and his attitude toward it. It tells how Basil, in the course of his travels in the Empire, had received thousands of complaints about "the powerful" who were buying up or seizing lands belonging to "the poor." He names names:

The patrician Constantine Maleinos and his son the magistros Eustathius have for a hundred years, or perhaps even a hundred and twenty, been in undisputed possession of lands unjustly acquired. It is the same way in the Phocas family, who, from father to son, for more than a century, have also succeeded in holding on to lands wrongly obtained. In more recent times certain newly-rich men have done the same. For example Philokales, a simple peasant who lived for a long while in poverty by the work of his hands and paid the same taxes as the other peasants his brothers, now has obtained various offices of the palace, because he had made a fortune . . . and acquired vast estates. He has not gone unpunished. When we arrived in the region where his property is located, and heard the complaints of those whom he had dispossessed we commanded that all the buildings he had built be razed and that the lands ravished from the poor be returned to them. Now this man is living again on the small piece of property which he owned at the start of his career, and has once more become what he was by birth, a simple peasant. Our imperial will is that the same should happen to all those of our subjects, whether of noble birth or not, who have in this way seized the land of the poor. It is for this reason that we proclaim what follows: Every estate which was established before the time of our maternal grandfather Romanos I (919-944) shall remain in the hands of its proprietor, provided that he can prove by authentic documents that his title goes back before that time. All estates acquired since, and contrary to my grandfather's laws, shall be considered to be illegally owned. . . . The peasants, the original owners, who were long since expelled by the owners of the large estates, have the right to reclaim the immediate and complete restitution of their property without being required to repay the sales price, or to pay for any improve-

ments which may have been installed by the proprietors who are about to be dispossessed.*

Shortly afterward, the Emperor, returning from a campaign in the Caucasus, visited the enormous estates in Asia Minor belonging to that very Eustathius Maleinos whom he had denounced in his law. Maleinos was able not only to entertain the Emperor himself in sumptuous style, but also to feed the entire army. On the pretext of wishing to repay his hospitality, Basil took this great potentate back to Constantinople with him. Once there, Maleinos was never allowed to go back to his estates, but was kept, like a bird in a cage, until he died. Thereupon, all his estates were seized by the Crown. As a final blow to "the powerful," Basil II ordained that they would have to pay all the tax arrears of the delinquent peasants, thus relieving the village communities of the heavy burden that was so difficult for them to bear, and placing it on the shoulders of the rich.

But a few years after Basil died, this law was repealed under the influence of "the powerful," and thenceforth they did indeed prove "more merciless than famine or plague." As the landlords got more and more of the free military peasants as tenants on their estates, their own military role grew more and more important, and they became virtual commanders of private armies. The only force on which the emperors after Basil could rely as a counterweight to the great landowners was the civil servants. The civil servants, in an effort to reduce the power of the landlords, tried to cut down the expenses of the army, in which the landlords were now playing the leading role.

Strife between these two parties weakened the imperial defenses. The Normans drove the Byzantines from the Italian peninsula by taking the great southern port of Bari in 1071. In the same year, after three

---

* G. L. Schlumberger, *L'Epopée Byzantine* (Paris, 1896-1905), II, 122. Our translation.

decades of raids across the eastern frontier of Asia Minor, the Seljuk Turks defeated the imperial armies at Manzikert in Armenia, and captured the Emperor Romanos IV. Asia Minor itself, mainstay of the Empire, now lay open to the Turks, who pushed their way to the Straits, and established their capital in Nicaea. Meanwhile other Turkic tribes, Pechenegs and Magyars, raided southward into the Balkans almost at will. In 1081, there came to the throne one of the "powerful" magnates of Asia Minor, Alexius I Comnenus. The story of the ways in which he and his successors built still another military and social system and staved off collapse for more than a century properly belongs to a later chapter.

V: Byzantium and the Slavs

Of all the achievements of the Byzantines, none is so remarkable as their impact on the Slavic world. Here we are dealing with the transfer of a civilization, substantially unmodified, from a more advanced to a less advanced group of peoples. Much as old Rome civilized and eventually Christianized large groups of "barbarians" in western Europe, so Constantinople, the new Rome, civilized and Christianized the Slavs. Many of the problems that beset the West today in its dealings with the Soviet Union arise from the fact that the Soviet Union is first and foremost Russia, a country in the Orthodox and not in the western Christian tradition, a country that still shows the effects of having experienced its conversion from Byzantium.

Conversion of the Bulgarians

The first of the Slavic peoples to fall under Byzantine influence were the Bulgarians, who were the product of a fusion between a Slavic population and a smaller group of Asiatic Bulgar invaders. From the time these barbarians crossed the Danube in the late seventh century, they engaged in intermittent warfare against the Byzantine Empire. In 811, the ruler of the Bulgarians, Krum, defeated the imperial forces, and the Emperor Nicephorus I (802-811) was killed, the first emperor to fall in battle since the death of Valens at Adrianople in 378. Krum took the skull of Nicephorus, had it hollowed out and lined with silver, and used it as a drinking-cup—behavior that vividly shows the level of Bulgarian civilization at the time. Bulgarian religion was primitive: the sun and moon and stars were worshiped, and were propitiated with sacrifices of horses and dogs. The overwhelming masses of the people were peasants living in huts.

Yet the rulers of this people had created a powerful state, which by the middle of the ninth century had reached the stage all barbarian tribes eventually reached—preparedness for conversion, for the reception of the religion that alone could accompany a position of prestige in the medieval world. Already Greek artisans were imported into Bulgaria to build the palaces of the native rulers. Since there was no Bulgarian alphabet, Greek letters had to be used in the royal inscriptions. Yet the Bulgarian rulers hesitated to accept missionaries from Byzantium, since this would surely mean the extension of Byzantine political power.

At the same time, a Slavic people called the Moravians, who lived far to the west in what is now Czechoslovakia, had also established a powerful state of their own and had reached a stage similar to that reached by the Bulgarians. Their rulers felt themselves ready for Christianity. But, just as the Bulgarians associated the religion with their powerful neighbors, the Byzantines, and feared Byzantine imperial political encroachment, so the Moravians associated it with their powerful neighbors the Germans, and feared both German and papal encroachment. In 862, the king of the Moravians began the process that was to culminate in the conversion of the Slavs. He sent to Byzantium, in order to avoid German or papal influence, and asked that a Greek missionary be sent to teach the Moravian people Christianity in their own Slavic language.

The Byzantine Emperor Michael III sent to Moravia two missionaries, Cyril (or Constantine) and his brother Methodius, called the "Apostles to the Slavs." They knew the Slavic tongue and had invented an alphabet in which it could be written. This is the alphabet still in use to this day by the Russians, the Bulgarians, and the Serbs, and still called Cyrillic after its inventor. Almost at once, as a countermove, Boris, ruler of the Bulgarians, asked for Christianity from the Germans. But these efforts on the part of the two Slavic rulers to avoid accepting conversion at the hands of their powerful neighbors and to obtain it instead from a less threatening distant court were doomed to failure. In spite of the efforts of Cyril and Methodius among the Moravians, German pressure and eventual papal reluctance to give final sanction to the conduct of church services outside the Latin tongue proved too strong. After some years, it was the German clergy and the Roman form of Christianity that triumphed in Moravia.

Similarly, despite Boris' negotiations with the Germans, and a long correspondence with the popes, during which the Roman pontiff on one occasion gave him advice about wearing trousers (permissible) and eating all his meals by himself (permissible but rude), the nearby power of Byzantium was too strong, and Roman Christianity had to yield. At first, the Byzantines forced their faith on Boris by the sword. Boris yielded, but the flood of Greek priests that followed, and the Byzantine attempts to prescribe the proper duties of the Christian prince, annoyed him and he turned to Rome. His flirtation with the papacy, however, ended in disillusionment when it became clear that Rome would not allow him to have an independent church of his own. He moved back to the Byzantine church, and this time the Byzantines did not repeat their mistakes. They permitted the Bulgarians virtual ecclesiastical autonomy. Only in the fold of the eastern church could Boris unify his country and consolidate his own autocratic power. The Byzantine patriarch, unlike the pope, made no temporal claims. In Bulgaria, then, from the late ninth century on, the language of the church was the native Slavonic tongue preached by followers of Cyril and Methodius.

Of course, the conversion of Bulgaria did not mean that an era of perpetual good relations was now established between Byzantium and the new converts. The ambitions of the Bulgarian rulers were too great for that. Under Symeon (889-927), second son of Boris, himself educated in Constantinople and called "half-Greek" by his contemporaries, there began a bitter hundred-years war, during which the Bulgarians tried to make themselves emperors by conquering Constantinople itself. Toward the end of the tenth century, the rivalry became more intense than ever under a Bulgarian ruler named Samuel. In 1014, Basil II (976-1025) captured fourteen or fifteen thousand Bulgarian prisoners, and savagely blinded ninety-nine out of every hundred. The hundredth man was allowed to keep the sight of one eye, so that he could lead his miserable fellows home. At the ghastly sight of his blinded warriors,

Samuel fell dead of shock. Basil II took the appropriate name of "Bulgar-slayer." Shortly afterward, Byzantine domination over Bulgaria became complete, and the country was ruled as a conquered province. But its inhabitants were never deprived of their own church, whose archbishop had just as much jurisdiction as he had had in the days of Bulgarian independence.

The great expenditures of money and manpower incidental to the long pursuit of the Bulgarian war played their part in weakening Byzantium for the military disasters that were to come at Manzikert and Bari (see above, pp. 239-240). But Boris' decision to accept Christianity from Constantinople, and the subsequent Byzantine military conquest of his country, helped to determine where the line between East and West would be drawn for all future history. The Bulgarians are an Orthodox people to this day, and their architecture, their literature, and their art throughout the Middle Ages directly reflected the overpowering influence of Byzantium. In much the same way, more than three hundred years later, the western neighbors of the Bulgarians, the Serbs, also took their faith from the Greek East after a flirtation with the Latin West. And the Serbs acted for the same reason: the attractions of Byzantium.

The Early Russian State

To the north and east of the Balkan Bulgarians lie the great plains between the Baltic and the Black seas, the plains of European Russia. Here movement is easiest by water, along the valleys of the rivers that flow north into the Baltic or south into the Black or Caspian seas. Beginning in the eighth century, the Scandinavians, whom we have already encountered in their invasions of England and of western Europe, expanded into Russia also. First taking control of the Baltic shore, they then began to move south along the Donets and the Don to the Sea of Azov and the northern Caucasus. Their name, in the period of expansion, was "Rus," which has survived in the modern term Russia. Gradually they overcame many of the Slavic, Lithuanian, Finnish, and Magyar peoples who were then living on the steppe. The details of this process are very little known. The story told in the Old Russian Primary Chronicle, compiled during the eleventh century, is suggestive of what may have happened among the inhabitants of Russia sometime in the 850's:

There was no law among them, but tribe rose against tribe. Discord thus ensued among them, and they [the native peoples] began to war one against another. They said to themselves 'Let us seek a prince who may rule over us and judge us according to the law.' They accordingly went overseas to the Varangian Russes . . . and said to the people of Rus, 'Our whole land is great and rich, but there is no order in it. Come to rule and reign over us.' *

This is the story of the "calling of the princes." The Chronicle goes on to tell how Rurik (who has now been successfully identified with a Danish warrior known from other sources) accepted the invitation, and settled in the town of Novgorod, already an important trading center. From Novgorod, within a few years, Scandinavian princes moved south along the Dnieper River. On the middle course of the Dnieper they seized the settlement called Kiev, still today the major city of the Ukraine, and made it the center of a state at first very loosely controlled and devoted especially to trade. And in 860, for the first time, a fleet of two hundred of their warships appeared off Constantinople, where they at first caused panic but were eventually repulsed. During the next two centuries there were three further attacks of

* Samuel H. Cross, *The Russian Primary Chronicle,* in *Harvard Studies and Notes in Philology and Literature,* XII (1930), 145.

varying seriousness, as well as other wars, which the Byzantines won.

But the normal state of affairs was not war between Byzantium and Russia. The texts of the trade treaties concluded between the two reflect close economic ties. We find the Byzantines promising to feed the visiting Russian traders and to furnish them baths, and ship supplies for the homeward voyage. The Russians agreed to live in a special quarter outside the city during their stay in Constantinople, and to be registered by imperial officials. "They shall not enter the city save through one gate, unarmed and fifty at a time, escorted by soldiers of the Emperor." This shows how anxious the Byzantines were to protect the lives and property of their citizens from the wild barbarians. At the same time, they were eager to obtain the merchandise that the Russians brought them.

Conversion of the Russians

Most important, however, was the continuing religious influence that Byzantium exercised upon the Russians. No doubt numerous individual Russians were converted from their primitive polytheistic faith simply as a result of their impressions during a visit to Byzantium. In the trade treaty of 945, we find that some of the Russian envoys are already Christians, and are already swearing by the Holy Cross to observe the provisions of the treaty. In the 950's, Olga, the ruling princess of Kiev, visited the Emperor at Constantinople:

'Olga came before him, and when he saw that she was very fair of countenance and wise as well, the Emperor wondered at her intellect. He conversed with her, and remarked that she was worthy to reign with him in his city. When Olga heard these words, she replied that she was still a pagan, and that if he desired to baptize her, he should perform this function himself: otherwise she was unwilling to accept baptism. The Emperor, with the assistance of the Patriarch, accordingly baptized her....

After her baptism, the Emperor summoned Olga and made known to her that he wished her to become his wife. But she replied, 'How can you marry me, after baptizing me yourself and calling me your daughter? For among Christians that is unlawful, as you must know.' Then the Emperor said, 'Olga, you have outwitted me.' *

The Russians were converted as a people during the late 980's in the reign of Vladimir. He felt the inadequacy of the old faith, about which we do not know very much except that the Russians worshiped forest and water spirits and a god of thunder. According to the partly legendary story in the Chronicle, Vladimir was visited by representatives of the different faiths, who told him about their beliefs. He discarded the faith of Mohammed, because "circumcision and abstinence from pork and wine were disagreeable to him. 'Drinking,' said he, 'is the joy of the Russes. We cannot exist without that pleasure.'" Judaism he rejected because the God of the Jews had not been strong enough to enable them to stay in their native Jerusalem. Roman Christianity he rejected because it required a certain amount of fasting, as of course did the Christianity of the Greeks. But the cautious Vladimir did not accept this fourth possibility, Orthodox Christianity, until he had sent a commission to visit the countries where all the faiths were practiced, and to report back to him.

The envoys reported, 'When we journeyed among the Moslems, we beheld how they worship in . . . a mosque. . . . , and there is no happiness among them but only sorrow and a dreadful stench. Their religion is not good. Then we went among the Germans [Roman Catholics], and saw them performing many ceremonies in their temples; but beheld no glory there. Then we went on to Greece [Byzantium], and the Greeks led us to the edifices where they worship their God, and we knew not whether we were in heaven or on earth. For on earth there is no such splendor or such beauty, and we are at a loss how to de-

---

* *Russian Primary Chronicle*, 168-169.

scribe it. We only know that God dwells there among men, and their service is fairer than the ceremonies of other nations. For we cannot forget that beauty.*

Shortly afterward, Vladimir was baptized, and married a Byzantine princess. Returning to Kiev, he threw down all the idols in the city, and in one day forcibly baptized the entire population in the waters of the Dnieper.

Despite its legendary features, the whole story reflects the various cultural influences to which the Kievan state was in truth exposed. It had Moslem, Jewish, and Roman and Greek Christian neighbors; but the most powerful and influential neighbor was Byzantium, and doubtless the marriage alliance with the Byzantine princess and the resulting gain in prestige played a part in Vladimir's decision. To secure the conversion of the Russians to the Byzantine form of Christianity was also important for the Byzantines, who needed to protect their possessions along the Black Sea and their capital itself against Russian attack.

Effects of Conversion

To the Russians, conversion meant great changes in their way of life. The church became an important social force in Kievan society, and the clergy formed an entirely new and highly influential social class. In spite of the fact that the Byzantines always asserted theoretical sovereignty over the Russian church, and in spite of the fact that the archbishops of Kiev in the early period were mostly Greeks, and appointed from Byzantium, the Russian church quite early asserted its practical independence. The church in Russia from the first became an important landowner, and, as in the Byzantine Empire, monasteries multiplied. The clergy came to have jurisdiction over all Christians in

---

* *Russian Primary Chronicle*, 199.

cases involving morals, family affairs, and religious matters. A new and more advanced concept that crimes should be punished by the state replaced the old primitive feeling that punishment was a matter of personal revenge. For the first time, formal education was established. The Cyrillic alphabet was adopted, and literature in Russian began to appear, almost all of it ecclesiastical. Byzantine art forms were

Early Russian architecture. Church of the Savior on the Nereditsa, Novgorod.

imported and imitated; the great church of Santa Sophia at Kiev is in its way as magnificent as its namesake in Constantinople. It is true that the old pagan faith persisted in the countryside, that enormous rural areas remained backward, and that culture was largely confined to the few cities and to the monasteries. In the main, however, the conversion of the Russians had a civilizing effect.

Yet the short-run gain may well have been outweighed by a long-run loss. The very use of the native language in the liturgy, which was so great an advantage to the Byzantines when, as missionaries, they sought to spread their faith without insisting on the use of their language, meant that the culture of Russia remained poor by contrast with that of the West. In the West, every priest and every monk had to learn Latin. As soon as he did so, he had the key to the treasures of Latin classical literature and the works of the Latin church fathers, who had themselves been formed in the schools of pagan rhetoric, philosophy, and literature. The educated man in the West, usually a cleric, had access to Vergil, to Ovid, to Cicero, and to a large number of lesser authors, some of whom may not have been in the least suitable for clerical reading, but all of whom gave the reader a sense of style, a familiarity with ancient taste and thought, and sometimes solid instruction. He had St. Jerome, who had gone to school to Cicero, and St. Augustine, whose *City of God* was the classic expression of Christian philosophy, written in magnificent Latin prose. The educated man in the West had a whole library of commentaries on the classical authors designed to reconcile them with Christian doctrine, and to make it legitimate to study them, to teach them, and to copy them for posterity. Not every priest and monk in the West could qualify as a professor of classics, but for those who had the leisure, the talent, the inclination, and the luck to find themselves in a monastery with a good library, the opportunity for learning and cultivation was open.

The fact that the Byzantines did not insist on the use of Greek in the liturgy meant that the Russian clergy did not automatically learn Greek, as French or English or German or Spanish priests had to learn Latin. A very few Russians did learn Greek, but by and large the great Greek classical heritage of philosophy and literature was not available to Russians. Sermons, saints' lives, some chronicles and

history, and certain other pieces of Byzantine literature, including both *Basil Digenes Akritas* and *Barlaam and Ioasaph*, were indeed translated and circulated in Slavonic. But these, as we have seen, were hardly substitutes for Plato and Aristotle, Homer and the dramatists. The conversion to Christianity from Byzantium thus had the effect of stunting the intellectual and literary progress of Russia. It is clear, of course, that the Kievan Russians of the tenth century were not ready for Plato and Aristotle, but when a time in their development came when they were ready, they were cut off from access to the treasure-house.

Indeed, in the nineteenth century a very influential group of Russian thinkers argued that conversion from Byzantium had led Russia into hopeless stagnation and wretched intellectual sterility, because it had cut Russia off from Rome, the fountainhead of the vigorous intellectual and spiritual life of the West, without providing a substitute. Their opponents argued just as vigorously that it was precisely the Orthodox faith accepted from Byzantium that gave modern Russia her high degree of spirituality, her willingness to bend to the will of God, and indeed all the virtues which they found in the Russian character and the Russian system. This difference of opinion persists, but it may be said without much fear of contradiction that modern Russia has shown a considerable cultural lag behind the development of western countries; that this cultural lag is partly attributable in the first place to the fact that Christianity was accepted from Byzantium; and that the very privilege of using Slavonic in the church services prevented the growth of a class of men educated in the wisdom of the ancient world.

It would be a grave mistake, however, to attribute the cultural lag solely to these factors. It was perhaps in even greater measure due to the effect on Russian development of the Tartar invasions and domination of the thirteenth and fourteenth centuries (see Chapter IX).

Kievan Russia

Kievan Russia itself, in spite of whatever drawbacks conversion from Byzantium may have had, developed a society not very unlike that in contemporary western medieval Europe. From being a mere Scandinavian war-band sworn to assist the prince in battle and entitled to divide the booty with him, the prince's entourage had now become that upper ruling group of councilors appropriate to a settled state. Law codes were formulated that reflect the social conditions of the time and place: arson and stealing horses were the worst crimes, more heavily punished than murder or mutilation. The penalty was the same for stealing a beaver out of another man's trap, for trespassing on his land, for knocking out his tooth, or for killing his slave. This was a society that put its emphasis on the value of property.

There has been some dispute among scholars over whether agriculture was more or less important than commerce in Kievan Russia. Although it is clear that farming played a large role, the emphasis should certainly be put upon trade. In this trade, with Byzantium in particular, the Russians sold mostly furs, honey, and wax, not products of agriculture at all, but of hunting and bee-keeping. Since the Byzantines paid in cash, Kiev had much more of a money economy than did western Europe. Viewed from the economic and social point of view, Kievan Russia was in some ways more advanced than backward manorial western Europe, where markets, fairs, and industries were only beginning to spring up in Flanders, along the Baltic shore, and in northern Italy.

During the period before the Tartar invasions, which began in the early 1200's, this Kievan state began to have close diplomatic and political relations with the West. Dynastic marriages were arranged between the ruling house of Kiev and the royal families of Sweden and France, and alliances were reached with the Holy Roman Empire of Germany. Merchants from the West appeared in Russia, especially at Novgorod in the north, and at Kiev itself. It is then conceivable that whatever handicap was imposed by Byzantine Christianity might have been overcome had Kiev been allowed to maintain its free lines of communications with the West. Its advance might have come through developing further this vigorous and valuable exchange. But as things turned out, Russia was denied this opportunity.

The Kievan state had internal political weaknesses, especially the failure to make any rules for the succession to the throne, and the practice of dividing up the land among the prince's sons as if it were the private property of the prince. The fragmentation of the Kievan state into mutually hostile provinces weakened it in the face of outside dangers. Beginning in the eleventh century the Turkish tribe of Polovtsy or Cumans appeared on the southern steppes of Russia just as the Huns had swept into Europe earlier. The Russian princes warring against each other made a tragic error by hiring bands of Polovtsy. Thus when the Mongol Tartars appeared in the early thirteenth century, Kievan Russia had been softened for the blow. The sole surviving heroic poem of the Kievan period, the *Song of the Expedition of Igor,* reproves the Russian princes:

Voices have grown mute, revelry has waned. . . . Lower your banners, sheath your damaged swords, for ye have already strayed far from the glory of your grandsire. For with your own treasons ye began to bring the infidels upon the Russian land. . . . For through civil strife came violence from the land of the Polovtsians.*

* *La Geste du Prince Igor*, H. Grégoire, R. Jakobson, and M. Szeftel, eds. (New York, 1948), 171. S. H. Cross, trans.

CHAPTER VI

Never entirely centralized politically, the Kievan state none the less strove for unity. It bequeathed the ideal of unity to the future Russian state that was to emerge after more than two centuries of Mongol domination. The common heritage of a literary language and of a single Christian faith laid the basis for a future unified state. It was this later state, the state of Moscow, that was to take from the Byzantines not only their form of religion, already deeply entrenched in the Russia of Kiev, but also their political theory of autocracy, and much of their political practice.

VI: Islam before the Crusades

Islam (the Arabic word means "submission") is the most recently founded of the world's great religions. Its adherents (Moslems, "those who submit") today inhabit the entire North African coast of the Mediterranean, part of Yugoslavia and Albania, Egypt, Turkey, the entire Near and Middle East, Pakistan, parts of India, the Malay Peninsula, Indonesia, and the Philippine Islands, to say nothing of Russian Central Asia and portions of China. From the point of view of western civilization, relationships with the Moslem world have been of crucial importance since Mohammed founded Islam in the early seventh century. In the Middle Ages, Islam was one of the three major cultural units to grow up west of India; the other two were Latin and Greek Christendom. In any balanced treatment of the entire subject of human civilization during the Middle Ages, Islam would probably deserve as much attention as either the Roman Catholic or the Greek Orthodox world. Yet, because our attention in this book is primarily centered on our own western civilization and its development, we must focus on the importance of Islam for our own society.

Mohammed

What we know of Mohammed is derived from Moslem authors who lived some time after his death; it is not easy to decide what is true and what is fictional in their accounts. The Arabia into which he was born about the year 570 was inhabited largely by nomad tribes, each under its own chief. These nomads lived on the meat and milk of their animals, and on dates from the palm trees. They raided each other's flocks of camels and sheep, and often feuded among themselves. The religion of the Arabs was pagan, centering around sacred stones and trees. Their chief center was Mecca, fifty miles inland from the coast of the Red Sea, where there was a sacred building called the Kaaba, or cube, in which the Arab worshipers did reverence to a large number of idols, especially to a small black stone fallen from heaven, perhaps a meteorite. To this place the pagan Arabs seem to have made a pilgrimage of some sort.

In the sixth century, Mecca was inhabited by a tribe called the Kuraish, a trading people who lived by caravan commerce with Syria. Mohammed was born into one of the poorer clans of the Kuraish. Early orphaned, he was brought up by relatives, and as a young man entered the service of a wealthy widow much older than himself, whom he later married, after successfully performing several trading missions for her. Now prosperous, Mohammed was free to devote himself to his divine mission. We do not know how he became convinced that

وقطع جمع علم انفوا الا خرج من بلادك من دال البني علا السلم ان ان الان كم الا عطا كم وظهكم لكن ان جرم جو
اولادكم ونركوا انوا لكم ون سلا حكم وصوا ئدكم ونركوا كا سوا الغر بون سنه نم با نلهم والمر لدمرس كا ن عاد ا عنا هم
اسلا فاطعو هم جمال الهد س وكان مسولى المحراج محمد سلمه فضوا اولادهم دنا اولاده مم وسمه محما للاه لادهد اد ه اله

Mohammed. In this miniature the Angel Gabriel appears to him in a vision, saying, "Thou art the Prophet of God."

he was the bearer of a new revelation. If he could read, which is uncertain, he certainly could read no language except Arabic, and there were no religious books written in it. His ideas and information on the beliefs of other religions must therefore have been derived from observations on his caravan journeys and from conversations with members of Christian and Jewish communities. In any case, he seems to have spent much time in fasting and in vigils, perhaps suggested by Christian practice. He surely suffered from nervousness and hysteria, and seems to have had paroxysms during which he suffered high fevers. He became convinced that God was revealing the truth to him, and had singled him out to be his messenger. The revelations came to him gradually over the rest of his life, often when some crisis arose. He probably wrote them down himself, in a rhythmic, sometimes rhyming prose, and included entertaining stories from the Old Testament of the Hebrews, and from popular and current Arabian folklore, such as the legends that had come to surround the memory of Alexander the Great.

The whole body of Moslem revelation was not put together until some little time after Mohammed's death. This is the Koran or "book." The chapters were not arranged in order by subject matter, but rather were put together mechanically by length, with the longest first. This makes the Koran difficult to follow, and the problem is not made easier by the fact that it is written in a peculiar style, full of allusions to things and persons who are not called by their right names. Readers are often puzzled by the Koran, and a large body of Moslem writings explaining it has grown up over the centuries. Mohammed regarded his revelation as the confirmation of Hebrew and Christian scriptures. Islam is a religion designed for all men, the perfection of both Judaism and Christianity, the final revelation of God's truth.

Mohammed was a firm monotheist. His God is the God of the Jews and Christians, yet Mohammed did not deny that his pagan fellow-Arabs had knowledge of God. He declared only that it was idolatry to worship more than one God, and he believed the trinity of the Christians to be three Gods and therefore idolatry. A major innovation for the Arabs was Mohammed's idea of an afterlife, which was to be experienced in the flesh. The delights of paradise for Mohammed are fleshly indeed, and the·punishments of hell are torture.

The requirements of Islam are not severe. Five times a day in prayer, facing toward Mecca, the Moslem must bear witness that there is no God but God and that Mohammed is his prophet. During the sacred month of Ramadan—perhaps suggested by Lent—he may not eat or drink between sunrise and sunset. He must give alms to the poor. And, if he can, he should at least once in his lifetime make a pilgrimage to the sacred city of Mecca. This was, and is, all, except for regulation of certain aspects of daily life—for example, the prohibition against strong drink, and other rules about food and its preparation, mostly taken from Jewish practice. The rest is social legislation: polygamy is sanctioned, but four wives are the most a man may have, save for the Prophet himself. Divorce was easy for the husband, who need only repeat a prescribed formula. The condition of women and of slaves was markedly improved by the new laws.

At first, Mohammed preached this faith only to members of his family; then he preached to the people of Mecca, who repudiated him scornfully. In 622, some pilgrims from a city called Yathrib, two hundred miles north of Mecca, invited Mohammed to come to their city to settle a local feud. He accepted the invitation. This move from Mecca is the famous *Hegira* from which the Islamic calendar has ever since been dated. 622 is the Moslem year 1. And Yathrib, to which he went, had its name changed to al-Medina, *the* city. Medina became the center of the new faith, which grew and prospered. The Jews of Medina, however, on whom Mohammed had been counting to become converted, did not do so, and aroused his hostility. He came to be more and more dependent upon the Arabs of the desert, the nomads, and became less and less universal in his appeal. God told him about the necessity for war against those who had not been converted. The holy war, or *jihad,* is a concept very like the Christian crusade: those who die in battle against the infidel die in a holy cause. In 630, Mohammed returned to Mecca as a conqueror, cleansed the Kaaba of all the idols except the black stone, and

incorporated it into his religion. Two years later, in 632, he died. Perhaps one-third of Arabia had by then become Moslem, but it seems clear that many of the Arabs had not even heard of the new faith. Yet only one century later, Charles Martel was having to battle Mohammed's co-religionists in far-off France; the great Byzantine Empire was locked in a struggle with them for its very existence; and Islam had reached India.

Expansion of Islam

Scholars used to feel that this startling expansion was due to the religious zeal of the converts to the new faith. Now, students of early Islam usually argue that overpopulation of the Arabian peninsula set off the explosion of the Arabs into so huge an area. In fact, Arabs had been quietly emigrating from Arabia for some time, to settle in Iraq, Palestine, and Syria. Now they had the new faith to serve as a symbol of their new unity, and the first stages of their advance took them into lands already infiltrated by fellow-Arabs. So the movement quickly gathered momentum: Islam might be its battle-cry, but its motives seems to have been the age-old ones of conquest for living-space and booty. Toward Christians and Jews the conquering Moslems generally were tolerant, regarding both as fellow monotheists and "peoples of the Book."

Syria and Persia were conquered almost simultaneously by two armies. The Syrian province, disaffected from Byzantium by Monophysitism, fell easily. And the Persians, because of their weakness after recent defeats at the hands of Heraclius, failed to put up the resistance that might have been expected. By 639, Jerusalem had been captured; in 641, the native Persian dynasty was ended. During 639-40, the Arabs added Egypt, the major Byzantine naval base, which was also Monophysite in religion and ripe for conquest. Launching ships,

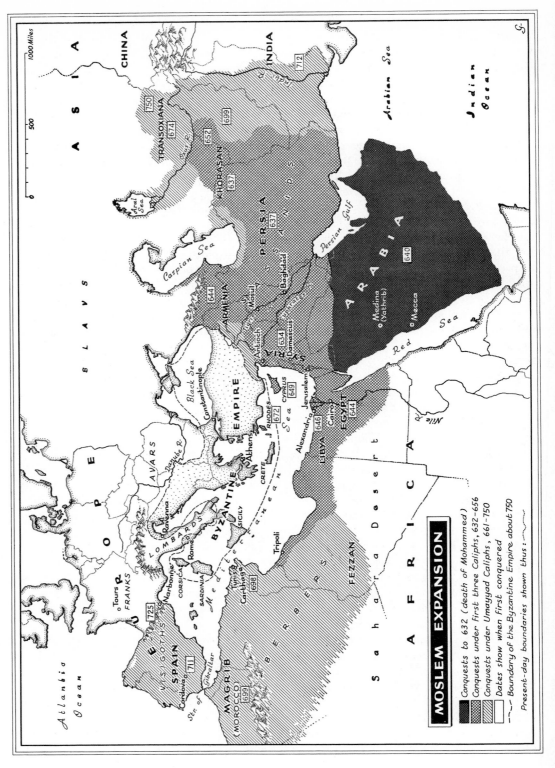

MOSLEM EXPANSION

- ■ Conquests to 632 (death of Mohammed)
- ▨ Conquests under first three Caliphs, 632–656
- ▧ Conquests under Umayyad Caliphs, 661–750
- Dates show when first conquered
- –– Boundary of the Byzantine Empire about 750
- Present-day boundaries shown thus: –·–

1000 Miles
500
0

ASIA

CHINA

INDIA

712

750 TRANSOXIANA
674
699

KHORASAN
652
637

PERSIA
637

ARMENIA
644

Baghdad
Mosul

ARABIA
640

Medina (Yathrib)
Mecca

Red Sea

Arabian Sea

Indian Ocean

Persian Gulf

Caspian Sea
Aral Sea

SLAVS

Black Sea
Constantinople

EMPIRE

Antioch
634 Damascus
SYRIA

Jerusalem
CYPRUS 649

RHODES 672

CRETE

Alexandria
646 Cairo
EGYPT 644

LIBYA

Nile R.

Sahara Desert

AFRICA

FEZZAN

BYZANTINE

Athens

Mediterranean Sea

Ravenna
Rome
SICILY
SARDINIA
CORSICA
Carthage
Tunis 698
Tripoli

LOMBARDS

AVARS

Danube R.

EUROPE

FRANKS
Tours 725
Narbonne

Atlantic Ocean

SPAIN
VISIGOTHS 711
Cordova

Str. of Gibraltar

MAGRIB
(MOROCCO) 699

BERBERS

they now seized the islands of Cyprus and Rhodes, and began attacking southern Italy and Sicily. Moving west across North Africa, they took Carthage in 698, and conquered the native Berber tribes, who had resisted Romans, Vandals, and Byzantines. In 711, with a mixed force of Berbers and Arabs, under the command of a certain Tarik, they launched the invasion of Spain across the Straits of Gibraltar. The very name Gibraltar is a corruption of Arabic words meaning "Rock of Tarik." By 725, the first Arabs had crossed the Pyrenees, to meet Charles Martel at Tours seven years later. Meanwhile, they had been spreading east from Persia throughout what is today Russian Turkestan, and in 724 they had reached the Indus and the western frontiers of China. Simultaneously, they moved south from Egypt and North Africa into the little-known and uncivilized desert regions of Central Africa. So far as the Mediterranean and Near Eastern world is concerned, these conquests of the first century of Islam were virtually final. Only the Mediterranean islands and Spain were reconquered by Christians over the centuries.

Disunity in Islam

The unity of these enormous conquests was of course more apparent than real. Not only did the peoples and customs of the lands from Spain to India vary widely from each other and from the Arabs, but the Arabs themselves were experiencing internal dissensions that made impossible the establishment of a unified state to govern the whole of the conquered territory. After Mohammed's death, there was disagreement over the succession. Finally, Mohammed's eldest companion, Abu Bekr, was chosen *khalifa* (caliph, the representative of Mohammed). Abu Bekr died in 634, and the next two caliphs were also chosen from outside Mohammed's family,

to the distress of many Moslems. Moreover, many Arabs resented the caliphs' assertion of authority over them, and longed for their old freedom as nomads. In 656, the third caliph was murdered. By then, those who favored choosing only a member of Mohammed's own family had grouped themselves around Ali, son-in-law of the prophet. This party also opposed all reliance on commentaries, or supplemental works explaining the Koran. They were thus fundamentalists with regard to the Koran. They were known as Shiites (the sectarians). Opposed to them were the Sunnites (traditionalists), who favored the election to the caliphate of any eligible person and approved of supplementing the Koran with commentaries called "traditions."

In 656, Ali was chosen Caliph; his period of office was marked by civil war between the two parties, and even before he was murdered in 661, his opponent Muawiya, leader of the Sunnites, had proclaimed himself, in 660, Caliph in Damascus. This marks the beginning of the so-called Umayyad Caliphate of Damascus, named after the family name of the ruling house. The Umayyads were caliphs in hereditary succession for ninety years, 660-750. On the whole, this was a period of prosperity, good government, brisk trade, and great cultural achievement along Byzantine lines, of which the famous "Dome of the Rock" mosque in Jerusalem is the outstanding example. The civil service was manned by Greeks, and Greek artists worked for the caliph; the Christian population, except for the payment of a poll tax, were on the whole unmolested and better off than they had been before.

Shiite opposition to the Umayyads, however, remained very strong. There was almost no difference between the two groups with regard to religious observances and law. But the Shiites felt it their duty to curse the first three caliphs, those who had ruled before their hero, Ali. These were men whom the Sunnites deeply revered. The

Interior of Umayyad Mosque, Damascus. From the eighth century.

Shiites were far more intolerant of the unbeliever than the Sunnites. They were ready to conspire in secret against the government, and were given to self-pity and to wild emotional outbursts of grief for Ali's son Husein, who was killed in 680. Southern Iraq was then the center of Shiite strength, although in modern times Persia has become the center.

From these eastern regions came the leadership of the plot which in 750 was responsible for the overthrow and murder of the last of the Umayyad caliphs at Damascus, together with ninety members of his family. The leader of the conspirators was Abu-'l Abbas, not a Shiite himself, but the great-grandson of a cousin of Mohammed. The caliphate was shortly afterward moved east to Baghdad, capital of present-

day Iraq, and was thereafter known as the Abbasid Caliphate. The days when Islam was primarily an Arab movement under Byzantine influence were over. At Baghdad, the caliphate took on more and more of the color of the Persian Empire, in whose former territory it was situated. But even now, its Christian subjects were on the whole well treated.

Meanwhile, the rest of the Moslem world fell away from its dependence upon the Abbasids. One of the few Umayyads to escape death in 750 made his way to Spain, and built himself a state centered around the city of Cordova. Rich and strong, his descendants declared themselves caliphs in 929. Separate Moslem states appeared in Morocco, in Tunis, and in Egypt, where still another dynasty, this time Shiite, built Cairo in the tenth century and began to call themselves caliphs. Rival dynasties also appeared in Persia itself, in Syria, and in the other eastern provinces. At Baghdad, though the state took much of its character and culture from its Persian past, the power fell gradually into the hands of Turkish troops. And it was the Seljuk Turks who emerged supreme from the confused struggle for power when they took Baghdad in 1055. Although the caliphate at Baghdad lasted down to 1258, when the Mongols finally ended it, the caliphs were mere puppets in Turkish hands.

Islamic Civilization

More interesting perhaps than the shifts in political and military fortunes of Islamic rulers is the extraordinary development of Islamic civilization. The Arab conquerors were moving into provinces that had an ancient tradition of culture, regions which, until the Arabs appeared, had been parts of the East Roman or Persian empires. The Arabs brought their new religion and their language to the peoples whom they conquered. The religion often stimulated new artistic and literary development, and, through its requirement of pilgrimage, brought about mobility among the Moslems, and encouraged the exchange of ideas with fellow-Moslems from the other end of the Moslem world. The language had to be learned by everybody who wished to read the Koran, since it was the rule that the Book might not be translated. Since Arabic is an extraordinarily flexible and powerful instrument, it became the standard literary language of the whole Islamic world. Indeed, the Moslems were highly conscious of its merits. They felt that incessant study of it was necessary for comprehension, and they gave the highest position among the arts to the composing of poetry, rating it even ahead of science. But aside from religion and language, the chief contribution to Moslem culture came from the civilizations of Persia and of the Greco-Roman world. Islamic government learned much from the Persian tradition; Islamic philosophy learned much from the classical tradition; and Islamic literature learned much from both.

Like both Roman and Greek Christianity, Islam was convinced of its superiority to all other religions and ways of life. Like Byzantium, Islam aspired to dominate the civilized world, which it thought of as divided between those lands already part of Islam, and those lands still to be conquered. Like the Byzantine emperor, the caliph was an absolute autocrat, a vicar of God, chosen by a mixture of election and the hereditary principle, who could not be mutilated and still keep the throne. The caliph, of course, could not add to or change the religious law, although we have seen the emperor pronounce on dogma. Both courts went in for show and ceremony.

Christians and Moslems, however strong their mutual hatred, felt themselves to be worshipers in two religions that were on the same level of intellectual advancement and parallel in many respects: in their attitude toward creation, human history, the last judgment, and the instability of everything mortal. When at peace with the Moslems, the Byzantines thought of them as the successors of the Persians, and as such the only other civilized nation. As a concession to the Moslem attitude toward women, diplomatic protocol prescribed that ambassadors from the caliph were not to be asked the customary question about the health of the ladies of the caliph's household. And the caliph's ambassadors had the highest places at the imperial table. Each had the highest respect for the other's attainments in science.

Science

The reign of Mamun (813-833) is often said to mark the high point in the civilization of the caliphate. In Baghdad, he built observatories, founded a university, and ordered the great works of Greek and Indian scientists and philosophers translated into Arabic. We hear of a young Byzantine geometry student who was taken prisoner by the Moslems and brought to Baghdad as a slave:

One day his master's conversation turned on the Caliph, and he mentioned Mamun's interest in geometry. 'I should like,' said the Greek youth, 'to hear him and his masters discourse on that subject.' . . . Mamun . . . eagerly summoned him to the palace. He was confronted with the Moslem geometers. They described squares and triangles; they displayed a most accurate acquaintance with the nomenclature of Euclid; but they showed no comprehension of geometrical reasoning. At their request he gave them a demonstration, and they inquired in amazement how many savants of such a quality Constantinople possessed. 'Many disciples like myself,' was the reply, 'but not masters.' 'Is your master still alive?' they asked. 'Yes, but he lives in poverty and obscurity.' Then Mamun wrote a letter to the master, Leo, inviting him to come to Bagdad, offering him rich rewards. . . . The youth was dispatched as ambassador to Leo. Leo discreetly showed the Caliph's letter to an imperial official, who brought the matter to the Emperor's attention.

By this means Leo was discovered and his value appreciated. The Emperor gave him a salary and established him as a public teacher. . . . Mamun is said to have communicated with Leo again, submitting to him a number of geometrical and astronomical problems. The solutions he received made him more anxious than ever to welcome the mathematician at his court, and he wrote to the Emperor begging him to send Leo to Bagdad for a short time, as an act of friendship, and offering in return eternal peace and 2,000 pounds of gold [about a million dollars]. But the Emperor, treating science as if it were a secret to be guarded like the manufacture of Greek fire, and deeming it bad policy to enlighten barbarians, declined.*

Although the charge that the Moslem mathematicians did not understand geometrical reasoning is surely an absurd invention, the story none the less reflects a real situation—the immense eagerness of the Moslems to acquire Greek learning, which seems to have served as a stimulus to the Byzantines to appreciate their own neglected men of science. In any case, the last portion of the story, showing how jealously guarded were not only the secret weapons of the Byzantines but also what we would call today their "basic research" in mathematics, has a modern ring indeed. Aristotle and the other philosophers and scientists of the ancient world were in any case available to the Arabs, whether in the original Greek or in Syriac or Persian translations. Under Harun al-Rashid (785-809), the Caliph of *Arabian Nights* fame, who walked about the streets of Baghdad in disguise looking for amusement and adventure, schools of translators were set up, and manuscripts were ordered from Constantinople and elsewhere. Even more was done by Mamun.

One of the chief fields of interest was medicine, which the Moslems developed beyond the standard works of the Greek masters. They wrote textbooks, for instance,

on diseases of the eye, on smallpox, and on measles, which remained the best authorities on the subject until the eighteenth century. Al-Razi, a Persian of the tenth century, wrote a famous twenty-volume compendium of all medical knowledge, and Avicenna (939-1037) was perhaps even more famous for his systematization of all known medical science. In physics, Al-Kindi wrote more than two hundred and fifty works, on such diverse fields as music, optics, and the tides.

Moslem scientists adopted the Indian numerals, the very ones that we use today and call "Arabic." The new numerals included the zero, a concept unknown to the Romans, without which it is hard to see how higher mathematical research could be carried on. The Moslems began on analytical geometry, and founded plane and spherical trigonometry. They progressed much further than their predecessors in algebra, which is itself an Arabic word like alcohol, cipher, alchemy, zenith, nadir, and many more.

Philosophy, Literature, and the Arts

On the philosophical side, the Moslems eagerly studied Plato, Aristotle, and the Neo-Platonists. Like the Byzantines and the western Europeans, the Moslems used what they learned to enable them to solve their own theological problems. These did not involve such questions as the relationships of the members of the Trinity to each other or the human and divine natures in Christ, but focused on the nature and the power of God and his relationship to the universe. Efforts to reconcile philosophy and religion occupied the great Spanish Moslem Averroes (*c.* 1126-1198), whose commentaries on Aristotle translated from Arabic into Latin were available to the Christian West before the original Greek text of Aristotle himself. Thus it was that

---

* Slightly adapted from J. B. Bury, *A History of the Eastern Roman Empire* (London, 1912), 437-438.

the Moslems came to share with the Byzantines the role of preserver and modifier of the classical works of philosophy and science. And eventually, in the twelfth century and later, when the West was ready and eager for the intellectual banquet of ancient learning, it was the Moslems in Sicily and in Spain, as well as the Greeks, who could set it before them.

Indeed, the process began even earlier in Spain, where the physical splendor and intellectual eminence of Cordova caused its fame to spread abroad. Cordova was only dimly known to non-Spaniards, but they were deeply aware of its superiority to their own cities. In Spain itself, a Spanish Christian in 854 complained that his fellow Christians were irresistibly attracted by Moslem culture:

My fellow-Christians delight in the poems and romances of the Arabs; they study the works of Moslem theologians and philosophers, not in order to refute them, but to acquire a correct and elegant Arabic style. Where today can a layman be found, who reads the Latin Commentaries on the Holy Scripture? Who is there that studies the Gospels, the Prophets, the Apostles? Alas! the young Christians who are most conspicuous for their talents have no knowledge of any literature or language save the Arabic; they read and study Arabian books with avidity, they amass whole libraries of them at immense cost, and they everywhere sing the praises of Arabian lore.[*]

These Arabic poems of which the Spaniard speaks went back in part to the pre-Islamic classical Arab tradition, and portrayed life in the desert, with its camels and horses, its warfare and hunting, its feasts and drinking-bouts. Love is a favorite subject, but it was bad form to mention a lady's real name unless she was a slave girl. Composition was governed by a strict code of convention. It was customary, for example, for the poet to praise himself, but not possible for him freely to portray human character. Still much understanding of fundamental human experience shines through. Here is a portion of a poetic treatise on the calamities of love, which describes the kinds of "avoidance" a lover encounters:

The first kind is the avoidance required by circumstances because of a watcher being present, and this is sweeter than union itself. Then there is the avoidance that springs from coquetry, and this is more delicious than many kinds of union. Because of this it happens only when the lovers have complete confidence in each other. Then comes avoidance brought about by some guilty act of the lover. In this there is some severity, but the joy of forgiveness balances it. In the approval of the beloved after anger there is a delight of heart which no other delight can equal. Then comes the avoidance caused by boredom. To get tired of somebody is one of the inborn characteristics of man. He who is guilty of it does not deserve that his friends should be true to him. Then comes the avoidance brought about when a lover sees his beloved treat him harshly and show affection for somebody else, so that he sees death and swallows bitter draughts of grief, and breaks off while his heart is cut to pieces. Then comes the avoidance due to hatred; and here all writing becomes confused, and all cunning is exhausted, and trouble becomes great. This makes people lose their heads.[*]

Arabic love poetry, especially as developed in Spain, deeply influenced the lyricists across the Pyrenees in Provence, in the south of France. "Earthly love" became an important element of medieval literature. The troubadours' songs spread to Germany, where the Minnesinger adopted this convention. Some of the greatest masterpieces of western love poetry thus find their ancestry in the songs of the Moslems of Spain.

Besides poetry there is a great deal of interesting autobiography and excellent history in Arabic, but no drama. The fiction is of a limited sort only—sad misfortunes of a pair of lovers, exciting incidents of urban life in the capital, with the caliph and the vizier participating, or the adventures of a rogue. These stories were collected in the celebrated *Arabian Nights*

[*] G. E. von Grunebaum, *Medieval Islam* (Chicago, 1946), 57-58.

[*] *Ibid.*, 269-270. Slightly adapted and abridged.

between 900 and 1500. Stories of Indian and Jewish origin are included, as well as some that derive from the Greek classics and from works of the Hellenistic period. Even when the plots are not so derived, much of the detail, especially geographical detail, is. Thus Sinbad the Sailor's famous *roc* with its enormous egg comes from the Greek romance of Alexander, and the *Odyssey* supplies the source of the adventure with the blinded giant.

In the arts, the Moslems developed their own adaptation of Byzantine churches in their mosques, which needed a front courtyard with a fountain, since Moslems must wash before entering. Because there were no priests or elaborate ritual, all that was necessary inside was a quiet and dignified place to pray and rest, with a small niche in the wall showing the direction of Mecca, and a pulpit from which the Koran might be read aloud. Since the faithful had to be summoned by the muezzin's call to prayer, slender towers or minarets were built next to the mosque. Beautiful and elaborate geometric patterns, in wood, stone, mosaic, and porcelain tile, characterize the interior decoration. Arabic script itself lends itself well to use in decoration; and the names

of the first four caliphs and passages from the Koran are regularly found. The great mosques of Damascus and Cairo, Jerusalem, and Cordova are perhaps the greatest surviving specimens, but there are thousands of others all over the Moslem world. The Gothic architecture of the West owes a still unexplored and largely unacknowledged debt to the pointed arches and ribbed vaults, the stone tracery (often called "arabesque") and the other striking features of these buildings. In the architecture of the Norman period in Sicily we can see direct traces of Moslem influence, as of course we can in Spain, whose entire civilization has been permanently shaped by the Moslems.

Finally, in music, we must point to a substantial Moslem contribution that is seldom recognized. The "Morris dance," for instance, is simply a "Moorish dance." Lute, tambourine, guitar, and fanfare are all words of arabic origin. From the Moslems of Spain across the Pyrenees into France and thence to the whole western European world came not only the poetry of courtly love but the instruments which the singer played while he sang of his beloved. Through Sicily and through Spain came

Interior of the mosque in Cordova, Spain.

Greco-Roman and Moslem science, philosophy, and art. When we consider the contributions of the Byzantines and the Moslems to the culture of our western society, we are altogether justified in saying that much light came from the East.

Reading Suggestions
on Eastern Christendom and Islam

(Asterisk indicates paperbound edition.)

GENERAL ACCOUNTS

G. Ostrogorsky, *History of the Byzantine State*, trans. J. Hussey (Rutgers Univ. Press, 1957). A brilliant historical synthesis, with rich bibliography.

A. A. Vasiliev, *History of the Byzantine Empire, 324-1453*, 2 vols. (* Univ. of Wisconsin Press, 1958). A good comprehensive work.

J. Hussey, *The Byzantine World* (Hutchinson's University Library, 1957). Useful shorter sketch.

V. O. Kluchevsky, *A History of Russia*, 5 vols. (Dent, 1911-1931). The greatest single work on Russian history, its usefulness impaired by a poor translation.

Michael Florinsky, *Russia: A History and an Interpretation*, Vol. I (Macmillan, 1953). A good textbook, solid and accurate.

H. A. R. Gibb, *Mohammedanism: An Historical Survey* (* Mentor, 1955). An excellent essay by the greatest western contemporary authority on the subject.

Bernard Lewis, *The Arabs in History*, 3rd ed. (Hutchinson's University Library (1956). A reliable short treatment.

P. K. Hitti, *History of the Arabs from the Earliest Times to the Present*, 6th ed. (St. Martin's, 1956). A detailed treatment, useful for reference.

G. E. von Grunebaum, *Mediaeval Islam*, 2nd ed. (Univ. of Chicago Press, 1954). A learned essay on Islamic culture, in part controversial.

SPECIAL STUDIES

A. H. M. Jones, *Constantine and the Conversion of Europe* (Macmillan, 1948, Teach Yourself History Library). A sensible and helpful introduction.

C. Diehl, *Byzantine Portraits* (Knopf, 1927). A collection of excellent essays on important Byzantine personalities.

J. B. Bury, *A History of the Later Roman Empire, 395-802*, 1st ed. 2 vols. (Macmillan, 1889). The first edition of a work later revised only down to 565. The second edition (*Dover, 1958) is the best work on the period 395-565.

J. B. Bury, *A History of the Eastern Roman Empire, 802-867* (Macmillan, 1912). Distinguished scholarly treatment.

G. Every, *The Byzantine Patriarchate, 451-1204* (S.P.C.K., 1947). A good summary.

J. M. Hussey, *Church and Learning in the Byzantine Empire, 867-1185* (Oxford Univ. Press, 1937). Good introduction to the subject.

G. Ostrogorsky, "Agrarian Conditions in the Byzantine Empire in the Middle Ages," and R. S. Lopez, "The Trade of Mediaeval Europe: The South," in *The Cambridge Economic History*, Vols. I and II, respectively. Brief modern discussions of these topics.

S. Runciman, *History of the First Bulgarian Empire* (Bell, 1930). A lively and reliable account.

A. Grabar, *Byzantine Painting* (Skira, 1953). Superb reproductions of mosaics and frescoes.

G. E. von Grunebaum, *Muhammadan Festivals* (Abelard-Schuman, 1958). Vivid picture of Islamic life.

G. Vernadsky, *Kievan Russia* (Yale Univ. Press, 1948). Vol. II of the Yale History of Russia, authoritative and complete.

G. F. Fedotov, *The Russian Religious Mind* (Harvard Univ. Press, 1946). A study of the Kievan period of Russian history from a most unusual point of view.

W. Muir, *The Caliphate*, rev. ed. (Grant, 1915); and G. Le Strange, *Baghdad during the Abbasid Caliphate* (Oxford Univ. Press, 1924). Standard works on these subjects.

SOURCES IN TRANSLATION

Procopius, H. B. Dewing, trans., 7 vols. (Loeb Classical Library, 1914-1940). The writings of a major historian who lived through the events he recounts. His work includes histories of Justinian's wars and of his activities as a builder, and also a scurrilous secret denunciation of Justinian.

Constantine Porphyrogenitus, *De Administrando Imperio*, G. Moravcsik, ed., and R. J. H. Jenkins, trans. (Budapest, 1949). A letter of advice written by an emperor to his son and heir, telling much about the various "barbarian" peoples on the imperial frontiers.

Michael Psellus, *Chronographia*, E. R. A. Sewter, trans. (Yale Univ. Press, 1953). A contemporary account of eleventh-century history.

Digenes Akrites, J. Mavrogordato trans. (Clarendon, 1956). The first English translation of the Byzantine frontier epic, with good introduction.

St. John Damascene: *Barlaam and Ioasaph*, G. R. Woodward and H. Mattingly trans. (Macmillan, 1914, Loeb Classical Library). The transformed life of Buddha discussed in the text above. The attribution to St. John of Damascus is highly controversial.

The Russian Primary Chronicle, Laurentian Text, S. H. Cross and O. P. Sherbowitz-Wetzor, eds. (Mediaeval Academy, 1953). Our oldest source for early Russian history.

The Koran, G. Sale, trans., 9th ed. (Lippincott, 1923).

HISTORICAL FICTION

W. S. Davis, *The Beauty of the Purple* (Macmillan, 1924). The career of Leo the Isaurian in eighth-century Byzantium.

F. Harrison, *Theophano* (Harper, 1904). Byzantium toward the end of the tenth century.

Monarchy in the Medieval West:

To the Early Fourteenth Century

CHAPTER VII

I: Introduction

ALL OF US have in our minds certain images of the way in which "typical" citizens of the major western European nations behave politically. We probably think of a Frenchman as intelligent and volatile, individualistic, disliking authority and regimentation, cynical about sweeping statements of principle, passionately patriotic, but hating his political opponents because they do not share his assumptions about the framework within which the country's destinies are to be worked out. He has become inured to unstable government. We probably think of an Englishman as sensible and calm, feeling the need to act on principle, devoted to political freedom, law-abiding, content with social inequality, and willing to work in harness with even his bitterest political enemy, since all agree on the basic assumptions about the country. He is accustomed to a political stability that is unparalleled elsewhere, and takes it entirely for granted. We probably think of a German as talented and docile, eager both to exercise authority over others and to have it exercised over him, convinced of his own superiority to men of other nations, disciplined but an easy prey for demagogues with glittering promises, dangerous and given to aggression against others.

Such standard mental pictures are called stereotypes, and of course they are altogether unscientific. But they would not even be recognizable if a great many people, on much or little evidence, had not reached these conclusions. If asked to explain historically why we think these peoples are the way we think they are, most of us would say of France: "France has been attacked three times by Germany since 1870, and has been weakened and disillusioned. Besides, ever since the Revolution of 1789 the French have never been able to agree on whether they shall have a democratic republic or not." Many would say of England: "In the eighteenth century the English were able to get such a head start in the industrial revolution that in the nineteenth century London became the economic capital of the world; economic power and a widespread empire have meant political stability." Many would say of Germany: "The Germans were not unified into one nation until the late nineteenth century, and when they were unified they accepted the traditional ideas of Prussian military discipline and absolute government. The defeat in World War I, the punitive Treaty of Versailles, and the depression were the things that made them fall for Hitler."

Now all these explanations are roughly true; but do they really explain anything? *Why* have a large number of Frenchmen never fully reconciled themselves to democracy? *Why* did the English get a head start in industrialization and colonial expansion? *Why* was German unity retarded? The trouble with all our answers is that they come out of the recent past, the period since the eighteenth century. They are good as far as they go, but they do not go far enough. We could answer our second set of questions accurately but inadequately with answers out of the sixteenth and seventeenth centuries, but a new set of unanswered questions would instantly present itself that could be answered only from a still earlier period. Until we get back to the time when there were no Frenchmen, Englishmen, or Germans in our modern sense, and then begin from the beginning and try to watch them develop along differing lines, we are not likely to come up with a set of satisfactory historical explanations for our stereotypes. This chapter begins in the tenth century, at a time when the national differentiation between the peoples of western Europe was still in its earliest stages. If our answers are to be found anywhere, this seems the place to look.

II: The Development of France, Hugh Capet to Philip the Fair

France is often considered to be the feudal country *par excellence,* the land where all the institutional complications inherently possible in feudal society developed most luxuriantly. Yet France was also the land where the monarch most successfully asserted his superiority over his vassals. In Germany, the kings were unable to make good this claim. In England,

having made it good, they were forced to watch it become diluted.

The Capetians

When Hugh Capet came to the throne of France in 987, there was little to distinguish him from the last feeble Carolingians. Yet he was different, if only because he was the first of a male line that was to continue uninterrupted for almost 350 years. Like the Byzantine emperors, but with better luck, the Capetians procured the election and coronation of the king's eldest son during his father's lifetime, and then took him into the government. When the father died, the son would already be king. After two centuries, when Philip II Augustus (1180-1223) decided for reasons of his own not to follow this practice, the hereditary principle had become so well established that the succession was no longer questioned.

For a hundred years before the accession of Hugh Capet, his ancestors had been rivals of the Carolingians for the throne. Now, as King of France, Hugh was recognized by all the feudal lords as their suzerain, but they were actually more powerful than he and could if necessary defy him with impunity. Thus he might not be able to collect the military service, the counsel, and the feudal dues which his vassals in theory owed him. He was also, of course, lord of his own domain, the Île de France. This was a compact strip of land including Paris and the land immediately adjacent, and extending south to Orléans on the Loire. The Île de France was far smaller than the domain of any of the great feudal lords: the Dukes of Normandy or Burgundy or Aquitaine, the Counts of Flanders, Anjou, Champagne, Brittany, or Toulouse. It may indeed have been for this very reason that Hugh was chosen to be king: he seemed less likely to be a threat than any of the better-endowed lords. Yet the Capetian domain was compact, not scattered, and central, not peripheral; it was easy to govern and was advantageously located. Hugh and his successors concentrated their attention on it.

In addition to their position as the suzerain of suzerains and as feudal lords of their own domain, the Capetians enjoyed the sanctity of kingship that came with coronation and unction with the holy oil, which tradition said a dove had brought down from heaven for Clovis at his baptism. In the eyes of his people this ecclesiastical ceremony brought the king very close to God. He could work miracles, it was soon believed. In this way the king was raised above all other feudal lords, however powerful: he had no suzerain. Further, the Church was his partner: he defended it, according to his coronation oath, and it assisted him. In the great sees near Paris, the king could nominate successors to vacant bishoprics and archbishoprics, and he could collect the income of bishoprics during vacancies. All through the West, as we shall see, these great powers of the lay lords, and especially of kings, in church affairs aroused the opposition of the papacy during the eleventh century. In France, the pope was eventually able to force the king to abandon lay investiture—the actual presentation of ring and staff (symbols of his office) to a new bishop. But the king retained his right of intervention in elections, and the bishops still took oaths of fealty to the king and accepted their worldly goods at his hands. This partnership with the Church greatly strengthened the early Capetian kings.

The history of the Capetians, during their first two centuries of rule in France, is on the surface far less eventful than the contemporary history of several of their great vassals, such as the Dukes of Normandy, who were conquering England, and whose vassals were establishing a great state in Sicily, or the Dukes of Burgundy, whose relatives were taking over the throne in Portugal. The Capetian kings stayed at home, made good their authority within their own domain, and, piece by piece, added a little neighboring territory to it. They put down the brigands who made a mockery of their authority on the roads. By the time of Louis VII (1137-1180), far-away vassals in the south of France and elsewhere, recognizing his prestige and authority, were appealing to him more and more often to settle local disputes. The king's duty to maintain peace throughout the realm had become more than a theoretical right.

Within the royal domain itself, the Capetians increased their control over the *curia regis*, the king's court, which consisted of an enlargement of the royal household. The great offices had at first tended to become hereditary, thus concentrating power in the hands of a few families. Under Louis VI (1108-1137) a single individual held the key household offices of chancellor and seneschal (steward) as well as five important posts in the Church. Louis VI put this man and his relatives out of their posts and made appointments of his own choosing. These new men were lesser nobles, lower churchmen, and members of the middle classes that were now emerging in the towns. Since these officials owed their careers to the Crown alone, they were loyal and trustworthy royal servants. Most important among them was Suger, the Abbot of St. Denis, a man of humble origin who efficiently served both Louis VI and Louis VII for several decades.

Besides insuring the loyalty and efficiency of the central administration, the Capetians replaced hereditary local officials. They introduced royal appointees known as *prévôts* (provosts) to administer justice and taxation in the lands of the royal domain. Further, Louis VI granted royal charters to rural colonists and to new towns, because he recognized that the colonization of waste lands and the growth of new towns would be advantageous to the monarchy. In these ways, the French kings began their long and significant alliance with the middle classes.

The Contest
with Normans and Angevins

The most important single factor in the development of Capetian France, how-

ever, was the relationship of the kings with their most powerful vassals, the Dukes of Normandy. By the mid-eleventh century, the Dukes had centralized the administration of their own duchy, compelling their vassals to render military service, forbidding them to coin their own money, and curbing their rights of justice. The viscounts, agents of the ducal regime, exercised local control. After Duke William conquered England in 1066 and became its king, he and his successors were still vassals of the Capetians for Normandy. But they became so much more powerful than their overlords that they did not hesitate to conduct regular warfare against them. Norman power grew even greater during the early twelfth century, when an English queen married another great vassal of the French king, the Count of Anjou. In the person of their son, King Henry II (1154-1190), England was united with the French fiefs of Normandy, Anjou, Maine, and Touraine in what is sometimes called the "Angevin" Empire.

But this was not all. King Louis VII of France had married Eleanor, the charming heiress of Aquitaine, a great duchy in the southwest of France. When he got the marriage annulled (1152) for lack of a male heir, Eleanor lost no time in marrying the Angevin Henry II and adding Aquitaine to his already substantial French holdings. When Henry became King of England in 1154, he was also lord of more than half of France. He added Brittany and still other French territories to his realm. This Angevin threat was the greatest danger faced by the Capetian monarchs, and it was their most signal achievement that they overcame it.

The first round in the victorious struggle was the achievement of Philip II, Philip Augustus (1180-1223), who quadrupled the size of the French royal domain. Shrewd, calculating, bald, one-eyed, and fierce-tempered, Philip first supported Henry II's rebellious sons against him. Then, on Henry's

MEDIEVAL FRANCE AND ENGLAND

Angevin Empire under Henry II, about 1180

French Royal Domain, 1180

Boundary of France, 1180

x Battle sites

Inset (top right)

0 Miles 50

Dover
Calais
Str. of Dover
Bruges
Antwerp
Ypres
Scheldt
FLANDERS
Lille
Brussels
Agincourt x
Arras
x Bouvines
Somme R.
Meuse R.
Amiens
VERMANDOIS
Rouen
Beauvais
Pierrefonds

Main map

SCOTLAND
Bannockburn
Edinburgh
Tweed R.
NORTHUMBERLAND
Carlisle
Durham
IRELAND
Dublin
LANCASTER
YORK
York
WALES
ENGLAND
Bosworth Field
Trent R.
Gloucester
Cambridge
Oxford
Runnymede
London
Thames R.
Canterbury
Salisbury
Southampton
Winchester

Atlantic Ocean

English Channel

Mont-St.-Michel
Bayeux
Caen
Seine R.
Rouen
Beauvais
ILE
Paris
St. Denis
NORMANDY
Rheims
CHAMPAGNE
LORRAINE
BRITTANY
MAINE
Chartres
Brétigny
DE
FRANCE
Troyes
Orleans
ANJOU
Nantes
Loire R.
BURGUNDY
Dijon
TOURAINE
Bourges
POITOU
FRANCE
Bay of Biscay

Clermont-Ferrand
Lyons
Geneva
AQUITAINE
GUIENNE
Bordeaux
Garonne R.
Avignon
GASCONY
Albi
TOULOUSE
Toulouse
Montpellier
Aigues-Mortes
Marseilles
LANGUEDOC
Narbonne
NAVARRE
ARAGON
CATALONIA

HOLY ROMAN EMPIRE
Rhine R.
Moselle R.
Meuse R.
Saône R.
Rhône R.
Marne R.

Mediterranean Sea

0 Miles 200

Inset (bottom left)

FRANCE AT THE DEATH OF PHILIP AUGUSTUS 1223

Royal domain

Under English rule

Paris
FRANCE

G.

263

death, he was seriously threatened by Henry's eldest son, Richard the Lionhearted, with whom he had gone on a crusade (see Chapter IX), but whom he worked against with all his might. During Richard's captivity in Austria (1191-1194), Philip plotted against him with Richard's younger brother, John. Philip even married a Danish princess with the idea of using the Danish fleet against England and making himself heir to the Danish claims to the English throne. When John succeeded Richard in 1199, however, Philip Augustus became his enemy, and as a matter of course strongly supported a rival claimant to the English throne—John's nephew, the young Arthur of Brittany.

Through legal use of his position as feudal suzerain, Philip managed to ruin John. In 1200, John foolishly married a girl who was engaged to somebody else. Her father, vassal of the King of France, complained in proper feudal style to Philip, his suzerain and John's. Since John would not come to answer the complaint, Philip declared his fiefs forfeit and planned to conquer them with young Arthur's supporters. When John murdered Arthur (1203), he played right into Philip's hands, lost his supporters on the Continent, and in 1204 had to surrender Normandy, Brittany, Anjou, Maine, and Touraine to Philip Augustus. Only Aquitaine was left to the English, who had been expelled from France north of the Loire. In 1214, at the famous battle of Bouvines in Flanders, Philip Augustus defeated an army of Germans and English under the Emperor Otto IV, John's ally. Unable to win back their former French possessions, the English confirmed this territorial settlement by treaty in 1259. England's remaining possessions in France were to be the cause of much future fighting. But John's great losses were added to the French royal domain. The kings now had possession of the efficiently run Duchy of Normandy, which they could use as a model for the rest of France.

The Albigensian Crusade and the Winning of the South

The conquest of large areas of southern France gave the Capetian domain its next great accession of territory. This was the rich and smiling land of Languedoc and Toulouse, the true Mediterranean south. It drew much of its culture from Moslem Spain, and spoke a dialect different from that in the north of France. And (this was its great misfortune) it was the seat of religious heresies. Most important was the "church" of the *Cathari* (Greek for "pure ones"), with its center at the town of Albi, whence its followers were called Albigensians.

The Albigensians believed that the history of the universe was one long struggle between the forces of light (good) and the forces of darkness (evil). The evil forces (Satan) created man and the earth, but Adam had some measure of goodness. Jesus was not born of woman, nor was he crucified, because he was wholly good, wholly of light. Jehovah of the Old Testament was the God of evil. The Albigensians had an elite of their own ("the perfect") who devoted themselves to pure living. Some of them forbade the worship of the cross; others forbade infant baptism, the celebration of the Mass, or the holding of private property. Many of them denied the validity of one or more of the sacraments. Some even said the Catholic Church itself was Satan's. The Albigensians were strongest among the lower classes, but they often had the support of nobles who adopted their views in order to combat the Church politically.

This heresy had had a long history. It had begun in the third century A.D. in Mesopotamia in the teachings of the Manicheans (see Chapter IV), whose doctrines appeared in the Byzantine Empire, spread thence to the Balkans, to northern Italy, and finally to France. The Church proclaimed a crusade against these heretics in 1208, after the Count of Toulouse had connived at the murder of a papal legate.

Philip Augustus did not at first participate in the expeditions of his nobles, who rushed south to plunder and kill in the name of the Catholic Church. By the year of his death (1223), however, after the war had gone on intermittently for fourteen years, the territorial issue had become confounded with the religious one. Northern French nobles were staking out their claims to the lands of southern French nobles who embraced the heresy; so Philip finally sponsored an expedition led by his son, Louis VIII (1223-1226). Assisted by a special clerical court called the Inquisition, which was first set up to extirpate this heresy, Louis VIII and his son Louis IX (1226-1270) carried on the campaign, which by the 1240's had driven the heresy underground. Languedoc itself was almost entirely taken over by the Crown, and it was arranged that the lands of Toulouse would come by marriage to the brother of the King of France, when the last count died. This happened in 1249.

Royal Administration

Administrative advance kept pace with territorial gain. Indeed, it is doubtful if Philip Augustus and his successors could have added to the royal domain if they had not overcome many of the disruptive elements of feudalism and if they had not asserted their authority effectively in financial, military, and judicial matters. Philip Augustus systematically collected detailed information on precisely what was owing to him from the different royal fiefs. He increased the number of his own vassals, and he reached over the heads of his vassals to *their* vassals, in an attempt to make the latter directly dependent on him.

He exacted stringent guarantees—such as a promise that if a vassal did not perform his duties within a month, he would surrender his person as a prisoner until the difficulty had been cleared up. Moreover, if a vassal did not live up to this agreement, the Church would lay an interdict upon his lands. This dreadful punishment meant that everyone resident on the lands was denied access to most of the sacraments and comforts of religion; the people naturally feared an interdict above all else.

Philip and his officials were alert to increase the royal power by purchasing new estates, by interfering as much as possible in the inheritance of fiefs upon the death of their holders, and by providing suitable husbands of their own choosing for the great heiresses. Since the men of those days led violent lives, a lady would sometimes outlast three or four husbands, inheriting from each, and thus each time becoming a more desirable prize, and offering the king a chance to marry her off with profit to himself.

The local officials of the Crown, the *prévôts,* had regularly been rewarded by grants of land, which, together with the office, tended to become hereditary. The Crown lost both income and power as well as popularity when a local *prévôt* made exactions on his own behalf. Early in his reign, Philip Augustus held an investigation and heard the complaints to which the system had given rise. He appointed a new sort of official, not resident in the countryside, but tied to the court, who would travel about, enforcing the king's rights in his domain, rendering royal justice on his behalf, and collecting moneys due to him. This official received no fiefs to tie him to a given region; his office was not hereditary. He was a civil servant appointed by the king, who paid him a salary and could remove him at will. In the north, where this system was introduced, he was called a *bailli* (bailiff), and his territory a *baillage* (bailiwick). In the south, to which the new system was extended, the official was called a *seneschal* (not to be confused with the

The Palais de Justice, Poitiers, France. The older building on the left was formerly the Palais des Comtes—a good example of the Gothic architecture of the twelfth century.

old officer of the household), and his district a *sénéchaussée*.

Like any administrative system, this one had its drawbacks: a *bailli* or *seneschal* far from Paris might become just as independent and unjust as the old *prévôt* had been, without the king's being aware of it. Louis IX (1226-1270) had to limit the power of these officials in two ways. He made it easy for complaints against them to be brought to his attention. And he appointed a new kind of official to take care of the caretakers. These were the *enquêteurs* or investigators, royal officials not unlike Charlemagne's *missi* (see Chapter V). The *enquêteurs* had supervisory authority over the *baillis* and seneschals, and traveled about the country inspecting their work. This whole complex of new civil servants introduced in the late twelfth and thirteenth centuries meant that the king was in a position to interfere with almost all local and private transactions, to exact his just due, and to supply royal justice at a price.

Naturally the king's court (*curia regis*) was so swamped with new business that the old haphazard feudal way of attending to it could no longer be followed. To depend on officers of the household, as the early Capetians had been able to do, would have been a little like the United States government of today trying to get along with no filing system except an old bureau belonging to George Washington. The administration of France in the thirteenth century was nowhere near as complicated as that of the United States in the twentieth, and there was plenty of time for gradual experiment and development.

What happened was something like this. The king's household differentiated itself into departments, most of which had little to do with government. Rather, they attended to the needs of the king and his court. This court consisted not only of retainers but of clerics and others who served as advisers on day-to-day problems. When a major policy question affecting the realm was up for decision, or when a major legal case needed to be tried, the king was entitled to summon his vassals (both lay and clerical) for counsel, and those he summoned were obliged to come. They joined the rest of the *curia regis* in a kind of enlarged royal entourage.

When the *curia regis* sat in judgment on a case, it came to be known as the *parlement,* a high judicial tribunal. Naturally, as law grew more complex, trained lawyers had to handle more and more of the judicial business. At first, they explained the law to the vassals sitting in judgment, and then, as time passed, they formed a court and arrived at decisions themselves in the name of the king. By the fourteenth century, this court was called the *Parlement de Paris,* because Paris was its headquarters. When the *curia regis* sat in special session on financial matters, auditing the reports of income and expenditure, it acted as a kind of government accounting department. By the fourteenth century, it was called the *chambre des comptes,* or chamber of accounts. Naturally enough, it engaged more and more professional full-time employees, clerks and auditors and the like.

Cash flowed to the Crown from the lands of the royal domain, from customs dues and special tolls, from fees for government services, and from money paid in by vassals in order to avoid rendering such outmoded feudal services as entertaining the king and his court. But, in spite of this variety of revenue, the King of France could not levy regular direct taxes on his subjects. During the twelfth century the regular collection of feudal aids accustomed the nobles to paying money to the Crown. Then a special levy was imposed on those who stayed home from the crusade of 1145. In 1188, Philip Augustus collected one-tenth of the movable property and one-tenth of a year's income from all who failed to join in a crusade. These extraordinary imposts, however, never failed to arouse a storm of protest.

Saint Louis

New advances in royal power came with Louis IX (1226-1270), in many ways the greatest of all medieval kings. Deeply pious, almost monastic in his personal life, Louis carried his own high standards over into his role as king. He wore simple clothes, gave alms to beggars, washed the feet of lepers, built hospitals, and created in Paris the beautiful Sainte Chapelle as a jewel-box of glowing stained glass to hold Christ's Crown of Thorns. The Church made him a saint in 1297, less than thirty years after his death.

One of his knights, the Sieur de Joinville, tells this characteristic story about St. Louis in his memoirs:

> Of his mouth he was so sober, that on no day of my life did I ever hear him order special meats, as many rich men are wont to do; but he ate patiently whatever his cooks had made ready.... In his words he was temperate; for on no day of my life did I ever hear him speak evil of any one; nor did I ever hear him name the Devil—which name is very commonly spoken throughout the kingdom, whereby God, as I believe, is not well pleased.
>
> He put water into his wine by measure, according as he saw that the strength of the wine would suffer it.... He asked me why I put no water into my wine; and I said this was by order of the physicians, who told me I had a large head and a cold stomach, so that I could not get drunk. And he answered that they deceived me;... if I drank pure wine in my old age, I should get drunk every night, and that it was too foul a thing for a brave man to get drunk.*

St. Louis was a dutiful husband and an energetic king. During the early years of his reign, when he was still a youth, his very able mother, Blanche of Castile, acted as regent on his behalf and kept the great lords from successful revolt. Louis was grateful to her, yet he resented her attempts to dominate his relations with his wife, Queen Margaret. Joinville recalls:

> The unkindness that the Queen Blanche showed to the Queen Margaret was such that she would not suffer, in so far as she could help it, that her son should be in his wife's company, except at night when he went to sleep with her. The palace where the king and his queen liked most to dwell was at Pontoise,

---

* *Joinville's Chronicle of the Crusade of Saint Lewis,* in *Memoirs of the Crusades,* Everyman ed. (New York, 1933), 139-140.

Aerial view of Carcassonne, a medieval walled town in southern France.

because there the king's chamber was above and the queen's chamber below; and they had so arranged matters between them that they held their converse in a turning staircase that went from the one chamber to the other; and they had further arranged that when the ushers saw the Queen Blanche coming to her son's chamber, they struck the door with their rods, and the king would come running into his own chamber so that his mother might find him there. . . . *

St. Louis did not let his own devotion to the Church stop him from defending royal prerogatives against every attempt of his own bishops or of the papacy to infringe upon them. For example, when the popes tried to enforce the theory that "all churches belong to the Pope," and to assess the churches of France for money and men for papal military campaigns, the King

---

* *Ibid.*, 288.

declared that church property in France was "for the requirements of himself and his realm," and was not to be despoiled by Rome (1247). Yet when he himself became deeply interested in the crusading movement (see Chapter IX), he found himself in need of papal support to enable him to tax the French clergy. Indeed, the clergy then complained to the Pope concerning the King's exactions.

In the towns, too, those old allies of the Capetian dynasty, there were difficulties during Louis' reign. These difficulties arose in large measure out of internal conflicts between the small upper class of rich merchants, who kept city government a kind of oligarchy, and the lower class of tradesmen and artisans, who felt oppressed and excluded from their own government. When the Crown intervened, it was out of concern not so much for the poor and humble

CHAPTER VII

as for the maintenance of order and the continued flow of funds to the royal coffers. Louis began to send royal officials into the towns, and in 1262 issued a decree requiring that the towns present their accounts annually.

This decree itself is a further instance of the King's assertion of royal prerogative. It was a new sort of enactment, the *ordonnance*, or royal command issued for all of France without the previous assent of all the vassals. Royal power and prestige had now progressed to the point where St. Louis did not feel the need to obtain all his vassals' consent every time he wished to govern their behavior. *Ordonnances* signed by some vassals governed all. Examples of St. Louis' *ordonnances* are his prohibition of private warfare, and his law providing that royal money was valid everywhere in France. Both show his advanced views as well as his determination to strengthen the power of the monarchy.

Royal justice had now become a widely desired commodity, and appeals flowed in to the *parlement* from the lower feudal courts. The royal court alone came to be recognized as competent to try cases of treason and of breaking the king's peace, and the extension of royal justice to the towns was secured by bringing in to the *parlement's* deliberations representatives of the middle classes: the king's *bourgeois*. So fair and reasonable was the King's justice felt to be that his subjects often applied to him personally for it. He made himself available to them by sitting under an oak tree in the forest of Vincennes, near Paris, and listening to the case of anybody, high or low, who wished to tell him his story. He maintained no royal protocol on these occasions, and there were no intermediaries. His justice was prized not only in France but also abroad. He settled quarrels in Flanders, Navarre, Burgundy, Lorraine, and elsewhere. He reached a reasonable territorial settlement with England in 1259, and in 1264 was asked to judge the dispute between King Henry III of England and the English barons (see below, p. 279).

Remarkable though he was, St. Louis was simply a remarkable man of the thirteenth century. In his devotion to the crusading enterprise, for instance, he was embracing wholeheartedly the highest ideals of the period. But he never seemed to realize that crusades were now no longer very practicable (see Chapter IX for details). Moreover, it cost France dear to have the King delayed abroad for years and to have him languish in captivity from which he was redeemed only at great expense. Yet, for all his human failings, St. Louis typifies the medieval ideal that the divine law of God's revelation was mirrored in our human law. As God ordered the universe, so human law established the proper relationships of men to one another in society. In human society, the king had his special role, and St. Louis, in his conception and enactment of that role, reached heights that had not been attained by other monarchs.

The System Hardens: Philip the Fair

After the death of St. Louis, the French kingship experienced the general change that was coming over the entire world of the Middle Ages during the late thirteenth and fourteenth centuries. Old conventions and forms persisted, but they seemed to be hardening, to be losing the possibility of fresh and vigorous new expression. In the political history of France, these tendencies begin with the reign of St. Louis' grandson, Philip IV (1285-1314). Called the "Fair" because he was handsome, Philip offered a striking contrast to St. Louis in personality and in character. Ruthlessly, he pushed the royal power and consolidated the royal hold; the towns, the nobles, and the Church all suffered invasions of their rights from his ubiquitous agents. Against the excesses of Philip the Fair, the medieval checks against tyranny, which had been successful against many other aggressive kings, failed to operate. His humiliation of the papacy alone helped as much as any other event of the Middle Ages to bring an end to the Christian commonwealth to which St. Louis had been so devoted. The multiplying *gens du roi,* "the king's men," used propaganda, lies, and trickery to undermine all authority except that of the king.

This undermining was a steady war that went on in a series of small engagements in local courts, with the king's lawyers pushing his rights. One of the devices used was *prévention:* a rule that if a case was started in a court, it had to be finished there, no matter what court was properly competent to try it. If the king's agents managed to bring a case into the royal court, it had to be completed there, even if the royal court was not the proper place for it. Another device was *défaute de droit:* a rule that if justice were refused in a lower court, the plaintiff had a right to appeal to his suzerain's court. The king's agents would urge plaintiffs to claim on any and all occasions that they had been denied justice in their lord's court, and to bring the case to the royal court. Still another device was *faux jugement:* a rule that if a man lost a suit he would be entitled to an appeal by challenging the judge, calling him "wicked and false." On the appeal, the judge would be the defendant in the next higher court. By using this device at the high level of the great lords' courts, the king's men would bring appeals into the royal courts. Indeed, skillfully used, this was a good start toward the absorption of the system of feudal justice into the system of royal justice.

With all the new business coming in, the *parlement* itself took on a new organization. It was still the *curia regis* sitting as a court of law, but it was becoming more specialized and professionalized. The *chambre des plaids* (chamber of pleas), where law-

yers actually argued the cases, rendered the judgments. The *chambre des requêtes* (chamber of petitions) handled all petitions for the royal court to intervene. The *chambre des enquêtes* (chamber of enquiries) would establish the facts in cases that were to come before the royal courts, and supervised the administration of the king's justice in the *baillages* and *sénéchaussées*. Members of the *parlement* now became itinerant justices, bringing royal justice to all parts of the royal domain, and in the great lordships local machinery was more and more taken over by the king's men.

Meanwhile, another important development was taking place—the formation of the central French representative assembly called the Estates General. The king's advisers in the *curia regis* were now dividing into two groups. The smaller group in the king's immediate entourage, who advised him on most issues, was now called the "narrow" or "secret" council. The larger group of advisers, consisting of all the lords, high clerics, and, after 1302, the representatives of the towns, was the "large" or "full" council. The meeting of the large council in 1302 was the first to include representatives of the towns. It is usually called the first Estates General, although the term itself was not used until after the reign of Philip the Fair. "Estate" is the old term for class: the first estate is the clergy, the second the nobility, and the third the townsmen. The lords and clergy in the Estates General acted as individuals, but the individual townsmen came as representatives of entire towns. Towns with executive officers of their own had often chosen their officials to represent them in negotiations with the local lord. But it was a new development to have a similar principle applied to the machinery of central government. The townsmen in the Estates General of Philip the Fair, it should be emphasized, represented municipal corporations; thus, they were not exactly like modern congressmen, who represent a district and all the people living in it.

Philip the Fair's Struggle for Money

War with England kept Philip pressed for cash during much of his reign. He summoned the estates to explain his need for money and to obtain their approval for his proceeding to raise it. He usually asked for funds in a general way, but did not fix the amount, since the groups whom he was asking to contribute always had the right to bargain. Since the medieval man felt that no action was proper unless it had always been customary, whenever the king wanted to do anything new he had to try to make it somehow seem like something old. A protest that such and such attempt to get money was an *exactio inaudita* (an unheard-of exaction) often was enough to frustrate the king's efforts. Philip tried all the known ways of getting money. One of the most effective was to demand military service of a man, and then permit him to escape by paying a specific amount assessed on his property. When protests arose, the king usually had to swallow them and retreat to more orthodox methods. Requests for revenue that had hitherto been irregular were made regular. Forced loans, debasement of the coinage, additional customs dues, and royal levies on commercial transactions also added to the royal income.

Need for money explains the two most celebrated incidents of Philip's reign, his quarrel with the papacy and his suppression of the Knights Templars. Philip claimed the right to tax the clergy for defense. In 1296, the vigorous Pope Boniface VIII (1294-1303) forbade kings and princes to tax the clergy of their countries without papal consent. Philip clapped an embargo on exports from France of precious metals, jewelry, and currency. The order threatened the elaborate financial system of the papacy so severely that under pressure from his distressed bankers, the Pope retreated, saying in 1297 that in an emergency the King of France could go ahead and tax the clergy without papal consent, and that the King would decide when an emergency had arisen.

But a new quarrel arose in 1300 over the trial in Philip's courts of a French bishop accused of treason. Although at the urging of his clergy Philip did send the case to Rome, the Pope was so angry that he made the mistake of giving Philip a public dressing-down in a bull entitled *Ausculta fili*, ("Listen, son"), in which he declared that when a ruler was wicked the Pope might take a hand in the temporal affairs of that realm. Philip replied in scornful and sarcastic language, calling the Pope "your fatuousness." When Boniface pushed his claims still further in a still more famous bull, which declared that it was necessary to salvation for every human creature to be subject to the Pope, and when he threatened to excommunicate the King, Philip issued a whole series of extreme charges against Boniface and sent a gang of thugs to kidnap him. They burst into the papal presence at the Italian town of Anagni (September 7, 1303), and threatened him brutally, but did not dare put through their plan to seize him. None the less, Boniface, who was over eighty, died not long after this humiliation. Philip then obtained the election of a French pope, who never went to Rome at all. Thus began the "Babylonian captivity" of the papacy at Avignon (1305-1378).

Philip used the docile papacy of Avignon in his attacks on the Knights Templars, a crusading order that had become a rich banking house. He owed them money, and to avoid paying it brought them to trial on a series of charges of vicious behavior. With papal co-operation he used as evidence against them confessions extorted by the Inquisition. In 1312, the order was abolished. Philip did not pay them what he owed, and took over their funds, while a rival order was allowed to annex the Templars' lands. Philip also proceeded against others with money, arresting the Jews, stripping them of their property, and expelling them from France in 1306. In 1311 he expelled the agents of Italian bankers. All debts owing the Jews and Italians were simply collected by royal agents, and the Crown kept the money.

Protest in France

Just before Philip died in 1314, his encroachments aroused a protest among the French nobility not unlike the protest that had arisen in England a century before and had culminated in Magna Carta (see below, p. 278). A series of local leagues was formed all over France, in which the towns joined with the lords in a kind of taxpayers' strike. What they were protesting against was that Philip had levied an aid for a war in Flanders, and then had made peace instead of fighting. Louis X (1314-1316) calmed the unrest by revoking the aid, returning some of the money, and making scapegoats of the more unpopular bureaucrats. He also issued a series of charters (instead of one great charter) to several of the great vassals, confirming their liberties.

Taxation, however, was still thought of as inseparably connected with military service, and military service was an unquestioned feudal right of the King. So the King was still free to declare a military emergency, to summon his vassals to fight, and then to commute the service for money, just as Philip the Fair had done. For this reason the charters of Louis X did not put an effective halt to the advance of royal power, and there was no committee of barons (as there had been in England) to make sure that the King lived up to his promises. As a consequence, the French monarch could continue to enjoy a position unique among the kings of western Europe.

III: The Development of England, 1066-1307

The Norman Conquest

The England that threatened the security of France had first become a major power as a result of the Norman conquest of 1066. In that year, William the Conqueror and his invading Normans defeated the Anglo-Saxon forces at Hastings on the south coast of England. William, Duke of Normandy, was a most aggressive and capable representative of an aggressive and capable people. His expedition of 1066, motivated in part by his personal claim to the English crown, was an important stage in the process of Norman expansion which spanned the tenth and eleventh centuries and reached from the British Isles to the south of Italy.

Fat, vigorous, intelligent, and violent, the Conqueror, as King William I of England (1066-1087), displayed the full Norman genius for government. In addition, he had the advantage of a conquered country to work in. Anglo-Saxon England had already developed its own institutions—its thirty-four shires and their sheriffs, its system of hundred and shire courts, its royal council or witenagemot, its royal tax of the Danegeld, and its national militia of the *fyrd* (see Chapter V). William could reshape these institutions as he saw fit. He had already established efficient ducal administration in Normandy; he now established efficient royal administration in England.

William completed the conquest by 1071. All the land in England belonged to him. About one-sixth he kept as royal domain. About half he gave to his great Norman barons in return for military service. Many of them proceeded to sub-infeudate, but their sub-vassals owed military service to the King alone. Thus William acquired the nucleus of a substantial feudal army, a new phenomenon in England. About a quarter of the land belonged to the Church, and William returned it, but bishops and abbots also held their lands of the King, and owed feudal services.

Because he was able to establish his own feudal system, William took precautions that the King of France had been unable to take. All vassals of his vassals swore primary allegiance to the King (Salisbury Oath, 1086). He asserted his right to claim all castles, and none could be built without his license. He forbade private war, and allowed only royal coinage. He continued to levy the Danegeld and to impose judicial fines, and summoned the national militia as well as the array of feudal knights. He kept the hundred, shire, and borough courts, and bound the sheriffs of the shires closely to him, giving them great local authority at the expense of the bishop and the earls.

Thus William the Conqueror maintained the local institutions of Anglo-Saxon England, respecting English custom and law, but superimposed the Norman feudal structure, with its mounted knight and its castle. The sheriffs remained the key link between the old English local government and the new Norman central administration. The Norman *curia regis*, replacing the Anglo-Saxon *witenagemot*, met regularly three times a year, but could be summoned at any time. It gave counsel and tried the cases of the great vassals, and its members could be ordered by the King to perform special tasks in their own shires. In 1086, at William's order, all landed property in England was carefully surveyed. The rec-

ord of the survey is the famous Domesday Book, which included for every piece of land a full statement of ownership, past and present, and a listing of all resources, so that the royal administration might ascertain whether and where more revenue could be obtained. Tenants, plows, forest land, fish ponds, all were listed in Domesday Book. Contemporary accounts reveal the thoroughness of William's inquiry and the resentment it caused:

> So very narrowly did he have it investigated, that there was no single hide nor a yard of land, nor indeed (it is a shame to relate but it seemed no shame to him to do) one ox nor one cow nor one pig was there left out, and not put down on his record: and all these records were brought to him afterward.

· · ·

> Other investigators followed the first; and men were sent into provinces which they did not know, and where they themselves were unknown, in order that they might be given the opportunity of checking the first survey and, if necessary, of denouncing its authors as guilty to the king. And the land was vexed with much violence arising from the collection of the royal taxes.*

No such monument was ever compiled for any other country in the Middle Ages.

William, with the assistance of the able Italian Lanfranc, whom he made Archbishop of Canterbury, established continental practices in the English church. But he refused the Pope's demand that feudal homage be done to him as overlord of England. Rightly maintaining that none of his predecessors on the English throne had ever acknowledged papal suzerainty, he agreed only to pay the accustomed dues to the Church of Rome. The English church recognized no new pope without the King's approval, and accepted no papal commands without his assent. When William died in 1087, the English monarchy was stronger

---

* "Anglo-Saxon Chronicle" and a note by the Bishop of Hereford, in D. C. Douglas and G. W. Greenaway, eds., *English Historical Documents, 1042-1189* (New York, 1953) II, 161, 851.

Harold's men are killed.   Harold is wounded by an arrow.

The Bayeux Tapestry:

than the French was to be for more than two hundred years.

Henry I and Henry II: Administration and Law

During the next sixty-seven years (1087-1154), William's system was both extended and subjected to serious dislocation. Under his son, Henry I (1100-1135), the household and *curia regis* increased in number and their functions became more highly specialized. Because lay administrators, when paid in land, tried to make their offices hereditary with their fiefs, and because clerical administrators were in part subject to papal jurisdiction, Henry more and more undertook to pay his officials fixed salaries out of the proceeds of the king's business. This made them dependent only on the king, and eager to extend his business. The king's immediate entourage became a "small council" within the *curia*, while the full body, now the "great council," met less often. As time went on, the secretarial work began to pile up, since as Duke of Normandy the King of England had extensive business on the Continent. To handle this work, the royal *chancery* or secretariat grew in size and complexity.

Henry I began the practice of accepting a money payment, scutage (literally, "shield-money"), instead of military service from his vassals, and of exempting the boroughs from the Danegeld in exchange for even heavier payments. With these and all his other sources of income, Henry felt the need for a specialized treasury department. This was the origin of the *exchequer,* which collected and checked on receipts. Great officers of the *curia regis* received the semi-annual audit of accounts, which was rendered by the clerks on a long table covered with a cloth divided into squares representing pounds, shillings, and pence. These checker-board squares gave the institution its name. It was typical that the first important new institution of the efficient and grasping Norman kings should have been designed to improve the collection of revenue and to ensure the king his due.

Because Henry's only legitimate son died before his father, the succession was disputed between Henry's daughter Matilda, wife of Geoffrey of Anjou, and Henry's nephew Stephen. A dreadful period of civil war (1135-54) between their partisans produced virtual anarchy in England, and showed what could happen when the strong royal hand disappeared from the helm. Yet the bases for the resumption of strong rule were never destroyed, and in

Harold is killed.

The English flee from the field.

William's defeat of the Anglo-Saxons led by Harold.

the person of the Angevin Henry II (1154-89), son of Matilda and Geoffrey, England got one of the greatest of her monarchs. We have already encountered him as the lord of half of France.

Stormy, energetic, scholarly, and quarrelsome, Henry II systematically cut at the roots of the anarchy: he had more than 1100 unlicensed castles destroyed. From the contemporary *Dialogue Concerning the Exchequer,* written by his treasurer, we learn how the money rolled in: from scutage plus special fees for the privilege of paying it, from fines, from aids, from tallage paid by the boroughs, and from a new tax collected from the knights who did not go on crusades. Even more important than this reestablishment and strengthening of the financial institutions was Henry's contribution to the law of England, built on that of Henry I.

In our own day, when the making of new laws is something we take for granted, it requires a real effort of the imagination to think of a period in which new law could not, in theory, be made at all. Law was what had always existed, and it was the job of the lawyers and government officials to discover what this was and proclaim it. Henry I and Henry II therefore did not fill whole statute books with new enactments: they could never have dreamed of such a

thing. Instead, Henry I claimed that he was ruling in accordance with the law of the Saxon King Edward the Confessor, and the law-books issued in his period contain a mixture of Anglo-Saxon and other materials, including, for example, fixed schedules of money payments imposed as penalties for crime. It was not by issuing laws that Henry I and Henry II transformed the legal practices of England. By developing old instruments in new combinations they created the new common law, law common to all of England because it was administered by the royal courts. Though the hundred and shire courts continued to exist, their jurisdiction had been diluted by that of the competing baronial courts, lay and ecclesiastical. Moreover, only the king could give Englishmen better ways of settling their quarrels among themselves than the old trial by ordeal or trial by battle. The chief instruments were writs, juries, and itinerant justices.

If, for example, somebody seized a subject's property, by the middle of Henry II's reign the victim could buy quite reasonably a royal writ: an order from the king directing a royal official to give the plaintiff a hearing. The official would assemble a group of twelve neighbors who knew the facts in the case; they took an oath, and were therefore called a jury (from *juré,* a man on oath); and then they told the truth as they knew it about whether dispossession had taken place, answering yes or no, and thus giving a verdict (from *veredictum*, a thing spoken truly). These early juries were *not* trial juries in the modern sense but men who were presumed to be in the best position to know the truth. By similar machinery, inheritances unjustly detained could be recovered, and a man unjustly held as a serf could win his freedom. Thus, though the use of a jury, or sworn inquest, dated back to the ninth-century Carolingians, and had come to England with the Conqueror, its application to civil cases between individuals was a new procedure, and so was the flexibility permitted by a variety of writs. No matter who won, the royal exchequer profited, since the loser had to pay a fine. Also, judgments rendered by royal judges in effect became new law without any new legislation in the modern sense.

Building on the practice begun by Henry I, Henry II also regularly sent itinerant justices out to the shires. On their travels they were instructed in each shire to receive reports from the local officials, and to try all cases pending in the shire court. Moreover, the sheriffs had to bring before the justices from each hundred and township a group of sworn men to report under oath all crimes that had occurred since the last visit of the justices, and to indicate whom they considered to be the probable criminal in each case. This is another use of the jury, the jury of "presentment," since it presented the names of suspect criminals. It is the ancestor of the modern grand jury ("grand" simply in the sense of large), consisting of greater numbers of men than the twelve that took part in the petty juries. Again, the treasury profited, as the itinerant justices imposed heavy fines. Again, blatant innovation was avoided; again, refinements and combinations of existing instruments produced new legal conditions. Of course, we are still in

the Middle Ages. The usual means of proof in a criminal trial was still under Henry II the ordeal by cold water: if the accused, with hands and feet tied, floated in a pool blessed by the Church, he was guilty; if he sank, he was innocent.

Henry II and Becket

Where Henry II failed was in an effort to limit the competing system of canon law. Confident that he would have a pliant assistant, he appointed his friend and chancellor, Thomas à Becket, to be Archbishop of Canterbury. But, once he had become Archbishop, Becket proved inflexibly determined not to yield any of the Church's rights, but rather to add to them whenever he could. The great quarrel between the two broke out over the question of "criminous clerks"—that is, clerics convicted of a crime. In publishing a collection of earlier customs relating to the Church (Constitutions of Clarendon, 1164), Henry included one provision that clerics convicted in the bishop's courts should be handed over to royal authorities for punishment. Before trial, they were also to be indicted in the royal court. Becket refused to agree to this part of the document, and appealed to the Pope for support.

Although the issue was compromised after a dispute that lasted six years, Henry, in one of his fits of temper, asked whether nobody would rid him of Becket. Four of his knights responded by murdering Becket in his own cathedral at Canterbury. Henry swore to the Pope that he was innocent of complicity in the murder, but he had to undergo a humiliating penance and, more important, he had to yield on the issue. The Church in England continued to have the sole right to punish its clergy—"benefit of clergy," the principle was called. Moreover, Henry had to accept the right of litigants in church courts to appeal to Rome direct, without royal intervention or license of any sort. This meant that the papacy had the ultimate say in an important area of English life. It was a severe defeat for Henry's program of extending royal justice. Yet the other clauses in the Constitutions of Clarendon were not challenged, and the King continued to prevent the Pope from taxing the English clergy directly. For his part, Becket was made a saint only two years after his death, and pilgrimages to his miraculous tomb at Canterbury became a standard part of English life.

Henry's reign was also notable for the reorganization of the old Anglo-Saxon *fyrd* by the Assize of Arms, 1181, which made each free man responsible, according to his income, to maintain suitable arms for the defense of the realm. Forests, floods, the ingredients and prices of bread and beer, and of course the warfare with France all occupied Henry's attention. Unfortunately, he could not control his own sons, who rebelled against him and made his last years miserable by attacking his possessions on the Continent. When he died, he is said to have turned his face to the wall and said, "Shame, shame on a conquered king!"

Richard I and John

Henry II's son, Richard the Lion-hearted (1189-1199), spent less than six months of his ten-year reign in England. But the country did not revert to the anarchy that had been characteristic of the reigns of Stephen and Matilda. Henry II hand done his work too well for that. The bureaucracy functioned without the presence of the King. Indeed, it functioned all too well for the liking of the population. For Richard needed more money than had ever been needed before to pay for his crusade, for his ransom from captivity, and for his wars against Philip Augustus of France. Heavy taxes were levied on income and on personal property; certain kinds of possessions, including silver plate, were simply confiscated; a large number of charters was sold to cities. Thus it was that Richard's brother, John (1199-1216), who was clever but unreliable, greedy, and tyrannical, succeeded to a throne whose resources had been squandered. John had the great misfortune to face three adversaries who proved too strong for him: Philip Augustus, who expelled the English from France north of the Loire (see above, p. 264), Innocent III, the greatest of medieval popes, and the outraged English baronage.

In 1206, the election to the Archbishopric of Canterbury was disputed between two candidates, one of whom was favored by John. The Pope refused to accept either, and in 1207 procured the election of a third, Stephen Langton. John exiled the members of the cathedral chapter of Canterbury and confiscated the property of the see. Innocent responded by putting all England under an interdict (1208) and by excommunicating John (1209). He threatened to depose John, and thought of replacing him with a Capetian; he corresponded with Philip Augustus, who prepared to invade England. Fearing with good reason that his own vassals would not stay loyal in the face of such an invasion, John gave in (1213). Not only did he accept Langton as Archbishop of Canterbury and promise to restore church property and to reinstate banished priests, but he also recognized England and Ireland as fiefs of the papacy, and did homage to the Pope for them. In addition, he agreed to pay an annual tribute to Rome. All this of course represented a startling papal victory. From now on, Innocent was on John's side in his quarrel with a large faction of the English barons —a quarrel that became acute after the French had won the battle of Bouvines (1214; see above, p. 264). "Since I have been reconciled to God, and have submitted to the Roman Church," John exclaimed when the news of Bouvines was brought to him, "nothing has gone well with me."

John and the Barons: Magna Carta

The quarrel with perhaps one-third of the English barons arose from John's ruthlessness in raising money for a campaign in France, and from his habit of punishing vassals without trial. At the moment of absolution by the Pope in 1213, John had sworn to Stephen Langton that he would "restore the good laws of his predecessors." But he violated his oath. After Bouvines, the barons hostile to John renounced their homage to him, and drew up a list of demands, most of which they forced him to accept on June 15, 1215, at Runnymede, one of the most celebrated occasions in all human history. The document that he agreed to send out under the royal seal to all the shires of England had sixty-three chapters, in the legal form of a feudal grant or conveyance. Known as Magna Carta, the Great Charter, it is often referred to by English and American historians and politicians as the foundation-stone of our liberties. But it contains, of course, no references to man's inalienable rights or to the free and equal birth of all men.

What one finds in Magna Carta is a feudal document, a list of specific concessions drawn up in the interest of a group of great barons at odds with their feudal lord, the King. The King promises reform in his exactions of scutage, aids, reliefs, and in certain other feudal practices. He makes certain concessions to the peasantry and the tradesmen (uniform weights and measures, town liberties) and to the Church (free elections to bishoprics and maintenance of liberties).

Certain provisions of Magna Carta have over the centuries proved particularly important. For example, the provision, "No scutage or aid, save the customary feudal ones, shall be levied *except by the common counsel of the realm*," meant only that the King must consult his great council (i.e., his barons and bishops) before levying extraordinary feudal aids. Yet this was capable of expansion into the later doctrine that all taxation must be by consent, that taxation without representation was tyranny. A similar history may be traced for the famous provision, "No freeman shall be arrested and imprisoned, or dispossessed or outlawed or banished or in any way molested; nor will we set forth against him, nor send against him, unless by the lawful judgment of his peers and by the law of the land." Originally, this seems to have meant only that the barons did not fancy trial by royal judges who were not their social equals, and that they wished to push back the aggressions of royal justice. Yet it was capable of later expansion into the doctrine of "due process of law" that everybody was entitled to a trial ("by his peers").

Although medieval kings of England reissued the charter with modifications some forty times, it was to be ignored under the Tudor monarchy in the sixteenth century, and Englishmen did not appeal to it until the revolt against the Stuarts in the seventeenth century (see Chapter XV). By then, the Middle Ages had long since been over, and the rebels against Stuart absolutism could read into the medieval clauses of Magna Carta many of the same modern meanings that we, just as inaccurately, see in them at first glance. Thus Magna Carta's lasting importance lies partly in what later interpreters were able to read into its original clauses. It also lies perhaps even more, however, in two general principles underlying the whole document: that the king was subject to the law and that he might, if necessary, be forced to observe it. This is why this document, more than seven centuries old, dealing with a now obsolete social system, still carries vitally important implications for us in the twentieth century.

As soon as John had accepted the Charter, he instantly tried to break his promises; the Pope declared the Charter null and void; and Langton and the barons opposed to John now took the Pope's former place as supporters of a French monarchy for England. Philip Augustus' son actually landed in England and occupied London briefly; but John died in 1216, and was succeeded by his nine-year-old son, Henry III (1216-1272), to whose side the barons rallied. The barons then expelled the French from England. It was not until 1258 that the King found himself again actually at open war with a faction of his own barons. Yet, during the interval, there were storm warning of future trouble.

Henry III and the Barons

In Henry's re-issue of Magna Carta (1216 and 1217), the clause requiring the great council to approve unusual taxation was omitted. In 1232, Henry appointed a favorite from Poitou in France to the highest post in his administration, replacing a loyal Englishman who had become identified with the barons' revolt. Frenchmen in high places in the state were now added to the host of Italians appointed by the Pope to high places in the English church. Since both the French and the Italian appointees were avaricious, many English nobles felt a deep resentment toward these foreigners. Henry's marriage to a French princess (1236) fanned the flames. The great council flatly refused to give Henry money for a campaign in France, and its members discussed plans for limiting the royal power. In 1254, Henry received from the Pope the crown of Sicily for his second son, and in 1257 he permitted his brother to seek election as Holy Roman Emperor. Both were highly expensive undertakings, since Sicily had to be conquered and the Empire had to be bought. Things came to a head in 1258, a year of bad harvest, when

Henry asked for one-third of the revenues of England as an extra grant for the Pope.

Now the barons openly rebelled. They came armed to the session of the great council, and secured the appointment of a committee of twenty-four of their number, which then issued a document known as the Provisions of Oxford. This document created a council of fifteen without whose advice the King could do nothing. The committee put its own men in the high offices of state. It also replaced the full great council with a baronial body of twelve. This provision clearly contained the seeds of a baronial tyranny perhaps worse than the King's own. The foreigners were expelled. But the barons were ridden by dissension among themselves; the Pope declared the Provisions null and void, and Henry III resumed his personal rule. Civil war broke out in 1263 between the King and the baronial party headed by Simon de Montfort. When St. Louis was called in to arbitrate, he ruled in favor of the King and against the barons. Simon de Montfort, however, would not accept the decision, took arms again, captured the King himself in 1264, and set up a regime of his own based on the restoration of the Provisions of Oxford. This regime lasted fifteen months. In 1265, Simon de Montfort called an assembly of his supporters, which, as we shall see, was a step in the evolution of Parliament. But in this same year, the heir to the throne, the lord Edward, defeated and killed Simon de Montfort, and restored his father, Henry III, to the throne. For the last seven years of Henry's reign (1265-1272), as well as for the next thirty-five years of his own rule (1272-1307), Edward I was the real ruler of England.

The Origins of Parliament

The revolts of the thirteenth century had given the barons experience in the practical work of government, and many of their reforms had been accepted by the royal governments that followed. Still more important, during the course of the struggle the local communities of England had emerged as significant elements in the operations of the central administration. Indeed, it is to these years of Henry III that historians turn for the earliest signs of the greatest contribution of the English Middle Ages to mankind: the development of Parliament.

The word "parliament" is French and simply means "a talking" or parley, a conference of any kind. The French historian Villehardouin (see Chapter IX) refers to a discussion between the French and Venetian leaders in the fourth crusade as a "*parlement.*" Joinville, the biographer of St. Louis, refers to his hero's secret conversations with his wife on the palace staircase as "*parlements.*" And we have already encountered the word as applied in France to that part of the *curia regis* which acted as a court. In England, during the thirteenth century, the word is found more and more often in reference to the assemblies summoned by the king, especially those that were to hear petitions for legal redress. In short, a parliament in England in the thirteenth century is much like the *parlement* in France: a session of the king's large council acting as a court.

The Anglo-Saxon witenagemot had been an assembly of the great churchmen and laymen of the kingdom who advised the king on taxation and on matters of policy, and who could also act as a supreme court in important cases. In these respects the great council of the Norman and Angevin kings was not much different from the witenagemot. Feudal law simply reinforced the king's right to secure from his chief vassals both aid (that is, military service) and counsel (that is, advice on law and custom and a share in judicial decisions). The Norman kings made attendance at sessions of the great council compulsory; it was the king's privilege, not his duty, to receive counsel, and it was the vassal's duty, not his privilege, to offer it.

But by requiring the barons to help govern England, the kings entirely unconsciously, and indeed contrary to their own intentions, actually strengthened the assembly of the vassals, the great council. The feeling gradually grew up that the king *must* consult the council; this feeling is reflected in the scutage and aid provision of Magna Carta. Yet the kings generally consulted only the small council of their permanent advisers; the great council met only occasionally and when summoned by the king. The barons who sat on the great council thus developed a sense of being excluded from the work of government in which they felt entitled to participate. It was this baronial discontent, perhaps as much as the issues we have already considered, that led to the troubles under Henry III. When the barons took over the government in 1258, they determined that the great council should meet three times a year, and they called it a "parliament." When Henry III regained power, he continued to use the small council and, significantly, he also continued to summon the feudal magnates to the great council, to parliament.

Knights of the Shire and Burgesses

The increasing prosperity of England in the thirteenth century had enriched many members of the landed gentry who were not necessarily the king's direct vassals, and might occupy a position fairly far down in the feudal pyramid. The inhabitants of the towns had also increased in number and importance with the growth of trade. Representatives of these newly important classes in country and town now began to attend parliament at the king's summons. They were the "knights of the shire," two from each shire, and the "burgesses" of the towns. Accustomed since Anglo-Saxon times to the compulsory participation in their local hundred and shire courts, the knights of the shire were landholders with local standing, and they were often rich men. By the time of Richard the Lionhearted, some were occasionally selected to bring court records to the judges. For other purposes (bringing in accounts or documents to show title) townsmen, too, had been chosen by the towns at royal command to appear before royal justices either on circuit in the shires or in London. In 1213, 1226, and 1227, knights of the shire had been summoned by the king to discuss current problems; in 1254 they were summoned to parliament for the first time. Meanwhile, burgesses or townsmen were also being summoned by the king to appear before his justices either on circuit in the shires or in London; they brought accounts or legal documents.

Although much controversy on the subject still rages, recent research has made it seem probable that the chief reason for the king's summons to the shire and town representatives was his need for money. By the thirteenth century the sources of royal income, both ordinary and extraordinary, were not enough to pay the king's ever-mounting bills. Thus he was obliged, according to feudal custom, to ask for "gracious aids" from his vassals. These aids were in the form of percentages of personal property, and the vassals had to assent to their collection. So large and so numerous were the aids that the king's immediate vassals naturally collected what they could from *their* vassals to help make up the sums. Since these sub-vassals would contribute such a goodly part of the aids, they, too, came to feel that they should assent to the levies. The first occasion when we can be sure that the king summoned sub-vassals for this purpose was the meeting of parliament in 1254, to which he called the knights of the shire. It should be emphasized that this was not exactly a great in-novation; the knights of the shire, as we have seen, were already accustomed to bringing information to the king and speaking on behalf of their shires.

The towns also came to feel that they should be consulted on taxes, since in practice they were often able to negotiate with the royal authorities for a reduction in the levy imposed on them. Burgesses of the towns were included for the first time in Simon de Montfort's parliament of 1265. Knights of the shire likewise attended this meeting, because Simon apparently wanted to muster the widest possible support for his program and believed that an assembly of the direct vassals would not be representative enough. But only known supporters of Simon were invited to attend the parliament. Scholars no longer believe, as they once did, that de Montfort had a twentieth-century democrat's devotion to representative institutions, or even that he regarded the assembly he was summoning as establishing a precedent for the future. Yet it did prove to be such a precedent, and the simultaneous presence of shire and town representatives made it the first true ancestor of the modern House of Commons. Not all subsequent parliaments had representatives from shire and town, and not all assemblies attended by knights and burgesses were parliaments. Knights and burgesses had no "right" to come to parliament; no doubt, they often felt it a nuisance and an expense to come, and not a privilege. But gradually they came to attend parliament regularly.

Edward I

Before continuing with the history of parliament under Edward I (1272-1307), we must briefly consider his other achievements. He tried to unite all Britain into a single kingdom. Wales, which had nominally been made subject by Henry II, became restless under Henry III, and revolted

Parliament under Edward I. Note the wool-sacks on which officials are sitting in the center.

under Edward. In 1283, Edward put down the rebels, executed the brother of the last native prince, and proclaimed his own infant son Prince of Wales. Ever since, this title has been reserved for the eldest son of the King of England. In the 1290's a disputed succession to the throne of Scotland, and the formation of a Franco-Scottish alliance, brought Edward to Scotland as invader. Although he declared himself King of Scotland in 1296, and carried off the Stone of Scone, the symbol of Scottish kingship, to Westminster Abbey, William Wallace's rebellion (1297-1305) required a second conquest of Scotland and led to the subsequent capture and execution of Wallace. Edward incorporated Scotland with England. However, the celebrated Robert Bruce now rebelled, and Edward I died while on an expedition against him (1307). Edward II (1307-1327) lost Scot-

land to Bruce at the battle of Bannockburn (1314). It was not until 1603 that England and Scotland were joined under the same king (James I), and he was a Scot who became King of England.

In the field of administration at home, Edward I's reign was especially memorable. In the thirteenth century the earlier medieval belief that law is custom, and that it cannot be made, was disappearing. Now the question was whether a single law-giver would emerge and declare the law, or whether the old feudal assemblies would be broadened so that new enactments would have a popular basis. In Edward I, England found a legislator who enacted a great series of systematizing statutes. These statutes were framed by the experts of the small council, who elaborated and expanded the machinery of government, and under whose rule parliament's function was more

CHAPTER VII

judicial than legislative or consultative. Each of the statutes was really a large bundle of different enactments. Taken together, they reflect declining feudalism, and show us an England in which the suzerain-vassal relationship was becoming more and more a mere landlord-tenant relationship, and in which the old duties of fighting were becoming less important than the financial aspects of the matter. The Second Statute of Westminster (1285), for example, was designed to assure the great landowner that an estate granted to a tenant could not be disposed of except by direct inheritance; this is what we would call entail. Similarly, the Statute of Mortmain (1279) prevented transfer of land to the Church without the consent of the suzerain. The Church placed a "dead hand" (*mortmain*) on land and could hold on forever to any land it received; lay landlords, therefore, found it highly unprofitable to see portions of their holdings transferred to clerical hands.

In addition to these statutes, all of which redounded to the interest of the landlord, Edward I commanded the barons to show by what authority (*quo warranto*) they held any franchise, such as a hundred court. Some franchises he revoked, but his chief aim was to assert the principle that all such franchises came from the king, and that what he had given he could take away. Under Edward the business of royal justice increased steadily, and specialized courts began to appear, all of them the offspring of the central *curia regis*. The Court of Common Pleas, which handled cases that arose between subjects, had begun to take shape earlier, but now crystallized into a recognizable, separate body. The new Court of King's Bench handled criminal and crown cases, and the special Court of Exchequer dealt with disputes pertaining to royal finance.

Edward I also regularized and improved existing financial and military practices. He made permanent the king's share in export duties on wool and leather, the burden of which fell mostly on foreigners, and in customs dues on foreign merchandise, which soon became the most important single source of royal income, eloquent testimony to the flourishing commerce of the period. At the behest of parliament, Edward expelled the Jews from England in 1290; they were not allowed to come back until the mid-seventeenth century. After their expulsion, the Italians assumed the role of moneylenders.

Edward required all freemen to be responsible for military service, and to equip themselves appropriately. The less well-off served as foot-soldiers. But those with a certain minimum amount of property were compelled to become knights (distraint of knighthood) and serve on horse-back, in part for financial reasons: once they had achieved knight's status the king could collect feudal dues from them. Edward's vigorous extension of royal power aroused the same sort of opposition that had plagued John and undone Henry III. In 1297, both the clergy (under the influence of Pope Boniface VIII; see above, p. 271) and the barons refused to grant the aid that Edward wanted; they were able to make him confirm Magna Carta, and promise not to levy any further taxes without first obtaining consent.

Edward I's parliament of 1295 is called the "Model Parliament," because it included all classes of the kingdom, not only barons, higher clergy, knights of the shire, and burgesses, but also representatives of the lower clergy. In the royal summons of 1295 we find a celebrated clause: "What touches all should be approved by all." This echoes a famous provision of Roman law, and pays at least lip service to the principle that consent to taxation was necessary. Again, in 1297, Edward declared that the "good will and assent of the archbishops, bishops, and other prelates, earls, barons, knights, burgesses, and other freemen of our realm" were *essential* to a royal levy of a tax. This principle was frequently re-asserted in later years, and parliament sometimes made its confirmation a condition for the grant of money. The regular presence of the knights and burgesses had gradually made them more and more nearly indis-pensable to the king's business. Unlike the French monarchs, the English had encountered a corporate baronial opposition, which by forcing consultation upon the king had begun to create brand-new institutions.

IV: The Development of Germany and the Empire, 911-1273

Dukes and King

In Germany, strong monarchy won a secure footing earlier than it had in either England or France. As the Carolingian Empire gradually disintegrated in the late ninth and early tenth centuries, five duchies arose in the East Frankish lands of Germany. They were Franconia, Saxony, Thuringia, Swabia, and Bavaria. These duchies were military units organized by the local Carolingian administrators, who took the title of duke (army commander). At first, these military leaders were loyal to the Carolingian monarchy, and, after the Carolingian dynasty had become extinct, they chose one of their own number, Conrad, Duke of Franconia, as their king in 911. The dukes felt that this was the best way to protect their lands against the threat of the Magyar invaders (see Chapter V). Conrad, however, could not claim the deference that his Carolingian predecessors had enjoyed. His efforts to exact it, coupled with his failure as a military leader, led the dukes for the first time to assert themselves as rivals to the Crown and to build up their duchies into petty kingdoms. Each duke made himself heredi-tary ruler and took control over the Church in his own duchy. Each tried to arouse the loyalty of his people and to dominate the local administrators of the king, the counts.

These decentralizing processes had only begun when Conrad died, having named as his successor the Duke of Saxony, who became King Henry I (919-936). A struggle with the duchies ensued, in which Henry and his descendants—notably Otto I (936-973) and Otto III (983-1002)—were able to reassert the power of the monarchy. They successfully combatted the ducal tendency to dominate the counts and to control the Church; they made the counts serve under the Crown and regained the right to appoint bishops. In 939, moreover, the Crown obtained the Duchy of Franconia; thenceforth the German kings, no matter what duchy they came from, would also have Franconia as the royal domain. Parts of Saxony, too, became crown land.

Saxon Administration

The Saxon dynasty established by Henry I relied on the Church to perform much of the work of governing Germany. Henry welcomed the alliance between Church and monarchy, partly because bishops, unlike counts, could not pass on their offices to their sons, and partly because bishops were better educated than laymen.

And the Church welcomed the alliance because a strong central government was its best guarantee of stability. In the tenth century the papacy itself recognized the rights of the German kings to appoint their own bishops. The later Saxon monarchs received church and abbey lands into their special protection, exempting them from the authority of the counts, and bringing them directly under the Crown. The bishops were given the right to administer justice within their own domain, and in fact were invested with the powers of counts. In 1007, for instance, the bishops of the great sees of Bamberg and Würzburg were given all the rights that had formerly belonged to counts.

In addition to efficient administration, the Church supplied the German king with much of his revenue, and tenants of church lands furnished three-quarters of his army. The Church also shared largely in the German expansion to the east—the celebrated *Drang nach Osten*—in the defeat of the Magyars (955), in the push into Slavic lands along the Elbe and Saale rivers, and in the advance into Silesia. New German bishoprics were set up, with Magdeburg as center, and subject sees were established east of the Elbe. The Church, in consequence, was now able to impose Christianity upon the vanquished Slavs.

The Empire

When King Otto I took the title of emperor in the year 962, he created for his successors a set of problems that far transcended the local problems of Germany, and that profoundly affected Germany itself. The old concept of the Roman Empire as the one true secular power was to continue unchanged in the eastern empire of Byzantium (see Chapter VI). In the Carolingian West, however, it had be-

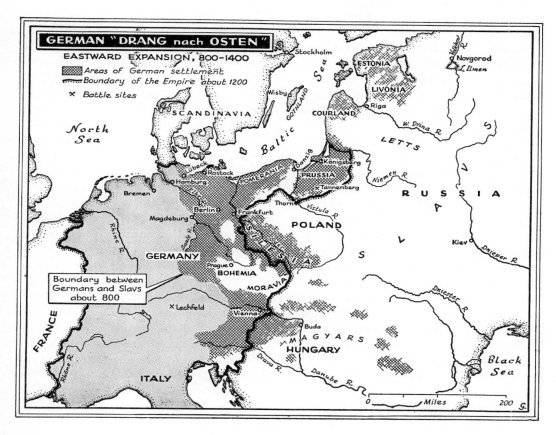

come much diluted, and "emperor" had come to mean a ruler who controlled two or more kingdoms, but who did not necessarily claim supremacy over the whole inhabited world. The kingdoms that the western emperor was likely to control were Germany, Burgundy, and Italy. Burgundy had grown up under ambitious rulers in the region between the eastern and western Frankish lands. Italy, on the other hand, was weak, divided, and open to invasion.

Thus the King of Germany had something to gain if he could secure even the diluted title of emperor. And, if he did not make himself emperor, he faced a real danger that somebody else would. That somebody might easily be the Duke of Swabia or of Bavaria, in which case the struggle of the Saxon kings to control the dukes would have proved unavailing. When viewed in this light, Otto I's fateful trip to Italy and his assumption of the imperial title appear not as a mere urge for conquest but as a move in self-defense. Moreover, it was the natural step for the heir to the Carolingians to take.

Otto I's grandson, the brilliant young Otto III (983-1002), used a seal with the words *Renewal of the Roman Empire.* In Rome itself he strove to restore a Roman imperial palace, Roman titles, and Roman glory, possibly acting under the influence of his Byzantine mother. But he tried to make imperial power real in Italy by putting German officials on church lands to keep these lands out of the hands of the Italian nobility, and by appointing German bishops to Italian sees in an effort to build up the sort of government he had at home. His Roman revival itself was calculated to win over the Roman aristocracy from their Byzantine sympathies. Moreover, Otto III did not ignore Germany; he paid careful attention to relations between Germany and the Slavs. German contemporaries seem to have felt that his intervention in Italy was proper and legitimate. The policy of Otto III was not aimed at dominating the entire West; it aimed, rather, at making good the title of emperor in the new dilute sense and at consolidating the rule of the Saxon dynasty in Italy, Burgundy, and Germany.

Italy benefited, now that her long period of anarchy had finally come to an end. The emperors raised the level of the papacy from the degradation it had reached in the tenth century. The imperial sponsorship of the Cluniac movement to reform the Church, however, began the work of making the papacy into a world power that was eventually to ruin later emperors (see Chapter IV). But German culture and German trade benefited from the Italian connection. Moreover, by the early eleventh century, the right of the German king to be King of Italy and emperor was taken for granted; even if a king had not yet been crowned emperor by the pope, he called himself "King of the Romans, still to be promoted to Emperor."

Salian Administration

The hereditary principle had by now been established in the German monarchy; regional barriers within Germany were disappearing; and a sense of German national unity was asserting itself, evidenced by the general use of the term *teutonici* (Teutons or Germans). In 1024, the Saxon dynasty died out, and was followed by the Salian dynasty, whose first emperor, Conrad II (1024-1039), was "designated" by the widow of the last of the Saxons. The new dynasty, which came from Franconia, produced some first-rate administrators. Conrad II modified the Saxon policy of entrusting the duchies and the great episcopal sees to members of the imperial family. He ruled instead through the counts, and permitted their offices to become hereditary, something that the greater nobles had opposed. Conrad thus experimented with a political alliance between the Crown and the lesser nobles (the counts) against the pretensions of the great lords (the dukes).

Yet this sort of alliance, which had been effective elsewhere in Europe, could not succeed in Germany. The counts, who did not usually feel oppressed by the dukes, were not ready to ally with the king against them; if anything, the counts felt more oppressed by the king and were more likely to ally with the dukes against the Crown. For Conrad II to permit the office of count to become hereditary was to establish a dangerous precedent. Thus the alliance with the counts was later abandoned by Conrad's successors, Henry III (1039-1056) and Henry IV (1056-1106).

But another of Conrad's administrative innovations was accepted and developed by his successors. This was the training of members of the lower class to serve as administrators—the *ministeriales,* who were employed first by churches to run their great estates, then by the kings to run the lands of the Crown. Though rewarded with land, the *ministeriales* did not hold true fiefs; they remained dependent directly on the Crown, and gradually established a new social status of their own that was not feudal and not quite like anything existing outside Germany. Conrad II employed one of these *ministeriales* as a kind of comptroller-general for revenue from the imperial estates; another, who occupied a similar post for Henry III, ended his career as a bishop. And under Henry IV, the great nobles actually began to complain that the King listened only to low-born fellows.

Under Henry III, the process of administrative consolidation was marked by the choice of the first permanent royal residence, Goslar in the Harz mountains. Previously, the court had moved from place to place. And under Henry IV the monarchy was strong enough to draw up a survey of crown lands in 1064-1065. This survey was less comprehensive than the English Domesday Book, but it was designed for the same purpose: to assure the Crown a regular income.

Indeed, from the standpoint of effective administration, the German state of the 1070's was almost comparable with Norman England. To find a French parallel, it would be necessary to look ahead more than a century to Philip Augustus. Moreover, Germany, unlike France, was not yet a fully feudalized country. In France, the Carolingian counts had become feudal lords, each in his own county, whereas in Germany the dukes had no such feudal position. Free men in Germany did not have to choose between becoming vassals of the dukes and ceasing to exist; both large and small estates continued to be owned outright by free men. Although the social distinction between the rich and poor was great, both were more often free of feudal ties than anywhere else in Europe. Technically, land that was still free was called an *allod* (from *allodium,* the opposite of *feudum,* a fief), and allods were far more numerous in Germany than elsewhere.

This situation, though curbing the growth of German feudalism, also contained a threat to the German monarchy. For a class of free landowners was maintained, holders of allods, bound neither by feudal nor by royal ties. So, when the attack came on the increasing centralization of the eleventh-century German monarchy, it came from these free landowners, a class that had no exact counterpart in France or England. They strengthened their position by becoming the guardians or "advocates" of monasteries, a process that was aided for a time by the Crown itself. In 973, there were in Germany 108 abbeys, probably all attached to the Crown; in 1075, there were more than 700, and almost all the new ones were attached to members of the landowner class. A new monastic foundation in Germany was not only a sign of the founder's piety. Monks opened up and colonized new lands, and the resulting revenues went to the founder of the house, who as "advocate" also had jurisdiction over the tenants.

These new monastic foundations, then, were the source of much wealth and power. To keep them out of royal hands, the German nobles often made them the legal property of the pope, who was far away and could not interfere as readily as the king could. Thus, side by side with what may be termed the "royal" church and its bishops, there grew up in Germany a "noble" church based largely on monastic foundations.

Opposition to the royal church, to the *ministeriales,* and to the trend toward monarchical centralization all led the German nobility to revolt. In 1073, the nobles rose in Saxony against the Emperor Henry IV; in 1075, Henry crushed the uprising. But only a few weeks later there began the open struggle with the papacy that gave the nobles new occasion to rebel. This was the Investiture Controversy, destined to last half a century and to end in the ruin of the German monarchy.

The Investiture Controversy to 1077

The origins of this struggle go back to the year 1049, when Emperor Henry III had installed Pope Leo IX, a close relative of his, on the papal throne. The Emperor had first intervened in Rome in 1046, at a moment when three rival popes were simultaneously in office while rival mobs of their supporters rioted in the streets. Henry deposed all three, and named a German, followed in a short time by a second German, and then, after only three years, by a third, Leo IX, who fought abuses bravely, and was thoroughly committed to the Cluniac program of monastic reform (see Chapter VIII). But Leo and especially his younger assistant, Hildebrand, also favored the extension of reform beyond the monasteries. The whole church hierarchy, they insisted, must be purged of secular influences, and over it all the pope

must reign supreme. Ironically enough, the imperial sponsorship of the reformers would spell grave danger to the imperial system of government in Germany.

In 1073, Hildebrand himself became pope as Gregory VII. He was determined to push ecclesiastical reform by insuring the canonical (regular) election of all bishops and abbots. This would mean sweeping away the system of royal selection and appointment, and the subsequent lay investiture—that is, the conferring of the prelate's insignia of office (for bishops, a ring and a staff) by a layman, the emperor. Yet the German royal administration largely depended on this royal appointment of prelates, which involved not only lay investiture but the sale of church offices and many other corrupt practices. Gregory VII now girded himself for the attack. And, though personally humble and saintly, he was a statesman of such vigor, shrewdness, intellect, and passion that modern historians agree with his contemporaries in judging him, with Gregory the Great and Innocent III, as one of the Church's greatest and most effective popes. He believed that, as the wielder of supreme spiritual authority, the pope had jurisdiction over temporal things as well, and that temporal princes who defied his command were followers of Antichrist.

In the great struggle with the Emperor, the Pope seemed to enjoy many advantages. The papacy had recently (1059) put the election of new popes into the hands of the College of Cardinals, thus depriving the emperors of their former role. Moreover, in its attacks on lay investiture and on the imperial administrative and ecclesiastical system in Germany, the papacy was assured of the support of the German nobles who had helped spread the Cluniac order in Germany. Also, the Pope was allied, after a long period of hostility, with the new Norman rulers of southern Italy.

Gregory VII took the offensive in 1075 by forbidding lay investiture. In 1076,

Henry IV and his bishops responded by declaring Gregory's election as pope null and void. Gregory then excommunicated Henry and declared him deposed, and deprived the bishops loyal to the emperor of their offices. Urged on by papal legates, Henry's noble opponents in Germany joined forces with the Pope, and made Henry promise to clear himself of the excommunication within four months, on pain of the loss of his crown, and meanwhile to accept the papal sentence and to withdraw from public life. Henry's opponents also invited the Pope to Germany.

To prevent this unwelcome visit, Henry himself secretly went to Italy in 1077, and appeared before the castle of Canossa, where Gregory was temporarily staying on his way north. Henry declared himself a penitent, and Gregory kept him waiting outside the castle for three days, barefoot and in sackcloth. When he was finally admitted he did penance, and Gregory absolved him. The drama and symbolism of this famous episode have often led historians to marvel at the power of the Pope. But it struck contemporaries the other way: by allowing himself to be publicly humiliated, Henry had actually forced Gregory's hand. The Pope had had to absolve him, and once absolved Henry could no longer be deposed.

The Investiture Controversy, 1077-1122

Before Henry returned home, his German opponents, in their resentment at his stealing a march on them, had elected a new ruler, an "anti-king," Rudolf of Swabia. This development resulted in a fearfully destructive civil war in Germany. By refraining for three years (until 1080) from making a decision between the rival kings, Gregory VII did what he could to prolong the civil war. When he did decide, it was in favor of Rudolf and against

Henry, whom he solemnly deposed and excommunicated once more. But the Pope's efforts failed. Rudolf was killed in battle, and a new anti-king commanded even less support. The German clergy again declared the Pope deposed, and Henry marched to Italy in 1081, took Rome in 1084, installed an anti-pope, and had himself crowned emperor by this anti-pope. Gregory summoned his Norman vassals and allies, but they did not arrive until after Henry had returned to Germany. Gregory died in defeat in 1085. By 1091, the last vestige of the revolt against Henry in Germany had been stamped out.

It must be realized that to many pious men of the Middle Ages Gregory's new claim that he could make and unmake kings seemed a dreadful thing. Implicit in it, they thought, lay future civil strife: the Pope was destroying something that had been established by God at the beginning of time. Thus the imperial theorists in the struggle were the conservatives, and the papal theorists were the revolutionaries.

Gregory VII's successors were reformers like him. They renewed his excommunication of Henry IV, supported civil war in Germany, and virtually put an end to imperial power in Italy. In 1106, Henry IV died and was succeeded by his son, Henry V (1106-1125). Just as Henry IV had tried to make his peace with the Church at Canossa in 1077 in the hope of defeating the princes, so now his son, Henry V, made his peace with the princes in the hope of defeating the Church. In doing so, he changed the character of the German monarchy. The nobles kept most of the gains they had won in the revolt of 1077. Consequently, feudal warfare continued in Germany, the ravaged royal lands could not be reassembled and put in order, and Henry V was unable to carry out the "Domesday Book" type of survey that he had planned (he was married to the daughter of Henry I of England). No final settlement was reached with the Church until the princes forced the issue and dictated imperial policy.

In the ecclesiastical settlement of 1122, the famous Concordat of Worms, Henry V renounced the practice of investing bishops with the clerical symbols of ring and staff. The Pope permitted imperial investiture with the *regalia* (worldly goods pertaining to the bishop's office). The investiture was to take place before the bishop was consecrated, thus assuring the Emperor of a previous oath of fealty from the bishop. Moreover, clerical elections in Germany were to be carried out in the presence of the Emperor (or his representatives), thus giving him an opportunity to exercise a strong influence over the decisions. In Italy and Burgundy, the Emperor retained less power; consecration was to take place *before* the *regalia* were conferred, and the Emperor could not attend clerical elections. The Concordat of Worms was a compromise that in effect ended the Investiture Struggle, despite its failure to settle many other issues.

The Investiture Controversy: Aftermath

As a result of this struggle, Germany had become feudalized. The princes and other nobles acted on the pretext that there was no king between 1076 and 1106, since the Pope had deposed him. They extended their powers, increasing the number of their dependents, and administering their land without reference to the monarchy. Feudal castles multiplied and became centers of administrative districts; free peasants fell into serfdom; the absence of central authority drove lesser nobles to become dependent on greater—in short, the familiar feudalizing process that had gone on in ninth- and tenth-century France now was operating in eleventh- and early twelfth-century Germany.

The princes had many assets in addition to their great allodial holdings. They employed *ministeriales* of their own, had a variety of vassals bound to them by feudal ties, and increased their power by combining and pyramiding their monastic "advocacies." The royal government did not extend outside the royal domains. The aristocracy were the "lords of the land," and their lands were their own. The foundations of the future German territorial principalities and of what is known as German *particularism* had been laid.

In Italy, the Investiture Controversy had seen the rise of the Norman kingdom of the south and had also been responsible for the growth of communes in the north. The communes had begun as sworn associations of lesser nobles, who banded together to resist the power of the local bishops. In Lombardy, the communes were favored by Gregory VII, and they took advantage of his support to usurp the powers of municipal government. In Tuscany, where the ruling house was pro-papal, the communes allied themselves with the Emperor, who granted them their liberties by charter. Thus, in Germany, the Crown faced a newly entrenched aristocracy; in Italy, it faced a new society of powerful urban communes.

The German nobles now controlled the election of the emperor. In 1138, they chose Conrad of Hohenstaufen, a Swabian prince, who became Emperor Conrad III (1138-1152). In so doing, they passed over another claimant, Henry the Proud, Duke of Bavaria and Saxony and Marquis of Tuscany in Italy, a member of the powerful Welf family. Because of their ancestral estate, the Hohenstaufens were often known as Waiblings; in Italian, Waibling became Ghibelline and Welf became Guelf. Thus, in the first half of the twelfth century, the Guelf-Ghibelline, or Welf-Hohenstaufen, feud—one of the most famous, lasting, and portentous in history—got under way. Henry the Proud, the Welf leader, refused homage to Conrad III; Conrad, in turn, deprived him of Saxony and Bavaria. Once more feudal warfare raged in Germany.

Frederick Barbarossa

In 1152, there came to the throne of this sadly divided Germany Frederick I Hohenstaufen (1152-1190), called Barbarossa ("red-beard"), who reorganized and rebuilt the monarchy. Using the Roman law as the source for his arguments, Frederick defended the power of the Empire against the Church, declaring that he was the lawful heir of the lands and titles that Charlemagne had won by conquest, and not merely king by God's grace. Frederick could not rely upon the great churchmen as administrators, as his predecessors had; the Investiture Controversy had made that impossible. Since his own landed possessions in Germany were not great enough to give him a basis for a full restoration of royal power, he focused his attention on Italy with its greater wealth, and on Burgundy, both of which were near his native Swabia.

Frederick married the heiress to Burgundy in 1156, and took possession of this great province, which had slipped out of imperial control during the Investiture Controversy. He made Switzerland the strategic center of his policy, since it was adjacent to Burgundy and Swabia and since it controlled the Alpine passes into Italy. For the first time, Germany, North Italy (Lombardy), and Burgundy were firmly united. Frederick tried to build in Swabia the sort of compact, well-run royal domain that the Capetians enjoyed in the Île de France. But the new royal power could be based only on feudal suzerainty over co-operative great vassals in Germany, and on an alliance with the North Italian communes—a pattern not unlike the one that Philip Augustus had worked out in France.

Frederick Barbarossa made six trips to Italy. He intervened first at Rome, where,

Frederick Barbarossa (1123-1190) portrayed as a crusader. From a Bavarian manuscript of 1188.

in 1143, a commune had risen up in protest against papal rule. The leader of the commune, Arnold of Brescia, strongly favored the Church's return to apostolic poverty and simplicity. Barbarossa won papal good will by offering the Pope assistance not only against Arnold but also against the Normans and against a Byzantine threat to southern Italy. He was crowned emperor in Rome in 1155, after a famous argument over whether he would hold the Pope's bridle and stirrup as well as kiss his foot (Frederick lost). At the Pope's request, the Emperor hanged and burned Arnold, whose death he is said to have regretted. The Pope, however, soon reached an accommodation with the Normans, and quarreled with Frederick once more (1157).

The Struggle
with the Italian Towns

Frederick returned to Italy in 1158 for the special purpose of subduing the leading North Italian commune, Milan. At Roncaglia (1158) he held a diet that was designed to define his *regalia*—that is, the rights of the emperor in the Italian towns. During the past three hundred years, these old imperial rights had been passed from the Frankish counts to the bishops, and had then been seized from the bishops by the communes. At stake were such matters as appointing dukes and counts, coining money, collecting a special tax to support the imperial army, and collecting customs-dues and other taxes. Although Frederick did not necessarily intend to resume exercising the *regalia*, he wanted it recognized that they really belonged to him, and that he alone could grant them to others. He was also prepared to appoint imperial officials "with the consent of the people" in those towns he did not trust; elsewhere he left the choice to the communes themselves.

But the Pope opposed this consolidation of imperial power, and so did the Lombard League of communes, headed by Milan. Frederick was forced into war against the Lombard League and the papacy. Although he defeated the Pope and occupied Rome in 1168, a devastating plague forced him to retreat. Then he was utterly defeated by the Lombard League at Legnano in 1176. In 1177, at Venice, Frederick reached an agreement with the Pope, and in 1183 he made the Peace of Constance with the Lombard towns.

The towns kept the *regalia* within their own walls; but outside the walls they retained only those rights which they had already purchased, or might in the future buy, from the Emperor. After free election by those towns which possessed the right, communal officials were to take an oath of fealty to the Emperor. Frederick retained the special tax to support the imperial army and recognized the Lombard League as a legitimate organization. The League paid a large sum of money in return for this peace. Although Frederick had made concessions of self-government to the communes, he had succeeded in establishing his claims as feudal suzerain.

The Peace of Constance enabled the Emperor to assert himself strongly in central Italy, where he established a direct imperial government rather than a feudal government, as he had in the north. Finally, in 1186, Frederick married his son, Henry, to the heiress of Norman Sicily. This was to prove one of the most important dynastic marriages of the Middle Ages. The papal territories, now in the hands of a weak pope, were gravely threatened by this union between the heir to Germany and northern Italy and the heiress to southern Italy. When a strong pope again came to the throne, it was clear that he would have to fight against this strangulation of his temporal power.

Barbarossa's German Policies

In line with his policy of consolidating his strength to the south, Frederick Barbarossa made certain concessions to the German princes. His great Welf rival, Henry the Lion (son of Henry the Proud), for example, obtained the right to invest the bishops of several important sees. Moreover, Henry was the leader of a great wave of German eastward expansion into the Slavic lands across the Elbe, where he ruled independently of his imperial overlord. He married the daughter of Henry II of England, received envoys from the Byzantine emperor, and conducted an almost independent foreign policy. By the 1160's Frederick was gradually beginning to counter this Welf threat by building up his own estates in Swabia and elsewhere. Then, when Frederick ran into trouble in Italy and needed reinforcements, Henry tried to bargain with the Emperor, and in general showed that he was not a loyal vassal. Frederick, in turn, determined to assert his authority as suzerain and punish Henry the Lion.

This he did by the same means that Philip Augustus had used against King John. He received complaints against Henry from his vassals, summoned Henry into the royal court to answer these complaints, and, when Henry refused, declared him contumacious and deprived him of his property (1180). The great territorial possessions of the Welf family were now broken up and divided among other smaller princes. The very act of parceling them out instead of adding them to the royal domain shows how feudalized Germany had become. Frederick could not hold onto these lands as Philip Augustus had held onto Normandy because he simply did not control his vassals as effectively as the French King did.

In the same year (1180), Frederick's immediate vassals were recognized as princes of the Empire. This step gave formal recognition to the new feudal order in Germany, by creating a new class that was jealous of its prerogatives. Other seeds of future crisis had been sown by Frederick's reliance on the resources of Italy, where resentment against German rule was strong, and especially by his tight organization of central Italy and his alliance with the Normans, both of which threatened the popes.

In 1190, Frederick was drowned in a river in Asia Minor while he was on the Third Crusade (see below, p. 356). His death in a far-off land, and his great achievements, led to the legend that he was not dead, but simply asleep in a mountain cave, with his great red beard flowing over the table on which his arm rested. Some day "the old Emperor" would come back, bringing glory and union to Germany. So Frederick joined King Arthur and Charlemagne's mighty peer, Holger the Dane, as heroes whom their people could not bear to lose.

Consequences of Henry VI's Sicilian Marriage

Barbarossa's son, Henry VI (1190-1197), changed the hitherto limited concept of the imperial role in the West. When Henry married Constance, the heiress of Sicily, he inherited an extraordinary kingdom. This kingdom had been built up in less than two centuries by the descendants of a small band of Norman adventurers, who in the early eleventh century had taken Apulia and Calabria (the heel and the toe of Italy) from the Byzantine Greeks. By 1091, the Normans had seized Sicily from the Moslems. Their great Roger II, who had been crowned King of Sicily in 1130, was an ally of the papacy. Ruling over a

Tomb of Duke Henry the Lion and his wife, Mathilde, in the cathedral in Brunswick, Germany (from about 1230-1250).

mixed population of Catholics, Orthodox Greeks, and Moslems, the small Norman upper class tolerated all faiths, and patronized and assimilated the Byzantine and Moslem cultures. Characteristically, they issued official documents in Arabic and Greek as well as in Latin.

The Norman kings of Sicily demonstrated the usual Norman gift for government. Ruling as absolute monarchs, and living the luxurious lives of Oriental potentates at their splendid capital of Palermo, they traded with the entire Mediterranean world. Their administration was professional, not feudal. The members of the *curia regis* were not hereditary vassals, but appointees of the king. Royal officials called justiciars gave justice to the provinces, and royal chamberlains supervised local financial administration. The army combined Arab professionalism with feudal Norman practice. It was this heritage to which Henry VI succeeded.

But Richard the Lionhearted of England united with the German Welfs and the papacy to back a rival to Henry for control over the Norman Sicilian kingdom. Henry dissolved the alliance through skillful use of his capture of Richard (1192) as a diplomatic weapon. He held Richard for ransom and applied pressure on Richard's German allies. He then forced Richard to become his vassal and used the ransom money to finance a campaign in Sicily. Sicily was won by 1194, and Henry refused to do homage to the Pope for it. Now Henry planned to acquire the Byzantine Empire, against which the Normans had waged intermittent warfare since the early eleventh century. He had secured the homage of the kings of Cyprus and Armenia, and he was building up a fleet to invade the eastern Mediterranean, when he died suddenly in 1197.

It was Henry VI's union of Germany, not only with Sicily, but also with the traditional Norman ambitions in the Mediterranean, that widened the hitherto limited western concept of empire—and that was to have such grave consequences for the structure that Frederick Barbarossa had reared so painfully. Henry's Sicilian policy required him to make further concessions to the German princes. He made still more during his efforts to get them to recognize the hereditary right of his son, Frederick, to succeed him, a problem that would not even have arisen in England or France. In this attempt, Henry offered the princes the same hereditary rights in their own fiefs that he asked of them. At Henry's death, then, the relationships between Crown and princes, and between Empire and Papacy, were thoroughly unsettled.

A protracted period of crisis followed, from 1197 to 1215, in which the rights of Henry's infant son, Frederick, were for long neglected. At first, the German princes rallied around Henry's brother, Philip of Swabia, who became king in 1198. But intervention by the new pope, Innocent III (1198-1216), and by Richard the Lionhearted touched off a new German civil war. Determined to destroy the German-Sicilian connection, which threatened to catch the papal lands in central Italy in an imperial pincers, Innocent revived the claim of Gregory VII that no emperor could rule without papal confirmation. He did everything he could to stir up trouble against Philip, who put forth the counter-thesis that an emperor duly elected by the princes was emperor with or without papal consent. Richard the Lionhearted, anxious to see an anti-French monarch on the German throne, backed his nephew, the son of Henry the Lion, the Welf Otto of Brunswick, who had been brought up in England. In order to get papal support, which Innocent extended to him in 1200, Otto sacrificed all that the Empire had won in the entire Investiture Controversy. Naturally, Philip Augustus of France backed Philip of Swabia, the enemy of the English-Welf coalition. The victory of Philip Augustus over John of England in Normandy

(1204) strengthened the cause of Philip of Swabia.

Even Innocent III was preparing to accept Philip of Swabia when Philip was assassinated in 1208. The princes elected Otto emperor, but in his new position, once he had been crowned by the Pope in 1209, Otto began to act like a Hohenstaufen instead of a protégé of the papacy. He undertook to conquer Sicily, the very thing Innocent III wanted most to prevent. So in 1210 the Pope excommunicated his old candidate, and turned to the young Frederick Hohenstaufen, son of Henry VI. Supported by the Pope and given money by Philip Augustus of France, Frederick reorganized the Hohenstaufen party in Germany, and was crowned king in 1212. When Otto was defeated at Bouvines by Philip Augustus in 1214, Frederick's position became more secure.

Frederick II

But to establish his authority, Frederick II (1212-1250) had to make more concessions to the princes, in order to win them from Otto, and to the Pope. He had to give up control of the German church, exactly as Otto had done, and he promised not to reunite Germany and Sicily. In 1215, Innocent III seemed to have won a resounding victory. Yet the possibilities for a reconstruction of the German monarchy lay open to a ruler who would devote himself to re-establishing his position in Germany. Frederick II, however, chose to give his attention to Sicily. It was in that civilized society that he felt at home; he disliked Germany and spent only nine years there.

Frederick II is perhaps the most interesting monarch of medieval history. Brilliantly intelligent and highly cultivated, he spoke Arabic and Greek as well as half a dozen other languages, took a deep interest in scientific experiment, collected wild animals and women, and wrote poetry in the Italian vernacular. He patronized the arts, wrote a great book on the sport of falconry, and was a superb politician. He was cynical, hard-boiled, a sound diplomat, an administrator with capacity and vision, and a statesman in the imperial mold, with his father's vision of a Mediterranean empire.

It was Germany's misfortune, however, that the base for his operations had to be his beloved Sicily. The Germans felt more and more that they had no stake in his empire. It was Frederick's own misfortune that he encountered, after the death of Innocent III, three successive popes—Honorius III (1216-1227), Gregory IX (1227-1241), and Innocent IV (1243-1254)—who were not only consistently determined to prevent him from achieving his aims but entirely competent to fight him on even terms. It is little wonder that Frederick could never extend to Germany the centralized administration he built in southern Italy, and that German particularism, already blossoming, came into full flower. Frederick's reign condemned Germany to six hundred years of disunity.

In 1220, Frederick obtained for his son, Henry, election as king of Germany and a promise that Henry would be the next emperor. To do this he granted great privileges to the bishops and abbots. These ecclesiastical princes were already elected without imperial interference. Now Frederick abandoned his right to set up mints and customs stations in their territories, together with royal rights of justice. He promised to exclude from imperial cities any serfs who might run away from church lands to try their fortunes in the towns, and he agreed to build no new towns or fortresses on church lands. Thus he made the mistake that the French and English kings had avoided from the first: he acted against the towns, failing to see that they were his natural allies. In 1231, the secular princes exacted from Frederick a privilege parallel to that which he had already granted to the great church magnates. As

North Sea

Miles 0 — 200

Danzig

PRUSSIA

POMERANIA

POLAND

Lübeck
Hamburg
Bremen

FRIESLAND

SAXONY

BRANDENBURG

Magdeburg

SILESIA

Meuse R.

Weser R.

Elbe R.

HARZ MTS.

Goslar

KINGDOM

Oder R.

Vistula R.

LOWER

Aachen
Cologne
THURINGIA

Frankfurt

Elbe R.

Prague

LORRAINE

Rhine R.

Trier
Mainz
Worms
PALATINATE
FRANCONIA

Bamberg
Würzburg
Main R.

BOHEMIA

MORAVIA

OF

UPPER
LORRAINE

Strasbourg

Saale R.

Ratisbon

Danube R.

Augsburg

AUSTRIA

Saône R.

SWABIA

GERMANY

BAVARIA

Vienna

Constance

STYRIA

K. OF BURGUNDY
(K. OF ARLES)

A L P S

CARINTHIA

TYROL

CARNIOLA

Trieste

Drava R.

Danube R.

HUNGARY

Rhône R.

Legnano ×

Brescia

Milan

LOMBARDY

Pavia

Venice

Po R.

Adige R.

Ferrara

Alessandria
Roncaglia
Genoa
Canossa
Bologna
Ravenna

OF

Zara

Avignon
Arles

ITALY

ROMAGNA

Ancona

Adriatic

SERBIA

Pisa
Florence
Siena
TUSCANY
Assisi

Ragusa

Sea

CORSICA
(To Pisa)

PAPAL
Rome
Tagliacozzo
Anagni

STATES

Bari

SARDINIA
(To Pisa and Genoa)

APULIA

Naples
Amalfi
Salerno
Melfi
Taranto

KINGDOM
OF THE
TWO SICILIES
(Hohenstaufen, 1194)

CALABRIA

Palermo

SICILY

Syracuse

MEDIEVAL GERMANY AND ITALY

AT DEATH OF FREDERICK II, 1250

Boundary of the Holy Roman Empire
Kingdom of the Two Sicilies
Papal States
Claimed by Papacy
Venetian possessions
× Battle sites

Mediterranean   Sea

g.

296

regarded royal justice, mints, runaway serfs, and the rest, the lay lords now enjoyed the same sort of rights as the clerical. Both the secular and the ecclesiastical princes had become virtually independent potentates.

In startling contrast is Frederick's administrative work in Sicily. Here, like William the Conqueror in England, Frederick assumed royal title to all property. In the Constitutions of Melfi, of 1231, he imposed his own completely centralized monarchical form of government upon his Italian subjects. Some of this centralization was a reassertion of the policies and programs of Frederick's Sicilian ancestor, Roger II. Much of the rest came from Roman law, with its extraordinary lofty conception of the emperor's position. Feudal custom was wiped out, and trial by battle was forbidden as antiquated and absurd. At Naples, Frederick founded a university, which became a state training school in which officials could be grounded in the Roman law. Frederick's army and navy were organized on a paid basis rather than on a feudal basis. Finances were regularized and modernized, and an imperial bureaucracy collected tariffs on incoming and outgoing merchandise. State monopolies like those at Byzantium (see Chapter VI) controlled certain key industries, such as silk. Frederick became rich and powerful—the nearest approach to a modern national monarch that the West produced in the Middle Ages.

Frederick II and the Papacy

Yet the keynote of Frederick II's reign was his tremendous and ultimately unsuccessful conflict with the papacy. The conflict began in the 1220's. During the Emperor's absence from Italy on a crusade (see Chapter IX for details), the Pope's newly hired mercenary armies attacked his southern Italian lands. When Frederick returned, he was able to make peace tempo-

rarily. But he soon created further trouble. After he had defeated the Lombard towns in 1237 for refusing to keep the Peace of Constance, he announced a new plan to extend imperial administration to all Italy, including Rome. So in 1239 the Pope excommunicated him, and war was resumed. Violent propaganda pamphlets were published and circulated by both sides. The Pope called Frederick a heretic who was trying to found a new religion. Frederick called the Pope a hypocrite, and urged all monarchs in Europe to unite against the pretensions of the Church. Hemmed in at Rome by the encroaching imperial system, the Pope summoned a church council, presumably to depose Frederick. But Frederick's fleet captured the entire council of more than one hundred high churchmen. Just as Frederick was about to enter Rome itself, Pope Gregory IX died (1241); Frederick tried to install a new pope favorable to himself, but failed. The new pope, Innocent IV, fled from Italy, summoned a council to Lyons in France (1244), and deposed Frederick. There followed five more years of struggle. Frederick died in 1250, before the conflict had been settled.

After Frederick's death, the papacy pursued his descendants with fury. His son, Conrad IV, died in 1254, leaving a young son who was called "Conradino," little Conrad. In 1255, Frederick's illegitimate son, the gifted and capable Manfred, gained control of Sicily, which the popes had been trying to give to the second son of Henry III of England. But in 1266 a long-maturing papal plan succeeded. St. Louis' brother, the ruthless and able Charles of Anjou, was brought into Italy as the papal candidate for the southern territories. He defeated and killed Manfred, and established himself as king in the south. When Conradino, aged fifteen, led an army south from Germany to combat the cruel and tyrannical régime of Charles, he was defeated and captured at the battle of Tagliacozzo in 1268, and soon afterward was executed at Naples. Angevin rule continued in Naples until 1435, although the Aragonese took Sicily in 1282.

In 1268, the breed of the Hohenstaufen was extinct. The Holy Roman Empire, begun by Frederick Barbarossa, and given an Italian rather than a German base by Henry VI and Frederick II, had been destroyed by the papacy. Yet within forty years of Charles of Anjou's entry into Italy as the instrument of papal vengeance, Charles' grand-nephew Philip the Fair was to puncture the inflated temporal claims of the papacy and take it off to Avignon.

In Germany, the imperial throne remained vacant from 1254 to 1272. The princes consolidated their power during this Interregnum by taking advantage of the large grants made by rival candidates to the throne, all foreigners, in the hope of receiving their support. But the princes were pleased for a time not to have an emperor; their usurpation of rights that had formerly belonged to the monarchy was now well on its way to completion. Meanwhile, the old links with Italy were virtually broken, and the earlier form of the imperial idea vanished. The allodial nobility, the investiture controversy, and the preoccupation with Italy had ensured that the princes would emerge as the real rulers of Germany.

V: Conclusion

Our examination of the history of three western peoples through these centuries of their medieval development suggests a preliminary set of explanations for the "stereotypes" about national character with which we began this chapter. Already, at the beginning of the fourteenth century, we can see, in the contrasting institutional development of France, England, and Germany, the emergence of national units somehow recognizable as the ancestors of the nations we know.

In France, the Capetian kings, beginning as relatively powerless and insignificant local lords, have extended the sway of their royal administration into the lands of their great vassals and created the institutions of a powerful centralized monarchy. The question of the English claims to large areas on the Continent remains to be settled in the grim struggle of the Hundred Years' War (see below, Chapter X). In England, on the other hand, the Norman conquerors have proved able to make the most of existing Anglo-Saxon institutions, and to superimpose effective feudal monarchy, while they and their Angevin successors have developed the common law, bringing not only money and power to the monarch but security to the subject.

Whereas in France the vassals are unaware of the danger to their position until it is too late, and are too divided by antagonism among themselves to unite in opposition to the monarch's aggressions, in England the vassals early recognize the need for presenting a united corporate opposition if they are to preserve their rights. And out of their opposition there have emerged the guarantees that limit the king: promises given in the first instance on behalf of the great vassals but later subject to much broader interpretation. By the early fourteenth century, out of the king's need to obtain assent for taxation and out of the custom of consultation between king and subject there is beginning to emerge Parliament, "incomparably the greatest gift of the English people to the civilization of the world."

In Germany, the monarchy, which effectively asserts itself in the earlier period, is fatally weakened by the prevalence of an allodial rather than a feudal nobility, which cooperates with the papacy in an assault upon the German administrative system. After the Investiture Controversy, once the country has been feudalized, the monarchy fails to realize, as both the French and the English have done, the advantages of an alliance with the towns, and is further weakened by the Sicilian marriage of Henry VI, the shift of the center of gravity to Sicily, and the virtual abandonment of power in Germany to the great princes.

Perhaps these rapid summaries help us begin to see through the fog of unfamiliar ideas and obsolete conceptions the first faint outlines of the France, England, and Germany we know in our own day.

Reading Suggestions on the West in the Later Middle Ages

(Asterisk indicates paperbound edition.)

FRANCE: GENERAL ACCOUNTS

A. Tilley, *Mediaeval France* (Cambridge Univ. Press, 1922). A collection of uneven essays, useful mainly for political history.

J. Evans, *Life in Mediaeval France* (Oxford Univ. Press, 1925). A good picture of medieval French society.

FRANCE: SPECIAL STUDIES

J. W. Thompson, *The Development of the French Monarchy under Louis VI le Gros* (Univ. of Chicago Press, 1895). A scholarly treatment.

A. Luchaire, *Social France at the Time of Philip Augustus* (Peter Smith, 1929). A well-written account, perhaps overemphasizing the seamy side of life.

A. R. Kelly, *Eleanor of Aquitaine and the Four Kings* (Harvard Univ. Press, 1950; *Vintage). A learned and lively treatment, the best in English.

ENGLAND: GENERAL ACCOUNTS

A. L. Poole, *From Domesday Book to Magna Carta, 1087-1216* (Clarendon, 1951); and F. M. Powicke, *The Thirteenth Century, 1216-1307* (Clarendon, 1953). These books are recent accounts by the most authoritative scholars.

D. M. Stenton, *English Society in the Early Middle Ages*, and A. R. Myers, *England in the Late Middle Ages* (* Penguin) are two useful introductory volumes in the "Pelican History of England" written at a popular level.

H. M. Cam, *England before Elizabeth* (Hutchinson's University Library, 1950), and F. M. Powicke, *Mediaeval England, 1066-1485* (Home University Library, 1948). Excellent short summaries.

ENGLAND: SPECIAL STUDIES

B. Wilkinson, *The Constitutional History of England, 1216-1399* (Longmans, Green, 1948-1952). Uses the latest scholarly investigations of a much-debated subject.

F. M. Powicke, *King Henry III and The Lord Edward* (Clarendon, 1947). A model of scholarship.

GERMANY: GENERAL ACCOUNTS

G. Barraclough, *The Origins of Modern Germany* (Blackwell, 1949). The best general treatment of mediaeval Germany in English.

J. Bryce, *The Holy Roman Empire*, rev. ed. (Macmillan, frequently reprinted). A brilliant undergraduate essay, whose conclusions have been somewhat modified by more recent investigation. Still a masterful synthesis.

GERMANY: SPECIAL STUDIES

G. Barraclough, *Mediaeval Germany, 911-1250*, 2 vols. (Blackwell, 1938). A series of scholarly essays by German historians, conveniently translated and commented upon.

T. F. Tout, *The Empire and the Papacy, 918-1273*, 8th ed. (Rivingtons, 1924). A standard work, though somewhat out-of-date in details.

J. W. Thompson, *Feudal Germany* (Univ. of Chicago Press, 1928). The only work on the subject in English.

E. Kantorowicz, *Frederick the Second, 1194-1250* (R. R. Smith, 1931). Scholarly and imaginative treatment; some scholars deplore the imagination, but none can deny the scholarship.

SOURCES

D. C. Douglas and G. W. Greenaway, eds., *English Historical Documents, 1042-1189* (Oxford Univ. Press, 1953). Volume II of a monumental series now in the course of publication.

The Chronicle of Jocelin of Brakelund, H. E. Butler, trans. (Nelson, 1949). Life in a medieval English monastery.

HISTORICAL FICTION

W. Bryher, *The Fourteenth of October* (Pantheon, 1952). A good novel about the Norman conquest of England.

H. Muntz, *The Golden Warrior* (Scribner's, 1949). Another well-written, historically sound novel of the Norman conquest of England.

Z. Oldenbourg, *The World Is Not Enough* (Pantheon, 1948). A highly successful effort to recapture in fiction the life, violence and all, of twelfth-century France.

Medieval Civilization in the West

CHAPTER VIII

I: Introduction

THE MEN AND WOMEN who lived between 500 and 1500 did not think of themselves as living in the Middle Ages or as being "medieval." The terms "Middle Ages" and "medieval" grow out of the attitudes held by scholars and men of letters in the years after the Renaissance and Reformation of the sixteenth century. These early modern men greatly admired the achievements of the Greeks and Romans, and they admired their own achievements almost as much. The centuries in between, roughly the thousand years from the fall of Rome to the discovery of America, they regarded as a kind of trough or depression between the great peaks of "ancient" and "modern." The Middle Ages seemed to them a period of disorder, ignorance, superstition, barbarism—in short, the "Gothic" night between the sunshine of the ancient and the modern days.

The nineteenth century, especially the Romantic generation of the early 1800's, showed a revived respect and admiration for the Middle Ages. But this revival did not destroy the old disparaging view of things medieval. To this day many of us, especially those of us who are of Protestant or secular upbringing, tend to think of the Middle Ages as a low state of human development. Yet most of us know vaguely

Opposite. THE VIRGIN WITH APOSTLES, *detail; window in the cathedral of Le Mans, France, about 1150. This early example of medieval stained glass suggests the astonishing colors of the medium. While it is not so delicate as some of the later Gothic glass, it conveys the solid, massive qualities of Romanesque art.*

that medieval cathedrals like those of Paris, Chartres, or Canterbury are very great human achievements—great even in engineering or economic terms. How were such achievements possible in the Middle Ages?

They were possible because the Middle Ages were one of the great times of flowering in the West. As we saw in Chapter V, the first few medieval centuries in some measure deserve the old tag of "Dark Ages." But by the beginning of the eleventh century the West is well on its way to that particular civilization called medieval. The culture, the "style," of the Middle Ages builds slowly up to a peak in the thirteenth century and then decays during the next two centuries. In Chapter X we shall note the process of hardening and sterility in the political life of France, England, and Germany, and in the present chapter we shall also find it obvious in art and philosophy. But, though the fourteenth and fifteenth centuries are full of civil strife and are in many ways a period of economic decline, they are also full of signs of renewal, even, if you like, of "progress." The "modern" emerges from the "medieval" with no such general breakdown as was recorded in Chapter V.

We may, then, look at the Middle Ages in two ways. If we look at them as a fully rounded culture, we see slow early growth, a peak, and a falling off. If we look at many aspects of their economic and political life, and indeed at some aspects of their thought, notably their natural science, we see them as a preparation, a seedbed, for our own society.

The Material Basis

The material basis of medieval life —that is, its basis in politics and economics —was adequate to sustain art and letters, the intellectual and emotional life of high culture. First of all, with the ending of the raids of the Northmen, the West was for centuries safe from outside attack. Indeed, with the eleventh century the West was able to take the offensive, and in the Crusades (see Chapter IX) the West could even try to turn the tables by invading the lands of Islam, which a few centuries earlier had been the source of some of the most menacing invasions. The Crusades might be regarded as a phase of western expansion or imperialism, but they were not in the long run successful imperialism. The West was simply not strong enough to do then what individual western states like France and Britain later did—actually conquer and hold for a long time parts of the Islamic world. But that the Crusades should have had even a temporary and incomplete success shows how much the West had strengthened itself since the low point of the Dark Ages.

Second, the feudal-manorial society of the Middle Ages gradually and partially solved the problem of large-scale organization that had been left as a challenge by the breakdown of the Roman Empire. This evolution can be traced in the mutually dependent fields of economics and politics. In economics, the almost self-sustaining manor gradually became a group of free or almost free agricultural workers producing for a money market. But we must not exaggerate. Not until today in America do we get the phenomenon of a farmer who sells nearly everything he raises and who buys nearly everything he uses. Only yesterday, with the housewife's "preserves," root-cellars, home-cured meats, homespun clothes, and even homemade shoes, the old-fashioned American farmer bought comparatively little. Long after the Middle Ages, the European farmer or peasant was still largely self-sustaining.

But the amount of goods produced for sale by the farmer did increase in the Middle Ages. On what he managed to save, which was often only a small sum, the peasant of western Europe was frequently able to buy from his lord exemption from this or that manorial duty, until at last he was no longer a serf. The process of emancipation of the serfs went on for centuries, and it ran different courses in different countries and regions. It was sometimes begun at the initiative of the lord himself, who needed ready money, and who often stood to gain by converting the complex manorial dues in money, labor, and produce into a straight economic rent. As early as 1400, the process had gone a long way in the West, without any formal enactment by governmental authority of the kind familiar to us in Lincoln's mass freeing of the slaves in 1863.

The evolution of the manor from self-sustaining agriculture to production for the market did not create a society that was made up entirely of independent peasant proprietors, although many families did attain such a status. Other peasants became either tenant farmers who paid money rent, or what in France were called *métayers*. *Métayage* was a tenure not unlike share-cropping, in which the landlord supplies tools and seeds as well as land, and the proceeds of the crop are divided between landlord and tenant. Still other peasants became agricultural laborers working for a money wage.

Admirers of the Middle Ages have certainly exaggerated the extent to which the manor took care of its own and gave each member, no matter how humble, a place of security. Disease in an age of the most rudimentary medical knowledge, famine in an age of poor transportation and feeble central government, and undernourishment in an age of fairly primitive technology meant that life was harsh and difficult for most people. There was an enormous difference between the material basis of our life and that of the western medieval man. In the Middle Ages the average life span, reduced especially by very high infant mortality, can hardly have been half that of mid-twentieth-century America, where it is nearly seventy years. It is probable, more-over, that approximately nine families had to work at producing food so that one family could do something else. In modern America one food-producing family can release at least five or six to do something else. It must be noted, however, that in terms of total economic production, measured perhaps most easily in such terms as available "horsepower," the sixteenth, seventeenth, and most of the eighteenth centuries were hardly superior to the medieval centuries. In command over material things, the great watershed in the West, as we shall see, was the late eighteenth century, in what has still to be called an industrial and scientific "revolution."

The Towns

Those who did the "something else" in the Middle Ages were the feudal nobility, the clergy (though village priests were often part-time farmers), and the townsmen. Throughout the Middle Ages the townsmen grew more numerous, which in itself is evidence of the rising productivity of medieval agriculture. The town was always hard to integrate into the feudal-manorial system. Townsmen could not be fitted so readily into the routine of shared labor as could peasants, and their mere numbers made them harder to control. In addition, the towns produced a class of people who depended for their livelihood on trade, craft production, and the beginnings of a credit system—this was the *bourgeoisie* or middle class we still hear so much about. The bourgeois merchants, especially, had contacts with a world beyond the purely local one.

Consequently, the towns were constantly quarreling with their feudal overlords. One of the central threads of medieval history is the process by which townsmen organized themselves politically and appealed to the top feudal authority of a given area, to a king or a duke, for a charter granting them special rights and privileges (see Chapter VII). The charter would set up the town as a corporate body, would allow it to hold a market, to have its own courts and its own local government, and would grant it exemption from feudal dues. In short, the charter would grant it something like the status of a modern municipality. Although these *communes,* as the privileged towns were called in France, the Low Countries, and Italy, were legally integrated into the fabric of feudalism, they tended to remain outside it and indeed hostile to it. Our modern assumption that kings belong with nobles *against* commoners is a product of the English Revolution of the 1640's and the French Revolution of 1789. It does not always make sense in the Middle Ages. In the last chapter we saw the French bourgeoisie allying itself with the central royal authority against the feudal landowning nobility to undermine the feudal-manorial system and to foreshadow the modern state.

The Growth of Central Authority

Thus the chief *economic* and *social* factors in the changing material basis of medieval life are the evolution of the manor, the growth of trade, and the partial emancipation of serfs and townsmen. The chief *political* factor is the development of a central governmental authority that deals directly with the individual, rather than through the complex feudal chain of authorities. The townsmen are already becoming "citizens" or "subjects" of a central government; they are already paying taxes instead of *feudal dues.* Chapter VII has shown that in England and France the central authority was national; it was the Crown. In Germany and Italy the effective authorities were regional or sectional, rather than national—the governments of Brandenburg and Austria, for example, or of Milan and other Italian communes. In Spain, as we shall see later (Chapter X), the central authorities were the crowns of Castile and Aragon.

In the modern world, central authorities are run largely by individuals who are *professionals* in the work of administration, and who hold their offices by appointment or election. In the Middle Ages, however, they were often run by individuals who were *amateurs,* and who held their positions by virtue of hereditary feudal status. Particularly in the earlier medieval world, most of the complex work of governing was carried on by men who thought of themselves not as employees of the government or as bureaucrats but as links in a chain of authority ultimately set up by God. Gradually, through the centuries from the eleventh to the sixteenth, central authorities turned to paid professional employees instead of to quasi-independent feudal authorities.

These last few paragraphs have anticipated the emergence of the modern political and economic state. The emergence was relatively complete in England, France, and West Europe generally by the sixteenth century, but it was much less complete in the rest of Europe. The material basis for the medieval culture we are about to study was, in fact, the product of a society that had already begun to emerge from Carolingian disintegration and feudal reconstruction. The West was part of the way along toward modernization in economic and political life before medieval culture came to full flower.

II: The Medieval Church

Medieval and Modern Christianity Contrasted

It is easy to write—and read—the commonplace that the Christian faith as embodied in the Church was supreme in the medieval West. But we moderns, no matter how good Christians we may be, need to exercise our imaginations to understand just what that statement means. For the medieval man, God made the weather, as he made everything else. God could and did interfere with the regular processes of nature. A lightning bolt was not an electrical discharge that could be simulated in the laboratory; it was an instrument in the hand of God, an instrument with which he could strike down a sinner. For the masses, God with his thunderbolt differed little from old Jupiter or Thor with theirs. Although the educated minority no longer held this crude view, even they thought of God as somehow working directly on natural forces.

In medieval times Christianity occupied a place very different from the place it holds in our culture. The separation of Church and State is for most Americans today an accepted fact. And though we hardly permit a man to belong to no state, we do permit him to belong to no church. Moreover, we readily accept the existence of many mutually exclusive churches, the so-called "denominations." In the medieval West there was but one church, and everybody, save the Jews, belonged to it. The Jews were penalized, as for instance by being obliged to live in a separate quarter (ghetto), but they also commonly had the privilege of worship of their religion, and other privileges of status. Heretics like the Albigensians (see above, p. 264) repudiated

some specific measures or beliefs of the Church, but they were, so to speak, religious outlaws who were not to be allowed to exist peacefully in society. The spiritual power and the temporal power were indeed regarded in the West as in a sense "separate," but that sense is very different from ours. For the medieval man, religious governance of humankind and political governance were both necessary instruments of the divine scheme for maintaining human society; they were, in medieval terms, the "two swords" of God. They were wielded by different sets of God's human agents, and they were *both* necessary.

The question of which sword was in fact the greater sword on this earth was a major source of dispute in medieval times. This was the issue in the Investiture Controversy, in the conflict between Henry II and Becket, and in the conflict between Philip the Fair and Boniface VIII (see Chapter VII). The question was not decided in medieval times; perhaps it has never really been decided. Certainly the spiritual power at times went so far as to claim that it was supreme. Here is a statement of Pope Innocent III in 1198:

The Creator of the universe set up two great luminaries in the firmament of heaven; the greater light to rule the day, the lesser light to rule the night. In the same way for the firmament of the universal Church, which is spoken of as heaven, he appointed two great dignities; the greater to bear rule over souls (these being, as it were, days), the lesser to bear rule over bodies (these being, as it were, nights). These dignities are the pontifical authority and the royal power. Furthermore, the moon derives her light from the sun, and is in truth inferior to the sun in both size and quality, in position as well as effect. In the same way the royal power derives its dignity from the pontifical authority: and the more closely it cleaves to

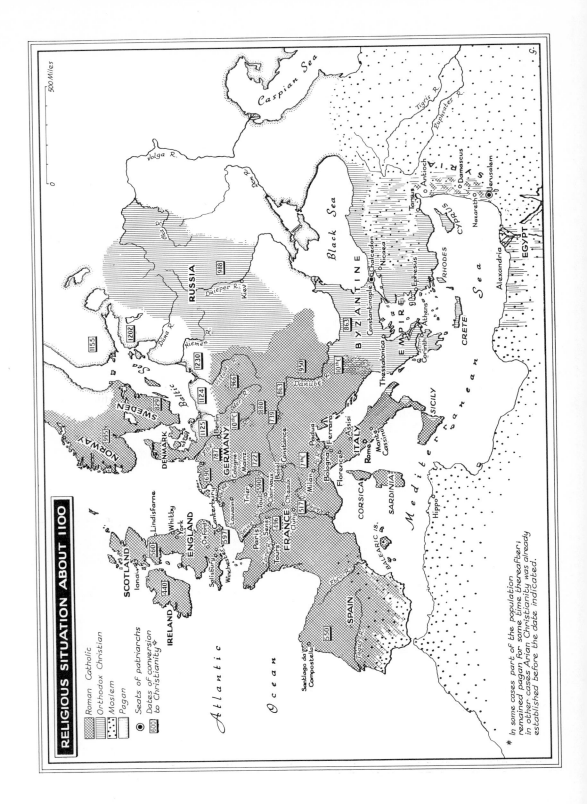

RELIGIOUS SITUATION ABOUT 1100

Roman Catholic
Orthodox Christian
Moslem
Pagan

● Seats of patriarchs
☐600☐ Dates of conversion to Christianity ✳

In some cases part of the population remained pagan for some time thereafter; in other cases Arian Christianity was already established before the date indicated.

✳

306

the sphere of that authority the less is the light with which it is adorned; the further it is removed, the more it increases in splendor.*

It is almost impossible to imagine a pope of Carolingian times making statements like these. The medieval Church, like medieval society as a whole, had to move beyond the disintegration of the Dark Ages; it had to develop its own organization into a wealthy, centralized, and powerful authority before it could use its great spiritual powers most effectively. Before we study the values, the ideals, of Christian life in the Middle Ages, we must study the *organization* of the Church which guided that life.

The Cluniac Reform Movement

The Church, like the State, sought to mold feudal-manorial society into something that was easier to control from the top—from Rome, and from the responsible agents of Rome who were the bishops, the archbishops, and the abbots. On the whole, this task was easier for the Church than for the State, and in fact it was pretty well accomplished by 1100. The base line from which the reform started we have sketched briefly in the preceding chapters. Simony, or the sale of church offices, frequent and open concubinage even among the clergy, control of church fiefs by laymen (the problem of lay investiture), corruption and decay of the originally strict Benedictine Rule, the loss of papal authority and prestige that followed the subjection of the papacy to local Roman politics—all were phases of the Church's involvement in the worldly scramble for wealth and power in the tenth century. The gap between Christian ideals and Christian practice had become too great for men who were at all sensitive to those ideals to bear. Reform

---

* *Documents of the Christian Church*, Henry Bettenson, ed. (New York, 1947), 157-158.

had to come, whether it came from within or from without.

It came, fortunately for the unity of western Christendom, from within. The reform movement was associated with the reformed Benedictine monastery founded in 910 at Cluny in France, and in particular with the great Cluniac reformer Hildebrand, who became Pope Gregory VII (1073-1085), the antagonist of the Emperor Henry IV in the investiture struggle. The Cluniac movement began as an attempt to restore the primitive simplicity and strict asceticism of St. Benedict's original Rule. Then Cluny and its affiliate monasteries, of which there were eventually more than three hundred, acted as a kind of organized pressure group, a catalyst or leaven for the whole process of clerical house-cleaning. Ultimately, the movement employed the full resources of the Church, from parish to papacy, and put through one of the most effective series of reforms in the history of the West.

The key reform was the definitive settlement, at the Lateran Synod of 1059, of the method of electing the pope. Soon the College of Cardinals was set up, a body of churchmen that was perpetuated constantly by regular appointments to vacancies. This body has continued to choose popes according to canonical rule ever since. Irregularities and rivalries of all sorts have indeed occurred since 1059; as we shall see, the Great Schism (1378-1417) produced two colleges of cardinals and two different lines of popes, the Avignonese line and the Roman line. But the chaotic conditions of the tenth century have never reappeared.

The victory of the reformers firmly established the principle of clerical celibacy. Although individual priests and monks have sometimes violated their vows of chastity since the eleventh century, these have been clear violations. Had it not been for the Cluniac movement, marriage of the lower clergy, in spite of the Latin tradition against it, might have taken root in the western Church as it did among the lower parish clergy in the eastern Orthodox Church. And if that had happened the Church in the West would probably not have been able to stand as firmly as it did against lay power and the temptations of localism and nationalism. Quite apart from the basic questions of theology, it is clear that the priest with children has more interests in the world of property rights and social prestige than the celibate priest has.

Against simony, the reformers had a comparable success; they made it a scandal, although they did not banish it entirely from this earth. With lay investiture we have already dealt in Chapter VII. Here again the reformers did not achieve perfect victory. But they met successfully the threat that was implicit in lay investiture, the threat that the Roman Catholic Church might dissolve into separate local or national churches with no more than vague international ties.

Significance of the Cluniac Movement

The Cluniac movement was the first of several great waves of reforming zeal that until the sixteenth century constantly renewed the spiritual strength of the Church without disrupting its organizational unity. The power of the medieval Church lay *both* in its other-worldly ideals *and* in its this-worldly skill in human government. Nothing is clearer evidence of this power than the Church's success in controlling these outbursts of desire to reform humanity, to have men and women everywhere and always behave like Christians.

Like almost all the great revivals of the Christian spirit, the Cluniac movement bore the stamp of Puritanism. Puritanism often relies on authoritarian rule, for it seems that the only way to get large groups of men to keep on denying the flesh for a long period of time is to police them. Perhaps the most striking thing about the Cluniac Order is not its revival of the strict Benedictine Rule but its enforcement of that rule through a centralized authority. The Abbot of Cluny was the theocratic ruler of the whole order. The daughter-houses enjoyed no real home rule; instead, they were held in firm obedience to the mother-house.

What happened to the Cluniac Order sets a pattern for later reforming orders. The ideal was poverty and humility; the result was riches and pride. By the twelfth century the Cluniac houses were becoming prodigiously wealthy, and their rule had relaxed. Perhaps this lapse was hastened by the very centralization of power in the mother-house and its abbot. Since everything depended on the personality of the ruler, a succession of weak or selfish abbots could do more harm than it would in an order that granted more home rule to the individual houses.

St. Bernard and the Cistercians

The Cluniac pattern of rigor followed by relaxation was repeated by the Cistercian Order. This order, an offshoot of the Benedictines, was founded at the very end of the eleventh century. The Cistercian pioneers built their monastery in a dismal, uncultivated waste at Cîteaux (Cistercium) in Burgundy, a site far from the distractions and temptations of worldly life. They set to work with the diligence of the first Benedictines, for whom hard work on the land was a prime need, and they eventually transformed the spot into a garden. The real founder of the Cistercian Order, however, was Bernard of Clairvaux (1098-1153), one of the greatest Christian leaders. In 1115, Bernard led a small band to Clairvaux, a nearby spot that was as unpromising as Cîteaux itself. From Clair-

Ruins of Fountains Abbey, Yorkshire, a great Cistercian house of the Middle Ages.

vaux he was to dominate his age in a way that we moderns, who so sharply separate in our minds political and spiritual rule, can hardly conceive.

St. Bernard not only upbraided clergymen for their laxity in observing ecclesiastical rules but also helped to organize a crusade to the Holy Land, advised the Kings of France, and chastened even the greatest feudal nobles. For example, the Duke of Aquitaine, the father of the famous Eleanor (see above, p. 262), had expelled the bishops from their sees. Bernard, after trying to win the Duke over in a conference, celebrated the Mass in his presence. Bearing aloft the sacred Host in the midst of the congregation, Bernard challenged the Duke to pit his will against God's. The Duke had armies, Bernard had none; but the Duke collapsed—literally, for he could not stand—and the bishops were restored.

The Cistercians, apparently warned by the overcentralization of the Cluniac system, gave the monasteries that were founded under their leadership genuine self-rule. As a result, their houses clung together far more successfully. Yet the Cistercians, too, failed to hold to the ideals of their founder. By the thirteenth century, the great Cistercian houses—Fountains Abbey in English Yorkshire, for instance, whose ruins are still impressive—were great and wealthy centers of agricultural and craft production. The expensive arts of architecture and sculpture were lavished on their buildings. They seem to have been places where men lived about as comfortably as they could in the Middle Ages. These Cistercian monasteries were great corporations, thoroughly tied into the increasingly complex web of economic life.

The Friars

The next wave of reform took on a new shape, and produced the wandering friars (from the Latin *fratres*, brothers) of the Franciscan and Dominican orders. They arose not so much to reform monasticism from within as to bring Christian charity to the new urban masses, who were not adequately served by the older ecclesiastical parishes. The wandering friars were in part—though they were much else—the first organized social workers among the new poor. Francis of Assisi (1182-1226) was a wellborn Italian who, after a youth of normal self-indulgence in things of the flesh, underwent a shattering—and restoring—religious conversion. Turning to the ascetic life, St. Francis gave up everything in this world, except his love of God and God's creation, men, animals, and flowers. We shall meet him again when we try to understand certain phases of medieval piety. Our concern here is with the order that he founded, in a sense almost unwillingly. St. Francis was fully aware that earlier monastic movements had rapidly outgrown their primitive asceticism, and had ended in wealth and power. He and his companions were not to fall into that trap. They were not to work in producing material things—not even books of learning. They were to own nothing, not even a corporate house of their own. Instead, they were to go among men preaching the word and the example of Jesus, and satisfying their simple needs by the alms of their fellow men. They were to take poverty as a bride. St. Francis followed as literally and as profoundly as any human being has ever done the words of Jesus: "He that findeth his life shall lose it; and he that loseth his life for my sake shall find it."

Domingo (Dominic de Guzman, 1170-1221), a Spanish contemporary of St. Francis, and like him wellborn, was the founder of the Dominican Order. The Dominicans, like the Franciscans, went directly to the people to spread the word of God. St. Dominic was not as radical a mystic as St. Francis; he had a vein of iron not found in the gentle Italian.

The thirteenth-century reform movement of these mendicant (begging) friars was directed, not toward a piety secluded from the world in a monastery, but toward a piety directly concerned with the lot of the masses. The mendicant orders were not "social revolutionaries" in a modern sense; to St. Francis poverty was a good, not an evil. He wanted his brethren to be wholly free of the encumbrances of this world. Like most mystics, he distrusted formal learning and the apparatus of the schools as impediments to true Christian humility. Here is an extract from his Rule:

The brethren shall nothing appropriate to them, neither in housing nor in lands, nor in rent nor in any manner of thing, but like pilgrims and strangers in this world, in poverty and meekness, serving Almighty God. They shall faithfully, boldly and surely and meekly go for alms. Nor they shall not nor ought to be ashamed, for our Lord made Himself poor in this world. . . .

· · ·

And those that be unlearned shall not busy themselves to be lettered and learned; but they should attend and take heed above all things, and desire to have the spirit of our Lord and his holy operation to pray always to almighty God with a pure spirit and a clean heart.[*]

The Franciscan, and to a lesser degree the Dominican, movements were a challenge to the established order of the medieval world. They were an appeal to the early Christian missionary spirit; they stirred things up. Yet they were quickly tamed and integrated into the complex organization of medieval Christendom, which was concerned with maintaining things as they were rather than with revolutionizing them. Within a generation of the death of St. Francis, his order had houses of its own and corporate possessions of its own. Far from disdaining formal learning, Franciscan scholars were in the forefront of medieval learning.

Lollards and Hussites

In the fourteenth and fifteenth centuries, manorial self-sufficiency continued

---

[*] Adapted from *Monumenta Franciscana*, R. Howlett, ed. (London, 1882), II, 69-70, 73.

to decline, and more and more people were thrown into a money economy with its unemployment and job displacement. Social problems became increasingly severe. The ravages of the Black Death, an epidemic which struck with particular force in the mid-fourteenth century, further disrupted the medieval order. Under these conditions, the Church was obliged to contend with reform movements that might be thought of as aiming at social revolution. The English priest, John Wiclif (see below, Chapter X), who died in 1384, and his Lollard followers mixed together religious, social, and economic aims; they were for the "people" and against those in power. The term Lollard means "babbler," and it is a good example of the common practice in all societies (which are normally conservative) of fastening a bad name on rebels. The Lollards had a part in stirring up the English Peasants' Revolt, one of the leaders of which was the priest John Ball. Its slogan has a "socialist" touch you will not find in St. Francis of Assisi:

> When Adam delved and Eve span
> Who was then the gentleman?

In the fifteenth century, a somewhat similar movement in Bohemia, the western province of modern Czechoslovakia, took its name from another religious leader, John Hus (1369-1415). The Hussite movement was a compound of religious and social aims, with a strong component of what we should call Czech nationalism. Hus wanted to end many clerical abuses, notably the domination of the Church in Bohemia by German prelates.

The Challenge of the New Dynastic States

The challenge to the unity of western Christendom was not confined to such social movements as those of Wiclif and Hus. Another challenge came from the newly developing dynastic states, fore-runners of the nation-states of modern times. When Boniface VIII came out second best in his encounter with Philip the Fair (see Chapter VII), the drive toward a Gallican church was greatly strengthened. *Gallicanism* did not aim to separate the Church in France (Gallia) from the Catholic communion, but it did aim to make it a national church that would be more under royal than papal control.

In Italy, the intervention of Philip the Fair had unleashed hostility against foreigners, and the city of Rome grew too disorderly for Boniface's successor, Benedict XI (1303-1304), who withdrew to Perugia. Benedict's successor, the Frenchman Bertrand de Got, was elected pope as Clement V (1305-1314); the cardinals hoped that he could somehow compromise with King Philip of France and restore papal prestige. Clement set up his residence at Avignon in what is now southern France, a papal possession on the river Rhône. From 1305 to 1378, the seat of the papacy remained at Avignon, a development that was a tremendous comedown for the holder of the See of Peter. This period was later known as the "Babylonian Captivity," a term coined by the Italian poet Petrarch in allusion to the captivity of the ancient Jews at Babylon.

In 1378, when the newly elected Urban VI announced his intention of returning to Rome, part of the College of Cardinals chose a rival pope, "Clement VII," who remained at Avignon. The Babylonian Captivity was followed by the Great Schism, 1378-1417, when there were two popes— one at Rome, the other at Avignon. The states of Europe gave their allegiance either to Rome or to Avignon, depending on their international alliances and enmities. For example, France was of course pro-Avignon; England, the enemy of France —this was in the midst of the Hundred Years' War—was pro-Rome; and Scotland, the enemy of England and the ally of France, was pro-Avignon.

The Conciliar Movement

Against the scandal of the Great Schism the Church rallied in the Conciliar Movement, a series of general councils beginning at Pisa, 1409, and continuing at Constance, 1414-1417, and at Basel, 1431-1449. The Council of Pisa failed so dismally that it actually chose a *third* claimant to the papal throne. But the Council of Constance at least solved the problem of the schism. With the election of Martin V in 1417, the unity of western Christendom was restored. But the schism had been an obvious symptom of more deep-seated troubles. Among these troubles were national rivalries; the decline and corruption of the monasteries; worldliness in the secular clergy, and especially in the upper clergy; the failure of the Church to keep in touch with the masses, who had been unsettled by the economic and social changes, the new "money economy," that were making the modern world—all the troubles, in short, that were to come to a head in the Protestant Reformation of the next century.

Against these difficulties the Conciliar Movement made little headway. Hus, in spite of an imperial guarantee of his safety, was tried at Constance for doctrinal heresy and was condemned to death in 1415. But the Hussite heresy was merely driven underground. The general councils attempted to supplant papal absolutism with a kind of constitutional government within the Church; the regular councils of the whole Church would be a parliament, and the pope would be a constitutional monarch. Could such councils with full powers have forestalled the Reformation by reforming the Church from within? The question is unanswerable, for the councils were never given the chance. Papal supremacy simply did not give way to constitutional government.

Our brief survey of the reform movements from the Cluniac to the Conciliar must not give the impression that medieval Christianity was weak and unstable. On the contrary, the very success of the medieval Church in absorbing rebels is proof of its strength and stability. For these movements were not suppressed by force, except for certain extremist movements like the Albigensian heresy of the twelfth and thirteenth centuries. Rather, they were softened, tamed, and absorbed into the unity of the Church. From them, the Church gained more than it lost; it gained in renewal of piety, in closer contact with the masses, in wealth, and in learning.

III: Medieval Thought

Education

The Church was not merely the center of intellectual life in the Middle Ages; it actually had a monopoly on formal education. For the first time in western society, there came to be a systematic, graded education under common control. The common control was not a single bureaucratic one, like that of an American state superintendent of education; it was exercised by the Church, with its numerous organs of education and administration. The education was not universal, but it was generally open to really bright, bookish boys (not, of course, girls), even from the lower classes. Formal education of this sort was not usually given to the upper classes (the knights), though through private tutors the young of the upper classes at least learned for the most part to read and write. They were trained also in the arts of war and the chase, and in the practice of running estates.

During the Middle Ages, the monasteries and cathedrals were generally recognized as under some obligation to provide for the education of the clergy; accordingly, at first under strong individual impulses, schools came into existence in various centers. Some of these schools survived the impulse given by the great and successful teacher, and began to grow as institutions. They taught elementary subjects, especially Latin, the language of the learned. The great educational institution of the later medieval West, and one of its great legacies to us, was the university. Many of these universities had their start early in the Middle Ages as church schools. By the twelfth and thirteenth centuries they had attained their characteristic form, which was a corporate whole known in Latin as a *universitas*. Bologna, an association or corporation of students who hired their teachers, set the type for Italy and the South. Paris, an association of teachers, set the pattern for the northern universities. The colleges were originally residence halls, but came to assume teaching functions as well. The English universities of Oxford and Cambridge, with their constituent residential teaching colleges, their university professors, lectures, examinations, and degrees, still preserve the basic structure of the north European medieval university.

The universities conferred degrees, after proper examination. The degree of Master of Arts qualified the recipient for most intellectual occupations, though the doctorate very soon became prerequisite for the highest posts. Since the Church both controlled and protected the universities, they enjoyed great freedom from political authorities. Accused teachers and students could demand trial in an ecclesiastical court, rather than in a secular one.

The Chapel, King's College, Cambridge (1446-1515).

The universities taught the higher subjects that formed the basis of formal medieval education—the liberal arts, divided into the *quadrivium* (arithmetic, music, geometry, astronomy), and the *trivium* (grammar, rhetoric, logic). These formal names conceal much of what still forms the basis of a liberal education. The experimental sciences were not taught, nor was the amazing variety of practical subjects, from the internal-combustion engine to success in marriage, that have got into the modern American curriculum. The medieval student, after becoming grounded in Latin as a living scholarly tongue and as a living literature, and in the mathematical sciences, could go on to study one of the two genu-

Scenes of student life in the Middle Ages (from *Statutenbuch des Collegium Sapentiae*).

inely learned professions, law or medicine. Or he could go on to what is basically the equivalent of our graduate work in philosophy and literature. Both the philosophy and the literature would seem restricted to a scholar used to the great list of courses offered by modern graduate schools. But, as we shall see, the formal thought of the Middle Ages grappled with all the major problems of learning.

By the thirteenth century, the learned career had come to be a fully recognized part of medieval social organization. There was *imperium,* the function of political administration, *sacerdotium,* the priestly function, and *studium,* the scholarly function. There was even, among the university students themselves, something we should recognize as college life. In those days, too, financial problems beset the student, and the letter home for money was a favorite subject for medieval writers, even poets.

This translation comes from fourteenth-century France:

Well-beloved father, I have not a penny, nor can I get any save through you, for all things at the University are so dear: nor can I study in my Code or my Digest, for they are all tattered. Moreover, I owe ten crowns in dues to the Provost, and can find no man to lend them to me; I send you word of greetings and money.

The Student hath need of many things if he will profit here; his father and his kin must needs supply him freely, that he be not compelled to pawn his books, but have ready money in his purse, with gowns and furs and decent clothing, or he will be damned for a beggar; wherefore, that men may not take me for a beast, I send you word of greetings and of money.[*]

The friction of "town" and "gown" dates from medieval times. The students played,

[*] Quoted in G. G. Coulton, *Life in the Middle Ages* (Cambridge, England, 1929), III, 113.

CHAPTER VIII

drank, sang, hazed freshmen, organized hoaxes and practical jokes, and staged riots that were often accompanied by bloodshed and injury to innocent bystanders. University authorities did not like this sort of thing, and passed many ordinances, usually in vain, against student sports and brawls. Student life in the Middle Ages was hard; it was little softened by what we call "activities." Here is a ducal ordinance of 1476 for the University of Louvain in the Low Countries:

The tutors shall see that the scholars rise in the morning at five o'clock, and that then before lectures each one reads by himself the laws which are to be read at the regular lecture, together with the glosses. . . . But after the regular lecture, having if they wish, quickly heard mass, the scholars shall come to their rooms and revise the lectures that have been given, by rehearsing and impressing on their memory whatever they have brought away from the lectures either orally or in writing. And next they shall come to lunch . . . after lunch, each one having brought to the table his books, all the scholars of the Faculty together, in the presence of a tutor, shall review that regular lecture; and in this review the tutor shall follow a method which will enable him, by discreet questioning of every man, to gather whether each of them listened well to the lecture and remembered it, and which will recall the whole lecture by having its parts recited by individuals. And if watchful care is used in this one hour will suffice.*

The Church and Public Opinion

Most of the members of the *studium* had taken holy orders, were in some sense a part of the Church. The great majority, however, were in "minor orders," such as that of deacon, not in "major orders," that is, those of priest and bishop, which officers of the Church alone could administer the sacraments. Since these teachers in minor orders did not have charge of a parish with

---

* H. Rashdall, *The Universities of Europe in the Middle Ages*, rev. ed. (Oxford, 1936), II, 341. Our translation.

the priestly duties of shepherd of the flock, the Church understandably was less strict in supervising their private lives than it was with parish priests. But to an extent we can hardly understand today, the Church penetrated and controlled all human activity, especially intellectual activity. In the Dark Ages, as we have seen, the ability to read was in itself taken as a sign that a man was a priest. Although this monopoly no longer existed in the later Middle Ages, the clergy even then bore a much larger part of the administrative work of the world than they do now.

In thousands of rural parishes, even in town parishes, the priest was the effective link with the outside world, the world of ideas as well as of wars, taxes, and intrigues. Although the sermon never became central in Catholic practice, still it was a way of spreading ideas. Indeed, the pulpit gave to the medieval Church a great comparative advantage over lay authorities in influencing public opinion. The temporal power was by no means helpless in such matters, especially toward the end of the medieval centuries, as the chancery court in England, Philip IV's quarrel with the pope, and many other instances show. Still the Church did have a hold on men's minds for which in our own free western "age of propaganda"—varied and confusing propaganda—there is no good parallel.

Finally, it is to the Church that we owe the preservation of Latin literature. Of course, extremists among the Christians thought of pagan literature as the devil's work and would have had it destroyed; even for the ordinary pious cleric, imaginative pagan literature held something of the attraction of forbidden fruit. Losses were great, especially during the long years of the breakup of the Roman Empire. Still, the monks collected and the monks copied —in modern terms, they "published." Nor was the work of the monastic copiers limited to the transmission of the classics. They also copied the Latin writings of contemporary medieval theologians and philosophers, the vernacular writings of medieval poets and storytellers. We owe to them not only Cicero but also Aquinas and the *Chanson de Roland*. And when, in the twelfth century, translations from the Greek and Arabic were made, it was the western Churchmen who read them first, and then passed them on.

Medieval Formal Thought

The content of medieval education, the formal thought of the age in theology, philosophy, political theory, and even natural science, seems strange to us today. Stranger still is the form in which it is cast. We are brought up in the tradition of experimentation, scientific skepticism, and devotion to the "practical." A great deal of medieval thought is unavoidably alien to us; we like to think we go first to the "facts," to "experience." Medieval formal thought was not exclusively "deductive," not unrelated to the "facts" of common sense. We may perhaps put the matter more safely this way: the medieval thinker *trusted* his mind to work logically, thought of it as a surer guide, in the long run, to God's plan of the universe than his direct sense-experience of the external world. Here, for instance, are bits of a minor work by the great medieval writer, Dante, the *Quaestio de Aqua et Terra*, which, since it deals with a scientific problem, seems even stranger than would a work dealing with politics or morals. Note particularly Dante's very last point (his II, 2b).

THE QUESTION: IS WATER, OR THE SURFACE OF THE SEA, ANYWHERE HIGHER THAN THE EARTH, OR HABITABLE DRY LAND?

AFFIRMATIVE ARGUMENT:

Reason 1. Geometrical Proof: Earth and Water are spheres with different centers; the center of the Earth's sphere is the center of the universe; consequently the surface of the Water is above that of the Earth.

Reason 2. Ethical Proof: Water is a nobler element than Earth; hence it deserves a nobler, or higher, place in the scheme of the universe.

Reason 3. Experimental Proof: based on sailors seeing the land disappear under their horizon at sea.

Reason 4. Economical Proof: The supply of Water, namely the sea, must be higher than the Earth; otherwise, as Water flows downwards, it could not reach, as it does, the fountains, lakes, etc.

Reason 5. Astronomical Proof: Since Water follows the moon's course, its sphere must be excentric, like the moon's excentric orbit; and consequently in places be higher than the sphere of Earth.

NEGATIVE ARGUMENT: These reasons unfounded.

I. REFUTATION BY OBSERVATION:
Water flows down to the sea from the land; hence the sea cannot be higher than the land.

II. REFUTATION BY REASONING:
  A. *Water cannot be higher than the dry land.*
     Proof: Water could only be higher than the Earth,
     1. If it were excentric, or
     2. If it were concentric, but had some excrescence.
        But since
          x. Water naturally moves downwards, and
          y. Water is naturally a fluid body:
     1. Cannot be true, for three impossibilities would follow:
          a. Water would move upwards as well as downwards;
          b. Water and Earth would move downwards in different directions;
          c. Gravity would be taught ambiguously of the two bodies.
        Proof of these impossibilities by a diagram.
     2. Cannot be true, for
          a. The water of the excrescence would be diffused, and consequently the excrescence would not exist:
          b. It is unnecessary, and what is unnecessary is contrary to the will of God and Nature.[*]

---

[*] Quoted in A. O. Norton, *Readings in the History of Education* (Cambridge, Mass., 1909), 117-118.

Nominalism and Realism

The formal philosophy of the Middle Ages is known as Scholasticism. Though the Scholastics had certain attitudes in common, and though they all accepted the truth of the doctrines of the Roman Church, they were genuine philosophers in their wide range of disagreement on matters of metaphysics, epistemology (theory of knowledge), and ethics. Notably, they differed over a very important technical philosophical problem known as the problem of universals. In medieval times there were two broad contrasting solutions of this problem, known as realism and nominalism. Although no attempted popular treatment of this difficult subject can be satisfactory, we must here attempt to see at least what the debate was about.

The central problem may be put this way: just what is the relation between certain *words* we human beings use and the *things* (or the *reality*, the *experiences*, *truths*) we use these words to refer to? These words are class-terms, of the kind we all use. We all use—and men of the Middle Ages used—the word "man," not just in the form meaning a specific man, but in the form meaning all mankind, man in general. A common Christian belief is that Christ atoned for the sins of "man." Now the extreme nominalist philosophers came to the conclusion that "man" is a mere word (*flatus vocis* in their Latin, a mere sound) and that there is no such "thing" as man—only individual men, whom we group together as "man" solely for convenience in talking and thinking, solely as a kind of shorthand of logic, to avoid repeating all their proper names.

But if there is no such "reality" as man, what becomes of phrases like "sins of man," even the familiar phrase "Son of man" as a designation for Jesus? The realists took a view opposite to that of the nominalists: they held that these words are signs indeed, but signs of a "reality" more real, more important, than that of individual existence as apprehended by our senses. Each individual man is but an imperfect part of (or but an imperfect representation or instance of, for these are difficult matters indeed, and words so inadequate!) a great whole, a perfect thing not to be apprehended by our unaided sense-perception. For the realist, "man" in the sense of "mankind" was in a sense *more real* than any individual John Doe.

In politics and political philosophy, the nominalist-realist problem comes out clearly. To the nominalist, society, the state, is just a collection of individuals, citizens or subjects, who alone are "real." To the realist, society, state, the collective unit, is the supreme reality, an "organism," a whole, of which individuals are merely parts, like the separate cells of an organism. The realist likes concepts such as that of a "group soul" or "style"; the nominalist dislikes such concepts.

In religion, extreme nominalism is very hard to reconcile with Christianity. It tends to the position that nothing exists except what can be apprehended by an individual through his senses. A man or a blade of grass is real to the nominalist. But God? Or even the Church, apart from the individuals who make it up? It may be difficult for the extreme nominalist to make either God or the Church very real. In fact, the *logical* implications of medieval nominalism put it in a class with what later came to be called materialism, positivism, rationalism, or empiricism. Medieval realism, also, had its dangers from the point of view of Christian orthodoxy. Realism took care of God and the Church, of justice and all the other moral "ideas." But like any other-worldly doctrine, it ran the risk, in the hands of a very logical, or a very mystical, thinker, of being pushed into a total denial of this material world of eating, drinking, working, calculating, and other un-Platonic activities. And the Catholic Church for two thousand years has been very concerned with ordinary men and women living in the material world. Therefore so successful a philosopher as St. Thomas Aquinas seeks to reconcile the nominalist with the realist position; and an ardent, innovating, logical mind like Abelard's seeks in "conceptualism" to have the best of both positions.

Peter Abelard (1079-1142), known to the modern general reader rather for his tragic love affair with his pupil Heloise than for his achievements as a philosopher and teacher, was one of the founders of the University of Paris. Basically, Abelard had tendencies toward rationalism, if not to what the American philosopher, William James, called "toughmindedness." His "Yes and No" (*Sic et Non*) is a collection of conflicting statements from earlier church fathers. He has long been a favorite with modern liberal thinkers, who see in him the eternally free and questing mind not tied to dogmatic beliefs. But Abelard was a medieval thinker, and accepted the Christian basis of medieval thought; indeed, he is one of the precursors of developed Scholasticism. His "conceptualism" was an attempt to solve the antithesis of nominalism-realism by maintaining that a general term like "man," though not "real" as John Doe is real, is nevertheless logically and psychologically a concept we can and must live with and work with, and is therefore not *just* a "mere" sound. The hostile critic, of course, can insist that Abelard himself is here no more than word-spinning.

It is unfortunate that what one may call the psychological or temperamental phases of this opposition (dualism) of realist and nominalist are probably best suggested to modern Americans by the contrast between "idealist" (that is, the medieval realist) and "realist" (that is, the medieval nominalist). Here "realist" quite reverses its meaning. The philosopher is suspicious of the validity of simple dualisms, rightly from his point of view, but to the historian they do help in understanding the attitudes of

ordinary educated and interested human beings in western history. Let us note as historians that some men tend to think-and-feel about these lofty matters as the medieval realist (modern idealist) does, that others think-and-feel in such matters as the medieval nominalist (modern realist) does. And let us further note that among medieval philosophers complete, radical "materialism" and complete, radical "skepticism" are both lacking; neither could come out in an age of Christian faith.

At any rate, it is a fact that many medieval Schoolmen belabored one another on the lecture platform and in writing quite as heartily as in any other great period of western philosophy. We must not be misled by terms like "medieval unity," or by the notion that the supremacy of the Church in the West stifled debate over basic philosophical issues. Medieval thought had room for the full philosophic spectrum, except perhaps, as we have just noted, for skepticism and systematic anti-intellectualism.

In Duns Scotus (1274-1308) we find a specific example of the dangers of Scholastic realism. This philosopher could never rest content with the imperfect arguments by which men prove that perfection exists. He wrote devastating criticisms of his predecessors, realists as well as nominalists. Duns Scotus spun out his own arguments for the realist position so that his works became a byword for oversubtlety, and added to the general discredit that came over Scholasticism at the end of the Middle Ages. William of Ockham (1270-1347), on the other hand, is the most famous of the extreme nominalists. His philosophical position, he came to see, made it impossible for him to accept as reasonable many of the essential doctrines of the Church. Accordingly—and like the good Englishman he was—Ockham chose to believe these doctrines anyway. Abandoning the characteristic medieval attempt to show that the truths of Christianity can be proved by human reason, he took a position very close to that of one of the early Fathers, Tertullian: *certum est quia impossibile est*—it's certain because it's impossible.

Saint Thomas Aquinas

But this was not the Scholastic way, and certainly not the way of the greatest of the Schoolmen, the Dominican St. Thomas Aquinas (1225-1274). Two of his books, the *Summa contra Gentiles* and the *Summa Theologica,* are encyclopedias of medieval learning and philosophy. They are not, however, mere collections of miscellaneous information put together, like a modern encyclopedia, in alphabetical order; everything in them is co-ordinated from a central point of view. That central point of view is orthodox Catholic Christianity interpreted by a moderate realist (in the medieval sense), an orderly logician never tempted to excess even in logic, a prodigious scholar who always kept in touch with the world of common sense.

Aquinas started with the authority of revealed faith, with those truths we possess directly from God. He believed that God designed this earth as a fit place for man, whom he created in his own image. Clearly, therefore, no such important human activity as thinking could be contrary to God's design. All our thinking, *if rightly done,* merely confirms the truths of faith, and helps us in daily life to apply them. In that eternal Christian problem of faith against reason (remember the "it's certain because it's impossible" of Tertullian) Aquinas took a firm stand: there is no problem, because there is no opposition between faith and reason rightly understood. If a man puts a series of arguments together and comes out with a conclusion contrary to what orthodox Christians believe, he is simply guilty of faulty logic, and the use of correct logic can readily show where he erred. Indeed, Thomas Aquinas, like most of the later Scholastics, delighted in the game of inventing arguments against accepted beliefs, matching them with a set of even more ingenious arguments, and then reconciling the two with an intellectual skill suggesting the trained athlete's ability in master timing and co-ordination.

Here is an example of the mind and method of Aquinas. It is a relatively unimportant part of the *Summa Theologica,* but it is fairly easy to follow, and it brings out clearly how close to common sense Aquinas can be. He is discussing the specific conditions of "man's first state," the state of innocence before the Fall. He comes to the question of what children were like in the state of innocence. Were they born with such perfect strength of body that they had full use of their limbs at birth, or were they like human children nowadays, helpless little wrigglers? In the Garden of Eden, one might think that any form of helplessness would detract from perfection, and that God might well have made the human infant strong and perfect, or might even have had men and women born adult. Aquinas did not think so; even his Eden was as "natural" as he could make it:

By faith alone do we hold truths which are above nature, and what we believe rests on authority. Wherefore, in making any assertion, we must be guided by the nature of things, except in those things which are above nature, and are made known to us by Divine authority. Now it is clear that it is as natural as it is befitting to the principles of human nature that children should not have sufficient strength for the use of their limbs immediately after birth. Because in proportion to other animals man has naturally a larger brain. Wherefore it is natural, on account of the considerable humidity of the brain in children, that the sinews which are instruments of movement, should not be apt for moving the limbs. On the other hand, no Catholic doubts it possible for a child to have, by Divine power, the use of its limbs immediately after birth.

Now we have it on the authority of Scripture that *God made man right* (Eccles. vii. 30), which rightness, as Augustine says, consists in the perfect subjection of the body to the soul. As, therefore, in the primitive state it was impossible to find in the human limbs anything repugnant to man's well-ordered will, so was it impossible for those limbs to fail in executing the will's commands. Now the human will is well ordered when it tends to acts which are befitting to man. But the same acts are not befitting to man at every season of life. We must, therefore, conclude that children would not have had sufficient strength for the use of their limbs for the purpose of performing every kind of act; but only for the acts befitting the state of infancy, such as suckling, and the like.*

This apparently trivial passage contains much that is typical of Thomism, as the philosophy of Aquinas is termed. It reveals the clear supremacy that is granted to "truths which are above nature," which we hold by faith and receive through divine authority; the belief that God usually prefers to let nature run its course according to its laws; the belief that there is a "fitness" in human action conforming to these laws of nature; and, finally, the appeal to authority, in this case the Old Testament and Augustine.

Political Thought

In dealing with problems of human relations, medieval thinkers again used a vocabulary that is different from ours. Yet they come fairly close in many ways to modern democratic thinking. Except for extreme realism, medieval thought was emphatically not totalitarian. To the medieval thinker the perfection of the kingdom of heaven could not possibly exist on earth, where compromise and imperfection are inescapable.

Full equality could not exist on earth. Medieval political thought accepts as its starting point an order of rank in human

society. The twelfth-century *Policraticus* ("Statesman's Book") of the English scholastic philosopher John of Salisbury (*c.*1115-1180), provides a complete statement of this social theory. The prince (or king) is the head of the body of the commonwealth; the senate (legislature) is the heart; the judges and governors of provinces are the eyes, ears, and tongue; the officials and soldiers are the hands; the financial officers are the stomach and intestines; and the peasants "correspond to the feet, which always cleave to the soil." This figure of speech, or, in more ambitious terms, this organic theory of society, is a great favorite with those who oppose change. For obviously the foot does not try to become the brain, nor is the hand jealous of the eye; the whole body is at its best when each part does what nature meant it to do. The field worker, the blacksmith, the merchant, the lawyer, the priest, and the king himself all have been assigned a part of God's work on earth.

Medieval thought thus distinguishes among vocations, but it also insists on the dignity and worth of all vocations, even the humblest. It accepts the Christian doctrine of the equality of all souls before God and holds that no man can be a mere instrument of another man. Even the humblest person on this earth could in the next world hope to enjoy a bliss as full and eternal as any king's. Furthermore, medieval political theory is by no means opposed to all change on earth. One might assume that it would have opposed any and all resistance to the acts of a superior. Certainly medieval thinkers were not democratic in the sense of believing that the people have a right to, or can, make their own institutions. But they did not hold that, since God has arranged authority as it now is in this world, we should preserve existing conditions, come what may. If existing conditions were bad, it was a sign that originally good conditions had been perverted. The

---

* *The "Summa Theologica" of St. Thomas Aquinas,* 2nd ed. (London, 1922), Vol. IV, Pt. I, Quest. XCIX.

CHAPTER VIII

Symbolic representation of medieval society. Above: to the left, clerics; center, the king; to the right, lay counselors and men at arms. Below: left, the bourgeoisie; right, peasants.

thing to do was to try to restore the original good, God's own plan.

A relatively rigid and authoritarian society needs a sovereign authority whose decisions are final. In ancient Sparta, for instance, there was no appeal from the decisions of the rulers, and in eastern Europe the Byzantine emperor, and his Russian successor, the tsar, were perhaps such final authorities (see Chapters VI and IX). But the medieval West never gave unquestioning acceptance to a single and final authority. At the very highest level, the popes and emperors each claimed supremacy in the West. Able and lucky emperors, like Otto the Great and Frederick Barbarossa, had tastes of such authority; Pope Innocent III very nearly attained it in the early thirteenth century. Both the imperial and the papal sides enlisted medieval thinkers. Dante spent a great deal of energy on a long political pamphlet, *De Monarchia* ("Concerning Monarchy"), in which he urged the world rule of the emperor as a solution for the evils of war. Thomas Aquinas concluded that the pope had "an indirect rather than a direct authority in temporal matters"—another example of his bent toward moderation.

In the strife of propaganda—for such it was—the imperialists insulted the papalists and the papalists insulted the imperialists. Each side, however, had to find backing for its claims to authority, and some of the backing came to have quite a modern look. Marsiglio of Padua (*c.* 1275-1343), the author of *Defensor Pacis* ("Defender of the Peace"), an imperialist pamphlet, found the only true source of authority in a commonwealth to be the *universitas civium*, the whole body of the citizens. Marsiglio probably did not mean to be as modern as this may seem. He still used medieval terms, and the constitutionalism, the notions of popular sovereignty, that have been attributed to him are a long way from our notion of counting heads to determine political decisions. But Marsiglio did in all earnestness mean what a great many other medieval thinkers meant: No man's place in the order of rank, even if he is at the top of it, is such that those of lower rank must always and unquestioningly accept what he commands.

Finally, the feudal relation itself, which held the nobility together as lords and vassals, is an admirable example of medieval insistence that the order of rank is not one of mere might. The feudal relation was a contract that was binding on *both* parties (see Chapter V). And the elaborate code of chivalry developed by this feudal class insisted on the personal dignity and standing of each initiate.

Economic Thought

In the stratified society of the Middle Ages, where every man had his rightful place, every man received, at least in theory, his just economic due. Medieval economic notions, therefore, have been greatly admired by modern intellectuals in revolt against what they regard as our crassly competitive business life. To the medieval theorist, work was a part of God's design for man. It was not a way of advancing the worker in the social scale; above all, one did not work to "make money" in the modern sense—for money could be made in this sense only by cheating someone else, by taking more than one's rightful share. A piece of work, say a pair of shoes made by a skilled craftsman, was not to be considered as a commodity on the open market, fetching what the buyer would pay for it—a high price if there was a scarcity of shoes at the moment, a low price, even at a loss, if there was a surplus of shoes. The shoes were worth a fixed price, their "just price." This just price included the cost of the raw materials, the amount needed to sustain the worker at his usual standards of life while making the shoes (*i.e.*, cost of labor), and a small item not so much of profit as of wages of management for the seller.

To ensure this economic justice, medieval society worked out an elaborate system of what we should now call controls. Merchants and artisans were both organized in trade associations called guilds. These guilds set prices and standards and controlled the admission of new workers and masters into the trade. They did not exactly set a quota for each firm in the trade, nor did they "plan" production in the modern sense of the word. Obviously in a static society a given firm (master and workmen) did the amount of business it had been doing from time immemorial; custom set its quota. As for planning, that had been done a long time ago by God himself. These customs and controls were reinforced by the regulations of local governments.

Finally, medieval society had in theory no place for finance capitalism; it had no fluid supply of money or credit from which the man who wished to expand his business could draw. Medieval theory—and here Aquinas is an especially clear and good source—regarded the taking of interest for money lent as getting something for nothing, as if the lender were exploiting the temporary needs of the borrower. If you lend a sum for twelve months and get back more than you lent, you are receiving unearned income. True, if the borrower does not pay within the time agreed, you may claim a kind of indemnity, since your plans are disturbed. But this and a few similar adjustments do not amount to a full recognition of the legitimacy of interest. Indeed, in the Middle Ages what we call interest was often regarded as the sin of usury.

The Law of Nature

Let us take one final illustration of medieval ways of thought. As we saw in Chapter VII, to the medieval mind, even to that of the lawyer, the law was not made but found. Law for common, everyday purposes was what we should call custom. On the manor, for instance, the customary arrangements for use of the field were found by consulting the men of the manor and learning what had been done time out of mind. Medieval thought also recognized something beyond custom, something beyond law in the sense of what people were used to doing. This was the *law of nature*, or natural law.

To the medieval thinker the law of nature was something like God's word translated into terms that made it usable by ordinary men on earth. It was the ethical ideal, the "ought to be," that was discernible by men of good will who were thinking rightly. This was not natural law as most modern scientists would interpret the term, for the scientist finds traditional moral distinctions vague and subjective, always open to dispute and misunderstanding. A thermometer, as well as common sense, can tell us when water becomes ice. But what instrument, what human faculty, can tell us in a similarly precise way when a man is acting in accordance with the law of nature, and when he is not?

The medieval thinker would answer that the thermometer, even common sense, can decide only limited questions of material fact. But, by using our full human faculties as God intended, we can answer with even more certainty the questions of right and wrong. To do so, we need the whole resources of the human community. We need the word of God as revealed in the Christian Church, the wisdom handed down to us by our ancestors, the skills and learning each of us has acquired in his calling, and the common sense of the community. Of course, due weight must always be given to those who are specially qualified by their position. Medieval opinion would insist that even though a common-sense test, or a thermometer, can give the correct answer, men will not necessarily take the right action. No instrument (that is, no scientific knowledge) can protect men from sin. Protection from sin is afforded only by being a full member of the Christian Church. Such a member will know right from wrong, natural from unnatural, by the fact of his membership.

The Medieval and the Modern Outlooks Contrasted

We have looked at three concrete instances of medieval attitudes—the notion of an organic stratified society in which each man plays the part God sent him to play, the concept of a just price and an economic order not dependent on the play of supply and demand, and the concept of a natural law to be understood by reason that regulates as well as explains human relations on earth. Behind all these ideas is the medieval idea of this earthly world as *static*. The Middle Ages thought that change was accidental and random, not what we call progress. No medieval person believed, or could believe, in progress in anything like our modern sense. Some changes, of course, did occur in the Middle Ages. Workmen improved their tools and indulged in that very modern form of change known as invention. Some merchants made money, often by methods that were not too different from those of today. In the last few medieval centuries, corruption, competition, and rapid social change were so visible that even the theorist saw them. Wiclif and many another rebel were fully aware of living in a changing society. Yet they thought that their society had lapsed from what God and natural law intended, not that it was progressing to new ideals.

The medieval intellectual, then, assumed that the universe was at bottom static; the modern intellectual assumes that it is at bottom dynamic. The one assumed that laws for right human action had been, so to speak, designed for all time by God in heaven, and that those laws were clear to the good Christian. The other assumes that laws for right human action are in fact worked out in the very process of living, that no one can be sure of them in advance, and that new ones are constantly being created. The medieval man, puzzled, tended to resolve his problem by an appeal to authority, the best or the natural authority in which he had been trained to put his faith. He turned to Aristotle if he was a Schoolman, to the customary law of the land if he was a lawyer, to his father's farming practices if he was a farmer. And—this is very important—he usually believed that no perfectly satisfactory solution of his problems would be available until he went to heaven. The modern man, puzzled, tends

at least to consult several different authorities and to compare them before he makes up his own mind. He may also try some experiments on his own. He usually feels that if he goes about it in the right way, he can in fact solve his difficulty. The right way for the medieval man already existed, and had at most to be *found;* the right way for the modern man may have to be *created.*

The foregoing pages summarize the central medieval view of theology, philosophy, and human relations. Two other sides of medieval thought, not as typical or as central as Scholasticism, must now be noted if we are to understand the variety and range of medieval intellectual activity. These are mysticism and science.

Mysticism

Although Scholasticism set faith above reason, nevertheless it held that the instrument of thought is a divine gift, and that it must be used and sharpened here on earth. This exaltation of reason the mystic cannot accept. Thus in 1140 St. Bernard secured the condemnation of the disputatious philosopher Abelard (see p. 318), for false teaching. Bernard was the mystic of action, a man in some ways like St. Paul, a great organizer and a commanding personality.

St. Francis was a very different kind of mystic. But for him, too, formal Scholastic thought was futile and harmful. Christ was no philosopher. Christ's way was the way of submission, of subduing the mind as well as the flesh. How Francis felt about learning is clear from the following:

My brothers who are led by the curiosity of knowledge will find their hands empty in the day of tribulation. I would wish them rather to be strengthened by virtues, that when the time of tribulation comes they may have the Lord with them in their straits—for such a time will come when they will throw their good-for-nothing books into holes and corners.[*]

The quality of Francis' piety comes out in this fragment of a work which is almost certainly by his own hand, the "Canticle of the Brother Sun":

Most High, omnipotent, good Lord, thine is the praise, the glory, the honour and every benediction;
To thee alone, Most High, these do belong, and no man is worthy to name thee.
Praised be thou, my Lord, with all thy creatures, especially milord Brother Sun that dawns and lightens us;
And he, beautiful and radiant with great splendour, signifies thee, Most High.
Be praised, my Lord, for Sister Moon and the stars that thou has made bright and precious and beautiful.
Be praised, my Lord, for Brother Wind, and for the air and cloud and the clear sky and for all weathers through which thou givest sustenance to thy creatures.
Be praised, my Lord, for Sister Water, that is very useful and humble and precious and chaste.
Be praised, my Lord, for Brother Fire, through whom thou dost illumine the night, and comely is he and glad and bold and strong.
Be praised, my Lord, for Sister, Our Mother Earth, that doth cherish and keep us, and produces various fruits with coloured flowers and the grass.
Be praised, my Lord, for those who forgive for love of thee, and endure sickness and tribulation; blessed are they who endure in peace; for by thee, Most High, shall they be crowned.
Be praised, my Lord, for our bodily death, from which no living man can escape; woe unto those who die in mortal sin.
Blessed are they that have found thy most holy will, for the second death shall do them no hurt.
Praise and bless my Lord, and render thanks, and serve Him with great humility.[†]

Such mystic feeling is an essential part of medieval life. If you are to understand the range of human experience in the Middle Ages, you must balance, or rather,

[*] Quoted in H. O. Taylor, *The Mediaeval Mind* (New York, 1930), I, 444-445.
[†] *Ibid.*, I, 455-456.

complement, Aquinas with Francis. Nearer than either Aquinas or Francis to the center of Christian experience, perhaps, is the best-known medieval work of piety, a work still read everywhere in the Christian world, the *Imitation of Christ*, attributed to the fifteenth-century German ecclesiastic, Thomas à Kempis. This work is an admirable example of a mysticism that consoles and fortifies the Christian instead of prodding him.

Science

Historians of science today by no means dismiss the Middle Ages as a period devoid of achievement in natural science. They have indeed revised downward the reputation of the Oxford Franciscan Roger Bacon (*c.* 1214-1294?) as a lone, heroic devotee of "true" experimental methods; but they have revised upward such reputations as those of Adelard of Bath (twelfth century), who was a pioneer in the study of Arab science, and Robert Grosseteste (*c.* 1170-1253), who clearly did employ experimental methods. No doubt much theological and philosophical thinking of the Middle Ages was concerned with forms of human experience that natural science is not concerned with; but in many ways even modern western science goes back at least to the thirteenth century.

First, especially in the late Middle Ages, real progress took place in the arts and crafts that underlie modern science—in agriculture, in mining and metallurgy, and in the industrial arts generally. Accurate clockwork, optical instruments, and the compass all emerge from the later Middle Ages. Even such sports as falconry, and such questionable pursuits as astrology and alchemy, helped lay the foundations of modern science. The breeding and training of falcons taught close observation of the birds' behavior; astrology involved close observation of the heavens, and complicated calculations; alchemy, though it was far short of modern chemistry, nevertheless brought the beginnings of the identification and a rough classification of elements and compounds. Second, mathematics, a deductive study quite in keeping with medieval intellectual proprieties, was pursued throughout the period; thanks in part to Arab influences, it had been fashioned into a tool ready for the use of early modern scientists. Through the Arabs, medieval Europeans learned to use the symbol for zero which originated apparently in India—a small thing, but one without which the modern world could hardly get along. If you doubt this, try doing long division with Roman numerals—dividing, say, MCXXVI by LXI. The process is difficult and time-consuming.

Finally, and of major importance, the intellectual discipline of Scholasticism, antagonistic as it often was to experimental science, formed a trained scholarly community that was accustomed to a rigorous intellectual discipline. Natural science uses deduction as well as induction, and early modern science inherited from the deductive Scholasticism of the Middle Ages the meticulous care, patience, and logical rigor without which all the inductive piling up of facts would be of little use to scientists. There was no direct "psychological" transfer of skills from the medieval philosophers to the early modern scientists; the transfer was the inheritance of an intellectual tradition of close, almost "unnatural" attentiveness and hard mental work that cannot grow up overnight.

IV: Lay Culture

Although learning rested throughout the Middle Ages essentially in the hands of the clergy, the feudal nobles by no means remained as illiterate as they had been in the Dark Ages. By the thirteenth century the king who, like Charlemagne, could not write was an exception. Few of the nobles and the rest of the lay population were intellectually "cultured" men. But we need to be reminded that the word "culture" does not mean simply bookishness or artiness. Culture is the whole way of life of a distinguishable group of human beings, whether literate or illiterate. In this sense there are many forms of culture in the Middle Ages. Indeed, one medieval characteristic was the subdivision of the West into small governmental units; as a result, small regions, even towns, had "cultures" of their own—customs, dishes, even weights and measures unique with them.

Early Chivalry

Although medieval culture abounded in local, regional, and eventually national differences, the feudal upper classes throughout the West shared the way of life we call *chivalry*. The term comes from *chevalier,* the French word for knight. The chivalric code began as the simple creed of fighting men, and like most things medieval it came into full maturity about the thirteenth century.

In the hard violence of feudal life, there was some suggestion of what we call "gangsterism." Certainly a French count of the tenth century was nearer to being a gangster than to being the "perfect gentle knight" of chivalry. He could neither read nor write. He mastered as a youth the necessary skills in horsemanship and swordsmanship. He could, and often did, leave to stewards and clerks the administrative dealings a ruling class usually has to take on in order to hold its power. He had, in short, a great deal of time on his hands, and plenty of opportunity to brood over insults, to take revenge, and to maintain his reputation, which he called his honor. He could have fits of ungovernable rage—one guesses that he sometimes cultivated them—and could in passion kill, maim, and seduce, violating most of the Christian precepts.

But this same tenth- or eleventh-century count believed in Christianity. He believed very much in heaven and especially in hell; and he had a conscience, not infrequently a bad conscience. The knight who had given way to his passions knew quite well that he had sinned. He might make an extravagant gesture of repentance. He might take the cross, mortgaging all his possessions in order to join a crusade to the Holy Land; he might give or will substantial property to the Church. Indeed, in the course of the Middle Ages the Church accumulated, from men of bad conscience as well as of good, such immense endowments of worldly goods that it became a major economic power.

The early medieval knights were not just unruly athletes who had somehow come into positions of power, and who were held to some minimum standard of conduct only by the fear of hell-fire. The ideal side of early European chivalry has been embodied in epics like the *Chanson de Roland.* Charlemagne and his paladins, as they are seen in this poem (and King Arthur and his knights, as they are seen in roughly similar poems), are still athletes. But they are simple, unsubsidized athletes who play the game fairly, even against the infidel, and who love God and the emperor in the old school spirit. Roland (Rollant, or Rollanz in this version) collects the corpses of his fallen comrades after the Moslem attack and brings them to receive the bene-

dictions of the dying Turpin, Archbishop of Rheims. Then:

So Rollant turns, goes through the field in
  quest;
His companion Oliver finds at length;
He has embraced him close against his breast,
To the Archbishop returns as he can best;
Upon a shield he's laid him, by the rest;
And the Archbishop has them absolved and
  blest:
Whereon his grief and pity grow afresh.
Then says Rollanz: 'Fair comrade Oliver,
You were the son of the good count Reinier,
Who held the march by th' Vale of Runier;
To shatter spears, through buckled shields to
  bear,
And from hauberks the mail to break and tear,
Proof men to lead, and prudent counsel share,
Gluttons in field to frighten and conquer,
No land has known a better chevalier.'

The count Rollanz, when dead he saw his
  peers,
And Oliver, he held so very dear,
Grew tender, and began to shed a tear;
Out of his face the colour disappeared;
No longer could he stand, for so much grief,
Will he or nill, he swooned upon the field.

· · ·

The count Rollanz wakes from his swoon once
  more,
Climbs to his feet, his pains are very sore;
Looks down the vale, looks to the hills above;
On the green grass, beyond his companions,
He sees him lie, that noble old baron;
'Tis the Archbishop, whom in His name
  wrought God;
There he proclaims his sins, and looks above;
Joins his two hands, to Heaven holds them
  forth,
And Paradise prays God to him to accord.
Dead is Turpin, the warrior of Charlon.
In battles great and very rare sermons
Against pagans ever a champion.
God grant him now His Benediction! *

Later Chivalry

Chivalry later came to have a rather more complex code of action, one that was better integrated into the elaborate series

* *The Song of Roland,* C. Scott Moncrieff, trans. (New York, 1931), 72-73.

of personal relations that made up medieval society at its height. This later chivalry is seen at its best in the memoirs of the Sieur de Joinville (1224-1317), crusading companion of the saintly King Louis IX of France (see Chapter VII). Joinville has the traditional feudal virtues: loyalty to his king, unquestioning faith in Catholic Christianity, above all that quality of athletic innocence we tried to convey above. He and his comrades fight as they have been trained to fight. Joinville is no intellectual, yet he is a sensible and practical man, a good handler of his fellows. In him, as in Aquinas, we get a sense of balance and moderation. That is by no means naive or primitive.

Joinville revered the memory of Louis IX, who, he noted, "so loved the truth that even when he dealt with the Saracens, he was not willing to go back on his word." But the saintly Louis could not quite take the younger man with him into absolute, otherworldly virtue. Joinville in a famous passage tells how Louis, after summoning two monks, began to talk to him:

'Now I ask you,' said he, 'which you would the better like, either to be a leper, or to have committed a mortal sin?' And I, who never lied to him, made answer that I would rather have committed thirty mortal sins than be a leper. And when the monks had departed, he called me to him alone, and made me sit at his feet, and said, 'How came you to say that to me yesterday?' And I told him that I said it again. And he answered, 'You spoke hastily and as a fool. For you should know that there is no leprosy so hideous as the being in mortal sin, inasmuch as the soul that is in mortal sin is like unto the Devil; wherefore no leprosy can be so hideous. . . . When a man dies, he is healed of the leprosy in his body; but when a man who has committed mortal sin dies, he cannot know of a certainty that he has, during his lifetime, repented in such sort that God has forgiven him; wherefore he must stand in great fear lest that leprosy of sin should last as long as God is in paradise. So I pray you,' said he, 'as strongly as I can, for the love of God, and for the love of me, so to set your heart that you prefer any evil that can happen to the body, whether it be leprosy, or any other sickness,

rather than that mortal sin should enter into your soul.' *

Joinville's recollections and the *Chanson de Roland* sounded two characteristic notes of medieval chivalry—Christian humility and knightly valor. A third note was struck by the minstrels who made the rounds of the feudal courts, the French troubadours and their German counterparts, the minnesingers. This third note was love, the love of the knight for his lady, the devotion of the warrior to the woman who inspired his exploits and for whom he would dare anything. The woman was seldom his wife, for marriage among the feudal nobility united "fiefs, not hearts." Sometimes the troubadours sang of violent passion and its fatal results, as in the illicit love of Tristan and Isolde (Tristram and Iseult) and in that of Lancelot and Guinevere.

The first and greatest home of chivalric love poetry was France, and particularly southern France in the twelfth century. Perhaps stimulated by the earlier love poetry of the Spanish Moslems, the troubadours of southern France produced many love songs, both passionate and light. The language of the troubadours was the vernacular Provençal, named for the area of Provence in southeastern France. The chief patroness of the troubadours was Eleanor of Aquitaine (1122-1204), the wife of Louis VII of France and of Henry II of England, the mother of two Kings of England, and always at heart a cultivated French noblewoman (see p. 262). Eleanor's grandfather, Duke William IX of Aquitaine, had been a celebrated troubadour. She herself received the troubadours with generous hospitality; she had their songs copied and made collections of them. She even held a "court of love," a cheerful parody of feudal courts at which she and her attendants sat in lenient judgment on

---

* *Joinville's Chronicle of the Crusade of Saint Lewis*, in *Memoirs of the Crusades*, Everyman ed. (New York, 1933), 141.

CHAPTER VIII

complaints of apparently hopeless or un-requited love.

Chivalry was much more than a code of courtly love. The knight admitted to the ranks of chivalry owed loyalty to his lord, devotion to the Church, and a duty to pursue all the long list of the great masculine and military virtues. He did not always live up to the code; but the medieval knight at his best, in Joinville, for instance, represents one of the great civilizing achievements of western culture.

The whole balance of chivalry, however, was precarious and brief. It was a way of life that lent itself readily to exaggeration, and that did not have an altogether graceful old age. The formalism, the hardening of the arteries of fashion, that seem to come upon all cultures in the West came rather quickly on this culture of chivalry. The chivalric virtue of consideration for inferiors, for the weak and unfortunate, degenerated into a maudlin pose; chivalry came to be a kind of protection for the nobleman's ego against the rising power of merchants and bankers. Most strikingly, the fighting that had perhaps once justified the existence of a feudal privileged class began to be quite frankly a game. With the rise of hired professional armies in the fourteenth century, feudal fighting decayed into the very complicated and rather dull game of the knightly tourney, or jousting. The rules grew very elaborate, the protective armor very strong, and no one suffered very much physical damage, although accidents did occur.

Chivalry, even at its most balanced, scarcely took a common-sense attitude toward love and women (if indeed there is a common sense of such matters). Decaying chivalry cultivated *romantic love*, the impossible, unearthly, unbedded love of the ideal woman, who was supposed somehow to ennoble her distant adorer. This was not the physical passion often sung by the troubadours, but the almost religious devotion to a paragon of feminine virtue. We cannot today read without a sense of strangeness even so moderate a statement of the ideals of courtly love as the "Knight's Tale" of Geoffrey Chaucer (1340-1400). In this poem from the *Canterbury Tales,* two Theban knights, the cousins Palamon and Arcite, both fall in love with the lovely Emelie, whom they have barely glimpsed from their prison. In the course of several years in prison and out, the two cousins, bound together though they are by blood and knightly honor, conduct a mortal feud over Emelie—and all this without knowing her at all, without any response from her. She finally learns of this strife for her love; but she never does anything much about it. In the final encounter of the two knights, Arcite wins glory and death, Palamon wins the maiden.

Chaucer's tale is moderate, but other late medieval romances were less bound to this earth. Lovers went through all the horrors and trials imaginable, indulged in abstract variations on the possible conflicts among Duty, Honor, and Love, and kept to their virtue as a Christian martyr kept to his faith. Yet in fairness we must note that decadent chivalry made a serious and often successful effort to police a phase of human activity which, especially in a privileged class, easily gets out of control and fosters a promiscuity disastrous to the discipline that such a class needs. Chivalry involved a real institutional sublimation of powerful sex drives. Moreover, the convention of courtly love has left its mark of unrealism upon our western culture. This tradition of romantic love is in many ways unique to our society; the Chinese, the Hindus, and many other peoples do not share it.

One final point, which is perhaps more central to the whole notion of chivalry than either religion or love, certainly more central to the decline of chivalry, is the point of honor. If early chivalry seems at bottom a code that tries to subdue the individual to the group, to make the fighting man into a member of the team, it nevertheless puts much emphasis on the individual. The knight was always acutely conscious of his honor, of himself as an individual and as final arbiter of what suited and what did not suit his dignity. In later chivalry, everything was focused on the point of honor, and the knight sometimes became a hysterically sensitive person quite cut off from the world of prosaic values. It is probably more than a coincidence that the nation whose aristocracy carried the point of honor furthest, the Spanish, also produced in Cervantes' *Don Quixote* a book that most of the world has taken to be a devastating attack on the ideals of chivalry (see Chapter XIII).

Popular Culture

We now turn from the culture of the medieval ruling classes to that of the people. The great mass of the population in the medieval West was rural. The small market towns and even the few larger cities like Paris, London, and Florence had farmlands at their gates and maintained constant relations with the nearby peasants, from whom they got most of their foodstuffs. Craftsmen living in towns might well be part-time farmers or gardeners. Popular culture was simple and relatively unchanging, but it was also worldly-wise. In the odds and ends of evidence on how the medieval masses felt, one is struck by a hard earthiness, an admiration for the cunning fellow, the successful hoodwinker of the gullible, a skepticism toward fine words and fine professions.

We should expect to find much coarseness in this culture, and indeed we do. The monosyllables which everyone knows and which only the very high-brow print nowadays appear even in Chaucer, at least when he has a commoner speak. Just as his "Knight's Tale" is a very good mirror of chivalry, so his "Miller's Tale" is an admirable literary reflection of popular taste.

It is a broad, farcical, bawdy tale, in which the jealous, stupid husband is properly cuckolded in the best traditions of folklore. It is so un-Christian that one never thinks of it in relation to Christian ideals. And yet there it is; and the miller, who tells it, is on his way to worship at the shrine of Canterbury, as are his companions, the gentle knight, the kindly clerk of Oxenford, the hearty wife of Bath, and all the rest of the Canterbury pilgrims.

Earthiness appears again in the bawdy French narratives called *fabliaux*, and in the Latin verse of the twelfth-century "Goliard poets." These poets, usually renegade scholars or clerics, purported to serve Golias, a sort of Satan, who perhaps was derived from Goliath in the Old Testament. Their verses mocked both the form and the values of serious religious poetry. Here is how the "Confessions of Golias," for example, defined the highest good:

My intention is to die
  In the tavern drinking;
Wine must be at hand, for I
  Want it when I'm sinking.
Angels when they come shall cry,
  At my frailties winking,
'Spare this drunkard, God, he's high,
  Absolutely stinking!'
Cups of wine illuminate
  Beacons of the spirit,
Draughts of nectar elevate
  Hearts to heaven, or near it.
Give me tavern liquor straight,
  Gouty lords may fear it—
Pah! their watered stuff I hate.
  Drawer, do you hear it? *

Sometimes the Goliards praised fleshly joys; sometimes, however, they sharply criticized the laxness of the clergy.

Anticlericalism was widespread in the Middle Ages. Often humorous and even goodnatured, some of the popular anticlericalism seems to have amused the clergy themselves. Visitors to medieval French

---

* "The Confession of Golias," in George F. Whicher, *The Goliard Poets* (Norfolk, Conn., 1949), 111.

churches are still shown carvings on the underside of their choir stalls, many of which show intimate and amusing details of daily life that seem to us somewhat out of place in a church. In Chaucer, who certainly knew what was going on in the popular mind, the men of God, with the exception of the clerk of Oxford, come off none too well. They have their full burden of human weaknesses. Toward the end of the Middle Ages, this earthy note took on the bitterness of social unrest. The Church was disliked as a wealthy corporation that was exploiting the poor.

But at its best, the medieval village or town was a community in which custom, backed by the authority of religion, had established a network of reciprocal rights and obligations. Within this community each man, from serf to feudal lord, could have the kind of security that comes with the knowledge that one has a place, a *status,* in a set of orderly rules of behavior resting on a well worked-out conception of the universe and of man's place in it. Of course, the peasant read neither Aquinas nor John of Salisbury; but something of the cosmology and the organic social theory of medieval intellectuals seeped down to him. Perhaps the simplest and most temperate way of putting it is this: In the Middle Ages life for the ordinary person in the West, though subject to much that we should find hardship or discomfort, indeed suffering, was psychologically more secure, *less competitive,* than life today; it was a life free from fundamental religious and ethical doubt and uncertainty.

V: Medieval Art

The Stamp of the Community

The contrast between medieval collective order and modern individualistic competition must not be exaggerated. The medieval baron sometimes built power and wealth for himself by methods quite as individualistic as those of a modern industrial baron. And, on the other side of the equation, a modern labor union can make its members conform to its rules as well as any medieval guild could. Still, the contrast is there, and it comes out well in medieval art. Admirers of the Middle Ages doubtless exaggerate when they claim that the medieval craftsman worked in complete anonymity, that he was content to carve or paint for the glory of God and the joy of creating beauty, and not for fame or money. We do not know the names of many medieval architects and sculptors, simply because the records have been lost. Yet the claim of selfless devotion for the medieval craftsman, though exaggerated, contains some truth. Both art and the artist seem to have been more closely tied to the community in the Middle Ages than they usually are in the modern world.

The greatest of medieval arts, architecture, clearly shows this community stamp. Only toward the end of the period, as great commercial fortunes begin to be made, do we find outstanding private houses, like that of the fifteenth-century French merchant Jacques Coeur in Bourges (see Chapter X). In a medieval town the cathedral, parish churches, town hall, guild halls, and other *public* buildings represent a greater proportionate expenditure of human effort and money than does the *private* property of all the citizens. You can see this concretely if you go to the cathedral of Chartres in France, which is often considered the

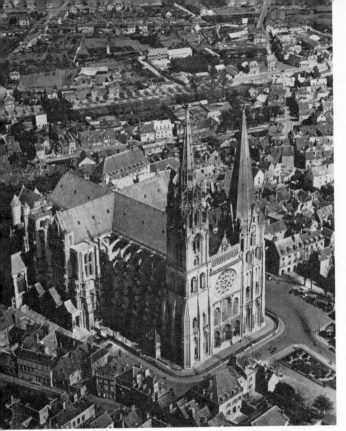

Air view of Chartres cathedral.

as a history of the Church for a population that could not read. The wealth of detail served not only to decorate but also to teach. Here the illiterate townsman or peasant could read in the universal language of art.

Gothic Architecture

The Gothic architecture of the Middle Ages develops according to the pattern common to most civilized art forms. It begins with youthful simplicity, attains a strong but graceful maturity, and trails off into an old age of overelaboration, pedantry, and striving for originality. Its immediate source is the style known as Romanesque, which prevailed in the West toward the end of the Dark Ages, and which was derived largely from the classical Roman basilica, a great hall roofed with the round arch perfected by the Romans. The Romanesque church is often built in the form of a cross. The east end, or *choir,* usually points in the general direction of the Holy Land, whence Christianity came. It contains the altar, which forms the center of worship, and places for the celebrants of the Mass. Usually the choir terminates in a semicircular *apse.*

finest medieval building. Even today, Notre Dame de Chartres dominates and embraces the little city much as it did in the Middle Ages.

The great medieval cathedrals were above all places of worship, and their almost universal cruciform (cross-shaped) plan was dictated by the needs of the Catholic cult. But they were also public gathering places, where people came to stroll, to get out of the rain, to gossip, to do business, even to court. In the quiet side chapels the worshiper could pray in peace while the people thronged the nave. As long as reasonable decorum was observed, no one thought that these activities profaned God's house; God did not expect his creatures to leave off their humanity in their dealings with him. Moreover, the statues, the paintings, the stained-glass windows, and the carvings served in effect as an illustrated Bible and

The long arm of the cross, which prolongs the choir toward the west, is the *nave,* where the congregation normally stays. The shorter arm of the cross makes up the *transepts,* north and south, and here too, though the view of the altar is not very good, there is room for a large congregation to overflow. The larger churches have *aisles,* with lower roofs, which extend outside the arms of the cross, and which follow its lines. Opening off these aisles there are sometimes—almost always in the great Gothic cathedrals—little chapels dedicated to the saints. At the crossing, where the nave and the transepts meet, many great churches have a central tower; but in the French cathedrals especially, the west end has two great towers, which, as in Notre Dame de Paris, dominate the exterior.

Since the medieval builder had no structural steel to work with, he had to support the stone ceiling and the heavy roof with masonry. The round arch of the Romanesque produced barrel vaulting, in which the ceiling presses down evenly all along the walls with great weight. To withstand this weight, the walls had to be strong, with a minimum of openings. Romanesque buildings often attain great dignity and solidity, as in the abbey church of St. Sernin at Toulouse in southern France, but since they have relatively little window space they are poorly lighted.

What freed the medieval Gothic builder to carry his buildings to soaring heights was a technical device, the pointed arch. By means of this device, the builder could carry the weight of a vaulted ceiling along masonry ribs to fall on four great supports. These supports could be pillars rather than walls, thus freeing space for large windows. A subsidiary device, the flying buttress, gave the builder a chance to provide for even more light and height. The walls of the more ambitious Romanesque churches had to be buttressed—that is, supported on the exterior by separate bits of wall at right angles to the main wall. But the Gothic builder began his buttress as part of the wall of the aisles. Then he threw out an arched support which braced that part of the masonry which held up the lofty vaults and roofs of nave, transepts, and choir. The effect is familiar to most of us, if only from postcards of Notre Dame de Paris, the apse of which has often been likened to a great galley, with the flying buttresses as oars.

With these devices, the medieval architect could indulge himself to the full in his passion for height. But this passion sometimes got out of hand; Frenchmen particularly tried to make loftier vaults with still loftier towers. The climax came

Nave of the Romanesque church of St. Sernin, Toulouse (from the early twelfth century).

with the late Gothic cathedral of Beauvais in northern France, where the best technical skills of vaulting and buttressing failed to support the ambitious central tower. The tower collapsed, and was never rebuilt. But even what remains of the apse, choir, and transepts today looks like a remarkable defiance of the law of gravity.

Gothic Architecture Evaluated

The Gothic buildings, from village church to great cathedral, represent the major effort of generations of western men to express in outward form some of their deepest feelings. They were built first of all for the glory of God on earth. They were built to serve what medieval men felt was the chief purpose of life in this world—to help toward salvation in the next world. But they were also public buildings in the full sense of the term, centers of community life. Into them went something of the spirit of community rivalry we know so well in America; each city tried to have a bigger and more splendid cathedral than other cities. Into them too there went the human desire to build permanently, impressively, and beautifully.

Most of these great buildings cost too much, in purely economic terms, for the limited resources of one city and its region in one generation. Many of them took several centuries to build, and in that period taste and fashion varied. The Gothic "style"

Cathedral of Notre Dame, Paris.

changed. For the layman, the easiest clue to these changes is the stone traceries of the windows. First comes the simple pointed arch—or lancet, as it is called in England. Gradually the traceries interweave in more complicated flowing patterns, especially in the great rose windows of French cathedrals. Finally these patterns become very complicated indeed as the windows get bigger. In France, the motif is flamelike, whence the name *flamboyant* for later French Gothic; in England, the emphasis was put on straight lines, and the later style is known as *perpendicular*. The aisles grow taller (in England they merely become longer), and the whole building becomes more and more elaborately decorated with statues, carvings, and traceries, until the west front of a flamboyant church like St. Maclou at Rouen looks like a wedding cake in stone. Since few great churches were built all of a piece, you will find in a single church perhaps a simple, pre-Gothic, round-arched crypt (a sort of basement church with shrines and chapels), an early choir, a middle-period nave, a perpendicular tower, or a flamboyant west front. The familiar west front of Chartres is a good example: it has two towers, one early and simple, one late and more ornate.

Yet, with all the mixture of primitive simplicity and late ornateness, these Gothic churches do hang together, they do give the modern observer a sense of looking at something unified. Occasionally there are failures, like the cathedral at Toulouse in France, where the later builders could not finish their work, and have left us with a building the nave of which literally does not fit the axis of the rest of the church. But, for the most part, even where a dozen generations have contributed something to the building, a Gothic cathedral remains a satisfying whole.

Gothic architecture is not wholly ecclesiastical. Yet its two other major manifestations—the great town halls and guild halls of medieval cities (at their best in the Low Countries), and the medieval castle—are both expressions of a community need. They are not merely private buildings. The best of the town halls are comparatively late. They are profusely decorated, usually with splendid towers and with at least one great room to express the medieval love of height. Many of the great castles are bound in part by military needs; these massive structures—the much-restored French castle of Pierrefonds will serve as an example— were first of all designed for the purpose of keeping the enemy out. But even these great fortresses often have a chapel and a hall that bear the mark of the Gothic love of light, height, and decoration.

If you are searching for the most complete, in a sense the most typical, Gothic building, you will find it not in the castles or town halls, nor even in the cathedrals, but in the great monastic abbeys. One of the best, though now no longer a religious

Interior of Beauvais cathedral, France, begun in 1247.

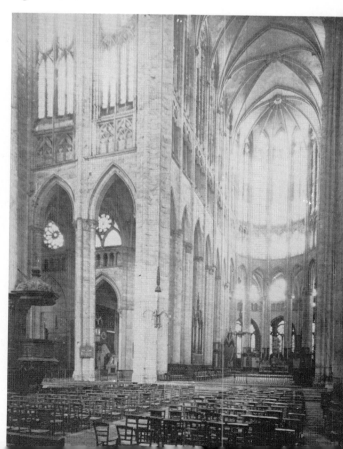

Flamboyant Gothic architecture. Church of Saint-Maclou, Rouen, France.

community but a mere museum piece, is the great abbey of St. Michel on the border of Brittany and Normandy. Mont-St.-Michel, a rocky islet tied to the mainland by a narrow causeway, is at once a fortress, a town, and a monastery. The late Henry Adams found in it, with some help from Chartres and the *Chanson de Roland*, the whole Middle Ages.

The Other Fine Arts

To these great community buildings the whole train of the fine arts—sculpture, painting, stained glass, carving, even music —contributed. Indeed up to the very last centuries of the Middle Ages these arts had hardly any other major outlet. Sculpture is a clear example. In the Middle Ages you do not find portrait busts in the great castles, cupids in the fountains of their courtyards, or even statues in the town squares. When you do find these things, you are passing out of the Middle Ages into the Renaissance.

Sculpture in the Middle Ages is subordinate to architecture. Statues and carvings are fitted into the design of the great churches, in niches on the fronts and porches, or on altars and shrines in the interior. The greatly admired statues on the early west front of Chartres are unnaturally elongated, but they fit all the better

336

into the builder's purpose of framing the entrance arch. Later, the statues—those at Rheims or Amiens, for example—are more "lifelike." But even this later Gothic sculpture, if only because it is bringing to life God, Christ, angels, saints—and devils—is never simply realistic in the way of the portrait bust, nor independently grand in the way of the equestrian statue. It is always a part of the "stone Bible." It almost always tells a story, as in the many representations of the Last Judgment, which is a favorite subject of the medieval sculptor. Finally, the sculpture of the Middle Ages is fond of the grotesque, as in the gargoyles of Notre Dame de Paris, which Victor Hugo and the postcard trade have combined to fix in all our minds.

Painting, too, is subordinated to the building. The medieval church had no place for the canvas designed to be hung for exhibition. Mosaics, wall painting, and above all stained glass contributed to the total de-sign. Time has dealt harshly with most of the paintings on walls and pillars, which were apparently brightly colored, almost gay. The stained glass, though suffering heavily from Protestant puritanism and from modern wars and revolutions, still survives as the great medieval achievement in painting. The glass was not really painted of course; each separate bit of the design was stained in the making, and the whole was pieced together as a mosaic of colored glass held in place by leaden tracery. Artists today have been unable to reproduce the colors of the great medieval rose windows of Chartres or Paris; but it is not clear whether this is because glass-staining is really a lost art, or because nothing can quite take the place of the long, slow, chemical action of time in the making of the glass.

The painting itself is at first stiff, whether in glass, murals, altar pieces, or in that characteristic medieval form, miniature paint-

The abbey of Mont-St. Michel.

West portals of Chartres cathedral, from about 1145-1170. Christ enthroned may be seen above the center doorway.

ing on illuminated manuscripts. Like the sculpture, the painting owes a great debt to the Byzantines (see Chapter VI). Again, as with sculpture, design later grows freer, more "naturalistic." Finally, the Italian painter Giotto (*c.* 1270-1337) and his successors begin to use highlights and the new science of geometrical perspective to suggest in the two dimensions of painting the three dimensions our eyes see in nature (see Chapter XI). But by the time of Giotto we are in a sense emerging from the medieval world into the modern world. Medieval men did not equate God and nature quite as we do; nor did they have the eye of the camera.

Wood-carver and stone-carver contributed their share—an important share—to the Gothic cathedral. Nothing is scamped or hasty in these buildings. A minor bit of vaulting, tucked away on the ceiling almost out of sight of the observer on the floor of the nave far below, is almost always done with loving care and perfection. The capi-

tals of the columns, unlike the Greco-Roman capitals from which they were probably derived, are carved in infinite variety, with motifs stemming from plant life but often interspersed with figures—human, animal, or purely fanciful.

Music

Medieval music fits the general pattern of medieval culture. Church music began in the sixth century with Gregorian chant or plain-song. Plain-song was simply a series of musical tones sung in unison, but with no set rhythmic interval between them. It was used in church services as a setting for the psalms and other prose. But apparently there were also hymns in metrical or verse form, which could be accommodated to a simple tune. As Europe emerged from the Dark Ages, music, like the other arts, grew more and more complex. Our present method of musical nota-

CHAPTER VIII

tion—the staff—was invented, or at any rate developed and taught, by an eleventh-century Italian monk, Guido d'Arezzo. Church music developed both melody and harmony—the sounding of two or more notes simultaneously—until the peak of balanced form and matter was reached in the thirteenth century. Later medieval church music sometimes became extremely complex musical puzzles. To understand them, the listener needs to have an elaborate technical education.

No doubt there had always been singing among the people. But conscious secular musical composition begins in the Middle Ages with the minstrels, who often elaborated popular tunes. By the end of the fourteenth century we get something like the modern composer, for example the Italian Landini, who wrote songs, called madrigals, set for two voices. As with architecture, the admirer of the Middle Ages makes much of the point that until the very eve of the Renaissance both church music and the music of the minstrels were anonymous, the product of community life. And again as with architecture, the cautious historian can only say that this anonymity may be simply a result of the gaps in our historical record.

Romanesque sculpture. Capital atop a pillar in the church at Vézelay, France, illustrating Ganymede being carried off by the eagle.

VI: Conclusion: The Medieval Way of Life

Looking back, we can see in the Middle Ages a seedbed of our own way of life, or even a kind of youth of which we are the apparent maturity. Modern economic organization by no means begins with the industrial revolutions of the years since 1750; it goes back to the breakup of self-sufficient manorialism and the rise of a money economy of trade and industry in the later medieval centuries. Our representative government, although it has been greatly modified since the Middle Ages, is clearly medieval in origin. So is modern nationalism, however much it has been strengthened by mass participation since the great revolutions of the seventeenth, eighteenth, nineteenth and twentieth centuries. More important, and less obvious, is the fact that our basic concept of law as something virtually sacred has its roots in medieval society. Whether we call this concept "natural law," or "higher law," or "constitutional law," it is one of our main bulwarks against totalitarianism. It has come down to us from Greco-Roman and Judaic sources, strengthened by the beliefs and the institutions of our medieval ancestors.

Yet it will not do to regard all medieval culture as simply a preparation for our own, or to view the men and women who made the art, literature, philosophy, and theology of the Middle Ages as merely "ourselves-when-young." The cathedral of Chartres, a *Summa* of St. Thomas, a romance of chivalry, a Gregorian chant are of course by no means beyond our powers of comprehension and enjoyment. But they remain in a sense alien and remote, the product of another time and another culture. Like the Magdalenian cave drawings, the Egyptian pyramids, the Greek temple, they have a "style" of their own.

That style is most apparent in the great poetic masterpiece of the high Middle Ages—the *Divine Comedy* of Dante Alighieri (1265-1321), which recounts the poet's trip through Hell, Purgatory, and finally Heaven. At the beginning of the *Comedy*, Dante, the narrator, is lost in a dark wood. He meets the Latin poet Vergil, who directs him:

Thou take me for thy guide, and pass with me,
Through an eternal place and terrible
Where thou shalt hear despairing cries, and see
Long-parted souls that in their torments dire
Howl for the second death perpetually.
Next, thou shalt gaze on those who in the fire
Are happy, for they look to mount on high,
In God's good time, up to the blissful quire;
To which glad place, a worthier spirit than I
Must lead thy steps. . . . *

Dante himself made the purpose of the *Divine Comedy* very plain in a letter to his patron:

The subject of the whole work, then, taken merely in the *literal* sense is 'the state of the

* *The Divine Comedy: Hell*, D. L. Sayers, trans. (Harmondsworth, Middlesex, 1949), Canto I, lines 113-121.

soul after death straightforwardly affirmed', for the development of the whole work hinges on and about that. But if, indeed, the work is taken *allegorically*, its subject is: 'Man, as by good or ill deserts, in the exercise of his free choice, he becomes liable to rewarding or punishing Justice.' *

Although we shall see later on (in Chapter X) that the *Divine Comedy* has qualities that reach beyond the Middle Ages into the Renaissance, its grand theme is medieval through and through, the Christian drama of the soul.

Now, as we have insisted, it is a mistake to think of this medieval "style" as primitive, childlike, or even youthful. Medieval culture has its own characteristic cycle of youth in the Dark Ages, maturity in the thirteenth century, decline and old age in the fourteenth and fifteenth. A word more about the centuries of decline and "hardening." In institutions, we may take as an example the papacy of the Babylonian Captivity: its claims are as large as ever, or larger, and the phraseology in which they are put is even more extravagant; but the popes by then faced a very complicated Europe—a Europe of rising dynastic states with new commercial ambitions; and they faced within the Church a series of intellectual and moral challenges that became the Conciliar Movement. They could not succeed as Innocent III succeeded. In Scholastic philosophy the techniques remain, but the inspiration and the capacity that led to Aquinas' great work in the thirteenth century have been replaced by rather futile debates over details. In architecture the great experiments all seem to have been made, and the late Gothic buildings often show what appears to be rather sterile elaboration on earlier forms, as in the contrast between the late and early towers of Chartres.

Yet, throughout, the style remains. Even in the masterpieces of medieval maturity,

* Quoted in *ibid.*, 15.

even in Chartres or in Dante, there is a note of simple recognition of the universe as something far transcending our poor human power of comprehension. Much of what we today seek to understand through the scientific study of nature the medieval man simply assigned to the realm of the supernatural, the realm of wonders, surprises, "miracles." Here is a single example: The mutterings and the odd behavior of a lonely old woman were not to medieval man a sign of senile degeneration of the central nervous system; they were signs of the influence of a supernatural being, the devil, and they meant that the woman was a "witch."

Put negatively, medieval men did not have our modern faith in the possibility of understanding and conquering the material world. They did not have the idea of progress. Put positively, what we have been saying is a clue to the serenity, the poise, and the wholeness of medieval culture. The medieval man did not expect physical comforts and luxuries, did not expect to avoid smallpox by vaccination, did not expect good roads, did not, in short, expect a thousand things that we take for granted. He was used to a hard life (in our terms), to violence and uncertainty. Nothing in his philosophy led him to expect that life on earth could actually be very different from what it had always been.

Such beliefs do not mean that the medieval man expected nothing, or that he was never discontented. A shrewish wife, for instance, was as unpleasant to live with in the thirteenth as in the twentieth century. But in no class of society, except occasionally among monarchs, would the thirteenth-century husband dream of trying to divorce his wife for "mental cruelty," or indeed for any other reason. Marriage was for him made in heaven, even if it had not been made well. God had made marriage indissoluble. So too with many other aspects of human life, which we tend to

"October," from *Les très riches heures du duc de Berry.*

regard as arrangements a man can make or unmake on his own. For the medieval man, much of his life was out of his own hands; it was, instead, in the hands of God working through society. We come back to the inescapable fact that medieval life was pervaded by the Christian attitude.

The Christian promise of salvation in an afterlife for the man or woman who lives on earth according to the precepts of the Church no doubt helps explain the Christian hold over the medieval mind. But the notion of religion as an opiate is a product of the modern mind, which thinks—or hopes—that human suffering is not in the order of things. Christianity for the medieval man not merely gave promise of a better life in the next world; it gave a meaning and purpose to this uncertain life on earth. More nearly than we, medieval man was *resigned* to a world he could not greatly change. He felt secure in the midst of what we should regard as insecurity precisely because he was keenly aware of his own weakness. He was neither ashamed nor disturbed by this weakness; it was not his fault, nor was it, humanly speaking, anyone's fault—certainly one could not be impious enough to attribute the fault to God. It is no accident that one of the best-known passages of Dante is

E'en la sua volontate è nostra pace:
    Ella è quel mare al qual tutto si move
    Ciò ch' ella crea, e che natura face.

"And in his will is our peace: that will is the ocean to which moves everything that it creates or that nature makes."

Reading Suggestions on Medieval Civilization in the West

(Asterisk indicates paperbound edition.)

GENERAL ACCOUNTS

H. O. Taylor, *The Mediaeval Mind*, new ed. (Harvard Univ. Press, 1949). A great, inclusive work by a modern American scholar. Both sympathetic and objective in its treatment of the Middle Ages.

H. Adams, *Mont-St.Michel and Chartres* (Houghton Mifflin, 1933; *Anchor). By a distinguished American of a generation back, very much disturbed by the machine age and attracted to the Middle Ages. An unreliable but highly stimulating introduction to the beauties of medieval architecture and literature.

G. C. Coulton, *Medieval Panorama* (Macmillan, 1938; *Meridian). This and other writings of Coulton are full of interesting details, but are basically "anticlerical" and unsympathetic toward much of medieval culture.

M. De Wulf, *Philosophy and Civilization in the Middle Ages* (Princeton Univ. Press, 1922; *Dover). Popular lectures by a great medieval scholar.

F. B. Artz, *The Mind of the Middle Ages*, A.D. 200-1500, 2nd ed. (Knopf, 1954). A very useful survey.

J. Huizinga, *Men and Ideas* (*Meridian, 1959). A collection of essays by a distinguished historian with special interest in the transitional period from medieval to modern times.

A. L. Poole, ed., *Medieval England*, 2 vols. (Oxford Univ. Press, 1958). Two nicely illustrated volumes, essentially a medley of essays by specialists, on such aspects of culture as landscape, communications, architecture, heraldry, education, recreation and other matters; uneven, but with much not elsewhere available to the general reader.

SPECIAL STUDIES

J. H. Clapham and E. Power, eds., *The Cambridge Economic History*, Vol. I, and M. Postan and E. E. Rich, eds., Vol. II (Cambridge Univ. Press, 1944, 1952). A definitive survey of many aspects of the material basis of medieval· civilization in the West.

CHAPTER VIII

P. Boissonade, *Life and Work in Medieval Europe* (Knopf, 1927). A good introduction to the social and economic life of villages, manors, countryside, and towns in the Middle Ages.

J. W. Baldwin, "The Medieval Theories of the Just Price," *Transactions* of the American Philosophical Society (July 1959). A study of characteristic twelfth- and thirteenth-century theories of what prices were legitimate.

H. Pirenne, *Medieval Cities* (Princeton Univ. Press, 1925; *Anchor). An excellent, readable, short essay.

S. Painter, *Mediaeval Society* (Cornell Univ. Press, 1951). A handy introduction designed for the beginning student.

S. Painter, *French Chivalry* (Johns Hopkins Univ. Press, 1940; *Cornell Univ. Press). A very good survey of the ideals and behavior of feudal society.

H. Rashdall, *The Universities of Europe in the Middle Ages,* new ed., 3 vols. (Clarendon, 1936). The classic account; full and readable.

C. H. Haskins, *The Rise of Universities* (Peter Smith, 1940; *Cornell Univ. Press). A delightful series of short essays. See also his *Renaissance of the Twelfth Century* (*Meridian, 1957). A reprint of the original of 1927.

L. Thorndike, *A History of Magic and Experimental Science,* 8 vols. (Macmillan, 1923-1956), and A. C. Crombie, *Augustine to Galileo: The History of Science, A.D. 400-1650* (Harvard Univ. Press, 1953). A detailed and a briefer account, both good.

S. Baldwin, *The Organization of Medieval Christianity* (Holt, 1929, Berkshire Studies). An introductory study.

A. C. McGiffert, *History of Christian Thought,* Vol. II (Scribner's, 1933). A good survey.

C. Dawson, *Religion and the Rise of Western Culture* (Sheed and Ward, 1950; *Image). An admirably sympathetic but also realistic survey in terms of cultural history.

E. Gilson, *The Spirit of Medieval Philosophy* (Scribner's, 1936). By a distinguished scholar, sympathetic to the Middle Ages.

P. Sabatier, *Life of St. Francis of Assisi* (Scribner's, 1912). A well-balanced biography of a personality hard to evaluate objectively.

A. Jessopp, *The Coming of the Friars* (Allen & Unwin, 1903). An old but still indispensable book, dealing mainly with England.

H. Waddell, *The Wandering Scholars* (Constable, 1927; *Anchor). A good study.

E. Troeltsch, *The Social Teaching of the Christian Churches,* 2 vols. (Macmillan, 1931). A subtle and rather difficult work of great significance.

C. R. Morey, *Medieval Art* (Norton, 1942). A good introduction.

C. H. McIlwain, *The Growth of Political Thought in the West* (Macmillan, 1932). An understanding and scholarly discussion.

HISTORICAL FICTION

There are many historical novels about the Middle Ages, a few of them quite good (see the suggestions for Chapters V and VII). But the best literary introduction to the many-sided human beings of the Middle Ages is provided by Chaucer's *Canterbury Tales*. E. Power's *Medieval People* (*Anchor) is an admirable set of brief biographical sketches of a half-dozen individuals from various walks of medieval life. Zoe Oldenbourg's *The Cornerstone* (Pantheon, 1955) is a remarkably frank novel about an early thirteenth-century French noble family. Helen Waddell's *Peter Abelard* (*Compass) is a novel about the famous love affair with Heloise.

CHAPTER VIII

The East:

Late Middle Ages

CHAPTER IX

I: The Main Threads

IN THE PAST FEW CHAPTERS we have been considering separately three great societies—Roman Christendom, Greek Christendom, and Islam. In the third quarter of the eleventh century, the relations between them entered upon a long period of crisis that was fundamentally important for the future of all three. Our first task in this chapter is to deal with the late medieval interaction of these three societies, particularly in the movement called the Crusades. Next, we shall consider the decline and final collapse of the Byzantine Empire. And, finally, we shall trace the fortunes down to the end of the seventeenth century of the two states that, in different senses, were its successors: the Ottoman Empire, and Muscovite Russia. In this introductory section we shall examine the main pattern of all these developments before discussing them in detail in subsequent sections.

By the eleventh century, each of the three societies had well-established relationships with the other two. Byzantium and the West had conducted diplomatic negotiations; the papacy had maintained regular official contact with the Byzantines even after the official break in 1054; and southern Italy had been a Byzantine outpost. The Byzantines had been involved in more or less continuous war and diplomacy with the caliphate and the local Moslem dynasties in Syria. Islam had touched Roman Christendom in Spain and Sicily, and western pilgrims had thronged, as we shall see, to the shrines of Christendom in Moslem Palestine. But after 1071, when the Normans took Bari and drove the Byzantines from Italy, and the Seljuk Turks won at Manzikert and battered their way into the central Byzantine stronghold of Asia Minor, the tempo of the relationship steadily quickened. For the next six centuries, the fate of each society became ever more closely bound up with the fate of the other two.

The Norman assault on the Byzantines now moved eastward from Italy across the Adriatic to the Balkan shores of the Empire itself. In order to ward it off, the Byzantine emperors, pressed as they were simultaneously by the Seljuks, in 1082 made an alliance with the booming port of Venice—once their vassal, now their equal. In exchange for naval assistance, they gave the Venetians commercial concessions in the Empire. Permitted to import and export at special tariff rates, and given a quarter in Constantinople itself, with warehouses, churches, and dwelling-places, the Venetians and later the Genoese joined the sailors of Amalfi and Pisa in taking over the carrying-trade of the eastern Mediterranean.

The Crusades

Meanwhile, the papacy, stimulated by Byzantine appeals for military assistance against the Seljuks, proclaimed a holy war against Islam. This concept had already become familiar in the Byzantine wars against the Moslems and in the Catholic attempts to reconquer Spain and Sicily. In 1095, Pope Urban II launched the great military movement of the crusade. The recovery of the Holy Sepulchre was the ultimate aim, and the Crusaders fought with the cross as their symbol. They were granted special privileges as soldiers of the Lord. From then on for a period of almost two hundred years, expedition after expedition was hurled against the Moslems, most often in Syria and Palestine, but also in Egypt, North Africa, and even Portugal. The armies were sometimes commanded by kings and emperors, sometimes by lesser nobles. Sometimes they came by sea, sometimes by land, sometimes by a combined land-and-sea route. Sometimes they scored successes, great or small; more often they met with partial or total failure. Reinforcements from the West flowed to the East in an almost continuous stream. Therefore, the practice of calling certain specific expeditions the "Second," "Third," or "Fourth" Crusade, and so on up to the "Eighth," is really not very accurate, though it is often useful.

As a result of the First Crusade, the westerners established in Moslem territory in Syria four independent states of their own, usually called the "Latin" states or "Frankish" states (to the Moslems all westerners were "Franks"). These states were ruled by Europeans of various origins, jealous of each other and often at odds. After the First Crusade, many of the later expeditions were directed toward meeting some emergency that had arisen in the Latin states. Here in the East, an interesting society sprang up in which western feudal practice could combine with Moslem local practice. Yet by 1187 the Moslems, overcoming their disunity, had swept away all but a remnant of the western outposts. After a century of epilogue, the process was complete by 1291.

Thereafter, although the crusading ideal continued to be preached in the West, no major expedition was ever again launched to reconquer the Holy Land, which remained in Moslem hands. In the fourteenth and fifteenth centuries some of the western expeditions against the Ottoman Turks took on various aspects of a crusade, but they were never the genuine article.

The Downfall of Byzantium

Most of the important crusading expeditions passed through Byzantium. From the first, the emperors were embarrassed by the presence of the often uncontrollable "barbarian" armies in their territory. Naturally, they tried to move the westerners as quickly as possible on to Moslem soil and into the combat against the infidel for which they had come. But the westerners tended to regard these precautions as "perfidy," and distrusted the Greeks. The vast material wealth of Constantinople appealed greatly to the greedy eyes of the western European military commanders. There were profound religious and social differences between the Greeks and Latins, and the Byzantines hated the Italian merchants resident among them as well as the western armies pouring through the capital. Tension mounted throughout the twelfth century. Internal disorder increased, signalized by a great increase in Byzantine feudal decentralization.

Finally, in 1204, the "Fourth" Crusade, which had set out from Venice by sea to fight in the Holy Land, was diverted for political reasons to Constantinople, and took the city by storm. This was the first time the Byzantine capital had been taken, and it marks a landmark in the history of the relations between eastern and western Christians. The westerners set up a "Latin Empire" in Constantinople, gained a foothold in Asia Minor, and founded feudal principalities throughout Greece and in the islands of the Aegean. Meanwhile, the Byzantines, driven from their capital, founded two Greek states in Asia Minor, Trebizond and Nicaea, and one in Europe, Epirus. All three eventually called themselves empires.

In 1261, the Latins, deprived of help from home, without roots, hated by the Greeks, were driven from Constantinople by the Greek Emperor of Nicaea, and the Byzantine Empire was restored. But from then on for the next two centuries, the Empire was merely a shadow of its former self. Though expelled as rulers from the capital, the westerners remained in Greece and on the islands. Venetians and Genoese retained and strengthened their privileged positions in Constantinople. In the Balkans, the Serbians rose to a position of power, and menaced Byzantium itself. It proved entirely impossible to restore the Byzantine military or economic system. Although its pretensions to being the only civilized state in the world and its theoretical aspirations to world-empire were never abandoned, Byzantium was now only a Balkan state. And, toward the end of the thirteenth century the Byzantine emperors became aware of how great a danger was presented by a new Turkish people, the Osmanlis, or Ottoman Turks. Moslems like the rest, the Ottoman Turks in only a few generations had been able to consolidate their power in northwestern Asia Minor, opposite Constantinople.

The Ottoman Turks

Themselves a product of a fusion between Greek natives and Turkish invaders, the Osmanlis crossed the Straits into Europe in the mid-fourteenth century, were invited to assist the parties in the ever-growing internal Byzantine strife, and gradually became a European power. They occupied most of the former Byzantine territory, except for the capital itself. A variety of efforts to reunite the eastern and western churches and to obtain assistance from the Roman Catholic West for the Byzantines, who were beleaguered by their Moslem enemy, all met with failure. In 1453, the Osmanlis besieged and captured the city of Constantine, and the Empire that proudly traced its origins to Augustus finally came to an end.

Yet the end, though definite enough, was

in some ways more of an appearance than a reality. The Ottoman Turks by 1453 had become a partly European people, and, though their system had many features that may be considered purely Turkish, they too, like so many of the earlier enemies of the Empire, were overwhelmed by their sense of its prestige. With Constantinople as their capital, the Ottoman sultans ruled like Byzantine emperors. Though Moslem, they permitted their Christian subjects to worship in their own way. Although the Christians suffered certain disabilities, the religious life of the Orthodox continued to be governed by the Patriarch of Constantinople, a Greek as always. Byzantine ways persisted throughout the Balkan region. In a real sense, the Ottoman Empire, despite its own peculiar institutions, was a successor state to Byzantium, and many of its inhabitants were descendants of the Byzantines.

Extraordinarily successful as a military power, the Turks, during the first two centuries of their domination at Constantinople, repeatedly threatened Europe. Twice they advanced as far as Vienna, and they fought naval wars all over the Mediterranean. Although a new general crusade against them was never launched successfully, many crusades were preached. The West did develop strong defenders, especially the Habsburg rulers of the Holy Roman Empire, now centered at Vienna, who in the end were able to resist the Ottoman onslaught. And meanwhile, after the end of the sixteenth century, the Ottoman system itself was in full internal decay. The astonishing thing is that it was able to forestall total disruption. By the end of the seventeenth century, European rulers were already beginning to discuss how they should divide the Turkish lands when the Empire fell apart. But contrary to all calculations, the Ottoman Empire, perhaps largely because its existence was valuable to some of the European powers, continued to exist down to the end of World War I in our own twentieth century.

Post-Kievan Russia

Although the Ottoman Empire represented a kind of successor state to Byzantium, it was still a Moslem state. There was, however, another state, which, though it occupied no Byzantine territory and never included within its borders more than a handful of Byzantine subjects, was also in its way a successor state to Byzantium, and which regarded itself as the new leader of the Orthodox world. This was Russia, whose story we left at the time of the decline of Kiev, when it was torn by internal dissension and a prey to invasion by the Mongol Tartars.

In the thirteenth, fourteenth, and early fifteenth centuries, the extreme western portions of the Kievan state fell under Polish and Lithuanian influence. At the same time, the city of Novgorod in the north continued to develop its trade with the West, chiefly Germany, and its municipal institutions. But the most striking feature of Russian development was the Tartar domination of the entire northeastern and eastern regions. The domination was exercised from afar, and, except for devastating raids, was not an occupation. Its most conspicuous feature was a levying of tribute. It was not until the fifteenth century that the princes of Moscow, who for a variety of reasons had emerged as the leading power in the region, were able to throw off this obligation, and even after this, the Tartars continued to have important settlements on Russian soil. The most important effect that the Tartar domination had on the future development of Russia was the cutting off of so vast an area from the West, and the consequent deepening of the cultural lag that we have already observed as one of the consequences of Kievan Russia's having been converted to Christianity from Byzantium.

Moreover, the princes of Moscow, in establishing themselves as supreme over the

Russian lands, received from the Orthodox Church, which was backing them in their endeavor, a full-fledged ideology: that Moscow was the successor of Byzantium, which had fallen to the Turks, and thus of Rome, which had fallen to the schismatic Roman Catholics. Moscow was thus the third and final Rome, and the rulers of Moscow were the direct heirs of the Byzantine emperors. The importance of this concept for future Russian historical development is sometimes disputed by scholars. But we shall try to show how deeply affected by it the Russian princes actually were, and how greatly it contributed to their absolutist rule in practice.

II: The Crusades

The Idea of a Holy War

In 964, the Byzantine Emperor Nicephorus Phocas (963-969) was about to go to war against the Arabs. He wrote a long letter to the Caliph, full of insults, threats, and boasts of his previous victories:

We have conquered your impregnable fortresses ... left piles of corpses with blood still pouring from them ... rendered your peasants and their wives helpless in the very midst of their flocks. Lofty buildings have been destroyed. ... When the owl hoots there now, echo answers. ... People of Baghdad, flee at once, and bad luck to you, for your weakened empire will not last. ... I shall march with all speed toward Mecca, bringing in my train a throng of soldiers black as night. I shall seize that city, and stay there a time at my ease, so that I may establish there a throne for the best of beings: Christ.*

Nicephorus' successor, John Tsimiskes (969-976), in 975 wrote a letter to his ally, the King of Armenia, in which he tells of his campaigns of that year against the Moslems in Syria. He had taken Damascus, he wrote, and Nazareth:

People came from Ramleh and Jerusalem, to beseech our majesty for grace. They asked of us a leader, and declared themselves to be our subjects. We gave them what they asked for.

It was our wish to free the holy tomb of Christ from the insults of the Moslems. ... If those accursed Africans [i.e., Egyptian Moslems] who now live in Caesarea on the seacoast had not taken refuge in the castles along the shore, we should have marched into the holy city of Jerusalem and should have been able to pray in those holy places.*

These two tenth-century Byzantine documents breathe the spirit of the later western movement known as the Crusades: a holy war against the Moslems for the possession of the Holy Places. Although the Byzantines never were able to fulfill their ambition, they had the will and the intention.

Similarly, in the West, the idea of a holy war was not new in 1095. In Spain, the fighting of Christian against Moslem had been virtually continuous since the Moslem conquest in the eighth century. The small Christian states of the north pushed southward when they could, and retreated again when they had to. Just after the year 1000, the great Cordovan Caliphate weakened, and the Spanish Christian princes of the north won the support of the powerful French abbey at Cluny (see pp. 307-308). Under prodding from Cluny, French nobles joined the Spaniards in warring on the Moslems. And soon the Pope offered an

* G. L. Schlumberger, *Nicéphore Phocas* (Paris, 1923), 348 ff. Our translation.

* G. L. Schlumberger, *L'Epopée Byzantine* (Paris, 1896), I, 287-288. Our translation.

indulgence to all who would fight for the Cross in Spain. In 1085, the Christians took the great city of Toledo, but a new wave of Moslem Berbers from North Africa set them back for a time. The Christian movement continued during the remainder of the eleventh century, and on into the twelfth. It recovered a large area of central Spain, and it was itself a crusade: a holy war against the infidel supported by the papacy. So too were the wars of the Normans in southern Italy against the Moslems of Sicily.

Pilgrimages

From the third century on, it had been a practice for Christians to visit the scenes of Christ's life. Constantine's mother, Saint Helena, visited Jerusalem, and discovered the True Cross and other relics of the Passion. Her son built the church of the Holy Sepulchre. Before the Moslem conquest in the seventh century, pilgrims came from Byzantium and the West, often seeking sacred relics for their churches at home. For a while after the Moslem conquest, pilgrimages were very dangerous, and could be undertaken only by the hardiest pilgrims. St. Willibald, an Englishman who made the journey between 722 and 729, encountered freezing cold and hunger in Asia Minor, captivity and imprisonment as a spy by Moslems in northern Syria, sickness on three different occasions, blindness at Gaza, a savage lion in the olive groves of Esdraelon, severe Moslem customs officers at Tyre (Willibald was smuggling at the time), and a volcanic eruption on an Italian island on the way home.

During the reign of Charlemagne, conditions improved for western pilgrims, largely because of the excellent relations between Charlemagne and the famous Caliph Harun al-Rashid (see above, p. 254). The Caliph made him a present of the actual recess in which Christ was buried. He also sent him a live elephant named Abu'l Abbas, who became a general favorite at Aachen, and a clock of gilded bronze with twelve mounted knights who on the stroke of noon emerged from twelve doors which shut behind them. Charlemagne was allowed to endow a hostel in Jerusalem for the use of pilgrims. He gave a splendid library to the Latin church of St. Mary, and sent money and bought land to support Christian foundations. So deep was Charlemagne's interest that there sprang up a legend that he had somehow acquired from Harun a "protectorate" over the Holy Land, and another that he had actually made a pilgrimage to the East in person. Neither of these stories is true, but they reflect the importance of the pilgrimage in Charlemagne's period.

In the tenth century, the belief grew that pilgrimage would procure God's pardon for sins. St. James (Santiago) of Compostella in Spain, and of course Rome itself, became favorite places of pilgrimage, but no place could compare in importance with the shrines of Palestine. As with the holy war in Spain, Cluny fostered pilgrimages. Now large organized groups replaced the individual journey. Great lords with suites of followers came, as well as humble clerics from all over Europe. We know of more than one hundred western pilgrimages during the eleventh century. On one occasion, contemporaries report 7,000 German pilgrims, all traveling together.

The Late-Eleventh-Century Crisis

Stable conditions in both Moslem and Byzantine dominions were essential for the easy and safe continuance of pilgrimages. Yet, with the death of the last ruler of the Macedonian house in 1057, there began at Byzantium an open struggle between the party of the court civil servants and the military party of the great Asia

Minor landowners (see above, p. 239). Simultaneously came Pecheneg invasions of the Balkans, Norman attacks on Byzantine southern Italy, and the rise in Asia of the Seljuks. By 1050, the Turks had created a state centering on Persia. In 1055, they entered Baghdad on the invitation of the Abbasid Caliph himself, and became the champions of Sunnite Islam against the Shiite rulers of Egypt. In the 1050's, Seljuk forces appeared in Armenia and Asia Minor; they raided deep into Anatolia, almost to the Aegean. Their advance culminated in the catastrophic Byzantine defeat of Manzikert in 1071, followed by the occupation of most of Asia Minor, and the establishment of a new sultanate with its capital at Nicaea. The Seljuks conquered not only much of Asia Minor but also Syria and Palestine. Jerusalem fell in the very year of Manzikert and Bari, 1071, and became part of a new Seljuk state of Syria.

Amid disorder and palace intrigue, with the Empire reduced in territory and the capital in danger, there came to the Byzantine throne in 1081 Alexius I Comnenus, a general and a great landowner, who was to found a dynasty that staved off disaster for over a century. Between 1081 and 1085, he held off the Norman attack on the Dalmatian coast by means of his alliance with Venice. He was at home in the slippery field of intrigue, playing one local Turkish potentate off against another, and slowly re-establishing a Byzantine foothold in Asia. Civil wars among the Turks and the multiplication of brigands on the highways in Anatolia and Syria made pilgrimage in the two decades after Manzikert a dangerous pursuit indeed, despite the relatively decent conditions in Palestine itself.

The schism between eastern and western churches provided the papacy with an additional incentive for intervention in the East. The vigorous reforming popes of the later eleventh century felt that the disunity of Christendom was intolerable, the rending of a seamless garment. In 1073, Pope Gregory VII sent an ambassador to Constantinople, who reported that the Emperor was anxious for a reconciliation and emphasized the dreadful conditions brought about for travelers by the Turkish conquests in Asia Minor. Gregory VII planned to extend the holy war from Spain to Asia, by sending the Byzantines an army of western knights. Even more striking, he intended to lead them himself, and thus put himself in a position to bring about a reunion of the churches. It was only the quarrel with the German Emperor (see Chapter VII) that prevented the Pope from carrying out this plan. But here, more than twenty years before the opening of the First Crusade, all the elements are combined: a holy war, to be fought in alliance with the Greeks against the Moslems in Asia, under the direct sponsorship of the papacy.

The First Crusade

Pope Urban II (1088-1099) was in the tradition of Gregory VII. To his Council at Piacenza in 1095 came envoys from Alexius, who asked for military help against the Turks. Turkish power was declining, and now would be a good time to strike. The Byzantine envoys also seem to have stressed the sufferings of the Christians in the East. In any case, eight months later, at the Council of Clermont (1095), Urban preached to the throng of the faithful. He emphasized the appeal received from eastern Christians, brothers in difficulty, and painted in dark colors the hardships that now faced pilgrims to Jerusalem. He summoned his listeners to form themselves, rich and poor alike, into an army, which God would assist. Killing each other at home should give way to fighting a holy war. Poverty at home would yield to the riches of the East (a theme especially important in view of the misery in which so many Europeans lived). If a man were killed doing this work of God, he would automatically be absolved of his sins and assured of salvation. The audience greeted this moving oration with cries of "God wills it." Throngs of volunteers took a solemn oath, and sewed crosses of cloth onto their clothes. Recruitment was under way. The First Crusade had been launched.

On the popular level, it was a certain Peter the Hermit, an unkempt old man, barefoot, who lived on fish and wine and was a moving orator, who proved the most effective preacher of the Crusade. Through France and Germany he recruited an undisciplined mob of ignorant peasants, including women and children, many of them serfs living wretched lives, suffering near-starvation as a result of crop-failure. Often they believed that Peter was leading them straight to heaven, the New Jerusalem, flowing with milk and honey, which they confused with the Jerusalem on earth. People less well-fitted for the tasks of the holy war can hardly be imagined.

In two installments, the rabble poured up the Rhine, across Hungary, where, among other incidents, 4,000 Hungarians were killed in a riot over the sale of a pair of shoes, and into Byzantine territory at Belgrade. The Byzantines, who had hoped for the loan of a few hundred well-trained knights, were appalled at the prospect of the enormous armies of human locusts about to descend on them from the West. They proceeded to arrange military escorts, and to take all precautions against trouble. Despite their best efforts, the undisciplined Crusaders burned houses, and stole everything that was not chained down, including the lead from the roofs of churches.

Once in Constantinople, they were graciously received by Alexius Comnenus (1081-1118), who none the less felt it necessary to ship them across the Straits as quickly as possible. In Asia Minor they quarreled among themselves, murdered the Christian inhabitants, scored no success against the Turks, and were eventually massacred. The trouble brought upon the Byzantines by this first mob of Crusaders was a symbol of future difficulties.

Meanwhile, at the upper levels of western society, no kings had enlisted in the Crusade, but a considerable number of great lords had been recruited, including a brother of the King of France, the Duke of Normandy, and the Count of Flanders. The most celebrated, however, were Godfrey of Bouillon (Duke of Lower Lorraine), and his brother Baldwin, Count Raymond of Toulouse, Count Stephen of Blois, and Bohemond, a Norman prince from southern Italy (see above, p. 239). Better equipped and better disciplined, the armies led by these lords now began to converge on Constantinople by different routes, arriving at intervals. Still, there was plenty of trouble for the people on the routes. "My lips are tight," wrote the distressed Byzantine archbishop of Bulgaria, through whose see so many of the Crusaders passed. "The passage of the Franks, on their invasion, or whatever you want to call it, has upset and gripped us all. . . . As we have grown accustomed to their insults, we bear trouble more easily than we used to. Time can teach a person to get used to anything." *

The Emperor Alexius was in a very difficult position. He was ready to have the western commanders carve out principalities for themselves from the Turkish-occupied territory which they hoped to conquer. But he wanted to assure himself that lands properly Byzantine would be returned to his control, and that whatever new states might be created would be dominated by him. He knew of the western custom of vassalage, and the importance attached to an oath taken to an overlord. So he decided to require each great western lord to take an oath of liege homage to him on arrival. To obtain these oaths, Alexius had to resort to bribery with splendid gifts, and to all

---

* J. P. Migne, *Patrologia Graeca* (CXXVI), 324-325. Our translation.

sorts of pressure, including in some cases the withholding of food supplies from the unruly crusading armies.

The armies were all ferried across the Straits. There was no supreme command, but the armies acted as a unit, following the orders of the leaders assembled in council. Nicaea, the Seljuk capital, was taken in June, 1097; the Turks surrendered at the last minute to Byzantine forces rather than suffer an assault from the Crusader armies. This the Crusaders bitterly resented, since they had not been informed of the negotiations for surrender, and had been looking

A battle between Crusaders and Moslems, 1099.

forward to plundering the town. Crossing Asia Minor, the Crusaders defeated the Turks in a battle at Dorylaeum, captured the Seljuk Sultan's tent and treasure, and opened the road to further advance. Godfrey's brother Baldwin, leaving the main army, marched to Edessa, a splendid ancient imperial city near the Euphrates, strategically situated for the defense of Syria from attacks coming from the East. Here, after negotiations with the local Armenian rulers, he became Count of

Edessa, lord of the first Crusader State to be established (1098).

Meanwhile, the main body of the army was besieging the great fortress city of Antioch, which finally was conquered by treachery after more than seven months. Antioch became the center of the second Crusader State, under the Norman Bohemond. The other Crusaders then took Jerusalem itself by assault in July, 1099, followed by a slaughter of Moslems and Jews, men, women, and children.

The Crusader States

The Lorrainer, Godfrey of Bouillon, was chosen, not king, for he would not consent to wear a royal crown in the city where Christ had worn the crown of thorns, but "defender of the Holy Sepulchre." The third Crusader State had been founded. When Godfrey died, not long afterward, his brother Baldwin of Edessa became first King of Jerusalem in 1100.

Venetian, Genoese, and Pisan fleets now assisted in the gradual conquest of the coastal cities, ensuring sea communications with the West and the vital flow of supplies and reinforcements. In 1109, the son of Raymond of Toulouse, from Provence, founded the fourth and last of the states, centering around the seaport of Tripoli. The King of Jerusalem was the theoretical overlord of the other three states, but was often unable to enforce his authority. The Byzantine emperors never relinquished the rights that had been secured to them by the oath that the Crusaders had made to Alexius, and were, especially in the case of Antioch, occasionally able to assert those rights successfully.

The holdings of the westerners lay within a long narrow coastal strip, extending from the Euphrates River to the borders of Egypt, more than five hundred miles long and seldom as much as fifty miles wide. From the Moslem cities of Aleppo,

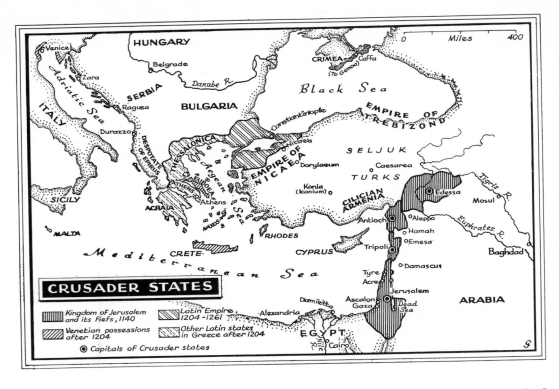

Hamah, Emesa, and Damascus, all just inland from the strip, and from Egypt to the southwest, danger constantly threatened. Yet measures essential to the common defense were repeatedly ignored. The great lords fought with one another, often in alliance with neighboring Moslems. In the circumstances, much reliance was put in the superb castles, among the finest ever built, which now sprang up at strategic places.

The government of the Crusader States was, as might have been expected, purely feudal—more pure, it is often said, than that of any country in western Europe. Its practices are found codified in the *Assizes of Jerusalem*, which were not written down until the thirteenth century, when the history of the Crusader States was almost at an end. The great officers of the realm were the officers of the king's household: seneschal, constable, marshal, and the like. The high court of the barons not only adjudicated disputes but acted as council of state for the king's business. The lords had rights of justice on their own fiefs. Police and civil cases were under the direction of the viscounts, royal officers in the towns, and there were special commercial and maritime courts. The Italian commercial cities, as colonial powers, had quarters of their own in the coastal cities, with privileged status. Revenues were raised by carefully collected customs dues, by monopolies on tanning and similar industries, by a poll tax on Moslems and Jews, and by a land tax on the native population. Yet in the early days especially, money was scarce, and the kings raided Moslem caravans or married rich wives in an effort to bolster their shaky finances. Ecclesiastical organization was quite complex—the two Latin patriarchs of Jerusalem and Antioch each had a hierarchy of Roman Catholic archbishoprics and bishoprics subject to them, and Greek, Syrian, and Armenian churches continued to exist, each with its own clergy, in addition to the Moslem and Jewish faiths.

CHAPTER IX

The Military Orders

Among the new creations of this new colonial world the "military orders" of knighthood are perhaps the most interesting. The first of these were the Templars, founded about 1119 by a Burgundian knight who sympathized with the hardships of the Christian pilgrims, and who banded together with several others in a group designed to afford protection to the helpless on their way to pray at the Holy Places. The knights took the vows of poverty, chastity, and obedience, and were given headquarters near the Temple of Solomon—hence their name of Templars. St. Bernard himself (see Chapter VIII) inspired their rule, which was based on the rules for his own Cistercians and was confirmed by the Pope in 1128. A second order, founded shortly after, was attached to the ancient Hospital of St. John of Jerusalem, and was therefore called the Hospitallers. Made up of knights, chaplains, and serving brothers, under the command of a master, with subordinate provincial commanders both in the East and at home in the West, the two orders put into the field the most effective fighting forces in the Holy Land. Each eventually obtained a special uniform, the Templars wearing red crosses on white, the Hospitallers white crosses on black. Later, a purely German group became the order of the Teutonic Knights, and wore black crosses on white.

After their establishment, the orders grew rapidly in wealth; they had fortresses and churches of their own in the Holy Land, and villages of which they obtained the produce. Moreover, western monarchs endowed them richly with lands in Europe. Their original purposes were soon dimmed or lost sight of, and they became another element in the complicated political, military, and ecclesiastical tangle in the Crusader States. They often allied themselves with Moslems when they thought such an alliance would be useful in pursuing their own quarrels with the nobility of the Holy Land, with its clergy, with new arrivals, with the Italian cities, and with one another. The original vows of poverty were so far forgotten that the orders engaged in banking and large-scale financial operations. In the early fourteenth century, the Templars were destroyed by Philip IV of France for political reasons of his own (see Chapter VII). The Teutonic Knights, most of whose fighting was done not in the Holy Land but against the pagans of the eastern Baltic shore, were disbanded only in 1525, and transmitted some of their lands and much of their outlook toward the world to the modern state of Prussia. The Hospitallers moved first to Cyprus, and then to Rhodes in the early fourteenth century. They were driven to Malta by the Turks in 1522, and continued there until Napoleon's seizure of the island in 1798.

The Moslem Reconquest

Tormented as the Crusader States were by the political disunity that was so characteristic of feudal society at its height, it is a wonder that they lasted so long. It was not the castles or the military orders that kept the Christian states alive so much as it was the disunion of their Moslem enemies. When the Moslems did achieve unity under a single powerful leader, the Christians suffered grave losses. Thus, beginning in the late 1120's, Zangi, governor of Mosul on the Tigris (the town that gives its name to our "muslin" cloth), succeeded in unifying the local Moslem rulers of the region. In 1144, he took Edessa, first of the Crusader cities to fall. It was never to be recaptured. Two years later, Zangi was assassinated, but the Moslem reconquest had begun.

As an answer to the loss of Edessa, St. Bernard himself preached the so-called "Second" Crusade in Europe. He aroused enormous enthusiasm, and for the first time western monarchs—King Louis VII of France and King Conrad III of Germany —came to the East. But the Second Crusade proved a shattering failure. As the German and French armies passed through Constantinople, relations with the Byzantines were worse than ever. It is quite likely that the Emperor, Manuel Comnenus (1143-1180), whose capital the Crusaders seriously considered attacking, mixed chalk with the flour that he sold them before he managed to get them across the Straits, and altogether possible that he was in touch with the Turks.

The western armies were almost wiped out in Asia Minor. When the remnants reached the Holy Land, they found themselves in hopeless conflict with the local lords, who feared that the newcomers would take over the kingdom, and who sabotaged what might otherwise have been a successful siege of the key Moslem city—Damascus. The Crusaders' failure to take Damascus in 1149 brought its own punishment—in 1154 Zangi's son, Nureddin, took it, and Moslem Syria was united against the Latins. St. Bernard had boasted of his success in recruiting the Crusade: "Because of my preaching, towns and castles are empty of inhabitants. Seven women can scarcely find one man." He now lamented:

We have fallen on evil days, in which the Lord, provoked by our sins, has judged the world, with justice, indeed, but not with his wonted mercy. . . . The sons of the Church have been overthrown in the desert, slain with the sword, or destroyed by famine. . . . The judgments of the Lord are righteous, but this one is an abyss so deep that I must call him blessed who is not scandalized therein.*

The next act of the Moslem reconquest was carried out in Egypt by a general of Nureddin's, who was sent in to assist one of the quarreling factions in Cairo. This general became vizier of Egypt, and died in

---

* Quoted in T. A. Archer and C. L. Kingsford, *The Crusades* (New York, 1895), 220.

1169, leaving his office to his nephew, the great Saladin. Saladin, celebrated in both history and legend, was the greatest single Moslem leader of the Crusade period. A vigorous and successful general, often moved by impulse, Saladin was also a chivalrous knight, whose humanity often prevailed over his natural enmity for the Christians.

Saladin brought the Moslem cities of Syria and Mesopotamia under his control and distributed them to faithful members of his own family. By 1183, his brother ruled Egypt, his sons ruled Damascus and Aleppo, and close relatives ruled all the other important centers. Internal decay in the Kingdom of Jerusalem and a squabble over the throne gave Saladin his chance, and a violation of a truce by an unruly Crusader lord gave him his excuse. In 1187 Jerusalem fell, and soon there was nothing of the kingdom left to the Christians except the port of Tyre.

The Later Crusades

These were the events that elicited the "Third" Crusade (1189-1192). The Holy Roman Emperor, Frederick Barbarossa, led a German force through Byzantium, and aroused the usual fears with the usual foundation. But Frederick was drowned in a river in Asia Minor (1190) before reaching the Holy Land. Some of his troops, however, continued to Palestine. There they were joined by Philip Augustus of France and Richard the Lionhearted of England, deadly rivals in the West (see Chapter VII). Each was at least as interested in thwarting the other as he was in furthering what was supposed to be the common cause. The main operation of the "Third" Crusade was a long siege of the seaport of Acre, which lasted a year and a half, and which finally successful in 1191. Jerusalem itself could not be recaptured, but Saladin signed a treaty with Richard allowing Christians

Krak des Chevaliers, a
Crusader fortress in
northern Syria.

to visit it freely. A small strip of seacoast
with Acre as center remained in the hands
of the Crusaders as a pitiful remnant of
the Kingdom of Jerusalem. The cities of
Tripoli and Antioch, their surrounding territories greatly shrunken, were also preserved.

Saladin died in 1193. His dominions were
divided among his relatives, and the Christians obtained a respite. But from the end
of the twelfth century on, the story of the
Crusades and of the Crusader States in
Syria is a mere epilogue to what has gone
before. Reinforcements from the West now
dwindled away to a very small trickle. Innocent III's great effort at a "Fourth" Crusade was, as we shall see, diverted from the
Holy Land against Byzantium, where the
foundation of the Latin Empire and of a
new series of states on Greek soil partly
distracted the attention of western knights.
They could now choose to crusade against
the schismatic Greeks instead of the infidel
Moslems. The failures in the East were
partly balanced by the successes in Spain,
where, by the end of the thirteenth century,
the Moslems were reduced to the Kingdom
of Granada in the southeastern corner of
the peninsula. Far to the northeast, the
pagan Lithuanians and Slavs received the

attention of the Teutonic Knights in the
Baltic region.

The zeal that had driven men toward the
Holy Land was diluted, perhaps most of all,
by the struggle between the papacy and its
European opponents: first, the Albigensian
heretics of southern France between 1208
and 1240, and second, the Emperor Frederick II between 1220 and 1250 (see Chapter VII). Now the Pope offered to give
those who would fight against a purely European and nominally Christian enemy the
same indulgence as he offered to those who
fought the infidel. All these factors no
doubt brought disillusionment, especially
when combined with the spectacle of repeated military failure and internal Christian dissension in the Holy Land itself.

The high point of tragic futility was the
famous "Children's Crusade" of 1212, when
throngs of French and German children
went down to the Mediterranean in the expectation that its waters would divide before them and open a path to the Holy
Land, along which they could march to a
bloodless victory. When this failed to happen, several thousand pushed on to Marseilles and other seaports, and many were
sold into slavery.

The more serious military efforts can be

quickly reviewed. The "Fifth" Crusade was an attempt at the conquest of Egypt, based on the sound theory that this was the center of Moslem strength. Although the fortress of Damietta on the Nile was captured late in 1219, the Crusaders could not continue to Cairo, and had to surrender Damietta in 1221. The "Sixth" Crusade has elements of great interest, since it was led by the highly intelligent western Emperor, Frederick II. The papacy excommunicated him once for failing to go on the Crusade, and again for going on it. No fighting was involved, partly because the Syrian Christians would not support a ruler at odds with the Pope, partly because Frederick was too sophisticated to fight when he could get what he wanted by diplomacy. Cultivated and tolerant, speaking Arabic and long familiar with the Moslems from his experiences in Sicily, he was able to secure more for the Christians by negotiation than any military commander since the First Crusade had secured by war. In 1229, he secured a treaty with Saladin's nephew, which actually restored Jerusalem to the Latins again, except for the site of the Temple, where stood the great mosque of the Dome of the Rock. Bethlehem and Nazareth were also handed over and a ten-year truce was agreed upon.

But the gains were mourned by the Moslems and not welcomed by the Christians, who put Jerusalem under an interdict when Frederick visited it to crown himself king. The Egyptian ruler now took into his service several thousand Turks from Central Asia, who had been displaced from their homes by the terrible invasions of Genghiz Khan and his Mongols, then raging through western Asia and eastern Europe. These Turks took Jerusalem in 1244, and shortly thereafter thoroughly defeated the Latins in a great battle at Gaza. Jerusalem remained in Moslem hands until 1917. The Mongols themselves appeared in the neighborhood of Antioch, and forced the ruler of the principality to pay tribute.

Now St. Louis, King of the French (see Chapter VII), and perhaps the very greatest of medieval Christian monarchs, launched the first of his two crusades, sometimes called the "Seventh." Aimed at Egypt, the expedition captured Damietta once again in 1249, but St. Louis himself was taken prisoner in the next year, and had to pay a very heavy ransom. His years in the East (1248-54) had little practical result.

In 1250, the household troops of the Egyptian sultan, called "Mamluks" or slaves, took power into their own hands in Egypt. Soon after, the Mongols, fresh from their victories in Asia, where they had finally extinguished the Abbasid Caliphate in Baghdad (1258), invaded Syria itself, and were defeated in an important battle in 1260 by the Mamluk general Baibars, who immediately proceeded to make himself sultan. Baibars, who had none of Saladin's chivalry, had much of his ability, and proceeded by degrees to reduce the number of strongholds remaining to the Crusaders, taking Antioch in 1268. He delayed his advance in fear of a new crusade (the "Eighth") of St. Louis in 1270, but resumed it when the King of France landed in Tunis and died there. The Moslems took Tripoli in 1289 and finally Acre in 1291, massacring 60,000 Christians. The century-long epilogue to the first hundred years of crusading fervor was now over, and the Christian settlements were wiped out. They were not deeply mourned even in the lands of western Europe, from which so much blood and treasure had flowed for their establishment and defense.

The Meeting of East and West

In the minds of the men who came out to the new Crusader States, the wish to make a pilgrimage and to win the indulgence that came with the war against the infidel was mixed, from the first with the wish for gain and the love of adventure.

Although many came only with the idea of returning home again, many others migrated with the intention of remaining. Although the population fluctuated, a new world neither eastern nor western but compounded of both was growing up in the narrow strip of Crusader territory. As one Crusader put it:

God has poured the West into the East; we who were Westerns are now Easterns. He who was a Roman or a Frank is now a Galilean or Palestinian. He who was from Rheims or Chartres is now a Tyrian or an Antiochene. We have all forgotten our native soil; it has grown strange unto us.°

Or if we look at it from the Moslem point of view, we find a Syrian warrior and cultivated gentleman of the twelfth century telling some revealing stories (remember as you read what follows that Mecca is *southeast* of Jerusalem):

Everyone who is a fresh immigrant from the Frankish lands is ruder in character than those who have become acclimatized and have held long association with Moslems. . . . Whenever I visited Jerusalem, I always entered the Aqsa Mosque . . . which was occupied by the Templars who were my friends. The Templars would evacuate the little adjoining mosque so that I might pray in it. One day I entered this mosque, repeated the first formula 'Allah is great,' and stood up in the act of praying, upon which one of the Franks rushed on me, got hold of me, and turned my face eastward saying 'This is the way thou shouldst pray!' A group of Templars hastened to him, seized him, and repelled him from me. I resumed my prayer. The same man, while the others were otherwise busy, rushed once more on me and turned my face eastward, saying 'This is the way thou shouldst pray!' The Templars again came in to him and expelled him. They apologized to me, saying 'This is a stranger who has only recently arrived from the land of the Franks and he has never before seen anyone praying except eastward.' Thereupon I said to myself, 'I have had enough prayer.' †

Yet, after a while, the "Franks" learn civilization:

Among the Franks are those who have become acclimatized and have associated long with Moslems. These are much better than the recent comers from the Frankish lands. But they constitute the exception, and cannot be treated as a rule. . . . We came to the home of a knight who belonged to the old category of knights who came with the early expeditions of the Franks. He had been by that time . . . exempted from service, and possessed in Antioch an estate, on the income of which he lived. The knight presented an excellent table, with food extraordinarily clean and delicious. Seeing me abstaining from food, he said, 'Eat, be of good cheer! I never eat Frankish dishes, but I have Egyptian women cooks and never eat except their cooking. Besides pork never enters my home.' °

Here in Usamah we find reflected the essential spirit of tolerance that moved both Christians and Moslems once they had begun to mix. Each side respected the valor of the other. The Latins were never numerous enough to cultivate the soil of Syria, and needed the labor of the Christian and Moslem peasants.

The natives were also most useful in commerce. As time passed, some westerners married easterners, and a race of half-breeds came into existence. Even those who did not intermarry often had their houses, palaces, or churches built by native craftsmen. They wore oriental clothes, let their beards grow, and ate squatting on carpets, eastern-style. Whenever they could get away with it, they liked to watch the Moslem dancing girls. They hired Moslem physicians, joined Moslems in tournaments and hunts, shared certain shrines, and debated the theology of each other's religions. The Prince of Antioch struck a coin showing himself wearing a Moslem turban, and another with a Greek inscription describing him as the "grand Emir." The Venetians in the Kingdom of Jerusalem struck coins bearing Arabic passages from the Koran.

° Fulcher of Chartres, quoted by Archer and Kingsford, *The Crusades,* 170.
† *Memoirs of Usamah Ibn-Munqidh,* P. K. Hitti, trans. (Princeton, 1930), 163-164.

° *Ibid.,* 169-170.

We have a respectful Arabic account of the main Christian customs house at Acre, where Arabic-speaking and Arabic-writing Christian officials sat on a carpeted platform behind gold-trimmed ebony desks, examining the merchandise arriving by caravan.

Impact of the Crusades on the West

These easternized westerners were suspect to their fellow countrymen who were freshly arrived from the West for a pilgrimage only. Yet the temporary visitors, by the mere fact of their numbers and their return to their homes in western Europe, probably had a greater effect on European society than those who stayed in the East. The number of those who went to the East and returned home was very large. From Marseilles alone, the ships of the Hospitallers and the Templars carried six thousand pilgrims a year, so many that the shipowners of the port sued the knightly orders for unfair competition. The result was what has been called a "small folk-migration," and "an active and peaceful binding together of Western Europe and Western Asia." Arabic words in western languages testify to the concepts and products borrowed by the westerners: in commerce, bazaar, tariff, the French *douane*, and the Italian *dogana* (a customs house, from the Arabic *diwan*, the sofa on which the officials sat); in foods, sugar, saffron, rice, lemons, apricots, shallots or scallions (both words derive from the city of Ascalon), melons, and pistachios; in manufactured goods, cotton, muslin, damask (from Damascus), and many others.

All the new products proved a stimulus to the markets and fairs, and to the growing commercial life of the West. Venice and Genoa, the ports from which much of the produce of the East was funneled into Europe, prospered exceedingly. So did the cities of Flanders, whose own manufacture of woolen goods was stimulated by the availability of eastern luxuries for trade. Letters of credit and bills of exchange became a necessity in an ever more complex commercial and financial system, stimulated by the vast numbers of men traveling and making financial arrangements for a journey and a long absence from home. Italian banking houses sprang up with offices in the Holy Land. The orders of knighthood—especially the Templars—played their own role in the money trade.

Thus the Crusades contributed to the introduction of new products, first luxuries and then necessities, and they helped create the conditions that called for the beginnings of modern methods of finance. In the long run, too, they probably stimulated the movement of population from the country to the towns, which in turn permitted the smaller rural population to live better on their lands and perhaps to improve their methods of agriculture. Yet these changes, though surely speeded by the Crusades, were under way before they began, as a result in part of contact with Islam in Spain and Sicily.

About the political and religious impact of the crusading experience upon western society, it is impossible to do more than speculate. Some historians believe that the Crusades helped to weaken and impoverish the feudal nobility and that therefore the monarchies benefited. It is certain that kings were able to tax directly for the first time as a result of the need to raise money for the expeditions to the Holy Land. The papacy was no doubt strengthened in its climb to leadership over all western Christendom by the initiative it took in sponsoring so vast an international movement and by the degree of control it exercised over its course; yet this short-run gain may have been outweighed by a long-run loss. The religious motive, never present unmixed even at the beginning, was more and more diluted by more worldly considerations. The spectacle of churchmen behaving like any layman in their human frailty, the misuse of the crusading indulgences for purely European papal purposes, and the cumulative effect of failure and incompetence piled upon failure and incompetence surely contributed to a disillusionment with the papal concept of the Crusades. Moreover, the mere discovery that all Moslems were not savage beasts, that profit lay in trade with them, and that living together was possible must have broadened the outlook of those who made the discovery and must have led them to question authoritative statements to the contrary even when these statements emanated from Rome.

On the whole, the influence of the Crusades upon western European art and architecture seems to have been relatively slight. It was greater in the writing of history and personal memoirs, especially in the vernacular language. In the thirteenth century, Villehardouin wrote his account of the "Fourth" Crusade, against Constantinople (see below, p. 363), and Joinville wrote his moving and vivid life of St. Louis, including an account of the "Seventh" Crusade. The stuff of poetry was greatly en-

riched by the crusading experience, and whole families of *chansons de geste* owe to it their theme, their scenery, and their appeal. Still more important was the great increase in geographical interest and knowledge; our first reliable maps and the beginnings of European journeys to the Far East date from the crusading period.

The fourteenth- and fifteenth-century Europeans who fought against the Ottoman Turks, who explored the West African coasts and rounded the Cape of Good Hope, emerging into the Indian Ocean and fighting Moslems there, who eventually crossed the broad Atlantic with the mistaken idea that they would find at the other side that old hypothetical ally against the Turks, the lord of the Mongols (see below, Chapter XIV), were the direct descendants of the Crusaders of the earlier period. It is perhaps as a medieval colonization movement, inspired, like all else in the Middle Ages, largely by the Church, that the Crusades are best considered. The westerners called the Crusader States in Syria *"Outremer,"* the "land beyond the sea." They were as truly overseas colonists as the followers of Columbus.

III: The Fortunes of Empire, 1081-1453

Western Influences at Byzantium

During its last 372 years, the fate of the Byzantine Empire became increasingly dependent upon the actions of western Europeans. The establishment of the Italian merchants and their increasing economic power robbed the emperors of their independence on the sea. The floods of Crusaders rendered the Byzantines first uneasy, then insecure. Popular hatred mounted on both sides, until, toward the end of the

twelfth century, it broke out in a series of violent acts, of which the Latin sack of Constantinople itself in 1204 was the climax. During the years between 1204 and 1261, while the Byzantine government was in exile from its own capital, its chief aim was to drive the hated Latin usurper out. But even after the Byzantine leaders had succeeded in 1261, they found themselves still unable to shake off the tentacles of the West. The economic and military dominance of westerners was such that twice— in 1274 and in 1439—the Byzantine emperors actually concluded a formal "union" with the Church of Rome, only to have it repudiated by the forces of Greek public opinion.

The western attitude is revealed in the crisp words of the great fourteenth-century Italian poet, Petrarch, who wrote:

I do not know whether it is worse to have lost Jerusalem or to possess Byzantium. In the former Christ is not recognized, in the latter he is neglected while being worshipped. The Turks are enemies but the schismatic Greeks are worse than enemies. The Turks openly attack our Empire [the Empire of the West]; the Greeks say that the Roman Church is their mother, to whom they are devoted sons; but they do not receive the commands of the Roman pontiff. The Turks hate us less because they fear us less. The Greeks both hate and fear us with all their souls.*

The corresponding attitude of the Greeks is shown by the famous remark of a fifteenth-century Greek churchman: that he would rather see the turban of the Turk in Constantinople than the red hat of a cardinal. Those who shared this attitude got their wish in 1453. Not even the Ottoman Turks themselves had so great a responsibility for the downfall of eastern Christian society as did the western Christians. Fraternal hatred spelled disaster.

Byzantine Feudalism

This great drama of the last centuries was played out to the accompaniment of internal decay. "The powerful," in the person of Alexius Comnenus, had captured the throne itself in 1081. Thereafter the accumulation of lands and tenants—who could serve as soldiers in the landlords' private armies—seems to have gone unchecked. With the weakening of the central government and the emergence of the local magnates, a form of feudalism became the characteristic way of life on Byzantine soil. As early as the middle of the eleventh cen-

---

* H. A. Gibbons, *Foundation of the Ottoman Empire* (New York, 1916), 133. Our translation.

tury we find the emperor granting land to be administered by a magnate in exchange for military service. Such a grant was called *pronoia*. Although it was not hereditary, and although no *pronoia* was held except from the emperor directly, these differences do not obscure the fundamental similarity between the *pronoia* and the western fief. Military service now depended on the holders of *pronoias*.

In the cities, imperial police officials or local garrison commanders often formed petty dynasties of their own, acting as virtually independent potentates. Many individual western knights entered imperial service. The concepts of feudalism on the western model are apparent as early as the oath exacted by Alexius from the Crusaders (see above, p. 352); and Alexius' successors acted as feudal suzerain of the Latin principality of Antioch. Manuel Comnenus (1143-1180), for example, was in some ways a strongly pro-Latin emperor, who had a fondness for the externals of western life, and especially enjoyed tournaments. But the prominence of individual westerners and the fashionable popularity of some western customs are only surface symptoms of the feudalizing tendencies hard at work within Byzantine society.

Along with political feudalism went economic ruin and social misery, which mounted steadily as the twelfth century wore on. Periodic re-assessment of the taxes gave the assessors unlimited opportunity for graft. They demanded food and lodging, presents and bribes. They would agree to turn in a fixed sum to the treasury, and would then pocket the difference between this and what they could squeeze out of the taxpayer. They would seize cattle on the pretext that they were needed for work on state projects, and then sell them back to the owners and keep the money for themselves. Irregular taxes for purposes of defense gave further chances to oppress the population. With the decline of the navy, piracy became a major problem of state.

The indented coasts of the Greek mainland and the numerous islands became nests of sea-raiders, preying not only on merchant shipping but upon the population on shore. Bands of wandering monks, at odds with the secular clergy, swarmed everywhere. They had no visible means of support and simply acted as brigands.

The Archbishop of Athens at the end of the twelfth century tells us that a large part of the population of the countryside had actually decamped, ruined by taxes and unable to bear the exactions any longer. Those free peasants who remained were selling their land to great landowners and were becoming serfs. The end of the free peasantry, as the Archbishop knew, meant economic ruin to the state.

Toward the end of the twelfth century, the processes we have been describing accelerated and rapidly reached a climax. In 1171, Manuel Comnenus made a desperate effort to rid the capital of Venetian merchants by suddenly arresting all he could lay his hands on in one day. More than ten thousand were imprisoned. But the economic hold of Venice was too strong, and the Emperor was soon forced to restore its privileges, though its rulers naturally remained angry with the Byzantines. In 1182, a passionate wave of anti-Latin feeling led to a savage massacre by the Constantinople mob of tens of thousands of westerners who were resident in the capital. In 1185, the Normans of Sicily, pursuing their century-old wars against the Empire, avenged the Latins by sacking Thessalonica, second city of the Byzantines. The last of the Comnenian dynasty, Andronicus I (1183-1185), was torn to pieces by the frantic citizens of Constantinople as the Norman forces approached the city walls. The weak dynasty of the Angeloi succeeded.

Four years later, in 1189-90, the crusading forces of the western Emperor Frederick Barbarossa (see above, p. 291) nearly opened hostilities against the Greeks. Frederick's son, Henry VI, married a Norman Sicilian princess, and inherited both her ancestors' feud with the Byzantines and his own father's frustrated wish to seize Constantinople. Henry prepared a great fleet designed for a major attack on Byzantium, but he died in 1197 just as it was about ready to sail. Against this background of smouldering hatred always on the point of bursting into the flames of open warfare, we can best understand the "diversion" of the "Fourth" Crusade.

The Fourth Crusade

In 1195, Alexius III Angelus deposed, blinded, and imprisoned his elder brother, Emperor Isaac Angelus (1185-1195). Just three years later, there came to the papal throne the great Innocent III, who soon called for a new crusade. No monarchs were to go on this expedition, but Count Baldwin of Flanders, and numbers of other powerful lords took the Cross. They decided to proceed to the Holy Land by sea, and applied to the Venetians for transportation and food. The Venetians agreed to furnish these at a high price, more than the Crusaders could pay, and also to contribute fifty armed warships, on condition that they would share equally in all future conquests. It is quite likely that the shrewd old Doge (Duke) of Venice, the eighty-year-old, blind Enrico Dandolo, intended from the first to use the Crusaders' indebtedness to him as an excuse to employ their military might for his own purposes. Indeed, he agreed to forgive the debt temporarily if the Crusaders would help him reconquer Zara, a town on the Dalmatian side of the Adriatic, down the coast from Venice, which had revolted against Venetian domination and had gone over to the King of Hungary. So the Crusade began with the sack and destruction of a Roman Catholic town, in 1202. Angrily, the Pope excommunicated the Crusaders. But worse was to follow.

The son of the blinded Isaac Angelus, known as the young Alexius, had escaped to the West, and was trying hard to recruit assistance to overthow his uncle, the usurper Alexius III, and to restore Isaac. The brother of the late Henry VI, Philip of Swabia, candidate for the western imperial throne, had married a daughter of Isaac, and welcomed his brother-in-law, the young Alexius, with sympathy not unmixed with the family's traditional ambitions. Philip had many followers among the Crusaders. At this moment, after the siege of Zara, the young Alexius offered to pay off the rest of the Crusaders' debt to Venice, and to assist their efforts in the Holy Land if they would go first to Constantinople and restore his father. This suited the ambitions of both the Venetians and the sympathizers of Philip of Swabia. Although many of the knights disapproved of the "diversion" and some left the Crusade to go on their own to Palestine, most went along with the decision.

Thus it was that in the spring of 1203 the Venetian fleet with the Crusaders aboard made its appearance in the Sea of Marmora:

Now you may know that those who had never before seen it gazed much at Constantinople; for they could not believe that there could be in all the world so mighty a city, when they saw those high walls and those mighty towers, with which it was girt all round, and those rich palaces and lofty churches, of which there were so many that no man could believe it unless he had seen it with his own eyes, and the length and breadth of the city, which of all others was the sovereign. And know well that there was no man so bold that his flesh did not creep, and this was no wonder; for never was so great an undertaking entered upon by human beings since the world was made.[*]

In July, 1203, the Crusaders took the city by assault. Isaac was set free and his son

the young Alexius was crowned as Alexius IV. Alexius III fled with as much treasure as he could carry. During the next few months, the Crusaders stayed in the neighborhood of the capital, waiting for Alexius IV to pay off his obligation to them. A great fire broke out, for which the Greek population blamed the Latins. A popular revolution put on the throne a new anti-Latin emperor, who strangled Alexius IV. In March, 1204, the Crusaders drew up a solemn treaty with their Venetian allies, agreeing to seize the city a second time, to divide up all the booty, to elect a Latin emperor, who was to have a quarter of the Empire, and to divide the other three-quarters evenly between the Venetians and the non-Venetians. If the emperor proved to be a Venetian, the non-Venetians were to name a Latin patriarch, and vice versa.

Then came the second siege, the second capture, and the dreadful sack of Byzantium. Here is the account of a Greek historian:

How shall I begin to tell of the deeds done by these wicked men? They trampled the images underfoot instead of adoring them. They threw the relics of the martyrs into filth. They spilt the body and blood of Christ on the ground, and threw it about. . . . They broke into bits the sacred altar of Santa Sophia, and distributed it among the soldiers. When the sacred vessels and the silver and gold ornaments were to be carried off, they brought up mules and saddle horses inside the church itself and up to the sanctuary. When some of these slipped on the marble pavement and fell, they stabbed them where they lay and polluted the sacred pavement with blood and filth. A harlot sat in the Patriarch's seat, singing an obscene song and dancing frequently. They drew their daggers against anyone who opposed them at all. In the alleys and streets, in the temple, one could hear the weeping and lamentations, the groans of men and the shrieks of women, wounds, rape, captivity, separation of families. Nobles wandered about in shame, the aged in tears, the rich in poverty.[*]

---

[*] G. de Villehardouin, *La Conquête de Constantinople,* E. Faral, ed. (Paris, 1938), I, 131. Our translation.

---

[*] Nicetas Choniates, *Historia,* I. Bekker, ed. (Bonn, 1835), 757 ff. Condensed; our translation.

The Pope himself fulminated against the outrages committed by the Crusaders. What was destroyed in the libraries of the capital we shall never know. Besides the relics, some of the most notable works of art were sent to the West, among them the famous gilded bronze horses from the Hippodrome still to be seen over the door of St. Mark's in Venice.

The Latin Empire

After the sack, the Latins set about governing their conquest. They elected Baldwin of Flanders as first Latin emperor, and the title continued in his family during the fifty-seven years of Latin occupation. The Venetians chose the first Latin patriarch, and kept a monopoly on that rich office. The territories of the Empire were divided on paper, since most of them had not yet been conquered. The Venetians secured for themselves the long sea route from Venice by claiming the best coastal towns and strategic islands. A strange hybrid state was created, in which the emperor's council consisted half of his own barons and half of members of the Venetian merchant colony under the leadership of their governor. Though in theory the Latin emperors were the successors of Constantine and Justinian, and wore the sacred purple boots, in practice they never commanded the loyalty of the Greek population, and could never make important decisions without the counsel of their barons.

They were not only surrounded by hostile Greeks but had as neighbor the new Bulgarian Empire, whose ruler promptly went to war against them, took Baldwin prisoner, and had him murdered in prison. Across the Straits, Greek refugees from Constantinople, under Theodore Lascaris, set up a state in Nicaea. The Latins could not concentrate upon the enemies in Asia because of the threat from Europe. Out-

numbered, incompetent as diplomats, slow to learn new military tactics, miserably poor after the treasures of Byzantium had been siphoned away, the westerners could not maintain their Latin Empire, especially after its main sponsors ceased to be able to assist it. When the popes became deeply involved in their quarrel with the western Emperor Frederick II (see Chapter VII), the Latin Empire was doomed. It was the Greeks of Nicaea who eventually recaptured their capital in 1261, and re-established the Byzantine Empire.

Meanwhile, however, the Latins had

These four horses of gilded bronze stood in the Hippodrome of Byzantium until the Crusaders looted it and sent them to Venice to stand over the portal of St. Mark's. Napoleon stole them from Venice, but after 1815 they were returned.

ΗΑΝΑΤΑCIC
ΙϹ ΧϹ

The Anastasis. Recently uncovered Byzantine fresco in the Church of the Chora (Turkish mosque of Kahrie Djami), Istanbul (fourteenth century). Note the locks, bolts, and hinges of the smashed gates of Hell, as Christ raises Adam and Eve from the dead.

fanned out from Constantinople, and also had made landings in continental Greece. Greece was divided into a whole series of feudal principalities. There were now French Dukes of Athens, worshiping in the Parthenon, which had been an Orthodox church of the Virgin, and now became a Roman Catholic shrine dedicated to her. The Peloponnesus, the southern peninsula of Greece, became the Principality of Achaia, with twelve great feudal baronies, and many minor lordships. Thessalonica became the capital of a new kingdom, which,

however, fell to the Greeks in 1224. In the islands of the Aegean a Venetian adventurer established the "Duchy of the Archipelago" (from the words meaning Aegean Sea), and other barons, mostly Italian, founded themselves tiny lordships among the islands. The Venetians held Crete and the long island of Euboea off the coast of Attica.

In the new world of Latin Greece, chivalry, castles, tournaments, all the externals of western feudal society, were so faithfully copied that in the 1220's Pope

Honorius III called it "as it were, New France." Templars, Hospitallers, and Teutonic Knights had lands there. The laws were codified in the *Assizes of Romania,* like the *Assizes of Jerusalem,* a valuable source book of feudal custom. As in the Latin states of Syria, intermarriage took place between Latins and Greeks, but the native population never really became reconciled to alien domination. As in Syria, the traces of Latin rule are seen most clearly only in the remains of the great castles and not in any lasting impression upon the native society. The feudal states of Greece lasted for varying periods, but most of them were wiped out during the long process of Turkish conquest in the fifteenth century, and none existed after the sixteenth.

Byzantium after 1261

When the Greeks of Nicaea, under Michael VIII Palaeologus (1261-1282), recaptured their capital, they found it depopulated and badly damaged, and the old territory of the Empire mostly in Latin hands. It was impossible for Michael and his successors to reconquer more than occasional fragments of continental Greece or the islands, to push the frontier in Asia Minor east of the Seljuk capital of Konia, or to deal effectively with the challenge of the Serbians in the Balkans. Michael VIII's diplomacy was distinguished for its subtlety even by Byzantine standards. He staved off the threat posed to his empire by Charles of Anjou, younger brother of St. Louis, to whom the popes had given the South Italian kingdom of the Normans and Hohenstaufens. Just as a new and powerful force appeared headed for Byzantium from Sicily, Michael helped precipitate the revolt of 1282, known as the "Sicilian Vespers." The French were massacred by the population, Charles of Anjou's plans had to be abandoned, and the way was open for the conquest of Sicily by the Aragonese from Spain.

So incompetent and frivolous were most of the successors of Michael VIII that they contributed materially to the decline of their own beleaguered empire. Wars among rival claimants for the throne tore the Empire apart internally at the very moment when the preservation of unity in the face of external enemies seemed of the utmost necessity. The social unrest that we noticed as characteristic of the period before the Latin conquest reappeared in even sharper form, as Thessalonica, second city of the Empire, was torn by civil strife. For a few years in the 1340's, Thessalonica was run as a kind of independent proletarian republic by a lower-class party known as the zealots. New theological controversy, which, as usual, barely concealed political disagreements, rent the clergy, already tormented by the choice between uniting with Rome or perishing. The currency, debased for the first time under the Comnenoi, was now allowed to drift.

At one moment in the 1350's, the leader of the Serbian state, the lawgiver King Stephen Dushan, proclaimed himself Emperor of the Serbians and Greeks (much as the Bulgarian Simeon, see above, p. 241, had done in the tenth century). In 1355, Dushan was about to seize Constantinople and make it the capital of a new Greco-Slavic state, when he suddenly died. The Genoese and the Venetians, usually at war with each other, interfered at every turn in the internal affairs of the Empire.

The Advance of the Ottoman Turks

It was the Ottoman Turks, however, who gave the Empire the final blow. These Turks were the ablest and luckiest of the groups to whom the Seljuk Empire in Asia Minor was now passing as it disintegrated. We find them in the last quarter of the thirteenth century settled on the borders of the province of Bithynia, across the Straits from Constantinople. This region had been the center of Greek resistance to the Latins during the Latin Empire, and the base of the movement for the reconquest of the capital. Economic and political unrest led the discontented population of this region to turn to the Turks in preference to the harsh and ineffectual officials of the Byzantine government. As a whole, the Turks were not fanatical Moslems, and they had no racial distaste for the Greek population, from whom, in fact, they were anxious to learn.

The Turks' conquest of Bithynia was a kind of gradual penetration, beginning with cattle-raids, and continuing with the acquisition of land. The farmers willingly paid tribute to the Turks, and as time went on many of them were converted to Islam in order to avoid the payment. They learned Turkish, and taught the nomadic Turkish conquerors some of the arts of a settled agricultural life; the Turks, in turn, adopted Byzantine practices in government. One interesting institution that probably speeded the process of assimilation of the two peoples was the Ottoman corporations of the Akhis, a curious combination of craft guild, monastic order, and social service agency. Highly tolerant, the Akhis were organized according to the craft or trade of their members. They were intensely pious Moslems who were determined to fight tyrannical government. In the towns of Anatolia they built hostels for travelers, where they gave religious dances and read the Koran. They presented Islam at its most attractive and thus aided the Christians to become converted. Within a generation or two it is likely that the original Ottoman Turks had become very highly mixed with the native Greeks of Anatolia.

Even before this process had got very far the Turks had begun to conquer the cities of Bithynia, and to engage in open warfare with the Byzantines. The Turks built a fleet and began raiding in the Sea of Marmora and the Aegean. It was not long before they were invited into Europe by one of the rival claimants to the Byzantine throne, who in 1354 allowed them to establish themselves in the Gallipoli peninsula. Soon they were occupying much of the neighboring province of Thrace. In 1363, they moved their capital to the European side of the Straits at the city of Adrianople. Constantinople was now surrounded by Turkish territory, and could be reached from the west only by sea. In order to survive at all, many of the later emperors had to reach humiliating arrangements with the Turkish rulers—in some cases becoming their vassals.

The Byzantine Empire survived down to 1453. But its survival was no longer in its own hands. The Turks chose to conquer much of the Balkan region first, putting an end to the independent Bulgarian and Serbian states in the 1370's and 1380's. The final defeat of the Serbs at the battle of Kossovo on June 28, 1389, has long been celebrated by the defeated Serbs themselves in poetry and song. June 28, St. Vitus' day, is their national holiday, and the day on which the Archduke Franz Ferdinand was assassinated by the Serb nationalists in 1914. A European "crusade" against the Turks was wiped out at Nicopolis on the Danube in 1396.

But Turkish conquests were delayed for half a century when a new wave of Mongols under Timur (celebrated in our literature as Tamerlane) emerged from Central Asia in 1402 and defeated the Ottoman armies at Ankara high in the Anatolian plateau, the present-day capital of Turkey. Like most Mongol efforts, this proved a temporary one, and the Ottoman armies and state recovered. In the 1420's and 1430's, the Turks moved into Greece, and the West, now thoroughly alarmed at the spread of Turkish power in Europe, tried to bolster the Byzantine defenses by proposing a union of the eastern and western churches in 1439 and by dispatching another "crusade" to Bulgaria in 1444. Both efforts proved futile.

CHAPTER IX

With the accession of Mohammed II to the Ottoman throne in 1451, the doom of Constantinople was sealed. His skillful Hungarian engineer cast for him an enormous cannon that fired great stone balls. It took two months to drag the cannon from Adrianople to the walls of Constantinople. New Turkish castles on the Bosphorus were able to prevent ships from delivering supplies to the city. In 1453, strong forces of troops and artillery were drawn up in siege array, and at one moment the Turks dragged a fleet of small boats uphill on runners, and slid them down the other side into the Golden Horn itself. As final defeat grew more and more inevitable, the Greeks and Latins inside the city took communion together inside Santa Sophia for the last time, and the last emperor, Constantine XI, died bravely defending the walls.

On May 29, 1453, with the walls breached and the Emperor dead, the Turks poured into the city. Mohammed II, the Conqueror, gave thanks to Allah in Santa Sophia itself, and ground the altar of the sanctuary beneath his feet. Thenceforth it was to be a mosque. When he passed through the deserted rooms of the imperial palace, he is said to have quoted a Persian verse on the transitoriness of human power: "The spider has become the chamberlain in the palace of the Emperor, and has woven her curtain before the door; the owl is now the trumpeter upon the battlements of Afrasiab." Shortly thereafter, he installed a new Greek patriarch, and proclaimed himself protector of the Christian Church. On the whole, during the centuries that followed the Orthodox Church accepted the sultans as successors to the Byzantine emperors.

IV: The Ottoman Successor-State, 1453-1699

Part of the Ottomans' inheritance no doubt came from their far-distant past in Central Asia, when, like other Turks, they had almost surely come under the direct or indirect influence of China, and had lived like other nomads of the steppe. Their fondness and capacity for war and their rigid adherence to custom may go back to this early period, as did their native Turkish language. From the Persians and the Byzantines, who themselves had been influenced by Persia, the Turks seem to have derived their exaltation of the ruler, their tolerance of religious groups outside the state religion, and their practice of encouraging such groups to form independent communities inside their state. Persian was always the literary language and the source of Turkish literature, both in form and in content. From Islam, the Turks took the sacred law and their approach to legal prob-

lems, the Arabic alphabet in which they wrote their Turkish tongue, and the Arabic vocabulary of religious, philosophical, and other abstract terms. All the well-springs of their inheritance—Asiatic, Persian-Byzantine, and Moslem—tended to make them an exceptionally conservative people.

A Slave System

The most unusual feature of Ottoman society was the advancement of slaves to the highest positions within the state. This practice was not original with the Ottoman Turks; we are reminded of the way in which the Mamluks (slaves) took over the actual rule in Egypt in the thirteenth century (see above, p. 358). Yet, as the Ottoman state developed, its slave system of government reached a height never approached before or since by any other important state. Except for the sultan himself, all the high officials of government, and of the sultan's household, as well as all the officers of the army and large bodies of picked troops, were slaves, almost always the children of Christians. They were picked in their early youth for their promising appearance and were especially educated for the sultan's service. As slaves, they owed all advancement to the sultan, and could be instantly removed from office and punished by death at any moment in their careers.

Since the sultan was entitled to one-fifth of all prisoners of war, he selected many of his slaves from that source. Sometimes they were bought, or were given as presents to the sultan. But perhaps a third or more were obtained through the regular levying of the "tribute of children" in the Balkan Christian provinces of the Ottoman Empire. Every four years until the early seventeenth century, specially trained officers, each with a quota of places to fill, visited the Balkan villages and selected and took away the strongest and ablest-appearing Slavic or Albanian youths, from ten to twenty years old, but usually between fourteen and eighteen. This practice has always aroused the natural horror of Christians. Yet two considerations make it less dreadful than it would seem at first. Since a married boy was ineligible, marriage was always an escape. Then too, unlimited opportunity for advancement within the system was open to the boys chosen. In poverty-stricken and remote Balkan villages, it is likely that being chosen was sometimes regarded as a positive privilege. We know of actual cases where Moslem families paid Christian parents to take their sons and pass them off as Christian in the hope that they would be selected.

Once taken, all these youths were converted to Islam. Some resisted conversion, or had certain reservations; occasionally one of them escaped. But most of them seem to have become good Moslems or to have been indifferent to religious matters. The Turks felt conversion to be absolutely essential before the youths were given government jobs. The system thus both fulfilled the missionary zeal of Islam and provided administrators and soldiers for the state. No born Moslem could in theory ever be recruited into the system, since the law said that no born Moslem could be a slave. This limited the choice to born Christians, and in theory meant that no child of a member of the system would be eligible to enter it himself. The sons of members would often be given fiefs, obliged to render military service, and thus transferred out of the system.

This ruling class of slaves was carefully educated. Of the seven or eight thousand chosen annually, all got systematic physical and military training. About one-tenth received higher education, and the very cream of the crop became pages in the sultan's own household and attended his palace school, where they were taught languages, Moslem and Turkish law, ethics, and theology, as well as horsemanship and military science. They were given an allowance, which was increased every year, and were carefully watched to see how their talents were developing. If a man who had not at first been selected for one of the higher schools showed any sign of ability, he would be shifted into one. All left school at the age of twenty-five, and the graduates of the picked schools were then given jobs in the administration; the rest became *spahis* or cavalry forces.

There was always plenty of room for advancement, since many were killed in war, and at the top levels many were demoted, dismissed, or executed for inefficiency or disloyalty. Splendid financial rewards awaited any man lucky enough to rise to one of the top posts. A typical career is that of one sixteenth-century Slav who graduated from the page corps as a gatekeeper, advanced to chief taster to the sultan, moved into the cavalry and became a general, was promoted to equerry, assigned to command the picked infantry corps, sent to Europe and then to Egypt as provincial governor, and then passed through the three grades of vizier, finishing his career as grand vizier, the very top office of the state.

At the lower level, the less intelligent slaves were often farmed out for agricultural work in Asia Minor on some estate, and then drafted into the so-called janissary troops (from the Turkish words *yeni cheri,* meaning new forces). Their training emphasized physical endurance, and they served not only as infantrymen in the army but as shipyard workers, palace gardeners, and the like. They lived in special barracks and had special privileges. A source of strength, they also posed a constant potential danger to the state. At the height of Turkish military successes, the Sultans could put into the field formidable armies, sometimes amounting to more than a quarter of a million men on the march. They were absolutely fearless in battle and were the terror of all opponents. An ambassador from the Habsburgs who spent eight years in Constantinople between 1554 and 1562 compares their endurance favorably with that of European troops. The Turks, he says:

. . . take out a few spoonfuls of flour and put them into water, adding some butter, and seasoning the mess with salt and spices; these ingredients are boiled and a large bowl of gruel is thus obtained. Of this they eat once or twice a day. . . . it is the patience, self-denial, and thrift of the Turkish soldier that enable him to face the most trying circumstances and come safely out of the dangers that surround him. What a contrast to our men! Christian soldiers on a campaign refuse to put up with their ordinary food and call for thrushes, and other such like dainty dishes. . . . It makes me shudder to think what the result of a struggle between such different systems can be. . . .*

---

* O. G. Busbecq, *Turkish Letters,* C. T. Forster and F. H. B. Daniell, trans. (London, 1881), I, 220-221.

The sultan's harem was a part of the slave institution, since all the women in it were slaves, together with all their household staffs and entertainers. The sultan's consorts, as slaves, gave birth to the heir to the Empire, so that each new sultan was always by birth half-slave. Every official, who was himself a slave, had a slave-family of his own in miniature, and often received as a wife one of the members of the sultan's harem who had not been chosen as a consort.

In Ottoman society there was no color line, and slavery carried no social taint. Rather, it was regarded as an accident of fortune. Relations between masters and slaves were often friendly, and masters often set their slaves free as a reward for service. The sultan picked his favorite, not necessarily his eldest, son to succeed him, and there was a law that the heir to the throne must kill all his brothers and half-brothers upon his accession. Every son of a sultan knew all the time he was growing up that he either must obtain the throne himself or be killed by whichever of his brothers or half-brothers did obtain it. In 1595, for instance, Mohammed III killed no fewer than nineteen brothers and half-brothers when he came to the throne.

The "Four Pillars" of Administration

Turkish writers thought of the state as a tent resting on four pillars. The first was the viziers, varying in number, to whom the sultan actually delegated many powers. The viziers presided over the council of state, kept the great seal, and could sometimes, when trusted, make decisions on policy. The council of state had no legislative power, all of which was vested in the sultan, but it did debate administrative or judicial questions. The second pillar was the financial officers, organized to collect revenues throughout the provinces. These revenues included the poll tax on the Christians, a tenth of all produce, and many of the old Byzantine taxes on commerce, as well as special levies of all kinds, including money realized by confiscating the great fortunes of disgraced officials. The third pillar was the chancery, a secretariat that affixed the sultan's signature to documents, and prepared, recorded, and transmitted them, whether they were statutes, diplomas, certificates of title, or appointments.

The fourth pillar, unlike the other three, was not a department of state manned by slaves born as Christians. It was the judges, who were all born Moslems, and thus part of the only non-slave portion of the Ottoman governing system. Islam itself had responsibility for all legal matters and for education. One-third of state lands were set aside as religious property. Each tract had its own purpose: the support of mosques, of charitable or educational institutions, and even of inns or public baths. Income from such property supported the entire class of *ulema,* learned men who were connected with Islam as an institution.

Among the *ulema* were the *muftis,* or jurists, who answered questions that arose in the course of lawsuits, and that were submitted to them by the judges. It was their function to apply the sacred law of Islam, and they usually gave short replies, without explanation. These replies settled the case. Thus they were a powerful class, and the grand *mufti* in Istanbul, whom the sultan himself consulted, was known as the *Sheikh-ul-Islam,* the ancient or elder of Islam, and outranked everybody but the grand vizier. Since he could speak the final word on the sacred law, he may even he said to have exercised a kind of check on the absolute power of the sultan himself. He alone could proclaim the beginning of war, or denounce a sultan for transgression of the sacred law, and summon his subjects to depose him. The opinions of the *muftis* were collected as a body of interpretative law, lying between the changeless, age-old

sacred law of Islam and the current enactments of the sultans. The general acceptance by all Moslems of the supremacy of the sacred law and the reluctance of the *muftis* to accept change were two of the factors that accounted for the failure of the Ottoman system to develop with the times. There are no "reformations" in Turkish history until the twentieth century.

The fourth pillar of the tent, the judges, were all members of the *ulema.* They were assigned to the various regions of the Empire. The chief justices for Europe and Asia were the two most important. These two were members of the council of state, the only two members who were born Moslems and non-slaves. Thus the council was the only place where the two chief Ottoman institutions were combined: the ruling institution of the sultan's slave-family that ran military affairs and civil affairs except for questions of law and justice, and the Moslem institution that ran religious, legal, and educational affairs. Of course, the sultan himself at the very top of the tent was the supreme head of both institutions.

Weaknesses of the Ottoman System

This remarkable system had inherent weaknesses, some of which leap instantly to the eye. First, the effectiveness of the entire structure depended upon the character of the sultan himself. Harem upbringing and the ruthless family antagonisms to which each sultan was exposed did not tend to produce sultans who could act as wise and mature statesmen. Rather, as time passed, more and more sultans were weaklings, drunkards, debauchees, and men of little experience or political understanding. Harem intrigue played a great role in the state.

Second, efficient operation of the administration depended upon maintaining the slave-system by excluding the born Moslem sons of the members of the slave ruling-class from participation, and upon recruiting only new slaves to do the work. But in practice this rigid exclusion broke down early, and born Moslems, often the sons of slaves high in the system who were attracted by the possibilities of gain and power, were admitted. They could not be regarded as slaves, and the chief restraints and fears that kept the machine running thus disappeared. Incompetent sultans and insubordinate soldiers together sped the decay of the state. Turbulent janissaries frequently deposed the sultan, and chose his successor from the ruling house.

Third, the whole concept of fixed, immutable, sacred law helped produce a society highly resistant to change, especially the change brought about by the impact of the West on the Ottoman Empire. This inflexibility did not begin to be seriously felt until the eighteenth century, but it was critically important thereafter.

Fourth, in a society where religion was the only test of nationality, all Orthodox Christians were automatically regarded as Greeks, and lived under the control of the patriarch. In the nineteenth century this was to prove a serious weakness, since it alienated many Slavs and Rumanians who might otherwise have been loyal subjects. Moreover, the disabilities placed on Christians ordinarily made it impossible for their talents to be used or their loyalties to be relied upon unless they were converted to Islam and became members of the slave-system.

Ottoman Expansion to 1566

By the end of the 1460's most of the Balkan Peninsula had been consolidated under Turkish rule, except for the tiny Slavic mountain region of Montenegro, which maintained a precarious independent existence. Thus the core of the new Ottoman state was Asia Minor and the Bal-kans, the same core around which the Byzantine Empire had been built. From this core before the death of Mohammed II in 1481, the Turks expanded across the Danube into modern Rumania, seized the Genoese outposts in the Crimea, and made this southern Russian region a vassal state under its Tartar rulers. They also fought against the Venetians and even landed forces in Italy. The limits of their expansion were marked by the great Hungarian fortress of Belgrade, key to a further advance into Central Europe, and the island fortress of Rhodes in the Mediterranean, stronghold of the Hospitallers and key to a further naval advance westward.

The next great advances were scored by Sultan Selim I (1512-1520), who nearly doubled the territories of the Empire, but almost exclusively in Asia, at the expense of the Persians, and in Africa, where Egypt was annexed in 1517 and the rule of the Mamluks ended. From them the Sultan inherited the duty of protecting Mecca and Medina. He also assumed the title of caliph, with the sacred insignia of office. It is doubtful whether this alone greatly enhanced his prestige, since the title had for centuries been much abused. At one moment in his reign, Selim contemplated a general massacre of all his Christian subjects. Only the refusal of the Sheikh-ul-Islam to grant his consent saved the Christians. This episode vividly illustrates the precariousness of Christian life under the Turks. It also demonstrates that the character of the Ottoman state was substantially altered by the acquisition of so much territory. It was now no longer necessary to appease the Christians by generous treatment, because the overwhelming majority of the population was Moslem. Moreover, most of the newly acquired Moslems were Arabs, more fanatical than the Ottoman Turks had hitherto been.

The advance into Europe was resumed in the reign of the next sultan, the greatest of them all: Suleiman the Magnificent (1520-

1566), contemporary of the western Emperor Charles V and of Francis I of France and Henry VIII of England (see Chapters XII and XIII). Indeed, the Ottoman Empire now became deeply involved in western European affairs. It participated in the dynastic wars between the imperial house of Habsburg and the French Valois, and affected the course of the Protestant Reformation in Germany by the threat of military invasion from the southeast. The newly consolidated national monarchies of the West had begun to outclass the old European enemies of the Turks, the Venetians and the Hungarians. Charles V had inherited Spain and now had to face the naval attacks of the Ottoman fleets. His younger brother, Ferdinand, as ruler of the Austrian and later the Hungarian territories, bore the brunt of the Turkish attacks on land. Cheering the Turks on were the French. Even though their king was the eldest son of the Church, their wars against the Habsburgs came first.

In 1521, Suleiman took Belgrade, and in 1522 Rhodes, thus removing the two chief obstacles to westward advance. In 1526, at Mohács in Hungary, he defeated the Christian armies, and the Turks entered Buda, the Hungarian capital on the middle Danube. In September, 1529, Suleiman besieged Vienna itself, posing a threat to Christendom greater than any since Leo III and Charles Martel had defeated the advance guard of the Arabs in the early eighth century (see above, p. 184). But the Turkish lines of communication were greatly overextended; Suleiman had to abandon the siege after two weeks. Finally, in 1533, Ferdinand recognized Suleiman as overlord of Hungary. In the years that followed Suleiman made good his claim to actual control over the south-central portion of Hungary, and added other lands north and east of the Danube. In North Africa he acquired Algeria, which remained an Ottoman vassal state in the western Mediterranean until the nineteenth century. In Asia he defeated the Persians, annexed modern Iraq, including Baghdad itself, and secured an outlet on the Persian Gulf. He even fought naval wars against the Portuguese in the Persian Gulf and the Indian Ocean.

In 1536, a formal treaty was concluded between France and the Ottoman Empire, the first of the famous "capitulations." It permitted the French to buy and sell throughout the Turkish dominions on the same basis as any Turk. They could have resident consuls with civil and criminal jurisdiction over Frenchmen in Turkey. In Turkish territory, Frenchmen were to enjoy complete religious liberty, and were also granted a protectorate over the Holy Places, the old aim of the Crusades. This was a great advance in prestige for the Roman Catholic Church. The Orthodox Church never accepted this settlement, and the same old dispute helped touch off the Crimean War in the nineteenth century. These "capitulations" gave the French a better position in the Ottoman Empire than that of any other European power and thus contributed to the wealth and prestige of France. They also brought the Turks into the diplomatic world of western Europe. And they are particularly interesting as parallels to the earlier Byzantine trade treaties with Venice and Genoa, who had received virtually the same privileges beginning at the end of the eleventh century (see above, p. 346). In this respect, as in so many others, the Ottoman sultans were behaving as the successors of the Byzantine emperors.

Ottoman Decline, 1566-1699

After Suleiman, the Ottoman system, already manifesting signs of weakness, deteriorated, despite occasional periods of Turkish success. The Ottoman capture of Cyprus in 1571 led to the formation of a western league against the Turk, headed by the pope, an enterprise as near to a crusade as the sixteenth century could produce. In 1571, the league won the great naval battle of Lepanto, off the Greek coast. It destroyed the Ottoman fleet but failed to follow up the victory, permitting the Turks to recover.

By the end of the century the sale of government offices had become a regular practice and the repeated rebellions of janissaries were jeopardizing the sultan's position. In 1606, a peace was signed that put an end to one of the perennial wars with the Habsburgs. Previously, all treaties with western states had been cast in the form of a truce granted as a divine favor from the sultan to a lesser potentate, and had been accompanied by a provision that the other party would pay tribute as part of the settlement. This time the Turks had to negotiate as equals. They gave the Habsburg emperor his proper title, and were unable to demand tribute.

Indeed, had it not been for the convulsion of the Thirty Years' War (1618-1648), which preoccupied the states of western Europe (see Chapter XIII), the Ottoman Empire might have suffered even more severely in the first half of the seventeenth century than it did. As it was, internal anarchy rent the state; troops rioted and several sultans were deposed within a few years; the Persians recaptured Baghdad; and rebellion raged in the provinces. In 1622, the British ambassador wrote to his government:

The Empire has become, like an old body, crazed through many vices. All the territory of the Sultan is dispeopled for want of justice, or rather by reason of violent oppression: so much so that in his best parts of Greece and Anatolia a man may ride three, four, and sometimes six days, and not find a village to feed him and his horse. The revenue is so lessened that there is not wherewithal to pay the soldiers and maintain the court.[*]

---

[*] Quoted by E. S. Creasey, *History of the Ottoman Turks* (London, 1854), I, 392-393.

Here we are already encountering what nineteenth-century statesmen two hundred years later were still calling the "sick man of Europe."

Yet a firm sultan, Murad IV (1623-1640), temporarily restored order through the most brutal means. Despite a temporary retrogression after his death, what looked like a real revival began with the accession to power of a distinguished family of viziers, the Köprülüs. The first Köprülü ruthlessly executed 36,000 people in a five-year period (1656-1661), hanged the Greek patriarch for predicting in a private letter that Christianity would defeat Islam, rebuilt the army and navy, and suppressed revolt. Between 1661 and 1676 the second Köprülü led the Ottoman navies to a triumph in Crete, which they took from Venice. The Turks temporarily won large areas of the Ukraine from the Russians and Poles, only to lose them again in 1681. In 1683, the Turks again penetrated the heart of Europe, and for the last time Vienna was besieged, with all Europe anxiously awaiting the outcome. For the second time in two centuries, the Turkish wave was broken, and now Europe began a great counteroffensive against the Turks. Although the Köprülüs had galvanized the warlike Ottoman armies into a last successful effort, they did not touch and could not touch the real evils of the Ottoman system.

The End of an Era

Now the Habsburgs drove the Turks out of Hungary, and the Venetians seized the Greek Peloponnesus. The Turks needed peace. In 1699, after an international congress at Karlovitz on the Danube, most of the gains of the European counteroffensive were recognized, including those of the Austrians, Poles, Venetians, and Russians. The Russians had appeared for the first time since the Tartar invasion on the shores of the Sea of Azov, which opens into the

Black Sea. The great territorial losses suffered by the Turks, the strengthening of the Habsburgs to the east, and the appearance of Russia as an important enemy of the Turks all mark this settlement as a landmark. From now on the western European powers could stop worrying about the Ottoman menace, which had preoccupied them ever since the fourteenth century, and which had replaced the Crusades as a great cause for which Christendom could occasionally be united. From now on, the importance of Turkey is no longer its military potential, but its diplomatic position as a power in decline over whose possible disintegration and division the states of Europe might squabble and negotiate. With Karlovitz, what we call the "eastern question" may be said to have begun.

With this shift from the military offensive, which had been their only policy since their arrival in Bithynia in the thirteenth century, to a new enforced policy of defensive diplomacy, the Ottoman Turks were forced to go outside their slave-family for administrators. Nobody trained in the old way had the proper equipment to act in the new. Thus it was that during the eighteenth century the Turks were forced, against their will, to rely more and more upon Christian Greeks to fill certain high offices of state. Born negotiators, with centuries of experience in commerce, and perhaps retaining the talents of their Byzantine ancestors, the Greeks now appear as the chief Ottoman diplomats. It is striking that the Turkish representative at Karlovitz should have been a Greek named Mavrogordato, from the island of Chios, who is said to have settled the disturbing question of protocol and precedence at the peace conference by inventing a round chamber with a door for each delegate, in the middle of which stood a round table. Each delegate could enter by his own door at the same moment, and sit in his own place at the round table with no question of higher and lower stations. This was a typically Greek idea, which no Turk could have had, and it signalized the opening of a new era.

V: Russia from the Thirteenth to the End of the Seventeenth Century

With the collapse of Kievan Russia about the year 1200, Russian development entered upon a confused and difficult period of about two hundred and fifty years. During this time, even the shrewdest contemporary observer would have been hard pressed to predict the future course of Russian history, or even the likely center for a future Russian state. There were at least four main centers of Russian national life, exposed to different enemies, undergoing different internal stresses, and shaping themselves in different ways.

The Western Lands

The southwestern portion of Russian territory, including the old capital at Kiev, became a virtually independent principality during the thirteenth century. It was distinguished by a particularly unruly nobility, which hampered all efforts of the princes to achieve consolidation in the face of the constant pressure from their Polish and Lithuanian neighbors. A parallel development took place in the northwest por-

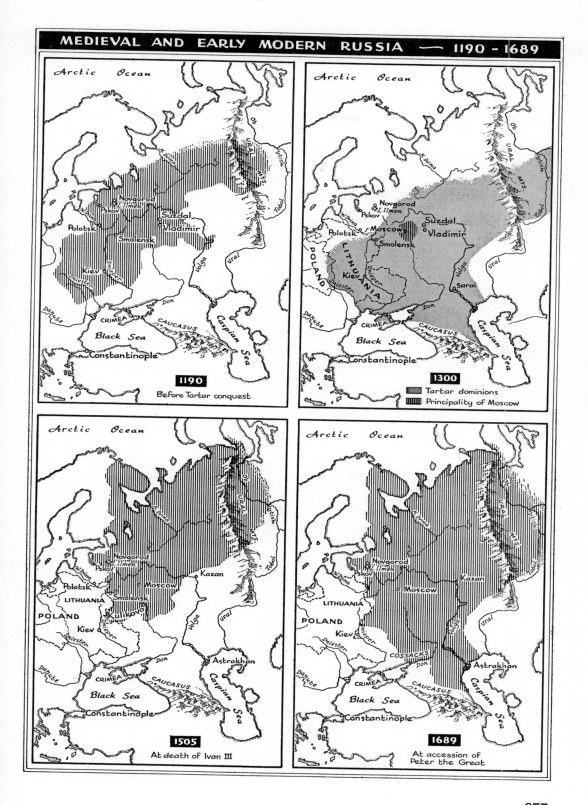

MEDIEVAL AND EARLY MODERN RUSSIA — 1190-1689

1190
Before Tartar conquest

1300
▨ Tartar dominions
▥ Principality of Moscow

1505
At death of Ivan III

1689
At accession of
Peter the Great

The Golden Gate in Vladimir, Russia, built in 1158.

Russian combination might just possibly have proved to be the center around which Russia could reunite. Yet even before the addition of the largely unassimilable Polish element, this region had become so feudal in character that its potential ability to unify Russia is extremely doubtful. Even under the Grand Duke of Lithuania, most of the lands nominally affiliated with his duchy were ruled without interference by local nobles bound to him only by an oath of fealty, and by their obligations to render military service. A parliament of nobles also limited the political authority of the Grand Duke. As in the West, the economic basis of the society in the western Russian lands was manorial. We find restrictions on the movement of the peasant farmer here long before we find them elsewhere in Russia.

The North

The northern regions of Russia, between the Baltic shore and Lake Ilmen, stretching far away to the north and northeast all the way to the Arctic Ocean and nearly to the borders of Siberia, were distinguished in this period by the growth of the town commonwealth of Novgorod (New-town). This city, stretched out along the banks of the Volkhov River where it flows out of Lake Ilmen, came to rule over the vast, empty, infertile northern regions, which were explored by armed merchants and pioneers in search of furs and other products of the forests.

In Novgorod even before the collapse of Kiev there grew up a tradition of municipal independence. The town council, or *veche*, (pronounced *vyé-che*) became very strong. The lifeblood of the city was its trade with the West: Russian furs, wax, honey, tar, and tallow were exchanged for German cloth and metal-work. The Germans had their own quarter in Novgorod, which they maintained for several centuries despite constant friction with the Russians. The

tion, centering around the cities of Polotsk and Smolensk. No Russian prince after the end of the thirteenth century was able to maintain himself in the face of these pressures.

By the early fourteenth century, the Grand Duke of Lithuania, with his capital at Vilna, ruled nominally over most of the western Russian lands. The culturally inferior Lithuanians, still mostly pagan, took over the language and manners of their more advanced Russian vassals. In 1386, in a celebrated dynastic marriage, Poland and Lithuania were united. The Polish Roman Catholic church and the Polish nobility now came to the fore. Had it not been for the antagonism between Orthodox Russians and Catholic Poles, and for the conflicting interests of the nobles of different religions and languages, the original Lithuanian-

town grew rich and strong. One might have expected that this city would have served as the agent to reunify Russia, although its territory was exposed to and suffered attack by the Teutonic Knights (see above, p. 355) and the Swedes.

But internally the class system of Novgorod was extremely rigid. The representatives of the richer merchants came to control the *veche*. A few powerful families concentrated the city's wealth in their hands and disputed with each other for political power. Economic discrepancies between rich and poor grew very wide. A man who could not pay his debts would be made a slave, and slaves frequently revolted and became brigands. Because the surrounding countryside had little good soil, the city depended upon the region to the southeast, around Moscow, for its grain. Yet its rulers did not have the sense to realize that Moscow possessed this weapon against them. When in the fifteenth century the Polish-Lithuanian state and the state of Moscow were competing, the class struggle inside Novgorod was reflected in the allegiances of the population. The upper classes were for the Poles and Lithuanians, the lower for Moscow. In 1478, the ruler of Moscow conquered the city, took away the bell, the symbol of its independence, and wiped out the upper classes. Novgorod may be compared with Venice and with other commercial patrician oligarchies in the West. But its inability to solve its own internal problems deprived it of its chance to unify Russia.

The Northeast: Moscow and the Tartars

Thus both western feudalism and western urban commercial development had their counterparts on Russian soil during the period after the collapse of Kiev. But it was the principality of Moscow, northeast of Kiev, east of Smolensk, and south-east of Novgorod, that succeeded where the other regions failed. Here neither feudality nor commercial oligarchy triumphed. This is the region where the prince was strong.

At the end of the Kievan period, the region of Moscow was still a frontier area, newly settled. Agriculturally poorer than the fertile southwest, it was richer than the north, could provide food enough for its people, and had flourishing forest industries. The cities remained small, and the pioneers turned neither to the nobility nor to the *veche*, since neither existed to any notable extent. Instead, they turned to the prince. This was also the region most exposed to the Tartar conquests of the thirteenth century.

By the early years of the thirteenth century, the celebrated Genghiz Khan had succeeded in consolidating under his command a large number of those Mongolian nomads of Central Asia who before, as Huns, Avars, and Polovtsy, had repeatedly erupted into Europe. Having conquered northern China and Asia from Manchuria to the Caspian Sea, Genghiz Khan led his savage Tartars across the Caucasus and into the steppes of southern Russia, defeating Russians and Polovtsy together in 1223, but retreating to Asia, where he died in 1227. His nephew Baty brought the Tartar hordes back again in the 1230's, sacked Moscow in 1237 and Kiev in 1240, and moved on into the western Russian regions and into Poland, Hungary, and Bohemia. Everywhere the Tartars went, the utmost devastation and slaughter marked their path.

Their success seems to have been due to their excellent military organization: unified command, general staff, clever intelligence service, and deceptive battle tactics. Though Baty defeated the Poles and the Germans in 1241, political affairs in Asia drew him eastward again, and the Tartars never again appeared so far to the west. Baty retreated across Europe, and at Sarai, near the great bend of the Volga, close to modern Stalingrad, he founded the capital of a new state. This was the "Golden Horde," which accepted the overlordship of the far-off central government of the Mongols, in Peking.

Other Mongol leaders were responsible for ending the Abbasid Caliphate in 1258 and were defeated by the Mamluks in 1260 (see above, p. 358). The enmity between Mongols and Moslems led the popes, St. Louis, and other leaders of western Europe to hope that they could bring the Mongol rulers into an alliance directed against the Moslems, and so crush the opponents of Christianity between eastern and western enemies. The existence of various Christian sects in distant Asia lent strength to the hope that the Khan himself could be converted. Considerable diplomatic correspondence was exchanged, and several embassies were sent to Mongolia and China during the thirteenth and fourteenth centuries with this end in view. But nothing ever came of all this, except a great increase in geographical knowledge derived from the extraordinarily interesting accounts of the European ambassadors, who were usually Franciscans or Dominicans. Their reports of their journeys into Asia and of their varied receptions at the court of the Mongol rulers rival any travel-books ever written.

The most lasting effect on Europe of the Tartar invasions is found in Russia. Here the Tartars' main purpose was the efficient collection of tribute. Although they laid waste the territory while they were in the process of conquering it, after the conquest had been achieved they shifted to a policy of exploitation. They took a survey of available resources, and assessed tribute at the limit of what the traffic would bear. It was not to their interest to disturb economic life, so long as their authority was recognized. They did draft Russian recruits for their armies, but after a while they made the local Russian princes responsible for the deliveries of men and money, and stayed out of Russian territory except occasionally to take censuses, survey property, and punish the recalcitrant. They had to confirm their tributary Russian princes, each of whom traveled to Sarai on his election to do homage. Some of them had to go all the way to China. Although no part of Russia was exempt from Tartar attacks during the period of conquest, thereafter the expensive burden of tribute and the humiliating sense of subservience fell most heavily upon the region of Moscow.

Toward the end of the fourteenth century, as the Mongol Empire itself grew feebler, the Russians became emboldened. The first Russian victories over the Tartars, scored by a prince of Moscow in 1378 and 1380, were fiercely avenged. Yet they served to show that the Tartars could be attacked and defeated. The Golden Horde did not disintegrate until the early fifteenth century, and even then the Tartars did not disappear from Russian life. Three separate khanates, or Tartar states, were formed from the debris of the Golden Horde: one at Kazan on the middle Volga, where it blocked the course of the river for another century and a half to Russian trade; one at Astrakhan at the mouth of the Volga on the Caspian; and one in the Crimea, where it later became a vassal of the Ottoman sultan.

Tartar Impact on Russian Civilization

Historians have long debated the effect upon the Russia of the "Tartar yoke"; one school has recently argued that the experience was somehow beneficial, because it eventually enabled the centralizing influence of the prince of Moscow, successor of the Tartar khan, to prevail. They add that trade with Asia helped Russia. They minimize the devastation wrought by the Tartar forces, and emphasize the fact that except for an occasional punitive expedition the Russian people never saw a Tartar after the conquest itself was over.

Yet it seems sure that the Tartar conquest also had a very serious negative effect on Russia. As the great nineteenth-century Russian poet, Pushkin, remarked, the Tartars brought to the Russians "neither algebra nor Aristotle." By this he meant to contrast the cultural impact of the Tartars on Russia with that of the Moslems on, let us say, Spain (see above, p. 255). Rule by an alien power is sometimes tolerable if the aliens are the bearers of a higher culture. But the Tartars, despite their military efficiency, were bearers of a lower culture than the Russians of the Kievan period had already achieved.

As we have seen (Chapter VI, above) there was no inherent reason why Russia in the late twelfth century should not have developed as a European state with highly individual characteristics of its own. After two centuries of Tartar domination, however, it had not advanced; rather, it had gone backward. Contemporaries felt that the Tartar yoke was a calamity, and historians have yet to demonstrate convincingly that it was anything else. When the Tartar power was finally shattered in the fifteenth century, Russian civilization was far behind that of the West. To the retarding effect of Byzantine Christianity there had been added the tremendous handicap of two centuries of cultural stagnation.

The Development of the Muscovite State

During these two centuries, the princes of Moscow asserted themselves and assumed leadership. Moscow had a favorable geographical position, near the great watershed from which the Russian rivers, always the great routes for trade, flow north into the Baltic or south into the Black Sea. Thus, when the Tartar grip relaxed and

Muscovite soldiers, sixteenth century.

trade could begin again, Moscow was advantageously located. Moreover, Moscow was blessed with a line of remarkably able princes, not so much warriors as grasping, shrewd administrators, anxious to increase their holdings and to consolidate their own authority within the steadily expanding borders of their principality. They married into powerful families, acquired land by purchase and by foreclosing mortgages, and inherited it by will. They established the principle of seniority, so that their domain was not divided among their sons in each generation, and the tragedy of Kiev was not repeated. Then too, they developed useful relations with their Tartar overlords. It was the princes of Moscow whom the Tartars chose to collect the tribute from other neighboring princes, and to deliver it at Sarai. Thus the princes were able to point to their success in excluding the Tartar agents from Russia, and to attract settlers to their lands. They were enabled to keep a close watch on the Tartars; so that when the moment of Tartar weakness came, it was they who could take advantage of it and marshal armies against them. They scored the first victories over the Tartars, and could truthfully claim to be the agents of liberation and the champions of Russia.

Finally, and very possibly most important, the princes of Moscow secured the support of the Russian Church. In the early fourteenth century the Metropolitan Archbishop transferred his see to Moscow, and made it the ecclesiastical capital of Russia. When the effective line of Muscovite princes faltered temporarily, it was the Metropolitan who administered the principality loyally and effectively until the royal house recovered. Thus the Russian Church deliberately bet on Moscow, and consciously decided to throw in its lot with the Muscovite house rather than with any other. The Metropolitan who first moved to Moscow is said by his biographer to have advised the prince as follows:

> If you build a church of the Virgin in Moscow, my son, and bury me in this city, so will you yourself become famous above the other princes, and also your sons and grandchildren from generation to generation. And this city will become celebrated above all the other Russian cities, and bishops will live here, and they will turn the city's forces against your enemies, and will praise God here.°

The Autocracy

By the middle of the fifteenth century, Moscow was a self-conscious Russian national state that was able to undertake successful wars against both the Polish-Lithuanian state and the Tartars. Ivan III (1462-1505) put himself forward as the heir to the princes of Kiev, and declared that he intended to regain the ancient Russian lands that had been lost to foreign

Poles and Tartars—a national appeal, although a purely dynastic one. Many nobles living in the western lands came over to him with their estates and renounced their loyalties to the Lithuanian-Polish state. In 1492, the Prince of Lithuania was forced to recognize Ivan III as sovereign of "all the Russias." This new national appeal was fortified by a religious appeal as well, for in addition to being sovereign Ivan was also the champion of Orthodoxy against the Catholic Poles and the Moslem Tartars. His wars took on the character of a purely Russian crusade. But he felt himself to be much more than a mere Russian prince.

In 1472, Ivan had married the niece of the last Byzantine emperor, Constantine XI, who had been killed fighting against the Turks on the battlements of Constantinople in 1453. Ivan adopted the Byzantine title of *autocrat,* used the Byzantine double eagle as his seal, and began to behave as a Byzantine emperor. He sometimes used the title tsar (Caesar). He no longer consulted his nobles, but reached decisions in solitude. Italian architects built him an enormous palace, the Kremlin, a building set apart, like the one at Byzantium. When the Holy Roman Emperor in the 1480's decided to make an alliance with Ivan III and to arrange for a dynastic marriage, Ivan responded:

> By God's grace we have been lords in our land since the beginning of time, since the days of our earliest ancestors. God has elevated us to the same position which they held, and we beg him to grant it to us and our children. We have never desired and do not now desire confirmation of this from any other source.°

Here is the claim to unlimited power derived directly from God that the Byzantine emperor had been accustomed to make.

When a rebellious noble fled Russia under the reign of Tsar Ivan IV, the Terrible (1534-1584), he wrote the Tsar from

° E. Golubinsky, *Istoriya Russkoi Tserkvi,* 2d ed. (Moscow, 1901-11), II, 1, p. 144. (Translation ours.)

° F. Adelung, *Kritisch-literarische Übersicht der Reisenden in Russland* (St. Petersburg and Leipzig, 1846), I, 153. Our translation.

abroad, denouncing him for failing to consult his nobles on important questions, as had been the custom in the days of Kievan Russia. Ivan replied that he was free to bestow favors on his slaves or inflict punishment on them as he chose. The Tsar thought of Russian nobles as his slaves. He scorned Queen Elizabeth of England for living among merchants, whom she permitted to influence her. In short, from the late fifteenth century on, we find the tsars calling themselves autocrats and acting like autocrats.

Part of the explanation for the immensely rapid growth of an autocratic theory and practice lies in the fact that Russia lived in a constant state of war or preparation for war. A national emergency prolonged over centuries naturally led to a kind of national dictatorship. Perhaps more significant is the fact that in Moscow's lands feudalism had not, as it had in the West, developed a united class of self-conscious nobles who would fight the rising monarchy for their privileges. Instead of uniting against the pretensions of the monarch, the Muscovite nobility produced various factions, with which the monarch could deal individually. Moreover, the absolutism of the Tartar khans probably helped furnish a model.

But most important of all was the ideology supplied by the Church and taken over largely from Byzantium. In the West, the Church itself was a part of feudal society, and jealous of its prerogatives. In Russia, as we have seen, it became the ally of the monarchy and something like a department of state. Russian churchmen were entirely familiar with Rome's claim to world-empire, and to Constantinople's centuries-long position as "new Rome." They knew many written Byzantine claims to world domination, and they were conscious of many historical legends that could be useful to them. With the fall of Constantinople (Tsargrad) to the Turks, they elaborated a famous theory that Moscow was the successor to the two former world capitals:

The Church of Old Rome fell because of its heresy; the gates of the Second Rome, Constantinople, have been hewn down by the axes of the infidel Turks; but the Church of Moscow, the Church of the New Rome, shines brighter than the Sun in the whole Universe. . . . Two Romes have fallen, but the Third stands fast; a fourth there cannot be.°

Russian churchmen spread the story that Rurik, the first political organizer of Russia (see Chapter VI), was descended from the brother of Augustus. They claimed that the Russian tsars had inherited certain insignia and regalia not only from the Byzantines but even from the Babylonians. All the tsars down to the last, in 1894, were crowned with a cap and clothed with a jacket that were actually of Byzantine manufacture, though of uncertain history. Thus the Church supplied the State with justification for its behavior. Imperial absolutism became one of the chief political problems of modern Russia.

Nobles and Serfs

Between the accession of Ivan III in 1462 and the accession of Peter the Great in 1689, the autocracy succeeded in overcoming the opposition of the old nobility. This was done in part by virtually creating a new class of military-service gentry who owed everything to the tsar. Their estates (pomestie) at first granted only for life in exchange for service, eventually became hereditary. The estates (vochina) of the old nobility, which had always been hereditary but for which they had owed no service, became service-estates. Thus, by the end of the period, the two types of noble and the two types of estate had by a gradual process become almost identical. The hereditary nobles often owed service. The military-service nobles often had hereditary land. During the eighteenth century this

° Quoted by A. J. Toynbee, in *Civilization on Trial* (New York, 1948), 171.

process was to be completed, and state service was to become universal. A central bureau in Moscow kept a census of the "service" men and of their obligations in time of war.

This tremendously important social process was accompanied by another, which is really the other side of the coin—the growth of serfdom. In a fashion familiar in earlier times in the West and in Byzantium, economic factors and political unrest had forced more and more peasants to seek out large landowners for dependence. The peasants would accept contracts that required rent in produce and service on the landlord's own land, and that involved the receipt of a money loan which had to be repaid over a period of years with interest or in the form of extra services. By the early seventeenth century it had become customary that the peasant could not leave his plot until he had paid off his debt. Since the debt was often too big for him to repay, he could in practice never leave.

The process was enormously speeded up when the tsars gave estates to the new military-service gentry. An estate was not much good unless there was farm labor to work it. In a period of bitter agrarian and political crisis such as the sixteenth and seventeenth centuries, it became advisable for the government to help the service gentry to keep their farmers where they were. Also, since the peasants paid most of the taxes, it was easier for the government to collect its own revenues if it kept the peasants where they were. Gradually it was made harder and harder for a tenant to leave his landlord, until by 1649 the avenues of escape were closed, and the serf was fixed to the soil. The landlord administered justice, and had police rights on the estate. He collected the serfs' taxes. He himself could sell, exchange, or give away his serfs. And the serf status became hereditary; children of serfs were enrolled on the estate's census books as serfs like their fathers.

The Russian serfs were not emancipated until 1861. Together with the absolute autocracy, the institution of serfdom is *the* most characteristic feature of Russian society. It affected every Russian, whether landowner, serf, or neither, for all the centuries it existed. In a very real sense, the consequences of Russian serfdom are still with us today, posing a great problem not only for the rulers of the Soviet Union but for all the world that has to deal with them. Russian serfdom became a fixed custom far later in time than did western European serfdom. In fact, it was most widely extended during the eighteenth century, at a moment when the serfs in western Europe had long been on their way to complete liberation. This is another illustration of the fact that Russia went through many of the same processes as the West, but with greater intensity and at a later time.

The Reign of Ivan the Terrible

Most of the disorders that distinguish Russian history in the sixteenth and seventeenth centuries have their origin in the long reign of Ivan IV, the Terrible (1534-1584). Pathologically unbalanced, Ivan succeeded to the throne as a small child. He experienced helplessly the indignities inflicted on him by the various rival groups of nobles who were maneuvering and intriguing for power. Devoted to the rites of the Church, and fancying himself as a theologian, Ivan was none the less horribly cruel. He had perhaps as many as seven wives; he murdered his own son in a fit of lunatic rage. Soviet historians have tried to turn him into a hero by explaining that his wrath was directed against the selfish nobles who were conspiring to take over Russia. But, though the nobles were selfish enough, the danger of their intrigues was surely hugely exaggerated by the Tsar.

When Ivan finally was strong enough, in 1547, to assume the crown and throw off the tutelage of the boyars, he embarked upon a period (1547-1560) usually regarded as one of sound government and institutional reform. He regulated the rapacity of the imperial administrators in the provinces, who had oppressed the population. He also convoked the first *zemski sobor* (land assembly), a consultative body consisting of nobles, clerics, and representatives from the towns, to assist with the imperial business, particularly with important questions of war and peace. Though comparable in its social composition to the various assemblies of the medieval western European world, the *zemski sobor* under Ivan seems to have met only once, and can in no sense be regarded as a parliamentary body.

When Ivan fell ill in 1553, the nobles refused to take an oath of allegiance to his son. This action apparently reawakened all his savagery, and upon his recovery he created a fantastic new institution: the *oprichnina*, or "separate realm." This was to belong to him personally, while the rest of Russia continued to be administered as before. The men whom Ivan now appointed to run the *oprichnina* (called *oprichniks*), grimly dressed in black and riding black horses, bore on their saddle-bows a dog's head (for vigilance) and a broom (symbolizing a clean sweep). They were the forerunners of the grim secret police forces that have long characterized Russian society. They waged a fierce, relentless war on the nobles, confiscating their estates, exiling them, killing them off. The Tsar, as was said, had divided his realm in two, and had set one part of it warring on the other. And in the diary of one *oprichnik* we find this revealing entry: "Today I did no harm to anyone: I was resting." The *oprichniks* took over the old estates of the men whom they were destroying. By the time of Ivan's death, many of the *oprichniks* themselves had been murdered at his orders, and Russian administration had degenerated to a state approximating chaos. Yet Ivan was able to extend Russian authority far to the

Ivan the Terrible, a contemporary portrait now in the National Museum of Denmark.

east against the Kazan and Astrakhan Tartars, thus for the first time opening the whole Volga waterway to Russian commerce, and facilitating expansion further east, into Siberia.

The Time of Troubles

Though the territory was wide and the imperial rule absolute, ignorance, illiteracy, and inefficiency weakened the structure of Russian society. The few foreign observers who knew the Russia of Ivan could foresee chaos ahead. And the Tsar himself had his own dire forebodings: "The body is exhausted, the spirit is ailing, the spiritual and physical wounds multiply, and there is no doctor to cure me," * he wrote in his last will. Though the old nobility had been dealt a series of blows, the

* Quoted by M. T. Florinsky, *Russia, A History and an Interpretation* (New York, 1953), I, 208.

new gentry had as yet no sense of corporate entity, and therefore was not firmly in control of the machinery. Ivan's son and heir, Fedor (1584-1598), was an imbecile, and with his death in 1598 the Moscow dynasty, descended from the rulers of the former Kievan state, died out. The cliques of rival nobles intrigued for power. Fedor's brother-in-law, Boris Godunov, emerged as the dominant figure in the state.

Though Boris Godunov was probably a man of talent, he could not overcome his handicaps: Ivan's legacy of disorder, the intrigues of the nobility, and the famine and plague that began in 1601. Bands of brigands roamed the countryside, and when in 1603 a pretender arose under the protection of the King of Poland and declared that he was a son of Ivan the Terrible —who had in fact died long before—he was able to capture the support of many of the discontented. Russia was launched on the decade known as the Time of Troubles (1603-1613).

After Boris Godunov's death (1605), the Pretender ruled briefly as Tsar. But within a year he was murdered, and was succeeded by a certain Shuisky, a representative of the ancient aristocracy. But new pretenders arose; the mobs of peasants and brigands were rallied once again; civil war continued, as Poles and Swedes intervened. Shuisky fell in 1610, and was succeeded by no one tsar but by a small group of nobles who planned that the heir to the Polish throne would become Tsar of Russia.

Polish forces took over in Moscow, and it soon appeared that the King of Poland intended not to turn over the power to his son but to reign in Russia himself. It was this specter of a foreign and Catholic domination that aroused the national sentiments of the Russians. In answer to a summons from the Patriarch, there assembled a kind of national militia, drawn largely from the prosperous free farmers of the middle Volga region, organized by a butcher named Kuzma Minin, and led by a nobleman named Dmitri Pozharsky. These two are the national heroes of the Time of Troubles. Under their command the militia won the support of other rebellious elements, and drove the Poles from Moscow in 1613.

The Role of the Zemski Sobor

A *zemski sobor* now elected Tsar Michael Romanov. From the election of Michael in 1613 to the Russian Revolution of 1917, the Romanov dynasty held the throne. Michael succeeded with no limitations placed upon his power by the *zemski sobor* or by any other body; he was that curious anomaly, an elected autocrat. For the first ten years of the reign of Michael Romanov, the *zemski sobor* stayed in continual session. Since it had picked the new Tsar in the midst of crisis, it had indeed performed a constitutional function. It even included some representatives of the free peasantry. It assisted the uncertain new dynasty to get under way by endorsing the policies of the Tsar and his advisers, and thus lending them the semblance of popular support. One might have supposed that this would be the beginning of a new kind of partnership, and that, as had sometimes happened in the West, representatives of the various social classes would gain more and more political self-confidence and power, and might even transform the *zemski sobor* from a consultative to some sort of legislative assembly, a parliament.

But this was not to be. After 1623, the *zemski sobor* was summoned only to help declare war or make peace, to approve new taxation, and to sanction important new legislation. It endorsed the accession of Michael's son Alexis (1645-1676), and in 1649 confirmed the issuance of a new law code, summarizing and putting in order past statutes. After 1653 Alexis did not summon it again, nor did his son and successor, Fedor (1676-1682). Its last meetings were in 1682.

No law abolished the *zemski sobor*. None had created it. The dynasty was simply entrenched and no longer needed it. Tsardom, autocratic tsardom, was taken for granted. No tsar need consult with any of his subjects unless he felt the need to do so. No subject had the right to insist on being consulted, though all subjects had the duty to give advice when asked for it. As the Romanovs became entrenched, they no longer felt the need to consult anybody's wishes except their own and those of their court favorites.

Individually, the early Romanovs were neither distinguished nor talented. The central government consisted of a number of bureaus or ministries or departments (*prikazy*), often with ill-defined or overlapping areas of competence. Provincial governors continued to milk the long-suffering population, and local efforts at self-government were in practice limited to the choice of officials obliged to collect and hand over taxes to the central authorities. Opposition to the system there certainly was, but it came not from articulate or literate citizens leveling criticism or offering suggestions for improvement. It came from below, from the oppressed and hungry peasantry. And it expressed itself in the only form of action the serf knew: large-scale or small-scale revolt, the burning of the manor house, the slaughter of the landlord or the tax-collector, the ill-directed march about in the vast flat countryside. Such affairs were a matter of yearly occurrence, the largest and most famous being that of Stenka Razin (1676), the "Russian Robin Hood." Such Russian uprisings were almost never directed against the tsar but against the landlords and officials, of whose misdeeds the tsar was supposed not to know. Often indeed the peasant leaders would arouse their followers *in the name* of the tsar. Sometimes, as during the Time of Troubles, the leaders pretended to be tsars in order to obtain more followers.

The Role of the Church

The Church remained the partner of the autocracy. The tsar controlled the election of the Metropolitan of Moscow, and after 1589 he controlled the election of the newly proclaimed Patriarch of Moscow, a rank to which the Metropolitan was elevated. In the seventeenth century, there were two striking instances when a patriarch actually shared power with the tsar. In 1619, the father of Tsar Michael Romanov, Filaret, became patriarch and was granted the additional title of "great sovereign." He assisted his son in all the affairs of state. In the next generation, Tsar Alexis (1645-1676), appointed a cleric named Nikon to the patriarchal throne, and gave him the same title and duties. Nikon proved so arrogant that he aroused protests from clergy as well as laity. He also seriously put forth the theory that the authority of the patriarch in spiritual affairs exceeded that of the tsar, and that, since the spiritual realm was superior to the temporal, the patriarch was actually superior to the tsar. This was a claim parallel to the one that was regularly made in the West by the more powerful popes, but that was almost never advanced in Byzantium or in Russia. In 1666, a church council deposed Nikon, who died a mere monk. These two experiments with two-man government ("dyarchy," it was called, in contrast with "monarchy") were never repeated, and they are interesting because they are the exceptions that prove the rule in Russia: the Church depends upon the State. Peter the Great was to abolish the patriarchate largely because he did not wish Nikon's claims ever to be repeated.

As in the Byzantine Empire, so in Russia, monasteries became immensely rich. By

St. Basil Cathedral, Moscow (1554-60).

literature and art of the Muscovite period. History was written by monks, in the form of chronicles. Travel literature took the form of accounts of pilgrimages to the Holy Land, although we have one secular travel book, a report by a Novgorod merchant who went to India on business. A handbook of etiquette and domestic economy, called *Household Management*, advises how to run a home and how to behave in company, revealing a conservative, well-ordered, solid, and smug society. Theological tracts attack the Catholics, and also the Protestants, whose doctrines were known in the western regions. This literature is limited, and it was still dominated by the Church several centuries after the West had made the break. Almost all of it was written in the Old Church Slavonic, the language of the liturgy and not the language of everyday speech. Though stately and impressive, Old Church Slavonic was not an appropriate vehicle for new ideas. There was no secular learning, no science, no flowering of vernacular literature, no lively debates on the philosophical level in the field of theology. In painting, the icon, inherited from Byzantium, did flourish mightily, and various local schools produced works of great beauty and character. The greatest are reminiscent of some of the "Italian primitives," which also were painted under the influence of Byzantium.

The Expansion of Russia

The sixteenth and seventeenth centuries saw the tremendous physical expansion of the Russian domain. Russian pioneers, in search of furs to sell and new land to settle, led the way, and the government followed. Frontiersmen in Russia were known as Cossacks (*Kazakh* is a Tartar word meaning "free adventurer"). It is a common error to suppose that they were somehow racially different from the mass of Russians. They were not; they were simply

1500, it is estimated that they owned more than one-third of the land available for cultivation. Opposition to monastic worldliness arose within the Church itself, and one might have supposed that the government would have supported this movement. But those who favored monastic poverty also wished to enforce the noninterference of the State in monastic affairs. To preserve their right to control the monasteries in other respects, the government of the tsar was obliged to oppose this reforming movement with respect to monastic property.

The Church, almost alone, inspired the

Russians living on the frontiers, organizing themselves for self-defense against the Tartars as our American pioneers did against the Indians. The Cossack communities gradually grew more settled, and two Cossack republics, one on the Dnieper, the other on the Don, were set up. These republics lived in a kind of primitive democracy relatively independent of Moscow; they fought Tartars and Turks quite at their own free will. As time passed, more Cossack groups formed in the Volga, in the Urals, and elsewhere.

A seventeenth-century house in Moscow.

The expansion movement took the Russians eastward into the Urals and on across Siberia—one of the most dramatic chapters in the expansion of Europe (see Chapter XIV). Far more slowly, because of Tartar, Turkish, and Polish opposition, the Russians also moved southeast toward the Caucasus and south toward the Black Sea. Repeated wars were fought with Poland over the old west-Russian territory of the Ukraine. Sometimes the Cossacks favored the Poles, and sometimes the Russians. But by 1682 the Poles were weakening, and were soon to yield. On the European fron-

tiers, it was the Swedes, still blocking the Baltic exit, against whom Russia's future wars would be fought. The struggle with the Tartars of the Crimea, whose lands extended far north of the peninsula, was also a constant feature. The Turks, overlords of the Tartars, held the key fort of Azov, controlled the Black Sea, participated in the wars over the Ukraine, and now for the first time became perennial enemies of the tsars.

Russia and the West

A final development of these two centuries was to prove of the utmost importance for the future Russia. This was the slow and gradual penetration of foreigners and foreign ideas, a process warmly welcomed by some Russians, deeply deplored by others, and viewed in a rather mingled light by still others, who prized the technical and mechanical learning they could derive from the West but feared western influence on Russian society and manners. This ambivalent attitude toward westerners and western ideas became characteristic of later Russians: they loved what the West could give, but they often feared and even hated the giver.

The first foreigners to come were the Italians, who helped build the Kremlin at the end of the fifteenth century. But they were not encouraged to teach Russians their knowledge and failed to influence even the court of Ivan III in any significant way. The English, who arrived in the mid-sixteenth century as traders to the White Sea, were welcomed by Ivan the Terrible, who had tried to attract German and other artisans, but who had been blocked by the Swedish control of the Baltic shore. He gave the English valuable privileges, and encouraged them to trade their woolen cloth for Russian timber and rope, pitch, and other naval supplies. These helped build the great Elizabethan fleets that sailed the seas and defeated the

Spanish Armada. The English were the first foreigners to penetrate Russia in any numbers and the first to teach Russians western industrial techniques. They got along well with the Russians and supplied a large number of officers to the tsar's armies, mostly Scotsmen. Toward the middle of the seventeenth century, the Dutch were able to displace the English as the most important foreign group engaged in commerce and manufacturing. The Dutch had their own glass, paper, and textile plants in Russia.

After the accession of Michael Romanov in 1613, the foreign quarter of Moscow, always called the "German suburb," grew rapidly. Foreign technicians of all sorts —textile-weavers, bronze-founders, clockmakers—received enormous salaries from the state. Foreign merchants sold their goods, much to the distaste of the native Russians, who begged the tsars to prevent the foreigners from stealing the bread out of their mouths. Foreign physicians and druggists became fashionable, though always suspected by the superstitious common people of being wizards. By the end of the seventeenth century, western influence is apparent in the life of the court. The first play in Russia was performed in 1672, and although it was a solemn biblical drama about Esther, it was at least a play. A few nobles began to buy books and form libraries, to learn Latin and French and German. People were eating salad and taking snuff, and shyly beginning to try their skills at some of the social arts, such as conversation. A few Russians went abroad to travel, and, of these few, all who could refused to go back.

The people, meanwhile, distrusted and hated the foreigners, looted their houses when they dared, and jeered at them in the street. As one intelligent writer of the seventeenth century put it:

Acceptance of foreigners is a plague. They live by the sweat and tears of the Russians.

The foreigners are like bear-keepers who put rings in our noses and lead us around. They are Gods, we fools, they dwell with us as lords. Our Kings are their servants.

The most dramatic outbreak of anti-foreign feeling took place, as might have been expected, in the field of religion. Highly educated clerics from the western lands (the Ukraine) and Greek scholars recommended to Patriarch Nikon that the Holy Books be revised and corrected in certain places where the texts were not sound. Resentment against this reform took the form of a great schism in the Russian Church itself. Given the deep Russian regard for the externals, the rite, the magic, rather than for the substance of the faith, we must not be surprised at the horror that was aroused when the Russians were told that for centuries they had been spelling the name of Jesus incorrectly and had been crossing themselves with the wrong number of fingers. As at Byzantium, the religious protest reflected a deep-seated hatred of change, particularly change proposed by foreigners. Declaring that the end of the world was at hand (since Moscow, the third Rome, had now itself become heretical), about 20,000 of the schismatics shut themselves up in their huts and burned themselves alive. When the world did not end, those schismatics who survived, always known as the "Old Believers," settled down and became sober, solid Russian citizens, many of them merchants and well-to-do peasants. Some later governments persecuted them, most did not; but, whatever the policies of the state might be toward them, the Russian Church was weakened as a result of the schism.

Peter the Great is usually thought of as the initiator of westernization for Russia. But before he had ever come to the throne, Russian society had been profoundly split at its heart, the Church, by the sixteenth- and seventeenth-century influx of foreigners and foreign ways.

VI: Conclusion

In this complex chapter we have handled as a unit events whose relationship is not often recognized by historians. Yet it has seemed to us that their true significance is comprehensible only if some of the more conventional dividing lines are disregarded. We have seen how, beginning in the last quarter of the eleventh century, the medieval West undertook a prolonged onslaught against the Moslem and Orthodox East. The crusades against Islam, the Norman and Hohenstaufen attacks on Byzantium, the ambitions of the Italian cities, the western distaste for the schism between the churches—all came together in the attack on Constantinople in 1204 and in the collapse of the Byzantine Empire, already deeply penetrated by the West. Yet the Crusader States founded on Syrian and Greek soil proved ephemeral. In Syria the Moslems had put an end to them by the close of the thirteenth century.

In the Byzantine world, though the Empire was re-established in 1261, the future lay with the Osmanli Turks, whose long slow rise to supremacy forms the central theme of the later Middle Ages in the southeast. Dominating the old Byzantine and Islamic worlds down to the end of the seventeenth century, their empire was the successor state to both. Meanwhile, Orthodox Russia —forced by the Tartar invasion to remain medieval long after the western European world had emerged into a new period—by the mid-fifteenth century took its character from Moscow, the Third Rome, and in its way proved itself also the heir of the Byzantine heritage. In dealing with the East, we perceive the fundamental continuities only by disregarding the conventional periods that are useful for the West: down to the end of the seventeenth century, the Ottoman Empire and Russia are still medieval.

Reading Suggestions
on the East in the Later Middle Ages

(Asterisk indicates paperbound edition.)

GENERAL ACCOUNTS

(See also listings for Chapter VI.)

S. Runciman, *A History of the Crusades*, 3 vols. (Cambridge Univ. Press, 1951-1954). The newest and the fullest treatment of the subject in English.

E. S. Creasy, *History of the Ottoman Turks*, 2 vols. (1854-56). Despite its age, still a good general account; based on a ten-volume German work.

H. A. R. Gibb and Harold Bowen, *Islamic Society and the West*, I, Parts 1 and 2 (Oxford Univ. Press, 1950, 1956). The most authoritative survey of Ottoman institutions.

SPECIAL STUDIES

J. L. LaMonte, *Feudal Monarchy in the Latin Kingdom of Jerusalem* (Mediaeval Academy, 1932). A study of the institutions of the Crusader States in the Levant.

W. Miller, *The Latins in the Levant, A History of Frankish Greece* (*1204-1566*) (John Murray, 1908), and *Essay on the Latin Orient* (Cambridge Univ. Press, 1921). Two good studies of the "Latins" in Greece.

A. S. Atiya, *The Crusade in the Later Middle Ages* (Methuen, 1938). A study of the propaganda and the expeditions that marked the decline of the crusading movement.

E. Pears, *The Destruction of the Greek Empire and the Story of the Capture of Constantinople by the Turks* (Longmans, Green, 1903). A solid work.

H. A. Gibbons, *The Foundation of the Ottoman Empire* (Century, 1916). An older work whose conclusions are again finding favor.

P. Wittek, *The Rise of the Ottoman Empire* (The Royal Asiatic Society, 1938). A suggestive essay on the elements that helped to advance the Ottoman state.

B. Miller, *Beyond the Sublime Porte* (Yale Univ. Press, 1931) and *The Palace School of Mohammed the Conqueror* (Harvard Univ. Press, 1941). Studies of the Ottoman imperial palace and the Ottoman educational system, respectively.

A. H. Lybyer, *The Government of the Ottoman Empire in the Time of Suleiman the Magnificent* (Harvard Univ. Press, 1913). A pioneering work on Ottoman institutions.

Dorothy M. Vaughan, *Europe and the Turk: A Pattern of Alliances, 1350-1700* (Liverpool Univ. Press, 1954). Role of the Ottoman Empire in European diplomacy.

G. Vernadsky, *The Mongols and Russia* (Yale Univ. Press, 1953). Volume III of the Yale History of Russia; authoritative and complete.

SOURCES IN TRANSLATION

Anna Comnena, *The Alexiad*, E. A. S. Dawes, trans. (Kegan Paul Trench, Trübner, 1928). The life and reign of Emperor Alexius Comnenus (1081-1118); by his daughter.

Fulcher of Chartres, *Chronicle of the First Crusade*, M. E. McGinty, trans. (Univ. of Pennsylvania, 1941).

An Arab-Syrian Gentleman and Warrior in the Period of the Crusades. Memoirs of Usamah ibn-Munqidh, P. K. Hitti, trans. (Columbia Univ. Press, 1929).

William, Archbishop of Tyre, *A History of Deeds Done Beyond the Sea*, E. A. Babcock and A. C. Krey, trans., 2 vols. (Columbia Univ. Press, 1943). The greatest of the contemporary accounts of the Crusaders' Levant.

Memoirs of the Crusades, including Villehardouin's chronicle of the Fourth Crusade and Joinville's of the crusade of St. Louis, F. T. Marzials, trans. (Dutton, 1933, Everyman ed.; *paperback edition by same publisher). Eyewitness accounts by prominent participants.

The Conquest of Constantinople, translated from the Old French of Robert of Clari, E. H. McNeal, trans. (Columbia Univ. Press, 1936). Eyewitness account by a humble participant in the events of 1204.

P. W. Topping, *Feudal Institutions as Revealed in the Assizes of Romania, The Law Code of Frankish Greece* (Univ. of Pennsylvania, 1949).

Kritovulos, *History of Mehmed the Conqueror,* C. T. Riggs, trans. (Princeton Univ. Press, 1954). A Greek life of Mohammed the Conqueror.

The Life and Letters of Ogier Ghiselin de Busbecq, C. T. Forster and F. H. Blackburne Daniell, eds., 2 vols. (C. K. Paul, 1881). Perceptive and amusing reports of a Habsburg ambassador to Suleiman the Magnificent.

The Correspondence between Prince A. M. Kurbsky and Tsar Ivan IV of Russia, 1564-1579, ed. and trans. J. L. I. Fennell (Cambridge Univ. Press, 1955). A fundamental source for the political theories of the Tsar and his noble opponents.

Politics

and

Economics:

Late Medieval West

CHAPTER X

I: Introduction

IN EASTERN EUROPE, as we have just seen, medieval institutions continued to flourish long after the final downfall of Byzantium in 1453, the date often cited as marking the end of the Middle Ages. For the next two centuries and more, the tsars in Moscow and the sultans in Istanbul acted in their different ways as the successors of Byzantium. The medieval pattern likewise persisted in religion and in the broad realm of culture. New, foreign ideas began to penetrate Russia only in the seventeenth century and the Ottoman Empire only in the eighteenth; by 1700, the typical medieval social and economic institution of serf-dom was still growing in Russia. In the long perspective of history the Middle Ages ended only yesterday in eastern Europe.

In western Europe, by contrast, the Middle Ages ended five centuries ago, with the accession of realistic national monarchs to the thrones of England, France, and Spain, with the discovery of America, and with the outbreak of the Protestant Refor-mation. This chapter surveys the political and economic forces that weakened and then destroyed feudal society. Succeeding chapters will examine the famous twin movements that disrupted the Christian cul-tural synthesis and religious unity of the

Middle Ages—the Renaissance and the Reformation.

Words like "destroyed" and "disrupted" should not suggest that the Middle Ages ended abruptly and that modern western civilization appeared with dramatic suddenness. The destruction and disruption did occur, but only as a long, gradual, complex process. The transition from medieval to modern spanned the history of the West from the fourteenth through the sixteenth centuries.

The Pattern of Late Medieval Politics

Two major trends stand out in the evolution of western politics during these centuries of transition. First, old medieval forms and attitudes persisted but became more rigid and less flexible, more sterile and less creative, as so often happens in an era of decline. Political leaders sometimes behaved as though they were living centuries earlier. In the early fourteenth century, the German Emperor Henry VII sought to straighten out the affairs of Italy in the old Ghibelline tradition, even though he possessed few of the resources that his Hohenstaufen predecessors had commanded. In France and England great nobles exploited the confusion produced by the Hundred Years' War (1338-1453) and built again the private armies and the great castles of the heyday of feudalism. They attempted to shift the locus of power back from the monarch to themselves; after transient success, they failed. The movement has been aptly termed "bastard feudalism," more artificial and less genuine than earlier feudalism. Manifestations like these have also been diagnosed as symptoms of senility, a hardening of the arteries in the body politic.

As bastard feudalism collapsed in the latter half of the fifteenth century, the second major trend of the political transition came to the fore. This was the emergence of the "new" monarch, not at all interested in faded feudal or imperial glories but very much concerned with the realities of rule, with what the twentieth century knows as power politics. The "new" monarchs of the fifteenth century did not, of course, invent power politics. The Norman monarchs of medieval England and Sicily had been hard-headed rulers; so had Philip Augustus and Philip the Fair of France. What distinguished the "new" monarchs of the fifteenth century from most of their medieval predecessors was the candor and efficiency of their operations. They were outspoken in their pursuit of power, naked and unadorned with medieval trappings; they developed better instruments of governing, better soldiers, diplomats, bureaucrats. In short, they made politics more professional.

Outstanding representatives of this new-model monarchy, as we shall shortly see, occupied the thrones of the states along the Atlantic seaboard. In the late 1400's Louis XI of France, Henry VII of England, and Ferdinand and Isabella of Spain set to work putting their respective states in order and increasing their central authority. In these three instances state and nation corresponded, and the monarchs profited by the developing nationalism of their kingdoms. Not all the "new" monarchs were actually kings or queens, however, nor were the new-model states always nations. Power politics flourished in late medieval Germany and Italy; its practitioners were usually to be found, however, not in the decadent office of Holy Roman Emperor but among the rulers of the particular German or Italian states. The German princes and, still more, the Italian despots accomplished on a sectional or regional basis what the Atlantic monarchs were achieving on the plane of the nation-state.

II: The Emerging National Monarchies

The Hundred Years' War: The First Round

At the death of Philip the Fair in 1314 the Capetian monarchy of France appeared well on the way to establishing a new-model state manned by efficient and loyal bureaucrats. Philip Augustus, St. Louis, and Philip the Fair had all consolidated the royal power at the expense of their feudal vassals, including the kings of England (see Chapter VII). Soon, however, France became embroiled in an almost interminable contest with England that crippled the monarchy for a century. This was the celebrated Hundred Years' War, 1338-1453.

The nominal cause of the war was a dispute over the succession to the French throne. For more than three hundred years, ever since Hugh Capet had been succeeded by his son, son had followed father as King of France. This remarkable streak of good fortune came to an end with the three sons of Philip the Fair. Each of them ruled in turn between 1314 and 1328, but none of them fathered a son who survived infancy. Consequently, the crown passed to Philip of Valois, Philip VI (1328-1350), a nephew of Philip the Fair and the first cousin of his sons; the Valois dynasty thereby succeeded the Capetian dynasty. In order to make the succession legal, the lawyers had to dispose of a dangerous claim to the throne—that of the King of England, Edward III (1327-1377), whose mother Isabella had been a daughter of Philip the Fair. As nephew of the last Capetian kings, did not Edward have a better right to succeed than their first cousin, Philip of Valois? To settle the question, French lawyers went all the way back to a Frankish law of the sixth century which said that a woman could not *inherit land*. Although this so-called "Salic" law had not applied in France for centuries, the lawyers now interpreted it to mean that a woman could not *pass on* the inheritance to the *kingdom*. The legal quibble was to serve Edward III as pretext for beginning the Hundred Years' War.

Edward's claim to the French throne was not, of course, the only reason for the outbreak of war. England's continued possession of the rich land of Aquitaine, with its lucrative vineyards, was an anomaly in an increasingly unified France. As suzerains over Aquitaine, the Kings of France encroached upon the feudal rights of the Kings of England. They encouraged the local knights to appeal to them over the head of the English king, and then cited him before their own court. The English, for their part, wished not only to keep what they had, but to regain Normandy and the other territories they had lost to Philip Augustus.

An immediate issue arose in Flanders. This small but wealthy area, which today lies on both sides of the frontier between Belgium and France, was ruled in medieval times by the Count of Flanders, a vassal of the King of France. The thriving Flemish cloth manufacturers bought most of their wool from England and sold much of their finished cloth there; the English crown collected taxes both on the exported wool and on the imported woolens. Inside Flanders, the artisans and tradesmen of the towns were in almost constant conflict with the rich commercial ruling class. The rich sought the backing of their lord, the Count of Flanders, and he in turn sought that of his overlord, the King of France; the poor

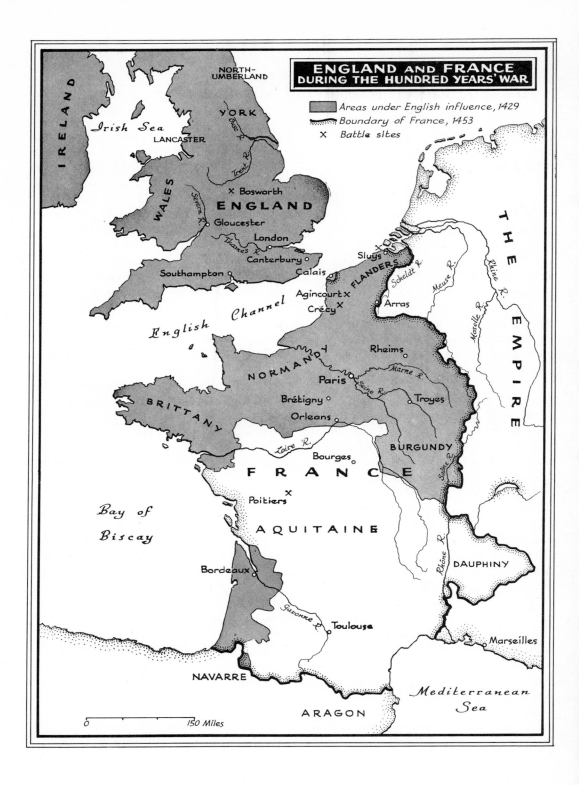

ENGLAND AND FRANCE
DURING THE HUNDRED YEARS' WAR

Areas under English influence, 1429
Boundary of France, 1453
X   Battle sites

IRELAND

Irish Sea

NORTH-
UMBERLAND

YORK

LANCASTER

WALES

ENGLAND

X Bosworth

Gloucester

London

Canterbury

Southampton

Calais

English Channel

Sluys

FLANDERS

Agincourt X

Crécy X

Arras

THE EMPIRE

NORMANDY

Rheims

Paris

BRITTANY

Brétigny

Orleans

Troyes

BURGUNDY

Bourges

FRANCE

Poitiers X

Bay of
Biscay

AQUITAINE

Bordeaux

DAUPHINY

Toulouse

Marseilles

NAVARRE

ARAGON

Mediterranean
Sea

0   150 Miles

got the help of the English, who feared the disruption of their lucrative trade. Warlike incidents multiplied during the early fourteenth century. In 1302, the Flemish town militias defeated Philip the Fair. In 1326, the Count of Flanders arrested and jailed all Englishmen on his lands; the King of England forbade the export of raw wool, or the import of finished goods, and caused a crisis in Flanders that brought the French armies back in 1328, this time to win a victory. King Edward III, however, allied himself with a Flemish merchant, Jacob van Artevelde, who threw out the ruling Flemish oligarchy and the French, and organized his own government of Flanders. It was in response to pressure from these Flemish allies that Edward III put forth his claim as King of France and precipitated war.

The war was synonymous with the history of France for a troubled century. The Valois kings, with the notable exception of Charles V, the Wise (1364-1380), were far less effective rulers than the Capetians had been. The English won all the greatest battles and gained by treaty huge amounts of French territory. France was racked by bubonic plague ("The Black Death," 1348-1350) and swept by social crisis and civil war. Yet in the end the French expelled the English and completed the unification of their country under a strong national monarchy. Under pressure, France developed a standing army and a system of direct taxation. The whole accomplishment depended in the long run upon the assistance rendered to the monarchy by the middle classes.

The first major operation of the war was an English naval victory at Sluys (1340), which gave the English command of the Channel for many years. When their Flemish ally, Van Artevelde, was killed in 1345, the English had to invade France itself to obtain a foothold on the Continent. In 1346 came the first of the great English victories, at Crécy. Despite inferior numbers, the English profited by the incompetent generalship of the French; from higher ground their archers with the longbow poured arrows down on a confused crowd of French cavalry and crossbowmen. Next, the English took Calais, which gave them a port in France. After an eight years' truce (1347-1355), marked by the ravages of the Black Death, open warfare was resumed. At Poitiers (1356), in western France, the English again compensated for inferior numbers by superior tactics. This time they captured the King of France himself (John, 1350-1364), and carried him off to England as a prisoner. His son, the future Charles the Wise, became regent, while John himself settled down to enjoy a carefree life in luxurious captivity. France's feudal armies had been shattered, and the machinery of government had been sadly weakened.

The Aftermath of Defeat in France

In these years the French monarchy faced not only a triumphant foreign enemy but also increasingly hostile criticism at home, focused in the central representative assembly, the Estates General (see above, p. 270). When summoned in 1355 to consent to a tax, the Estates General insisted on fixing its form: it was to be raised by a general levy on sales and a special levy on salt. They demanded also that their representatives rather than those of the Crown be allowed to collect it. Moreover, the Estates for the first time scheduled their own future meetings "to discuss the state of the realm." Here was a new spirit of responsibility and assertion of rights.

After the defeat at Poitiers, the Estates demanded that the regent Charles dismiss and punish the royal advisers, and substitute for them twenty-eight delegates chosen from the Estates. When Charles hesitated to accept the demands of the Estates, their leader, Étienne Marcel, a bourgeois of Paris, led a general strike and revolution in the capital, the first of many in French history, and forced Charles to consent. In his *grande ordonnance* of 1357, he accepted the Estates' demands for a complete administrative housecleaning.

But this was as far as the success of the Estates went. Marcel made two cardinal mistakes. He allied himself with a rival claimant to the throne, and he assisted a violent peasant revolt, the Jacquerie (so-called from the popular name for a peasant, Jacques Bonhomme—James Goodfellow), which broke out early in 1358 with murders of nobles and burnings of chateaux. The royal forces, in disarray though they were, put down and massacred the peasants. Thus, in the pinch, the country failed to support the more radical Parisians—this, too, was to be a familiar pattern in later French history. In the final flare-up, Marcel was killed, and Charles won his struggle.

Although the Estates had in effect run France for two years during 1356 and 1357, they had imposed no principle of constitutional limitation upon the king; they had not made themselves permanent or necessary to the conduct of government. After all, France was in danger of invasion, and even the rebellious wished to meet the emergency by strengthening rather than weakening the royal power. They were willing to criticize its methods but not to limit them. Moreover, the opponents of the Crown—nobles, clergy, townsmen—had conflicting class interests and mistrusted one another; even members of a single estate were divided by the regional interests of the provinces from which they came. Class and local antagonisms gave the Crown an advantage which Charles the Wise was not slow to take. As early as 1358, then, the reasons for the failure of the Estates General ever to become a real French Parliament are clear.

The Hundred Years' War: The Second Round

In 1360 the war again came to a halt, with the Treaty of Calais. Edward III renounced his claim to the French crown, but only in exchange for all southwestern France (Aquitaine plus Poitou) and lands bordering the Channel near Calais. The King of England was to annex these lands outright, not simply hold them as the vassal of the King of France. An enormous ransom was agreed upon for the captive French King John. But John broke his parole, and relations deteriorated once more. When the war was resumed in 1369, the French made impressive gains under Charles the Wise, a capable king with capable advisers from the middle class. By his death in 1380, they had ejected the English from all but a string of seaports, including Bordeaux and Calais. For the first time since the beginning of the war, the French fleet was able to sail freely in the Channel and raid the English coasts. Charles also continued the policies that had helped defeat the brief bid of the Estates for power. He regularized the salt tax and in 1369 secured an agreement from the Estates that other existing taxes were to be made permanent.

But, instead of initiating a period of reconstruction and recuperation, the military victories against the English and the royal consolidation of financial power under Charles the Wise were only the prelude to a period of still worse suffering. Charles VI (1380-1422) went insane, and never ruled effectively. A struggle broke out between one of the King's uncles, the Duke of Burgundy, and the King's brother, the Duke of Orléans, for control of France. The whole conflict illustrated the danger of a king's giving provinces (called *appanages*) to any of his sons other than the heir to the throne himself. Such a son might himself be loyal, but within a generation or two his heirs would be remote enough from the royal family to feel themselves rivals. It was essentially this pattern that had ruined the Carolingians. In 1361 King John revived the practice and opened the door to bastard feudalism by assigning the important Duchy of Burgundy as the *appanage* of his youngest son, Philip. He thus revived the old political entity of Burgundy in a new form that was to threaten France herself.

The rivalry between Burgundy and Orléans led to the murder of the Duke of Orléans in 1407 by assassins hired by the Burgundians. The Orléanists, now led by the father-in-law of the new Duke, Count Bernard of Armagnac, were known thereafter as the Armagnacs. They commanded the loyalty of much of southern and southwestern France, while the Burgundians controlled the north and east. The Armagnacs were strongest among the great nobles, and were professedly anti-English; the Burgundians, who in 1381 had inherited Flanders and had thus become immensely rich, were pro-English, and had the support of the upper bourgeoisie in the towns.

Under these circumstances, the English reopened the war in alliance with the Burgundians. Their king, Henry V, won the celebrated battle of Agincourt (1415), and undid the work of Philip Augustus and Charles the Wise by reconquering Normandy. The Burgundians took over in Paris, massacring partisans of the Armagnacs, whose party fled in disorder to set up their own rival regime south of the Loire, with the heir to the throne, the future Charles VII, as its nominal head. When the English took the Norman capital, Rouen (1419), the alarmed Burgundians tried to patch up a truce with the Armagnacs. But the Duke of Burgundy, the head of their party, was assassinated at a peace conference in 1419, in an act of vengeance for the murder of the Duke of Orléans in 1407. There followed the Treaty of Troyes (1420), in which Charles VI cast off his own son as illegitimate, and adopted Henry V of England as heir and as his regent during his lifetime. Henry married Charles VI's daughter, and was allowed to retain as his own all the conquests north of the Loire until he should inherit all of France on the death of Charles VI.

This fantastic settlement, which gave the English a position in France even higher than it had been under the Angevins, and which threatened to put an end to French national sovereignty altogether, was supported by the Burgundians, the Estates General, and the University of Paris. Had Henry V lived, it is barely possible that the entire future would have been changed. But French national consciousness was now aroused; the rightful king, the pitiful Charles VII (1422-1461), ruled at Bourges with Armagnac support. England, too, was torn with faction (see below, p. 407) and could not or would not supply enough troops to hold down conquered northern France. In any case, Henry V and Charles VI both died during 1422, and the regent for the infant English King Henry VI prepared to move south against Charles VII.

At this juncture, the miracle of Joan of Arc saved France. The wretched, demoralized forces of Charles VII were galvanized into action by the visionary peasant girl who reflected the deep patriotism of the French, and who touched a responsive chord at a moment when all seemed lost. The story is well known: how saints and angels told Joan that she must bring Charles VII to be crowned at Rheims, traditional coronation place for the Kings of France; how she was armed and given a small detachment that drove the English out of Orléans; how the King was crowned, Joan taken prisoner by the Burgundians, sold to the English, turned over to the French Inquisition, and burned at Rouen (1431). The papacy itself undid the verdict against her in 1456, and made her a saint in 1919.

Against heavy odds the French monarchy

managed to sustain the impetus provided by the martyred Joan. In 1435, at Arras, Charles VII and Burgundy concluded a separate peace which made it impossible for the English to win the war. Charles now recovered Paris (1436), but for ten years the countryside was ravaged and pillaged by bands of soldiers organized into private companies. They were known as the "flayers" (*écorcheurs*), a term indicating vividly their mode of treating the peasantry. Moreover, leagues of nobles, supported by the heir to the throne, the future Louis XI, revolted in 1440. The Estates General, however, in 1439 granted the King not only the right to have an army, but also the *taille*, a tax to be levied directly on individuals and collected by royal agents.

With this instrument ready to his hand, with financial aid from the great merchant prince, Jacques Coeur (below, p. 432), and with assistance from professional military experts, Charles VII embarked on military reforms which at last ended the medieval system that had for so long shown itself inadequate. Twenty companies of specialized cavalry were organized, 1200 to a company, under commanders of the King's personal choice. These companies were assigned to garrison the towns. Professionals supervised the introduction of artillery, which became the best in Europe.

The new French equipment and the newly organized French force drove the English out of Normandy in 1449-1450, and out of Aquitaine in 1450-1451. Calais alone in France remained in English hands when the Hundred Years' War finally ended in 1453. The standing army, based on direct taxation that had been granted by the Estates as a royal right, had enabled France to overcome the English threat.

Meantime, Charles had scored against another institution, the Church, that might have weakened the Crown. In 1438, he regulated Church-State relations by the Pragmatic Sanction of Bourges ("pragmatic sanction" is simply a name for a solemn royal pronouncement). This document laid down the policy known as Gallicanism, claiming for the Gallican, or French, church a virtually autonomous position within the Church Universal. It greatly limited papal control over ecclesiastical appointments and revenues in France and asserted the superiority of church councils over popes. Despite these achievements, however, when Charles VII died in 1461 rebellious vassals were still defying his authority in large areas of the kingdom.

France: Louis XI

Louis XI (1461-1483), the son of Charles VII, pursued energetically the unfinished business left by his father. By no means a model son, Louis had repeatedly intrigued against his father; at his accession he was already a mature and practiced politician. This crafty monarch, who despised the pageantry of kingship, liked a simple tavern meal better than elaborate royal fare, and preferred secret diplomacy to open war, soon gained the nickname of the "Universal Spider." One of his aides, the statesman and historian Philippe de Comines (1445-1509), drew a notable portrait of the wily Louis:

... He was the wisest Prince in winding himself out of trouble and adversity, the humblest in words, the plainest in apparel, and greatest traveller to win a man that might do him service or harm that ever I knew.... Never Prince gave audience to so many men, never Prince was inquisitive of so many matters, nor desirous to be acquainted with so many strangers as he.... And by these virtues preserved he his estate, which stood in great danger at his first coming to the crown, because of the enemies himself had procured to himself. .

... And I think verily he should never have wound himself out of those troubles had not his education been better than noblemen's commonly is in this realm, who are brought altogether in wantonness and dissoluteness, as well in their apparel as in their talk, they are utterly unlearned, there is not one wise man about them. . . .*

Louis returned to the strong monarchical tradition of Philip Augustus and Philip the Fair. He forced his protesting subjects to pay higher taxes, then sweetened the dose, at least for the men of the middle class, by granting them favors and by giving them responsible posts in his administration. He propitiated the Pope by withdrawing the Pragmatic Sanction of 1438 but in practice continued most of its restrictions on papal intervention in the Gallican Church. He enlarged the army bequeathed him by his father yet conserved its use for the direst emergencies only. And he countered the greatest single feudal threat to the French monarchy since the days of Philip Augustus.

The threat came from Burgundy. The

---

* *The History of Comines,* Thomas Danett, trans., Bk. I, Ch. X. Translation somewhat modernized.

BURGUNDIAN DOMINIONS
AT THE DEATH OF CHARLES THE BOLD, 1477
Boundary between France and the Empire

authority of its dukes reached far beyond the Duchy of Burgundy in eastern France and the adjoining Free County (Franche Comté) and encompassed a large portion of the Low Countries. This sprawling Burgundian realm almost deserved to be called an emerging national state. But it was a divided state: the two main territorial blocs in eastern France and the Low Countries were separated by the non-Burgundian lands of Alsace and Lorraine. And it was a personal state, for Duke Philip the Good (1419-1467) had assembled it as much by good luck as by good management, inheriting some lands and acquiring others by conquest or negotiation. Yet it was also a menacing state, which might have interposed itself permanently as a middle kingdom between France and Germany. Philip had been allied with England in the Hundred Years' War, as we have seen. He could draw on the wealth of the Flemish and Dutch towns, and his resources at least equaled those of his feudal suzerains, the King of France and the Holy Roman Emperor.

The decisive trial of strength between France and Burgundy took place under Philip's successor, Charles the Bold (1467-1477). Where Louis XI was cautious, Charles was bold to the point of folly. The policies and temperaments of the two men made a striking contrast. Comines' characterization of Louis may be flanked by his portrait of Charles:

. . . Never was Prince more desirous to entertain noble men, and keep them in good order than he. His liberality seemed not great, because he made all men partakers thereof. Never Prince gave audience more willingly to his servants and subjects than he. . . . In his apparel and all other kind of furniture he was wonderful pompous, yea somewhat too excessive. He received very honorably all ambassadors and strangers, feasting them sumptuously, and entertaining them with great solemnity. Covetous he was of glory, which was the chief cause that made him move so many wars: for he desired to imitate those ancient Princes, whose fame continueth till this present. Lastly, hardy he was and valiant, as any man that lived in his time: but all his great enterprises and attempts ended with himself, and turned to his own loss and dishonor; for the honor goeth ever with the victory.[*]

Charles determined to build a true middle kingdom by bridging the territorial gap between Burgundy and the Low Countries and seizing Lorraine and Alsace. But, since Alsace in those days was a confused patchwork of feudal jurisdictions overlapping northern Switzerland, his designs threatened the largely independent Swiss confederation. Subsidized by Louis XI, the Swiss defeated Charles three times in 1476 and 1477; in the last of the battles Charles was slain.

Since Charles left no son, his lands were partitioned. The Duchy of Burgundy passed permanently, and the Franche Comté temporarily, to France; the Low Countries went to Mary, the daughter of Charles. Mary married Maximilian of Habsburg, who later became Holy Roman Emperor; their son was to marry the daughter of Ferdinand and Isabella of Spain. The son of this latter union, the emperor Charles V, was to rule Germany, the Low Countries, Spain, and the fast-growing Spanish empire overseas, and to threaten the kingdom of France with hostile encirclement (see Chapter XIII).

Louis XI, though he did not keep all the Burgundian inheritance out of the hands of potential enemies, did shatter the prospect of a middle kingdom. More than that, he doubled the size of the royal domain and completed the task of rebuilding the strength and prestige of the Crown. His work was solid enough to survive the reigns of his mediocre successors and to give them a base for adventurous expeditions to Italy (see Chapter XIII). The France of Louis XI was not yet a full-fledged national monarchy; the forging of the French people into a proud, cohesive, confident nation was to be the accomplish-

ment of subsequent centuries. But he did lay the indispensable foundations for the later achievement by his consolidation of territorial unity and by his competent central administration. At his death in 1483 it is fair to say that France was passing from medieval to modern times, was indeed an emerging national monarchy.

England: Edward II and Edward III

England, too, was emerging as a national monarchy at the close of the fifteenth century. There were many other parallels between the experience of England and that of France during the last two centuries of the Middle Ages. In England, also, the royal authority went slack when it was exercised by mediocre rulers. There, too, social and political dissension accompanied the Hundred Years' War, and bastard feudalism threatened anarchy until finally Henry VII (1485-1509) reasserted the royal power, much as Louis XI had done in France. But there was also an all-important difference between the experiences of the two countries: whereas in France the Estates General were becoming the docile servant of the monarchy, the English Parliament was slowly setting the precedents and acquiring the powers that would one day make it in fact the master of the monarchy.

One more parallel, however, may be noted: as the fourteenth century opened, the thrones of both countries were occupied by strong and ambitious kings, Philip the Fair and the English Edward I (for details, see Chapter VII). After the death of Edward I in 1307 the political tide turned abruptly against the monarchy. His son, Edward II (1307-1327), was weak and inept, dominated by his favorites and by his French queen. In 1314 he lost the battle of Bannockburn to the Scots, and with it the short-lived English hegemony over Scot-

---

[*] *The History of Comines*, Bk. V, Ch. IX.

land. Meantime, Edward II faced baronial opposition much like that which had harassed his grandfather, Henry III (see above, p. 279). In 1311, the barons virtually re-enacted the Provisions of Oxford of 1258. This time they set up as the real rulers of England twenty-one "Lords Ordainers," who had to consent to royal appointments, to declarations of war, and to the departure of the king from England. But, as under Henry III, the barons were as selfish as the king's bureaucrats had been. In the end, Edward's queen, Isabella, led a revolt against Edward, who was imprisoned and murdered. He was succeeded on the throne by their fifteen-year-old son, Edward III (1327-1377), a knightly and vigorous figure.

The headline incidents of Edward III's reign were the opening of the Hundred Years' War, and the great English victories in France. The reign also saw a great economic crisis, arising in part out of the ravages of the Black Death (1348-1349), which killed about three-eighths of the population. A terrible shortage of manpower resulted; crops rotted in the fields and good land dropped out of cultivation.

The agricultural laborers of England, aware of their suddenly increased bargaining power (and of the enhanced wealth gained by their masters from the French war), demanded better working conditions, or left home and flocked to the towns. In 1351, Parliament passed the Statute of Laborers, an attempt to fix wages and prices as they had been before the plague. It also included regulations forbidding workmen to give up their jobs, and requiring the unemployed to accept work at the old rates. The law was not a success, and the labor shortage hastened the end of serfdom and paved the way for the disorders that took place under Edward's successor. A striking item in medieval literature is a verse satire of Edward's reign, *Piers Plowman*, which denounces the corruption of the officials, especially of the Church, and pleads the cause of the poor peasant. Here is a representative passage:

There I found friars of all the four orders,
Who preached to the people for the profit of their bellies,
And glossed the gospel to their own good pleasure;
They coveted their copes, and construed it to their liking.
Many master-brothers may clothe themselves to their fancy,
For their money and their merchandise multiply together.
Since charity has turned chapman to shrive lords and ladies,
Strange sights have been seen in a few short years.
Unless they and Holy Church hold closer together
The worst misery of man will mount up quickly.

* * *

Because parishes were poor since the pestilence season,
Parsons and parish priests petitioned the bishops
For a licence to leave and live in London
And sing there for simony, for silver is sweet.

Bishops and bachelors, both masters and doctors,
Who have cures under Christ and are crowned with the tonsure,
In sign of their service to shrive the parish,
To pray and preach and give the poor nourishment,
Lodge in London in Lent and the long year after;
Some are counting coins in the king's chamber,
Or in exchequer and chancery challenging his debts
From wards and wardmotes, waifs and strays.
Some serve as servants to lords and ladies
And sit in the seats of steward and butler.
They hear mass and matins and many of their hours
Are done without devotion. There is danger that at last
Christ in his consistory will curse many.*

Edward III's reign also provided evidence of the growth of English national feeling. Hostility to the papacy was increasing, largely for the nationalistic reason that the popes now resided at Avignon and

---

* *The Vision of Piers Plowman*, modern English version, Henry Wells (Sheed & Ward, 1945), 4-6.

were thought to be under the thumb of England's enemy, France. In 1351 Parliament passed a statute restricting the appointment of aliens to Church offices in England; two years later, another statute checked the appeal of legal cases to the papal *curia*. The dislike for the papacy, the widespread economic discontent, and the growing nationalist awareness were all reflected in England's first real heresy, which appeared at the close of Edward III's reign. This was the doctrine preached by John Wiclif, an Oxford scholar who died in 1384. Advocating a church without property, in the spirit of the early Christians, Wiclif called for the direct access of the individual to God, and for the abolition or weakening of many of the functions of the priest. He and his followers were also responsible for the preparation and circulation of an English translation of the Bible. Wiclif's views were heretical, for the Church had long insisted that the priest was the indispensable intermediary between man and God, and that the Bible should remain in its Latin version, the famous Vulgate, and should not be translated into the vernacular. Meanwhile, though French was still used in documents, English became the language of the courts in 1362. As the years passed, English was taught in the schools, and in 1399 it was used to open Parliament. The growing sense of national identity expressed itself in the increased use of the English language, which in turn must have quickened national feeling.

Another English institution of a different kind made its appearance under Edward III—the "justices of the peace," appointed originally to enforce the Statute of Laborers. They were all royal appointees selected from the gentry in each shire. Since they received no pay, they accepted office from a sense of duty or from a fondness for prestige. In later centuries, and down almost to our own times, the justices of the peace acted virtually as the rulers of rural England, while the old shire and hundred courts disappeared.

The Evolution of Parliament

The most significant constitutional development of Edward's long reign, however, was the evolution of Parliament, both in organization and in function. The division of Parliament into two houses, the Lords and the Commons, was beginning to appear in the fourteenth century, although the terms House of Commons and House of Lords were not actually used until the fifteenth and sixteenth centuries, respectively. Edward I's "Model Parliament" of 1295 (see above, p. 283) had assembled not only barons, the higher clergy, knights of the shire, and burgesses but also representatives of the lower clergy. It did not prove to be an exact model for later parliaments, since the lower clergy soon dropped out, preferring to limit their attendance to the assembly of the English church known as Convocation. But all the other groups present in 1295 continued to appear. The higher clergy, the lords spiritual, also attended Convocation, but as vassals of the king they had to come to Parliament too. As time wore on, this group coalesced with the earls and barons, the lords temporal, to form the nascent House of Lords. The knights of the shire and the burgesses coalesced to form the nascent House of Commons.

The gradual coalescence of knights and burgesses was an event of capital significance—an event that laid the social foundation of the future greatness of the House of Commons. It brought together two elements, the one representing the lower level of the second estate and the other representing the third estate, which always remained separate in the assemblies of the continental monarchies. Little is known about the precise reasons for this momentous development. We do know that in the fourteenth century the knights of the shire were far from feeling a sense of social unity with the burgesses; instead they felt closer to the great lords, with whom they had many ties of blood and common interests in the countryside. But we also know that some of the smaller boroughs were represented by knights from the countryside nearby. At any rate, the king regarded both knights and burgesses as separate from the great lords, and during the reign of Edward III the two groups regularly deliberated together. By the end of the fourteenth century the important office of Speaker of the House was developing, as the Commons chose one of their members to report to the king on their deliberations. The parliamentary coalition of knights and burgesses evidently came well before their sense of social closeness.

In the fourteenth century the chief business of Parliament was judicial. From time to time the knights and burgesses employed the judicial device of presenting petitions to the king; whatever was approved in the petitions was then embodied in statutes. This was the faint beginning of parliamentary legislative power. Under Edward III, furthermore, the growth of parliamentary power was stimulated by Edward's constant requests to Parliament for new grants of money to cover the heavy expenses of the Hundred Years' War. More and more, Parliament took control of the purse strings, while Edward, who had little interest in domestic affairs other than finances, let the royal powers be whittled away imperceptibly. Thus were laid the political foundations of the future greatness of the House of Commons.

Richard II

When Edward III died, his ten-year-old grandson succeeded as Richard II (1377-1399). Richard's reign was marked by mounting factionalism on the part of the royal relatives and their noble followers and by an outbreak of social discontent on the part of the peasants. Both conflicts strongly resembled their French counterparts, the strife between Burgundy and Armagnac, and the Jacquerie of 1358.

The social disorders arose out of protests against the imposition of poll (that is, head) taxes in 1378, 1379, and 1380. Unless it is graduated, a poll tax falls equally upon rich and poor. In 1380, the poor bitterly resented paying their shilling a head for each person over fifteen, whereas the rich scarcely noticed it. Riots provoked by attempts to collect the tax led to the Peasants' Revolt of 1381. First the peasants burned manor records to destroy evidence of their obligations, and then they marched on London. Here the fifteen-year-old king interviewed them personally and promised to meet their demands, notably the ending of serfdom and the seizing of clerical wealth. These demands revealed Wiclif's widespread influence among the lower classes. Richard II managed to save his own life by offering to lead the peasants himself, but he failed to keep his promises. Reprisals against the rebels were severe, and had it been economically possible to restore serfdom, the King and Parliament would have done so. Wiclif, discredited by the excesses of the peasants, retired to private life.

Under Richard II and his successors factional strife mounted to a critical point, although interludes of peaceful, constitutional rule did occur. The baronage, which still dominated the scene, had become a smaller, richer class of great magnates. The older feudalism at its height had succeeded in keeping society going by its system of mutual guarantees. But now, at the very moment when it was disappearing, the new bastard feudalism made its appearance, and threatened to tear society apart.

During the fourteenth century the relationship of the great lords to their vassals grew to be based more and more on cash, and less and less on military service and protection. These lords recruited the armed following they still owed to the king, not by bringing into his increasingly professional army their tenants duly armed as knights, but by hiring private armies to go to war for them. These mercenaries were not social equals of the lords bound to them by the old feudal ties; rather, they were social inferiors bound by "written indenture and a retaining fee." The custom was known as "livery and maintenance," since the lord provided uniforms for his retainers, who, in turn, "maintained" the lord's cause, especially in judicial disputes. Though forbidden by statute in 1390, this practice continued to flourish. The danger from private armies became greater at each interlude of peace in the war with France. Each time, mercenaries used to plundering

for a livelihood in a foreign country were suddenly turned loose in England. The climax came immediately after the end of the Hundred Years' War, with the outbreak of the Wars of the Roses in 1455.

The trouble had begun during the last years of Edward III when effective control of the government passed to one of his younger sons, John of Gaunt, Duke of Lancaster, and his corrupt entourage. John of Gaunt's faction persisted after the accession of Richard II, and new factions appeared, centered on two of the young king's uncles, the Dukes of York and Gloucester. In 1387 Gloucester defeated Richard II's supporters in battle. Then, in a packed Parliament (1388), which was called either the "wonderful" Parliament or the "merciless" Parliament, depending on one's factional ties, Gloucester disposed of the remaining royal

The Peasants' Revolt in England, 1381. Rebels marching under leadership of Wat Tyler. Fifteenth-century Flemish miniature.

ministers by having them condemned for treason. The baronage seemed now to control the Crown: it commanded superior armies, it put its own people into royal administrative commissions, and it packed Parliament. Richard II took no steps against Gloucester until 1397, when he arrested him and moved against his confederates. The King now packed Parliament in his own favor, and had it pass extraordinary new anti-treason laws, many of which were retroactive. He grew tremendously extravagant and imposed heavy exactions. His confiscation of the estates of his first cousin, Henry of Bolingbroke, son of the late John of Gaunt, precipitated a revolution. The success of this revolution rested not so much on Henry's popularity as on the great alarm created by Richard's doctrine that the king could control the lives and property of his subjects. Henry's conspiracy against Richard and his landing in England, therefore, gained wide support. Richard was defeated, was forced to abdicate in 1399, and was later murdered.

Lancaster and York

Henry now became Henry IV (1399-1413), first monarch of the House of Lancaster. To recover from the upheavals of Richard II's reign and to check the growth of bastard feudalism, England badly needed a long period of stable royal rule. But this the Lancastrian dynasty in the long run was unable to provide. Henry IV owed his position to Parliament, and Parliament in turn, mindful of the experience with Richard II, was very sensitive about allowing any assertion of the royal authority. Inevitably, Henry and Parliament did not get on very smoothly. Moreover, Henry faced a whole series of revolts—by dispossessed supporters of Richard, by the Welsh aristocracy, and by the great northern border family of the Percies in Northumberland. And, as if this were not enough, the

last years of his reign were troubled by his own poor health and by the hostility of his son, the "Prince Hal" made famous by Shakespeare.

The son came to the throne as King Henry V (1413-1422) and embarked on a policy of royal assertiveness. At home, he persecuted vigorously the followers of Wiclif in an attempt to suppress the social and religious discontent that had caused the Peasants' Revolt. Abroad, as we have seen, he renewed the Hundred Years' War and won spectacular victories. But his untimely death in 1422 ended the brief period of Lancastrian success, for it brought to the throne Henry VI (1422-1461), an infant nine months old on his accession, who proved mentally unstable as he grew up.

The reign of this third Lancastrian king was a disaster for England. Across the Channel her forces went down to defeat in the last campaigns of the Hundred Years' War. At home, meanwhile, serious quarrels broke out between Henry's wife, Margaret of Anjou, and her noble English allies on the one side, and, on the other, Richard, Duke of York, a great-grandson of Edward III, and heir to the throne until the birth of Henry's son in 1453. These quarrels led directly to the dreary Wars of the Roses (1455-1485), named for the red rose, the badge of the House of Lancaster, and the white rose, the badge of the House of York.

For thirty years the aristocrats slaughtered each other in droves, livery and maintenance ran riot, Parliament became the tool of rival factions, and the kingdom itself changed hands repeatedly. In 1460 Richard of York was killed, and the ambitious Earl of Warwick, the "Kingmaker," took over the leadership of the Yorkist cause. In the next year Warwick forced the abdication of Henry VI and placed on the throne the son of Richard of York, Edward IV (1461-1483). The King and the Kingmaker soon fell out, and in 1470-1471 Warwick staged an abortive revolution that

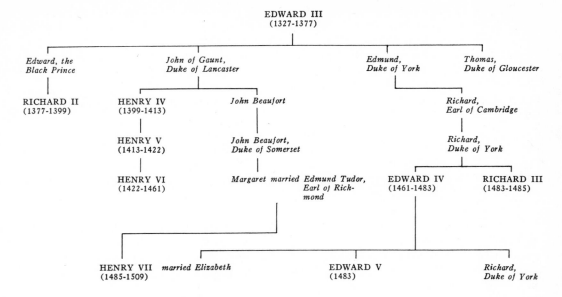

EDWARD III
(1327-1377)

Edward, the
Black Prince

John of Gaunt,
Duke of Lancaster

Edmund,
Duke of York

Thomas,
Duke of Gloucester

RICHARD II
(1377-1399)

HENRY IV
(1399-1413)

John Beaufort

Richard,
Earl of Cambridge

HENRY V
(1413-1422)

John Beaufort,
Duke of Somerset

Richard,
Duke of York

HENRY VI
(1422-1461)

Margaret married Edmund Tudor,
Earl of Rich-
mond

EDWARD IV
(1461-1483)

RICHARD III
(1483-1485)

HENRY VII   married Elizabeth
(1485-1509)

EDWARD V
(1483)

Richard,
Duke of York

restored the throne briefly to the hapless Henry VI. Edward IV quickly regained control and Henry VI and Warwick were killed. With Edward securely established, firm royal government seemed at last to have returned to England.

Again, however, the prospect of stability faded, for Edward IV died in 1483 at the threshold of middle age. The crown passed momentarily to his young son, Edward V, and then to the older Edward's brother, Richard III (1483-1485), last of the Yorkist kings. Able and ruthless, Richard III may not have been quite the villainous figure indelibly imprinted on history by Shakespeare's play. There is still controversy over whether or not he was responsible for the death of the "little princes of the Tower"— Edward V and his younger brother. In any case, factional strife flared up again as Richard's opponents found a champion in the Lancastrian leader, Henry Tudor. In 1485, on Bosworth Field, Richard III was slain, and the Wars of the Roses at last came to an end. The battle gave England a new monarch, Henry VII (1485-1509), and a new dynasty, the Tudors (1485-1603).

Henry VII: The First Tudor

As the descendant of a bastard branch of the Lancastrian family, Henry VII had only a tenuous hereditary claim to the throne. His right to be king really derived from his victory at Bosworth and from his subsequent confirmation by Parliament. The new king, however, had excellent qualifications for the job of tidying up after the dissipations of civil war. Shrewd and economical, able but far from heart-warming, Henry VII bore many resemblances to Louis XI of France.

Henry formally healed the breach between the houses of the rival roses by marrying the Yorkist heiress Elizabeth, daughter of Edward IV. Some of the magnates attempted to continue the old factional strife by supporting Perkin Warbeck, an imposter who claimed to be Elizabeth's brother, the younger of the "little princes of the Tower." Henry dealt very firmly with this rebellion and with other uprisings. He disarmed the nobles by forbidding livery and maintenance, thereby ending the vicious institution of private armies. He also banned the nobles' old habit of interfering at will in the royal courts to intimidate the litigants.

Measures like these had been tried by Henry's predecessors but had ultimately failed for lack of enforcement. Henry, however, enforced his measures most vigorously through an administrative court known as the Star Chamber, from the star-painted

The first Tudor monarch of England, King Henry VII.

ceiling of the room in which it met. The Star Chamber was a special committee of the King's Council, charged with the task of seeing that the apparatus of the law should not be used to back up local privileges, local abuses, local resistance to what Henry wanted. To make justice swift and implacable, the Star Chamber bypassed the customary procedures of the common law, including trial by jury. It could trample on the rights of defendants and engage in

the other arbitrary practices that have made "star-chamber proceedings" a term of reproach, synonymous with the abuse of judicial authority. The court, however, did not fully acquire its bad reputation until the seventeenth century (see Chapter XV). During the reign of Henry VII the Star Chamber and the rest of the royal administration usually served purposes approved by the nation, or, more precisely, by Englishmen concerned with affairs of state.

The men who did Henry's work for him were for the most part new men, men of the prosperous urban merchant class, or men who had worked their way up in the Church and who owed their careers to him, like the able lawyer Morton, who became Archbishop of Canterbury. Henry rewarded many of his advisers with lands confiscated from his opponents at the end of the Wars of the Roses. The King and his councilors more than doubled the revenues of the central government, partly by using such high-handed methods as "Morton's Fork." This fund-raising scheme, attributed (though probably wrongly) to Archbishop Morton, victimized prelates when they were summoned to make payments to the King. Those who dressed magnificently in order to plead exemption on the grounds of the cost of high ecclesiastical office were told that their rich apparel argued their ability to make a large payment. The other "tine" of the fork caught those who dressed shabbily to feign poverty, for their demonstrated talent for economy argued that they, too, could afford a large contribution. Such practices enabled Henry to avoid a clash with Parliament, because he seldom had to raise taxes requiring parliamentary sanction. The King's obvious efficiency, moreover, won him support in the increasingly significant business community. Since foreign vessels still carried the bulk of England's trade, Henry dared not revoke the special privileges of foreign merchants. But he used the threat of revocation to gain trading privileges for

English merchants abroad, especially in Italy. And he buttressed his financial success by keeping England out of war.

Henry VII left a well-filled treasury and a prosperous country; he had re-established law and order in an England weary of rebellion and civil war. His policies set the stage for the more dramatic reigns of his illustrious successors, Henry VIII and Elizabeth I (see Chapter XIII). He restored the prestige of the monarchy, made it the rallying point of English nationalism, and fixed the pattern for the Tudor policy toward Parliament, a policy often called "Tudor absolutism." This last term is, however, misleading. Henry VII and his successors were indeed strong monarchs but they were not absolute in the sense that they attempted to trample over Parliament. Henry, as we have just seen, asked Parliament for money as infrequently as possible; the later Tudors were to manage their parliaments but not to ignore them. Parliament, though somewhat eclipsed by the belated feudal aristocrats of the fifteenth century and by the strong personalities of the Tudors, remained very much a going concern. Its vitality was to make it "incomparably the greatest gift of the English people to the civilization of the world" and to make the English monarchy differ fundamentally from Continental monarchies. At the death of Henry VII precedents for limiting a monarch's authority were not entirely forgotten; they lay at hand ready for use, if the time again should come when a tyrannical king needed to be curbed.

Spain

The accomplishments of Henry VII and Louis XI, impressive though they were, were overshadowed by those of their great Spanish contemporaries, Ferdinand and Isabella. Henry and Louis ruled kingdoms which, however racked by internal dissensions, had long been well-defined states with established central institutions. Ferdinand and Isabella inherited a Spain that had never really been united; they had to build the structure of central government from the very foundations.

The decisive event in the early medieval history of the Iberian Peninsula was the Moslem conquest, starting in the year 711 (see Chapters V and VI). The whole peninsula, with the exception of the extreme north, came under Moslem control. In the eighth and ninth centuries Christian communities free of Moslem domination survived only in the Carolingian March of Catalonia and in the tiny states of Galicia, the Asturias, Leon, and Navarre. From the ninth century through the fifteenth, the Christian states of the north pressed southward until the Moslem remnant at Granada fell in 1492. This slow expansion by Catholic Spaniards has often been likened to a crusade more than five hundred years long. It was indeed a crusade, and the proud, militant, intolerant spirit of the crusader left a permanent mark upon the Spanish "style." The reconquest of Spain, like the great Crusades to the Holy Land, was a disjointed movement, undertaken in fits and starts by rival states that sometimes put more energy into combating each other than into fighting the Moslem.

Three Christian kingdoms dominated the Iberian Peninsula in the middle of the fifteenth century. Castile, the largest and most populous, occupying the center of the peninsula, had originated as a frontier province of Leon and had assumed the leadership of the reconquest. The capture of Toledo in central Spain (1085) and the great victory over the Moslems at Las Navas de Tolosa (1212) were landmarks in its expansion southward. The power of the Castilian kings, however, did not grow in proportion to their territory. The powerful organization of sheep-ranchers, the *Mesta*, controlled vast stretches of Castilian territory and constituted a virtual state within the state. Both the nobility and the towns, which played a semi-independent part in the reconquest, maintained many rights against the royal authority. Both were represented, together with the clergy, in the Cortes, the medieval Castilian counterpart of the English Parliament and the French Estates General.

To the west of Castile, along the Atlantic coast, lay the second Christian kingdom, Portugal. Once a Castilian province, Portugal had won independence in the twelfth century. Though still retaining close links with Castile, the Portuguese were gradually maturing their own particular national interests, especially in exploration and commerce overseas (see Chapter XIV).

those limiting the Crown—the Cortes, the nobility, and the towns, particularly the thriving Catalonian city of Barcelona. Moreover, two of Aragon's provinces on the Spanish mainland, Catalonia and Valencia, enjoyed many autonomous privileges.

Ferdinand and Isabella

In 1469, Ferdinand, later King of Aragon (1479-1516), married Isabella, later Queen of Castile (1474-1504), and thus made the dynastic alliance that eventually consummated the political unification of Spain. The obstacles confronting them were immense. Not only was the royal

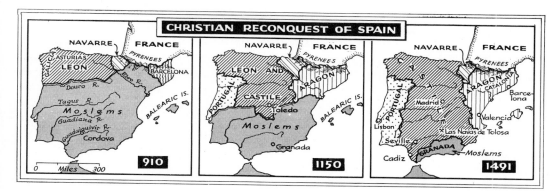

CHRISTIAN RECONQUEST OF SPAIN

The third kingdom, located in northeastern Spain, was Aragon, which was as much a Mediterranean power as a Spanish one. Its kings controlled the Balearic Islands, ruled lands along the Mediterranean on the French side of the Pyrenees, and had an important stake in southern Italy. In the breakup of the Hohenstaufen Empire (see Chapter VII) Aragon took the island of Sicily (1282). King Alfonso the Magnanimous (1416-1458) added the mainland territories of Naples (1435); at Alfonso's death his inheritance was divided: Sicily and Aragon went to his brother, John (1458-1479), and Naples to his illegitimate son, Ferrante. In Aragon, as in Castile, the oldest established political institutions were

power weak in both states; the inhabitants of Castile and Aragon did not even speak the same language, a difference still evident today in the distinction between the Castilian spoken in Madrid and the Catalan of Barcelona. Aragon looked toward the Mediterranean, Castile toward the Atlantic; thus in some respects the union of Castile with Portugal would have been more natural. Finally, Ferdinand and Isabella themselves did not make a perfect political team. He was a wary realist of the stamp of Louis XI and an ardent promoter of Aragon's ambitions in Italy, where he successfully strove to regain Naples. Though given the honorific title of "The Catholic" by the Pope, he was skeptical and tolerant in religion. Isabella, on the other hand, adored the pomp and circumstance of the throne. In religion she was devout to the point of fanaticism, and in policy she was wholly absorbed in the task of consolidating her authority over Castile.

The welding of Castile and Aragon into a single Spanish nation was a formidable undertaking; even today it is incomplete, and regional feeling, in Catalonia, for example, remains strong. Ferdinand and Isabella, however, made an impressive beginning at the task of building a Spanish national monarchy. This they did, above all, by creating a strong central government in Isabella's Castile. The Queen summoned the Cortes as infrequently as she dared and entrusted much executive power to a potent new instrument of absolutism staffed by royal appointees, the Council of Castile. She allied herself with the middle class against the nobles and drew military support more from town militias than from feudal levies. Her sovereignty was jeopardized by the existence of three large military brotherhoods controlled by the Castilian nobility and founded in the twelfth century to advance the reconquest. Isabella imposed royal authority on all three brotherhoods by the simple device of insisting that Ferdinand be made the head of each.

Last and most important, Ferdinand and Isabella enlisted the aid of the Church. The Queen was pious, but she was also determined to bring the Church under royal discipline and prescribed a thorough purge of ecclesiastical corruption. The purified Spanish church was later to assume leadership of the Catholic Reformation (see Chapter XII). The Spanish monarchs also obtained from the papacy the right to dispose of ecclesiastical appointments and part of the ecclesiastical revenue in their dominions. Like the Gallican church, the Spanish church was half-independent of Rome; far more than the Gallican church, it was the prop of royal absolutism.

An individual and an institution cemented the alliance of Church and State in Spain. The individual was Cardinal Ximenes (or Jiménez; 1436-1517), the Archbishop of Toledo, and Isabella's chief minister. Ximenes executed her policies of purifying the Church, curbing the aristocracy, and making an alliance with the towns. The institution was the Inquisition, brought into Spain in 1478. The Spanish Inquisition was from the first a royal rather than a papal instrument; it sought to promote Spanish nationalism by enforcing universal Catholicism, to create loyal subjects of the Crown by obliging men to be obedient children of the Church.

The chief targets of the new policy were the two important Spanish religious minorities—the Moslems and the Jews. Both groups had long enjoyed toleration; both owned some of the most productive farms and businesses in Spain; their wealth, independence, and religious faith all alarmed Isabella and Ximenes. In 1492 persecution of the Jews began when they were offered the alternatives of immediate baptism into the Christian faith, or immediate exile with loss of their property. Ten years later, it was the turn of the Moslems who were given no choice but baptism. Catholicism thereby won many apparent converts from Judaism and Islam, nominal Christians who conformed only because they feared the tortures and burnings which the Inquisition could prescribe if they wavered in their new faith. Isabella and Ximenes had secured religious uniformity but at the cost of suppressing some of the most productive elements in Spain.

The year 1492, therefore, is the critical date in the whole history of Spain. It was the year when Ferdinand and Isabella seized the last fragment of Moslem Spain and Columbus laid the first stones of the great Spanish Empire in the New World (see Chapter XIV). But it was also the year when intensive religious persecution began. The Spanish national monarchy, though only in its infancy, already bore the stamp of the bigoted nationalism that was to be at once its strength and its weakness in generations to come.

III: Particularism in Germany and Italy

The German Interregnum and Its Results

Germany had monarchs but no national monarchy in the later Middle Ages, as power shifted steadily from the emperor to the princes of the particular states. Once, indeed, for a span of almost two decades there was no emperor at all. The imperial throne became vacant in 1254 at the death of Conrad IV, the son of Frederick II (see Chapter VII). Since it remained unfilled until 1273, these were the years between reigns, the Interregnum. The princes were pleased for a time not to have an emperor; their usurpation of rights that had formerly belonged to the monarchy was now well on the way to completion. They also enhanced their power by taking advantage of the large grants made by rival foreign candidates for the imperial throne in the hope of receiving princely support. Meanwhile, the old links with Italy were virtually broken, and the earlier form of the imperial idea vanished.

The imperial title, however, did not vanish. It went to the Emperor Rudolf of Habsburg (1273-1291), first to be chosen after the Interregnum. Scion of a family of lesser German nobility, whose landed estates lay mostly in Switzerland, Rudolf cared nothing for imperial pretensions. What he wanted was to establish a hereditary monarchy for his family in Germany, and to make this monarchy as rich and as powerful as possible. He added Austria to the family holdings, and his descendants ruled at Vienna until 1918. Since Habsburg inter-

ests were focused on the southeastern part of the Empire, Rudolf was willing to make concessions to the French in the western imperial territories in order to get their support for the new Habsburg monarchy.

After 1270, consequently, the French moved into imperial territories that had once belonged to the old Carolingian "middle kingdom." They thus secured lands east of the Rhone and a foothold in Lorraine. The German princes, however, especially the great archbishops of the Rhine Valley, opposed the Habsburg policy of propitiating the French. Thus, during the century following the Interregnum, two parties developed in Germany. There was a Habsburg party, anti-imperial (in the sense of being indifferent to the territorial integrity of the Empire), in favor of a strong hereditary monarchy, eastern-based, and therefore pro-French. And there was an opposition party, pro-imperial, opposed to a strong hereditary monarchy, western-based, and therefore anti-French. Since both parties on occasion elected emperors, the imperial office was no longer monopolized for long periods by one family but was held at various times by the houses of Nassau, Luxembourg, Bohemia, and Habsburg, and by the Wittelsbach family of Bavaria.

This division on the imperial question helped prevent any real development of German national unity. German political life, like that of contemporary France and England, now showed some of the sterility and concern for empty forms that characterized the later Middle Ages. Thus the Emperor Henry VII (1308-1313) inter-

Top. The Pope (center) receives the key from St. Peter; the Emperor is at the left.

Bottom. The Pope and Emperor embrace as a symbol of the coordination of spiritual and temporal power.

would help them add to their own possessions. As each German emperor strove to achieve family territorial aims, the position of the monarchy became simply that of another territorial princedom. The pursuit of such aims engaged all the princes, whether their houses happened to be in temporary control of the imperial throne or not. Thus, toward the middle of the fourteenth century, the principle of elective monarchy finally triumphed and the princes as a class secured a great victory.

Top. The three ecclesiastical electors, the Archbishops of Mainz, Trier, and Cologne, point to the Emperor.

Middle. Three lay electors, with their symbols of office, and the Emperor. The electors are, from left to right, the Count Palatine of the Rhine, the Duke of Saxony, and the Margrave of Brandenburg.

Bottom. Other princes (four laymen and five bishops) and the Emperor.

vened in Italy just as if he could still perform the miracle of uniting that divided country, and just as if the imperial dreams which the Hohenstaufens had pursued in vain could be made realities without the resources and the loyalties which the Hohenstaufens had commanded. Similarly, in a long conflict between the papacy and the Emperor Louis of Bavaria (1314-1347), the "captive" pope at Avignon put forth pretensions which Gregory VII and Innocent III had striven in vain to make good, long after the possibility of such achievement had disappeared.

Elective Monarchy: The Golden Bull of 1356

Rudolf of Habsburg had pursued territorial aims in order to strengthen the monarchy. But in time, as the crown passed from hand to hand, matters were reversed: the princes wanted the crown because it

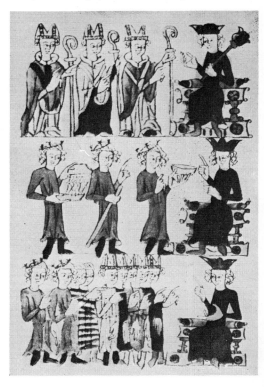

CHAPTER X

Their victory was embodied in the famous Golden Bull of 1356, issued by the Emperor Charles IV (1347-1378). The Golden Bull reaffirmed what the German princes had themselves declared in 1338 during Louis of Bavaria's conflict with the papacy: that the imperial dignity was of God, that the German electoral princes chose the emperor, and that the choice of the majority of the electors needed no confirmation by the pope. In 1356, it was expressly stated that a candidate receiving the majority of electoral votes had been unanimously elected emperor. Further, the position of the electors was now regularized: they were to be the Archbishops of Mainz,

The Pope consecrates the Emperor; six electors look on at the left.

Trier, and Cologne, and the Count Palatine of the Rhine, the Duke of Saxony, the Margrave of Brandenburg, and the King of Bohemia. The rights of the four lay electors were to pass to their eldest sons and could never be divided. Each of the seven electors was to be all but sovereign in his own territory, with full rights of coinage and of holding courts from which there was no appeal.

The Consolidation of Princely Power

During the fourteenth century the German princes inside their own principalities had been facing the threat of a new political fragmentation. This came especially from their own *ministeriales* (see above, p. 287), who had turned their lands and powers into feudal rights, had assumed knighthood, and had virtually merged with the old nobility. It appeared as if a permanent state of feudal anarchy might prevail within the German states. To levy taxes, the princes had to obtain the consent of the nobles and knights along with that of the other "estates." Knights, towns, and clergy, often leagued together, won privileges from the princes in exchange for money. As late as 1392 in Brunswick, for example, the estates forced the duke to give them far-reaching concessions, which amounted to establishing them as rival rulers of the duchy. This period of increasing power of the estates also saw the rise of the famous Hanse of North German commercial towns (see below, p. 427). But the rise of the estates meant also a rise in public disorder as urban-rural antagonism increased, robber barons infested the roads, and wars between rival leagues became common.

By about 1400, the power of the estates had reached its height; then it slowly yielded to other forces that had begun to operate after the enactment of the Golden Bull. The princes who were not electors gradually adopted for their own principalities the rules of primogeniture and indivisibility which the Golden Bull had prescribed for the electoral principalities. The princes were assisted in their assertion of authority by the spread of Roman law. As the Roman law had helped the emperors in ages past, it now helped the prince to make good his claims to absolute control of public rights and offices. Gradually, in half a hundred petty states, orderly finance, indivisible princely domains, and taxation granted by the estates became typical.

By the end of the fifteenth century, then, the German princes had achieved on a local or regional scale the kind of stability

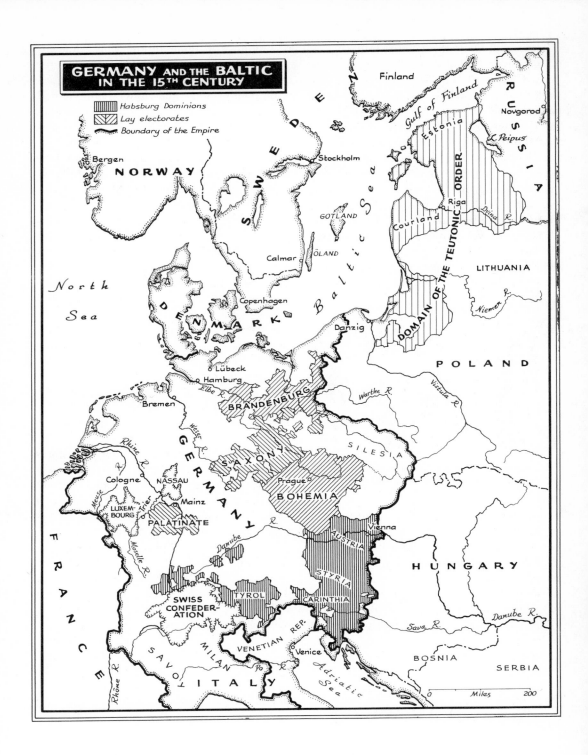

GERMANY AND THE BALTIC
IN THE 15TH CENTURY

|||| Habsburg Dominions
//// Lay electorates
~~~~ Boundary of the Empire

RUSSIA

Finland

Novgorod

L. Peipus

Gulf of Finland

Estonia

Riga

DOMAIN OF THE TEUTONIC ORDER

Courland

Dvina R.

LITHUANIA

S W E D E N

Stockholm

GOTLAND

ÖLAND

Calmar

Niemen R.

Bergen

N O R W A Y

POLAND

North
Sea

D E N M A R K

Copenhagen

Danzig

B a l t i c   S e a

Vistula R.

Lübeck

Hamburg

Warthe R.

Bremen

BRANDENBURG

Elbe R.

SILESIA

Weser R.

G E R M A N Y

Rhine R.

SAXONY

Cologne

NASSAU

Prague

BOHEMIA

Trier

Mainz

LUXEM-
BOURG

PALATINATE

Vienna

Meuse

AUSTRIA

Moselle R.

Danube R.

STYRIA

H U N G A R Y

SWISS
CONFEDER-
ATION

TYROL

CARINTHIA

F R A N C E

Danube R.

Sava R.

SAVOY

MILAN

VENETIAN REP.

BOSNIA

SERBIA

Rhône R.

I T A L Y

Po R.

Venice

Adriatic
Sea

Miles   200

416

and constitutional balance which the king of France had first achieved in his kingdom two centuries earlier. As in England, the estates sometimes aired their grievances at meetings and obtained redress. Instead of mutual hostility between them and the princes, there was now co-operation. This was the pattern that was to typify German political life for the centuries ahead.

With a host of sovereign princes firmly installed in their particular states, the Empire itself had become almost meaningless. In the two centuries following the Interregnum it had lost control not only over the western lands taken by France but also over other frontier areas, notably Switzerland. In 1291 three forest cantons in the heart of the country had made a successful bid for effective self-rule. By the early sixteenth century the number of confederated cantons had quadrupled, and the Swiss, backed by France, had checked both Burgundian and German attempts to subjugate them. The Swiss Confederation, though nominally still subject to the Empire, was in fact an independent entity, with boundaries beginning to resemble those of present-day Switzerland. Another national state was emerging, but one distinguished by the absence of a strong central authority. Indeed, the Swiss federal government was extremely weak, and the individual cantons enjoyed many prerogatives of the kind that Americans know as "states' rights."

As territorial losses and other visible signs of the Empire's weakness multiplied, the Germans themselves began to undergo a national awakening. The emperor would have been the natural rallying point of emerging national feeling, if that office had not already become an instrument to advance the interests of particular dynasties. In 1438 the emperorship, though still elective, passed permanently to the house of Habsburg. Forty-five years later a most attractive scion of that house, Maximilian I (1493-1519), became emperor. He was a gentleman and a scholar, and an athlete

and warrior as well, and he had acquired great riches by marrying Mary of Burgundy, the heiress of the Low Countries (see above, p. 402). Under his weak predecessors, the Habsburg position in central Europe had deteriorated; Maximilian reestablished firm Habsburg power in Austria and its dependencies. He also arranged for his children and grandchildren marriages that promised to add vast new territories to the family possessions and that in fact would make his grandson, Charles V, the ruler of half of Europe. On the other hand, Maximilian's projects for reforming the Empire came to little not only because of the vested interests of German particularism but also because of Maximilian's own dynastic concerns. German nationalism was still awaiting a leader.

The Italian States

Italy, too, lacked an effective central authority, and had lacked even the shadow of control by the emperor since the disintegration of the Hohenstaufen Empire. Italy, too, experienced the advance of particularism and the emergence of powerful local and regional rulers. In Germany the fifteenth century was the Age of the Princes; in Italy it was the Age of the Despots, power politicians *par excellence*, brilliant, ruthless, cultivated rulers who did much to set the style of the Renaissance.

Despots had not always ruled in Italy. As we saw in Chapter VII, the medieval struggle between popes and emperors had promoted the growth of independent communes or city-states, particularly in northern Italy. In the twelfth and thirteenth centuries, the communes were oligarchic republics, dominated by the nobility and by the newly rich businessmen. The ruling oligarchies, however, were torn by the strife between the pro-papal Guelfs and the pro-imperial Ghibellines. Meantime, something close to class warfare arose be-

RENAISSANCE ITALY
ABOUT 1494

tween the wealthy; on the one hand, and the small businessmen and wage-earners, on the other. In town after town, from the thirteenth century on, social and political dissensions grew so bitter that arbitrary one-man government seemed to be the only remedy. Sometimes a despot seized power; sometimes he was invited in from outside by the contending factions. Often he was a *condottiere*, a captain of the mercenaries whom the states hired to fight their wars. The *condottieri*, who fought for no cause save personal advancement and adventure, were representative figures of the age.

By the fifteenth century, the fortunes of politics and of war had worked significant changes in the map of Italy. Many small city-states that had been important a century or two earlier were sinking into po-

litical obscurity, victims of their stronger neighbors. Although some small city-states and principalities maintained their independence, a few larger states now dominated Italy. These were the Two Sicilies in the south, the States of the Church in the center, and Milan, Florence, and Venice in the north.

The Two Sicilies comprised the island of Sicily and the mainland territory of Naples, confusingly named the "Kingdom of Sicily." Both territories had long been subject to foreign domination, Byzantine and Arab, Norman and Hohenstaufen. In 1268 Charles of Anjou, the brother of St. Louis, conquered them from the grandson of the Emperor Frederick II. Sicily revolted against Angevin rule in the bloody uprising known as the "Sicilian Vespers" (1282) and passed to the control of Aragon, and eventually to the Spain of Ferdinand and Isabella. Naples remained Angevin until 1435, when it was taken by Alfonso the Magnanimous of Aragon. In 1458 it became an independent state again, ruled by Alfonso's illegitimate son Ferrante (Ferdinand, 1458-1494), a particularly ruthless despot. Under Angevin and Aragonese rule the Two Sicilies never fully recovered the vigor, the prosperity, and the cultural leadership they had enjoyed in their great medieval days. But their eclipse was by no means total; Alfonso the Magnanimous was a generous patron of art and learning, and Naples played a role in the Renaissance.

Like the Two Sicilies, the States of the Church suffered a material decline. They virtually disintegrated as a political unit during the fourteenth century and the first half of the fifteenth, when the popes sustained the successive blows of the Babylonian Captivity, the Great Schism, and the struggle with the Councils (see Chapter VIII). The city of Rome relapsed into the hands of rival princely families; the outlying territories fell to local feudal lords or despots.

After 1450, the popes once more concentrated their attention on central Italy. Beginning with Nicholas V (1447-1455), a scholar and librarian, and Pius II (1458-1464), an accomplished writer, the papacy was held by a series of able men, often highly cultivated, and often highly ambitious and corrupt. They restored Rome to its old importance as a center of art and learning, and they began the reconquest of the papal dominions. The Borgia pope, Alexander VI (1492-1503), greatly aided by his aggressive and unscrupulous son, Caesar, made notable progress in subjugating the lords of central Italy and in breaking the power of the Roman princely families. Caesar Borgia employed almost any means—treachery, violence, assassination by poisoning—to gain his ends. His success ended on the death of his father in 1503,

but the next pope, Julius II (1503-1513), was a statesman and general who commanded his troops in person and who consolidated further the temporal, though hardly the spiritual, authority of the papacy. Soon, however, the double blow of the Reformation and the Habsburg-Valois Wars shattered the popes' political ambitions (see Chapters XII and XIII).

Milan

By the closing centuries of the Middle Ages the focus of Italian political life had shifted to the north. Neither the States of the Church nor the Two Sicilies could effectively challenge the supremacy of Milan, Florence, and Venice. Located in the midst of the fertile Lombard plain, within sight of the Alps, Milan occupied a site of great strategic and economic value. It was the center of the bread-basket of Italy and the terminus of trade routes through the Alpine passes from northern Europe. It was also a textile and metallurgical center, famous for its velvets and brocades, its weapons and armor. Many traces of Milan's old significance survive today, for it is still the financial and industrial capital of Italy and calls itself the most modern city in Europe.

In politics, Milan had begun to play a major role in the twelfth century, when it headed the Lombard League in a successful contest with Frederick Barbarossa (see Chapter VII). At that time its territories reached from Lake Como in the Alps south to Pavia on the Po River. Later, the Milanese extended their dominions southward into Tuscany and threatened to annex both Florence and Genoa. Twelfth-century Milan was a republic, run by the nobility in conjunction with a *Parlamento,* or great council, in which all citizens of modest means could participate. This combination of aristocracy and democracy, however, proved awkward and unworkable; it could not prevent the seizure of power by the noble Visconti family in 1277. These henchmen of the powerful Archbishops of Milan soon secured recognition by the emperor as hereditary Dukes of Milan; their high-handed methods, together with the great prosperity of the city, gave them an income larger than that of many kings. The age of despotism had begun in Milan.

When the direct line of the Visconti died out in 1447, the ducal title was soon usurped by Francesco Sforza (1450-1466), the husband of an illegitimate daughter of the last Visconti duke. An energetic *condottiere,* Francesco quickly overcame the efforts of a group of Milanese citizens to revive the old republic. He maintained the Visconti tradition of arbitrary rule but made it more tolerable by his soldierly efficiency and by his many public works. He founded a great hospital in the city, completed its cathedral, and extended irrigation canals throughout the duchy.

The most famous of the Sforza dukes was a younger son of Francesco, Ludovico Il Moro, 1479-1500 (Lewis "the Moor"—the nickname has been traced both to Maurus, his middle name, and to his dark, "Moorish" appearance). Like his father, Il Moro was a usurper; he seized the government from his weak and sickly nephew. He assembled a retinue of outstanding artists and intellectuals, headed by the renowned Leonardo da Vinci, and made the court of Milan perhaps the most brilliant in all Europe. Il Moro had the reputation of being the craftiest diplomat of the age. All his craftiness, however, did not suffice to defend him against the armies of France and Spain (see Chapter XIII). Driven from his throne in 1500, Il Moro died in a French prison eight years later. The Duchy of Milan came under direct Spanish rule in 1535 and remained under the control of Spain for almost two hundred years. The Sforzas were thus true *condottieri,* soldiers of fortune who gained power—and lost it—almost overnight.

Florence

Not *condottieri* but bankers and merchants governed the Republic of Florence, a pioneer in industry and finance (see below, pp. 430-1). Class conflicts largely determined the course of politics in this city on the banks of the Arno in Tuscany, midway between Milan and Rome. By the thirteenth century the struggle between Guelfs and Ghibellines had become a contest for power between the wealthy and the older feudal nobility. In the late 1200's, the Guelf plutocrats won out over the Ghibelline aristocrats. The victorious Guelfs now revised the constitution of the Republic so that a virtual monopoly of key government offices rested with the seven major guilds, which were controlled by the great woolen masters, bankers, and exporters. They denied any effective political voice to nobles, Ghibellines, common laborers, or the small businessmen and shopkeepers of the fourteen lesser guilds. Feuds soon divided the dominant Guelfs and sowed a new crop of political exiles, among them the poet Dante, whose attempts to heal the divisions among his fellow Guelfs resulted in his permanent banishment (1302) and his subsequent adoption of the lost Ghibelline cause of imperial rule for divided Italy.

Throughout the fourteenth century and into the fifteenth, factionalism continued to torment Florentine politics, though it did not prevent the remarkable cultural burgeoning of the city, as we shall see in the next chapter. The politically unprivileged sought to make the Republic more democratic; they failed, not only because of the power of the entrenched oligarchy, but also because of the hostility between the lesser guilds and the poor workmen, between what we would term the lower middle class and labor. In the 1340's bank failures aggravated social and political tension. Unrest reached a climax in 1378 with a revolt of the woolen workers, who obtained, but soon lost, the right to form their own guilds and to have a minor say in politics. Finally, in the early 1400's, a new rash of bankruptcies and a series of military reverses weakened the hold of the ruling clique. In 1434, some of its leaders were forced into exile, and power fell to a political champion of the poor, Cosimo de' Medici.

The Medici ran Florence for the next sixty years (1434-1494). Their championing of the poor had its ironic side, for they had large woolen and banking interests and were perhaps the wealthiest family in all Italy; yet they introduced a "soak-the-rich" tax program and did a good deal to im-prove the status of the lower classes. The Medici were despots, but despots who operated quietly behind the façade of republican institutions. Cosimo kept himself in the background and seldom held public office. It was an old custom that the municipal executives should be chosen every two months by a sort of political lottery, by random selection from leather bags containing the names of eligible citizens. All Cosimo had to do to control the outcome of these "elections" was to arrange that only the names of his supporters get into the leather bags. Since, however, the incessant turnover of personnel hardly promoted political stability, Cosimo's grandson made a

A view of Florence during the Renaissance. The religious reformer Savonarola (see pp. 473-74) is being burnt at the stake.

Lorenzo de' Medici (1449-1492). Detail from a painted terra cotta bust by Andrea del Verrocchio.

new council with permanent membership the real center of administration.

The grandson of Cosimo was Lorenzo the Magnificent, the most famous of the Medici, ruler of Florence from 1469 to 1492. Machiavelli, who came to hate some of the later Medici, drew an admiring portrait of Lorenzo:

It was throughout his aim to make the city prosperous, the people united, and the nobles honored. He loved exceedingly all who excelled in the arts, and he showered favors on the learned. . . . Lorenzo delighted in architecture, music, and poetry. . . . To give the youth of Florence an opportunity of studying letters he founded a college at Pisa, to which he had appointed the most excellent professors that Italy could produce. . . . His character, prudence, and good fortune were such that he was known and esteemed, not only by the princes of Italy, but by many others in distant lands. . . . In his conversation he was ready and eloquent, in his resolutions wise, in action swift and courageous. There was nothing in his conduct, although inclined to excessive gallantry, which in any way impaired his many virtues; it is possible he found more pleasure in the company of droll and witty men than became a man of his position; and he would often be found playing among his children as if he were still a child. To see him at one time in his grave moments and at another in his gay was to see in him two personalities, joined as it were with invisible bonds. . . . There had never died in

CHAPTER X

Florence—nor yet in Italy—one for whom his country mourned so much, or who left behind him so wide a reputation for wisdom.*

Lorenzo possessed in abundance many of the qualities most admired in his time. He was tolerant, and he was devoted to sports and rural pleasures; he had great charm; he had a most decided way with women; and he lavished money on the beautification of the city of Florence. Neither his looks (he had a deformed nose) nor his policies were perfect, however. Lorenzo's neglect of military matters and his financial carelessness left Florence ill prepared for war.

Like the story of Milan after Il Moro, the story of Florence after Lorenzo is one of rapid political decline. Following the death of Lorenzo in 1492, the Florentines made two short-lived attempts to drive the Medici from power and to reestablish a genuine republic. In 1512 and again in 1530 the Medici returned. In 1569 they converted the Florentine Republic, now a minor state, into the Grand Duchy of Tuscany, with themselves as hereditary Grand Dukes.

Venice

The third great north Italian state, Venice, enjoyed a political stability that contrasted sharply with the turbulence of Florence and Milan. By the fifteenth century the Republic of St. Mark, as it was called, was in fact an empire. Its territories included the lower valley of the Po River, the Dalmatian shore of the Adriatic Sea, and part of the Greek islands and mainland. The Venetian Empire reflected the Republic's leadership in the eastern trade and in the "fourth" crusade (see above, Chapter IX); the Venetian government likewise reflected the paramount importance of the Republic's commercial interests.

* Machiavelli, *Florentine History*, W. K. Marriott, trans. (New York, 1909), 359-360.

The Venetian constitution assumed its definitive form in the early fourteenth century. Earlier, the chief executive had been the doge or duke, originally appointed by the Byzantine emperor, subsequently an elected official; the legislature had been a general assembly of all the citizens, somewhat resembling the *Parlamento* of Milan. The Venetian merchants, however, feared that a powerful doge might establish a hereditary monarchy, and they found the assembly unwieldy and unbusinesslike. Accordingly, they relegated the doge to an ornamental role like that of a constitutional monarch today. Conveyed in a gorgeously outfitted barge, and attended by a host of citizens and foreign visitors, the doge annually cast a huge "wedding ring" into the Adriatic. He thus "married" the sea and paid yearly tribute to the source of Venetian wealth. At the same time the merchants made the old assembly into the Great Council, a closed corporation whose membership was limited to the individuals whose names appeared in a special "Golden Book." The Great Council, in turn, elected the Doge and the members of the smaller councils which really ran the government. Foremost among these was the secret Council of Ten, charged with maintaining the security of the Republic.

This system, therefore, vested a permanent monopoly of political power in the old merchant families listed in the Golden Book, about 2 per cent of the total population. It accounts for the label "Venetian oligarchy," often pinned on any government that seeks to perpetuate the privileges and profits of the few. The oligarchs of Venice, however, while denying the many a voice in politics and sternly repressing all opposition, did institute many projects for the general welfare, from neighborhood fountains on up to the great naval Arsenal (see below, p. 431). They treated the subject cities of the empire with fairness and generosity, and they were pioneers—at least in the western world—in the development of a corps of diplomats to serve the far-reaching concerns of a great commercial power. Though they were unable to prevent the eventual decline of the city, they did pursue their business aims with single-minded efficiency for several hundred prosperous years. Venice was unique among Italian states for its political calm and order: there were no upheavals, no sudden seizures or losses of power by rival factions or ambitious despots. Seldom in history have political means been so perfectly adapted to economic ends.

The "School of Europe"

The Italian states of the fifteenth century have been called the "school of Europe," instructing the other European states in the new realistic ways of power politics. Despots like Il Moro, Caesar Borgia, Lorenzo the Magnificent, and the oligarchs of Venice might well have given lessons in statecraft to Henry VII of England or Louis XI of France. They were the most hard-boiled rulers in a hard-boiled age. In international affairs, Venetian reliance on diplomacy was soon imitated by the other Italian states and then by the national monarchies farther north. Italian reliance on *condottieri* foreshadowed the general use of mercenaries and the abandonment of the old feudal levies. The rival Italian states, though their mutual competition often led to open conflict, yet learned to co-exist in a precarious balance of power. This balance, particularly its precarious quality, served as a kind of model for the European monarchies in later centuries.

This very example, however, also reveals that Italy was the "school of Europe" in a negative sense, for she furnished a compelling object lesson in how not to behave politically. By the close of the fifteenth century it was evident that the balance established among the several Italian states was not adequate to preserve their independ-ence. Beginning with the French invasion of 1494, Italy became a happy hunting-ground for the new national and dynastic imperialists of France, Spain, and the Habsburg realm (see Chapter XIII for details). The national monarchy was the wave of the future, at least of a successful political future; the city-state, even though ruled by an efficient despot, was not. The Italians of the Renaissance, like the ancient Greeks whom they so often resembled, were victimized by stronger neighbors and were penalized for their failure to form "one Italy."

Machiavelli

These lessons from the "school of Europe" were first drawn by Niccolò Machiavelli (1469-1527). A diplomat who served the restored Florentine Republic in the early 1500's, Machiavelli was exiled when the Medici returned in 1512. Soon after, he wrote *The Prince* and dedicated it to the Medici ruler in the vain hope of regaining political favor. This essay on power politics, for all its notorious reputation, often makes rather dull reading; but in it may be found the statements that have given the word "Machiavellian" its sinister significance. Machiavelli has a low opinion of human nature:

For it may be said of men in general that they are ungrateful, voluble, dissemblers, anxious to avoid danger, and covetous of gain; as long as you benefit them, they are entirely yours; they offer you their blood, their goods, their life, and their children, . . . when necessity is remote; but when it approaches, they revolt.*

One might term this a secular adaptation of original sin, a transfer of Christian pessimism about mankind from the realm of religion to that of social and political psy-

_____
* *The Prince*, Ch. 17. This and succeeding quotations from Machiavelli are from the Modern Library edition of *The Prince and the Discourses* (New York, n.d.).

chology. The politics of *The Prince* follow directly from its estimate of human nature:

A prudent ruler ought not to keep faith when by so doing it would be against his interest, and when the reasons which made him bind himself no longer exist. If men were all good, the precept would not be a good one; but as they are bad, and would not observe their faith with you, so you are not bound to keep faith with them. . . .*

Accordingly, Machiavelli praises the vigorous and unscrupulous absolutism of Francesco Sforza, of Lorenzo the Magnificent, and, above all, of Caesar Borgia. After surveying the bad faith and deception practiced by Caesar Borgia to tighten his hold on the States of the Church, Machiavelli concludes:

I find nothing to blame, on the contrary, I feel bound . . . to hold him up as an example to be imitated by all who by fortune and with the arms of others have risen to power.†

Here it should be noted that a minority of scholars believe *The Prince* to be pure satire and argue that Machiavelli really meant the opposite of what he seemed to say. At any rate, Machiavelli had a very particular end in mind, the strengthening of Italy and the expulsion of the French, Spanish, and Habsburg intruders. Italy is "without a head, without order, beaten, despoiled, lacerated, and overrun," he wrote in the last chapter of *The Prince*, the one emotion-charged section of the book. *The Prince* was, first and last, a tract for the times, a drastic prescription against the severe political maladies afflicting Italy in the early 1500's.

Machiavelli wrote a second major political work, *The Discourses on the First Ten Books of Titus Livius* (the Roman historian Livy). Here he addressed not the immediate Italian crisis but the enduring problem of building a lasting government, and he reached significantly different conclusions.

To achieve lasting stability, *The Discourses* argue, the state requires something more than a single prince endowed with power, more power, and yet more power. In a chapter entitled "The People Are Wiser and More Constant than Princes," Machiavelli writes:

I say that the people are more prudent and stable, and have better judgment than a prince. . . . We also see that in tne election of their magistrates they make far better choice than princes; and no people will ever be persuaded to elect a man of infamous character and corrupt habits to any post of dignity, to which a prince is easily influenced in a thousand different ways. . . . We furthermore see the cities where the people are masters make the greatest progress in the least possible time, and much greater than such as have always been governed by princes; as was the case with Rome after the expulsion of the kings, and with Athens, after they rid themselves of Pisistratus; and this can be attributed to no other cause than that the governments of the people are better than those of princes.*

In *The Discourses*, Machiavelli thus presents both an estimate of human nature and a political program seemingly in conflict with the statements of *The Prince*. But the conflict is perhaps more apparent than real. *The Discourses* concerned people, like the Athenians and Romans of old, who had great civic virtues and were capable of self-government. *The Prince* concerned people, Machiavelli's Italians, who in his view had lost their civic virtues and therefore required the strongest kind of government from above.

Machiavelli blamed the Church for this loss of civic spirit. He attacked the papacy in particular for preventing Italian unity because of its temporal interests, and then questioned the values of Christianity itself:

Reflecting now as to whence it came that in ancient times the people were more devoted to liberty than in the present, I believe that it resulted from this, that men were stronger in those days, which I believe to be attributable

---

* *The Prince*, Ch. 18.
† *The Prince*, Ch. 7.

* *The Discourses*, Bk. I, Ch. 58.

to the difference of education, founded upon the difference of their religion and ours. For, as our religion teaches us the truth and the true way of life, it causes us to attach less value to the honors and possessions of this world; whilst the Pagans, esteeming those things as the highest good, were more energetic and ferocious in their actions. . . . The Pagan religion deified only men who had achieved great glory, such as commanders of armies and chiefs of republics, whilst ours glorifies more the humble and contemplative men than the men of action. Our religion, moreover, places the supreme happiness in humility, lowliness, and a contempt for worldly objects, whilst the other, on the contrary, places the supreme good in grandeur of soul, strength of body, and all such other qualities as render men formidable. . . .*

* *The Discourses,* Bk. II, Ch. 2.

Machiavelli believed that the purpose of government was not to prepare men for the City of God but to make upstanding citizens of this world, ready to fight, work, and die for their earthly country.

In defending nationalism Machiavelli was exalting the doctrine that was to contribute so much to shaping the modern world. In defending secularism and power politics Machiavelli preached what others had already practiced. Henry VII, Louis XI, Ferdinand of Aragon, and the Italian despots, in their different ways, were all good Machiavellians. The businesslike character of politics, in turn, was intermeshed with the increasingly businesslike character of economic life during these centuries of transition.

IV: Economic Changes

Trade

In the 1430's an unknown Englishman wrote a rhymed pamphlet, *The Libel of English Policy,* which may serve as an almanac of fifteenth-century commerce. *The Libel* states that among English imports from Spain

Bene fygues, raysns, wyne bastarde, and dates;
And lycorys, Syvyle ole [Seville oil], and grayne,
Whyte Castelle sope, and wax. . . .

And so on through "iren" and "wolle," "saffron" and "quiksilver." * *The Libel* deals tartly with the "commodities and nycetees . . ." brought in by Italian galleys:

The great galees of Venees and Fflorence
Be wel ladene wyth thyinges of complacence,

* *Political Poems and Songs Relating to English History,* Thomas Wright, ed. (London, 1861), II, 160.

Alle spicerye and of grocers ware,
Wyth swete wynes, alle manere of chaffare [merchandise],
Apes, and japes, and marmusettes taylede,
Nifles, trifles, that litelle have availede,
And thynges wyth whiche they fetely blere our eye,
With thynges not enduryng that we bye;
Ffor moche of thys chaffare that is wastable
Might be forborne for dere and dyssevable.*

The spelling is almost the only item of quaintness here; most of the wares mentioned still circulate in international trade today. Note the modern-sounding implication that people might do better to buy British rather than let Italian merchants "fetely blere" (cleverly dazzle) their eyes with shoddy goods.

Many of these items might also have appeared on a list for the twelfth century. To preserve food, the West had long imported salt from Spain, Italy, and Germany; to

* *Ibid.,* 172-173.

make food tasty if it had begun to spoil, the West had long sought the spices of the East. Since drafty medieval buildings made warm clothing essential, the furs of eastern Europe, the wool of England and Spain, and the woolen cloth of Flanders and Italy all commanded good markets. At the close of the Middle Ages supplies of palatable food and comfortable clothing were steadily increasing. Salt fish, for example, was a cheap food, easily kept from spoiling. In the fourteenth century a great boom occurred in the herring fisheries along the narrow Baltic waters between Denmark and Sweden. According to the exaggerated report of one traveler, the Baltic fisheries employed 300,000 people in catching fish, salting them down, and making the barrels to pack them in.

It is, then, essential to observe that the difference between the trade of the twelfth century and that of the fifteenth was one of degree, not of kind. It was the difference between some commerce and more commerce, rather than between no commerce and a reborn commerce. Nor did the expansion of trade proceed at a uniform rate; the Black Death of the mid-fourteenth century caused a disastrous drop in population and brought on a severe economic depression. By the fifteenth century, however, the trade of the West was for the first time beginning to compare in volume and variety with that of Rome in the days of the Empire, of Byzantium at its tenth-century peak, and of Norman and Hohenstaufen Sicily. During the 1300's and 1400's, therefore, western merchants developed more elaborate commercial procedures and organizations. One can follow these developments most readily in the Hanseatic towns of the Baltic and the trading cities of Italy.

The Hanse

The great Hanse (the German word means a league or confederation) of North German trading towns flourished in the fourteenth and fifteenth centuries. Among its leaders were Lübeck, Hamburg, Bremen, and Danzig; its membership included at one time or another almost a hundred towns. By its own initiative and also by reason of the weakness of the Empire, the Hanse exerted extensive political and military influence in addition to its economic power. After 1500, the fortunes of the Hanse declined rapidly. The shifting of trade routes from the Baltic to the Atlantic sapped the prosperity of the Hanseatic towns to the advantage of Holland and England. The loosely organized Hanse was no match for the stronger monarchical governments that were growing up along the rim of its old Baltic preserve in Sweden, in Russia, and even, with the development of Brandenburg-Prussia, in Germany itself.

The Hanse was not the first important confederation of commercial towns in Europe, nor was it the first to throw off control by a higher political authority. In ancient times the Greek city-states had formed defensive leagues, like the Delian confederation promoted by Athens. Earlier in the Middle Ages the "free cities" of Germany had sometimes made good their right to virtual autonomy, and alliances of communes in Lombardy and in Flanders had blocked the ambitions, respectively, of Hohenstaufen emperors and French kings. The Hanse, however, operated on a grander scale. Its ships carried Baltic fish, timber, furs, metals, and amber to London, to Bruges in Flanders, and to other western European markets. For a time, Hanseatic vessels controlled the lucrative business of transporting wool from England to Flanders. Hanseatic merchants, traveling overland with carts and pack-trains, took their Baltic wares to Italy. The Hanse maintained especially large outposts at Venice, at Bruges, at Russian Novgorod, and at London, where its headquarters was known as the Steelyard. At the Norwegian port of

Bergen, the Hanseatic contingent was said to number 3,000 individuals. These outposts enjoyed so many special rights, and they were so largely ruled by their own German officials and their own German laws, that they were Hanseatic colonies on foreign soil.

The Hanse had all the appurtenances of political independence. Its policies were determined by meetings of representatives from the member towns, held usually in the guildhall at Lübeck. It had its own flag, its own diplomats, and its own legal code, the "Law of Lübeck." It made treaties, declared war, and sometimes used the weapon of undeclared war. When English merchants attempted to get a foothold at Bergen, the Hanseatic colony there destroyed the intruders' property and then ejected them by force. In 1406, to teach a forceful lesson to English vessels fishing in the teeming waters off Norway, Hanseatic captains seized ninety-six English seamen, bound them hand and foot, and threw them overboard to drown.

The Hanseatic complex almost added up to an independent power of the first magnitude—almost, but not quite. The kind of jealous local spirit that had bedeviled the Greek city-states also bedeviled the Hanseatic towns. Rivalries between member towns and between competing merchant families blunted the power of the League. Only a minority of the towns belonging to the Hanse usually sent representatives to the deliberations in Lübeck, and scarcely any of the members could be counted on for men and arms in an emergency. Trading was carried on by a multitude of individuals rather than by a few relatively large firms; it has been estimated that about two hundred and fifty independent merchants engaged in the transport of English wool to Flanders. The truly big business of the last medieval centuries was to be found in the cities of the Mediterranean world, especially Venice.

Venice

Many of the Mediterranean cities were already thriving veterans of trade, toughened and enriched by the Crusades. In Italy, besides Venice, there were Genoa, Lucca, Pisa, Florence, Milan, and a dozen others; in southern France there were Narbonne, Montpellier, and Marseilles; and in Spain there was Barcelona. Venice, however, was not merely first among equals, not just Queen of the Adriatic, but the undisputed mistress of Mediterranean trade through most of the fourteenth and fifteenth centuries. In the 1300's she settled accounts with her strongest rival, Genoa, and thus won a long feud that had gone on during the Crusades and the spoliation of the Byzantine Empire. Her empire, as we have seen, was strung all along the sea route from the northern Adriatic to Byzantium.

The trade that enriched the merchants of Venice was the East-West traffic—spices, silks, cotton, and sugar from the East; wool, cloth, and other wares from the West. The area of Venetian business was enormous, stretching from Flanders and England in the West to the heart of Asia. In the thirteenth century the Venetian Marco Polo reached China after a great journey overland.

The main carrier of Venetian trade was the galley. By 1300, the designers of the Arsenal, the great government-operated shipyard, had improved the traditional long, narrow, oar-propelled galley of the Mediterranean into a swifter and more capacious merchant vessel, relying mainly on sails and employing oarsmen chiefly for getting in and out of port. In the fifteenth century these merchant galleys had space for 250 tons of cargo. This figure is unimpressive in our day, when the capacity of freighters is computed in thousands and tens of thousands of tons, but remember that spices and luxuries were small in bulk

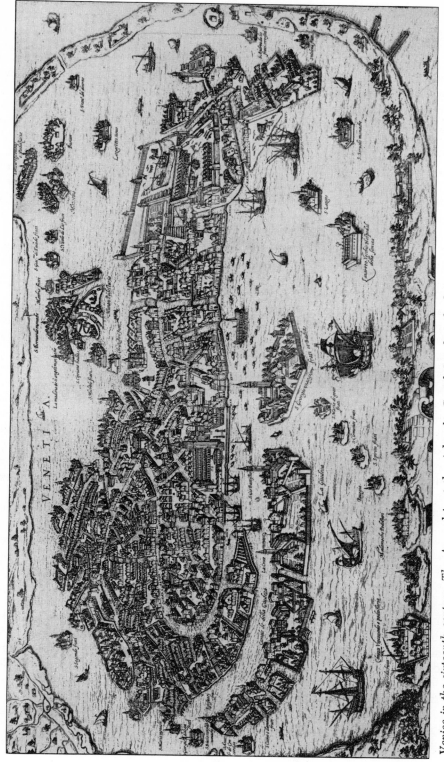

Venice in the sixteenth century. The Arsenal is at the right, the Grand Canal at the left.

and large in value. Records from the early fifteenth century show approximately forty-five galleys sailing annually, among them four to Flanders, four to Beirut on the Lebanon coast, three to the Black Sea, three to Alexandria, two to southern France, and two or three transporting pilgrims to Jaffa in the Holy Land. The Flanders galleys touched both at Sluys, the harbor of Bruges, and at the English ports of London and Southampton. First sent out in 1317, and making an annual voyage thereafter, the Flanders fleet was a very important European economic institution. It provided the first regular all-water service between Italy and northwestern Europe, and made shipments between the two cheaper and more secure than they had been on the older overland route.

The state supervised the activities of these galleys from the cradle to the grave. Since the average life of galleys was ten years, government experts tested their seaworthiness periodically, and the Arsenal undertook systematic replacements. The government provided for the defense of the galleys and their cargoes by requiring that at least twenty of the crew be bowmen. The captains of the Flanders galleys were directed to protect the health of the crew by enlisting a physician and a surgeon, and to maintain the prestige of the city with two fifers and two trumpeters. For the Flanders fleet the government also determined the time of sailing (the spring), the number of galleys (usually four to six), and the policies of the captains (avoid "affrays and mischiefs" in English ports, even if the crew have to be denied shore leave, and, above all, get to Bruges before the Genoese do). Officials back home were furious when, as occasionally happened, merchants from Genoa did get to Bruges first and skimmed the cream off the Flemish market. To smooth the way for her merchants, Venice maintained an ambassador in England, a pioneering experiment in formal diplomatic representation.

Industry

The expansion of trade stimulated the industries that furnished the textiles, metals, ships, and other requirements of the merchants. By 1300 the towns of Flanders and Italy had developed the weaving of woolen cloth into a big business, with a large production, large numbers of workmen, and large profits for a relatively few entrepreneurs. In the early fourteenth century, it is estimated, 200 masters controlled the wool guild of Florence, which produced nearly 100,000 pieces of cloth annually and employed 30,000 men. The older medieval idea that all artisans should belong to the guild was giving way to the modern division into capital and labor.

It should be emphasized, however, that the last centuries of the Middle Ages did not experience a true industrial revolution. In 1500, according to an informed estimate, industry employed less than 5 per cent of the European population. Manufacturing continued to be what the Latin roots of the word suggest that it was—making by hand—though many hand tools were ingenious and efficient. Power-driven machines did not exist, except for an occasional experimental device operated by water or by draft animals. The modern aspects of late medieval industry, confined largely to a few advanced crafts, were the increase in output, the trend toward mass production of standardized articles, and the complementary trend toward the specialization of the labor force.

In Lübeck, Hanseatic capitalists promoted the mass production of rosaries by supplying materials and wages to bead-makers and by promoting a standardized product. In the Habsburg lands of Central Europe, the silver mines developed the modern practice of dividing their labor force into three parts, each working an eight-hour daily shift. In Florence, thirty different specialized crafts participated in woolen manufacture—washing, combing, carding, spinning, weaving, dyeing, and many others. Probably the largest industrial establishment in Europe was the Venetian Arsenal, which normally employed a thousand men, and many more in time of emergency. These workmen, called *Arsenalotti*, formed a kind of pyramid of skills. At the bottom were the stevedores, helpers, and other unskilled laborers; then came the sawyers, who cut the timbers for the galleys, and the caulkers, who made the wooden hulls seaworthy; then the pulley-makers and mast-makers; and finally, at the top, the highly skilled carpenters, who did the all-important work of shaping the lines of the hull. Supervisors, like modern foremen, disciplined the *Arsenalotti*, checking on their presence at their posts during the working day; anyone who reported late, after the Arsenal bell had ceased tolling its summons to work, forfeited a day's pay. By the sixteenth century the process of adding a superstructure to the hull and outfitting the vessel was so efficiently arranged that the *Arsenalotti* could complete and equip a hundred galleys for a campaign against the Turks in the space of two months.

Banking

The expansion of industry and trade promoted the rise of banking. New enterprises required new money, which in turn was supplied by merchants anxious to invest the excess capital they had accumulated. The risks of lending were great; kings in particular, we shall see, were likely to repudiate their debts. But the potential profits were also very large. Florentine bankers were known to charge 266 per cent annual interest on an especially risky loan, and in 1420 the Florentine government vainly tried to put a ceiling of 20 per cent on interest rates. The high rate of interest also reflected the demand for money. Kings,

popes, and lesser rulers needed it for war and administration; businessmen needed it to finance trading voyages.

Bankers were money-changers as well as money-lenders. Only an expert could establish the relative value of the hundreds upon hundreds of coins in circulation, varying in reliability, and minted by every kind of governmental unit from the big monarchy down to the small city and the tiny feudal principality. Bankers also facilitated the transfer of money over long distances. Suppose an English exporter, A, sold wool to an Italian importer, Z; it would be slow and risky for Z to pay A by sending actual coins on the perilous trip between the two countries. Now suppose that two other businessmen enter into the transaction—Y, an Italian woolen manufacturer who has shipped cloth to B, an English importer. Obviously it is safer and often far swifter if Z pays Y in Italy what he really owes to A in England, and if B pays A what he really owes to Y. This sort of transaction became commonplace through the commercial device of bills of exchange, which bankers bought and sold.

Despite the widespread popular belief to the contrary, Jews did *not* play a leading part in these banking activities except in Spain, and there only until 1492, when they were expelled from the kingdom. The great European bankers after the crusading Templars (see above, p. 271) were Italians, the so-called "Lombard" bankers, though many of them came not from Lombardy but from Florence, Siena, and other towns in Tuscany. By the late 1200's Italian bankers had become the fiscal agents of the pope, charged with the transfer of papal revenues from distant countries to Rome. Florence was the Wall Street of the early fourteenth century, literally the "Evil Street," for the great import-export houses were grouped into the *Arte di Calimala* (The Guild of the Evil Street), named after a thoroughfare once notorious for riffraff. The beautiful florins minted by the city were the first gold coins made outside Byzantium to gain international currency. The great Florentine banking families of the Bardi and the Peruzzi advanced large sums to the kings of England and France. Then, when the expenses of the Hundred Years' War led Edward III of England to default on his debts to the Bardi and the Peruzzi, both firms failed in the 1340's. Florentine banking rallied in the fifteenth century under the dynamic Medici, whose thriving firm maintained branches in sixteen cities in Italy and abroad.

Meantime, successful banks and wealthy bankers had appeared elsewhere. Barcelona established an important municipal bank in 1401. The Bank of St. George, founded at Genoa in 1407, eventually took over much of the Mediterranean business once done by Spanish Jews. In London, "Dick" (Sir Richard) Whittington, a merchant and money-lender, was Lord Mayor for three terms around 1400 and the subject of a rags-to-riches legend foreshadowing the fortunate newsboys and bootblacks of **Horatio Alger.**

Jacques Coeur and the Fuggers

The little city of Bourges in France contributed a great millionaire, Jacques Coeur (1395-1456). This "moneyman," the son of an ordinary craftsman, used private wealth to secure public office, and public office to augment his private wealth. And he employed both for the greater glory of France and of the Church. Coeur made a fortune by trading with the Moslem Near East and by running a ship service for pilgrims to the Holy Land. King Charles VII of France sent him on diplomatic missions and made him the chief royal fiscal agent; Coeur, indeed, financed the final campaigns of the Hundred Years' War. Aided by the royal favor, Coeur acquired a string of textile workshops and mines, bought landed estates from impoverished nobles, lent money to half the dignitaries of France, and obtained noble husbands and high church offices for his own middle-class relatives. At Bourges he met the cost of embellishing the cathedral and built himself a private palace, one of the showplaces of France.

Coeur demonstrated dramatically the wealth and the power that a mere bourgeois could attain. Yet it was all too good to last. Coeur's success seemed to threaten the established order of things; too many highly placed people owed him too much money. He was disgraced on the trumped-up charge of poisoning the favorite royal mistress. A refugee from France, Coeur was starting to recoup his losses when he died while leading a papal expedition against the Turks.

Even richer and more powerful than Jacques Coeur in his prime was the Fugger family of southern Germany, often accounted the most influential single family in the history of finance. The Fuggers

House of Jacques Coeur, Bourges, France (fifteenth century).

Jacob Fugger of Augsburg (1473-1523).

made the little Bavarian city of Augsburg an international financial center from about 1450 to 1600. The founder of the family fortune was a prosperous linen-weaver. His sons and grandsons sold textiles and luxuries, began buying up mines, and in the late 1400's became bankers to the papacy and to the Habsburgs. With the Fuggers, as with Jacques Coeur, wealth bred more wealth, power, and eventual ruin. Through Habsburg favor they secured silver, iron, and copper mines in Hungary and the Tyrol. At the peak of their prosperity in the 1540's, the family fortune is estimated to have reached a figure worth about a quarter of a billion of our present-day dollars. Then the Fuggers made the mistake of extending repeated loans to a very poor risk, the Habsburg Philip II of Spain (see Chapter XIII). The Spanish monarch did not honor his debts, and in 1607 the firm went bankrupt.

Two quotations will convey something of the personality of these German bankers. First, there is the prideful note of rugged individualism in the epitaph that Jacob Fugger composed for his own tomb in the early sixteenth century:

To the best, greatest God! Jacob Fugger of Augsburg, the ornament of his class and people, imperial councillor under Maximilian I and Charles V, who was behind no one in the attainment of extraordinary wealth, in generosity, purity of morals, and greatness of soul, is, as he was not comparable with anyone in his lifetime, even after death not to be counted among the mortals.*

But the haughty Fuggers were not just "robber barons," and so there is a note of philanthropy in the inscription at the entrance to the "Fuggerei," a charming garden village that they built for the poor of Augsburg:

Ulrich, George, and Jacob Fugger of Augsburg, blood brothers, being firmly convinced that they were born for the good of the city, and that for their great prosperity they have to thank chiefly an all-powerful and benevolent God, have out of piety, and as an example of special generosity founded, given, and dedicated 106 dwellings, both buildings and furnishings, to those of their fellow citizens who live righteously, but are beset by poverty.†

The Social Impact of Economic Change

Augsburg, with its special housing development for low-income families, begins to seem very much like a contemporary city. Yet we must not exaggerate its apparent modernity, for the total population of Augsburg at the zenith of Fugger power probably never exceeded 20,000. In fact, none of the centers of international economic life five or six hundred years ago was really a big city at all. None of them was

---

* Quoted by Miriam Beard, *A History of the Business Man* (New York, 1938), 239-240.
† J. Strieder, *Jacob Fugger the Rich* (New York, 1931), 176.

Fuggerei in Augsburg.

comparable with our own metropolises or with Hellenistic Alexandria, imperial Rome, or tenth-century Byzantium. One set of estimates for the fourteenth century puts the population of Venice, Florence, and Paris in the vicinity of 100,000 each; that of Genoa, Milan, Barcelona, and London at about 50,000; and that of the biggest Hanseatic and Flemish towns between 20,000 and 40,000. At the close of the Middle Ages the great majority of Europeans still lived on the land.

The urban minority, however, was beginning to bring important changes to the life of the rural majority. In those days, we should remember, farms usually came right up to the city walls. Ties between town and countryside tightened in those areas where towns were especially numer-

ous—Lombardy, Tuscany, Flanders, the Rhine Valley, and northern Germany. Merchants often invested their wealth in farm properties, and peasants often moved to town as workmen or became part-time artisans on the farm itself. Rural laborers made prayer beads for the capitalists of Lübeck and spun woolen yarn for the guild masters of Florence. Town governments sometimes improved adjacent farmland on the pattern established by the medieval communes of Milan and Siena, which had drained marshes nearby to increase the area under cultivation.

Moreover, the growth of trade and the increased use of money partly transformed the agrarian institutions of western Europe. Many manors, no longer largely self-sufficient, now specialized in a single crop, like grain or wool; consequently, they had to purchase the necessities that they themselves no longer produced. The lords of these one-crop manors, depending increasingly on a monetary income, thus became capitalists, usually on a very modest scale. The most enterprising, however, wanted to sweep away what seemed to them inefficient medieval survivals. They demanded that their peasants pay their rent in money rather than in commodities or in work on the demesne land. The sheep-raising capitalists of sixteenth-century England were to secure the right of enclosure, of fencing off for their own flocks common lands where the peasants had traditionally pastured their own livestock. In Spain, the great guild of sheep-raisers called the *Mesta* secured comparable exclusive rights to vast tracts of pasture.

Businessmen, too, attacked medieval economic customs. They wanted property in a form that they might readily buy and sell, free from the restrictions of feudal tenure. And they wanted a labor force that they could hire and fire and move to new jobs at will, free from the restrictions of serfdom.

In sum, at the heart of economic and social relationships the cash nexus of the capitalist was beginning to replace the medieval complex of caste and service. These new developments blurred the old lines between classes. The ordinary individual very probably made a gain in real income by becoming a wage-earning laborer instead of a serf. Yet he also lost something—the security, the inherited job, the right to certain lands—which he had possessed in the days of manorialism. Hence the undercurrents of despair and discontent which came to the surface in peasant rebellions like the Jacquerie and the English rising of 1381. Finally, in the towns and cities, a new social cleavage was appearing, between the actual workmen and the wealthy businessmen. Sometimes the social tensions that resulted were kept under effective control, as in Venice. But sometimes they became so acute that they exploded, as in fourteenth-century Florence or in Flanders on the eve of the Hundred Years' War.

The Political and Cultural Impact of Economic Change

The most immediate political result of the economic changes we have been surveying was the newly enlarged political role of the business class, the celebrated bourgeoisie. Sometimes the bourgeois themselves ruled, as did the Medici in Florence and the merchants in Venice and the Hanse. Sometimes the bourgeois provided monarchs with the money or the professional skills, or both, to further dynastic and national interests. Men of the middle class helped Henry VII bring law and order back to England; Fugger money supported the Habsburgs; Jacques Coeur was, at least for a time, indispensable to Charles VII of France. This last example may serve as a reminder that the bonds between economics and politics were not indis-

soluble. The holders of political power could always ruin the holders of economic power, as Charles VII disgraced Coeur and Edward III bankrupted the Bardi and Peruzzi. By and large, however, the ties between the realms of statecraft and business were tightening.

The economic leaders made their impact not only on politics but also on the whole "style" of the age. The medieval outlook on man was undergoing a significant change: witness the extreme of worldly pride asserted in the epitaph of Jacob Fugger (see above, p. 433). No medieval man, except perhaps such a very rare specimen as the Emperor Frederick II, would have been so presumptuous, so self-centered, so lacking in humility. The bourgeois were beginning to invade the Church's near-monopoly of the support of culture. The Fuggers, the Medici, Jacques Coeur, and the well-to-do in general were undertaking the patronage of art and learning, and financing the building of public monuments. The palace or the library of the rich man challenged the monastery or the Church-dominated university as a center of scholarship. In the late 1400's, for example, the intellectual life of Florence revolved around the Platonic Academy, a project of the Medici.

The Church itself, the very keystone of medieval civilization, threatened to crack under the impact of the new economic forces and the new secularism. The popes of the later 1400's, like their contemporaries in the business world, were great admirers and amassers of material wealth; they, too, were connoisseurs of art. In fact, there was little to distinguish the rich and cultivated prelate from the rich and cultivated layman. By 1500, even the Church seemed less Christian and more worldly than it had been in the Middle Ages. It was indeed the age of the Machiavellians—the age of the Renaissance.

Reading Suggestions
on Politics and Economics in the Late Medieval West

(Asterisk indicates paperbound edition.)

GENERAL ACCOUNTS

E. P. Cheyney, *The Dawn of a New Era, 1250-1453* (Harper, 1936), and M. Gilmore, *The World of Humanism, 1453-1517* (Harper, 1952). The first two volumes of the important series, "The Rise of Modern Europe," edited by W. L. Langer; good introductory accounts, with full bibliographies.

W. Durant, *The Story of Civilization*, Vol. V: *The Renaissance* (Simon and Schuster, 1953). An informative survey directed to the general public.

The New Cambridge Modern History, Vol. I: *The Renaissance, 1493-1520* (Cambridge Univ. Press, 1957). A detailed work by many scholars; useful for reference.

FRANCE

E. Perroy, *The Hundred Years War* (Oxford Univ. Press, 1951). The standard work on the subject and the best introductory volume to French history in the fourteenth and fifteenth centuries.

P. Champion, *Louis XI* (Dodd, Mead, 1929). A solid, popular account.

J. Huizinga, *The Waning of the Middle Ages* (*Anchor, 1954). A remarkable recreation of the atmosphere of an entire period in European history, with particular stress on France and the Low Countries.

ENGLAND

A. R. Myers, *England in the Late Middle Ages* (*Penguin). A useful brief survey.

E. F. Jacob, *Henry V and the Invasion of France* (Macmillan, 1950). A good popular account.

C. W. S. Williams, *Henry VII* (Barker, 1937). A solid study of the first Tudor.

S. B. Chrimes, *English Constitutional History*, 2nd ed. (Oxford Univ. Press, 1953). A reliable guide to a complex and controversial subject.

B. Wilkinson, *The Constitutional History of England, 1216-1399* (Longmans, Green, 1948-1952). A detailed, scholarly account.

SPAIN

R. B. Merriman, *The Rise of the Spanish Empire in the Old World and the New*, Vol. II (Macmillan, 1918). Still perhaps the best treatment in English of Ferdinand and Isabella.

GERMANY

G. Barraclough, *The Origins of Modern Germany* (Blackwell, 1949). The best general treatment of late medieval Germany in English.

ITALY

L. Olschki, *The Genius of Italy* (Cornell Univ. Press, 1954). Thoughtful essays on many aspects of Italian history at the close of the Middle Ages:

H. Baron, *The Crisis of the Early Italian Renaissance: Civic Humanism and Republican Liberty in an Age of Classicism and Tyranny*, 2 vols. (Princeton Univ. Press, 1955). A scholarly monograph affording many insights into Italian political life.

F. Schevill, *A History of Florence from the Founding of the City through the Renaissance* (Harcourt, Brace, 1936), and *The Medici* (Harcourt, Brace, 1949). Two useful detailed studies.

C. M. Ady, *Lorenzo dei Medici and Renaissance Italy* (English University Press, 1955). A brief, popular account.

E. Armstrong, *Lorenzo de' Medici* (Putnam, 1941). A standard biography of the famous Medici.

D. Noyes, *The Story of Milan* (1908). The most comprehensive account in English.

R. Sabatini, *The Life of Cesare Borgia* (Houghton Mifflin, 1924). A biography by the author of colorful historical novels.

H. Butterfield, *The Statecraft of Machiavelli* (Bell, 1940). Presents the traditional, rather unfavorable view of the famous Florentine.

F. Chabod, *Machiavelli and the Renaissance* (Bowes and Bowes, 1958). A celebrated and more sympathetic interpretation.

ECONOMIC AND SOCIAL HISTORY

The Cambridge Economic History of Europe, Vol. II: *Trade and Industry in the Middle Ages* (Cambridge Univ. Press, 1954). An advanced scholarly study; a mine of information.

H. Heaton, *Economic History of Europe*, rev. ed. (Harper, 1948). A first-rate textbook survey.

G. Renard and G. Weulersse, *Life and Work in Modern Europe* (*Fifteenth through Eighteenth Centuries*) (Knopf, 1926). A useful, scholarly account.

M. Beard, *A History of the Business Man* (Macmillan, 1938). Contains good sketches of Renaissance millionaires.

R. Ehrenberg, *Capital and Finance in the Age of the Renaissance: A Study of the Fuggers and Their Connections* (Harcourt, 1928).

A. W. O. von Martin, *Sociology of the Renaissance* (Oxford Univ. Press, 1941). An instructive study of Italian society in the 1300's and 1400's.

F. C. Lane, *Venetian Ships and Shipping of the Renaissance* (Johns Hopkins Univ. Press, 1934). An unusually interesting monograph.

SOURCES

J. Froissart, *The Chronicles*, adapted by H. P. Dunster (Dutton, 1906). The great narrative source for French history in the later Middle Ages.

The History of Comines, T. Danett, trans. (D. Nutt, 1897). The famous contemporary account of the reign of Louis XI.

W. Langland, *The Vision of Piers Plowman* (many editions).

ECONOMICS: LATE MEDIEVAL WEST

Machiavelli, *The Prince and the Discourses,* Max Lerner, ed. (*Modern Library).

G. T. Matthews, ed., *News and Rumor in Renaissance Europe* (* Capricorn, 1959). Reports to the Fuggers by their agents.

G. B. Shaw, *St. Joan* (*Penguin). A most successful dramatization of Joan, perhaps sounder as theater than as history.

W. Scott, *Quentin Durward* (many editions). The France of Louis XI is the setting of this tale by the famous Romantic novelist.

V. Hugo, *Notre Dame* (many editions). The celebrated novel about the 'hunchback' by the French Romantic writer; set in the age of Louis XI.

T. B. Costain, *The Moneyman* (Doubleday, 1951). Jacques Coeur interpreted by a highly popular modern historical novelist.

C. Reade, *The Cloister and the Hearth* (many editions). A famous novel set in Continental Europe in the late 1400's; based on scholarly research.

Josephine Tey, *The Daughter of Time* (Macmillan, 1952; * Berkley). A fascinating attempt to rehabilitate Richard III, by an expert writer of detective fiction.

N. Balchin, *The Borgia Testament* (Houghton Mifflin, 1949). A fictional autobiography, as Caesar might have written it.

The
Renaissance

CHAPTER XI

I: Introduction: The Problem of the Renaissance

THE RENAISSANCE was one of the great periods of cultural and intellectual achievement in the West, a literary, artistic, and philosophical flowering that filled the centuries of transition from the medieval to the modern world. The Renaissance began in the 1300's and came to an end during the 1500's and early 1600's, as Europe passed into the ages of the Reformation and of dynastic and religious wars. The first writer to show some of the marks of the Renaissance "style," though he belonged primarily to the Middle Ages, was the Italian poet, Dante, who lived at the turn of the thirteenth century to the fourteenth. The last major figure of the Renaissance was Shakespeare, who lived three centuries after Dante, or perhaps John Milton, who came later still, in the mid-seventeenth-century England of revolution and civil war. The homeland of the Renaissance was Italy, the Italy of aggressive and cultivated businessmen and politicians. As time went on, the movement reached France, Germany, and the Low Countries as well as England, but it did not flourish everywhere in the West. It scarcely touched the Scandinavian states, and it affected Portugal and Spain only slightly.

439

These chronological and geographical definitions, however, do not hint at the basic historical problem posed by the Renaissance. Like many simple labels attached to broad historical movements, like the "Fall of Rome" or the "Dark Ages," the term Renaissance has aroused lively controversy among scholars, calling forth a bewildering variety of interpretations and reinterpretations. The word itself means "rebirth," the rebirth of the classical culture of ancient Greece and Rome. But what in actual fact was the Renaissance? Was Greco-Roman culture truly reborn? What accounted for the remarkable productivity of the writers, the sculptors, the painters, and all the other artists of the Renaissance?

Only a few decades ago, most educated men would have offered simple answers to these questions. The chief reason for the classical revival appeared to be the capture of Constantinople by the Turks in 1453 and the subsequent flight of Greek scholars to Italy and other countries of western Europe. The Renaissance seemed a blaze of light after nearly a thousand years of unrelieved gloom. The views of the eighteenth-century historian, Gibbon, still attracted many adherents:

Before the revival of classical literature, the barbarians in Europe were immersed in ignorance; and their vulgar tongues were marked with the rudeness and poverty of their manners. The students of the more perfect idioms of Rome and Greece were introduced to a new world of light and science; to the society of the free and polished nations of antiquity; and to a familiar converse with those immortal men who spoke the sublime language of eloquence and reason. Such an intercourse must tend to refine the taste, and to elevate the genius, of the moderns. . . . °

Today, however, these simple answers no longer suffice. We cannot attribute such exaggerated importance to the fall of By-

zantium. Well before 1453 knowledge of Greek writings was filtering into the West from Moslem Spain, from Sicily, and from Byzantium itself. Moreover, Greek influence was by no means the only decisive factor in promoting the Renaissance. The businessmen and politicians of the Italian states impressed upon the culture of their day the stamp of their own individualism. Today, most of all, we can no longer accept the old contrast between medieval darkness and Renaissance light. A great Christian civilization had in fact come to maturity during the Middle Ages, and culture, even in the narrow sense of the heritage from classical antiquity, had never actually disappeared from the medieval West. It is both inaccurate and presumptuous to speak of a literal "rebirth" of culture at the close of the Middle Ages. Some historians have contended that the cultural rebirth had occurred much earlier than the 1300's, with the "Carolingian Renaissance" (see Chapter V), for example, or with the chivalric poetry of the troubadours at the court of Eleanor of Aquitaine, the so-called "Renaissance of the twelfth century" (see Chapter VIII).

But to find that the germ or the foundation of everything characteristic of the Renaissance had already existed long before 1300—to deny any originality to the Renaissance, as a few historians do—is to push the pendulum of reinterpretation too far. Unquestionably, the men of the Renaissance owed a large debt to the scholarship and art of their medieval predecessors, as we shall see. Unquestionably, the men of the Renaissance were often religious, credulous, and caste-conscious. But they were also materialistic, skeptical, and individualistic to a degree unknown in the Middle Ages. The Renaissance most decidedly had a style of its own, neither fully medieval nor fully modern but a transition between the two. To examine in more detail the nature of that style is the task of this chapter.

° Edward Gibbon, *The Decline and Fall of the Roman Empire,* Ch. LXVI.

The task will not be easy, since we are confronting a complex era of transition, swept by contradictory currents and cross-currents. In politics, for instance, the fifteenth century was torn between the old and the new, between "bastard feudalism" and the emerging national monarchy (see Chapter X). One scholar has suggested a comparable division in culture and thought, between "Renaissance" elements that incorporated the Christian values of the Middle Ages and "Counter-Renaissance" elements that denied or subverted those values. Although the two labels may seem somewhat illogical, the division they make is a useful one. The distinguished Italian historian, Professor Federico Chabod, has observed that the new secular elements may be summarized as "art for art's sake, politics for politics' sake, science for science's sake." * In other words, men were

* F. Chabod, *Machiavelli and the Renaissance* (London, 1958), 184.

attempting to do things and study things as an end in itself, not as the means to the glorification of God and the salvation of humanity, much as Machiavelli divorced political thought from theology or as Machiavellian rulers cultivated power politics.

We shall now survey these attempts, first in literature and thought, then in art and science. The new secular elements will be found intermingled with the old, not neatly isolated or compartmentalized. The thinkers and the artists of the Renaissance expressed the nationalism and the materialism of their time; yet they also continued the age-old examination into the mysteries of nature and the personality of man. Moreover, the world of culture, though never wholly separate from the workaday world of business and politics, is never wholly the same as that world. Parallels between the two exist, but they must not be pushed too far. Our inquiry begins with the instrument of so many Renaissance writers, the vernacular languages.

II: Literature and Thought

The Rise of the Vernaculars

The term "vernacular" means native or local and applies particularly to the languages of the western European countries. Everywhere the vernaculars developed slowly, arising deep in the Middle Ages as the spoken language of the people, then extending gradually to popular writing and later to formal and official works. Many of the vernaculars developed from Latin. These were the Romance (Roman) languages—Spanish, Portuguese, Italian, and French. Castilian, the core of modern literary Spanish, attained official status early; the King of Castile ordered that it

be used for government records in the thirteenth century. Italian, on the other hand, scarcely existed as a literary language until the very eve of the Renaissance, when Dante composed the *Divine Comedy*.

In medieval France two families of vernaculars appeared. Southern Frenchmen spoke the *langue d'oc,* so called from their use of *oc* (the Latin *hoc*) for "yes"; their northern cousins spoke the *langue d'oïl,* in which "yes" was *oïl,* the ancestor of the modern *oui.* The epic verses of the *Song of Roland,* the rowdy *fabliaux,* and the chronicles of Villehardouin and Joinville were all composed in the *langue d'oïl,* while the troubadours entertaining the court of Eleanor of Aquitaine sang in Provençal, a variety of the *langue d'oc*. By 1400, the *langue d'oïl* of the Paris region was well on its way to replacing Latin as the official language of the kingdom. One reminder of the *langue d'oc* survives in the name for a region of southern France, Languedoc. Another survival is the Catalan language, still spoken on both the French and Spanish sides of the Pyrenees.

In Germany and in England the vernaculars were derived ultimately not from Latin but from an ancient Germanic language. The minnesingers of thirteenth-century Germany (see above, p. 328) composed their poetry in Middle High German, the immediate ancestor of modern literary German. The Anglo-Saxons of England had spoken a dialect of Low German which incorporated some words of Scandinavian or Celtic origin and later added many borrowings from Norman French and Latin to form the English vernacular. As we have already seen (p. 404, above), English achieved official recognition in the fourteenth century; meantime, it was coming into its own as a literary language with such popular works as *Piers Plowman* and Chaucer's *Canterbury Tales*. For us today the English of 1400 is stranger and more difficult than the Shakespearean English of 1600, but it is still recognizable as English. Glance back at the passages quoted in Chapter X from the *Libel of English Policy*, which was almost contemporary with Chaucer.

The rise of vernaculars often paralleled and assisted the growth of nationalism. Use of a common language undoubtedly aroused in Englishmen a common sense of national purpose and a common mistrust of foreigners who did not speak the King's English. The vernaculars quickened the emergence of distinctive national "styles" in England, in France, and in Spain. The vernaculars, however, could not by themselves create national political units; witness the triumph of particularism in fifteenth-century Germany and Italy. Nor did the vernaculars divide western culture into water-tight national compartments. Translations kept ideas flowing across national frontiers, and some of the vernaculars themselves became international languages. In the Near East, for instance, the Italian that had been introduced by the Crusaders was the *lingua franca*, the western tongue that almost everyone could understand.

Humanism

In spite of the rise of the vernaculars, Latin remained the international language of the Church and the academic world. Scholars worked diligently to perfect their Latin and, in the later Renaissance, to learn at least the rudiments of Greek. They called themselves humanists. It may seem surprising that many avowed humanists both revered the classics and employed one of the vernaculars with great skill. This is an example of the Renaissance transition, the old and the new side by side. Indeed, generations of vernacular writers since the Renaissance have studied the classical masters to improve their own style.

Humanism, however, was far more than a linguistic term. The humanist was more than a classical scholar, for he also studied the great men, the great ideas, and the great art of classical antiquity. The humanist came to cherish the values of antiquity, pagan though they were, almost as much as the traditional Christian values; indeed, he sometimes cherished them even more. To cite an extreme example, Machiavelli found more virtues in pre-Christian Greece and Rome than he did in the Christian society of his own day. Other humanists, however, sought a kind of common denominator in the best ancient moral teaching and in the highest Christian aspiration, as we shall see.

Altogether, humanism revolutionized men's attitudes toward the classical heritage. The medieval schoolmen had not disdained this heritage; rather they had transformed it to fortify their own Christian views, finding in Vergil's *Aeneid*, for instance, not only the splendor of epic poetry but also an allegory of man's sojourn in this vale of tears. The humanists of the Renaissance, in turn, in the more secular spirit of their own age and in the light of their own more extensive knowledge of the classics, transformed their medieval heritage. They began to study the classics for their own sake, not just to embellish or enrich their religious faith. The two literary trends we have been sketching, the rise of the vernaculars and the evolution of humanism, may now be traced in more detail through the great writers of the later Middle Ages and early Renaissance, beginning with Dante Alighieri (1265-1321).

Dante

Much of Dante's writing, above all the *Divine Comedy*, was firmly rooted in the Middle Ages (see Chapter VIII). The chivalric concept of disembodied love inspired his love poems to Beatrice, who was married to another and whom he seldom saw. No Ghibelline was more romantic, less realistic, about the unpromising Holy Roman Emperors of the time. Though hostile to the political ambitions of Pope Boniface VIII, Dante was no Machiavellian anticlerical but a good Christian who simply wanted the Pope to keep out of politics.

Yet Dante also foreshadowed developments that were to characterize the Renaissance. He championed the vernacular, writing in Latin a plea for its toleration by pedants who refused to read Italian. For the *Divine Comedy* he deliberately chose the vernacular of his native Tuscany over the more respectable Latin, and he modeled his style on the popular poetry of the Provençal troubadours rather than on the loftier epic verse of the classics. In other respects, however, he gave the classics their full due. Among the characters of the *Comedy* are

a host of classical figures, both real and mythological. The Trojan Hector, Homer, Vergil's Aeneas, Vergil himself, Euclid, Plato, Socrates, Caesar, and other virtuous pagans dwell forever in Limbo on the edge of Hell, suffering only the hopelessness of the unbaptized who can never reach God's presence. Dante took from ancient mythology the tormentors of the damned—the Minotaur, the Furies, and Cerberus, the three-headed hound of Hell and the symbol of gluttony.

Moreover, the concerns of this world are constantly with Dante in the other world. Thus, when he and Vergil board a boat to cross an infernal marsh, he observes that Vergil, being a shade, has no weight:

So then my guide embarked, and at his call
  I followed him; and not till I was in
  Did the boat seem to bear a load at all.[*]

The lost souls are real people, from Judas through corrupt medieval clerics down to Dante's own fellow Florentines. Finally, Dante was not one of the medieval intellectuals who withdrew from society to the sanctuary of holy orders. He was deeply involved in practical politics and, as a political refugee (see above, p. 420), adopted the good Renaissance expedient of obtaining the patronage of a minor despot, the ruler of Verona. As a man of letters, he achieved a remarkable popular success during his lifetime. Half a century after his death, a group of Florentine citizens honored the memory of their exiled compatriot by founding a public lectureship for a person "well trained in the book of Dante."

Petrarch

Popular fame and classical enthusiasm positively obsessed the next important Italian literary figure, Francesco Petrarca

---

[*] *The Divine Comedy: Hell,* Canto, VIII, lines 25-27, D. L. Sayers, trans. (Penguin Classics, 1949).

(1304-1374), better known as Petrarch. Petrarch set a lasting example for scholarly research by his zeal for collecting and copying the manuscripts of ancient authors. He assembled a splendid private library and found in an Italian cathedral some dusty and forgotten letters by Cicero which threw new light on that Roman's political career. Petrarch so admired the past that he addressed a series of affectionate letters to Cicero and other old masters, and composed a Latin epic in the manner of the *Aeneid* to celebrate Scipio Africanus, the hero of the Second Punic War (see Chapter III). Although he never learned Greek well enough to read it, he could at least gaze reverently at his manuscripts of Homer and Plato.

Petrarch's attainments, even as a young man, led the Senate of Rome (then a kind of municipal council) to crown him with a wreath of laurel. This elaborate ceremony revived the Greco-Roman custom of extending official recognition to artistic excellence. The new poet laureate reveled in it. He wanted desperately to win lasting renown, to rank with the Romans to whom he addressed his letters. Petrarch achieved fame, but, ironically, the writings of his that are most admired in modern times are not those in his beloved Latin but those which he himself esteemed the least, the beautiful vernacular love poems to his adored Laura. In these lyrics Petrarch perfected the verse form known as the Italian sonnet, fourteen lines long, divided into one set of eight lines and another of six, each with its own rhyme scheme. The word "sonnet" literally means a little song, and Petrarch developed his sonnets from vernacular folk-songs. Almost despite himself, therefore, he proved to be one of the founders of modern vernacular literature.

Petrarch exemplified the emerging humanism of the Renaissance not only in his reverence for the classics but also in his deep feeling for the beauties of this world.

Here is his account of climbing the summit of Mount Ventoux in southern France:

At first I stood there almost benumbed, overwhelmed by a gale such as I had never felt before and by the unusually open and wide view. I looked around me: clouds were gathering below my feet, and Athos and Olympus grew less incredible, since I saw on a mountain of lesser fame what I had heard and read about them. From there I turned my eyes in the direction of Italy, for which my mind is so fervently yearning. The Alps were frozen stiff and covered with snow—those mountains through which that ferocious enemy of the Roman name once passed, blasting his way through the rocks with vinegar if we may believe tradition.*

But then the story takes a medieval turn:

I admired every detail, now relishing earthly enjoyment, now lifting up my mind to higher spheres after the example of my body, and I thought it fit to look into the volume of Augustine's *Confessions*. . . . I happened to hit upon the tenth book of the work. My brother stood beside me, intently expecting to hear something from Augustine on my mouth. I ask God to be my witness and my brother who was with me: Where I fixed my eyes first it was written: 'And men go to admire the high mountains, the vast floods of the sea, the huge streams of the rivers, the circumference of the ocean, and the revolutions of the stars— and desert themselves.' I was stunned, I confess. I bade my brother, who wanted to hear more, not to molest me, and closed the book, angry with myself that I still admired earthly things.†

The story may sound too pat; but it is known that Petrarch did possess a small manuscript of Augustine which could have fitted handily into a climber's kit.

In fact, Petrarch admired Augustine as much as he admired Cicero. From the religious teachings of the one and the Stoic philosophy of the other he hoped to make himself a better Christian. Petrarch found no conflict between his neoclassical learn-

---

* Quoted in E. Cassirer, P. O. Kristeller, J. H. Randall, Jr., *The Renaissance Philosophy of Man* (Chicago, 1948), 41.
† *Ibid.*, 44.

ing and older Christian doctrine: both should make their contribution to enrich the human spirit. This was an attitude taken by many humanists, an excellent instance of the fusion of new and old in the Renaissance. Furthermore, Petrarch disliked the scholastic philosophers of the Middle Ages for their rationalism, their preoccupation with detail. In their concern with the letter of Christianity he felt that they missed its spirit—they "desert themselves," as he read in Augustine on Mount Ventoux. This hostility to scholasticism is also an attitude characteristic of the humanists.

Boccaccio

Another humanist attitude, less frequently held but still significant in the Renaissance, was taken by Petrarch's friend and pupil, Giovanni Boccaccio (1313-1375). This was the light-hearted and matter-of-fact view of human frailty assumed in Boccaccio's famous *Decameron*. The *Decameron* recounts, in the Italian vernacular, the stories told by a company of gay young people to enliven their exile in a country villa where they have fled to escape the Black Death in Florence in 1348. Here is the gist of one of the stories:

You must know, then, that there was once in our city a very rich merchant called Arriguccio Berlinghieri, who . . . took to wife a young gentlewoman ill sorting with himself, by name Madam Sismonda, who, for that he, merchant-like, was much abroad and sojourned little with her, fell in love with a young man called Ruberto.*

Arriguccio discovers his wife's infidelity and gives her the beating of her life—or so he thinks. The beating occurs in a darkened room, Sismonda has directed her maid to

---

* This and the following quotations are from the eighth story of the seventh day, as translated in the Modern Library edition of the *Decameron* (New York, n.d.).

take her place, and it is actually the maid whom Arriguccio has thrashed. He, ignorant of the deception, plays the wronged husband to the hilt and summons Sismonda's brothers to witness her disgrace. "The brothers,—seeing her seated sewing with no sign of beating on her face, whereas Arriguccio avouched that he had beaten her to a mummy,—began to marvel." Sismonda immediately accuses her hapless husband of "fuddling himself about the taverns, foregathering now with this lewd woman and now with that and keeping me waiting for him . . . half the night." The result: the brothers give Arriguccio a thorough beating. And Boccaccio's moral:

Thus the lady, by her ready wit, not only escaped the imminent peril but opened herself a way to do her every pleasure in time to come, without evermore having any fear of her husband.

Boccaccio did not invent all the stories of the *Decameron;* he reworked some of the bawdy *fabliaux* of medieval France, particularly those exposing the sins of the clergy. But what he did do for the first time was to give these earthy tales a kind of literary respectability. From now on, the gay, un-Christian story occupies a small but acknowledged place in European literature. Boccaccio here reflected in part the worldly, rather frivolous outlook of the court of the Angevin monarchs at Naples, where he spent part of his youth.

Boccaccio himself, however, was no frivolous worldling but a serious humanist scholar. He aided Petrarch in the search for ancient manuscripts and found a copy of Tacitus in the Benedictine abbey at Monte Cassino; he was more successful than his master in learning Greek; he taught at the University in Florence and held the Dante memorial lectureship there. He was anticlerical in the sense that he criticized the corruption of the clergy, but he was not anti-Christian. As the son of a Florentine banker, he turned to letters after a disillusioning apprenticeship in banking. He came to hate what he felt to be the gap between the sharp business practices and the professed Christian ideals of wealthy Florentines. Note that the cuckolded husband in the tale above is a rich merchant; Boccaccio, in his way, was a moralist.

Preservation of the Classics

The men of letters who followed Petrarch and Boccaccio may be divided into three groups. First, there were the conservers of classical culture, the bookworms, scholars, cultivated despots and businessmen, all the heirs of Petrarch's great humanistic enthusiasm for classical antiquity. Second were the vernacular writers who took the path marked out by the *Decameron*, from Chaucer at the close of the fourteenth century down to Rabelais and to Cervantes in the sixteenth. And third there were the synthesizers, headed by Pico and Erasmus, who endeavored to fuse Christianity, classicism, and much else into a universal philosophy of man.

The devoted antiquarians of the fifteenth century uncovered a really remarkable number of ancient manuscripts. They ransacked monasteries and other likely places, in Italy and Germany, in France and Spain. They pieced together the works of Cicero, Tacitus, Lucretius, and other Latin authors. Collecting Greek manuscripts became a regular business, transacted for Italian scholars and patrons by agents who were active in Constantinople both before and after the city's fall in 1453. They did their work so thoroughly that almost all the Greek classics we now possess reached the West before 1500.

To preserve, catalogue, and study these literary treasures, the first modern libraries were created. Cosimo de' Medici supported three separate libraries in and near Florence and employed forty-five copyists. The humanist popes founded the library of the Vatican, today one of the most important collections in the world. Even a minor state might have a major library, as was the case with the small duchy of Urbino in northern Italy.

Greek scholars also made the journey from Byzantium to Italy. Manuel Chrysoloras, one of the earliest of them, taught at Florence during the last few years of the fourteenth century; now men willing to persevere could learn Greek thoroughly. The revival of Greek reached maturity in 1462, when Cosimo de' Medici founded the Platonic Academy at Florence. Nevertheless, Greek did not attain the popularity of Latin. Many humanists found it easier to study Plato in a Latin translation than in the difficult original, and almost all of them neglected the Greek drama because they found the plays so hard to translate.

The classicists of the fifteenth century made a fetish of pure and polished Latin. The learned composed elaborate letters designed less for private reading than for the instruction of their colleagues. Papal secretaries began to make ecclesiastical correspondence conform to what we should call a manual of correct style. At their worst, these men were not humanists but pedants, exalting manner over matter, draining vitality from the Latin language. At their best, they were keen and erudite scholars who applied to classical studies the kind of critical spirit that Machiavelli would bring to politics.

Lorenzo Valla (*c.* 1405-1477) represented classical scholarship at its best. One of the few important figures of the Italian Renaissance not associated with Florence, Valla spent most of his life at Naples and Rome. Though petty and quarrelsome, and fond of exchanging insults with rival humanists, he also commanded both immense learning and the courage to use it. His *Elegancies of the Latin Language* went through sixty printings within a century, and he even dared to criticize the supposedly flawless prose of Cicero. His historical reputation rests above all on his demonstration that the "Donation of Constantine" (see Chapter V), long a basis for sweeping papal claims to temporal dominion, was actually a forgery.

Valla proved his case against the authenticity of this famous document by showing that both its Latin style and its references dated from an era several centuries after Constantine. For example, the Donation (here called the "privilege") mentioned Constantinople as the seat of a patriarch:

> How in the world . . . could one speak of Constantinople as one of the patriarchal sees, when it was not yet a patriarchate, nor a see, nor a Christian city, nor named Constantinople, nor founded, nor planned! For the 'privilege' was granted, so it says, the third year after Constantine became a Christian; when as yet Byzantium, not Constantinople, occupied that site.*

When Valla published this exposure in 1440, he was secretary to Alfonso the Magnanimous (see above, p. 419), whose claim to Naples was being challenged by the Pope on the basis of the Donation itself. The Pope might well have been expected to condemn Valla as a heretic. Nothing of the kind occurred, and Valla soon accepted a commission to translate Thucydides under papal auspices, with no strings attached. The climate of opinion had indeed changed since the high Middle Ages: one cannot picture a Gregory VII or Innocent III treating Valla so indulgently.

Chaucer and Rabelais

Our second group of literary men, the vernacular writers, illustrate once again the broad range of the Renaissance. The Englishman, Geoffrey Chaucer (c. 1340-1400), like Dante, belongs both to the Middle Ages and to the Renaissance. As we

*The Treatise of Lorenzo Valla on the Donation of Constantine, C. B. Coleman, ed. (New Haven, 1922), 95.

saw in Chapter VIII, his *Canterbury Tales* have a medieval setting; they are told by pilgrims on their way to the shrine of the martyred Becket, not by the gay young people of the *Decameron*. Yet Chaucer's tales are not unlike Boccaccio's: he, too, uses the vernacular; he, too, borrows stories from the *fabliaux*. Although Chaucer apparently had not actually read the *Decameron*, he was familiar enough with other writings of Boccaccio to use one as the basis for his Knight's Tale and another for *Troilus and Criseyde*, his long narrative poem about two lovers in the Trojan War. The Clerk's Tale, he reveals, "I Lerned at Padowe of a worthy clerk . . . , Fraunceys Petrark, the laureat poete," and the Wife of Bàth mentions "the wyse poete of Florence That Highte Dant."

Chaucer came to know Italian literature in the course of several trips to Italy on official business for the English king. He led a busy and prosperous life in the thick of politics, domestic and international. Coming from a family of well-to-do merchants, he eventually became Controller of Customs and Clerk of the King's Works, posts more important than their titles may suggest. The writings of Chaucer showed that the English vernacular was coming of age; his own career revealed the increasing secularization of the profession of letters, which was no longer almost monopolized by the clergy.

A century and a half later, when we come to the Frenchman, François Rabelais (c. 1494-1553), the medieval values still evident in Chaucer are beginning to disappear. Rabelais contributed far more to literature than the pornography for which he is famous. He studied the classics, particularly Plato and the ancient medical writers; practiced and taught medicine; and created two of the great comic figures of letters, Gargantua and his son Pantagruel. The two are giants, and everything they do is on the heroic scale. The abbey of Theleme, which Gargantua helps to found, permits its residents a wildly un-monastic existence:

> All their life was spent not in lawes, statutes or rules, but according to their own free will and pleasure. They rose out of their beds, when they thought good: they did eat, drink, labour, sleep, when they had a minde to it, and were disposed for it. . . . In all their rule, and strictest tie of their order, there was but this one clause to be observed,

> DO WHAT THOU WILT.*

But Rabelais recommends more than self-indulgence; Gargantua seeks to endow his son with the insatiable appetite for knowledge shown by so many men of the Renaissance. He exhorts Pantagruel to learn everything. He is to master Arabic in addition to Latin, read the New Testament in Greek and the Old in Hebrew, and study history, geometry, architecture, music, and civil law. He must also know "the fishes, all the fowles of the aire, all the several kinds of shrubs and trees," "all the sorts of herbs and flowers that grow upon the ground: all the various metals that are hid within the bowels of the earth." "In brief," Gargantua concludes, "let me see thee an Abysse, and bottomless pit of knowledge." †

The Platonic Academy

Our third group of writers, the philosophical humanists, aspired not only to universal knowledge but also to a kind of universal truth and faith. The Platonic Academy, an informal intellectual club subsidized by the Medici, made Florence a center of philosophical studies in the late fifteenth century. The outstanding member of the Academy was Pico della Mirandola (1463-1494), one of those dazzling prodigies who crowded much into a brief life. He knew Arabic and Hebrew and studied Jewish allegory, Arab philosophy, and me-dieval Scholasticism. Pico's tolerance was as broad as his learning. In his short *Oration on the Dignity of Man,* he cited approvingly Chaldean and Persian theologians, the priests of Apollo, Socrates, Pythagoras, Cicero, Moses, St. Paul, St. Augustine, Mohammed, St. Francis, St. Thomas Aquinas, and many others. In all the varied beliefs of this galaxy Pico hoped to find the common denominator of faith, the key to man and the universe.

Naturally he failed. Yet there is something very appealing about the man who strove to capture the essence of all truth. He helped found the great humane studies of comparative religion and comparative philosophy. And, though ambitious, Pico was also disarmingly modest. "I have wished to give assurance," he wrote, "not so much that I know many things, as that I know things of which many are ignorant." *

Erasmus

The man who brought to maturity the humanist endeavor to draw on all wisdom was not Italian but Dutch. Erasmus (1466-1536), the "Prince of Humanists," dominated the intellectual life of Europe as few other men have done. He was in fact a cosmopolitan, the foremost citizen of the Republic of Letters. He studied, taught, and lived at Oxford, Cambridge, and Paris, and in Italy, Switzerland, and Germany. He knew Greek so well that he published a scholarly edition of the Greek New Testament. He carried on a prodigious correspondence in Latin and compiled a series of *Adages* and *Colloquies* to give students examples of good Latin composition. Because Erasmus never regarded elegance of style as an end in itself, he assailed the "knowledge-factories" of the grammarians.

---

* Rabelais, *Gargantua and Pantagruel,* Urquhart trans. (New York, 1883), Bk. I, Ch. 57.
† *Ibid.,* Bk. I, Ch. 8.

* Pico della Mirandola, "Oration on the Dignity of Man," in E. Cassirer, P. O. Kristeller, J. H. Randall, Jr., *Renaissance Philosophy of Man* (Chicago, 1948), 254.

Erasmus, by Dürer.

that they alone, of all mortal men, are not barbarians. . . . The Greeks, as well as being the founders of the learned disciplines, vaunt themselves upon their titles to the famous heroes of old.*

Erasmus played no favorites; he satirized any group or class inflated by a sense of its own importance—merchants, churchmen, scientists, philosophers, courtiers, and kings.

In appraising human nature, however, Erasmus tempered criticism with geniality. In what proportions, he asks in an ironic passage, did Jupiter supply men with emotion and reason?

Well, the proportions run about one pound to half an ounce. Besides, he imprisoned reason in a cramped corner of the head, and turned over all the rest of the body to the emotions. After that he instated two most violent tyrants, as it were, in opposition to reason: anger, which holds the citadel of the breast, and consequently the very spring of life, the heart; and lust, which rules a broad empire lower down. . . .†

So, Erasmus concludes, we must cherish particularly the few outstanding individuals who have led great and good lives. Christ heads his list of great men; Cicero and Socrates rank very high. Plato's account of the death of Socrates moved Erasmus so deeply that he almost cried out, "Pray for us, Saint Socrates."

Erasmus possessed most of the main attributes of Renaissance humanism. He coupled a detached view of human nature with faith in the dignity of man, or at least of a few individuals. He joined love of the classics with respect for Christian values. While he was both testy and vain, he had little use for the finespun arguments of Scholasticism and was a tireless advocate of what he called his "philosophy of Christ," the application, in the most humane spirit, of the doctrines of charity and love taught by Jesus. Yet, though Erasmus always considered himself

As for those stilted, insipid verses they display on all occasions (and there are those to admire them), obviously the writer believes that the soul of Virgil has transmigrated into his own breast. But the funniest sight of all is to see them admiring and praising each other, trading compliment for compliment, thus mutually scratching each other's itch.*

The *Adages* and *Colloquies*—in fact, most of his enormous output—contain penetrating comments on human weaknesses. Erasmus was one of the very first to detect the pretensions and hypocrisies of nationalism:

And now I see that it is not only in individual men that nature has implanted self-love. She implants a kind of it as a common possession in the various races, and even cities. By this token the English claim . . . good looks, music, and the best eating as their special properties. The Scots flatter themselves on the score of high birth and royal blood, not to mention their dialectical skill. Frenchmen have taken all politeness for their province. . . . The Italians usurp *belles lettres* and eloquence; and they all flatter themselves upon the fact

* Erasmus, *Praise of Folly*, H. H. Hudson, trans. (Princeton, 1941), 71-72.

* *Ibid.*, 61.
† *Praise of Folly*, 23.

a loyal son of the Church, he nevertheless helped to destroy the universality of Catholicism. His edition of the Greek New Testament raised disquieting doubts about the correctness of the Vulgate and therefore of Catholic Biblical interpretations. His attacks on the laxity of the clergy implied that the wide gap between the professed ideals and the corrupt practices of the Church could not long endure. A famous sixteenth-century epigram states: "Where Erasmus merely nodded, Luther rushed in; where Erasmus laid the eggs, Luther hatched the chicks; where Erasmus merely doubted, Luther laid down the law." Erasmus was still in his prime when Luther "laid down the law" in 1517 and launched the Protestant revolt.

III: The Arts: Painting

Main Characteristics of Renaissance Art

The Renaissance wrought a revolution in the fine arts. Both the humanistic enthusiasm for classical antiquity and the growing secularism of the age carried over into the realm of the arts. Exploiting these new forces, and aided by technical advances, men of genius produced an extraordinary number of masterpieces. In particular, they released painting and sculpture from their subservience to architecture, "queen of the arts" in the medieval West. In the era of the Romanesque and the Gothic, sculptors, the painters of altarpieces, and the superb craftsmen who made stained-glass windows, had all enhanced the glory of the cathedrals and other splendid buildings. But at most they had made only a contribution to the beauty of the whole structure. In the Renaissance, architecture lost its old aesthetic predominance, and painting and sculpture came into their own, often still closely allied with architecture, but often functioning as "free-standing" arts. The individual picture or statue won fresh importance as an independent work of art rather than as a part of a larger whole. The celebrated individualism of the Renaissance was replacing the stamp of the community found in the medieval West (see Chapter VIII).

Reflecting the classical revival, the fashion in building changed from the soaring Gothic to adaptations of the ancient Roman temple, emphasizing symmetry and the horizontal line. The contrast may be observed by comparing a Gothic cathedral like Chartres with a Renaissance monument like St. Peter's at Rome. Reflecting the expanding wealth and materialism of the age, palaces and private residences began to rival cathedrals and churches in magnificence.

The arts as a whole, like society and culture in general, became less Christian and more secular than they had been in the Middle Ages. For patrons, artists turned increasingly to men of state and business; for subjects they chose not only the traditional Virgin, Christ, and saints but also pagan gods and their own patrons. Interest in the things of this world, however, did not exclude concern with the next world; the Renaissance was *both* worldly *and* otherworldly. The fame of Leonardo, for instance, rests both on the profoundly religious Last Supper and the quite unreligious portrait of Mona Lisa.

The artists of the Renaissance, even more than its writers and thinkers, displayed an extraordinary range of talents and interests. They produced both secular and sacred works; they copied ancient classical models and launched bold new experiments in artistic expression; they took pride in their individual achievements, even boasted of them. Some of the very greatest were also the most versatile. Michelangelo executed heroic frescoes and heroic statues, and helped to plan St. Peter's. Giotto painted, designed, and ornamented buildings, wrote verses, and did handsomely in business. Leonardo was a jack of all trades and a master of many—painter and sculptor, musician and physicist, anatomist and geologist, inventor and city-planner.

The Renaissance, in sum, was one of the truly great ages in the history of art. In sculpture, it rivaled the golden centuries of Greece. In painting, it was more than a rebirth; it transformed an old and rather limited medium of expression into a thrilling new aesthetic instrument. These wonders, of course, did not take place overnight. In the arts, as in literature, a distinctive Renaissance style began to emerge about 1300; after a long development the arts reached their fullest flowering two hundred years later. For example, the most celebrated names in painting—Leonardo, Michelangelo, Titian, Dürer—belong to the "High Renaissance" of the late fifteenth and early sixteenth centuries. But the great forerunner of these masters was Giotto, a contemporary of Dante.

Giotto

Before 1300, Italian painters had generally followed the lead of Byzantium. Their work was impressively religious and highly decorative, but it was also flat and two-dimensional, lacking in depth. Giotto (c. 1270-1337), though not entirely forsaking the Byzantine tradition, experimented to make painting more lifelike and less austere. He learned much from the realistic statues of Italian sculptors, who, in turn, had been influenced by those striking sculptures decorating the portals of French Gothic cathedrals. We may take as examples the frescoes Giotto executed for the Arena Chapel at Padua. In the "Return of Joachim to the Sheepfold," the dog greets his returned master with his right forepaw raised to scratch a welcome. In the "Entombment of Christ," the mood of grief is intensified by the lamentations of the mourners on the ground, and still more by the angels flying above the dead Christ. They did not glide placidly but seem to be beating their wings in a transport of distraction and sorrow.

Medieval artists had used the same tone of color throughout a picture, and this uniformity of tone intensified the flat quality of the painting. Giotto, on the other hand, varied the brightness of his colors and attempted contrasts of light and shade, the technique that goes by the Italian name of *chiaroscuro* ("bright-dark"). Through these experiments with highlights Giotto achieved a three-dimensional quality, an illusion of depth.

As a person, Giotto anticipated the proud and versatile man of the Renaissance bent on worldly success. He was no anonymous craftsman, dedicated and withdrawn, content to work in obscurity, but a many-sided man, hungry for fame, and famous in his own day for his verses and his witty remarks as well as for his artistic accomplishments. His artistic commissions netted him a sizable fortune, which he augmented through a variety of business enterprises: lending money, running a debt-collection service, and renting looms (at stiff fees) to poor woolen-weavers. Giotto had many connections with the great and wealthy; he won the patronage of Roman cardinals, the King of Naples, and the guilds and millionaires of Florence. The richest man in Padua, Enrico Scrovegni, following a custom prevalent in the later Middle Ages, commissioned him to paint the frescoes in the Arena Chapel on behalf of his father's soul. (The senior Scrovegni had been a notorious money-lender, and

Giotto, "The Lamentation" (1305-6). Fresco in the Arena Chapel, Padua.

Dante's *Divine Comedy* had assigned his soul to Hell.)

Patronage, Subject Matter, and Technique

Thus in the time of Giotto art was beginning to attract the patronage of secular individuals in addition to that of the churchmen who had been its chief sponsors in the Middle Ages. During the next two centuries, more and more despots, kings, and merchant princes joined the ranks of patrons. This is one of the developments to follow in surveying the history of Renaissance painting. A second is the introduction of humanistic and secular themes into the world of art. A final development is technical: the advances in the use of *chiaroscuro*, perspective, color, oils, precise anatomical detail—all the techniques that gave the medium more expressive power.

By 1500, almost all the Italian states, and many states outside Italy, had their court painters. In Florence, the government, the guilds, the wealthy magnates, and the churches and monasteries had all been patronizing artists since the time of Giotto, participating in what the twentieth century would term a prolonged campaign for civic beauty and political prestige. Lorenzo the Magnificent subsidized a great painter like Botticelli as well as the humanists of the Platonic Academy. "Il Moro," the Sforza usurper in Milan, made Leonardo in effect his Minister of Fine Arts, Director of Public Works, and Master of the Revels. After the collapse of Il Moro's fortunes, Leonardo found new patrons in Caesar Borgia, the Pope, and the French kings, Louis XII and Francis I, ambitious rulers all. The popes employed Leonardo, Botticelli, Michelangelo, and many other leading artists. The popes had a keen appreciation of aesthetic values, and they favored projects that would brighten the luster of their rule. They intended to make St. Peter's the largest and the most resplendent church in Christendom, and to make Rome the artistic capital of the world.

The mixture of secular and religious motives was evident in the subject matter of art. Time and again the painters of the Renaissance executed Madonnas, the Na-

tivity, the Crucifixion, and all the rest of the grand Christian themes. But they interpreted them in their own individual ways, realistically or piously. And they applied equal skill to scenes from classical mythology, portraits of their secular contemporaries, and other subjects remote from the Christian tradition. Often the sacred and the secular could be found in the same picture. In a Florentine chapel, for instance, Giotto placed around a religious fresco a border of medallions portraying the sponsors, the banking family of the Peruzzi. Giotto's successors often introduced into a sacred painting the person who had commissioned it, and they sometimes brought in the whole family (see illustration facing p. 439). Usually the patron assumed a duly reverent posture, but there was often more than a hint of the acumen and ambition that had won him worldly success and permitted him to afford the luxury of commissioning a work of art. It is hard to tell whom such paintings were intended to honor, God or the donor.

Botticelli, "Primavera" (Spring).

Ambiguities also complicated the treatment of pagan and classical themes in Renaissance painting. At first artists took figures like Jupiter and Venus out of their Olympian context and made them just another lord and lady of the chivalric class; the sense of historical appropriateness was conspicuously missing. Later painters attempted to depict the gods and goddesses in a proper classical setting, sometimes in a pagan state of undress. Even so, the result was seldom pagan in the sense of a glorification of the flesh.

There is nothing crude or carnal in the *Primavera*, the pagan allegory of Spring painted by Botticelli (1445-1510), another figure in the long file of great Florentines. The figures in the *Primavera* are, from left to right, Mercury, the messenger of the gods; the lightly clad Three Graces; a surprisingly wistful Venus; the goddess Flora, bedecked with flowers; and Spring herself, blown in by the West Wind. They are all youthful, slender, indeed almost dainty, with their tiny feet; almost all have the air of otherworldly sweetness for which Botticelli is famous.

It may be argued that Botticelli was to painting what the mystics of the Platonic Academy were to humanism. He seems to have moved in the circle of Pico della Mirandola at Florence, and his paintings often suggest an aspiration to some lofty Platonic realm. Yet Botticelli also knew the drive of raw religious emotion. He rallied to the reforming friar, Savonarola, who briefly imposed a puritanical regime on Florence in the 1490's (see below, pp. 473-474). And when Savonarola prescribed the burning of all worldly "vanities," so the story has it, Botticelli threw some of his own paintings of nudes onto the flames.

The most significant contributor to the technique of painting after Giotto was Masaccio (1401-c.1428), yet another Florentine genius. Masaccio made bold experiments with *chiaroscuro* and emphasized anatomical realism. In painting the expul-

Masaccio, "Expulsion of Adam and Eve from Eden."

sion from the Garden of Eden, he conveyed the shame·and the sorrow of Adam and Eve both by their facial expressions and by the forlorn posture of their bodies. And he intensified the dramatic impact of the scene by using somber colors, appropriate to the tragedy, and by employing bold contrasts of light and shadow on the bodies. Masaccio had the rare gift of reducing a situation to its essentials.

Where Masaccio stressed human nature, other artists strove for the more faithful representation of the natural environment. A botanist can identify the plants and flowers in Botticelli's *Primavera*. Where Masaccio relied, as it were, on mass to achieve his artistic effects, others turned to line and to color. Botticelli was a superb colorist, and such a painstaking draughtsman that he seems to have brushed in every single hair on a human head.

A great step forward in the use of color came with the introduction of oil paints, developed first in Flanders and brought to Italy in the latter part of the fifteenth century. Until then, painters had generally worked in fresco or tempera or a combination of the two. Fresco, the application of pigments to the wet plaster of a wall, required the artist to work swiftly before the surface dried and set. Tempera (or distemper) painting, in which the pigments were mixed with a sizing, tended to be muddy-looking. Oils overcame the disadvantages of fresco and tempera; they allowed the artist to work more slowly and assured him clearer and more lasting colors.

The major trends we have been following in patronage, subject matter, and technical proficiency reached a climax with the masters of the High Renaissance. Three of them—Leonardo, Michelangelo, and Titian —may illustrate this mature age of Italian painting.

Leonardo

Compared with other great masters, Leonardo da Vinci (1452-1519) completed relatively few pictures. His scientific activities (see below, p. 468) and his innumerable services of every kind for his patrons demanded a large part of his time

and energies. Few of his paintings survive today, and some of them are badly damaged, notably the "Last Supper," executed on the damp wall of a monastery in Milan. Fortunately, Leonardo's superb talent and his extraordinary range of interests may also be sampled in the voluminous collections of his drawings and notebooks. The drawings include every sort of sketch, from preliminary work for paintings through realistic human embryos and fanciful war-machines to mere "doodles." From the notebooks comes this characteristic advice of Leonardo:

... Since, as we know, painting embraces and contains within itself ... whatever can be comprehended by the eyes, it would seem to me that he is but a poor master who makes only a single figure well.

For do you not see how many and how varied are the actions which are performed by men alone? Do you not see how many different kinds of animals there are, and also of trees and plants and flowers? What variety of hilly and level places, of springs, rivers, cities, public and private buildings; of instruments fitted for man's use; of divers costumes, ornaments and arts?—Things which should be rendered with equal facility and grace by whoever you wish to call a painter.

• • •

The painter will produce pictures of little merit if he takes the works of others as his standard; but if he will apply himself to learn from the objects of nature he will produce good results.[*]

Leonardo followed his own advice about studying nature afresh. He investigated plants, animals, and fossils. From his intensive study of human anatomy he drew up rules for indicating the actions of human muscles and for establishing the proportions between the parts of the human body. He made many sketches of the deformed and of people suffering intense strain and anguish. He combined a zeal for scientific precision with a concern for the grotesque that recalls the gargoyles of a Gothic cathe-

---

[*] *The Notebooks of Leonardo da Vinci*, Edward MacCurdy, ed. (New York, n.d.), II, 256, 276.

Leonardo da Vinci, "The Madonna of the Rocks" (Louvre, Paris).

dral. And to all this Leonardo added an interest in revealing the character and personality of human beings.

For example, he made the "Last Supper" in part an exercise in artistic geometry, arranging the apostles in four groups of three men each, around the central figure of Christ, and keeping the background de-liberately simple to accent the lines of perspective. Yet he did not make the picture superficially realistic; it would have been physically impossible for thirteen men to have eaten together at the relatively small table provided by Leonardo. Older painters had usually shown the group at the solemn yet peaceful moment of the final com-

CHAPTER XI

munion, and had suggested the coming treachery of Judas by placing him in isolation from the others. Not Leonardo. He chose the tense moment when Jesus announced the coming betrayal, and he placed Judas among the apostles, relying on facial and bodily expression to convey the guilt of the one and the consternation of the others.

Serenity pervades the picture by Leonardo illustrated on page 456, the "Madonna of the Rocks," now in the Louvre in Paris. The background is almost Gothic in its fantasy, while the plants and flowers have the accuracy of plates in a textbook. The arrangement of the figures in a pyramid, the foreshortening of the arms, the fineness of the hair, and the careful painting of the folds in the draperies show Leonardo's geometrical sense and his expert draughtsmanship. Transcending these details, Leonardo quietly insists on the religious beauty of the scene, as the angel (on the right) supports the infant Jesus and points to the young St. John, kneeling reverently.

Michelangelo and Titian

Leonardo got on fairly amicably with his patrons; his strong-minded contempo-

rary, Michelangelo Buonarotti (1475-1564), had a very different experience. He quarreled repeatedly with the imperious Pope Julius II (1503-13); it took all the Pope's high-handedness to persuade Michelangelo to complete a fresco for the ceiling of the Sistine Chapel in the Vatican. The Sistine ceiling is in every respect a prodigious piece of work. The area is approximately fourteen yards by forty, and Michelangelo covered it with 343 separate figures. He executed the whole in the space of four years, working almost single-handed, assisted only by a plasterer and a color-mixer, painting uncomfortably on his back atop a scaffolding, sometimes not bothering to descend for his night's rest, and arguing stormily with the impatient Pope, who dared to complain of the painter's slow rate of progress.

For this massive undertaking Michelangelo boldly chose not a simple subject but a series of the grandest scenes from Genesis—the creation of the sun and moon, God hovering over the waters, the creation of Adam and of Eve, the eating of the forbidden fruit, and the expulsion from Paradise. Throughout, the recurring form is that most appropriate to a master sculptor-painter, the human nude. In this vast gallery of nudes in all types of poses Michel-

Michelangelo, "Creation of Adam," from ceiling of Sistine Chapel, Rome.

angelo summed up all that Renaissance art had learned about perspective, anatomy, and motion. More astonishing still, the Sistine ceiling also comes close to summarizing man's concepts of God; no medieval artist would have dared to represent the deity so directly. God appears repeatedly, draped in a mantle, an everchanging patriarch. Hovering over the waters, he is benign; giving life to the motionless Adam, or directing Eve to arise, he is gently commanding; creating the sun and moon, he is the all-powerful deity, formidable and urgent as a whirlwind.

Both Michelangelo and Leonardo, had received their artistic training in Florence; Titian (1477-1576) was identified with Venice. In some respects Titian had the most remarkable career of any artist in that remarkable age, or any age. For eighty years he enjoyed almost unbroken professional success and produced an average of one picture a month! Even a partial listing of the commissions that he received underscores again the wide range of Renaissance painting and patronage. At the start of his career in Venice, Titian was hired to do frescoes for the headquarters of the German merchant colony. Then he undertook portraits for rich merchants, altarpieces and madonnas for churches and monasteries, and a great battle scene for the palace of the Doge. In the middle decades of the sixteenth century, Titian had become so famous that he received offers from half the despots of Italy and crowned heads of Europe. Pope Paul III, the Habsburg Emperor Charles V, and Charles' son, Philip II of Spain, became his patrons.

Titian transferred to paint much of the flamboyance and pageantry identified with Venice. Rich, intense colors, particularly reds and purples, are his hallmark. He likewise accomplished wonders of design and characterization. When he painted the Assumption of the Virgin for a place high up in a church, he distorted the figures so that they would seem right to the viewers

below and would at the same time direct their eyes upward. The Virgin herself was a majestic figure, ascending to Heaven effortlessly. A gallery of Titian's portraits would make a splendid introduction to the high politics of the sixteenth century. There is Paul III, one of the last of the Renaissance popes, ambitious and authoritative; there is a *condottiere* from the successful family of the della Rovere, at once handsome and worn, cultivated and shrewd. Titian even accomplished the feat of making the undistinguished-looking Charles V appear reasonably imperial (see illustration facing p. 479).

Northern European Painting

The fame and influence of Titian and many other Italians reached far beyond Italy itself and helped to stimulate the flowering of northern European painting in the sixteenth century. This northern Renaissance, however, also grew out of native traditions of Gothic art passed down from the Middle Ages. It centered chiefly in southern Germany and in the Low Countries. Its leading artists were Albrecht Dürer (1471-1528) and Hans Holbein (c. 1497-1543), Germans both, and Pieter Breughel the Elder (c. 1520-1569), who was born near Brussels. These northern artists, too, won the patronage of the mighty. Dürer received commissions from the Emperor Maximilian; Breughel had the support of businessmen in Antwerp and Brussels; armed with an introduction from Erasmus, Holbein moved to England, where he soon won the custom of humanists, aristocrats, and the court of King Henry VIII.

Holbein executed handsome portraits of his benefactors (see his likeness of Henry VIII, p. 492); his portrait of Erasmus, as the humanist sits writing, suggests his wit and intelligence. Dürer was in many ways the Leonardo of Germany. His realistic yet compassionate portrait of his aged and

Pieter Breughel the Elder, "Peasant Wedding" (about 1565). Now in Kunsthistorisches Museum, Vienna.

homely mother might almost have been taken from da Vinci's sketch book. He collected monkeys and other tropical specimens, painted the Virgin in the unusual pose of a "Madonna with Many Animals," and, in the closing years of his career, wrote treatises on perspective and human proportions. By sensitive use of line and shading Dürer revolutionized the hitherto primitive techniques of copper engraving and woodcuts. These innovations permitted the reproduction of drawings in many copies and enabled artists to illustrate whole editions of volumes prepared by the new process of printing. They brought Dürer closer than any Italian painter to the rapidly expanding public of readers; they made him in effect the first artist in history to become a "best-seller."

Northern painters did not always share Italian tastes in subject matter; often they were more down-to-earth. Breughel, for example, delighted in scenes of peasant life—weddings, dances, and festivals, executed with Rabelaisian gusto. He also painted a series of lovely landscapes showing the cycle of farming activities during the various months of the year. Here Breughel was not striving deliberately to be popular, as Dürer sought popularity through the mass production of engravings and woodcuts; wealthy individuals commissioned most of Breughel's plebeian subjects.

Lastly, northern art retained the old medieval fascination with the monstrous and the supernatural. Dürer showed this Gothic strain in a series of sixteen woodcuts depicting the Four Horsemen and the other grim marvels of the Apocalypse. In Breughel, the strain is almost obsessive. His "Tower of Babel" is a nightmarish skyscraper, decayed, hideous, and unclean. His bizarre "Battle of the Angels and the Demons" is full of "things" whose nearest relatives populate the science fiction and the surrealist art of the twentieth century—coats-of-arms that actually fight, shellfish that fly, hybrids with insect wings, artichoke bodies, and flower heads. Most of these fantasies were designed to teach a moral lesson; they were sermons in paint or ink, almost as the Gothic cathedrals had been sermons in stone. The painting of northern Europe demonstrates once more the absurdity of the old notion that the men of the Renaissance had somehow managed to cast off completely all the traditions and values of the Middle Ages.

IV: The Other Arts

Sculpture

In the Renaissance, sculpture and painting maintained a close organic relationship; they were, so to say, the two faces of a single artistic coin. Italian pictures owed their three-dimensional qualities partly to the painters' study of the sister art; some of the finest painters were also accomplished sculptors—Giotto, Leonardo, Michelangelo. Sculptors, too, turned to classical models and secular themes, studied human anatomy, and experimented with new techniques.

Many of these innovations are evident in Donatello (*c.* 1386-1466), a Florentine and the first great name in Renaissance sculpture. Donatello's equestrian statue of the *condottiere*, Gattemalata, in Padua is a landmark in artistic history. The subject is secular; the treatment is classical (Gattemalata looks like the commander of a Roman legion); and the material is bronze, not the stone that sculptors had been accustomed to use during the Middle Ages. In free-standing statues of religious figures Donatello sometimes stressed physical realism and beauty to the exclusion of any spiritual quality; his bronze David is a handsome youth rather than the divinely inspired slayer of Goliath. In a masterpiece like the statue of Mary Magdalen, however, Donatello transcended literal realism and heightened the dramatic and emotional effect by exaggeration. A critic has called the saint "an emaciated monster." Emaciated the figure certainly is, all skin and

Donatello, "*Equestrian Monument of Gattamelata*" (1445-50), *Padua.*

Donatello, "Mary Magdalen," about 1455.

bone, lank hair, and tattered clothing; but everything about it accents the vertical line and contributes to its extraordinary quality. Mary Magdalen is a saint who looks the part.

Half a century after Donatello, the genius of Michelangelo brought sculpture to the highest summit it had reached since the Age of Pericles, perhaps the highest in the whole record of the art. The man who painted the Sistine ceiling brought the same daring conceptions and concentrated energy to his sculptures. Early in his career, when the government of Florence offered him the exacting task of creating something beautiful from an enormous chunk of marble that another artist had already seemingly spoiled, Michelangelo produced the renowned colossal statue of David. Late in his career, Michelangelo met another outstanding challenge to his skill when he made the four figures that adorn the tombs of the Medici family in Florence—Dawn, Day, Dusk, and Night. The figures recline on sloping cornices, and a lesser artist would have made them look precarious, about to slide off. Michelangelo gave them repose and yet suggested tremendous latent power, especially in the exuberantly muscled nudes of Day and Dusk. Even more than Donatello, Michelangelo gave his best work a realism surpassing the merely literal. His remarkable statue of Moses makes a good counterpart to his depictions of God on the Sistine ceiling: one side of the prophet's face shows compassion, the other reveals the stern and wrathful law-giver. In portraying the Virgin grieving over the dead Christ (see illustration on p. 462), Michelangelo brilliantly solved the difficult technical problem of posing a seated woman with a corpse lying across her lap, and he triumphantly called attention to his feat by executing the work in highly polished marble. The face of Mary is sorrowful yet composed, and younger than that of the dead Christ. She is the eternal Virgin, Michelangelo explained, and so is always

youthful and does not grieve as an earthly mother would.

Architecture

In 1546, at the age of seventy, Michelangelo shouldered one more artistic burden: he agreed to be the chief architect of St. Peter's. Michelangelo died long before the great Roman basilica was finally completed in 1626, and his successors altered many of his details. But the great dome, the key feature of the whole structure, followed his basic design. St. Peter's shows most of the characteristics that separate the architectural style of the Renaissance from the Gothic of the High Middle Ages. Instead of great spires and towers, it has Michelangelo's dome, which rises 435 feet above the floor below, yet is dwarfed in mass by the immense building underneath. Gothic structures, with their great windows, pointed arches, and high-flung vaults, create an impression of strain and instability. St Peter's, on the other hand, with its round arches, heavier walls, and stout columns, seems to have been built for eternity.

St. Peter's also has the symmetry so admired by Renaissance builders; everything about it fits into a tidy geometrical pattern. Michelangelo cast that pattern in the shape of a Greek cross, which has four arms of equal length, whereas the Gothic cathedral had taken the form of a Latin cross, with the nave in the long arm. Though the Greek-cross design was later modified, St. Peter's still retains many traces of the original plan. The balanced character of the whole edifice is enhanced by the magnificent curving colonnades which were built in the early seventeenth century in the great square outside the basilica and which sweep the eye of the approaching visitor straight to the church of the pope.

The architects of the Renaissance thus adapted many elements used in the buildings of ancient Rome—domes, columns, round arches, geometrical symmetry. They also had some knowledge of humanistic learning, particularly the Platonic and Pythagorean concepts of perfect ideas and perfect geometric forms. Palladio, the foremost architectural theorist of the age, praised the Greek-cross plan for churches because of its symbolic values. If the apses (at the ends of the four arms) were rounded, and if the spaces between the arms were filled with rounded chapels, then the whole structure became an almost perfect circle. And the circle, according to Palladio, "demonstrates extremely well the unity, the infinite essence, the uniformity, and the justice of God." [*] Some scholars have taken the change in the plan of the church structure from the Latin cross to the circled Greek cross to symbolize a shift in religious emphasis. The Gothic stress on the sacrifice of Christ yields to the Renaissance celebration of the perfection of God.

The total architectural record of the Renaissance includes a large number of palaces, chateaux, villas, and other purely secular buildings. This conspicuous display of worldly wealth was partly a matter of the decline of medieval values and the rise of materialism, political ambition, and other forms of secular pride. But it was also a simple question of economics and security. The expansion of business gave private individuals the money to finance the construction of lavish residences. The gradual growth of effective government meant that, even in the country, a man's home could be a showplace and no longer had to be, quite literally, his castle.

[*] Quoted by Rudolf Wittkower, *The Architectural Principles of the Age of Humanism* (London, 1949), 21.

Elaborately symmetrical villas now ornamented the countryside; in the cities the characteristic structure was the *palazzo* or palace, usually not a royal or official establishment but an imposing private town house combining business offices and residential apartments. Palaces by the dozen went up in Rome and Florence; in Venice they lined the Grand Canal, the chief thoroughfare, almost solidly from one end to the other. The usual *palazzo* was three-storied and rectangular, with its windows arranged in symmetrical rows. Architects relieved the effect of monotonous regularity by a variety of decorative devices, such as pillars, pilasters, and cornices, and by using a different finish of stone for each story, with the roughest at the bottom. The largest of the *palazzi* in their dimensions even rivaled the monuments of ancient Rome. The Pitti Palace, for example, which was erected in Florence by a millionaire rival of the Medici, was 475 feet long and 114 feet high.

The fame of Italian builders soon spread throughout Europe, even to distant Moscow, where Italian experts supervised the remodeling of the Kremlin for Ivan III (see above, p. 382). Most countries did not copy the Italian style straight-out, but grafted it onto the older native architecture. The resulting compound produced some very striking buildings, particularly the great chateaux of central France. The "chateau country" of the Loire Valley contains perhaps the most graceful and elegant private residences ever constructed. The tasteful combination of elements taken from the Gothic church, the feudal castle, and the Italian palace gives these chateaux some of the magic and the unreality of a fairy tale (see the illustration of Chenonceaux, p. 546).

Music

The structure of music is often called architectural. A musical composition, like a building, has its basic skeleton or form, its over-all line, and also its surface decora-

St. Peter's Cathedral, Rome.

Renaissance architecture. The Grimani Palace, Venice.

tions and embellishments. The sacred music of the Middle Ages (see Chapter VIII), had achieved very complex and elaborate combinations of form, line, and decoration. Piling voice upon voice in complicated harmony, fusing a multitude of parts into a single whole, these ecclesiastical compositions have sometimes been compared to Gothic cathedrals. The center of Gothic music in the late Middle Ages was northern France and the Low Countries. By the fifteenth century French and Flemish musicians were journeying to Italy, where a process of mutual influence developed. The northerners took up the simple tunes of folk songs and dances; the Italians, in turn, added a strain of Gothic complexity to the austere plain-song, which had long been the mainstay of their sacred music. The end-product was the beautiful sacred music of the Italian composer, Palestrina (*c.* 1525-1594), which was at once intricate in the northern manner and devout in the Italian.

Although the secularism and individualism of the Renaissance probably exerted less influence on music than on the other arts, the influence was still conspicuous. The Flemings based their most sacred works, their Masses, on popular tunes, even rowdy ones. Moreover, Renaissance music was losing some of the anonymous quality associated with the Middle Ages. The era of prima donnas and other "stars" had not quite arrived, but the day of the celebrated individual composer, like Palestrina, was at hand. In addition, the composers and performers of music shared the taste for experiment of their colleagues in the other arts. They developed or imported a variety of new instruments—the violin, double-bass, and harpsichord; the organ, with its complement of keyboards, pedals, and stops; the kettle-drum, which was adopted from the Polish army; and the lute, which had originally been developed in medieval Persia and reached Italy by way of Moslem Spain.

Music played its role at almost every level of Renaissance society. The retinue of musicians became a fixture of court life, with the Dukes of Burgundy, Philip the Good and Charles the Bold, leading the way. Castiglione, an authority on etiquette, thought music proper for every social station:

We may see it used in the holy temples to render laud and thanks unto God, and it is a credible matter . . . that He hath given it unto us for a most sweet lightening of our travails and vexations. So that many times the boisterous laborers in the fields, in the heat of the sun, beguile their pain with rude and carterlike singing. With this the unmannerly countrywoman, that ariseth before day out of sleep to spin and card, defendeth herself and maketh her labor pleasant. This is the most sweet pastime after rain, wind, and tempest unto the miserable mariners. With this do the weary pilgrims comfort themselves in their troublesome and long voyages.*

The "boisterous laborers" of German towns called themselves "mastersingers" and organized choral groups. The most famous of them, Hans Sachs, a cobbler in Nuremberg in the 1500's, was later immortalized in Wagner's opera, *Die Meistersinger.*

But the mastersingers followed directly in the tradition of the thirteenth-century minnesinger. And princely patronage of music went back at least to the twelfth-century court of Eleanor of Aquitaine and its chivalric troubadours. The troubadours themselves, musicians as well as poets, had sung of the great secular subjects, war and love. In sum, the history of music underlines again the important fact that the Renaissance did not break sharply with the past but built on the legacy it had received from the Middle Ages.

----

* Castiglione, *The Courtier,* T. Hoby, trans., modernized (1907), 77.

V: Science

The Place of the Renaissance in the History of Science

Science is a field of human endeavor where the term "Renaissance" must be used with great caution. A scientific revolution did take place in early modern times, but it came in the seventeenth century of Galileo and Newton when the Renaissance had run its course (see Chapter XV). In the history of science the late medieval and Renaissance centuries—the fourteenth, fifteenth, and sixteenth—were a time of preparation. Men of science absorbed, enlarged, criticized, and modified the body of scientific knowledge handed down to them from the Middle Ages, and antiquity. The followers of the old scholastic tradition, the new humanists, and artists and craftsmen of every kind, all contributed to this important work of preparation.

As we saw in Chapter VIII, medieval Scholasticism was by no means anti-scientific. The intellectual discipline of the Schoolmen, their habit of close work, and their enthusiasm for Aristotle made them, in a sense, precursors of the scientific revolution. These Scholastic traditions remained very much alive after the eclipse of Scholasticism toward the close of the Middle Ages. Aristotelian studies continued to be pursued vigorously at two universities in particular: Paris, and Padua, in northern Italy. Meantime, the humanists were steadily increasing the amount of ancient scientific writing available to the scholarly world; Galen, Ptolemy, Archimedes, and others were for the first time translated from Greek into the more accessible Latin.

Humanism, however, also thwarted the advance of science; the worship of classical antiquity tended to put old authorities high on a pedestal, beyond the reach of criticism. Few men of the Renaissance believed it possible to improve on the astronomy taught by Ptolemy during the second century A.D., or on the medicine taught by Galen in the same century. Galen, for example, had advanced the erroneous theory that the blood moved from one side of the heart to the other by passing through invisible pores in the thick wall of tissue separating the two sides of the organ. Actually, as Harvey was to discover in the seventeenth century, the blood gets from

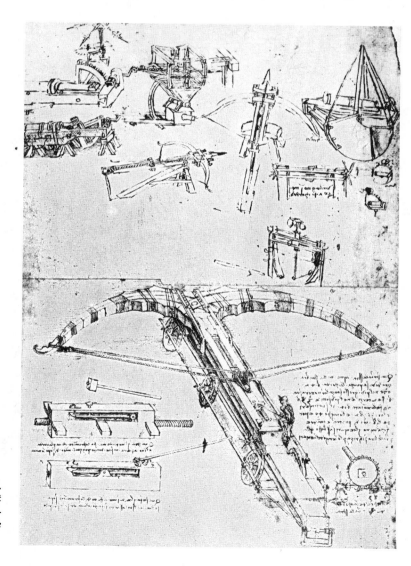

Leonardo da Vinci. Drawing of a giant crossbow and other military machines, from his notebooks.

the one side to the other by circulating through the body and lungs. Galen's theory of invisible pores, however, was enough to keep Leonardo from anticipating Harvey. Leonardo's anatomical studies led him up to the brink of discovery; then he backed away, for he was certain that Galen could not have been wrong.

Leonardo, in fact, illustrates both the shortcomings and the achievements of Renaissance science. On the one hand, he took notes in a hit-or-miss fashion, and in a secretive left-handed writing which must be held up to a mirror to be read. He did not have the modern scientist's concern for the systematic cataloguing of observations and the frequent publication of findings and speculations. On the other hand, Leonardo also showed the real scientific contribution that could be made by the inspired artist and craftsman. Witness his inventiveness: he projected lathes, pumps, war machines, flying machines, and many other contraptions, not all of them workable, to be sure, but all of them highly imaginative. Witness, too, his passionate curiosity for anatomy and proportions, and for almost everything about man and nature. Finally, Leonardo did not always bow before established authority, as he did before Galen. His geological studies convinced him that the earth was far older than the men of his time thought it to be. The Po River, he estimated, must have been flowing for about 200,000 years to wash down the sediments forming its alluvial plain in northern Italy.

Leonardo, then, participated in the major areas of Renaissance scientific activity—technology and invention, anatomy and medicine—with the one exception of astronomy. Our survey of Renaissance science will be centered on these areas, beginning with technology and invention.

Technology and Invention

Most of the advances recorded in the applied sciences during the Renaissance had started during the Middle Ages. An instructive case history is provided by the chain of events leading up to the invention of the printed book. The revolution in book production began when medieval Europeans imported paper from China and found it to be cheaper than the lambskin or sheepskin previously used by copyists. The next step came when engravers, pioneering in the methods later used by Dürer, made woodcuts or copper plates that could produce many copies of the same drawing. Then sentences were added to the cuts or plates to explain the sketches. Finally, almost certainly in the German Rhineland, during the 1440's movable type was devised. Each piece of type was simply a minute bit of engraving; it could be combined with other pieces to form words, sentences, a whole page, and then salvaged to be used over and over again. This crucial invention used to be credited to Gutenberg; he has now become the focus of a scholarly controversy that has partly "debunked" his old heroic reputation.

The new invention soon gained wide popularity. By 1500, Italy alone had seventy-three presses employing movable type. The most famous of them was the Aldine Press in Venice, named for its founder, Aldus Manutius (1450-1515). The Aldine Press won its reputation by selling at reasonable prices scholarly editions of the classics printed in a beautiful type-face which, reportedly, was based on the handwriting of Petrarch. Everywhere the printing press suddenly made both classical and vernacular literature available to large numbers of people who could never have afforded hand-copied manuscripts. Without the perfection of printing, Erasmus might not have become the acknowledged arbiter of European letters. Without it, Luther could not have secured the rapid distribution of his anti-papal tracts, and the Protestant Reformation might not have rent Christian Europe asunder.

Although no other single invention can

be compared with printing on the score of quick and decisive effects, many innovations ultimately had comparable influence. Gunpowder, for example, brought from China to medieval Europe, was used in the fighting of the early 1400's, notably the later campaigns of the Hundred Years' War. The long, slow improvement of firearms and artillery doomed both the feudal knight and the feudal castle, for both were vulnerable to the new weapons. In navigation, as we have seen, the Venetians made galleys swifter, more capacious, and more seaworthy. At the same time important aids to navigation came into general use, particularly the magnetic compass and the sailing charts which, at least for the Mediterranean, established a high level of accuracy. By the close of the fifteenth century, Europeans possessed the equipment needed for the oncoming age of world discovery (see Chapter XIV).

On land, the mining industry scored impressive technological advances. The engineers of the late medieval centuries solved some of the problems of extracting and smelting silver, iron, and other ores. Then, in 1556, a German mining expert published a comprehensive treatise on the practices of the industry. Following the custom of the day, he called himself Agricola, a Latinized version of his German name, Bauer, which means peasant. His treatise, *De Re Metallica* ("all about metals"), was translated from Latin into English in 1912 by a famous American mining engineer and his wife, Mr. and Mrs. Herbert Hoover. Agricola's treatise was an early specimen of those handbooks that are indispensable to the engineer. And its detailed observations on soil structures also made it a pioneer study in geology.

Medicine and Anatomy

Medical knowledge advanced very unevenly during the Renaissance. Though anatomical studies moved ahead, the practical application of this knowledge to suffering humanity lagged, often very badly. Many so-called physicians were outright quacks; many teachers of medicine simply repeated for their classes the demonstrations that Galen had made more than a thousand years before, without attempting to test the validity of his findings. A striking exception to this rule was furnished by the physicians and scholars of the University of Padua. Protected against possible ecclesiastical censorship by the overlordship of Venice, which controlled the city, they maintained a lively tradition of scientific inquiry that presaged the seventeenth-century triumphs of the experimental method.

In 1537, a young Belgian named Vesalius took a teaching post at Padua. Vesalius (1514-1564) repeated the dissections of Galen, but always with an open mind, always on the lookout for errors. Thus, he rejected Galen's notion of invisible pores in the wall of tissue within the heart, because he could not find such pores. In 1543, Vesalius published *De Humanis Corporis Fabrica* (Concerning the Structure of the Human Body). In this great anatomical study he largely confirmed the teachings of older authorities, but he also pointed out some of their shortcomings. He prepared the work with admirable concern for accuracy and detail, and the elaborate woodcuts established a new standard of excellence in scientific illustration.

Astronomy

The year 1543 was a landmark in the history of scientific publication. Not only did it mark the appearance of Vesalius' treatise; it was also the year in which Copernicus launched modern astronomical studies with *De Revolutionibus Orbium Coelestium* (Concerning the Revolutions of Heavenly Bodies). Born in Poland, of German extraction, Copernicus (1473-1543) studied law and medicine at Padua and other Italian universities, spent thirty years as canon of a cathedral near Danzig, and made his real career in mathematics and astronomy. His scientific work led him to attack the traditional hypothesis of the *geocentric* (earth-centered) universe derived from Ptolemy and other astronomers of antiquity. In its place, he advanced the revolutionary new hypothesis of the *heliocentric* (sun-centered) universe.

The concept of the geocentric universe generally accepted in the sixteenth century included an elaborate system of spheres. Around the stationary earth there revolved some eighty spheres, each, as it were, a separate sky containing some of the heavenly bodies, each moving on an invisible circular path, each transparent so that we mortals could see the spheres beyond it. This imaginative and symmetrical picture of the universe had already come under attack before the time of Copernicus. Now and again scientists had had trouble making it agree with the observable behavior of heavenly bodies. Copernicus used both these earlier criticisms and his own computations to arrive at the heliocentric concept. He prefaced this explanation to *De Revolutionibus:*

> . . . What moved me to consider another way of reckoning the motions of the heavenly spheres was nothing else than my realisation that Mathematicians were not agreed about the matter of their research. . . . In setting out the motions of the Sun and Moon and of the five other planets they did not in each case employ the same principles, assumptions and demonstrations of apparent revolutions and motions. For some used concentric circles only, others eccentrics and epicycles, by which, none

the less, they were not able to fully arrive at what they sought. . . .

> And so after long consideration of the uncertainty of the mathematical traditions about the inferring of the motions of the spheres, it began to vex me that no more certain system of the motions of the machine of the world . . . could be agreed upon by the philosophers. . . .

> I . . . began to think about the mobility of the earth. And although it seemed an absurd opinion, . . . I discovered by much and long observation, that if the motions of the rest of the planets are compared with the motion of the earth, . . . not only do their appearances follow therefrom, but the system moreover so connects the orders and sizes both of the planets and of their orbits, and indeed the whole heaven, that in no part of it can anything be moved without bringing to confusion the rest of the parts and the whole universe.[*]

Once Copernicus had reversed the roles of the sun and the earth, his universe retained many Ptolemaic characteristics. Its heavens were still filled with spheres revolving along their invisible orbits. Only they now moved about a stationary sun, instead of the stationary earth, and Copernican astronomy required only thirty-four of them, not eighty. The revolution in astronomy begun by Copernicus did not reach its culmination for a hundred and fifty years. The *circular* orbits of Copernicus had to yield to *elliptical* orbits; the scheme of thirty-four spheres had to be modified; and a theory explaining the forces that kept the universe together had to be put forward. And all these developments had to await the genius of Galileo and Newton, and the detailed observations made possible by the invention of the telescope.

[*] Quoted in F. S. Taylor, *A Short History of Science and Scientific Thought* (New York, 1949), 83-84.

VI: Religion

The Relationship between the Renaissance and Religion

Although Copernicus dedicated his great book to the pope himself, Christendom did not welcome a theory that overturned the old orthodox view of the earth-centered and man-centered universe. By the time Copernicus published, however, western Christendom was split into the warring factions of Catholic and Protestant. To what extent was the Renaissance responsible for the shattering religious crisis of the Reformation? There is no simple answer to this question. The next chapter will examine in more detail the reasons for the Protestant revolt; here, meantime, we may suggest a few conclusions about the relationship between the Renaissance and religion.

First, the Renaissance did not make the Reformation *inevitable*. It is an oversimplification to suppose that the religious individualism of Luther arose directly out of the more general individualism of the Renaissance. If we look back over the checkered culture of the age, we do find some elements that are hard to reconcile with traditional Christian values. These are materialism, self-indulgence, power politics, and the other elements sometimes grouped under the label "Counter-Renaissance." If pushed to extremes, they could indeed become anti-Christian; but they were seldom pushed to extremes. Even the most ruthless *condottieri* of politics and business, men like Caesar Borgia and the Fuggers, remained nominal Christians. Also a pronounced anti-clerical like Machiavelli reserved his most stinging criticism for the pope's claim to temporal authority, not his claim to ecclesiastical supremacy. And, in rebuking the

pope for political maneuvering, he was following the example of that profound Christian, Dante.

Second, the most characteristic intellectual movement of the Renaissance—humanism—did not propose to replace the traditional Christian values of the Middle Ages with a whole new set of values. On a lower level, much of the fun in the *Decameron* derives from that time-honored object of satire, often lampooned in the Middle Ages, the misbehaving cleric. On a higher level, men like Pico and Erasmus proposed to enrich or purify Christianity; they did not intend to subvert it. Erasmus, in particular, the most representative thinker of humanism, was too strongly attached to Catholicism and too moderate in temperament to be a revolutionary.

Third and finally, a religious crisis was gathering during the Renaissance, but that crisis was, so to speak, more internal than external. That is, the Church was only to a limited extent the innocent victim of outside forces operating beyond its control, like the challenge presented to its old international dominion by the new national monarchies. If the Church of the 1400's had been strong and healthy, it might have met such external challenges successfully. Except in Spain (see above, p. 412), the Church was neither strong nor healthy.

The Condition of the Church

The Renaissance Church as a whole exhibited a low moral tone, although many honorable exceptions to the prevailing laxity and backwardness could be found. Priests were often illiterate and immoral, ill prepared for the effective exercise of their parochial responsibilities. Many bishops—following good medieval precedent, it must be admitted—behaved as politicians, not as churchmen. Perhaps the worst shortcomings existed at the top, in the papacy itself. In the fourteenth and early fifteenth centuries, the papacy experienced a series of crises—the Babylonian Captivity, the Great Schism, and the Conciliar Movement (see Chapter VIII). It emerged from the ordeal with its power reinvigorated, notably by its victory over the reformers who sought to make church councils a check against unlimited papal absolutism. The triple crisis, however, had gravely damaged the spiritual prestige of the office.

The popes of the High Renaissance did little to repair the damage. From Nicholas V (1447-1455) through Leo X (1513-1521), the See of Peter was occupied by a series of men who scored many brilliant worldly successes. We have already encountered the Borgia pope, Alexander VI, and Julius II (see above, p. 419); other popes of the period were cultivated humanists and generous patrons of art and learning. The modern world is indebted to these popes for the Vatican Library, the Sistine Chapel, and the beginning of the Basilica of St. Peter's. Yet their magnificence cost immense sums of money and increased the burden of ecclesiastical taxation, and with it increased the resentment that higher taxes usually arouse. Their indifference to their spiritual functions enfeebled the Church at a time when it needed firm and dedicated control. The Church was ruled by connoisseurs and *condottieri* when it needed reformers.

Intellectually, too, the clergy were losing the vitality they had possessed in the age of Abelard and Aquinas. Some of the monks and friars on university faculties hardly qualified as teachers; they blindly defended a decadent Scholasticism against the new humanist studies. These reactionary educators provoked the most blistering satire of the Renaissance, *The Letters of Obscure Men*. The story began when John Reuchlin

(1455-1522), a German humanist, studied with Pico della Mirandola at Florence. Catching Pico's enthusiasm for comparative religious studies, Reuchlin learned Hebrew in order to ponder the great books of Judaism. On his return to Germany, Reuchlin aroused the wrath of theological faculties by suggesting that a knowledge of Hebrew and of the sacred Jewish writings might enable a man to be a better-informed Christian. Arraigned in an ecclesiastical court, Reuchlin assembled in his defense testimonials from leading humanists, *The Letters of Eminent Men*. Then, in 1516 and 1517, a couple of his friends published *The Letters of Obscure Men*, supposedly exchanged between Reuchlin's clerical opponents but actually a hoax designed to laugh the opposition out of court. One of the "obscure men," for instance, related the experience he had had in a Roman tavern:

For you must know that we were lately sitting in an inn, having our supper, and were eating eggs, when on opening one, I saw that there was a young chicken within.

This I showed to a comrade; whereupon

Michelangelo, "Moses," in S. Pietro in Vincoli, Rome; commissioned by Pope Julius II for his tomb.

quoth he to me, 'Eat it up speedily, before the taverner sees it, for if he mark it, you will have to pay for a fowl.'

In a trice I gulped down the egg, chicken and all.

And then I remembered that it was Friday!

Whereupon I said to my crony, 'You have made me commit a mortal sin, in eating flesh on the sixth day of the week!'

But he averred that it was not a mortal sin— nor even a venial one, seeing that such a chickling is accounted merely as an egg, until it is born.

Then I departed, and thought the matter over.

And by the Lord, I am in a mighty quandary, and know not what to do.

It seemeth to me that these young fowls in eggs are flesh, because their substance is formed and fashioned into the limbs and body of an animal, and possesseth a vital principle.

It is different in the case of grubs in cheese, and such-like, because grubs are accounted fish, as I learnt from a physician who is also skilled in Natural Philosophy.

Most earnestly do I entreat you to resolve the question that I have propounded. For if you hold that the sin is mortal, then, I would fain get shrift here, ere I return to Germany.[*]

Never had the futility of theological hair-splitting come in for more withering scorn; but Reuchlin still lost his case.

Proposals for Reform

Dedicated Christians, both from the clergy and the laity, were aware that the Church needed a thorough cleansing. But their proposals for reform were either ignored or else actively combated by the popes of the High Renaissance. Thus the influence of the ecclesiastical renovation initiated by Queen Isabella and Cardinal Ximenes was restricted to Spanish territories. Thus fresh attempts within the secular hierarchy to increase the powers of representative church councils again failed in the face of papal opposition.

Meantime, a deeper transformation of

[*] Adapted from *Epistolae Obscurorum Virorum*, F. G. Stokes, ed. (New Haven, 1925), 445-447.

existing Christianity was implicit in the activities of the association called the Brethren of the Common Life. Founded in the Low Countries about 1375, the Brethren followed a spiritual discipline resembling that of the monastic organizations. More than discipline, however, they emphasized service to one's fellow men as a means whereby individuals might attempt to realize in practice the high ideals of Christianity. They ran schools, in one of which Erasmus received his early education. Erasmus himself reflected the goals of the Brethren in his "philosophy of Christ," with its belief that men should be guided in their daily lives by the example and the teaching of Jesus. This kind of appeal was essentially quietist, directed to the high-minded layman rather than to the Church. While it exerted a profound influence on such individuals as Erasmus, its total impact on the Christian community was limited.

Quite different in character was the turbulent current of reform identified with Savonarola (1452-1498). A Dominican friar, Savonarola preached in Florence and led the sort of moral crusade that we call puritanical. He won the favor of the Medici through the influence of Pico della Mirandola; his eloquent sermons and reputed gift of predicting future events soon made him the most popular preacher in Florence. Savonarola spared no clerics in his strictures on un-Christian conduct:

You Christians should always have the Gospel with you, I do not mean the book, but the spirit, for if you do not possess the spirit of grace and yet carry with you the whole book, of what advantage is it to you? And again, all the more foolish are they who carry round their necks Breviaries, notes, tracts and writings, until they look like pedlars going to a fair. Charity does not consist in the writing of papers. The true books of Christ are the Apostles and saints, and true reading consists in imitating their lives. But in these days men are like books made by the Devil. They speak against pride and ambition and yet they are immersed in them up to their eyes. They preach chastity and maintain concubines. They enjoin fasting and partake of splendid feasts. . . . Only look to-day at the prelates. They are tied to earthly vanities. They love them. The cure of souls is no longer their chief concern. . . . In the Primitive Church the chalices were made of wood and the prelates of gold—to-day—chalices of gold, prelates of wood! *

He particularly abominated the reigning pope, Alexander VI, whom he cursed for "a devil" and "a monster" presiding over what he labeled a "ribald" and "harlot" Church.

In the political confusion following the death of Lorenzo the Magnificent (1492), Savonarola rapidly gained power and prestige in Florence. He attracted many enthusiastic supporters, among them Botticelli and Michelangelo. By 1497, he was virtual dictator of the republic and organized troops of boys and girls to tour the city, collect all "vanities," from cosmetics to pagan books and paintings, and

---

* Quoted by Piero Misciatelli, *Savonarola* (New York, 1930), 60-61.

burn them on public bonfires. This hysterical pitch of zeal could not be sustained for long, however. Alexander VI excommunicated Savonarola, and his popular following began to disperse, especially after he had failed in his promise to induce a miracle. He would demonstrate his divine inspiration by going unscathed through the ordeal by fire, but his political opponents secured the cancellation of the spectacle at the last moment. Within a short time, Savonarola was condemned for heresy; on May 23, 1498, he was hanged and his body was burnt.

Savonarola perished not only by the hands of his political and ecclesiastical enemies but also through his own uncompromising violence. He did not know what a truly great reformer would have known: that morals could not be restored overnight. Like most extreme puritans, Savonarola was more a fanatic than a saint; he was in a sense too unworldly to survive. But the Church that he sought to purge was too worldly to survive without undergoing the major crisis of the Reformation.

VII: Conclusion: The Renaissance Style

It is not easy to define the style of an era as complex as the Renaissance. No definition in fact can take in all its currents and cross-currents or encompass such extraordinarily different personalities as Erasmus and Savonarola. No single man of the time, no single masterpiece of art or literature, was fully typical of the Renaissance. And yet there is something about most of its great men and most of its great books, paintings, and sculpture that sets them apart from the great figures and works of other ages. Humanists like Petrarch, Pico, and Erasmus do differ from St. Thomas Aquinas; Caesar Borgia, Lorenzo the Mag-

nificent, and Louis XI of France have very little in common with Louis IX; the sculpture of Michelangelo does not resemble that of Chartres; St. Peter's belongs to an era unlike that of Mont-Saint-Michel or Notre Dame. The men of the Renaissance lived in a world no longer medieval but not yet fully modern. Their changing values and ideals were presented most sympathetically and disarmingly in a dialogue on manners published in 1528, *The Courtier* by Castiglione.

A solid book of etiquette may often reveal much about a way of life. Castiglione knew his subject inside out; he had spent years on diplomatic missions and at the highly civilized court of Urbino. He begins his delineation of the ideal courtier with a group of traits differing very little from those commended in the paladins of medieval chivalry:

I will have this our Courtier to be a gentleman born and of a good house. For it is a great deal less dispraise for him that is not born a gentleman to fail in the acts of virtue than for a gentleman.

I will have him by nature to have not only a wit and a comely shape of person and countenance, but also a certain grace, and, as they say, a hue, that shall make him at the first sight acceptable and loving unto who so beholdeth him.

I judge the principal and true profession of a Courtier ought to be in feats of arms, the which above all I will have him to practise lively.[*]

The chivalry of Castiglione, however, never gets out of hand; it is restrained by the sense of balance and grasp of reality that we have already found in some of the humanists. In love, the perfect gentleman should adore in his lady "no less the beauty of the mind than of the body." In duels and private quarrels, he should be far more moderate than the medieval knight was ever supposed to be. He should excel in sport, like the knight of old, should hunt, wrestle, swim, "play at tennis." Then, again, Castiglione sounds the note of balance:

Therefore will I have our Courtier to descend many times to more easy and pleasant exercises. And to avoid envy and to keep company pleasantly with every man, let him do whatsoever other men do.[†]

The courtier should also receive a good education

... in those studies which they call Humanity, and to have not only the understanding of the Latin tongue, but also of the Greek, because of the many and sundry things that with

great excellency are written in it. Let him much exercise himself in poets, and no less in orators and historiographers, and also in writing both rhyme and prose, and especially in this our vulgar tongue.[*]

Here in *The Courtier* once again we encounter the celebrated Renaissance concept of the "universal man" that we have already met in the writings of Pico and Rabelais and in the wide-ranging careers of Giotto, Leonardo, and Michelangelo. Castiglione is both reviving the old classical ideal of the well-rounded individual, "the sound mind in the sound body," and is anticipating modern champions of the humanities and a liberal education.

Finally, when Castiglione praises beauty, he puts into words more eloquently than any of his contemporaries the style of the Renaissance:

Behold the state of this great engine of the world, which God created for the health and preservation of everything that was made: The heaven round beset with so many heavenly lights; and in the middle the Earth environed with the elements and upheld with the very weight of itself.... These things among themselves have such force by the knitting together of an order so necessarily framed that, with altering them any one jot, they should all be loosed and the world would decay. They have also such beauty and comeliness that all the wits men have can not imagine a more beautiful matter.

Think now of the shape of man, which may be called a little world, in whom every parcel of his body is seen to be necessarily framed by art and not by hap, and then the form altogether most beautiful.... Leave Nature, and come to art.... Pillars and great beams uphold high buildings and palaces, and yet are they no less pleasureful unto the eyes of the beholders than profitable to the buildings.... Besides other things, therefore, it giveth a great praise to the world in saying that it is beautiful. It is praised in saying the beautiful heaven, beautiful earth, beautiful sea, beautiful rivers, beautiful woods, trees, gardens, beautiful cities, beautiful churches, houses, armies. In conclusion, this comely and

---

[*] Adapted from Castiglione, *The Courtier*, T. Hoby, trans., modernized (1907), 21, 23, 26.
[†] *Ibid.*, 35.

---

[*] *Ibid.*, 70.

holy beauty is a wondrous setting out of everything. And it may be said that good and beautiful be after a sort one self thing. . . .*

A medieval man might also have coupled the good and the beautiful, but he would

---
* *Ibid.*, 348-349.

have stressed the good, the mysterious ways in which God led man to righteousness. Medieval man had a vision of God's world. The age of Leonardo and of humanism, which Castiglione interpreted so movingly, had a vision not only of God's world but also of nature's world and man's world.

Reading Suggestions
on the Renaissance

(Asterisk indicates paperbound edition.)

GENERAL ACCOUNTS

W. K. Ferguson, *The Renaissance* (Holt, 1940). A brief introduction by a sound scholar.

See also the general accounts listed for Chapter X.

INTERPRETATIONS

W. K. Ferguson, *The Renaissance in Historical Thought: Five Centuries of Interpretation* (Houghton Mifflin, 1948). A useful and stimulating monograph.

F. Chabod, *Machiavelli and the Renaissance* (Bowes and Bowes, 1958). The chapter entitled "The Concept of the Renaissance" and the bibliography together furnish a meaty up-to-date survey of the problem of interpretation.

J. Burckhardt, *The Civilization of the Renaissance in Italy*, 2 vols. (*Harper Torchbooks, 1958). A classic statement of the old view that the Renaissance was unique.

J. A. Symonds, *Renaissance in Italy* (Modern Library). Another older interpretation.

L. Olschki, *The Genius of Italy* (Cornell Univ. Press, 1954). Essays on many aspects of the Renaissance.

LITERATURE, THOUGHT, AND RELIGION

G. Highet, *The Classical Tradition: Greek and Roman Influences on Western Literature* (*Oxford Univ. Press Galaxy Books, 1949). A lively and scholarly study.

H. O. Taylor, *Thought and Expression in the Sixteenth Century*, rev. ed. (Macmillan, 1930). A sound and suggestive work.

F. de Sanctis, *History of Italian Literature*, Vol. I (Harcourt, Brace, 1931). A standard account.

P. O. Kristeller, *Studies in Renaissance Thought and Letters* (Edizioni di Storia e Letteratura, 1956). Includes some thoughtful essays on humanism.

J. Huizinga, *Erasmus and the Age of the Reformation* (*Harper Torchbooks, 1957). Excellent analysis by a distinguished Dutch scholar.

N. A. Robb, *Neoplatonism of the Italian Renaissance*. (Allen & Unwin, 1953). A good solid study.

A. Hyma, *The Christian Renaissance* (Appleton-Century-Crofts, 1924). A study of an aspect of the Renaissance often overlooked.

P. Misciatelli, *Savonarola* (Appleton-Century-Crofts, 1930). A sound biography of the Florentine reformer.

THE FINE ARTS

H. Wölfflin, *Classic Art: The Great Masters of the Italian Renaissance* (Phaidon, 1952). New edition of an old and celebrated work.

B. Berenson, *The Italian Painters of the Renaissance* (*Meridian). Essays by one of the foremost authorities on the subject.

F. Antal, *Florentine Painting and its Social Background* (Kegan, Paul, 1948). An attempt to relate art to economic and social currents.

E. Panofsky, *Studies in Iconology: Humanistic Themes in the Art of the Renaissance* (Oxford Univ. Press, 1939). By a distinguished modern scholar.

K. M. Clark, *Leonardo da Vinci* (*Penguin Books, 1958). A learned and lively analysis of Leonardo as an artist.

E. MacCurdy, *The Mind of Leonardo da Vinci* (Dodd, Mead, 1928). Standard work by an expert on Leonardo.

O. Benesch, *The Art of the Renaissance in Northern Europe* (Harvard Univ. Press, 1945). A study of the interrelations of artistic, religious, and intellectual history.

E. Panofsky, *The Life and Art of Albrecht Dürer* (Princeton Univ. Press, 1955). Standard work on the great German artist.

R. Wittkower, *Architectural Principles in the Age of Humanism*, 2nd ed. (A. Tiranti, 1952). A notable attempt to examine the connections between humanism and architecture.

MUSIC

P. H. Láng, *Music in Western Civilization* (Norton, 1941). A detailed general history endeavoring to illuminate the relationship between music and other historical currents.

C. Gray, *The History of Music*, 2nd ed., (Knopf, 1947). Brief, opinionated, and lively survey.

E. J. Dent, *Music of the Renaissance in Italy* (British Academy, 1935). Informative lecture by a great authority.

SCIENCE

H. Butterfield, *The Origins of Modern Science, 1300-1800,* rev. ed. (Macmillan, 1957). A work of major significance; rather disparages the contribution of the Renaissance to science.

A. R. Hall, *The Scientific Revolution, 1500-1800* (*Beacon, 1956). A solid account.

G. Sarton, *Six Wings: Men of Science in the Renaissance* (Univ. of Indiana Press, 1956). By a distinguished historian of science.

J. B. Conant, *Science and Common Sense* (Yale Univ. Press, 1951). The origins of modern science reviewed by the notable chemist and educator.

F. S. Taylor, *A Short History of Science and Scientific Thought* (Norton, 1949). A useful introductory manual.

A. C. Crombie, *Medieval and Early Modern Science*, 2 vols. (° Anchor). A good brief account.

A. Wolff, *A History of Science, Technology, and Philosophy in the Sixteenth and Seventeenth Centuries*, 2 vols. (° Harper Torchbooks, 1959). A standard detailed treatment.

L. Thorndike, *Science and Thought in the Fifteenth Century* (Columbia Univ. Press, 1929). Important study by a major historian of science.

A. Castiglioni, *A History of Medicine*, 2nd ed. (Knopf, 1947). An excellent manual.

SOURCES

E. Cassirer and others, *The Renaissance Philosophy of Man* (° Phoenix Books). Most useful selections from the writings of Petrarch, Pico, Valla, and other humanists, with helpful editorial comments.

Erasmus, *The Praise of Folly*, H. H. Hudson, trans. (Princeton Univ., 1941).

Three Renaissance Classics: Machiavelli's Prince, Castiglione's Courtier, More's Utopia (Scribner's, 1953).

Rabelais, *Gargantua and Pantagruel* (many editions). The most admired translation is by Urquhart.

E. MacCurdy, ed., *The Notebooks of Leonardo da Vinci*, 2 vols. (Reynal and Hitchcock), and A. H. Popham, ed., *The Drawings of Leonardo da Vinci* (Reynal and Hitchcock). The fascinating records left by the great artist-scientist.

Epistolae Obscurorum Virorum ("Letters of Obscure Men"), F. G. Stokes, ed. (Chatto and Windus, 1909). A classic of humanist satire.

HISTORICAL FICTION

D. Merejkowski, *The Romance of Leonardo* (Modern Library). By all odds the best work of fiction treating the culture of the Italian Renaissance; highly romantic, yet based on extensive scholarship.

The Protestant Reformation

CHAPTER XII

I: Protestant Origins—Luther

I F THE PAST means anything at all to us, it must engage our feelings. We hate or love, or more mildly like or dislike, Socrates or Alexander or Caesar, Greek or Egyptian art. But until we reach the subject of this chapter, most of us westerners are not fully committed by our birth and upbringing to one side or another. With the issues between Protestantism and Catholicism it is different. Complete detachment is impossible, even for the historian. The conventional titles he must use commit him. For the Protestant, the phrase "Protestant *Reformation*" comes naturally; for the Catholic, "Protestant *Revolt*." Nor can the modern secularist truly say he belongs to neither side and feels the same way toward each. In the western tradition, such non-Christians almost inevitably feel that Protestantism, if only because it broke up medieval Catholic unity, is somehow nearer to them, somehow prepared the way for them. Inevitably, there are still alive the exaggerations, indeed the slanders, that emerged from the fierce partisan struggles of the times, notions such as that Luther led a revolt against the Church so that he, a monk, might marry; that the Catholic clergy actually *sold* salvation; that Henry VIII of England broke with the Pope so that he might marry Anne Boleyn; and many, many more.

Opposite. THE EMPEROR CHARLES V, *by Titian (1477-1576), Venetian (see above, p. 458); painted in 1548; The Prado, Madrid. Titian has made his subject appear suitably majestic without, however, glossing over the weak features of the Habsburg face.*

479

The End of Medieval Religious Unity

Protestant beginnings can be precisely dated, in the sense, for instance, that one can date the beginning of the American Revolution with the battles of Lexington and Concord, April 19, 1775. The great date is October 31, 1517, when the Augustinian monk Martin Luther nailed his Ninety-Five Theses to the door of the court church at Wittenberg in the German state of Saxony. The actual term "protestant" dates from April 19, 1529, when a group of German princes professing Lutheran doctrines lodged a formal "protest" at the Diet of Spires against the annulment of an earlier imperial decree. This decree had promised that a general council would consider the whole problem that Luther's activities had set. But of course the origins of the American Revolution go well back of the battle at Concord, and the origins of the Protestant movement go well back of Luther's Ninety-Five Theses. As we saw in Chapter VIII, the medieval Catholic Church had faced many reform movements—the Cluniac, the Cistercian, the Franciscan, and, in the century or so before Luther, movements like those of Wiclif and Hus which had anticipated Protestant doctrines and had almost ended by setting up separate, or *schismatic,* religious bodies. The Conciliar Movement of the fifteenth century, though it failed to set general councils above the pope, brought into open discussion the question of papal authority.

The Protestant Reformation was, in fact, a major social, economic, and intellectual revolution. Major leaders such as Luther and Calvin, let alone Henry VIII of England, can hardly have intended such a revolution; indeed, it is important for us to note that these leaders did not conceive themselves as initiators, as beginning *new* churches, but as going back to the true old Church.

The Reformation came in a time of great religious ferment, of economic change, of violence, uncertainty, even a sense of doom —in short, in times well described by the phrase of the distinguished Dutch historian Huizinga as "the autumn of the Middle Ages." Men everywhere were seeking something, characteristically not usually specific political or economic reforms, but something less readily definable or understandable by most of us today—spiritual salvation, renewal, the better world of Christian promise. Luther, notably, appealed from what he held to be existing evil to a possible—indeed, in men's souls already real—good. Hence the Lutheran appeal from *works,* from the conventions of established things, to *faith,* to something not evident to the outward eye, but there, inside us all, if we could but see it. Hence, too, much of the attractiveness to the religious temperament of many Protestant movements; the Protestants appealed from the spotted reality to the promise of a better future, in heaven but also on earth.

Although Luther, when he posted his theses, had no clear intention of setting up a separate religious body, he did live to see a church, now called the Lutheran, organized outside the Catholic communion. The Lutheran was but the first of such Protestant churches. Within the very generation that had seen the posting of the Ninety-Five Theses, there were organized dozens of churches or sects or denominations—Anglican, Calvinist, Anabaptist, and many others. The medieval unity of Catholic Christendom had given way to the multiplicity of churches we know so well that we often think such multiplicity "natural." In this country, churches, sometimes even Roman Catholic churches, have their denomination duly posted on signboards in front of them. In the Middle Ages this labeling would of course have been inconceivable, not so much because most people could not read as because no such labeling was necessary.

Luther and the Ninety-Five Theses

Martin Luther (1483-1546) was a professor of divinity at the University of Wittenberg. When he posted his theses in 1517, he had recently experienced a great religious awakening, in effect a conversion, after a long period of spiritual despair. Luther's parents were peasants; his father became a miner and in time a prosperous investor in a mining enterprise. He sent Martin to study law, but in 1505 the young man had a shattering experience. Caught in a severe thunderstorm, the terrified Luther prayed to Saint Anne for help and pledged himself to become a monk. He joined the order of Augustinian canons in fulfillment of his pledge and then soon found himself in a major personal religious crisis.

Luther was convinced that he was a lost soul, a sinner without hope of salvation. None of Luther's good works, neither the monastic discipline of his order nor his pilgrimage in 1510 to Christian shrines in Rome, could free him of the gnawing feeling that he could not attain God's grace and was destined for hell. Finally, a wise confessor advised the desperate young man to study the Bible and to become a teacher of scripture. Through his reading in the Epistles of St. Paul and the writings of St. Augustine, Luther at last found a positive answer to his anxiety. The answer was that man should have faith in God, faith in the possibility of his own salvation. This answer had indeed long been the answer of the Roman Church; what later separated Luther doctrinally from this Church was his emphasis on *faith alone, to the exclusion of works.*

Fortified by his intense personal conviction of the great importance of faith, Luther questioned Catholic practices which in his view were abuses and tended to corrupt or weaken faith. He cast his questions in the form of the Ninety-Five Theses, written in Latin and in the manner of medieval Scholasticism as a challenge to academic debate. A casual observer who saw the manuscript on the door of the Wittenberg church might well have thought that here was another professor "sounding off." Yet this apparently academic exercise in Latin was the trigger-pull for revolution.

The specific abuse that Luther sought to prove un-Christian in the Ninety-Five Theses was what he called the "sale" of indulgences, and in particular, the activities of a talented ecclesiastical fund-raiser named Tetzel. Basically, Tetzel was conducting a "campaign" or "drive" for voluntary contributions of money to help fill the treasury of a great institution, an institution which like the state possessed taxing powers, but which like many modern states could not in fact extend those taxing powers to keep up with the rising costs of an era of inflation and luxurious living. Tetzel was raising money to rebuild the great basilica of

Martin Luther, by Cranach (1521).

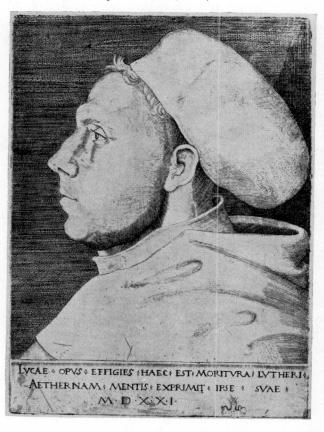

St. Peter's in Rome, and he had papal authorization for his campaign.

The theory of indulgences concerned the remission of the punishment of sins. Only God can forgive a sin, but the repentant sinner also has to undergo punishment on earth in the form of penance and after death in purgatory, where sinners repentant on earth atone by temporary but painful punishment for their sins and are prepared for heaven. Indulgences did not assure the forgiveness of sins, according to the theory advanced by the medieval Schoolmen, but they could remit penance and part or all of the punishment in purgatory. The Church claimed authority to grant such remission by drawing on the Treasury of Merit, a storehouse of surplus good works accumulated by the holy activities of Christ, the Virgin, and the saints. Only the priest could secure for a layman a draft, as it were, on this heavenly treasury. The use of the word "sale" in connection with indulgences was a form of propaganda useful for the Protestants; the Catholics insist that indulgence was "granted" by the priest, and any monetary contribution thereupon made by the recipient was a free-will offering. The theory of indulgences, we may note, is of great theological subtlety. It is not a theory scientifically verifiable.

The doctrine of indulgences was thus a complex matter, too complex for the ordinary layman to grasp completely. To the man in the street in sympathy with the reformers, it must have looked as though a sinner could obtain not only remission of punishment but also forgiveness of sin if only he secured enough indulgences. Men like Tetzel, by making extravagant claims for the power of their indulgences, strengthened this popular feeling. Luther objected not only to Tetzel's perversion of indulgences but also to the whole doctrine behind them. He phrased his objections with great vehemence in the Ninety-Five Theses:

20. The pope by his plenary remission of all penalties does not understand the remission of all penalties absolutely, but only of those imposed by himself.

21. Therefore those preachers of indulgences are in error who allege that through the indulgences of the pope a man is freed from every penalty.

22. For he remits to souls in purgatory no penalty which they had been bound, according to the canons, to pay in this life.

23. If any complete remission of penalties can be given to anyone it is sure that it can be given only to the most perfect; that is, to very few.

24. And therefore it follows that the greater part of the people is deceived by this indiscriminate and liberal promising of freedom from penalty.*

At the highest level of formal theological thought, Luther's quarrel with his ecclesiastical superiors was over one of the oldest and most abiding tensions of Christian thought, the tension between faith and good works (see Chapter IV). Faith is inward and emotional belief, and good works are the *outward* demonstration of that belief by doing good deeds, by partaking of the sacraments, and by submitting to the discipline of penances. Indulgences, certainly to the ordinary believer, permitted men to secure extra good works by drawing on those stored up in the Treasury of Merit. Now Christian practice usually insists on the need for *both* faith and good works. But at times of crisis some men pursue one extreme, others the other. In the years of crisis immediately after the posting of the Ninety-Five Theses, the challenged papal party stiffened into a resistance that in turn drove the Lutherans into further resistance. Moreover, Luther's own increasing hostility to things-as-they-were in his Germany drove him to emphasize things-as-they-ought-to-be—that is, drove him to minimize, and at his most excited moments to deny, the uses of the outward, the visible, the here-and-now which is works, earthly ecclesiastical organization, priestly ways of doing things; and to insist

* *Documents of the Christian Church*, Henry Bettenson, ed. (New York, 1947), 265.

CHAPTER XII

on the inward, the spiritual, the Church invisible which is faith.

Luther's Revolt

In Luther's personal spiritual struggle, as we have seen, faith had helped him immensely, and good works had helped him not at all. In the Ninety-Five Theses, he did not attack all works, but only those he felt to be wrong:

43. Christians are to be taught that to give to the poor or to lend to the needy is a better work than the purchase of pardons.
44. And that because through a work of charity, charity is increased and a man advances in goodness; whereas through pardons there is no advance in goodness but merely an increased freedom from penalty.*

The theses, however, as our earlier quotation from them shows, put great stress on the abuses, and Luther made some very harsh statements about the pope. Soon, in the rapid march of events, Luther took a more extreme position on works: men are saved by *faith alone.* Soon, he was driven to deny that the priest is at all necessary—that is, to the doctrine of the priesthood of all true believers, or, in our vulgar American phrase, the doctrine of "every man his own priest."

The Roman Church quickly sensed the high importance of the issues that Luther had raised. In 1518, at Augsburg, Luther was summoned before a papal legate, Cardinal Cajetan, and was directed to recant some of his propositions on indulgences; Luther defied the legate. In 1519, at Leipzig, a learned theologian, John Eck, taxed Luther in debate with disobeying the authoritative findings of popes and church councils. Luther denied that popes and councils were necessarily authoritative and, carrying his revolt further, explicitly declared adherence to some of Hus' teachings. These teachings had been declared

* *Ibid.,* 267.

heretical by the Council of Constance. In 1520, Luther brought his defiance to its highest pitch by publishing a pamphlet, *The Appeal to the Christian Nobility of the German Nation,* which stated in part:

There has been a fiction by which the Pope, bishops, priests, and monks are called the 'spiritual estate'; princes, lords, artisans, and peasants are the 'temporal estate.' This is an artful lie and hypocritical invention, but let no one be made afraid by it, and that for this reason: that all Christians are truly of the spiritual estate, and there is no difference among them, save of office. As St. Paul says (1 Cor. xii), we are all one body, though each member does its own work so as to serve the others. This is because we have one baptism, one Gospel, one faith, and are all Christians alike; for baptism, Gospel, and faith, these alone make spiritual and Christian people.*

Luther's adherence to justification by faith had now led him to deny totally the central Catholic doctrine of works, that only the priest had the God-given power to secure for the layman remission of punishment for sin. In *The Appeal to the Christian Nobility* he swept aside the distinction between clergy and laity and declared the priesthood of all believers. The complete break between the rebel and the Church was now at hand. Late in 1520, Pope Leo X (1513-1521) issued a bull condemning Luther's teachings; Luther burnt the bull. In 1521, Luther was excommunicated and made an outlaw, the political equivalent of being excommunicated. The Emperor Charles V and the imperial diet passed the sentence of outlawry in a most dramatic session at Worms. Luther was asked, once again, if he would recant. His reply contained his most famous words:

Your Imperial Majesty and Your Lordships demand a simple answer. Here it is, plain and unvarnished. Unless I am convicted of error by the testimony of Scripture or (since I put not trust in the unsupported authority of Pope or of councils, since it is plain that they have often erred and often contradicted them-

* *Documents,* 274.

selves) by manifest reasoning I stand convicted by the Scriptures to which I have appealed, and my conscience is taken captive by God's word, I cannot and will not recant anything, for to act against our conscience is neither safe for us, nor open to us.

Hier stehe ich. Ich kann nicht anders. Gott helff mir. Amen. [On this I take my stand. I can do no other. God help me. Amen.] [*]

The empire and the papacy took their drastic actions in vain. Luther was already gathering a substantial following and becoming a national hero. He had the protection of the ruler of his own German state, the Elector Frederick the Wise of Saxony (1463-1525), and was soon to secure the backing of other princes. In the next few years he translated the Bible into vigorous and effective German and remodeled the church in Saxony according to his own views. His revolt was a success.

The Reasons
for Luther's Success

More than theology was at issue in Luther's revolt. The Catholic Church that Luther attacked was, as many Catholic historians grant, at the time in one of its more worldly states. Especially in its center at Rome, it had come under the influence of the half-pagan Renaissance. New wealth had come to Italy, and new fashions of good living. The papacy, triumphant over the councils, had been drawn into Italian politics (see Chapter X), and the Rome Luther visited in his younger days was a shocking spectacle of intrigue, display, and corruption. Some part of Luther's success lies in the fact that he was attacking practices revolting to decent men.

There is a second great reason for his success: in the name of good Germans he was attacking the practices of Italians and Italianate Germans. Tetzel was in the eyes of Luther and his followers not only extend-

[*] *Ibid.*, 285.

ing an abuse theologically and morally outrageous; the money he was raising was going to enrich Italy, and that was one more step in the exploitation of Germans by Italians.

For Rome is the greatest thief and robber that has ever appeared on earth, or ever will.... Poor Germans that we are—we have been deceived! We were born to be masters,

The Pope in Hell. Anti-papal German woodcut, 1521.

and we have been compelled to bow the head beneath the yoke of our tyrants.... It is time the glorious Teutonic people should cease to be the puppet of the Roman pontiff. [*]

In terms that come natural to us today, the nationalistic and economic factors present in the Lutheran movement help explain its success. But a word of warning is necessary. These political and economic factors *help* explain Lutheran success; they do not in and of themselves wholly account for it. As always in human affairs, ideas and ideals

[*] *Documents*, 278-279.

worked together with material interests to move the men of the Reformation.

The princes who supported Luther stood to gain financially, not only by the cessation of the flow of German money to Italy, but by the confiscation of Catholic property, especially monastic property, which was not needed for the new Lutheran cult. Luther gave them a new weapon in the eternal struggle against their feudal overlord, the emperor. The princes were also moved by Luther's German patriotism. Some, like Frederick the Wise of Saxony, sympathized with many of his ideas. Philip of Hesse found Luther helpful in a very personal problem of his relations with women: he had decided on the somewhat un-Christian and indeed unpromising solution of trying bigamy. Though Luther did not precisely like this solution, he condoned it, much to the salving of Philip's conscience.

Nor must Luther's personality be left out of account. It is true enough that what he started was soon taken out of his hands by the German princes who joined the reform movement in part to strengthen their political power against the emperor, and to strengthen their treasuries by confiscating the possessions of the Catholic Church. Yet Lutheranism without Luther is inconceivable, save perhaps to single-minded devotees of the economic interpretation of history. He wrote the pamphlets that did for this revolution what Tom Paine and the Declaration of Independence did for ours. He put his *Appeal to the Christian Nobility of the German Nation* in the vernacular German, not the academic Latin, so that it became a "best-seller" overnight. His defiance of the papal legate Cajetan, of the papal champion Eck, and of the Pope himself—indeed all his actions—helped to focus German sentiments on what was, in spite of rather primitive techniques of communication, a mass movement. Luther's translation of the Bible made that book a part of German life, and made Luther's language one of the bases of modern literary

German. His marriage to a former nun and his raising of a large family dramatized the break with Rome. And back of all this was Luther's passionate conviction that he was doing what he had to do: *"Ich kann nicht anders."*

Moreover, Luther's doctrine of justification by faith alone was, as we have noted, attractive to many religious dispositions. St. Paul at the very beginnings of Christianity set up the contrast between the Spirit—invisible, in a sense private to the believer—and the Letter—only too visible, only too public. Established churches have always tended to balance spirit and letter, invisible and visible, internal and external, faith and works; but to the ardent, crusading Christian even a working successful balance of this sort seems a yielding to a gross materialism. He will have none of this compromise, but will imperiously assert the primacy of the spirit. In Luther's day, the established Roman Church had lost its medieval balance; the world was too much with it. The Lutheran felt the new church offered him something he could not get in the old.

The Opposition to Luther

A final reason for Luther's success lay in the relative weakness of the forces that opposed him. The opposition may be divided into the religious and the political, though the two were really inseparably connected. Clerical opposition centered in the top levels of the Catholic bureaucracy; Pope Leo X did not so much head it as prove its willing instrument. Moderate Catholics, anxious to compromise and avert a schism, existed both within the Church and on its margin among the humanist scholars of the Renaissance. It is tempting to agree with the great liberal Catholic historian, Lord Acton, that had there been at the head of the Catholic Church a pope willing to reform in order to conserve, willing to make concessions that did not destroy the basic position of the Church as God's chosen instrument on earth, even Luther might have been reconciled. Luther's ablest associate, Melanchthon, was a moderate. Yet the historian can hardly avoid comparing this revolution with other great modern revolutions, the English, the French, the Russian, and noting that in all of them the moderates —gifted, numerous, and active though they were—could not hold up against the extremists. Once Leo X had excommunicated Luther in 1520, the way to compromise was probably blocked, for Luther's associates could have been won away from him only by concessions too great for a Catholic to make.

Politically, the opposition in these critical early years centered in the young Emperor Charles V, who came to the imperial throne in 1519. Charles of Habsburg was the fruit of a series of marriages that gave rise to the famous epigram: "Let others wage war; thou, happy Austria, marry." The combined inheritance of his Austrian father and Spanish mother made Charles ruler of the German Empire, the Low Countries, Spain, the Spanish Indies, Hungary, and parts of Italy. This looks on the map like the nearest thing to a real European superstate since Charlemagne, and Charles wanted very much to make it such a state in reality. The activities of Luther's princely German supporters seemed to him a threat to his hold over Germany, and might in themselves have sufficed to turn him against Luther. But Charles, though by no means a mere papal instrument, was by upbringing a good conventional Catholic, in no state of mind to throw his great influence on the side of the moderate group within the Catholic Church. He decided to fight—and had to fight the rest of his reign, thus gainsaying the famous epigram about his house.

Charles V entrusted the government of the Germans to his younger brother Ferdinand, who formed alliances with Bavaria and other Catholic German states to op-
pose the Lutheran states. Thus began a long series of alliances and combinations within the Germanies, the fruits of which were the religious wars of the next few generations, and the territorial division of Germany into, roughly, a Protestant north and east and a Catholic south and west, which has endured to this day (see Chapter XIII). The fact that Charles himself did not directly lead the fight in Germany gives another clue to the success of the Protestant movement in breaking down the unity of western Christendom. Charles had too many other fights on his hands to concentrate on Germany. His huge inheritance was a threat to the only remaining great power on the continent, France, which moreover was still committed to the Italian adventures Charles VIII had begun (see p. 521). Four general wars between Charles V and Francis I of France, really one great war, prevented anything like the forcible suppression of the German Protestants by imperial Habsburg power.

The Lutheran Church

Thus far, Luther has appeared in the role of the great revolutionary. But on some issues he also took a fundamentally conservative stand. He did not, for example, push his doctrines of justification by faith and the priesthood of all believers to their logical extreme, which is anarchy. If religion is wholly a matter between each man and his maker, an organized church becomes unnecessary if not impossible, or else there are as many churches as there are individuals. Reformers inspired by Luther, but more radical, attempted to apply these anarchical concepts to the churches of Saxony; the consequences were immense confusion and popular unrest. Luther and his moderate followers, who had no sympathy with such anarchistic experiments, intervened in Saxony. They organized a church that permitted its clergy to marry, but that did

possess ordained clergymen, ritual, dogmas, even some sacraments—a whole apparatus of good works.

And, most important for us to understand, the Lutherans did not found this church as an alternative choice to the Roman Catholic, but as the *one true church*. Where a Lutheran church was founded, a Catholic church ceased to be; indeed, the Lutherans commonly just took over the church building. Stimulated by Luther and his clerical and academic disciples, this process at first went on among the people of Germany almost spontaneously, without the intervention of political leaders.

But very soon the lay rulers of certain of the half-independent, or rather nine-tenths independent, German states took a hand. In Saxony, in Hesse, soon in most of northern Germany, princes and their ministers superintended and hastened the process of converting the willing to Lutheranism, and evicting the unwilling. Here, as so often in any process of change, the formula "either . . . or" does not serve well for sensible interpretation. The Lutheran Church was not invented by Luther and the princes and

Rebelling German peasants, 1525.

foisted on the people; nor on the other hand was it the spontaneous work of the German people. *Both* people and princes had a share in the complex process of the Protestant Reformation.

Knights' War and Peasants' Rebellion

It was not only the great and near-great German princes who took advantage of the Lutheran movement to assert themselves. Just beneath the princes, lay and ecclesiastical, in the German social pyramid and like them a legacy of the Middle Ages were the knights, the lesser nobility. Some of them held a castle and a few square miles direct from the emperor, and were in theory as "independent" as an Elector of Saxony; others were simply minor feudal lords. Many were younger sons, landless but still gentlemen, who could hardly have a career save that of arms. The class as a whole was caught in the squeeze of rising prices and the need for maintaining aristocratic standards of living. Luther's challenge to the established order, above all the chance it seemed to give for taking over ecclesiastical holdings, was too good an opportunity for many of these knights to miss. Under the leadership of Ulrich von Hutten and Franz von Sickingen, they rose in 1522 in what is called the "Knights' War." They were put down by the bigger lords, but only after a struggle, and their rising added to the confusion of the time.

The really bitter social struggle of the early German Reformation was the Peasants' Rebellion of 1524-25. Now peasant risings were not unknown in the Middle Ages. In many ways, the German rising resembles the peasant revolts of the fourteenth century in England and France (see Chapter X). Like them, it was directed against the burdens of the manorial system; like them, it lacked co-ordination and effective military organization and was cruelly put down by the possessing classes who did have command over military power. Like them, too, it was a rising, not of peasants who were in the very lowest state of oppression, but of peasants who were beginning to enjoy some gain from the slowly rising standards of living of medieval society, who had enough to know they wanted more. The German Peasants' Rebellion centered not in those eastern parts of the country where serfdom was most complete, where the status of the peasant was lowest, but in the southwestern parts where the peasant had at least the beginnings of the status of a landowning farmer and were beginning capitalist farming.

Yet in one very important respect this sixteenth-century German rising looks more modern, more democratic, than its medieval counterparts in western Europe. Even more clearly than the English Peasants' Revolt, which had been influenced by Wiclif and the Lollards, it was led by educated men who were not themselves peasants and who had a program, a set of revolutionary ideas of what the new social structure should be. Their leaders drew up a set of demands known as the "Twelve Articles," which were given various regional forms. They are generally moderate enough, and are usually couched in Biblical language, which shows clearly their relation to the Reformation. Important articles demanded that each parish have the right to choose its own priest, that the tithes paid to the clergy and the taxes paid to the lord be reduced, and that the peasants be allowed to take game and wood from the forests.

Luther's reaction to the Peasants' Rebellion was thoroughly conservative. He was horrified at what the peasants' leaders had found in the Bible he had translated into German so that they might read it. He turned against them, directing at them impassioned abuse that sounds even stronger than his abuse of the Catholics. From this time on, he turned definitely to the princes, and the church he founded became itself an established church, respectful toward civil authority. Luther indeed is quoted in his *Table Talk* as saying: "The princes of the world are gods, the common people are Satan."

In fairness to Luther, it may be said that his conservatism in social, economic, and political matters is by no means inconsistent with his fundamental spiritual position. For if the visible, external world is really wholly subordinate to the invisible, spiritual world, the most one can hope for in this world of politics is that it be kept in as good orderliness, in as little imperfection as possible so that the spiritual may thrive. Authority, custom, law, existing institutions combine to provide this orderliness. Kings and princes are better for this wretched world than democratically chosen representatives of the people; obedience better than discussion.

Luther's conservative views on social and political questions had two important results. First, he won increasing support from kings and princes. By the mid-sixteenth century, Lutheranism had become the state religion in most of the principalities of northern Germany and in the Scandinavian kingdoms, Sweden and Denmark, together with the Danish dependency of Norway. The Scandinavian monarchs, in particular, appear to have been attracted to the Reformation for secular reasons, for the opportunities it presented to curb unruly bishops and confiscate monastic wealth. Second, it is hardly surprising that after the Peasants' Rebellion the popular initiative in the Protestant movement passed to other hands.

II: Protestant Origins—Zwingli, Calvin, and Other Founders

As we have seen (Chapter VIII), there was in the fourteenth and fifteenth centuries in movements like those of Wiclif in England and Hus in Bohemia, to say nothing of earlier revolts against the worldly success of the Church, much that anticipates the Protestantism of the sixteenth century. Moreover, many of the things that had troubled Luther had long been troubling his contemporaries in Germany, France, England, and elsewhere. The great humanist Erasmus (see Chapter XI), the Englishman Thomas More (author of *Utopia*), the Frenchman Lefèvre d'Etaples, and many others were in revulsion against the worldliness and corruption of the Church and against the oversubtleties of late Scholasticism. They had been seeking in their writing and preaching for a renewal of evangelical Christianity, for a return to what most of them held to be an earlier and better faith that had somehow gone wrong. Many of these reform-minded men wanted the Catholic Church to be reformed from within. They were shocked by Luther's intransigent revolt, and sought to tame the movement he had unloosed. Others, however, went on to a break even more complete in many ways than Luther's. Of these other founders of Protestantism the first in time was Zwingli and the first in importance was Calvin.

Zwingli

Almost contemporaneously with Luther's spectacular revolt, another German, Ulrich Zwingli (1484-1531), had begun in Switzerland a quieter reform, one that produced no great single organized church, but that nevertheless extended and deepened some of the fundamental theological and moral conceptions of Protestantism, and had a wide influence on the less "enthusiastic," less "fundamentalist," forms of Protestantism. Zwingli was a scholarly humanist trained in the tradition of Erasmus. Like Luther, he was aiming to destroy what seemed to him the perversion of primitive Christianity which made the consecrated priest an agent, indeed a sharer, of a miraculous power not possessed by the layman. But, where the doctrine of the priesthood of the true believer drove the emotional Luther to the edge of anarchism, the humanistic Zwingli saw that individuals might achieve a common discipline that would promote righteous living. This discipline would arise from the social conscience of enlightened and emancipated people led by their pastors.

Zwingli believed in a personal God and in the miraculous origin of the Christian religion. Indeed, his God was a highly transcendental one, so powerful, so real, and yet so far above this petty world of sense experience that to Zwingli he was not to be approached by mere sacraments. Hence Zwingli is fundamentally, basically, anti-sacramental in a way Luther was not. Hence Zwingli distrusted what many Protestants feel is the continuous appeal of the Catholics to "superstition," to belief in saints, to the use of images, to incense and candles, and of course to indulgences. Zwingli began the process of making the church building an almost undecorated hall, of making the service a sermon and responsive reading, of abolishing the Catholic liturgy. He thus started on the way toward the puritanical simplicity of the later Calvinists.

A good concrete example of Zwingli's attitude is his doctrine of the Eucharist. The Catholic doctrine of *transubstantiation* holds that by the miraculous power of the priest the elements, the bread and the wine, become in *substance* the body and blood of Christ, although their *accidents*, their make-up as far as chemistry or indeed common sense sees them, remain those of bread and wine. Luther stubbornly refused to eliminate the miraculous completely, and adhered to a difficult and confusing compromise doctrine called *consubstantiation.* Zwingli, however, went all the way to what is the usual Protestant doctrine that when we partake of the elements in communion we are indeed commemorating Christ's last supper with his disciples, but only in a symbolic way. We are not, in short, sharing through a sacrament in a miracle; we are merely sharing anew the eternal memory of Christ's stay on earth.

Ulrich Zwingli.

Calvin

Zwingli attracted adherents in the German-speaking parts of Switzerland. The independent French Swiss city of Geneva came under the domination of the French-born Jean Cauvin (1509-1564), better known in the Latin form of his name as Calvin. Under Calvin, the Protestant movement was shaped as a faith, a way of life, that gave it a European and not merely a German basis. The historian finds it useful to take Calvinism as the middle—to borrow a political term, the Center—of Protestant beliefs. In Germany and Scandinavia the Lutherans, and in England the Anglican Church, remained in doctrine what we may call to the Right of Calvinism. In England, the Low Countries, and Germany there grew up radical sects like the Anabaptists, to whom we shall shortly come, who were to the Left of Calvinism.

With the moral and theological ideas of Calvin we shall deal in the next section of this chapter. Here we may note that in his *Institutes of the Christian Religion,* published in 1536, he laid a firm doctrinal basis for a Protestantism that, like Zwingli's, breaks completely with Catholic church organization and with Catholic ritual. Calvin had been trained as a lawyer. His system had a logical rigor and completeness that gave it great conviction. He had also a base from which to work, a town that was to become a Protestant Rome, Geneva, where after a temporary rejection in 1538 he returned in 1541 to organize his City of God. To Geneva came Protestant refugees from many parts of Europe, there to receive indoctrination in Calvin's faith, and to return, sometimes at the risk of their lives, to spread the word in their own countries. Within a generation or two, Calvinism had spread to Scotland, where it was led by a great preacher and organizer, John Knox; to England, whence it was brought to Plymouth in New England; and even to Hungary and Poland.

In the Low Countries, Calvinism had by the second half of the sixteenth century found a foothold, especially in cities like Antwerp. The Low Countries, both north and south, belonged to the Burgundian inheritance of Charles V, and passed on to his heir, the austerely ardent Catholic Philip II. When Philip attempted to suppress the revolt of the Netherlands, the patriotism of the Dutch in the northern provinces was welded together with Calvinism into one of the firmest of spiritual alloys—a metal which resisted heavy Spanish pressures (see Chapter XIII).

In France—where the intellectual classes have long been very serious-minded, and not at all as common opinion conceives Frenchmen, gay and irresponsible—concern over the worldliness of the Catholic Church was strong. From Jean Gerson, one of the leaders of the Conciliar Movement, to Lefèvre d'Etaples, Frenchmen had been seeking ways of reform. Calvin's ideas found ready acceptance among many Frenchmen, and soon there were organized Protestant churches called Huguenot (perhaps a corruption of a German word, *Eidgenossen*, "covenanted") especially in the southwest. But France was a centralized monarchy. King Francis I (1515-1547) was not anxious, as so many of the German princes were, to stir up trouble with Rome. In 1516, he had signed with the Pope the Concordat of Bologna, an agreement that increased the royal authority over the Gallican Church. In the mid-sixteenth century, only a very few intellectuals could even conceive of the possibility of citizens or subjects of the *same* political unit professing and practicing *different* religious faiths. Protestantism in France had to fight, not for toleration, but to succeed Catholicism as the established religion of Frenchmen. The attempt failed, but only after the long hard struggle of the French wars of religion, only after Protestantism had left its mark on the French conscience (see Chapter XIII).

The English Reformation

In strict chronology, the first great sixteenth-century religious overturn outside the Germanies was in England. The signal for the English Reformation was something very different from the Ninety-Five Theses of Luther. It was the desire of King Henry VIII (1509-1547) to put aside his wife, Catherine of Aragon, who had given him no male heir. The house of Tudor had only recently achieved the Crown, and Henry felt more strongly than was usual even in those days that a male heir was essential. He rested his case on the fact that Catherine had been married to his deceased brother Arthur, and that marriage with a deceased brother's widow is against canon law. Henry's case was hardly strengthened by the circumstance that he had taken nearly twenty years to discover the existence of an impediment. Moreover, Catherine was aunt to the Emperor Charles V, whom the Pope could scarcely risk offending by granting an annulment. Nevertheless Henry tried hard, through his minister Cardinal Wolsey, who was dismissed in disgrace for his failure. Henry then put his case to universities in England and on the Continent, and got a few favorable replies. Finally, he married Anne Boleyn, and Cranmer, the obliging Archbishop of Canterbury whom Henry had recently appointed, pronounced the annulment of the marriage (*not* the divorce) of Henry and Catherine. The Pope excommunicated Henry and declared the annulment invalid. Henry's answer was the Act of Supremacy in 1534, which set the king up as supreme head of the Church in England.

More than the private life of Henry VIII was involved in this English Reformation. Henry could not have secured the Act of Supremacy and other Protestant legislation from Parliament if there had not been a considerable body of English opinion favorable to the breach with Rome, particularly among the sizable and prosperous middle classes. Anti-papal sentiment, which was an aspect of English nationalism, had long existed; it had motivated the fourteenth-century statutes of Edward III (see Chapter X), which limited the right of the pope to intervene in the affairs of the English church. Anticlericalism went back to the days of Wiclif; in the days of Henry VIII it was aimed particularly at the monasteries, which were still wealthy landowners but had become corrupt since their great medieval days. In the eyes of many Englishmen, the monasteries had outlived their purpose and needed to be reformed or indeed abolished. Moreover, the ideas of Luther and other continental Protestants quickly won a sympathetic hearing in England. Many English scholars were in touch with continental reformers; one of them,

Tindal, studied with Luther and published an English translation of the New Testament in 1526.

Henry VIII sponsored measures in addition to the Act of Supremacy which found favor with Protestant opinion in England. Most important, he closed the monasteries, confiscated their property, and distributed much of the loot among the nobility and the country gentry. Thus Henry gave influential subjects good reason to be grateful to him and to the Tudor dynasty. Moreover, this policy, by increasing the wealth of the landed aristocracy, amounted to a social and economic revolution. It is another illustration of how closely the religious and the secular threads were interwoven in the Reformation.

Yet Henry VIII did not really consider himself a Protestant. The church set up by

Henry VIII, by Hans Holbein the Younger (1540). Now in National Gallery, Rome.

the Act of Supremacy was in his eyes—and remains today in the eyes of some of its communicants—a Catholic body. Henry hoped to retain Catholic doctrines and ritual, doing no more than abolish monasteries and deny the pope's position as head of the Church in England. Inevitably, his policies aroused opposition. Part of that opposition was Roman Catholic, for some Englishmen greatly resented the break with Rome. And part, the more pressing and the larger part, was militantly Protestant. Hardly had Henry given the signal for the break with Rome when groups began even within the new Church of England to introduce such Protestant practices as marriage of the clergy, use of English instead of Latin in the ritual, abolition of auricular confession, abolition of the invocation of saints.

Henry used force against the Catholic opposition, and executed some of its leaders, notably Thomas More. He tried to stem the Protestant tide by appealing to a willing Parliament, many members of which were enriched by the spoliation of the Catholic Church. In 1539, Parliament passed the statute of the Six Articles, reaffirming transubstantiation, celibacy of the priesthood, confession, and other Catholic doctrines and ritual, and making their denial heresy. By this definition, indeed by almost any possible definition, there were far too many heretics to be repressed. The patriotic Englishman was against Rome and all its works. England from now on was to be a great center of religious variation and experimentation, much (though not all) of it peaceful. The Church of England, substantially more Protestant than Henry had intended, became a kind of central national core of precarious orthodoxy.

The Anabaptists

One major item is left to consider in this survey of Protestant origins. Socially and intellectually less "respectable" than the soon-established Lutheran and Anglican churches, or the rapidly sobered Calvinists, was a whole group of radical sects, the left wing of the Protestant revolution. In the sixteenth century, most of them were known loosely as Anabaptists, from the Greek for "baptizing again." Some of Zwingli's followers had come to believe that the Catholic sacrament of baptism of infants had no validity, since the infant could not possibly be said to "believe" or "understand." Here again the relation to Luther's basic doctrine of faith as a direct relation between the believer and God is clear—only for the Anabaptist it is a relation of rational understanding by the believer; here also can be seen one of the clearest elements of much Protestantism, an appeal to individual "reason" or "understanding." Yet note carefully that this appeal is not to "scientific" or "common-sense" reason, as it was with the eighteenth-century Enlightenment; and it is an appeal to reason that in these wilder sects is in fact quite congruous with very excited, "enthusiastic," evangelical practices, indeed, with what Americans know as "holy rolling."

The Anabaptists in these early years "baptized again" when the believer could hold that he was voluntarily joining the company of the elect. Later generations were never baptized until they came of age, so the prefix "ana" was dropped, and we have the familiar Baptists of our time. The Anabaptists split under the pressure of persecution and with the spread of private reading of the Bible. Indeed, for some Catholic observers, the proliferation of Protestant sects seems due inevitably to the Protestant practice of seeking in the Bible for an authority they refused to find in the established dogmas of Catholic authority. The Bible is—from the historian's point of view—a complex record of several thousand years of Jewish history, and it contains an extraordinary variety of religious experience. Especially the apocalyptic

How Anabaptists were reported to carry on. May-dance at Münster, 1535.

books of the Old Testament and the Revelation of St. John the Divine of the New can be made to yield almost anything a lively imagination wants to find. Many of the leaders of these new sects were uneducated men with a sense of grievance against the established order. They were seeking to bring heaven to earth, quickly.

Their best-known early manifestation in the Reformation gave the conservatives and moderates as great a shock as had the German Peasants' Rebellion, in which these same radical religious ideas had also played a large part. In the mid-1530's, a group of Anabaptists under the leadership of John of Leyden, a Dutch tailor, got control of the city of Münster in Germany, and set up a Biblical Utopia. They were put down by force, their leaders executed, and the faithful dispersed. We know about them chiefly from their opponents, who certainly exaggerated their doctrines and practices. Still, even if we allow for the distortions of propaganda, it seems clear that the Anabaptists of Münster were behaving in ways that

western traditions do not permit large groups to adopt. For one thing, they preached, and apparently practiced, polygamy. They pushed the Lutheran doctrine of justification by faith to its logical extreme in anarchism, or in theological language, *antinomianism,* from the Greek "against law." Each man was to be his own law, or rather, to find God's universal law in his own conscience, not in *written* law and tradition. They did not believe in class distinctions or in the customary forms of private property. They were disturbers of an established order that was strong enough to put them down.

The great majority of Anabaptists were very far from being such wild fanatics as the men of Münster. Many Anabaptist groups sought to bring the Christian life to earth in quieter and more constructive ways. They established communities where they lived as they thought the primitive Christians had lived, in brotherhood, working, sharing, and praying together. These communities bore many resemblances to monasteries, though their members had taken no vows and did not observe celibacy. As we shall see in the next section of this chapter, some of the Anabaptist ideas—quietism, asceticism, the high sense of community—made a lasting contribution to the Protestant tradition. This sober majority of Anabaptists, too, met violent persecution in the sixteenth century. But something of their spirit lives on today in such diverse groups as the Baptists, the Quakers, the Hutterites of Canada, and the Mennonites and the Amish of the Pennsylvania "Dutch."

Unitarianism

A Protestant strain close to Anabaptism was that of Unitarianism, the denial of the Trinity and of the full divinity of Christ. Today, Unitarianism is usually identified with the rejection of the Trinity on the grounds that it is an unreasonable concept and with the view that Christ was simply a particularly inspired human being. But this version of Unitarianism derives largely from the rationalistic Enlightenment of the

eighteenth century. Sixteenth-century Unitarianism was a very different matter and much more mystical in outlook. Its most famous advocate, the Spanish physician Servetus (1511-1553), believed that though Christ was not eternal, he was indeed the Son of God. His concept made Christ, as it were, less removed from man but not less removed from God. Thereby Servetus hoped to make it easier for humanity to acquire a mystic identification with Christ and to achieve salvation.

Even this mystic doctrine of Unitarianism greatly alarmed not only Catholics but also many Protestants. Servetus was finally prosecuted for heresy at Geneva by Calvin himself and burnt at the stake in 1553. The doctrines of Servetus, however, contributed to the teachings of another Unitarian, Socinus (in Italian, Sozzini, 1539-1604). This far-traveling Italian theologian gained a considerable following among the peoples of eastern Europe, particularly in Poland, Hungary, and Transylvania. The Socinians, too, suffered vigorous persecution at the hands of both Catholics and Protestants, but they were never to be fully stamped out.

III: Protestant Beliefs and Practices

Common Denominators

It is very difficult to establish a common denominator for Protestant beliefs. Henry VIII (who almost certainly never thought of himself as a Protestant), Luther, Zwingli, Calvin, John of Leyden, and Servetus make a most disparate group. Obviously they all, even the Anglican High Churchmen, repudiated the claim of the Roman Catholic Church to be the one true faith. They were all hostile to the Church of Rome.

One other generalization is almost as universally valid, if less obvious today. In these early days, each Protestant sect was convinced that it was the one true faith, that it and not Rome was the true successor of Christ and his apostles. Even the Antinomians, who believed that each man carried the truth in his own bosom, believed that if all the perversions that custom, education, and bad environment generally had set up as obstacles to the penetration of truth were swept away, each man would find the *same* truth in his bosom. Some early Protestants held that, though their own belief was the sole true belief, its ultimate prevailing on earth must be the slow process of educating men, of convincing them, of converting them. Others, however, could not wait for this slow process. Though they had once been persecuted themselves, they did not hesitate to persecute in their turn when they rose to power. Witness Calvin's condemnation of Servetus.

At this point, indeed, it must be emphasized that what we nowadays in the United States accept as normal—that is, the peaceful co-existence of many different churches, "freedom of religion," "separation of Church and State"—were certainly not normal, widespread concepts in the sixteenth-century, nor even in the seventeenth-century, western world. Religious toleration itself is a complex matter, based at one extreme on mere opportunism (the sheer impossibility of bringing the sects together) and at the other extreme on a belief that religious divergences are in themselves good, and toleration a positive benefit for all.

Only with the late seventeenth- and early eighteenth-century Enlightenment does the doctrine of religious toleration emerge into *full* prominence; and in that period many "enlightened" individuals were essentially non-believers in Christianity, for whom toleration was a way of letting Christianity wither on the vine. Nevertheless, the era of the Renaissance and Reformation does see the gradual emergence of a characteristic form of positive belief in religious toleration—that is, the belief that although there *is indeed* a single true religion which men may one day find, each man must find his own way to it freely, unforced by any external pressures. Therefore there must be no established church, no enforced conformity, no persecution. Many humanists held this view. One of them, Sebastian Castellio, or Châteillon, wrote in 1554 a book in Latin on "whether heretics are to be persecuted," attacking Calvin for the execution of Servetus in 1553. In this book one may discern clearly the positive doc-trine of religious toleration: force must never be used to attempt to change a man's ideas about religion. But, as the experience of Roger Williams in seventeenth-century New England was to show, such ideas were only very slowly accepted in the western world. As denial of the wisdom and rightness of actual persecution, religious toleration is now firmly established in the West; there is still debate as to whether religious variation, and religious indifference, are in themselves good.

Finally, even the conservative established churches of the Reformation—the Anglican and the Lutheran—shared with the more radical Protestants certain reductions in ritual and other external manifestations of belief. All reduced somewhat the seven sacraments; a general Protestant minimum was to retain baptism and communion. But the Protestant theological justification of these sacraments could range very widely, from consubstantiation to the symbolic view of the Eucharist, from an almost Roman *acceptance* of the miraculous to an almost secularist *denial* of the miraculous. Veneration of saints, pilgrimages, rosaries, amulets, and such "papist" practices disappeared even among the right-wing Protestants; the left wing also banished music, painting, indeed all the arts except the oratorical arts.

To these outward signs there corresponds an inner link that ties Protestantism together, loosely indeed, and often uncomfortably. All Protestants were rebels in origin. They had *protested* almost always in the name of an older, purer, primitive church, almost always maintaining that *Rome* was the real innovator, the wicked revolutionist. (This attempt of the rebel not to seem to be rebelling often recurs in western history.) The Protestants had appealed from an established order to a "higher law" not concretely established in the flesh, in institutions, on this earth. That is to say, all Protestantism has at least a tinge of the Lutheran appeal from works to faith, in the terms of St. Paul, from the "letter" of the law to the "spirit"; it has at least a tinge of *individualism*. This individualism is what early Protestantism bequeathed to the modern world.

The divergent beliefs of the separate Protestant churches may most conveniently be arranged in order of their theological distance from Roman Catholicism, beginning with those nearest Rome. But it must be noted that the political and social distance is not always the same as the theological.

Anglicanism

The Church of England, as we have already noted, contains communicants who think of themselves as Catholics; they represent the "High Church" point of view. But the Church of England also includes members who take a "Low Church" view; they are more Protestant in outlook, and some come very close to being Unitarians. The Church of England keeps a modified form of the Catholic hierarchy, with archbishops and bishops, though of course without acknowledging the authority of the pope. On the other hand, it permits its clergy to marry and, although it does have orders of monks and nuns, it does not put anything like the Catholic emphasis on the regular clergy. Indeed, historically speaking, the Church of England has somehow managed to contain elements from almost the whole range of Protestant belief, though Anglicans have not been very cordial toward the more publicly demonstrative types of Protestantism, toward "holy rolling."

Perhaps the central core of Anglicanism has been a tempered ritualism, a tempered belief in hierarchy, in discipline from above, a tempered acceptance of this imperfect world—a moderate attitude really not very far from the Catholicism of St. Thomas Aquinas. Indeed, Richard Hooker, who wrote a great defense of the Anglican Church in the 1590's (*The Laws of Ecclesiastical Polity*), relied heavily on Aquinas. It is significant, too, that Hooker is usually called "the judicious Hooker," because of his efforts to reconcile divergent points of view and adjust them to Anglicanism.

On the other hand, there has also always been a strong puritanical or evangelical current in the broad stream of Anglicanism. The Puritans for the most part only reluctantly left the Anglican communion in the late sixteenth and early seventeenth century, and many of them stayed within it. This is not so much what later became the "Low Church" strain in Anglicanism or, in America, Episcopalianism, as it is a strain of earnest, evangelical piety, social service, plain living and high thinking—in short, Puritanism.

The Church of England assumed its definitive form during the reign of Henry VIII's daughter, Elizabeth I (1558-1603). The Thirty-Nine Articles enacted by Parliament in 1563 were a kind of constitution for the Church. They illustrate the essential conservatism of the Anglican Church and the compromises on which it is founded. The Thirty-Nine Articles rejected the more obvious forms of Romanism—the use of Latin, auricular confession, clerical celibacy, the allegiance to the pope. The thirtieth article took a firm Protestant stand on one of the great symbolic points at issue. The Church of England gave communion in both kinds, both wine and bread, to the layman, where the Catholic Church gave only the bread. Yet the articles also sought to compromise on some of the greater issues, and notably to avoid the anarchistic dangers of the doctrines of justification by faith and the priesthood of the believer. The article on the Lord's Supper was firm in its rejection of Catholic transubstantiation, but equally firm in its rejection of Zwinglian symbolism; the Anglican really was to receive the Eucharist as body and blood of Christ.

The Church of England has always

Die Zehen Gebot/Wie sie
ein Haußvatter seinem Gesinde
einfeltiglich fürhal-
ten sol.
Diese Figur stehet im Andern Buch
Mosi/am xxii.Cap.

Das Erst Gebot.
Du solt nicht ander Götter haben.
Was ist das? Antwort.
Wir sollen GOTT ober alle ding
fürchten/lieben vnd
vertrawen.
    B   Diese

Page from A Catechism for the People, Pastor, and Preacher, *by Martin Luther. Printed in Frankfurt, 1553. The text reads, in part: "The Ten Commandments; as the father of the family should impress them on his household, in a simple manner.... The First Commandment. Thou shalt have no other gods. What does this mean? Answer. Above all else we must fear, love, and trust in God."*

seemed to its enemies, and even to some of its friends, a bit too acquiescent in face of civil authority. In what was once a word of abuse, the Church of England has seemed

Erastian. The term comes from the name of a sixteenth-century Swiss theologian and physician named Erastus (not to be confused with the Dutch humanist Erasmus), who by no means held the doctrine attributed to him. This doctrine in the abusive sense—and it has hardly any other—holds that the State is all-powerful against the Church, that the clergy are but the moral police force of the State, in short, that the government in power is always right. This extreme statement is indeed a caricature of Anglican practice. But a touch of subservience to political authority, a modified Erastianism, does remain in the Church of England. It is evident in the English civil and religious struggles of the seventeenth century (see Chapter XV).

Lutheranism

The first section of this chapter has already presented the main beliefs of the other great conservative Protestant church, the Lutheran. Once it had become established, Lutheranism preserved many practices which seem to outsiders Catholic in origin, but which to Luther represented a return to early Christianity before the corruption by Rome. Lutheranism preserved the Eucharist, now interpreted according to the mysterious doctrine of consubstantiation. It also preserved the notion of hierarchy, bishops, gowns, and something of the plastic arts. The tradition of good music in the church was not only preserved but greatly fortified.

Luther, like so many others upon whom character and fate have thrust rebellion, was at heart a conservative about things of this world, as we have seen. In his own lifetime he really wanted the forms of Lutheran worship to recall the forms he was used to. The Lutheran Church, like the Anglican, had its high or conservative party. Yet it also had a strong evangelical party and a tradition of Bible reading. To outsiders, the Lutheran Church has seemed even more Erastian than the Anglican. As the state church in much of North Germany and in Scandinavia, it was often a docile instrument of its political masters. And in its close association with the rise of Prussia —though Prussia's Hohenzollern rulers later became Calvinist—it was inevitably brought under the rule of the strongly bureaucratic Prussian state.

Calvinism: Predestination

The Protestant Center is Calvinism, and the main theological problem of Calvinism is not so much Luther's problem of faith against good works as the related problem of predestination against free will. It is a problem that must seem tortured, unreal to many people, but the historian must record the fact that it keeps cropping up in western history—even in Marxism. The problem is an old one in Christianity, already evident in the fifth-century struggle over the heresy of Pelagius (see Chapter IV). It arises from the Christian concept that God is all-powerful, all-good, all-knowing. If this is so, he must will, must *determine,* everything that happens. He must will that the sinner shall sin. For if he did not so will, the individual would be doing something God did not want him to do, and God would not be all-powerful. But there is a grave moral difficulty here. If God wills that the sinner sin, the sinner cannot help himself, cannot be "blamed" for his sin. We seem to be at a dead end, where the individual can always say, no matter what he does, that he is doing what God makes him do. We seem, in short, to have cut the ground from individual moral responsibility. And—at least from their enemies' reports—that is just what John of Leyden and his Antinomians (see p. 494) did. When they took several wives at once, they argued that God must want them to, since they wanted to.

The dilemma is clear: if the individual can choose for himself between good and evil acts, if in theological terms he has *free will* to do what God does not want him to do—then it looks as if God were not all-powerful; if he has no such choice, if in theological terms he is subject to *predestination*—then it looks as if the individual were morally irresponsible. *Both* these conclusions are repugnant to the general nature of historical Christianity.

To an outsider, it looks as if most Christians most of the time solved the dilemma by embracing both horns at once—by holding that God determines every human act, and yet that human beings may do things God does not want them to do. Theologians do not of course put the matter this way. Most of their basic solutions preserve the moral responsibility of the individual by asserting the profound distance between God and man, a distance that the miracle of faith alone can, in a sense, bridge. In terms of everyday life, this means that for the individual to claim that whatever he does is what God wants him to do is to make the incredibly presumptuous claim that he *knows* God's will, that his petty human understanding is on a par with God's. The individual can never be *certain* that what he wants to do is what God wants him to do. Therefore he should look about him and see what signs he can, limited though his vision be, of God's intentions. These he will find in Christian tradition and Christian history. To be concrete: if the individual is tempted to commit adultery, he will not follow the Antinomian and say that God wants him to do so; he will follow Christian tradition, and recognize the adulterous desire as an indication that he is being tempted to do wrong, and that if he does it he will not be saved, but damned.

Calvin himself, though he would not have put it this way, would have reached the same conclusion. But he was, as we have noted, a logician. Both his temperament and his environment led him to reject *what he believed* to be the Catholic emphasis on easy salvation by indulgences and the like. He put his own emphasis on the hard path of true salvation, on the majesty of God and the littleness of man. He evolved therefore a very extreme form of the doctrine of predestination.

In Calvin's system, Adam's original sin was unforgivable. God, however, in his incomprehensible mercy, sent Jesus Christ to this earth to make salvation possible for some of Adam's progeny, stained though they were by original sin. Very few indeed, the elect, could attain this salvation, and that through no merit of their own, and certainly not on the wholesale scale the Roman Catholic Church of the sixteenth century was claiming. The elect were saved only through God's free and infinite grace, by means of which they were given the strength to gain salvation. Grace is not like anything else that touches human life on earth. It is not of a piece with law, morals, philosophy, and other human ways of relating man to his environment—to hold that it is, was to Calvin one of the errors of the Catholic. But it is not wholly divorced from these earthly relations—to hold that it is, is the error of the Antinomian. The elect actually tend to behave in a certain way, an identifiable way, a way not wholly misrepresented if it is called *puritanical*.

Calvinist Practice: Puritanism

Calvinism as a way of life is one of the forms of idealistic or other-worldly Christianity. It has often been reproached for un-Christian exclusiveness, for holding that the elect are no more than a tiny minority. Yet in fact it represents an attempt to extend to life in this world something of the ideals which the Catholic Church had long reserved for the monastic and the secular clergy. The Calvinist would

not let sinners sin freely if he could help it, even though in strict logic it might be maintained that God obviously intended the sinner to sin. Where the Calvinists were in complete control of an area (as in sixteenth-century Geneva) or in partial control of larger areas (as in England, Scotland, the Netherlands, or Puritan Massachusetts), they censored, forbade, banished, and punished behavior they thought sinful. They were in fact petty tyrants and universal busybodies, denying the individual much of his privacy, pleasure, and individualism. But in their own minds they were clearly God's agents, doing God's work. These firm believers in the inability of human efforts to change anything were among the most ardent of workers toward getting men to change their behavior. To an amazing extent, they succeeded. They helped make the industrial revolution and the modern world.

Classroom sketches of Calvin by one of his students.

CHAPTER XII

The note of Christianity the Calvinists most clearly emphasized is that of asceticism, or at least, austerity. The Calvinist did not seek to annihilate the senses but sought rather to select among his worldly desires those that would further his salvation, and to curb or suppress those that would not. The Calvinist thought the world a very serious place indeed, in which laughter was somewhat out of order. This world is for most of us, the Calvinist believed, an antechamber to hell and eternal suffering; if you really feel this, you are not likely to be much amused. The Calvinist thought that many pleasures to which the human race is addicted—music, dancing, gambling, fine clothes, drinking, and playgoing, among others—were the kind of thing Satan liked. Although the Calvinist did not hold that all sexual intercourse is sinful, he believed firmly that the purpose God had in mind in providing sexual intercourse was the continuation of the race, and not the sensuous pleasures of the participants. Those pleasures are all the more dangerous since they may lead to extramarital indulgence, which is a very great sin.

Calvinism also sounded very loudly the ethical note of Christianity. The Calvinist had a high moral code; he was always trying to live up to his code, and to see that other people did so too. Both inward and outward directions of this effort are important. The Calvinist certainly felt the "civil war in the breast," the struggle between what has become famous as the Puritan conscience and the temptations of this world. This notion of a higher part of human consciousness that can and should censor and suppress the promptings of a lower part has left a firm imprint on the West, an imprint especially strong where Calvinism has set the dominant tone.

In its outgoing direction, this Calvinist ethical concern has taken many forms other than that of the outright, police-enforced prohibition the critics of Puritanism single out for condemnation. The early Calvinists certainly prohibited dancing, the theater, and other pleasures—the more naturally because, as we shall see, they had no democratic worries about the freedom of the individual. But the Calvinist also believed in persuasion; he made the sermon a central part of his worship. He believed in hell-fire and in the moral uses of fear of hell-fire; he believed in emotional conversion, and was a good missionary, though not at his best among primitive peoples.

Calvinism appears in pure or diluted form in many sects, Presbyterian and Congregational in Britain, Reformed on the Continent. It influenced almost all the other sects, even the Anglican and the Lutheran. Theologically, its main opponent is a system of ideas in name almost as remote from us as the Erastian, but like Erastian a fighting word as late as the eighteenth-century beginnings of the United States. This is Arminianism, so-called from James Arminius, a late sixteenth-century Dutch divine. Arminianism may be classified among the free-will theologies, for Arminius held that election (and of course damnation) were conditional in God's mind—not absolute as Calvin had maintained—and that therefore what a man did on earth could change God's mind about the man's individual fate. Generally, Arminianism was more tolerant of the easy ways of this world than Calvinism, less "puritanical," more Erastian.

Calvinism can hardly be accused of being Erastian. Where it did become the established state church—in Geneva, in the England of the 1650's, in Massachusetts, for instance—the Calvinist Church ran or tried to run the state. This is *theocracy*, not Erastianism. Where Calvinism had to fight to exist, it preached and practiced an ardent denial of the omnipotence of the state over the individual, made affirmations of popular rights which later generations turned to the uses of their own struggle against kings—and churchmen. In this sense, Calvinism helped make democracy possible, but in its original form it is by no means democratic in spirit.

The French Calvinists, the Huguenots, not only challenged royal absolutism. They often by their conduct challenged a form of absolutism then less clear than it became later—that is, the doctrine that the nation-state is the supreme form of human allegiance, the doctrine of "my country, right or wrong." Here is a letter from the French Huguenot Hotman, in which he clearly has no feeling whatever that he is being "treasonous," though he is a Frenchman inviting help from the English enemy:

We have received letters from some papists of Lyons who tell us that the people of La Rochelle [a Protestant town] have torn down the royal banners everywhere, and demanded their former independence. . . . Rumor has it that the Rochellois are thinking of allying themselves, or rather of giving themselves, to the English. If you could write to England in their favor, I believe that you would render a great service to our unhappy brothers.*

The Left Wing

The sects of the Protestant Left were usually greatly influenced by Calvinist theology and by Calvinist example. The Anabaptists and the others generally arose among humble people, more often in cities or small towns than in open farming country. They broke sharply with Catholic forms of worship, in which the congregation, if not quite passive in the presence of age-old rites, was at least quiet and orderly. In the new sects, the congregation sometimes shouted and danced, and always sang hymns with great fervor. Preaching was even more important than in more conservative forms of Protestantism, and more emotionally charged with hopes of heaven

John of Leyden (1536), as King of Münster.

and fears of hell. Many of the sects were wildly chiliastic—that is, they expected the Second Coming of Christ at once. Many were in aim, and among themselves in practice, economic equalitarians, communists of a sort. They did not share wealth, however, so much as the poverty that had seemed to St. Francis and now seemed to them an essential part of the Christian way.

Almost all of them had some beliefs, some goals, that alarmed many ordinary, conventional men and women. Many refused to take oaths on grounds of conscience. Most distrusted the state, regarding it as a necessary instrument operated by sinners to punish other sinners, an institution from which true Christians should hold aloof. What is most striking about these sects is the extraordinary range of their ideals and behavior. Some of them really behaved as badly—as insanely—as their conservative enemies have charged. John of Leyden, crowned at Münster as "King David" with two golden, jeweled crowns, one kingly, one imperial, with his "Queen Divara" and a whole harem in attendance,

---

* Hotman to Bullinger, 12 December, 1572, quoted in B. Reynolds, *Proponents of Limited Monarchy in Sixteenth-Century France* (New York, 1931), 62-63.

CHAPTER XII

seems a mad parody of the Protestant appeal to the Bible. Yet the Anabaptists already scattered about northwestern Europe at the time were shocked by what went on in Münster; and if one examines their ideas and practices one finds, for the most part, pious and earnest pacifist Christians, living simply and productively as do their modern successors, Mennonites, Baptists, and Quakers.

These left-wing sects often display an illogical and magnificent combination of pacifist principles and ardent combativeness (as long as the weapons are not physical ones, conventional means of inflicting bodily harm). These men are fighting to end fighting. Here is Jacob Hutter, who founded the Hutterite sect of Moravian Anabaptists, addressing the Governor-General of Moravia, Ferdinand of Habsburg, a good Catholic who was ruling the Germanies for his brother Charles V:

Woe, woe! unto you, O ye Moravian rulers, who have sworn to that cruel tyrant and enemy of God's truth, Ferdinand, to drive away his pious and faithful servants. Woe! we say unto you, who fear that frail and mortal man more than the living, omnipotent, and eternal God, and chase from you, suddenly and inhumanly, the children of God, the afflicted widow, the desolate orphan, and scatter them abroad. . . . God, by the mouth of the prophet, proclaims

that He will fearfully and terribly avenge the shedding of innocent blood, and will not pass by such as fear not to pollute and contaminate their hands therewith. Therefore, great slaughter, much misery and anguish, sorrow and adversity, yea, everlasting groaning, pain and torment are daily appointed you.*

Given the pacifist basis of most Anabaptist cults, the violence of this letter is extraordinary, even for the time. Yet these men did know how to die. They, too, were martyrs. And they were persecuted by the more moderate reformers with a violence as firm and principled as that which Protestant tradition attributes to the Catholic Inquisition.

It must not be concluded that all sectarians of the Left were as violently non-violent as Hutter. An even stronger and more long-lasting note is that sounded by a man like the English John Bunyan (1628-1688), whose *Pilgrim's Progress* has long been read far beyond the circles of the Baptist sect of which he was a lay preacher. This book is an allegory of life seen as a pilgrimage toward a happy end, and the joys of Beulahland, a pilgrimage full of trials, but not by any means a series of horrors. It is written in simple language, and its view of life is quite untortured.

* J. T. van Braght, *Martyrology*, I, 151-153, quoted in R. J. Smithson, *The Anabaptists* (London, 1935), 69-71.

IV: The Catholic Reformation

The dominant early Catholic response to the challenge of the Protestant Reformation was to stand pat and try to suppress the rebels. Such, basically, was the papal policy toward Luther. Yet the fact remains that the religious ferment out of which Protestantism emerged was originally a ferment *within* the Catholic Church. To that ferment many who remained within

the Church had contributed. Erasmus and other Christian humanists (see p. 449) greatly influenced the early stages of what has come to be called the Catholic Reformation. Notably in Spain, but spreading throughout the Catholic world, there was a revival of deep mystical impulses and a corresponding increase in popular participation in religion.

Within a long generation, the Catholic Church was to rally its spiritual and material forces, achieve a large measure of reform from within, and, by winning back areas in Germany, Bohemia, Hungary, and Poland, establish the territorial limits of Protestantism in the West substantially where they now are. This Catholic Reformation, in Protestant historical writing often called the Counter-Reformation, was no mere negative defense, but a positive spiritual renewal in its own right. It did not restore the medieval unity of Christendom, but it did preserve and reinvigorate fundamental Catholic beliefs and practice.

They were not preserved without the aid of the secular arm. Both the Catholic and the Protestant Reformations were inseparably tied up with domestic and international politics, as we shall see in detail in the next chapter. The powerful House of Habsburg, both in its Spanish and its German branches, was the active head of political Catholicism in the next few generations. The French monarchs, though their support was perhaps rather more political than religious, none the less helped greatly to preserve France as a Catholic land. Moreover, in France itself the seventeenth century was to witness a firm Catholic revival, led by such great preachers as Massillon, Bossuet, and Fénelon. This religious revival, as is not uncommon, produced diverging strains as well as orthodox ones—the almost Calvinistic Jansenism of Port Royal, the quietism of Madame Guyon. In many parts of Germany and its Slavic borderlands, and in Italy, the reigning princes and their nobilities were powerful influences behind the old religion.

Nor were Catholic fundamentals preserved without special organization. Once more, as with the Cluniacs, the Cistercians, the mendicant orders, this renewal of Catholic strength, this need to achieve in the name of the old something quite new, produced a series of new orders of the regular clergy, a revival of the old monastic ideals

of austere simplicity and social service. The reforming current was already gathering strength when the papacy was still in the lax hands of Leo X, Luther's opponent. During Leo's pontificate an earnest group formed at Rome the Oratory of Divine Love, dedicated to the deepening of spiritual experience through special services and religious exercises. In the 1520's, the Oratory inspired the foundation of the Theatines, an order aimed particularly at the education of the clergy. In the 1520's also, a new branch of the Franciscans appeared, the Capuchins, to lead the order back to Francis' own ideals of poverty and preaching to the poor. During the next decade or so, half a dozen other new orders were established.

The Jesuits

The greatest of these by far was the Society of Jesus, founded in 1540 by the Spaniard Ignatius Loyola (1491-1556). The founder, until he turned to religion after a painful wound received in battle, had been a soldier, and the Jesuit order was from the beginning the soldiery of the Catholic Church. Loyola set the rules for his order in his *Spiritual Exercises*. The following extracts bring out admirably two major characteristics of the Jesuits: first, the absolute (for once the word must be taken literally) obedience to higher authority, to the Catholic Church as embodied in its hierarchy; and second, the realistic, middle-of-the-road estimate of what can be expected of ordinary human beings in this world:

1. Always to be ready to obey with mind and heart, setting aside all judgment of one's own, the true spouse of Jesus Christ, our holy mother, our infallible and orthodox mistress, the Catholic Church, whose authority is exercised over us by the hierarchy.
13. That we may be altogether of the same mind and in conformity with the Church herself, if she shall have defined anything to be

black which to our eyes appears to be white, we ought in like manner to pronounce it to be black. For we must undoubtedly believe, that the Spirit of our Lord Jesus Christ, and the Spirit of the Orthodox Church His Spouse, by which Spirit we are governed and directed to Salvation, is the same; . . . .

Ignatius Loyola.

14. It must also be borne in mind, that although it be most true, that no one is saved but he that is predestinated, yet we must speak with circumspection concerning this matter, lest perchance, stressing too much the grace or predestination of God, we should seem to wish to shut out the force of free will and the merits of good works; or on the other hand, attributing to these latter more than belongs to them, we derogate meanwhile from the power of grace.*

Born in controversy, the Jesuits have always been a center of controversy. To their hostile critics, who have been numerous both within and without the Catholic Church, the Jesuits have seemed unscrupulous soldiers of the pope. Though they have

* *Documents of the Christian Church*, Henry Bettenson, ed. (New York, 1947), 363, 364-365.

rarely been accused of the simpler vices common gossip has long alleged against the monk—fondness for food and drink, laziness, laxity with women—they have been accused of a subtler devotion to worldly power, to success in a quite unspiritual sense. They have been accused of preaching and practicing the doctrine that the end justifies the means, that as soldiers of the one true Church they may indulge in dirty fighting as long as such tactics seem likely to bring victory.

This is indeed a slander, for even at the purely worldly level, Jesuit devotion to Catholic tradition is too deep for them to make the mistake of underestimating the hold the moral decencies have on human beings. And the historical record leaves no doubt of Jesuit success in bolstering the spiritual as well as the material credit of Catholicism in these critical days of the sixteenth and seventeenth centuries. Jesuits were everywhere, in Hungary, in Poland, in England, in Holland, trying to win back lost lands and peoples from the Protestants. They were winning new lands and peoples on the expanding frontiers of the West, in India, in China, in Japan, in North America. They were martyrs, preachers, teachers, social workers, counselors of statesmen, always disciplined, never lapsing into the kind of fleshly worldliness that had been the fate of other monastic orders.

The Inquisition

The Jesuits were the chief new instruments of the Catholic Reformation. An old instrument of the Church was also employed—the Inquisition, a special ecclesiastical court which in its papal form began in the thirteenth century as part of the effort to put down the Albigensian heresy (see Chapter VII), and in its Spanish form began in the fifteenth century as part of the effort of the new Spanish monarchy to enforce religious uniformity on its subjects (see Chapter X). Both papal and Spanish inquisitions were medieval courts, which used medieval methods of torture. Both were employed against the Protestants in the sixteenth century.

Protestant tradition sometimes makes both the Inquisition and the Jesuits appear as the promoters of a widespread and veritable reign of terror. Certainly the Jesuits and their allies made full use of the many pressures and persuasions any highly organized society can bring to bear on nonconformists. And the Inquisition did perpetrate horrors against former Moslems in Spain and against Catholics-turned-Protestants in the Low Countries. But the Inquisition does not appear to have been a really major force in stemming the Protestant tide. It was most active in countries of southern Europe—Italy, Spain, Portugal—where Protestantism was never a real threat. And in the regions where the Catholic Reformation was most successful in winning back large numbers to the Roman faith—the Germanies, the Slavic and Magyar marches of the West—sheer persecution was not a decisive factor.

The Council of Trent

The Catholic Reformation was not a change of dogma, not a change of spiritual direction. If anything, revulsion against the Protestant tendency toward some form of the "priesthood of the believer" hardened Catholic doctrines into a firmer insistence on the miraculous power of the priesthood. Protestant variation promoted Catholic uniformity. Not even on indulgences did the Church yield; interpreted as a spiritual return for spiritual effort, not as a money transaction, indulgences were reaffirmed by the Council of Trent. The work of this council ties together the various measures of reform, and illustrates clearly the fact that what the Catholic Reformation reformed was not doctrine but practice.

The Council of Trent was called in 1545 by Paul III (1534-1549), the first of a line of popes devoted to the task of combatting realistically the inroads of Protestantism. To liberals—including liberal Catholics—it has seemed no true general council, but an instrument in the hands of the popes and the Jesuits, a mere rubber stamp. Certainly in conception it was meant to provide at least a chance for reconciliation with the Protestants. Leading figures in the more conservative Protestant groups were invited, but they never attended. The French clergy, with their Gallican tradition, did not co-operate freely, and indeed part of the work of the Council of Trent was not accepted in France for some fifty years. The Council was caught in the web of the religious wars and intrigues of high politics, and its work was several times interrupted. Nevertheless it continued to meet off and on for twenty years until it completed its work of re-affirming and codifying doctrine in 1564.

On matters of doctrine, the Council of Trent took a stand that ruled out all possibility of a compromise with the Protestants on the major issues separating them from Catholics. It reaffirmed the essential role of the priesthood, reaffirmed all seven sacraments, reaffirmed the great importance of *both* faith and works, reaffirmed that *both* the Scriptures and the spokesmen of the Church were authorities on theology. The uncompromisingly traditional stand taken by the Council is evident in the *Professio Fidei Tridentine* (the Trent Profession of Faith), which for long was subscribed to by converts to Catholicism. It runs in part:

I most firmly acknowledge and embrace the Apostolical and ecclesiastical traditions and other observances and constitutions of the same Church. I acknowledge the sacred Scripture according to that sense which Holy Mother Church has held and holds, to whom it belongs to decide upon the true sense and interpretation of the holy Scriptures, nor will I ever receive and interpret the Scriptures except

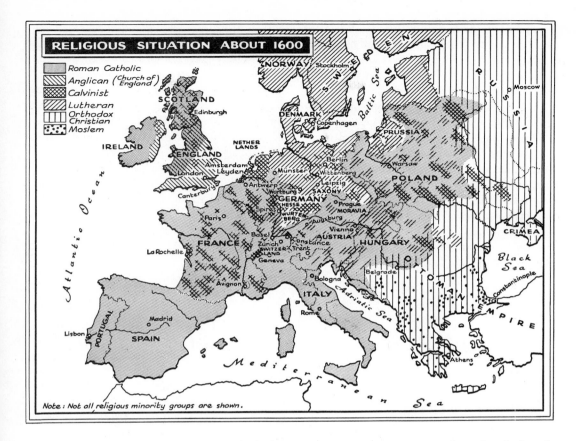

RELIGIOUS SITUATION ABOUT 1600

Roman Catholic
Anglican (Church of England)
Calvinist
Lutheran
Orthodox Christian
Moslem

Note: Not all religious minority groups are shown.

according to the unanimous consent of the Fathers.

• • •

I profess likewise that true God is offered in the Mass, a proper and propiatory sacrifice for the living and the dead, and that in the most Holy Eucharist there are truly, really and substantially the body and the blood, together with the soul and divinity of our Lord Jesus Christ, and that a conversion is made of the whole substance of bread into his body and of the whole substance of wine into his blood, which conversion the Catholic Church calls transubstantiation.*

The Council of Trent and the reforming popes of the later sixteenth century effected in Catholic practice the kind of change that had been achieved under Cluniac auspices five hundred years earlier. The Council insisted on the strict observance of clerical vows and on the ending of abuses.

─────────
* Bettenson, *Documents*, 374-375.

It took measures against the sale of church offices and against non-residence of prelates. It called for the establishment of seminaries to give priests better training. To promote discipline among the laity, it imposed censorship on a large scale, issuing the *Index*, a list of books that Catholics were not to read because of the peril to their faith. The *Index* included not only the writings of heretics and Protestants but also the works of such anticlericals as Machiavelli and Boccaccio.

Under Pius V, Pope from 1566 to 1572, a standard catechism, breviary, and missal were drawn up to embody for purposes of instruction the codifying work of the Council of Trent. In short, the whole structure of the Church, both for the training of the priesthood and for the training of the layman, was tightened up, given a new spirit. The papal court was no longer just another Italian Renaissance court. It is true that, especially among the upper clergy in countries like France, a certain laxity had again crept in by the eighteenth century. But the widespread corruption against which Luther and his fellows inveighed never again prevailed in the West.

The strength of the Catholic Reformation is shown by the fact that, once it was well launched, the Protestants made few further territorial inroads. Within a century of Luther's revolt, the broad lines of the territorial division in the West between areas dominantly Catholic and areas dominantly Protestant were established much as they are today. England, Scotland, Holland, northern and eastern Germany (with a southward projection in Wurtemberg and Switzerland), and Scandinavia were predominantly Protestant. Ireland, Belgium, France, southern Germany (with a northern projection in the valley of the Rhine), the Habsburg lands, Poland, Italy, and the Iberian Peninsula were predominantly Catholic. But only predominantly. There were Catholic minorities in England, Scotland, and Holland, and the two faiths interpenetrated most confusedly in a greatly divided Germany; there were Protestant minorities in Ireland, France, and even in some of the Habsburg lands the Jesuits had won back.

V: The Place of Protestantism in History

Protestantism and Progress

Protestants and secularists sometimes interpret the Reformation as something peculiarly "modern," a decisive break with a "medieval" past, something forward-looking and even "democratic" as distinguished from the stagnant and status-ridden Middle Ages. This notion seems to gain support from the obvious fact that those parts of the West which in the last three centuries have been economically most prosperous, which have worked out most successfully democratic constitutional government, and which have made the most striking contributions to modern western culture, especially in the natural sciences, were predominantly Protestant. Moreover, the powers which, since the decline of Spanish power after 1600, have risen to a kind of preponderance of power and prestige in the West—namely France, the British Empire, Germany, and now the United States—have been with one exception predominantly Protestant. And the one exception, France, has had since the eighteenth century a strong, at times a leading element which, though not in the main Protestant, is strongly secularist and anticlerical. It looks as if the nations that went Protestant also went modern and progressive.

This notion that Protestantism is somehow a cause or at least an accompaniment of political and cultural leadership in the modern West needs to be examined carefully. It has, of course, the kind of truth certain modern philosophers have called the truth of the "myth." That is, for a good many years a good many Protestants and secularists in these prosperous countries have believed that their Protestantism was a major part of what made them prosperous. To the average Victorian Englishman, for instance, at the height of British power and wealth, the fact that his country had gone Protestant in the sixteenth century was at least as important as Magna Carta—and the existence of good deposits of coal and iron—in producing the prosperous England of which he was so proud. The historian must record the acceptance of the myth; but he must also attempt to go back to the events that were used to construct the myth.

We find that Protestantism in the sixteenth century looks in many ways quite different from Protestantism seen from the nineteenth and twentieth centuries, just as Magna Carta in the thirteenth century looks quite different from Magna Carta looked back at from the nineteenth. First, as we have already noted, sixteenth-century Protestants were not rationalists. They were, to use an unfavorable word, almost as "superstitious" as the Catholics. Luther actually threw his ink bottle at the devil, or so they tell the tourists at the castle of the Wartburg; the Calvinists burned witches, or at any rate hanged them. To put the matter more favorably, the Protestants for the most part shared with their Catholic opponents very fundamental Christian conceptions of original sin, the direct divine governance of the universe, the reality of heaven and hell, and—most important—they had no more than did the Catholics a general conception of life on this earth as improving, as progressing to an even better life for coming generations.

Second, these early Protestants were by no means tolerant, by no means believers in the separation of Church and State. When they were in a position to do so, they used governmental power to prevent public worship in any form other than their own. Many of them persecuted those who disagreed with them, both Protestants of other sects and Catholics—that is, they banished them or imprisoned them or even killed them. The classic instance is Calvin's condemnation and execution of Servetus, and there are many other instances.

Third, these early Protestants were hardly democratic, at least in most of the senses that loose (but indispensable) word has for twentieth-century Americans. Logically, the Protestant appeal from the authority of the pope backed by Catholic tradition to the conscience of the individual believer fits in with notions like "individualism," "rights of man," and "liberty." Some historians have even found a correlation between the Protestant appeal to the authority of the Bible and the later characteristic American appeal to the authority of a written constitution. But most of the early Protestant reformers certainly did not hold that all men are created equal; they were not social and economic equalitarians. Rather, they believed in an order of rank, in a society of status. Lutheranism and Anglicanism were clearly conservative in their political and social doctrines. Calvinism can be made to look very undemocratic indeed if we concentrate on its conception of an elect few chosen by God for salvation and an unregenerate majority condemned to eternal damnation. And in its early years in Geneva and in New England Calvinism was in fact a theocracy, a rule of the "saints."

In the long run, however, Calvinism favored the domination of a fairly numerous middle class. As we shall see shortly, the most persuasive argument for a causal relation between Protestantism and modern western democratic life does not proceed directly from the ideas of the early Protestants about men in society, but from the way Protestant moral ideals fitted in with the strengthening of a commercial and industrial middle class. Finally, among the Anabaptists and other radical sects, we do find even in the sixteenth century demands for political, social, and economic equality. But where these demands are made, they are cast in Biblical language and rest on concepts of direct divine intervention quite strange to us. Moreover, many of these sects tended not so much toward active social revolt to improve earthly standards of living as toward a peculiarly Protestant form of withdrawal from things of this earth, toward a pacifism and a mysticism quite compatible with leaving the unregenerate majority in possession of this unworthy sense-world.

The Protestant Reformation, then, did not create modern society single-handed. But it did challenge those in authority in many parts of Europe and did start all sorts of men, some of them in humble circumstances, thinking about fundamental problems of life in this world as well as in the next. It was one of the great destroyers of the medieval synthesis. Its most important positive action can best be traced through its part in forming the way of life of the middle classes who were to lay the foundations of modern western democracy. The relation between Protestant ethics and the "spirit of capitalism" has been admirably traced in the work of a modern German sociologist, Max Weber.

Protestantism and Capitalism

In a simplified form, Weber's thesis runs as follows: Capital is the produced means of further production—not, in these early days, power-driven machines and factories, but tools, the division of labor, the production of specialized items for exchange. The accumulation of capital requires abstention from immediate consumption. A worker who has to grow all his own food can barely take time out to improve his tools. But if he can save or borrow enough to feed himself and keep warm while he is working on his tools, he can ultimately produce a better crop, more than is needed to keep him alive. The surplus he can sell for money, which he can use to make further improvements, to increase his capital. As we have seen, not even in the Dark Ages were manorial groups wholly reduced to living from hand to mouth. In a sense, there has always been in the historic West *some* "capitalism," some division of labor, some production for exchange. But toward the later Middle Ages, this process was greatly speeded up,

and a class of men arose who traded on a fairly large scale, and who made large profits. The more they could "plough back" those profits into the business, especially if by so doing they could reduce the cost of the items they made or sold, the more capital they accumulated, and the bigger their business became.

Now this "ploughing back" of course meant not spending on immediate goods for their own consumption. It might also mean in part squeezing more work for the same or less pay from their workers. But at least this process could not go beyond the point where it ruined the effectiveness of the labor. It meant also that the capitalist, the businessman who worked very hard at his job, who spent all his time "making money," did in fact add to the total productiveness of the society. In very simple terms, hard work and no play, all along the line, but especially at the top, meant more actual production.

Protestantism, especially its Calvinist form, encouraged this sort of life. It encouraged hard work. The devil lies in wait for idle hands. Work keeps a man from temptation to run after women, or play silly games, or drink, or do many other things unpleasing to the Calvinist God. More, work is positively a good thing, a kind of tribute we pay to the Lord. Luther, too, glorified work of all kinds and preached the doctrine of the dignity of the vocation a man is called to, be it ever so humble. In almost all forms of Protestantism we find this feeling, so contrary to the contempt for work of the field and countinghouse evident in the tradition of chivalry.

It is for action that God maintaineth us and our activities; work is the moral as well as the natural end of power. . . . It is action that God is most served and honoured by. . . . The public welfare or the good of the many is to be valued above our own.°

° *Richard Baxter's Christian Directory*, quoted in Max Weber, *The Protestant Ethic and the Spirit of Capitalism*, Talcott Parsons, trans. (London, 1930), 260.

So much for the work, for the positive side of the equation. But on the negative side, Protestantism, and in particular Calvinism, discouraged many kinds of consumption which took energies away from the large-scale production that is the essence of the modern economic system. The Calvinist, to put it mildly, discouraged the fine arts, the theater, the dance, expensive clothes, what the American economist Veblen has called "conspicuous consumption" generally. The Calvinist represents a new development of the perennial Christian ascetic tradition. This is not the asceticism of the hermits of the desert:

Question: But may I not cast off the world that I may only think of my salvation? Answer: You may cast off all such excess of worldly cares or business as unnecessarily hinder you in spiritual things. But you may not cast off all bodily employment and mental labour in which you may serve the common good. Everyone as a member of Church or Commonwealth must employ their parts to the utmost for the good of the Church and the Commonwealth. To neglect this and say: I will pray and meditate, is as if your servant should refuse his greatest work and tie himself to some lesser, easier part. And God hath commanded you some way or other to labour for your daily bread and not to live as drones of the sweat of others only.*

A society with many Calvinists tended to produce much, to consume solidly but without "waste" (we are speaking here in terms of economics, not in terms of art or morals). Therefore, under competitive conditions, its business leaders accumulated the kind of surplus we call capital, which they could invest in the methods of production that have so enriched the West. All work and no play—well, not much—made the Calvinist society an economically prosperous one.

The Scots, the Dutch, the Swiss, the Yankees of New England—all of them markedly Calvinistic peoples—have long had a popular reputation for thrift, diligence,

---

* Ibid., 261-262.

and driving a hard bargain. And it is surprising how many concrete bits of evidence reinforce the Weber thesis. The Protestant societies at once cut down the number of holy days—holidays without work. They kept Sunday very rigorously as a day without work, but the other six were all work days. The Calvinists even eliminated Christmas, and, since there were as yet no national lay equivalents of the old religious festivals, no Fourth of July or Labor Day, the early modern period in most Protestant countries had a maximum of work days per year. This is a marginal matter, but it is by such margins that economic superiority is won. Many Protestant theologians rejected the medieval Catholic doctrine that regarded interest on investments beyond a low, "just" rate as usury, an illegitimate and immoral thing. In general, they rejected most of the medieval doctrines suggested by the term "just price" (see p. 322) in favor of something much closer to our modern notions of free competition in the market. In the market, God would certainly take care of his own.

Moreover, it would appear that the Weber thesis can be extended to include a certain rough parallel between the flourishing of Protestantism, especially of the Calvinist kind, and the flourishing of science-with-technology. This does not mean that Catholic countries produced no great scientists, or that there is anything in Catholic beliefs that inhibits the scientist in his work. It is rather, as with capitalism, that the Protestant ethic gave a slight extra push to the scientist and technologist in their pursuit of so this-worldly a concern as the detached study of natural phenomena.

Finally, the firm Calvinist retention of the other world as the supreme, but for the individual never *certain*, goal reinforced the class-consciousness of the middle class. It helped shield the individual wealthy Calvinist from the great temptation of the newly rich—that is, assimilation to the standards of life of a loose-living, spendthrift upper class. Family fortunes founded by hard work and inconspicuous consumption tended to hold together for several generations.

Weber's thesis must not be taken as the sole explanation of the rise of capitalism in early modern times. It is but one of many variables in a complex situation. In the first place, the stirrings of modern economic life far antedate Luther and Calvin, and are clearest and most important in many regions—Italy, southern Germany, Belgium—which were not actually won over to Protestantism. Banking begins in northern Italy under Catholic rule—in Florence, for instance—when the theoretical official prohibition of usury still prevails. Almost certainly relaxation of rules against usury would have received official Catholic theological sanction even had there been no Protestant Reformation. In the second place, there is no perfect co-ordination between Protestantism and industrial development on one hand and Catholicism and industrial backwardness (or notably slower development) on the other. Belgium, the German Rhineland, Piedmont, and Lombardy are striking examples of Catholic regions which on the whole have kept in modern times well up to the fore in general productiveness and prosperity. Protestant East Prussia, on the other hand, remained a basically rural region. In the third place, no sensible explanation of the rise of modern industrial economy can neglect the simple facts of geography and natural resources. Suppose, contrary to all likelihood, Italy had turned solidly Calvinistic; this still would not give Italy the coal and iron that Calvinist, or at least Protestant, England had.

Yet the "Protestant ethic" remains an important element in the economic transformation of modern Europe. It gave perhaps the extra fillip, the margin that started the West on its modern path—along with that opening up of Europe overseas which helped the Atlantic nations over the Mediterranean nations, along with the natural resources of northern and western Europe, along with the damp, temperate climate that made hard work easier than in the Mediterranean, along with much else.

Protestantism and Nationalism

One final big generalization about the Protestant Reformation is much less disputable than attempts to tie that movement with modern individualism, democracy, and industrialism. After the great break of the sixteenth century, both Protestantism and Catholicism became important elements in the formation of modern nationalism. Here again we must not fall into the trap of one-way causation. That Protestants were not always patriots we have seen in the letter from the French Huguenot, Hotman, seeking help from the English enemy. Much besides the Reformation goes into the formation of the modern state-system of the West and its cementing patriotism. "French-ness" and modern "German-ness" perhaps began as far back as the Strasbourg oaths of the ninth century. But where a specific form of religion became identified with a given political unit, religious feeling and patriotic feeling each reinforced the other. This is most clear where a political unit had to struggle for its independence. Protestantism heightened Dutch resistance to the Spaniard; Catholicism heightened Irish resistance to the Englishman. But even in states already independent in the sixteenth century, religion came to strengthen patriotism. England from Elizabeth I on has, despite the existence of a Catholic minority, proudly held itself up as a Protestant nation. Spain has with at least equal pride identified itself as a Catholic nation. In the great wars to which we must now turn, religion and politics were inextricably mixed.

Reading Suggestions
on the Reformation

GENERAL ACCOUNTS

See also the titles listed after Chapter X.

L. von Ranke, *History of the Reformation in Germany* (many editions). A very famous work, more than a century old.

R. H. Bainton, *The Reformation of the Sixteenth Century* (* Beacon, 1952). By a sound Protestant historian, fully abreast of modern research.

E. H. Harbison, *The Age of Reformation* (Cornell Univ. Press). Admirable introduction.

G. L. Mosse, *The Reformation* (Holt, 1952. A Berkshire Study). A very brief account.

H. J. Grimm, *The Reformation Era, 1500-1650* (Macmillan, 1954). A good American text book with a very thorough critical bibliography.

W. Durant, *The Reformation* (Simon & Schuster, 1957). The sixth part of the distinguished popularizer's "Story of Civilization," a by no means unsympathetic study made from a rationalist position. The bibliography marks works on the history of religious questions with C, P, J, and R after an author's name to indicate respectively Catholic, Protestant, Jewish, and Rationalist.

G. R. Elton, ed., *The Reformation, 1520-1559* (Cambridge Univ. Press, 1958). This is Vol. II of the *New Cambridge Modern History*. A collaborative work, the latest standard work of reference in the field. Unfortunately, the full bibliographies of the old *Cambridge Modern History* (1902-1912) are in this new one to be postponed to a later companion volume for the whole series.

H. Holborn, *A History of Modern Germany:* Vol. I, *The Reformation* (Knopf, 1959). Scholarly, readable, up-to-date.

SPECIAL STUDIES

R. H. Bainton, *Here I Stand: A Life of Martin Luther* (Abingdon-Cokesbury, 1950; * New American Library). Sympathetic, scholarly, and readable.

H. Belloc, *Characters of the Reformation* (* Image). Lively, suggestive partisan writing by an English Catholic.

H. Grisar, *Martin Luther, His Life and Works* (Herder, 1930). From the Catholic point of view.

E. G. Schwiebert, *Luther and His Times* (Concordia, 1952). Particularly useful for the setting and the effects of Luther's revolt.

S. M. Jackson, *Ulrich Zwingli: The Reformer of German Switzerland* (Putnam's, 1900). An old work, but indispensable.

G. Harkness, *John Calvin, The Man and His Ethics* (Holt, 1931; * Apex). A good short introduction.

J. Huizinga, *Erasmus and the Age of Reformation* (* Harper Torchbook). A distinguished work by the great Dutch historian.

J. Mackinnon, *Calvin and the Reformation* (Longmans, Green, 1936); and W. Walker, *John Calvin, the Organizer of Protestantism* (Putnam's, 1906). Solid, longer studies.

T. M. Parker, *The English Reformation to 1558* (Oxford Univ. Press, 1950. Home University Library). Excellent short account.

F. M. Powicke, *The Reformation in England* (Oxford Univ. Press, 1941). A scholarly study.

E. B. Bax, *The Rise and Fall of the Anabaptists* (Macmillan, 1903). Old-fashioned socialist bias. A major treatise on this subject is needed, but see R. H. Bainton, "The Left Wing of the Reformation," *Journal of Religion*, XXI (1941).

L. Pastor, *History of the Popes from the Close of the Middle Ages* (Herder, 1923-1953). The classic account; in many volumes.

B. J. Kidd, *The Counter-Reformation* (Society for Promoting Christian Knowledge, 1933) and P. Janelle, *The Catholic Reformation* (Bruce, 1951) are two modern scholarly accounts, the first by an Anglican, the second by a Catholic.

T. J. Campbell, *The Jesuits, 1534-1921* (Encyclopaedia Press, 1921). Written from the Catholic standpoint.

H. Boehmer, *The Jesuits* (Castle, 1928). From the Protestant point of view.

M. Weber, *The Protestant Ethic and the Spirit of Capitalism*, T. Parsons, ed. (Scribner's, 1930; ° paperback edition by same publisher). A famous and controversial work on the interrelationship of religion and economics.

E. Troeltsch, *Protestantism and Progress* (Putnam's, 1912; ° Beacon). By one of the most important religious philosophers of modern times.

R. H. Tawney, *Religion and the Rise of Capitalism* (° Mentor). A modified English version of the Weber thesis, written by a leading intellectual associated with the Labor party.

J. W. Allen, *Political Thought in the Sixteenth Century*, 3rd ed. (Barnes & Noble, 1951). The best account of the subject in English, though not easy reading.

SOURCES

H. S. Bettenson, *Documents of the Christian Church* (Oxford Univ. Press, 1947). This admirably arranged compilation is particularly useful for the Reformation.

R. H. Bainton, *The Age of the Reformation* (Van Nostrand, 1956; ° Anvil). A comprehensive selection from the great men and great works of the period.

Châteillon, *Concerning Heretics*, R. H. Bainton, ed. (Columbia Univ. Press, 1935). One of the earliest tracts urging religious freedom, not just toleration.

Dynastic and Religious Wars

CHAPTER XIII

I: International Politics— The Modern European State-System

Historians influenced by national traditions, their own interests, and much else, have chosen a number of different dates, usually in the last half of the fifteenth century, to mark the watershed between "medieval" and "modern." Americans, for understandable reasons, like to think of 1492 as the great date. In the kingdoms of western Europe, the historian singles out the appearance of strong and ambitious monarchs—1485, the first Tudor, Henry VII in England; 1461, Louis XI in France; 1469, the marriage of Ferdinand of Aragon and Isabella of Castile. Some historians feel that Luther's posting of the Ninety-Five Theses in 1517 is the real break with the Middle Ages. Others, focusing on what we now call international relations, choose a date obscure to most Americans—1494. In that year, Charles VIII of France led his army over the Alps toward the conquest of Italy, in what some consider the "first modern war."

All such dates are of course somewhat arbitrary. As we have seen (Chapter X), the watershed between medieval and modern culture cannot be placed in a single country or a single year. Moreover, as we shall see later, it can be argued that what *really* makes the modern world modern—that is, new, different from preceding worlds—is the combination of rationalism, natural science, technology, and economic organization which has given men a new power over natural resources. If the standard of change is an economic and technological one, the great change comes as late as the eighteenth century, and the sixteenth and seventeenth centuries are but preparation.

The Competitive State-System

Still, for the historian of international relations, a difference between the medieval and the modern organization of the European state-system is noticeable as early as the late fifteenth century. First of all, there *was* a state-system, indeed in some senses a society of states. Some propagandists for world government in our own day like to insist that relations among states claiming to be "sovereign" or "independent" are really no relations at all, that the modern state-system is simply anarchic chaos. Actually, all political units whose citizens have frequent relations of any kind—trade, travel, study, sport, war—with citizens of other units are perforce members of the same state-system. Rome and China in 100 A.D. were not members of the same system, for though there are traces of some relations, some traffic across Asia between the two, these are slight indeed. But France, Spain, England, and indeed all the nations of Europe belonged to one system in the sixteenth century.

This state-system had no common central political or ecclesiastical institution. In theory, in the West during the Middle Ages, there was on earth but one Christian society, headed by Pope and Emperor, each wielding one of the swords of God. In practice, the eastern Orthodox Church was wholly separate from Rome; and the Holy Roman Emperor never had any real hold on England, France, or, in the Middle Ages, the Iberian Peninsula. Medieval unity was an aspiration rather than a fact. Still, the pope was a fact, and Roman Catholic unity was a fact in the late Middle Ages. Protestantism and the rise of strong dynastic states made the later disunity, the lack of any central institutions, even more obvious.

The West, then, is in early modern times a group of states, big, middle-sized, and little, each striving to grow, usually in a quite concrete way by annexing others in whole or in part, or at least by bringing them under some sort of control. In practice, at any given moment some states are on the offensive, trying to gain land, power, and wealth; others are on the defensive, trying to preserve what they have. Historically, some few of these units have been so small, so self-contained, that they have never tried to expand. Yet even the model small democracies of the twentieth century, like Sweden and Denmark, have taken the offensive at some time in the past five hundred years.

The constituent units of this system of competing states may be called "sovereign" or "independent." There is never a perfect achievement of sovereignty or independence; since by definition the states are in competitive relations, no one can ever be unaffected by the behavior of the others. But we may roughly call a state sovereign if its rulers have an armed force they can use against others. In this sense, there has been since the height of feudal disintegration, perhaps in the tenth century, a continuous though irregular process of reducing the number of sovereign states, until today the whole world contains no more than eighty-odd. If a feudal lord with his own armed retainers is called "sovereign," since he could and did make war on his own initiative, then the tenth-century West had thousands of such units. As we have seen in Chapter VII, the situation was never quite so bad as this. The successor states of the Roman Empire in the West did preserve some kind of formal national or at least provincial unity. By the end of the Middle Ages, however, over large parts of the West the little feudal units had been absorbed into much bigger states and local wars had become impossible—or if they did occur, they were risings of barons against the big ruler, and were felt to be *civil wars*. The great but shadowy unity of western Christendom was destroyed at the end of the Middle Ages; but so too was the real disunity of numerous local units capable of organized war among themselves.

As the modern state-system began to shape up in the fifteenth and sixteenth centuries, the three well-organized monarchies of Spain, France, and England dominated the western part of Europe. The smaller states of Scotland, Portugal, and Scandinavia generally played a subordinate role. In Central Europe, the Holy Roman Empire, with its many quasi-independent member states, did not have the kind of internal unity enjoyed by the Atlantic powers. Yet, under the leadership of the Austrian Habsburgs, the Empire proved capable of taking a leading part in international competition. Between the French and Habsburg power centers lay the zone of fragmentation where the Burgundian dukes of the fifteenth century had tried to revive the middle kingdom (see Chapter X). Out of this zone have come the modern small nations of Holland, Belgium, Luxembourg, Switzerland, and the larger (but never quite major) power, Italy. To the southeast was a new factor in international relations, Turkey, the Moslem successor to the old Byzantine Empire, with European lands right up to and beyond the Danube. To the east, the great state of Muscovite Russia was beginning to be formed, and Poland was already great at least in size. But save for Turkey, which sought to expand northwestward, and which was therefore ac-

tively anti-Habsburg, the eastern and southeastern states of Europe were not yet really integrated into high politics.

Save for the overseas expansion of Europe, we have here a picture that is not worlds apart from the present one. Italy is today one political nation instead of a dozen, the German power-unit is in normal times one unified nation instead of the decentralized Holy Roman Empire, and on the east Russia is a very great power indeed, Poland a lesser one. Still, on the whole, the European state-system has the broad lines it had five centuries ago. Its units are still "sovereign."

This comparative stability has not been maintained without threats to destroy it. In succession, certain states have attempted to break it down—sixteenth-century Spain, the France of Louis XIV in the seventeenth century and of the Revolution and Napoleon at the turn from the eighteenth to the nineteenth, the Germany of the Kaiser and Hitler in the twentieth. They have tried to absorb the other states, or at the very least to control them to a point where they were scarcely "sovereign." Each time, the threatened units sooner or later joined together in a coalition that was able to beat the armies of the aggressive power and maintain the system. Each time, England, which after the late medieval venture of the Hundred Years' War never attempted to absorb lands on the Continent of Europe (save for the few square miles of Gibraltar), sooner or later intervened to bolster, often to lead, the coalition against the aggressor. To use a time-honored phrase, the system was maintained through the workings of the "balance of power." This principle is not primarily a moral one, though some writers have defended it as basically moral in the sense that it tends to preserve the independence of organized states. "Balance of power" is, rather, a descriptive principle, a thread through the intricacies of international politics in the modern West. We must take up this thread in 1494.

Dynastic State
and Nation State

First, however, we must examine briefly the nature of the political units that make up the competitive state-system. It is the fashion to call them *dynastic* states up to about the end of the eighteenth century and *nation* states thereafter. The distinction is a good rough working one. In the early modern period, many states were loose agglomerations of formerly independent units that were sometimes separated from each other by foreign territory, that sometimes spoke separate languages, and that were tied together almost solely by the ruling dynasty. The Habsburg realm is a good example. In war and diplomacy the dynastic ruler and his circle of nobles and bureaucrats were a team, but the different peoples in the state had relatively little sense of patriotism, of common national effort and ambitions. Early modern wars were less than total wars. Except in their disastrous effects on government finances and on taxes, they scarcely touched the lives of the common people who were not actually in the way of contending armies. In the peace settlements, no one talked about "national self-determination of peoples," or worried greatly about transferring areas and populations from one ruler to another.

The distinction between dynastic and nation states must not be exaggerated or oversimplified. Especially in the great monarchies of Spain, England, and France a degree of national patriotism existed as early as the sixteenth century. Many of the obvious signs of "national" feeling are clear, in spite of all the local variations common to these countries. The English had long known the French scornfully as "frogs," and the French had retaliated by calling the English *les godons,* the French mispronunciation of a favorite English blasphemy. In the great war between England and Spain which culminated in the defeat of the Spanish Armada, all the signs of intense popular patriotic feeling were clearly present in England. It is true that mingled with nationalist there were religious feelings; the Englishman hated and feared the Spaniard not only as a foreigner but as a Catholic. But this mingling of nationalism and religion was to last right down to our own time.

Even in divided Germany, Luther could count on Germans to dislike Italians. Hatred of the foreigner binds men together at least as effectively as love of one another. Nor does the custom, so strange to us, of transferring political units by marriage of ruling families really affect the basic similarity between the state-system of early modern times and our own. Perhaps the accidents of marriage account for the unusual combination of Germany and Spain under Charles V; but for the most part the alliances and alignments of the sixteenth century conform extremely well to conditions of geography, resources, tradition, and culture.

Indeed, the differences between our late modern and the early modern state are generally exaggerated by most of us today. The differences are real and they make these dynastic wars seem petty and confusing; but they are differences of degree of efficiency, centralization, ability to command vast numbers of men and great resources, rapidity of movement, not differences of kind. Possibly by 1960 such differences, embodied in the possibilities of total war, push-button execution, biological warfare, fusion bombs and the like did amount to differences in kind. But this does not hold of the past right up to the immediate present, including World War II. Such a truth justifies the study in our next few chapters of these bewildering wars, big and little, the uncertain treaties of peace, the dubious diplomacy of early modern times. Such a study should at the very least give us some perspective on our present troubles. Politically and morally, if not technologically, they are much the same troubles our forefathers have known for four centuries.

By 1500, then, almost all these states possessed in at least a rudimentary form most of the social and political organs of a modern state. They lacked only a large literate population brought up in the ritual and faith of national patriotism. Notably they had two essential organs, a diplomatic service and an army, both professional, both usually controlled from a common governmental center.

Diplomacy

Some forms of diplomacy can be traced back into the Middle Ages, and indeed into ancient times. But the fifteenth and sixteenth centuries saw the full development of modern diplomatic agencies and methods. Governments established central foreign offices and sent diplomats on regular missions to foreign courts. Espionage and the secret services developed under the cover of open diplomacy. Formal peace conferences were held, and formal treaties were signed, to the accompaniment of the ceremony and protocol we now associate with such occasions. Finally, a set of rules governing all these formal relations began to take shape, a set of rules that can be called international law.

The apparatus of international politics developed most fully and soonest in Renaissance Italy, and found its classic expression in the admirably organized diplomatic service of the Republic of Venice. The detailed reports Venetian ambassadors sent back to the Senate from abroad are among the first documents of intelligence work we have. They are careful political and social studies of the personalities and lands involved rather than mere gossipy cloak-and-dagger reports. Here is an excerpt from the report of the Venetian ambassador to England in the reign of the Catholic Mary Tudor. If its estimate of English political psychology seems strange, remember that in less than twenty-five years the English had changed their religion officially three times.

But as for religion, speaking generally, your Highness may be sure that the example and the authority of the prince can here achieve everything. For as the English think highly of religion, and are moved by it, so they satisfy their sense of duty towards the prince, living as he lives, believing as he believes, and finally doing all he tells them to. In all this the English rather conform externally, in order not to be in disfavor with their ruler than follow any inner light, for they would conform in the same way to the Mohammedan or Jewish faith were the King to adopt such a faith and want them to, and indeed they would accommodate themselves to anything, but the more readily to something that seemed to promise them more freedom of living—or more utility.[*]

In those days, the diplomat abroad was a most important maker of policy in his own right. With rapid travel impossible, his government could not communicate with him in time to prescribe his acts minutely, and he had often to make important decisions on his own responsibility. Good or bad diplomacy, good or bad intelligence about foreign lands, made a vital difference in a state's success or failure in the struggle for power.

The Armed Forces

The armed forces made still more difference. These early modern centuries are the great days of the professional soldier, freed from the limitations of feudal warfare and not yet tied to the immense economic requirements and the inhuman scale of our modern warfare. The officer class in particular could plan, drill, and campaign on a fairly large but quite manageable scale; they could do more than the

---

[*] E. Alberi, *Relazione degli Ambasciatori veneti*, Series I (Florence, 1839 ff.), II, 362. Our translation.

Sixteenth-century cannon. Engraving by Dürer.

interminable jousting of late medieval times. They could, so to speak, handle warfare as an art and sometimes as a pleasure. The common soldiers had a less agreeable life. But they too, for the most part, were paid professionals; indeed the word "soldier" comes from *solidus,* the Latin for a "piece of money." Recruited usually from among the poor and dispossessed, sometimes by force, they became inured to many hardships and were on the whole rather more secure in food, clothing, and housing than their poorer civilian relatives. Certainly they rarely revolted.

The armed forces were the ruler's forces, no longer mere feudal levies. They were paid professionals, often trained to parade, to dress ranks, to keep discipline. They were whipped if they broke discipline, although threats of punishment did not always prevent desertions when pay was late or rations inadequate. Each regiment, troop, or unit commonly wore the same uniforms; whole armies, however, usually displayed such an extraordinary variety of costume that in battle recognition of friend and foe was not easy. Tactics and strategy in the field were under the control of a formal officer hierarchy that culminated in a general in command, who in turn was at least somewhat controlled by the central government through a ministry of war. In short, though these armies would look anarchic to a modern professional of the spit-and-polish school, they were far better organized and better disciplined than feudal levies had been.

Yet the early modern armies also show many feudal survivals, many forms of entrenched privilege, many ways of twisting away from centralized control. The officer class continued to preserve many of its old habits of chivalry, such as the duel, which often seriously menaced internal discipline.

If the feudal lord no longer brought his own knights for the forty days of allotted time, his descendant as regimental colonel often raised his own regiment and financed it himself. Weapons were of an extraordinary variety. Reminders of the old hand-to-hand fighting survived in the sword and in the pike, the long shaft used by foot soldiers against the armored knight and his mount. Hand firearms—arquebus, musket, and many others—were slow-loading and slow-firing, and usually not even capable of being aimed with any accuracy. The cannon, quite unstandardized as to parts and caliber, and heavy and hard to move, fired solid balls, rather than exploding shells.

Armies on the march lived mostly off the land, even when they were in home territory. But they were beginning to develop the elaborate modern organization of supply and the modern service of engineers. Both the growth of military technology and differences of national temperament were reflected in the shift of military predominance from Spain to France about 1600. Spain, the great fighting nation of the sixteenth century on land, excelled in infantry, where the pike was a major weapon. France, the great fighting nation of the seventeenth and early eighteenth centuries on land, excelled in artillery, engineering, and fortification, all services that were more plebeian, less suited to the former feudal nobility than infantry and cavalry.

Meanwhile, the first modern navies were also growing up. In the later Middle Ages, Venice, Genoa, and Pisa had all begun to assemble fleets of galleys disciplined both in the running of each ship and in maneuvers as a fleet. In the Renaissance, Venice took the lead with its Arsenal and its detailed code of maritime regulations (see Chapter X). Naval organization, naval supply, the dispatch and handling of ships, all required more orderly centralized methods than an army. They could not tolerate the survival of rugged feudal individualism, indiscipline, and lack of planning. The officer class, as in the armies, was predominantly aristocratic, but it came usually from the more adventurous, the less custom-ridden part of that class. During the sixteenth century, naval supremacy passed out of the Mediterranean to the Atlantic, where it rested briefly with Spain, and thence passed in the seventeenth century to the northern maritime powers of England, Holland, and France.

II: Habsburg and Valois

The Italian Wars
of Charles VIII and Louis XII

Charles VIII of France (1483-1498) inherited from his parsimonious father Louis XI a well-filled treasury and a good army (see Chapter X). He added to his kingdom by marrying the heiress to the Duchy of Brittany, which had long been largely independent of the French crown. Apparently secure on the home front, Charles decided to expand abroad. As the remote heir of the Angevins who had conquered Naples in the thirteenth century, Charles disputed the right of the Aragonese Ferrante (see Chapter X) to hold the Neapolitan throne. He chose Italy, however, not only because he had this tenuous genealogical claim but also because Renaissance Italy was rich, held romantic attractions for the northerners, and was divided into small rival political units—it looked, in short, to be easy picking. So it was at first, for in the winter of 1494-95 Charles paraded through to Naples in triumph. But Charles' acquisition of Brittany had already disturbed his neighbors, and his possession of Naples threatened the balance of power in Italy. The French intrusion provoked the first of the great modern coalitions, the so-called Holy League of the Papacy (which, remember, was also an Italian territorial state), the Empire, Spain, Venice, Milan, and soon England. This coalition forced the French armies out of Italy without much trouble in 1495.

Charles was followed on the French throne by his cousin of the Orléans branch of the Valois family, Louis XII (1498-1515). Louis married Charles' widow to make sure of Brittany, and then tried again in Italy, reinforced by another genealogical claim, this time to Milan. Since his grandmother came from the Visconti family, Louis regarded the Sforza dukes as simple usurpers; he proceeded to drive Il Moro from Milan in 1499 (see Chapter X). In this second French invasion, the play of alliances was much subtler and more complicated, quite worthy of the age of Machiavelli. Louis tried to insure himself from the isolation that had ruined Charles by allying in 1500 with Ferdinand of Aragon, with whom he agreed to partition Naples. Then, in 1508, Louis helped form one of those cynical coalitions that look on paper at though they could break the balance-of-power principle, because they are the union of the strong against a much weaker victim. This was the League of Cambray, in which Louis, Ferdinand, Pope Julius II, and the Emperor Maximilian joined to divide up the lands held in the lower Po Valley by the rich but militarily weak Republic of Venice.

The practical trouble with such combinations is that the combiners do not really trust one another, and usually fall to quarreling over the pickings. All went well for the despoilers at first, though the Venetians rallied and re-took their mainland stronghold of Padua. Then Ferdinand, having taken the Neapolitan towns he wanted, decided to desert Louis. The Pope, frightened at the prospect that France and the Empire might squeeze him out entirely, in 1511 formed another "Holy League" *with* Venice and Ferdinand, later joined by Henry VIII of England and the Emperor Maximilian, *against* France. Despite some early successes in the field, the French could not hold out against such a coalition, for they now had a war on two fronts. Henry attacked the north of France and won at Guinegate in 1513 a battle that has always been a sore spot with Frenchmen. It was called (by the English) the "battle of the spurs" from the speed with which the French cavalry departed from the battlefield. In Italy too the French were defeated, and Louis XII, like Charles VIII, was checkmated.

Charles V and Francis I: The First Round

These two efforts were, however, merely preliminaries. The important phase of this first great modern test of the balance of power was to follow immediately, and to take a basically different form. For there were now really two aggressors: the French House of Valois, still bent on expansion, and the House of Habsburg. When the Habsburg Charles V succeeded his grandfather Maximilian as emperor in 1519, he was a disturber by the mere fact of his existence rather than by temperament or intent. As we have already seen in Chapter XII, he had inherited Spain, the Low Countries, Germany (that is, the imperial headship of the Holy Roman Empire), and the preponderance in Italy. He apparently had France squeezed in a perfect vise.

The vise almost closed. The French king, Francis I, was badly defeated by the imperial—mostly Spanish—forces at Pavia in 1525. Francis himself was taken prisoner and held in Madrid until he signed a treaty giving up all his Italian claims, and ceding the Duchy of Burgundy. This treaty he repudiated the moment he was safely back on French soil. It is probable that Charles V would not have "eliminated" France entirely even had he been able to. These early modern wars were in no sense "total" wars, and there were accepted limits to what may decently be done to the defeated. Certainly these people convey the impression of engaging in a kind of professional athleticism that was often bloody and unscrupulous but by no means without rules. The players sometimes changed sides. In fact, one of the imperial commanders at the battle of Pavia in which the French were so badly beaten was the Constable de Bourbon, a great French noble at odds with his king.

Two years after Pavia, an incident occurred that burnt deeply into the minds of contemporaries—the sack of Rome in 1527 by the Spanish and German mercenaries of the emperor, led by the Frenchman Bourbon. These mercenaries had become infuriated by delays in pay and supplies. In a sudden shift of alignment, Pope Clement VII, a Medici and a good Italian at heart, had turned against the foreign Charles, and had allied himself with Francis and the other main Italian powers in the League of Cognac in 1526. The siege of Rome was part of Charles' reply, but the sack was a horror that he had not planned, and that lay heavily on his conscience as a good Catholic. This was one of the horrors of war that outrage public opinion in all but the most hardened partisan circles.

Charles was now at the height of his power. By the end of the decade, he had made peace with the Pope and with Francis. In 1530, he was crowned by the Pope as Emperor and as King of Italy, the last ruler to receive this double crown, this inheritance of Charlemagne and the ages, with the full formality of tradition. But the western world over which he thus symbolically ruled was a very different world

Francis I of France.

from Charlemagne's, and Charles was in fact no emperor, but a new dynast in a new conflict of power.

Charles V and Francis I: The Second Round

France was still in the vise between the Spanish and the German holdings of Charles, and Francis I was no man to accept for long so precarious a position—above all, a position in which he lost face. He used the death of the Sforza ruler of Milan in 1535 to reopen the old claim to Milan and to begin the struggle once more. Neither Francis nor Charles lived to see the end even of this particular phase of the Habsburg-Valois rivalry. Neither side secured decisive military victory. In 1559, the important Treaty of Cateau-Cambrésis confirmed Habsburg control of Milan and Naples. It marked the failure of France to acquire a real foothold in Italy, but it also marked the failure of the Habsburgs to lessen the real strength of France. The vise had not been closed; the war had been stalemated.

It had not closed because France proved militarily, economically, and politically strong enough to resist the pressure. But the vise itself was a most imperfect instrument. Charles was not as strong as he looked on the map to be. His German arm was paralyzed by the political consequences of the Protestant Reformation. Even in the decade of the 1520's, when the power of Charles was at its height, the Protestant princes of Germany had formed the League of Torgau to resist him. All the rest of his life, Germany was to be in a state of civil war, marked by truces indeed, and by attempts to settle the religious question, but never permitting the Emperor to count on a united Germany against France.

The last phase of the personal duel between the aging rivals, Charles and Francis, is a concrete example of how many variables enter the play of balance of power. Francis, to gain allies, did not hesitate to turn to Charles' rebellious German subjects. Although head of a Catholic state, a "most Christian" king, he allied himself with the Protestant Duke of Cleves. He did not even stop with Protestants, but concluded an alliance with the Moslem Sultan Suleiman of Turkey (see Chapter IX), who attacked Charles in the rear in Hungary. At the death of Francis in 1547, his son Henry II continued the Protestant alliance.

One other participant in the complex struggles of the first half of the sixteenth century was England. Though not yet a great power, she was already a major element in international politics. The men who guided English policy were perhaps moved by a consciously held theory of the balance of power which told them to intervene in Europe always on behalf of the group that was being beaten, that seemed weaker at the time. But other factors were also involved. For one thing, England after 1534 was deeply involved in her own religious troubles; moreover, she had on her northern border an independent Scotland, which tended to side with France. Finally, to English statesmen, with memories of the long medieval struggles with the French, the great hereditary enemy was always France. Yet in a pinch the English were quite capable of allying with the hereditary French enemy if they thought Charles was too strong. This happened in 1527, after Charles had won at Pavia and had taken Rome. The English minister, Cardinal Wolsey, in that year worked out an alliance with France.

But the English were quite capable of reversing themselves. In 1543, when Charles was beset by Protestants and Turks, Henry VIII came to his aid against Francis. But not too vigorously. In the campaign of 1544, something like a Christian revulsion against the French alliance with the heathen Turk had brought the Germans together for the moment, and a German army was actually on its way to Paris along the Marne Valley route. The English had landed on the Channel coast; had they really pressed matters in co-operation with the Germans, Paris itself might have fallen. But they rather deliberately besieged the Channel port of Boulogne, and Francis escaped with his capital city intact.

The Peace of Augsburg

Charles V, beset by Protestants, French, and Turks, allowed in 1555 the very important German religious settlement known as the Peace of Augsburg. By this peace, the Protestants were formally recognized as established in the regions they had consolidated. Augsburg marks the formal

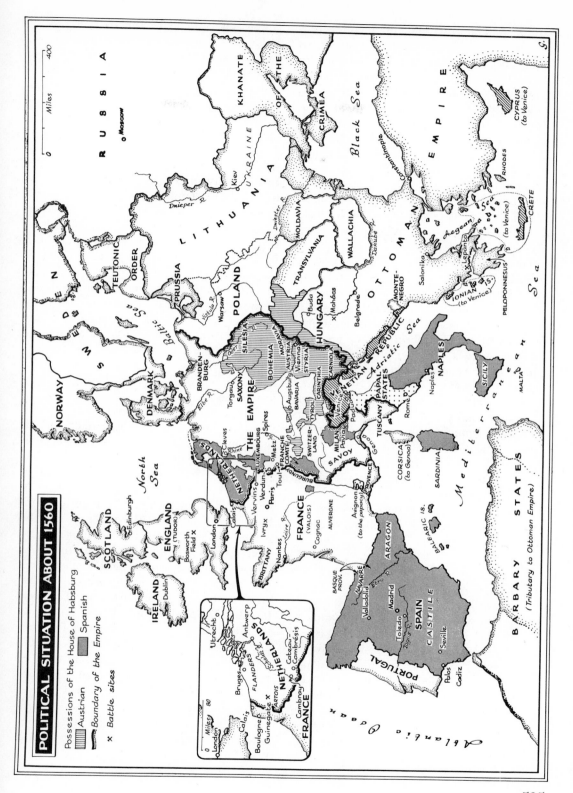

POLITICAL SITUATION ABOUT 1560

Possessions of the House of Habsburg

||||| Austrian

▨ Spanish

····· Boundary of the Empire

× Battle sites

end of the first great effort to keep the Empire wholly Catholic. But it by no means established full toleration in the modern sense. Its guiding principle is in the Latin phrase *cuius regio eius religio,* freely translated as *whoever rules an area may establish the religion of that area.* The ruler of Saxony is Lutheran: then all Saxons are practicing Lutherans. The ruler of Bavaria is Catholic: then all Bavarians are practicing Catholics. To work, this settlement would have had to mean that all the many German states were self-sealed little blocks of one religion, which was quite impossible.

Two concrete failures of the Augsburg settlement made a renewal of religious strife almost certain. First, no solution was reached concerning "ecclesiastical reservation," the problem of what happened to the property of the Church in a given region if its ruler were a Catholic prelate who was converted to Protestantism. Second, by recognizing formally only the Catholic and Lutheran faiths, the settlement ignored the growing numbers of militant Calvinists who were bound to press for equal treatment. Still, with all its weaknesses, Augsburg made possible the permanent establishment of Protestantism on a peaceful footing in Germany. Together with the Treaty of Cateau-Cambrésis, it brought to an end the first great Habsburg effort to dominate Europe.

The Wars of Philip II

The second effort at domination of Europe was less Habsburg than Spanish. In 1556, Charles V abdicated both his Spanish and imperial crowns and retired to a monastery, where he died two years later. His brother, Ferdinand I (1556-1564), secured the Austrian Habsburg complex of territories and, by election, the Empire. His son, Philip II (1556-1598), got Spain and the colonies, the Burgundian inheritance of the Netherlands, and the Italian holdings of Milan and Naples. Philip's realm was no mere national state; even without the Germanies, it was a supranational state threatening France, England, and the whole balance of power.

Like his father, Philip II found Protestantism and the concept of many separate Christian political units intolerable. He sought, if not world conquest, at least the forced unity of the West. Philip's attempt to invade England and restore Catholicism there has left him as one of the villains of Anglo-Saxon tradition. He was indeed no bright, jovial Renaissance monarch, but he was hardly the cold-blooded "Devil of the south" he appeared to Protestants and moderate Catholics to be. He was a serious, hard-working administrator, and certainly no lover of war for its own sake. He saw Protestantism as an intolerable divisive force that must be wiped out by force if necessary. He was a doctrinaire chained to a past no one could restore, committed to a lost cause.

Philip's major points of involvement were: (1) Italy, which as long as it remained divided was to be a major source of difficulties in the play of balance of power; (2) the Netherlands, where the revolt of his Dutch Protestant subjects was soon to involve Philip not only with them but with Protestant England; (3) France, where the second half of the century brought a series of civil wars of religion in which Philip was bound to appear as the Catholic champion, (4) the Mediterranean, where the Turks, now at the height of their naval power, threatened Spanish control; (5) finally, as we shall see in the next chapter, England and France were beginning to challenge the monopoly Spain and Portugal had tried to set up in the newly discovered Americas and in Asia. Since this New World as well as the Old World was at stake in Philip's wars, there is some justification for considering these as in fact the first "world wars."

The Dutch Revolt

The dramatic focal point of these struggles is the revolt of the Netherlands. When the Burgundian inheritance had come to the Habsburgs, Charles V had made no attempt to absorb these provinces into a unified superstate. They were simply parts of a great dynastic holding, parts that were essentially autonomous, with their own complex of feudal privileges confirmed by their new ruler. They had medieval estates or assemblies, representing privileged groups, which raised taxes and armies. Like most northern lands, the Low Countries had felt the full force of the Protestant Reformation. In mid-sixteenth century, the religious situation was still fluid. In resistance to Philip, the northern provinces became firmly Calvinist.

Philip II was bound to antagonize his subjects in the Low Countries. Charles V had liked the Low Countries and had made Brussels his favorite place of residence, but Philip was thoroughly Spanish in outlook. For all his medievalism, he had up-to-date ideas about centralized, efficient rule and curtailed the political liberties of the Netherlands. And he hated all forms of Protestantism. Finally, the economic element was also present, for the Dutch were a seafaring commercial people, desirous of conducting a trade freed from the jealous restrictions of Spanish mercantilism.

This explosive mixture of religion, politics, and economics produced the revolt. Philip sent Spanish garrisons to the Netherlands, and attempted to enforce edicts against heretics. Opposition, which centered at first in the privileged classes who had been most affected by Philip's political restrictions, soon spread to the common people. In the riots that broke out, Catholic churches ·were destroyed; a league was formed against the Spaniards, proudly taking on the name of "Beggars," which had first been used by a scornful conserva-

Philip II of Spain.

tive; indeed all the apparatus of revolution made its appearance. When in 1567 Philip dispatched to the Netherlands an army of twenty thousand Spaniards headed by the unyielding, politically stupid Duke of Alba, the revolt had fully begun.

The Spanish infantry was in those days incomparably the best in Europe, and the Dutch were ill-armed and ill-prepared. The Dutch resistance, successful in the long run, was a heroic achievement against great odds, fully deserving the praise sympathetic historians have given it. It was, however, no extraordinary victory of weakness over strength, but rather a victory in full accord with what has until the twentieth century at least been a general rule of western political life—that no thoroughly disaffected population can be long held down by force alone. Alba had the force, and he set up a Council of Troubles, which applied executions, confiscations, and severe taxation on a large scale. The Council has received from history the significant title of the "Council of Blood." Yet all that this repression accomplished was to unite opposition against Alba, for the southern provinces of the Netherlands, which we know as Belgium, now joined the northern provinces. Both the ordinarily peaceful merchants and the great nobles like William the Silent, Prince of Orange, stood with the populace and with the adventurous "Beggars," who turned to a sort of naval guerrilla warfare. Alba gave up in despair in 1573, but it was not until the Duke of Parma was sent out in 1578 that Philip's policy showed signs of the essential element of statesmanship, a willingness to compromise in the face of facts.

Under Parma, the southern provinces at least were won back by political concessions to their old privileges of self-rule; they remained basically Catholic. But it was too late to win back the northern provinces, except perhaps by radical religious concessions which Philip was by temperament utterly unable to make. By the Union of Utrecht, the Dutch tightened their organization and in 1581 took the decisive step of declaring themselves independent of the Spanish Crown. They made good that declaration by their courageous use of their now much better-organized land forces. But they were greatly helped by three facts. First, Philip, like most of the great aggressors, had been drawn into fighting on more than one land front. He had to cope with Turks, the French Protestants, and the anti-Spanish moderate French Catholics, as well as with grave internal economic problems. Second, fate gave the Dutch that invaluable spiritual aid, a martyr. And last and most important, they acquired a major ally.

The martyr was William the Silent, who was assassinated in 1584 by an individual moved either by religious hatred or by the reward Philip had set upon the outlawed Dutchman's head, or by both. William's death deprived the Dutch of the first great leader in their national history, but the assassination did not profit the Spanish cause. It made William, who was a western European nobleman without strong religious feeling, a Protestant and Dutch hero. The ally was England, now under Elizabeth I firmly Protestant and from the start sympathetic with the Dutch cause. Elizabeth, however, was no crusader, and her kingdom appeared to be no match for powerful Spain. She had been hesitant to come out openly on the Dutch side, the more since in the uncertain condition of French politics in the midst of internal religious wars, a Franco-Spanish alliance seemed by no means impossible. Here too Philip showed himself incapable of diplomacy. He permitted France to maneuver into neutrality, and provoked England by fomenting Catholic plots against Elizabeth. The English in turn, provoked Spain. For years they had been preying on Spanish commerce on the high seas, and Hawkins, Drake, and other English sailors had been raiding Spanish possessions in the New World. When an English army came to the aid of the Dutch in 1585, Philip decided to make formal war on England, though he still had the Dutch on his hands.

The End of Philip II

The great Spanish Armada of unwieldy men-of-war which he sent out to invade England was defeated in the English Channel in July, 1588, by a skillfully maneuvered lighter English fleet, and was utterly destroyed afterward by a great storm. The battle was the beginning of the end of Spanish preponderance, the beginning of English greatness in international politics, and the decisive step in the achievement of the independence of the Dutch

The battle between the English fleet and the Spanish Armada, 1588.

Republic. These portentous results were not as evident in 1588 as they are now, but even at the time the defeat of the Armada was seen as a great event. Protestants everywhere were greatly heartened, and the great storm that finished the destruction of the Spanish fleet was christened the "Protestant wind."

Philip II died in 1598 after a long and painful illness, in the great, severe palace of the Escorial he had built near Madrid. He had ordered an open coffin put beside his bed, and a skull with a crown of gold. Save for the seven northern provinces of the Netherlands—and even these he had never officially given up—the great possessions with which he had begun to reign were still his. Indeed, he had added Portugal in 1580 at the death of the Portuguese Cardinal-King Henry and had made the whole Iberian Peninsula formally if briefly one. Yet he knew almost as clearly as we

know that his life had been a failure. He left his kingdom, as we shall see, worn out, drained of men and money. And, whatever his aims in international politics had been, whether a Spanish hegemony, a revived western Empire, or merely the extinction of the Protestant heresy, he had realized none of them. Under his illegitimate half-brother Don John of Austria, the Spanish fleet had indeed participated in the great naval victory over the Turkish fleet at Lepanto in 1571 (see above, p. 375). But Lepanto was at most a checking of Turkish expansion, not a great gain for the Spaniards. It was no balance for the loss of the great Armada.

The Dutch Republic

After Philip's death, the fighting went on in Holland in a desultory way until a truce in 1609 established the virtual independence of the United Provinces—or United Netherlands, as the Dutch Republic was termed. This independence was confirmed as part of international law by the Peace of Westphalia in 1648. In those days the Dutch were one of the great powers of Europe, a major factor in international politics (see Chapter XV), and the leaders in some highly significant developments. In religion, for instance, a wide toleration was practiced, and Holland became a refuge for persecuted Jews from Portugal and Spain and even from Poland and Lithuania. In government the United Provinces were decentralized, preserving the local self-government that had long persisted. The central government was usually at the mercy of the provincial governments, though the office of stadholder, held by a prince of the House of Orange, provided a symbol of national unity.

In spite of the lack of a firm national central government, the Netherlands reached in the seventeenth century the high point of their cultural, economic, and political power and prestige in the world. In economic life, above all, the Dutch were the pace-setters of seventeenth-century Europe. They managed government finances as adroitly and efficiently as they managed their private businesses; the state borrowed money at 2½ per cent interest, an amazingly low figure for the time. They made life insurance into a big business by putting it on a firm actuarial basis, and in the Bank of Amsterdam they fostered a great commercial institution that went far to make Amsterdam the financial capital of Europe. Highly successful specialized industries grew up in the cities and towns of Holland—diamond-cutting at Amsterdam, shipbuilding at Zaandam, the distilling of gin at Schiedam, and around Haarlem the growing of tulip bulbs, which set off a wild financial speculation. Abroad, Dutch ships played a large part in the international carrying trade, and the Dutch East India Company assembled and exploited a commercial empire (see Chapter XIV).

The Dutch of this seventeenth century made major contributions to western culture. In painting, they produced in Rembrandt (1606-1669) one of the greatest of masters; and a whole school of artists painted technically admirable, "realistic" scenes of everyday life for the homes of prosperous businessmen. In science, Christian Huygens (1629-1695), son of a dis-

Portrait of a Dutch family by Maerten van Heemskerk (sixteenth century).

tinguished poet, was a major figure in the advance of mathematics and physics; in biological studies, Jan Swammerdam (1637-1680) pioneered in the use of the microscope and probably discovered the red corpuscles in the blood; and Anton van Leeuwenhoek (1632-1723), with a microscope of his own making, first described protozoa and bacteria. In philosophy, Baruch (or Benedict) Spinoza (1632-1677), a Jew rejected by his fellow religionists for his unorthodoxy, laid the basis for much modern philosophical thought by his self-conscious, high-minded, rigorous rationalism. Indeed. one of his books has the remarkable title: *Ethics Mathematically Demonstrated.*

The Dutch style at this flowering time is hard to define. It is solid, reasonable, sober, but far from colorless, and by no means puritanical in any ascetic sense. Perhaps the Dutch at their height are the best evidences for the Weber thesis of Protestant ethics (see Chapter XII). Certainly this little nation, through intelligence, hard work, adventurous exploration, and hard trading, and, as we shall see in the next chapter, some rather unscrupulous exploitation of non-European peoples, made for itself a great place in the world. But by 1700 the great days of Holland were coming to an end. The Dutch Republic declined, not absolutely, but relatively to the great powers around it—Britain, France, and Prussia. The Dutch simply did not have a home base extensive enough or populous enough to support the status of a great power.

III: The Thirty Years' War

Nature and Causes

We have now seen two of the great conflicts of early modern times—the Habsburg-Valois struggle between Charles V and Francis I, and the wars of Philip II. The third great conflict, the Thirty Years' War of 1618-1648, was fought largely in Germany and takes us a bit beyond the chronological limits of this chapter. But it was a war in which religion bore a part at least as great as it had in the wars of Charles and Philip, and its focus was still a Habsburg focus. The Austrian Emperor, Ferdinand II (1619-1637), scarcely aspired to universal rule, but he did make the last serious political and military effort to unify Germany under Catholic rule. The Thirty Years' War began as a conflict between Catholics and Protestants; it ended as an almost purely political struggle to reduce the power of the Habsburgs in favor of France and a newcomer to high international politics, Sweden.

As we have already noted, the Augsburg Peace of 1555 did not bring complete religious peace to Germany. It did not recognize Calvinism, to say nothing of the more radical Protestant sects, and it left unsettled the problem of ecclesiastical reservation. On this latter issue, an imperial decree provided that if a Catholic prelate were converted to Protestantism the property formerly under his control should remain in Catholic hands. But this was a one-sided proclamation; it had not been formally negotiated with the Protestants and it was naturally much resented by them.

By the opening of the seventeenth century, the religious situation in Germany was becoming increasingly unsettled. Incidents of violence between Catholics and Protestants, especially Calvinists, were multiplying. In 1608, Calvinist elements formed the

Protestant Union, which in turn prompted the creation of the Catholic League in 1609. Thus Germany was split into rival camps a decade before the outbreak of war. From the start, moreover, both the Protestant Union and the Catholic League had political as well as religious ambitions. Both really represented the interests of German particularism—that is, of the individual German states—against those of the Empire, even though the Catholic League and its leader, Maximilian of Bavaria, were to ally with the Emperor Ferdinand.

The Bohemian Period, 1618-1625

The war broke out in Bohemia, now part of Czechoslovakia, then a Habsburg crown land, with a strong Protestant minority known as the Utraquists. This name brings up one of the main quarrels between Protestants and Catholics, that of the actual administration of the Eucharist. In Catholic worship, the layman receives the bread but not the wine, the body but not the blood of Christ; only the officiating priest takes the wine. The Utraquist, from the Latin for "both," took both the wine and the bread in communion. As with the Hussite movement two centuries earlier, Utraquism was in part Czech nationalism. The Czech nationalists wanted local independence from the rule of Germans and of Vienna, and they caused the incident that actually provoked war, the "defenestration of Prague" in 1618. Rebels headed by Count Matthias of Thurn seized control of the Bohemian capital city and in an excited conference threw two royal governors out of a palace window. Though the victims fell seventy feet, they landed on a pile of dung and escaped with their lives.

The emperor-to-be, Ferdinand II (he was formally elected in 1619), was not prepared for civil war. The rebels, aided by Protestant forces from Germany, gained control in Bohemia and deposed Ferdinand as King of Bohemia. To fill his place, an assembly of the Bohemian estates chose the youthful Frederick V, Elector of the Palatinate in western Germany, and head of the Protestant Union. Although Frederick was the son-in-law of James I of England and as a Protestant very popular there, England did not come to his aid, nor in effect did the Protestant Union. The Spaniards, however, did come in on the Catholic side and sent an army to the Palatinate, frightening the Protestant Union into a declaration of neutrality. In Bohemia, Frederick was defeated by the army of the Catholic League at the battle of the White Mountain (1620) and was forced to flee his new kingdom. The Protestant Union was dissolved, and small Protestant remnants were beaten by the imperial general Tilly.

The Danish Period, 1625-1629

At this low point in Protestant fortunes, a champion arose outside Germany proper in Denmark, where King Christian IV (1588-1648) took over the leadership of the Protestant forces. A vigorous and ambitious monarch, Christian had increased his royal power by taking full advantage of the increased authority that Lutheranism gave to the king. When he intervened in the war, he sought not only to defend his co-religionists but also to extend Danish political and economic hegemony over northern Germany.

Still another factor now entered the struggle, the famous—and infamous—private army of Wallenstein (1583-1634). This general, though born of a German Protestant family in Bohemia, was reared a Catholic, and fought on the imperial side. His army was recruited and paid by himself, and lived off the land by requisitions and plunderings, sometimes at the expense of imperial and Catholic sympathizers. Wallenstein was in fact a German *condottiere,* a private citizen seeking to become a ruling prince, perhaps even dreaming of a united German empire, no longer the old medieval successor to Charlemagne's empire, but a fine, new-model monarchy. He never came close to success, but his army was a major factor in the war at its most critical period. Tilly's and Wallenstein's armies were enough to dispose of Christian IV. They overran Christian's North German lands and pushed into the Danish peninsula.

Then, at the height of the imperial and Catholic success, Ferdinand and his advisers overreached themselves. By the Edict of Restitution and the Treaty of Lübeck in 1629, they sought to take the fullest advantage of their victories. The Edict of Restitution not only reaffirmed the Augsburg exclusion of the Calvinists and Protestant radicals from toleration but also demanded the restoration of all ecclesiastical estates that had passed from Catholic to Lutheran hands since 1551, three generations before. The Treaty of Lübeck allowed Christian IV to recover his lands, but it exacted from him a promise not to intervene in Germany. This seemed to the outside world a sign that the Habsburg power was actually spreading to the Baltic, to a region thoroughly Protestant and hitherto only on the margin of imperial control. The old pattern was, then, repeated. The Habsburgs on the wave of success went outside the bounds of their customary spheres of influence; those upon whose spheres they thus encroached fought back against the trespass; the trespasser was finally forced to withdraw.

The Swedish Period, 1630-1635

In 1630, at the height of Catholic Habsburg success, Gustavus Adolphus, Protestant King of Sweden (1611-1632), landed with a Swedish army on the North German coast. A new champion of the Protestants, a much stronger one than Christian of Denmark, had come out of the North. Once again, religious and secular motives were thoroughly intermixed. Gustavus was a strong Lutheran, who led an army of hymn-singing soldiers. In Sweden, as in Denmark, the coming of the Reformation had consolidated royal authority. Like Christian, Gustavus Adolphus had ambitions for political control in northern Germany, and he hoped, too, that Sweden might take over the old economic leadership of the Hanseatic League, hoped, indeed, to make the Baltic Sea a Swedish lake. He had already won territories along the eastern Baltic by waging successful wars against Russia and Poland. Significantly, his army, large and well equipped for so relatively poor a country as Sweden, was now in part paid for by subsidies received from the French monarchy through negotiations with its minister Richelieu, a cardinal of the Roman Catholic Church. For France, too, the great success of the old Habsburg enemy seemed a trespass, and those who guided French policy were eager to help Protestant Sweden beat Catholic Austria.

Gustavus Adolphus was a very skillful general whose intervention was to alter the whole course of the war—but not before a Catholic victory that probably did more to harm the Catholic cause than a defeat. The fall and sack of Magdeburg, the "Maiden City" of the Protestants and a great symbol of their cause, is one of those events that should warn the student of international politics that he must not leave moral forces out of his calculations. Magdeburg was taken by storm by the imperialists in May, 1631, and was almost wholly destroyed by fire and pillage. The imperial general Pappenheim, who commanded at the storming of the walls, estimated that twenty thousand people were killed. Each side sought to blame the sack on the other and to enlist in its cause public opinion all over Europe. A volume issued in 1931 on the three-hundredth anniversary of the sack of

Magdeburg takes forty-six pages to list contemporary accounts in European newspapers (then in their infancy), pamphlets, broadsides, popular songs, and cartoons. The Protestants accused the imperial commander-in-chief, Tilly, of actually planning the destruction of the city and the killing of its inhabitants, an accusation from which most historians absolve him, for the imperial troops clearly got out of hand. The Catholics countered by accusing the Protestants of setting the fires themselves as a deliberate "scorched-earth" policy. But the Protestants were the sufferers, and in the long run, as the outpourings of the press took effect, their cause was strengthened. In the field, the Swedes won two decisive victories at Leipzig in 1631 and at Lützen in 1632. Gustavus Adolphus was killed at Lützen, but his coming had turned the tide. Wallenstein withdrew into winter quarters, and began negotiations that have baffled historians ever since. Certainly he was trying to set himself up as a mediator between the Protestants and the extremist wing of the imperial party, the Court at Vienna, the wing that had called in the Spaniards. Perhaps he was at heart a great patriot, striving to unite divided Germany. Whatever he was planning was cut short by his assassination in 1634, an assassination almost certainly not directly planned by the Emperor Ferdinand, but from which he cannot be dissociated, since he rewarded the assassins.

The Swedish and French Period, 1635-1648

Though the two great antagonists, Gustavus and Wallenstein, were dead, the war went on. Swedish affairs were in the able hands of the chancellor Oxenstierna, aided by two good generals, Baner and Torstenson. In 1642, the Swedes won a second battle at Leipzig and threatened the core of Habsburg power, the hereditary lands of Bohemia and Austria. But these Swedish successes had begun to seem more Swedish than Protestant and drew from Christian IV of Denmark, the recent champion of Protestantism, a response not uncommon in the history of balance-of-power politics. Now more fearful of the nearby Swedes than of the distant Austrians, Christian went to war with Sweden, and saw his lands once more successfully invaded.

Meanwhile, however, the ultimately decisive force was entering the bewildering struggle. The French had decided that subsidies to German and Swedish opponents of the Habsburg power were not enough, and that they would have to fight. French armies crossed the Rhine and struck at the imperialists through South Germany. Theirs was by no means a triumphal march, and bitter fighting took place in the last years of the war, from 1643 to 1648. Although the hard-pressed imperial armies gained an occasional victory, they lost on the whole. In 1645, the Danes gave up and made a separate peace. In 1648, a series of peace conferences met in the northwestern German region in Westphalia—the first of the great general peace conferences of modern times. The Habsburgs were the vanquished; the French and Swedes were the victors.

In its last years the Thirty Years' War had in fact become a general war. On the seven seas the French and Spanish were at odds. In Italy, the French had tried to split communication between the Austrian and the Spanish Habsburgs by controlling the Alpine passes. This general war had, however, one striking difference from all others of modern times: the balance of power had to be achieved without one of its main factors, England. England kept out of the war for the obvious reason that in all these years she was facing domestic crisis and civil war (see Chapter XV).

Effects on Germany

The defeat of the Habsburgs in 1648, though it did not end in the sheer collapse

The siege of Magdeburg during the Thirty Years' War, 1631.

of the defeated power, left the Germanies in a fearful state. Although the engines of destruction available to men in the seventeenth century were feeble in comparison with those available to us, it may well be that in terms of human suffering and material destruction the Thirty Years' War was quite as disastrous to Germany as the Second World War of the twentieth century. One obvious point: if we today can destroy more easily, we can also mend more easily. In the seventeenth century, the rebuilding of a destroyed town was a long process. On the human side, deaths from wounds, disease, and famine could not in the defective state of medicine and transport be effectively checked as they are today.

Religious and political passions combined to make each side unsparing of the other. Worse yet, much of the fighting was done by mercenaries hardened to the cruelties of war, badly disciplined, and forced by the inadequacies of military administration to live off the country of friend and foe alike. Here from a satirical novel, *Simplicissimus,* written by a man named Grimmelshausen, himself captured as a ten-year-old during the war, is a passage that gives the flavor of the times:

Now this same foraging is neither more nor less than attacking of villages (with great pains and labour: yea, often with danger to life and limb), and there threshing, grinding, baking, stealing, and taking all that can be found; harrying and spoiling the farmers, and shaming of their maids, their wives, and their daughters. And if the poor peasants did murmur, or were bold enough to rap a forager or two over the fingers, finding them at such work (and at that time were many such guests in Hesse), they were knocked on the head if they could be caught, or if not, their houses went up in smoke to heaven. Now my master had no wife (for campaigners of his kidney be not wont to take ladies with them), no page, no chamberlain, no cook, but on the other hand a whole troop of grooms and boys which waited both on him and his horse; nor was he himself ashamed to saddle his own horse or give him a feed; he slept ever on straw or on the bare ground, and covered himself with a fur coat. So it came about that one could often see great fleas or lice walk upon his clothes, of which he was not ashamed at all, but would laugh if any one picked one out.*

By the end of the war, men had got so used to constant warfare that armies were whole little societies in themselves. It is estimated that although the imperial armies at the end of the war numbered about 40,000, the regular camp followers, wives, mistresses, children, servants, sutlers, and the like, numbered 140,000, and were kept in some kind of order by imperial officers known unofficially as "provosts of the harlots." Such details are more revealing than attempts at statistical estimates of the losses in men and things, which are not very trustworthy.

Some historians trace to this disastrous war aspects of modern Germany that have made her a disturbing influence in the modern world. They point to a national sense of inferiority heightened by her delayed achievement of national unity, a lack of the slow ripening in self-government that a more orderly growth in early modern times might have encouraged, a too strong need for authority and obedience brought out in response to the anarchic conditions of the seventeenth century. These are dangerously big generalizations that are at most suggestive; they can by no means be proved. And yet though modern scholarship sometimes tends to question the traditional view, there is little doubt that the Thirty Years' War was highly destructive, even if not so horrible as scholars used to think.

The Peace of Westphalia

The reality of 1648 was that Germany had reached a low point of political and cultural disintegration. In the great set-

---

* H. J. C. von Grimmelshausen, *Simplicissimus,* A. T. S. Goodrick, trans. (New York, 1912), 110.

tlements of Westphalia, though some of the separate German states came out well, Germany herself was a major victim. The French got bits of land toward their northeast frontier, notably a foothold in Alsace. Sweden got lands south of the Baltic, on the German mainland, and a real start toward her ambitious goal of controlling the Baltic area. Due compensations and adjustments were made among the major German states. In particular, Brandenburg, though damaged by the cessions to Sweden on the mainland, got valuable compensations in lands around Magdeburg, and in the next two centuries was to recover some of the cessions made to Sweden. Indeed, the beginning of the greatness of Brandenburg-Prussia is commonly dated from this Westphalian settlement of 1648.

Still more important, the Peace of Westphalia formally recognized the "independence" of the constituent elements of the German Empire. From now on, the German states could enter into alliances with one another and with foreign powers, as long as they were not directed against the emperor. This last was a face-saving for the Habsburgs, but the fact that the constituent states now had their own foreign services, their own armies, their own finances—three obvious earmarks of "independence" in our state-system—is clear evidence that the Holy Roman Empire of the German nation was no longer a viable political entity. The Westphalian settlement also formally recognized the independence of two small states—the United Netherlands of the Dutch, already independent in fact for more than half a century, and the Swiss Confederation, the nucleus of which had first broken away from Habsburg control during the later Middle Ages.

Finally, the ecclesiastical provisions of the treaties really did settle matters, leaving German religious differences henceforth to take their relatively peaceful modern form of missionary and educational struggles. The Thirty Years' War was the last formal war between Protestants and Catholics, though by no means the last war in which their religious antagonism played a part. Calvinists now secured the same recognition as Catholics and Lutherans. Princes could still "determine" the faith of their territories, but the right of dissidents to emigrate was recognized. In most of Protestant Germany, multiplicity of sects was in fact accepted. The boundary between Protestant and Catholic regions recognized the Catholic gains made since the Catholic Reformation, and is today much as in 1648. On the vexed question of ecclesiastical reservation the year 1624 was taken as the *annus normalis,* the year from which ownership of ecclesiastical property was to be measured; as things were on January 1 of that year, so they were to be in the future. After thirty years of trying to exterminate each other, Catholics and Protestants in Germany gave up the effort.

The simple "hard" explanation of this fact is that Protestants and Catholics were driven to mutual toleration by exhaustion and sheer despair of imposing their will on their opponents. The simple "soft" explanation is that at last men saw the light and came to believe in freedom of worship as an individual right. Neither explanation is fully true. By 1648, an intellectual minority had for some time been urging toleration as a good; men of peaceful disposition had been attacking the horrors of war and the futility of religious persecution. Another minority, thoroughly committed to the struggle, clearly accepted the peace as a mere truce. The majority, after all these years of war, were simply tired out. But once the settlement was made, once men grew used to the existence of Protestants and Catholics side by side, or at least in adjoining territories, such an arrangement came on the whole to seem entirely normal.

EUROPE IN 1648

Legend:
- Brandenburg–Prussia
- Austrian } Habsburg Lands
- Spanish }
- Swedish possessions
- Venetian possessions
- Ottoman Empire
- Boundary of the Holy Roman Empire
- × Battle sites

NORWAY
Oslo
Stockholm

SCOTLAND
Edinburgh × × Dunbar
× Berwick

North Sea

DENMARK
Copenhagen
Baltic
Lübeck
Hamburg

ULSTER
IRELAND
× Drogheda
Dublin
Wexford ×

Preston × Marston Moor
ENGLAND
Nottingham
Worcester × × Naseby
London

TEXEL ×
UNITED NETHERLANDS
Bremen
Osna-brück
Münster
WEST-PHALIA
THE
Magdeburg
Berlin
BRANDENBURG
Lützen ×
SAXONY

WHITE MT.
SILES
Prague
BOHEMIA
MORAVIA
AUSTRIA
Vienna

Approximate division line between Puritans [▨] and Cavaliers in England, May, 1643

SPANISH NETHERLANDS
Seine R.
Paris
Verdun
Metz
Toul
PALATINATE
Heidelberg
ALSACE
Strasbourg
EMPIRE
Danube
BAVARIA
STYRIA
CARINTHIA

Nantes
Orleans
Loire R.
FRANCHE COMTE
SWITZER-LAND
VALTELLINE
Geneva
FRANCE
Bordeaux

Rhone R.
SAVOY
PIEDMONT
MILAN
Venice
VENETIAN REPUBLIC
TYROL
CARNIOL
HU

Avignon (to the papacy)
Marseilles
Genoa
Florence
PAPAL STATES
Rome
Adriatic
Rag

Burgos
Ebro R.
Madrid
Lisbon
PORTUGAL
Tagus R.
SPAIN
Barcelona
Valencia
Guadalquivir R.
Seville
Granada

BALEARIC IS.
CORSICA (to Genoa)
SARDINIA
NAPLES
Naples

Mediterranean

ALGIERS
(Tributary to Ottoman Empire)
TUNIS

Palermo
SICILY
MALTA

Atlantic Ocean

G.

538

FINLAND

DEN

Sea

L. Onega

L. Ladoga

G. of Finland

INGRIA

ESTONIA

LIVONIA

COURLAND

Novgorod

Pskov

Volga R.

Moscow

RUSSIA

Oka R.

Miles

0   500

55

50

W. Dvina R.

LITHUANIA

Smolensk

Königsberg

Vilna

PRUSSIA

Don R.

Volga R.

Ural R.

45

Caspian Sea

Warsaw

POLAND

Kiev

Dnieper R.

Vistula R.

Dniester R.

TRANSYLVANIA

MOLDAVIA

ARY

C R I M E A

SEA

Belgrade

WALLACHIA

Danube R.

OTTOMA

Black   Sea

40

MONTE-
NEGRO

Morava R.

Constantinople

Salonika

Vardar R.

EMPIRE

Tigris R.

IONIAN IS.
(Venice)

Aegean Sea

Athens

35

Euphrates R.

RHODES

CYPRUS

Sea

20

CRETE
(to Venice)

30

35

40

IV: The New Monarchies—Spain and France

The "Age of Absolutism"

The sixteenth century sees all over the West an uneven working out of the new political aims and methods of the Renaissance. The states that took part in the dynastic and religious wars we have just traced were all to a degree centralized states with paid professional armies and paid professional civilian bureaucrats. They had a central financial system with some control over taxation and the supply of money, a central legal system that made some attempt to apply the same kind of law to all individuals within the state, and a central authority—king, king and council, king and parliament, estates, Cortes, or other assembly—that could actually make new laws. Phrases like "Age of Absolutism" and "Divine Right of Kings" are frequently used of the early modern centuries, and not without reason. All over Europe, the control of central administration usually rested with a monarch who inherited his throne and claimed the right to make the kind of final decisions that modern democracies make by some sort of popular vote, or at least through legislatures.

But it is of major importance to note that everywhere in the sixteenth century there were strong survivals of the old medieval local privileges, of local ways of life quite different from the standards set by the court or the capital. The early modern governments were less "absolute," in at least one very significant sense of the term, than the government of a modern democracy like the United States. They could not possibly make *and enforce* the kind of regulation which federal and state agencies nowadays can make and enforce—public health regulations like pure food and drug

acts, licensing the practice of medicine, setting of standards of measure, even the kind of standardization of higher education we have achieved in the training of teachers, for instance, by accreditation and other controls. This last instance suggests that standardization, the efficient application of general rules to large areas and large groups, is in the United States partly a matter of voluntary control from *below*. Generally speaking, such collaboration from below was not attained in these first modern centuries. The standardization came from *above*, from a small group that had been won over to these new methods of governing, which did increase their power. It is this active attempt of a minority to achieve "streamlining" that justifies our use of terms like absolutism for these centuries.

Power and Limits of Spanish Absolutism

Spain provides a clear-cut example of the difference between the concepts of absolutism with which this minority worked and the varied and often successfully recalcitrant groups on which this minority sought to impose its standardized rules. The reigns of the two hard-working Spanish monarchs, Charles V (technically, Charles I of Spain, 1516-1556) and Philip II (1556-1598), span almost the whole sixteenth century. Charles was rather a medieval survival than a modern king. He did little to remodel the instruments of government he inherited from his grandparents, Ferdinand and Isabella (see Chapter X). Brought up in the Low Countries, Charles came to Spain a stranger, with a Flemish following that already had the modern northern

European contempt for "backward" Spain, and showed it. His election to the imperial throne made him further suspect in Spain. In 1520, a group of Spanish cities, led by Toledo, rose up in the *comuneros*. This revolt, like most such uprisings, was compounded of many elements. The municipalities disliked the growth of central control; the aristocrats were restless in the face of the new monarchical dignity, no longer just like their own; the poor and the middling had class feelings and grievances. The *comuneros* were put down in 1521, but Charles had been frightened out of what reforming zeal he may have had, and did his best not to offend his Spanish subjects. His son, at least, grew up a Spaniard first of all.

Philip II was much more willing and able to build a new-model centralized state in Spain. He did devise a system of consultative councils, topped by a council of state, and manned by great nobles; but these councils could do no more than advise. Philip made the final decisions, and the details were worked out by a series of private secretaries and local organs of government, not manned by nobles. Furthermore, Philip reduced the representative assemblies, the Cortes, to practical impotence, especially in Castile. Nobles and priests, because they did not pay direct taxes, no longer attended the sessions of the Cortes, and the delegates of the cities

were left as a powerless rump. Above all, Philip had assured sources of income—his tax of a fifth of the precious cargoes from America, direct taxes from the constituent states of his realm, revenues from the royal estates and from the sale of offices and patents of nobility, revenues from the authorized sale, at royal profit, of dispensations allowed by the pope (permission to eat meat on Fridays and in Lent, and even something very close to the very indulgences that had raised Germany against the pope). Philip, like most monarchs of his time, had no need to worry over representative bodies with control of the purse. Yet he was always heavily in debt, and at his death in 1598 left his government almost bankrupt.

Even in this matter of revenue, where Philip's power at first sight looks so complete and unchecked, the actual limitations of the absolute monarch of early modern times are clear. Except by borrowing and hand-to-mouth expedients like the sale of offices, he could not notably increase his income. He could not summon any representative group together and get them to vote new monies. In the first place, the constituent parts of his realm, Castile, Aragon, Navarre, the Basque Provinces, the Italian lands, the Low Countries, the Americas, and the newest Spanish lands, named after the monarch himself, the Philippine Islands, had no common organs of consul-

Escorial, near Madrid, Spain. This palace-monastery - mausoleum was built by Philip II in the sixteenth century.

tation. Each had to be dealt with as a separate problem. For the most part the nobility and clergy were tax-exempt, and could not be called upon for unusual financial sacrifices. Add to all this the difficulty of collection, the opportunities for graft, and the lack of a long accumulated administrative and financial experience, and one can see why Philip could not have introduced a more systematic general taxation.

Outside the financial sphere, the obstacles to really effective centralization were even more serious. The union of the crowns of Aragon and Castile, achieved by the marriage of Ferdinand and Isabella, had by no means made a unified Spain. To this day, regionalism—to call it by a mild name—is perhaps more acute in Spain than in any other large European state. In those days, some of the provinces did not even have extradition arrangements for the surrender of common criminals within the peninsula. Many of them could and did levy customs dues on goods from the others. The old northern regions, which had never been well conquered by the Moslems, preserved all sorts of *fueros* or privileges. Aragon still preserved the office of *justicia mayor,* a judge nominated, it is true, by the Crown, but for life, and entrusted with an authority something like that of the United States Supreme Court.

What the Habsburgs might have accomplished in Spain had they been able to expend their full energies on the task of uniting and developing their lands can never be known. What they did do was exhaust the peninsula, and weaken the lands overseas, in their effort to secure hegemony over Europe and to subdue the Protestant heresy. This was indeed the great age of Spain, the age when both on land and on sea the Spanish were admired and envied as the best fighters, the age when Spain seemed destined to be mistress of both the Americas, the age when Spain seemed the richest of states, the age of Loyola and Cervantes, the golden age of Spanish religion, literature, and art. But it was a brief flowering, and Spanish greatness largely vanished in the seventeenth century.

The Spanish Economy

Spain is a classical example of a great political unit that failed to maintain a sound economic underpinning for its greatness. The peninsula is mountainous, and its central tableland is subject to droughts, but its agricultural potentialities are greater, for example, than those of Italy, and it has mineral resources, notably in iron. Moreover, Spain was the first of the great European states to attain lands overseas, and a navy and merchant marine to integrate the great resources of the New World with an Old World base. Yet all this wealth slipped through Spain's fingers in a few generations. Certainly a major factor in this decline was the immense cost of the wars of Charles V and Philip II. The Low Countries, which had brought in a large revenue to Charles, were a pure drain on Philip's finances. The famous Spanish infantry had to be paid everywhere it went, and the money thus spent went out of Spain forever, with nothing in the long run to show for it. Philip took over from his father a heavy debt, which grew heavier through his long reign.

Now governmental expenditure on armed forces, though in itself unproductive, is not necessarily fatal to a national economy. If such expenditure stimulates even greater productivity within the nation and its dependencies, then the nation may bear it, and even grow in wealth, as did imperial Germany after 1870. But this was not true of sixteenth-century Spain. She drew from the New World vast amounts of silver and many articles—sugar, indigo, tobacco, cocoa, hides—without which she could hardly have carried on her European wars at all. But it was not enough to pay for world dominion. The bullion passed through Spanish hands into those of bankers and merchants in other European countries, partly to pay for the Spanish armies and navies, partly to pay for the manufactured goods Spain had to send to the New World.

In accordance with an economic policy common to other colonial powers of the time, Spain forbade industrial production in her colonies and sought to supply them with manufactured goods. *But she could not, or did not, develop her own industrial production to take care of this need.* Her merchants had by royal decree a monopoly on trade with the Indies. But as the century wore on, they were more and more reduced to the role of mere middlemen, sending to the Indies goods increasingly imported from the rest of Europe—and paid for with the bullion of the Indies. The English, the Dutch, and other competitors smuggled goods into Spanish overseas territories on a large scale. To use a favorite modern term, Spain's governmental expenditures were not used to "prime the pump" for increased national productivity—or, more accurately, the pumps they primed were not Spanish, but foreign, pumps. By 1600, Spanish home industry was on the decline.

The free-trade economists of the nineteenth century offered a simple explanation for this failure of Spain to make good use of her economic opportunities—monopoly under government supervision. Sixteenth-century Spain was certainly moving toward that economic policy called *mercantilism,* which reached its fullest development in seventeenth-century France (see Chapter XV). Although Spain lacked the true mercantilist passion for building national wealth under government auspices, she used many mercantilist techniques, the endless regulation in general and the narrow channeling of colonial trade in particular. The Spanish system left little room for individual economic initiative. In Castile, a single institution, the famous *Casa de Contratación* (House of Trade), controlled every trans-

action with the Indies, and licensed every export and import. The amount of sheer paper work, in an age unblessed by typewriters and mimeographs, was enormous.

Yet bureaucratic methods and monopolies were not the sole source of difficulty. The whole direction of Spanish civilization turned Spanish creative energies into other channels than the industrial. Warfare, politics, religion, art, traditional farming, or simply living like an *hidalgo* (*hijo de algo,* "son of somebody," hence nobleman, gentleman) were respectable activities. What Americans broadly understand by "business" was, if not disgraceful, certainly not an activity on which society set a premium. Not that as a nation the Spanish were lazy; the lower classes especially had to work very hard. That epitome of so much we think of as Spanish, Don Quixote, was hardly a lazy man, but his activity was not exactly productive of material wealth. If we take into consideration the numerous holidays, the habit of the siesta, the large numbers of beggars, soldiers, priests, monks, and *hidalgos,* as well as the lack of encouragement to new enterprises and techniques and the heavy hand of an inefficient bureaucracy—if we put all this together, it becomes clear that the total national effort was bound to be inadequate in competition with nations better organized for modern economic life. Spain, in short, presents almost the antithesis of the picture of what goes into the "capitalist spirit" drawn by Weber and his school (see Chapter XII).

The Spanish Style

Yet the Spanish supremacy, though short-lived, was real enough, and has helped make the world we live in. Half the Americas speak Spanish (or a rather similar tongue, Portuguese) and carry, however altered, a cultural inheritance from the Iberian Peninsula. French, Dutch, and English national unity and national spirit were hardened in resistance to Spanish aggression. The Spanish character, the Spanish "style," was set—some may say hardened—in this Golden Age, which has left to the West some magnificent paintings and one of the few really universal books, the *Don Quixote* of Cervantes (1547-1616). This Spanish style is not at all like those of France and Italy, so often tied with Spain as "Latin"—a term that is very misleading if used to contrast these nations with "Nordic" or "Germanic" nations. Perhaps the term is most misleading when it groups these lands and their peoples together as "sunny." For the Spanish spirit is among the most serious, most darkly passionate, most unsmiling, in the West. It is a striving spirit, carrying to the extreme the chivalric "point of honor," the religious pain of living in this flesh, the desire for something more.

The Spanish spirit stands out in the painting reproduced in color at the opening of this chapter. The artist was not a native Spaniard at all, but El Greco, "the Greek" (1541-1614). Born Domenico Theotokopouli on the island of Crete, trained both in the Byzantine tradition of the Aegean world and at the school of Titian in Venice, he settled at Toledo, the religious capital of Castile, when he was approaching the peak of his career. Despite his cosmopolitan background, El Greco belongs completely to the Spain of Philip II and the Catholic Reformation, not at all to the Renaissance.

The subject of the painting is a Spanish legend, the burial of the Count of Orgaz. This fourteenth-century Castilian nobleman had built a church at Toledo to honor Saint Augustine and Saint Stephen. When he died, the two saints miraculously appeared to bury his body. In the painting, the two saints (Augustine is the bearded one) gently lift the Count, and the aristocratic mourners gravely witness the miracle as an angel conveys the Count's soul to the Virgin, to Christ, Saint Peter, and the host of the blessed waiting above. The whole

effect is heightened by El Greco's characteristic distortion of human figures, with their long, thin heads, their great eyes turned upward. The painting stretches toward heaven like the pinnacles of a Gothic cathedral; it is a most extraordinary effort to record the mystic's unrecordable experience.

Spain is indeed the land of passionate religious will to overcome this world in mystical union with Christ. St. Theresa of Avila (1515-1582) and St. John of the Cross (1542-1591) bring back the tortured ecstasies of the early Christian ascetics, and add a dark, rebellious, note of their own. Theirs was no eastern attempt to withdraw from the world of sense and common sense, but a heroic effort to combat this world of the senses and thus transcend it. They were both familiar figures to the Spanish common people, who in their own way identified themselves with these saints in their struggle. Here is a portion of a modern writer's account of the funeral of St. John of the Cross:

Hardly had his breath ceased than, though it was an hour past midnight, cold and raining hard, crowds assembled in the street and poured into the convent. Pressing into the room where he lay, they knelt to kiss his feet and hands. They cut off pieces from his clothes and bandages and even pulled out the swabs that had been placed on his sores. Others took snippings from his hair and tore off his nails, and would have cut pieces from his flesh had it not been forbidden. At his funeral these scenes were repeated. Forcing their way past the friars who guarded his body, the mob tore off his habit and even took parts of his ulcered flesh.*

The creations of Cervantes, in their very different way, carry the mark of the Spanish style. Spain is Don Quixote tilting with the windmills, aflame for the Dulcinea he has invented, quite mad. But it is also the knight's servant, Sancho Panza, conven-

---

* Gerald Brenan, "A Short Life of St. John of the Cross," in *The Golden Horizon*, ed. by Cyril Connolly (London, 1953), 475-476.

tional, earthy, unheroic, and sane enough, though his sanity protects him not at all from sharing his master's misadventures. Cervantes almost certainly meant no more than an amusing satire of popular tales of chivalry. But his story has got caught up in the web of symbolism we live by, and the Don and his reluctant follower are for us Spain forever racked between ambitious heroism and reluctant common sense.

This tension runs all through *Don Quixote.* Chivalry is indeed silly, and worth satire—gentle satire:

'I would inform you, Sancho, that it is a point of honor with knights-errant to go for a month at a time without eating, and when they do eat, it is whatever may be at hand. You would certainly know that if you had read the histories as I have. There are many of them, and in none have I found any mention of knights eating unless it was by chance or at some sumptuous banquet that was tendered them; on other days they fasted. And even though it is well understood that, being men like us, they could not go without food entirely, any more than they could fail to satisfy the other necessities of nature, nevertheless, since they spent the greater part of their lives in forests and desert places without any cook to prepare their meals, their diet ordinarily consisted of rustic viands such as those that you now offer me. And so, Sancho my friend, do not be grieved at that which pleases me, nor seek to make the world over, nor to unhinge the institution of knight-errantry.'
'Pardon me, your Grace,' said Sancho, 'but seeing that, as I have told you, I do not know how to read or write, I am consequently not familiar with the rules of the knightly calling. Hereafter, I will stuff my saddlebags with all manner of dried fruit for your Grace, but inasmuch as I am not a knight, I shall lay in for myself a stock of fowls and other more substantial fare.' *

The extreme of pride—pride of race, of faith, of nation—has seemed to the outside world the mark of Spain. Perhaps there is little to choose among the triumphant prides of nations in triumph. Yet as the "shot heard

---

* *Don Quixote,* Samuel Putnam, trans. (New York, 1949), I, 78-79.

round the world" sounds very American, so the Cid, the legendary hero of the reconquest, is very Spanish in these verses as he goes off to his crusade:

Por necesidad batallo
Y una vez puesto en la silla
Se va ensanchando Castilla
Delante de mi caballo

[I fight by necessity: but once I am in the saddle, Castile goes widening out ahead of my horse.]

The French Monarchy

North of the Pyrenees another of the new monarchies had emerged in the fifteenth century. Perhaps no province of France—not even Brittany with its Celtic language and autonomous traditions, not even Provence with its language of the troubadours, its ties with Italy, its long history as a separate unit—shows the intense awareness of its own separateness that is to be found in Aragon or the Basque Provinces of Spain. Moreover, unlike Greece, Italy, and the Iberian Peninsula, France for the most part is not cut up by mountain ranges into relatively isolated regions; the mountain barriers are mostly on her borders. Even so, France was but imperfectly tied together under Francis I (1515-1547), contemporary of Charles V and Henry VIII. Provinces like Brittany, which had only recently come under the Valois crown, retained their own local representative bodies (estates), their own local courts (*parlements*), and many other privileges. The nobility held on to feudal memories and attitudes, though it had lost most of its old governmental functions to royal appointees. The national bureaucracy was most rudimentary, a patchwork that could hardly fit into a modern administrative chart, with its little boxes showing who consults with whom, who obeys whom in a chain of authority.

As we have seen, however, the kingdom

Chenonceaux Chateau, built over the River Cher, in the Loire Valley, France.

of Francis I possessed strength enough to counter the threat of encirclement by Charles V. The King himself was not another Louis XI. Self-indulgence weakened his health and distracted him from the business of government; his extravagant court and, far more, his frequent wars nearly wrecked the finances of the state. Yet in many respects Francis was a good Renaissance despot, thoroughly at home in the age of Machiavelli. In adversity he had courage: witness his successful recovery after the disaster at Pavia in 1525. In diplomacy he was unscrupulous and flexible: witness his alliance with the Turks and with the German Protestants. Good-looking (at least until his health broke down), amorous, courtly, lavish, Francis comported himself as many people expect royalty to behave. He did things on the grand scale; it is reported that it took 18,000 horses and pack animals to move the King and his court on their frequent journeys. Francis built the famous chateaux of Chambord and Fon-

tainebleau, two of the masterpieces of French Renaissance architecture. In Paris he remodeled the great palace of the Louvre and founded the Collège de France, second only to the university (the Sorbonne) as an educational center. He patronized men of letters and artists, among them numerous Italians including Benvenuto Cellini and Leonardo da Vinci.

The artistic and humanist Renaissance spread gradually northward from Italy in the sixteenth century, taking on somewhat different characteristics in various countries. In France, the architecture of the Renaissance still bears the stamp of late Gothic, as at Chambord, or, as in the smaller chateaux like Chenonceaux, is classically French in its restraint and graceful ornamentation. French humanists are scholarly indeed, French poets conscious adapters of Latin and Greek concepts and language. Two very great sixteen-century French writers point up this national stamp, which is by no means without paradoxical contrasts, on a classic Renaissance ground: Rabelais (1494-1553), once a monk, exuberant, fleshly, optimistic, unreasonable, indecent, excited, undisciplined (but very learned), a perpetual reminder that not all French writers are logical, conventional adherents to literary standards of clarity and orderliness (see also above, pp. 447-448); and Montaigne (1533-1592), essayist, reasonable skeptic—very reasonable, a worried self-analyst, in his own way a seeker, and as a stylist one of the chief makers of the rigorously disciplined, orderly, conventional French literary language (another, Blaise Pascal, we shall encounter in Chapter XV).

Francis was the last strong king of the House of Valois. After his death in 1547, his son Henry II and his grandsons, strongly under the control of Catherine de' Medici, their mother, were barely able to maintain the prestige of the Crown. Possibly not even a greatly gifted ruler could have prevented the disorders of the second half of the sixteenth century, disorders that seriously crippled France in the international rivalries of the day. These are the years of the French religious wars, the crisis that almost undid the centralizing work of Louis XI and his successors.

The French Wars of Religion, 1562-1598

Obvious parallels exist between the French religious wars and the German Thirty Years' War. In both regions, important elements among the upper and middle classes welcomed the intellectual and spiritual concepts of Protestantism. In both regions, religious toleration at first found few supporters, and the result was endemic civil war. In both regions, the weakness of a land devoured by civil war involved it in the international strife between Catholic and Protestant and invited and secured foreign intervention. In both regions, exhaustion of the struggling parties brought with it in the end a perhaps reluctant official policy of religious toleration.

Yet the differences between the French and the German experience of wars of religion are striking and important. The French experience was briefer, and less crippling. Passions ran high, and the French wars laid one of the great blots on the historical record: the massacre of St. Bartholomew's Day (August 23-24, 1572). On that day, the Protestant leader Coligny was murdered in Paris and thousands of other Protestants in Paris and in the provinces were dragged from their beds and killed according to a prearranged plan. Yet armies were small, and the great masses of the French people went on living not too badly. By the end of the sixteenth century, in spite of the recent chaos, France was on the threshold of its own era of preponderance.

In France, Protestantism scarcely touched the great peasant masses except for parts of the South, notably Languedoc. The Huguenots, as the French Protestants came to be known, were strong among the nobility and among the new classes of capitalists and artisans. The religious map of France also showed a territorial as well as a class division, an exception to the rule that in Europe the North tends to be Protestant and the South Catholic. The northernmost sections of France, up against the Low Countries, though affected by Lutheranism at first, remained ardently Catholic, as did Brittany, most of Normandy, and the region of Paris. By the latter sixteenth century the Protestants were strongest in south-central France, above all in the lands of the old Albigensian heresy (see Chapter VII), and in the southwest. Even in these regions, however, the employer class was more likely to be Protestant, the workers to be Catholic. The French nobility took up with Protestantism in part for political reasons; the old tradition of local feudal independence among the nobles encouraged resistance to the centralized Catholic monarchy and its agents.

For the Valois kings remained firm, though hardly pious, Catholics. Francis I had extended the royal gains made at papal expense in the Pragmatic Sanction of Bourges of 1438 (see Chapter X). In the Concordat of Bologna, 1516, the pope allowed the king a very great increase in control over the Gallican Church, including the important right of choosing bishops and abbots. The German princes in revolt had everything to gain in a worldly way by confiscation of church property and establishment of an Erastian Lutheran Church (see Chapter XII). But the French kings after 1516 had everything to lose by a Protestant movement that strengthened their restive nobility and that in its Calvinist form was the very opposite of Erastian, was indeed anti-monarchical.

The most striking development to come out of the French religious wars was the establishment of the French Crown and its bureaucrats as a mediating power between the extreme Catholics and the Protestants. At the outbreak of the wars in 1562, the Queen-Mother, Catherine de' Medici, firmly opposed the growing Protestant party, if only because the great nobles who headed that party seemed to threaten the Crown itself. As the wars went on, however, the Huguenots, in spite of St. Bartholomew's Day and defeats in the field, remained strong. The Catholic nobles organized a threatening league headed by the powerful Guise family, and both sides took to negotiating with foreigners for help, the Catholics with Spain and the Protestants with England. Thus the French rulers found themselves pushed into opposition to *both* groups.

Henri IV (Henry of Navarre) (1553-1610).

The Victory of Henry of Navarre

The wars culminated in the "War of the Three Henries" (1585-1589)—named for Henry III, the actual King of France and the last of the grandsons of Francis I; Henry, Duke of Guise, head of the Catholic League; and Henry of Navarre, the Protestant cousin and heir-apparent of the childless king. The mere threat that a Protestant, Henry of Navarre, would succeed to the throne pushed the Catholic League to the extreme of proposing a deliberate violation of the rules of succession by making an uncle of Henry of Navarre, the Catholic Cardinal of Bourbon, king. But in an established monarchy rules of succession are in fact what we call "constitutional" laws and have behind them the full force of public opinion. Moderate French public opinion, already disturbed by the extremes of both Catholics and Protestants, now turned against the Catholic League.

Paris, however, was a strong Catholic city, and a popular insurrection there, the "Day of the Barricades" (May 12, 1588), frightened Henry III out of the city, which triumphantly acclaimed Guise. Henry III took the weak man's way out, and connived at—indeed almost certainly planned—the assassination of the two great men of the Catholic League, Henry of Guise and his brother Louis. Infuriated, the League rose in full revolt, and King Henry was forced to take refuge in the camp of his Protestant cousin, Henry of Navarre, where he in turn was assassinated by a monk.

Henry of Navarre was now by law King Henry IV (1589-1610), first of the House of Bourbon. The Catholics set up the aged Cardinal of Bourbon as "King Charles X," but in the decisive battle of Ivry in March, 1590, Henry won a great victory, and laid siege to Paris. Long negotiations now followed, and Henry was persuaded that if he would abjure his own Protestant faith he could rally the moderate Catholics and secure at least tolerated status for the Protestants. He turned Catholic in 1593, and Paris was surrendered, giving rise to the probably apocryphal tale that he had remarked, "Paris is well worth a Mass." With the Edict of Nantes in 1598, the French religious wars were ended, but full religious freedom was not achieved. The Huguenots were allowed the exercise of their religion in certain areas, and their great nobles were permitted it in their own households; but notably at Paris and its environs, and in episcopal and archiepiscopal cities, the Huguenots were forbidden public worship. Nevertheless the Edict of Nantes was a major symbol of religious toleration. In the same year, 1598, the Treaty of Vervins with Spain put an end to Spanish intervention, and restored to the French Crown all Spanish conquests in France.

The Politiques

Henry of Navarre was a gifted leader, a realist rather than a cynic—in spite of his alleged remark about Paris being worth a Mass—and, as we shall see in Chapter XV, the restorer of the French mon-archy. He was fortunate in coming on the scene after the passions of civil war were nearing exhaustion; he could hardly have succeeded in his work of pacification had France not been ready for it. The intellectual preparation for the Edict of Nantes and the revived French monarchy had been in large part the work of a group of men known by the untranslatable French term, *politiques*, which is nearer to "political moralist" than it is to our "politician." The greatest of them, Jean Bodin, who died in 1596, has been rather unfairly labeled a proponent of absolute monarchy. He did indeed hold that the sole possibility of order in a divided France lay in obedience to a king above petty civil strife. But he was far from preaching that the king must be obeyed no matter what he did. He was rather a moderate who believed in acceptance of the limitations imposed by history and tradition on any practical program of politics. The *politiques* were convinced that under the supremacy of the French state Frenchmen could be allowed to practice different forms of the Christian religion.

Some of the *politiques* were unreligious persons; but the best of them, like Michel de l'Hospital, were Christians who held firmly to the belief that the basic aim of those who fought the religious wars—to put down by force those who disagreed with them in matters religious—was un-Christian. Here is l'Hospital addressing the Estates-General in 1560:

If they are Christians, those who try to spread Christianity with arms, swords, and pistols do indeed go contrary to their professed faith, which is to suffer force, not to inflict it. . . . Nor is their argument, that they take arms in the cause of God, a valid one, for the cause of God is not one that can be so defended with such arms. . . . Our religion did not take its beginnings from force of arms, and is not to be kept and strengthened by force of arms.

Yet l'Hospital is a good child of his age, and he cannot conceive that men can really practice different religions in the same political society:

It is folly to hope for peace, quiet and friendship, among persons of different religions. And there is no opinion so deeply planted in the hearts of men, as opinion in religion, and none which so separates one from another.

He can but hope that as good Frenchmen they will sink their quarrels in a common Frenchness and a common Christianity:

Let us pray God for the heretics, and do all we can to reduce and convert them; gentleness will do more than harshness. Let us get rid of those devilish names of seditious factions, Lutherans, Huguenots, Papists: let us not change the name of Christian.*

---

* P. J. S. Dufey, *Oeuvres complètes de Michel de l'Hospital* (Paris, 1824), I, 395-402. Our translation.

V: The New Monarchies—England

Henry VIII, 1509-1547

In England, the first Tudor, Henry VII, had already established the new monarchy on a firm footing (see Chapter X). He left his son, Henry VIII, a full treasury and a well-ordered kingdom. That Henry VIII did not run through his heritage and leave an exhausted treasury was not because he lacked the will to spend lavishly. Henry, unlike his father, loved display, and all the trappings of Renaissance monarchy. His summit conference (to use a modern term) with Francis I near Calais in 1520 has gone down in tradition as the "Field of the Cloth of Gold."

Henry did not, however, seriously weaken England's finances, and for many reasons. Basically, we must make a distinction between the finances of a government and the economy of a whole society. We may sometimes, as on the eve of the great French Revolution of 1789, find a poor, even bankrupt, government in a *relatively* prosperous society; we may even, as in eighteenth-century Prussia, find a prosperous, well-run government in a society *relatively* poor. Tudor England had the good fortune to enjoy *both* solvent government finances and a prosperous society. No doubt the great enclosures of land for sheep-farming and other factors helped create a new poor, but the middle classes and the new upper classes continued on the whole to thrive. Moreover, this national material wealth was not unduly expended in foreign wars, the really major cause of disastrous financial difficulties of modern governments. Good democrats have often accused European royalty of ruinous expenditures on palaces, retinues, pensions, mistresses, and high living of all sorts; yet the fact seems to be that such expenditures were but a very small part of the total outlay of society. Henry's wives— he had six—his court, his royal progresses, did not by any means beggar his country; the wars of Charles V and Philip II did beggar Spain.

Henry VIII made war in a gingerly manner, never really risking big English armies on the Continent, and contenting himself with playing a rather cautious game of balance of power. He made full use of the opportunities afforded him by the English Reformation (see Chapter XII) to add to royal revenues by confiscation of monastic property, and, even more important, by rewarding his loyal followers with lands so confiscated. Henry thus followed in the footsteps of his father in helping create a new upper class, which was soon actually a titled or noble class. In these critical years of English development, the new class was, in contrast to France, on the whole loyal to the Crown and yet, in contrast to some of the German states, by no means subservient to the Crown, by no means a mere ennobled bureaucracy. Henry continued the administrative policies of his father, strengthening his central administration and maintaining adequate supervision over the justices of the peace, who were the keystone of English local government.

Tudor Parliaments

Most important of all, Henry was able to get what he wanted from his Parliaments, including statutes that separated the English Church from Rome, and grants for his wars and conferences. Henry's Parliaments were very far from being elected legislatures based on wide suffrage. The Tudor House of Lords had a safe majority of men—titled nobles and, after 1534, bishops of the Anglican Church—who were in fact of Tudor creation or allegiance. The House of Commons, as we have seen in Chapters VII and X, was composed of the knights of the shire, chosen by the freeholders of the shires, and of the burgesses, representatives of incorporated towns or boroughs (not by any means all towns). In most boroughs, a very narrow electorate chose these members of Parliament. Since the majority of the people of the shires were agricultural workers or tenants, rather than freeholders of land, the county franchise, too, was limited. In fact, the knights of the shire were chosen from among, and largely by, the squires and the lesser country gentlemen. Royal favor and royal patronage, as well as the patronage of the great lords, could pretty well mold the shape of a House of Commons.

Still, even the Tudor Parliaments are nearer a modern legislative assembly than the parallel assemblies, or estates, of the Continent. The great point of difference lies in the composition of the House of Commons, which had emerged from the Middle Ages not as a body representing an urban bourgeoisie but as a composite of the rural landed gentry and the bourgeoisie of the towns, meeting in one body. On the Continent, the assemblies corresponding to the English Parliament were *estates* (*Stände* in German, *états* in French). They usually sat in three distinct houses—one representing the clergy, another all the nobles, great and small, and a third the lay commoners. Some countries, as for instance Sweden, had four estates—clergy, nobles, townsmen, and peasants. In England, moreover, the nobility were a small group, the eldest sons who had actually inherited the title. Younger sons, even of earls and dukes, had no title of nobility and, unless they were ennobled by the Crown, had nothing to do with the House of Lords. They fell back into the class of gentry, which was represented in the Commons. On the Continent, by contrast, all legitimate descendants of nobles were themselves generally noble, members of a definite caste.

Finally, in England Parliament came out of the Middle Ages with the power to make laws or statutes, including money laws. These laws did indeed require royal consent. But at the end of the fifteenth century Parliament had already obtained much more than the merely advisory powers which were all that the French Estates-General, for instance, really had.

Purely in terms of constitutional structure, then, the Tudor Parliaments could have quarreled as violently with the Crown as did the Stuart Parliaments in the next century see (Chapter XV). Although the Tudor monarchs had their spats and difficulties with Parliament, on the whole they got what they wanted out of Parliament without serious constitutional crises. This was particularly true of Henry VIII and Elizabeth I. The monarchs succeeded in part, as we have noted, because their Parliaments, if not precisely packed, were generally recruited from men favorable to the Crown, to which they owed so much. But they also succeeded because they were skillful rulers, willing to use their prestige and gifts of persuasion to win the consent of Parliament, careful to observe the constitutional and human decencies. Moreover, both Henry and Elizabeth were good hearty persons, sure of themselves and their dignity, immensely popular with all classes of their subjects. Both were fortunate enough to be able to incorporate in their persons strong national feelings of patriotic resistance to the hated foreign foes, the Roman church and Spain.

The course of Tudor domestic history did not run with perfect smoothness. Henry VII had faced two pretenders; Henry VIII met opposition to his religious policy. A Catholic minority, strong in the north, continued throughout the sixteenth century to oppose the Protestant majority, sometimes in arms, sometimes in intrigues. The death of Henry VIII in 1547 marked the beginning of a period of really extraordinary religious oscillation.

Religious Difficulties

Henry was succeeded by his only son, the ten-year-old Edward VI. Led by his uncle, the Duke of Somerset, Edward's government pushed on into Protestant ways. The Six Articles (see p. 493), by which Henry had sought to preserve the essentials of Roman Catholic theology, worship, and even church organization, were repealed in 1547. The legal title of the statute commonly called the Six Articles had been "An Act for Abolishing Diversity in Opinion." The goal was still uniformity, and in the brief reign of Edward VI an effort was made to prescribe uniformity of religious worship through a prayer book and articles of faith duly imposed by Parliament. Cranmer, Archbishop of Canterbury, was a convinced Protestant, and had committed himself by marrying—as did Luther—to a clear, symbolic break with Roman Catholicism. Under his supervision, the patient bulk of the English people was pushed into Protestant worship.

Then, in 1553, the young king, Edward VI, always a frail boy, died. Protestant intriguers vainly attempted to secure the crown for a Protestant, Lady Jane Grey, a great-granddaughter of Henry VII and a quiet, scholarly young woman with no ambitions. But Edward VI was followed by his older sister Mary, daughter of the Catholic Catherine of Aragon whom Henry VIII had put aside. Mary had been brought up a Catholic, and at once began to restore the old ways. Of course there was a rebellion, which flared into the open when Mary announced a marriage treaty by which she was to wed Philip II of Spain. Yet Mary prevailed against the rebels, and Lady Jane Grey was executed for a plot she had never really shared in. The Catholic Cardinal Pole was made Archbishop of Canterbury, under Rome, and Cranmer was burned at the stake. Catholic forms of worship came back to the parishes, but significantly the land settlement of Henry VIII remained undisturbed.

Mary, too, died after a short reign, in 1558. The last of Henry's children left was Elizabeth, daughter of Anne Boleyn. She had at her father's request been declared illegitimate by Parliament in 1536. Henry's last will, however, rehabilitated her, and she now succeeded as Elizabeth I (1558-1603). She had been brought up a Protestant, and once more the ordinary English churchgoer was required to switch religion. This time the Anglican Church was firmly established; the prayer book and Thirty-Nine Articles of 1563 issued under Elizabeth (see Chapter XII) have remained to this day the essential documents of the Anglican faith.

The Elizabethan settlement, moderate and permanent though it was, did not fully settle the religious problem. England still had a Catholic party. Spain, especially after the repudiation of Catholicism, was a serious enemy; it seemed hardly likely that the heavy expenses of a real war could be long avoided. Moreover, Scotland could always be counted on in those days to take the anti-English side. The new Queen of Scotland was Mary Stuart, granddaughter of Henry VIII's sister, Margaret, and therefore the heir to the English throne should Elizabeth I die without issue. Mary did not wait for Elizabeth's death, but on the ground that Elizabeth was in fact illegitimate, herself assumed the title of "Queen of England and Scotland."

Finally, the English Catholics were by no means the most serious of Elizabeth's religious difficulties; Protestant groups not satisfied with the Thirty-Nine Articles were coming to the fore. Broadly, these people are called "Puritans," since they wished to "purify" the Anglican Church of what they considered papist survivals in belief, ritual,

and church government. Actually, the Puritans ranged from moderates to radicals. The moderates would be content with a simpler ritual but would retain bishops. The Presbyterians were Calvinists who would substitute councils (synods) of elders, or presbyters, for bishops, and would adopt the full Calvinist theology. The Brownists, named for their leader Browne, were the radical wing of Puritanism; they wanted to have each congregation an independent body.

Elizabeth the Queen

Thus Elizabeth faced a decidedly grim prospect during the early years of her reign. The troubles of the reigns of Edward and Mary had undone some of the work of the two Henries; dissension seemed all around her. Yet she was to reign for nearly fifty years, and to give her name to one of the greatest times of flowering of English culture.

The personality of Elizabeth is hardly heart-warming. She was vain (or simply proud), not altogether proof against flattery, but too intelligent to be led astray by it in great matters. She was a good Renaissance realist (a better one than Machiavelli himself), somewhat too overpowering and impressive for a woman, but very effective in the pageantry and posing of public life. She was loved by her people if not by her intimates. She never married, a fact that has unleashed a good deal of not very sound medical and psychological explanation. But in the early years of her reign she played off foreign and domestic suitors one against another with excellent results for her foreign policy, in which she was always trying to avoid the expenses and dangers of war, trying to get something for nothing. One may believe that her spinsterhood settled on her at first as no more than a policy of state, and later as a convenient habit. She had male favorites, but hardly lovers.

Elizabeth I.

Under such able ministers as Burleigh and Walsingham, her government was put in excellent order. Thanks to skillful diplomacy, which made full use of the French and Dutch opposition to Spain, the showdown with Philip was postponed until 1588, when the kingdom was ready for it. Mary Queen of Scots proved no match at all for her gifted cousin, not merely because she was not a good politician, but even more because she had no sure Scottish base to work from. Mary was a Catholic, and Scotland under the leadership of John Knox was on its way to becoming one of the great centers of Calvinism. Mary managed everything wrong, including, and perhaps most important in a puritanical land, her love affairs. Her subjects revolted against her, and she was forced in 1568 to take refuge in England, where Elizabeth had her put in confinement. Mary alive was at the very least a constant temptation to all who wanted to overthrow Elizabeth. Letters, which Mary declared were forged, and over which historians still debate, involved her in what was certainly a very real conspiracy against Elizabeth, and she was tried, convicted, and executed in 1587, to become a romantic legend.

The dramatic crisis of the reign was the war with Spain, resolved in the defeat of the great Spanish Armada in 1588. But Elizabeth's old age was not to be altogether quiet. In Ireland, the native masses were ruled by an Anglo-Irish landed class out of touch with the people. In 1542, the country had been made a kingdom, but by no means an independent one, since the crowns of England and Ireland were held by the same person. An earlier act, the Statute of Drogheda (Poynings' Act), in 1495 had put the Irish Parliament firmly under English control, and had made laws enacted in the English Parliament applicable to Ireland. The native Irish had remained firmly Catholic. The stage was set for the perennial Irish Problem, the long struggle for Irish national independence.

In 1597, the Irish rose under the leadership of Hugh O'Neill, Earl of Tyrone. The revolt had temporary success, but was put down bloodily in 1601 after the favorite of Elizabeth's old age, the Earl of Essex, had failed dismally to cope with it. Essex, too, involved himself in a plot against his mistress, and was executed after its discovery and suppression. But the Elizabethan settlement of Ireland's troubles was no settlement, and we shall return to this running sore, closed only in the 1930's, in Chapter XV.

The Elizabethan Age, then, was no age of quiet, but rather one of wars, rebellions, personal and party strife, and intense competition. None the less, it never reached the fatal depths of destruction of a Thirty Years' War, though for a while it threatened to do so under Mary Tudor. There was a solid foundation under the state and society that produced the literature, music, architecture, science, and wealth and victories of the Elizabethan Age. That foundation was in part a good administrative system, itself based on a substantial degree of national unity, or, negatively, on the absence of the extreme local differences and conflicts of the Continent. It was in part general economic prosperity, based on individual enterprise in many fields—enterprise often unscrupulous and, as far as raids on the commerce of foreigners like the Spaniards went, piratical. It was certainly something not simply material, a common sentiment that kept Englishmen together, and that traced for most of them limits beyond which they would not carry disagreement. Elizabeth herself played a large part in holding her subjects together; her religious policy, for example, was directed at stretching the already broad principles and practices of the Church of England so that they would cover near-Catholicism and near-Congregationalism. But there was a limit to this stretching, and Elizabeth "persecuted" Catholics on the Right and Brownists on the Left.

Tudor architecture. Compton Wynyates.

The English Renaissance

The Age of Elizabeth I was a flowering of English culture symbolized for all of us by Shakespeare (1564-1616). Elizabeth's actual reign, from 1558 to 1603, by no means measures the Age accurately. Much of her father's reign belongs to the flowering, as do the first ten or fifteen years of the reign of her successor, James I, the first Stuart king.

This is the English Renaissance, tardiest of the great classical Renaissances. It has the range and variety we have found in other lands, and the same clear admiration for, the same dependence on, the old Greeks and Romans we have found elsewhere. It is hard to pick up a poem, an essay, a play, any piece of writing not purely religious, without coming very soon upon a classical allusion. Yet the English Renaissance did not imitate classical an-

tiquity, so to speak, photographically. It holds on to much that could be grown only in the climate of the island. Tudor and early Stuart architecture is a clear case in point. The new palaces and manor houses are no longer much like the medieval castles; they are more open, more elegant. But they preserve all sorts of Gothic habits, mullioned windows, tracery and carving, traditional woodwork.

Painting, sculpture, the plastic arts in all their range—music itself—are for England in these years at a high level. Elizabethan ladies and gentlemen cultivated all the muses, sang madrigals, played the lute, appreciated modern paintings, had their houses built in the modern style, dressed as did ladies and gentlemen in the center of European culture of this sort, Italy. Yet the commonplace is unavoidable: England is not a land of great original creation in music and the plastic arts. The greatness of Elizabethan England, when it is not in the deeds of Drake, Hawkins, Wolsey, Burleigh, the Tudors themselves, lies in the words of St. Thomas More, Shakespeare, Francis Bacon, Spenser, Ben Jonson, and many others who are part of the formal higher education of English-speaking people all over the world.

They are a hard group to generalize about. They are established "classics" and have suffered the popular admiration and neglect as well as the academic working-over that go with the status of classics in our culture. They belong to a culture now four hundred years past, and they wrote English before its structure and its word-order were tamed, partly by the influence of French prose, into their present straight-forward simplicity. They are much easier to read about than to read. Finally, they have been targets for some debunking, but on the whole they have survived intact as classics. Shakespeare, notably, continues even outside the English-speaking world to be a kind of George Washington of letters, above reproach. He is the necessary great writer of a great people, as is Dante for the Italians, Goethe for the Germans, Pascal or Molière or Racine for the French, Tolstoy for the Russians.

These Elizabethans are overwhelmingly exuberant. They are exuberant even in refinement, full-blooded even in erudition. Above all, they are anxious to get in that something more, that transcending something that makes words more than words, and possibly more than sense. To a later generation, the tame, orderly admirers of measure and sense in the late seventeenth and eighteenth centuries, these Elizabethans were somewhat uncouth, undisciplined. To the nineteenth-century Romantics, they were brothers in romance, sharing the desire of the moth for the star. And indeed this exuberance, this love of the excessive, is obvious in much Elizabethan writing, in the interminable, allusion-packed, allegory-mad stanzas of Spenser's *Faerie Queene*, in the piling up of quotations from the ancient Greeks and Romans, in Shakespeare's love of puns and all kinds of rhetorical devices, in the extraordinarily bloody nature of their tragedies—remember the end of *Hamlet*, which finds the stage littered with corpses.

There is, however, a balancing quality in the Elizabethans. They had a good carnal appreciation of this earth; they seemed even to have enjoyed their gloom and depth when they left the world of the fleshly enjoyments for their brief trips into transcendence. The absurd notion that Shakespeare's works were written by Bacon—a notion apparently based on the assumption that Shakespeare was not formally and academically well enough trained to write the plays, which is nonsense—has at least some meaning in terms of the spirit of the age. Francis Bacon, lawyer and humanist, philosopher of inductive science (see Chapter XV), and rather bad practitioner of experimental science, was at bottom a heaven-stormer, intent on solving the problems of the ages. Yet he was at the same time an earth-bound Tudor gentleman, quite capable of enjoying himself in this harsh world. So, too, was Shakespeare, who has the dying Hamlet tell his friend Horatio:

> If thou didst ever hold me in thy heart,
> Absent thee from felicity a while
> And in this harsh world draw thy breath in
>   pain
> To tell my story.

Bacon and Shakespeare have at least this in common: they are hearty of mind and spirit, wide-ranging, bound by no narrow formulas of literary or philosophic taste, really willing to accept the world about them without drying up into conformity, willing to get beyond that world without indulging in complaint or rebellion.

However men may vary in their attempts to define the climate of Elizabethan opinion and the quality of its culture, there can be no doubt that the Elizabethans were good English patriots, lovers of their country in the first flush of its worldly success. Here is one of the most famous of quotations from Shakespeare, in itself an admirable sample of the English Renaissance, right down to the inevitable, and in this case rather flat, allusion to Greco-Roman mythology:

This royal throne of kings, this scepter'd isle,
This earth of majesty, this seat of Mars,
This other Eden, demi-paradise,
This fortress built by Nature for herself
Against infection and the hand of war,
This happy breed of men, this little world,
This precious stone set in the silver sea,
Which serves it in the office of a wall
Or as a moat defensive to a house,
Against the envy of less happier lands,
This blessed plot, this earth, this realm, this England.[*]

---

[*] *Richard II*, Act II, Scene i.

Reading Suggestions
on the Dynastic and Religious Wars

(Asterisk indicates paperbound edition.)

GENERAL ACCOUNTS

D. Ogg, *Europe in the Seventeenth Century*, 6th ed. (Black, 1948); and G. N. Clark, *The Seventeenth Century*, 2nd ed. (Clarendon, 1947). Two good general histories, ranging in part well beyond the subject of this chapter.

C. J. Friedrich, *The Age of the Baroque, 1610-1660* (Harper, 1952). This volume, in the "Rise of Modern Europe" series, is unusually firm and provocative. Emphasizes culture and political theory. NOTE: The important bibliographies of these "Rise of Modern Europe" volumes are undergoing revision. Especially for earlier volumes published between 1934 and 1946, users should note from the beginning of the bibliographical section whether it has been revised.

C. Petrie, *Earlier Diplomatic History, 1492-1713* (Macmillan, 1949). A useful manual of the history of international relations.

SPECIAL STUDIES: ENGLAND

C. Read, *The Tudors* (Holt, 1936). A most readable introduction by a sound historian.

S. T. Bindoff, *Tudor England* ([*] Penguin, 1952). A brief, popular account.

J. D. Mackie, *The Earlier Tudors, 1485-1558* (Clarendon, 1952); and J. B. Black, *The Reign of Elizabeth, 1558-1603* (Clarendon, 1936). These two volumes in the "Oxford History of England" are scholarly and comprehensive.

G. R. Elton, *The Tudor Revolution in Government* ([*] Cambridge Univ. Press, 1953). An important study of the shift to the "new-model" bureaucratic state.

D. L. Keir, *The Constitutional History of Modern Britain, 1485-1937*, 4th ed. (Black, 1950). A good introduction to an important and difficult subject.

A. F. Pollard, *Henry VIII*, new ed. (Longmans, Green, 1951). An old and highly respected study.

J. E. Neale, *Queen Elizabeth* (Harcourt, Brace, 1934; [*] Anchor). Generally considered the best single volume on the famous queen. The author has also written several specialized works on aspects of political life under Elizabeth.

C. Read, *Mr. Secretary Walsingham and the Policy of Queen Elizabeth* (Harvard Univ. Press, 1925). A thorough study of a key figure in Tudor government.

A. L. Rowse, *The Expansion of Elizabethan England* (St. Martin's, 1955), and *The England of Elizabeth: The Structure of Society* (Macmillan, 1950). These complementary studies are the work of a "maverick" English scholar in rebellion against academic caution.

E. Jenkins, *Elizabeth the Great* (Coward-McCann, 1959). Deservedly a best-seller; focused on the queen as a person.

G. Mattingly, *The Armada* (Houghton Mifflin, 1959). A fascinating narrative.

SPECIAL STUDIES:
PRIMARILY ON SPAIN, SWEDEN, GERMANY, AND THE NETHERLANDS

R. B. Merriman, *The Rise of the Spanish Empire in the Old World and the New* (Macmillan, 1918-1934). Volumes III and IV of this detailed work deal with Charles V and Philip II.

R. Trevor Davies, *The Golden Century of Spain* (Macmillan, reprinted 1954). A standard shorter study of sixteenth-century Spain.

K. Brandi, *The Emperor Charles V* (Jonathan Cape, 1939). A very complete study of the man who first tried to secure something like control over the European state-system.

M. Roberts, *Gustavus Adolphus: A History of Sweden, 1611-1632,* 2 vols. (Longmans, Green, 1953-58). Sympathetic biography which is also a full history of these important years for Sweden.

C. V. Wedgwood, *The Thirty Years' War* (Jonathan Cape, 1938). A full and generally well-balanced account.

S. R. Gardiner, *The Thirty Years' War* (Scribner's, 1874). A much older account, brief and good.

H. Holborn, *A History of Modern Germany: The Reformation* (New York: Knopf, 1959). First volume of a projected two-volume history by a distinguished scholar. This volume is not confined to The Reformation in a narrow sense, but is an excellent general, yet reasonably detailed, history of Germany from the late Middle Ages to 1648. A promised second volume will bring the account to the present.

C. J. Cadoux, *Philip of Spain and the Netherlands* (Lutterworth Press, 1947). A modest restatement of the Protestant and liberal thesis with interesting reflections on moral judgments in history.

P. Geyl, *The Revolt of the Netherlands, 1555-1609* (Williams and Norgate, 1945) and *The Netherlands Divided, 1609-1648* (Williams and Norgate, 1936). Very good studies by a leading modern Dutch scholar.

C. V. Wedgwood, *William the Silent* (Yale Univ. Press, 1945). An enthusiastic biography.

L. von Ranke, *Civil Wars and Monarchy in France in the Sixteenth and Seventeenth Century* (Harper, 1853). An old and famous work by one of the greatest nineteenth-century historians; may still be read with profit.

SPECIAL STUDIES: FRANCE

A. J. Grant, *The Huguenots* (Butterworth, 1934. Home University Library). A brief and reasonably dispassionate account.

J. E. Neale, *The Age of Catherine de' Medici* (Jonathan Cape, 1943). A solid study.

J. W. Thompson, *The Wars of Religion in France, 1559-1576* (Univ. of Chicago Press, 1909). A detailed narrative.

de L'Estoile, Pierre, Selections from his *Mémoires-Journaux*, trans. and ed. by Nancy Lyman Roelker under the title, *The Paris of Henry of Navarre* (Harvard Univ. Press, 1958). A fine translation; a rich source of information on Henry IV.

Q. Hurst, *Henry of Navarre* (Appleton-Century-Crofts, 1938). A standard biography in English of King Henry IV of France.

SPECIAL STUDIES: OTHER TOPICS

G. Mattingly, *Renaissance Diplomacy* (Houghton Mifflin, 1955). Indispensable for the topic.

H. Nicholson, *The Evolution of Diplomatic Method* (Macmillan, 1954). A brief survey, which goes back to the Greeks, and is especially good on the techniques and spirit of early modern diplomacy.

G. H. Sabine, *A History of Political Theory*, rev. ed. (Holt, 1950). This admirably sane and lucid treatment has very useful sections covering topics dealt with in this chapter.

J. W. Allen, *Political Thought in the Sixteenth Century*, 3rd ed. (Barnes and Noble, 1951). A more detailed and difficult account of the subject.

F. L. Nussbaum, *A History of the Economic Institutions of Modern Europe* (Appleton-Century-Crofts, 1933). Incorporates the views of the important German economic historian, Sombart.

G. Renard and G. Weulersse, *Life and Work in Modern Europe (Fifteenth through Eighteenth Centuries)* (Knopf, 1926). Useful for the general economic background.

(*Note:* For other useful works on economics and political theory, consult the titles listed at the close of chapters X and XII).

C. W. C. Oman, *A History of the Art of War in the Sixteenth Century* (Dutton, 1937). A highly interesting study of an aspect of history often neglected.

J. F. C. Fuller, *A Military History of the Western World*, 3 vols. (Funk & Wagnalls, 1954-1956). By an informative and rather unorthodox general; Vols. I and II include material relating to this chapter.

L. Goldscheider, *El Greco* (Phaidon, 1954). An excellently illustrated book on the painter who expresses so well the Spanish "style."

Cervantes, *Don Quixote,* S. Putnam, trans., 2 vols. (Viking, 1949). Widely considered the best translation of this great classic.

H. J. C. von Grimmelshausen, *Simplicissimus* (Dutton, 1924). This novel of the Thirty Years' War, written in the seventeenth century, is an important document of social history. Good reading, despite its rather strange form.

W. Scott, *Kenilworth* (many editions). Elizabethan England is the scene of this novel by the famous Romantic writer of the early nineteenth century.

CHAPTER XIII

The Expansion of Europe:

Fifteenth Through Seventeenth Centuries

CHAPTER XIV

I: Introduction

MOST HISTORICAL GEOGRAPHIES provide a series of maps showing what they commonly call the "known world" at certain periods—starting usually from the known world of Homer, little more than the eastern Mediterranean and its fringes. Next come the known worlds of Alexander the Great and the Romans, centered still on the Mediterranean, hazy or blank for much of interior Europe and Africa, with only the western fringes of Asia known, and with the Americas still unsuspected. Then from late medieval explorations through the great modern discoveries, the series goes on to the full fruition of geographical knowledge, which happened only yesterday. There is a revealing symbolism in that phrase "known world," for we really mean "known to interested members of Greco-Roman society and its Christian successor states of the West." The Chinese, too, had a "known world," and even the Red Indians.

Ancient and Modern Expansion Contrasted

Men have always moved about on this planet. In the prehistoric ages of movement and migration, which include such daring feats as the Polynesian settlement of

561

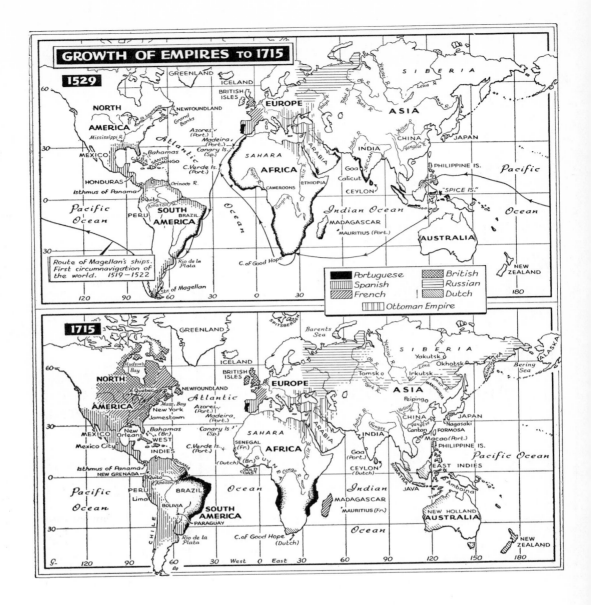

GROWTH OF EMPIRES TO 1715

1529

Route of Magellan's ships. First circumnavigation of the world. 1519–1522

Portuguese · British · Spanish · Russian · French · Dutch · Ottoman Empire

1715

the Pacific islands, the movers kept no written records and no concrete ties with their place of origins. They were not societies in expansion, but groups of individuals on the move, carrying no more than traditions, habits, and tools. The expansion of the West was a very different thing. From the very start in ancient Greece and Rome, records were kept, indeed maps were made, and the nucleus always remained in touch with its

offshoots. Western society has expanded *as a society*, often as a group of states.

The western expansion, which began in the mid-fifteenth century, however, differed in important ways from the expansion that had carried the cultures of the ancient Near East as far as western and northern Europe. In the first place, this modern expansion was much faster and covered more ground. Although some secrets of the Arctic and

562

the Antarctic, some details of the wilder interiors of the world, were not known to us until the twentieth century, it is broadly true that the whole world was revealed to Europeans within the two and a half or three centuries after 1450—within four long lifetimes. In the second place, this modern expansion was the first time our western society crossed oceans. Ancient and medieval navigation had clung to the narrow seas and the shorelines. The ancients had even commonly drawn up their boats on land to spend the night. Now westerners crossed Atlantic and Pacific, far from the protecting land. In the third place, this expansion carried westerners well outside the orbit of relations with Byzantines and Mohammedans, who were also successors to the cultures of Socrates and Christ, into relations with a bewildering variety of races, creeds, and cultures, from naked savages to cultivated Chinese. Not since the Germanic peoples had been tamed and converted in the Dark Ages had westerners come into close contact with primitive peoples. Finally, and of very great importance, expanding Europe possessed a margin of superior strength that lasted in some respects up to our own time, a margin that enabled western society to do what no society had ever done before—extend its influence around the world.

An important element of that margin was the possession of firearms; yet firearms could be legally or illegally acquired by non-Europeans, and very soon were. The strength by which Europeans overcame the world was not quite so simple as the possession of firearms. It was a compound of technological and economic superiority and of superior political and social organization, which in turn permitted superior military organization. This superiority was not exercised from a common western center, but rather by half a dozen competing western nations, each anxious to cut the others' throats, and quite willing to arm and organize natives against its western competitors.

Frenchmen in North America armed the savages against the English, and the English armed them against the French. Yet not even the Iroquois were able to maintain themselves against white society. French, English, Portuguese, Dutch, Spaniards, and later Germans and Americans all intrigued against one another in the Far East, and yet not until the mid-twentieth century did any Asiatic nation (save only Japan, and Japan not until about 1900) really compete successfully in war and politics with a western land. So great was western superiority that the rivalries of competing powers did not delay the process of expansion but probably stimulated and hastened it.

How far this physical superiority in the expansion of the West throughout the world was—and is—also a spiritual and moral superiority is a problem we in the West today cannot answer as firmly as did our fathers. But you will not understand the successful expansion of Europe if you do not realize that those who carried out the expansion, though moved often by greed, by love of adventure, by sheer despair over their lot at home, and by many other motives, were also moved by the conviction that they were doing God's work, the work of civilization, that they were carrying with them a better way of life. They were confident and energetic people, capable of great endurance and courage, and they have made over the face of the globe.

The Motives and Nature of Modern Expansion

Why did men living on the Atlantic coasts of Europe in the second half of the fifteenth century venture out on an ocean that ancient and medieval mariners had not seriously tried to penetrate? We cannot answer the question with finality. Indeed, though it is rather a question of fact than a question of value-judgments, it is still a most difficult one. The Americas, Africa south of the Sahara, Australia, all were there for the Phoenicians or the Greeks or the Romans to find. Yet it was left for Europeans in the fifteenth and the sixteenth centuries to find them, systematically and surely.

The great explorations were part of the Renaissance, part of a general stirring of European nations, of an era of adventure and the energetic pursuit of new things. So small a thing as the magnetic compass helped make ocean voyages possible. Without the compass, earlier mariners had been helpless, except when clear weather gave them sun or stars as guides. The actual origins of the compass are obscure, but we know that by the beginning of the fifteenth century it was familiar to European sailors, and was a normal part of navigation by the time of Columbus. Better instruments and better methods of determining a ship's position at sea were also fully in hand by the late fifteenth century. Shipbuilders were getting away from older types of traditional Mediterranean ships, building somewhat longer and narrower vessels that could stand the long swells of the ocean, deliberately trying to find the kind of ship that could be handled in these unknown waters. Technologically, the way was ready for the great explorations.

Politically, the blocking or at least hindering of the usual trade routes in the Near East by the new and still unsettled Turkish power turned men's minds to the search for another way to India and China. Yet the Italians, especially the Venetians and Genoese, had installed themselves in the Near East and were making arrangements with the Turks in spite of difficulties. More important, actually, was the fact that Spain, Portugal, France, and England were all rising in political and economic activity, all on the way up that had been shown them by the Italians. Blocked in the Near East, in part by Italians, they eyed the unoccupied Atlantic. Those addicted to Marxist or other variants of the innocent economic interpretation of everything can answer our question readily: Renaissance men discovered new worlds because the economic drives natural to nascent capitalism sent them on their way.

Yet technology and the politics of the trade routes had to be taken advantage of by men, men in the state of mind that sent Columbus out across the unknown ocean— to see with his own eyes what was there, to test in experience a set of concepts. Columbus deliberately sought to prove his theory that because the earth is round one can travel from Europe westward and reach Asia. No sensible person would maintain that even the first voyage of Columbus can be explained entirely in such purely intellectual terms; but neither can it be explained without such terms. One of the essential characteristics of the explorations and the subsequent expansion of Europe is that this is a movement guided in part by the new spirit of empirical science, the spirit that impelled men, if for instance they heard about the existence of unicorns, to go out and try to find some. Their medieval predecessors did not need to see a unicorn to believe in its existence. This new scientific spirit, however, did not immediately banish unicorns, mermaids, and sea serpents from men's minds, and has not yet done so now that the whole world has been thoroughly explored. Indeed, the first news of these strange worlds resulted in a whole new set of wonders, some real or merely exaggerated, which the publishing of accounts of travel brought to all Europe.

Nothing makes more clear the consecutive, planned, deliberately scientific nature of these early modern explorations and settlements than the contrast with the sporadic, unplanned, and perhaps wholly mythical, earlier oceanic navigation. Tradition is full of these early voyages, and of Atlantis, a lost continent, now sunk beneath the waves, but once inhabited, which Plato and later commentators tell about. Irishmen, Norsemen, Breton fishermen, and others have all been credited with the "discovery" of America, a discovery that was never widely spread abroad in the medieval West. Of all these tales of pre-Columbian discovery, that of the Vikings' reaching the North American continent about the end of the tenth century is most likely. There is not the slightest doubt that Norsemen reached Iceland and settled it for good, and that they had outpost settlements in Greenland. Their traditional literature, the heroic poems known as sagas, credit Leif Ericson with reaching a Wineland (or Vineland), which most experts believe to have been some part of the New England or Nova Scotian coast. It is quite possible that all during the Middle Ages, more probably toward their close, fishermen from northwest Europe fished the Grand Banks off the coast of Newfoundland.

And yet it is rather surprising that, especially in the case of the Norsemen, who were an organized group, there has not yet been discovered in North America a single unquestionably authentic artifact of European origin universally accepted as originating before Columbus. It seems amazing that these adventurers, traveling light though they may have been, have not left for us to stumble on a single spoon or spearhead or discarded pot or any of the human detritus that even Neanderthal man has left. Perhaps a naive American desire to push our pedigree here on this continent farther back is responsible for such great efforts to prove the pre-Columbian voyages to America. A stone tower in Newport, Rhode Island, which was claimed to be of Norse origin, turned out on excavation to have bits of clay pipe of seventeenth-century manufacture underneath it. Other pre-Columbian artifacts of European origin remain at best controversial. The main thing for us to understand is this: even if hundreds of Europeans reached the New World before Columbus, they did not establish a permanent link between the two worlds; they were not explorers of the kind we are about to talk about, and they were, above all, not supported by the organized social purpose we are about to encounter.

II: East by Sea to the Indies

Prince Henry and the Portuguese

There is, as the historically minded would expect, abundant medieval background for the great explorations we are about to describe. The overland voyages to China of the Venetian Marco Polo (*c.* 1264–*c.*1324) were widely known through manuscripts of his own account of his travels. But there were other less well-known travelers in the late Middle Ages, which were years of ferment and search for the new and the striking.

The first of the great names in modern expansion is not that of a bold explorer or *conquistador*, but that of an organizing genius who directed the work of others—in fact, in modern terms, a "planner." Prince Henry of Portugal, known as "the Navigator," lived from 1394 to 1460. He was a deeply religious man, and he may well have been moved above all by a desire to convert the populations of India and the Far East, whose existence had been well known to westerners since the travels of Marco Polo. Indeed, there was a widespread conviction in the West that these distant peoples were in fact already Christian, and needed only to be brought in direct contact with the Roman Catholic Church. One of the great medieval legends was that of Prester (that is, Priest) John, a powerful Christian ruler somewhere out in the vague East. Fragments of one of the very early heretic sects, the Nestorians (see Chapter IV), had indeed survived in the East, and there were Coptic Christians in Ethiopia. But Prester John was never found, and the Portuguese in India were soon disabused of their first notion that the Hindus —since they were not Mohammedans—must be Christians.

Prince Henry and his fellow workers presumably wanted to promote Portuguese commerce and national power as well as the Christian faith. They must also have felt pride in Portugal the homeland, which now appears for the first and last time as a major factor in the broad story of western civilization. They went about their work carefully, planning and sending out frequent expeditions equipped with the best technical means they could devise. Gradually, these expeditions crept southward along the harsh desert coast of Africa where the Sahara meets the Atlantic, until in 1445 Cape Verde was doubled, and the land began to grow greener and to trend hopefully eastward. Whether Henry himself believed that Africa could be circumnavigated is not absolutely certain, but according to ancient tradition the Phoenicians had done it, and Greco-Roman geographers had believed that Africa was surrounded by the ocean.

By 1472, after Henry's death, the Portuguese reached the end of the bulge of West Africa at the Cameroons, and faced the disheartening fact that the coast was once more trending southward, not eastward. But they kept on, stimulated by royal patronage, and in the next generation two great explorers finished the job. In 1488, Bartholomew Diaz, blown far south by a great storm, turned northeast and found that he had rounded the great cape we call

the Cape of Good Hope. He was followed by Vasco da Gama, who set out in 1497 with four ships to reach India. He rounded the Cape of Good Hope, thanks to the previous discoveries of Diaz, and worked northward along the east coast of Africa, coming soon to an area of Arab trading where the route to India was well known. Despite Arab jealousy of the intruder, da Gama secured a pilot and reached the Malabar coast of India at Calicut ten months and fourteen days out from Lisbon. The Portuguese now had an ocean route to the East.

On the next great voyage toward India, the Portuguese made a lucky strike that was to break the Spanish monopoly in South America and to bring it about that one of the great Latin-American states would be Portuguese in language and culture. Pedro Cabral, in 1500, started out to repeat da Gama's voyage to India. But by now the Portuguese were used to long voyages on the open ocean, far from sight of land, and they no longer needed to creep around the coast of Africa. Cabral kept boldly southward from the bulge of Africa, and was apparently blown somewhat westward of his course so that he made a landfall on the bulge of the South American continent in what is now Brazil. He at once detached a ship and sent it home to announce his discovery. Now the voyages of Columbus were of course well known to navigators by this time, and some geographers think that in fact Cabral set out deliberately to see what he could find south of the route Columbus had taken. Six years previously, in 1494, Spain and Portugal had by the Treaty of Tordesillas agreed to partition these new lands along a north-south line three hundred and seventy leagues (about a thousand miles) west of the Azores, so that Brazil came quite definitely into the Portuguese sphere.

The main Portuguese push, however, was toward India and the Far East. The explorer was succeeded by that other characteristic agent of European expansion, the trader. But the trader by no means worked alone. He was aided and protected by the power of the state, which aimed to set up for its nationals a monopoly of trade with the newly discovered lands. The great figure of early Portuguese imperialism is Alfonso de Albuquerque, governor of the Indies from 1509 to 1515, under whom the Portuguese set up a firm base in their capital at Goa in India, and from that base organized regular trade routes toward southeastern Asia and China. By 1557, the Portuguese had established a base at Macao in China near Canton, and they had begun trade with the Japanese. Portugal had assembled a colonial empire.

Africa

The two new worlds thus opened to Europeans were very different both from Europe and from each other. Africa was hot, relatively thinly populated, relatively poor by current European standards. India, China, and much of southeastern Asia were even then thickly populated, with great wealth accumulated in a few hands, with much that the Europeans wanted in the way of silks, spices, and luxury goods. Africa was in a sense by-passed, though the many coastal stations that the Europeans founded carried on a flourishing trade in Negro slaves. These African tribes, at least in the northern center and along the bulge of the continent westward, had not been wholly out of touch with the more efficient societies to the north. They had long been in contact overland with the Arabs, who had found them a good source of slaves, and who had brought Islam and some of the wares of civilization with them. But, for the most part, the tribes in central and southern Africa were, in terms of their command over material goods, still in the Stone Age. They were primitives, men without cities and states, men with cultures so different from those of Europe that few Europeans made any effort to understand them. Nor did the Europeans, at least in these centuries, do much to undermine these primitive cultures. Save for the enforced mass migration of Negroes as slaves, most of them to the Americas, save for some trade in ivory and other tropical goods, Africa had for years little effect on Europe, and Europe had little effect on Africa.

India

The India that Europeans thus reached around Africa had been marginally in touch with Europe for several thousand years. Alexander the Great had actually

The Polo brothers with their caravan, about 1270.

campaigned in northern India, and throughout the Middle Ages the Arabs had served as a link in trade, and, in at least vague general knowledge, as a link between the West and India. But now a direct link was forged, never to be loosened. The link was not of course a form of union or assimilation, and especially in these early modern centuries, West and East hardly communicated at the higher levels of cultural interchange. Indeed, the Portuguese were contemptuous of the Indians, once they discovered that the inhabitants of India were not, as they had believed, the Christians of Prester John or some other Christian leader. Among the Dutch, French, and English who followed the Portuguese to India, this attitude of contempt became set in the conventional idea of white superiority. This feeling of European superiority among all the many agents of the West in India has probably been exaggerated both in our western literary tradition and in the minds of educated Indians quick to take offense. Still, this sense of superiority was there, perhaps most clearly reflected centuries later in Kipling's too famous

> Oh, East is East and West is West, and never the twain shall meet,
> Till Earth and Sky stand presently at God's great judgment seat. . . .°

Inescapably, this western superiority was at bottom a superiority on the battlefield. In the last analysis, and long after the initial European monopoly of firearms had ended, a European or European-trained and commanded native army or navy could always beat a native Asiatic army or navy. In India, at least, this European domination was greatly helped by the political and military disunity of the subcontinent. The Portuguese reached India at the time when in the north Moslem invaders were consolidating a foreign rule of the sort which, from the earliest Mesopotamian civ-

° R. Kipling, *Ballad of East and West.*

ilization, had periodically brought comparative order to these regions. This Mogul (Mongol) Empire in the north had little hold on regions of the south where the Europeans got firm footholds. Local Indian rulers, whether they were Moslem or Hindu in faith, were in intense rivalry and were a ready prey to European promises of aid. All the European powers found it easy, not merely to get Indian princes on their side, but to raise and train on their own responsibility native armies to fight under Portuguese, French, Dutch or British flags.

Perhaps the lack of political and social integration in India is the basic reason why a few handfuls of Europeans were able to dominate the country until 1945. China, too, saw her armed forces beaten whenever they came into formal military conflict with European or European-trained armies or fleets; China, too, was forced to make to European nations all sorts of concessions—treaty ports, and above all extraterritoriality, that is, the right of Frenchmen or Englishmen, for instance, to be tried in French or English courts for offenses committed on Chinese soil. Yet China, unlike India, was never "annexed" by a European power, never lost its "sovereignty." For China preserved a fairly strong central government, and had many strands of ethical and political unity that India lacked.

Indeed, the variety and range of Indian life are extraordinary. Some of the more isolated parts of India in the Deccan or southern peninsula were inhabited by tribesmen of no higher level than many African tribesmen. Some, on the northern edges, were warrior tribesmen much like those of the highlands of Central Asia. In the great valleys of the Indus and the Ganges, and in the richer parts of the Deccan, there was a wealthy, populous society basically Hindu in culture, though when the Europeans arrived, it was dominated in many areas by Central Asiatic invaders of Moslem faith and culture. Hindu society itself was the result of an amalgamation between earlier native stocks and invaders from the north who certainly spoke a language closely related to Greek, Latin, and indeed our own, and who probably were white "Indo-Europeans" or "Aryans." The early history of India, however, is most confusing, and we cannot tell how many these invaders were, or just where they came from, though the invasion apparently had taken place between 2000 and 1200 B.C. It seems almost certain that the white invaders' consciousness of differing from the natives is responsible basically for the characteristic Indian institution of *caste*.

According to the laws of caste, men and women were by the fact of birth settled for life in a closed group which pursued a given occupation and occupied a fixed position in society. When the Europeans reached India, there were apparently something over a thousand castes, including a group at the bottom without caste, the "untouchables." The ruling groups were of two main castes, the Brahmins or priests, and the Kshatriya or warriors. The great multiplicity of castes lay in the third group, the Vaisya or commonalty, and was based largely on vocation or trade. In theory, marriage between members of different castes was forbidden, as was change of caste through social mobility. In fact, in the centuries since the invasion by the "Indo-Europeans" considerable human intermixture had undoubtedly occurred. Yet even today the upper classes in most of India are of a lighter color than the lower.

The most striking thing about Indian culture was the high place occupied by the priestly caste, the Brahmins. The Brahmin faith has strains of a most other-worldly belief in the evils of the life of the flesh and the attainment of salvation by a mystic transcendence of the flesh in ascetic denial. With this is a doctrine of the transmigration of souls, in which sinful life leads to reincarnation in lower animal life, and virtuous life leads, at least in some

forms of Hindu belief, to ultimate freedom from flesh of any sort and reunion with the perfect, the ineffable. But official Brahminism became a series of rigid and complicated rituals, and the religion of the common people became, or rather retained from earlier times, an elaborate polytheism lush with gods and goddesses by no means ethereal, but fleshly indeed. Against all these corruptions there rose in the sixth century B.C. a great religious leader, Gautama Buddha, himself of noble stock. Buddhism is in origin one of the great higher religions of the world. It accepts the basic Brahminical concept of the badness of this world of the flesh, but it finds salvation, the *nirvana* of peaceful release from the chain of earthly birth and rebirth, in a life ascetic but not withdrawn, a life of charity and good works. Buddhism died out in the land of its birth, but it spread to China, Japan, and southeastern Asia.

In these lands it took two forms, still existing. In the northern lands of Tibet, China, Japan, the Mahayana (Great Vehicle) continued in theology to emphasize Buddha's strong ethical desire to make salvation (*nirvana*) available to all. In southeastern Asia and Ceylon, the Hinayana (Lesser Vehicle) prevailed. In theory, the Hinayana relies more on ritual, and its monks are wholly detached from the world. In fact, the two vehicles are not in our times clearly distinguished as *popular religions*. Buddhism remains a great world religion, which has made some converts among western intellectuals.

The religious thought of India has left a residue of greater other-worldliness, of greater emphasis on a mystical subduing of the flesh, on a revulsion from struggle for wealth, satisfaction of the common human appetites, worldly place and power, than has Christianity or Islam. In the practice of Indian life even before the Europeans came to India, there was plenty of violence, plenty of greed, cruelty, and self-indulgence. Except as superstition and tabu

Chinese Art. Ma Yüan, "Sage under a Pine Tree" (Sung Dynasty).

and ritual, little of the higher religions of India had seeped down to the masses. To certain types of western minds, indeed, the educated classes of India have seemed to take refuge in other-worldly doctrines as a psychological defense against the worldly superiority of the West and the poverty and superstition of their own masses. But the fact remains that for three hundred years educated Indians have insisted that they feel differently about the universe and man's place in it than do we, that theirs is a higher spirituality.

China

China, too, resisted the West, and in many ways more successfully than did India. A very old civilization that goes back several millennia before Christ, and becomes reasonably historical about 1000 B.C., was established in the valleys of the Yangtze and the Yellow rivers. Like the other civilizations on the outskirts of the great nomadic reservoir of the Eurasian heartland, the Mesopotamian, the Indian, the European, it was subject to periodical incursions of the Eurasian tribesmen. It was against such incursions that the famous Great Wall of China was built in the third century B.C. On the whole, however, the Chinese protected their basic institutions against the nomads, whom they absorbed after a few generations. At just about the time when the first Europeans were setting up permanent trade relations with China, the last of these "barbarian" conquests took place. Early in the seventeenth century, Mongolian tribes established a state of their own in eastern Manchuria, to the north of China Proper. In 1644, they seized

CHAPTER XIV

the Chinese capital of Peking (today Pei-ping) and established the Manchu dynasty that lasted until 1911. But the Manchus, like other outsiders before them, left Chinese institutions almost untouched.

Chinese history is by no mean the uneventful record of a "frozen" and unchanging society that some westerners have thought. It is filled with the rise and fall of dynasties, with wars and plagues and famines, with the gradual spread of Chinese culture southward and eastward, to the region of Canton, to Korea, to Japan. It has periods of effective governmental centralization, and periods of "feudal" disintegration. Its art and techniques were subject to periods of flourishing and decay. But there were many elements of continuity.

First of all, at the base of Chinese social life was a communal village organization, held together by very strong family ties, a cult of ancestor worship, and hard work guided by traditional agricultural techniques. The Chinese village, basically unchanged until the communist reforms of our own day, was one of the oldest socio-economic organizations in the civilized world. Second, at the top of this society was an emperor, Son of Heaven, the "natural" ruler of a great state. The Chinese were conditioned to at least formal imperial unity in somewhat the same way early medieval westerners were conditioned to the unity of Roman Catholic Christendom. Third, the business of running this vast empire was entrusted to one of the most remarkable ruling classes history has ever recorded, the *mandarins*, a bureaucracy of intellectuals, or at any rate of men who could pass literary and philosophical examinations in classics, examinations that required a rigorously trained memory.

This class proved not very resilient in the face of the challenge of new ideas from Europe, and it was except at its brief best by no means free from what we know as graft and nepotism. But it had served the state for several millennia, and its existence

is one of the reasons for the extraordinary stability of Chinese society. In theory, the class was one open to talents, even for the great mass of poor peasants. But for most of these long years, the necessary education was too expensive and too hard to acquire for any but a very few gifted and persistent poor boys.

Just as in India, there were in China an immense population at the very margin of existence, and a small upper class that enjoyed gracious living of a kind hardly available to the medieval western upper classes. The Chinese millions had their superstitions, their demons, their other-world. The earlier periods of Chinese cultural flowering show traces of mystic beliefs among the educated, traces of the eternal Platonism of the human spirit. Still, everyone who has known the Chinese, even the casual traveler who makes some effort to appreciate what is going on about him, finds in the Chinese a lack of mysticism, other-worldliness, "tender-mindedness." Or, in positive terms, he finds a sense of worldly realism, an acceptance of the universe as it appears to common sense, or at least to the "tough-minded," a concern with human relations, with politeness, decorum, and the like, and an absence of theology, sacraments, and faith in a supranatural god which we in the West expect in a higher religion.

It has been commonly said that China never had a religion, in the sense that Buddhism, Christianity, and Islam are religions with a firm doctrine of salvation in an order of existence quite different from that of our daily lives on earth. The conventional Confucianism of the upper classes is indeed a code of manners and morals, not a sacramental religion, not a religion in which the faithful undergo the miracle of sharing in something ineffable. Confucius, a sage who flourished early in the fifth century B.C., was no mystic, no prophet, but a moralist who taught an ethical system of temperance, decorum, obedience to the wisdom of the wise and the good. This lack of commitment to an other-worldly religion, however, has hitherto by no means made the Chinese more receptive to western ideas. At least until our own times, China has resisted westernization more effectively than has any other great culture.

The Portuguese Empire

The empire that the Portuguese founded in Asia and Africa was a trading empire, not an empire of settlement. They established along the coasts of Africa, India, and China a series of posts, or "factories," over which they hoisted the Portuguese flag as a sign that they had annexed these bits of territory to the Portuguese Crown. From these posts they traded with the natives. As all the European colonial powers did later, they offered relatively cheap and relatively mass-produced articles—guns, knives, gadgets of all sorts, cheap cloth, and a great deal else. In return, they got gold and silver (when they could), spices, still essential for meats in those days without refrigeration, silks and other luxuries, and, finally, raw ma-terials such as cotton and slaves, and, in the New World, tobacco and sugar.

Two guiding principles of this trade were accepted by almost all contemporaries, whether in the mother country or in the colonies, as simple facts of life. First, in this trade the mother country was the determining element, and would naturally produce goods and services while the colony produced raw materials. Second, foreigners, nationals of other European lands, were ex-cluded from this trade; they could not deal directly with the colony or take part in the commerce between mother country and colony. The Portuguese, in sum, followed a policy of *mercantilism*.

Armed forces were essential to the establishment and maintenance of this colonial system. Relatively small land forces proved sufficient both to keep the natives under control and to ward off rival European powers from the trading posts. A large and efficient navy was, however, necessary, for the easiest way to raid a rival's trade was to wait until its fruits were neatly concentrated in the hold of a merchant vessel, and then take it at sea as a prize. Such deeds are known as piracy, a very common

Lisbon. Departure of an exploration trip to America (by De Bry).

activity in these early modern centuries. Sometimes, especially in the eighteenth century, these pirates became in fact outlaws, men of no nation, willing to rob nationals of any country. In these earlier centuries, they were often openly an unofficial adjunct of a given navy, operating only against enemies or neutrals, never against their own nationals. A navy was, then, essential to protect the sea routes of a colonial power. The Portuguese fleet was not only a merchant fleet; under the command of governors like Albuquerque, it was a great military fleet that brushed aside Arab opposition and for a few decades ruled the oceans of the Old World.

The Portuguese made no serious attempt to settle large numbers of their own people either in the hot coast lands of Africa or in the already densely populated lands of India and the Far East. Nor, save in the single respect we are about to encounter, did they attempt to make over these natives into pseudo-Portuguese. There were of course useful places for Portuguese in the colonial services, both civilian and military; many of the natives were enlisted in the armed forces or used as domestic help and in subordinate posts such as clerks. These natives inevitably picked up, however imperfectly, the language and culture of the colonial power. But neither among the primitive Negro tribes of Africa nor among the Indian and Chinese masses did this process of Europeanization go very fast or far.

Nor did the Portuguese attempt to rule directly, to alter the political, social, or economic structure of native life. They left the old ruling chiefs and the old ruling classes pretty much as they had found them. In the total lives of these millions, the imported European wares played extremely little part in these early days. The native upper classes monopolized most of these wares, and Europe could not yet flood non-European markets with cheap manufactured goods made by power-driven machinery. Nothing western touched these masses of natives in the sixteenth century, nothing tempted them away from their millennial ways of life, in anything like the degree our twentieth-century West attracts and tempts the East.

There is one exception. The Portuguese and the Spanish, and even their relatively secular-minded rival nations in eastern Asiatic regions, the English, Dutch, and French, did attempt to Christianize the natives. From the very first, much sincerity, devotion, and hard work went into the Christian missionary movement. The earliest missionaries no doubt underestimated the difficulties they were to encounter. Many of them were in a sense partly converted themselves; that is, they came to be very fond of their charges, and convinced that they were in fact almost Christians already. Some of the Jesuits in China, the first European intellectuals to live in this very civilized country, seriously believed that with just a bit more effort the full reconciliation between Christianity and Confucianism could be achieved.

From the start, difficulties arose between the missionaries, anxious to protect their charges, and the traders and colonial officials, driven by their very place in the system to try to exploit the natives. Finances were always a serious problem, with so many tens of millions to convert and to tend, and with so few men, so little money, to do the work. Certainly, measured in statistical terms, the Christianizing of India and the Far East did not make a serious impression on the masses. Christianity has been part of the whole influence of the West on the East, not to be measured in terms of actual Christian church memberships in the East. Christian influence on the upper and the intellectual classes has been far greater than on the masses. Still, in the balance, the confident words of one of the pioneer Jesuits in China in the sixteenth century, Father Ricci, now sound most unrealistic:

Jesuit missionary in China, about 1660.

Against this monster of Chinese idolatry . . . which has for so many thousands of years tyrannized without contradiction over so many millions of souls and sent them to the abyss of Hell, our Company of Jesus has, in conformity with its constituted purpose, arisen to make war, coming from distant lands and crossing many kingdoms and seas to deliver these unfortunate souls from eternal damnation. And trusting to the mercy of God, the Jesuits did not let themselves be frightened by the dangers and difficulties of gaining entrance to an empire so carefully closed to foreigners and so full of a multitude of people who would defend their erroneous beliefs; indeed, to the kingdom and the arms of the holy cross no force in this world or in Hell can make resistance.*

---

* Quoted in Henri Bernard, *Le Père Matthieu Ricci* (Tientsin, 1937), I, 1. Our translation.

The Portuguese, though first in the field in the East, very soon had to yield to newer rivals—French, Dutch, English. A trading empire depends on naval protection and on an enterprising trading community at home, and in both these critical matters the Portuguese were unable to keep up the pace they had set. Like the Spaniards, they suffered from an inadequate, or at any rate inadequately run, home industry; their banking, their business methods, their initiative—if not their scruples—were not up to competition with the aggressive expanding powers of northwest Europe. After the sixteenth century, they ceased to add to their empire and their wealth, and took a decidedly secondary place in international politics. A great poem, *The Lusiads* (1572) of Camoens, is their monument.

Yet the Portuguese by no means lost their empire, which remained strong along the old trade route around Africa to Goa and other stations in India, Timor in Indonesia, and Macao in China. In Africa, it has counted nearly 800,000 square miles. It has not been a flourishing empire, but it has continued to exist. That it should have endured so long, and against such active and hungry rivals as the French, Dutch, and British, is in part evidence of the existence of a force in history difficult for modern Americans to recognize—that of inertia. It is very hard, or until the present totalitarian age it has been very hard, to destroy outright any going territorial concern. Portugal's more successful rivals took away Portuguese leadership, but left her a participant in the competition. Still, the survival of the Portuguese Empire was greatly aided by the fact that the most successful of the European imperial powers, England, remained through modern times in alliance with Portugal. The complete victory of France or the Netherlands in the colonial scramble might possibly have meant the eventual annihilation of the Portuguese Empire. At any rate, as of 1960, the Portuguese Empire was still there.

CHAPTER XIV

III: West by Sea to the Indies

Columbus

In the earliest days of concerted effort to explore the oceans, the Spanish government had been too busy disposing of the last Moslem state in the peninsula, Granada, and uniting the disparate parts of Spain to patronize scientific exploration as the Portuguese had done. But individual Spanish traders were active, and Spain was growing in prosperity. As long ago as the end of the fourteenth century and the beginning of the fifteenth, Portuguese mariners had found the three groups of Atlantic islands, Azores, Madeira, and Canaries, well out in the stormy ocean, but still essentially European rather than American. By papal decree, the Canaries were assigned to the Crown of Castile, the others to Portugal. Once the marriage of Ferdinand and Isabella had united Aragon and Castile, the Spanish government wanted to catch up with the Portuguese. So it commissioned Columbus to try out his plan to reach India by going west.

Columbus (1451-1506) was an Italian, born in Genoa. He was essentially self-educated, but, at least in navigation and geography, had educated himself very well. His central conception, that it would be possible to reach the Far East—"the Indies" —by sailing westward from Spain, was certainly not uniquely his. That the earth is a globe was a notion entertained by ancient Greek geographers, and revived with the renaissance of the classics. Toscanelli at Florence in 1474, Behaim at Nuremberg in the very year of Columbus' voyage, published maps that showed the earth as a globe —but without the Americas, and with the combined Atlantic and Pacific much narrower than they are in fact. To act on this notion by deliberately sailing west on the Atlantic had become with the growth of oceanic navigation a clear possibility. But it was still a strikingly novel idea—an idea that was not acceptable to conservative minds. It took a persistent, innovating personality to get support for such an expedition.

Columbus met with many rebuffs, but finally, with the support of the wealthy Spanish trading family of Pinzon, was able to get the help of Queen Isabella. Indeed, with the sole aim of reaching the Indies he might not have been able to set out. But, as his commission shows, he was also charged to discover and secure for the Spanish Crown new islands and territories, a mission that probably reflects the importance of ancient and medieval legends about Atlantis, St. Brendan's isle, and other lands beyond the Azores. Even if he did not reach the

Christopher Columbus, painted by Sebastiano del Piombo.

Indies, there seemed a chance that he would reach something new.

He reached a New World. Setting out from Palos near Cadiz on August 3, 1492, in three ships so small that they could all be propped up comfortably on the deck of a modern airplane carrier, he made a land-fall on a Bahaman island on October 12 of the same year, and eventually went on to discover the large islands we know as Cuba and Santo Domingo. On a second voyage, in 1493, he went out with seventeen ships and some fifteen hundred colonists, explored further in the Caribbean, and laid the foundations of the Spanish Empire in America. On his third voyage in 1498-1500, he reached the mouth of the Orinoco in South America but encountered difficulties among his colonists, and was sent home in irons by the royal governor Bobadilla, who took over the administration of the Indies for the Crown. He was released on his return to Spain, and in 1502-1504 made a fourth and final voyage, in which he reached the mainland at Honduras. He died in comparative obscurity at Valladolid in Spain in 1506, totally unaware that he had reached, not Asia, but a new continent.

That continent was, by a freak of history, not destined to bear his name, though it is now liberally sprinkled with other place-names in his honor. News of Columbus' voyages soon spread by word of mouth in Europe. But printing was still in its infancy; there were no newspapers or geographical institutes; the international learned class—the humanists—were more interested in Greek manuscripts than in strange lands; and, from early Portuguese days on, governments had done their best to keep their discoveries as secret as possible. The most effective spreading of the word in print about the New World was done by another Italian in the Spanish service, Amerigo Vespucci, who wrote copiously about his explorations in the immediate footsteps of Columbus. Scholars still dispute whether or not Vespucci really made all the

discoveries, from the southeastern United States to the tip of South America, that he claimed to have made. But his letters came to the attention of a German theoretical geographer, Martin Waldseemüller, who in 1507 published a map blocking out a land mass in the southern part of the New World which he labeled, from the latinized form of Vespucci's first name, America. The map was read and copied, and though Waldsee-müller in a new map of 1531 removed it in favor of a noncommittal "Terra Incognita" (unknown land), he had successfully chris-tened two new continents.

Later Explorers

From now on, the roster of discov-ery grows rapidly. Ponce de León reached Florida in 1512, and Balboa in 1513 crossed the Isthmus of Panama and saw a limit-less ocean, on the other side of which the Indies did indeed lie, for it was the Pacific. Many other Spaniards and Portu-guese in these first two decades of the six-teenth century explored in detail the coasts of what was to be Latin America. It was now quite clear that an immense land mass lay athwart the westward route from Eu-rope to Asia, and that even the narrow isth-mus of Panama was an obstacle not readily to be overcome by a canal. Maritime ex-ploration was therefore turned to the prob-lem of getting around the Americas by sea and into the Pacific. North America proved an obstacle indeed, for none of the great estuaries—Chesapeake, Delaware, Hudson—promising though they looked to the first explorers, did more than dent the great con-tinent, the breadth of which was totally un-known. The St. Lawrence looked even better, for to its first French explorers it seemed like the sought-for strait. But even the St. Lawrence gave out, and the rapids near Montreal, which showed it was only another river after all, received the ironic name of Lachine (China) Rapids, for this was *not* the way to China. Not until the mid-nineteenth century was the usually ice-choked "Northwest Passage" discovered by the Englishman Sir John Franklin, who died in the Arctic wastes before he could return to civilization.

The "Southwest Passage" was found only a generation after Columbus, in the course of an expedition that is the most extraordinary of all the great voyages of discovery. Ferdinand Magellan, a Portuguese in the Spanish service, set out in 1519 with a royal commission bidding him to find a way westward to the Spice Islands of Asia. Skirting the coast of South America, he found and guided his ships through the difficult fog-bound passage that bears his name, the Straits of Magellan, reached the Pacific, and crossed it in a voyage of incredible hardship. Scurvy alone, a disease we now know to be caused by lack of vitamin C, and a standard risk in those early days, meant that he and his men had to surmount torturing illness. After he had reached the islands now known as the Philippines, Magellan was killed in a skirmish with the natives. One of his captains, however, kept on along the known route by the Indian Ocean and the coast of Africa. On September 8, 1522, the "Victoria" and her crew of eighteen men —out of five ships and 243 men that had sailed in 1519—landed at Cadiz. For the first time, men had sailed around the world, and had proved empirically that the world is round.

What these explorations cost in terms of human suffering, what courage and resolution were needed to carry them through, is very hard for our easy-traveling generation to imagine. Here, from the bare report the sailor Pigafetta gives of Magellan's expedition, is a firsthand account of one of the crises:

Wednesday, the twenty-eighth of November, 1520, we came forth out of the said strait, and entered into the Pacific sea, where we remained three months and twenty days without taking in provisions or other refreshments, and we only ate old biscuit reduced to powder, and full of grubs, and stinking from the dirt which the rats had made on it when eating the good biscuit, and we drank water that was yellow and stinking. We also ate the ox hides which were under the main-yard, so that the yard should not break the rigging: they were very hard on account of the sun, rain, and wind, and we left them for four or five days in the sea, and then we put them a little on the embers, and so ate them; also the sawdust of wood, and rats which cost half-a-crown each, moreover enough of them were not to be got. Besides the above-named evils, this misfortune which I will mention was the worst, it was that the upper and lower gums of most of our men grew so much that they could not eat, and in this way so many suffered, that nineteen died.[*]

Such accounts could be multiplied for every part of the newly discovered world and for every nation taking part in the expansion of the West.

The Foundation of the Spanish Empire

As a by-product of Magellan's voyage, the Spaniards who had sent him out got a foothold in the Far East, which they had reached by sailing west. As we have seen, by the Treaty of Tordesillas in 1494 Spain and Portugal had divided the world —the world open to trade and empire— along a line that cut through the Atlantic in such a way that Brazil became Portuguese. This same line, extended round the world, cut the Pacific so that some of the islands Magellan discovered came into the Spanish half. Spain conveniently treated the Philippines as if they also came in the Spanish half of the globe, though they are just outside it, and colonized them from Mexico.

Up to now, we have concerned ourselves mostly with maritime explorations and the

---

[*] Lord Stanley of Alderly, *The First Voyage Round the World by Magellan,* translated from the accounts of Pigafetta, and other contemporary writers (London, 1874), 64-65.

founding of coastal trading stations. The Spaniards in the New World, however, very soon explored by land, and acquired thousands of square miles of territory. To the explorer by sea there succeeded the *conquistador*, half explorer, half soldier and administrator, and all adventurer. Of the *conquistadores* two, Hernando Cortés and Francisco Pizarro, have come down in history with a special aura of tough romance. With a handful of men they conquered the only two civilized regions of the New World: the Aztec empire of Mexico, conquered by Cortés in 1519, and the Inca empire of Peru, conquered by Pizarro in 1531-33. The narrative of these conquests, whether in the classic nineteenth-century histories of the American Prescott or in the narratives of actual participants, remains among the most fascinating if not among the most edifying chapters of western history. A book of this scope cannot possibly do justice to the drama of the conquerors of Mexico and Peru, nor to the many other

Machu Picchu, Peru, ancient Inca city in the Andes.

Spaniards who in search of glory, salvation, gold, and excitement toiled up and down these strange new lands—Quesada in New Granada (later Colombia), Coronado, de Soto, and Cabeza de Vaca in the southwest of what became the United States, Mendoza in the La Plata (the lands around the River Plate), Valdivia in Chile, Alvarado in Guatemala, and many others. These are the men who opened up the New World for Spain, as our own North American pioneers from Captain John Smith to Lewis and Clark and Kit Carson opened up the New World for the English-speaking peoples.

Unlike the great cultures of the Middle and Far East, the pre-Columbian cultures of the Americas went down pretty completely before the Europeans. It is certainly true that from Mexico to Bolivia and Paraguay there survive millions of men and women of Indian stock, true that for a full understanding of the Latin-American republics one needs to know something about the traditions and the folkways of many tribes and peoples. That Mexican artists and intellectuals have in our day proudly held up their. Indian heritage against the Yankees, and against their own Europeanized nineteenth-century rulers, is important for us to know. But the structure of the Aztec or the Inca empire has simply not survived. The sun-god in whose name the Inca ruled, the bloody Aztec god of war, Huitzilopochtli, are no longer a part of the lives of men, as Confucius and Buddha are. Perhaps someday social scientists can tell us what part—if any—the old civilizations of Peru and Central America play in the behavior of present-day Latin Americans. But now it looks as though these old civilizations are chiefly of interest as specimens, fossils, no longer alive. At most, knowledge of them may help us establish a kind of genetics or evolutionary theory of civilization. In themselves, however, these cultures are fascinating examples of the variety of human life on this earth. And the fact that they existed at all, as organized, large territorial states,

Coatlicue. Stone statue of the Aztec Goddess of Earth and Death (fifteenth century).

and that they made high achievements in the arts and the sciences, is further evidence against naive western notions of racial superiority.

The First True Colonial Empire

Well before the end of the sixteenth century, the work of the *conquistadores* had been done, and in Latin America the first of the true colonial empires of Europe—in contrast to the trading empires in Africa and Asia—had been founded. Nowhere, save in the region of the La Plata and in central Chile, were the natives eliminated and replaced by a population almost en-

tirely of European stock. Over vast reaches of Mexico and Central and South America, a crust of Spanish or Portuguese formed at the top of society, and made Spanish or Portuguese the language of culture; a class of mixed blood, the *mestizos,* was gradually formed from the union, formal or informal, of Europeans and natives; and in many regions the native Indians continued to maintain their stock and their old ways of life almost untouched. Finally, wherever as in the Caribbean the Indians were exterminated under the pressure of civilization, or as in Brazil they proved inadequate as a labor force, the importation of Negro slaves from Africa added another ingredient to the racial mixture.

Moreover, geography and the circumstances of settlement by separate groups of adventurers in each region combined to create a number of separate units of settlement tied together only by their dependence on the Crown, and destined to become the independent nation-states of Latin America today. Geography alone was perhaps a fatal obstacle to any subsequent union of the colonies, such as was achieved by the English colonies that became the United States of America. Between such apparently close neighbors as the present Argentine and Chile, for instance, lay the great chain of the Andes, crossed only with great difficulty by high mountain passes. Between the colonies of the La Plata and the colonies of Peru and New Granada lay the Andes and the vast tropical rain-forests of the Amazon Basin, still essentially unconquered today. The highlands of Mexico and Central America are as much invitations to local independence as were the mountains of Hellas to the ancient Greeks, and to this day the Isthmus of Panama remains almost impassable the long way, at right angles to the canal. Cuba and the other Caribbean islands have the natural independence of islands. And even had the coastal fringes of Brazil not been settled by Portuguese, men of a different language from the Spaniards, these regions have no easy land connections with the rest of Latin America. Geography alone would probably have made Brazil independent.

The Spanish used the centralized administrative institutions that were then the rule among the new monarchies of Europe. At the top of the hierarchy were two vice-royalties, that of Peru with its capital at Lima and that of New Spain with its capital at Mexico City. From Lima the viceroy ruled for the Crown over the Spanish part of South America, save for Venezuela. From Mexico City the viceroy ruled over the mainland north of Panama, the West Indies, Venezuela, and the Philippines. Each capital had an *audiencia,* a powerful body operating both as a court of law and as an advisory council, and there were *audiencias* in such major centers as Guatemala, New Granada (modern Colombia), Quito, and the Philippines.

The Balance Sheet of Latin-American Empire

This was certainly a centralized, paternalistic system of government, which has rightly enough been contrasted with the "salutary neglect" in which the North American colonies were generally left by the home government until the crisis that led to the American Revolution. But it was not —given the vast areas and the varied peoples under its control, it could not be— as rigid in practice as it was in theory. The rudiments of popular consultation of the Spanish colonists existed in the *cabildos abiertos* or assemblies of citizens. Moreover, as time went on the bureaucracy itself came to be filled largely with colonials, men who had never been in the home country, and who developed a sense of local patriotism and independence. Madrid and Seville were simply too far away to enforce all their decisions. Notably in the matter of trade, it proved impossible to maintain the rigid

monopolies of mercantilistic theory, which sought to confine trade wholly to the mother country, and to prohibit, or severely limit, domestic industry in the colonies. Local officials connived at a smuggling trade with the English, Dutch, French, and North Americans which in the eighteenth century reached large proportions.

The hand of Spain was heaviest in the initial period of exploitation, when the rich and easily mined deposits of the precious metals in Mexico and Peru were skimmed off for the benefit both of the Spanish Crown, which always gots its *quinto,* or fifth, and of the *conquistadores* and their successors, Spaniards all. This gold and silver did the natives no good, but in the long run it did no good to Spain, since it went to finance a vain bid for European supremacy. By the seventeenth century, the Latin-American colonial economy and society had settled down in a rough equilibrium. It was not a progressive economy, but neither was it a hopelessly backward one. Colonial wares—sugar, tobacco, chocolate, cotton, hides, and much else—flowed out of Latin America in exchange for manufactured goods and for services. Creoles (American-born of pure European stock) and mestizos were the chief beneficiaries of this trade. The Indians remained at the bottom of the social pyramid.

Certainly the two great Indian civilizations, the Mexican and the Peruvian, were wiped out by the Spaniards. Certainly all over Latin America the natives fell to the bottom of a caste system based on color, a system never quite as rigid as it became in North America, but still a system that damaged the native's pride and self-respect. Yet Spanish imperial policy toward the natives was in aim by no means ungenerous, and even in execution holds up well in the long and harsh record of contacts between whites and non-whites all over the globe. Especially in the Caribbean, but to a degree everywhere, the whites tried to use native labor. The first result was disastrous for the natives; new diseases, to which the natives had no immunity, decimated their ranks. Here, as with the gold and silver, some ironic spirit of history seems to have taken revenge on the whites: though the question of the origin of syphilis is still disputed, many historians of medicine believe that it was brought from the West Indies, where it was mild, to western civilization, where it has been deadly. The attempt to regiment native labor in a plantation system, or to put it on a semi-manorial forced-labor system, known as the *encomienda*, proved almost as disastrous. Negro slavery was an inevitable result. Finally, the colonial whites tended toward the aggressive, the insensitive, the hard-boiled; by and large, the gentle souls stayed at home.

Yet, against all these forces making for harshness and cruelty, there were counteracting forces. The natives were regarded as wards of the Crown, and their actual enslavement was prohibited by the New Laws of 1542. The central Spanish government passed a good many laws to protect the Indians, and though these were often flouted in the colonies—a phenomenon not unknown in the English colonies—they put a limit to wholesale exploitation of the natives. Their cause was championed by men of great distinction, and notably by Bartholomew de Las Casas (1474-1566), "Father of the Indians," Bishop of Chiapas in Mexico. The kind of man he is is clear even in these brief passages from his *Short Report on the Indies* (1542):

God has created all these numberless people [Indians] to be quite the simplest, without malice or duplicity, most obedient, most faithful to their natural Lords, and to the Christians, whom they serve; the most humble, most patient, most peaceful, and calm, without strife nor tumults; not wrangling, nor querulous, as free from uproar, hate and desire of revenge, as any in the world.

• • •

Their food is so poor, that it would seem that of the Holy Fathers in the desert was not scantier nor less pleasing. Their way of dress-

ing is usually to go naked, covering the private parts; and at most they cover themselves with a cotton cover, which would be about equal to one and a half or two ells square of cloth. Their beds are of matting, and they mostly sleep in certain things like hanging nets, called in the language of Hispaniola *hamacas* [hammocks].[*]

Unlike the Asian and African masses, the Indians were formally converted to Christianity. Church and State in the Spanish and Portuguese colonies in the New World worked hand in hand, undisturbed for generations by the troubles roused in Europe by the Protestant Reformation and the rise of a secular anti-Christian movement. The Jesuits in Paraguay set up among the Guarani Indians a remarkable society, a benevolent despotism, a utopia of good order, good habits, and eternal childhood for the Guarani. On the northern fringes of the Spanish world, where it was to meet the Anglo-Saxons, a long line of missions in California and the Southwest held the frontier. Everywhere save in wildest Amazonia and other untamed areas the Christianity of the Roman Catholic Church brought to the natives something of the western tradition, made them in some sense part of this strange new society of the white men.

In the main, the Portuguese settlements in Brazil have a character much like those of the Spaniards elsewhere in Latin America. The Portuguese, perhaps because of the proximity of Brazil to European waters, had more serious trouble with rival nations than the Spanish did. Indeed, the existence of those fragments of imperial hopes, French, British, and Dutch Guiana just north of Brazil on today's map, is a witness to the fact that the northern maritime nations made a serious effort to settle in what became Brazil. The race mixture in Brazil came also in colonial times to be somewhat different from that in most Spanish colonies,

---

[*] Francis Augustus MacNutt, *Bartholomew de Las Casas* (New York, 1909), 314-315.

except Cuba. A large number of Negroes were imported into tropical Brazil, and, because the white males drew no sexual color line, were thoroughly mixed with the rest of the population. But in its mercantilist economics, its close tie with the home country, its close union of Church and State, Brazil resembled the Spanish colonies.

IV: The Latecomers—France, Holland, England

Early French and English Activity

Spain and Portugal enjoyed a generation's head start in exploration and in founding empires of trade, and a whole century in founding empires of settlement. Without this head start, which they owed in part to their position as heirs of the Mediterranean trade, Spain and Portugal could scarcely have made the great mark in the world that they have made. For the northern Atlantic states soon made up for their late start. As early as 1497 the Cabots, father and son, Italians in the English service, saw something of the North American coast, and gave the English their exploration-based claims. Another Italian, Verrazzano, and the Frenchman Cartier gave France a claim based on exploration, claims reinforced by the early seventeenth-century detailed explorations of Champlain. Dutch claims began with the voyages of Henry Hudson, an Englishman who entered their service in 1609.

The English did not immediately follow up the work of the Cabots. Instead, they put their energies in the mid-sixteenth century into the profitable business of breaking into the Spanish trading monopoly. John Hawkins, in 1562, started the English slave trade, and his nephew, Francis Drake, penetrated to the Pacific, reached California, which he claimed for England under the name of New Albion, and returned to England by the Pacific and Indian oceans, completing the first English circumnavigation of the globe. By the end of the century, the great fishing grounds off northeastern North America had become an important prize, and under Sir Humphrey Gilbert in 1583 the English staked out a claim to Newfoundland which gave them and their later colonists a firm place in these valuable fisheries.

The Thirteen Colonies: Settlement

In 1584, Sir Walter Raleigh attempted to found a settlement on Roanoke Island (in the present North Carolina) in a land the English named, from their Virgin Queen Elizabeth, Virginia. Neither this, nor a colony sent out in 1587, managed to survive. But early in the next century the English got two permanent footholds, at Jamestown in Virginia, 1607, and at Plymouth in New England, 1620. Both were to become colonies of settlement, regions in which the sparse native population was exterminated and replaced by men and women for the most part of British stock. But in their inception both were nearer the pattern of trading posts set by the Spanish and Portuguese. Both were established by chartered trading companies with headquarters in England; both, and especially the Virginian, cherished at first high hopes that they would find, as the Spaniards had, great stores of precious metals. Both were disappointed in these hopes, and managed to sur-

An early map of America (1587).

vive the first terrible years of hardship by the skin of their teeth. Tobacco, first cultivated in 1612, and the almost legendary Captain John Smith, explorer and man of resourcefulness, saved the Virginia colony, and furs, notably beaver, codfish, and Calvinist toughness saved Plymouth. Both colonies gradually built up an agricultural economy, supplemented by trade with the mother country and interloping trade with the West Indies. Neither received more than a few tens of thousands of immigrants from abroad. Yet both these and the later colonies expanded by natural increase in a country of abundant land for the taking. The thirteen colonies by 1776 were a substantial series of settlements with almost three million inhabitants.

Before these English colonies were completed, one important and one very minor foreign group had to be pushed out. The Dutch, after their successful resistance to Spain (see Chapter XIII), had come into the competition for commerce and empire. They had founded a trading colony at New Amsterdam at the mouth of the Hudson, and had begun to push into the fur trade. This made them rivals of both the French and the English. They lacked an adequate home base to be a great power, however, and in a war with England in the 1660's they lost New Amsterdam, which was annexed by the English in 1664 and became New York. The Dutch, though very few in numbers, were destined to supply some important families to the future United States, as names like Stuyvesant, Schuyler, and Roosevelt suggest.

The Swedes, too, were now making a bid for greatness, and in 1638 they founded Fort Christiana on the Delaware. But New Sweden was never a serious competitor, and in 1655 Fort Christiana was taken over by the Dutch, who in turn were ousted by the English. Pennsylvania, chartered to the wealthy English Quaker, William Penn, in 1681, filled the vacuum left by the expulsion of the Swedes and the Dutch from the

Delaware, and was to be the keystone colony before it became the keystone state.

By the early eighteenth century, the English settlements formed a continuous string from Maine to Georgia. Each of the thirteen was founded separately. None had quite identical charters. Perhaps American popular tradition exaggerates the differences between the southern and the northern group. Massachusetts was not settled wholly by democratic plain people, "Roundheads," nor was Virginia settled wholly by great English landowners, gentlemen or "Cavaliers." Both colonies—and all the others—were settled by a varied human lot, which covered most of the range of social and economic status in the mother country, save for the very top. Dukes and earls did not emigrate. But the poorest could and did, as indentured servants or as impressed seamen who deserted ship. The middling men came, and everywhere, even in New England, a solid sprinkling of the well-to-do.

Still, it is true that New England was for the most part settled by Calvinist Independents (Congregationalists), already committed to wide local self-government and to a distrust of a landowning aristocracy; and it is true that the southern colonies, especially tidewater Virginia, were settled for the most part by Anglicans used to the existence of frank social distinctions and to large landholdings. In Virginia, the Church of England became the established church; in Massachusetts, the Puritan Congregationalists, nonconformists in the homeland, almost automatically became conformists in their new home, and set up their own variety of state church. Geography, climate, and a complex of social and economic factors, drove the South to plantation monoculture of tobacco, rice, indigo, or cotton even in colonial days, and drove New England and the Middle Colonies to small farming by independent farmerowners and to small-scale industry and commerce. Yet note that in the Piedmont sections of Virginia and the Carolinas, there were small farmers, Presbyterians, "Scotch-Irish," Germans from Pennsylvania, a very northern mixture. Some historians hold that the natural environment, and not any original difference of social structure and beliefs, accounts for the diverging growths of North and South and their eventual armed conflict.

The Thirteen Colonies: Institutions

To us who are their heirs, it has seemed that these English colonists brought with them the religious freedom, the government by discussion, and the democratic society of which we are so proud. So they did, though they brought the seeds, the potentialities, rather than the fully developed institutions. These colonists came from an England where the concept of freedom of religion was only beginning to emerge from the long struggles of the sects. It was quite natural for the Virginians and the New Englanders to set up state churches. Yet, just as in contemporary England, these immigrants represented too many conflicting religious groups to enforce anything like the religious uniformity that prevailed to the south among the Spanish colonists and to the north among the French. Even in New England, "heresy" appeared from the start, with Baptists, Quakers, and even Anglicans, who seeped into New Hampshire and eventually even into Boston. Moreover, some of the colonies were founded by groups which from the first practiced religious freedom and separated Church and State. In Maryland, founded in part to give refuge to the most distrusted of groups at home, the Catholics; in Pennsylvania, founded by Quakers who believed firmly in the separation of Church and State; in Rhode Island, founded by Roger Williams and others unwilling to conform to the orthodoxy of Massachusetts Bay—in all these colonies there was something like the complete religious freedom that was later embodied in the Constitution of the United States, and, as the eighteenth century came on, the characteristic modern freedom not to belong to any formal religious organization.

The seeds of democracy, too, existed, although the early settlers, not only in Virginia but even in the North, accepted class distinctions more readily than we now do. No formal colonial nobility ever arose, and the early tendency to develop a privileged gentry or squirearchy in the coastal regions was balanced by the equalitarianism of the frontier and the career open to talents in the towns. Government by discussion was firmly planted in the colonies from the start. All of them, even the so-called proprietary colonies like Pennsylvania, which were granted to a "proprietor," had some kind of colonial legislative body.

Here we come to the critical point of difference between the English and the Spanish and French governments in the New World. The Spanish and French governments were already centralized bureaucratic monarchies; their representative assemblies were no more than consultative and had no power over taxation. Royal governors in Latin America and in New France could really run their provinces, leaning on men they appointed and recalled, and raising funds by their own authority. England was indeed a monarchy, but a parliamentary monarchy, torn by two revolutions in the seventeenth century. Though the Crown was represented in most colonies by a royal governor, the English government had no such bureaucracy as the Spanish and French had. Royal governors in the English colonies had hardly even a clerical staff and met with great difficulty in raising money from their legislative assemblies. The history of the colonies is full of bickerings between governors and assemblies, in which the governor, with little local support, and with but sporadic backing from the home government, was often stalemated. Moreover, in the local units of government—towns in New England, counties in the rest of the colonies—there was the same participation of the people—the established landowners, merchants, and professional men, if not everywhere all the people—and the same absence of an authoritative bureaucracy. Finally, the settlers brought with them the common law of England, with its trial by jury, and its absence of bureaucratic administrative law.

In sum, not only the opportunities of an almost empty land—the frontier—but also English traditions and ideas and the weakness of the central government were major factors in the growth of American democracy. Frenchmen and Spaniards did not bring to their colonies what the English brought to theirs.

New France

To the north, in the region about the Bay of Fundy and in the St. Lawrence Basin, the French built on the work of Cartier and Champlain. New France was to be for a century and a half a serious threat to the English North American colonies. The St. Lawrence and the Great Lakes gave the French easy access to the heart of the continent, in marked contrast to the Appalachians which stood between the English and the Mississippi. The French were also impelled westward by the fact that the fur trade was by all odds their major economic interest, and furs are goods of very great value and comparatively little bulk, easily carried in canoes and small boats. Moreover, led by the Jesuits, the Catholic French gave proof of a far greater missionary zeal than did the Protestant English. The priest, as well as the *coureur des bois* (trapper), led the push westward. Finally, the French in North America were guided in their expansion by a conscious imperial policy directed from the France of the Bourbon monarchs, *la grande nation* at the height of its prestige and power.

The result was that not the English but the French explored the interior of the continent. By 1712 they had built up a line of settlements—or rather, isolated trading posts, with miles of empty space between, thinly populated by Indians—which completely encircled the English colonies on the Atlantic coast. The story of these French explorers, missionaries, and traders, admirably told by the American historian Francis Parkman, is one of the most fascinating pages of history. The names of many of them—La Salle, Père Marquette, Joliet, Frontenac, Cadillac, Iberville—are a part of our American heritage. From Quebec, one line of outposts led westward, and from Mobile and New Orleans, in a colony founded at the beginning of the eighteenth century and named after Louis XIV, Louisiana, lines led northward up the Mississippi to join with those from Canada and Illinois.

Yet, impressive though this French imperial thrust looks on the map, it was far too lightly held to be equal to the task of pushing the English into the sea. It was a trading empire with military ambitions, and save in Quebec it never became a true colony of settlement. And even there it never grew in the critical eighteenth century beyond a few thousand inhabitants. Frenchmen simply did not come over in sufficient numbers, and those who did come spread themselves out over vast distances as traders and simple adventurers. Frenchmen who might have come, the Huguenots who might have settled down as did the Yankee Puritans, were excluded by a royal policy bent on maintaining the Catholic faith in New France.

The Indies, West and East

The northwestern European maritime powers intruded upon the pioneer Spanish and Portuguese both in the New World and in the Old. The French, Dutch, and English all sought to gain footholds in South America, but had to settle for the unimportant Guianas. They broke up thoroughly the Spanish hold on the Caribbean, however, and ultimately made that sea of many islands a kaleidoscope of colonial jurisdictions and a center of constant naval wars and piracy. These West Indian islands, though today for the most part a seriously depressed area, were in early modern times one of the great prizes of imperialism.

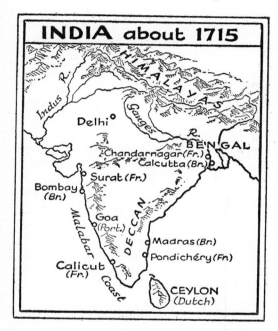

INDIA about 1715

Here the cheap Negro slave labor that had replaced the exterminated Caribs raised for their masters on the plantations the great staple tropical crops, tobacco, fruits, coffee, and, most basic of all, cane sugar, which had as yet no rival in beet sugar.

The French, Dutch, and English began as well to raid the trading empires the Iberian powers had set up in the Old World. They also raided each other, both in times of official peace and in wartime. By 1715, the bases of their trading and colonial empires had been firmly laid in Asia and Africa.

India proved in these early modern centuries to be the richest prize, and the most ardently fought for. The Mogul Empire

(see above, p. 568) was not strong enough in southern India to keep the Europeans out, but it did prove strong enough to confine them on the whole to the coastal fringes. Gradually, in the course of the seventeenth century both the French and the English established themselves in India on the heels of decaying Portuguese power and wealth. The English defeated a Portuguese fleet in 1612, and immediately thereafter got trading rights at Surat on the western coast. Although the able and active Mogul emperor, Aurangzeb, tried to revoke their rights in 1685, he soon found their naval and mercantile power too much to withstand. In 1690, the English founded in Bengal in eastern India the city they were to make famous, Calcutta. Meanwhile, the French had got footholds on the south coast near Madras, at a place called Pondichéry, and soon had established other stations. By the beginning of the eighteenth century, the stage was set in India as in North America for the decisive struggle for overseas empire between France and Britain.

Both countries operated in India, as they had initially in North America, by means of chartered trading companies, the English East India Company and the French *Compagnie des Indes Orientales*. The companies traded, and in trading were backed up by their governments when it was clear that bits of land around the trading posts had to be held, and that the whole relation with India could not be a purely commercial one. Gradually, both countries became involved in support of their companies in Indian politics and wars. But neither country made an effort to found a New England or a New France in the East.

The Dutch, too, entered vigorously into the competition. Their own East India Company, founded in 1602, succeeded in the next few decades in pushing the Portuguese out of Ceylon. But the great Dutch effort rather bypassed India to concentrate on southeastern Asia, and especially the East Indies. Here again they pushed the Portuguese out, save for part of the island of Timor; they also discouraged English interlopers. In spite of their rapid political decline as a great power in the eighteenth century, they got so firm a hold in Java and Sumatra that their empire in the Netherlands East Indies was to last until our own day.

Africa

All three of the northern maritime powers needed to use the same basic ocean route around Africa that the Portuguese had pioneered in the fifteenth century. All three got African posts. The Dutch put themselves in a good strategic situation by occupying the southern tip of Africa, the Cape of Good Hope, in 1652. The Cape was for them essentially a fitting station for their ships on the long voyage to Indonesia and the Far East, but it was empty except for primitive tribes, and its climate was suitable for Europeans. Though immigration was never heavy, a colony of settlement did grow up, the nucleus of the Afrikaners of South Africa today. Here, notably, the French Huguenots were welcomed. In West Africa, the Dutch took from the Portuguese some posts on the Gold and Guinea coasts, and got a share of the increasingly lucrative slave trade.

The French also worked down the African coast, which was not held in the blocks of territory seen on the map today, but in separate posts which gave ample room for interlopers. In 1626, the French were in Senegal in West Africa. In the Indian Ocean they were on the island of Madagascar, formally annexed by Louis XIV in 1686, and in 1715 they took the island of Mauritius from the Dutch, rechristening it the Isle de France. The British broke into the competition by securing a foothold at the mouth of the Cambia River in West Africa (1662), later followed by other acquisitions at French and Dutch expense. Thus a map of Africa and adjacent waters in the eighteenth

century shows a series of coastal stations controlled by the various European imperial powers. But the interior remained untouched, save by the slavers and native traders, and was to all intents and purposes unexplored. Only in the nineteenth century was the "Dark Continent" opened up to European expansion.

The Far East

China, long established as a great empire, was better able to withstand European pressure for territory. Somehow, even in the decay of their imperial power, the Portuguese were able to cling to Macao, and the Dutch, on their heels as always, obtained a station on Formosa in 1624. The Jesuits, bringing with them European instruments and learning that interested the Chinese, were able in the seventeenth century to get tolerated positions in China, but they made little real headway against rooted Chinese ways of life. Indeed, the Chinese, convinced that their own land was the "Middle Kingdom"—that is, *central* in a spiritual and cultural sense—of the whole world, regarded the Europeans as ignorant barbarians who should be paying them tribute. They kept open only the slender privileged trade from Canton and Macao. This trade was indeed enough to keep Chinese and Europeans in firm contact, but the real opening of China was not yet.

In Japan, the European penetration started much as in China. In 1549, the great Jesuit missionary, St. Francis Xavier, had begun work with the Japanese. In the sixteenth century the Portuguese, and in 1609 the Dutch, won trading footholds. General trade with the Europeans was carried on from Nagasaki. But the Japanese reacted even more strongly than did the Chinese. Though Christianity did not make wholesale conversions, it did make considerable headway. The Tokugawa family, the feudal military rulers of Japan from 1600 to 1868,

Courtyard of the Hōryūji Monastery, Japan (seventh century).

feared Christianity not only as a threat to national traditions but also as a threat to their own rule, because of the opportunities it might give European powers to intervene in Japanese politics and intrigue with the enemies of the Tokugawa. The Tokugawa therefore decided to close their land entirely to foreign dangers. In the early seventeenth century, they suppressed Christianity by force and literally sealed off Japan. Foreign-ers were refused entry, and Japanese were refused exit. Even the building of large ships capable of sailing the ocean was forbidden. The Dutch, strictly supervised, were allowed to cling to an island in Naga-saki harbor, where after 1715 they were limited to two ships a year. Not until the American Perry came to Japan in 1853 was this amazing self-blockade really broken and Japan thrown open to the world.

V: The Beginnings of One World

The expansion of Europe in these early modern centuries was not restricted to the Atlantic maritime powers. Although our own American tradition naturally centers on the Columbuses, the Magellans, the Captain John Smiths, general history must find a place for the extraordinary Russian exploration and conquest of Siberia. It offers all sorts of parallels with European expansion in the New World, from the chronological (the Russians crossed the Urals from Europe into Asia in 1483) to the political, for the expanding Muscovite state of Russia was a "new" monarchy, newer in some ways than the Spain of Charles V and Philip II or the England of Elizabeth I.

By 1715, the expansion of Europe was beginning to affect almost every part of the globe. European explorers, missionaries, traders, proconsuls of empire, had spread out in all directions. Even Arctic exploration, stimulated by the hope of finding a Northwest or a Northeast Passage that would shorten the route to the Far East, had already gone a long way by the beginning of the eighteenth century. Henry Hudson had found not only the Hudson River but also Hudson's Bay in the far north. In the late seventeenth century, English adventurers and investors formed an enterprise that still flourishes in Canada today—the Hudson's Bay Company, originally set up for fur trading along the great bay to the northwest of the French settlement in Quebec. In the late sixteenth century, the Dutch under Barents had penetrated far into the European Arctic, had discovered Spitsbergen, and had ranged across the sea named after their leader, the Barents Sea. Finally, the Russians under government patronage explored most of the long Arctic coasts of their empire early in the eighteenth century.

The Black Side of the Record

The record of European expansion contains pages as grim as any in history. The African slave trade, begun by the Portuguese and entered by other peoples for its financial gains, is a series of horrors, from the rounding up of the slaves by native chieftains in Africa through their transportation across the Atlantic to their sale in the Indies. What strikes a modern most of all is the matter-of-fact acceptance of this trade, as if the Negroes were literally so much livestock. The Dutch slave trader *St.*

Jan (note the irony of the saint's name) started off for Curaçao in the West Indies in 1659. Her log records every day or so deaths of slaves aboard, in parallel columns for Men, Women, Children, until between June 30 and October 29 a total of 59 men, 47 women, and 4 children have died. But there are still 95 slaves aboard when disaster strikes, thus simply and unmovingly recorded:

Nov. 1. Lost our ship on the Reef of Rocus, and all hands immediately took to the boat, as there was no prospect of saving the slaves, for we must abandon the ship in consequence of the heavy surf.

4. Arrived with the boat at the island of Cuaraçao; the Hon'ble Governor Beck ordered two sloops to take the slaves off the wreck, one of which sloops with eighty four slaves on board was captured by a privateer.*

Americans need hardly be reminded of the fact that we virtually exterminated the native Red Indian population east of the Mississippi, and that if they massacred us when they could, we replied in kind often enough, and with superior means. There were, of course, exceptions to this bloody rule. In New England, missionaries like John Eliot did set up little bands of "praying Indians," and in Pennsylvania, the record of the relations between the Quakers and the Indians was excellent. The white man's diseases, which in those days could hardly have been controlled, and the white man's alcoholic drinks, which were surely quite as hard to control, did more to exterminate the red men than did fire and sword.

The Economic Record

Seen in terms of economics, the expansion of Europe in early modern times was by no means the pure "exploitation"

---

* *Documents Illustrative of the History of the Slave Trade to America,* Elizabeth Donnan, ed. (Washington, D. C., 1930), I, 143.

and "plundering" it sometimes appears to be in the rhetoric of anti-imperialists. There was robbery, just as there was murder or enslavement. There was, in dealing with the natives, even more giving of slight or nominal value in exchange for land and goods of great value. Just as all Americans are familiar with the slogan, "The only good Indian is a dead Indian," so they are familiar with a dozen variants of how little the Indians sold the island of Manhattan for. Finally, the almost universally applied mercantilist policy kept money and manufacturing in the hands of the home country. It relegated the colonies to the production of raw materials, a role not as well rewarded, generally speaking, as other economic roles, and one that tended to keep even colonies of settlement in a relatively primitive and certainly economically dependent condition.

Still, with all these limitations granted, the expansion of Europe was in economic terms an expansion of the total wealth produced here on earth. Although Europeans certainly took the lion's share in these early days, the expansion added to the goods available to non-Europeans. Although few Europeans settled in India or in Africa, their wares, and especially their weapons, began gradually the process of Europeanizing, or westernizing, the rest of the world. By the eighteenth century this process was only beginning, and in particular few of the improvements in public health and sanitation that Europeans were to bring to the East had yet come about; nor had any greater public order come to India and Africa. But over the whole world, in the New World especially, there were signs of the Europeanization, or "modernization," to come.

Effects of Expansion on the West

The West has in its turn been greatly affected by its relations with other peoples.

The list of items that have come into western life since Marco Polo and Columbus is long. It includes foodstuffs above all; utensils and gadgets, pipes for smoking, hammocks and pyjamas; styles of architecture and painting, bungalows and Japanese prints; and much else. Some of the novelties caught on more quickly than others. Tobacco, brought into Spain in the mid-sixteenth century as a soothing drug, had established itself by the seventeenth century as essential to the peace of mind of many European males. Potatoes, on the other hand, though their calory content is high and though they are cheaper to grow than the staple breadstuffs, did not immediately catch on in Europe. In France, where they are now a necessity of life, potatoes had to be popularized in a regular campaign which took generations to be effective. Tomatoes, the "love-apples" of our great-grandfathers, were long believed to be poisonous and were cultivated only for their looks.

Among westerners, knowledge of non-European beliefs and institutions eventually penetrated to the level of popular culture, where it is marked by a host of words—powwow, kowtow, tabu, totem, for instance. At the highest level of cultural interchange, that of religion and ethical ideas, however, the West took little from the new worlds opened after Columbus. The first impression of westerners, not only when they met the relatively primitive cultures of the New World, but even when they met the old cultures of the East was that they had nothing to learn from them. Once the process of interchange had gone far enough, some individuals were impressed with the mysticism and other-worldliness of Hindu philosophy and religion, and with the high but quite this-worldly ethics of Chinese Confucianism. Others came to admire the dignity and simplicity of the lives of many primitive peoples. But for the most part what struck the Europeans—when they bothered at all to think about anything more than money-making and empire-building—

A fifteenth-century European's fantastic conception of people in unknown lands.

was the poverty, dirt, and superstition they found among the masses in India and China, the low material standards of primitive peoples everywhere, the heathenness of the heathens.

Yet certainly exposure to these very different cultures acted as a stimulus in the West and broadened our horizons. The mere accumulation of so much new information gave the western mind something new to occupy itself with. Perhaps the first effect was no more than to increase the fund of the marvelous, the incredible. The early accounts of the New World are full of giants and pygmies, El Dorados where the streets are paved with gold, fountains of eternal youth, wonderful plants and animals. All this was a great stimulus to the literary and artistic imagination. From the island of Shakespeare's *Tempest* to the Xanadu of Coleridge's *Kubla Khan* you will find in our own literature the clear mark of all these new worlds.

But science, too, was stimulated. A dip into any of the early collections of voyages,

say the famous and easily available voyages edited in English by Richard Hakluyt in 1582, gives an impression more of the realistic sense and careful observation of these travelers than of their credulity and exaggerations. Here is modern geography already well on the way to maturity, and here too is the foundation of the modern social sciences of anthropology, comparative government, even of economics. Here, as well as in the work of a Bacon or a Galileo, you will find the origins of that important modern western contribution to the culture of our world, natural science. A good example is the following attempt to report on the puzzling Hindu institution of caste. It is from the travels of Pietro della Valle, an early seventeenth-century Italian:

The whole Gentile-people of *India* is divided into many sects or parties of men, known and distinguisht by descent or pedigree, as the Tribes of the Jews sometimes were; yet they inhabit the Country promiscuously mingled together, in every City and Land several Races one with another. 'Tis reckon'd that they are in all eighty four; some say more, making a

CHAPTER XIV

more exact and subtle division. Every one of these hath a particular name, and also a special office and Employment in the Commonwealth, from which none of the descendants of that Race ever swerve; they never rise nor fall, nor change condition: whence some are Husbandmen, others Mechanicks, as Taylers, Shoemakers and the like; others Factors or Merchants, such as they whom we call *Banians,* but they in their Language more correctly *Vania;* others, Souldiers, as the *Ragiaputi;* . . . so many Races which they reckon are reduc'd to four principal, which, if I mistake not, are the Brachmans, the Souldiers, the Merchants and the Artificers; from whom by more minute subdivision all the rest are deriv'd, in such number as in the whole people there are various professions of men. In the substantial points of Religion all agree together; all believe the Transmigration of Souls, which according to their merits and demerits (as they think) are sent by God into other bodies, either of Animals more or less clean, and of more or less painful life, or else of men more or less noble and handsome, and more or less pure of Race, wherein they place not a little of their vain superstition; accounting all other Nations and Religions besides themselves unclean, and some more than others, according as they more or less differ from their Customs.°

It may well be that the intellectual effects of the great discoveries were on the whole *unsettling, disturbing.* They helped, along with the new astronomy, the new mechanics, the Protestant Reformation, and much else, to break the medieval "cake of custom." They helped, literally, to make a New World of ideas and ideals. Such changes are always hard on ordinary human beings, for they demand that men change their minds, something which most of us, in spite of current American belief to the contrary, find it very hard to do.

One great effect of the discoveries is quite clear, and of much importance to us. However uncertain the degree of economic change or dynamism may be for the late Middle Ages (see Chapter X), for the sixteenth and seventeenth centuries there can be no doubt. The great new supplies of gold and silver from the Americas set in motion a secular trend toward price rises —toward, in current terms, inflation. This inflation accompanied, perhaps indeed "caused" or at least helped, general economic expansion. In this process, which has continued with ups and downs to the present, some groups gained, and others lost. In general, the merchants, financiers, "businessmen" in the broadest sense, gained; those on fixed incomes suffered; and wage-earners, peasants, and the like generally until very recent years did not receive additional income as fast as prices rose. In short, here as elsewhere, the effects of expansion were unsettling, often indeed harsh, as well as stimulating.

A distinguished contemporary American historian, Walter P. Webb, has made a still more sweeping generalization about the effects of these extraordinary discoveries. The vast new lands of the "frontier" in the New World were, he maintains, a bonanza or windfall, and supplied the real force behind the great increase in man's power to get more out of his natural environment with less sacrifice, the real force behind the great novelty of modern western civilization—its *wealth and power.*°

Here it must be noted again that the attempt to find a *single, one-way* causative factor in the great movements of history is a dangerous one. The great opportunities for expansion that the discoveries of the explorers gave to Europeans were certainly a factor in the rapid growth of productivity, population, and technical skills that characterizes the modern world. The great and easily acquired supplies of gold and silver from the New World were in the late sixteenth century a specific and useful "pump-priming" that furthered the growth of modern capitalism in northwest Europe. But the "frontier theory" of modern western capitalist society is no more to be taken as a

---

° *The Travels of Pietro della Valle in India,* Edward Grey, ed. (London, 1892), I, 78-79.

° Walter P. Webb, *The Great Frontier* (Boston, 1952).

sole explanation than, say, the Marxist theory of economic determinism or the Weber theory of the spirit of Protestant ethics. Most obviously, the roots of the discoveries themselves, like the roots of Protestantism and modern science, lie deep in the Middle Ages. Before the new worlds could be available to Europeans at all, trade, navigation, government organization—all had to arrive at the point where Henry the Navigator, Columbus, da Gama, and the others could proceed methodically to the discoveries and conquests that after all had been there for the Greeks, the Phoenicians, the Romans or the Vikings to make, had they been able and willing.

The One World of 1700

By the beginning of the eighteenth century, there were still blank spots on the map of the world, especially in the interior of Africa and in our Pacific Northwest. Yet, in spite of this and in spite of the insignificance of the impression made by Europe on China and Japan, it was already clear that only one system of international politics existed in the world. From now on, all general wars tended to be world wars. They were fought, if only by privateers, on all the Seven Seas, and, if only by savages and frontiersmen, on all the continents. Sooner or later, any considerable transfer of territory anywhere, any great accession of strength or wealth anywhere, had its effect on the precarious international equilibrium that we call the balance of power. From the eighteenth century on, there was One World.

This was certainly not One World of the spirit. There was no common authority of any kind that could reach all men. There were pockets of isolated peoples. And the masses of the world, even at its center in Europe, were ignorant enough of what really went on in the hearts and heads of men elsewhere. But already western goods penetrated almost everywhere, led by firearms, but followed by a great many other commodities, not all of them "cheap and nasty." Already an educated minority was growing up all over the world from professional geographers to journalists, diplomatists, and men of business, who had to deal with what are now for the first time quite literally the affairs of the whole world and its peoples.

Reading Suggestions on the Expansion of Europe

(Asterisk indicates paperbound edition.)

GENERAL ACCOUNTS

P. Sykes, *A History of Exploration from the Earliest Times to the Present* (Routledge, 1934). A comprehensive treatment of the subject.

C. R. Beazley, *The Dawn of Modern Geography*, 3 vols. (John Murray, 1897-1906). An authoritative account; stops in 1420 but useful for the background of this chapter.

J. H. Parry, *Europe and a Wider World, 1415-1715* (Hutchinson's University Library, 1949). A good, up-to-date general study.

C. E. Nowell, *The Great Discoveries* (Cornell Univ. Press, 1954). A handy introductory manual.

W. P. Webb, *The Great Frontier* (Houghton Mifflin, 1952). A daring series of generalizations about the role of the New World in western history.

J. H. Rose and others, eds., *The Cambridge History of the British Empire,* Vol. I (Cambridge Univ. Press, 1929). A convenient account of development up to 1783.

H. I. Priestley, *France Overseas through the Old Regime* (Appleton-Century-Crofts, 1939). A rather pedestrian study, but the best available in English.

SPECIAL STUDIES: PRIMARILY ON EXPLORERS AND NAVIGATORS

E. Prestage, *The Portuguese Pioneers* (Black, 1933). Stresses the early Portuguese work.

E. Sanceau, *Henry the Navigator* (Norton, 1947). A good biography of the Portuguese sponsor of exploration.

S. E. Morison, *Admiral of the Ocean Sea,* 2 vols. (Little, Brown, 1942). The best book on Columbus; Professor Morison retraced Columbus' route in a small ship as part of his preparation for writing.

H. H. Hart, *Sea Road to the Indies* (Macmillan, 1950). Deals with Da Gama and other Portuguese explorers.

C. McK. Parr, *So Noble a Captain* (Crowell, 1953). A very scholarly treatment of Magellan and his circumnavigation.

J. B. Brebner, *The Explorers of North America, 1492-1806* (Macmillan, 1933; *Anchor). A good account.

E. Heawood, *History of Geographical Discovery in the Seventeenth and Eighteenth Centuries* (Cambridge Univ. Press, 1912). Best work on the opening of the Pacific.

C. Lloyd, *Pacific Horizons* (Allen & Unwin, 1946) and *Captain Cook* (Faber and Faber, 1952). Together these most readable books give a modern review of early Pacific explorations.

SPECIAL STUDIES: PRIMARILY ON ASIA AND THE EAST

The Cambridge History of India, 5 vols. (Macmillan, 1922-1937). A fully detailed account.

R. Grousset, *The Civilizations of the East,* 4 vols. (Knopf, 1931-34). Vol. III (China) is particularly good on Chinese culture. The other volumes deal with the Near and Middle East, India, and Japan.

W. A. Fairservis, Jr., *The Origins of Oriental Civilization* (*New American Library, 1959). A good introduction to the prehistory and archaeology of China and Japan.

K. S. Latourette, *The Development of China,* new ed. (Houghton Mifflin, 1956). Probably the best single introductory volume on the subject.

G. B. Sansom, *Japan: A Short Cultural History* (Appleton-Century-Crofts, 1943). Perceptive book by a distinguished British expert on the subject.

G. B. Sansom, *A History of Japan,* Vol. I (Stanford Univ. Press, 1958). The first volume of a first-rate detailed history in course of publication.

A. L. Basham, *The Wonder That Was India* (* Evergreen, 1959). A more sober and careful survey of Indian history and culture up to the Moslem invasions than the title would indicate.

Jawaharlal Nehru, *The Discovery of India* (* Anchor, 1959). As valuable as an index of Nehru's mind as for the history of India.

B. H. M. Vlekke, *Nusantara: A History of Indonesia,* rev. ed. (Lorenz, 1959). Good introduction to the study of an important but often neglected area.

A. Hyma, *The Dutch in the Far East* (Wahr, 1942). Emphasizes social and economic developments.

SPECIAL STUDIES: PRIMARILY ON THE AMERICAS

W. H. Prescott, *The Conquest of Mexico* and *The Conquest of Peru* (many editions). Two classic accounts, written a century ago, by a famous American historian.

C. H. Haring, *The Spanish Empire in America* (Oxford Univ. Press, 1947). The best general study of the subject.

J. F. Rippy, *Latin America* (Univ. of Michigan Press, 1958). An authoritative new survey, one of a forthcoming series of fifteen volumes written with a focus on world, as opposed to European, history.

S. E. Morison, ed., *The Parkman Reader* (Little, Brown, 1955). A convenient selection from the celebrated multi-volumed *France and England in North America* by Francis Parkman.

G. M. Wrong, *The Rise and Fall of New France,* 2 vols. (Macmillan, 1928). Sound study by a Canadian.

A. P. Newton, *The European Nations in the West Indies, 1493-1688* (Black, 1933). The best account.

R. Hofstadter, W. Miller, D. Aaron, *The American Republic,* 2 vols. (Prentice-Hall, 1959). Vol. I of this excellent textbook summarizes the development of the thirteen English colonies.

O. T. Black and H. T. Lefler, *Colonial America* (Macmillan, 1958). A good up-to-date American textbook.

D. J. Boorstin, *The Americas: The Colonial Experiment* (Random House, 1958). A provocative treatment.

L. B. Wright, *Cultural Life in the American Colonies, 1607-1763* (Harper, 1957). An excellent volume in Harper's current New American Nation Series.

HISTORICAL FICTION

N. Shute, pseud., *An Old Captivity* (Morrow, 1940). On the Viking explorer, Leif Ericson.

L. Wallace, *The Fair God* (Osgood, 1873). A real thriller, unduly forgotten, on the Aztecs of Mexico; by the author of *Ben-Hur.*

S. Shellabarger, *Captain from Castile* (Little, Brown, 1945). On Cortés and the conquest of Mexico. The "cloak and bosom" school of historical fiction, but based on sound scholarship.

C. S. Forester, *To the Indies* (°Bantam). An excellent novel on Columbus.

R. Sabatini, *The Sea Hawk* (Houghton Mifflin, 1923). A good melodramatic novel of adventures on the sea in the late sixteenth century.

C. Kingsley, *Westward Ho!* (many editions). Rather juvenile in tone, but gives a good picture of the excitement of English exploration.

W. Cather, *Shadows on the Rock* (Knopf, 1931). Sensitive re-creation of life in New France by a distinguished modern American novelist.

Divine-Right Monarchy —and Revolution

CHAPTER XV

I: International Politics— France as Aggressor

BY THE mid-seventeenth century it was clear that neither the Spanish nor the Austrian Habsburgs were going to break down the European state-system and set up a new form of that haunting old institution, the Roman Empire. Yet for several generations, and in spite of Spain's reputation as a decaying power, men still feared a possible Spanish aggression. The actual aggressor in the great wars of the later seventeenth and early eighteenth centuries was France, the real victor in the Thirty Years' War. Well recovered from the wounds of her own religious wars, prospering economically and politically, with a young and ambitious king, Louis XIV (1643-1715), on the throne, France was ready for expansion.

As always in attempts to describe what the aggressor wanted, there is some exaggeration in attributing to Louis designs for "world conquest." He clearly wanted French culture, French taste in the arts, French social ways, to influence all Europe, which to an amazing extent they did in the late seventeenth century. Yet neither he nor his ministers can possibly have envisaged an organized world-state in which everyone was a subject of Louis XIV. In North

597

America, however, in India, in Holland, on the Rhine, in dozens of other places, the agents of Louis were hard at work trying to increase their master's power and prestige—the latter a vague but very real and important word. Other peoples believed that France was threatening something they held dear—life, property, independence, self-respect. Under this threat, most of the European states finally united against the French aggressor, and beat him.

Before Louis XIV: Henry IV and Sully

Other kings in other days, like Louis XI of France and Henry VII of England, had accomplished the restoration of law and order. But only Henry of Navarre (Henry IV, 1589-1610) made the restorer a genuinely popular hero. Witty, dashing, with a pronounced taste for pretty women and bawdy stories, he was the most human king the French had had for a long time, and the best-liked monarch in their whole history. His court casually included his wife, his mistresses, and his children, legitimate and otherwise. He made jokes about his financial difficulties. And, most of all, he convinced his subjects that he was really concerned for their welfare. Among ordinary Frenchmen, Henry IV is still remembered as the king who remarked that every peasant should have a chicken in his pot on Sunday.

Henry's economic experts reclaimed marshes for farm land, encouraged the luxury crafts in Paris, and planted thousands of mulberry trees to foster the culture and manufacture of silk. They extended canals and launched a program of building roads and bridges that eventually won France the reputation of maintaining the best highways in Europe. Faced with a heavy deficit when he first took office, Henry's great minister, Sully (1559-1641) systematically lowered it until he brought government income and expenditure into balance.

In 1610, when a madman assassinated Henry IV in the prime of his career, the new king, Louis XIII (1610-1643), was only nine years old. The succession of a child presents grave difficulties in a monarchy where the king really rules; in France, the reins of government went slack during the minority of Louis XIII. The queen-mother, Marie de' Medici, attempted to rule but showed little of her famous family's political skill. Her Italian favorites and French nobles, Catholic and Huguenot both, carried on a hectic competition which threatened to undo all that Henry IV had accomplished. In the course of these troubles, the French representative body, the Estates-General, met at Blois in 1614 for what was destined to be its last meeting until 1789 on the eve of the great French Revolution. Finally, Louis XIII came of age and, though incapable himself of asserting a strong rule, in 1624 picked a minister who could.

Before Louis XIV: Richelieu and Mazarin

The minister was Cardinal Richelieu (1585-1642), Bishop of Luçon, a sincere but certainly not an ardent Catholic, and also efficient and ambitious, a born administrator. As the virtual ruler of France for the next eighteen years, Richelieu proved to be a good Machiavellian and a good *politique*. He subordinated religion and every nonpolitical consideration to *raison d'état* (literally, reason of state), a phrase that he probably coined himself.

Raison d'état determined Richelieu's policy toward the Huguenots. The Edict of Nantes had given them certain political privileges, notably the right to govern some hundred fortified towns located mostly in the southwestern quarter of France. To Richelieu these Protestant towns formed a state within the state, a block to his program of strong centralization; they were to him a hundred centers of potential rebellion that should be brought under control. Alarmed, the Huguenots did in fact rebel. It took the royal forces fourteen months to besiege and take their chief stronghold, the port of La Rochelle, which finally fell in 1628. Richelieu thereupon canceled the political clauses of the Edict of Nantes but left its religious provisions intact.

The siege of La Rochelle lasted fourteen months, because France scarcely possessed a navy worth the name. In the next ten years, Richelieu created a fleet of thirty-eight warships for the Atlantic and a dozen galleys, manned by slaves (an exception to the rule that white men were never enslaved), for the Mediterranean. Meanwhile, he skillfully guided France through the Thirty Years' War, his eye always on the greatness of France, husbanding French resources carefully, committing them only when concrete gains for France seemed possible. Richelieu was one of the great practitioners of realistic power politics in international relations.

Raison d'état, indeed, motivated all his policies. He lived in elaborate style, accompanied on his travels by his private choir and corps of musicians, not just because he was fond of music but because he believed such a retinue befitted the chief minister of a great and splendid kingdom. In 1635, he founded the *Académie*, the famous French Academy, to compile a dictionary of the French language and to set the standards and style of the national culture. He tried to curb the factious nobles, though with only middling success, by ordering the destruction of some of their châteaux and forbidding the favorite aristocratic indulgence of private duels. More significant was his transfer of effective supervision over the local administration from the nobles to the more reliable *intendants*. These royal officials had existed earlier but had only minor functions; now they received greatly increased powers, particularly in the vital work of apportioning and collecting taxes.

Richelieu was unquestionably a great

Cardinal Richelieu.

statesman, a man largely responsible for building *la grande nation* of Louis XIV. Historians have always differed in their estimates of how good for France in the long run his work was to prove. For royalists generally, his work was sound, an efficient, centralized state. For others, he built in a sense too well, made the French government so centralized, so professionally bureaucratic, that it had no place for the give and take of politics, for government by discussion, above all, no political place, save for a few bureaucrats, for the new and ambitious middle classes.

Richelieu himself had picked and schooled his successor, the Italian-born Mazarin (1602-1661). Mazarin, too, was a cardinal and a past master of *raison d'état*. He, too, was careless about the finances of the French state and, unlike Richelieu, amassed an immense personal fortune during his public career. Soon after taking over, Mazarin faced the emergency of a long minority and regency. When the thirteenth royal Louis died in 1643, the fourteenth was a boy of four and a half. The feudal nobles resented being excluded from the regency by a foreigner; the judges and other high officials, who had invested heavily in government securities, particularly disliked Mazarin's casual way of borrowing money to meet war expenses and then letting the interest payments on government borrowings fall into arrears. The discontent boiled over in the uprising of the Fronde, 1648-1653, named for the slingshot used by Parisian children to hurl mud at passers-by.

The narrative history of the Fronde is a complicated set of plots, interspersed with some very mild battles and Mazarin's repeated flights from the capital. Its upshot was to confirm Mazarin in his power, and to pave the way for the personal rule of Louis XIV. The youthful king got a bad fright when the *frondeurs* actually broke into the room where he was feigning sleep, and he resolved to hold firmly to the reins of state. The Fronde failed essentially because it had no real roots in the country, not even in the rising middle classes. It was a struggle for power between Mazarin and his new bureaucracy, and two privileged groups, the old nobles and the newer official nobles of the law courts. Each of the noble groups distrusted the other, and in the long run Mazarin successfully applied the old Roman adage: Divide and rule.

The Successes of Louis XIV

Richelieu and Mazarin had seldom gone beyond the point of maintaining French power and prestige; they attempted

little actual French expansion in Italy or in Germany and the Low Countries. Louis XIV, however, definitely did attempt to add to French territories. His main effort was no longer, as had been that of the Valois kings, toward Italy, but northeast toward Germany and Holland. He sought also to secure Spain, if not quite as a direct annexation, at least as a French satellite with a French ruler. Finally, French commitments overseas in North America and in Asia drove him to attempt, against English and Dutch rivals, the establishment of a great French empire outside Europe.

The first actual war of Louis XIV was a minor affair, but it showed how he was going to move. When he married the daughter of Philip IV of Spain, his bride had renounced her rights of inheritance. Now Louis claimed that, since her dowry had never been paid, her renunciation was invalid. His lawyers dug up an old family rule, the *right of devolution,* which Louis claimed gave his wife lands in what is now Belgium. In the ensuing "War of Devolution" with Spain, the great French general, Turenne, won various victories, but Louis was feeling his way and did not press them. A compromise peace at Aix-la-Chapelle in 1668 settled little and left the Dutch quite rightfully alarmed for the independence they had won from Spain.

In 1672, Louis began his war on the Dutch, against whom he eventually secured a fair number of allies, notably England, bought off in 1670, Sweden, and some of the German states. The Dutch, however, resisted stoutly under their strong leader, William III of Orange, a descendant of William the Silent. Even without William, Europe would probably have responded to the threat of French domination by an anti-French alliance. As it was, Spain, the Holy Roman Empire, and a still not very important German state, Brandenburg-Prussia, joined against France and her allies. The anti-French coalition was not very effective, and French diplomacy separated the allies at the treaties of Nijmegen (Nimwegen) in 1678-79. Holland was left intact at the cost of promising neutrality; Spain yielded to France the Franche Comté (County of Burgundy) and some towns in the Spanish Netherlands; Prussia, which had won a crucial battle against Sweden at Fehrbellin in 1675, was obliged by French pressure to give the Swedes back their Baltic German lands.

The French had not only succeeded to the military preponderance Spain had once enjoyed; they had improved upon it. The French armed forces were strong not only in the conventional field forces but also in artillery, engineering, and siege techniques. The French navy had expanded around the nucleus provided by Richelieu. And behind these efficient armed forces the ministries maintained an adequate service of supply. It is true, as we have noted of Spanish organization, that the fighting arms of this "absolute" French monarchy were by modern standards inefficient and loosely organized. Everything moved slowly and ponderously. There was still a great deal of leeway in the armies and civilian bureaus for semi-feudal independence; there was still nothing like the modern standardization of munitions, supplies, and channels of command. For manpower, Louis increasingly depended either on foreign mercenaries, who were expensive, or on Frenchmen drafted, not according to any broad system of universal military service, but chiefly from the poorer classes and by methods that allowed wide scope for favoritism and bribery. Leadership, however, was largely professional. At the best period of the reign, in the 1670's and 1680's, the officers were, for an old society, chosen and promoted to an extraordinary degree for ability rather than for family ties.

The power and prestige of France were now at their peak. Louis' place in Europe rested by no means solely on his armed forces. He was well served by a diplomatic corps trained in the niceties of *raison d'état.*

Above all, he enjoyed to an unusual degree the position of leader and exemplar of culture and taste. Rulers all over Europe, and in particular the host of princes and princelets in the Germanies, aped the standards of Louis' court at Versailles. French manners, French language, French clothes, French dishes, French art, were all the fashion. The prestige of France was not diminished by those who hated while they envied her; France was hardly loved, but she was admired and imitated. All in all, France in 1680 enjoyed assets Spain had never enjoyed. She was now *la grande nation,* adding to material power the very great power of cultural prestige.

The Failures of Louis XIV

Yet in the last three decades of Louis' reign most of these assets were dissipated, especially the concrete ones of wealth and efficient organization. Not content with the prestige he had won in his first two wars, Louis embroiled himself with most of the western world in what looked to that world like an effort to destroy the independence of Holland and most of western Germany, and to bring the great Iberian Peninsula under a French ruler. The third of his wars, the War of the League of Augsburg, broke out in 1688 basically over the continued French nibbling at bits of territory in western Germany. Louis' assertion of a dynastic claim to most of the lands of the German Elector Palatine was the last straw. The league against him was largely put together by his old foe, William of Orange, who after 1688 shared the throne of England with his wife Mary, daughter of James II of England. Thenceforth, England was thoroughly committed to take sides against Louis. The great sea victory of the English over the French at Cape La Hogue in 1692 showed that England, not France, was to be mistress of the seas. But on land the honors were more nearly even. William was beaten in battle in the Low Countries time and again, but he was never decisively crushed. In Ireland, French attempts to intervene on behalf of the deposed English king, James II, were foiled at the battle of the Boyne in 1690.

Louis was growing old, and perhaps for the moment he had had enough. The Peace of Ryswick, concluded in 1697, was one of those comparatively rare peaces without victory, a general agreement to keep things as they were. It lasted barely four years, for in 1701 Louis, after much personal soul-searching, took a step that led to the great world war over the Spanish succession. His brother-in-law, the Habsburg king of Spain, Charles II, died in 1700 without a direct heir. For several years the diplomatists of Europe had been striving to arrange by general consent a succession that would avoid putting on the Spanish throne either a French Bourbon or an Austrian Habsburg. They had agreed on a Bavarian prince; but he had died in 1699, and the whole question was reopened. New plans were made, partitioning the Spanish inheritance between Habsburgs and Bourbons. But Charles II of Spain made a new will, giving his lands intact to Philip of Anjou, the grandson of Louis XIV, and then died. Louis could not withstand the temptation. He accepted on behalf of Philip, despite the fact that he had signed the treaty of partition. The threat to the balance of power was neatly summarized in the remark a gloating Frenchman is supposed to have made, "There are no longer any Pyrenees" (the great mountain chain that separates France and Spain). England, Holland, the Empire, and many German states formed the Grand Alliance to preserve the Pyrenees.

In the bloody war that followed, the French were gradually worn down in defeat. Their North American possession of Acadia (Nova Scotia) was taken by the English. In four great European battles, Blenheim (1704), Ramillies (1706), Oudenarde (1708), and Malplaquet (1709), the French were beaten by the Allies under two great generals, the English John Churchill, Duke of Marlborough, ancestor of Winston Churchill, and the Savoyard Prince Eugene. But the French were not annihilated. The last of the great Allied victories, Malplaquet, had cost the Allies 20,000 casualties, and somehow, by scraping the bottom of the barrel for men and money, the French managed even after Malplaquet to keep armies in the field.

Moreover, the Grand Alliance was weakening. The English, now following their famous policy of keeping any single continental power from attaining too strong a position, were almost as anxious to prevent the union of the Austrian and Spanish inheritances under a Habsburg as to prevent the union of the French and the Spanish inheritance under a Bourbon. At home, they faced a possible disputed succession to the throne, and some of the mercantile classes were sick of a war that was injuring trade, and that seemed unlikely to bring any compensating gains. In 1710, the Tory party, inclined toward peace, won a parliamentary majority and began negotiations that culminated in a series of treaties at Utrecht in 1713.

The Utrecht Settlement

Utrecht was a typical balance-of-power peace. France was contained but by no means humiliated. She lost to England Newfoundland, Nova Scotia, and the Hudson's Bay territories, but she preserved Quebec and Louisiana, as well as her Caribbean islands. Louis gained in a sense what he had gone to war over, for Philip of Anjou was formally recognized as King Philip V of Spain and secured the Spanish lands overseas. The French and Spanish crowns were not, however, ever to be held by the same person; so the Allies, too, had won a point. Furthermore, England took from Spain the Mediterranean island of

Minorca, which she handed back later in the century, and the great Rock of Gibraltar guarding the Atlantic entrance to the Mediterranean. The English also gained by what is called the Asiento the right to supply Negro slaves to the Spanish colonies, a right that gave them a chance also at interloping trade or just plain smuggling.

The Austrian Habsburgs, denied the main Spanish succession, were compensated with the former Spanish Netherlands, the modern Belgium. Holland was granted the right to maintain garrisons in certain fortified towns in these Austrian Netherlands for better defense against possible French aggression. Savoy, an Italian state that had been true to the Grand Alliance, was rewarded with Sicily; though diplomatic jockeying substituted for this prize in 1720 the lesser island of Sardinia, the Duke of Savoy was able to call himself King of Sardinia and thus started the long process that united Italy under the crown of Savoy in the nineteenth century. The Elector of Brandenburg-Prussia, too, was rewarded with a royal title, King *in* Prussia (not *of*, for Prussia proper was outside the Holy Roman Empire).

In all the general European settlements of modern times—Westphalia, Utrecht, Vienna, Versailles—historians discern the elements, the imperfections, that led to subsequent unsettlement and another general war. Utrecht is no exception, even though of all the great modern settlements it is the one in which victors and vanquished seem closest. First of all, the rivalry between France and England for empire overseas was not at all settled. In India, as in North America, each nation was to continue after Utrecht as before the effort to oust the other from land and trade. In Europe, the Dutch were not really protected from French expansion by the right to garrison forts in the Austrian Netherlands. The Austrian Habsburg leader, now the Emperor Charles VI, never forgot that he had wanted to be "Charles III" of Spain and never quite gave

up hope that somehow he could upset the decisions made at Utrecht. No one seemed to have quite what he wanted, which is one of the difficulties of working out reasonable, compromise solutions. The distribution of Italian lands satisfied nobody, Italian or outsider, and the next two decades were filled with intrigues, negotiations, and very mild wars over Italy.

French Aggression in Review

In retrospect, this first period of French aggression seems one of the less violent and critical tests of the European state-system. True, these wars caused horrors enough, especially in the deliberate French devastation of the German Palatinate during the War of the League of Augsburg. Their total cost in human and in economic resources was very great. The French were sometimes hated as foreigners and aggressors. These wars were not simply struggles among professional armies directed by professional politicians; they were in part wars among peoples, wars that brought out feelings of patriotism and hatred for the foreigner.

Yet in comparison with the wars of religion that had preceded them, and with the wars of nationalism and revolution that were to follow, the wars of Louis XIV seem to have lacked the all-out qualities of human drives toward both good and evil. Louis set himself up as a champion of Catholicism, especially after the revocation of the Edict of Nantes in 1685, and much was made of William of Orange as a Protestant champion. In the end, however, the coalition against Louis was a complete mixture of Catholic and Protestant, in which religion played a comparatively minor role. On the other hand, no lay substitute for the crusading religious spirit had yet emerged. Unlike such later aggressors as Napoleon and Hitler, Louis XIV was not the product

EUROPE IN 1715

Brandenburg – Prussia
Austrian Habsburg Lands
Swedish possessions
Venetian possessions
Ottoman Empire
Boundary of the Holy Roman Empire
× Battle sites

NORWAY

Oslo

SWEDEN

Stockholm

North Sea

DENMARK

Copenhagen

Baltic

SWEDISH POMERANIA

Hamburg

BRANDENBURG

Danzig

Berlin

THE EMPIRE

SAXONY

SILESIA

Prague

BOHEMIA

MORAVIA

AUSTRIA

Vienna

STYRIA

CARINTHIA

CARNIOLA

HUN

SCOTLAND

Edinburgh
Berwick

ULSTER

Limerick
IRELAND
Boyne
Drogheda
Dublin

ENGLAND

London

KINGDOM OF GREAT BRITAIN

Ocean

Atlantic

Tor Bay
C. La Hogue

Dover

UNITED NETHERLANDS
Bremen
Ryswick
Utrecht
Nimwegen
AUSTRIAN NETHERLANDS
Oudenarde
Ramillies
Aachen
WESTPHALIA
Malplaquet

Rhine

Paris
Versailles
Verdun
Metz
Toul
Orleans
Blois
Nantes
Loire R.

Rastadt
Strasbourg
ALSACE
LORRAINE

Blenheim
Augsburg
BAVARIA

FRANCE

FRANCHE COMTÉ

Geneva

SWITZERLAND

TYROL

Venice

VENETIAN REP.

Adriatic Sea

Ragusa

PORTUGAL

Lisbon

Burgos
Ebro R.

Madrid

SPAIN

Tagus R.

Seville
Guadalquivir R.
Granada

Valencia

Barcelona

Gibraltar (Br.)

Bordeaux

Rhone R.

Avignon (to the papacy)

Marseilles

SAVOY

MILAN

Genoa

Florence

PAPAL STATES

Rome

NAPLES

Naples

BALEARIC IS.

MINORCA (Br.)

CORSICA (to Genoa)

SARDINIA (to Austria, 1714; to Savoy, 1720)

Mediterranean

Palermo

SICILY

(to Savoy, 1714; to Austria, 1720)

MALTA

ALGERIA

TUNIS

Miles

0   500

G.

604

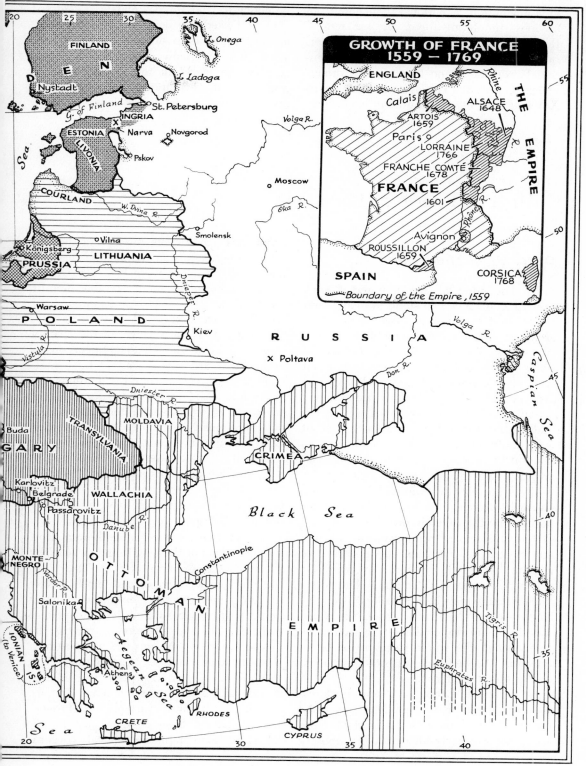

FINLAND

D   E   N

Nystadt

L. Onega

L. Ladoga

G. of Finland

St. Petersburg

INGRIA

Narva

Novgorod

ESTONIA

X

LIVONIA

Pskov

Sea

COURLAND

W. Dvina R.

Königsberg

Vilna

PRUSSIA

LITHUANIA

Volga R.

Moscow

Smolensk

Oka R.

Warsaw

Vistula R.

P   O   L   A   N   D

Dnieper R.

Kiev

R   U   S   S   I   A

x Poltava

Volga R.

Caspian Sea

Dniester R.

MOLDAVIA

TRANSILVANIA

Buda

GARY

Don R.

CRIMEA

Karlovitz

Belgrade

WALLACHIA

Passarovitz

Danube R.

Black   Sea

MONTE-
NEGRO

O   T   T   O   M   A   N

Vardar R.

Salonika

Constantinople

E   M   P   I   R   E

Tigris R.

IONIAN
(to Venice)
Is.

Aegean Sea

Athens

Euphrates R.

Sea

CRETE

RHODES

CYPRUS

20   30   35   40

GROWTH OF FRANCE 1559 — 1769

ENGLAND

Calais

Rhine

THE EMPIRE

ALSACE
1648

ARTOIS
1659

Paris

LORRAINE
1766

FRANCHE COMTÉ
1678

FRANCE

1601

Avignon

Rhone R.

ROUSSILLON
1659

SPAIN

CORSICA
1768

Boundary of the Empire, 1559

55

50

45

40

35

of a revolution, a national awakening, an obvious stimulating force. He was indeed the "Sun King," a great and admired ruler, but he was the legitimate, even conventional, ruler of a land long used to prominence in Europe. The aggression of Louis XIV was thus, like the culture of his France, a moderate, measured, "classical" aggression. It lacked the heaven-storming fervor of aggressions born of revolution; aggressions that are really crusades, efforts to remake the world in the image of some exalted ideal; revolutionary nationalist, or fascist, or communist aggressions.

II: The France of Louis XIV

Divine-Right Monarchy

The admired and imitated French state of Louis XIV can stand in many ways as the best example of divine-right monarchy, the absolute monarchy of early modern times. We have for the France of Louis' prime one of those convenient but certainly oversimplified tags that history furnishes so abundantly. Perhaps Louis never actually said *L'Etat, c'est moi* (I am the State), but the phrase has stuck, and it is certainly not altogether misleading as an attempt to summarize a state of mind and an ideal. In theory, Louis was for his subjects the earthly representative of God on earth—or at least, in France. He held this position by the divinely ordained workings of the principle of primogeniture; he was not elected by his subjects, nor did he acquire his throne by force of arms. He was born to a position God had planned for the legitimate male heir of the tenth-century Hugh Capet. As God's agent, his word was final, for to challenge it would be to challenge the whole structure of God's universe. Disobedience was both a political and a religious offense.

Now though Louis has been dead less than three centuries, the ideas and sentiments centered on this divine-right monarchy are so utterly alien to contemporary Americans that it takes an effort of the historical imagination not to dismiss them as nonsense. There they were, however, clearly enough believed by many sensible men of the day. Two clues may help us understand why they were held so widely and so firmly. The first clue is the survival of the characteristic medieval view that right decisions in government are not arrived at by experiment and discussion, but by "finding" the authoritative answer provided for in God's scheme of things (see Chapter VIII). In the days of Louis XIV men still believed that God through his chosen agents directly managed the state. Men were indeed beginning to question this idea, but the full force of their questioning was not to come for another generation or two on the continent of Europe.

A second clue lies in the deliberate effort by the makers of the new French monarchy to cope with specific problems. Their central problem we have already noted: How to bring men together into those larger political units necessitated by the course of technological and economic growth, the overseas discoveries, and the pressure of a slow but steady increase of population. How to make men who were used to thinking, feeling, and behaving as Normans, Bretons, Flemings, Alsatians, Burgundians, Provençaux, Gascons, Basques—even just as villagers or members of a medieval "corporative" society (see Chapter VIII)—think, feel, and behave as *Frenchmen*. The makers of the new French monarchy could not rely on a common language, for only a minority spoke standard French; the fifteen or twenty millions who had to get along together as Frenchmen spoke several dozen mutually incomprehensible languages or at least dialects. And of course they could not rely on a common educational system, a common press, common participation in political life; all that lay in the future. They could, and did, attempt to set up at least a symbol of common Frenchness, a King of France who was king for Celtic-speaking Bretons as for Catalan-speaking southerners. That king collected taxes, raised armies, touched in a hundred ways the lives of ordinary men who had to feel somehow that the king had a right to do all this, had to feel that he was indeed doing this *for* them, rather than *to* them. A king who was, if not like the old Roman emperors a god himself, at least the agent of God, was the kind of king they could understand and accept.

Divine-right monarchy, with its corollary of obedience on the part of subjects, is thus one phase of the growth of the modern centralized nation-state. It was an institution that appealed to very old theological ideas, such as the Biblical admonition to obey the powers that be, "for the powers that be are ordained of God." But it was an institution that was also inspired by the newer ideas of binding men together in a productive, efficient state. In practice, naturally, the institution did not wholly correspond to theories about it. Louis XIV was not the French state, and his rule was not absolute in any full, logical sense of that word. He simply did not have the physical means for controlling in detail what his subjects did. Such control is actually much more completely possible under modern techniques of communication, propaganda, and administration than it ever was in days of "absolute" monarchy.

The early modern monarchy in France and throughout the West was subject to many limitations besides those set by the physical possibilities of supervision. Medieval survivals made for diversities of many sorts, in language, laws, customs, even in weights and measures. All stood in the way of the uniformity, the administrative neatness and exactness, that are essential to the smooth working of a chain of command. Important groups still clung to medieval privileges—that is, to rights, immunities, a status, which they felt did not depend on the king's will, which were, certainly in the minds of those who enjoyed them, legal limitations on the power of the King. Many of these groups were corporations—municipal boards, judicial boards, economic groups such as guilds—which usually possessed written charters and traditional privileges very difficult for the government to override. Two of these groups, the old nobility and the clergy, deserve special mention.

The Nobility

In all the important countries the feudal nobility maintained themselves into early modern times. The degree to which they were integrated into the new machinery of state was of crucial importance in the development of modern Europe. In Habsburg Spain, as indeed in the Habsburg lands of Central Europe, the old nobility generally accepted the new strength of the Crown, but maintained much of their privilege and all their old pride of status. In Prussia, they were most successfully integrated in the new order, becoming on the whole faithful servants or soldiers of the Crown, but with a social status that set them above bourgeois bureaucrats. In England, as we shall shortly see, the nobility achieved a unique compromise with the Crown. In France, they were in effect shoved aside by the Crown and deprived for the most part of major political functions, but they were allowed to retain social and economic privileges and important roles as officers in the king's army.

This process of reducing the old French nobility to political powerlessness had begun during the fifteenth century, and had been hastened by the religious and civil wars of the sixteenth century. An important part of the nobility, perhaps nearly half, had espoused the Protestant cause, in large part from sheer opposition to the Catholic Crown. The victory of Henry IV, purchased by his conversion to Catholicism, was a defeat for the nobility. The process was completed by the increasing use under Richelieu and Louis XIV of commoners in the task of running the government, from the great ministers of state, through the *intendants,* down to local administrators and judges. These commoners were usually elevated to a status technically noble, a status that came to be hereditary, but they were known by a special term, the *noblesse de la robe* (from the robes or gowns worn by judges and other officials). This official bureaucratic nobility did not, however, have at first the social prestige of the old nobility of the sword, the *noblesse de l'épée.* The old nobles felt a contemptuous envy toward the newcomers of the gown; they knew they were shelved.

The Clergy

In medieval times, the clergy had been a separate order, backed by the supranational power and prestige of the papacy, and possessing privileges not wholly in the control of the Crown. In the new centralized France, however, the Crown had fostered a national Gallican Church which was indeed Catholic but also under good control by the monarchy. Under Louis, this Gallican union of throne and altar reached a high point, and the greatest of his bishops, Bossuet (1627-1704), wrote firmly in support of royal absolutism. Yet even under Louis XIV the French clergy continued to possess important corporate privileges. They were not subject to royal taxation; they contributed of their own free will a gift of money which they voted in their own assembly.

Moreover, Louis was by no means wholly master of the religious beliefs and practices of his subjects. Whereas Richelieu had attacked only the political privileges of the Huguenots, Louis attacked their fundamental right of toleration and finally abolished it. Pressed by the clergy, he revoked the Edict of Nantes in 1685. After the revocation, fifty thousand Huguenot families fled abroad, notably to Prussia, Holland, Belgium, England, and the new colonial lands of British North America. The practical skills and intellectual gifts of these early "refugees" greatly strengthened the lands that received them. Some Huguenots also remained in France, where they continued to worship underground in spite of persecution.

Within the Catholic Church itself, Louis had to contend with two important elements that refused to accept his Gallicanism. The Quietists, a group of religious enthusiasts led by Madame Guyon, sought for a more mystical and emotional faith. The Jansenists, sometimes called the "Puritans of the Catholic Church," were a high-minded group whose most distinguished spokesman was the scientist and philosopher, Pascal. Named for Cornelius Jansen, Bishop of Ypres in the early seventeenth century, the Jansenists took an almost Calvinistic stand on the issue of predestination. They stressed the need to obey the authority of God rather than that of man, no matter how exalted the position of the particular man might be. They therefore questioned both the authority of the pope (and of his agents, the Jesuits) and that of the king. On the surface, Louis was successful in repressing both Quietists and Jansenists, but the latter in particular survived to trouble his successors in the eighteenth century.

Palace at Versailles.

The Royal Administration

Louis did not quite succeed in building up an administrative machine wholly under royal control. It was not for want of application that he fell short. When he began his personal rule in 1661, he was only twenty-two years old but had already impressed a seasoned observer of the court with his earnestness:

As the single desire for glory and to fulfill all the duties of a great king occupied his whole heart, by applying himself to toil he began to like it; and the eagerness he had to learn all the things that were necessary to him soon made him full of that knowledge. His great good sense and his good intentions now made visible in him the rudiments of general knowledge which had been hidden from all

who did not see him in private; for he suddenly appeared like a politician in affairs of the State, a theologian in those of the Church, precise in matters of finance, speaking with justice, taking always the right side in council, sensitive to the interests of private persons, but an enemy to intrigue and flattery, and stern towards the grandees of his kingdom whom he suspected of a desire to govern him.

He was agreeable personally, civil and easy of access to every one; but with a lofty and serious air which impressed the public with respect and awe . . . , though he was familiar and gay with ladies.*

Louis continued to be "familiar and gay" with the ladies until finally, after the death of his Spanish queen, he settled down to a proper middle-aged marriage with Madame

---

* *Memoirs of Madame de Motteville,* K. P. Wormeley, trans. (Boston, 1902), III, 243.

de Maintenon, a devout Catholic who had been the governess of his illegitimate children. Meanwhile, he had provided himself a setting worthy of the Sun King by building a few miles outside Paris the celebrated Palace of Versailles, which was more than a third of a mile long and housed a court of ten thousand.

At Versailles, Louis met regularly with his ministers, who headed departments essentially like those of any modern state—War, Finance, Foreign Policy, Interior. The ministers were responsible directly to him, and not to any legislative body. The Estates-General never met during his lifetime. From the top, a reasonably clear chain of command proceeded down through the *intendants*, who were now the heads of *généralités* (big administrative units roughly corresponding to the older provinces), thence through smaller units to the town or village. Even the indefatigable Louis, however, could do no more than exercise general supervision over the affairs of his large and complex kingdom. And he probably could not have achieved even partial success without the invention of printing. For the familiar government printed forms to be filled out were already in existence. And they are still there, duly filled out and filed in their hundreds of thousands in the local archives of France.

In practice, naturally, the royal administration was full of difficulties and contradictions. There were many superimposed and often conflicting jurisdictions, survivals of feudalism and the medieval struggle to control feudalism. The officials of Louis XIV, by the very fact of being nobles of the gown, possessed a privileged status which they could hand down to their heirs. They, too, tended to form a corporation, tended even as individuals to be more their own masters in their own bailiwicks than the theory of royal absolutism would allow. The key provincial administrators, the *intendants,* may seem to have been no more than agents of the Crown. Yet anyone who pursues in local history the detailed records of what the *intendants* actually did sees that many of them exercised considerable initiative and were by no means rubber-stamp officials. Nor was the old administrative device of moving the *intendants* about from one *généralité* to another sufficient to overcome this centrifugal tendency.

Still another set of institutions gave trouble. These were the *parlements*, the supreme courts of appeal in the various provinces, of which one, the Parlement of Paris, enjoyed special prestige and power from its place at the capital and from the size of its territorial jurisdiction, almost half of the kingdom. The judges who staffed the courts headed the nobility of the gown, owned their offices, and were not removable at the will of the king. In addition to the usual work of a court of appeals, the *parlements* claimed through their function of registering royal edicts something very close to what in American usage is called the right of judicial review. That is, they claimed to be able to refuse to register an edict if they thought it "unconstitutional," not in accord with the law of the land. The claim, of course, negated theoretical royal absolutism.

Actually, Louis got around the difficulty in his own lifetime. The Parlement of Paris had already lost a round in its struggle with the royal power by entering the lists against Mazarin in the Fronde. Now Louis successfully utilized another old institution, the *lit de justice* (literally, "bed of justice"), in which he summoned the Parlement of Paris before him in a formal session and ordered the justices to register a royal edict. In this way, for instance, he enforced measures against Jansenism which was strong among the judges. But the *parlements*, too, were to plague his eighteenth-century successors.

Mercantilism in Theory

Just as divine-right monarchy was not peculiarly French, so the mercantilism identified with the France of Louis XIV was common to many other westerns states in the early modern period. But, like divine-right rule, mercantilism flourished most characteristically under the Sun King. Its most famous exponent was one of Louis' greatest ministers, Colbert (1619-1683).

Mercantilism comprised a set of economic aims and practices, particularly in the field of relations between government and business. The central doctrine of mercantilism is that hard money, gold and silver, is the basic wealth, that a given state should aim to acquire as much hard money as possible, and that therefore it should aim always at a "favorable balance of trade." It encourages exports to bring in money from abroad and discourages imports to prevent money from being paid out; it puts high protective tariffs against imports, and perhaps even places bounties on exports. In this simple form, the doctrine can readily be made absurd. A country that took in huge amounts of gold and silver would thereby simply increase prices within its borders, for gold and silver are merely media of exchange. No one can eat the precious metals or even find much practical use for them.

But mercantilism was much more than an oversimple and perhaps mistaken theory of international trade. It was part and parcel of the early modern effort to construct strong, efficient, political units. The mercantilists quite frankly aimed to make a given nation as self-sustaining as possible, as independent as possible of the need to import from other nations, which were its rivals and its potential enemies. As a policy, it is not entirely remote from us today; indeed, there are those who maintain that the policy of most twentieth-century nations is "neo-mercantilism."

Within a given nation, the mercantilists held that national production should provide the necessities of life for a hard-working population, and the necessities of power for a nation able to fight and win wars. These ends and the means for achieving them, they believed, demanded planning and control from above. They did not think that the old traditional ways of manor and guild, the old standard of the "just price," brought out the energies and abilities needed in an expanding economy. They were all for sweeping away these remnants of medieval controls. But they did not believe, as the free-trade economists after them were to believe, that all that was necessary was to destroy these controls and leave individual businessmen free to do whatever they thought would enrich them most as individuals. Instead, the mercantilists would channel the national economic effort by government subsidies, by grants of monopolies, by direct production in government-run industries, by encouraging scientific and technological research, and of course by protective tariffs.

At this point we come back to a phase of the expansion of Europe. Already in the seventeenth century many foodstuffs and raw materials were more easily available overseas than in Europe. The colonies could supply necessities that could not be so well produced at home, but that thanks to the existence of the colonies need not be imported from a rival. Thus the mercantilist viewed France overseas as a special part of France, a part that should be run from the homeland by a strong government, as indeed the homeland itself should be managed. Since the homeland produced industrial goods and the colonies produced raw materials, the two were mutually supplementary, and free trade between the two would give each partner what it needed. This mercantilistic attitude toward colonies was held not only by absolutist France and Spain, but by the more limited governments of England and Holland.

Mercantilism in Practice: Colbert

The great practitioner of mercantilism, Colbert, never quite attained the supremacy reached by Richelieu and Mazarin; he was the collaborator, never the master, of Louis XIV. Other great ministers, Louvois for military affairs especially, stood in the way of his supremacy. Yet Colbert was influential in all matters affecting the French economy, most interested in foreign trade and in the colonies, and therefore in the merchant marine and in the navy. His hand was in everything, in invention, in technological education, in attracting enterprising foreigners to settle in France, in designing and buildings ships, in founding and encouraging industries. The eight big volumes of his Letters, Instructions, and Memorials, published in the nineteenth century, gave an admirable general view of the activities of this first great modern exponent of the controlled economy—not yet by any means the "welfare state."

Whether the great prosperity France achieved in the first thirty years of Louis' reign came about because of, or in spite of, the mercantilist policies of Colbert is a question difficult to answer. The convinced adherent of laissez-faire doctrines will argue that France would have done even better had her businessmen been left alone. But this was not the seventeenth-century way, not even in England and Holland. Under the mercantilist regime, France did attain an undoubted leadership in European industry and commerce. That lead she lost, in part because the last two wars of Louis XIV were ruinously expensive, in part because from the eighteenth century on France's rival, England, took to the new methods of power machinery and concentrated on large-scale production of inexpensive goods. France remained largely true to the policies set by Colbert—relatively small-scale production of a variety of goods, often luxuries, and predominantly consumers' goods. But the difference between French and English industry was not so much a difference of economic theory as a difference of natural resources—coal, iron, and water power were more easily exploited in England than in France—and, even more, a difference in the focus of national energies. France in early modern times, like Spain before her, spent an undue proportion of her national product in the ultimately unfruitful effort to achieve the political domination of Europe and the overseas world by force of arms.

These late seventeenth-century wars bring up a still unsolved problem: does—or at any rate, until the present, did—modern warfare act as a stimulant, or as a depressive on economic life? Did they more than balance their destructiveness by creating demand for goods, for new techniques, by giving "full employment" if only as soldiers? It is pretty clear that the late seventeenth century was in general a period of economic decline or crisis in Europe. But it is not clear that Louis' wars were a "cause" of these economic difficulties. Sufficient perhaps here for us to note that France, in particular, carried the heavy debt burden of these wars into the eighteenth century, which was to culminate in the great French Revolution.

III: England in Revolution

The Constitutional Tradition

To the men of the seventeenth century, France seemed the home of a stable government and society, and England seemed the land of violence and change. Within the century, to the scandal of continental Europeans living under divine-right monarchies, the English cut one king's head off and drove another into exile. It is hard for us today, to whom the English seem the most orderly of people, to realize that they were once regarded as politically disorderly, as hard to govern. Yet they ushered in with considerable turmoil an important modification of the new-model state, a modification that was to make its way with greater or less success, and greater or less deviation from the English original, all through western civilization by the end of the nineteenth century.

This modification should not yet in the seventeenth century be given the name of "democracy"; it is more safely called constitutional, representative or parliamentary government. To the extent that such government used to the full the new methods of professional administration developed in the fifteenth and sixteenth centuries, it may be considered just as "absolute" as any divine-right monarchy. But representative government has grown in the West under historical conditions that have provided a check on the potential absolutism it shares with divine-right monarchy. This check is the concept of a "constitution," a set of rules, written or traditional, not to be altered by the ordinary processes of government. These rules are in the modern western tradition felt to be limitations on the authority even of a government elected by the majority of the people, a guarantee to the individuals and to groups that they may do certain things even though men in governmental posts of authority do not want them to. Without these rules and habits of constitutionalism, or "civil rights," the machinery of parliamentary government could be as ruthlessly absolute as the machinery of Soviet Russian government.

English-speaking people throughout the world have come to believe that England has always had a representative and constitutional government; or, put negatively, that England never went through the stage of divine-right absolute monarchy most of the continental states went through. This belief is partly correct. But it would be better stated as follows: England in the fifteenth and sixteenth centuries began, as did the continental states, to develop a new-model centralized monarchy; but the development in the seventeenth century was checked and modified by the continued growth of representative institutions at both the local and the national level. In France, for instance, cardinals and kings were able to raise money and govern without the Estates-General. In England, Parliament met in 1629 and quarreled violently with King Charles I. For eleven long years, until 1640, Charles too governed without calling Parliament. But in 1640 he felt obliged to call Parliament and, though he dismissed it at once when it proved recalcitrant, he had to call another in that same year. This was the famous Long Parliament, which sat—with changes of personnel and with interruptions—for twenty years, and which made the revolution that ended the threat of absolute monarchy in England. If we understand why Charles, unlike his French counterpart, was obliged to call Parliament, we have gone a long way toward under-

King Charles I, by Van Dyck.

standing why England had a head start in modern representative government.

One very basic reason goes back to later medieval history. As we have already seen, the English Parliament diverged in one important detail of organization from continental parliaments. The House of Commons represented two different social groups not brought together in one house on the Continent, the aristocratic "knights of the shire" and the largely middle-class "burgesses" of the towns and cities. The strength of the Commons lay in the practical working together of both groups, which intermarried quite freely and, in spite of some economic and social tensions, tended to form a single ruling class with membership open to talented and energetic men from the lower classes.

The Middle Ages left another important heritage—the persistence in local government of magistrates who were not directly dependent on the Crown. We must not exaggerate: England, too, had its bureaucrats, its clerks and officials in the royal pay. But

whereas in France and in other continental countries the new bureaucracy tended to take over almost all governmental business, especially financial and judicial affairs, in England the gentry and the higher nobility continued to do important local work. The Elizabethan Poor Law of 1601 put the care of the needy not under any national ministry but squarely on the smallest local units, the parishes, where decisions lay ultimately with the amateur, unpaid justices of the peace, recruited from the gentry. In short, the privileged classes were not, as in France, shelved, thrust aside by paid agents of the central government; nor did they, as in Prussia, become themselves mere agents of the Crown. Instead, they preserved a firm base in local government and an equally firm base in the House of Commons. When Charles I tried to govern without the consent of these privileged classes, when he tried to raise from them and their dependents money to run a bureaucratic government without these privileged amateurs, they had a solid institutional basis from which to resist.

The Role of the Crown

But they had to struggle. They had to fight a civil war. No matter how much emphasis the historian may put on the social and institutional side, he cannot ignore what looks like the sheer accident of human personality. The Tudors from Henry VII to Elizabeth I, with some faltering under Edward VI and Mary, had been strong personalities and had been firmly—quite as firmly as any Valois or Habsburg—convinced that they were called to absolute monarchy. They had slowly built up a very strong personal rule, handling their Parliaments skillfully, giving in occasionally in detail, but holding the reins firmly. Henry VIII and his daughter Elizabeth both commanded the kind of devotion from their subjects that can be built in time into formidable personal rule; they could hold the emotional loyalty of the English. Their successors could not. Elizabeth I was childless, and in 1603 she was succeeded by the son of her old rival and cousin, Mary Queen of Scots. James Stuart, already King of Scotland as James VI, became James I of England (1603-1625), thus bringing the two countries, still legally separate, under the same personal rule. James was a pedant by temperament, very sure of himself, and above all sure that he was as much a divine-right monarch as his French cousins. He was a Scot—that is, a foreigner—and as such an object of distrust to his English subjects. He lacked entirely the Tudor heartiness and tact, the gift of winning people to him.

His son, Charles I (1625-1649), under whom the divine-right monarchy came to an end, was by no means as unattractive a monarch and, partly because of his martyrdom, has had his ardent partisans among historians. But if he had many of the graces of a monarch, it is still true that Charles I was no man to continue the work of the Tudors. He was quite as sure as his father had been that God had called him to rule England, and he could never make the happy compromises the Tudors made.

Issues between Crown and Parliament

The fundamental fact about the actual break between the first two Stuarts and their parliamentary opponents is that *both* were in a sense revolutionaries. Both were seeking to bend the line of English constitutional growth away from the Tudor compromise of a strong Crown working with and through a late medieval Parliament based on the alliance of gentry and commercial classes. James and Charles were seeking to bend the line toward divine-right monarchy of the continental type; the parliamentarians were seeking to bend it toward something quite as new in England

and in the world, the establishment of a legislative body possessing the final authority in the making *and carrying out* of law and policy.

Behind this struggle lay the fact that the business of state was gradually growing in scope and therefore in money cost. Foreign relations, for instance, which had been most rudimentary in the Middle Ages, had by the end of the sixteenth century begun to take on modern forms, with a central foreign office, ambassadors, clerks, and the like, all needing money and personnel. The money required by Stuarts—and indeed by Bourbons, Habsburgs, and the rest of the continental monarchs—did not simply go for high living by royalty and the support of parasitic nobles. It went to run a government that was beginning to take over the many functions of the new-model state. Basically, James I and Charles I failed to get the money they needed because those from whom they sought it, the ruling classes, succeeded in placing the raising and spending of it in their own hands through parliamentary supremacy. The Parliament that won that supremacy was in fact a committee —a big one, but still a committee—of the ruling classes. It was not a democratic legislature.

One final fact in the background of this struggle between Crown and Parliament: religion played a major part in welding both sides into cohesive fighting groups. The struggle for power in England was in part a struggle to impose a uniform worship on Englishmen. The royalist cause was identified with High Church Anglicanism, that is, with an episcopalian church government and a liturgy and theology that makes it a "sacramental" religion relatively free from the "liberal" or "rationalist" touches of other forms of Protestantism, and quite free from "holy rolling." The parliamentary cause, at first supported by many moderate Low Church Anglicans, also attracted a strong Puritan or Calvinist element. Later, it came under the control of the Presbyterians and then of the extreme Puritans, the Independents or Congregationalists.

The term "Puritanism" in seventeenth-century English history is a confusing one, and must remain so to those who demand simple, clear-cut definitions. For it was used as a blanket term to cover a wide variety of religious experience, from that of moderate Anglicans to that of the radical splinter sects of the 1640's and 1650's. Its core went back to Zwingli and Calvin, to the repudiation of Catholic sacramental religion and the rejection of music and the adornment of the church. It placed a positive emphasis on sermons, on simplicity in church and out, and on "purifying" the tie between the worshiper and his God of what the Puritans thought of as Catholic "superstitions" and "corruptions."

The Reign of James I
(1603-1625)

In the troubled reign of James I, we may distinguish three major threads of the struggle in which his son was to go under —money, foreign policy, and religion. In all three issues, the Crown and its opposition each tried to bend the line of constitutional development in its own direction. In raising money, James sought to make the most of revenues which he did not need to ask Parliament to grant. Parliament sought to make the most of its own control over the purse strings by insisting on the principle that any new revenue-raising had to be approved by Parliament. On the whole, James got along, though he levied some taxes without parliamentary grant. One of these, on the somewhat insignificant commodity of imported dried currants, was refused by an importer named Bate. Bate's case was decided in favor of the Crown by the Court of Exchequer, and the decision attracted much attention because the judges held the King's powers in general to be absolute. Then a royal "benevolence"—a euphemism

for a direct imposition on an individual—was resisted by a certain St. John, and his appeal was sustained by the Chief Justice, Sir Edward Coke. James then summarily dismissed Coke from office and thereby once again focused the attention of his subjects on his broad use of the royal prerogative.

Foreign affairs had been regarded by the Tudors as strictly a matter of royal prerogative. The delicate problem of marriage for Elizabeth I, for instance, had indeed concerned her Parliaments and the public. But Parliament made no attempt to dictate a marriage, and Elizabeth was most careful not to offend her subjects in her own tentative negotiations. On the other hand, when James I openly sought a princess of hated Spain as a wife for his son Charles, his subjects did more than grumble. The Commons in 1621 made public petition against the Spanish marriage. When James rebuked them for what he considered meddling, the House drew up the Great Protestation, the first of the great documents of the English Revolution, in which they used what they claimed were the *historic* liberties, franchises, privileges, and jurisdictions of Parliament to assert what was in fact a *new* claim for parliamentary control of foreign affairs. James responded by dissolving Parliament and imprisoning four of its leaders. The Spanish marriage fell through, but the betrothal of Charles in 1624 to a French princess, also a Catholic, was hardly more popular with the English people.

In religion, the policy of Elizabeth I had been broad and moderate. Though she persecuted—that is, refused to permit open religious services of—both extremes of Catholics and Puritans, she allowed much variety of actual practice within the Anglican Church. James neatly summed up his religious policy in the phrase, "No bishop, no king"—which meant that he believed the enforcement of the bishops' monarchical power in religion was essential· to the maintenance of his own monarchical power. James at once tightened up on nonconformity. He called a conference at Hampton Court in 1604, at which he presided in person and used the full force of his pedantic scholarship against the Puritans. The conference dissolved with no real meeting of minds, and royal policy continued to favor the High Church, anti-Puritan party. In spite of James' failure to achieve anything like religious agreement among his subjects, his reign is a landmark in the history of Christianity among English-speaking peoples. In 1611, after seven years' labor, a committee of forty-seven ministers authorized by him achieved the English translation of the Bible that is still used among all the astounding variety of Protestant sects in the English-speaking world. The King James Version remains a masterpiece of Elizabethan prose, perhaps the most remarkable literary achievement a committee has ever made.

The Troubles of Charles I

Under Charles I, all his father's difficulties came to a head very quickly. England had been maneuvered into war against Catholic Spain, always a popular kind of war among Englishmen of the time. Though English forces were small, any war costs money; Charles found Parliament most reluctant to grant him funds, even though the members hated Spain. Meanwhile, in spite of his French queen, Charles got involved in a war against France. This he financed in part by a forced loan from his wealthier subjects, and by quartering his troops in private houses at the householders' expense. Consequently, Parliament in 1628 passed the Petition of Right, in which some of the most basic rules of modern constitutional government are first explicitly stated: No taxation without the consent of Parliament; no billeting of soldiers in private houses; no martial law in time of peace; no one to be imprisoned except on a specific charge and subject to the

protection of regular legal procedure. Note that all the principles set forth in this Stuart Magna Carta are limitations on the Crown.

Charles, to get money in new subsidies from Parliament, consented to the Petition of Right. But he also collected duties not authorized by Parliament. Parliament protested by resolutions, not only against his unauthorized taxes but also against his High Church policy. The King now veered from conciliation to firmness; he dissolved Parliament in 1629 and then had Sir John Eliot, mover of the resolutions, and eight other members arrested. Eliot died in prison in the Tower of London, the first martyr on the parliamentary side.

For the next eleven years (1629-1640), Charles governed without a Parliament. He squeezed every penny he could get out of the customary royal revenues, never quite breaking with precedent by imposing a wholly new tax, but stretching precedent beyond what his opponents thought reasonable. Ship money illustrates how Charles worked. It had been levied by the Crown before, but only on coastal towns for naval expenditures in wartime; Charles now imposed ship money on inland areas, and in peacetime. A very rich gentleman named John Hampden from inland Buckinghamshire refused to pay it. In 1637, he lost his case in court by a narrow margin, but he directed public attention to the new expedient.

In religious matters, Charles was under the sympathetic guidance of a very High Church archbishop of Canterbury, William Laud, who systematically enforced Anglican conformity and deprived even moderate Puritans of their pulpits. In civil matters, Charles made use of an opportunist conservative, Thomas Wentworth, Earl of Strafford, who had deserted the parliamentary side.

As with all modern revolutions, including our own American one of 1776, there arises this problem: just what were the tensions of this society, just who were hurt, oppressed—or felt so—what changes were being promoted by whom, resisted by whom? In other words, we face the old problem of the causes of a great successful revolution. Americans tend to seek some economic explanation, even if it is exalted into a moral issue such as "taxation without representation is tyranny." Certainly in seventeenth-century England the great changes of the sixteenth century—confiscation of monastic lands, the shift to sheep farming, enclosures, the new commerce, inflation, the legacy of the Wars of the Roses, the many "squeezes" on those with fixed possessions —all this had hurt many people, put them in a mood to blame "the government," to support parliamentary attacks on royal prerogative.

England was seething with repressed political and religious passions underneath the outward calm of these years of personal rule. Yet England was certainly prosperous, at least as prosperous as she had been under Tudor rule. The total weight of the taxation that offended so many Englishmen was, as far as one can tell from the imperfect statistics of early modern times, less than on the Continent. The Englishmen who resisted the Crown by taking arms against it were clearly not downtrodden, poverty-stricken people revolting from despair, but hopeful, self-assertive people out to get the things they wanted—power, wealth, their own form of religious worship, their own newly conceived *rights*.

The Road to Civil War, 1638-1642

The English revolution actually began in Scotland. If Charles I had not had to contend with his fellow Scots, he could perhaps have weathered his financial difficulties for a long time. But in Scotland Laud's attempt to enforce the English High Church ritual and organization came up against the three-generations-old Scots Pres-

byterianism. In 1638, a Solemn League and Covenant banded the Presbyterians of the Scottish Kirk to resist Charles by force if need be. Charles marched north against the Scots but concluded a temporizing pacification in 1639. Even this mild campaign had been too much for the treasury, and Charles, facing an empty treasury, called an English Parliament in 1640. This Short Parliament, firmly denying any money until the piled-up grievances of nearly forty years were settled, was dissolved at once. Then the Scots went to war again, and Charles, defeated in a skirmish, bought them off by promising them £850 a day until peace was made. Since he could not raise £850 a day, he had to call another Parliament, which became the famous Long Parliament of the revolution.

Holding the unpaid Scots army as a club over Charles' head, the Long Parliament put through a great series of reforms that struck at the royal power. It abolished ship money and other disputed taxes. It disbanded the unpopular royal administrative courts, like the Star Chamber (see Chapter X), which had become symbols of Stuart absolutism. The Star Chamber, operating as it did without the safeguards for the accused afforded by common law courts, had most certainly been used by the Stuarts in ways contrary to English traditions. Up to now, Parliament had been called and dismissed at the pleasure of the Crown; the Triennial Act of 1640 made obligatory the summoning of future Parliaments every three years, even if the Crown did not wish to do so. Parliament also attacked the royal favorites, whom Charles reluctantly abandoned. Archbishop Laud was removed, and Strafford, having been declared guilty of treason, was executed in May, 1641.

Meanwhile, Strafford's unfeeling policy toward the Irish had borne fruit in a terrible rebellion that resulted in the massacre of thousands of Protestants in northern Ireland. Parliament, unwilling to trust Charles with an army to put down this rebellion, drew up in 1641 the Grand Remonstrance summarizing all its complaints. Charles now made a final attempt to repeat the tactics that had worked in 1629. Early in 1642, he ordered the arrest of five of his leading opponents in the House of Commons, including Hampden of the ship-money case. The five took refuge in the privileged political sanctuary of the City of London, where the king could not reach them. Charles I left for the north and in the summer of 1642 rallied an army at Nottingham; Parliament simply took over the central government. The Civil War had begun.

Signs were already evident during these first years of political jockeying that strong groups in England and in Parliament wanted something more than a return to the Tudor balance between Crown and Parliament, and between religious conservatives and religious radicals. In politics, the Nineteen Propositions that Parliament submitted to the King in June, 1642, and that he of course rejected, would have firmly established parliamentary supremacy and left Charles a rather weak "constitutional" monarch much like the present English queen. In religion, the Root and Branch Bill, introduced in 1641 but not enacted, would have radically reformed the whole Church of England, destroying, "root and branch," the bishops and much of what had already become traditional in Anglican religious practices. The moderates in politics and religion were plainly going to have trouble defending their middle-of-the-road policies among the extremists of a nation split by civil war.

The Civil War, 1642-1649

England split along lines partly territorial, partly social and economic. The royalist strength lay largely in the north and west, relatively less urban and less prosperous than other parts and largely controlled by country gentlemen loyal to throne and altar. Parliamentary strength lay largely in the south and east, especially in the great city of London and in East Anglia, where even the gentry were firm Puritans (see map on p. 538). The Scots were always in the offing, distrustful of an English Parliament but quite as distrustful of a king who had sought to foist episcopacy on their Kirk.

In the field, the struggle was at first indecisive. The royalists, or "cavaliers," recruited from gentlemen used to riding, had at first the important advantage of superior cavalry. What swung the balance to the side of Parliament was the development under a Puritan gentleman named Oliver Cromwell (1599-1658) of a special force, recruited from ardent Puritans of the eastern counties, and gradually forged under strict discipline into the famous "Ironsides." At Marston Moor in 1644, Cromwell won a crucial battle. The parliamentary army, now reorganized into the "New Model Army," staffed by radicals in religion and politics, stood as "Roundheads" (from their short-cropped hair) against the cavaliers. At the battle of Naseby in 1645, the New Model was completely victorious over the King, and Charles in desperation took refuge with the Scots army, who turned him over to the English Parliament in return for £400,-000 back pay.

Now there arose a situation that was to be repeated, with variations for time and place, in the French Revolution in 1792 and the Russian Revolution in 1917. The group of moderates who had begun the revolution and who still controlled the Long Parliament were confronted by the much more radical group who controlled the New Model Army. In religion, the moderates, seeking to retain some ecclesiastical discipline and formality, were Presbyterians or Low Church Anglicans; in politics, they were constitutional monarchists. The radicals, who were opposed to disciplined churches, were Independents or Congregationalists, and they already so distrusted Charles that they were able at least to contemplate that extraordinary possibility, an

England under a republican form of government. The situation was complicated by the Scots, firmly Presbyterian and hostile to the radical Roundheads, whom they regarded as religious anarchists.

The years after 1645 are filled with difficult negotiations, during which Charles stalled for time to gain Scots help. In 1648, Cromwell beat the invading and now royalist Scots at Preston, and his army seized the King. Parliament, with the moderates still in control, now refused to do what the army wanted, to dethrone Charles. The Roundhead leaders then ordered Colonel Pride to exclude by force from the Commons ninety-six Presbyterian members. This the Colonel did in December, 1648, in true military fashion, with no pretense of legality. After "Pride's Purge" only some sixty radicals remained of the more than five hundred members originally composing the Long Parliament; they were known henceforth as the Rump Parliament. The Rump brought Charles to trial before a special high court of trustworthy radicals, who condemned him to death. On January 30, 1649, Charles I was beheaded.

Cromwell
and the Interregnum, 1649-1660

England was now a republic, under the government known as the Commonwealth. But the radicals did not dare call a free election, which would almost certainly have gone against them. From the start, the Commonwealth was in fact the dictatorship of a radical minority come to power through the tight organization of the New Model Army. From the start, too, Cromwell was the dominating personality of the new government. He was, in a sense, an unwilling dictator. In religion an earnest and sincere Independent, but no fanatic, a patriotic Englishman, strong-minded, stubborn, but no pathological luster after power, by no means unwilling to compromise, he

was nevertheless a prisoner of his position.

Cromwell faced a divided England, where the majority were no doubt royalist at heart and certainly sick of the fighting, the confiscations, the endless changes of the last decade. He faced a hostile Scotland and an even more hostile Ireland. The disorders in England had encouraged the Catholic Irish to rebel once more against the Protestant English "garrison." Finally, Cromwell faced a war with Holland, brought on largely by the Navigation Act of 1651, a typically mercantilist measure. By forbidding the importation of goods into England and the colonies except in English ships or in ships of the country producing the imported goods, the Navigation Act deliberately struck at the Dutch carrying trade.

By 1654, Cromwell had mastered these foes. He himself went to Ireland and suppressed the rebellion with bloodshed that is still not forgotten. In the so-called "Cromwellian Settlement," he dispossessed native

Oliver Cromwell dissolving Parliament, 1653.

CHAPTER XV

Irish landholders in favor of Protestants; he achieved order in Ireland, but not peace. Charles II, eldest son of the martyred Charles I, landed in Scotland, accepted the Covenant—that is, guaranteed the Presbyterian faith as the established Scottish Kirk —and led a Scots army once more against the English. Once more the English army proved unbeatable, and at the battle of Worcester in September, 1651, the hope of the Stuarts went down for the time. Charles took refuge on the Continent, after a romantic escape in disguise. The Dutch War was almost wholly a naval one, and ended victoriously for the English in 1652. Cromwell also waged an aggressive war against Spain, from whom the English acquired the rich Caribbean sugar island of Jamaica. Even in this time of troubles, the British Empire kept on growing.

Cromwell, however, could not master the Rump Parliament, which brushed aside his suggestions for an increase of its membership and a reform of its procedures. In April, 1653, he forced its dissolution by appearing in Parliament with a body of soldiers. In December, 1653, Cromwell took the decisive step of setting himself up as Lord Protector of the Commonwealth of England, Scotland, and Ireland, with a written constitution—the only one England has ever had—known as the Instrument of Government. Under this constitution an elected Parliament of 460 members was provided for. It was in fact chosen by Puritan sympathizers, for no royalist dared vote. Even so, the Lord Protector had constant troubles with his Parliaments, and in 1656 yielded to pressure and accepted some modifications to his dictatorship. Oliver Cromwell died in 1658, and was succeeded as Lord Protector by his son Richard. But Richard Cromwell was a nonentity, and the army soon seized control. By now some army leaders saw in the restoration of the Stuarts the best hope of putting an end to the chronic political turbulence. To insure the legality of the move, General Monk, com-

mander of the Protectorate's forces in Scotland, summoned back the Rump and readmitted the living members excluded by Pride's Purge. This partially reconstituted Long Parliament enacted the formalities of restoration, and in 1660 Charles Stuart came back from exile to reign as Charles II.

The Revolution in Review

It is no doubt misleading to say that there was a Reign of Terror in the English Revolution. Much of the bloodshed was the respectable bloodshed of formal battle between organized armies, not the revolutionary bloodshed of guillotine, lynching, and judicial murder. Still, Charles I was beheaded; Strafford, Laud, and others suffered the death penalty; royalists had their properties confiscated. Above all, the Puritans at the height of their rule in the early 1650's attempted to enforce on the whole population the difficult, austere life of the Puritan ideal. This enforcement took the familiar form of "blue laws," of prohibitions on horse-racing, gambling, cock-fighting, bear-baiting, dancing on the green, fancy dress, the theatre, on a whole host of ordinary phases of daily living.

This English Reign of Terror and Virtue, coming too early for modern techniques of propaganda and control over the masses, was in fact very different from the absolutism, say, of the communist minority in the Russian Revolution. Many an Anglican clergyman, though officially "plundered"— that is, deprived of his living—kept up his worship in private houses; many a cock fight went on in secluded spots. Nevertheless, the strict code was there, with earnest persons to enforce it, and with implacable enemies to oppose it. The famous remark of the historian Macaulay—that the Puritans prohibited bear-baiting, not because it gave pain to the bear, but because it gave pleasure to the spectators—is a sample of the deep hostility that still survives in England toward the reign of the Puritan "Saints." So too is the popular doggerel of the time:

> To Banbury came I, O profane one,
> Where I saw a Puritane-one,
> Hanging of his cat on Monday
> For killing of a mouse on Sunday.*

Many Englishmen have seemed rather ashamed of their great revolution, preferring to call it the "Civil War" or the "Great Rebellion," and recalling instead as their "Glorious Revolution" the decorous movement of 1688-89, to which we shall come in a moment. Yet the events of 1640-1660 are of major importance, not only in the history of England, but in the history of the West. Here for the first time the absolute monarchy was firmly challenged, and a constitutional and representative government was set up, based on a legislature backed by politically active private citizens. Though the Stuarts were restored, no English king ever again could hope to rule without a Parliament or restore the Court of Star Chamber or take ship money, benevolences, and other controversial taxes. Parliament thenceforward retained that critical weapon of the legislative body in a limited monarchy, ultimate control of the public purse by periodic grants of taxes.

Moreover, minority groups had gone much further, and in their extraordinary fermentations had foreshadowed much modern social thought and action. One such group, the Levellers, though they never attained power, won considerable sympathy from the revolutionary army. They put forward a program later carried by emigrants to the American colonies. The Levellers anticipated much of what we now call political democracy—universal suffrage, regularly summoned Parliaments, progressive taxation, separation of Church and State, protection of the individual against arbitrary arrest, and the like. There are even

---

* Richard Brathwaite, *Barnabee's Journal* (London, 1774), Pt. I.

hints of the "socialistic" drive toward economic equality, though in those days it was tied up closely with Biblical ideas. The Diggers, for example, were a small sect that preached the sharing of earthly goods in a kind of communism. They actually dug up public lands in Surrey near London and began planting vegetables. They were driven off, but not before they had got their ideas into circulation. The Fifth Monarchy men, the Millennarians, and a dozen other radical sects preached the Second Coming and the achievement of some kind of utopia on earth.

Still more important, there emerged from these English struggles, even more clearly than from the religious wars on the Continent, the conception of religious toleration. The Independents, while they were in opposition, stood firmly on the right of religious groups to worship God as they wished. Though in their brief tenure of power they showed a willingness to persecute, they were never firmly enough in the saddle to make of England another Geneva or Boston. Moreover, many of the Puritans sincerely believed that compulsion should not be exercised to secure conformity.

At least one of the sects held to the idea and practice of religious toleration as a positive good. The Quakers, led by George Fox (1624-1691), were Puritans of the Puritans. They themselves eschewed all worldly show, finding even buttons ostentatious, the names of days and months indecently pagan, the polite form "you" in the singular a piece of social hypocrisy and legal oaths or oathtaking most impious. Hence they met for worship not on the day of the pagan sungod, but on First Day; they addressed any man as "thee" or "thou"; and they took so seriously the basic Protestant doctrine of the priesthood of the believer that they did entirely without a formal ordained ministry. In the Religious Society of Friends, as they are properly known, any worshiper who felt the spirit move might testify in what in other sects would be a sermon. But

Quakers felt too deeply the impossibility of forcing the inner light in any man, were too sure that conversion is the work of God alone, to try to *make* men Quakers. They would abstain entirely from force, particularly from that shocking kind of force we call war, and would go their own Christian way in peace, in the hope that in God's good time men would freely come to God's way.

Still another of our basic freedoms owes much to this English experience. Freedom of speech was a fundamental tenet of the Puritans, though again at the height of their power they by no means lived up to it. The pamphlet literature of the early years of the great turmoil is a lively manifestation of free speech in practice. And it received a classic statement in the *Areopagitica* of the poet, John Milton, who was the secretary of the Commonwealth.

The Restoration, 1660-1688

The Restoration of 1660 kept Parliament essentially supreme, but attempted to undo some of the work of the Revolution. Episcopacy was restored in England and Ireland, though not as a state church in Scotland. Against the "dissenters," as Protestants who would not accept the Church of England were then termed, the so-called Clarendon Code set up all sorts of civil liabilities and obstructions. For instance, by the Five-Mile Act all Protestant ministers who refused to subscribe to Anglican orthodoxy were forbidden to come within five miles of any town where they had previously preached. Yet the dissenters continued to dissent without heroic sufferings. In characteristically English fashion, the Test Act of 1672, which prescribed communion according to the Church of England on all officeholders, local as well as national, was simply got around in various ways, though it was not actually repealed until 1828. One way was "occasional conformity," by which a dissenter of not too

strict conscience might worship as a Congregationalist, say, all year, but might once or twice take Anglican communion. Another, developed in the eighteenth century, was to permit dissenters to hold office, and then pass annually a bill of indemnity legalizing their illegal acts. Dissenters remained numerous, especially among the artisans and middle-class merchants, and as time went on they grew powerful, so that the "non-conformist conscience" was a major factor in English public life.

The Restoration was also a revulsion against Puritan ways. The reign of Charles II (1660-1685) is a period of moral looseness, of gay court life, of the Restoration drama with its indecent wit (the Puritans in power had closed the theaters), of the public pursuit of pleasure, at least among the upper classes. But the new Stuarts had not acquired political wisdom. Charles II dissipated some of the fund of good will with which he started by following a foreign policy that seemed to patriotic Englishmen too subservient to the wicked French King Louis XIV. The cynic is tempted to point out that, if Charles's alliance with Louis in 1670 was most un-English, it did result in the final extinction of any Dutch threat to English seapower. And it sealed a very important English acquisition, that of New Amsterdam, now New York, first taken in the Anglo-Dutch War of 1664-1667.

What really undid the later Stuarts and revealed their political ineptitude was the Catholic problem. Charles II had come under Catholic influence through his French mother and very possibly embraced the Roman religion before he died in 1685. Since he left no legitimate children, the crown passed to his brother, James II (1685-1688), who was already a declared Catholic. In the hope of enlisting the support of the dissenters for the toleration of Catholics, James II issued in 1687 a "Declaration of Indulgence," granting freedom of worship to *all* denominations, Protestant dissenters

Jack, with the superimposed crosses of St. George for England and St. Andrew for Scotland, was henceforth to be the national flag of Great Britain. The union, most necessary to insure the carrying out of the Hanoverian succession in both kingdoms, met with some opposition in both. But on the whole it went through with surprising ease, so great was Protestant fear of a possible return of the Catholic Stuarts. And, in spite of occasional sentimental outbreaks of Scottish nationalism even as late as our own day, the union has worked very well. With the whole of England and the colonies open to Scots businessmen, the nation famed for its thrifty and canny citizens achieved a prosperity it had never known before.

The Glorious Revolution did not, however, settle one other perennial problem— Ireland. The Catholic Irish rose in support of the exiled James II and were put down at the battle of the Boyne in 1690. William then attempted to apply moderation in his dealings with Ireland, but the Protestant "garrison" there soon forced him to return to the severe spirit of Cromwellian policy. Although Catholic worship was not actually forbidden, all sorts of galling restrictions were imposed on the Catholic Irish, including the prohibition of Catholic schools. Moreover, economic persecution was added to the religious, as Irish trade came under stringent mercantilist regulation. This was the Ireland whose misery inspired a great writer, Jonathan Swift, to make his bitter "modest proposal" that the impoverished Irish solve their economic problems by selling their babies as articles of food.

IV: The Century of Genius

In the seventeenth century the cultural, as well as the political, hegemony of Europe passed from Italy and Spain to France, England, and Holland. Especially in literature, the France of Racine, Molière, Boileau, Bossuet, and a host of others set the imprint of a style on the West. Yet the men who achieved the abiding effect of the seventeenth century on our culture were truly international in origin and outlook, and were rather philosophers and scientists than men of letters. When the twentieth-century philosopher, Alfred Whitehead, christened the 1600's the "century of genius," he was thinking above all of men like Galileo, Harvey, Newton, Descartes, Huyghens, and Pascal.

Natural Science

The Renaissance had certainly prepared the way for modern science, first by its successful attack on the abstract, deductive, over-refined late medieval philosophy, and second by its emphasis on this world, on the life of the senses (see Chapter XI). But the seventeenth century made the great advances that established the natural sciences as part of our common heritage. The Englishman Francis Bacon (1561-1626) bore a major part in the rise of modern science. Though he himself experimented in a somewhat random and unproductive fashion, he was the tireless proponent of one of the essentials of scientific achievement—observation of phenomena, the patient accumulation of data. If you observe enough facts, he seems to say, they will somehow make sense of themselves in a process called "induction," which he contrasts with the medieval "deduction" he was attacking:

There are and can be only two ways of searching into and discovering truth. The one [deduction] flies from the senses and particulars to the most general axioms, and from these principles, the truth of which it takes for settled and immovable, proceeds to judgment and to the discovery of middle axioms. And this way is now in fashion. The other [induction] derives axioms from the senses and particulars, rising by a gradual and unbroken ascent, so that it arrives at the most general axioms last of all. This is the true way, but as yet untried.*

Both deduction and induction are essential in science, but Bacon's emphasis on induction was a necessary corrective in his time and helped to set modern science on its way.

Progress along that way was facilitated by the invention of new instruments, by the establishment of scientific societies, and by the advance of mathematics. Both the great figures of the "century of genius" and scores of unknown or now forgotten individuals contributed to the new instruments that permitted more exact measurements and more detailed observations. For instance, Dutch glassmakers probably first put two lenses together and discovered that they could thus obtain a greater magnification. By 1610, the Italian Galileo was using the new device in the form of a telescope to observe the heavens, and by about 1680 the Dutchman Van Leeuwenhoek was using it in the form of a microscope to discover tiny creatures—protozoa—hitherto unknown. Working from a discovery made by Galileo, another Italian, Torricelli, invented the barometer. The Frenchman Pascal (1623-1662), using Torricelli's invention, proved by measuring the height of a column of mercury at the base and then at the top of a mountain that what we call air pressure diminishes with altitude, and went on to show that a vacuum is possible, in spite of the old adage "Nature abhors a vacuum."

Two important organizations promoting scientific investigation were the English Royal Society for Improving Natural Knowledge, founded in 1662, and the French *Académie des Sciences*, founded in

1666. The one, in characteristic English fashion, was a private undertaking; the other, sponsored by Colbert for the greater glory of Louis XIV and the mercantilistic state, was a government enterprise. Both financed experiments and both published scientific articles in their "house organs," the *Philosophical Transactions* and the *Journal des Sçavans* (savants). Scoffers sometimes mocked their activities; Charles II, for example, roared with laughter at the news that the Royal Society was weighing the air. But ultimately the scientific societies exerted a strong affirmative influence, at least on the community of learned men. It would be hard even today to improve on the Royal Society's statement of purpose, in which it promised "to examine all systems, theories, principles, hypotheses, elements, histories and experiments" and "to question and canvass all opinions, adopting nor adhering to none, till by mature debate and clear arguments, chiefly such as are deduced from legitimate experiments, the truth of such experiments be demonstrated invincibly."

Meanwhile mathematics took a great leap forward. In 1585, Stevin, a Fleming, published *The Decimal, Teaching with Unheard-of Ease How to Perform All Calculations Necessary among Men by Whole Numbers without Fractions*. A generation later, Napier, a Scot, offered *The Marvelous Rule of Logarithms* (1616), which provided the principle of the slide rule and a wonderful short cut in the laborious processes of multiplying, dividing, and taking square root. Next, the Frenchman Descartes worked out analytical geometry, which brings geometry and algebra together, as in the plotting of an algebraic equation on a graph. The mathematical achievements of the century culminated in the perfection of a method of dealing with variables and probabilities. Pascal had made a beginning with his studies of games of chance, and Dutch insurance actuaries had devised tables to show the life expectancy

---

* Bacon, *The Great Instauration.*

of their clients. Then Newton and the German Leibniz, apparently quite independently of one another, invented the calculus. The detailed description of the new invention must be left to the experts, but its practical value is indicated by the fact that without the calculus, and indeed without Cartesian (from Descartes) geometry, Newton could never have made the calculations supporting his revolutionary hypotheses in astronomy and physics.

The Englishman Isaac Newton (1642-1727), building on the work of earlier astronomers, especially Copernicus, Kepler, and Galileo, made the great theoretical generalization that is now, of course in simplified form, part of every schoolboy's picture of the astronomical universe. This is the law of gravitation. The sun, the planets, and their satellites are, according to this theory, held in their orbits by the force of mutual attraction. Newton stated the formula that this force is proportional to the product of the masses of two bodies attracted one to the other, and inversely proportional to the square of the distance between them. Modified by Einstein, the law still holds.

The law of gravitation is a part of physics as well as of astronomy. Physics too came of age in the seventeenth century, and like astronomy is capped by the work of Newton. Here too Galileo is of importance, though recent research has shown that a devoted follower may have invented the story of how by dropping balls of different weights from the Leaning Tower of Pisa he disproved Aristotle's theory that objects fall with velocities proportional to their weight. Galileo's studies of projectiles, pendulums, and falling and rolling bodies helped to establish modern ideas of acceleration. Newton, building on Galileo's work, formulated the three classic Laws of Motion:

1. That a body will continue in a state of rest, or of uniform motion in a straight line, until compelled to change its state by some force impressed upon it;

2. That every change of motion is proportional to the force that makes the change;

3. That to every action there is always an equal reaction.

Newton also contributed to optics, using a prism to separate sunlight into the colors of the spectrum. He demonstrated that objects only appear to be colored, that their color is not intrinsic but depends on their reflection and absorption of light. Newton first hit on some of his great discoveries when he was an undergraduate at Cambridge, but published them only many years later in the *Principia* (1687—"The Mathematical Principles of Natural Philosophy" is the English translation of the full Latin title). He won fame early and held it long, gaining successively a professorship at Cambridge, a knighthood, the presidency of the Royal Society, and a well-paid government post as Master of the Mint.

Meanwhile, the mechanical views of the physicists were invading the science of life itself, biology. In 1628, Harvey, the physician of Charles I, published his demonstration that the human heart is in fact a pump, and that the human blood is driven by the heart along a system of circulation. And in 1679 the Italian Borelli showed that the human arm is a lever, and that the muscles do mechanical "work."

The Implications of Scientific Progress

All these investigations in the various sciences tended to undermine the older Aristotelian concept of something "perfect." Instead of perfect circles, Keplerian and Newtonian astronomy posited ellipses. Instead of bodies moving in straight-forward fashion of themselves, Newton's laws of motion pictured bodies responding only to forces impressed upon them. All these investigations, in short, suggested a new major scientific generalization, a law or uniformity that simplified and explained, that co-ordinated many separate laws into one general law summing up millions of man-hours of investigation. The new law was not final and unalterable, and would almost certainly be modified, given time and further investigation. But still it would be a *relatively* permanent resting place, a plateau. Galileo almost made this achievement, and a dozen other major figures made essential contributions to the big generalization. It was Newton, however, who drew

Descartes, by Frans Hals.

everything together into that grand mechanical conception that has been called the "Newtonian world-machine."

The Newtonian world-machine and, indeed, the whole of the new science had very important theological and philosophical implications. Natural science, strictly speaking, does not deal with the great problems of theology and philosophy. It does not give men *ends*, purposes, but rather *means*, and the theories it provides are always *explanations*, not *justifications*. Yet, historically speaking, the rise of modern science has been associated with a very definite world-view and system of values, for which the best name is perhaps *rationalism*. This is a wide term. It is perhaps possible to be at the same time a rationalist and a believer in a supernatural God. Again, however, historically, the balance of the influence of rationalism in the West has been to banish God entirely, or at any rate reduce him to a First Cause that started this Newtonian world-machine going, but does not —indeed cannot—interfere with its working.

For the rationalist took as his model the neatly integrated mathematical universe that the scientists had worked out. He would not start with the revealed truths of Christianity, as the Schoolmen had done, but would question all formulations until he had something to start with as clear and as certain as the axioms of Euclidean geometry. Here is how the most influential of these philosophers, the Frenchman Descartes (1596-1650), began to put himself straight:

I thought . . . that I ought to reject as downright false all opinions which I could imagine to be in the least degree open to doubt— my purpose being to discover whether, after so doing, there might not remain, as still calling for belief, something entirely indubitable. Thus, on the ground that our senses sometimes deceive us, I was prepared to propose that no existing thing is such as the senses make us image [*sic*] it to be; and because in respect even of the very simplest geometrical questions some men err in reasoning . . . , I therefore rejected as false (recognising myself to be no less fallible than others) all the reasonings I have previously accepted as demonstrations; and, finally, when I considered that all the thoughts we have when awake can come to us in sleep (none of the latter being then true), I resolved to feign that all the things which had entered my mind were no more true than the illusions of my dreams. But I immediately became aware that while I was thus disposed to think that all was false, it was absolutely necessary that I who thus thought should be somewhat; and noting that this truth *I think, therefore I am,* was so steadfast and so assured that the suppositions of the sceptics, to whatever extreme they might all be carried, could not avail to shake it, I concluded that I might without scruple accept it as being the first principle of the philosophy I was seeking.[*]

From this start, Descartes arrived finally at God—but a God who in his mathematical orderliness, in his remoteness from this confusing world, must seem most unreal to any believer in a personal God.

Scientist and rationalist helped greatly to establish in the minds of educated men throughout the West two complementary concepts that were to give the Enlightenment of the eighteenth century a pattern of action toward social change, a pattern still of driving force in our world. These were first, the concept of a regular "natural" order underlying the apparent irregularity and confusion of the universe as it appears to unreflecting man in his daily experience; and second, the concept of a human faculty, best called "reason," buried and obscured in most men by their faulty traditional upbringing, but capable of being brought into effective play by a good—that is, rational—upbringing. Both these concepts can be found in some form in our western tradition at least as far back as the Greeks. What gives them novelty and force at the end of the seventeenth century is their being welded into the doctrine of progress—the belief that all human beings can attain here on earth a state of happiness, of perfection, hitherto in the West thought to be possible only for Christians in a state of grace, and for them only in a heaven after death.

Two literary movements of the end of the seventeenth century are neatly symptomatic of the coming Enlightenment—the quarrel of the "ancients" and the "moderns" in France, the "battle of the books" in England. In both these literary disputes the issue was fundamentally the same. Can any "modern" write or paint or do anything better than the Greeks and Romans? Or,

in terms of our own day, can we *progress* beyond those giants of old, beyond their Golden Age? It is significant that most Americans today would unhesitatingly answer that we *have* progressed far beyond the ancients. And it is significant of the turn the eighteenth century was to take that most of the educated public of the day generally considered the "moderns" to have won this battle of the books.

The Classical Spirit

Art and letters as well as science and philosophy had a part in setting the pattern of the Enlightenment. The characteristic style of the seventeenth century, which flowered in the France of Louis XIV, is often known as *l'esprit classique*. The classical spirit leans toward measure, toward discipline, toward conformity with "those rules of old discover'd, not deviz'd," toward a dignified eloquence, toward an aristocratic refinement and avoidance of the undignified that could forbid so vulgar an object as a handkerchief to the heroine in tears—that could in fact rather dislike even the tears. There seems something paradoxical in maintaining that devotees of the classical tradition could have aided in setting up attitudes that undermined the veneration paid those classics of classics, the Greeks and Romans. The paradox is heightened by the fact that the writers and artists of the Age of Louis XIV were generally pillars of the established order, supporters of authority and tradition, politically conservative.

The paradox, however, diminishes when you realize that the best writers of the age found in their classical models not a confirmation of existing standards but a better, simpler set of standards that the eighteenth century could later easily express in terms of nature and reason. Boileau (1636-1711), the chief literary critic of the day, who set the rules for writing poetry, issued the pronouncement, "Que toujours le bon sens

---

[*] *Discourse on Method,* Pt. IV, in *Descartes' Philosophical Writings,* N. K. Smith, ed. (London, 1952), 140-141.

CHAPTER XV

s'accorde avec le rhyme" (Always have good sense agree with the rhyme). The great French dramatists, in particular, were trying to find in the infinite variety of men and manners something universal, something typical of all men and all times. Molière (1622-1673) makes the main characters of his satirical comedies not only individuals but also social types—the miser in *L'Avare*, the hypocrite in *Tartuffe*, the boastful and ignorant newly rich man in *Le Bourgeois Gentilhomme*. Corneille (1606-1684) and Racine (1639-1699) followed the classical canons of tragedy. They took subjects from mythology and wrote in the rhymed couplets of Alexandrine verse. To observe the rigid rules governing time, place, and action—the "unities" derived from Aristotle's *Poetics*—they pruned the dramatic action of irrelevance and restricted it to one place and a time-span of twenty-four hours. But within this rigid form Corneille and Racine created moving portraits of human beings seeking exalted ideals of honor or crushed by overwhelming emotions. The French tragedies of the seventeenth century may be ranked next to the Greek tragedies of antiquity, not so much because of their classical form, but rather because of their psychological insight and emotional power.

Even in its broadest sense, the term "classical spirit" does not do justice to the full range of seventeenth-century literature. La Rochefoucauld (1613-1680) mastered an epigrammatic prose of classic simplicity but used it for devastatingly cynical maxims far removed from the lofty ethical decencies of the classics:

We all have enough strength to bear the misfortunes of others.... We generally give praise only in order to gain it for ourselves. ... Virtue in woman is often the result of love of reputation and ease.... We always find something not altogether displeasing in the misfortunes of our friends.°

_____
° *The Maxims of La Rochefoucauld*, F. G. Stevens, trans. (London, 1939), 9, 49, 65, 173.

With the seventeenth century the business of printing, as distinguished from the art of printing, began to take on some of the attributes of bigness. The number of people who could read increased all through the West, though most strikingly in northwestern Europe. From now on, there is a printed literature in all the main languages of the West, and a full history of ideas in the West would not neglect any of them. Yet seen in broad outline, German literature, though in bulk sufficient to occupy plenty of modern scholars, had not attained greatness or wide influence, and Spanish and Italian literature had passed their Renaissance peaks. The seventeenth was, as we have seen, the great century of French literary flowering. As yet, English remained a tongue peripheral to European culture, and English writers, even Shakespeare, and most certainly the Milton of *Paradise Lost,* were not generally known abroad. England by her political example, by her great contributions to natural science, and at the end of the century by her political and philosophical writers, Locke above all, had indeed entered fully into the current of the common culture of the West. But the most important work of the two great English scientists Newton and Harvey, as well as the most important theorizing of Francis Bacon, was first published in Latin.

Yet to all of us to whom English is a mother-tongue the seventeenth century produced one of the great classics, Milton. We have already noted his famous defense of freedom of the press, the *Areopagitica. Paradise Lost* is the only epic written in English in the grand style that still finds readers—and it does find them, not all of them compelled by the formalities of higher education. Milton must be tagged a Christian humanist; both terms are important. His classical erudition is to a twentieth-century American staggering, and he needs copious footnoting. He was an active worker on the Puritan side in the Great Revolution, and has left many incidental prose writings, all of which seem now in style extremely difficult.

For to the historian of culture the major fact of English writing in the seventeenth century is not Milton, classic though he is, nor the brilliant, witty, and indecent comedies of the Restoration stage, but the simplification, the clarification, the modernization of English prose style that was achieved in the last half of the century. At the level of high formal culture, and perhaps above all under the influence of the poet Dryden (1631-1700), English began to model itself on French, on its straightforward word-order, on its comparative brevity, and on its polish, neatness, and clarity. But also at a level addressed to the common man, and exemplified in the prose of John Bunyan (1628-1688) of *The Pilgrim's Progress* and later, in that of Daniel Defoe (c.1660-1731) of *Robinson Crusoe*, English began to simplify itself. Even a modern American can read a piece of English prose picked at random from writings of 1700 and not feel he is reading something strange; this would hardly be true of a random choice from a mere fifty years earlier, which would seem almost another language.

The Arts

The term "classical spirit" hardly expresses the full achievement of seventeenth-century art. The France of Louis XIV did indeed produce neoclassical monuments like the balanced and columned *exterior* of Versailles or of the wings of the Louvre in Paris. But the *interior* of Versailles has acres of ceiling painted with smirking cherubs. This lavish embellishment is one aspect of Baroque, the foremost artistic style of the century.

Baroque added a profusion of detail and fantastic and theatrical effects to the basic geometrical patterns of Renaissance design. Sir Christopher Wren used a moderate Baroque style, still somewhat under classical restraints, for St. Paul's Cathedral in London, the only major church building ever designed and completed by a single architect. The dramatic qualities of Baroque are evident at Rome in the vast open spaces and eye-catching colonnades of St. Peter's Square, and at Versailles in the Hall of Mirrors, the majestic Staircase of the Ambassadors, and the elaborate gardens, lagoons, and fountains. Baroque at its most fantastic produced the *baldacchino*, the twisting bronze canopy rising to a height of eight stories above the altar of St. Peter's. Though not Gothic in origin, the Baroque style yet achieved a kind of translation of Gothic decorative richness into classical terms. Some of its most interesting monuments are Mexican churches.

In painting, the late sixteenth-century master, El Greco, had achieved a thoroughly Baroque effect in his distorted and mystical canvases (see Chapter XIII). Velasquez (1599-1660), the outstanding Spanish painter of the seventeenth century, however, followed the secular and realistic aspects of the Renaissance tradition. A court painter, he did forty portraits of the Habsburg king, Philip IV, and in some of his best work he produced what one critic has called "optical," as opposed to "photographic," realism. Velasquez depicts what the eye sees at a glance, rather than what is actually there.

In the Low Countries, the chief centers of northern European painting, artists planted themselves thoroughly in the workaday world of business, farming, taverns, and even almshouses. The Fleming Rubens (1577-1640) not only received commissions from French and English royalty but also made a fortune from his art and established a studio with two hundred students, a veritable factory of painting. The rosy, fleshy nudes for which Rubens is famous have the exuberance of Baroque, and he himself worked on the grand scale, contributing, it has been estimated, at least in part to more than two thousand pictures. Most of the Flemish and Dutch masters of the seven-

The Baldacchino, St. Peter's, Rome.

Velasquez, "The Maids of Honor."

teenth century, however, seem rather apart from Baroque theatricality and still further apart from the "classical spirit." They were quite willing to paint handkerchiefs and even less dignified objects, and by their quiet realism they made the commonplace uncommonly lovely. In the hands of the greatest Dutch painter, Rembrandt (1609-1669), the commonplace—the municipal Night Watch, the Syndics of the Cloth Hall, even the Anatomy Lesson of Dr. Tulp—receives a transcendental glow that already deserves to be called "romantic." (See also Chapter XIII.)

In music, the term Baroque conveys much of the accomplishment of the seventeenth century. Here Italy took the lead, following in the paths laid out by the musicians of the Renaissance (see Chapter XI). In Rome, Frescobaldi (1583-1644) released the dramatic potentialities of that most Baroque instrument, the organ, and attracted thousands to his recitals at St. Peter.'s In Venice, Monteverdi (1567-1643), contending that

"speech should be the master of music, not its servant," backed his contention in practice by writing the first important operas. This Baroque compound of music and the theater gained immediate popularity. Venice soon had no fewer than sixteen opera houses, which were already establishing the tradition of slighting the chorus and orchestra to pay for the "stars." The star system reached its height at Naples, the operatic capital of the later 1600's. There conservatories (originally institutions for conserving orphans) stressed voice training; composers provided operatic vehicles that were little more than loose collections of arias; and the crowning touch of unreality came with the Neapolitan custom of having the male roles sung by women and the female by *castrati*—that is, eunuchs, permanent boy sopranos.

Seventeenth-century opera at its best rose above the level of stilted artificiality. Purcell (1658-1695), the organist of Westminster Abbey and virtually the only significant native composer of opera in English musical history, produced a masterpiece for the unpromising occasion of graduation at a girls' school. This was the beautiful and moving *Dido and Aeneas*. In France, Louis XIV realized the potentiality of opera for enhancing the resplendence of the Sun King, and from Italy imported Lully (1632-1687), musician, dancer, speculator, and politician extraordinary, who vied with Molière for the post of "cultural director" at court. Lully's operatic exercises on mythological themes are for the most part now forgotten, but the overtures and dances that he wrote for them live on as a prelude to the great eighteenth-century achievement in instrumental music.

Seventeenth-Century Culture in Review

The "century of genius," then, produced a rich and complex culture, at once scientific, classical, Baroque, and much else besides. It is the complexity that must now be underscored once more. In religion, for example, the seventeenth century was not simply a preparation for the toleration and the diluted "natural religion" of the eighteenth-century Age of Prose and Reason. Against the practical toleration resulting in England from the Glorious Revolution must be set the savage persecutions still prevailing in Ireland and Louis XIV's revocation of the Edict of Nantes. Remember, too, the variety of religious sects that flourished in revolutionary England, the heaven-stormers, the Quakers, whose other-worldly beliefs were to prove so disconcertingly compatible with material success in this world, the Independents, and all the others. In France, along with a conventional Gallican like Bossuet, there flourished the Quietists and the Jansenists, groups who went well beyond orthodoxy into mystical beliefs that conformists were already damning with one of the Enlightenment's favorite words of reproach—"enthusiasm." In Germany, the spiritual descendants of the Anabaptists were laying the foundation of that evangelical appeal to human emotions which in the very midst of the Age of Prose and Reason was to flourish in German Pietism and English Methodism, and which, carried to the shores of the New World by immigrants, was to play so important a part in the early religious history of our own country.

The contrasts presented by the seventeenth century, this fecund "century of genius," come out in one of its great men, the Frenchman Pascal (1623-1662). As mathematician and physicist, Pascal has an important place in the history of science. His barometric experiment on Mt. Puy-de-Dôme and his other experiments to prove the possibility of a vacuum we have already noted (see above, p. 627). And in this-worldly activity Pascal was wide-ranging and very modern. He made contributions to pure mathematics, invented and tried not very successfully to market a calculating machine, forerunner of our modern ones, and started the first omnibus line—horse-drawn, of course—in Paris. Yet Pascal was also a profoundly other-worldly man, who spent the last years of his life in religious meditation, defended the Jansenists against the Jesuits—incidentally in lively, epigrammatic modern French, with the skill, fervor, and one-sidedness of the born pamphleteer—and left unfinished at his death one of the most remarkable works of Christian apologetics in existence, the fragments known as the *Pensées* (thoughts). Here he could write:

Man is but a being filled with error. This error is natural, and, without grace, ineffaceable. Nothing shows him the truth: everything deceives him. These two principles of truth, reason and the senses, besides lacking sincerity, reciprocally deceive each other. The senses deceive reason by false appearances; and just as they cheat reason they are cheated by her in turn: she has her revenge. Passions of the soul trouble the senses, and give them

Rubens, self-portrait with Isabella Brant, his first wife (1609-10). Pinakothek, Munich.

Rembrandt, "The Night Watch."

false impressions. They emulously lie and deceive each other.[*]

These are hardly the words of a rationalist. Nor is one of his best-known aphorisms: "Cleopatra's nose: if it had been shorter, the whole face of the earth would have been changed." The "century of genius" was no mere prelude to the Enlightenment, but an age in which men were "voyaging on strange seas of thought."

The seventeenth century, and not the sixteenth, is perhaps the clearest point of time where the "modern" comes fully into existence. In this century the new science, the new technology, the new economic life finally make possible—indeed among the educated, common—a belief in progress, in steadily increasing human command over

material resources, in steadily increasing and widening possibilities of happiness for most men and women right here on earth. In this century Christianity meets in this new spirit of belief in progress the sternest challenge to new adaptations it has met in nearly two millennia. And yet, as we see with much of its classical literature, with much baroque art, with the new religious movements, the seventeenth century was keenly aware of mystery, of horror, of emotion, of the apparently insoluble paradoxes that face man, this "reed, but a thinking reed." Once more to quote Pascal, the seventeenth century was aware, far more than the eighteenth was to be, of *both* the *esprit de finesse* (the hunch, the immeasurable gift of measure) and the *esprit de géométrie* (mathematics, reason cold, clear, always summonable, always the same).

[*] Pascal, *Thoughts, Letters, and Opuscules*, O. W. Wright, trans. (Boston, 1882), 192.

CHAPTER XV

Reading Suggestions
on Divine-Right Monarchy and Revolution

(Asterisk indicates paperbound edition.)

GENERAL ACCOUNTS

D. Ogg, *Europe in the Seventeenth Century,* 6th ed. (Black, 1952); and G. N. Clark, *The Seventeenth Century,* 2nd ed. (Clarendon, 1947). Two very readable general accounts. Clark's is perhaps the more useful, since it is organized by topics and centers on developments in France.

C. J. Friedrich, *The Age of the Baroque, 1610-1660* (Harper, 1952); F. L. Nussbaum, *The Triumph of Science and Reason, 1660-1685* (Harper, 1953); and J. B. Wolf, *The Emergence of the Great Powers, 1685-1715* (Harper, 1951). These three volumes in the "Rise of Modern Europe" series provide a treatment of the seventeenth century fully abreast of modern scholarship. Each contains an exhaustive bibliography.

SPECIAL STUDIES: PRIMARILY ECONOMIC AND MILITARY

E. F. Heckscher, *Mercantilism,* 2 vols., rev. ed. (Macmillan, 1955). A famous work, the subject of much scholarly controversy; indispensable for a thorough examination of the topic.

H. Heaton, *Economic History of Europe,* rev. ed. (Harper, 1948); and S. B. Clough and C. W. Cole, *Economic History of Europe,* 3rd ed. (Heath, 1952). Two good general economic histories.

C. Petrie, *Earlier Diplomatic History, 1492-1713* (Macmillan, 1949). A useful manual on international affairs.

A. Vagts, *A History of Militarism* (Norton, 1937); E. M. Earle, ed., *Makers of Modern Strategy* (Princeton Univ. Press, 1943); J. F. C. Fuller, *Military History of the Western World* (Funk & Wagnalls, 1954-1956). Three general books on military history containing useful material on seventeenth-century developments.

A. T. Mahan, *The Influence of Sea Power on History, 1660-1783* (Little, Brown, 1890; *Saga). A most celebrated book, but no longer a very reliable guide to the subject.

E. Barker, *The Development of Public Services in Western Europe, 1660-1930* (Oxford Univ. Press, 1944). Attempts to treat an important topic usually totally neglected.

F. L. Nussbaum, *A History of Economic Institutions of Modern Europe* (Crofts, 1933). An abridgment of Sombart's *Moderne Kapitalismus,* with its argument that war is economically *creative.*

J. U. Nef, *War and Human Progress* (Harvard Univ. Press, 1950). An answer to Sombart above, arguing that war is economically *destructive.*

SPECIAL STUDIES: FRANCE

L. von Ranke, *Civil Wars and Monarchy in France* (Harper, 1853). This great old classic continues to be worth reading for the seventeenth century.

A. Guérard, *The Life and Death of an Ideal,* new ed. (Braziller, 1956). Perhaps the best single volume in English on the Age of Louis XIV; most suggestive, and does full justice to the cultural side.

C. V. Wedgwood, *Richelieu and the French Monarchy* (Macmillan, 1950), and M. P. Ashley, *Louis XIV and the Greatness of France* (Macmillan, 1947). Two good brief accounts in the "Teach Yourself History Library."

L. B. Packard, *The Age of Louis XIV* (Holt, 1929. A Berkshire Study). Very short and very good.

W. H. Lewis, *The Splendid Century* (Sloane, 1954; *Anchor). A well-written account with emphasis on French society.

J. E. King, *Science and Rationalism in the Government of Louis XIV* (Johns Hopkins Univ. Press, 1949). A significant monograph.

P. R. Doolin, *The Fronde* (Harvard Univ. Press, 1935). Interesting not only for the topic dealt with but for the thesis that the so-called absolute monarchy in France was really not so absolute.

C. W. Cole, *Colbert and a Century of French Mercantilism,* 2 vols. (Columbia Univ. Press, 1939). A solid, detailed study.

SPECIAL STUDIES: ENGLAND

L. von Ranke, *A History of England,* 6 vols. (Clarendon, 1875). Another classic account by the great German historian.

S. R. Gardiner, *History of England, 1603-1642,* 10 vols.; *History of the Great Civil War, 1642-1649,* 4 vols.; and *History of the Commonwealth and Protectorate, 1649-1656* (Longmans, Green, 1904-1913). A really major work of detailed history.

G. Davies, *The Early Stuarts, 1603-1660,* and G. N. Clark, *The Later Stuarts, 1660-1714,* new eds. (Clarendon, 1949). These two volumes in the "Oxford History of England" provide a briefer scholarly account.

C. H. Firth, *Oliver Cromwell and the Rule of the Puritans in England* (Putnam's, 1900). Often considered the best of the very many books on Cromwell.

C. V. Wedgwood, *The King's Peace, 1637-1641,* and *The King's War, 1641-1647* (Macmillan, 1955, 1959). The first two volumes of a detailed study of the Great Rebellion by the best contemporary specialist. Miss Wedgwood is the acknowledged expert of our generation, an excellent writer, and a conservative historian untainted by sociological leanings.

G. Davies, *The Restoration of Charles II, 1658-1660* (Huntington Library, 1955). An authoritative monograph completing the work of Gardiner and Firth.

A. Bryant, *King Charles II* (Longmans, Green, 1931). An unusually sympathetic account.

F. C. Turner, *James II* (Macmillan, 1948). A balanced treatment of a highly controversial figure.

G. M. Trevelyan, *The English Revolution, 1688-1689* (Butterworth, 1938. The Home University Library). A very good study by a historian who has written several famous works on the Stuart period.

D. L. Keir, *The Constitutional History of Modern Britain, 1485-1937,* 4th ed. (Black, 1950). A good introduction.

J. R. Tanner, *English Constitutional Conflicts of the Seventeenth Century* (Cambridge Univ. Press, 1928). A full and scholarly account.

C. Brinton, *The Anatomy of Revolution*, rev. ed. (°Vintage, 1957). Generalizations based on England's 17th-century revolution, France's 18th-century one, and Russia's 20th-century one. Selected bibliographies for each revolution.

W. Notestein, *The English People on the Eve of Colonization, 1603-1630* (Harper, 1954). An admirable piece of social and intellectual history.

G. P. Gooch, *English Democratic Ideas in the Seventeenth Century*, H. J. Laski, ed. (Cambridge Univ. Press, 1927; °Harper Torchbook, 1959). Essential for understanding the scope of the English revolution.

E. Bernstein, *Cromwell and Communism: Socialism and Democracy in the Great English Revolution* (Allen and Unwin, 1930). The second part of the title of this significant study is the more accurate.

Everybody's Pepys, O. F. Morshead, ed. (Harcourt, Brace, 1926). A useful abridgment of the famous diary kept during the 1660's; a fascinating document of social history.

SPECIAL STUDIES: THE CENTURY OF GENIUS

C. Brinton, *Ideas and Men* (Prentice-Hall, 1950); and J. H. Randall, Jr., *Making of the Modern Mind*, rev. ed. (Houghton Mifflin, 1940). Two general books on intellectual history with useful sections on the seventeenth century.

P. Smith, *A History of Modern Culture*, Vol. I (Holt, 1930). A mine of information on topics often passed over in general histories.

B. Willey, *The Seventeenth Century Background* (°Anchor). Reprint of a modern classic; essays on Descartes, Hobbes, Milton, and other major figures in the intellectual and religious life of the century.

P. Hazard, *The European Mind, 1680-1715* (Hollis and Carter, 1953). A significant reëvaluation of the intellectual history of the period.

Ernest Mortimer, *Blaise Pascal* (Harper, 1959). A sympathetic study, admirably written.

Arnold Zweig, *The Living Thoughts of Spinoza* (°Fawcett World Library, 1959). A good selection in a useful series.

A. N. Whitehead, *Science and the Modern World* (°Mentor). A major essay by a great philosopher and mathematician; not easy reading.

Charles Singer and others, eds., *A History of Technology* (Oxford Univ. Press, 1954-1958). The third volume of this magnificently designed and expensive work covers this period. The authoritative work of our time on the subject.

A. Wolf, *A History of Science, Technology, and Philosophy in the Sixteenth and Seventeenth Centuries*, rev. ed. (Allen & Unwin, 1950; °Harper Torchbooks). A standard, detailed account. See also the works by H. Butterfield and A. H. Hall cited for Chapter XI.

M. F. Bukofzer, *Music in the Baroque Era* (Norton, 1947); and H. Leichtentritt, *Music, History, and Ideas* (Harvard Univ. Press, 1938). Both are useful introductions to the development of music in the period; see also the works of P. Láng and C. Gray cited in the reading suggestions for Chapter XI.

H. J. C. Grierson, *Cross-Currents in English Literature of the 17th Century* (°Harper Torchbook, 1958). Important studies in the history of ideas.

S. E. Bethell, *The Cultural Revolution of the Seventeenth Century* (Roy, 1951). Another study of the literature with fruitful suggestions for the historian of social and political ideas.

A. Dumas, *The Three Musketeers, Twenty Years After, The Vicomte de Bragelonne* (many editions). The famous "D'Artagnan" trilogy, set in seventeenth-century France; properly swashbuckling, yet based on sound research.

T. Gautier, *Captain Fracasse* (Bigelow, Smith, 1910). A good picaresque tale, based on conscientious research; set in the France of Louis XIII.

A. Manzoni, *The Betrothed,* A Colquhoun, trans. (Dutton, 1951). Milan about 1630; a famous Italian novel.

N. Hawthorne, *The Scarlet Letter* (many editions). The best introduction to the Puritan spirit through fiction.

R. Graves, *Wife to Mr. Milton* (Creative Age, 1944). A good novel, though not very kind to Milton.

W. M. Thackeray, *Henry Esmond* (many editions). A famous novel, set in England about 1700.

Index

A

Aachen, 181, 187, 205 (see also Aix-la-Chapelle)
Abbasid Caliphate, 252, 358
Abbeys, 335-336; illus., 337
Abelard, Peter, 318, 324
Abraham, 42
Absolutism: Age of, 540; challenged in English Civil War, 622; of Louis XIV, 606-607; Spanish, 540-542
Abu Bekr, 251
Abu-'l Abbas, 252
Académie des Sciences, 627
Academy: at Athens, 80; French, 599
Achaemenid Empire, 40
Achilles, 55
Acre, 360: siege of, 356
Acrocorinth, 57
Acropolis, 57, 69, 72; illus., 71
Act of Settlement, 625
Act of Supremacy, 491, 492
Acton, Lord, 485-486
Adams, Henry, 208, 336
Adelard of Bath, 325
Adrianople, 368
Aegean civilization, 51-53
Aegean Sea, 49, 51
Aeneid, 95, 128
Aeschylus, 69, 71, 72, 73
Aëtius, 179
Africa, 106, 566, 567; European expansion in, 588; prehistoric men in, 13-14; Roman possessions in, 117; slave trade, 588, 590
Afrikaners, 588
Afterlife, 71: Christian, 144; Egyptian, 28; Jewish, 44, 45; Mesopotamian, 37; Moslem, 248
Agamemnon, 53, 54, 55, 73
Agincourt, battle of, 399
Agricola, 469
Agriculture: in ancient Egypt, 23-24; in Greece, 50-51; in late Roman Empire, 136; under manorialism (see Manorialism)
Ahura-Mazda, 40
Aix-la-Chapelle, compromise peace of, 600
Akhis, 368
Akkadians, 34
Alamanni, 182
Alans, 180

Alaric, 177
Alba, Duke of, 527, 528
Albigensian Crusade, 264-265
Albigensians, 305, 357
Albright, W. F., 42
Albuquerque, Alfonso de, 567
Alchemy, 326
Alcibiades, 85
Aldine Press, 468
Aldus Manutius, 468
Alexander the Great, 25, 86-88: empire of, 88 (map); illus., 87
Alexander VI, Pope, 419, 474
Alexandria, 36, 87, 89, 90, 92, 229, 230, 234
Alexiad, 233
Alexis Romanov, Tsar, 387
Alexius, the young, 364
Alexius I Commenus, 233, 240, 351, 352-353
Alexius III Angelus, 363, 364
Alfonso the Magnanimous, 411, 418-419, 447
Alfred the Great, 193
Algebra, 254
Algeria, 374
Ali, son-in-law of Mohammed, 251
Al-Kindi, 254
Allods, 201, 287
Alphabet, 22-23, 41: Cyrillic, 196, 241, 244, 245
Al-Razi, 254
Amazon Basin, 579
Amenophis, 29
America: discovery of, 565; early map of, 583; English colonies in, 584-586; French colonies in, 586; naming of, 576; Spanish possessions in, 577-582
Amish, 495
Amon, 29
Amorites, 34
Amsterdam, Bank of, 530
Anabaptists, 480, 493-495, 502, 503, 509, 635
Anabasis, 86
Anastasis, illus., 366
Anatolia, 237
Anatomy, 32, 469
Andes Mountains, 579
Andronicus I, 363
Angevin Empire, 262-264
Anglican church, 480, 497-498, 509, 614
Anglo-Dutch War, 623
Anglo-Saxons, 180, 189

Animals, domesticated, 12
Anna Commena, 233, 362
Annals of Ashurbanipal, 38-39
Anne, Queen, 624, 625
Anthropology, 11
Anthropomorphism of Greek deities, 70
Anticlericalism: English, 492; medieval, 330-331
Antigone, 73
Antinomianism, 494
Antioch, 89, 229, 230: as Crusader state, 353
Anti-Semitism, medieval, 272, 283
Antoninus Pius, 116
Antony, Mark, 25, 112
Antwerp, 490
Apache Indians, 14
Apes and man, 10, 11
Aphrodite, 70
Apocrypha, 154
Apollo, 70
Apology, of Plato, 80
Apostolic succession, doctrine of, 154
Appeal to the Christian Nobility of the German Nation, The, 483, 485
Apse, 332
Apuleius, 151
Aqueduct, Roman, illus., 122
Aquinas, St. Thomas, 318, 319-320, 322
Aquitaine, 177, 264, 395: Eleanor of, 262, 328
Arabesques, 256
Arabia, 20
Arabian Nights, 255-256
Arabic language, 253
Arabic numerals, 254
Arabs: northward invasions of, 217; in time of Mohammed, 246-247
Aragon, 411, 542
Arcadius, 234; illus., 235
Arches: pointed, 333, 335; Roman, 123-124; round, 333
Archimedes, 91
Architecture: ancient, 23; Byzantine, 216; French Renaissance, 546; Gothic, 332-336; Greek, 75-76; Moscow, illus., 388, 389; Renaissance, 450, 463-464; Romanesque, 332, 333; Russian, early, 244; Tudor, illus., 555

Archons, 63
Arctic, explorations in, 590
Arena Chapel, 451; *illus.*, 452
Areopagitica, 623, 631
Ares, 70
Arianism, 163-164, 229
Aristarchus, 90
Aristophanes, 69, 74, 80
Aristotle, 57, 67, 69, 82-83, 86, 254, 631
Armada, Spanish, 518, 528-529, 554; *illus.*, 529
Armagnacs, 399
Armenia, 229, 294: annexation of, by Byzantium, 238-239
Arminianism, 501
Arminius (Dutch theologian), 501
Arminius (German hero), 115, 117
Army, 469: Byzantine, 219; early modern, 519-521; English, 397; feudal, 273; French, 601; New Model, 620; Roman, 98-99; 110, 114, 132-133, 135
Arnold of Brescia, 291
Arsenal, of Venice, 428, 430, 431; *illus.*, 429
Art: Baroque, 632-634; Byzantine, 216-217, 227, *illus.*, 366; Chinese, *illus.*, 570; of Dark Ages, 175, 205-206; early Christian, *illus.*, 143, 149, 159, 162, 170; Egyptian, 27, 31; Etruscan, *illus.*, 97; Greek, 61, 75-77; Hellenistic, *illus.*, 90; medieval, 331-333; Minoan, 52; Moslem, 256; Muscovite, 388; patronage of, 452-455, 458; prehistoric, *illus.*, 15-16; Renaissance, 450-464; Roman, 123-124
Artevelde, Jacob van, 397
Arthur of Brittany, 264
Artifacts, of prehistoric man: *illus.*, 11-12; in New World, 14
Art of Love, The, 128
Asceticism, 168, 501: Brahmin, 569; early Christian, 156, 157
Ashurbanipal, Annals of, 38-39
Asia: Central, 20; prehistoric men in, 13-14
Asiento, 603
Aspasia, 66
Assembly: Athenian, 63, 64, 65; of Roman Republic, 100, 101, 110, 111, 114
Assize of Arms, 277
Assizes of Jerusalem, 354
Assizes of Romania, 367
Assyria, 20, 21, 35, 38-40, 43
Astrakhan, 380
Astrology, 34, 325
Astronomy: Greek, 23, 34, 36; Renaissance, 469-470; seventeenth-century, 628
Ataulf, 177
Athanasius, 164
Athena, 55, 70
Athens, 53, 69, 89: democracy in, 64-67; early history of, 63-64; empire of, 68-69, 84-85; institutions of, 62-63; in Peloponnesian War, 84-86; in Persian Wars, 67-68

Atlantis, 564-565
Atoms, 79, 126
Aton, 29, 44
Attic dialect, 69
Attila the Hun, 156, 179
Audience Hall of Darius, 39 (*illus.*)
Audiencias, 580
Augsburg, 433-434: Peace of, 524-526
Augustan Age, literature of, 127
Augustine, St., 166-167
Augustus (Octavian), 112-114, 116
Aurangzeb, Emperor, 587
Aurignacian Age, 16
Ausculta fili, 271
Australopithecines, 13
Austria, 185 (*see also* Holy Roman Empire *and* Vienna)
Autocracy: of Byzantine Emperor, 224, 225; Russian, 382-383
Autokrator, 223
Avars, 185, 217, 235, 236
Averroes, 254
Avicenna, 254
Avignon: "Babylonian Captivity" in, 35, 311, 340; seat of papacy in, 271-272
Azores Islands, 575
Azov, 389
Aztec empire, 578-579

B

Baalbek, temple at, 124; *illus.*, 123
Babel, Tower of, 34, 37
Babylon, 20, 21, 34, 36, 40 (*see also* Mesopotamia)
Babylonian captivity, of Jews, 35
"Babylonian Captivity," of papacy, 311, 340
Bacon, Francis, 556, 626-627
Bacon, Roger, 325
Baghdad, caliphate of, 252, 253
Baibars, 358
Bailiff, 265, 266
Balance of power, 517
Balboa, Vasco N. de, 576
Baldacchino, 632; *illus.*, 633
Baldwin of Flanders, 352, 353, 363, 365
Balearic Islands, 411
Balkans, the, 20, 46, 236-237, 373
Ball, John, 311
Baner, General, 534
Banking, 512: origins of, 431-432
Bank of Amsterdam, 530
Bank of St. George, 432
Bannockburn, battle of, 282, 402
Baptism, 160, 162, 493
Baptists, 493, 495
Barbarossa, Frederick, 292, 293, 363; *illus.*, 291; and third crusade, 356, 357, 359
Bardi family, 432
Barents, W., 590
Barents Sea, 590
Barlaam, 215
Barlaam and Ioasaph, 245
Barons, English, 278
Baroque style, 632-634
Basil I, 238

Basil II, 239, 241-242
Basil, St., 157
Basil Digenes Akritas, 213-214, 245
Basileus, the title, 223
Basilics, 225
Basque Provinces, 541
"Battle of the Angels and the Demons," 460
Baty (Tartar leader), 379
Bauer, Bruno, 142
Bavaria, 284
Bayeux Tapestry, *illus.*, 193, 274, 275
Beauvais Cathedral, 333; *illus.*, 335
Becket, Thomas à, 276-277
Behaim, 575
Belgae, 176
Belgium, 508, 512, 517, 603
Belgrade, 373, 374
Benedict XI, Pope, 311
Benedictine order, 307
Benefice, 198, 199
Berengar, 221
Bergen, 428
Bering Strait, 14
Bernard of Armagnac, 399
Bernard of Clairvaux, St., 308-309, 324: and Second Crusade, 355-356
Bible: "higher criticism of," 42; King James Version of, 617; Luther's translation of, 485
Bill of Rights, English, 625
Bills of Exchange, 431
Bishops, 154, 159, 228
Bithynia, Turkish conquest of, 368
Black Death, 311, 403
Blanche of Castile, 267
Blenheim, battle of, 602
Blues, Byzantine political party, 225-226
Bobadilla, 576
Boccaccio, Giovanni, 445-446
Bodin, Jean, 550
Bohemia, 379: and Thirty Years' War, 532
Bohemond, 233, 352, 353
Boileau, N., 630-631
Boleyn, Ann, 491
Bologna, Concordat of, 491
Bologna, University of, 313
Boniface (Roman governor), 178-179
Boniface VIII, Pope, 271, 283, 311
Book of Kells, 194
Book of the Dead, 25, 28
Borelli, G., 628
Borgia, Caesar, 419, 453
Borgia, Pope Alexander VI, 419, 474
Boris (Bulgarian ruler), 241
Bosporus, 57
Bossuet, Bishop, 504, 608
Bosworth Field, battle of, 408
Botticelli, 454-455; *illus.*, 453
Bourbon, house of, 549
Bourgeoisie, 303-304, 435
Bourges, Pragmatic Sanction of, 400, 401
Bouvines, battle of, 264, 277
Boyars, 385

Boyne, battle of the, 626
Brahmins, 569
Brandenburg, 537
Brandenburg-Prussia, 600
Brazil, 579-580, 581-582: discovery of, 566
Breasted, J. H., 28
Bremen, 427
Brethren of the Common Life, 473
Brian of Munster, 194
Britain: abandonment of, by Rome, 180; Anglo-Saxon invasion of, 180; Christianity brought to, 189; Roman conquest of, 111, 116, 117
Brittany, 545
Bronze Age, 11
Brownists, 553
Bruce, Robert, 282
Brueghel, Pieter, the Elder, 459, 460; *illus.,* 459
Bruges, 427
Brutus, 112
Bryce, James, 186-187
Buddha, Gautama, 215, 569
Buddhism, 569
Bulgaria, 368
Bulgarian Empire, 365
Bulgarians, 196, 230, 231, 240-242
Bulgars, 217, 218
Bunyan, John, 503, 632
Bureaucracy: ancient, 21; in ancient Egypt, 28; Byzantine, 239; Capetian, 265-267; Roman, 119
Burgesses, English, 280-281
Burgundians, 180
Burgundy, 286, 291, 399: dominions of, 517; *map,* 401
Burial: in Egypt, 27, 28; of prehistoric man, 16
Burleigh, 554
Buttress, flying, 333
Byzantine Empire: after *1261,* 347, 364-365, 367; art of, 216-217, 227, *illus.,* 366; church and state in, 227-229; conquest of, by Ottomans, 368-369; diplomacy of, 220-221; economic prosperity of, 221-223; Emperors of, 212, 223-224, 225, 228; gold coinage of, 222; feudalism in, 362-363; history of, 212-213, 233-240; impact of, on Slavs, 240-246; international relations of, 345-347; in Italy, 183; law, 224-225, 229; literature of, 213-216; *map,* 220; military achievements of, 217-220; monasticism in, 230-231, 237; religion, 241-242; reorganization of, in 7th-8th centuries, 236-238; under rule of Alexius I Commenus, 351; and Russia, 241-242
Byzantium, 57, 58: as preserver of classics, 213

C

Cabot, John and Sebastian, 582
Cabral, Pedro, 566
Cadillac, Antoine de la Mothe, 586

Caesar, Julius, 111: writings of, 127
Caesarean operation, 121
Caesarism, 111
Caesaropapism, 159, 229, 230
Cairo, Egypt, 252
Cajetan, Cardinal, 483
Calais, 397: Treaty of, 398
Calculus, 628
Calcutta, 587
Calendar, 23-24: Islamic, 249; Julian, 112
California, 581, 582
Caligula, Emperor, 115
Caliphate: Abbasid, 252; Umayyad, 251-252
Calvin, John, 490-491, 495: student sketch of, *illus.,* 500
Calvinism: predestination in, 499-500; Puritanism in, 500-502; spread of, 490-491
Calvinist church, 480, 489, 490-491, 509
Cambray, League of, 522
Cambridge University, *illus.,* 313
Canaries, the, 575
Candidate, origin of word, 100
Cannae, Roman defeat at, 103-104
Cannon, sixteenth-century, 521; *illus.,* 520
Canon, Christian, 154
Canon law, 120-121
Canossa, Peace of, 289
Canterbury Tales, 329, 442, 447
"Canticle of the Brother Sun," 325
Canute, King, 193
Cape La Hogue, sea battle of, 601
Cape of Good Hope, 566, 588
Capet, Hugh, 195, 260-261
Capetian rule, in France, 260-272
Cape Verde, 566
Capitalism: early, 434-435; after European exploration, 593-594; and Protestantism, 510-512
Capitularies, of Charlemagne, 199
Capitulations of French and Turks, 374
Capuchins, 504
Caracalla, baths of, 124
Carbon *14,* 10, 12, 13
Carcassonne, *illus.,* 268
Cardinals, College of, 159, 288, 307
Carolingian Empire, 185-187 (*see also* Charlemagne): decay of, 188-189; establishment of, 183-188; in Germany, 194-195; *map,* 187
Carolingian Renaissance, 204
Carthage, 41, 58: Islamic conquest of, 251; and Rome, 103-104
Cartier, Jacques, 582
Casa de Contratación, 543
Caste (*see also* Social classes): Hindu, 569, 592-593
Castellio, Sebastian, 496
Castiglione, Conte Baldassare, 466, 474-476
Castile, 410-411, 543
Castilian language, 441
Castles, medieval, 335
Castrati, 634
Catacombs, art in, *illus.,* 149

Catalan language, 442
Catalonia, 410, 411
Cateau-Cambrésis, Treaty of, 524, 526
Cathari, 264
Catharsis, in tragedy, 72-73
Cathedrals, medieval, 331-335
Catherine of Aragon, 491
Catholic Church (*see* Roman Catholic Church)
Catholic League, 532, 533, 548, 549
Catholic Reformation, 503-508: Council of Trent, 506-508; the Inquisition, 505-506; Jesuits in, 504-505, 506
Cato, 104, 107, 122
Cavaliers, 619
Cave paintings, 15
Celibacy, clerical, 157, 207, 307-308, 493
Cellini, Benvenuto, 546
Celts, 193
Censors, Roman, 100
Central America, 579
Central Asia, 20
Cervantes, Miguel de, 330, 544, 545
Chabod, Federico, 441
Chadwick, John, 53
Chaeronea, 86
Chalcedon, Council of, 165, 230
Chaldea, 20
Champagne, Counts of, 201
Champlain, Samuel de, 582
Champollion, J., 25
Chancery, Ottoman, 372
Chanson de Roland, 327, 328
Chansons de geste, 361
Charlemagne, 184, 205; attempt to restore culture, 204; expansion of empire under, 185-187; as man, 187-188 (*illus.*); pilgrimages in time of, 350; political institutions of, 198-199
Charles I, Emperor (*see* Charlemagne)
Charles I (England), 613, 614, 615: *illus.,* 614; reign of, 617-620
Charles I (Spain) (*see* Charles V, Emperor)
Charles II (England), 621, 622
Charles II (Spain), 602
Charles II, the Bald (France), 188, 189
Charles V, Emperor (Spain), 374, 402, 417, 458, 483, 486, 522-524, 540-541
Charles V, the Wise (France), 397, 398
Charles VI (France), 398
Charles VII (France), 399, 400, 432
Charles VIII (France), 521-522
Charles X, "King" (France), 549
Charles Martel, 183, 217
Charles of Anjou, 297-298, 367, 418
Charles the Bold (Duke of Burgundy), 401-402
Charters, town, 303-304

Chartres, Cathedral of, 331-332, *illus.*, 335, 338
Chaucer, Geoffrey, 329, 330, 331, 447
Chenonceaux Chateau, *illus.*, 546
Cheops, 25
Chiaroscuro technique, painting, 451, 452
Children, tribute of, in Ottoman state, 370
Children's Crusade, 357
China, 516, 588: early life in, 18, 19; history and institutions of, 570-572; Jesuit missionaries in, 573-574, 588; Portuguese trade with, 567
Chivalry, 326-330: code of, 199, 208, 322
Christian IV (Denmark), 532-533, 534
Christianity, 46, 127 (*see also* Missionaries): in Britain, 185; Bulgarian, 240-242; Byzantine, 227-228; Coptic, 566; and decline of Rome, 136-137; doctrine of salvation, 161; early art of, *illus.*, 143, 149, 159, 162, 170; the Eucharist, 160-161, 162; German, 185; and Gnosticism, 163; heresies of, 162, 166; Jesus (*see* Jesus); medieval, 305-306; Russian, 243-246; St. Paul, 145-147; schism of *1054*, 231-232; even sacraments, 160-162; and sex, 168; syncretistic nature of, 152, 207; the Trinity, 163-164; triumph of, 150-152; western, way of life in, 167-171
Christians, early, 118, 144-147: government of, 158-160; organization and hierarchy of, 152-155; persecutions of, 115, 147, 148-150
Chrysoloras, Manuel, 446
Church (*see also* Heresy, Reformation, Saints, *and individual denominations*): architecture, 155; Celtic, 193-194; Cistercians, 308-309; clergy (*see* Clergy); Cluniac reform, 307-309; Conciliar Movement, 340; in Dark Ages, 205; music, 498; religious situation (c. *1100*), *map,* 306; religious situation (c. *1600*), *map,* 507; Russian, 159
Church and state, separation of, 305, 496
Churchill, John, 602
Church of England, 493 (*see also* Anglican church)
Cicero, 109, 126, 127
Cid, the, 545
Cimbri, 176
Cincinnatus, 99, 100
Circumcision, 145
Cistercian Order, 308-309
Cities: establishment of, 18-19; Hellenistic, 88-89; population of, fourteenth century, 433-434
Citizenship, Roman, extension of, 102, 119
City of God, 166-167, 177

City-state: Greek, 56-57; colonization by, 58
Civilization: in ancient Near East, 21-22; and river valleys, 18-20
Civil War, in England, 618-620
Clarendon Code, 623
Classical spirit, of seventeenth century, 630-632
Classics, Renaissance, preservation of, 446-447
Claudius, Emperor, 115
Cleisthenes, 64-65
Clement V, Pope, 311
"Clement VII," Pope, 311, 523
Cleopatra, 25, 111, 112
Clergy: and anticlericalism, 330-331; in divine-right monarchy, 608; of early Christian Church, 156-158; medieval, 303, 315: in Russia, 244
Clermont, Council of, 351
Clontarf, battle of, 194
Clouds, The, 74, 80
Clovis, King, 182
Cluniac, order, 288: reform movement, 307-309
Cluny, Abbey of, as supporter of crusades, 349-350
Clytemnestra, 73
Cnossos: excavations at, 52; fresco from palace at, *illus.*, 50
Coatlicue, *illus.*, 579
Code of chivalry, 199, 208, 322
Code of Hammurabi, 36-37
Code of Justinian, 224
Coeur, Jacques, 331, 400, 432-433: house of, *illus.*, 432
Cognac, League of, 523
Coinage, 59, 61: Athenian, 64; Byzantine, 222; of Crusader states, 359-360; Florentine, 431-432
Coke, Sir Edward, 616
Colbert, Jean, 611-612
Coligny, Gaspard, 547
Collectivism, manorial, 202-203
College of Cardinals, establishment of, 159, 288, 307
Colombia, 580
Coloni, 201
Colonies, American, 584-586
Colonization: ancient Greek, 57-59; Roman, 102
Colosseum, 131 (*illus.*)
Columbus, Christopher, 412, 564, 575-576; *illus.*, 575
Comedy, Greek, 74-75: New, 90
Comines, Philippe de, 400-402
Commentaries on the Gallic Wars, 111, 127
Commodus, Emperor, 132
Common law, English, 121
Common Pleas, Court of, 283
Commons, House of, 404-405, 614
Commonwealth, of England, 620-621
Communes, Italian, 417-418
Communion, 162
Compagnie des Indes Orientales, 587
Compass, 325: magnetic, 564
Compton Wynyates, *illus.*, 555
Conceptualism, 318

Conciliar Movement, 340
Concordat of Bologna, 548
Concordat of Worms, 290
Condottieri, 418, 424
Confessions, of St. Augustine, 166
Confirmation, 162
Confucianism, 571-572
Confucius, 571
Congregational church, 501
Conquistador, 565, 578
Conrad I (of Franconia), 195, 284
Conrad II, 286, 287
Conrad III, 290, 356
Conrad IV, 297, 413
Conradino, 297
Constance: Council of, 312; Peace of, 282
Constance, Queen, 293
Constantine I, Emperor, 133, 149, 212, 229, 235, 361: Donation of, 184-185, 447; *illus.*, 228
Constantine VII Porphyrogenitus, 232
Constantine XI, 369
Constantinople, 57, 133: as Byzantine capital, 225-226; capture of, by Crusaders, 347; capture of, by Ottoman Turks, 347
Constitution: concept of, 613; Roman, 99-102; of Venice, 423
Constitutional government, 622
Constitutions of Clarendon, 276, 277
Constitutions of Melfi, 297
Consubstantiation, 490, 498
Consuls, Roman, 98-99, 100
Consumption: conspicuous, 511; and Protestantism, 510
Contract, feudal, 199-200
Convocation (English assembly), 404
Copernicus, Nicholas, 469-470
Coptic Christians, 566
Cordova, Spain, 252, 254
Corinth, 57, 58
Corinthian order, 75
Corneille, Pierre, 631
Cornelia, 130
Coronado, Francisco, 578
Cortés, Hernando, 578
Cortes, of Spain, 411, 412, 541
Cosmology, 90-91
Cossacks, 388-389
Council of Basel, 312
Council of Blood, 528
Council of Chalcedon, 165, 230
Council of Clermont, 351
Council of Constance, 312
Council of Ephesus, 165
Council of Nicaea, 228, 229, 230
Council of Piacenza, 351
Council of Pisa, 312
Council of the Areopagus, 63
Council of Trent, 506-508
Council of Troubles, 528
Counter-Reformation (*see* Catholic Reformation)
Counts, the title, 198
Courtier, The, 474-476
Court of Common Pleas, 283
Court of Exchequer, 283
Court of King's Bench, 283

Court of love, 328
Courts: Athenian, 66; Roman, 100
Cranmer, Archbishop, 491, 552
Crécy, battle of, 397
Credit, 360
Creoles, 580
Creon, 73-74
Crete, 41, 237, 238, 366: excavations at Cnossos, 50, 52; Minoan culture of, 50-53
Crimea, 373, 380
Crimean War, 374
Croats, 196
Cro-Magnon man, 13 (illus.)
Cromwell, Oliver, 619, 621; illus., 620
Cromwell, Richard, 621
Cromwellian Settlement, 620-621
Crown of Saint Stephen, 217
Crusade, Albigensian, 264-265
Crusader states: establishment of, 353-354; map, 354
Crusades, 268, 269, 302, 349-361, 391: attack on Byzantium, 218, 219; Children's Crusade, 357; eighth, 358; fifth, 356; first, 351-353; fourth, 346, 347, 363-365; as holy war, 349-350; illus., 353; impact on West, 358-360; knighthood orders, 271-272, 355; second, 355-356; seventh, 358; sixth, 358; third, 356-357
Cuba, 576, 579
Cults: fertility, 16, 29; mystery, 91
Culture, 17, 326 (see also Renaissance, Style, and individual countries): of Dark Ages, 204-205, 208-209; Hellenistic, 90-91; medieval, 326-331
Cumans, 217, 246
Cuneiform writing, 23
Curia regis, 134-135, 262, 266, 267, 270: English, 273
Custom: in medieval manors, 202-203; as natural law, 323
Customs, duties, in England, 283
Cyprus, 251, 294, 374
Cyrenaica, 117
Cyril and Methodius, 241
Czechoslovakia, Hussite movement in, 311
Czechs, 196, 532

D

Dacia, 117
Damascus, 356
Damasus I, Pope, 156
Damietta, 358
Dandolo, Enrico, 363
Danegeld, royal tax, 272, 273
Danelaw, 193
Danes, 189 (see also Northmen)
Dante Alighieri, 314, 322, 340-342, 420, 439, 441, 443
Danzig, 427
Dardanelles, 57, 211-212
d'Arezzo, Guido, 339
Darius I, 35-36, 46, 67; Audience Hall of, illus., 39
Dark Ages, 157, 173-208: culture in, 204-205, 208-209; documentation on, 196; Germany in, 194-195; Italy in, 194-195; losses in, 174-176; Northmen in, 190-193
Dead Sea Scrolls, 142
Decameron, 445
Declaration of Indulgence, 623-624
Decline and Fall of the Roman Empire, History of the, 136
Deduction, 326, 626-627
Defensor Pacis, 322
Defoe, Daniel, 632
De Humanis Corporis Fabrica, 469
Deification: of Byzantine Emperor, 223; of Roman Emperor, 116, 133-134, 147-148
Delaware, 584
Delian Confederation, 68
Delphi, 70
Delphic oracle, 70
Demesne, of lord, 202
Demeter, 71
Democracy: Athenian, 64-67; after English Civil War, 622-623; origins of, 46
Democritus, 79
De Monarchia, 322
Denmark, 196, 488, 516: and Thirty Years' War, 532-533, 534
De Re Metallica, 469
De Rerum Natura, 125
De Revolutionibus Orbium Coelestium, 469, 470
Descartes, René, 627, 629-630; illus., 629
de Soto, Hernando, 578
Despots, ancient, 21-22
Devolution, War of, 600
Dialogue Concerning the Exchequer, 275
Diaspora, 42
Diaz, Bartholomew, 566
Dictator, Roman, 99-100
Dido and Aeneas, 634
Die Meistersinger, 466
Diffusion, 23
Digest of Justinian, 224
Diggers, the, 622
Diocletian, Emperor, 124, 132-135, 222
Dionysus, 72
Diplomacy, 519
Discobolus, 76-77 (illus.)
Divination, 97
Divine Comedy, The, 340
Divine right of kings, 540, 597-636
Divorce: Moslem, 249; Roman, 130
Dome, Roman, 124
Domesday Book, 273
Dominican order, 309-310
Dominic de Guzman, 310
Domitian, 115
Donatello, illus., 460, 461
Donation of Constantine, 184-185, 447
Donation of Pepin, 184
Donatism, 165, 179
Don Quixote, 330, 544, 545
Dorians, 54-55
Doric order, 75-76
Draco, code of, 63
Drake, Sir Francis, 582
Drama (see also Literature): Elizabethan, 556-557; Greek, 72-74; Russian, 390
Drang nach Osten, German, 285
Druids, 193
Dryden, John, 632
Duchy of the Archipelago, 366
Due process of law, 278
Duke, the title, 198
Duns Scotus, 318
Dürer, Albrecht, 458-460; illus., 449, 520
Dushan, Stephen, 367
Düsseldorf, fossils found near, 13
Dutch East India Company, 530
Dutch Revolt, 527-528
Dutch War, 621 (see also Holland)
Dyarchy, in Rome, 113; in Russia, 387
Dynasty III, of ancient Egypt, 25

E

Earth, age of, 6-7
East (see Crusades, Ottoman state and eastern countries)
Easter, 152, 194
Eastern Orthodox Church, 231-232
East India Company: Dutch, 587-588; English, 587
East Indies, Netherlands, 587, 588
Eck, John, 483
Economic thought, medieval, 322-323
Edessa, 353, 355
Edict of Nantes, 549, 598, 599, 608
Edict of Restitution, 533
Education: Byzantine, 213; in Dark Ages, 175; medieval, 312-314, 316; Roman, 131; scholasticism, 317; universities, 313-314, 467
Edward I, 279, 281-284
Edward II, 282, 402-403
Edward III, 395, 397, 398, 403-404
Edward IV, 407
Edward V, 408
Edward VI, 552
Edward the Confessor, 193
Egypt, 20, 21, 23-33, 229, 230, 373 (see also Alexandria): art of, 27, 31, 32; Coptic Christians, 566; Crusade against, 358; culture of, 31-32; dynasties of, 25-26; economy of, 22, 28; Islamic conquest of, 249-250; Lower, 23; Middle Kingdom, 27; Old Kingdom, 25; people of, 24-25; under Ptolemies, 88, 89; religion of, 28-30; Roman acquisition of, 112; society of, 27-28; style of, 32-33; Upper, 23
Einhard, 186, 187, 188, 206
Ekloga, 224-225
El Dorado, 592
Eleanor of Aquitaine, 262, 328
Elect, doctrine of, 500
Electra, 73

Elephants, in Punic War, 103
Eleusinian Mysteries, 71, 72
Eleusis, 71
El Greco, 544, 632
Eliot, Sir John, 590, 617
Elizabeth I, 497, 528, 552-556, 614, 615, 616
Embalming, 32
Emperors: Byzantine, 212, 223-224, 225, 228, 229; of Holy Roman Empire, 285-289; of Roman Empire, 116, 133-134, 147-148
Empress, Byzantine, 223-224
Enclosure, 434
Encomienda, 581
Engineering, Roman, 122-123
England, 505, 508: Charles I, 613, 614 (*illus.*), 615; Civil War in, 618-620; colonization in New World by, 582-586; Commonwealth of, 620-621; Constitutional tradition of, 613-614; Cromwell and Interregnum, 619-621, *illus.,* 620; development of (1066-1307), 272-284; under Edward II and Edward III, 402-404; under Elizabeth I, 552-556; Glorious Revolution, 624-625; government of, 274; under Henry VIII, 550-552; international politics of, sixteenth century, 524; Lancaster and York, 407-408; Magna Carta, 200, 278, 283; medieval, *map,* 263; nationalism in, 518; Norman conquest of, 191-193, 272-274; Parliament (*see* Parliament); Petition of Right, 617; Reformation, 491-493; Renaissance, 555-557; Restoration, 622-624; trade with Muscovite Russia, 389-390; Tudor accession, 408; union with Scotland, 625-626
English East India Company, 587
English language, 137, 442, 632
English Reformation, 550
Enlightenment, the, 496
Enquêteurs, 266
Eoliths, 12
Eparch, 225-226
Ephesus, Council of, 165
Ephors, Spartan, 60
Epic: Byzantine, 213-214; Greek, 55; medieval, 208
Epicureanism, 91, 125-126
Epicurus, 91
Epidaurus, theater at, 76; *illus.,* 73
Epirus, 54, 347
Episcopalian church, 480, 497-498
Epistemology, 33
Equites, Roman, 107, 108, 109, 114
Erasmus, Desiderius, 80, 448-450, 473; *illus.,* 449
Erastus, 498
Eratosthenes, 91, 121
Ericson, Leif, 565
Eschatology: Christian, 144; Jewish, 44
Escorial, *illus.,* 541
Eskimos, 15
Essenes, 142
Essex, Earl of, 554

Estates General, 270-271, 397-398, 610
Ethiopia, 20, 229
Etruscans, 96-97
Eucharist: doctrines about, 490, 497, 498, 532; sacrament of, 160-161, 162
Euclid, 91
Eugene, Prince, 602
Eunuchs, Byzantine, 225
Euphrates, 33-34
Euripides, 69, 72
Europe: modern state system, 516-518; political situation, *1560, map,* 525; prehistoric culture of, 12-14; in *1648, map,* 538-539; in *1715, map,* 604-605
European expansion, 561-564 (*see also* America *and* Slave trade): economic record of, 590-591; impact on West, 590-594; and missionaries, 505, 573-574
Evans, Sir Arthur, 52
Evolution, doctrine of, 16-17
Exarchs, 236
Exchequer, British, 274, 275
Exchequer, Court of, 283
Exploration: of Columbus, 575-576; later, 576-577
Extraterritoriality, 568
Extreme Unction, 162

F

Fabius the Delayer, 104
Fabliaux, 330, 441, 445, 447
Factories, Portuguese, 572
Faerie Queene, 556
Faith, Christian, 169-170, 319: and works, 161, 482, 483, 485, 493, 506
Falconry, 325
Far East (*see* China, India, *and* Japan)
Fedor, 386
Fehrbellin, battle of, 601
Fellaheen, Egyptian, 27
Fénelon, 504
Ferdinand I (Two Sicilies), 419
Ferdinand II, Emperor (Austria), 531, 532
Ferdinand of Aragon, 349, 411-412, 419, 522, 526
Ferdinand of Habsburg, 503
Fertile Crescent, 20
Fertility cults, 16, 29
Feudal contract, 199-200
Feudalism: Byzantine, 362-363; definition of, 197-198; early, institutions of, 199-201; medieval, 302; new "bastard," 394, 405-406; of Northmen, 191; vassals, lords, 199-200
Fief, 199, 200
Fifth Monarchy men, 622
Filaret, 387
Filioque controversy, history of, 231-232
Five-Mile Act, 623
Flanders, 360, 395-396, 430: fleet, 430

Flemish painting, 632, 634
Flood, Great, 37
Florence, 420-423: art of, 452-453; banking in, 431-432; *illus.,* 421
Fontainebleau, 546
Font-de-Gaume, cave paintings at, 15 (*illus.*)
Fontechevade, fossils found at, 13-14
Formosa, 588
Fort Christiana, 584
Fossils, 10
Fountains Abbey, England, *illus.,* 309
Fox, George, 622
France: Albigensian Crusade, 264-265; army of, 521; and Burgundy, 286, 291, 399, 401 (*map*), 517; colonization in America by, 585, 586; Estates General, 270-271, 397-398, 610; under Francis I, 545-547; founding of, 195; under Henry IV, 598; Huguenots (*see* Huguenots); in Hundred Years' War, 395-400; under Louis XI, 400-402; under Louis XIV, 600-602; medieval, *map,* 263; Normans and Angevins, 262-264; Philip the Fair, 269-272, 298; Reformation in, 491; religious wars (*1562-1598*), 547-548; Renaissance, 546-547; royal administration under Capetians, 260, 265-267; in Thirty Years' War, 533, 534
Francis I (France), 486, 491, 522-524, 546
Franciscan order, 309-310
Francis of Assisi, St., 310
Franconia, 284
Franklin, Sir John, 577
Franklins, 204
Franks, 174, 177 (*see also* Charlemagne *and* Merovingians): alliance of, with Pope, 184-185; empire of, 180-189
Franz Ferdinand, Archduke, 368
Fredegund, Queen, 182-183
Frederick Barbarossa (Frederick I), 291, 292, 293, 363: *illus.,* 291; and third crusade, 356, 357, 359
Frederick II (Germany), 295-297, 297-298, 357, 358
Frederick V, Elector of the Palatinate, 532
Frederick the Wise, Elector of Saxony, 484, 485
Freedom of speech, 623
Free will, 499-500
Frescobaldi, 634
Fresco painting, 455
Friars, 309-310
Friends, Religious Society of, 154-155, 622-623, 635
Friezes, Greek, 76
Frogs, The, 74
Fronde, uprising of, 600
Fugger, Jacob, *illus.,* 433
Fuggerei, 433; *illus.,* 434
Fugger family, 432-433
Fulcher of Chartres, 359

Fur trade, French, 586
Fyrd, 277

G

Gaiseric, 179
Galen, 122, 467-468
Galerius, Emperor, 133, 149
Galicia, 410
Galileo, 627
Galleys, Venetian, 428, 430
Gallicanism, 311, 400
Gallic Wars, 111
Gama, Vasco da, 566
Gargantua, 447, 448
Gargoyles, 337
Gattemelata statue, *illus.,* 460
Gaul, 116: as Roman province, 117-118
Gauls, 102
Gaza, battle of, 358
Genesis, 42
Geneva, 490, 495, 500
Genghiz Khan, 358, 379
Genoa, 353, 360, 428, 521
Geography, 206, 361, 561, 575, 576, 592
Geometry: analytical, 627; in Dark Ages, 206; Moslem, 253-254
George I (England), 625
Georgics, 128
Germania, 128-129
Germany: in Dark Ages, 194-195; development of, *911-1273,* 284-298; *Drang nach Osten,* 285; feudalism in, 290; Frederick Barbarossa, 291, 292, 293, 356, 357, 359, 363; Frederick II, 295-298, 357, 358; and Golden Bull of *1356,* 415; Hanseatic League, 415, 427-428; Interregnum, 413; Investiture controversy, 288-291; Knights' War and Peasants' Rebellion in, 487-488; Lutheran revolt in, 484-486; medieval, *map,* 296; particularism in, 413-416, 537; in Thirty Years' War, 531-532, 535-536
Gerson, Jean, 491
Ghibellines, 290, 417, 420
Gibbon, Edward, 136, 137, 212, 440
Gibraltar, 251, 517, 603
Gilbert, Sir Humphrey, 582
Gilgamesh, epic of, 37-38, 55
Giotto, 338, 451-452, 460; *illus.,* 452
Gizeh, pyramids at, 25; *illus.,* 24
Glaciers, 13
Glorious Revolution of *1688-1689,* 624-625
Gluttony, 168
Gnosticism, 163
Goa, 574
God (*see* Monotheism)
Godfrey of Bouillon, 352
Gods and goddesses: Egyptian, 29; Greek, 54; Roman, 125
Godunov, Boris, 386
Golden Age, belief in, 16

Golden Ass, 151
Golden Bull of *1356,* 415
Golden Gate, in Vladimir, Russia, *illus.,* 378
Golden Horde, state of, 380
Goliard poets, 330
Goslar, 287
Gospels: message of, 151; synoptic, 142
Gothic architecture, 332-336
Goths, 176
Government: representative, 339; Roman, 99-102; by slaves, in Ottoman Empire, 369-371
Gracchi, reforms of, 107-108
Grace, Calvinist doctrine, 500
Granada, 410
Grand Remonstrance, 619
Gravestones, 205 (*illus.*)
Gravitation, law of, 628
Great Britain, formation of, 625
Great Protestation, 616
Great Wall of China, 570
Greco, El, 544, 632
Greece (*see also* Athens *and* Sparta): age of colonization in, 57-59; agriculture, 50-51; ancient, 50 (*map*); architecture, 75-76; art, 61, 75-77; city-states of, 56-57; early forms of government of, 59; early history of, 53-59; everyday life in, 82; Hellenistic epoch, 88-92; Homeric age, 53, 55-56, 69, 70; language, revival of, 442 (*see also* Renaissance); literature, 72-74, 213; medieval, 366; Peloponnesian War, 69, 84-85; philosophy, 79-83; physical setting of, 49-51; religion of, 70-72; science, 77-79; style, 83-84; theater, 70, 72-74
Greek fire, 220
Greek Orthodox Church, 231-232
Greenland, 565
Greens, Byzantine political party, 225-226
Gregorian chant, 338
Gregory VII, 288-289, 290, 307, 351-352
Gregory IX, Pope, 295, 297
Gregory of Tours, 174, 182-183, 206, 208
Gregory the Great, Pope, 156, 158, 159
Grey, Lady Jane, 552
Grimani Palace, *illus.,* 465
Grimmelshausen, H. J. C., 536
Grosseteste, Robert, 325
Guarani Indians, 581
Guatemala, 580
Guelfs, 290, 417, 420
Guianas, 587
Guild halls, 335
Guild of the Evil Street, 431
Guilds: Byzantine, 222, 226; medieval, 322
Guinegate, battle of, 522
Guinevere, 328
Gunpowder, 469
Gustavus Adolphus, 533, 534
Gutenberg, Johann, 468
Guyon, Madame, 504, 608

H

Habsburgs, 504, 518 (*see also* Charles V *and* Thirty Years' War): wars with Turks, 375-376
Habsburg-Valois rivalry, 521-522
Hades, 37
Hadrian, Emperor, 116
Hakluyt, Richard, 592
Hals, Frans, *illus.,* 629
Hamburg, 427
Hamitic languages, 25
Hamlet, 556
Hammurabi, Code of, 23, 36-37
Hampden, John, 617
Hanging Gardens of Babylon, 34
Hannibal, 103-104
Hanover, House of, 625
Hanseatic League, 415, 427-428
Harem, of sultan, 371, 372
Harun al-Rashid, 254, 350
Harvey, W., 467-468, 628, 631
Hastings, battle of, 272
Hawkins, John, 582
Hector, 55
Heemskerk, Maerten van, *illus.,* 530
Hegira, 249
Helena, Saint, 350
Hellenes, 46
Hellenistic Age: culture of, 90-91; Greek states in, 88-90; style of, 91-92
Hellespont, 57
Heloise, 318
Helots, 60
Henry, Duke of Guise, 548, 549
Henry I (England), 274, 275
Henry I (Saxony), 284-285
Henry II (England), 262-264, 275-277
Henry II (France), 524
Henry III (England), 279
Henry III (France), 548, 549
Henry III (Germany), 287
Henry IV (England), 407
Henry IV (Germany), 287, 288-289
Henry IV (of Navarre), 548, 549-550, 598; *illus.,* 548
Henry V (England), 399, 407
Henry V, Emperor of Germany, 289
Henry VI (England), 363, 399, 407, 408
Henry VI (Germany), 293-295
Henry VII (England), 394, 402, 408-410; *illus.,* 409
Henry VII (Germany), 413
Henry VIII (England), 491, 492, 493, 524, 550-552; *illus.,* 492
Henry the Lion, 292-293; *illus.,* 293
Henry the Navigator, 565-566
Henry the Proud, 290
Hephaestus, 55
Heraclius, 225, 230, 236
Heresy, 156: in Byzantine world, 229-230; in early Christian church, 162-166
Heriot, 203
Herodotus, 36, 84
Herod the Great, 142, 143

Hibernia, 193 (*see also* Ireland)
Hildebrand, 288
Hinayana Buddhism, 569
Hindu society, 568-569
Hippocrates, 69, 78
Hippodrome, 226, 227
Historicism, 4
History: Christian attitude to, 166-167; detachment in, 479; new, 6; uses of, 3-4
Hitler, Adolf, 517
Hittites, 41
Hohenstaufen family, 295, 298
Holbein, Hans, 458; *illus.,* 492
Holland, 505, 508, 517: Dutch Republic in, 529-531; industries of, 530; revolt of, against Philip II, 527-528; trade with Russia, 390; wars of Louis XIV with, 600-601; war with England, 621
Holy League of the Papacy, 522
Holy Roman Empire, 187, 517: creation of, 285-288; end of, 298, 357
Holy Sepulchre, Church of, 350
Homer, 53, 55-56, 69, 70
Hominids, 11, 13
Homo neandertalensis, 13-14 (*illus.*)
Homo sapiens, 9, 13, 14, 16-18
Homosexuality, Greek, 58
Honor, chivalric, 329-330
Honorius, Emperor, 177, 234; *illus.,* 235
Honorius III, Pope, 295, 367
Hooker, Richard, 497
Hoover, Herbert, 469
Hoover, Mrs. Herbert, 469
Horace, 127, 128
Horse, the, 41
Horus, 29
Hospitallers, 355, 367
Hospitals, Roman, 122
Hotman, François, 502
Household Management, 388
House of Commons, 281, 404-405, 551, 614
House of Lords, 404, 551
Hubris, 73
Hudson, Henry, 582, 590
Hudson's Bay Company, 590
Huguenots, 491, 502, 547, 548, 608: and Richelieu, 598-599
Huitzilopochtli, 578
Huizinga, J., 480
Humanism, 442-443, 471
Humbert, Cardinal, 232
Hundred Years' War (*1338-1453*), 394, 395-397
Hungary, 490, 495, 504, 505: Tartar invasions of, 379; Turkish conquest of, 374
Huns, 176, 177, 217: European invasion by, 179-180
Hurrians, 39
Hus, John, 311, 312
Husein, 252
Hutten, Ulrich von, 487
Hutter, Jacob, 503
Hutterites, 495
Huygens, Christian, 530-531
Hyksos kings of Egypt, 27, 41

I

Iberian Peninsula (*see* Portugal *and* Spain)
Iceland, 565
Icons, 228: controversy over, 230, 231, 237-238; Russian, 388
Ideas, Platonic, 80-81
Ikhnaton, 29-30 (*illus.*), 44
Île de France, 261
Iliad, 53, 55-56
Illyricum, 231
Imitation of Christ, 325
Immortality (*see* Afterlife)
Inca empire, 578-579
Incest, 37
Index, Catholic, 507
India, 587, 603: caste system, 569, 592-593; history and institutions of, 567-570; *map,* 587; Portuguese trade with, 567
Indians, American, 578-579, 590
Indies: East, 587, 588; West, 587
Individualism, in Christian thought, 168-169, 497
Indo-European languages, 25
Induction, 626-627
Indulgences, sale of, 481-482
Industry, 430-431
Indus Valley, 18
Infanticide, Greek, 58, 60
Inflation, of sixteenth century, 593
Innocent III, Pope, 277, 294, 295, 304-305, 322
Innocent IV, Pope, 295, 297
Innovations, 5-6
Inquisition, 265, 271, 412, 505-506
Institutes, of Justinian, 224
Institutes of the Christian Religion, 490
Instrument of Government, 621
Instruments, musical, 466
Intendants, 599, 610
Interest, medieval attitude toward, 323
International politics, 594
Interregnum, German, 413
Invasions: from Asia, 217-218; of Europe, 7th-11th centuries, 192 (*map*); Germanic, in early Middle Ages, 173-174, 176, *map,* 178; of Moslems, 190; of Northmen, 190-193
Invention, Renaissance, 468-469
Investiture, of vassal, 199
Investiture Controversy: to *1077,* 288-289; *1077-1122,* 289-290; aftermath of, 290-291, 307, 308
Ioasaph, 215
Ion, 70
Ionia, 55
Ionic order, 75
Iraq, 20, 34, 252, 374
Ireland, 508, 602, 626: *Book of Kells* of, 194; early culture of, 193-194; in Elizabethan Age, 554; nationalism, 512
Iron Age, 11, 12
Iroquois Indians, 563
Irrigation, 23, 36
Isaac Angelus, Emperor, 363

Isabella of Castile, 394, 412, 575
Isaiah, Book of, 44-45
Isis, 28, 29: cult of, 151
Islam, 152, 236, 247: civilization of, 252-253; expansion of, 248-251, *map,* 250; extent of, 346; the Koran, 248; Mohammed, 246-249; music, 256; philosophy and science, 253-255
Israel, 35, 43
Istanbul, 57, 211
Italy, 506, 508: arts during Renaissance, 450-458, 460-466; banking in, 431-432; Baroque music of, 634; in Dark Ages, 194-195; Greek colonies in, 58, 69, 102; growth of communes in, 290-291; under Holy Roman Empire, 286; intervention of Franks in, 183-184; medieval, *map,* 296; particularism in, 417-424; Renaissance, *map,* 418; as school of Europe, 424
Ivan III, Tsar, 382
Ivan IV (the Terrible), 382-383: *illus.,* 385; reign of, 384-385
Ivry, battle of, 549

J

Jacquerie, the, 398
Jamaica, 621
James I (England), 282, 615, 616-617
James II (England), 602, 623-624
James, William, 318
Jamestown, Virginia, 582
Janissaries, 371
Jansenism, 504, 608, 635
Japan, European penetration of, 567, 588-589
Java, 12-13, 588
Jehovah, 43, 44
Jerome, St., 154, 156
Jerusalem, 35, 43, 236, 249, 251, 351: as Crusader state, 353, 357; destruction of, 117
Jesuits, 504-505, 506: in China, 573-574, 588; in Paraguay, 581
Jesus, Society of (*see* Jesuits)
Jesus Christ, 168: disputes over nature of, 164-165; life of, 142-143; teachings of, 143-144
Jewelry, of Dark Ages, 206; *illus.,* 205
Jews, 20, 431: Babylonian Captivity of, 35; expelled from England, 283; expelled from France, 272; history of, 41-43; persecution of, in Spain, 412; refuge for, in Holland, 530; religion of, 43-45; after Roman conquest, 117, 118; status of, in Middle Ages, 305; in time of Jesus, 142; uniqueness of, 43-44
Joan of Arc, 399
Job, Book of, 42, 45-46
John, Don, of Austria, 529
John, King (England), 200, 264, 277, 278-279
John II (France), 397, 398, 399

John of Gaunt, 406
John of Leyden, 494, 499; *illus.*, 502
John of Salisbury, 320
John Tsimiskes, 349
Joinville, Sieur de, 267-268, 280, 328, 361, 441
Journal des Sçavans, 627
Judah, Kingdom of, 43
Judea, 20
Julian the Apostate, 150
Julius II, Pope, 419, 457
Jury, English, origin of, 275-276
Justices of the peace, 404
Justinian, 120, 178, 179, 213, 216, 230: administration of, 234-236; *Code* of, 224; *illus.*, 228; Nika revolt under, 226-227
Jutes, 180
Juvenal, 127, 128

K

Kaaba, 247, 249
Karlovitz, congress of, 374-375
Karnak, temple of, *illus.*, 31
Kassites, 34-35
Kazan, 380
Kemal Attaturk, 6
Kempis, Thomas à, 325
Khalifa, succession of, 251
Kievan Russia, 242-243, 246-247, 379
King James Version of Bible, 617
King's Bench, Court of, 283
Kipling, Rudyard, 568
Knights, 283 (*see also* Feudalism)
Knights of the Shire, 280-281
Knights Templars, 271-272, 355
Knights' War, 487-488
Knox, John, 490
Köprülüs, the, 375
Koran, 248
Kossovo, battle of, 368
Krak des Chevaliers, *illus.*, 357
Kremlin, 382, 464
Krum, Bulgarian ruler, 240
Kshatriya, 569
Kuraish, 247
Kuzma Minin, 386

L

Laborers, Statute of, 403
Labyrinth, 52
Lachine Rapids, 576
Lagash, 34
Lancaster, house of, 407-408
Landini, 339
Lanfranc, Archbishop of Canterbury, 273
Langton, Stephen, 277, 278, 279
Languages: ancient Egyptian, 25; English, 137, 442, 632; Greek, 442; Latin, 127, 137, 175, 206, 245, 442, 631; Old Church Slavonic, 241, 245; rise of vernacular, 441-442, 443; Romance, 441
Langue d'oc, 441-442
Languedoc, 264, 265; *map,* 263
Langue d'oïl, 441-442

La Rochefoucauld, François de, 631
La Rochelle, siege of, 599
Lascaris, Theodore, 365
Las Casas, Bartholomew de, 581
Lateran Synod of *1059,* 307
Latifundia, Roman, 106-107, 108, 136, 201
Latin America (*see* America)
Latin Empire, established by Crusaders, 365-367
Latin language, 127, 137, 175, 206, 245, 442, 631
Latin states, in Syria, 346
Laud, William, 617, 618
Law, 23: Athenian, 63-64; Byzantine, 224-225, 229; canon, 120-121; constitutional, 339-340; of Edward I, 282-283; English common, 275-276; French, 270; international, 519; of Lübeck, 428; Mesopotamian, 36-37; natural, 120, 323; Ottoman, 372, 373; Roman, 101, 120; Russian, early, 246
League of Chambray, 522
League of Cognac, 523
League of Torgau, 524
Lechfeld, battle of, 195
Lecky, W. E. H., 621
Leeuwenhoek, Anton von, 531
Lefèvre d'Etaples, 489, 491
Leibniz, Gottfried W. von, 628
Leo I, Pope (the Great), 156, 165, 179
Leo III, Emperor (the Isaurian), 217, 234, 237
Leo III, Pope, 186
Leo IV, Emperor, 231
Leo VI, Pope, 225
Leo IX, Pope, 288
Leo X, Pope, 472, 483, 485, 486
Leon, Ponce de, 576
Lepanto, battle of, 375, 529
Letters of Eminent Men, The, 472
Letters of Obscure Men, The, 472-473
Levant (*see* Near East)
Levellers, 622
l'Hospital, Michel de, 549-550
Libel of English Policy, The, 426
Libraries: in Dark Ages, 175; Hellenistic, 90; Renaissance, 446
Licinius, 149
Lighthouse, at Alexandria, 90
Linear B, 53-54, 55
Lingua franca, 442
Lisbon, *illus.*, 572
Literature: ancient, preservation of, 315-316; Arabic, 254-255; Egyptian, 32; Elizabethan, 556-557; Greek, 72-74; Hellenistic, 90; humanistic, 442; inspired by Crusades, 361; inspired by exploration, 592; Muscovite, 388; Renaissance, 441-450; Roman, 127-129; seventeenth century, 631-632
Lithuania, 378, 382
Lithuanians, 357
Liudprand, of Cremona, 221, 224, 232-233

Locke, John, 631
Logarithms, 627
Logic, of Aristotle, 82
Lollards, 311
Lombard bankers, 431
Lombard League, 292
Lombards, 180, 183-184, 231, 236, 237
Lombardy, 238, 512
Lords, House of, 404
Lords, in feudalism, 199-200
Lords Ordainers, 403
Lorenzo the Magnificent, 422-423; *illus.,* 422
Louis I (the Pious), 188
Louis II (the German), 188, 189
Louis III (the Child), 195
Louis IV of Bavaria, Emperor, 414, 415
Louis VI (France), 262
Louis VII (France), 261-262, 356
Louis VIII (France), 265
Louis IX (France) (St. Louis), 265, 266, 267-269, 358
Louis X (France), 272
Louis XI (France), 394, 400-402
Louis XII (France), 522
Louis XIII (France), 598
Louis XIV (France), 597: absolutism, 606-607; administration of, 609-610; reign of, 600-602, 603
Louis XVI (France), 195
Louisiana, 586, 602
Louvain, University of, 314
Louvois, 612
Louvre, 546
Love: in Arabic and medieval literature, 255; in chivalric poetry, 328-329; romantic, 329
Low Countries (*see* Belgium *and* Holland)
Loyola, Ignatius, 504-505; *illus.,* 505
Lübeck, 427, 428, 430: Treaty of, 533
Lucretius, 125-126, 127
Lully, Jean Baptiste, 634
Lute, 466
Luther, Martin, 468, 480: *illus.,* 481; and Ninety-Five Theses, 481-483; opposition to, 485-486; revolt of, 483-485; writings of, 483, 485
Lutheran church, 480, 486-487, 509
Lutheranism, 498-499
Luxembourg, 517
Lyceum, 82
Lycurgus, 60, 70
Lysistrata, 74

M

Macao, 567, 574
Macaulay, W., 621
Macedonia, 104, 106: after death of Alexander, 88; rise of, 86
Macedonian dynasty, of Byzantium, 238
Machiavelli, Niccolò, 422-423, 424-426, 442

Madagascar, 588
Madeira, 575
Madonna of the Rocks, 457; *illus.,* 456
Maecenas, 127-128
Magdalenian culture, 15
Magdeburg, sack of, 533-534; *illus.,* 535
Magellan, Ferdinand, 577
Magic, prehistoric, 16
Magna Carta, 200, 278, 283
Magna Graecia, 58, 69, 102
Magnates, 198, 199, 201
Magyars, 179-180, 195, 217, 240, 285
Mahayana Buddhism, 569
Maintenon, Mme. de, 610
Maison Carrée, 116 (*illus.*)
Maleinos, Eustathius, 239
Malplaquet, battle of, 602
Malta, 335
Mamluks, 358, 369
Mamun, Caliph, 253
Man: evolution of, 16-17; prehistoric, 10-16; races of, 17, 24-25
Manchuria, 570
Mandarins, 571
Manfred, son of Frederick II, 279
Manicheism, 166
Manorialism, 434: definition of, 197-198; medieval, 302-303; plan of manor, *illus.,* 202; society under, 203-204
Manuel Commenus, 356, 363
Manuscripts, illuminated, 194, 205-206, 217, 337-338
Manzikert, battle of, 240, 346, 351
Marathon, 41, 67
Marcel, Étienne, 398
Marcus Aurelius, 116, 126-127: death of, 132
Marduk, 37
Margaret, Queen, 267-268
Margraves, of Charlemagne, 198-199
Marius, 110
Marlborough, Duke of, 602
Marseilles, 57-58
Marshall, Gen. George, 5
Marsiglio of Padua, 322
Marston Moor, battle of, 619
Martel, Charles, 183, 217
Martin V, Pope, 312
Martyrs, Christian, 149
Mary II, Queen, 624, 625
Maryland, 584
Mary Queen of Scots, 553, 554
Mary Tudor, Queen, 568
Masaccio, 454-455; *illus.,* 454
Massachusetts, 500, 501, 584
Massacre of St. Bartholomew's Day, 547, 548
Massilia, 58
Massillon, 504
Mathematics, 23, 34, 36, 78, 91: in Dark Ages, 206; Islamic, 253-254; medieval, 326; 17th century, 627-628
Mathilde, wife of Henry the Lion, *illus.,* 293
Matilda, Queen, 275, 276
Matrimony, 162

Matthias of Thurn, 532
Mauretania, 117
Mauritius, 588
Mavrogordato, 376
Maximilian I, Emperor, 402, 417
Mazarin, Cardinal, 599-600
Mecca, 247, 249
Medes, 35
Medici, Catherine de', 547, 548
Medici, Cosimo de', 421-422, 446
Medici, Lorenzo de', 422-423; *illus.,* 422
Medici, Marie de', 598
Medicine, 32: Greek, 78; Moslem, 254; Renaissance, 469
Medieval civilization (West), 301-341: anticlericalism, 330-331; architecture, 332-336; art, 331-333; chivalry, 326-330; economic thought, 322-323; education, 312-314, 316; guilds, 322; lay culture, 326-331; manorialism, 302-303; music, 338-339, 465; mysticism, 325-326; as term, 301-302
Medina, 249
Meditations, of Marcus Aurelius, 126-127
Megara, 58
Melanchthon, 486
Melfi, Constitutions of, 297
Menander, 90
Mencken, H. L., 151
Mendoza, Pedro de, 578
Mennonites, 495
Mercantilism, 543, 572, 591: of Colbert, 611-612; theory of, 611
Merchants, ancient, 21, 22 (*see also* Trade)
Merchet, 203
Merovingians, rule of, 181-183, 205
Mesopotamia, 20, 23: culture of, 36-38; history, 33-36; science, 36
Messiah, concept of, 44, 142
Mestizos, 579
Métayage, 303
Methodist church, 635
Metics, 66-67
Metropolitan of Moscow, 382
Mexico, 19, 578, 579
Mexico City, 580
Michael III, Emperor, 241
Michael VIII Palaeologus, 367
Michael Romanov, Tsar, 386
Michelangelo, 451, 453, 457, 458: *illus.,* 457, 472; as sculptor, 460-461
Microscope, 531, 627
Middle Ages (Early) (*see also* Dark Ages): church, status of, 205; feudalism (*see* Feudalism); Germanic invasions in, 173-174, 176, *map,* 178
Middle class, and Protestantism, 509-510
Middle East (*see also* Near East)
Middle Kingdom, 27
Midland, Texas, fossils found at, 14
Migration, of prehistoric man, 14
Milan, 304, 419-420, 523: as head of Lombard League, 292

Millennarians, 622
Milton, John, 439, 623, 631-632
Mining industry, Renaissance, 469
Ministeriales, German, 287
Minnesingers, 255, 328, 442, 466
Minoan civilization, 51-53
Minorca, 603
Minos, King, 51
Minstrels, 328, 339
Missing link, 11
Missionaries: to East, 573-574; Jesuit, 505
Mitanni, 41
Mithraism, 91, 151
Mithridates, 109, 110
Mobility, social, 22
Mogul Empire, 568, 587
Mohács, battle of, 374
Mohammed, 246-249; *illus.,* 248
Mohammed II, Sultan, 369
Mohammed III, Sultan, 371
Molière, 631, 634
Monarchs: English, 410; German election of, 414-415, *illus.,* 414; in late Middle Ages, 394; national, 402
Monasteries: Byzantine, 230-231, 237; Cistercian, 309; in Dark Ages, 207; German, 287-288; in Ireland, 194; Russian, 387-388
Monasticism: evaluation of, 157-158; origins of, 156-157
Mongols, 358, 368, 380: in China, 570-571; in India, 568
Mongol Tartars (*see* Tartars)
Monk, General, 621
Monophysite controversy, 165, 229, 230, 234
Monotheism: early Christian, 148; and Gnosticism, 163; of Ikhnaton, 29; Jewish, 43-45; of Mohammed, 248; of Plato, 87
Montaigne, Michel de, 547
Montenegro, 373
Monteverdi, Claudio, 634
Montfort, Simon de, 279
Mont-St.-Michel, 336; *illus.,* 337
Moravians, 240-241
More, Thomas, 489, 493
Morocco, 252
Morton, Archbishop, 409
Mosaics: Byzantine, 216, *illus.,* 228; Roman, 124-125 (*illus.*)
Moscow: as center of consolidation, 379-380; church in, 377-378; development of state in, 380-384; German suburb of, 390; princes of, 381-382; as third Rome, 348-349, 383
Moses, 42, 43
Moslems (*see also* Islam): European invasions of, 190, 217; factions and disunity among, 251-252; importance of, 247; in Spain, 410, 412
Mosques, Turkish, 216, 251; *illus.,* 252, 256
Motion, laws of, 628
Mount Olympus, 55
Muawiya, Caliph, 251
Muftis, 372
Mummies, Egyptian, 28

Münster, Anabaptists at, *illus.*, 494
Murad IV, Sultan, 375
Music: Baroque, 634; church, 498; in Dark Ages, 205; medieval, 338-339, 465; Moslem, 256; Renaissance, 464-466
Mycenae, 53
Mycenaean civilization, 54
Myron, 76, 77
Mystery cults, 91, 125
Mysticism: Hindu, 569; medieval, 325-326

N

Nagasaki, 588, 589
Nantes, Edict of, 549, 598, 599, 608
Napier, John, 627
Naples, 58, 418: opera in, 634; university of, 297
Naseby, battle of, 619
Nationalism, 339, 518: English, 404; growth of, 442; and Protestantism, 512
Nature, law of, 120, 323
Navigation, Renaissance, 469, 564
Navigation Act of *1651*, 620
Navy: Byzantine, 219-220; French, 599; modern, 521; Roman, 114; under mercantilism, 572-573
Neanderthal man, 13-14 (*illus.*)
Near East: achievements of, 22-23; common religious beliefs of, 45; early civilizations in, 20-22; Norman settlements in, 191; Old Stone Age in, 12; Roman possessions in, 117
Nebuchadrezzar I, 35
Nebuchadrezzar II, 43
Nefertiti, Queen, 29; *illus.*, 30
Negroes, in slave trade (*see* Slave trade)
Nehemiah, 43
Neolithic Age, 11, 12, 21
Neolithic revolution, 12
Neoliths, *illus.*, 12
Neo-Platonism, 87, 152, 214, 254
Nero, Emperor, 115: persecution of early Christians by, 147, 148
Nerva, Emperor, 115-116
Nestorian Church, 165, 566
Nestorius, Bishop, 164-165
Netherlands, United, 530, 537 (*see also* Holland)
Newfoundland, 565, 582, 602
New France, 586
New Laws of *1542* (Spanish), 581
Newport, Rhode Island, tower in, 565
New Stone Age, 11, 12
New Testament, 142, 492 (*see also* Bible)
Newton, Sir Isaac, 628, 631
New York, 584, 623
Nicaea: Byzantine kingdom of, 365, 367; Council of, 228, 229, 230; Empire, 347
Nicene creed, 234
Nicephorus I, Emperor, 240
Nicephorus Phocas, 232-233, 349

Nicetas Choniates, 364
Nicholas V, Pope, 419, 472
Nijmegen, treaties of, 601
"Nika" revolt, Byzantine, 226
Nile Valley, 18, 19, 23, 24
Nîmes, 116
Nineveh, 35, 39
Nirvana, 569
Nobiles, Roman, 101-102
Nobles: in reign of Louis XIV, 607-608; Russian, 383-384
Noblesse de la robe, 608
Noblesse de l'épée, 608
Nominalism, 33, 317-319
Nomisma, 222
Noricum, 117
Normandy, 191: strength of Dukes of, 201, 262
Normans: contest with Angevins, 262, 264; in England, 272-274; in Italy, 239; sack of Thessalonica by, 363
Northmen, 218: invasions of, 190-193; in North America, 565
Norway, 196, 488
Notre Dame, Cathedral of, 337; *illus.*, 334
Nova Scotia, 602
Novels, of Justinian, 224
Novgorod, 242, 246, 348, 378-379, 427
Numbers, cult of, 78
Numerals, Arabic, 254
Numidia, 117
Nureddin, Sultan, 356

O

Ockham, William of, 318-319
Octavia, 112
Octavian (*see* Augustus)
Odovacar, 177-178
Odyssey, 55
Oil paints, 455
Old Believers, 390
Old Kingdom, of Egypt, 25, 27
Old Russian Primary Chronicle, 242
Old Stone Age, 11
Old Testament, 32, 41-42, 44
Olga, Princess, 243
Oligarchy: Spartan, 60; Venetian, 423
Olympia, 70-71
Olympic games, 70, 72
O'Neill, Hugh, 554
One World, concept of, 594
Opera, 634
Oprichnina, 385
Optics, 628
Optimates, Roman, 109, 110
Oracle, Delphic, 70
Oration on the Dignity of Man, 448
Oratory of Divine Love, 504
Orders: mendicant, 309-311; military, 355
Ordination, 162
Ordonnances, 269
Oreopithecus, 11
Oresteia, 73

Orgaz, Count of, burial (legend), 544
Original sin, 161, 165, 168
Orthodox Church, schism of, from West, 159-160
Osiris, 28-29
Osmanlis (*see* Ottoman Turks)
Ostracism, Athenian, 65
Ostrogoths, 177-178, 235
Otto I, 195, 232, 284, 285
Otto III, 284, 285
Ottoman state, 369-376: administration of, 371-373; expansion of, 373-374; slave system of, 369-371
Ottoman Turks, 347-348: advance of, 367-369; in Hungary, 374; at Karlovitz peace conference, 374-375
Otto of Brunswick, 264, 294, 295
Oudenarde, battle of, 602
Outremer, 361
Overpopulation, Greek, 58-59
Ovid, 127, 128
Oxenstierna, Chancellor, 534
Oxford, Provisions of, 403
Oxford University, 313

P

Pacific Ocean, discovery of, 576
Padua, University of, 467, 469
Paestum, Temple of Poseidon at, 57 (*illus.*)
Painting (*see also* Art): cave, *illus.*, 15; chiaroscuro technique, 451, 452; medieval, 337-338; oil, 455; Renaissance, 450-460; wall, 11
Palaces, Renaissance, 464
Palais de Justice, Poitiers, *illus.*, 266
Paleolithic Age, 11, 15
Paleoliths, 12 (*illus.*)
Palermo, 294
Palestine, 20, 117 (*see also* Jews): in time of Jesus, 142
Palestrina, 465
Palladio, 463
Panathenea, 71, 72
Pannonia, 117
Pantagruel, 447, 448
Papacy, 195, 261: alliance of, with Franks, 184-185, 186; "Babylonian Captivity," 271-272; in Dark Ages, 207; and election of German monarch, 414, 415; and England, 273-274, 277; and Frederick II, 297-298; Great Schism, 231-232; Holy League of the, 522; and Philip the Fair, 270, 271; in Renaissance, 419, 472; as sponsor of Crusades, 351
Pappenheim, 533
Papyrus, 25
Paradise Lost, 631
Paris, University of, 313, 467, 469
Parkman, Francis, 586
Parlamento, of Milan, 419
Parlement, 269, 270: Capetian, 266-267

Parlement under Louis XIV, 610
Parliament, 298: evolution of, 404-405; *illus.*, 282; under James I, 616-617; Long, 613-614, 618; Model, 283-284, 404; origins of, 279-280; Rump, 620, 621; Short, 618; Tudor, 551-552
Parthenon, 69, 75-76; *illus.*, 71, 76
Pascal, Blaise, 608, 627-628, 635
Patriarch of Constantinople, 229, 232
Patricians, Roman, 99, 100-101
Patrick, St., 193
Patroclus, 55
Patronage, of art, in Renaissance, 452-455, 458
Paul, St., 145-146, 147
Paul III, Pope, 458, 506
Pavia, battle of, 522-523
Pax Romana, 96, 115, 130, 138
Peace: of Aix-la-Chapelle, 600; of Augsburg, 524-526; conferences, Thirty Years' War, 602-603; of Constance, 282; of Ryswick, 602; of Westphalia, 530
Peasant rebellions, 435: German, 487-488, *illus.*, 487
Peasants' Revolt, English, 311, 405; *illus.*, 406
Pechenegs, 217, 240, 351
Pelagianism, 165, 167
Peloponnesian League, 61, 84
Peloponnesian War, 69, 84-85
Penance, 162
Penn, William, 584
Pennsylvania, 584, 585
Pensées, 634-635
Pepin the Short, 183-184
Pergamum, 91
Pericles, 62, 65-66, 68, 85
Perioikoi, Spartan, 60
Perry, Admiral M., 589
Persepolis, 40; *illus.*, 39
Persia, 20, 21, 252: capture of Jerusalem by, 236; Islamic conquest of, 249-250; Persian Empire, 35, 40, 85, 87; wars with Turks, 374, 375
Persian Gulf, 374
Persian language, 25
Persian Wars, 67-68
Peru, 19, 580
Peruzzi banking family, 432, 453
Peter, St., 146, 147, 155
Peter the Great, 387
Peter the Hermit, 352
Petition of Right, 617
Petrarch, 362, 443-445
Phaedo, 80
Phalanx, 98
Pharisees, 142-143
Phidias, 69, 76
Philip II Augustus (France), 261, 262, 264, 267, 277, 356, 540, 552
Philip II of Macedon, 86
Philip II (Spain), 433, 491, 526-527; *illus.*, 526
Philip IV, the Fair (France), 269-272, 298, 355
Philip V of Anjou (Spain), 602
Philip VI of Valois (France), 395

Philip of Hesse, 485
Philip of Swabia, Emperor, 294, 295, 364
Philippine Islands, 541, 580
Philip the Good, Duke of Burgundy, 401
Philosophical Transactions, 627
Philosophy: Greek, 79-83; Hellenistic, 91; Islamic, 254-255; Roman, 125-127
Phocaea, 58
Phocas, Emperor, 236
Phoenicia, 20, 22
Phoenicians, 41; *map*, 50
Physics, 254, 628
Piacenza, Council of, 351
Pico della Mirandola, 448
Picts (*see* Scotland)
Piedmont, 512
Piers Plowman, 403, 442
Pietà, of Michelangelo, 461-462; *illus.*, 462
Pietism, 635
Pilgrimages, 350 (*see also* Crusades)
Pilgrim's Progress, 503, 632
Piltdown man, 14
Pindar, 75
Piracy, 572-573
Pisa, 353, 521: Council of, 312
Pisistratus, 64, 72
Pithecanthropus erectus, 12; *illus.*, 13
Pitti Palace, 464
Pythagoras, 69, 78, 80
Pius II, Pope, 419
Pius V, Pope, 507
Pizarro, Francisco, 578
Plain-song, 338
Plataea, 67
Plato, 57, 69, 79, 80-82, 254
Platonic Academy of Medici, 435, 446, 448, 453
Plebeians, Roman, 99, 101-102
Pleistocene period, 11
Pliny the Elder, 121, 127
Pliny the Younger, 127, 148-149
Plymouth, Massachusetts, 582, 584
Poetics, of Aristotle, 82, 631
Poetry: Arabic, 254; Greek, 74; Latin, 127
Poitiers, battle of, 397
Poland, 490, 495, 504, 505, 508, 517: Tartar invasions of, 379; united with Lithuania, 378
Pole, Cardinal, 552
Poles, 196
Police, secret, 385
Political organization: ancient, 21; in ancient Near East, 22; medieval, 304, 394; modern state-systems of, 516-518
Politics, international, 518, 594
Politics, of Aristotle, 82
Politiques, French, 549-550
Polo, Marco, 428, 565; *illus.*, 567
Polovtsy, 246, 379
Polybius, 98-99, 103
Polygamy: of Anabaptists at Münster, 494; Moslem, 249
Polyneices, 73-74
Polytheism: Egyptian, 29; Greek

(*see* Religion, Greek); Roman, 125
Pomestie, 383
Pompeii, 130 (*illus.*)
Pompey, 111
Pondichéry, 587
Pontifex maximus, 125
Poor Law of *1601*, 614
Pope, Alexander, 16
Pope, in Church hierarchy, 153-154, 155 (*see also* Papacy)
Populares, Roman, 109
Population: pressure of, Greek, 58-59; shortage of, in Rome, 135-136
Port Royal, 504
Portugal, 374, 411, 439, 506, 508, 517, 529, 564:* expansion of, 565-567; trade empire of, 572-574
Portuguese language, 44
Postal system, Persian, 36
Potatoes, 591
Power, balance of, 517
Poynings' Act, 554
Pozharsky, Dmitri, 386
Praetor, 100
Pragmatic Sanction of Bourges, 400, 401, 548
Prague, defenestration of, 532
Predestination, 499-500, 608
Prehistoric man: art, 15-16; characteristics of, 17-18; chronology of, 10-14; culture of, 14-16; tools of, 12 (*illus.*)
Presbyterian church, 501
Presbyterians, 553, 615-616, 618
Presbyteries, 154
Prester John, legend of, 566
Prévôts, 265
Pride, Colonel, 620
Priesthood: Christian, 154; Roman, 125
Primavera, 454; *illus.*, 453
Primitive culture, 11, 14
Principia, of Newton, 628
Printing: business of, 631; press, 468, 610
Procopius, 216, 234-235
Progress, doctrine of, 630
Pronoia, 362
Prophets, Jewish, 42
Protestant Reformation, 479-503: conditions preceding, 480, 484-485, 487-488; in England, 491-493; in Germany, 484-488 (*see also* Luther, Martin); left wing, 502-503; as revolution, 480
Protestant Union, 532
Protestantism: Anglicanism, 480, 497-498, 509, 614; beliefs and practices of, 495-503; Calvinism, 480, 489, 497-492, 509; and capitalism, 510-512; in France, 491, 547; Lutheranism (*see* Luther; Lutheran church); and nationalism, 512; and progress, 508-510; and Thirty Years' War, 537
Provençal, 441
Provinces, Roman, 117-118
Provisions of Oxford, 279, 403

Provosts of the harlots, 536
Prussia, 537, 607
Prussia, East, 512
Pseudepigraphia, 154
Ptolemies, dynasty of, 25, 89
Punic Wars, 103-104
Purcell, Henry, 634
Puritanism, 497, 616: Calvinist, 500-502; of Cluniac reform, 308; in iconoclastic controversy, 237-238; Jewish, 44, 45; of Savonarola, 453, 473-474
Puritans, 553, 584, 621
Pushkin, Alexander, 381
Pyramids, 22, 25; of Gizeh, *illus.*, 24
Pyrrhus, 102

Q

Quaestio de Aqua et Terra, 316
Quakers (Religious Society of Friends), 154-155, 622-623, 635
Quebec, Province of, 586, 602
Queen Mary's Psalter, illus., 197
Quesada, Jimenez de, 578
Quietists, 608, 635
Quito, 580

R

Rabelais, François, 447-448, 547
Races, of man, 17, 24-25
Racine, Jean Baptiste, 631
Radiocarbon, 10, 12, 13
Raetia, 117
Raleigh, Sir Walter, 582
Ramadan, 249
Rameses, 27
Ramillies, battle of, 602
Rationalism, 629
Ravenna: Byzantine exarchate at, 236, 237; churches of, 216
Realism, 33: medieval, 317-319
Redemption, 73
Reformation, Protestant (*see* Protestant Reformation)
Relief, 200
Religion (*see also* Christianity): about *1100, map,* 306; ancient, 23; of ancient Egypt, 28-30; Buddhist, 569; Bulgarian, 240; Byzantine, 227-228; Chinese, 571-573; early Christian, 144-147; in Europe, about *1600, map,* 507; freedom of, 496; freedom of, in American colonies, 585; Greek, 70-72; Hellenistic, 91; Hindu, 569; Jewish, 43-46; of Mesopotamia, 37; Moslem, 248-249; monotheism (*see* Monotheism); Persian, 40; polytheism, 29, 125; prehistoric, 16; in Renaissance, 471-474; Roman, 125-127; Russian, 390; seventeenth-century, 635
Religious toleration, 537, 622-623
Rembrandt, 530, 634; *illus.*, 636
Renaissance: architecture of, 450, 463-464; art, 450-464; banking, 431-432; Carolingian, 204; English, 555-557; in France, 546-547; historical problem of, 439-441; humanism, 442-443, 471; industry, 430-431; literature, 441-442; medicine, 469; music, 464-466; painting in, 450-460; preservation of classics in, 446-447; religion in, 471-474; science of, 466-470; sculpture of, 460-462; style of, 474-476
Representative government, 339
Republic, The (Plato), 80, 81-82
Republic of St. Mark, 423
Resignation, medieval, 342
Restitution, Edict of, 533
Restoration, English, 622-624
Reuchlin, John, 472-473
Revolution, Glorious, 622, 624-625
Rhode Island, 585
Rhodes, 89, 251, 373, 374
Ricci, Father Matthew, 573-574
Richard I the Lionhearted, 264, 277, 294, 356
Richard II, 405-407
Richard III, 408
Richard of York, 407
Richelieu, Cardinal, 533, 598-600; *illus.,* 599
Ripuarian Franks, 187
Ritual, in Byzantine church, 230-231
River valleys, and civilization, 18-20
Roads, Roman, 123
Roanoke Island, 582
Robinson, James H., 6
Roger II, 293-294
Roland, Chanson de, 327, 328
Roman Catholic Church, 138 (*see also* Papacy): canon law, 120-121; Cluny reform of, 286; College of Cardinals, 288, 307; in Dark Ages, 175; Investiture Controversy, 288-291, 307, 308; in Ireland, 194; and medieval public opinion, 314-316; monasticism in (*see* Monasteries; Monasticism); reform by Gregory VII, 288-289; reform movements in, 473-474; Reformation in, 503-508; relations of, with German kings, 284-285; in Renaissance, 471-474; Rome as center, 155-156; and schism, 231-232; status of, in Middle Ages, 206
Roman Empire, 96, 112-118 (*see also* Byzantium *and* Invasions, Germanic): administration of, 117-119; Augustus, and creation of, 112-115; and Christianity, 136-137; decline of, 132-136; emperors, 115-116, 132-135; end of, 177-178; provinces of, 116-117; succession in, 132
Roman Republic, 97-108: army of, 98-99; beginnings of autocracy in, 110-112; Caesarism and end of, 111-112; class structure, 99-101; economic crisis of, 106-107; expansion of, in Italy, 102-103; government of, 99-101; rise of, 97-98
Romance languages, 441
Romanesque church, *illus.,* 333
Romanos IV, 240
Romanov, Alexis, 386-387
Romanov, Michael, 386
Rome, 89, 129, 131, 133; abandonment of, 228; and Carthage, 103-104; as center of Christianity, 155-156; and China, 516; civilization of, 119-138; founding of, 95-96; frontier wars of, 109; geography of, 96; and Hellenistic World, 104-106; importance of, 137-138; Renaissance, 419; sack of, 177, 179, 523; standard of living in, 129-132
Romulus Augustulus, 177-178
Root and Branch Bill, 619
Rose windows, 337
Roses, Wars of the, 406, 407-408
Rosetta Stone, 25; *illus.,* 26
Rostovtsev, M., 136-137
Roundheads, 619
Royal Society for Improving Natural Knowledge, 627
Rubens, P., 632, 634; *illus.,* 635
Rubicon River, 111
Rudolf of Habsburg, Emperor, 413, 414
Rudolf of Swabia, 289
Rumania, 373
Runnymede, 278
Rurik, 242, 383
Rus, 242
Russia, 196, 218, 230, 375, 517: and Byzantium, 241-242; church in, 159, 243-246; conversion of, 243-246; development of Muscovite state, 380-384; early state of, 20, 242-243; imperial absolutism in, 382-383; Kievan, 246-247; literature, 388; monarchy and early modern, *maps,* 377; monasteries in, 387-388; Moscow becomes center of, 379-380; northern lands of, 378-379; Old Believers in, 390; and Poland, 389; post-Kievan, 348-349; and relations with West, 389-390; serfs, 384; Tartars in, 348-349, 379-381; Time of Troubles in, 385-388; western lands of, 377-379
Russian Orthodox Church, 159, 387-388
Ruth, Book of, 42
Ryswick, Peace of, 602

S

Sachs, Hans, 466
Sacraments: Byzantine, 231; Protestant, 496, 497; seven Christian, 160-162
Sadducees, 142
Sagas, Norse, 565
Sahara Desert, 20
St. Anthony, 157
St. Augustine, 166-167
St. Bartholomew's Day, massacre of, 547, 548
St. Basil, 157

St. Basil, Cathedral of, *illus.,* 388
St. Benedict, 157
St. Bernard of Clairvaux, 308-309, 324, 355-356
St. Columban, 194
St. Francis of Assisi, 310, 324-325
St. Francis Xavier, 588
St. Helena, 350
St. James of Compostella, 350
St. Jerome, 154, 156
St. John of the Cross, 544
St. Lawrence River, 576
St. Louis (*see* Louis IX)
St. Maclou, Church of, 335; *illus.,* 336
St. Mark's Cathedral, 216; *illus.,* 218, 219, 365
St. Patrick, 193
St. Paul, 145-146, 147
St. Paul's Cathedral, London, 632; *illus.,* 625
St. Peter, 146, 147, 155
St. Peter's, Rome, 453, 463; *illus.,* 464; *illus.,* 633
St. Sernin, Church of, *illus.,* 333
St. Simeon Stylites, 156
St. Theresa of Avila, 544
St. Thomas Aquinas, 318, 319-320
St. Willibald, 350
Sainte Chapelle, 267
Saints, lives of, 206, 214-215
Saite dynasty, Egypt, 27
Saladin, Sultan, 356-357
Salamis, battle of, 67
Salian Franks, 181, 286-288
Salisbury Oath, 273
Salvation, personal, 71, 91, 161, 341
Samuel, Bulgarian ruler, 241-242
Sancho Panza, 544-545
Sanskrit, 23, 25
Santa Maria Maggiore, *illus.,* 155
Santa Sophia, Church of, *illus.,* 216, 228
Santa Sophia, at Kiev, 244
Santo Domingo, 576
Sappho, 69, 75
Sarai, 379, 380
Sardinia, 603
Satire, 74-75, 128
Savonarola, 454, 473-474
Savoy, 603
Saxony, 284
Scandinavians (*see* Northmen)
Schism, church, 231-232, 307, 311
Schliemann, Heinrich, 53, 54
Scholasticism, 317, 466-467
School of the Patriarch, 213
Science: ancient, 23; in Dark Ages, 206; Dutch, 530-531; after European exploration, 592-593; Greek, 77-79; Hellenistic, 90; Islamic, 253-254; medieval, 324-325; in Mesopotamia, 36; natural, in seventeenth century, 626-630; and Protestant ethic, 511; in Renaissance, 466-470; Roman, 121-123
Scipio Africanus, 104, 107
Sciri, 180
Scotland, 282, 490, 508, 517, 524: Calvinism in, 554; in Civil War,

618-620; in Dark Ages, 195; union of, with England, 625-626
Scrovegni, Enrico, 451
Sculpture: Assyrian, 38 (*illus.*); Egyptian, 31, 32; Greek, 76-77; Hellenistic, 90 (*illus.*); medieval, 336-337; Minoan, 52 (*illus.*); Renaissance, 460-462; Roman, 124 (*illus.*); Romanesque, 339
Scutage, 274, 278
Seleucid Empire, 88-89, 104
Selim I, Sultan, 373
Seljuk Turks, 240, 351, 353
Semitic languages, 25
Senate, Roman, 99, 100-101, 107, 113-114
Seneca, 126
Senegal, 588
Seneschal, 265, 266
Septuagint version, of Bible, 154
Serbia, 368
Serbs, 196, 218, 242, 347, 367
Serfs, 203-204, 488: Byzantine, 222-223; emancipation of, 303; in Russia, 384
Servetus, 495
Settlement, Act of, 625
Sex, Christian view of, 168, 501
Sforza, Francesco, 420
Sforza, Ludovico Il Moro, 420
Shakespeare, William, 439, 555, 556-557, 631
Sheikh-ul-Islam, 372
Sheol, 37
Shiites, 251-252
Shuisky, 386
Siberia, 389: Russian conquest of, 589-590
Sic et Non, 318
Sicilian Vespers, 367, 418-419
Sicilies, Two, 418-419
Sicily, 106, 191, 603: administration of Frederick II, 295, 297; Moslems in, 217, 237; Norman, 293-295
Sickingen, Franz von, 487
Silk: Byzantine, 221-222; state monopoly of, 297
Silver Age, Roman, 127
Simony, 207, 307, 308
Simplicissimus, 536
Sin, original, 161, 165, 168
Sistine Chapel, 457-458
Six Articles, 493, 552
Slavery, 130: Athenian, 67, 89-90; and government, in Ottoman Empire, 369-371; in New World, 580, 581; Roman, 120; true, 203-204
Slave trade, 588, 590
Slavonic language, 241, 245, 388
Slavs, 218, 235, 236, 357: in Dark Ages, 195, 196; impact of Byzantium on, 240-246
Sluys, victory at, 397
Smith, Capt. John, 584
Social classes (*see also* Feudalism *and* Middle Class): ancient Near East, 18, 21-22; and Christianity, 150; India, 569, 592-593; Sparta, 60-61
Social mobility, 22

Society of Friends, 154-155, 622-623, 635
Society of Jesus, 504-505, 506
Socinus, 495
Socrates, 69, 74, 79-80
Solomon, King, 43
Solon, 63-64
Song of Roland, 185, 208, 441
Song of the Expedition of Igor, 246
Sonnet form, 44
Sophocles, 69, 72, 73-74
Sorbonne, the, 546
South America, 579
Sovereignty, of modern states, 516-517
Spain: 103, 104, 106, 116, 304, 410-411, 439, 506, 508, 517, 564 (*see also* Ferdinand of Aragon *and* Isabella of Castile): absolutism in, 540-542; Crusades in, 357; in Dark Ages, 177, 195-196; economy of, 542-543; infantry, 521; *map,* 411; Moslems in, 217, 254; and Naples, 418-419; regionalism of, 542; as Roman province, 117-118; 17th century style, 543-545; wars of Philip II, 526-529; wars with Louis XIV, 600-601
Spanish Armada, 528-529; *illus.,* 528
Spanish Empire in America, 577-582
Spanish language, 441
Sparta, 66-67: evaluation of, 61-62; in Peloponnesian War, 84-85; régime of, 60-61, 102
Spinoza, Baruch, 531
Spiritual Exercises, 504-505
Spitsbergen, 590
Stained glass, medieval, 337-338
Star Chamber, 409, 618
State-system: European, 516-521; balance of power in, 517; competitive, 516-517; dynastic, 518-519; diplomacy, 518; sovereign, 516-517
Statute of Drogheda, 554
Statute of Laborers, 403
Statute of Mortmain, 283
Statute of Westminster, Second, 283
Steelyard, 427
Stenka Razin, 387
Stephen Dushan, King, 367
Stephen, of England, 277
Stephen II, Pope, 183
Stereotypes, of national character, 259-260, 298-299
Stevin, Simon, 627
Stilicho, 177
Stoics, 91, 120, 126
Stone Age, 11, 12
Stone of Scone, 282
Strabo, 129, 131
Strasbourg Oaths, 188-189
Strepsiades, 74
Stuart, James, 615
Stuart, Mary, 553, 554
Student life, medieval, 313-314; *illus.,* 313

Style: Egyptian, 32-33; Greek, 83-84; Hellenistic, 91-92; Medieval, 302, 340-341; Renaissance, 474-476; Roman, 119-138
Subinfeudation, 200
Succession: of Byzantine Emperors, 223; problem of, in Roman Empire, 115-116
Sudan, 20
Suevi, 180
Suger, Abbot of St. Denis, 262
Suleiman the Magnificent, 373-374, 524
Sulla, 110
Sully, Duc de, 598
Sumatra, 588
Sumerians, 22, 34
Summa Contra Gentiles, 319
Summa Theologica, 319
Sunnites, 251
Supremacy, Act of, 491, 492
Surgery, Roman, *illus.,* 121
Swabia, 284
Swammerdam, Jan, 531
Sweden, 196, 389, 488, 516, 531, 584, 600, 601: and Thirty Years' War, 533-534, 537
Swift, Jonathan, 626
Swiss Confederation, 537
Switzerland, 402, 417, 508, 517
Syagrius, General, 182
Symeon, 241
Syncretism: of early Christianity, 152, 207; in Greek religion, 70
Synod of the Lateran, 159
Synod of Whitby, 194
Synoptic Gospels, 146
Syphilis, 581
Syracuse, 58
Syria, 20, 217, 229, 230: Islamic conquest of, 249-250; Seleucid dynasty in, 88-89, 104

T

Table Talk, of Luther, 488
Tacitus, 114-115, 127, 128-129, 148
Tagliacozzo, battle of, 297
Tamerlane, 368
Tammuz, 37
Tarquin the Proud, 97
Tartars, 389: invasion of Russia by, 245-246; in Russia, 348-349, 379-380
Taurobolium, 151
Taxation: ancient, 21, 22; under Augustus, 114; Byzantine, 222, 237, 362-363; by consent, in Magna Carta, 278, 283-284, 298; in Crusader states, 354; under Diocletian, 134-135; English, 274; of Frederick II, 297; French, 397, 400; French, under Capetians, 267, 272; medieval, 304; Ottoman, 372; with representation, 617
Taylor, Henry O., 206
Technology, 12, 15, 17: Renaissance, 468-469
Teeth, human, 14-15
Telescope, 627
Tell el Amarna, 29

Tempera painting, 455
Templars, Knights, 355, 367, 431
Tertullian, 319
Test Act of *1672,* 623
Tetzel, J., 481, 482, 484
Teutones, 176
Teutonic Knights, 355, 356, 367
Theater, Greek, 70, 72-74 (*illus.*)
Theatines, 504
Thebes, 29, 30, 85, 87
Themes, 236-237
Themistocles, 67
Theocracy: Byzantine, 229; Puritan, 501-502
Theodora, Empress, 226, 234
Theodore of Sykeon, 215
Theodoric, 178
Theodosius the Great, Emperor, 150, 234; *illus.,* 235
Theology, controversies over, in Byzantine Christianity, 214, 227, 229-230 (*see also* Heresy)
Theophilus, 225
Thermopylae, 67
Thessalonica, 363, 366, 367
Thirty-Nine Articles, 497, 552
Thirty Years' War, 375, 531-539, 547: Bohemian Period, 532; Danish Period, 532-533; and Germany, 534-536; nature and causes of, 531-532; peace of Westphalia, 536-537; Swedish Period, 533-534
Thomas the Slav, 238
Thomism, 320
Thrace, 36
Thucydides, 62, 69, 84
Thuringia, 284
Thutmosis III, 25, 27
Tiberius, 115
Tigris-Euphrates Valley, 18, 19, 33-34
Tilly, Johann, Count of, 532, 533, 534
Timor, 574
Tindal, William, 492
Titian, 458
Tobacco, 591
Tokugawa family, 588-589
Toledo, Spain, 350, 410
Toleration, religious, 495-497
Tomatoes, 591
Tools, of prehistoric man, 12 (*illus.*), 15, 17
Tordesillas, Treaty of, 566, 577
Torgau, League of, 524
Tories, origins of, 624
Torricelli, Evangelista, 627
Torstenson, General, 534
Toscanelli, 575
Totemism, 29
Toulouse, 177, 264, 265
Tours, 217: battle of, 183
Tower of Babel, 34, 37, 460
Town halls, 335
Towns, as allies of kings, 303-304
Trade (*see also* Mercantilism): ancient, 21, 22-23; Byzantine, 221-222; after Crusades, 360; in East Indies, 587; fur, 586; Greek, 51, 61; of fifteenth century, 426-427; Hanseatic, 427-

428; in Kievan Russia, 246; with Muscovite Russia, 389-390; of Novgorod, 378-379; Portuguese, with East, 567, 570, 572; slave, 567, 582, 588, 590-591; Venetian, 428-430; wool, 430-431
Tragedy: French, seventeenth-century, 631; Greek, 72-74
Trajan, Emperor, 116, 148-149
Transepts, 332
Transmigration of souls, 569
Transubstantiation, 490
Transylvania, 495
Treasury of Merit, 482
Treaties of Nijmegen, 601
Treaty of Cateau-Cambrésis, 524, 526
Treaty of Lübeck, 533
Treaty of Tordesillas, 566, 577
Treaty of Troyes, 399
Treaty of Vervins, 549
Treaty ports, 568
Trebizond, 351
Trent, Council of, 506-508
Tribal Assembly, 101
Tribunes, Roman, 101, 110, 111, 114
Tribute of children, 370
Triennial Act of *1640,* 618
Trinity: Arian heresy concerning, 163-164; Moslem view of, 248
Tripoli, as Crusader state, 353
Tristan and Isolde, 328
Tri-theism, 164
Troilus and Criseyde, 447
Trojan War, 53, 54, 55
Troubadours, 255, 328, 411, 466
Troyes, Treaty of, 399
Tsar, the title, 382
Tsargrad, 212
Tsimiskes, John, 349
Tudor, Edward VI, 552
Tudor, Elizabeth I (*see* Elizabeth I)
Tudor, Henry VII, 394, 402, 408-410
Tudor, Henry VIII, 491, 492, 493, 524, 550-552
Tudor, Mary, 568
Tudors, accession of, 408
Tunis, 252
Turenne, Vicomte de, 600
Turkestan, Russian, 251
Turkey, 20
Turks, origins of, 369-370: Seljuk, 240, 351, 353
Turks, Ottoman (*see* Ottoman Turks)
Tutankhamen, 27, 30
Twelve Articles, 488
Twelve Tables, 101, 120
Tyler, Wat, *illus.,* 406
Tyranny, Greek, 59, 64-65
Tyrone, Hugh O'Neill, Earl of, 554

U

Ukraine, 375, 389
Ukrainians, 196
Ulema, 372
Ulfilas, 164

Ulpian, 120
Ulysses, 55
Umayyad Caliphate, 251-252
Union of Utrecht, 528
Unitarianism, 164, 495
United Netherlands, 530, 537
Universal man, concept of, 475
University: at Athens, 213; at Bologna, 313; Cambridge, *illus.*, 313; at Constantinople, 213; of Louvain, 314; medieval, 313-314; of Naples, 297; Oxford, 313; of Padua, 467; Paris, 313, 467, 469
Ur, of the Chaldees, 33, 34 (*illus.*)
Ural Mountains, 389
Urban II, Pope, 346, 351
Urban VI, Pope, 311
Urbino, 446
Usamah Ibn-Munqidh, 359
Ussher, Archbishop, 9
Usury, 323, 512
Utraquists, 532
Utrecht: treaties of, 602-603; Union of, 528

V

Vaca, Cabeza de, 578
Vaisya, 569
Valdivia, Pedro de, 578
Valencia, 411
Valens, Emperor, 177
Valerian, Emperor, 132
Valla, Lorenzo, 184-185, 446-447
Valle, Pietro della, 592-593
Valleys, river, and origins of cities, 18-20
Valois, House of, 522
Valois-Habsburg rivalry, 521-522
Vandals, 174, 178-179, 235
Vase, Greek, 62 (*illus.*), 77
Vassals, 199-200
Vatican, 457: library of, 446
Veblen, Thorstein, 511
Veche, of Novgorod, 378, 379
Velasquez, 632; *illus.*, 634
Venezuela, 580
Venice, 216, 353, 360, 366, 423-424, 521: Arsenal of, 428, *illus.*, 429, 430, 431: and commercial ties to Byzantium, 363; diplomatic service of, 519; galleys of, 428, 430; and Latin Empire, 364; as oligarchy, 423; as trade center, 428-429; treaty with Byzantium, 346
Ventris, Michael, 53
Vergil, 95, 127-128: in *Divine Comedy*, 443
Vernacular languages, 441-442
Verrazzano, Giovanni da, 582
Verres, Gaius, 109
Versailles, Palace of, 610, 632; *illus.*, 609
Vervins, Treaty of, 549
Vesalius, 469

Vespasian, Emperor, 115, 124 (*illus.*)
Vespucci, Amerigo, 576
Vesuvius, 121
Vézelay, church at, *illus.*, 339
Vienna, 374, 375
Vikings (*see* Northmen)
Village life: Chinese, 571; Neolithic, 21
Villehardouin, 280, 361, 364, 441
Vinci, Leonardo da, 420, 450, 451, 453, 455-457, 460, 546: *illus.*, 456; as scientist, 468, *illus.*, 467
Vineland, Ericson in, 565
Virginia, 584
Visconti family, 420
Visigoths, 177, 235
Viziers, duties of, 371
Vladimir, Emperor, 243-244
Vochina, 383
Voltaire, 6
Vulgate, 154, 450

W

Wagner, Richard, 466
Waldseemüller, Martin, 576
Wales, 281-282: in Dark Ages, 195
Wallace, William, 282
Wallenstein, 532, 533, 534
Wall paintings, 11
Walsingham, 554
War, of early man, 14, 18
Warbeck, Perkin, 408
War of Devolution, 600
War of the League of Augsburg, 601, 602
War of the Spanish Succession, 602-603
War of the Three Henries, 548-549
Wars: Dutch, 621; Hundred Years', 394, 395-397; of Louis XIV, 600-601, 603; Peloponnesian, 69, 84-85; Persian, 67-68; Punic, 103-104; Thirty Years', 531-537
Wars of the Roses, 406, 407-408
Warwick, Earl of, 407-408
Weapons, 563: Roman, 98; in sixteenth century, 521, *illus.* 520
Webb, Walter P., 593
Weber, Max, 510, 511, 512
Wei Valley, 18
Welf family, 292
Wentworth, Thomas, 617
West (*see also* Europe): impact of Crusades on, 358-360; influence of Byzantium on, 213; influence of Islam on, 247, 346
West Indies, 587
Westminster, Second Statute of, 283
Westphalia, Peace of, 534, 536-537
Wheel, invention of, 12, 23
Whigs, in Glorious Revolution, 624
Whitby, Synod of, 194

Whitehead, Alfred, 626
White Mountain, battle of, 532
Whittington, Richard, 432
Wiclif, John, 311, 404, 405
Will, free, 499-500
William III of Orange, 600, 601, 602, 624, 625
William IX, Duke of Aquitaine, 328
William of Ockham, 318-319
Williams, Roger, 496, 585
William the Conqueror, 193, 262, 272-273
William the Silent, 528
Willibald, Saint, 350
Wilson, Woodrow, 36
Witenagemot, 272, 273, 280
Wolsey, Cardinal, 491, 524
Women, status of, 97: Athenian, 66; as Byzantine rulers, 223-224; Islamic, 249, 253; Roman, 130; Spartan, 61; in sultan's harem, 371
Woodcuts, 459
Wool trade, 430-431
Worcester, battle of, 621
Work, in Protestant thought, 510, 511
Works and faith, 482, 483, 485, 506
Worms: Concordat of, 290; diet, 483-484
Wren, Christopher, 632; *illus.*, 625
Writing, invention of, 18, 22-23
Württemberg, 508

X

Xavier, St. Francis, 588
Xenophon, 86
Xerxes, 67
Ximenes, Cardinal, 412

Y

Yahweh, 43
Yathrib, 249
York, house of, 407-408

Z

Zangi, 355
Zara, 363, 364
Zarathushtra, 40
Zealots, 367
Zemski sobor, 385: in time of troubles, 386-387
Zeno, Emperor, 230
Zero, concept of, 254, 326
Zeus, 54, 71, 91
Ziggurat, 34, 35 (*illus.*)
Zoroaster, 40
Zuñi Indians, 14
Zwingli, Ulrich, 489-490; *illus.*, 490

Year	Event
1214	Bouvines: victory of Philip Augustus of France and Emperor Frederick II; defeat of John of England
1215	Magna Carta in England
	Fourth Lateran Council in Rome: papal power at height under Innocent III
1227	Death of Genghiz Khan, Tartar conqueror
1250	Death of Frederick II: decline of Hohenstaufen Empire
1272	Death of St. Thomas Aquinas, greatest of medieval Schoolmen
c. 1300	Dante and Giotto flourishing: dawn of the Renaissance
1303	Philip IV of France against Pope Boniface VIII: prelude to "Babylonian Captivity" of papacy
1415	Burning of John Hus, Czech forerunner of Protestantism
1453	In the West, close of the Hundred Years' War (France victorious)
	In the East, capture of Byzantium by Ottoman Turks
1472	Grand-Duke Ivan III of Muscovy takes Byzantine wife: Moscow as "third Rome"
1485	Bosworth Field: end of Wars of Roses; Henry VII (Tudor) King of England
1492	Capture of Granada by Ferdinand and Isabella: end of Moslem Spain
	First voyage of Columbus: start of Spanish empire overseas
1494	French invasion of Italy: beginning of "modern" power politics